G000296733

STREET ATLAS
Greater Manchester

Contents

PHILIP'S

First edition published 1997
Reprinted 1997, 1999 by

Ordnance Survey®   and   George Philip Ltd, a division of
Romsey Road   Octopus Publishing Group Ltd
Maybush   2-4 Heron Quays
Southampton   London
SO16 4GU   E14 4JP

ISBN 0-540-06485-8 (hardback)
ISBN 0-540-06486-6 (spiral)

To the best of the Publishers' knowledge, the information in this atlas was
correct at the time of going to press. No responsibility can be accepted
for any errors or their consequences.

The representation in this atlas of a road, track or path is no evidence
of the existence of a right of way.

**The mapping between pages 1 and 171 (inclusive) in this atlas is
derived from Ordnance Survey® OSCAR® and Land-Line® data, and
Landranger® mapping.**

Ordnance Survey, OSCAR, Land-line and Landranger are registered trade
marks of Ordnance Survey, the national mapping agency of Great Britain.

Printed and bound in Spain by Cayfosa

Key to map symbols

22a	**Motorway** (with junction number)
	Primary route (dual carriageway and single)
	A road (dual carriageway and single)
	B road (dual carriageway and single)
	Minor road (dual carriageway and single)
	Other minor road
	Road under construction
	Railway
	Tramway, miniature railway
	Rural track, private road or narrow road in urban area
	Gate or obstruction to traffic (restrictions may not apply at all times or to all vehicles)
	Path, bridleway, byway open to all traffic, road used as a public path
	The representation in this atlas of a road, track or path is no evidence of the existence of a right of way

142	**Adjoining page indicators** (The colour of the arrow indicates the scale of the adjoining page – see scales below)
130	
141	**The map area within the pink band is shown at a larger scale on the page indicated by the red block and arrow**

	British Rail station
(M)	**Metrolink station**
	Private railway station
	Bus, coach station
	Ambulance station
	Coastguard station
	Fire station
	Police station
+	**Casualty entrance to hospital**
+	**Church, place of worship**
H	**Hospital**
i	**Information centre**
P	**Parking**
PO	**Post Office**
St Matthews CE Prim Sch	**Important buildings, schools, colleges, universities and hospitals**
	County boundaries
River Roch	**Water name**
	Stream
	River or canal (minor and major)
	Water
	Tidal water
	Woods
	Houses

Acad	**Academy**	Mon	**Monument**
Cemy	**Cemetery**	Mus	**Museum**
C Ctr	**Civic Centre**	Obsy	**Observatory**
CH	**Club House**	Pal	**Royal Palace**
Coll	**College**	PH	**Public House**
Ex H	**Exhibition Hall**	Resr	**Reservoir**
Ind Est	**Industrial Estate**	Ret Pk	**Retail Park**
Inst	**Institute**	Sch	**School**
Ct	**Law Court**	Sh Ctr	**Shopping Centre**
L Ctr	**Leisure Centre**	Sta	**Station**
LC	**Level Crossing**	TH	**Town Hall/House**
Liby	**Library**	Trad Est	**Trading Estate**
Mkt	**Market**	Univ	**University**
Meml	**Memorial**	YH	**Youth Hostel**

■ The dark grey border on the inside edge of some pages indicates that the mapping does not continue onto the adjacent page

■ The small numbers around the edges of the maps identify the 1 kilometre National Grid lines

The scale of the maps on pages numbered in blue is 5.52 cm to 1 km (3½ inches to 1 mile)

0		¼		½		¾		1 mile
0	250m	500m	750m	1 kilometre				

The scale of the maps on pages numbered in red is 11.04 cm to 1 km (7 inches to 1 mile)

0		220 yards		440 yards		660 yards		½ mile
0	125m	250m	375m	½ kilometre				

IV

Key to map pages

New Longton · Much Hoole · Bretherton · Croston **A581** · Eccleston · Mawdesley · Heskin Green · LEYLAND · Clayton-le-Woods · Euxton · CHORLEY · Abbey Village · HASLINGDEN · Hoddlesden · DARWEN · Edgworth · Stubbins

M6 · **M61** · **A674** · **A666** · **A675** · **A676** · **A59** · **A581** · **A49** · **A5106**

Egerton · Toppings · Bradshaw · Tottington · Ainsworth · Little Lever

Coppull · ADLINGTON · STANDISH · Blackrod · Rivington · HORWICH · Haigh · Aspull · Wingates · WIGAN · WESTHOUGHTON · BOLTON · FARNWORTH · KEARSLEY · Walkden · SWINTON · Worsley · ECCLES · URMSTON

Appley Bridge · Shevington · SKELMERSDALE · ORRELL · Higher End · HINDLEY · INCE-IN-MAKERFIELD · ATHERTON · TYLDESLEY · Astley Green

RAINFORD · Billinge · Bryn · ASHTON-IN-MAKERFIELD · ABRAM · LEIGH · GOLBORNE · HAYDOCK · Lowton · Culcheth · Glazebury · IRLAM · Partington · Hollinfare · ALTRINCHAM · Little Bollington

ST HELENS · PRESCOT · Rainhill · NEWTON-LE-WILLOWS · Croft · Burtonwood · Bold Heath · WARRINGTON · Grappenhall · LYMM · Broomedge

Ditton · WIDNES · Moore · Daresbury · Stretton · New Mills

RUNCORN · FRODSHAM · Preston Book · Dutton · Antrobus · KNUTSFORD · Pickmere · Mobberley · Plumley

Helsby · Kingsley · Acton Bridge · NORTHWICH · Comberbach · Little Leigh

Roads: A59, A577, A570, A580, A572, A557, A5300, A562, A558, A56, A533, A49, A559, A574, A57, A6144, A50, A560, A673, A58, A56, A579

Page grid references: 18/19, 20/21, 22/23, 24/25, 26/, 8/9, 10/, 142/143, 144/145, 148, 146/147, 42/43, 35, 36/37, 38/39, 40/41, 53, 150/151, 54/55, 56/57, 58/59, 60/61, 78/79, 71, 72/73, 74/75, 76/77, 13, 89, 90/91, 92/93, 94/95, 105, 106/107, 117, 118/119, 128/

Page Scale
105	These pages are at 3½ inches to the mile
148	These pages are at 7 inches to the mile

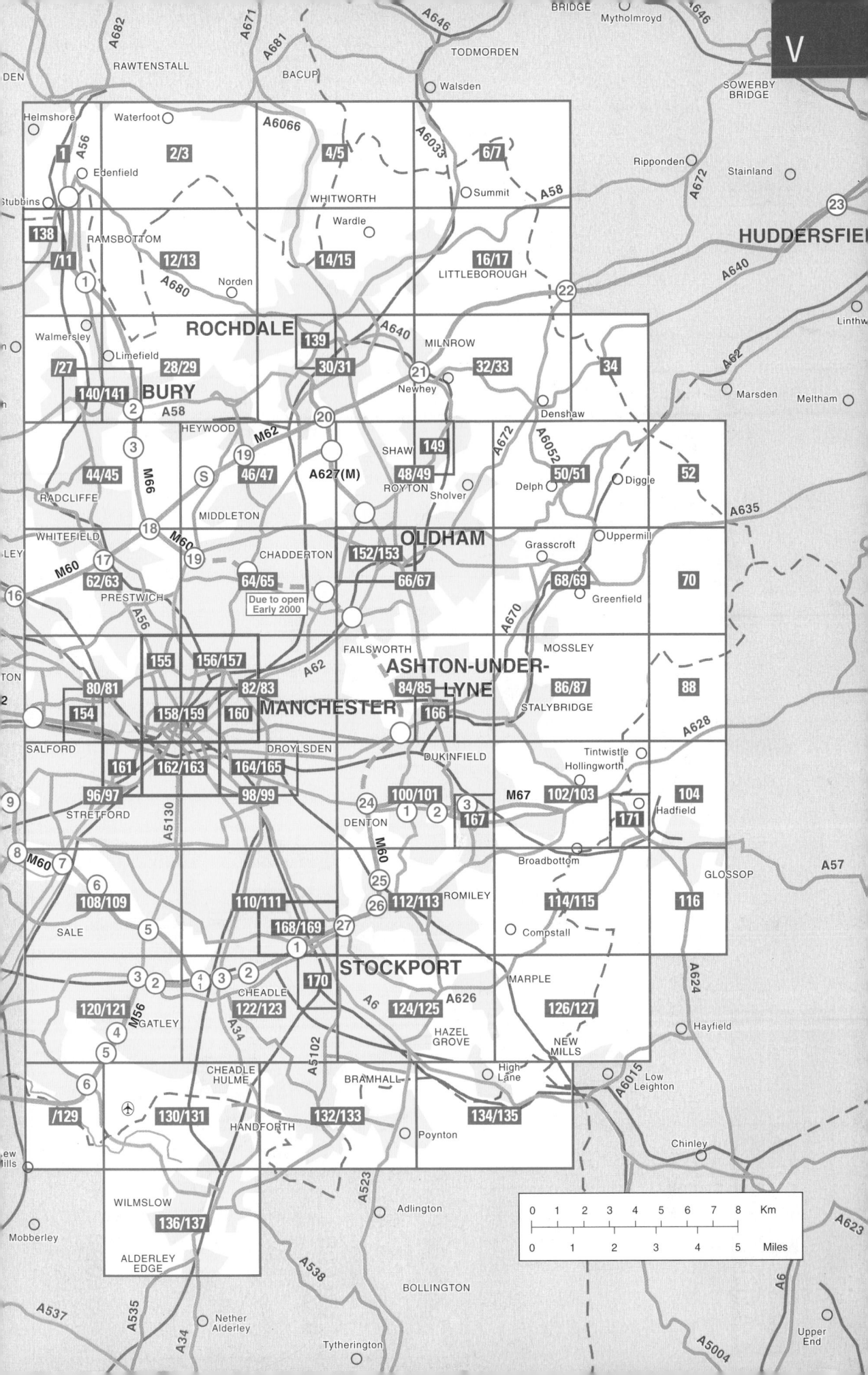

V
BRIDGE
Mytholmroyd
A646
TODMORDEN
Walsden
RAWTENSTALL
A682
A671
A681
BACUP
SOWERBY
BRIDGE
Helmshore
Waterfoot
A6066
A6033
A56
1
2/3
4/5
6/7
Edenfield
Stubbins
WHITWORTH
Summit
A58
Ripponden
Stainland
A672
23
HUDDERSFIE
138
RAMSBOTTOM
/11
12/13
14/15
16/17
Wardle
LITTLEBOROUGH
Norden
A680
A640
22
Walmersley
ROCHDALE
139
Limefield
/27
28/29
30/31
32/33
34
MILNROW
21
Newhey
140/141
BURY
A58
A62
Marsden
Meltham
Linthw
Denshaw
HEYWOOD
M62
20
SHAW
149
A672
A6052
52
44/45
46/47
48/49
50/51
A627(M)
ROYTON
Sholver
Delph
Diggle
M66
RADCLIFFE
MIDDLETON
A635
WHITEFIELD
M60
18
19
S
OLDHAM
CHADDERTON
152/153
Grasscroft
Uppermill
17
62/63
64/65
66/67
68/69
70
16
PRESTWICH
Due to open
Early 2000
Greenfield
A56
A670
FAILSWORTH
MOSSLEY
155
156/157
ASHTON-UNDER-
LYNE
80/81
82/83
84/85
86/87
88
A62
154
158/159
160
MANCHESTER
166
STALYBRIDGE
A628
SALFORD
DROYLSDEN
DUKINFIELD
Tintwistle
Hollingworth
161
162/163
164/165
96/97
98/99
100/101
M67
102/103
104
171
167
Hadfield
STRETFORD
A5130
24
DENTON
M60
Broadbottom
GLOSSOP
A57
8
7
6
108/109
25
26
112/113
ROMILEY
114/115
116
110/111
168/169
27
SALE
Compstall
5
STOCKPORT
170
3
2
CHEADLE
MARPLE
120/121
122/123
124/125
126/127
A626
A6
A624
M56
GATLEY
A34
HAZEL
GROVE
Hayfield
NEW
MILLS
A5102
CHEADLE
HULME
BRAMHALL
High
Lane
Low
Leighton
A6015
/129
130/131
132/133
134/135
HANDFORTH
Poynton
Chinley
A523
Adlington
WILMSLOW
136/137
Mobberley
ALDERLEY
EDGE
0 1 2 3 4 5 6 7 8 Km
0 1 2 3 4 5 Miles
A538
BOLLINGTON
A623
A6
A537
A535
A34
Nether
Alderley
Tytherington
A5004
Upper
End

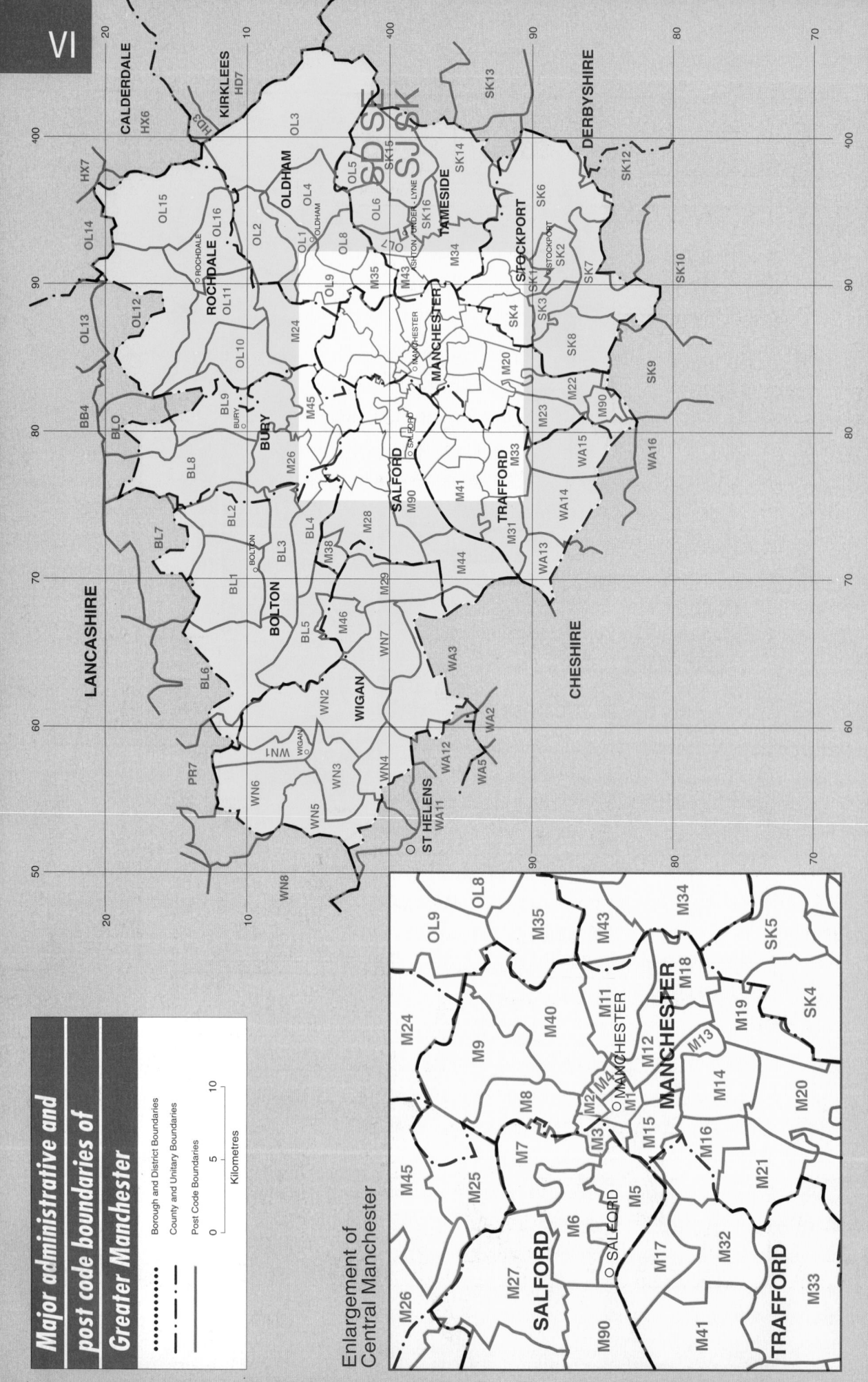

VI

Major administrative and post code boundaries of Greater Manchester

- ••••••• Borough and District Boundaries
- —•—•— County and Unitary Boundaries
- ———— Post Code Boundaries

Kilometres
0   5   10

Enlargement of
Central Manchester

2

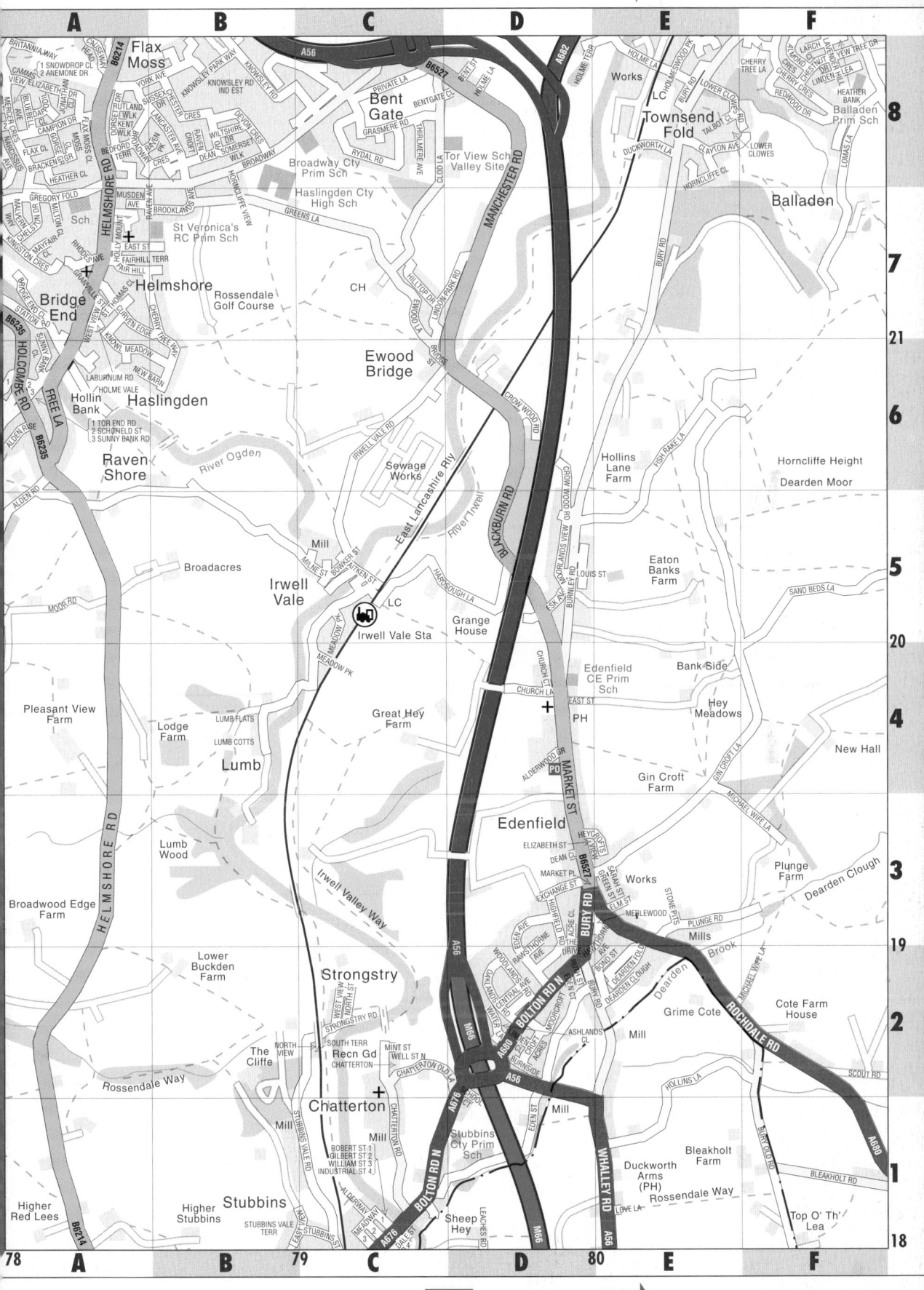
Flax Moss
Bent Gate
Townsend Fold
Balladen
Helmshore
Bridge End
Haslingden
Hollin Bank
Raven Shore
Ewood Bridge
Irwell Vale
Irwell Vale Sta
Edenfield
Lumb
Strongstry
Chatterton
Stubbins
Broadway Cty Prim Sch
Haslingden Cty High Sch
Tor View Sch Valley Site
St Veronica's RC Prim Sch
Rossendale Golf Course
Balladen Prim Sch
Horncliffe Height
Dearden Moor
Hollins Lane Farm
Eaton Banks Farm
Broadacres
Grange House
Pleasant View Farm
Lodge Farm
Great Hey Farm
Edenfield CE Prim Sch
Bank Side
Hey Meadows
New Hall
Gin Croft Farm
Lumb Wood
Broadwood Edge Farm
Plunge Farm
Lower Buckden Farm
Grime Cote
Cote Farm House
The Cliffe
Recn Gd
Stubbins Cty Prim Sch
Duckworth Arms (PH)
Bleakholt Farm
Higher Red Lees
Higher Stubbins
Sheep Hey
Top O' Th' Lea
Rossendale Way
Irwell Valley Way
River Ogden
River Irwell
East Lancashire Rly
Dearden Clough
Dearden Brook
HELMSHORE RD
MANCHESTER RD
BLACKBURN RD
MARKET ST
BURY RD
BOLTON RD N
ROCHDALE RD
WHALLEY RD
A56
A682
A680
A676
M66
B6527
B6214
B6235
A B C D E F
8 7 6 5 4 3 2 1
21 20 19 18
78 79 80

11
2

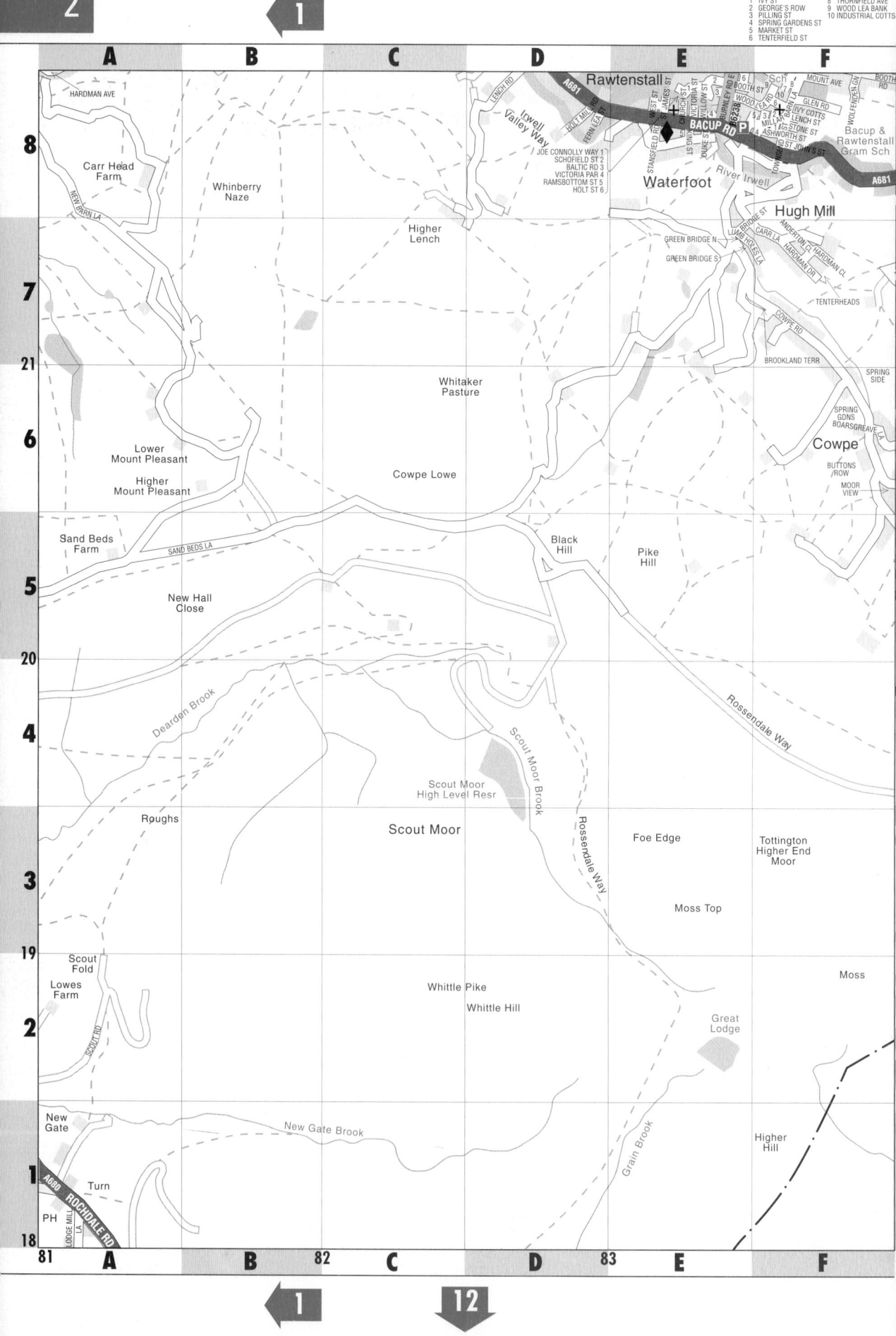

F8
1 IVY ST
2 GEORGE'S ROW
3 PILLING ST
4 SPRING GARDENS ST
5 MARKET ST
6 TENTERFIELD ST

7 YARE ST
8 THORNFIELD AVE
9 WOOD LEA BANK
10 INDUSTRIAL COTTS

A   B   C   D   E   F

8

Hardman Ave

Carr Head
Farm

Whinberry
Naze

Higher
Lench

New Barn La

LENCH RD

Irwell
Valley Way

A681

Rawtenstall

HOLT MILL RD
FERN LEA ST
B6238

JOE CONNOLLY WAY 1
SCHOFIELD ST 2
BALTIC RD 3
VICTORIA PAR 4
RAMSBOTTOM ST 5
HOLT ST 6

WEST ST
ST JAMES ST
CHURCH ST
VICTORIA ST
WILLOW ST

STANSFIELD RD E

BACUP RD P

Waterfoot

Sch
BOOTH RD E
BOOTH ST

WOOD ST
LS SM
JONES ST

MOUNT AVE
GLEN RD
IVY COTTS
STONE ST
LENCH ST
ST JOHN'S ST

BOOTH
RD

WOLFENDEN CL

Bacup &
Rawtenstall
Gram Sch

A681

River Irwell

Hugh Mill

GREEN BRIDGE N
GREEN BRIDGE S

LUMB HOLES LA
BRIDGE END
CARR LA

ANDERTON CL HARDMAN CL
HARDMAN DR

TENTERHEADS

COWPE RD

BROOKLAND TERR

SPRING
SIDE

7

21

Whitaker
Pasture

Lower
Mount Pleasant

Higher
Mount Pleasant

Cowpe Lowe

SPRING
GDNS
BOARSGREAVE

Cowpe

BUTTONS
ROW

MOOR
VIEW

6

Sand Beds
Farm

SAND BEDS LA

New Hall
Close

Black
Hill

Pike
Hill

5

20

Dearden Brook

Rossendale Way

4

Scout Moor
High Level Resr

Scout Moor Brook

Roughs

Scout Moor

Rossendale Way

Foe Edge

Moss Top

Tottington
Higher End
Moor

3

19

Scout
Fold

Lowes
Farm

SCOUT RD

Whittle Pike

Whittle Hill

Great
Lodge

Moss

2

New
Gate

New Gate Brook

Grain Brook

Higher
Hill

1

A680

Turn

ROCHDALE RD

PH

LODGE MILL LA

18

81   A   B   82   C   D   83   E   F

4

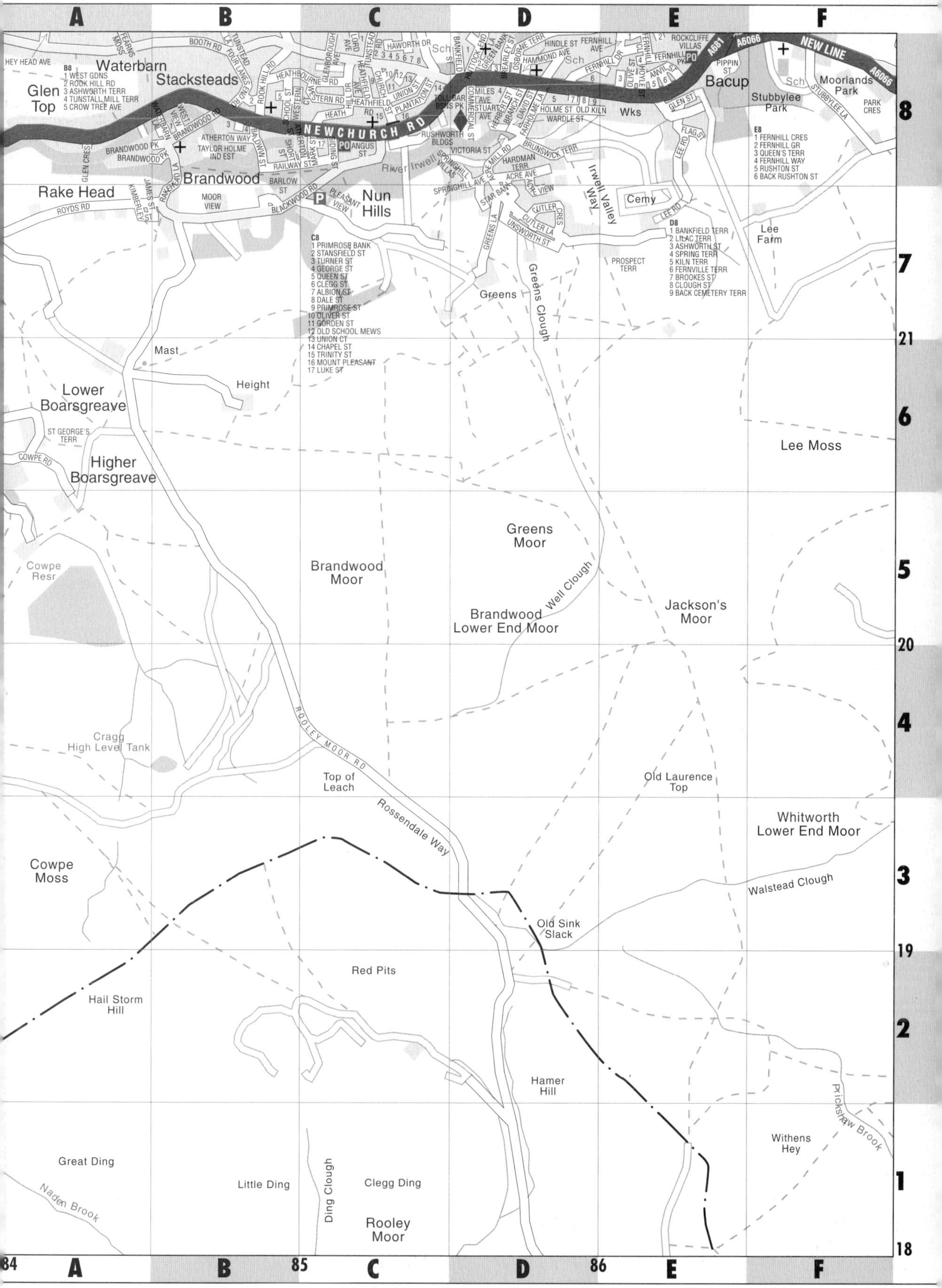

A B C D E F
Glen Top
Waterbarn
Stacksteads
HEY HEAD AVE
B8
1 WEST GDNS
2 ROOK HILL RD
3 ASHWORTH TERR
4 TUNSTALL MILL TERR
5 CROW TREE AVE
BOOTH RD
NEWCHURCH RD
ATHERTON WAY
TAYLOR HOLME IND EST
BRANDWOOD PK
Brandwood
Rake Head
ROYDS RD
MOOR VIEW
BLACKWOOD RD
PLEASANT VIEW
Nun Hills
RAILWAY ST
ANGUS ST
River Irwell
TOLL BAR BSNS PK
RUSHWORTH BLDGS
VICTORIA ST
HARDMAN TERR
BRUNSWICK TERR
ACRE AVE
SPRINGHILL AVE
STAR BANK
CUTLER CRES
CUTLER LA
UNSWORTH ST
GREENS LA
HINDLE ST
HAMMOND AVE
FERNHILL AVE
HOLME ST
OLD KILN
WARDLE ST
Wks
ROCKCLIFFE VILLAS
PIPPIN ST
GLEN ST
FLAG ST
LEE RD
Bacup
NEW LINE
A681
A6066
Stubbylee Park
STUBBYLEE LA
Moorlands Park
PARK CRES
E8
1 FERNHILL CRES
2 FERNHILL GR
3 QUEEN'S TERR
4 FERNHILL WAY
5 RUSHTON ST
6 BACK RUSHTON ST
Irwell Valley Way
Cemy
PROSPECT TERR
D8
1 BANKFIELD TERR
2 LILAC TERR
3 ASHWORTH ST
4 SPRING TERR
5 KILN TERR
6 FERNVILLE TERR
7 BROOKES ST
8 CLOUGH ST
9 BACK CEMETERY TERR
Lee Farm
C8
1 PRIMROSE BANK
2 STANSFIELD ST
3 TURNER ST
4 GEORGE ST
5 QUEEN ST
6 CLEGG ST
7 ALBION ST
8 DALE ST
9 PRIMROSE ST
10 OLIVER ST
11 GORDEN ST
12 OLD SCHOOL MEWS
13 UNION CT
14 CHAPEL ST
15 TRINITY ST
16 MOUNT PLEASANT
17 LUKE ST
Greens
Greens Clough
Mast
Height
Lower Boarsgreave
ST GEORGE'S TERR
COWPE RD
Higher Boarsgreave
Lee Moss
Greens Moor
Brandwood Moor
Well Clough
Brandwood Lower End Moor
Jackson's Moor
Cowpe Resr
ROOLEY MOOR RD
Cragg High Level Tank
Top of Leach
Old Laurence Top
Rossendale Way
Whitworth Lower End Moor
Cowpe Moss
Walstead Clough
Old Sink Slack
Red Pits
Hail Storm Hill
Hamer Hill
Prickshaw Brook
Withens Hey
Great Ding
Little Ding
Ding Clough
Clegg Ding
Rooley Moor
Naden Brook
8 7 21 6 5 20 4 3 19 2 1 18
84 85 86

13

4

3

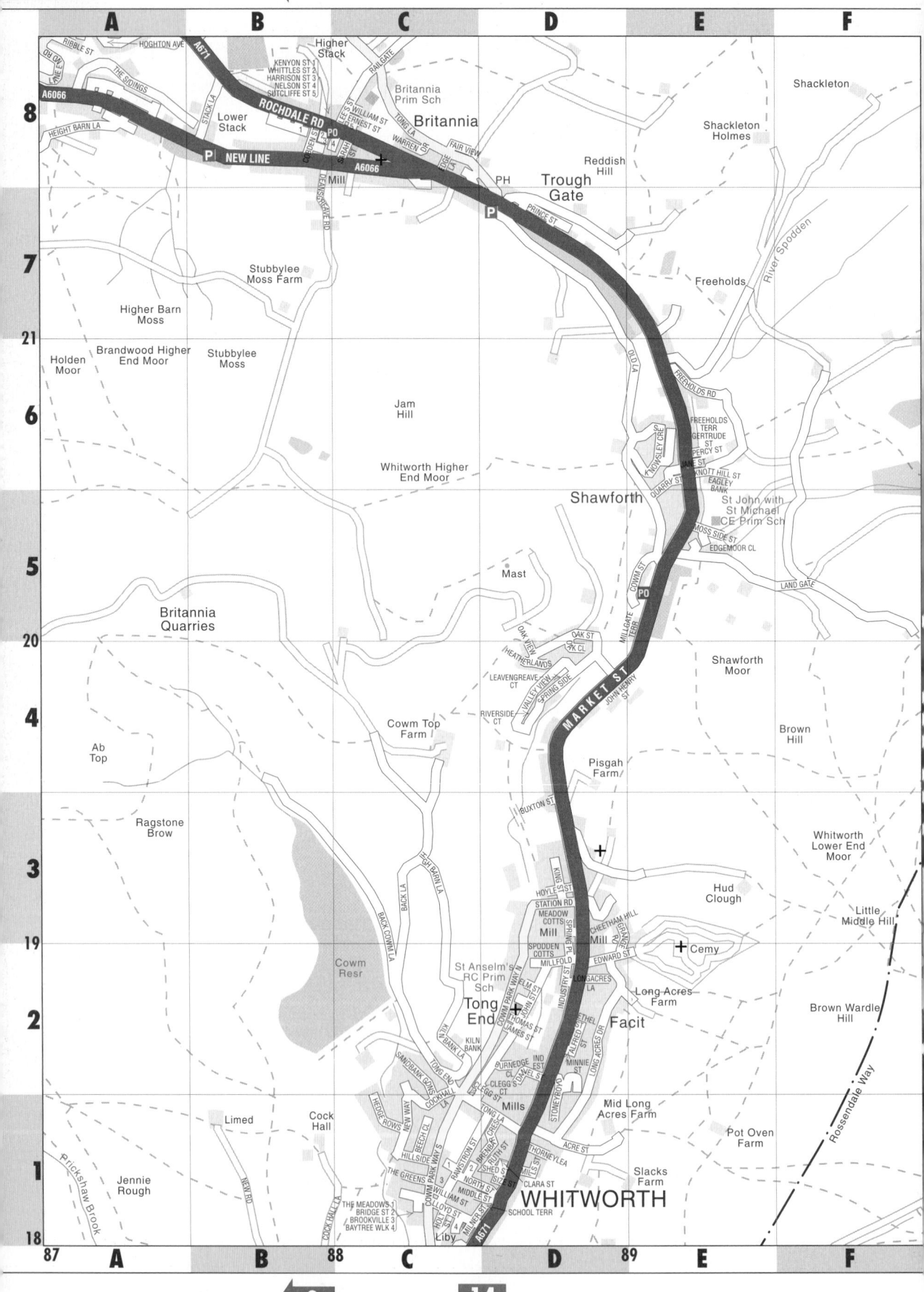
Britannia
Higher Stack
Lower Stack
Britannia Prim Sch
Trough Gate
Reddish Hill
Shackleton
Shackleton Holmes
Freeholds
River Spodden
Stubbylee Moss Farm
Higher Barn Moss
Holden Moor
Brandwood Higher End Moor
Stubbylee Moss
Jam Hill
Whitworth Higher End Moor
Shawforth
St John with St Michael CE Prim Sch
Mast
Britannia Quarries
Shawforth Moor
Cowm Top Farm
Brown Hill
Ab Top
Pisgah Farm
Ragstone Brow
Whitworth Lower End Moor
Hud Clough
Little Middle Hill
Cowm Resr
St Anselm's RC Prim Sch
Tong End
Facit
Cemy
Long Acres Farm
Brown Wardle Hill
Rossendale Way
Limed
Cock Hall
Mid Long Acres Farm
Pot Oven Farm
Prickshaw Brook
Jennie Rough
Slacks Farm
WHITWORTH
ROCHDALE RD
NEW LINE
MARKET ST
A671
A6066
A B C D E F
8 7 21 6 5 20 4 3 19 2 1 18
87 88 89

3
14

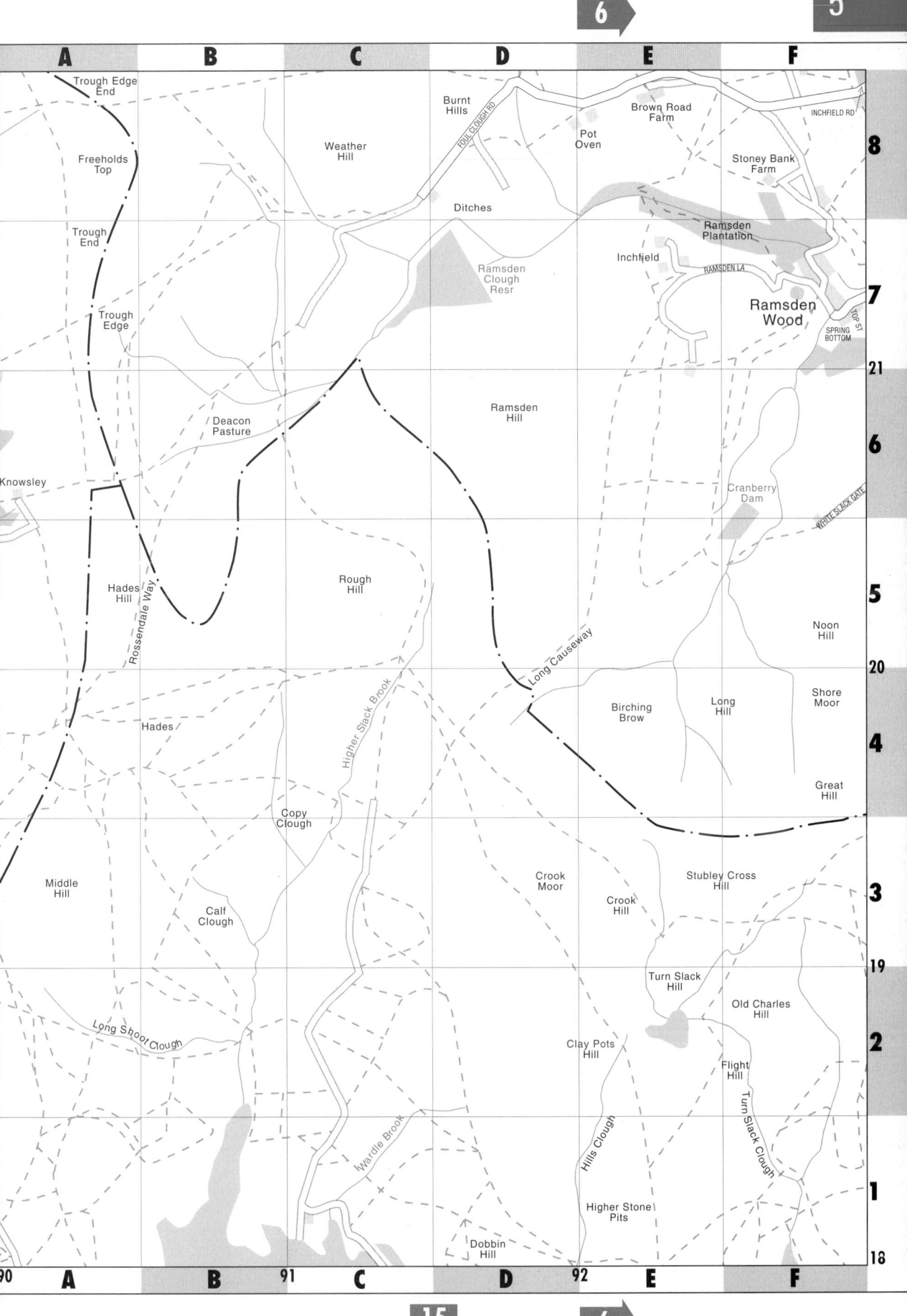

A B C D E F

Trough Edge
End

Burnt
Hills

Brown Road
Farm

INCHFIELD RD

8

Weather
Hill

Pot
Oven

Freeholds
Top

Stoney Bank
Farm

FOUL CLOUGH RD

Ditches

Ramsden
Plantation

Trough
End

Ramsden
Clough
Resr

Inchfield

RAMSDEN LA

7

Ramsden
Wood

Trough
Edge

TOP ST

SPRING
BOTTOM

21

Ramsden
Hill

6

Deacon
Pasture

Knowsley

Cranberry
Dam

WHITE SLACK GATE

5

Rough
Hill

Hades
Hill

Noon
Hill

Rossendale Way

20

Long Causeway

Shore
Moor

Birching
Brow

Long
Hill

Hades

Higher Slack Brook

4

Great
Hill

Copy
Clough

Crook
Moor

Stubley Cross
Hill

3

Middle
Hill

Crook
Hill

Calf
Clough

Turn Slack
Hill

19

Old Charles
Hill

Long Shoot Clough

Clay Pots
Hill

2

Flight
Hill

Wardle Brook

Hills Clough

Turn Slack Clough

1

Higher Stone
Pits

Dobbin
Hill

18

90 A B 91 C D 92 E F

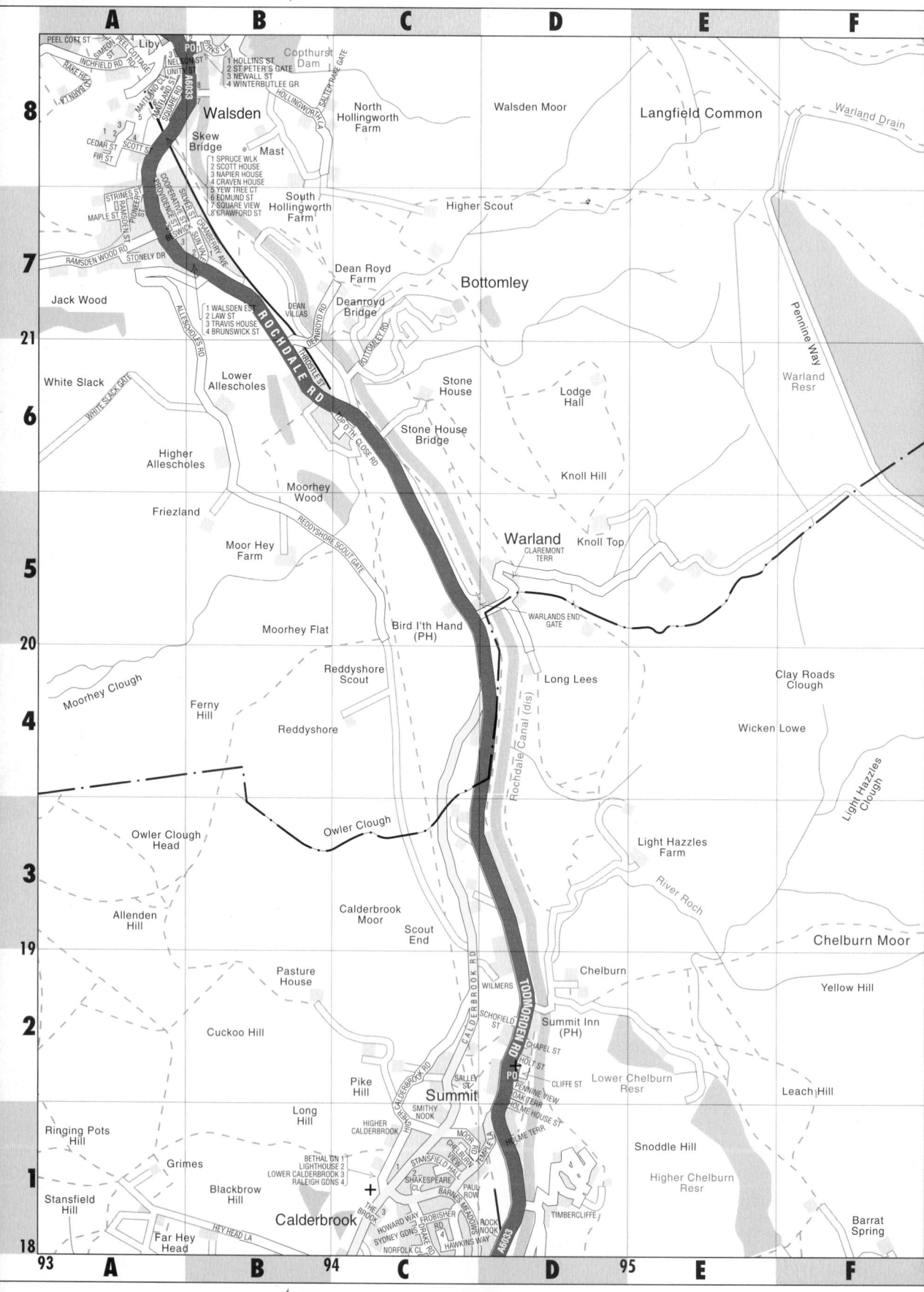

A B C D E F

8 Walsden
Skew Bridge
Mast

North Hollingworth Farm

Walsden Moor

Langfield Common

Warland Drain

7 Jack Wood

Dean Royd Farm

Deanroyd Bridge

Dean Villas

Bottomley

Higher Scout

Pennine Way

21 White Slack

Lower Allescholes

Stone House

Lodge Hall

Warland Resr

6 Higher Allescholes

Moorhey Wood

Stone House Bridge

Knoll Hill

Friezland

Moor Hey Farm

Warland
CLAREMONT TERR

Knoll Top

5 Moorhey Flat

Bird I'th Hand (PH)

WARLANDS END GATE

Clay Roads Clough

20 Moorhey Clough

Reddyshore Scout

Long Lees

Wicken Lowe

4 Ferny Hill

Reddyshore

Light Hazzles Clough

Owler Clough Head

Owler Clough

Light Hazzles Farm

River Roch

3 Allenden Hill

Calderbrook Moor

Scout End

Chelburn Moor

19 Pasture House

WILMERS

Chelburn

Yellow Hill

2 Cuckoo Hill

SCHOFIELD ST

Summit Inn (PH)

CHAPEL ST

Lower Chelburn Resr

Leach Hill

Pike Hill

Long Hill

Summit

SMITHY NOOK

Higher Calderbrook

CLIFFE ST

Snoddle Hill

1 Ringing Pots Hill

Grimes

Blackbrow Hill

BETHAL GDN 1
LIGHTHOUSE 2
LOWER CALDERBROOK 3
RALEIGH GDNS 4
SHAKESPEARE

Higher Chelburn Resr

Barrat Spring

Stansfield Hill

Far Hey Head

HEY HEAD LA

Calderbrook

TIMBERCLIFFE

18

A   B   C   D   E   F

Warland Drain

Bird Nest Hill

Turley Holes and Higher House Moor

Middle Moor

Blake Moor

White Holme Drain

Little Dove Lowe

White Holme Moss

Turvin Clough

Round Hills

Light Hazzles Resr

White Holme Resr

Little Moor Clough

Saw Gill Hollow

BLACKSTONE EDGE RD

B6138

Little Moor

Round Hill

Captains Mark Hill

Soyland Moor

Light Hazzles Edge

Farther Hill

Knave Holes Hollow

Knave Holes Hill

Utley Edge

Pennine Way

Middle Hill

Byron Edge

Cold Laughton Drain

TURVIN RD

Nigher Hill

Hassock

Cow Head Drain

Black Castle Drain

Rush Bed Hill

Blackstone Edge Resr

A58

Cow Head

B6138

ROCHDALE RD

Fairy Hill

Slate Pit Hill

A58   HALIFAX RD

A   97   B   C   D   98   E   F

8
7
21
6
5
20
4
3
19
2
1
18

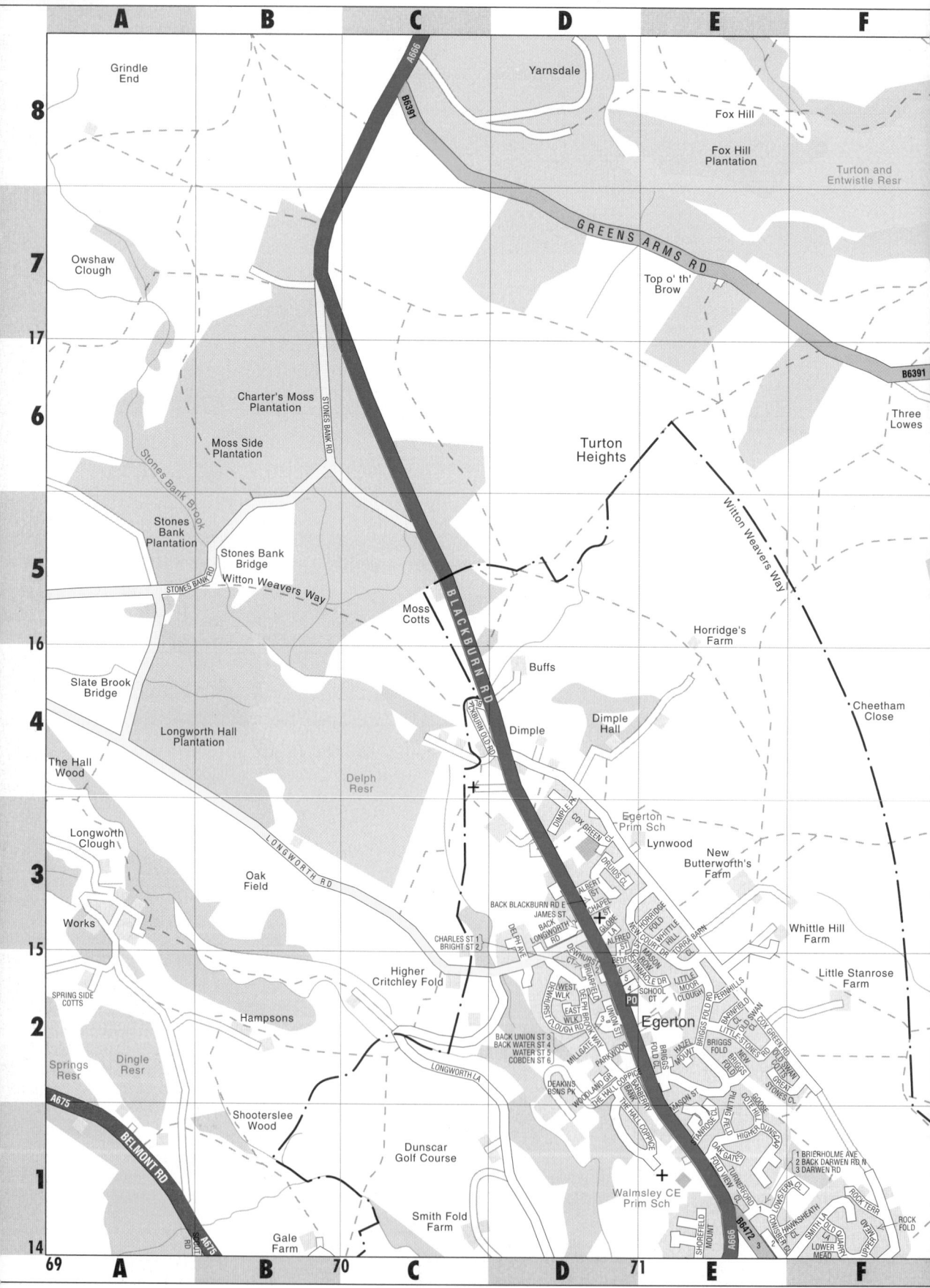

Grindle
End

Yarnsdale

Fox Hill

Fox Hill
Plantation

Turton and
Entwistle Resr

8

GREENS ARMS RD

Owshaw
Clough

7

Top o' th'
Brow

17

Stones Bank Brook

Charter's Moss
Plantation

Three
Lowes

B6391

6

Moss Side
Plantation

STONES BANK RD

Turton
Heights

Witton Weavers Way

Stones
Bank
Plantation

Stones Bank
Bridge

5

STONES BANK RD

Witton Weavers Way

Moss
Cotts

Horridge's
Farm

16

BLACKBURN RD

Buffs

Slate Brook
Bridge

Dimple
Hall

Cheetham
Close

4

Longworth Hall
Plantation

Dimple

BLACKBURN OLD RD

The Hall
Wood

Delph
Resr

Egerton
Prim Sch

LONGWORTH RD

Longworth
Clough

Oak
Field

DIMPLE PK
COY BREEN CL

Lynwood

New
Butterworth's
Farm

3

DRUIDS CL

Whittle Hill
Farm

Works

ALBERT
ST

CHAPEL
ST

HORRIDGE
FOLD

WHITTLE
HILL

Little Stanrose
Farm

BACK BLACKBURN RD E
JAMES ST

NEW COURT DR
ALFRED
ST

TORRA BARN

15

SPRING SIDE
COTTS

CHARLES ST 1
BRIGHT ST 2

BACK
LONGWORTH
RD

MASON
ST

BEDFORD CL

PINNACLE DR

LITTLE
MOOR
CLOUGH

FERNHILLS

Higher
Critchley Fold

DELPH AVE

SCHOOL
CT

2

Hampsons

DEWHURST
CLOUGH RD

WEST
WLK

EAST
WLK

DELPH BROW WAY

PO

Egerton

OLD SWAN

COX GREEN RD

LITTLE STONES

BRIGGS FOLD RD

GARFIELD

Springs
Resr

Dingle
Resr

LONGWORTH LA

MILLGATE

PARKWOOD

BRIGGS
FOLD CL

HAZEL
MOUNT

BRIGGS
FOLD

NEW

GREAT
STONES CL

A675

BACK UNION ST 3
BACK WATER ST 4
WATER ST 5
COBDEN ST 6

DEAKINS
BSNS PK

WOODLAND GR

THE HALL COPPICE

BARKERTY

BEASON ST

STANROSE CL

COTE HILL
FIELD

HIGHER DUNSCAR

GORSE
DR

BELMONT RD

Shooterslee
Wood

THE HALL COPPICE

OAK GATE

THUNDERFORD

1 BRIERHOLME AVE
2 BACK DARWEN RD N
3 DARWEN RD

1

Dunscar
Golf Course

FOLD VIEW RD

Walmsley CE
Prim Sch

LONGSHAW

ROCK TERR

A675
SCOUT

Smith Fold
Farm

SHOREFIELD
MOUNT

A666

B6472

HAWKSHEATH

SMITH LA

OLD QUARRY
RD

COBSLEY CT

LOWER
MEAD

ROCK
FOLD

14

Gale
Farm

10

A B C D E F
8 7 17 6 5 16 4 3 15 2 1 14
Hill Top
Entwistle Sta
Dingle Farm
Pleasant View
Wheatsheaf Farm
EDGE LA
New House Farm
Strawbury Duck (PH)
OVERSHORES RD
RAILWAY TERR
ENTWISTLE HALL LA
SCHOOL VIEW
SCHOOL LA
Hob Lane Farm
HOB LA
CROW TREES LA
Isherwood Fold
BLACKBURN RD
BROADHEAD RD
Hazel Clough Farm
PLANTATION RD
Entwistle
HOLLY BANK
Witton Weavers Way
ISHERWOOD FOLD
Horrocks Fold Farm
Greenthorne
GREENTHORNE CL
FOXDALE CL
BATRIDGE RD
HORROCKS RD
CROWNDALE
AINSDALE AVE
GREENACRES
CROWN POINT
Nabbs Farm
Armsgrove Farm
THOMASON FOLD
MOORFIELD
HEATHERFIELD
MAY ST
PH
Edgworth
Wayoh Resr
SHARPLES MEADOW
SHARPLES GN
LOWER MEADOW
WAYOH CROFT
MEADOW WAY
Mill
GREENS ARMS RD
OVER HOUSES
BARN MEADOW
HARBOUR LA
MARS ST
BARLOW CT
MARLED HEY
BENSON ST
PARK RD
Temple Farm
Spring Bank Farm
BRANDWOOD FOLD
BOLTON RD
Edgworth CE/Meth Prim Sch
HAWORTH ST
BURY RD
Higher Barn Farm
Billy Brook
MOUNT PLEASANT
BACK SANDY BANK RD
BEECH ST
SANDY BANK RD
EMBANKMENT RD
Fir Trees
CHAPEL GRANGE
Chapeltown
Clough House Farm
Chetham Arms Hotel (PH)
TOWER CT
MARTIN ST
Pallet Farm
CHAPEL FIELDS
CHARLOTTE ST
KAY ST
BANK ST
HIGH ST
STATION RD
Victoria Mill
WELLINGTON RD
YALE ST
Turton Bottoms
BIRCHES RD
KNOTTS BROW
LC
BACK HIGH ST
Bradshaw Brook
Birches
Quarlton Fold Farm
BOTTOM O' TH' KNOTTS BROW
Turton Tower (Mus)
Tower Farm
Lithermans Bridge
Jumbles
Walves Resr
BURY RD
Horrobin Lodge
Bull's Head Inn (PH)
RAMSBOTTOM RD A676
TOTTINGTON RD B6213
Torra Barn
THE COPSE
LEES COTTS
Jumbles Country Pk
Turton Heights (PH)
HORROBIN LA
THE SPINNEY
CHAPELTOWN RD
WATLING ST
Hazelhurst Brook
HORROBIN FOLD
Jumbles Resr
King William Inn (PH)
WALSH FOLD
CH
Turton Golf Course
Lamb Inn (PH)
BRADSHAW RD
Toye Farm
Top of Turton
Last Drop Village
Holts Fold
BROMLEY CROSS
GLEDHILL WAY
HAYDOCK LA
B6391
HILLSIDE AVE
GRANGE RD
A676
72 73 74

25
10

9

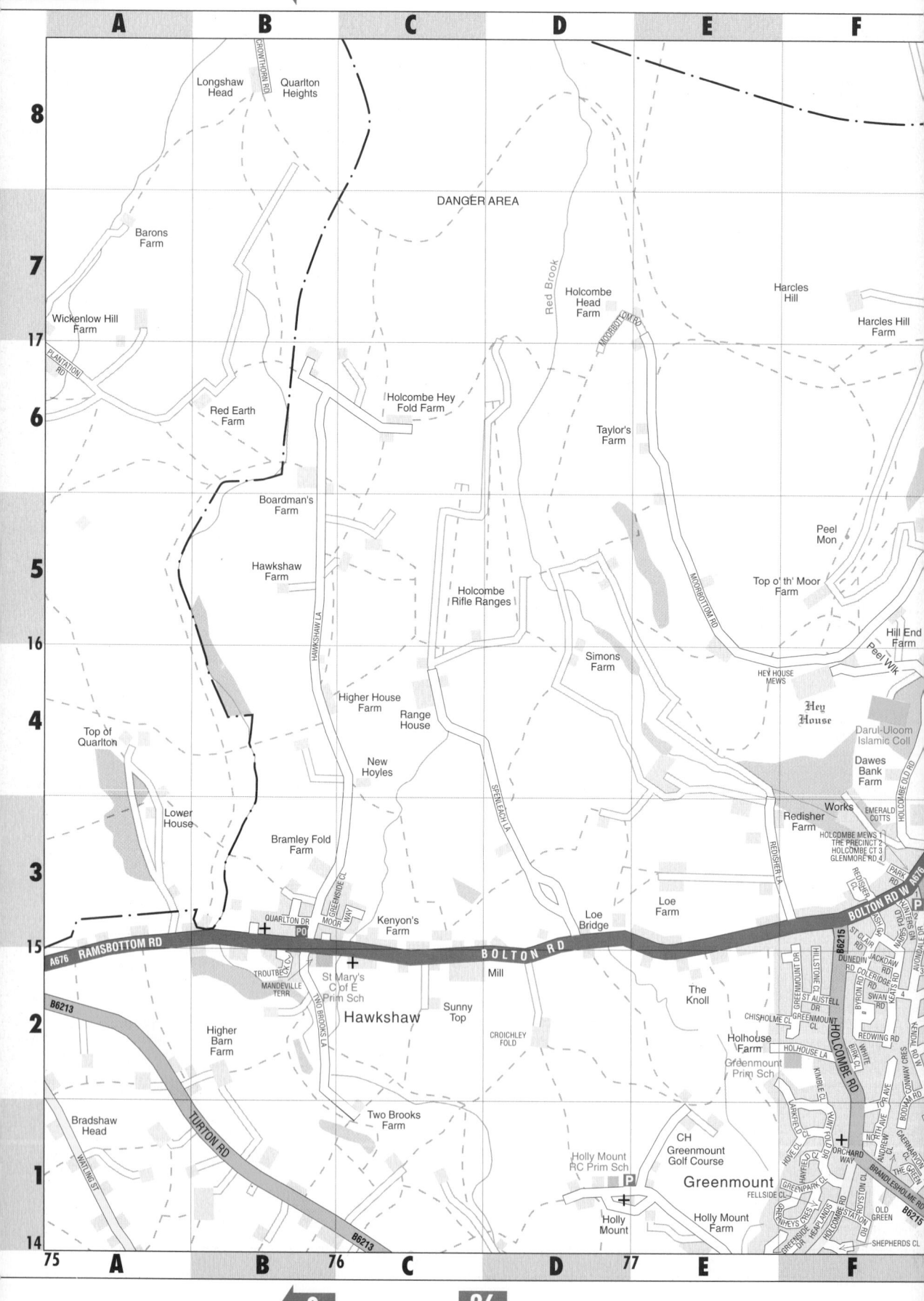

DANGER AREA
Longshaw Head
Quarlton Heights
CROWTHORN RD
Barons Farm
Wickenlow Hill Farm
PLANTATION RD
Red Earth Farm
Holcombe Hey Fold Farm
Red Brook
Holcombe Head Farm
MOORBOTTOM RD
Harcles Hill
Harcles Hill Farm
Taylor's Farm
Boardman's Farm
Hawkshaw Farm
Holcombe Rifle Ranges
Peel Mon
Top o' th' Moor Farm
Hill End Farm
Peel Wlk
HEY HOUSE MEWS
Hey House
Darul-Uloom Islamic Coll
Simons Farm
HAWKSHAW LA
Higher House Farm
Range House
Top of Quarlton
New Hoyles
SPENLEACH LA
Dawes Bank Farm
HOLCOMBE OLD RD
Lower House
Works
EMERALD COTTS
Redisher Farm
HOLCOMBE MEWS 1
THE PRECINCT 2
HOLCOMBE CT 3
GLENMORE RD 4
Bramley Fold Farm
REDISHER LA
REDISHER CL
PARK RD
GREENSIDE CL
QUARLTON DR
MOOR WAY
PO
Kenyon's Farm
Loe Bridge
Loe Farm
BOLTON RD W A676
A676 RAMSBOTTOM RD
BOLTON RD
TROUTBECK CL
MANDEVILLE TERR
St Mary's C of E Prim Sch
Mill
The Knoll
B6215
HILLSTONE CL
GREENMOUNT DR
ST CLAIR RD
DUNEDIN RD
JACKDAW RD
COLERIDGE RD
BYRON RD
SWAN RD
KEATS RD
ST AUSTELL DR
GREENMOUNT CL
CHISHOLME CL
B6213
TWO BROOKS LA
Hawkshaw
Sunny Top
CROICHLEY FOLD
Higher Barn Farm
Holhouse Farm
HOLHOUSE LA
Greenmount Prim Sch
REDWING RD
WHITE
BIRK CL
HOLCOMBE RD
KIMBLE CL
KENDAL RD W
CONWAY CRES
BODIAM RD
Bradshaw Head
TURTON RD
Two Brooks Farm
CH
Greenmount Golf Course
LARKFIELD CL
HUNT FOLD DR
HOVE CL
HAYFIELD CL
ORCHARD WAY
ANDREW CL
CAERNARVON CL
THE GREEN
BRANDLESHOLME RD
WATLING ST
Holly Mount RC Prim Sch
P
Greenmount
FELLSIDE CL
GREENPARK CL
ROYSTON CL
Holly Mount
Holly Mount Farm
HEADLANDS
STATION RD
HOLCOMBE RD
OLD GREEN
B6215
GREENSIDE DR
SHEPHERDS CL
B6213
A B C D E F
8 7 6 5 4 3 2 1
17 16 15 14
75 76 77

9
26

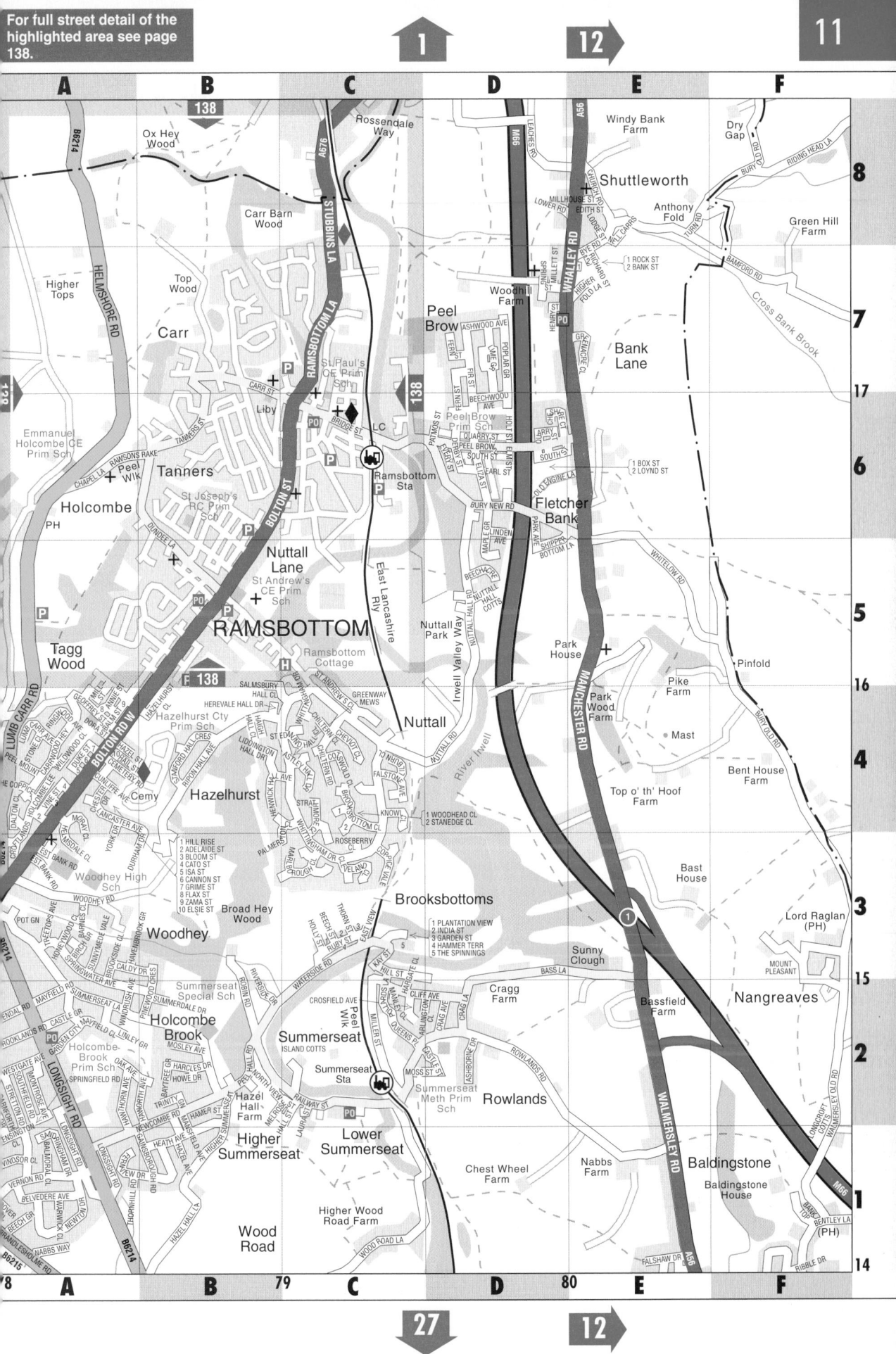

For full street detail of the highlighted area see page 138.

11

11
2

A
B
C
D
E
F
8
7
17
6
5
16
4
3
15
2
1
14
81
82
83
RIDING HEAD LA
A680
Mill
Smithy Carr
Farm
Kay Close
Farm
Rossendale Way
COAL RD
Fecit
Farm
FECIT LA
FECIT LA
Turf Moor
ROCHDALE RD
Man Road Ditch
Cheesden
Pasture
Rossendale
Sch
BLACK LA
Moor Side
Farm
MOOR SIDE LA
Close Nooks
Farm
Cheesden Brook
BAMFORD RD
Gate
House
Harden Brook
Tom
Hill
Cheesden
Bridge
Cheesden
Wham
Hill
Harden Moor
Wham Hill
Farm
Lumb
Bridge
New Inn
(PH)
Owd Betts
(PH)
EDENFIELD RD
Ashworth
Moor
Throstle
Hill
Croston
Close
Mam Hill
Croston
Close
Bottoms
Ridshaw
Farm
Far Buckhurst
Brow
Kirkby's
CROSTON CLOSE RD
Ashworth
Moor
Resr
A680
Buckhurst
Brow
BUCKHURST RD
Snape
Hill
Buckhurst
Farm
Rough
Lee
Far Croft
Head
Closes
SALES'S LA
Sales's
Farm
Top o' th' Hill
Farm
Whitewall
Farm
Lark
Mount
DEEPLY VALE LA
Deeply
Vale
Deeply
Hill
ASHWORTH RD
Wind Hill
Bird
Fields
Stand
Lees
Farm
Wind Hill
Farm
Copped Hill
Farm
Cob House
Nab
Gindles
Farm
Copped
Hill
BENTLEY LA
Cob House
Farm
M66
WHITE CARR LA
Shepherd
Hey
A
B
C
D
E
F

11
28

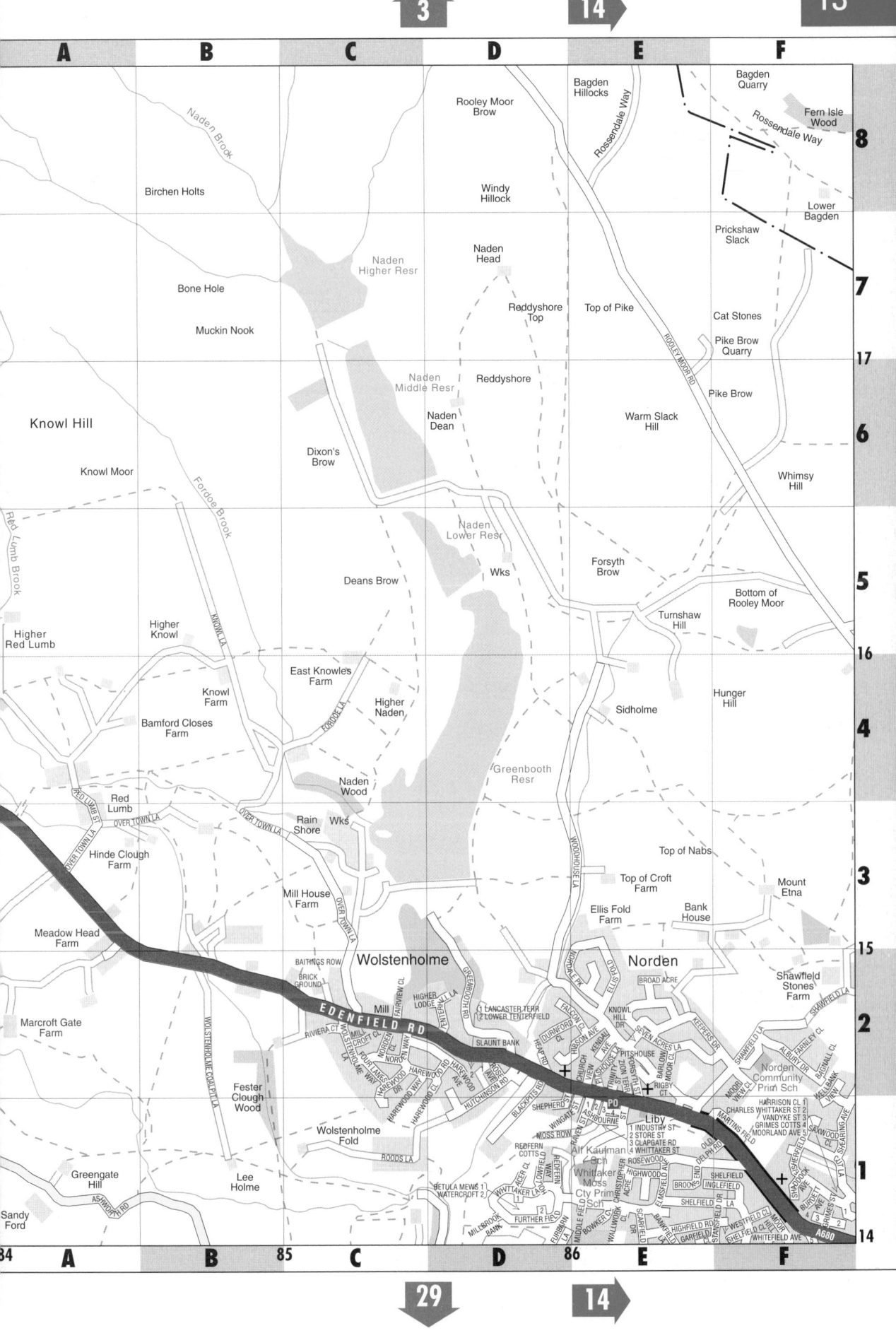

A B C D E F

Bagden Hillocks
Rossendale Way
Bagden Quarry
Fern Isle Wood
8

Naden Brook

Birchen Holts

Rooley Moor Brow

Windy Hillock

Rossendale Way

Lower Bagden

Prickshaw Slack

7

Bone Hole

Naden Higher Resr

Naden Head

Reddyshore Top

Top of Pike

Cat Stones

Pike Brow Quarry

17

Muckin Nook

Naden Middle Resr

Reddyshore

Pike Brow

6

Knowl Hill

Naden Dean

Warm Slack Hill

Knowl Moor

Fordoe Brook

Dixon's Brow

Whimsy Hill

Red Lumb Brook

Naden Lower Resr

Wks

Forsyth Brow

Bottom of Rooley Moor

5

Deans Brow

Turnshaw Hill

16

Higher Red Lumb

Higher Knowl

East Knowle's Farm

Higher Naden

Sidholme

Hunger Hill

4

KNOWL LA

Knowl Farm

FORDOE LA

Bamford Closes Farm

Greenbooth Resr

Red Lumb

Naden Wood

WOODHOUSE LA

Top of Nabs

Mount Etna

3

OVER TOWN LA

Rain Shore

Wks

Top of Croft Farm

Bank House

Hinde Clough Farm

Ellis Fold Farm

OVER TOWN LA

Mill House Farm

15

Meadow Head Farm

BAITHINGS ROW

Wolstenholme

Norden

BROAD ACRE

Shawfield Stones Farm

SHAWFIELD LA

Marcroft Gate Farm

WOLSTENHOLME COALPIT LA

BRICK GROUND

Mill

HIGHER LODGE

GREENBOOTH RD

PENTER ST LA

EDENFIELD RD

KNOWL HILL LA

KEEPERS DR

2

1 Lancaster Terr
2 Lower Tenterfield

FALCON CL

SLAUNT BANK

SEVEN ACRES LA

ALBURY DR

Fester Clough Wood

RIVIERA CT

MILLCROFT CL

NORDEN WAY

HAREWOOD WAY

HAREWOOD AVE

HUTCHINSON RD

BLACKPITS LA

HEAP RD

CHURCH VIEW

PITSHOUSE

TRINITY ST

ZION TERR

RIGBY CT

BARLOW MOOR CL

SHAWFIELD LA

MOOR VIEW CL

Norden Community Prim Sch

HARRISON CL 1
CHARLES WHITTAKER ST 2
VANDYKE ST 3
GRIMES COTTS 4
MOORLAND AVE 5

SAXWOOD CL

SHEARING AVE

Wolstenholme Fold

ROODS LA

SHEPHERD

WINGATE

NOSS ROW

ASHLINE ST

ASHBOURNE

STORE ST

Liby

1 INDUSTRY ST
2 STORE ST
3 CLAPGATE RD
4 WHITTAKER ST

MARTINS FIELD

OLD DELPH RD

SHADSWORTH

WELLBANK

RANDALL CL

1

Greengate Hill

ASHWORTH RD

Lee Holme

MILLBROOK BANK

BETULA MEWS 1
WATERCROFT 2

WHITTAKER LA

FURTHER FIELD

REDFERN COTTS

LOWFIELD

Alf Kaufman Sch

Whittaker Moss Cty Prim Sch

MIDDLE FIELD

HIGHFIELD

BOWKER ST

ROSEWOOD

CHRISTOPHER

ELMSFIELD

BANKFIELD

HIGHFIELD RD

SHELFIELD

Inglefield

SHELFIELD DR

SHELFIELD DR

CALDER

SHADSWORTH

A680

14

Sandy Ford

FURBRINN

MILLBROOK BANK

ACRE ST

WHITTAKER LA

WALLWORK

WIGHWOOD

SCARFIELD

GARFIELD

WESTFIELD LA

WHITEFIELD AVE

84 A 85 B C 85 D 86 E F

13
4

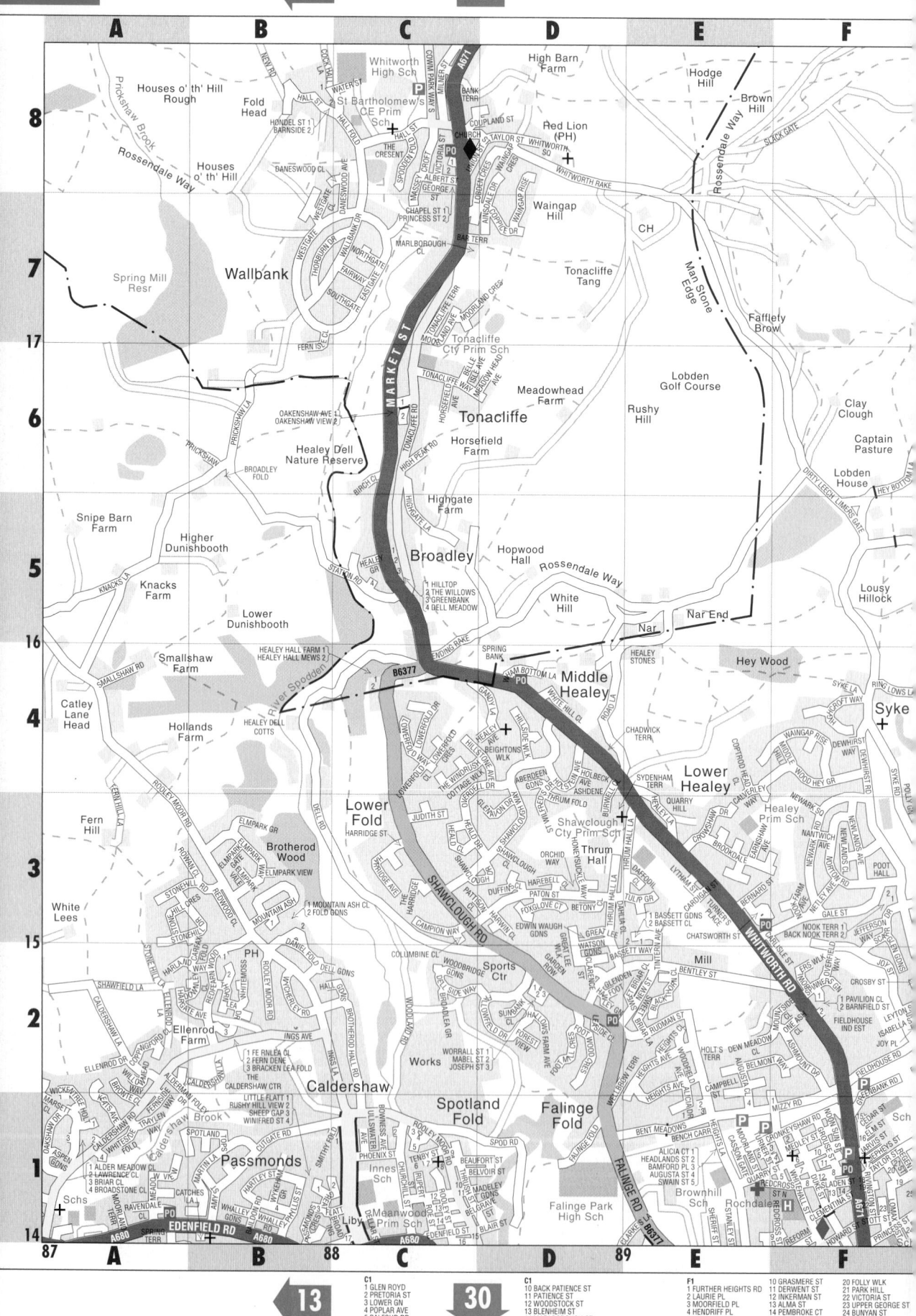

C1
1 GLEN ROYD
2 PRETORIA ST
3 LOWER GN
4 POPLAR AVE
5 BALFOUR RD
6 TENBY GR
7 TRENGROVE ST
8 AIR HILL TERR
9 BENTINCK ST

13
30

C1
10 BACK PATIENCE ST
11 PATIENCE ST
12 WOODSTOCK ST
13 BLENHEIM ST
14 MARLBOROUGH ST
15 MEANWOOD BROW
16 PRESTON ST
17 LISBON ST

F1
1 FURTHER HEIGHTS RD
2 LAURIE PL
3 MOORFIELD PL
4 HENDRIFF PL
5 SAWYER ST
6 MILFORD ST
7 DENTON ST
8 INDUSTRY RD
9 HENLEY ST
10 GRASMERE ST
11 DERWENT ST
12 INKERMAN ST
13 ALMA ST
14 PEMBROKE CT
15 DAVID ST N
16 DAVID ST
17 JEPHEYS PL
18 TAYLORS PL
19 WELLINGTON ST
20 FOLLY WLK
21 PARK HILL
22 VICTORIA ST
23 UPPER GEORGE ST
24 BUNYAN ST
25 ALMA IND EST

5
16

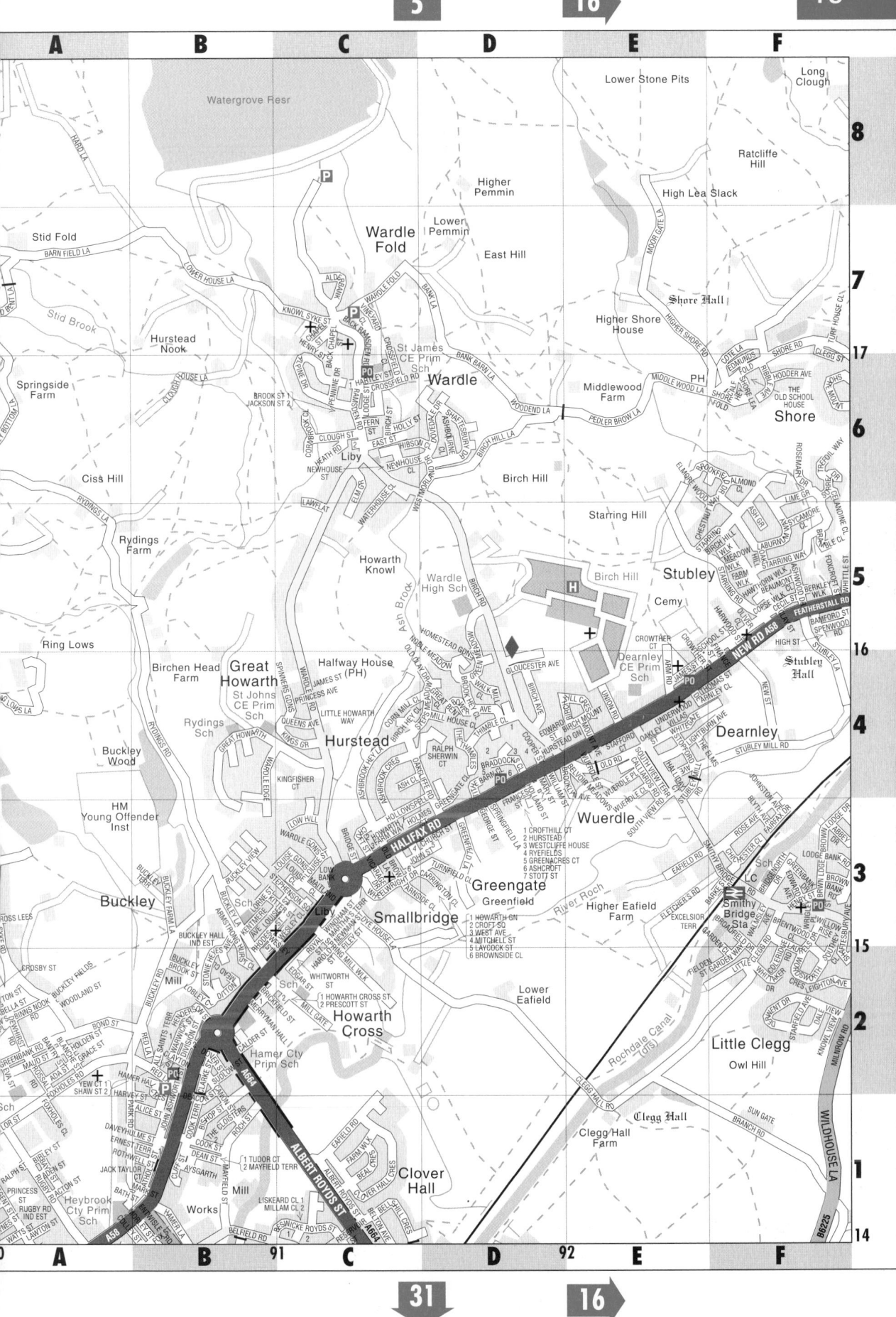
A
B
C
D
E
F
8
7
17
6
5
16
4
3
15
2
1
14
91
92
Watergrove Resr
Lower Stone Pits
Long Clough
Ratcliffe Hill
Higher Pemmin
High Lea Slack
Lower Pemmin
Wardle Fold
East Hill
Stid Fold
Stid Brook
Hurstead Nook
Shore Hall
Higher Shore House
St James CE Prim Sch
Wardle
Springside Farm
Middlewood Farm
Shore
Liby
Ciss Hill
Birch Hill
Starring Hill
Rydings Farm
Howarth Knowl
Wardle High Sch
Birch Hill
Stubley
Cemy
Ash Brook
Ring Lows
Birchen Head Farm
Great Howarth
Halfway House (PH)
Dearnley CE Prim Sch
Stubley Hall
St Johns CE Prim Sch
Rydings Sch
Hurstead
Dearnley
Buckley Wood
HM Young Offender Inst
Wuerdle
Greengate
Greenfield
Buckley
Smallbridge
River Roch
Higher Eafield Farm
Smithy Bridge Sta
Lower Eafield
Howarth Cross
Hamer Cty Prim Sch
Rochdale Canal (dis)
Little Clegg
Owl Hill
Clegg Hall
Clegg Hall Farm
Clover Hall
Heybrook Cty Prim Sch
Works
Mill
HALIFAX RD
NEW RD A58
ALBERT ROYDS ST
WILDHOUSE LA
A58
A664
B6225

31
16

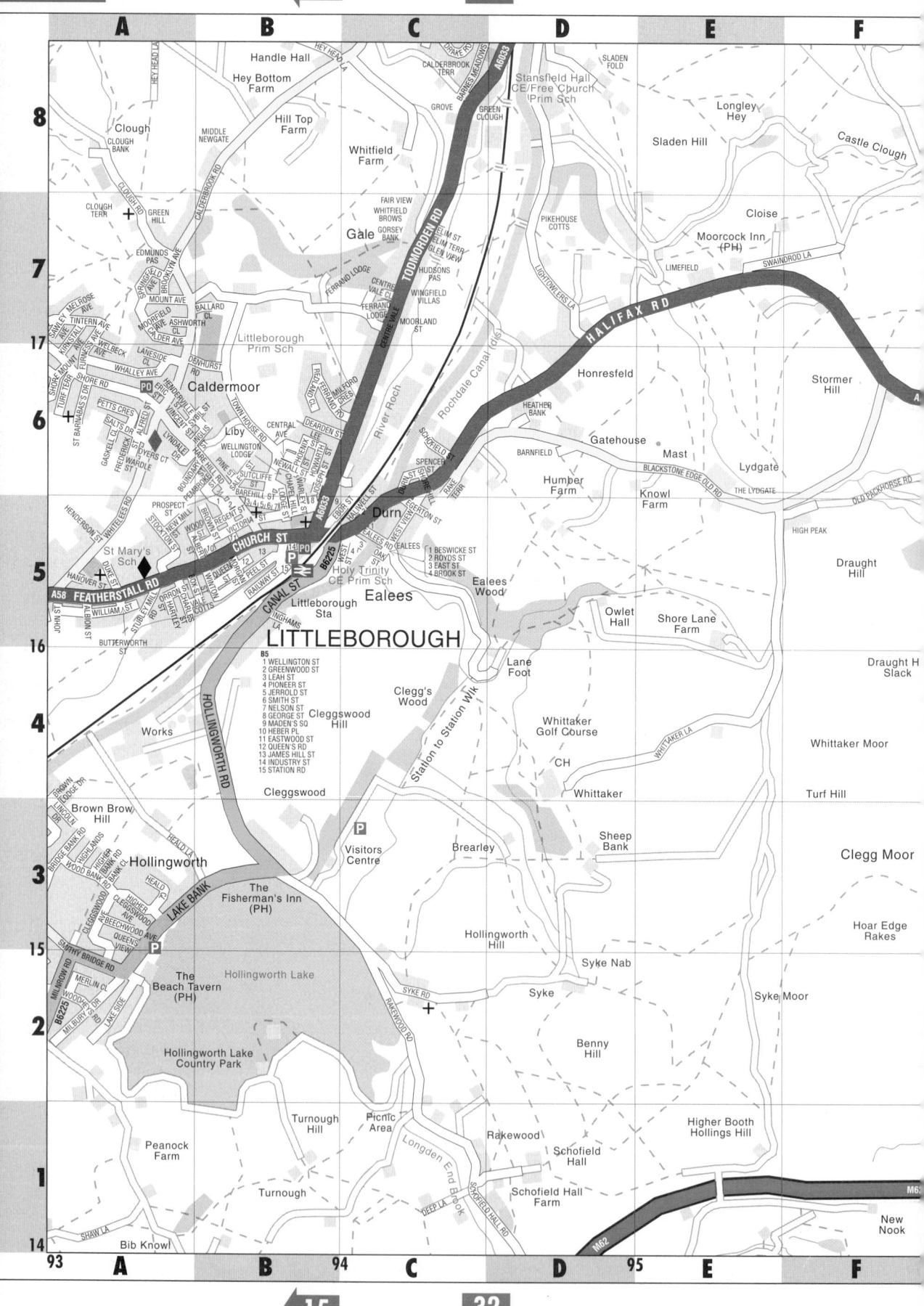
A
B
C
D
E
F
8
7
17
6
5
16
4
3
15
2
1
14
93
94
95
Handle Hall
Hey Bottom Farm
Hill Top Farm
Whitfield Farm
Clough
CLOUGH BANK
MIDDLE NEWGATE
CALDERBROOK RD
HEY HEAD LA
HEY HEAD LA
CALDERBROOK TERR
DRAKE ST
BARNES MEADOWS
A6033
Stansfield Hall CE/Free Church Prim Sch
SLADEN FOLD
Longley Hey
Sladen Hill
Castle Clough
GROVE
GREEN CLOUGH
CLOUGH TERR
GREEN HILL
CLOUGH RD
FAIR VIEW
WHITFIELD BROWS
GORSEY BANK
Gale
TODMORDEN RD
ELIM ST
ELIM TERR
GLEN VIEW
HUDSONS PAS
WINGFIELD VILLAS
PIKEHOUSE COTTS
Cloise
Moorcock Inn (PH)
SWAINDROD LA
LIMEFIELD
EDMUNDS PAS
BROOKLYN AVE
SPRINGFIELD AVE
MOUNT AVE
FERRAND LODGE
CENTRE VALE CL
MOORLAND ST
LIGHTOWLERS LA
HALIFAX RD
MELROSE AVE
TINTERN AVE
SAWLEY AVE
KIRKSTALL AVE
FURNESS AVE
WELBECK AVE
MOORFIELD AVE
CALDER AVE
ASHWORTH CL
BALLARD CL
Littleborough Prim Sch
CENTRE VALE
Honresfeld
Stormer Hill
LANESIDE CL
WHALLEY AVE
DENHURST RD
REDLAND CL
FERRAND RD
MILFORD CRES
SHORE MOUNT
TURF TERR
SHORE RD
ST BARNABAS'S DR
Caldermoor
River Roch
Rochdale Canal
HEATHER BANK
PETTS CRES
SALTS DR
GASKELL CL
FREDERICK ST
ALFRED ST
DYERS CT
WARDLE ST
LYNDALE DR
HENDERVILLE ST
ERIC ST
VINCENT ST
SYBIL ST
INGLIS ST
Liby
TOWN HOUSE RD
WELLINGTON LODGE
CENTRAL AVE
DEARDEN ST
LEE ST
PHOENIX ST
HOWARTH ST
NEWALL ST
CHAPEL HILL
HARLEY ST
JOSEPH ST
SCHOFIELD ST
SPENCER ST
Gatehouse
Mast
BARNFIELD
BLACKSTONE EDGE OLD RD
Lydgate
THE LYDGATE
OLD PACKHORSE RD
Humber Farm
Knowl Farm
HENDERSON ST
WHITELEES RD
PROSPECT ST
NEW MILL ST
STOCKTON ST
BOUNDARY ST
PEMBROKE ST
HARE HILL RD
PINE ST
SUTCLIFFE ST
BAREHILL ST
LODGE ST
DURN ST
SHORE HILL
RAKE TERR
EBOR ST
HALIWELL ST
Durn
EGERTON ST
WEST VIEW
HIGH PEAK
REGENT ST
VICTORIA ST
WOOD ST
BROWN ST
CHURCH ST
B6225
A6033
St Mary's Sch
HANOVER ST
DUKE ST
A58
FEATHERSTALL RD
QUEEN ST
WINTON ST
MORGAN ST
PEEL ST
RAILWAY ST
WEST ST
OAK ST
EALEES RD
EALEES
1 BESWICKE ST
2 ROYDS ST
3 EAST ST
4 BROOK ST
Draught Hill
Holy Trinity CE Prim Sch
Ealees
Ealees Wood
ORRON ST
HARTLEY ST
CHARLES ST
VALE COTTS
CANAL ST
WILLIAM ST
JOHN ST
ALBION ST
STUBLEY MILL RD
Littleborough Sta
INGHAMS LA
Owlet Hall
Shore Lane Farm
BUTTERWORTH ST
LITTLEBOROUGH
Lane Foot
Draught H Slack
B5
1 WELLINGTON ST
2 GREENWOOD ST
3 LEAH ST
4 PIONEER ST
5 JERROLD ST
6 SMITH ST
7 NELSON ST
8 GEORGE ST
9 MADEN'S SQ
10 HEBER PL
11 EASTWOOD ST
12 QUEEN'S RD
13 JAMES HILL ST
14 INDUSTRY ST
15 STATION RD
Clegg's Wood
Cleggswood Hill
Station to Station Wlk
Whittaker Golf Course
WHITTAKER LA
Whittaker Moor
HOLLINGWORTH RD
Works
CH
Whittaker
Turf Hill
BROWN LODGE DR
Cleggswood
LINCOLN DR
Brown Brow Hill
Visitors Centre
Brearley
Sheep Bank
BRIDGE BANK RD
HIGHLANDS
WOOD BANK RD
HIGHER BANK RD
BANK CL
HEALD LA
Hollingworth
Clegg Moor
HEALD CL
LAKE BANK
The Fisherman's Inn (PH)
CLEGGSWOOD AVE
HIGHER CLEGGSWOOD AVE
BEECHWOOD AVE
QUEENS VIEW
Hollingworth Hill
Hoar Edge Rakes
SMITHY BRIDGE RD
Syke Nab
MILNROW RD
MERLIN CL
The Beach Tavern (PH)
Hollingworth Lake
SYKE RD
Syke
Syke Moor
WOODHOUSE LA
MILBURY DR
LAKE SIDE
B6225
RAKEWOOD RD
Benny Hill
Hollingworth Lake Country Park
Turnough Hill
Picnic Area
Higher Booth Hollings Hill
Peanock Farm
Rakewood
Schofield Hall
Longden End Brook
Turnough
DEEP LA
SCHOFIELD HALL RD
Schofield Hall Farm
M62
New Nook
SHAW LA
Bib Knowl
M62

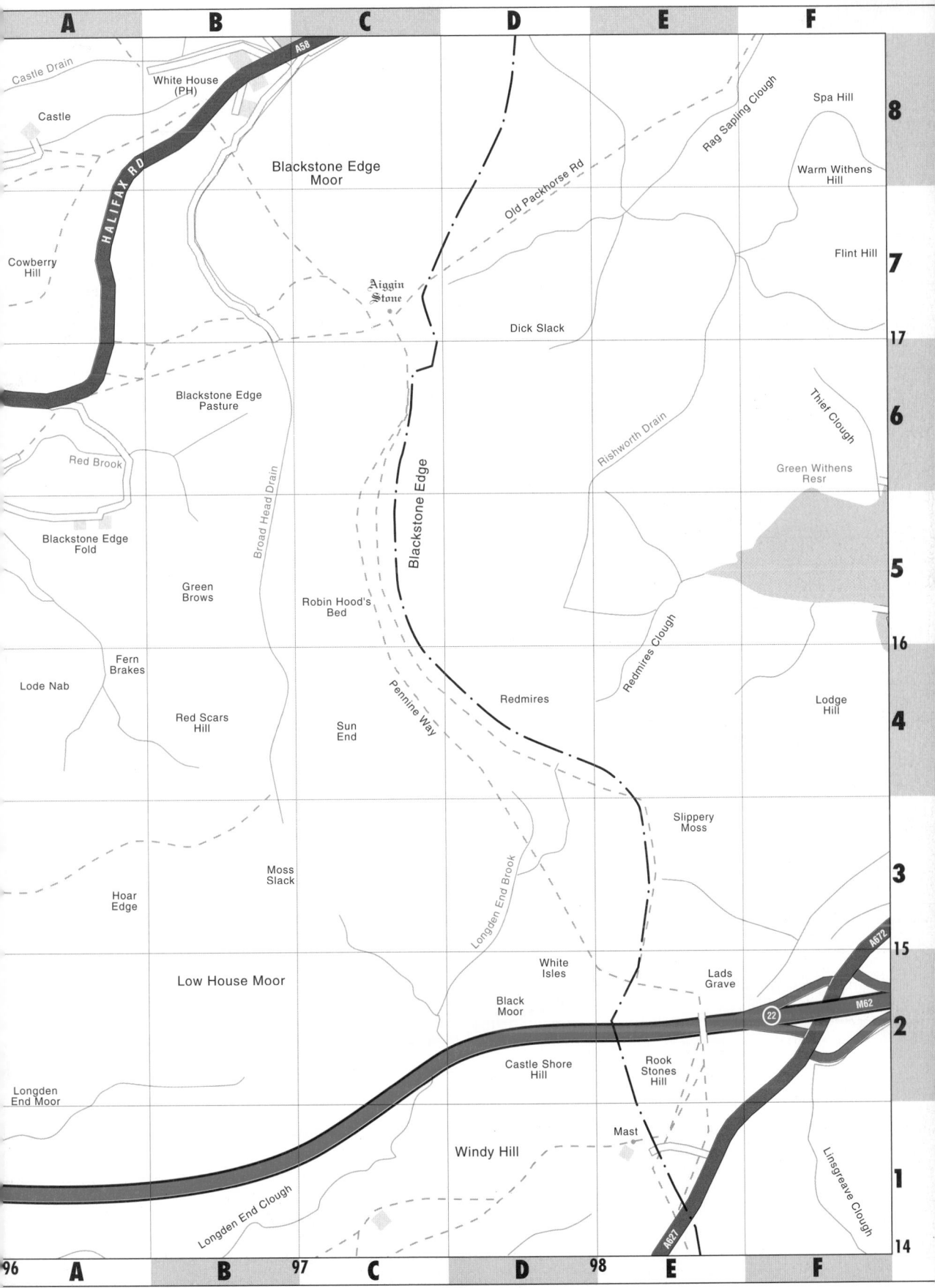

A B C D E F

8

7

17

6

5

16

4

3

15

2

1

14

Castle Drain

White House (PH)

Castle

Blackstone Edge Moor

Old Packhorse Rd

Rag Sapling Clough

Spa Hill

Warm Withens Hill

Flint Hill

HALIFAX RD

A58

Cowberry Hill

Aiggin Stone

Dick Slack

Thief Clough

Green Withens Resr

Blackstone Edge Pasture

Rishworth Drain

Red Brook

Broad Head Drain

Blackstone Edge

Blackstone Edge Fold

Green Brows

Robin Hood's Bed

Redmires Clough

Fern Brakes

Lode Nab

Red Scars Hill

Sun End

Pennine Way

Redmires

Lodge Hill

Slippery Moss

Moss Slack

Hoar Edge

Longden End Brook

A672

Low House Moor

White Isles

Lads Grave

22

M62

Black Moor

Longden End Moor

Castle Shore Hill

Rook Stones Hill

Mast

Windy Hill

Linsgreave Clough

Longden End Clough

A627

Sanderson House
Charity Farm
Higher Wrennall
High Hopes
Dwerry House
Harrock Hill
Harrock Old Windmill
Wrights Coverts
North Tunley
Toogood Farm
Cowling's Farm
Scarisbrick Arms (PH)
Copyhold Farm
Sandhole Farm
Wrightington Bar
Mast
Butteries Wood
Hill House Fold
Hesketh House
Stone Leach
Higher Barn
Pine Covert
Mossy Lea
Mossy Lea Cty Prim Sch
Hind's Head (PH)
Diglake Farm
South Tunley Farm
Lathom's Charity Farm
Tunley Brook
Tunley Moss Farm
Lassell House Farm
Robin Hood
High Moor Farm
Boggart House
Moss House Farm
Hunger Hill
Robin Hood Farm
Bury Hey Wood
Boar's Den Farm
Tunley Moss
Primrose Woods
Wrightington Hotel
Black Field Plantation
Dangerous Corner
Parbold Hall
Fairy Glen
Sprodley Brook
The Rookery
Wrightington Pond
Wrightington
The Dingle
Delf House
Delf House Wood
Big Wood
Nursery
All Saints CE Prim Sch
SANDERSON LA
COOPER'S LA
BARMSKIN LA
SMITHY BROW
CHURCH LA
B5250 WOOD LA
CARR HOUSE LA
BROADHURST LA
TOOGOOD LA
HILL HOUSE LA
HILL HOUSE FOLD LA
HARROCK LA
COURAGE LOW LA
TUNLEY LA
TUNLEY MOSS
MOSSY LEA RD
HIGH MOOR LA
MOSS LA
ROBIN HOOD LA
B5250
MOSSY LEA FOLD
A5209 SPARROW HILL
HALL LA
CROW ORCHARD RD
A5209
B5375
APPLEY LA N
GLENSIDE
SPRODLEY DR
GRAHAM DR
NORTH AVE
SOUTH DR
THE GROVE
STONEYGATE LA
FINCH LA
DOBSON CL
BACK LA
SKULL HOUSE LA
CHISNALL AVE
MANSE AVE
A B C D E F
8 7 6 5 4 3 2 1
13 12 11 10
51 52 53

35

A B C D E F

8

Wet Oaks Wood

Vause Farm

Elmhurst Farm

Coppull Moor Farm

Blainscough Hall

Coppull

Chapel Way

Church Fold

PH

Green La

7

Coppull Cross Rds

Jolly Tar La

Bridge Farm

Chisnall Wood

Patrick Farm

CHISNALL LA

Alison Arms (PH)

St John's CE Prim Sch

BELMONT PL

Coppull Moor

COPPULL MOOR LA

13

Coppull Hill

6

CHISNALL LA

The Grange

SPRINGS BROW

PRESTON RD

CRANE ST

BOGBURN LA

Moorhouse Farm

HIC BIBI LA

Bogburn Hall Farm

Stars Brook

Langtree Old Hall Farm

New Seven Stars (PH)

5

12

Lone Farm

St Joseph's RC Prim Sch

Chadwick Farm

Cross Farm

Gorse Hall

4

Potters Farm

Thompson House

Pepper Lane Farm

PEPPER LA

ROBIN HILL LA

QUAKERS TERR

PENHURST AVE

LANGTREE LA

Langtree Hall

MOSSY LEA FOLD

MOSSY LEA RD

BOUNDARY LA

Shevington Moor

MARPLE CL

CLIVETON GR

HARRIS RD

LUDLOW ST

Saddle Hill Farm

WHITWELL CL

KENYON RD

Standish Comm High Sch

MARWICK

MOORES LA

NORTHWAYS

WOODLANDS

LANGLEY CL

SHELDON AVE

EDALE DR

STERNDALE AVE

BRADLEY LA

STANDISH

2

B5250

27

CROW ORCHARD RD

SHEVINGTON LA

B5206

Chamberlain's Farm

RIPPLE GATE

ASHURST RD 1 GREENSWARD CL 2

ALMOND BROOK RD

Black Horse Farm

ARBOUR LA

ST STEPHEN'S RD

A5209

SCHOOL LA

HIGH ST

A49

RECTORY LA

B5239

Liby

Lark Hill

Hill

11

1

10

A   B   C   D   E   F

8

Coppull
Old Hall

Coppull Hall
Wood

Coppull
Hall

Green Lane
Farm

GREEN LA

COPPULL HALL LA

7

Pear Tree
Farm

JOLLY TAR LA

Coppull Brow
Farm

WIGAN LA

A5106

Eller Brook

WESTHOUGHTON RD

A6

CHATSWORTH CT

Allanson
Hall

Rigshaw
Bridge

13

Sand Pit

STONER RD
CARRINGTON RD
SANDS
CROOK ST
HOLDEN
CHAPEL ST
SMITH ST

Adlington
Cty Prim
Sch

6

Holt
Farm

Grey Horse
(PH)

Moss Ditch

Sand Pit

CASTLE HOUSE LA
SANDBIRMINGHAM CL
LEWIS CL
PARK RD
ACRESFIELD
GRAFTON ST
RICKMANW
WINDSOR
BALMORAL

THE POPLARS HAT LA

Buckow Brook

Mill Bridge
Farm

White Cross
Hotel (PH)

Rigby House
Farm

CASTLE DR

THE COMMON
OLD SCHOOL LA
CRANFORD AVE

5

Talbot House
Farm

Leeds and Liverpool Canal

12

Refuse
Tip

Bores
Farm

BORES HILL

Adlington Hall
Farm

COMMON END
STONEY LA

Aberdeen
Bridge

4

Wrennalls
Farm

PLATT LA

Adlington
Park

Crawshaw
Hall

River Douglas

Aberdeen
Farm

BLUNDEL LA

3

BRADLEY LA
HUTTON ST

Crown
Hotel
(PH)

Bradley Brook

CHORLEY RD

11

BRADLEY HILL
TRAD EST

Worthington
Hall

Hotel

Arley Wood

ARLEY LA

2

Wigan
Golf Course

CH

Hollins
Head

Refuse
Tip

Worthington Lakes
(Resrs)

CANAL ROW

Worthington
Farm

PENNINGTON LA
PENNINGTON LA

1

Rectory
Farm

RECTORY LA

B5239

BROOKSIDE RD
CORNWALL
CRES
DORSET
RD
WESSEX CL
SUSSEX
DEVON DR
A5106

Works

Water Works
Farm

LAKE SIDE
COTTS

MAYFAIR
COTTS

Pennington
Farm

10

A   B   C   D   E   F

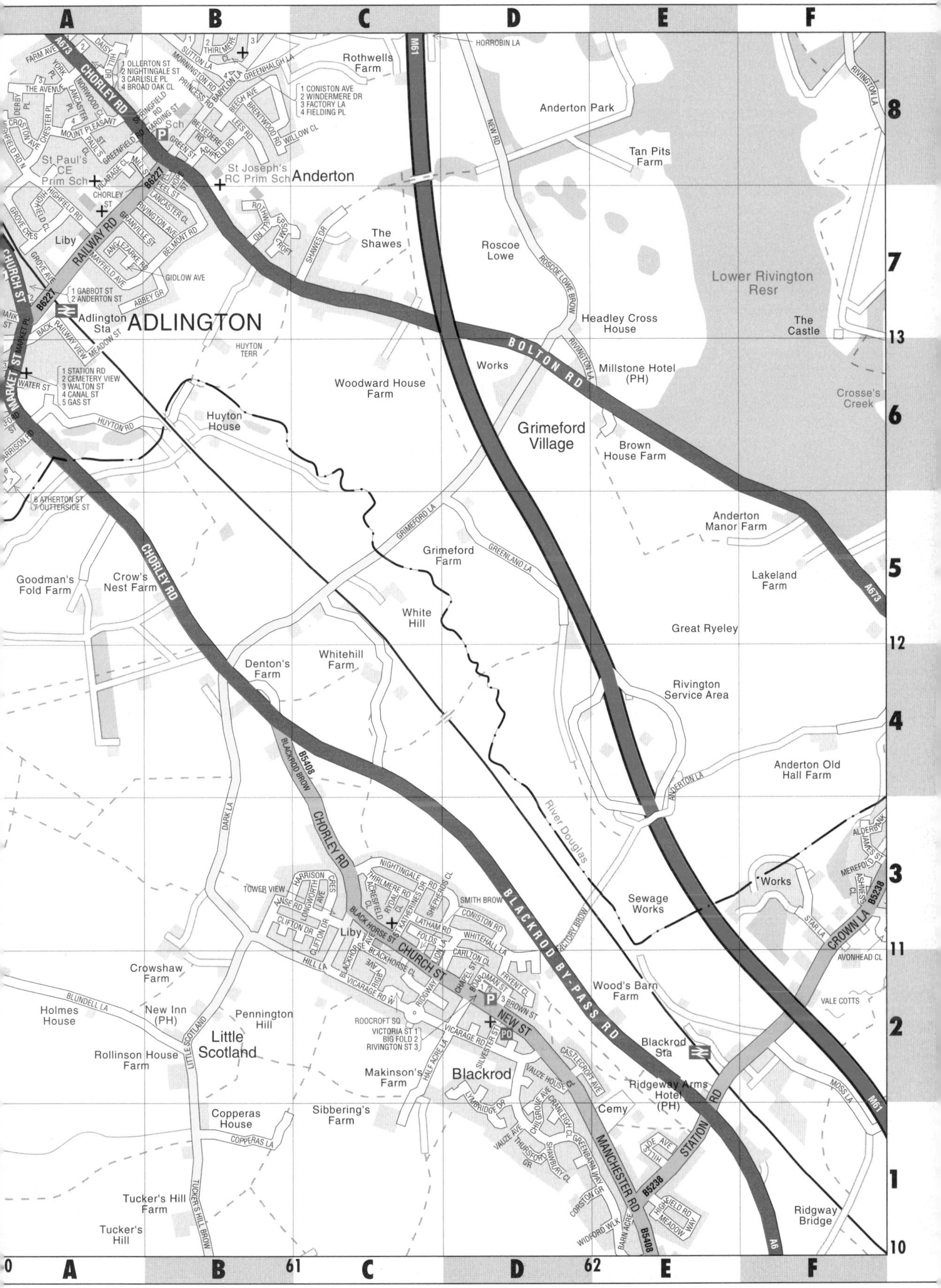

8

FARM AVE
DAISY ST
YORK
LANCASTER ST
MORWOOD CL
CHESTER PL
MOUNT PLEASANT
GREENFIELD RD
THE AVENUE
DERBY PL
HIGHFIELD RD
GROVE CRES
CHORLEY RD
SUTTON LA
THIRLMERE
MORNINGTON RD
PRINCESS RD
GREENHALGH LA
BELVEDERE
BEECH AVE
BRENTWOOD CL
WILLOW CL
ASHFIELD
GREEN'S ST
BABYLON LA
FIELDING RD
Sch

Rothwells Farm
M61
HORROBIN LA

1 CONISTON AVE
2 WINDERMERE DR
3 FACTORY LA
4 FIELDING PL

Anderton Park

St Paul's CE Prim Sch
St Joseph's RC Prim Sch
Anderton

Tan Pits Farm

Liby
CHORLEY
CHORLEY RD
RAILWAY RD
MILL
PEEL ST
LANCASTER CL
GRANVILLE ST
BELMONT RD
ANN CL
MAYFIELD AVE
ZARKE ST
GIDLOW AVE
ABBEY GR
ROTHWELL RD
KIRKSIDE
SHAWES DR

The Shawes

Roscoe Lowe
NEW RD
ROSCOE LOWE BROW

Lower Rivington Resr

CHURCH ST
B6227
Adlington Sta
ADLINGTON
HUYTON TERR

Headley Cross House
BOLTON RD
RIVINGTON LA

The Castle
13

1 GABBOT ST
2 ANDERTON ST

MARKET ST
WATER ST
HARRISON RD
HUYTON RD
Huyton House
BACK RAILWAY VIEW
MEADOW ST

Woodward House Farm

Works
Millstone Hotel (PH)

Crosse's Creek
6

1 STATION RD
2 CEMETERY VIEW
3 WALTON ST
4 CANAL ST
5 GAS ST

Grimeford Village

Brown House Farm

8 ATHERTON ST
7 OUTTERSIDE ST

CHORLEY RD

Anderton Manor Farm

A673
5

Goodman's Fold Farm
Crow's Nest Farm

GRIMEFORD LA
Grimeford Farm
GREENLAND LA

Lakeland Farm

Great Ryeley
12

White Hill

BLACKROD BROW
B5408

Denton's Farm
Whitehill Farm

Rivington Service Area

DARK LA

River Douglas

Anderton Old Hall Farm
4
ANDERTON LA

Works
ALDERBY
JAMES ST
ASHNESS
MEREFOLD
B5238
3

TOWER VIEW
HARRISON
NIGHTINGALE
THIRLMERE DR
KATHERINE'S
SHEPHERDS CL
SMITH BROW
CONISTON RD
WHITEHALL LA
Sewage Works

CHORLEY RD
CHESTERFIELD
LATHAM RD
CRES
VALSE ST
CLIFTON DR
BLACK HORSE LA
FOLDS RD
Liby
CHURCH ST
CARLTON RD
BROWN ST

CROWN LA

Crowshaw Farm
New Inn (PH)
Pennington Hill
BLACKHORSE AVE
BLACKROD BY-PASS RD
PORTSMOUTH BROW
Wood's Barn Farm

AVONHEAD CL
VALE COTTS
11

BLUNDELL LA
Holmes House
HILL LA
VICARAGE RD W
ROOCROFT SQ
VICTORIA ST 1
BIG FOLD 2
RIVINGTON ST 3
VICARAGE RD
ROWBOTHAM
RIGSBY
ADMAN ST
PRYOR CL
NEW ST
PO
P
CASTLECROFT AVE
Blackrod Sta

2
Little Scotland
LITTLE SCOTLAND
Rollinson House Farm

Makinson's Farm
Blackrod
VAUZE HOUSE LA
Ridgeway Arms Hotel (PH)
Cemy
STATION RD
MOSS LA
M61

Copperas House
COPPERAS LA
Sibbering's Farm
VAUZE AVE
THURSBY
SHAWBURY CL
CRANLEIGH CL
GREENBANK
HIGHRIDGE
RIDGE AVE
JADE AVE
HILL
HIGHFIELD RD
MEADOW WAY
B5238
MANCHESTER RD

Ridgway Bridge
1

Tucker's Hill Farm
TUCKER'S HILL BROW
CORSTON GR
BARN ACRE
WIDFORD WLK
B5408
A6

Tucker's Hill
10

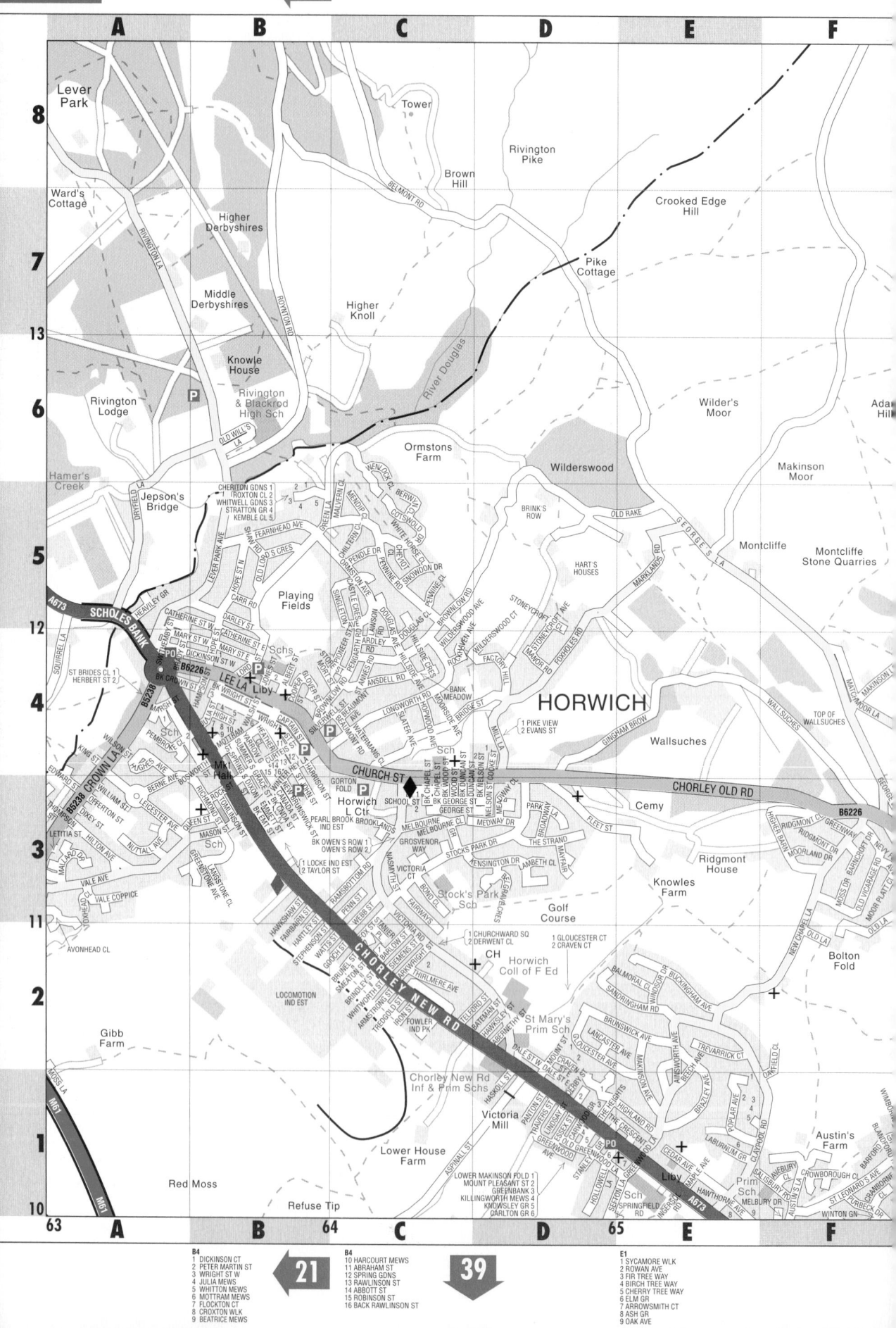

B4
1 DICKINSON CT
2 PETER MARTIN ST
3 WRIGHT ST W
4 JULIA MEWS
5 WHITTON MEWS
6 MOTTRAM MEWS
7 FLOCKTON CT
8 CROXTON WLK
9 BEATRICE MEWS

B4
10 HARCOURT MEWS
11 ABRAHAM ST
12 SPRING GDNS
13 RAWLINSON ST
14 ABBOTT ST
15 ROBINSON ST
16 BACK RAWLINSON ST

E1
1 SYCAMORE WLK
2 ROWAN AVE
3 FIR TREE WAY
4 BIRCH TREE WAY
5 CHERRY TREE WAY
6 ELM GR
7 ARROWSMITH CT
8 ASH GR
9 OAK AVE

A B C D E F

8

Smithills Moor

Whimberry Hill

7

Lomax Wifes
Farm

13

Holden's
Farm

Gilligant's
Farm

COAL PIT RD

Green Nook

Haslam's
Farm

Brown
Lowe

6

Sheep Cote Green
Farm

Chadwick's Close
Farm

Smithills Dean

Burnt Edge

Hampsons
Farm

NEW COLLIER'S
ROW

Cunliffe's
Farm

White
Brow

BURNT EDGE LA

Slack Hall

COLLIER'S
ROW

COLLIERS ROW RD

Higher
Tongs

Pendlebury's
Farm

5

Walker Fold

Walker Fold
Farm

LONGSHAW FORD RD

Lower Tongs

EDGE LA

12

Mast

Hole Hill
Farm

Little Dakins
Farm

Dakin's Brook

BARROW BRIDGE RD

P

4

MATCHMOOR LA

Fleet's Moor

Old Harts
Farm

WALKER FOLD RD

Old Links
Golf Course

Barrow
Bridge

BRN LEA TERR

FOURTH ST
FIFTH ST
THIRD ST
SECOND ST
FIRST ST
BAZLEY
BARROWDENE
HOUSE
RIVERS EDGE
CL

Horwich
Moor

Harpers

Harwood's
Farm

3

GEORGE'S

SHEPHERD'S DR

Ivy Model
Farm

Blundell Arms
(PH)

Yate Fold

Bob's Smithy Inn
(PH)

CH

WHALLEY AVE
CHATBURN RD
DUNSOP DR
LIGHTBOUNDS RD
WORSTON AVE
SLATER

Johnson
Fold Cty
Prim
Sch

BOTTOM O' TH' MOOR

OLD LA

CHORLEY OLD RD

MONTSERRAT BROW

ROMNEY RD

BOWLAND DR

MONTSERRAT RD
CHIPPING RD
GARGRAVE AVE

Johnson Fold A58

11

Bottom o' th' Moor

Green
Hill

Grundy
Fold

B6402

CRAVEN PL
PATTERSALL AVE
SHACKETON GR
GISBURN AVE
SABDEN AVE

LONGRIGG
CRES
OAKENCLOUGH
DR
SMITHILLS
DR

HARROWBY
RD

2

Colemans

Coal
Brow

Rants
Farm

Delph Hill

LYMSON FOLD DR
SABDEN AVE

PO

KNOTT
LA
MARLD CRCS
BEASDALE
MARLOW
MARLWOOD
RD

WODSLEY
RD

NEW CHURCH
RD

BK ARNOLD
TERR

B6226

Hawthorn
Plantation

DELPH HILL
DELPH HILL CRES

BOOT LA

MOSS BANK WAY

Doffcocker

DOFFCOCKER LA

MILLSTONE

1

Wilson Fold
Farm

High Rid
Resr

OLD KILN LA

Doffcocker Lodge

THORNBECK RD 1
THORNBECK DR 2
BK MARKLAND HILL LA 3
LEVI ST 4
BK MARKLAND HILL LA W 5
BK MARKLAND HILL LA E 6
BK CHORLEY OLD RD 7
HEXHAM AVE 8
BK CHORLEY OLD RD S 9

HEATON AVE

THORNTON
AVE

RIPON LA

INA AVE

CALDER

MARKLAND HILL

GREENMOUNT

BLANDFORD RISE

Fall
Birch

High Rid
Farm

HIGH RID LA

OLD HALL LA

Old
Hall

NEW HALL
MEWS

THE HIGHGROVE

B6402

A58

TOWNCROFT LA

OLD KILN LA

HEATON
MOUNT

Sch

LINGARCR

10

H

23
8

F6
1 BK PARK VIEW
2 PARK VIEW
3 PARK ROW
4 KELLETT ST
5 WRENBURY DR
6 BRAMLEY RD
7 CRUNDALE RD
8 ASHOVER CL
9 SHARPLES HALL
10 LAKENHEATH CL
F8
1 BK COX GREEN RD S
2 COX GREEN RD
3 BK COX GREEN RD N
4 BK KING ST N
5 KING ST
6 BK MILL ST N
7 BK MILL ST S
8 SMITH LA

23
41
For full street detail of the highlighted area see pages 142 and 143.

A B C D E F

8

7

13

6

5

12

4

3

11

2

1

10

72 73 74

Major labels:

Moss Hill Farm
Water Field
Brown Barn Farm
Inst of Islamic Higher Ed
Toppings
Eagley Inf Sch
Eagley Jun Sch
Bromley Cross
Toppings Gn
Harry Fold
Cromptons
Turton High Sch
Blake St
Bromley Cross Rd
Bromley Cross Sta
Top o' th' Knotts
Lower Knotts
Meadow Barn
Birtenshaw Farm
Birtenshaw Hall Sch
Top o' th' Brow
Old Gn
Side of the Moor
Hill Farm
St Maxentious Sch
Bradshaw Chapel
Harwood Lee
Sharples Sch
Sharples Prim Sch
Bank Top
Great Oak Farm
Bradshaw
Kershaw St
Cottage Croft
Moor Gate
Lee Gate
Liby
Longsight
Brook Fold
Harwood
Greenwoods La
Playing Field
Canon Slade Sch
Hall i' th' Wood
Eagley Brook
Longsight City Prim Sch
St Brendan's RC Prim Sch
Works
Mus
Bradshaw Brook
Longworths
Newbridge Gdns
Old Nursery Fold
Hawthorn Bank
Four Lane Ends
Harwood Vale
Hardy Mill Cty Prim Sch
Prospect Hill
Hall i' th' Wood Sta
Firwood Fold
Hillsdale Gr
Springwater Cl
Carlton Cl
High Mount
Brook Bank
Jolly Brows
Spinney Nook
Christ Church La
Sch
Castle Hill
Bewick St
Frogley St
Rowton St
Nesbit St
Colmore St
Ashwell St
Castle Hill
Elsinore St
Castle Hill Cty Prim Sch
Hartwell Cl
Firwood Sch
Christ Church CE Prim Sch
Earls
Withins Farm
Withins Sch
Withins Sports Ctr
Denvale Mills
Britannia Way
Glaisdale St
Castle Hill St
Furness Gr
Saddle St
Haverhill Gr
Wealostone Gr
Dalymount Cl
Connaught Sq
Top o' th' Brow
Top o' th' Brow Prim Sch
Works
Tonge Moor
River Tonge
Slater La
Ryefield St
Bk Ryefield St
Grassington Pl
Liby
Priory Pl
Fountains Ave
Thicketford Brow
Thicketford Brow
Bridson La
Red Lane Cty Prim Sch

42 26

Index B1:
1 APPLEBY GDNS
2 BARRINGTON WLK
3 WADRIDGE CL
4 NEWHAVEN WLK
5 TONBRIDGE PL
6 EMSWORTH CL
7 BRADWELL PL
8 ELSDON GDNS
9 SHORNBROOK WLK
10 HILLFIELD WLK
11 LANSDOWNE CL
12 LOWERWOOD LA
13 OLAF ST
14 BK OLAF ST
15 BK STONE ST
16 HORSA ST
17 BK HORSA ST N
18 EGHAM CT
19 BK BEACONSFIELD TERR
20 WELLING ST
21 SCOWCROFT ST
22 BK SCOWCROFT ST
23 ANGLE ST
24 GEORGE BARTON ST
25 BK GEORGE BARTON ST
26 HUNTROYDE AVE
27 HARWOOD GR
28 ECCLESTON AVE
29 WEMSLEY GR

Index F1:
1 MARDALE DR
2 MARDALE CL
3 HIGHWOOD CL
4 ENNERDALE AVE

25

10

A B C D E F

8 Affetside
Buckley Close Farm
Windmill Farm
Ferns
B6213
TURTON RD
Old Kays
Brook House Bridge
BROOK HOUSE CL 1
BROOKSIDE CRES 2
GREENSIDE DR 3
SHEPHERDS CL 4
Brookhouse Farm
SHEPHERD ST
Brookhouse Mill

Pack Horse Inn (PH)
Stormer Hill House
Recn Gd
HOLCOMBE RD
OSWESTRY CL
QUAKERS FIELD
MILL ST

7 Mum's Harris Farm
Meadowcroft Farm
Howarth's Farm
Stormer Hill Closes
CAIRN ST
WOODSTOCK DR
THORNFIELD RD
HIGH CL
CLAYBANK
ZLIFF AVE
PRIMROSE BANK
CRIMPOSE
VICTORIA ST
NORLEY ST
HARWOOD CRES
WESLEY ST
P P P
MARKET ST
BANK ST
CHAPEL ST
ROYDS ST
SHERWOOD ST
GREEN
OLD DOCTORS
LABURNUM CT
KIRKLEES CL
LABURNUM
BAR AVE
BURGUNDY DR
RHINE
AVALLON CL 1
PROSPECT CT 2

13 Hoyle's Fold
Old Ned's
HARWOOD WLK
WESLEY CT
SPRING VALE PL
SPRING CL
SPRING TERR
SPRING VALE RD
LAUREL ST
NEW ST
SOUTH ROYD ST
Tottington High Sch

Raikes
TOTTINGTON RD
White Paddock Farm
Gorsey Clough
Tottington
Hey Head
HILLTOP DR
SUNNY BOWER ST
RICHMOND CL
FIRST AVE
WELLBANK ST
MEADOW WAY
SANDBROOK
BURY RD B6213

6 Hill End Farm
Bowstone Hill
Isherwood's Farm
HARWOOD RD
Birchen Bower Farm
MOORSIDE RD
CROFT DR
BRAMMAY DR
HILDA AVE
Tottington South Cty Prim Sch
HESWALL
SOUTH LYNDON CL
KENYON WAY
BOOTH HALL
SYCAMORE

Castle Farm
Bowstone Hill Rd
Four Lane Ends
BRADSHAW RD
SHEEP GATE DR
COPTHORN WLK 1
GORSEY CLOUGH WLK 2
ACRESBROOK WLK 3
BIRCHEN BOWER WLK 4
WALSHAW WLK 5
BOOTH WAY
PRENTON WAY
ACRES ST
SCOBELL ST

5 Asmus Farm
The Height
Height Barn
Walshaw Hall
HOLTHOUSE RD
HESWALL DR
NESTON RD
MOOSE AVE
PARKGATE DR
UPTON WAY
CHURCH ST
COLLINS ST
PLEASANT
Christ Church (VA) Prim Sch
HIGHBAN H

12 Greenwoods La
Old Holts
High Crompton
HALL ST
HAWORTH ST
PENNINGTON CL
GRASSINGTON
GRANBY ST
WALSHAW BROOK CL
WALSHAW RD
SHARPLES DR

4 FAIRWAY AVE
Harwood Golf Course
BENTLEY HALL RD
Bentley Hall
Walshaw
Bentley Fold
BURTON AVE
SHORROCKS ST

BRAMHALL AVE
DAVENPORT AVE
GLEAVES AVE
BRIGHTFIELD
AIRE
PRIMROSE
LINKS RD
FELLSIDE
ROADING BROOK RD
CH
Higher Bury Meadows
SUDREN ST

B6196
HARDY MILL RD
DAVENPORT FOLD
PO
3 STITCH LANE
Nab Gate Farm
SHILLINGSTONE CL
Harwood Lodge
ARTHUR LA
Barrack Fold
Meadow Croft
GISBURN DR
BENTHAM CL
SLAIDBURN DR
STAINFORTH CL
BOWLAND
WRIGGLESWORTH CL
DOW FOLD

11 Arthur Lane Farm
Old Barn
SETTLE CL
WHITECROFT DR
CLITHEROE DR
KEIGHLEY
WHALLEY CL
WADDINGTON
MUTTON
LOWERFORD
HASLAM HEY CL

2 Resr
Knowsley
KNOWSLEY RD
Lowerbrook Cty Prim Sch
Starling
HARROGATE SQ 1
SELBY WLK 2
B6196 AINSWORTH RD
PLEASINGTON DR
WHITBY CT
PENDLE
SWANSEA CL
STARBECK
SWINSIDE CL
WHITBY CT
BELLINGHAM CL
SOWERBY
CHANTON
ASHINGTON

Resr
BARNSDALE CL 1
BROOKFIELD AVE 2
1 METCALF TERR
2 LAURIA TERR
3 CHURCHILL AVE
4 SALOMBE AVE
5 KINGSBRIDGE AVE
6 THURLESTONE AVE

1 Breightmet Golf Course
BURY OLD RD
Christ Church Ainsworth CE Prim Sch
WELL ST
Mill
Cockey Moor
COCKEY MOOR RD
CHORLEY
FULWOOD
BLACKROD CL
CLAYTON
STARLING RD
B6292
FRECKLETON
HAMBLETON
PREESALL CL
BISPHAM
BLACKROD

Red or Middle Brook Bridge
CH
Dearden Fold Farm
CHURCH ST
DELPH
PO
BRADLEY FOLD
DEVON DR
WOOD TERR
NEWMAN AVE
SUMNER AVE
MOORSIDE AVE

RED LA
10 SLUMBRIDGE CL
Red Bridge Inn (PH)
RED BRIDGE
Ainsworth
HASLAM HEY CL
AINSWORTH HALL RD
GREENSIDE LA
BANKFIELD
BROOMFIELD CL
Liby
ROSEDALE AVE
HARLEY AVE
THOMPSON AVE

75 A B 76 C D 77 E F

25

43

11
28

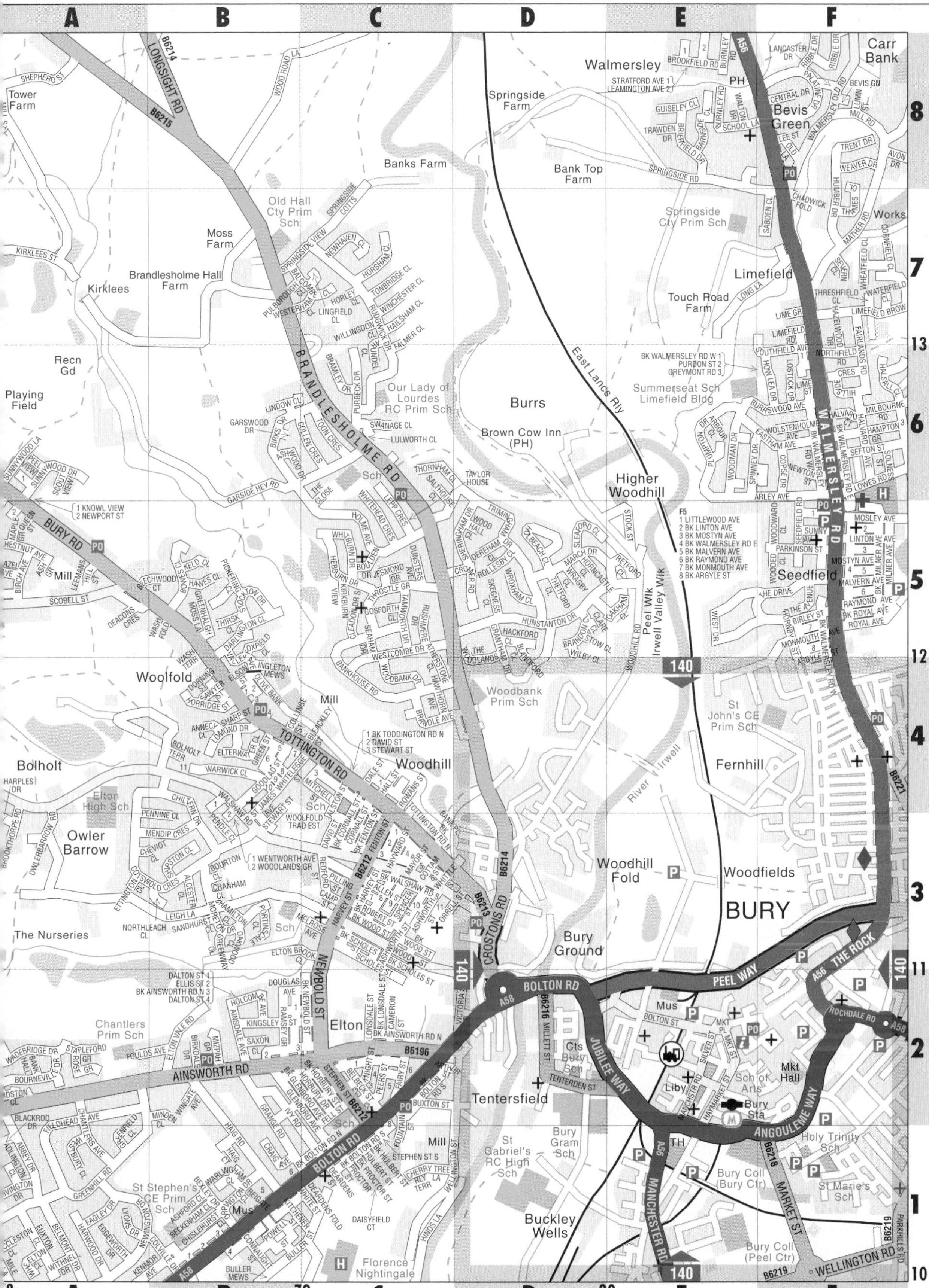

1
WOLSELEY ST
WARREN ST
LUTON ST
CHIRMSIDE ST
WELLINGTON SQ
WELLINGTON CT

1 WALMSLEY ST
2 BK OLIVE BANK

3 HILL'S CT
4 MILL LA
5 BK TOTTINGTON RD
6 BK GOODLAD ST
7 SMETHURST ST
8 BK BYROM ST
9 BYROM ST
10 BK BYROM ST S
11 BONHOLT IND EST

C2
1 BK AINSWORTH RD S
2 BK STEPHEN ST
3 BK BELBECK ST
4 BK KNIGHT ST
5 BK PEERS ST
6 DAISY ST
7 STEPHEN CL
8 BELBECK ST S

C3
1 BK TOTTINGTON RD S
2 BK HAYWARD ST
3 BK WALSHAW RD N
4 BK MAYOR ST
5 BK COTTAM ST
6 BK WHITTLE ST
7 HILLYARD ST
8 NEW GEORGE ST
9 BK NEW GEORGE ST
10 BK ASHWORTH ST
11 BOOTHFIELD

44
28
For full street detail of the highlighted area see page 140.

27
12

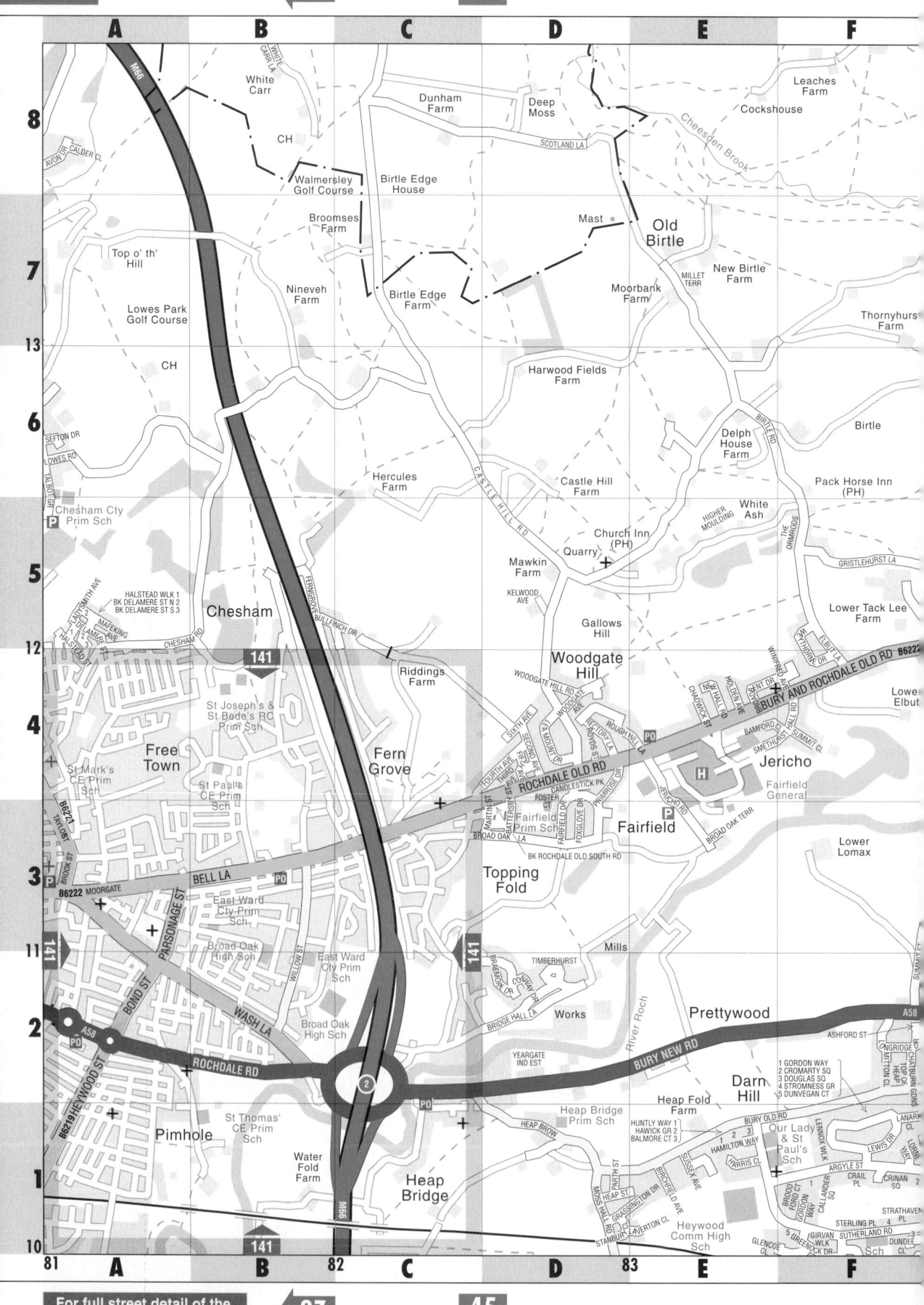
White Carr
Dunham Farm
Deep Moss
Leaches Farm
Cockshouse
Cheesden Brook
SCOTLAND LA
CH
Walmersley Golf Course
Birtle Edge House
Broomses Farm
Mast
Old Birtle
Top o' th' Hill
Nineveh Farm
Birtle Edge Farm
Moorbank Farm
New Birtle Farm
MILLET TERR
Lowes Park Golf Course
Thornyhurst Farm
Harwood Fields Farm
Birtle
Delph House Farm
BIRTLE RD
Hercules Farm
Castle Hill Farm
CASTLE HILL RD
Pack Horse Inn (PH)
Chesham Cty Prim Sch
White Ash
HIGHER MOULDING
THE ORMRODS
Church Inn (PH)
Quarry
Mawkin Farm
GRISTLEHURST LA
KELWOOD AVE
Chesham
Lower Tack Lee Farm
Gallows Hill
Woodgate Hill
Riddings Farm
CHESHAM RD
FERNGROVE
BULLFINCH DR
HALSTEAD WLK 1
BK DELAMERE ST N 2
BK DELAMERE ST S 3
MAFEKING AVE
DELAMERE ST
HALSTEAD ST
St Joseph's & St Bede's RC Prim Sch
Free Town
St Mark's CE Prim Sch
Fern Grove
St Paul's CE Prim Sch
BURY AND ROCHDALE OLD RD
B6222
Lower Elbut
Jericho
Fairfield General
ROCHDALE OLD RD
Fairfield Prim Sch
Fairfield
Lower Lomax
Topping Fold
BELL LA
MOORGATE
B6222
East Ward Cty Prim Sch
PARSONAGE ST
Broad Oak High Sch
East Ward Cty Prim Sch
Mills
TIMBERHURST
WASH LA
Works
Prettywood
River Roch
Broad Oak High Sch
BRIDGE HALL LA
ROCHDALE RD
A58
BURY NEW RD
YEARGATE IND EST
Darn Hill
Heap Fold Farm
Heap Bridge Prim Sch
St Thomas' CE Prim Sch
Pimhole
Water Fold Farm
Heap Bridge
Our Lady & St Paul's Sch
Heywood Comm High Sch
M66
141
For full street detail of the highlighted area see page 141.

27
45

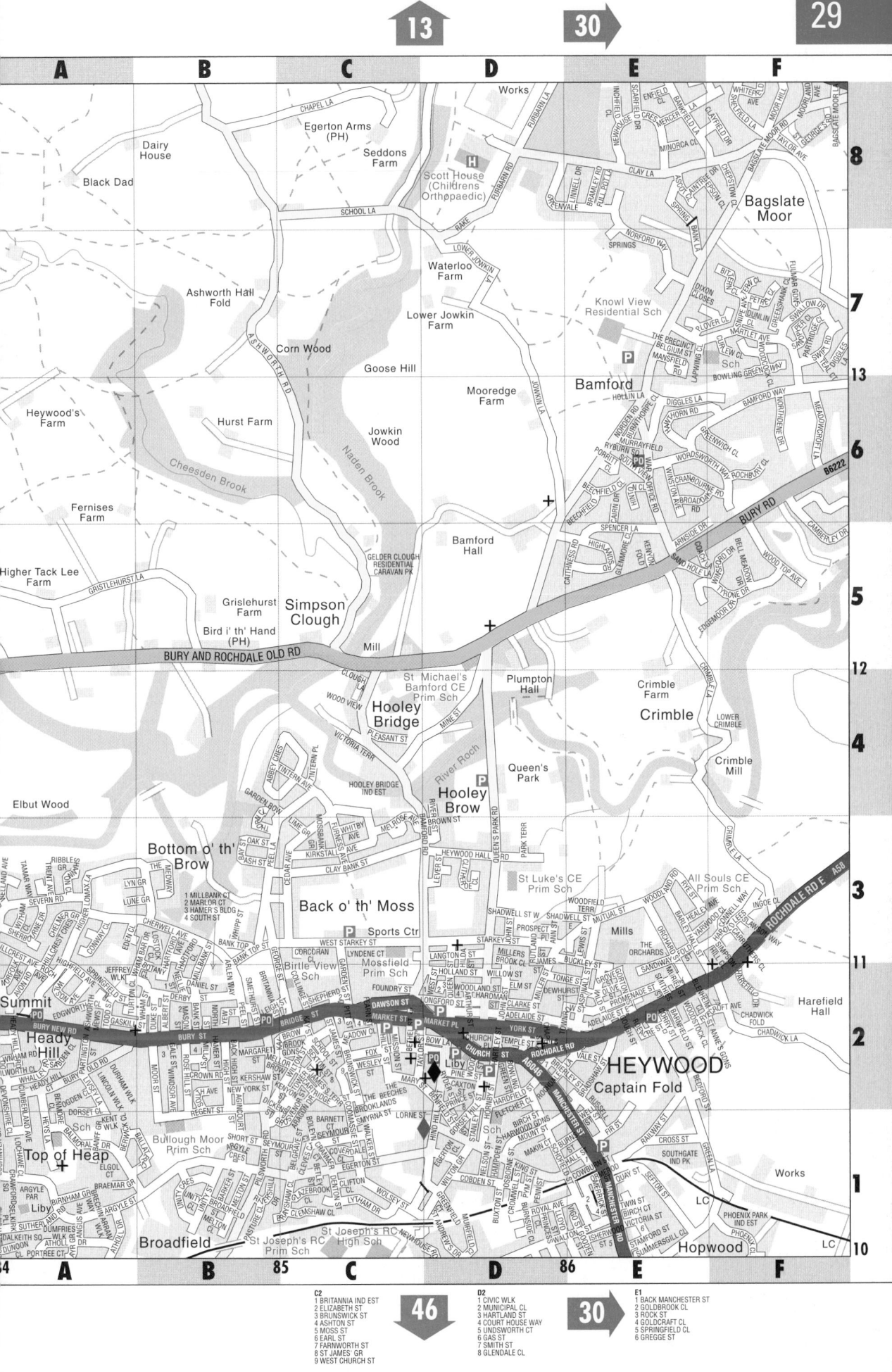
29
13
30
46
A
B
C
D
E
F
8
7
6
5
4
3
2
1
13
12
11
10
84
85
86
Works
Chapel La
Egerton Arms (PH)
Dairy House
Seddons Farm
Black Dad
Scott House (Childrens Orthopaedic)
School La
Clay La
Bagslate Moor
Springs
Norford Way
Waterloo Farm
Lower Jowkin La
Ashworth Hall Fold
Knowl View Residential Sch
Lower Jowkin Farm
Corn Wood
Ashworth Rd
Goose Hill
Bamford
Mooredge Farm
Heywood's Farm
Hurst Farm
Jowkin Wood
Jowkin La
Cheesden Brook
Naden Brook
Fernises Farm
Bury Rd
B6222
Bamford Hall
Gelder Clough Residential Caravan Pk
Higher Tack Lee Farm
Gristlehurst La
Grislehurst Farm
Simpson Clough
Bird i' th' Hand (PH)
Mill
Bury and Rochdale Old Rd
St Michael's Bamford CE Prim Sch
Plumpton Hall
Crimble Farm
Crimble
Hooley Bridge
Lower Crimble
Victoria Terr
Crimble Mill
River Roch
Queen's Park
Hooley Bridge Ind Est
Hooley Brow
Elbut Wood
Bottom o' th' Brow
Heywood Hall Rd
Queen's Park Rd
St Luke's CE Prim Sch
All Souls CE Prim Sch
Rochdale Rd E
A58
Back o' th' Moss
Sports Ctr
Mills
The Orchards
Birtle View Sch
Mossfield Prim Sch
Summit
Heady Hill
Bury New Rd
Bury St
Market Pl
Church St
Rochdale Rd
Harefield Hall
Chadwick Fold
Chadwick La
Liby
HEYWOOD
Captain Fold
Manchester Rd
A6046
Bullough Moor Prim Sch
Top of Heap
Sch
Southgate Ind Pk
Works
Phoenix Park Ind Est
Broadfield
St Joseph's RC Prim Sch
St Joseph's RC High Sch
Hopwood
LC
1 MILLBANK CT
2 MARLOR CT
3 HAMER'S BLDG
4 SOUTH ST
C2
1 BRITANNIA IND EST
2 ELIZABETH ST
3 BRUNSWICK ST
4 ASHTON ST
5 MOSS ST
6 EARL ST
7 FARNWORTH ST
8 ST JAMES' GR
9 WEST CHURCH ST
D2
1 CIVIC WLK
2 MUNICIPAL CL
3 HARTLAND ST
4 COURT HOUSE WAY
5 UNDSWORTH CT
6 GAS ST
7 SMITH ST
8 GLENDALE CL
E1
1 BACK MANCHESTER ST
2 GOLDBROOK CL
3 ROCK ST
4 GOLDCRAFT CL
5 SPRINGFIELD CL
6 GREGGE ST

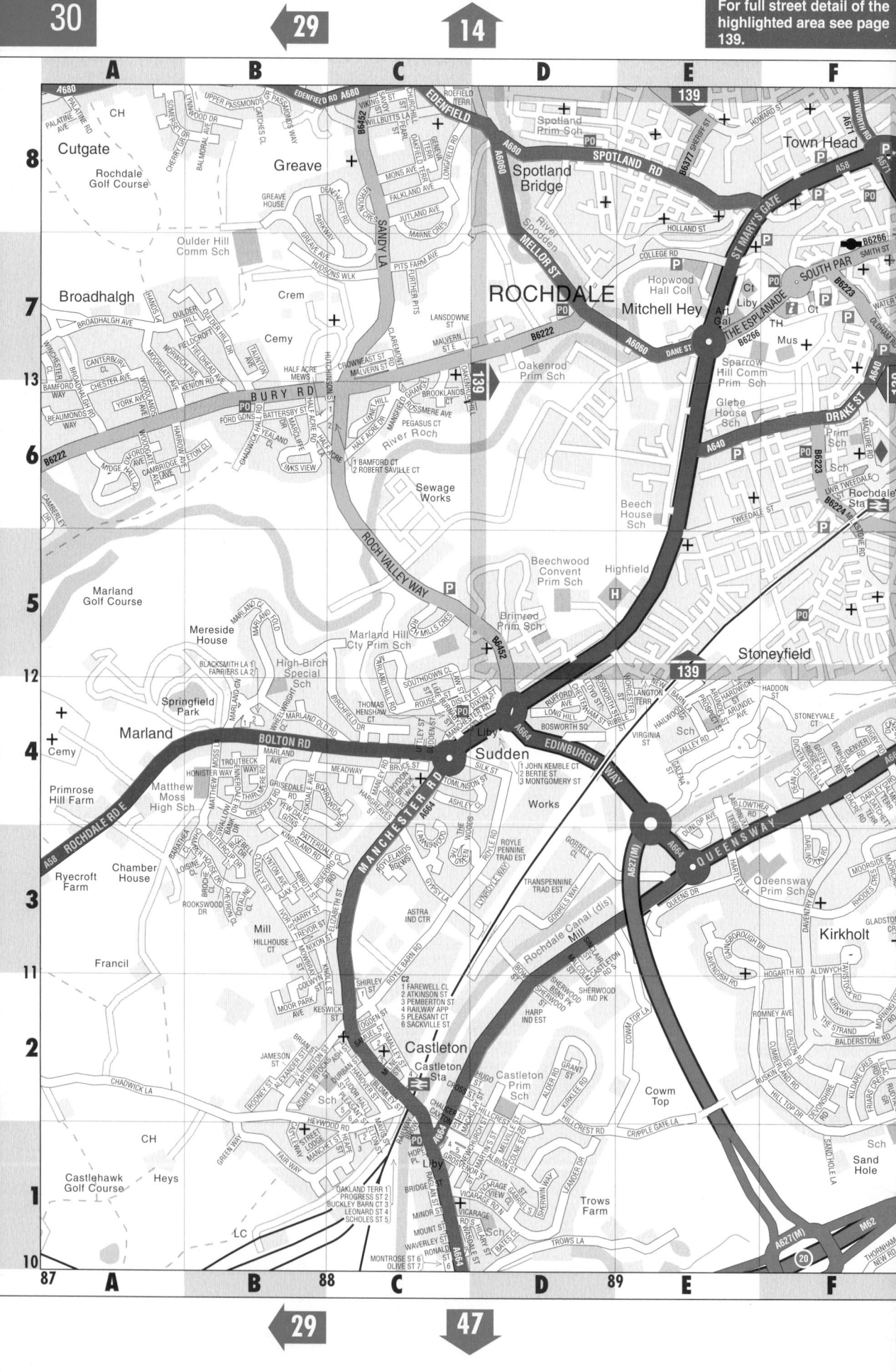

31
A8
1 WATTS ST
2 REGENT ST
3 LISLE ST
4 FLANNEL ST
5 JAMES ST
6 BRITON ST
7 BACK BRADSHAW ST
8 THOMAS ST
9 BRADSHAW ST
10 JACK McCANN CT
11 SOUTH PL
12 BUCKINGHAM ST
13 WELLINGTON PL
14 KITCHEN ST
15 ROBERT ST
16 CROOK ST
17 GARDEN LA
18 BAILLIE ST E
19 RAMSAY TERR
20 COPENHAGEN SQ
B6
1 SHEPHERD CT
2 GUINNESS HOUSE
3 ST JOHN'S DR
4 ST JOHN'S CT
5 VAVASOUR CT
6 JAMES BUTTERWORTH CT
7 SYKES ST
8 SKYES CT
9 JAMES BUTTERWORTH ST
10 SARAH BUTTERWORTH ST
11 SARAH BUTTERWORTH CT
12 CLARA GORTON CT
13 CLEMENT CT
15
B6
14 GRAFTON CT
15 CHANNING CT
16 ROWLAND ST
17 ROWLAND CT
18 LAUREL CT
19 IVEAGH CT
32
B6
20 WINDMILL ST
21 WINDMILL CT
22 OULDFIELD CL
23 MORNINGSIDE CL
24 LYEFIELD WLK
25 CHANNING SQ
26 Mc NAUGHT ST
A B C D E F
8
7
13
6
5
12
4
3
11
2
1
10
90 91 92
Newbold Brow
Belfield Prim Sch
L Ctr
Belfield
Mill
Newbold
Plumb House
Wild House
Croft Head Farm
Works
Firgrove
Sacred Heart RC Prim Sch
Ind Est
Lower Moss Side Farm
Moss Side Farm
Dixon Green
The Kingsway (PH)
Spring Hill High Sch
MILNROW
Milnrow Sta
Lower Lane Farm
Lady House
Lowerplace Cty Prim Sch
Lower Place
Mayfields Farm
Fenns
Turf Hill
Castle Farm
Near Moor Bank Farm
Ellenrod Farm
Spring Inn (PH)
Liby
Balderstone Comm High Sch
Buersil
Springhill Hospice
Green Gate
Broad Shaw
Garside Farm
Dig Gate Farm
Balderstone
Dean Farm
Chadwick Fold
Pleasant View
Old Barn Farm
The Fairview Inn (PH)
Bryney Heyes Farm
Hill Top Cty Prim Sch
St Cuthbert's RC High Sch
Oldham Way Crompton Circuit
Buersil Head
Gerrard Hey Farm
Burnedge
Greenhill Farm
Fentons Farm
KINGSWAY
ROCHDALE RD
MILNROW RD
OLDHAM RD
ELIZABETHAN WAY
QUEENSWAY
BROAD LA
NEW BROAD LA
ALBERT ROYDS ST
MOLESWORTH ST
DURHAM ST
M62
A4
1 WINBY ST
2 WILLIAM HENRY ST
3 SUTCLIFFES PL
4 WHEATHILL ST
5 WAREINGS YD
6 MARCROFT PL
7 CALF HEY N
8 CALF HEY S
9 MAY PL
10 CHAPEL ST
11 FIELD ST
12 BURLINGTON ST
13 HARVARD ST
14 ARGYLE ST
15 LOWER ST
A5
1 TENNYSON ST
2 LETCHWORTH AVE
3 ANNE LINE CL
4 GORREL ST
5 WELLFIELD PL
6 WELL ST
7 CLIFTON ST
8 HEALING ST
9 GORDON ST
10 ALBANY ST
11 NEW BARN ST
12 SOUTH TERRACE CT
13 CROWN GDNS
14 OXFORD PL
15 BACK ROYDS ST
16 ROYDS PL
17 BRIGHT ST
18 VINCENT ST
19 HEREFORD ST
20 FALMOUTH ST
A6
1 HALFPENNY BRIDGE IND EST
2 LINCOLN CLOSE IND EST
48
A6
3 EQUITABLE ST
4 PIONEERS ST
5 SARAH ST
32

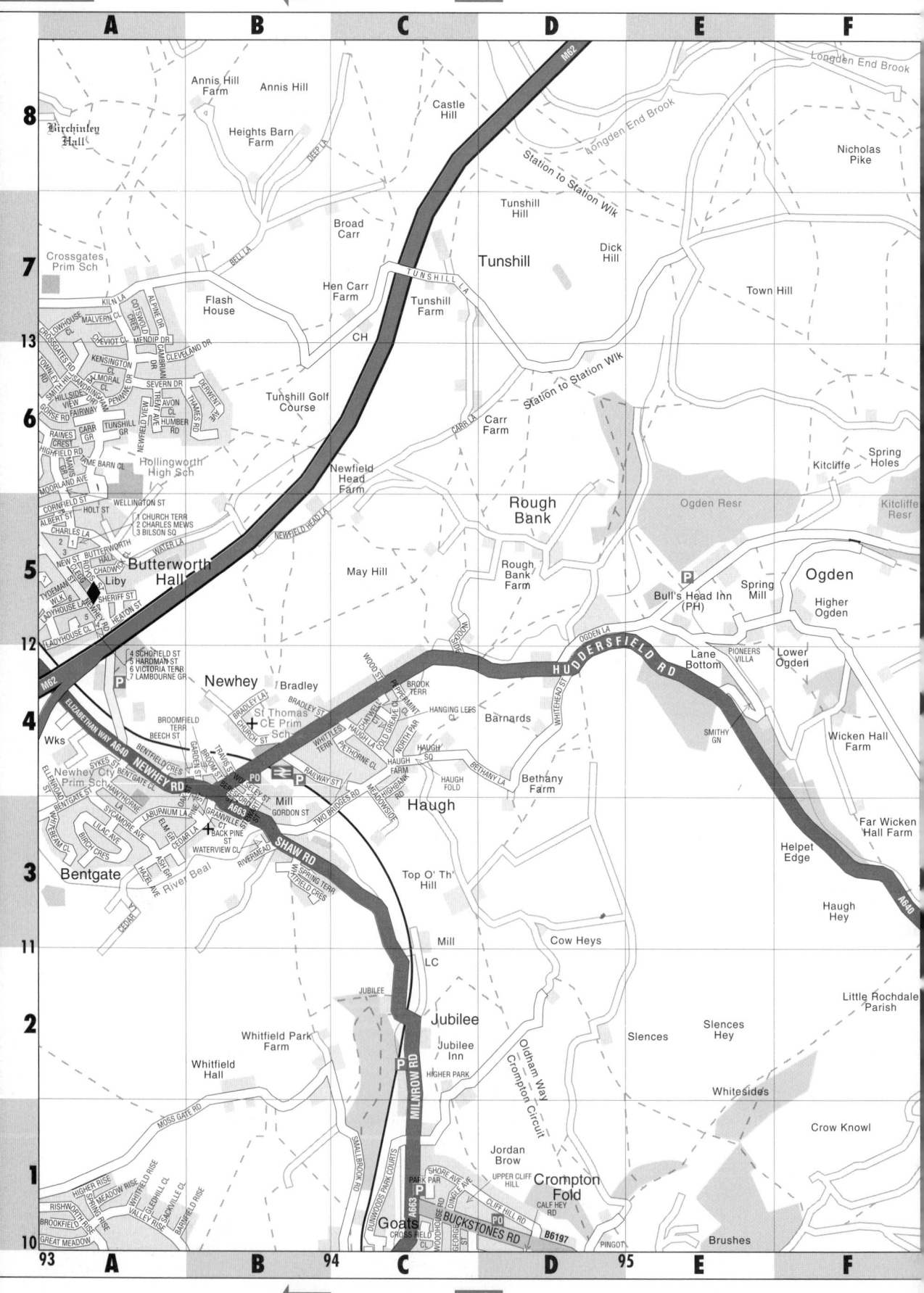

A   B   C   D   E   F

Longden End Brook

8   Birchinley Hall

Annis Hill Farm   Annis Hill

Castle Hill

Heights Barn Farm

DEEP LA

Nicholas Pike

Station to Station Wlk

7   Crossgates Prim Sch

Broad Carr

Tunshill Hill

Dick Hill

Town Hill

BELL LA

KILN LA

Flash House

Hen Carr Farm

Tunshill

13   COWHOUSE
CROSSGATES ST
TOWN LA   MALVERN CL
CLEVELAND DR
MENDIP DR   CAMBRIAN DR   DERWENT DR
CHEVIOT CL   ALPINE DR   COTSWOLD CRES
KENSINGTON CL   PENNINE DR
BALMORAL DR   CAMBRIAN DR
SEVERN DR

CH

TUNSHILL LA

Tunshill Farm

6   SMITH HILL
HILLSIDE VIEW   FAIRWAY
GORSE RD
RAINES CREST   CARR GR
TUNSHILL GR
HIGHFIELD RD   ACRE BARN CL
MOORLAND AVE   AVON CL   HUMBER RD
NEWFIELD VIEW   TRENT AVE   THAMES AVE

Tunshill Golf Course

CARR LA

Carr Farm

Spring Holes

Kitcliffe

Ogden Resr

Kitcliffe Resr

CORNFIELD ST
ALBERT ST   HOLT ST   WELLINGTON ST

Newfield Head Farm

NEWFIELD HEAD LA

Rough Bank

5   CHARLES LA
NEW ST   BUTTERWORTH HALL
WILKS ST   CHADWICK ST
TYObeam   Liby   SHERIFF ST
LADYHOUSE LA   SEATON CL

Butterworth Hall

May Hill

Rough Bank Farm

P Bull's Head Inn (PH)

Spring Mill   Ogden

Higher Ogden

Lower Ogden

LADYHOUSE CL

12

M62

4   Wks
ELIZABETHAN WAY A640
Newhey City Prim Sch
ELLENROAD ST   HAWTHORNE LA   BENTGATE ST   NEWHEY RD

4 SCHOFIELD ST
5 HARDMAN ST
6 VICTORIA TERR
7 LAMBOURNE GR

P

Newhey

BROOMFIELD TERR
BEECH ST
BROOMFIELD CRES
GRAVES ST   TRAVIS ST

Bradley
BRADLEY LA   BRADLEY ST
St Thomas CE Prim Sch   CHURCH ST
WHITLEY TERR
PIETHORNE CL   WOOD ST
PEPPERMINT
COLD GREAVE CL   BROOK TERR

Hanging Lees CL

Barnards

WHITEHEAD ST   OGDEN LA

HUDDERSFIELD RD

Lane Bottom   PIONEERS VILLA

SMITHY GN

Wicken Hall Farm

3   BENTGATE ST
SYCAMORE AVE   LABURNUM LA
BIRCH CRES   LILAC AVE   ELM ST   GRANVILLE SQ
HAZEL AVE   ASH GR   CEDAR LA   BACK PINE ST
WATERVIEW CL
CEDAR LA

Mill   Gordon St
WOODEARD ST   RAILWAY ST
A663   NEWHEY RD

SHAW RD

Riverhead   SPRING TERR   WHITFIELD CRES

Top O' Th' Hill

HAUGH SQ   NORTH PAR
HAUGH FARM
HAUGHBANK   HIGHBANK
MEADOWSIDE
HAUGH FOLD

Haugh

BETHANY LA   Bethany Farm

Far Wicken Hall Farm

Helpet Edge

A640

Bentgate   CEDAR ST

River Beal

Mill   LC

Cow Heys

Haugh Hey

11

2   Whitfield Park Farm
Whitfield Hall

JUBILEE

Jubilee

Jubilee Inn

Higher Park

MILNROW RD

Oldham Way   Crompton Circuit

Slences

Slences Hey

Little Rochdale Parish

Whitesides

Crow Knowl

MOSS GATE RD

1   Higher Rise   MEADOW RISE   WHITFIELD CL   GLEDHILL CL
RISHWORTH ST   BANKFIELD RISE
BROOKFIELD ST   VALLEY RISE
GREAT MEADOW

SMALLBROOK RD

DUNWOODS PARK COURTS

PARK PAR   SHORE AVE
A663   DINGLE AVE
George st   CLIFF HILL RD

Goats   Cross Field
WOODHOUSE RD   BUCKSTONES RD
B6197

Jordan Brow

UPPER CLIFF HILL

Crompton Fold   CALF HEY RD

PINGOT

Brushes

10

93   A   B   94   C   D   95   E   F

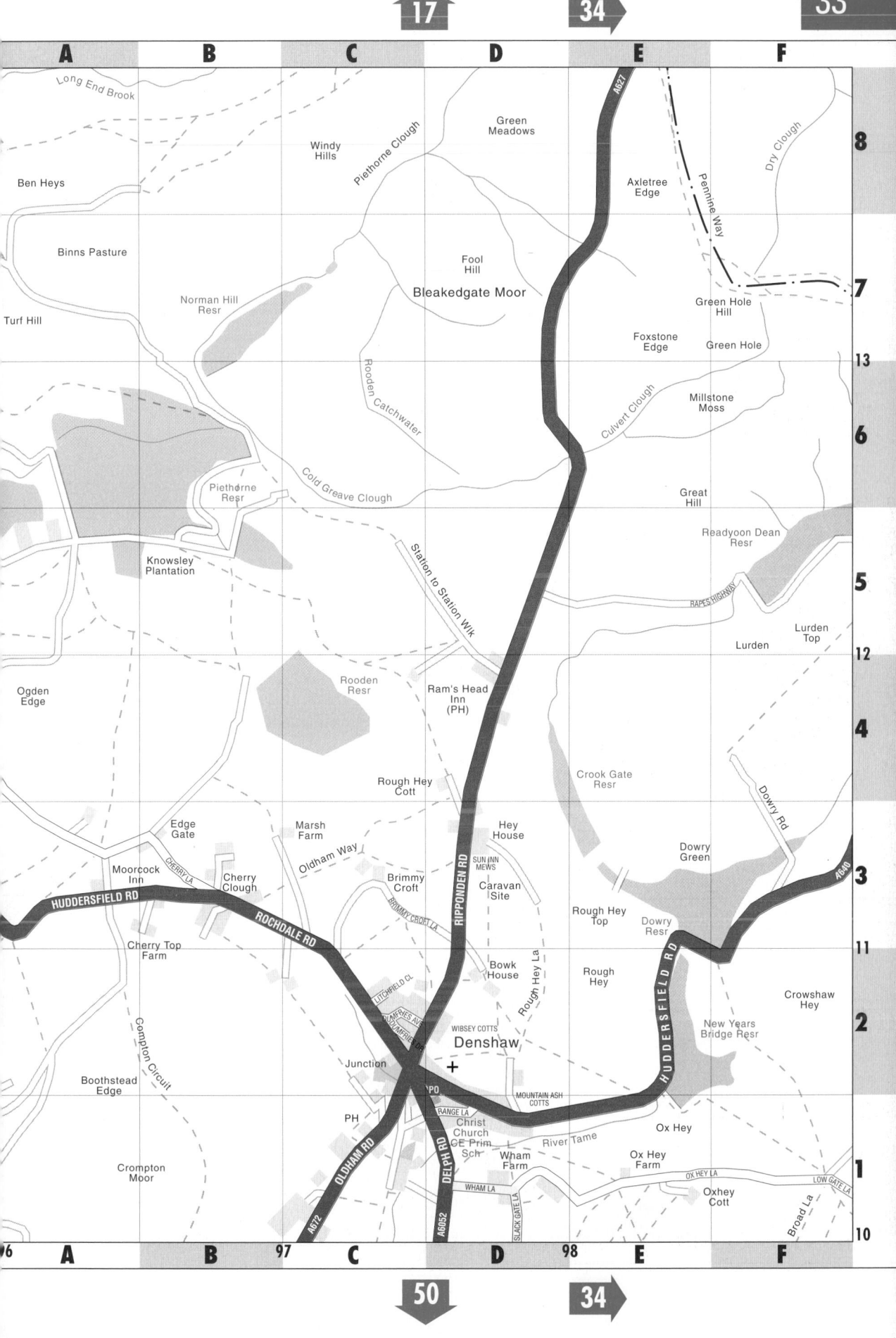

17
34
50
34
A
B
C
D
E
F
8
7
13
6
5
12
4
3
11
2
1
10
96
97
98
Long End Brook
Ben Heys
Binns Pasture
Turf Hill
Windy Hills
Piethorne Clough
Green Meadows
Axletree Edge
Pennine Way
Dry Clough
Fool Hill
Bleakedgate Moor
Norman Hill Resr
Green Hole Hill
Foxstone Edge
Green Hole
Rooden Catchwater
Culvert Clough
Millstone Moss
Piethorne Resr
Cold Greave Clough
Great Hill
Readyoon Dean Resr
Knowsley Plantation
Station to Station Wlk
RAPES HIGHWAY
Lurden
Lurden Top
Ogden Edge
Rooden Resr
Ram's Head Inn (PH)
Crook Gate Resr
Rough Hey Cott
Dowry Rd
Edge Gate
Marsh Farm
Hey House
Dowry Green
Moorcock Inn
CHERRY LA
Cherry Clough
Oldham Way
SUN INN MEWS
Brimmy Croft
Caravan Site
HUDDERSFIELD RD
ROCHDALE RD
RIPPONDEN RD
BRIMMY CROFT LA
Rough Hey Top
Dowry Resr
A640
A627
Cherry Top Farm
Bowk House
Rough Hey La
Rough Hey
Crowshaw Hey
LITCHFIELD CL
DUMFRIES AVE
DUMFRIES DR
WIBSEY COTTS
Denshaw
Compton Circuit
New Years Bridge Resr
Junction
Boothstead Edge
PO
MOUNTAIN ASH COTTS
RANGE LA
PH
Christ Church CE Prim Sch
River Tame
Ox Hey
Ox Hey Farm
OX HEY LA
Crompton Moor
OLDHAM RD
DELPH RD
Wham Farm
WHAM LA
Oxhey Cott
LOW GATE LA
Broad La
A672
A6052
SLACK GATE LA

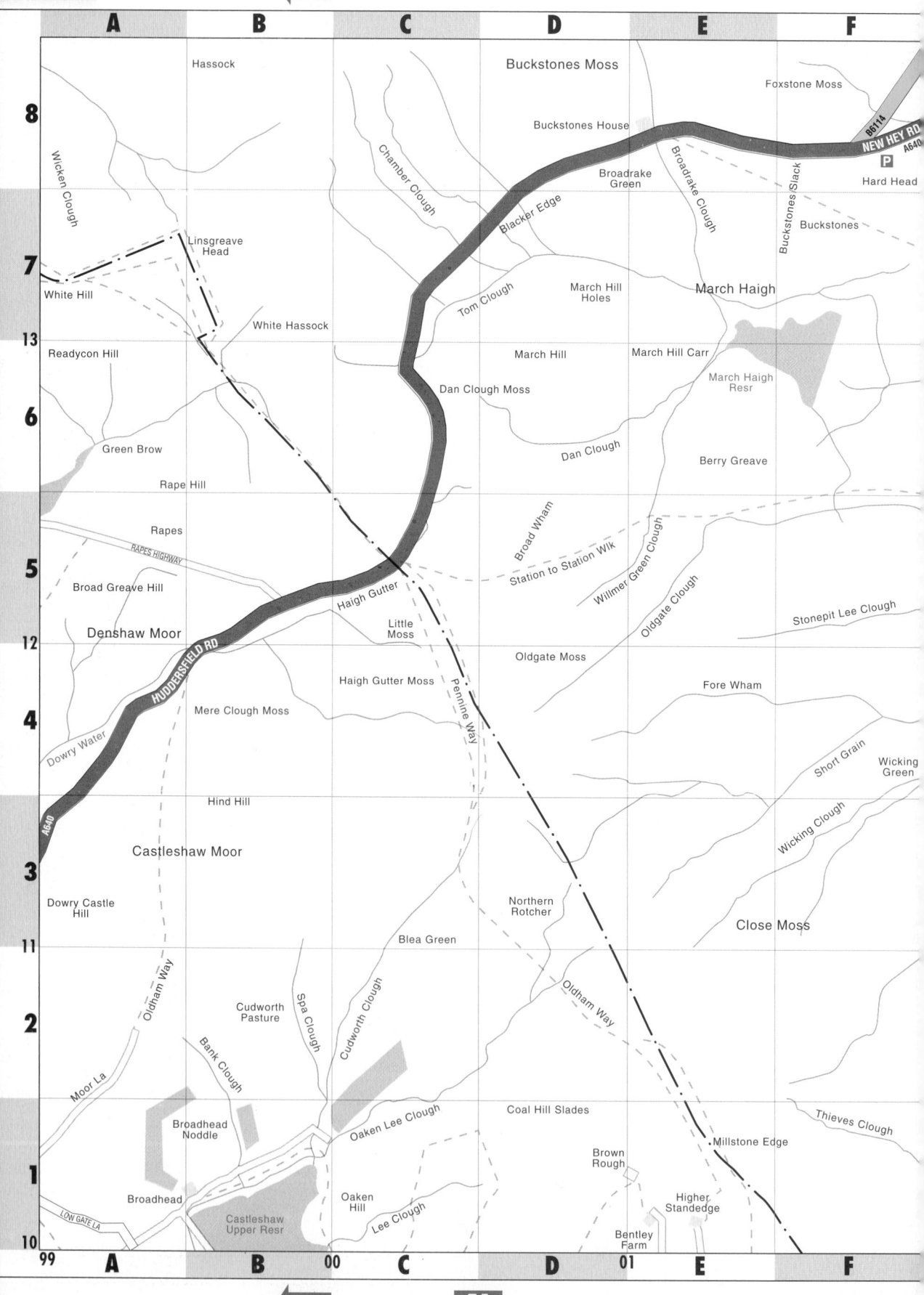

8

7

13

6

5

12

4

3

11

2

1

10

Hassock

Buckstones Moss

Foxstone Moss

Buckstones House

Broadrake Green

Chamber Clough

Blacker Edge

Broadrake Clough

B6114

NEW HEY RD

A640

Hard Head

Buckstones Slack

Buckstones

Wicken Clough

Linsgreave Head

White Hill

White Hassock

Tom Clough

March Hill Holes

March Haigh

March Hill Carr

Readycon Hill

March Hill

March Haigh Resr

Dan Clough Moss

Green Brow

Dan Clough

Berry Greave

Rape Hill

Broad Wham

Rapes

RAPES HIGHWAY

Station to Station Wlk

Willmer Green Clough

Oldgate Clough

Stonepit Lee Clough

Broad Greave Hill

Haigh Gutter

Denshaw Moor

Little Moss

Oldgate Moss

Fore Wham

HUDDERSFIELD RD

Haigh Gutter Moss

Pennine Way

Mere Clough Moss

Dowry Water

Short Grain

Wicking Green

Hind Hill

Wicking Clough

A640

Castleshaw Moor

Northern Rotcher

Close Moss

Dowry Castle Hill

Blea Green

Oldham Way

Cudworth Pasture

Spa Clough

Cudworth Clough

Coal Hill Slades

Thieves Clough

Moor La

Oldham Way

Bank Clough

Oaken Lee Clough

Brown Rough

Millstone Edge

Broadhead Noddle

Oaken Hill

Higher Standedge

Broadhead

LOW GATE LA

Castleshaw Upper Resr

Lee Clough

Bentley Farm

18
36

A
B
C
D
E
F
Appley Bridge
Shevington Vale
Refuse Tip
East Quarry
Appley Bridge Sta
The Railway (PH)
The Inn Between (PH)
Martin's Farm
Halliwell Farm
Douglas Bank Farm
Holland Lees
Quarry
Hullet Hole Wood
Shevington Vale Prim Sch
Calico Wood Farm
Shevington Prim Sch
Broadridings Farm
Forest Fold Farm
CH
Ayrefield Farm
Coppice Bank Wood
Gathurst Golf Course
Lees Wood
Green Alley Wood
Bank Top
Ayrefield House
Star Inn (PH)
Roby Mill
Walthew Green
Roby Mill CE Prim Sch
Cemy
Gathurst
Golf Course
Fox Inn (PH)
Walthew Green Farm
Johnson's Farm
Convent
Pearson's Farm
Dean Wood
The Kingfisher (PH)
Quarry (dis)
Rough Park Wood
Walthew Park
St Joseph's Con Ctr
Collage Farm
Jollies i'th Dean
Orrell House Farm
St John Rigby RC Coll
St Teresa's RC Prim Sch
Golf Course
River Douglas
Leeds & Liverpool Canal
Dean Brook
M6
B5375
B5206
SKULL HOUSE LA
MILES LA
NEW MILES LA
GATHURST RD
APPLEY LA N
APPLEY LA S
BANK BROW
BANK RD
AYREFIELD LA
ROBY MILL
FARLEY LA
SCHOOL LA
WHITLEY RD
LAFFORD LA
STONEY BROW
COLLEGE RD
LEES LA
STONE HALL LA
LONG HEYS LA
BACK LA
MILL LA
HART'S LA
CANAL BANK
SPEAKMANS DR
HEYES ST
TAN PIT COTTS
ST GABRIEL CL
SPRING RD
HOUGHTON LA
8
7
6
5
4
3
2
1
09
08
07
06
51
52
53

53
36

35
19

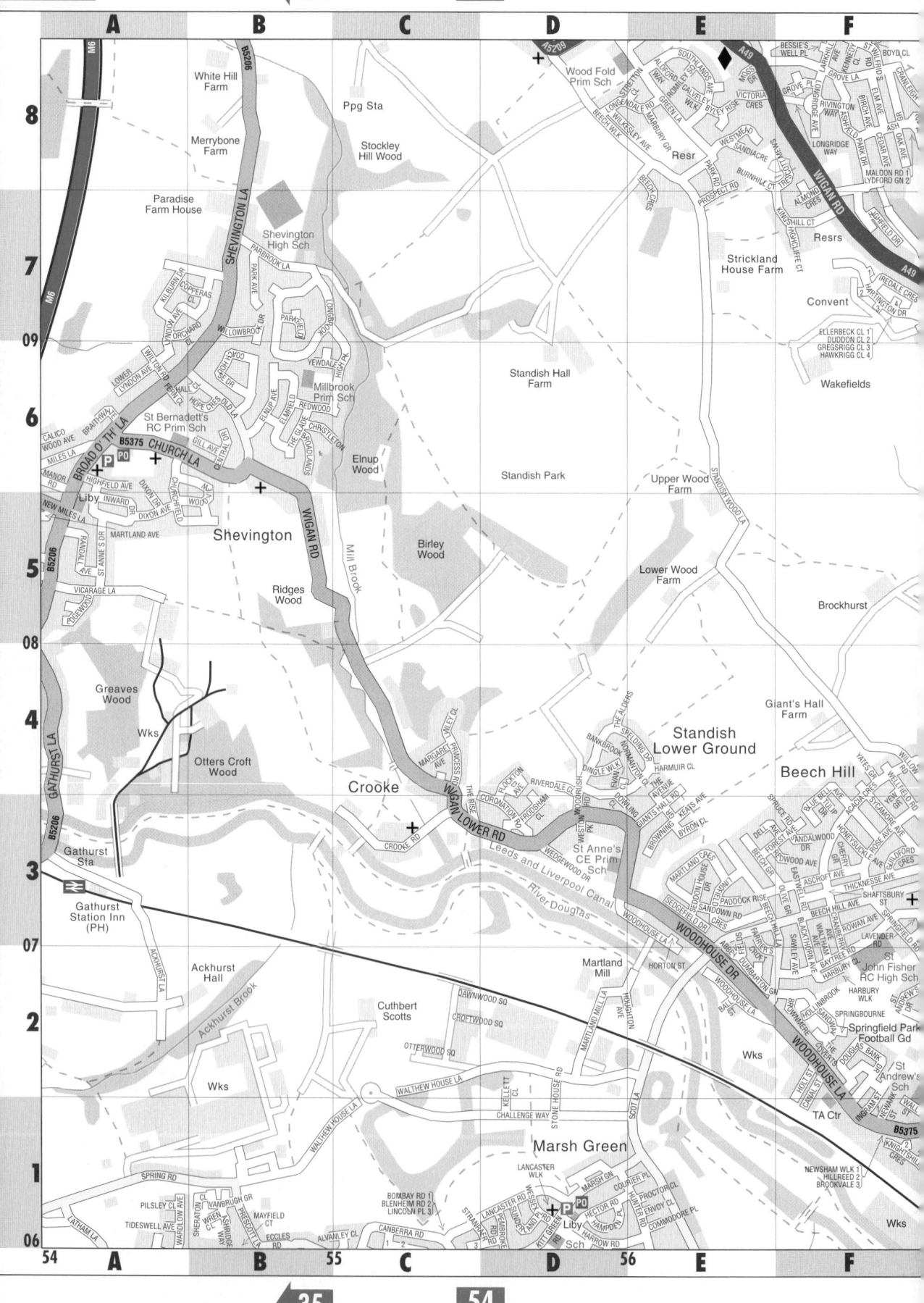
A
B
C
D
E
F
8
7
09
6
5
08
4
3
07
2
1
06
54
55
56
White Hill Farm
Merrybone Farm
Paradise Farm House
Ppg Sta
Stockley Hill Wood
Wood Fold Prim Sch
Resr
Resrs
Shevington High Sch
Strickland House Farm
Convent
Wakefields
Millbrook Prim Sch
St Bernadett's RC Prim Sch
Standish Hall Farm
Elnup Wood
Standish Park
Upper Wood Farm
Liby
Shevington
Birley Wood
Mill Brook
Ridges Wood
Lower Wood Farm
Brockhurst
Greaves Wood
Wks
Otters Croft Wood
Giant's Hall Farm
Standish Lower Ground
Beech Hill
Crooke
Gathurst Sta
Gathurst Station Inn (PH)
St Anne's CE Prim Sch
Leeds and Liverpool Canal
River Douglas
Martland Mill
St John Fisher RC High Sch
Ackhurst Hall
Ackhurst Brook
Cuthbert Scotts
Springfield Park Football Gd
St Andrew's Sch
TA Ctr
Marsh Green
Sch
SHEVINGTON LA
B5206
B5375 CHURCH LA
BROAD O' TH' LA
GATHURST LA
WIGAN RD
WIGAN LOWER RD
WOODHOUSE DR
WOODHOUSE LA
STANDISH WOOD LA
A49
A5209
M6

35
54

A B C D E F

8
09
6
5
08
4
07
3
2
1
06

57 A 58 B C 59 D E F

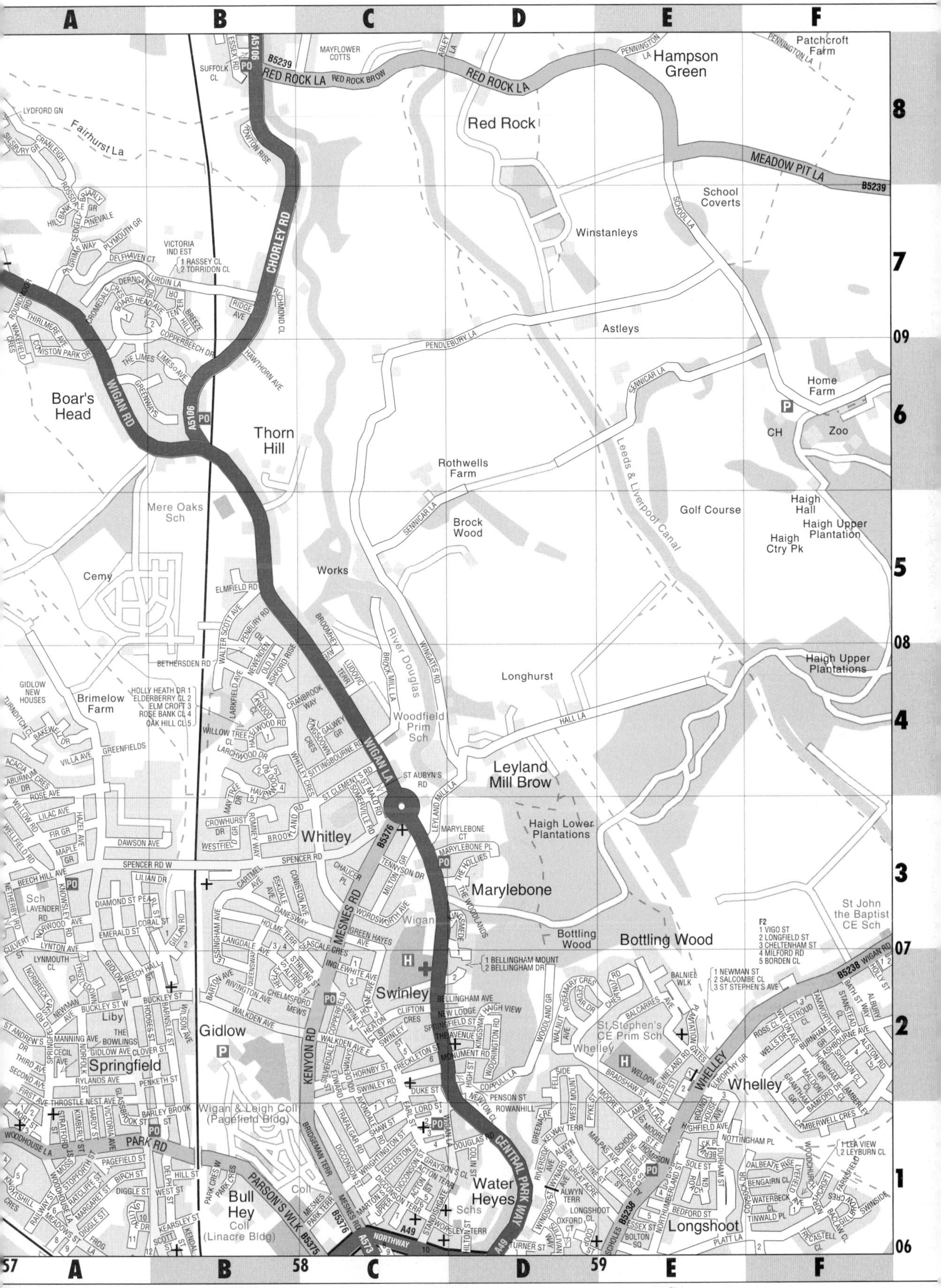

A1
1 HEARDMAN AVE
2 WHITESIDE AVE
3 WATERLOO ST
4 BROOKVALE
5 HEDGEMEAD
6 FOSTER ST
7 PAGEFIELD CL
8 BERESFORD ST
9 GORMAN ST
10 NIGHTINGALE CT
11 FALCONWOOD CL
12 LOWER ST STEPHEN ST

B3
1 RIPON AVE
2 PATELEY SQ
3 YEWDALE CRES
4 MONTON MEWS

C1
1 SANDYCROFT AVE
2 CHARLES ST
3 SCARISBRICK ST
4 CLIFTON ST
5 LITTLE LONDON
6 DICCONSON CRES
7 BRICK KILN LA
8 BK MESNES ST
9 MESNES TERR
10 POWELL ST

C2
1 INGLEWHITE CRES
2 INGLEWHITE PL
3 WARNFORD ST
4 EVEREST PL
5 ASHLAND AVE
6 MONUMENT MANSIONS
7 ST MICHAEL'S CT

E1
1 SALMON ST
2 CUMBERLAND ST
3 WESTMOORLAND ST
4 PERCH ST
5 WINDERMERE ST
6 WRIGHT ST
7 SEDWYN ST

37 21

A B C D E F
8 7 09 6 5 08 4 3 07 2 1 06
60 61 62
Nightingale's Farm
Willoughby Farm
Harts
MEADOW PIT LA
B5239
RILEY LA
HILL BROW
TUCKERS
TODDINGTON LA
Toddingtons
Freezeland Farm
Haigh & Aspull (St David's) CE Prim Sch
Haighlands
HAIGH RD
Haigh
COPPERAS LA
SCHOOL LA
Windmill
CHURCH ST
HENLEY ST
VICTORIA CL
CROSS ST 1
THOMAS ST 2
PROSPECT COTTS
Gorses Farm
STANLEY LA
Stanley Nook Farm
Aspull
HAIGH RD
ST DAVID'S CRES
ST JOHN'S RD
ST ELIZABETH'S RD
ST MARY'S RD
SMITH ST
SHOEMAKER GDNS
Our Lady's RC Sch
Liby
P
PO
LINDSAY TERR
HOLLY RD
CRAWFORD AVE
CRAWFORD CL
HIGHFIELD GR
BALCARRES RD
MANOR GR
Hilton Farm
NEW RD
Haigh Country Park
1 EDINBURGH WLK
2 BRAEMAR WLK
3 CARLISLE WAY
4 INVERNESS CL
EPHRAIM'S FOLD
SCOT LA
Walkers Higher Farm
Walkers Lower Farm
Shepherds Farm
Borsdane Brook
MOORSIDE
STANMOOR DR
HEATON ST
SUMNER ST
HAROLD ST
LINCOLN DR
EXETER DR
BELMONT DR
WARWICK
WINDSOR CRES
DEVON CL
ALNWICK CL
RENFREW RD
CORFE CL
RESTORMEL AVE
CRICCIETH AVE
OLD FOLD RD
CONWAY DR
BOLTON RD
Aspull Church Sch
THE FIELDS
CRAWFORD ST
Shaw's Fold Farm
SIMM'S SQ
ASHWORTH ST
Landlord's Farm
B5239
DICCONSON LA
PO
WIGAN RD
HIGHER LA
HIGH ST
SOUTHERN'S FOLD
WOODFIELD ST
BRIDGE ST
Rugby Football Gd
Ainscow's Farm
RESERVOIR ST
HOPE ST
WOODVALE AVE
WILLOWCROFT AVE
LEIGH ST
MILL LA
ILKESTON DR
Dodd's Farm
New Springs
B5238
HAWKSHAW ST
KIRKLESS ST
BOLNEY ST
ARMSTRONG ST
ASH LA
Sch
Leeds & Liverpool Canal
SENECAR CL
ARLEY CL
HILL ST
ALBION ST
Top Lock
1 ANDERTON WAY
2 LIVERPOOL ST
LONGFIELD ST
Holy Family RC Inf Sch
CAMBERWELL CRES
KIRKLESS VILLAS
MARCHBANK
MONTFORD RISE
HOLMSFIELD
BURLTON GR
ASHBOURNE AVE
BROMLEY CL
BOTANY CL
CALE LA
ALBION DR
Kirkless Hall Inn (PH)
WITHINGTON LA
Commercial Inn (PH)
FARM LA
Works
FINCHLEY CRES
1 SILVINGTON WAY
2 DRYTON WLK
Kirkless Hall
Bradshaw Hall
HALL LA
Marsh Farm
PEMBERLEI RD
GERRARD CL
MAYFAIR DR
PENNINGTON GREEN LA
PENNINGTON CL
BAGSHAW LA
FIRS COTTAGES
FIRS PARK CRES
Pennington Green
School Farm
The Firs Farm
Borsdane Wood
Hindley Hall Golf Course
Bank House Farm
Borsdane
RATHEN AVE
BRANTHWAITE
KIRKLESS LA
GREENBARN WAY
B5408
Blackrod Cty Prim Sch
A6
BLACKROD BY-PASS RD
HOPE ST
MANCHESTER RD
Park Hall Farm
Scot Lane End Sch
THE CHEETHAMS
MILLER ST
ESKDALE AVE
NEWLANDS DR
B5238
DORNING ST
B5408
Yate's Farm
Scot Lane End
CHORLEY RD
Hotel
Works

37 56

22
40

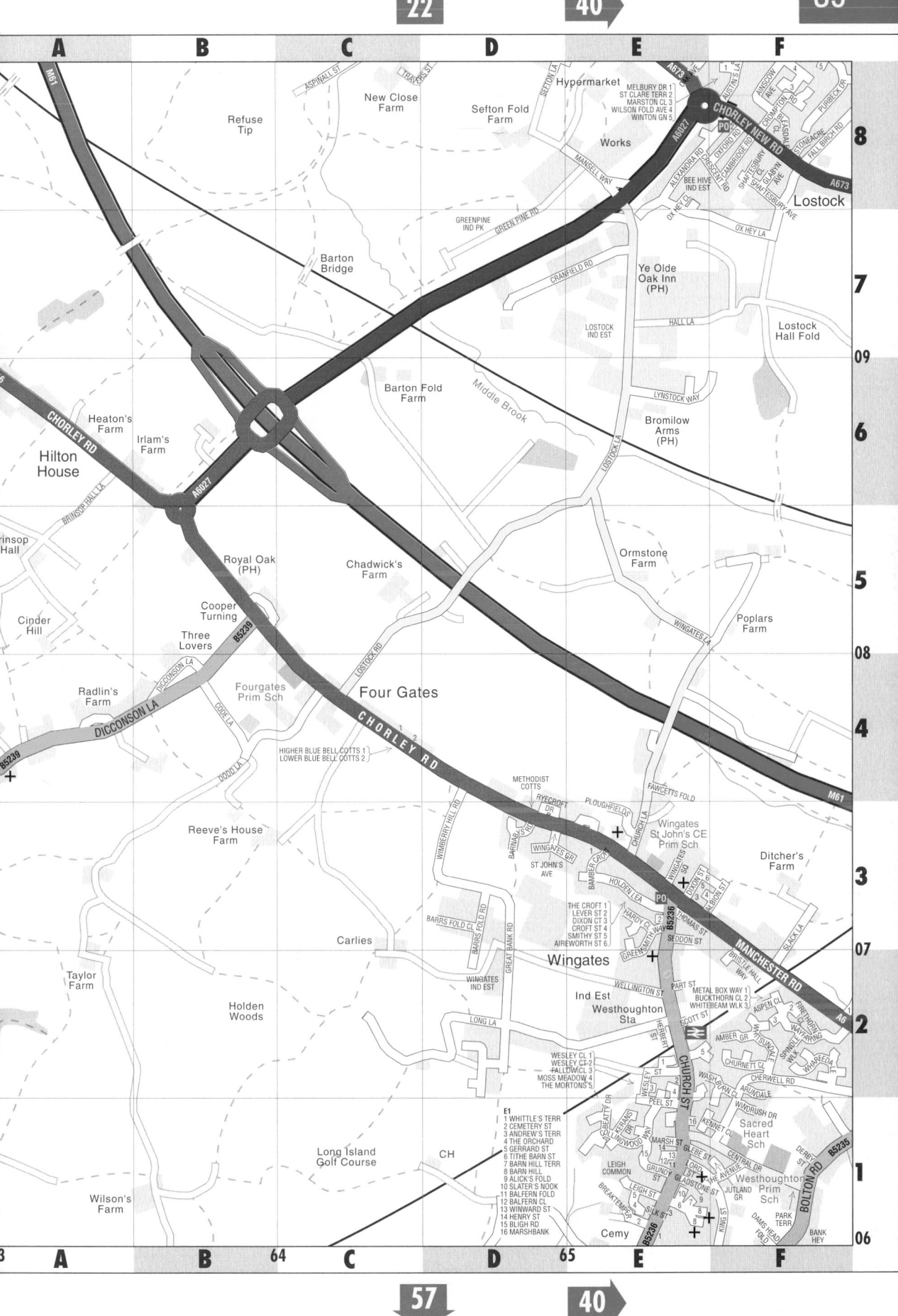
A
B
C
D
E
F
8
7
09
6
5
08
4
3
07
2
1
06
64
65
M61
A6027
A673
A6
B5239
B5236
B5235
Refuse Tip
New Close Farm
Sefton Fold Farm
Hypermarket
Works
Lostock
Barton Bridge
GREENPINE IND PK
Ye Olde Oak Inn (PH)
LOSTOCK IND EST
Lostock Hall Fold
Barton Fold Farm
Middle Brook
Bromilow Arms (PH)
Heaton's Farm
Irlam's Farm
Hilton House
Brinsop Hall
Royal Oak (PH)
Chadwick's Farm
Ormstone Farm
Cooper Turning
Cinder Hill
Three Lovers
Poplars Farm
Radlin's Farm
Fourgates Prim Sch
Four Gates
CHORLEY RD
CHORLEY NEW RD
DICCONSON LA
HIGHER BLUE BELL COTTS 1
LOWER BLUE BELL COTTS 2
METHODIST COTTS
Reeve's House Farm
Wingates St John's CE Prim Sch
Ditcher's Farm
THE CROFT 1
LEVER ST 2
DIXON CT 3
CROFT ST 4
SMITHY ST 5
AIREWORTH ST 6
Carlies
Wingates
WINGATES IND EST
Ind Est
Westhoughton Sta
MANCHESTER RD
METAL BOX WAY 1
BUCKTHORN CL 2
WHITEBEAM WLK 3
Taylor Farm
Holden Woods
WESLEY CL 1
WESLEY CT 2
FALLOW CL 3
MOSS MEADOW 4
THE MORTONS 5
E1
1 WHITTLE'S TERR
2 CEMETERY ST
3 ANDREW'S TERR
4 THE ORCHARD
5 GERRARD ST
6 TITHE BARN ST
7 BARN HILL TERR
8 BARN HILL
9 ALICK'S FOLD
10 SLATER'S NOOK
11 BALFERN FOLD
12 BALFERN CL
13 WINWARD ST
14 HENRY ST
15 BLIGH RD
16 MARSHBANK
MELBURY DR 1
ST CLARE TERR 2
MARSTON CL 3
WILSON FOLD AVE 4
WINTON GN 5
Long Island Golf Course
CH
LEIGH COMMON
Sacred Heart Sch
Westhoughton Prim Sch
Cemy
Wilson's Farm
CHURCH ST
BOLTON RD

39
23

A
B
C
D
E
F
8
7
09
6
5
08
4
3
07
2
1
06
66
67
68
Fall Birch
HIGH RID LA
FALL BIRCH RD
Bolton Golf Course
CH
A673
THE KILPHIN
PRINCESS RD
THE HAMLET
HIGH BANK LA
Beaumont
HOLLY DENE DR
THE WOODLANDS
OLD HALL CLOUGH
WHINSLEE CT
WHINSLEE
WHINS CRES
DALEGARTH AVE
RAVENSDALE RD
LOWER HOUSE DR
CHORLEY NEW RD
LOSTOCK PARK DR
LINKS RD
LINKS DR
ST ANDREWS RD
REGENT DR
MEADOWFIELD
NEW MEADOW
BROADWOOD
BRYANT'S ACRE
ROSEBANK
BRIKSDAL WAY
ACRESDALE
GREEN DR
LOSTOCK JUNCTION LA
THE MEADOW
MALLOWDALE CL
RAVENHURST DR
MARTINSCLOUGH
GREENLEAS
GLENGARTH DR
DENTDALE CL
Municipal Golf Course
YEW TREE DR
REGENT RD
SUDBURY DR
Lostock Cty Prim Sch
SANDFIELD DR
THORNEYHOLME CL
BESSYBROOK CL
ASHBRIDGE
RUMWORTH RD
STONEBRIDGE CL
KILSBY CL
DUNCHURCH CL
MIDDLEBROOK DR
PRINCETHORPE CL
PAULTON CL
WESTBANK RD
MERIDEN GR
WILMCOTE CL
OVERDALE CL
MORRIS FOLD DR
HEATON RD
PENDENNIS AVE
KILWORTH DR
MILVERTON CL
WHITESTONE CL
ASHCOTT CL
JUNCTION RD W
Morris Fold Farm
Lostock Sta
PO
Lostock Junction
TEMPEST RD
Lostock Park Sch
Middle Brook
Golf Course
A58
STAPLETON AVE
TOWNCROFT LA
VERDURE AVE
Markland Hill Prim Sch
KINGWOOD AVE
ALBERT RD W
FELSTED
LINGMELL CL
LINDALE AVE
VICTORIA RD
MARKLAND HILL
EASTWOOD TERR
OAKWOOD DR
BEAUMONT CT
Markland Hill
NORTHWOLD DR
MARSHDALE RD
BRECKLAND DR
RAVENSWOOD DR
ASH LEIGH DR
THE BOWANS
NEYLAND CL
WAVERSLEA DR
Edmund Potter
HEATON COURT
RAVENS WOOD
THE LANE
THE GLEN
LADY BRIDGE LA
OAKLEY PK
Woodside Schs
OAKLANDS
FERN CLOUGH
HILLSIDE CT
WOODS LA
A673
BEAUMONT RD
LADY BRIDGE LA
ASHBANK AVE
ARMADALE RD
CULROSS AVE
LOMOND PL
LAXFORD GR
RUTHERGLEN DR
GLENDALE DR
CAITHNESS DR
KILDONAN DR
HELMSDALE
WINSFORD GR
BEAUMONT DR
KINTYRE DR
THE WALKWAY
SANDRAY GR
CHESTERTON DR
KILMAINE DR
GLENLUCE WLK
Ladybridge Prim Sch
LAKELANDS DR
Beaumont Prim Sch
CROSSHILL WLK
WENDOVER DR
BROADGATE
KINROSS DR
BROADFORD RD
St Bernard's RC Prim Sch
GREENOCK CL
BIRKENHILLS DR
AMBERLEY CL
ERRINGTON CL
GALLOWAY CL
BRAESIDE GR
GLENDEVON CL
New York
JUNCTION RD
ERSKINE CL
CAIRNGORM DR
CROSSFORD DR
MARNLAND GR
WHITBURN CL
WINTON GR
NORWICK CL
1 DALKEITH GR
2 HAMBLEDEN CL
3 BARRISDALE CL
Sch
The Deane Sch
Fernhill Gate
KINCRAIG CL
BIRCHFIELD GR
LANGSIDE DR
SALTERGATE
CRINGLE CL
KILDALE CL
BLAKEY CL
BRANSDALE CL
OLDSTEAD GR
GREENHILL LA
A676
HOLMFIELD GN
SUTTON RD
ADDINGTON RD
THISTLETON RD
PH
Rumworth Lodge Resr
Moss Hall Farm
ST JOHNS WOOD
TEMPEST CHASE
NEW TEMPEST RD
CHULSEY GATE LA
GOLDSTEIN RD 1
BACK MIREY LA 2
COWDALS RD
HAVISHAM CL
PH
ST JOHN'S RD
COPPERFIELDS
TEMPEST RD
Chew Moor
Seddon Fold
LOCK LA
M61
POCKET NOOK RD
MEADOWBROOK CL
Morris Farm
Hunger Hill
WIGAN RD
Knutshaw Bridge
TURNBERRY
BEAUMONT CHASE
MUIRFIELD CL
GLENEAGLES
RENFREW DR
STONEHAVEN
WINSLOW RD
HIGHGATE
TAYWOOD RD
HILLSIDE CL
CARTMEL CL
BOLTON RD
HORNBY DR
PO
KNUTSHAW CRES
DOYLE RD
HUNGER HILL AVE
MOSSLAND GR
PENDLEBURY FOLD
SNYDALE WAY
5
METAL BOX WAY
CHEW MOOR LA
Monks Farm
Works
UPPER BROOM WAY
HEATONS GR
SNYDALE CL
BOLTON RD
CALVER HEY CL
WHITE HORSE GR
Snydale Gate Farm
Garnet Fold Farm
HORRIDGE FOLD AVE
BROOM WAY
B5235 BOLTON RD
MANCHESTER RD
SNYDALE WAY
A58
HALL LEE DR
COW LEES
FIELDBROOK WLK
BROOK MEADOW
SELBOURNE CL
CAPTAIN LEES RD
BARNFIELD DR
BROADHEATH
REDSTOCK CL
MOLYNEUX RD
LODGE DR
Motel
MANLEY CRES
St Thomas Prim Sch
BEEHIVE GN
SINGLETON GR
FAIRHAVEN AVE
PO
PARK RD
BRANCKER ST
Chequerbent
MANCHESTER RD
A6
M61

39
58

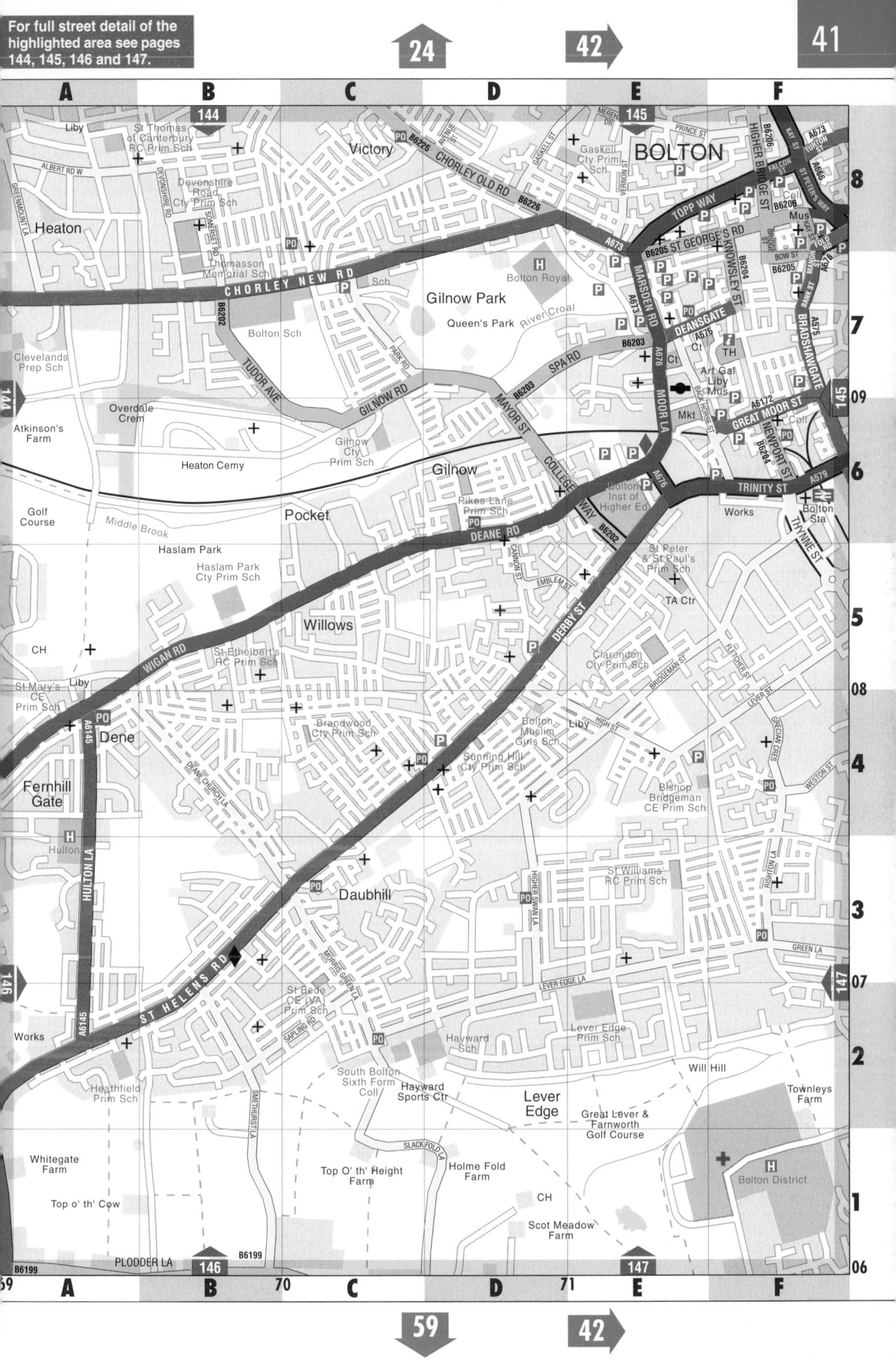

For full street detail of the highlighted area see pages 144, 145, 146 and 147.

42

41 25

For full street detail of the highlighted area see page 148.

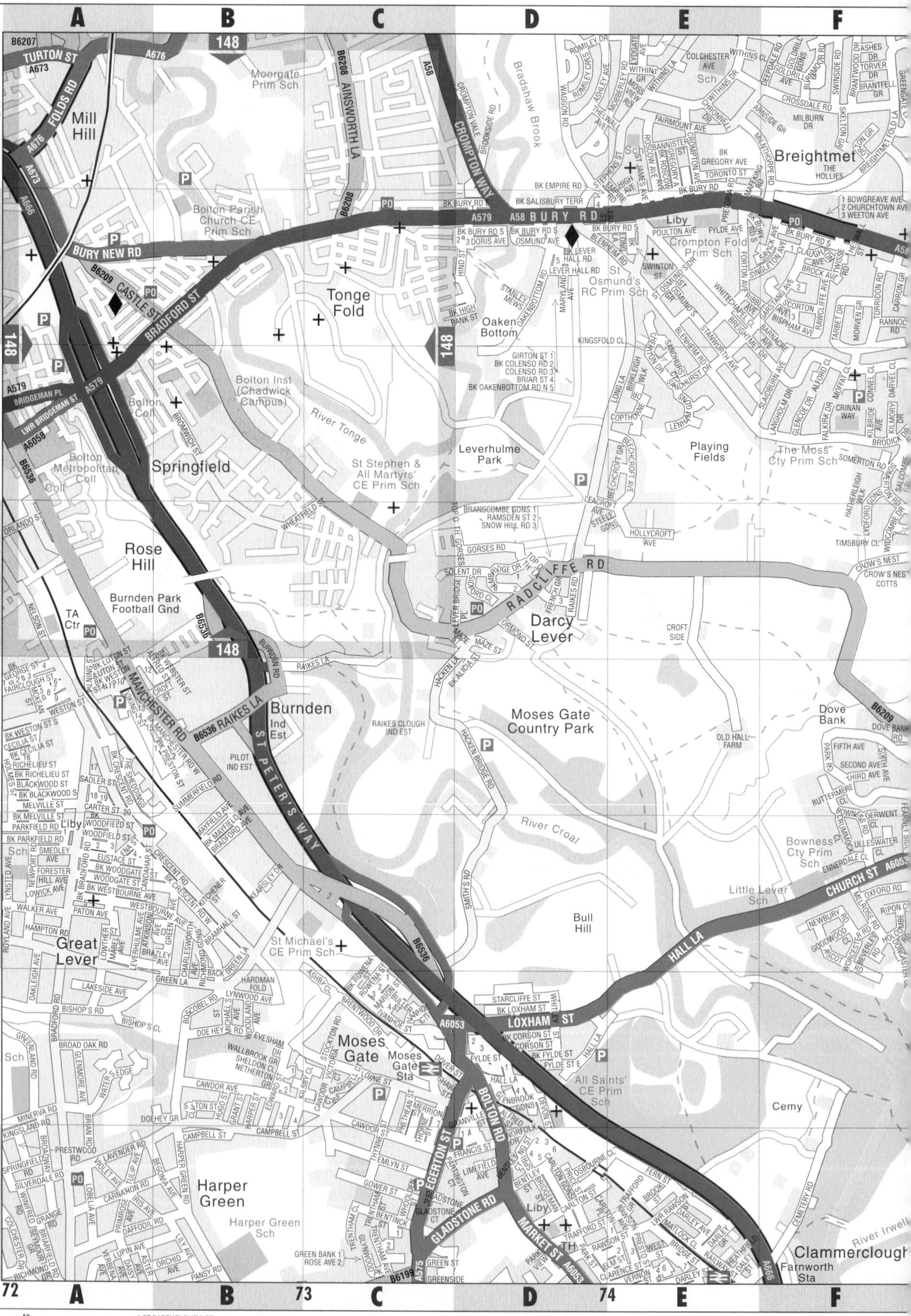

TURTON ST
A673 A676
FOLDS RD
Mill Hill
Moorgate Prim Sch
AINSWORTH LA
148
A676 A579
BURY NEW RD
CROMPTON WAY
Bradshaw Brook
Breightmet
The Hollies
Bolton Parish Church CE Prim Sch
CASTLE ST
BRADFORD ST
A579 A58 BURY RD
Liby
Crompton Fold Prim Sch
BK EMPIRE RD
BK SALISBURY TERR
BK BURY RD
Tonge Fold
148
St Osmund's RC Prim Sch
Oaken Bottom
Kingsfold Cl
Bolton Inst (Chadwick Campus)
River Tonge
Leverhulme Park
The Moss City Prim Sch
Bolton Coll
Bolton Metropolitan Coll
Springfield
St Stephen & All Martyrs' CE Prim Sch
Playing Fields
CRINAN WAY
Rose Hill
Burnden Park Football Gnd
RADCLIFFE RD
Darcy Lever
CROFT SIDE
CROW'S NES COTTS
TA Ctr
148
RAIKES LA
Burnden Ind Est
Moses Gate Country Park
Old Hall Farm
Dove Bank
Dove Bank
MANCHESTER RD
RAIKES LA
ST PETER'S WAY
Raikes Clough Ind Est
PILOT IND EST
River Croal
Bowness City Prim Sch
Liby
Great Lever
St Michael's CE Prim Sch
Bull Hill
Little Lever Sch
CHURCH ST
HALL LA
Moses Gate
STARCLIFFE ST
BK LOXHAM ST
LOXHAM ST
A6053
All Saints' CE Prim Sch
Harper Green
Moses Gate Sta
BOLTON RD
Cemy
EGERTON ST
GLADSTONE RD
MARKET ST A6053
Liby
TH
Clammerclough
Farnworth Sta
Harper Green Sch
River Irwell
B619

A3
1 BK BRADFORD RD W
2 BK EUSTACE ST
3 ASIA ST
4 BK ENA ST
5 PATON MEWS
A4
1 BK AUGUSTUS ST W
2 BK AUGUSTUS ST
3 AUGUSTUS ST

4 ST BARTHOLOMEW ST
5 BK McKEAN ST N
6 HILDA ST
7 GILDERDALE ST
8 BK McKEAN ST
9 BK WESTON ST N
10 BK MANCHESTER RD S
11 BK VIKING ST N
12 BK ALFRED ST
13 SPRINGFIELD ST

14 BK SPRINGFIELD ST
15 SOUTHFIELD ST
16 BK NEWPORT RD
17 BRADFORD CRES
18 BK BRADFORD RD
19 BK CARTER ST
20 BK DOBIE ST
B2
1 BARWELL SQ
2 GLENFIELD SQ

B2
3 GEORGIANA ST
4 VICTORIA ST
5 CLIFTON CT
B4
1 BK SOUTHFIELD ST
2 PRESTON ST
C2
1 BK MANCHESTER RD
2 BK MARION ST

3 BK IVANHOE ST
4 BK MARION ST S
5 CAMPBELL ST
6 CAWDOR WLK
7 LOMAX ST
D1
1 JOSEPH ST
2 LEYBURN GR
3 BURNHAM WLK
4 ASTON GDNS

5 ARNCLIFFE CL
6 BENTHAM CL
D2
1 HALL ST
2 MOSES GATE WORKSHOPS
3 GLADYS ST
4 BROADGREEN GDNS
E1
1 ENTWISTLE ST
2 MOSS ST

3 CHARLES ST
4 LEACH ST
5 EASTCOTE WLK
6 REDBROOK CL
7 LIGHTWOOD CL

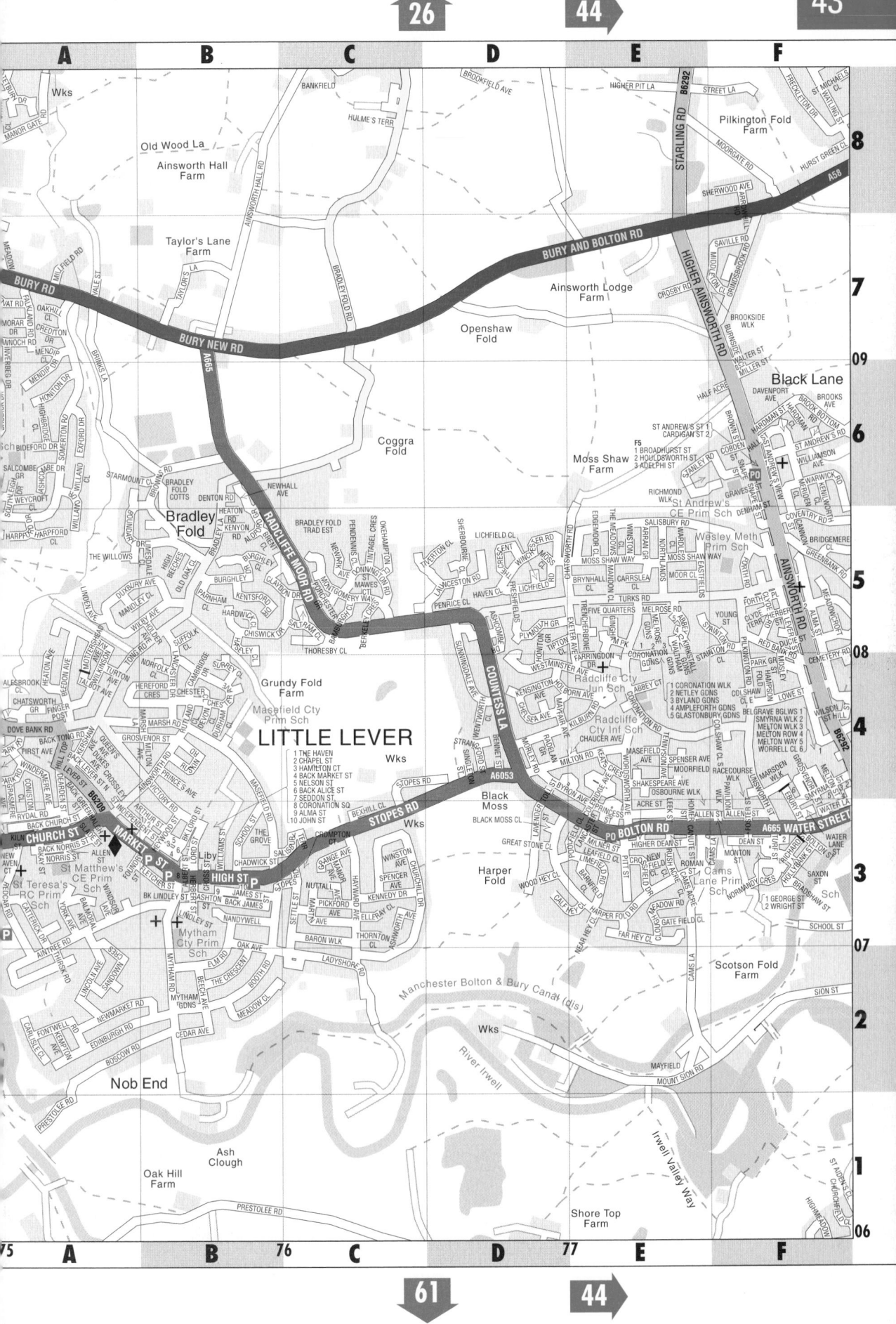
26
44
A
B
C
D
E
F
8
7
09
6
5
08
4
3
07
2
1
06
75
76
77
Wks
Old Wood La
Ainsworth Hall Farm
Taylor's Lane Farm
BANKFIELD
HULME'S TERR
BROOKFIELD AVE
HIGHER PIT LA
B6292
STREET LA
Pilkington Fold Farm
STARLING RD
MOORGATE RD
HURST GREEN CL
A58
SHERWOOD AVE
AINSWORTH HALL RD
BRADLEY FOLD RD
BURY AND BOLTON RD
SAVILLE RD
HIGHER AINSWORTH RD
GRINDSBROOK RD
CROSBY RD
Ainsworth Lodge Farm
BROOKSIDE WLK
BURY RD
MILLFIELD RD
VALE ST
TAYLOR'S LA
BURY NEW RD
A665
Openshaw Fold
WALTER ST
MILLER ST
Black Lane
DAVENPORT AVE
BROOKS AVE
HALF ACRE
BRINKS LA
HONITON DR
HIGHBRIDGE CL
SOMERTON RD
EXFORD DR
BIDEFORD DR
SALCOMBE GR
WEYCROFT CL
HARPFORD CL
Coggra Fold
Moss Shaw Farm
ST ANDREW'S ST 1
CARDIGAN ST 2
F5
1 BROADHURST ST
2 HOULDSWORTH ST
3 ADELPHI ST
COBDEN ST
STANLEY RD
ST ANDREW'S RD
WILLIAMSON AVE
WARWICK RD
RICHMOND WLK
St Andrew's CE Prim Sch
DENHAM ST
COVENTRY RD
STARMOUNT CL
BRADLEY FOLD COTTS
DENTON RD
NEWHALL AVE
Bradley Fold
HEATON RD
KENYON RD
RADCLIFFE MOOR RD
BRADLEY FOLD TRAD EST
PENDENNIS CL
TINTAGEL CRES
OKEHAMPTON CL
SHERBOURNE CL
LICHFIELD CL
SALISBURY RD
Wesley Meth Prim Sch
BRIDGEMERE CL
GREENBANK RD
THE WILLOWS
HIGH BEECHES
OLD OAK CL
BURGHLEY
MOSS SHAW WAY
BRYNHALL CL
CARRSLEA CL
MOOR CL
AINSWORTH RD
LAUNCESTON RD
HAVEN CL
LICHFIELD
TURKS RD
MEADOWCROFT
DUXBURY AVE
MANDLEY CL
PARNHAM CL
KENTSFORD
MONTGOMERY WAY
PENRICE CL
FIVE QUARTERS
MELROSE RD
YOUNG ST
ALMA ST
HARDWICK CL
CHISWICK DR
SALTRAM CL
THORESBY CL
BERKELEY CRES
PLYMOUTH GR
TIPTON CL
STAINTON RD
RED BANK RD
CEMETERY RD
SUFFOLK CL
NORFOLK CL
CAMBRIDGE DR
SURREY CL
FARRINGDON DR
CORONATION GDNS
PARK GR
TURTON AVE
HEREFORD CRES
CHESTER AVE
Grundy Fold Farm
COUNTESS LA
WESTMINSTER AVE
Radcliffe Cty Jun Sch
ABBEY CT
1 CORONATION WLK
2 NETLEY GDNS
3 BYLAND GDNS
4 AMPLEFORTH GDNS
5 GLASTONBURY GDNS
COLSHAW CL E
LOWE ST
CHATSWORTH GR
FINGER POST
Masefield Cty Prim Sch
KENSINGTON AVE
HOLBORN AVE
CHELSEA AVE
KILBURN RD
Radcliffe Cty Inf Sch
BELGRAVE BGLWS 1
SMYRNA WLK 2
MELTON WLK 3
MELTON ROW 4
MELTON WAY 5
WORRELL CL 6
WILSON ST
HILL ST
DOVE BANK RD
BACK TONG RD
MARSH RD
LITTLE LEVER
CHAUCER AVE
GROSVENOR ST
RUSKIN RD
PRINCE'S AVE
1 THE HAVEN
2 CHAPEL ST
3 HAMILTON CT
4 BACK MARKET ST
5 NELSON ST
6 BACK ALICE ST
7 SEDDON ST
8 CORONATION SQ
9 ALMA ST
10 JOHN ST
Wks
STRANGFORD ST
SINGLETON ST
MILTON RD
MASEFIELD AVE
SPENSER AVE
MOORFIELD
RACECOURSE WLK
MARSDEN WLK
FIRST AVE
LEVER ST
B6209
MASEFIELD RD
STOPES RD
A6053
BYRON AVE
SHAKESPEARE AVE
OSBOURNE WLK
Black Moss
BLACK MOSS CL
ACRE ST
ALLEN ST
WATER LA
RYDAL RD
BACK CHURCH ST
MARKET ST
VICTORY RD
THE GROVE
STOPES RD
BEXHILL CL
Wks
CROMPTON CT
BOLTON RD
A665 WATER STREET
CHURCH ST
BACK NORRIS ST
NORRIS ST
ALLEN ST
Liby
CHADWICK ST
SALISBURY TERR
GRANGE AVE
WINSTON AVE
GREAT STONE CL
MILNER ST
HIGHER DEAN ST
DEAN ST
WATER LANE ST
St Matthew's CE Prim Sch
St Teresa's RC Prim Sch
FLETCHER ST
HIGH ST
JAMES ST
BACK JAMES
SPENCER AVE
NUTTALL AVE
Harper Fold
WOOD HEY CL
LEAFIELD CL
LIMEFIELD
ROMAN ST
Cams Lane Prim Sch
MONTON ST
NORMANDY CRES
SAXON ST
BK LINDLEY ST
ASHTON ST
PICKFORD AVE
KENNEDY DR
ELLERAY CL
CALF HEY
HARPER FOLD RD
MEADOW RD
GATE FIELD CL
1 GEORGE ST
2 WRIGHT ST
BRADSHAW ST
Sch
NANDYWELL
SETTLE ST
BARON WLK
THORNTON CL
FAR HEY CL
NEAR HEY CL
SCHOOL ST
Mytham Cty Prim Sch
AINTREE RD
OAK AVE
LADYSHORE RD
Scotson Fold Farm
MYTHAM RD
ELM RD
THE CRESCENT
BOOTH RD
CAMS LA
LINCOLN AVE
SANDOWN CRES
Manchester Bolton & Bury Canal (dis)
SION ST
NEWMARKET RD
MYTHAM GDNS
BEECH AVE
MEADOW CL
FONTWELL RD
KEMPTON AVE
EDINBURGH RD
CEDAR AVE
Wks
River Irwell
BOSCOW RD
MAYFIELD
MOUNT SION RD
Nob End
PRESTOLEE RD
Irwell Valley Way
Ash Clough
Oak Hill Farm
PRESTOLEE RD
Shore Top Farm
ST AIDEN'S CL
CHURCHFIELD CL
HIGHMEADOW
61
44

43

27

E8
1 BK HORNE ST N
2 BK DEVON ST N
3 WALKER ST
4 BK PARKHILLS RD S
5 MOSS PL

F8
1 BK NELSON ST S
2 BK DEVON ST S
3 BK PARKHILLS RD S
4 BK PARKHILLS RD N
5 BK NELSON ST N
6 NELSON ST
7 LINCOLN DR
8 MIDDLESEX DR

A B C D E F

8 7 09 6 5 08 4 3 07 2 1 06

Lower Hinds
Fishpool
Bury CE High Sch
Florence Nightingale
The Derby High Sch
Higher Spen Moor
Lower Spen Moor
Elton Resr
Club
Old Hall Farm
Hogside LC
Doffer Fold
Withins Resr
Brook Bottom Farm
Manchester Bolton & Bury Canal (dis)
Crow Trees Farm
Cemy
Redvales
St Peter's CE Prim Sch
Works
Millwood Sch
Irwell Valley Way
St Mary's RC Sch
Gorsefield Prim Sch
Coney Green Sch
Sewage Works
Blackford Bridge
Bealey
River Roch
Radcliffe Sta
RADCLIFFE
Radcliffe High Sch
River Irwell
Liby
New Church Coll
Lily Hill
Prim Sch
High Sch
St John's CE Prim Sch
Chapelfield Prim Sch
Chapel Field
Stand Golf Course
Bury Coll (Stand Ctr)
Whitefield Sta
BOLTON RD
WELLINGTON RD
MANCHESTER RD
DUMERS LA
BURY ST
CROSS LA
SPRING LA
WATER ST
PILKINGTON WAY
NEW RD
RADCLIFFE NEW RD
BURY NEW RD
DALES LA

78 A B 79 C D 80 E F

A3
1 VICARAGE ST
2 WEST ST
3 ELIZABETH ST
4 FOUNDRY ST
A4
1 GRINDROD ST
2 SIDDALL ST
3 CO-OPERATIVE ST
4 WATER LANE ST
5 HAMPSON SQ
B2
1 PEEL ST
2 MELLOR ST
3 MILLTOWN CL
4 IRWELL CL
5 REGAN ST
6 BRIDGE CL
B3
1 DARBYSHIRE WLK
2 SEYMOUR CT
3 HOWARTH WLK
4 SEYMOUR WLK
5 NEWCHURCH WLK
6 NEWCHURCH CT
7 BRIDGEFIELD WLK
8 HOWARTH CT
9 CROOK ST

43

C1
1 CHURCH MEWS
2 OAK ST
3 BEECHFIELD AVE
4 WALKER ST
5 ROSSALL AVE
6 NORTH WOODLEY
C4
1 ASHWORTH CT
2 EASTBROOK AVE

62

C4
3 CALEDONIA ST
4 HUTCHINSON ST
5 WELLINGTON ST
6 CARRBROOK TERR
7 GINGHAM CT
8 EDMUND ST
E1
1 BLEAKLEY ST
2 DEVON MEWS
3 SILVER CT
4 GROSVENOR RD
5 GROSVENOR AVE
F2
1 MALTON CL
2 THE PARADE
3 ELMS FARM
4 THE ELMS
5 RIPON CL
6 MELROSE CL

28
46

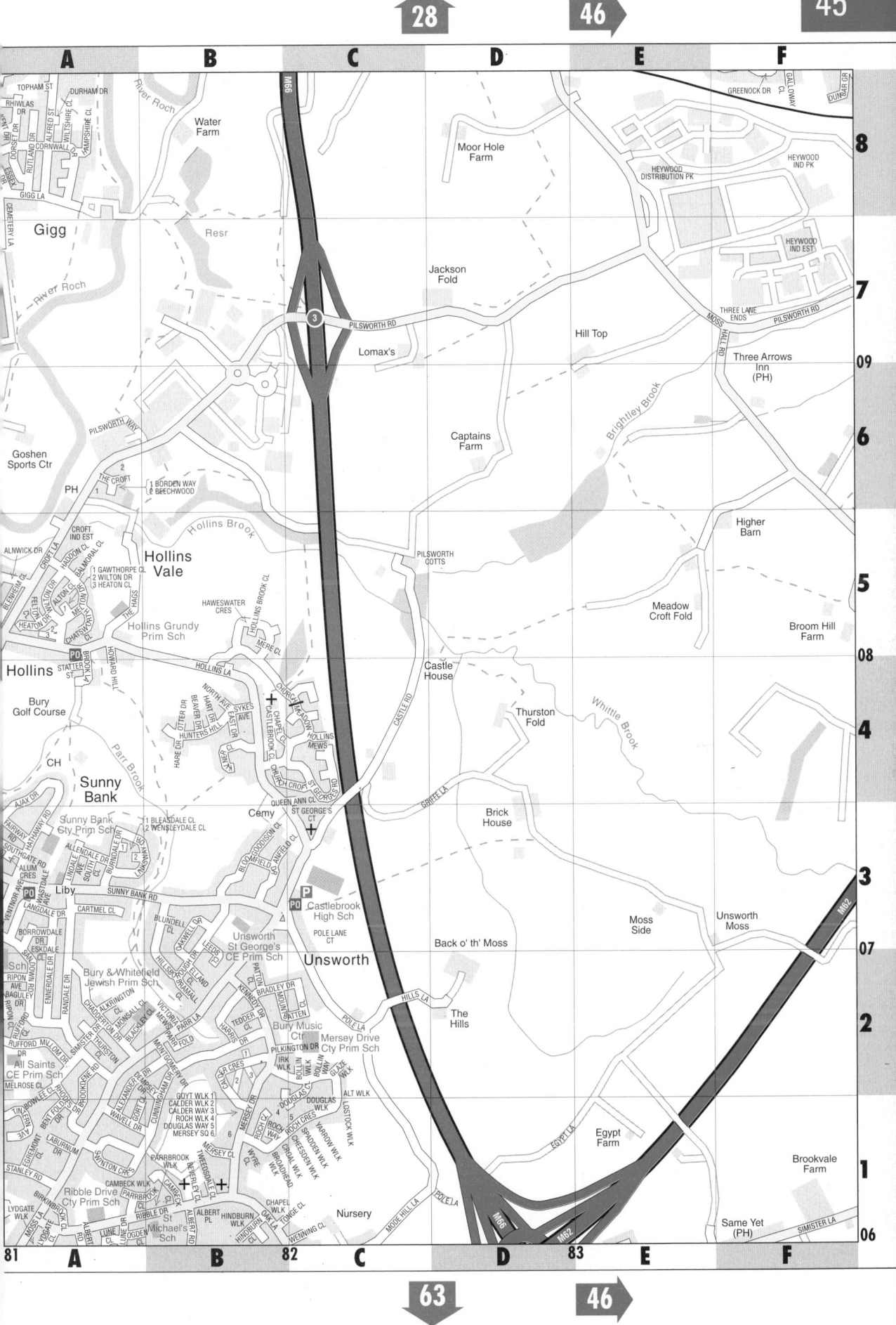
A
B
C
D
E
F
8
7
09
6
5
08
4
3
07
2
1
06
81
82
83
M66
M62
TOPHAM ST
DURHAM DR
RHIWLAS DR
DORSET DR
RUTLAND DR
ALFRED ST
WILTSHIRE CL
HAMPSHIRE CL
CORNWALL DR
ESSEX DR
GIGG LA
CEMETERY LA
Gigg
River Roch
Water Farm
Resr
Moor Hole Farm
GREENOCK DR
GALLOWAY CL
DUNBAR GR
HEYWOOD DISTRIBUTION PK
HEYWOOD IND PK
HEYWOOD IND EST
Jackson Fold
PILSWORTH RD
Lomax's
Hill Top
THREE LANE ENDS
MOSS HALL RD
Three Arrows Inn (PH)
PILSWORTH WAY
Goshen Sports Ctr
Captains Farm
Brightley Brook
THE CROFT
1 BORDEN WAY
2 BEECHWOOD
PH
CROFT IND EST
Hollins Brook
Hollins Vale
ALNWICK DR
CROFT LA
HADDON CL
BALMORAL CL
1 GAWTHORPE CL
2 WILTON DR
3 HEATON CL
BLENHEIM CL
FELTON CL
ALTON CL
MELTON CL
CHATSWORTH CL
HEATON CL
THE HAGS
HAWESWATER CRES
HOLLINS BROOK CL
MERE CL
Hollins Grundy Prim Sch
PILSWORTH COTTS
Higher Barn
Meadow Croft Fold
Broom Hill Farm
Hollins
PO
STATTER ST
BROOK LA
HOWARD HILL
HOLLINS LA
Castle House
CASTLE RD
Thurston Fold
Whittle Brook
Bury Golf Course
NORTH AVE
HART DR
BEAVER DR
OTTER DR
HUNTERS HILL
SYKES AVE
EAST DR
HARE DR
KAYE CL
CHURCH CL
MEADOW CL
CHAPEL CL
CASTLEBROOK CL
HOLLINS MEWS
CHURCH CROFT
ST GEORGES RD
CH
Sunny Bank
Parr Brook
QUEEN ANN CL
ST GEORGE'S CT
Cemy
GRIFFE LA
Brick House
AJAX DR
HATHAWAY RD
FAIRWAY RD
Sunny Bank Cty Prim Sch
1 BLEASDALE CL
2 WENSLEYDALE CL
SOUTHGATE RD
ALLENDALE DR
BURNDALE DR
ALUM CRES
LINDALE AVE
SOUTH CL
GOODISON CL
BLOOMFIELD DR
ANFIELD CL
VENTNOR AVE
WASDALE AVE
Liby
SUNNY BANK RD
P
Castlebrook High Sch
LANGDALE DR
CARTMEL CL
BLUNDELL CL
OAKWELL DR
BORROWDALE DR
ESKDALE DR
POLE LANE CT
Unsworth St George's CE Prim Sch
Unsworth
Back o' th' Moss
Moss Side
Unsworth Moss
Sch
RIPON AVE
BAGULEY DR
RIPON CL
ENNERDALE DR
RANDALE DR
Bury & Whitefield Jewish Prim Sch
ALKRINGTON CL
CHADDERTON DR
MONSALL CL
BLACKLEY CL
VICTORIA MEWS
PARR LA
ELLAND CL
HILLSBOROUGH DR
BRAMALL CL
LEEDS CL
PATTON CL
BRADLEY DR
KENNEDY DR
MOUNTBATTEN CL
HILLS LA
The Hills
POLE LA
TEDDER CL
HARRIS DR
Bury Music Ctr
Mersey Drive Cty Prim Sch
RUFFORD CL
RUFFORD DR
MILLOM DR
SIMISTER DR
THURSTON CL
MONTGOMERY DR
PARR FOLD
PILKINGTON DR
IRK WLK
BOLLIN WLK
BOLLIN WAY
GLAZE WLK
All Saints CE Prim Sch
MELROSE CL
BOWLEE CL
RHODES DR
BROOKDENE RD
ALEXANDER DR
CALDER CRES
ALT WLK
DOUGLAS CL
DOUGLAS WLK
LOSTOCK WLK
GOYT WLK 1
CALDER WLK 2
CALDER WAY 3
ROCH WLK 4
DOUGLAS WAY 5
MERSEY SQ 6
WAVELL DR
CUNNINGHAM DR
MERSEY DR
ROCH CL
ROCH WAY
ROCH CRES
YARROW WLK
SPADDEN WLK
CHEESDEN WLK
TINTERN AVE
BENT FOLD DR
EGREMONT CL
LABURNUM DR
SWINTON CRES
PARRBROOK WLK
TWEEDSDALE CL
MERSEY CL
WYRE CL
BROADHEAD WLK
CROAL WLK
EGYPT LA
Egypt Farm
Brookvale Farm
STANLEY RD
CAMBECK WLK
BEVERLEY CL
CAMBECK CL
Ribble Drive Cty Prim Sch
RIBBLE DR
ALBERT PL
HINDBURN WLK
HINDBURN CL
CHAPEL WLK
OAK LA
TONGE CL
Nursery
MODE HILL LA
LYDGATE WLK
BIRKINBROOK CL
MOSS LA
LYDGATE CL
ALBERT RD
LUNE CL
LUNE DR
OGDEN CL
St Michael's Sch
WENNING CL
Same Yet (PH)
SIMISTER LA

63
46

E2
1 DUFTON WLK
2 DUDDON WLK
3 SEASCALE WLK
4 MOWBRAY WLK
5 HAWESWATER MEWS
6 WINSTER DR
7 D'OLIVERA CT
8 DOVEDALE CT
9 ST BEES WLK

F1
1 THROSTLE HALL CT
2 NINIAN CT
3 EXETER CT
4 KID ST
5 WATER ST
6 MARKET ST
7 CHAPEL ST
8 WOOD ST
9 CROSS ST

10 CHISHOLM CT
11 WEAVERS CT
12 GREAT ARBOR WAY
13 SCHOLARS WAY

D2
1 LAKELAND CT
2 LONGTHWAITE CL
3 KESWICK CT
4 MILLBECK CT
5 BOWNESS CT

A1
1 WATER ST
2 SADLER ST
3 ST LEONARD'S SQ
4 BARROWFIELD WLK
5 ASSHETON ST

A2
1 WALTON ST
2 WHITE HART MEADOW
3 CHURCH STREET IND EST
4 BREWSTER ST
5 NORMAN WEALL CT
6 BACK SPRING GDNS
7 LOWER BAMFORD CL
8 PETERLOO TERR
9 ASSHETON ST
10 ST STEPHEN'S GDNS
11 WICKHAM TERR

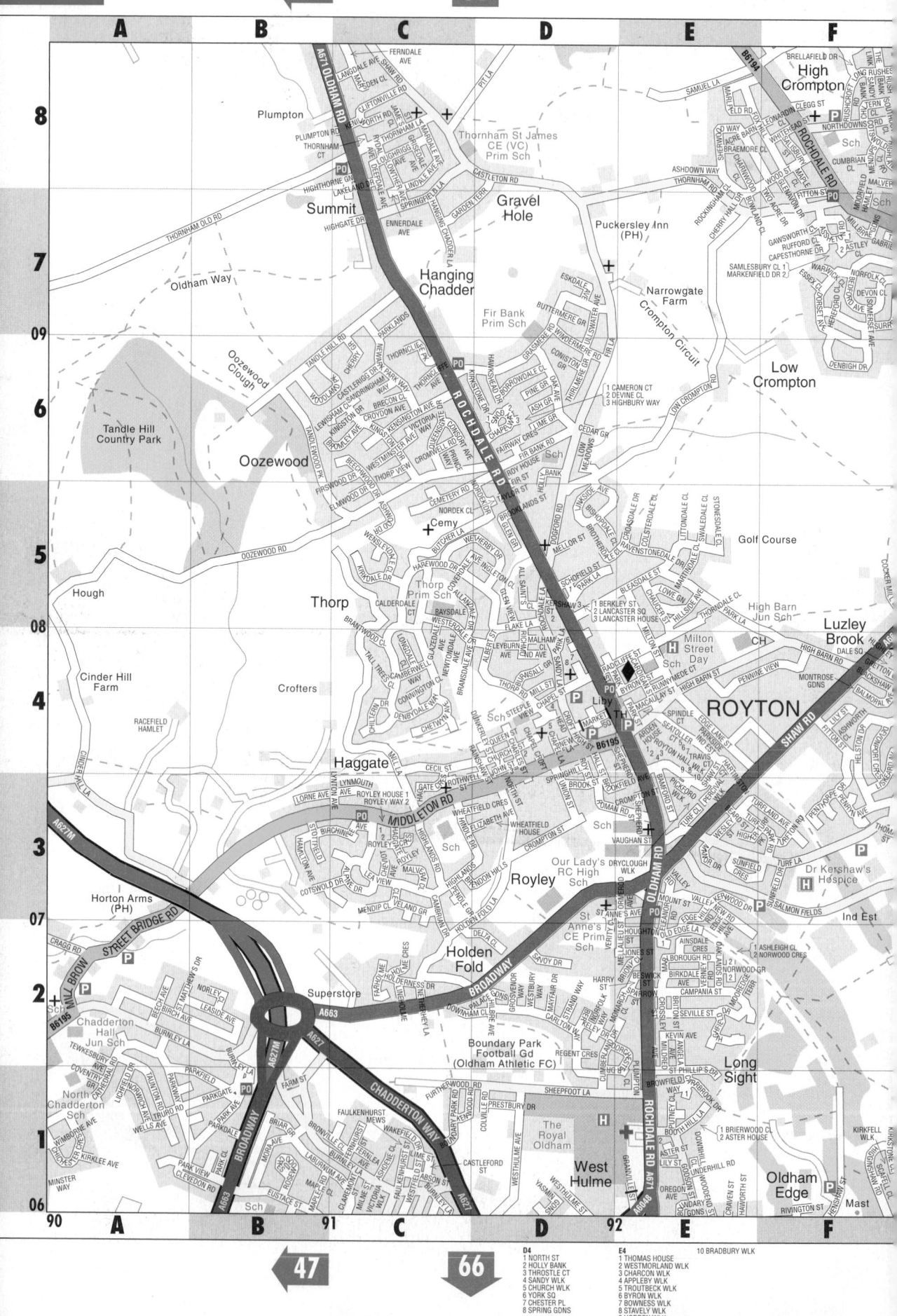

A B C D E F

8
7
09
6
5
08
4
07
3
2
1
06

90 A B 91 C D 92 E F

High Crompton
Plumpton
Summit
Gravel Hole
Thornham St James CE (VC) Prim Sch
Hanging Chadder
Puckersley Inn (PH)
Narrowgate Farm
Low Crompton
Oldham Way
Fir Bank Prim Sch
Crompton Circuit
Oozewood Clough
Tandle Hill Country Park
Oozewood
Cemy
Golf Course
Thorp Prim Sch
Thorp
High Barn Jun Sch
Luzley Brook
Hough
Milton Street Day
Cinder Hill Farm
Crofters
ROYTON
Racefield Hamlet
Haggate
MIDDLETON RD
Royley
Our Lady's RC High Sch
Dr Kershaw's Hospice
Horton Arms (PH)
STREET BRIDGE RD
Ind Est
Chadderton Hall Jun Sch
Superstore
Holden Fold
BROADWAY
St Anne's CE Prim Sch
North Chadderton Sch
Boundary Park Football Gd (Oldham Athletic FC)
Long Sight
CHADDERTON WAY
The Royal Oldham
West Hulme
Oldham Edge
Minster Way
Mast

D4
1 NORTH ST
2 HOLLY BANK
3 THROSTLE CT
4 SANDY WLK
5 CHURCH WLK
6 YORK SQ
7 CHESTER PL
8 SPRING GDNS

E4
1 THOMAS HOUSE
2 WESTMORLAND WLK
3 CHARCON WLK
4 APPLEBY WLK
5 TROUTBECK WLK
6 BYRON WLK
7 BOWNESS WLK
8 STAVELY WLK
9 HORDEN WLK

10 BRADBURY WLK

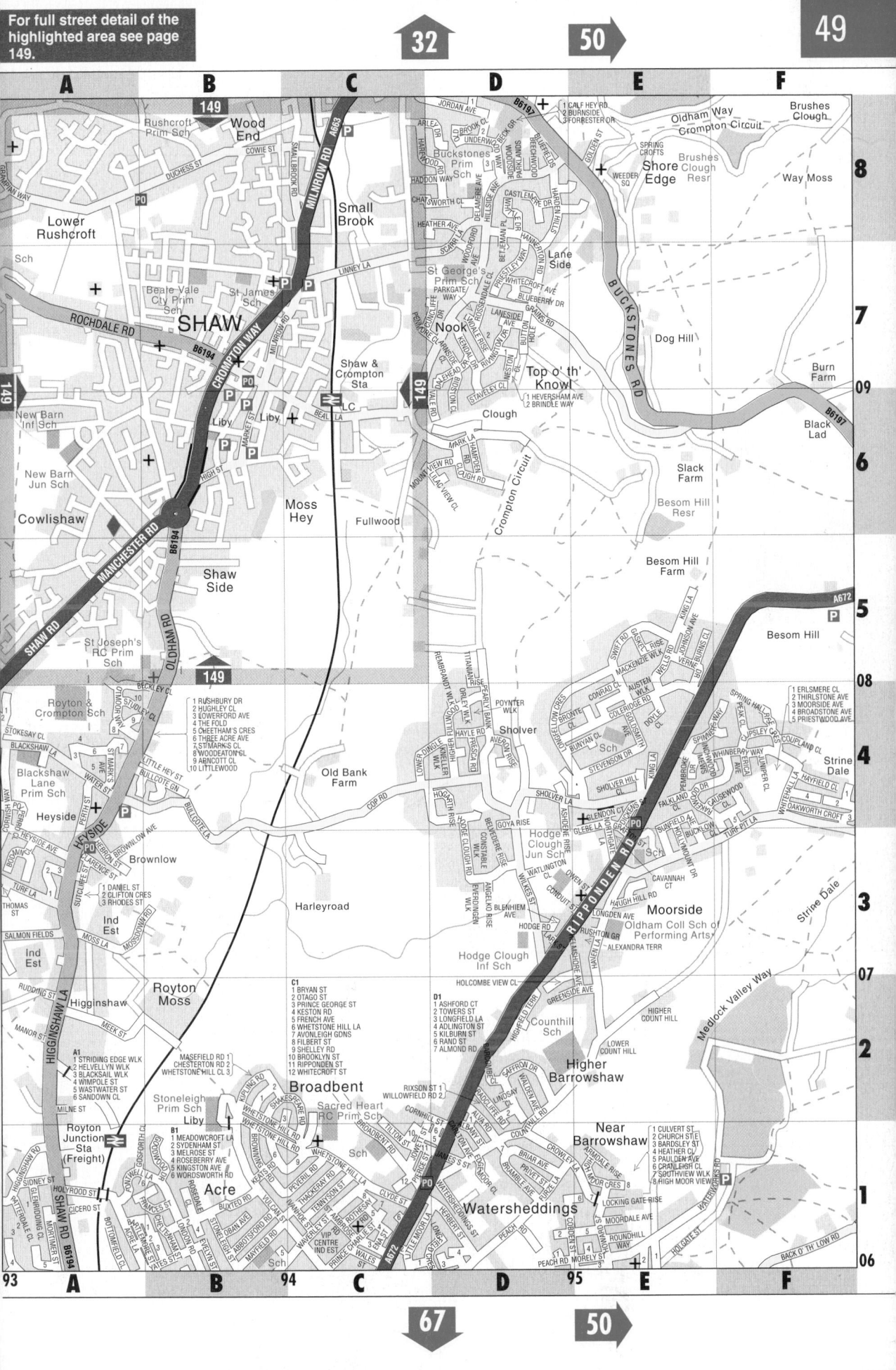

49 33

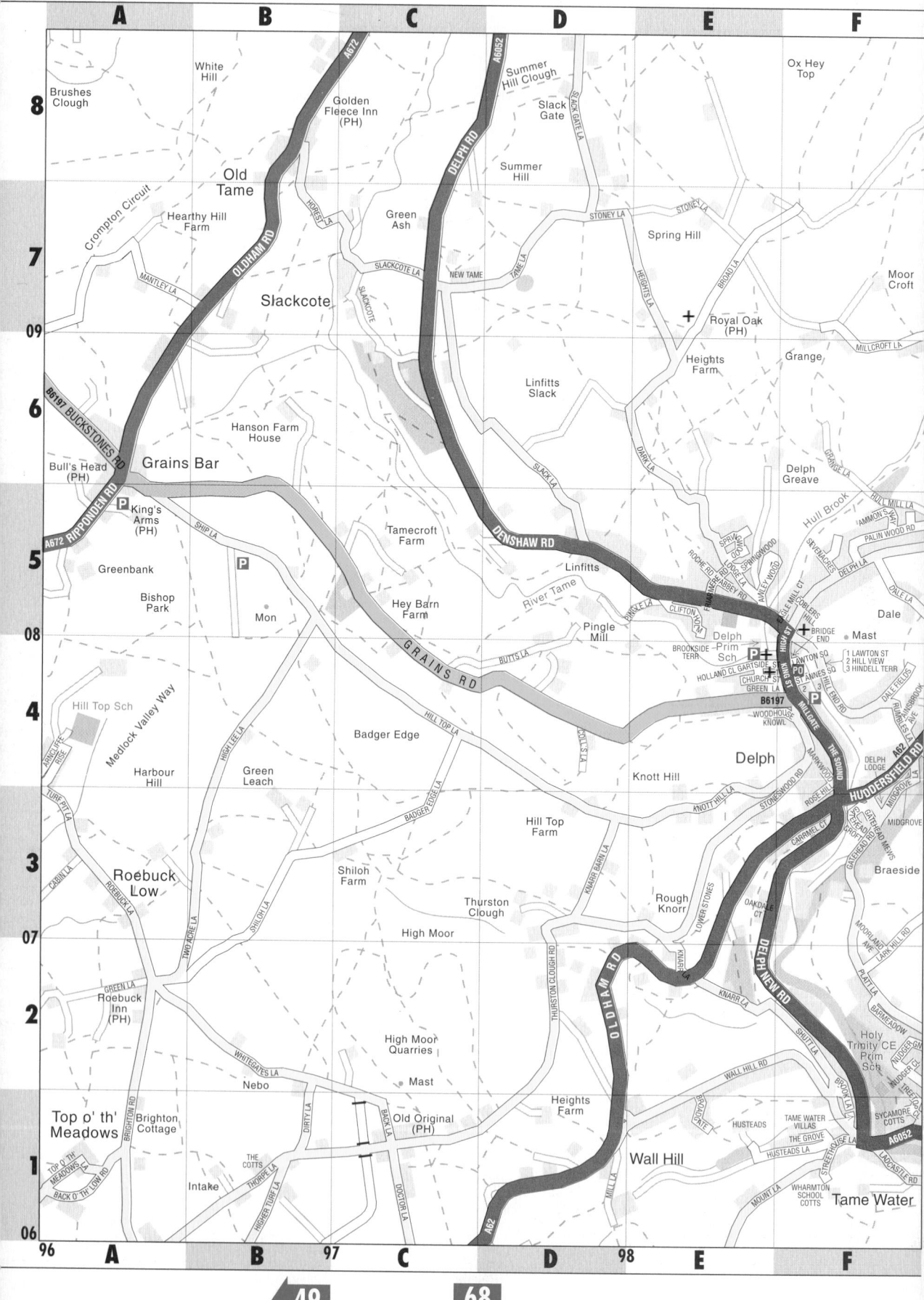
A
B
C
D
E
F
8
7
09
6
5
08
4
3
07
2
1
06
96
97
98
Brushes Clough
White Hill
A672
A6052
Summer Hill Clough
Golden Fleece Inn (PH)
Slack Gate
SLACK GATE LA
DELPH RD
Ox Hey Top
Summer Hill
Old Tame
Crompton Circuit
Hearthy Hill Farm
HORES LA
Green Ash
STONEY LA
Spring Hill
OLDHAM RD
SLACKCOTE LA
NEW TAME
TAME LA
HEIGHTS LA
BROAD LA
Moor Croft
MANTLEY LA
Slackcote
SLACKCOTE
Royal Oak (PH)
MILLCROFT LA
Heights Farm
Grange
Linfitts Slack
B6197 BUCKSTONES RD
Hanson Farm House
DARK LA
SLACK LA
Delph Greave
GRANGE LA
Bull's Head (PH)
Grains Bar
Hull Brook
HULL MILL LA
AMMON'S WAY
PALIN WOOD RD
A672 RIPPONDEN RD
King's Arms (PH)
SHIP LA
Tamecroft Farm
DENSHAW RD
SPRINGWOOD
SEVENACRES
DELPH LA
Greenbank
Linfitts
ROCHE RD
FRIARMERE RD
ABBEY RD
AWLEY WOOD
EAGLE MILL CT
COBLERS HILL
DALE LA
Bishop Park
Hey Barn Farm
River Tame
PINGLE LA
CLIFTON HOLM
Dale
Mon
Pingle Mill
Delph Prim Sch
BRIDGE END
Mast
GRAINS RD
BUTTS LA
BROOKSIDE TERR
HIGH ST
LAWTON SQ
ST ANNES SQ
1 LAWTON ST
2 HILL VIEW
3 HINDELL TERR
HOLLAND CL
GARTSIDE ST
CHURCH ST
GREEN LA
KING ST
PO
HILL END RD
DALE FIELDS
Hill Top Sch
Medlock Valley Way
B6197
WOODHOUSE KNOWL
MILLGATE
RUMBLES LA
AINSBROOK AVE
ARNCLIFFE RISE
HILL TOP LA
Badger Edge
COLLS LA
Delph
THE SOUND
A62
HUDDERSFIELD RD
DELPH LODGE
Harbour Hill
HIGH LEE LA
Green Leach
Knott Hill
STONESWOOD RD
MARKWOOD
ROSE HILL
KNOTT HILL LA
MIDGROVE LA
TURF PIT LA
BADGER EDGE LA
Hill Top Farm
CARMEL CT
GATEHEAD RD
GATEHEAD MEWS
GATEHEAD CROFT
MIDGROVE
KNARR BARN LA
Roebuck Low
Shiloh Farm
Braeside
CABIN LA
ROEBUCK LA
LOWER STONES
Thurston Clough
Rough Knorr
OAKDALE CT
SHILOH LA
TWO ACRE LA
High Moor
MOORLAND AVE
LARK HILL RD
DELPH NEW RD
KNARR LA
GREEN LA
Roebuck Inn (PH)
THURSTON CLOUGH RD
OLDHAM RD
PLATT LA
BARMEADOW
Holy Trinity CE Prim Sch
High Moor Quarries
SHUTT LA
WHITEGATES LA
WALL HILL RD
Mast
Nebo
Heights Farm
BROADGATE
BROOK LA
DIRTY LA
BACK LA
Old Original (PH)
HUSTEADS
TAME WATER VILLAS
THE GROVE
SYCAMORE COTTS
Top o' th' Meadows
Brighton Cottage
BRIGHTON RD
HUSTEADS LA
STREETHOUSE LA
A6052
TOP O' TH' MEADOWS LA
THE COTTS
THORPE LA
Wall Hill
LADCASTLE RD
BACK O' TH' LOW RD
Intake
HIGHER TURF LA
DOCTOR LA
MILL LA
MOUNT LA
WHARMTON SCHOOL COTTS
Tame Water
A62

49 68

34
52

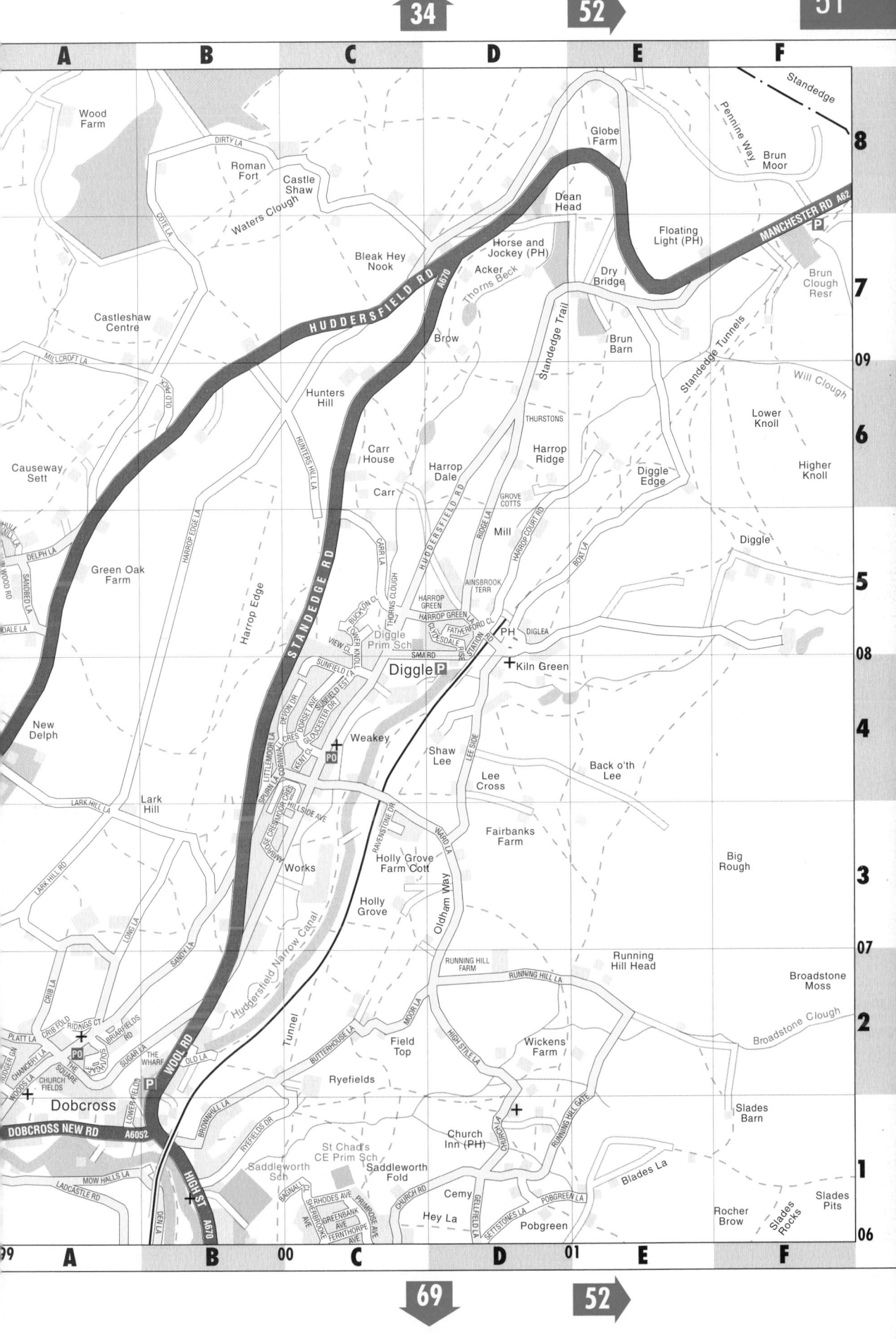
Standedge
Pennine Way
Wood Farm
Roman Fort
Castle Shaw
Waters Clough
Globe Farm
Brun Moor
Dean Head
Floating Light (PH)
MANCHESTER RD A62
Horse and Jockey (PH)
Bleak Hey Nook
Acker
Thorns Beck
Dry Bridge
Brun Clough Resr
HUDDERSFIELD RD
A670
Castleshaw Centre
Brow
Standedge Trail
Brun Barn
Standedge Tunnels
MILLCROFT LA
Will Clough
Hunters Hill
Lower Knoll
THURSTONS
Carr House
Harrop Dale
Harrop Ridge
Diggle Edge
Higher Knoll
Causeway Sett
Carr
HUNTERS HILL LA
HARROP EDGE LA
GROVE COTTS
Mill
DELPH LA
Diggle
Green Oak Farm
STANDEDGE RD
Harrop Edge
AINSBROOK TERR
HARROP GREEN
PH
DIGLEA
Diggle Prim Sch
Kiln Green
Diggle
New Delph
Weakey
Shaw Lee
Lee Cross
Back o'th Lee
LARK HILL LA
Lark Hill
Fairbanks Farm
Works
Holly Grove Farm Cott
Big Rough
Holly Grove
Oldham Way
Huddersfield Narrow Canal
RUNNING HILL FARM
RUNNING HILL LA
Running Hill Head
Broadstone Moss
Broadstone Clough
Tunnel
Field Top
Wickens Farm
WOOL RD
Dobcross
DOBCROSS NEW RD A6052
Ryefields
Slades Barn
Church Inn (PH)
St Chad's CE Prim Sch
Saddleworth Sch
Saddleworth Fold
Blades La
HIGH ST A670
Cemy
Hey La
Pobgreen
Rocher Brow
Slades Rocks
Slades Pits
A B C D E F
8 7 09 6 5 08 4 3 07 2 1 06
99 00 01

69
52

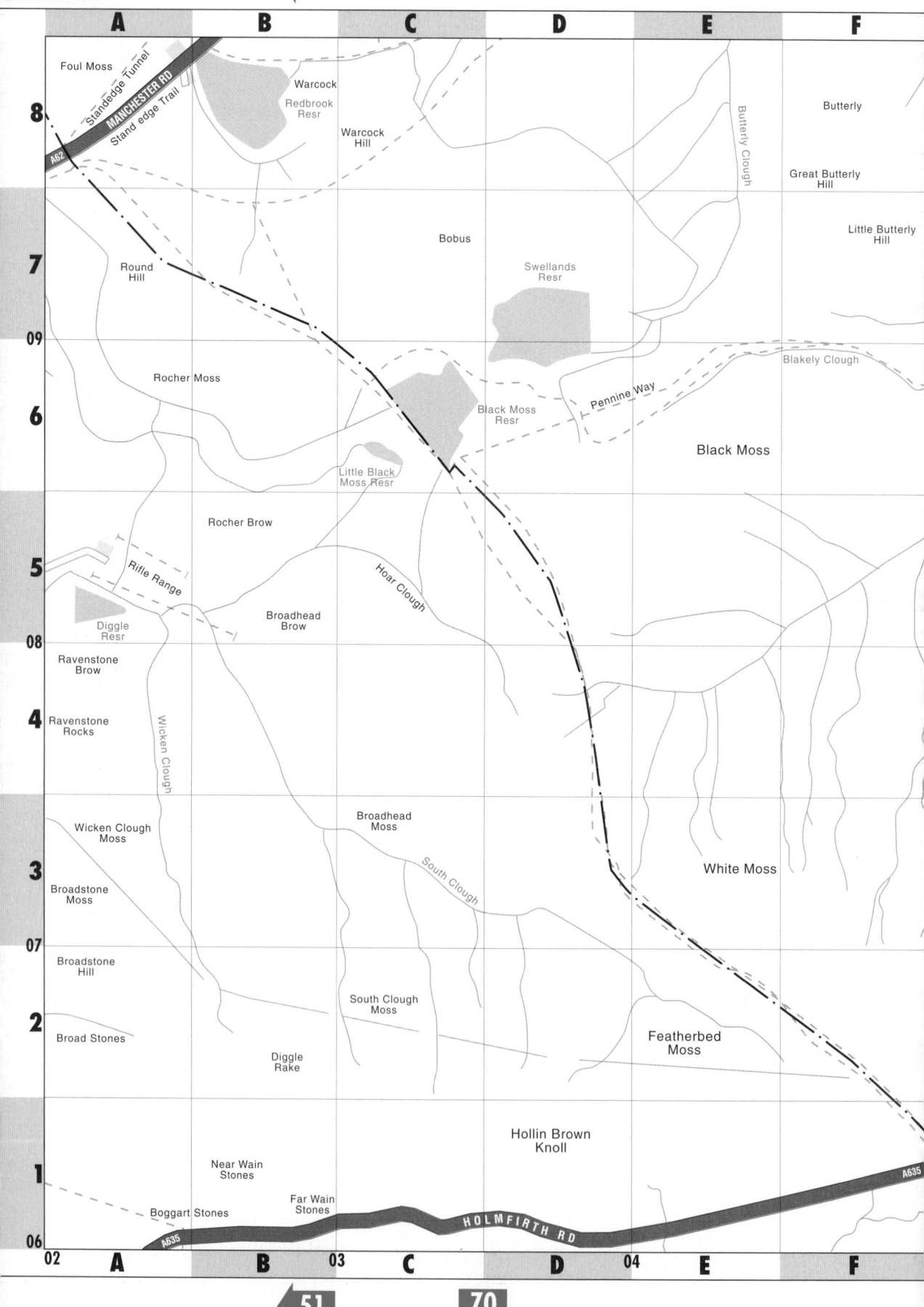

A   B   C   D   E   F

8

7

09

6

5

08

4

3

07

2

1

06

02   A   B   03   C   D   04   E   F

Foul Moss

Standedge Tunnel

MANCHESTER RD

Stand edge Trail

A62

Warcock

Redbrook Resr

Warcock Hill

Butterly Clough

Butterly

Great Butterly Hill

Little Butterly Hill

Round Hill

Bobus

Swellands Resr

Blakely Clough

Rocher Moss

Black Moss Resr

Pennine Way

Black Moss

Little Black Moss Resr

Rocher Brow

Hoar Clough

Rifle Range

Broadhead Brow

Diggle Resr

Ravenstone Brow

Ravenstone Rocks

Wicken Clough

Broadhead Moss

White Moss

South Clough

Wicken Clough Moss

Broadstone Moss

Broadstone Hill

South Clough Moss

Featherbed Moss

Broad Stones

Diggle Rake

Hollin Brown Knoll

Near Wain Stones

Far Wain Stones

Boggart Stones

A635

HOLMFIRTH RD

A635

35
54
A
B
C
D
E
F
8
7
6
5
4
3
2
1
05
04
03
02
52
53
71
ORRELL
Hall Green
Newgate
Up Holland
Orrell Post
Tontine
Far Moor
Higher End
Longshaw
Brownlow
Windmill (dis)
Works
Dean Wood Golf Course
Hotel
CH
St Thomas Sch
Higher Tower Hill Farm
Mast
Well Cross Farm
The Lawns Farm
Upholland Tunnel
Lower Pimbo
Higher Pimbo Farm
Pimbo Bushes
Up Holland High Sch
Orrell St James' Rd Cty Jun & Inf Sch
St James' RC Prim Sch
Orrell Holgate Prim Sch
Orrell Sta
St Peter's RC High Sch
Orrell Water Park
Farrar's Farm
Winstanley Coll
Greenslate Farm
Billings
Moss Wood
Bispham Hall
Mountains Farm
Heaton House
Brownlow Farm
Promised Land Farm
Longshaw Bottom
New House Farm
BISPHAM HALL BSNS PK
ORMSKIRK RD
GROVE RD
DINGLE RD
PARLIAMENT ST
SCHOOL LA
ORRELL RD
GATHURST RD
MOOR RD
ST JAMES' RD
GANTLEY RD
UPHOLLAND RD
SMETHURST RD
WINSTANLEY RD
TOWER HILL RD
CINNAMON BROW
TONTINE RD
SPENCER'S LA
HALL LA
PARK RD
EDGE HALL RD
B5206
A577
M58
M6
26

53
36

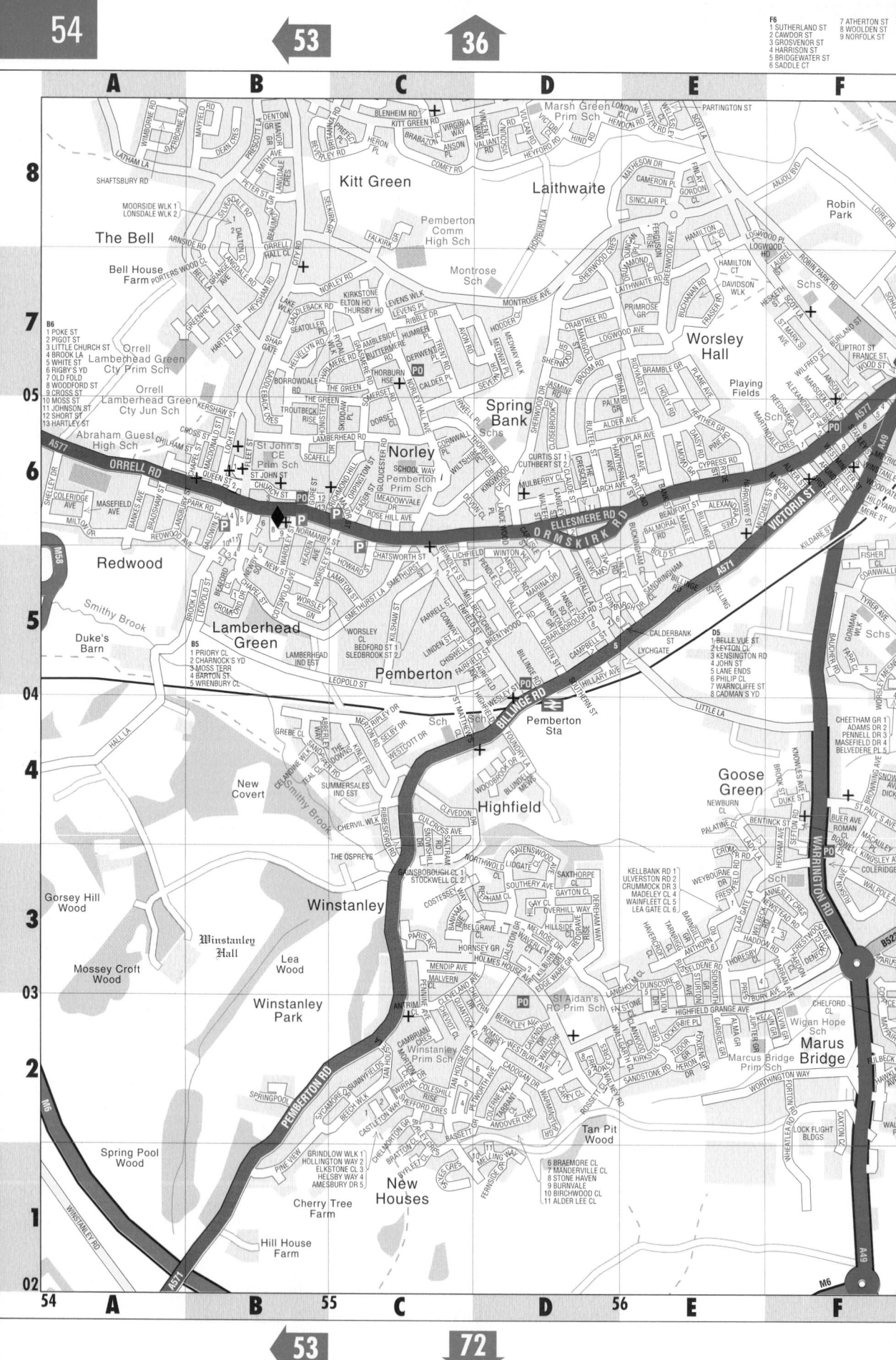
F6
1 SUTHERLAND ST
2 CAWDOR ST
3 GROSVENOR ST
4 HARRISON ST
5 BRIDGEWATER ST
6 SADDLE CT
7 ATHERTON ST
8 WOOLDEN ST
9 NORFOLK ST
A
B
C
D
E
F
8
7
05
6
5
04
4
3
03
2
1
02
54
55
56
Kitt Green
Laithwaite
Marsh Green Prim Sch
Robin Park
The Bell
Bell House Farm
Pemberton Comm High Sch
Montrose Sch
Worsley Hall
Playing Fields
Schs
B6
1 POKE ST
2 PIGOT ST
3 LITTLE CHURCH ST
4 BROOK LA
5 WHITE ST
6 RIGBY'S YD
7 OLD FOLD
8 WOODFORD ST
9 CROSS ST
10 MOSS ST
11 JOHNSON ST
12 SHORT ST
13 HARTLEY ST
Orrell Lamberhead Green Cty Prim Sch
Orrell Lamberhead Green Cty Jun Sch
Abraham Guest High Sch
St John's CE Prim Sch
Spring Bank
Norley
School Way Pemberton Prim Sch
Redwood
Lamberhead Green
Duke's Barn
Smithy Brook
B5
1 PRIORY CL
2 CHARNOCK'S YD
3 MOSS TERR
4 BARTON ST
5 WRENBURY CL
Lamberhead Ind Est
Pemberton
Pemberton Sta
D5
1 BELLE VUE ST
2 LEYTON CL
3 KENSINGTON RD
4 JOHN ST
5 LANE ENDS
6 PHILIP CL
7 WARNCLIFFE ST
8 CADMAN'S YD
CHEETHAM GR 1
ADAMS DR 2
PENNELL DR 3
MASEFIELD DR 4
BELVEDERE PL 5
New Covert
Summersales Ind Est
Highfield
Goose Green
Winstanley
Gorsey Hill Wood
Winstanley Hall
Lea Wood
Mossey Croft Wood
Winstanley Park
GAINSBOROUGH CL 1
STOCKWELL CL 2
KELLBANK RD 1
ULVERSTON RD 2
CRUMMOCK DR 3
MADELEY CL 4
WAINFLEET CL 5
LEA GATE CL 6
St Aidan's RC Prim Sch
Winstanley Prim Sch
Wigan Hope Sch
Marcus Bridge Prim Sch
Marus Bridge
Tan Pit Wood
Spring Pool Wood
GRINDLOW WLK 1
HOLLINGTON WAY 2
ELKSTONE CL 3
HELSBY WAY 4
AMESBURY DR 5
6 BRAEMORE CL
7 MANDERVILLE CL
8 STONE HAVEN
9 BURNVALE
10 BIRCHWOOD CL
11 ALDER LEE CL
New Houses
Cherry Tree Farm
Hill House Farm
ORRELL RD
ORMSKIRK RD
VICTORIA ST
BILLINGE RD
PEMBERTON RD
WARRINGTON RD
A577
A571
A49
B5238
M58
M6

53
72

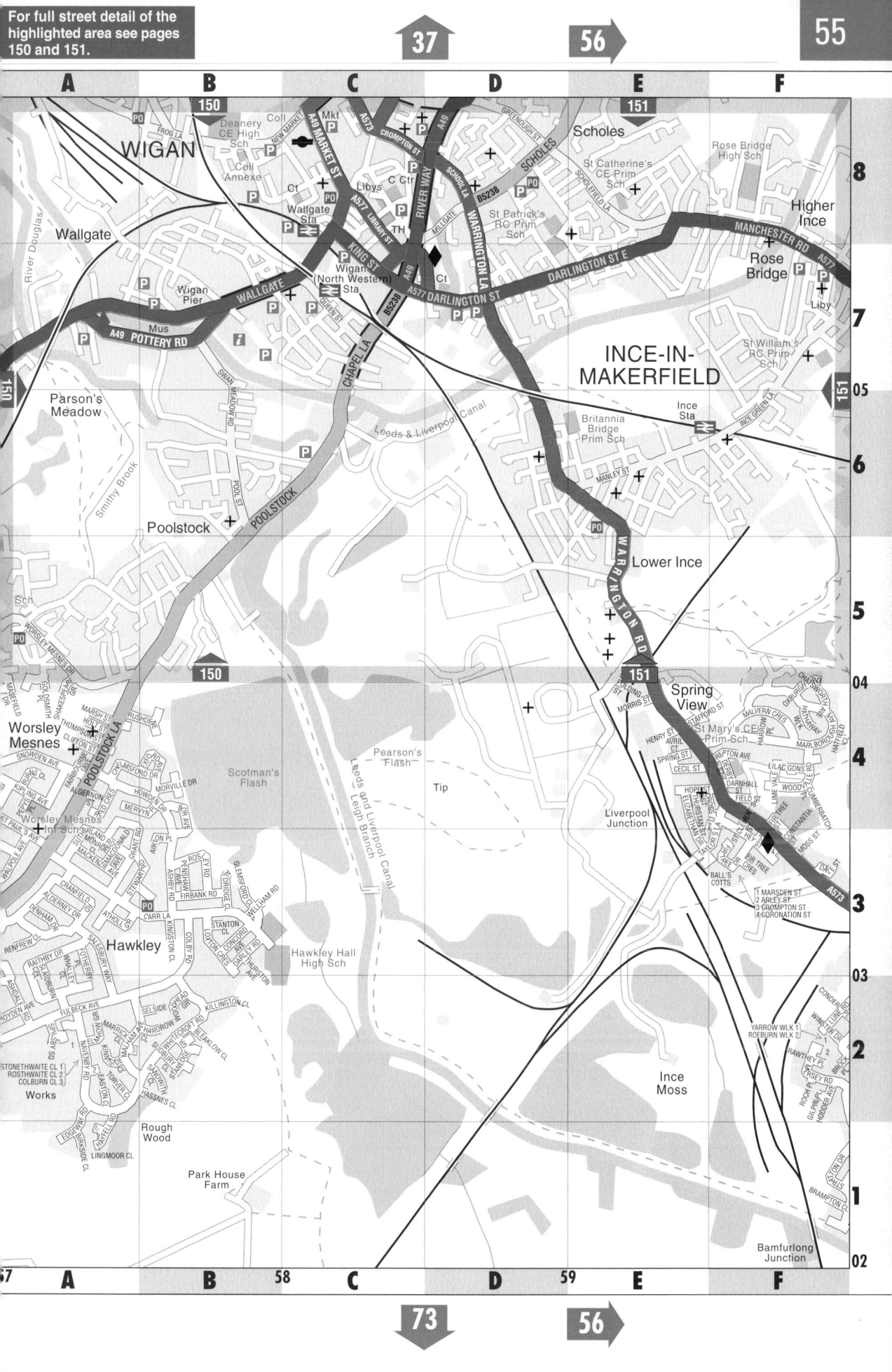

55
38

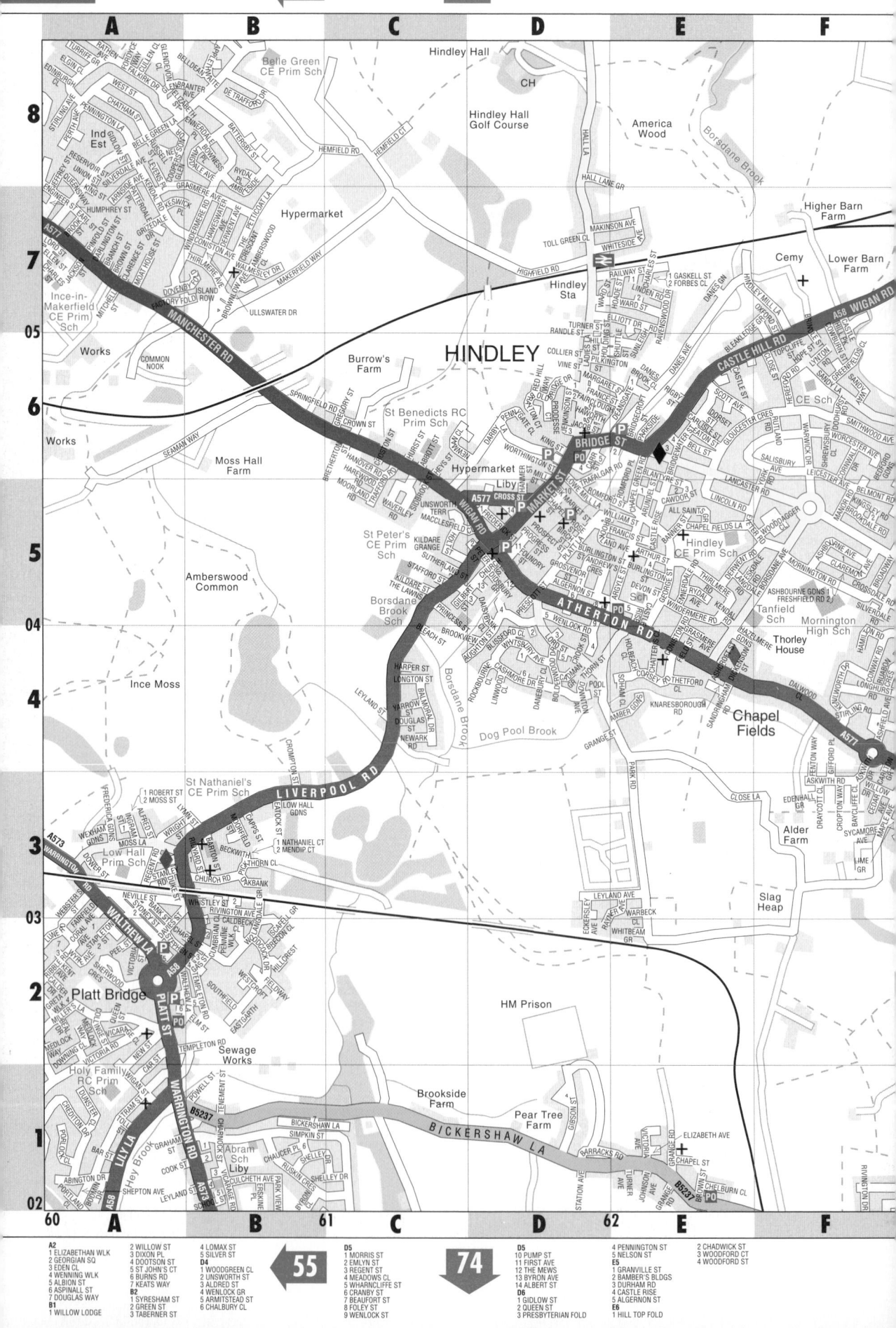

A2
1 ELIZABETHAN WLK
2 GEORGIAN SQ
3 EDEN CL
4 WENNING WLK
5 ALBION ST
6 ASPINALL ST
7 DOUGLAS WAY
B1
1 WILLOW LODGE
2 WILLOW ST
3 DIXON PL
4 DOOTSON ST
5 ST JOHN'S CT
6 BURNS RD
7 KEATS WAY
B2
1 SYRESHAM ST
2 GREEN ST
3 TABERNER ST
4 LOMAX ST
5 SILVER ST
D4
1 WOODGREEN CL
2 UNSWORTH ST
3 ALDRED ST
4 WENLOCK GR
5 ARMITSTEAD ST
6 CHALBURY CL

55

D5
1 MORRIS ST
2 EMLYN ST
3 REGENT ST
4 MEADOWS CL
5 WHARNCLIFFE ST
6 CRANBY ST
7 BEAUFORT ST
8 FOLEY ST
9 WENLOCK ST

74

D5
10 PUMP ST
11 FIRST AVE
12 THE MEWS
13 BYRON AVE
14 ALBERT ST
D6
1 GIDLOW ST
2 QUEEN ST
3 PRESBYTERIAN FOLD
4 PENNINGTON ST
5 NELSON ST
E5
1 GRANVILLE ST
2 BAMBER'S BLDGS
3 DURHAM RD
4 CASTLE RISE
5 ALGERNON ST
E6
1 HILL TOP FOLD
2 CHADWICK ST
3 WOODFORD CT
4 WOODFORD ST

39
58

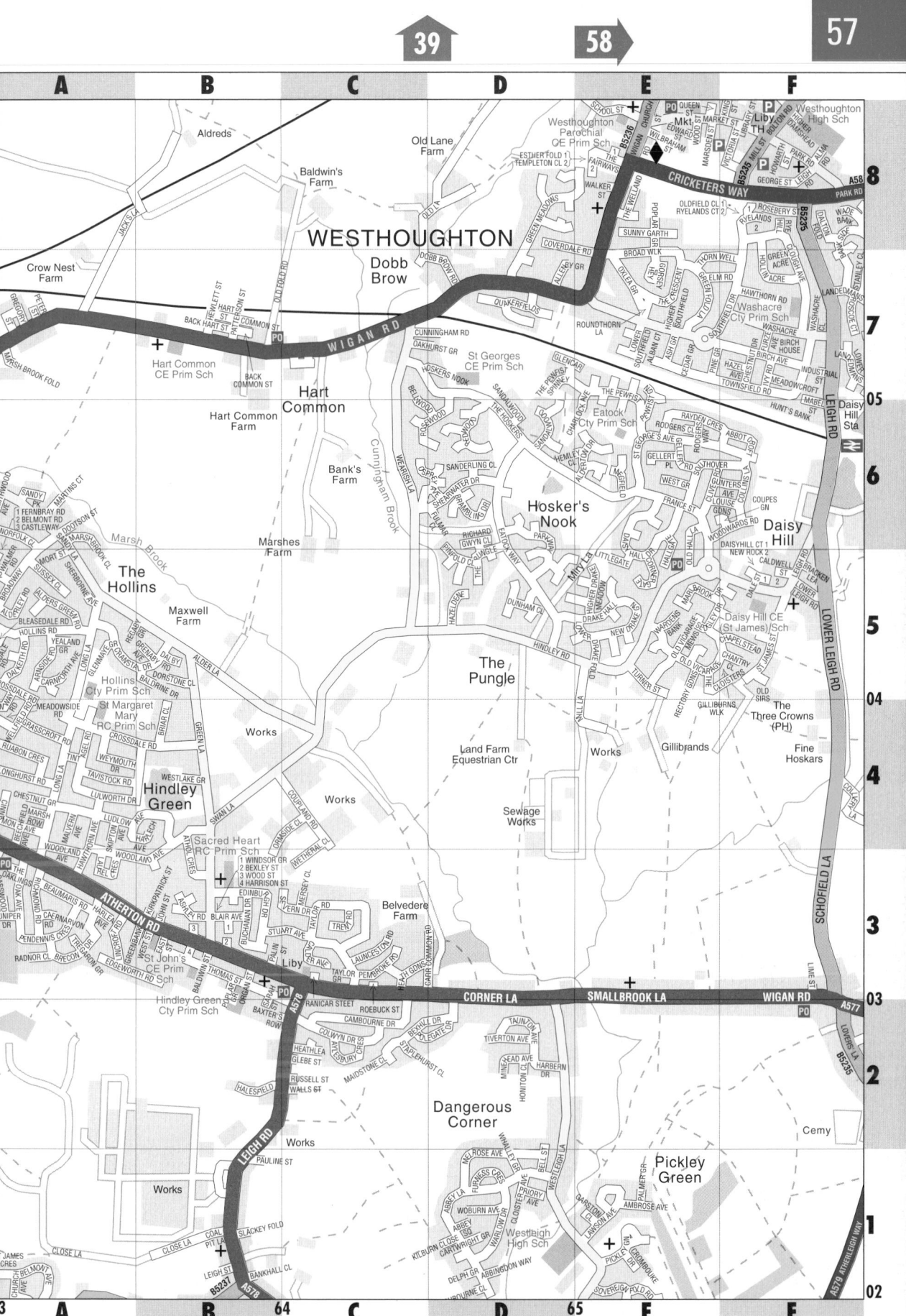
WESTHOUGHTON
Aldreds
Old Lane Farm
Baldwin's Farm
Westhoughton Parochial CE Prim Sch
Westhoughton High Sch
Mkt
Liby
TH
CRICKETERS WAY
Crow Nest Farm
Dobb Brow
WIGAN RD
Hart Common CE Prim Sch
Hart Common
Hart Common Farm
St Georges CE Prim Sch
Washacre Cty Prim Sch
Eatock Cty Prim Sch
Daisy Hill Sta
Bank's Farm
Cunningham Brook
Hosker's Nook
Daisy Hill
Marshes Farm
Marsh Brook
The Hollins
Maxwell Farm
Daisy Hill CE (St James) Sch
The Pungle
Hollins Cty Prim Sch
St Margaret Mary RC Prim Sch
Works
Land Farm Equestrian Ctr
Gillibrands
The Three Crowns (PH)
Fine Hoskars
Hindley Green
Sewage Works
Sacred Heart RC Prim Sch
Belvedere Farm
ATHERTON RD
St John's CE Prim Sch
Hindley Green Cty Prim Sch
CORNER LA
SMALLBROOK LA
LOWER LEIGH RD
SCHOFIELD LA
LEIGH RD
Dangerous Corner
Cemy
Pickley Green
Westleigh High Sch
A B C D E F
8 7 6 5 4 3 2 1
05 04 03 02
64 65

75
58

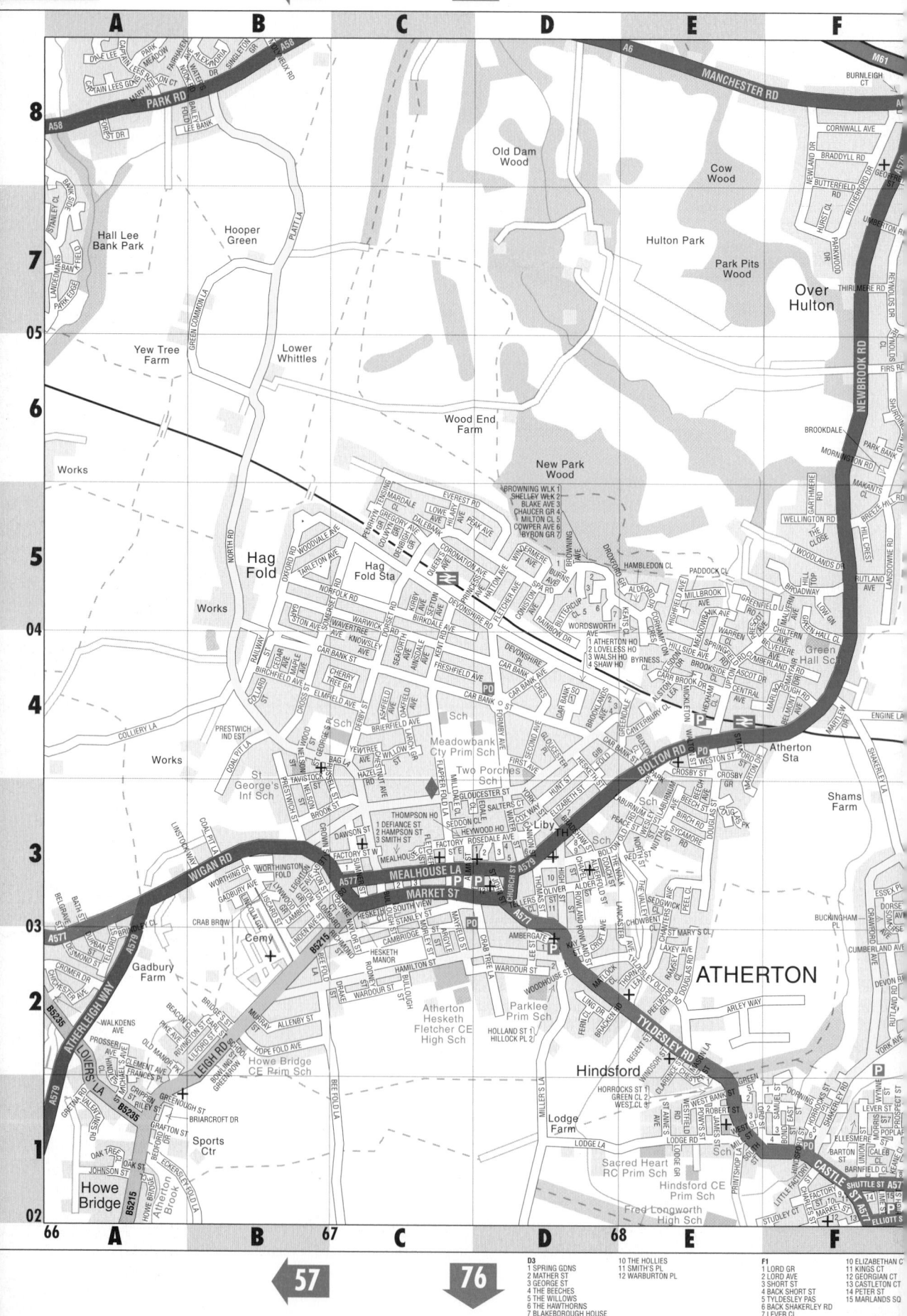

D3
1 SPRING GDNS
2 MATHER ST
3 GEORGE ST
4 THE BEECHES
5 THE WILLOWS
6 THE HAWTHORNS
7 BLAKEBOROUGH HOUSE
8 MARTIN ST
9 BRAMPTON ST

10 THE HOLLIES
11 SMITH'S PL
12 WARBURTON PL

F1
1 LORD GR
2 LORD AVE
3 SHORT ST
4 BACK SHORT ST
5 TYLDESLEY PAS
6 BACK SHAKERLEY RD
7 LEVER CL
8 MORT ST
9 ALFRED ST

10 ELIZABETHAN CT
11 KINGS CT
12 GEORGIAN CT
13 CASTLETON CT
14 PETER ST
15 MARLANDS SQ

A1
1 PARK ST
2 ASH ST
3 BIRCH ST
4 ELM ST
5 PINE ST
6 HENRY ST
7 JOHN ST
8 GREEN ST
9 PATCHETT ST
10 MEANLEY ST
11 BLOSSOM ST
12 WESTON ST
13 COBDEN ST
14 ROBINSON ST
15 WHEWELL ST
16 DERBY ST

F3
1 SHILLINGTEN CL
2 WHITE LADY CL
3 CLOCK TOWER CL
4 WOOD COTTAGE CL
5 ICE HOUSE CL
6 NARCISSUS WLK
7 BUTTERCUP AVE
8 PETUNIA WLK
9 FREESIA AVE
10 HAREBELL AVE
11 WICHEAVES CRES
12 ASPINALL GR
13 WICHBROOK RD

59

C8
1 THOMAS GARNET CT
2 PHILIP ARNOLD CT
3 SUTHERLAND ST
4 WESTMINSTER WLK
5 LONSDALE GR
6 KENTFORD GR

42

C8
7 LIDGATE GR
8 ASHLEY GR
9 ALMOND ST
10 ORMROD ST
D8
1 JANE BARTER HOUSE
2 BARNES HOUSE
3 ELLESMERE WLK
4 WILCOCKSON HOUSE
5 HESKETH WLK

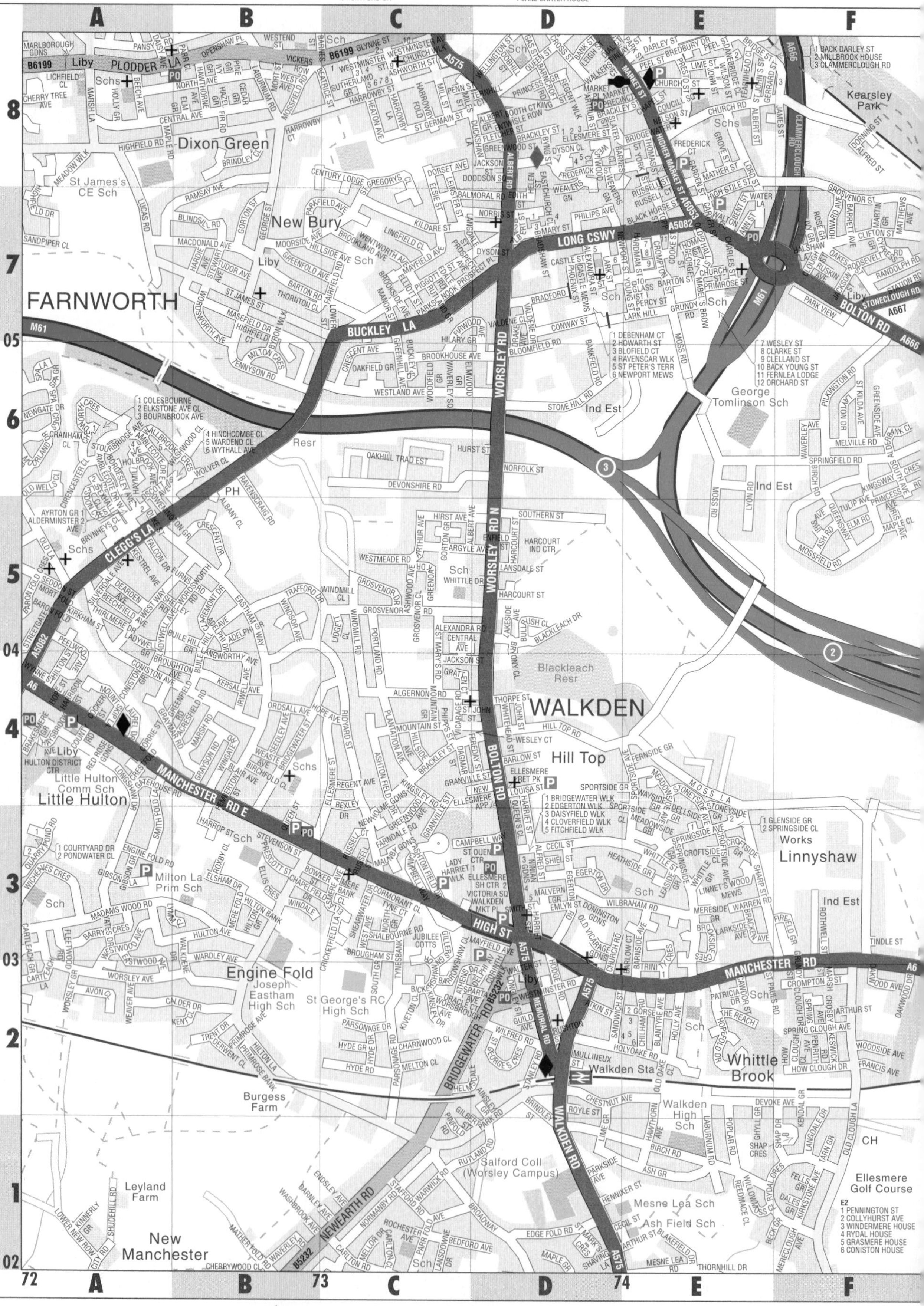

FARNWORTH
WALKDEN
Dixon Green
New Bury
Little Hulton
Hill Top
Linnyshaw
Engine Fold
Whittle Brook
New Manchester
Kearsley Park
Blackleach Resr
Burgess Farm
Leyland Farm
Ellesmere Golf Course
Salford Coll (Worsley Campus)
Walkden Sta
Walkden High Sch
Mesne Lea Sch
Ash Field Sch
St George's RC High Sch
Joseph Eastham High Sch
Milton La Prim Sch
Little Hulton Comm Sch
George Tomlinson Sch
St James's CE Sch
M61
A6
A575
A5082
A666
A667
B6199
B5232
WORSLEY RD
WORSLEY RD N
BOLTON RD
MANCHESTER RD E
MANCHESTER RD
WALKDEN RD
BUCKLEY LA
CLEGG'S LA
LONG CSWY
HIGH ST
BRIDGEWATER RD
NEWEARTH RD
PLODDER LA
1 BACK DARLEY ST
2 MILLBROOK HOUSE
3 CLAMMERCLOUGH RD
1 DEBENHAM CT
2 HOWARTH ST
3 BLOFIELD CT
4 RAVENSCAR WLK
5 ST PETER'S TERR
6 NEWPORT MEWS
7 WESLEY ST
8 CLARKE ST
9 CLELLAND ST
10 BACK YOUNG ST
11 FERNLEA LODGE
12 ORCHARD ST
1 COLESBOURNE
2 ELKSTONE AVE CL
3 BOURNBROOK AVE
4 HINCHCOMBE CL
5 WARDEND CL
6 WYTHALL AVE
1 BRIDGEWATER WLK
2 EDGERTON WLK
3 DAISYFIELD WLK
4 CLOVERFIELD WLK
5 FITCHFIELD WLK
1 GLENSIDE GR
2 SPRINGSIDE CL
1 COURTYARD DR
2 PONDWATER CL
E2
1 PENNINGTON ST
2 COLLYHURST AVE
3 WINDERMERE HOUSE
4 RYDAL HOUSE
5 GRASMERE HOUSE
6 CONISTON HOUSE

59

78

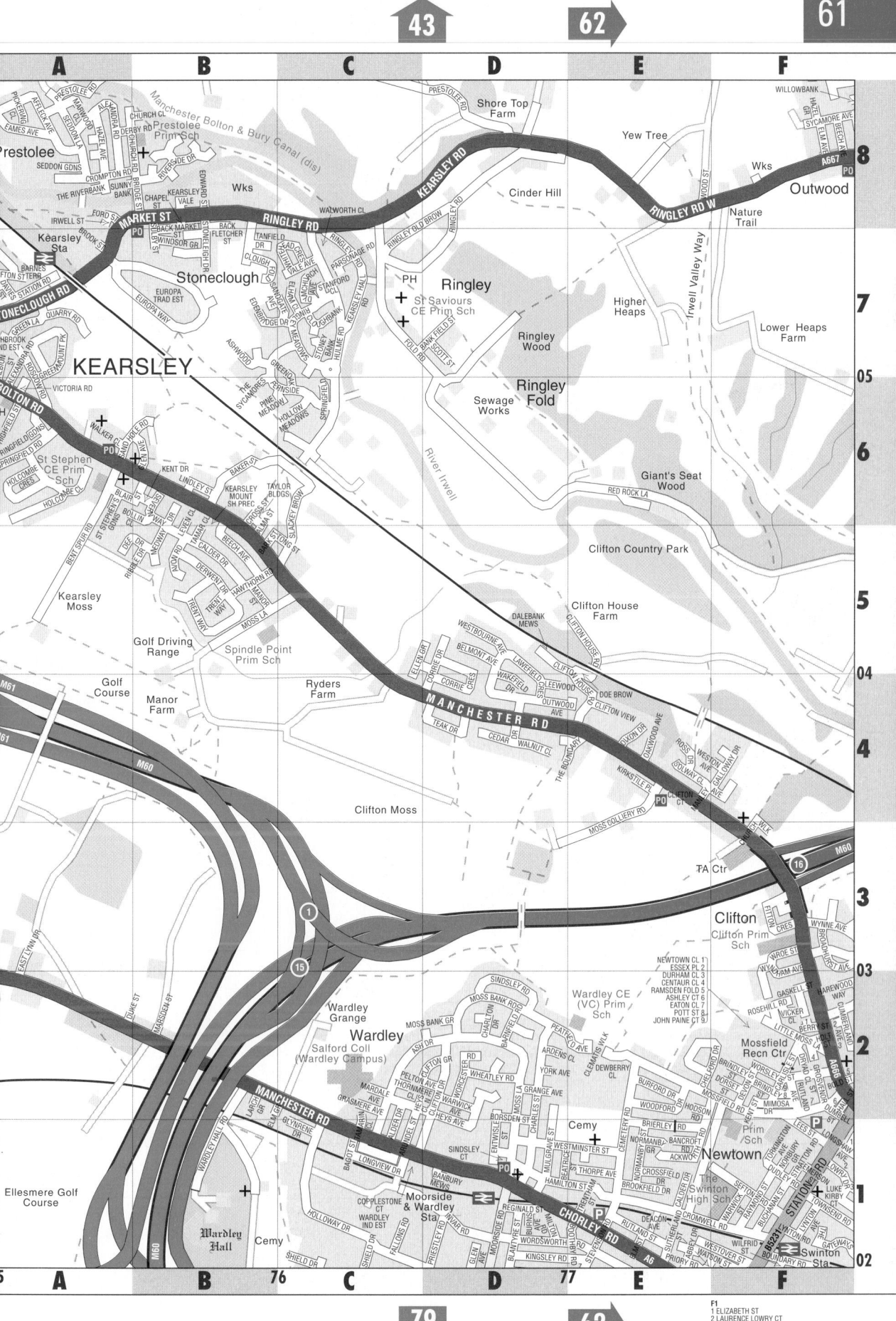
Prestolee
Kearsley Sta
Stoneclough
KEARSLEY
Ringley
Ringley Fold
Shore Top Farm
Yew Tree
Cinder Hill
Outwood
Nature Trail
Higher Heaps
Lower Heaps Farm
Ringley Wood
Sewage Works
Giant's Seat Wood
Clifton Country Park
Clifton House Farm
Kearsley Moss
Golf Driving Range
Spindle Point Prim Sch
Golf Course
Manor Farm
Ryders Farm
Clifton Moss
Clifton
Clifton Prim Sch
Wardley Grange
Wardley
Salford Coll (Wardley Campus)
Wardley CE (VC) Prim Sch
Mossfield Recn Ctr
Newtown
The Swinton High Sch
Moorside & Wardley Sta
Swinton Sta
Ellesmere Golf Course
Wardley Hall
Cemy
KEARSLEY RD
RINGLEY RD
RINGLEY RD W
MARKET ST
MANCHESTER RD
CHORLEY RD
STATION RD
M60
M61
A666
A667
A6
B5231
River Irwell
Irwell Valley Way
Manchester Bolton & Bury Canal (dis)
F1
1 ELIZABETH ST
2 LAURENCE LOWRY CT
3 HENDERSON AVE

61
44

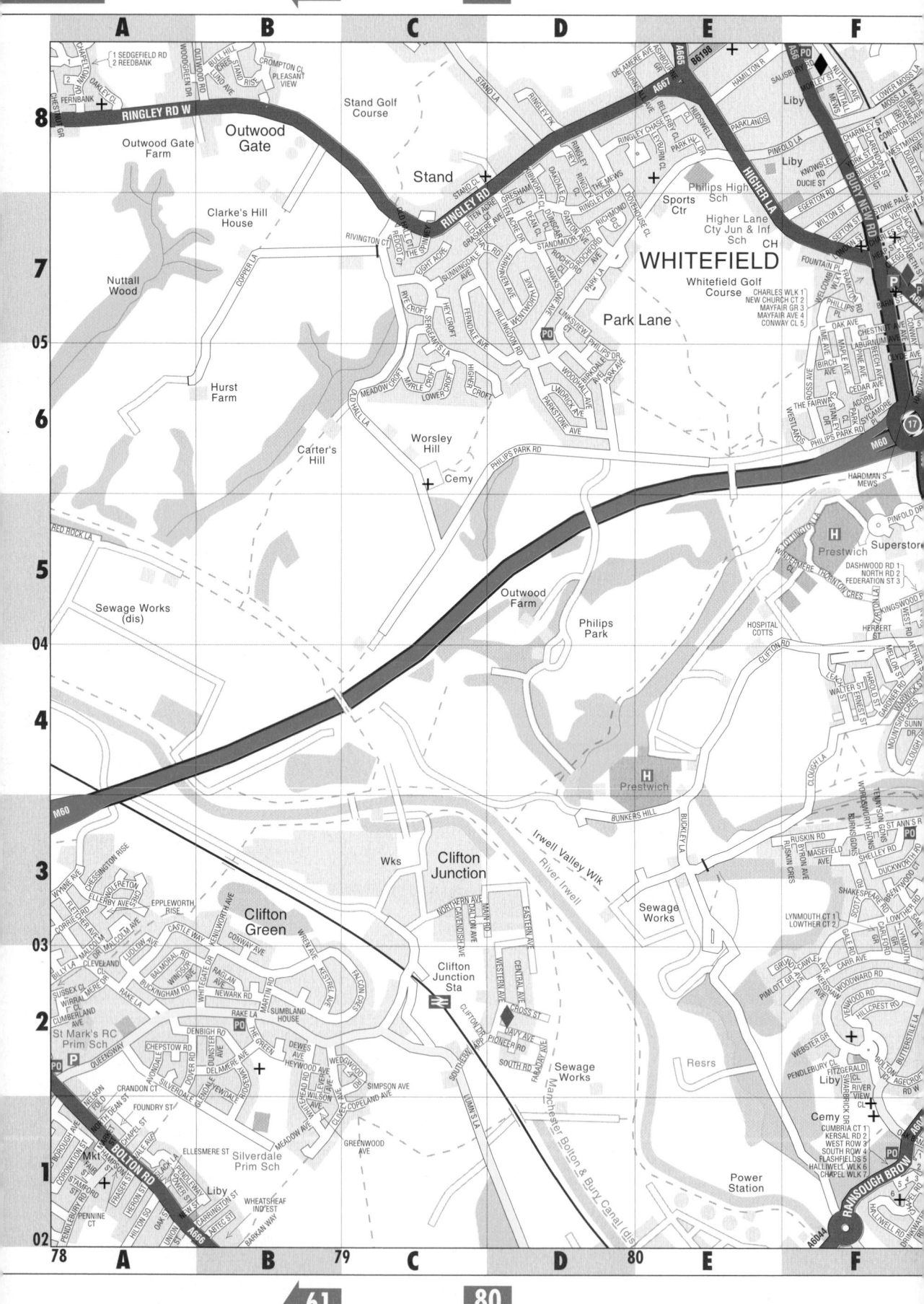
A
B
C
D
E
F
8
7
05
6
5
04
4
3
03
2
1
02
78
79
80
RINGLEY RD W
Outwood Gate
Outwood Gate Farm
Stand Golf Course
Stand
RINGLEY RD
Clarke's Hill House
Nuttall Wood
Hurst Farm
Carter's Hill
Worsley Hill
Cemy
PHILIPS PARK RD
WHITEFIELD
Whitefield Golf Course
Park Lane
Sports Ctr
Philips High Sch
Higher Lane Cty Jun & Inf Sch
CH
Liby
HIGHER LA
BURY NEW RD
A665
A667
B6198
A56
M60
Sewage Works (dis)
RED ROCK LA
Outwood Farm
Philips Park
Prestwich
Superstore
HOSPITAL COTTS
CLIFTON RD
BUNKERS HILL
Irwell Valley Wlk
River Irwell
Wks
Clifton Junction
Clifton Junction Sta
Clifton Green
Sewage Works
Resrs
Power Station
Manchester Bolton & Bury Canal (dis)
St Mark's RC Prim Sch
Silverdale Prim Sch
Mkt
BOLTON RD
A666
RAINSOUGH BROW
A6044
Cemy
Liby
CHARLES WLK 1
NEW CHURCH CT 2
MAYFAIR GR 3
MAYFAIR AVE 4
CONWAY CL 5
DASHWOOD RD 1
NORTH RD 2
FEDERATION ST 3
LYNMOUTH CT 1
LOWTHER CT 2
CUMBRIA CT 1
KERSAL RD 2
WEST ROW 3
SOUTH ROW 4
FLASHFIELDS 5
HALLIWELL WLK 6
CHAPEL WLK 7
1 SEDGEFIELD RD
2 REEDBANK

61
80

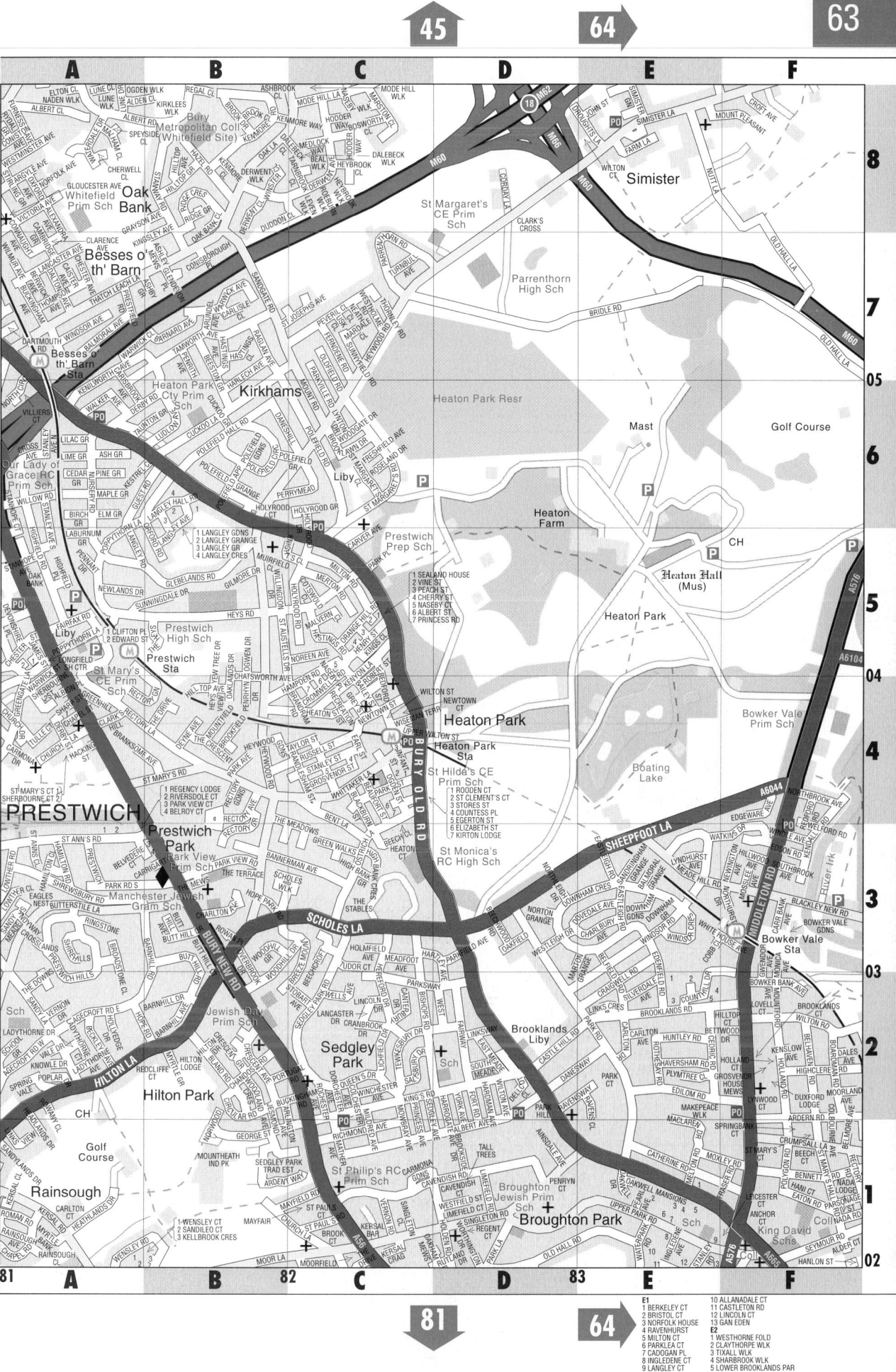

E1
1 BERKELEY CT
2 BRISTOL CT
3 NORFOLK HOUSE
4 RAVENHURST
5 MILTON CT
6 PARKLEA CT
7 CADOGAN PL
8 INGLEDENE CT
9 LANGLEY CT

10 ALLANADALE CT
11 CASTLETON RD
12 LINCOLN CT
13 GAN EDEN
E2
1 WESTHORNE FOLD
2 CLAYTHORPE WLK
3 TIXALL WLK
4 SHARBROOK WLK
5 LOWER BROOKLANDS PAR

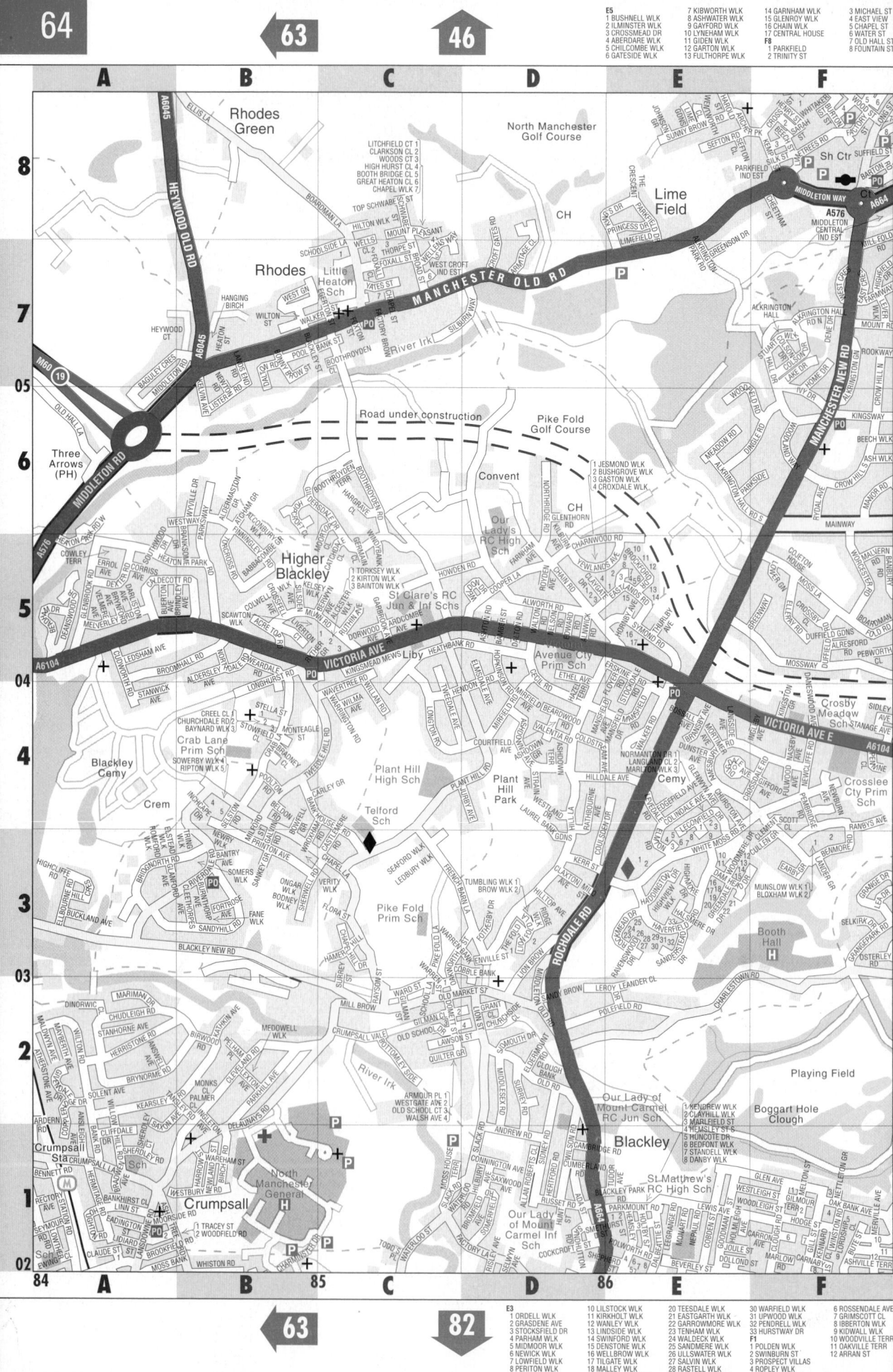

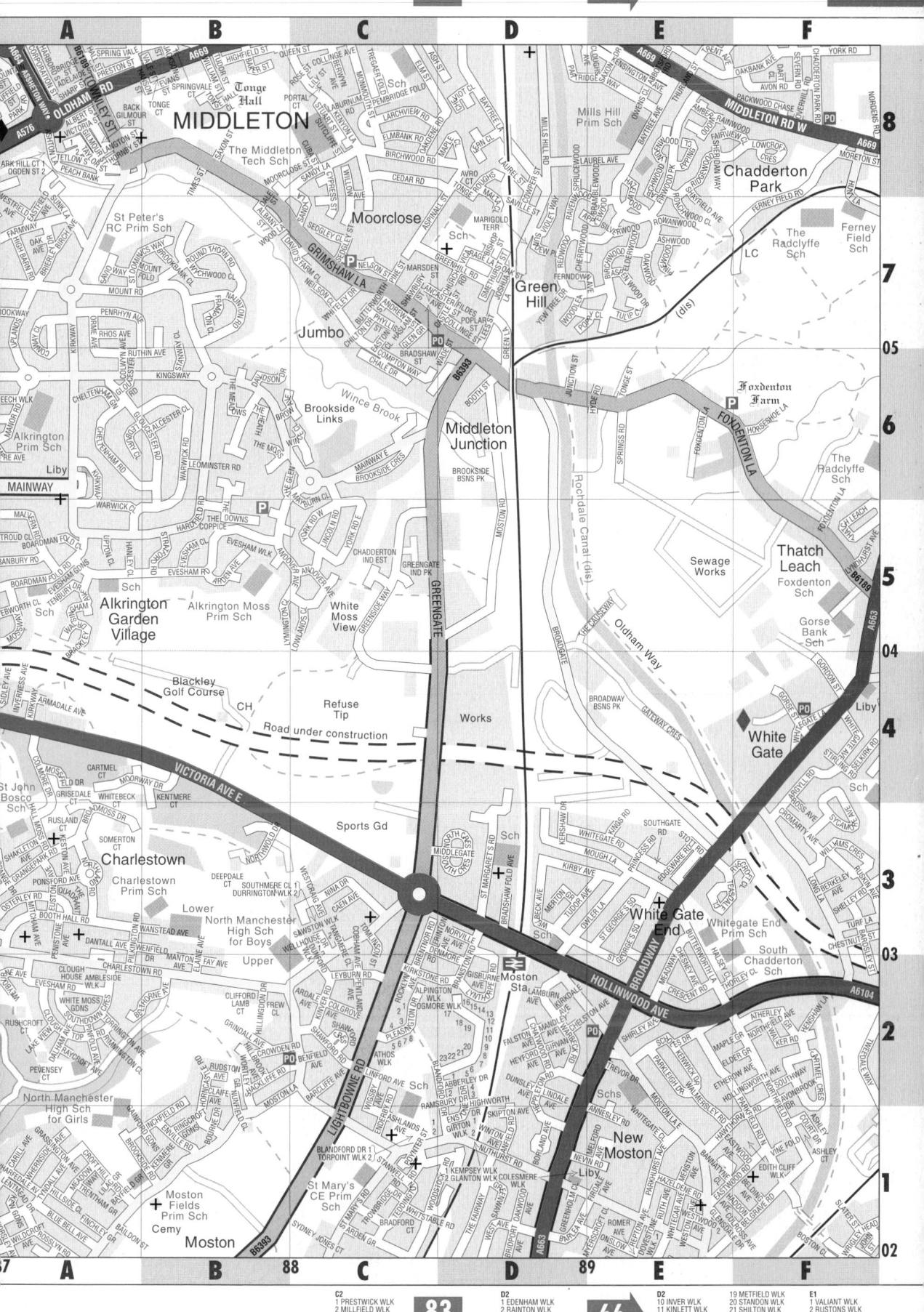

83 66

C2		D2		D2		19 METFIELD WLK	E1
1 PRESTWICK WLK		1 EDENHAM WLK		10 INVER WLK		20 STANDON WLK	1 VALIANT WLK
2 MILLFIELD WLK		2 RAINTON WLK		11 KINLETT WLK		21 SHILTON WLK	2 RUSTONS WLK
3 WOOLTON CL		3 PITMORE WLK		12 KIRKHILL WLK		22 SHAFTON WLK	
4 SNOWDEN WLK		4 HALLKIRK WLK		13 TEDBURN WLK		23 SCORTON WLK	
5 ANCASTER WLK		5 OTTERY WLK		14 THORNFORD WLK			
6 ROCKLAND WLK		6 FONTWELL WLK		15 TONGLEY WLK			
7 BARNWAY WLK		7 GAYTON WLK		16 TETSWORTH WLK			
8 AMPORT WLK		8 GLENCAR DR		17 OXHILL WLK			
		9 HENLOW WLK		18 ROXBY DR			

65 48

For full street detail of the highlighted area see pages 152 and 153.

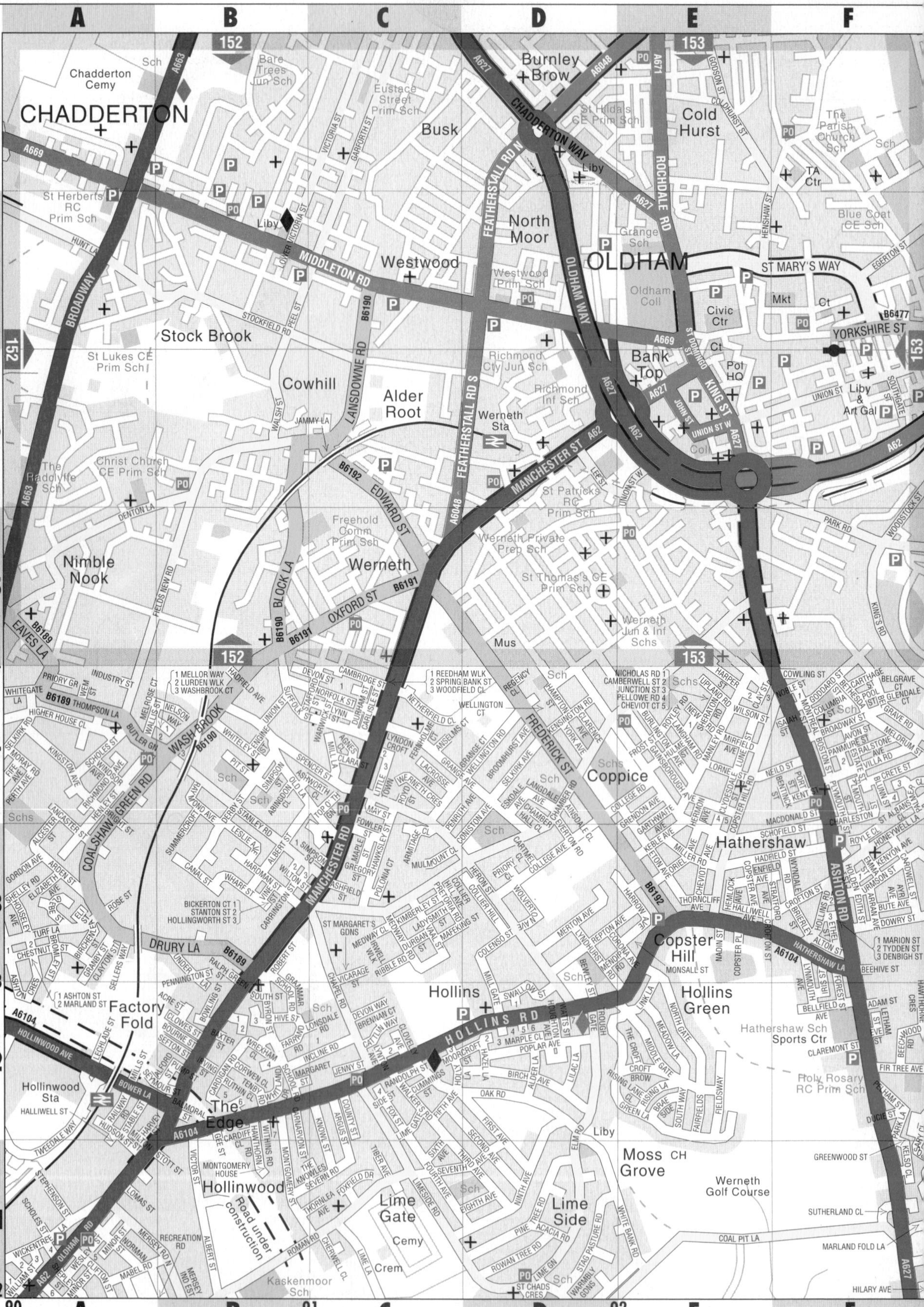

A B C D E F

152   153

CHADDERTON

Chadderton Cemy

Bare Trees Jun Sch

Busk

Burnley Brow

Cold Hurst

The Parish Church Sch

Blue Coat CE Sch

St Herberts RC Prim Sch

Liby

North Moor

OLDHAM

Westwood

Westwood Prim Sch

Oldham Coll

St Mary's Way

Mkt

Ct

Yorkshire St

Stock Brook

St Lukes CE Prim Sch

Civic Ctr

Pot HQ

Liby & Art Gal

Cowhill

Richmond Cty Jun Sch

Richmond Inf Sch

Bank Top

Alder Root

Werneth Sta

Christ Church CE Prim Sch

The Radclyffe Sch

Freehold Comm Prim Sch

St Patricks RC Prim Sch

Nimble Nook

Werneth

Werneth Private Prep Sch

St Thomas's CE Prim Sch

Werneth Jun & Inf Schs

Mus

152   153

1 MELLOR WAY
2 LURDEN WLK
3 WASHBROOK CT

1 REEDHAM WLK
2 SPRING BANK ST
3 WOODFIELD CT

NICHOLAS RD 1
CAMBERWELL ST 2
JUNCTION ST 3
PELLOWE RD 4
CHEVIOT CT 5

Coppice

Hathershaw

WASH BROOK

1 BICKERTON CT 1
2 STANTON ST 2
3 HOLLINGWORTH ST 3

DRURY LA

1 ASHTON ST
2 MARLAND RD

Factory Fold

St Margaret's Gdns

Hollins

Copster Hill

Hollins Green

Hathershaw Sch Sports Ctr

HOLLINS RD

Holy Rosary RC Prim Sch

Hollinwood Sta

HALLIWELL ST

The Edge

Montgomery House

Hollinwood

Road under construction

Lime Gate

Cemy

Crem

Lime Side

Moss Grove

Werneth Golf Course

Kaskenmoor Sch

90 A B 91 C D E 92 F

65 84

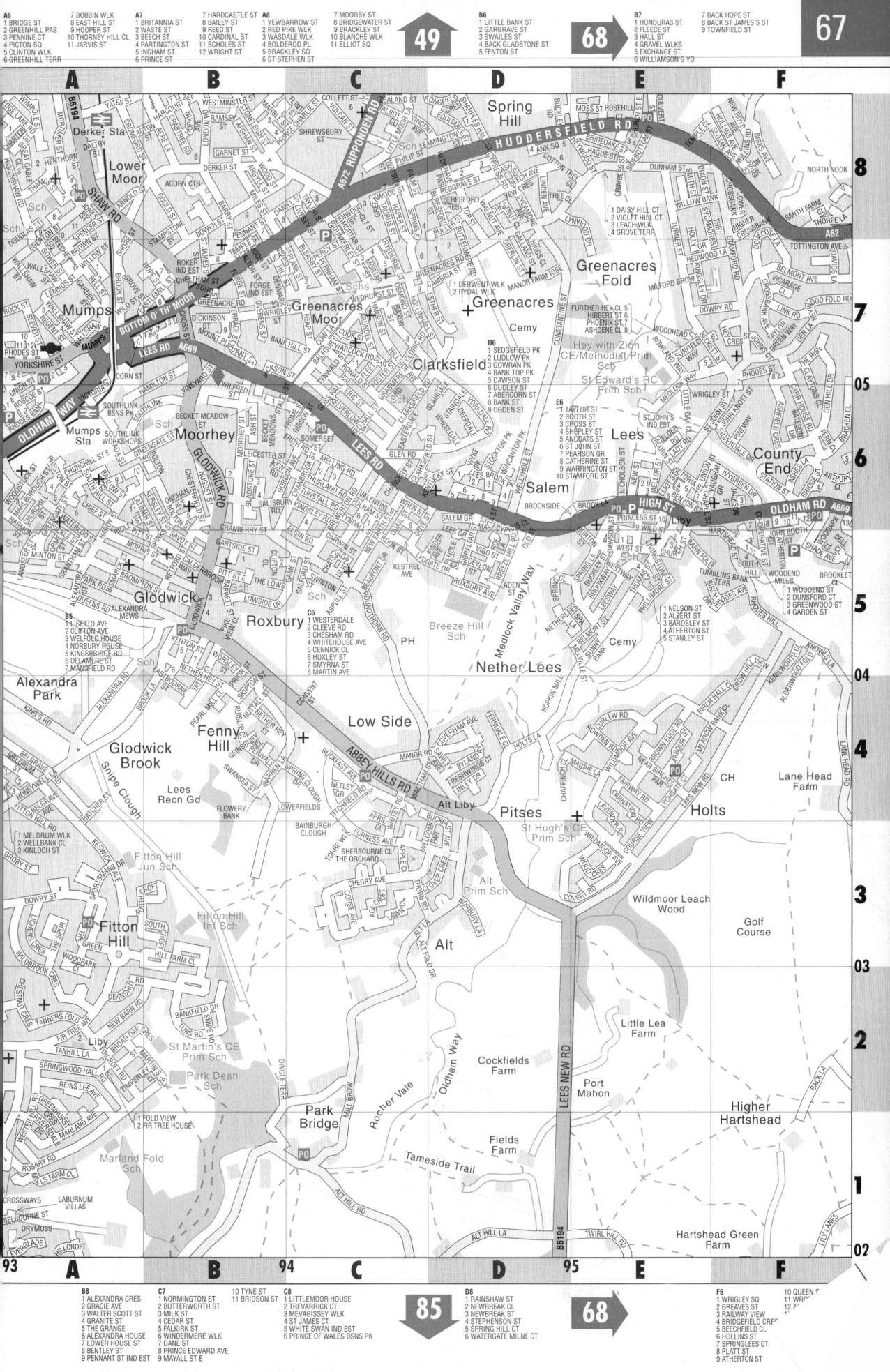
67
49
68
85
A6
1 BRIDGE ST
2 GREENHILL PAS
3 PENNINE CT
4 PICTON SQ
5 CLINTON WLK
6 GREENHILL TERR
7 BOBBIN WLK
8 EAST HILL ST
9 HOOPER ST
10 THORNEY HILL CL
11 JARVIS ST
A7
1 BRITANNIA ST
2 WASTE ST
3 BEECH ST
4 PARTINGTON ST
5 INGHAM ST
6 PRINCE ST
7 HARDCASTLE ST
8 BAILEY ST
9 REED ST
10 CARDINAL ST
11 SCHOLES ST
12 WRIGHT ST
A8
1 YEWBARROW ST
2 RED PIKE WLK
3 WASDALE WLK
4 BOLDEROD PL
5 BRACKLEY SQ
6 ST STEPHEN ST
7 MOORBY ST
8 BRIDGEWATER ST
9 BRACKLEY ST
10 BLANCHE WLK
11 ELLIOT SQ
B6
1 LITTLE BANK ST
2 GARGRAVE ST
3 SWAILES ST
4 BACK GLADSTONE ST
5 FENTON ST
B7
1 HONDURAS ST
2 FLEECE ST
3 HALL ST
4 GRAVEL WLKS
5 EXCHANGE ST
6 WILLIAMSON'S YD
7 BACK HOPE ST
8 BACK ST JAMES'S ST
9 TOWNFIELD ST
Spring Hill
Lower Moor
Mumps
Derker Sta
Mumps Sta
Greenacres Moor
Greenacres
Greenacres Fold
Clarksfield
Moorhey
Lees
Salem
County End
Glodwick
Roxbury
Nether Lees
Alexandra Park
Low Side
Fenny Hill
Glodwick Brook
Pitses
Holts
Fitton Hill
Alt
Wildmoor Leach Wood
Golf Course
Lane Head Farm
Little Lea Farm
Cockfields Farm
Port Mahon
Higher Hartshead
Park Bridge
Fields Farm
Tameside Trail
Hartshead Green Farm
HUDDERSFIELD RD
OLDHAM RD
LEES RD
ABBEY HILLS RD
LEES NEW RD
GLODWICK RD
B8
1 ALEXANDRA CRES
2 GRACIE AVE
3 WALTER SCOTT ST
4 GRANITE ST
5 THE GRANGE
6 ALEXANDRA HOUSE
7 LOWER HOUSE ST
8 BENTLEY ST
9 PENNANT ST IND EST
C7
1 NORMINGTON ST
2 BUTTERWORTH ST
3 MILK ST
4 CEDAR ST
5 FALKIRK ST
6 WINDERMERE WLK
7 DANE ST
8 PRINCE EDWARD AVE
9 MAYALL ST E
10 TYNE ST
11 BRIDSON ST
C8
1 LITTLEMOOR HOUSE
2 TREVARRICK CT
3 MEVAGISSEY WLK
4 ST JAMES CT
5 WHITE SWAN IND EST
6 PRINCE OF WALES BSNS PK
D8
1 RAINSHAW ST
2 NEWBREAK CL
3 NEWBREAK ST
4 STEPHENSON ST
5 SPRING HILL CT
6 WATERGATE MILNE CT
F6
1 WRIGLEY SQ
2 GREAVES ST
3 RAILWAY VIEW
4 BRIDGEFIELD CRES
5 BEECHFIELD CL
6 HOLLINS ST
7 SPRINGLEES CT
8 PLATT ST
9 ATHERTON ST

67
50

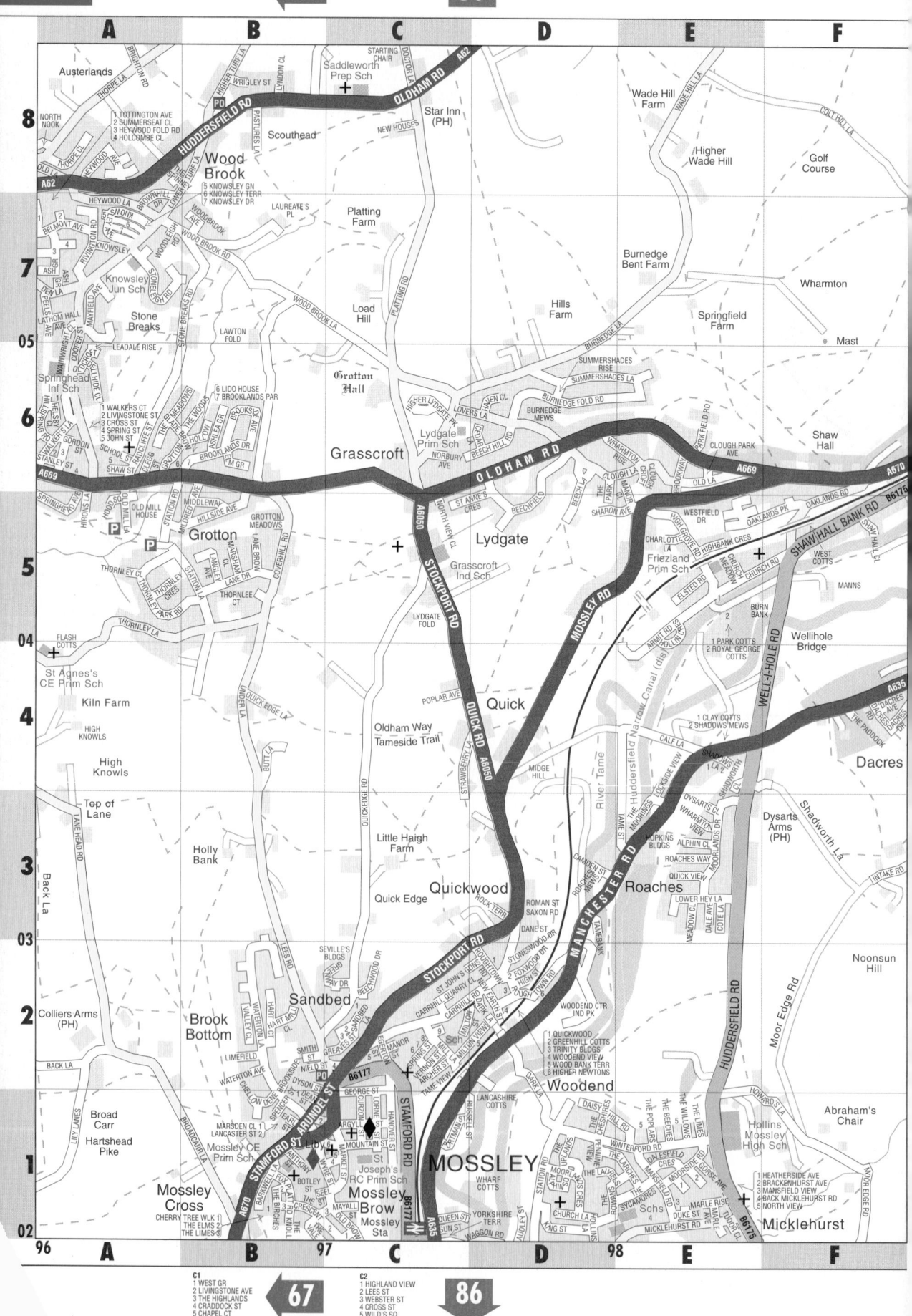

C1
1 WEST GR
2 LIVINGSTONE AVE
3 THE HIGHLANDS
4 CRADDOCK ST
5 CHAPEL CT
6 CHAPEL ST

67

C2
1 HIGHLAND VIEW
2 LEES ST
3 WEBSTER ST
4 CROSS ST
5 WILD'S SQ
6 SPRING COTTS
7 BACK MILL LA
8 HAWTHORN TERR
9 WOODMEADOW CT

86

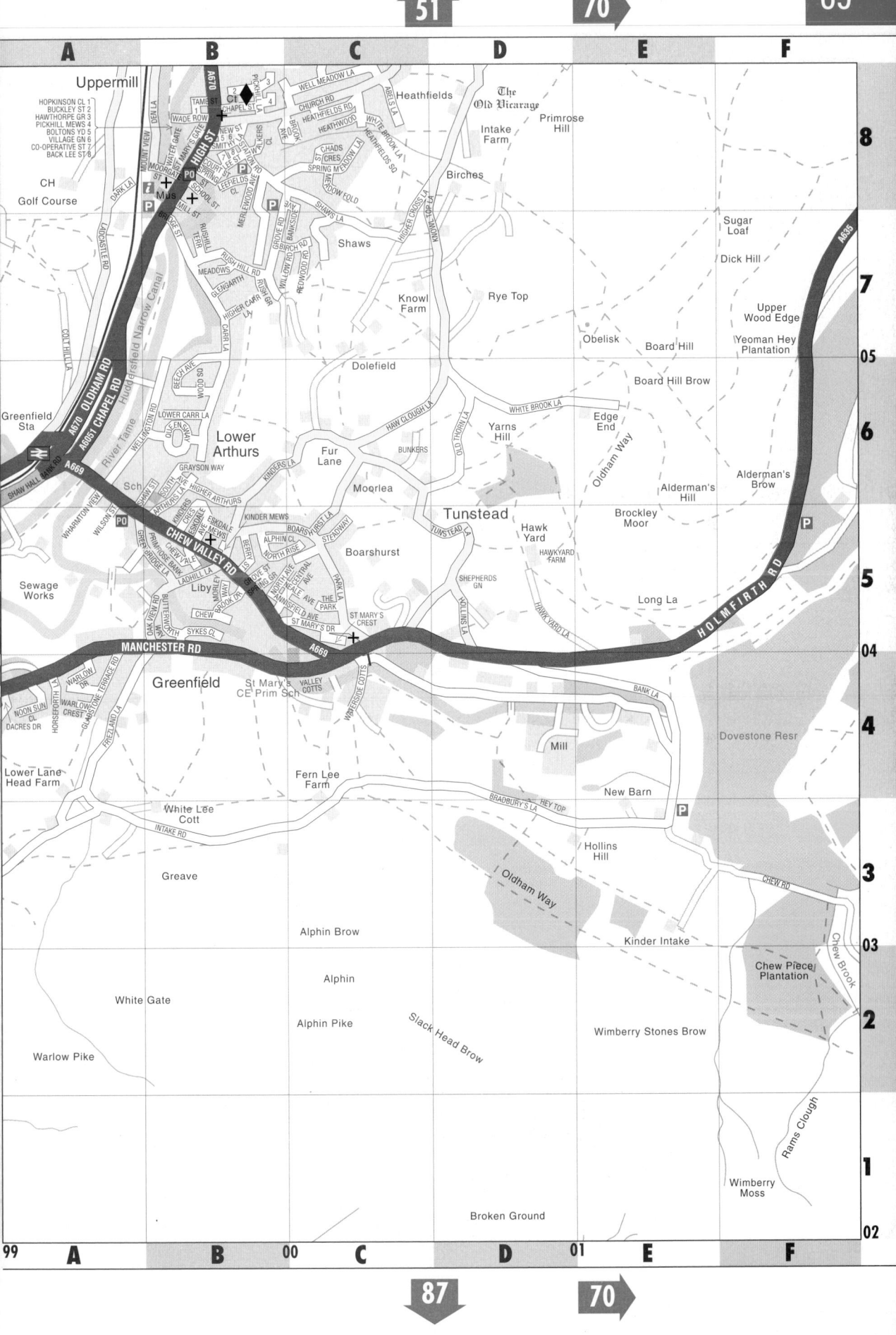

A B C D E F

Uppermill

HOPKINSON CL 1
BUCKLEY ST 2
HAWTHORPE GR 3
PICKHILL MEWS 4
BOLTONS YD 5
VILLAGE GN 6
CO-OPERATIVE ST 7
BACK LEE ST 8

WELL MEADOW LA

Heathfields

The Old Vicarage

Primrose Hill

Intake Farm

CH
Golf Course

Mus
PO

HIGH ST
A670

Shaws

Birches

Sugar Loaf

Dick Hill

Knowl Farm

Rye Top

Upper Wood Edge

Yeoman Hey Plantation

Obelisk

Board Hill

A635

Greenfield Sta

Dolefield

WHITE BROOK LA

Board Hill Brow

Lower Arthurs

Fur Lane

HAW CLOUGH LA

BUNKERS

Yarns Hill

Edge End

Oldham Way

Alderman's Brow

River Tame

Moorlea

Tunstead

Hawk Yard

Alderman's Hill

Brockley Moor

Sewage Works

Boarshurst

Liby

CHEW VALLEY RD

Hawkyard Farm

SHEPHERDS GN

Long La

HOLMFIRTH RD

MANCHESTER RD
A669

A669

Greenfield

St Mary's CE Prim Sch

VALLEY COTTS

BANK LA

Dovestone Resr

Mill

Lower Lane Head Farm

Fern Lee Farm

BRADBURY'S LA

HEY TOP

New Barn

Hollins Hill

CHEW RD

White Lee Cott

INTAKE RD

Greave

Oldham Way

Kinder Intake

Chew Piece Plantation

Chew Brook

Alphin Brow

Alphin

White Gate

Alphin Pike

Slack Head Brow

Wimberry Stones Brow

Warlow Pike

Rams Clough

Wimberry Moss

Broken Ground

8
7
05
6
7
05
04
5
04
4
3
03
2
1
02

69
52

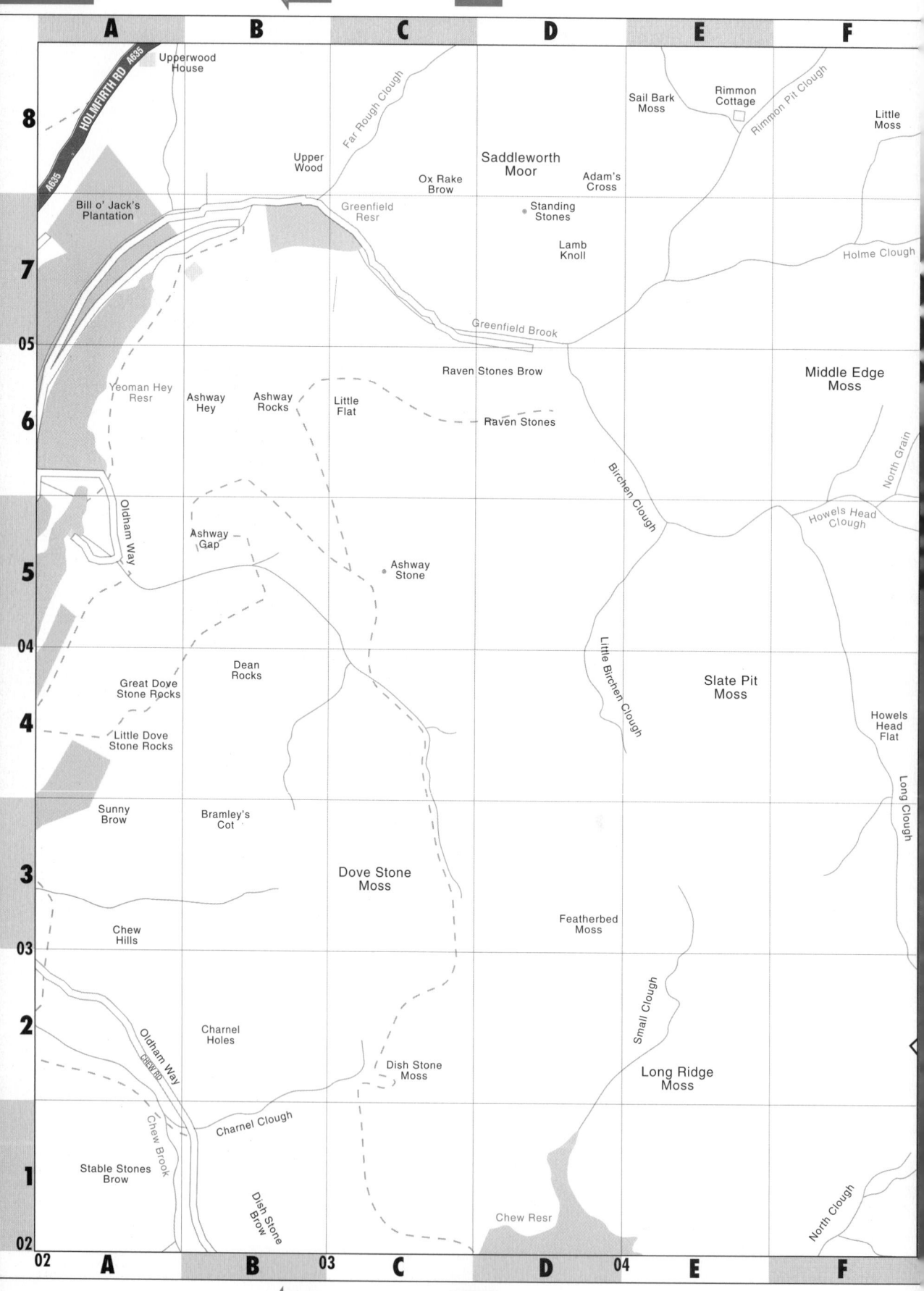
A
B
C
D
E
F
8
7
05
6
5
04
4
3
03
2
1
02
02
03
04
HOLMFIRTH RD
A635
Upperwood House
Far Rough Clough
Sail Bark Moss
Rimmon Cottage
Rimmon Pit Clough
Little Moss
Upper Wood
Saddleworth Moor
Ox Rake Brow
Adam's Cross
Bill o' Jack's Plantation
Greenfield Resr
Standing Stones
Lamb Knoll
Holme Clough
Greenfield Brook
Raven Stones Brow
Middle Edge Moss
Yeoman Hey Resr
Ashway Hey
Ashway Rocks
Little Flat
Raven Stones
North Grain
Birchen Clough
Oldham Way
Ashway Gap
Howels Head Clough
Ashway Stone
Little Birchen Clough
Dean Rocks
Great Dove Stone Rocks
Slate Pit Moss
Little Dove Stone Rocks
Howels Head Flat
Long Clough
Sunny Brow
Bramley's Cot
Dove Stone Moss
Featherbed Moss
Chew Hills
Small Clough
Charnel Holes
Oldham Way
CHEW RD
Dish Stone Moss
Long Ridge Moss
Charnel Clough
Chew Brook
Stable Stones Brow
Dish Stone Brow
Chew Resr
North Clough

69
88

53
72

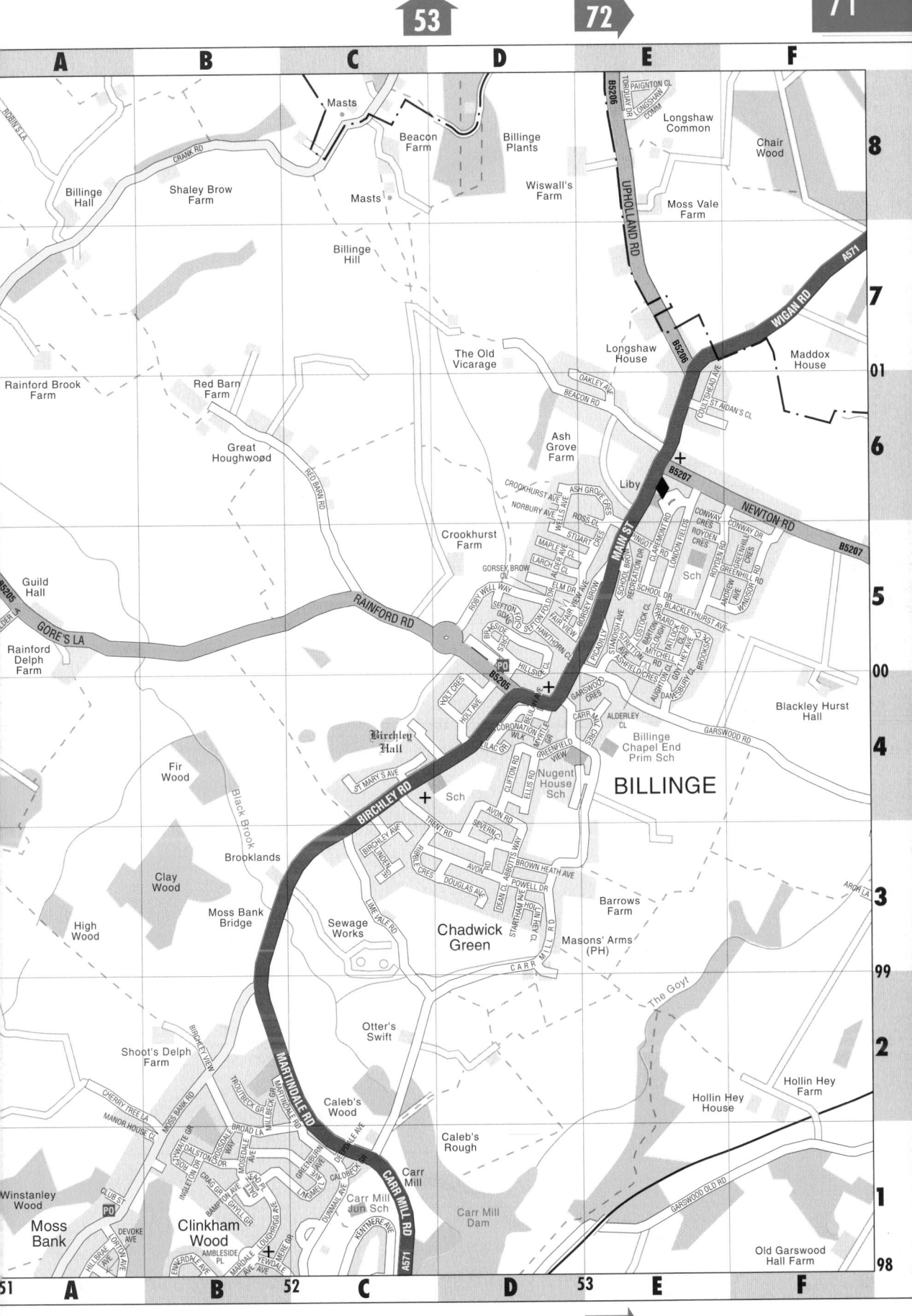
A
B
C
D
E
F
8
7
01
6
5
00
4
3
99
2
1
98
51
52
53
Masts
Beacon Farm
Billinge Plants
Longshaw Common
Chair Wood
Billinge Hall
Shaley Brow Farm
Masts
Wiswall's Farm
Moss Vale Farm
UPHOLLAND RD
B5206
Billinge Hill
WIGAN RD
A571
The Old Vicarage
Longshaw House
Maddox House
Rainford Brook Farm
Red Barn Farm
Great Houghwood
RED BARN RD
Ash Grove Farm
Liby
B5207
NEWTON RD
Crookhurst Farm
MAIN ST
Sch
Guild Hall
B5205
GORE'S LA
RAINFORD RD
Rainford Delph Farm
Blackley Hurst Hall
GARSWOOD RD
Birchley Hall
Billinge Chapel End Prim Sch
Fir Wood
Nugent House Sch
BILLINGE
BIRCHLEY RD
Sch
Black Brook
Brooklands
Clay Wood
Barrows Farm
High Wood
Moss Bank Bridge
Sewage Works
Chadwick Green
Masons' Arms (PH)
The Goyt
Otter's Swift
Shoot's Delph Farm
MARTINDALE RD
Hollin Hey Farm
Hollin Hey House
Caleb's Wood
Caleb's Rough
Carr Mill
CARR MILL RD
Winstanley Wood
Carr Mill Jun Sch
Carr Mill Dam
GARSWOOD OLD RD
Moss Bank
Clinkham Wood
Old Garswood Hall Farm

72

71
54

Windy Arbour
Windy Arbour Farm
Sandyforth Farm
Cranberry Ley
Cranberry Hotel
HASLEMERE IND EST 1
LANDGATE IND EST 2
HILLSIDE AVE 3
PARKSIDE AVE 4
BROOKSIDE AVE 5
THE BUNGALOWS 6
WINSTANLEY RD
PEMBERTON RD
WIGAN RD
A571
M6
A49
ASHTON RD
BROCSTEDES RD
Low Brooks Farm
DRUMMER'S LA
Rosehill Sch
Drummersfield Farm
Rose Hill
Opencast Workings
Ryecroft Farm
Brocstedes Farm
Barton Clough
Mine
Gladden Hey Brow
Downall Green RC Jun Sch
DOWNALL GREEN RD
St Peter's CE Prim Sch
B5207
Bryn
Tatlock's Hillock
Leyland Green
Down Brook
LEYLAND GREEN RD
Rectory CE Prim Sch
North Ashton
NEWTON RD
Billinge Lane Farm
Simm's Lane End
Downall Green
BILLINGE RD
Mill Farm
F5
1 ELMSBURY ST
2 COLUMBUS ST
3 BEVINGTON ST
4 RUFFORD ST
5 HADDON ST
6 CLARENCE ST
7 POULTON DR
KELVIN CL 1
RANMORE AVE 2
Weathercock Hill Farm
Weathercock Hill
Senely Green Farm
Garswood Cty Prim Sch
MELROSE CRES
Stag Hotel (PH)
OLD COLLIERY YD
Montrey Resr
Charity Farm
Montrey House
Arch Lane Farm
ARCH LA
Garswood
Garwood Sta
GARSWOOD RD
LOW BANK RD
PETERHOUSE WLK
WOLFSON SQ 1
CAMPION GR 2
Long Covert
LEDMORE GR
CAMP RD
GIBBON'S RD
PARK IND EST
A58
Tithe Barn Hillock
TITHEBARN RD
Tithe Barn Farm
Ashton Cross
Garswood Park
CH
Ashton-in-Makerfield Golf Course
LIVERPOOL RD
THE FAIRWAYS
Carter's Fold Farm
GARSWOOD OLD RD
Old Garswood Park
MILLFIELD LA
Millfield Farm
Oil Depot
HAYDOCK LA
HAYDOCK LANE IND EST
WINCHESTER RD
Old Garswood Hall Farm
Pewfall

71

55
74

A
B
C
D
E
F
8
7
01
6
5
00
4
3
99
2
1
98
57
58
59
Land Gate
Land Gate Farm
Perry Brook Community Prim Sch
Bryn Hall
Bryn Hall Farm
Three Sisters Recn Area
Bamfurlong
Bryn Gates
Abram Bryn Gates Prim Sch
LILY LA
A58
BRYN GATES LA
LAND GATE LA
THREE SISTERS RD
SOUTH LANCASHIRE IND EST
KINGFISHER CT
REDGATE RD
LOCKETT RD
KESTREL DR
BEAVER CT
Bryn Sta
BRYN RD
WIGAN RD
ASHTON-IN-MAKERFIELD
Lily Lane Farm
Lily Farm
Stubshaw Cross
Stubshaw Cross CE Prim Sch
Rose Farm
Harrow Inn
Nan Holes Brook
BOLTON RD
B5207
Potter's Farm
Cansfield Comm High Sch
L Ctr
Town Green
St John Southworth RC Prim Sch
Jameson's Farm
GOLBORNE RD
Edge Green Farm
EDGE GREEN RD
RIDING LA
LOCKER LA
DAM LA
RL Hughes Prim Sch
Down Brook
St Thomas CE Prim Sch
Liby
St Oswald's Prim Sch
TH
Sewage Farm
Edge Green
ASHTON RD
Edge Green Common
LIVERPOOL RD
BRYN ST
GERARD ST
WARRINGTON RD
Ashton Heath
Ashton Heath Farm
St Edmund Arrowsmith RC High Sch
Byrchall High Sch
Stables
Haydock Park Race Course
Park House Farm
LODGE LA
A49
M6
THE PARKS
HAYDOCK PARK GDNS

89
74

73
56

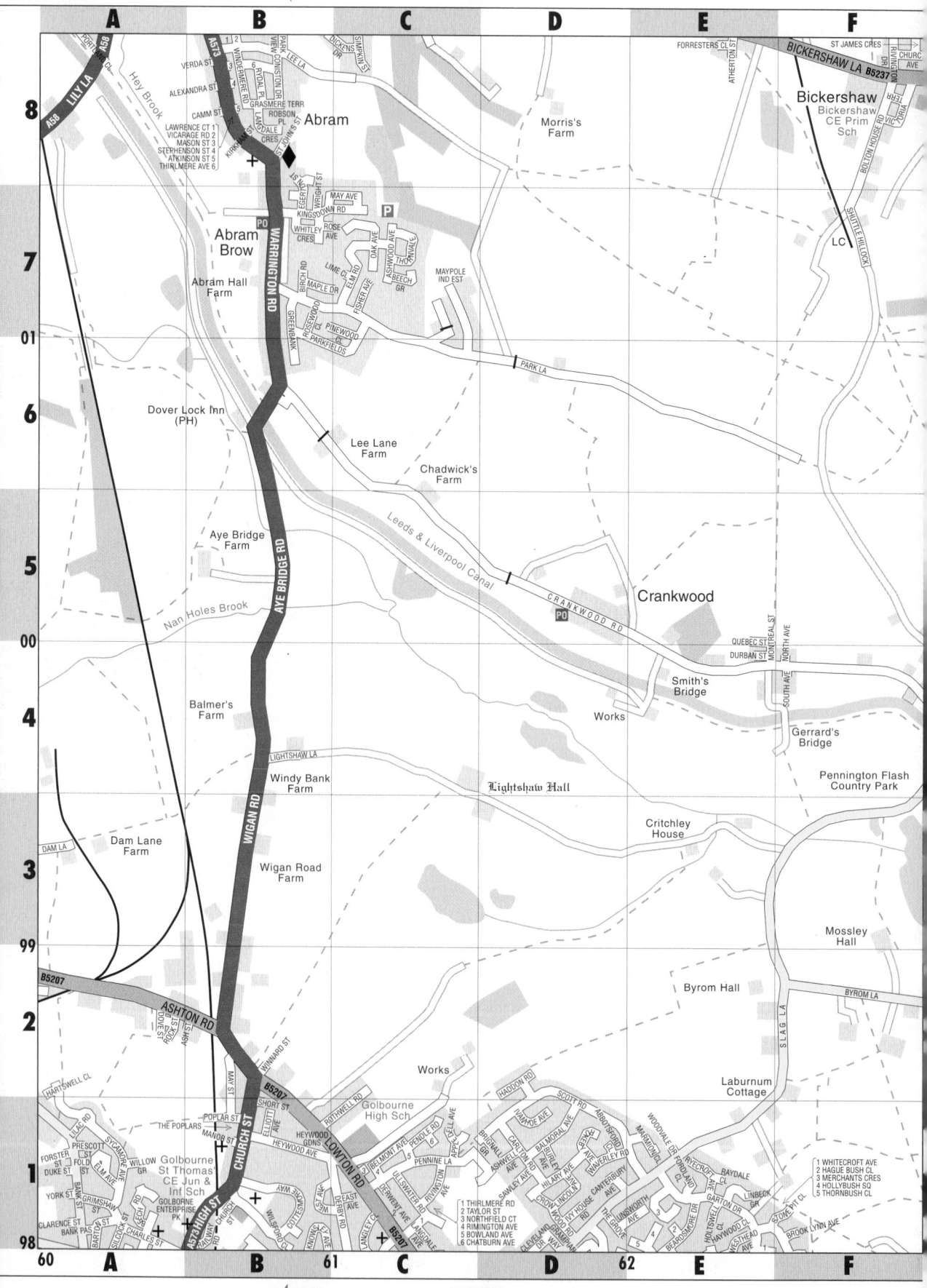
Abram
Abram Brow
Abram Hall Farm
Dover Lock Inn (PH)
Lee Lane Farm
Chadwick's Farm
Morris's Farm
Bickershaw
Bickershaw CE Prim Sch
Aye Bridge Farm
Leeds & Liverpool Canal
Crankwood
Nan Holes Brook
Hey Brook
Balmer's Farm
Smith's Bridge
Works
Gerrard's Bridge
Windy Bank Farm
Lightshaw Hall
Pennington Flash Country Park
Dam Lane Farm
Critchley House
Wigan Road Farm
Mossley Hall
Byrom Hall
Laburnum Cottage
Golbourne High Sch
Golbourne St Thomas' CE Jun & Inf Sch
WARRINGTON RD
AYE BRIDGE RD
WIGAN RD
ASHTON RD
CHURCH ST
LOWTON RD
CRANKWOOD RD
PARK LA
BICKERSHAW LA
LIGHTSHAW LA
SLAG LA
BYROM LA
LILY LA

73
90

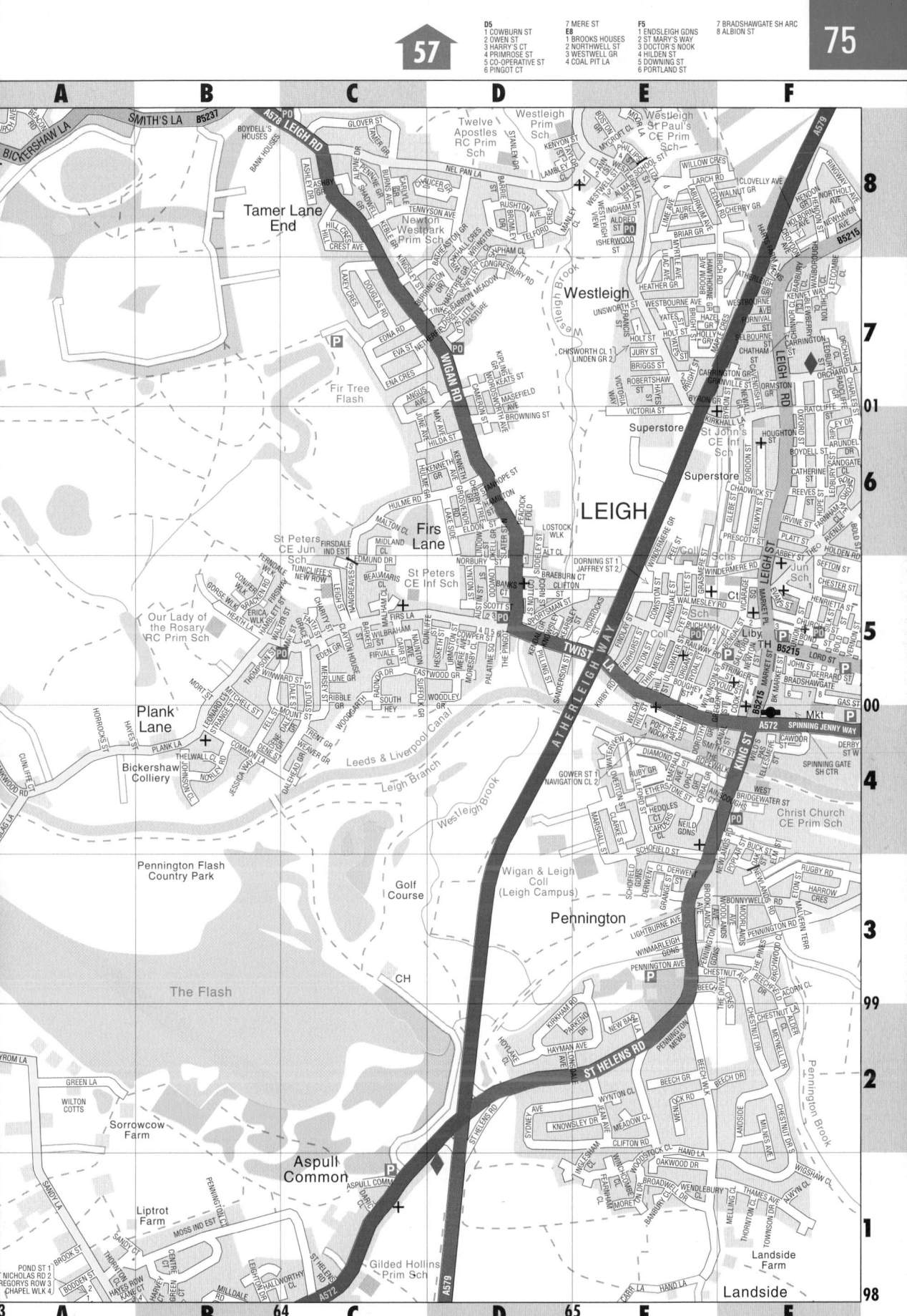

57

75

D5
1 COWBURN ST
2 OWEN ST
3 HARRY'S CT
4 PRIMROSE ST
5 CO-OPERATIVE ST
6 PINGOT CT

7 MERE ST
E8
1 BROOKS HOUSES
2 NORTHWELL ST
3 WESTWELL GR
4 COAL PIT LA

F5
1 ENDSLEIGH GDNS
2 ST MARY'S WAY
3 DOCTOR'S NOOK
4 HILDEN ST
5 DOWNING ST
6 PORTLAND ST

7 BRADSHAWGATE SH ARC
8 ALBION ST

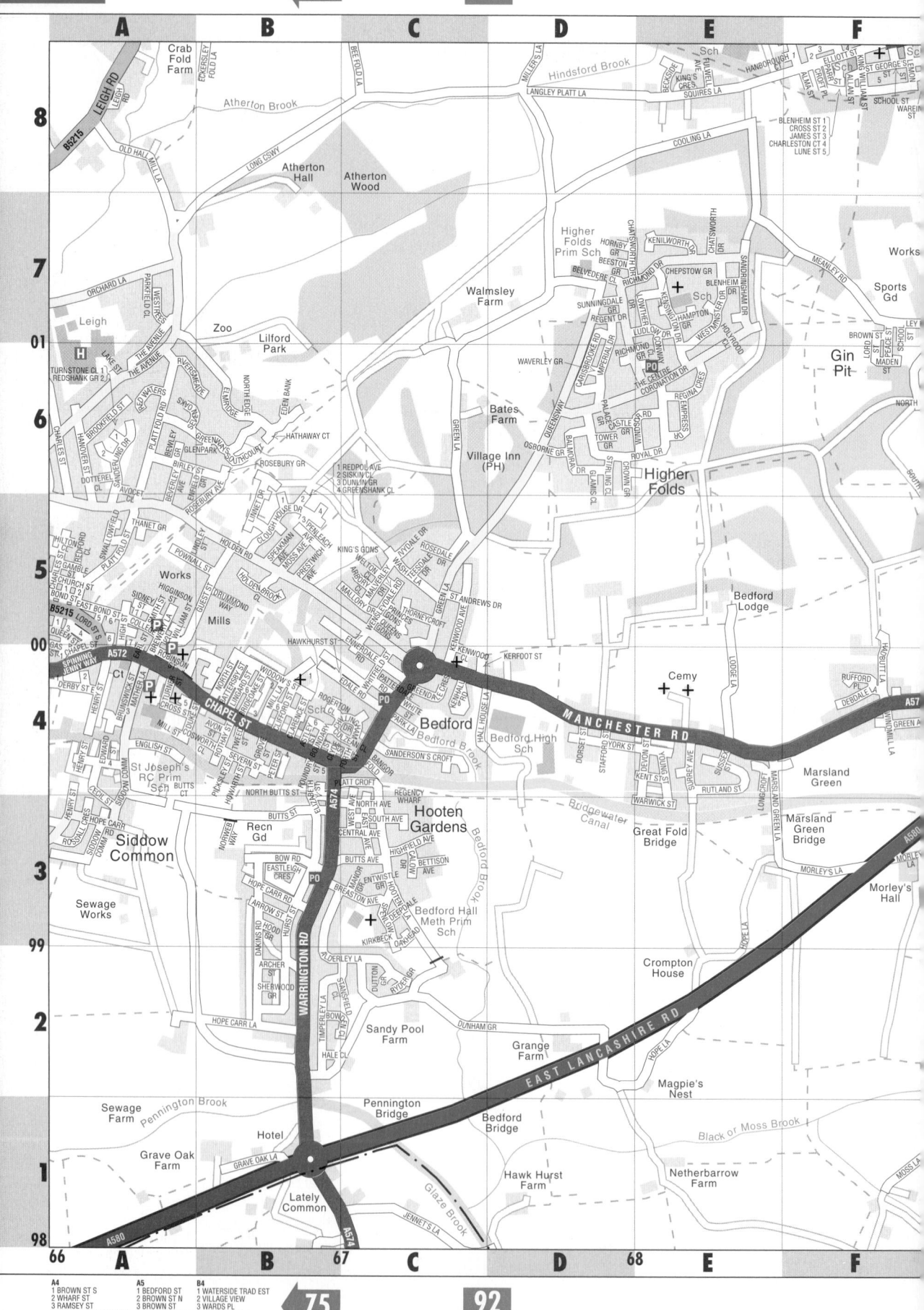

A4
1 BROWN ST S
2 WHARF ST
3 RAMSEY ST
4 EAST BRIDGEWATER ST
5 SIZE HOUSE PL

A5
1 BEDFORD ST
2 BROWN ST N
3 BROWN ST
4 BACK QUEEN ST
5 PRINCESS ST
6 DUKINFIELD ST
7 NOBLE ST

B4
1 WATERSIDE TRAD EST
2 VILLAGE VIEW
3 WARDS PL
4 LANCASTER CT
5 GEORGIAN CT
6 FARNWORTH ST

59
78

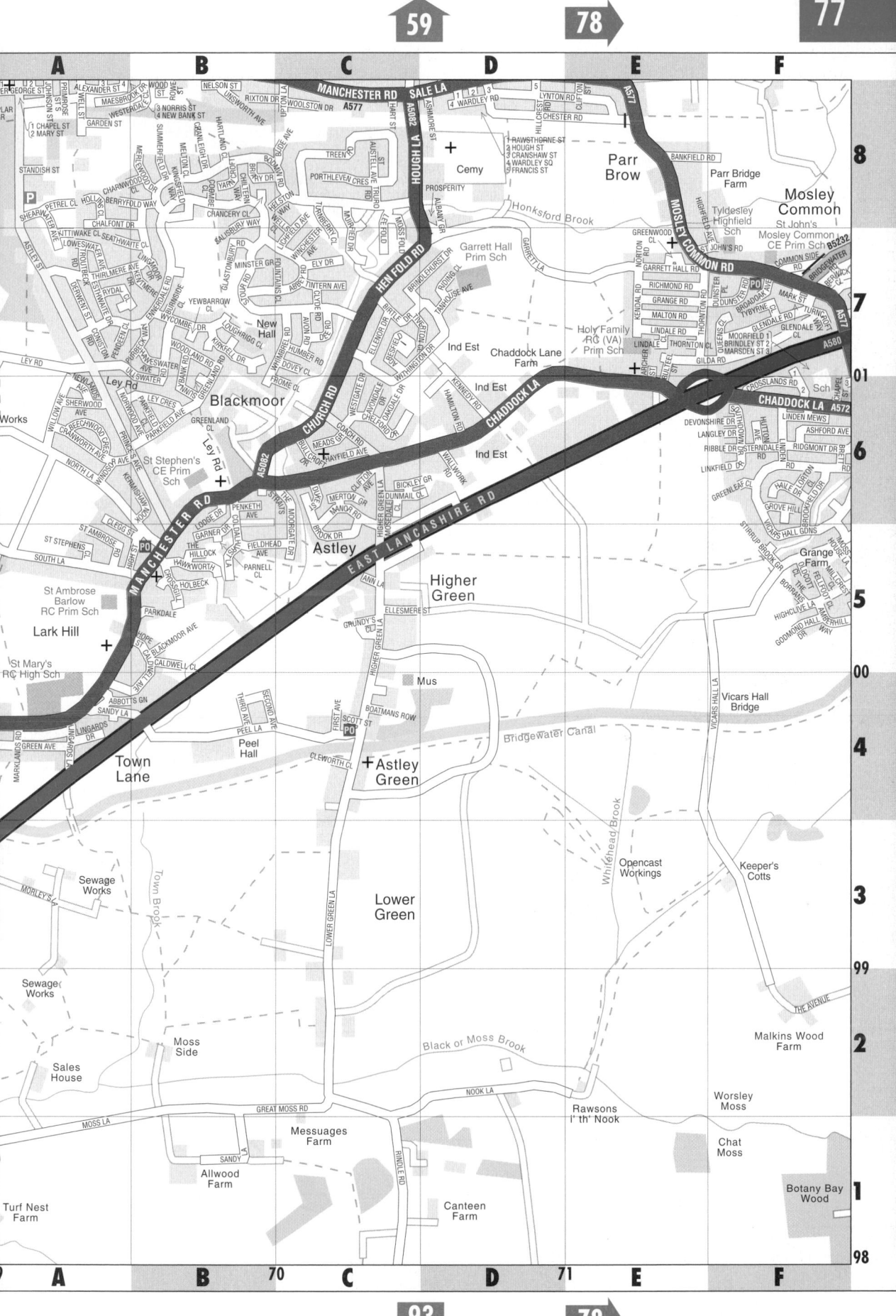
A
B
C
D
E
F
MANCHESTER RD
SALE LA
A577
HOUGH LA
A5082
HEN FOLD RD
CHURCH RD
CHADDOCK LA
EAST LANCASHIRE RD
MOSLEY COMMON RD
CHADDOCK LA
A572
A580
B5232
Cemy
Parr Brow
Parr Bridge Farm
Mosley Common
Tyldesley Highfield Sch
St John's Mosley Common CE Prim Sch
Honksford Brook
Garrett Hall Prim Sch
New Hall
Ind Est
Chaddock Lane Farm
Holy Family RC (VA) Prim Sch
Blackmoor
Ley Rd
St Stephen's CE Prim Sch
Works
Astley
Higher Green
St Ambrose Barlow RC Prim Sch
Lark Hill
St Mary's RC High Sch
Mus
Peel Hall
Town Lane
Astley Green
Bridgewater Canal
Vicars Hall Bridge
Grange Farm
Sewage Works
Town Brook
Lower Green
Whitehead Brook
Opencast Workings
Keeper's Cotts
Malkins Wood Farm
Black or Moss Brook
Moss Side
Sales House
Messuages Farm
Rawsons i' th' Nook
Worsley Moss
Chat Moss
Allwood Farm
Turf Nest Farm
Canteen Farm
Botany Bay Wood
GREAT MOSS RD
MOSS LA
NOOK LA
RINDLE RD
LOWER GREEN LA
VICARS HALL LA
THE AVENUE
8
7
01
6
5
00
4
3
99
2
1
98
70
71

93
78

77
60

A
B
C
D
E
F
8
7
01
6
5
00
4
3
99
2
1
98
72
73
74
Ellenbrook
WORSLEY
THE MEWS
Boothstown
Liby
Lady Hill
Old Hall Farm
Worsley Old Hall
Meml
St Mark's CE Prim Sch
St Andrew's Sch
Prim Sch
Booth's Bank Farm
Middle Wood
Boating Lake
Nurseries
Marina
Bridgewater Canal
Hollin Wood
Moss House Farm
Keepers Cottage
The Grange
Chat Moss
Worsley Moss
Botany Bay Wood
Shaw Brook
Barton Moss
Eccles CE High Sch
EAST LANCASHIRE RD
LEIGH RD
SIMPSON RD
BRIDGEWATER RD
NEWEARTH RD
WALKDEN RD
WORSLEY BROW
WORSLEY RD
THE AVENUE
ROCK RD
BUCKTHORN LA
OLD CLOUGH LA
CRAWFORD AVE
OLD HALL LA
WOODLANDS RD
KEMPNOUGH HALL RD
GREENLEACH LA
LUMBER LA
AVIARY RD
BARTON RD
MOSS HOUSE LA
CITY RD
NEW CITY RD
MOSLEY COMMON RD
CHADDOCK LA
BRETT RD
VICARS HALL LA
HIGHGROVE
SANDRINGHAM RD
LEIGH RD
ELLENBROOK RD
STETCHWORTH DR
HOLLINSWOOD RD
FALCONWOOD CHASE
BOOTHSBANK AVE
BOOTH'S HALL RD
VALDENE DR
KINGSWAY
DUCHY AVE
LYNTON CRES
CHALFONT DR
THORNHILL DR
CROSSFIELD DR
BODDINGTON RD
STANNARD RD
NORTHFLEET
A580
A572
A575
A577
B5232
B5211
M60
M62
13
1 ASHLANDS AVE
2 BERWICK CL
CHERRYWOOD CL 1
MATHER FOLD RD 2
1 ELVINGTON CRES
2 GAMBLESIDE CL
3 WOODSHAW GR
4 WILDERS MOOR RD
5 SPINDLEPOINT DR
6 LADYHILL VIEW
7 SMALLBRIDGE CL
8 SIXPOOLS GR
9 DOEFIELD AVE
1 CHAPEL MEADOW
2 CROMBOUKE FOLD
3 PENRICE FOLD
4 REDPOLL CL
5 STONECHAT CL
6 GOLDCREST CL
1 SPRINGBURN CL
2 LECKENBY CL
3 ASHFORD AVE
4 RIDGMONT DR
1 ARNFIELD DR
2 BOOTH'S HALL GR
3 SADDLEBACK CL
1 VICTORIA CL
2 IRVINE AVE
3 BRINDLEY AVE
4 STANDFIELD CTR
5 THE CHADDOCK LEVEL
6 BLEASEFELL CHASE
7 CASTERTON WAY
8 THORNS VILLA GDNS
9 REDINGTON CL
10 REDWATER CL
11 BRIDGEFOOT CL

77
94

61 80

E7
1 BEDFORD AVE
2 PADDISON ST
3 STOCKTON ST
4 THORNFIELD DR
5 ALBERMARLE RD
6 COLLIER ST
7 LINCOLN RD

F7
1 GORSEFIELD DR
2 WAGGONERS CT
3 ROSETTE WLK
4 MAIDEN MEWS
5 LIGHTBOURNE AVE

SWINTON
Roe Green
Hazelhurst
Egerton Park
Moorside
Deans
Broad Oak
Broadoak Park
Light Bourne Green
Dales Brow
Broadoak Park Golf Course
Golf Course
Chorlton Fold
Alder Forest
Monton
Ellesmere Park
Westwood Park
Winton
Winton Park
Patricroft
ECCLES

B1
1 SARAH ST
2 WINIFRED ST
3 BEECH HOUSE
4 ATHERTON WAY
5 HAMPSON CL
6 GREEN ST

C1
1 WILLOW TREE CT
2 CORNWALL ST
3 CHAPEL ST
4 ELIZA ANN ST
5 SPOONER RD

95 80

D1
1 ST JOHN ST
2 BRADBURN CL
3 MOORFIELD CL
4 BRADBURN AVE
5 BRADBURN GR
6 DORNING ST
7 WILHAM AVE
8 WADE HOUSE
9 WALKER HOUSE
10 O'KANE HOUSE
11 UVEDALE HOUSE
12 PITCAIRN HOUSE
13 DE TRAFFORD HOUSE
14 ELLESMERE ST

F2
1 CHAPEL WLK
2 THIRKHILL PL
3 KEMBALL
4 NORTHWAY
5 THE MALL
6 SHUTTLE ST
7 SOUTHWAY
8 BOOTHWAY
9 BACK CHAPEL ST
10 COLLEGE CROFT
11 ST MARY'S RD
12 EWOOD
13 CRAUNTON

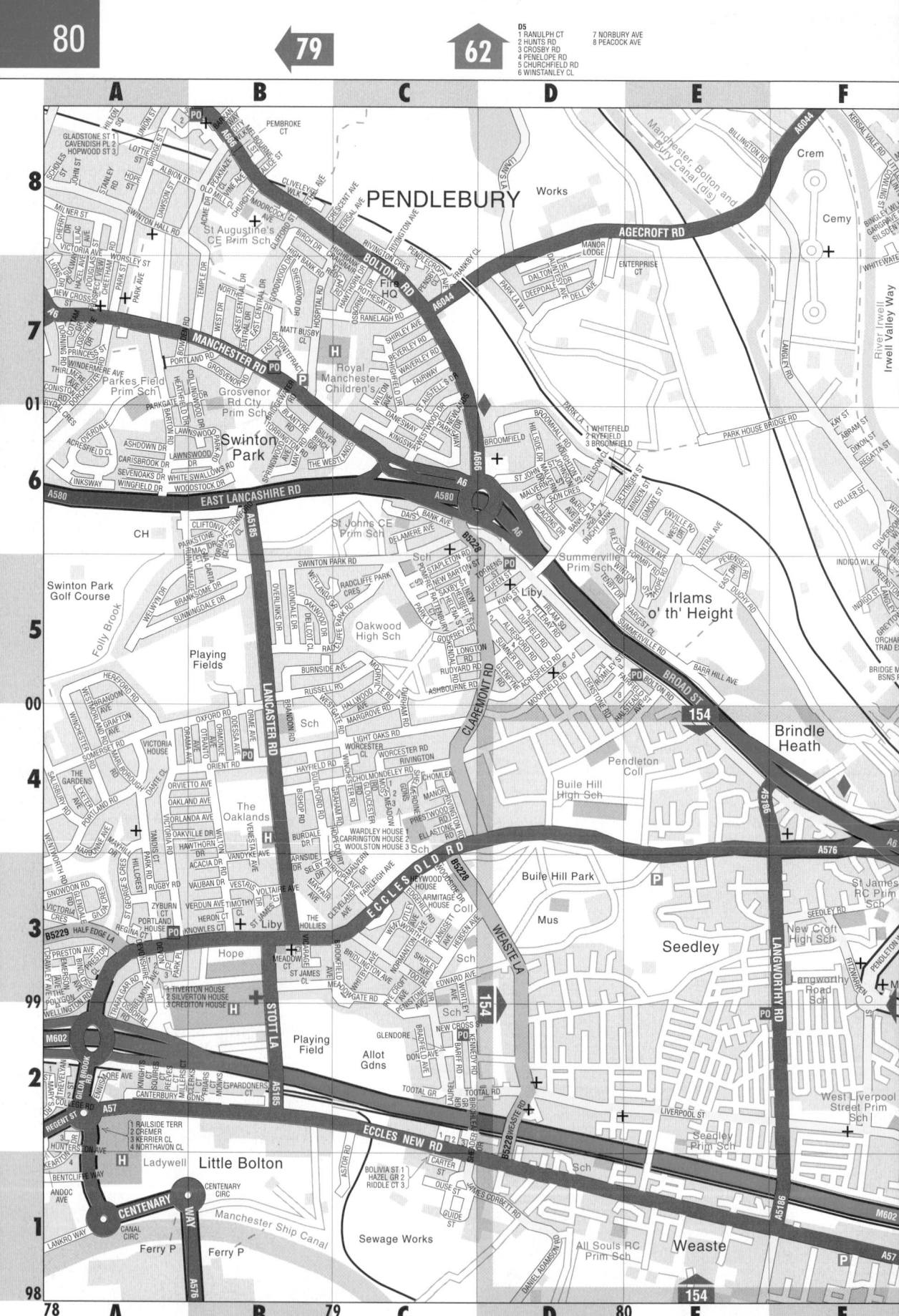

79

62

D5
1 RANULPH CT
2 HUNTS RD
3 CROSBY RD
4 PENELOPE RD
5 CHURCHFIELD RD
6 WINSTANLEY CL
7 NORBURY AVE
8 PEACOCK AVE

79

96

For full street detail of the
highlighted area see page
154.

For full street detail of the highlighted area see pages 155 and 158.

63

82

81

A   B   C   D   E   F

8
7
01
6
5
00
4
3
158 99
2
1
98

Kersal High Sch

St Pauls CE Prim Sch

Kersal

Beis Yaakov High Sch

Lower Kersal

Playing Fields

Sports Gd

Jewish Cassel Fox Prim Sch

Kersal Dale

Brentnall Prim Sch

Cheetham CE Comm Sch

Mandley Park Sch

Liby

Marlborough Road Prim Sch

Higher Broughton

The Cliff

Lower Kersall Prim Sch

St Boniface RC Prim Sch

Grecian Prim S

Castle Irwell Student Village

Great Cheetham St W

Great Cheetham St E

Lawry High Sch

Lower Broughton

Ascension CE Prim Sch

Cheetwood Prim Sch

Charlestown

Charlestown Prim Sch

Pendleton Sta

HM Prison Strangeways

Strangeways

Recn Gd

Peel Park

Univ of Salford

The Friars Prim Sch

Pendleton

Liby

Wallness

Salford Crescent Sta

Liby

Playing Field

Univ of Salford

SS. Peter & John RC Prim Sch

Lowry Heritage Ctr (Art Gal & Mus)

Salford Royal

Cath (RC)

Coll of Art & Tech

SALFORD

St Philips CE Prim Sch

Salford Central Sta

Cath (CE)

Recn Ctr

New Windsor

ECCLES   NEW RD

Granada TV Ctr

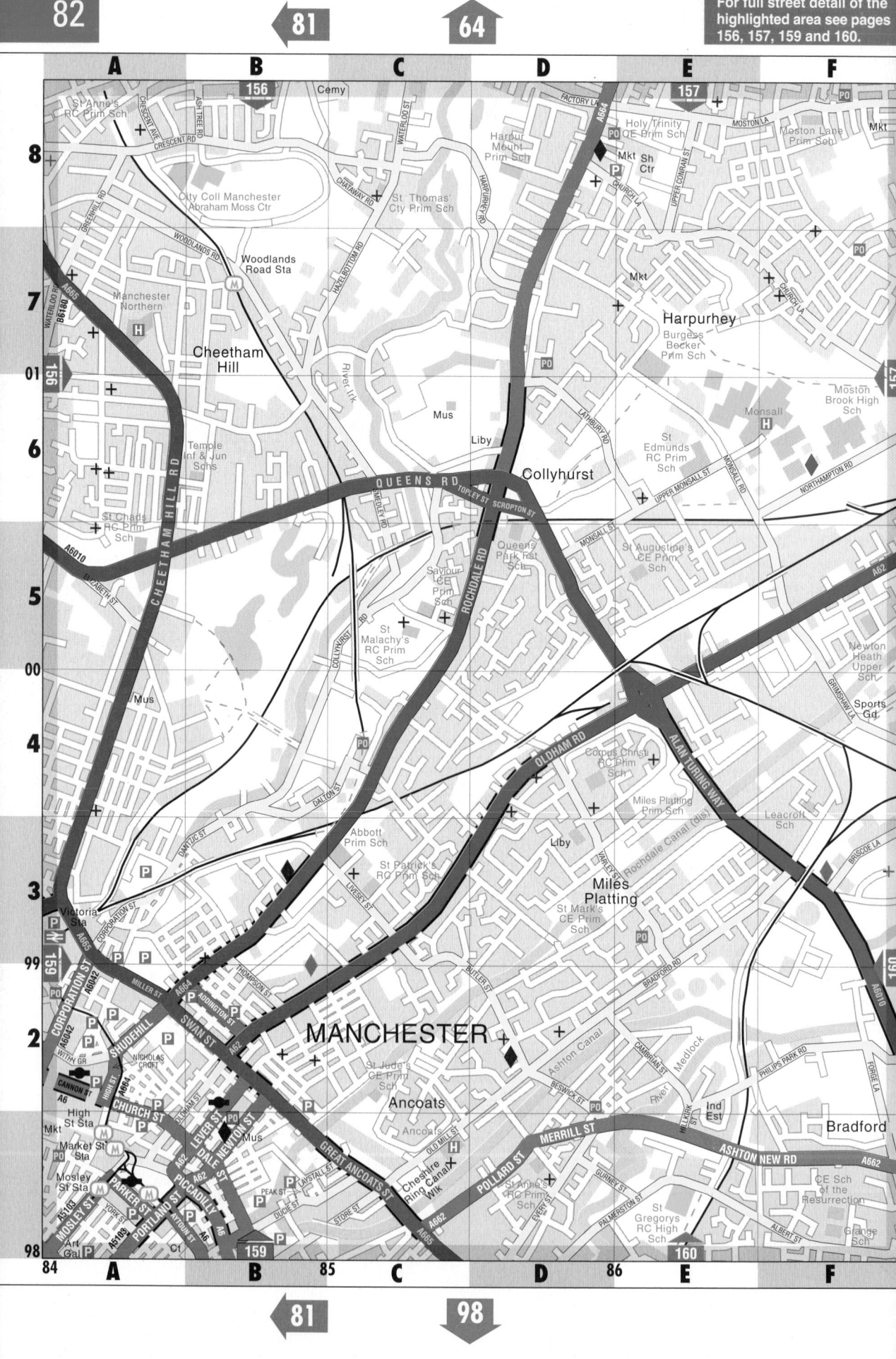

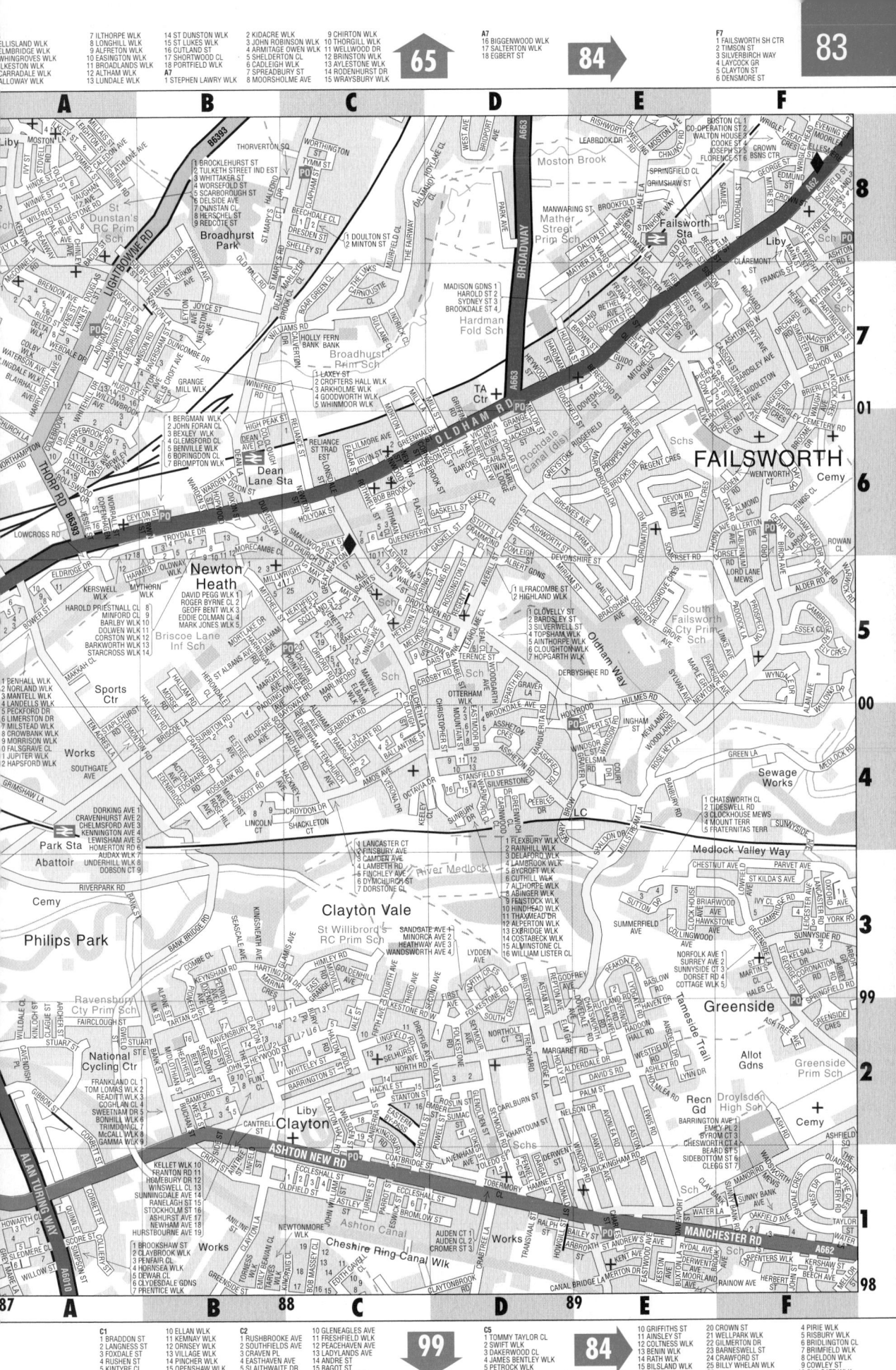

83
66

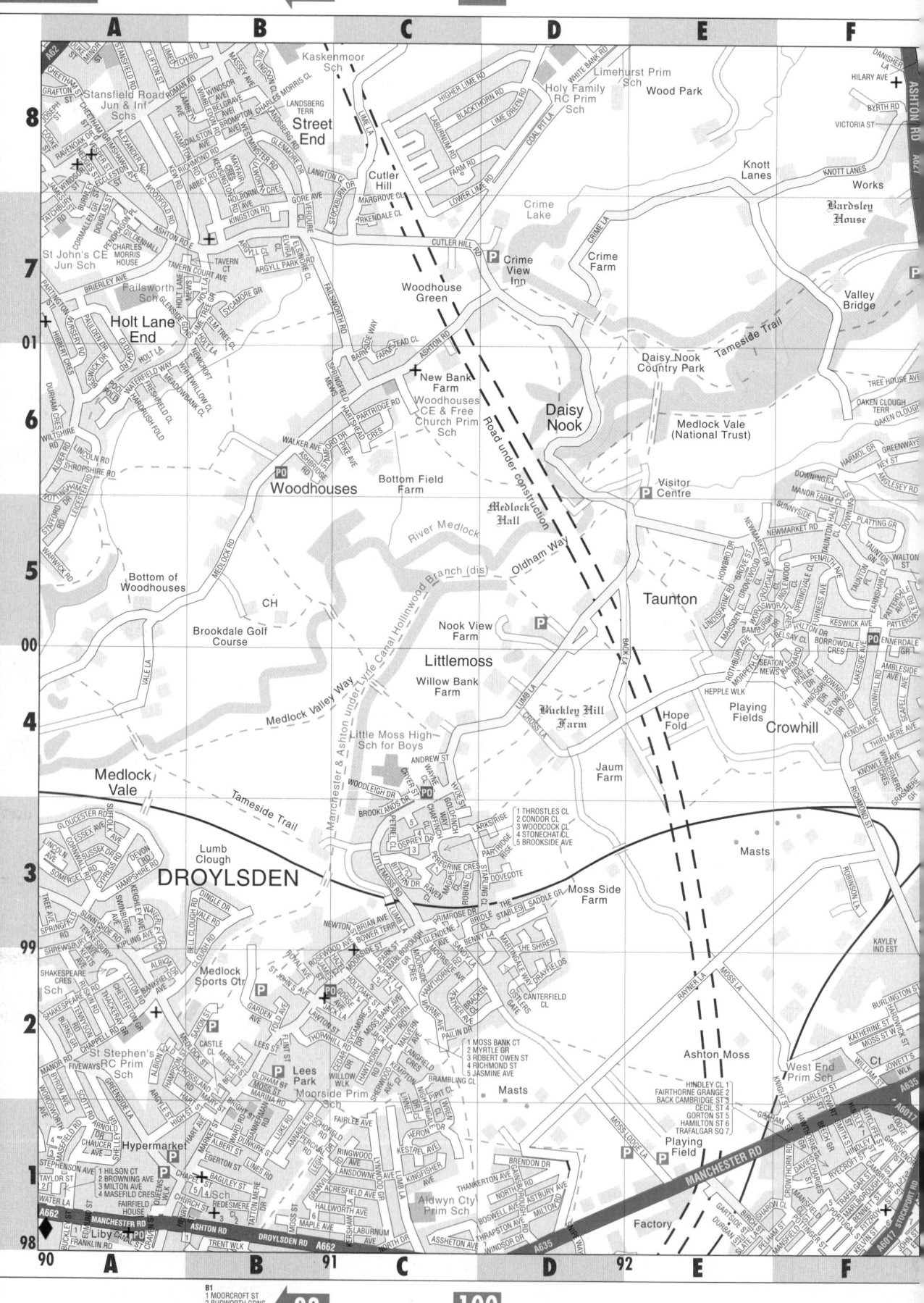

B1
1 MOORCROFT ST
2 BUDWORTH GDNS
3 TABLEY GDNS
4 PICKMERE CL
5 BESWICK ST
6 MERLEWOOD AVE

83
100

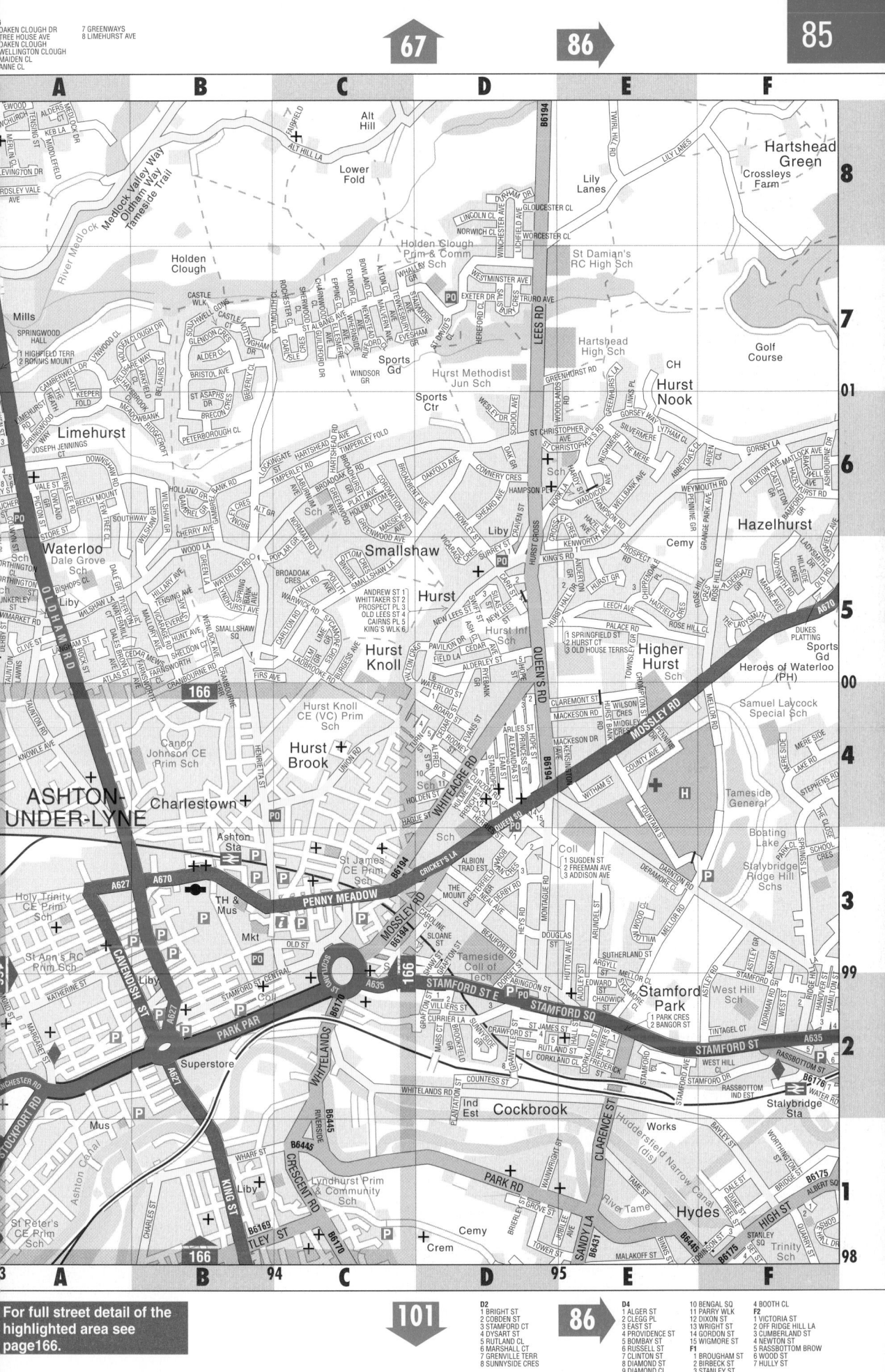
OAKEN CLOUGH DR
TREE HOUSE AVE
OAKEN CLOUGH
WELLINGTON CLOUGH
MAIDEN CL
ANNE CL
7 GREENWAYS
8 LIMEHURST AVE
67
86
A
B
C
D
E
F
8
7
01
6
5
00
4
3
99
2
1
98
Alt Hill
Lower Fold
Lily Lanes
Hartshead Green
Crossleys Farm
Medlock Valley Way
Oldham Way
Tameside Trail
River Medlock
Holden Clough
Holden Clough Prim & Comm Sch
St Damian's RC High Sch
Hartshead High Sch
Golf Course
Mills
Sports Gd
Hurst Methodist Jun Sch
Sports Ctr
Hurst Nook
Limehurst
Waterloo
Dale Grove Sch
Smallshaw
Hurst
Hurst Knoll
Hurst Inf Sch
Higher Hurst
Hazelhurst
Cemy
Heroes of Waterloo (PH)
Samuel Laycock Special Sch
Hurst Knoll CE (VC) Prim Sch
Hurst Brook
Canon Johnson CE Prim Sch
ASHTON-UNDER-LYNE
Charlestown
Ashton Sta
St James' CE Prim Sch
Tameside General
Boating Lake
Stalybridge Ridge Hill Schs
Holy Trinity CE Prim Sch
TH & Mus
Mkt
St Ann's RC Prim Sch
Tameside Coll of Tech
Stamford Park
West Hill Sch
Superstore
Ind Est
Cockbrook
Works
Stalybridge Sta
Huddersfield Narrow Canal (dis)
River Tame
Hydes
Lyndhurst Prim & Community Sch
St Peter's CE Prim Sch
Ashton Canal
Cemy
Crem
Trinity Sch
OLDHAM RD
LEES RD
QUEEN'S RD
MOSSLEY RD
PENNY MEADOW
STAMFORD ST E
STAMFORD SQ
STAMFORD ST
PARK PAR
CAVENDISH ST
KING ST
WHITELANDS RD
CRESCENT RD
PARK RD
CLARENCE ST
STOCKPORT RD
HIGH ST
WHITEACRE RD
166
94
95
For full street detail of the highlighted area see page166.
101
86
D2
1 BRIGHT ST
2 COBDEN ST
3 STAMFORD CT
4 DYSART ST
5 RUTLAND CL
6 MARSHALL CT
7 GRENVILLE TERR
8 SUNNYSIDE CRES
D4
1 ALGER ST
2 CLEGG PL
3 EAST ST
4 PROVIDENCE ST
5 BOMBAY ST
6 RUSSELL ST
7 CLINTON ST
8 DIAMOND ST
9 DIAMOND CL
10 BENGAL SQ
11 PARRY WLK
12 DIXON ST
13 WRIGHT ST
14 GORDON ST
15 WIGMORE ST
F1
1 BROUGHAM ST
2 BIRBECK ST
3 STANLEY ST
4 BOOTH CL
F2
1 VICTORIA ST
2 OFF RIDGE HILL LA
3 CUMBERLAND ST
4 NEWTON ST
5 RASSBOTTOM BROW
6 WOOD ST
7 HULLY ST

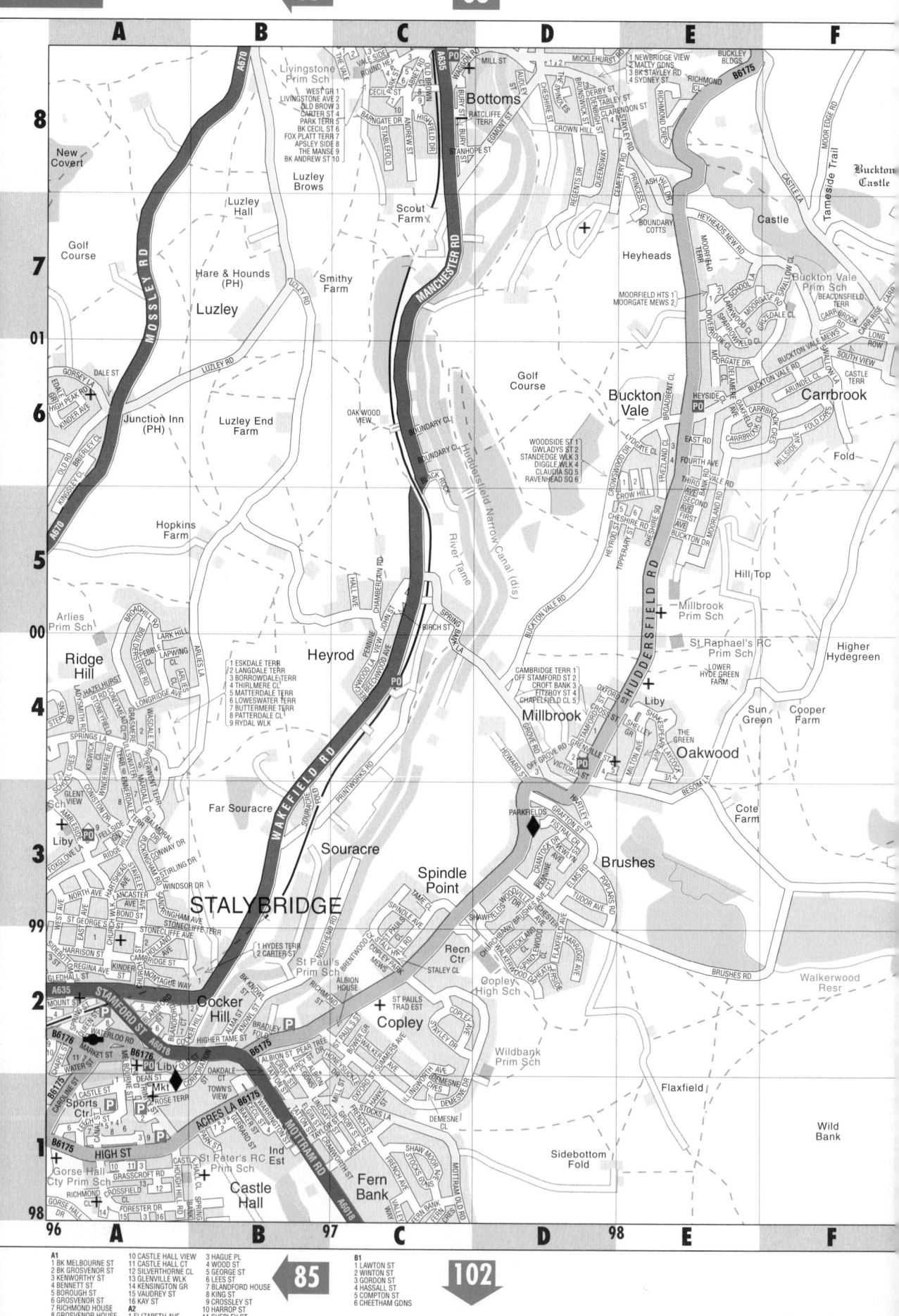

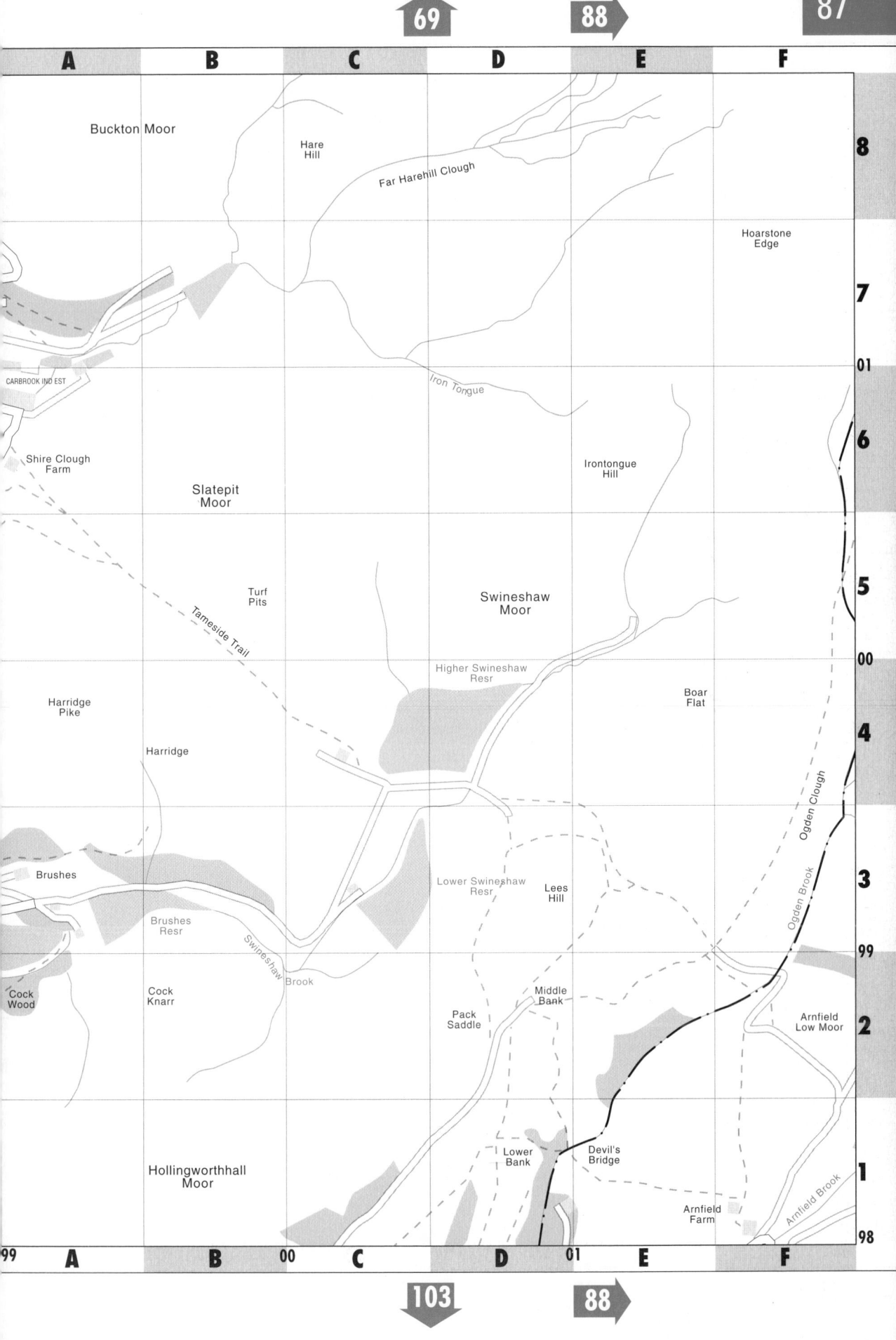

A B C D E F

8
7
01
6
5
00
4
3
99
2
1
98

Buckton Moor

Hare Hill

Far Harehill Clough

Hoarstone Edge

CARBROOK IND EST

Iron Tongue

Shire Clough Farm

Slatepit Moor

Irontongue Hill

Turf Pits

Swineshaw Moor

Tameside Trail

Higher Swineshaw Resr

Boar Flat

Harridge Pike

Harridge

Brushes

Brushes Resr

Lower Swineshaw Resr

Lees Hill

Ogden Clough

Ogden Brook

Swineshaw Brook

Cock Wood

Cock Knarr

Pack Saddle

Middle Bank

Arnfield Low Moor

Lower Bank

Devil's Bridge

Arnfield Farm

Hollingworthhall Moor

Arnfield Brook

A   B   C   D   E   F

8

01

7

6

5

00

4

3

99

2

1

98

Chew Green

Dish Stone Rocks

Chew Brook

CHEW RD

Chew Hurdles

Wilderness

Chew Resr

South Clough

Green Grain

Dry Clough

Blindstones Moss

Blindstones

Bowerclough Head

Ormes Moor

Featherbed Moss

Windgate Edge

Mount Skip

Arnfield Flats

Robinson's Moss

Milestone Rocks

Arnfield Gutter

Arnfield Clough

Black Gutter

Shooting Cabins

Arnfield Brook

Tintwistle Knarr

Rawkins Brook

Arnfield Moor

Didsbury Intake

Arnfield Covert

A628

Tintwistle Low Moor

Rhodeswood Resr

Round Intake

A628

Longdendale Trail

02   A   B   03   C   D   04   E   F

73
90

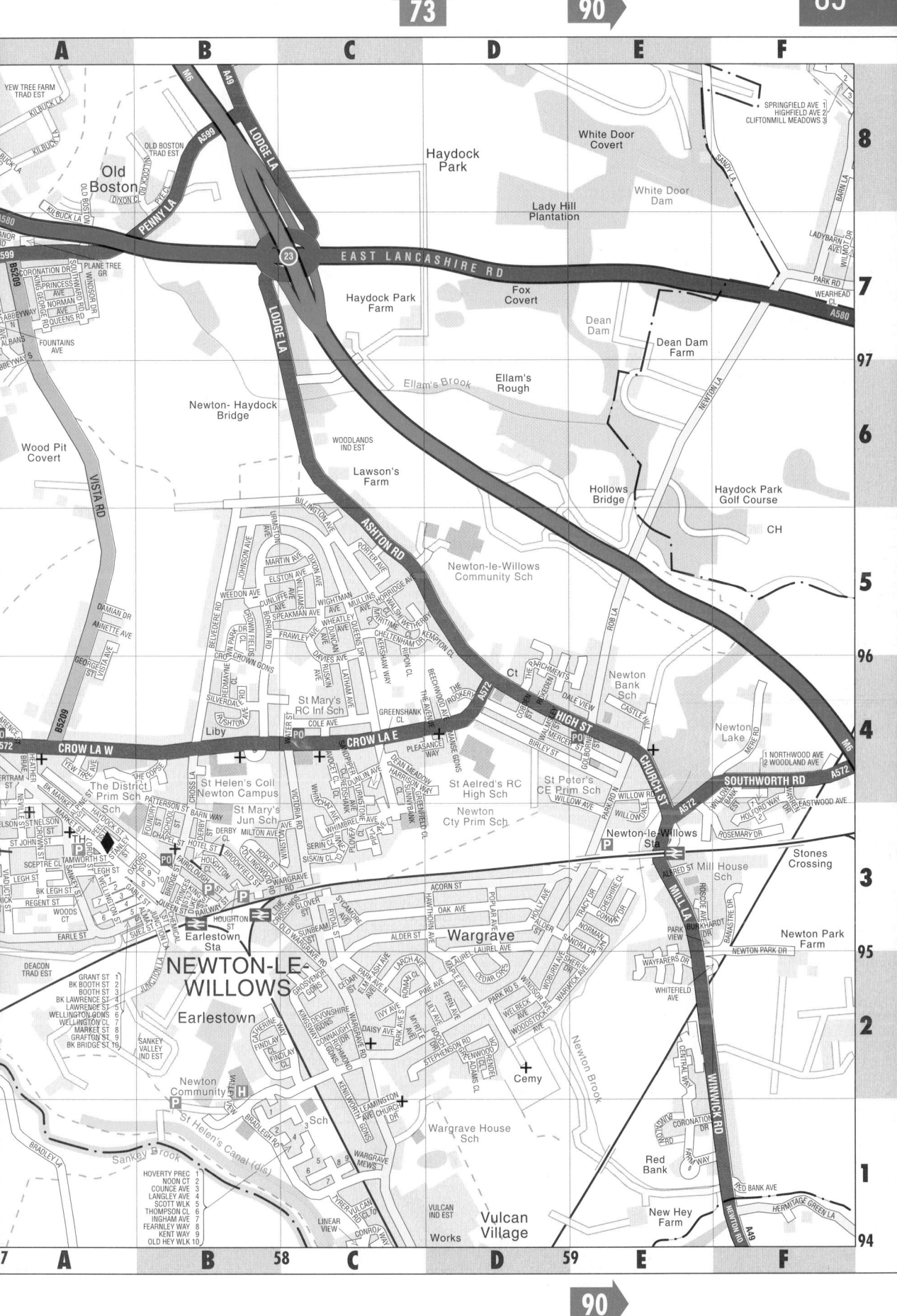
A
B
C
D
E
F
8
7
97
6
5
96
4
3
95
2
1
94
58
59
YEW TREE FARM TRAD EST
KILBUCK LA
Old Boston
OLD BOSTON TRAD EST
PENNY LA
A599
LODGE LA
A49
M6
Haydock Park
White Door Covert
White Door Dam
Lady Hill Plantation
SPRINGFIELD AVE 1
HIGHFIELD AVE 2
CLIFTONMILL MEADOWS 3
SANDY LA
BARN LA
LADYBARN AVE
WILMOT DR
EAST LANCASHIRE RD
A580
23
PARK RD
WEARHEAD CL
CORONATION DR
PLANE TREE GR
PRINCESS AVE
NORMAN AVE
QUEENS RD
KING GEORGE RD
SOUTHWARD RD
WINDSOR DR
ABBEYWAY N
ABBEYWAY S
FOUNTAINS AVE
B5209
Haydock Park Farm
Fox Covert
Dean Dam
Dean Dam Farm
Ellam's Brook
Ellam's Rough
NEWTON LA
Newton- Haydock Bridge
Wood Pit Covert
VISTA RD
WOODLANDS IND EST
Lawson's Farm
Hollows Bridge
Haydock Park Golf Course
CH
BILLINGTON AVE
ASHTON RD
Newton-le-Willows Community Sch
JOHNSON AVE
URMSTON AVE
MARTIN AVE
DIXON AVE
ELSTON AVE
PORTER AVE
WEEDON AVE
CUNLIFFE AVE
WILLIAMS
WIGHTMAN AVE
MULLINS AVE
HORRIDGE AVE
SPEAKMAN AVE
WHEATLEY AVE
QUEENS DR
WETHERBY
MARITIME CL
CHELTENHAM DR
KEMPTON CL
FRAWLEY AVE
DUNCAN AVE
KERSHAW WAY
RIPON CL
BELVEDERE RD
CROWN FIELDS
CROWN GDNS
BORRON RD
DAVIES AVE
RUSKIN AVE
LATHAM AVE
DAMIAN DR
ANNETTE AVE
GEORGE ST
VISTA AVE
REDMAYNE CL
SILVERDALE RD
RUSHTON AVE
St Mary's RC Inf Sch
GREENSHANK CL
COLE AVE
WATER ST
BEECHWOOD AVE
THE AVENUE
THE ROOKERY
A572
Ct
COBDEN ST
ROKEDEN
THE PARCHMENTS
DALE VIEW
Newton Bank Sch
CASTLE HILL
ROB LA
HIGH ST
MERCER ST
BIRLEY ST
WALMSLEY ST
GOLBORNE ST
Newton Lake
MERE RD
1 NORTHWOOD AVE
2 WOODLAND AVE
M6
CROW LA W
CROW LA E
Liby
PO
PLEASANCE WAY
MANSE GDNS
CHURCH ST
SOUTHWORTH RD
A572
HEATHER BRAE
YEW TREE AVE
THE COPSE
CROSS LA
St Helen's Coll Newton Campus
SANDPIPER CL
AVOCET CL
REDSHANK AVE
DUNLIN AVE
TURNSTONE
DEAN MEADOW
HARRISON WAY
SUNNYBANK
GREENFIELD CL
St Aelred's RC High Sch
St Peter's CE Prim Sch
WILLOW RD
WILLOW AVE
WILLOWDALE
PARK RD N
HOLFORD WAY
EASTWOOD AVE
ROSEMARY DR
The District Prim Sch
BK MARKET ST
PINE ST
HAYDOCK ST
PATTERSON ST
BARN WAY
St Mary's Jun Sch
VICTORIA RD
WHINCHAT AVE
WHIMBREL AVE
Newton Cty Prim Sch
NELSON ST
CROWN ST
ST JOHN ST
SCEPTRE CL
TAMWORTH ST
LEGH ST
BK LEGH ST
REGENT ST
WOODS CT
EARLE ST
LORD ST
STANLEY ST
SANKEY ST
WELLINGTON ST
TH
FOUNDRY ST
SCHOOL ST
CHAPEL ST
DERBY ST
HOTEL ST
HOLDEN CL
DERBY CL
MILTON AVE
HOPE ST
COLLINGWOOD RD
BROOKFIELD ST
WARGRAVE RD
SERIN CL
SISKIN CL
Newton-le-Willows Sta
Stones Crossing
Mill House Sch
ALFRED ST
MILL LA
ROSCOE AVE
BANASTRE DR
BURKHARDT DR
PARK VIEW
Newton Park Farm
NEWTON PARK DR
WAYFARERS DR
WHITEFIELD AVE
OXFORD ST
BRIDGE ST
FAIRCLOUGH ST
KING ST
QUEEN ST
RAILWAY ST
GABLE ST
CHEMICAL ST
JUNCTION LA
SUEZ ST
Earlestown Sta
HOUGHTON ST
THE CROSSINGS
OLD WARGRAVE RD
GLOVER ST
SUNBEAM ST
RYDAL ST
SYCAMORE AVE
ACORN ST
OAK AVE
HAWTHORN AVE
POPLAR AVE
HOLLY AVE
ALDER ST
Wargrave
ALDER ST
LAUREL AVE
LAUREL
CEDAR CRES
MAPLE AVE
TRACY DR
CHESHIRE CL
CONWY DR
NORMAN AVE
SANDRA DR
SHERI DR
WOBURN AVE
WARWICK AVE
WINDSOR AVE
PARK RD S
WELBECK AVE
WOODSTOCK AVE
DEACON TRAD EST
NEWTON-LE-WILLOWS
GROSVENOR GDNS
CEDAR AVE
ELM AVE
ASH AVE
LARCH AVE
ROMAN CL
PINE AVE
FERN AVE
LILY AVE
IVY AVE
PARK AVE S
MYRTLE AVE
DAISY AVE
GOOCH DR
STEPHENSON RD
GREENWOOD CT
ADAMS CL
RENDEL CL
Cemy
Newton Brook
GRANT ST 1
BK BOOTH ST 2
BOOTH ST 3
BK LAWRENCE ST 4
LAWRENCE ST 5
WELLINGTON GDNS 6
WELLINGTON CL 7
MARKET ST 8
GRAFTON ST 9
BK BRIDGE ST 10
Earlestown
SANKEY VALLEY IND EST
CATHERINE WAY
FINDLAY CL
KINGSWAY
DEVONSHIRE GDNS
CONNAUGHT DR
RICHMOND GDNS
WARGRAVE RD
Newton Community
H
P
VALLEY VIEW
BRADLEGH RD
Sch
KENILWORTH GDNS
LEAMINGTON AVE
CHURCH DR
Wargrave House Sch
CENTRAL WAY
CORONATION DR
BUCKLOW RD
FARM WAY
WINWICK RD
St Helen's Canal (dis)
Sankey Brook
BRADLEY LA
WARGRAVE MEWS
Red Bank
RED BANK AVE
HERMITAGE GREEN LA
HOVERTY PREC 1
NOON CT 2
COUNCE AVE 3
LANGLEY AVE 4
SCOTT WLK 5
THOMPSON CL 6
INGHAM AVE 7
FEARNLEY WAY 8
KENT WAY 9
OLD HEY WLK 10
LINEAR VIEW
TYRER RD
VULCAN CL
CONROY WAY
VULCAN IND EST
Works
Vulcan Village
New Hey Farm
NEWTON RD
A49

90

89
74

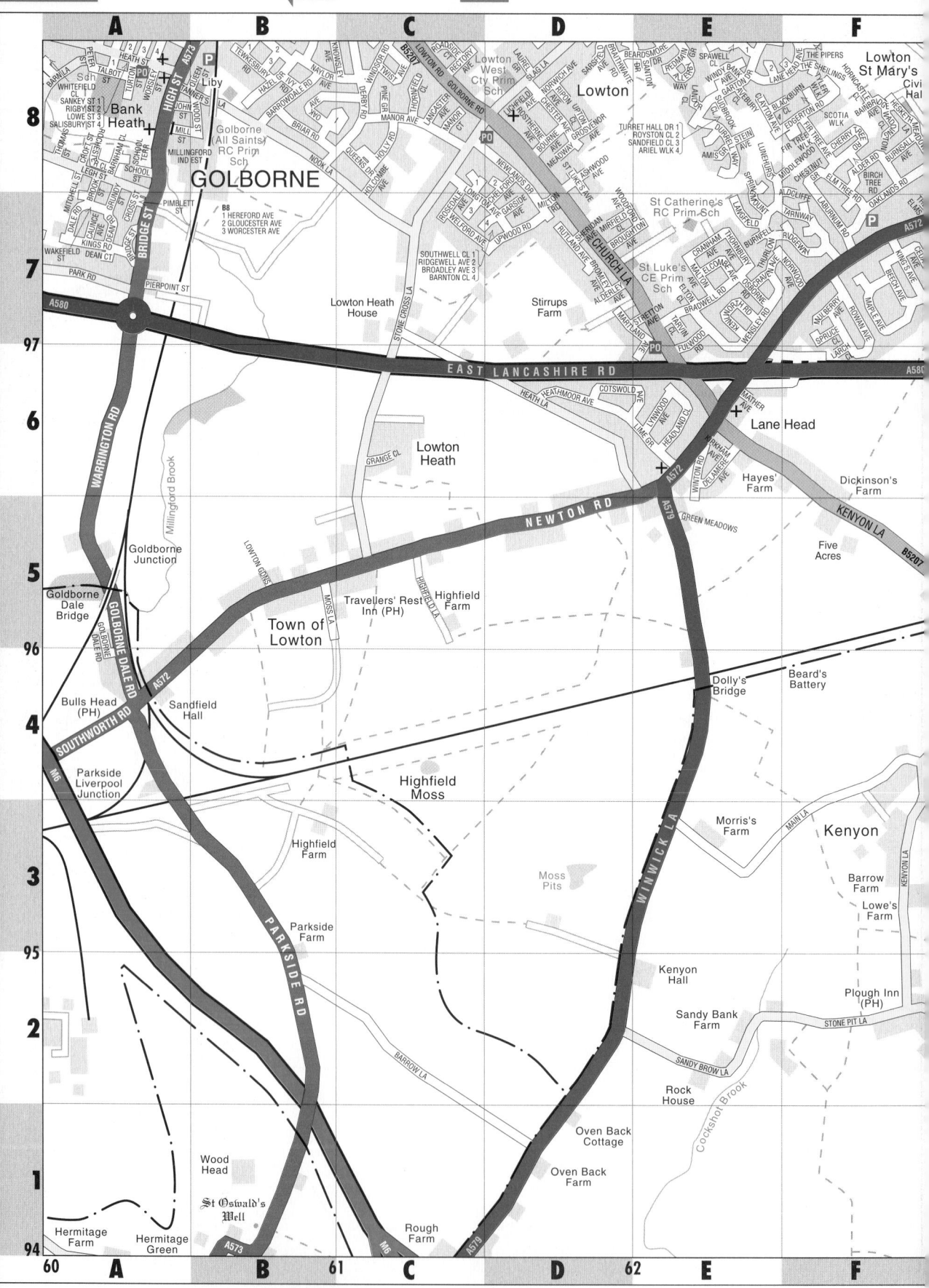
A
B
C
D
E
F
8
7
97
6
5
96
4
3
95
2
1
94
60
61
62
GOLBORNE
Lowton
Lowton St Mary's
Bank Heath
Golborne (All Saints) RC Prim Sch
Lowton West Cty Prim Sch
St Catherine's RC Prim Sch
St Luke's CE Prim Sch
MILLINGFORD IND EST
Liby
B8
1 HEREFORD AVE
2 GLOUCESTER AVE
3 WORCESTER AVE
SOUTHWELL CL 1
RIDGEWELL AVE 2
BROADLEY AVE 3
BARNTON CL 4
TURRET HALL DR 1
ROYSTON CL 2
SANDFIELD CL 3
ARIEL WLK 4
WHITEFIELD CL
SANKEY ST 1
RIGBY ST 2
LOWE ST 3
SALISBURY ST 4
HIGH ST
BRIDGE ST
WARRINGTON RD
GOLBORNE DALE RD
SOUTHWORTH RD
PARKSIDE RD
EAST LANCASHIRE RD
NEWTON RD
CHURCH LA
WINWICK LA
KENYON LA
LOWTON RD
GOLBORNE RD
STONE CROSS LA
HEATH LA
HEATHMOOR AVE
MOSS LA
HIGHFIELD LA
LOWTON GDNS
GRANGE CL
GREEN MEADOWS
BARROW LA
SANDY BROW LA
STONE PIT LA
MAIN LA
PIERPOINT ST
PARK RD
A580
A572
A573
A579
B5207
M6
Lowton Heath House
Stirrups Farm
Lowton Heath
Lane Head
Hayes' Farm
Dickinson's Farm
Five Acres
Goldborne Junction
Goldborne Dale Bridge
Millingford Brook
Town of Lowton
Travellers' Rest Inn (PH)
Highfield Farm
Bulls Head (PH)
Sandfield Hall
Parkside Liverpool Junction
Highfield Moss
Dolly's Bridge
Beard's Battery
Morris's Farm
Kenyon
Barrow Farm
Lowe's Farm
Moss Pits
Parkside Farm
Kenyon Hall
Sandy Bank Farm
Plough Inn (PH)
Rock House
Cockshot Brook
Oven Back Cottage
Oven Back Farm
Wood Head
St Oswald's Well
Rough Farm
Hermitage Farm
Hermitage Green

89

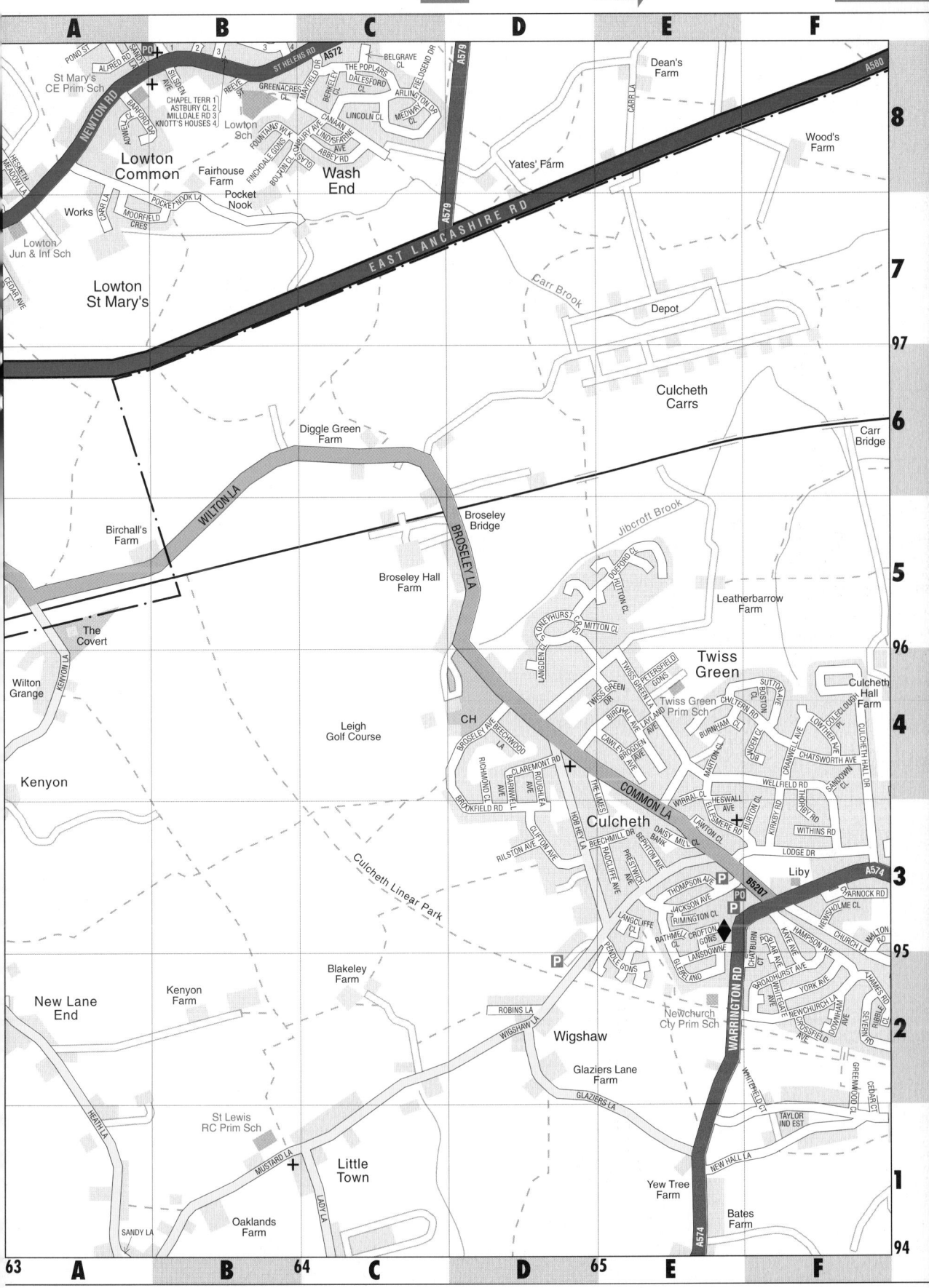

A B C D E F

8

7

97

6

5

96

4

3

95

2

1

94

91
76

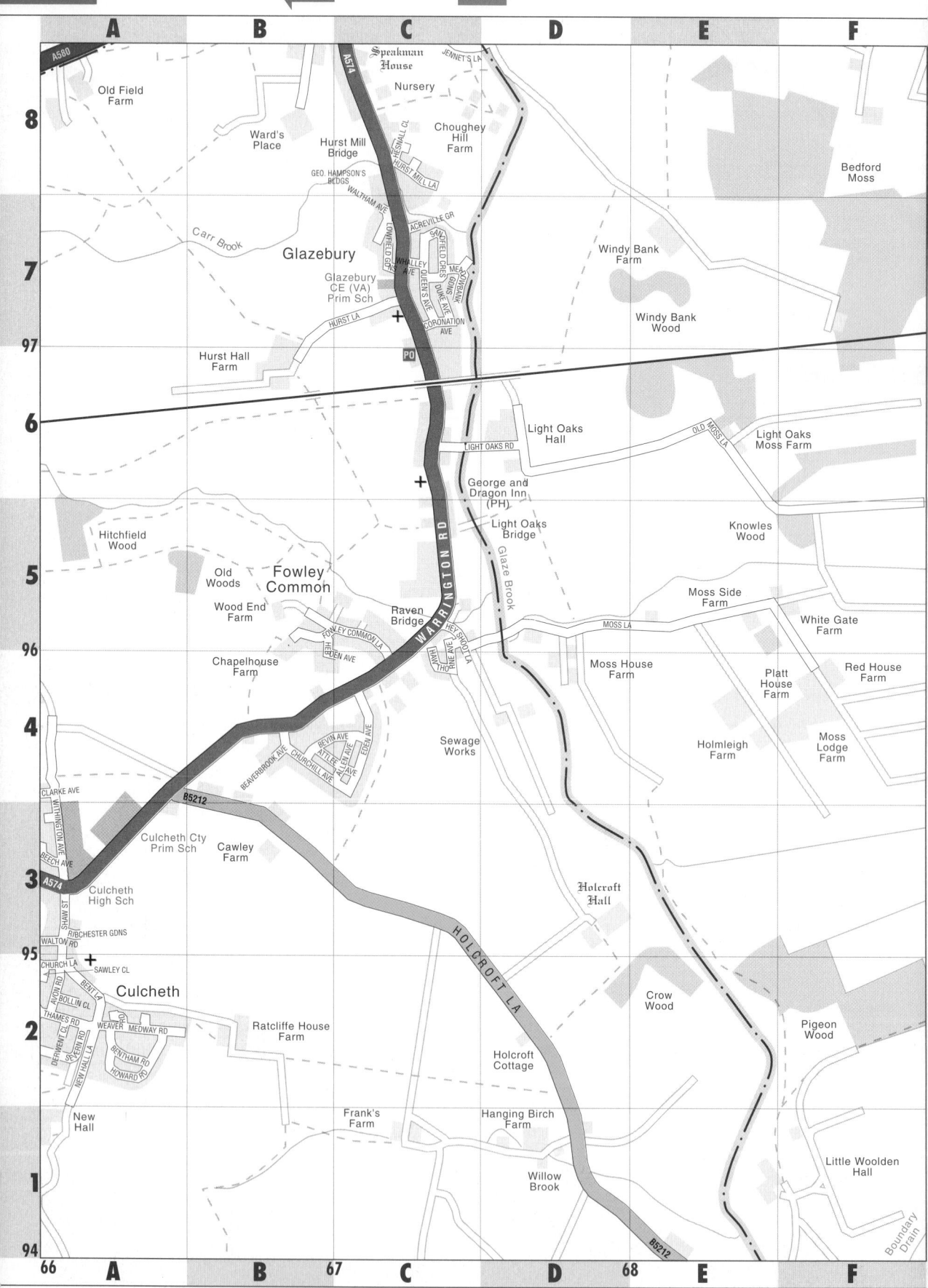
A B C D E F
8
7
97
6
5
96
4
3
95
2
1
94
66 67 68
A580
A574
Speakman House
Jennet's La
Nursery
Old Field Farm
Ward's Place
Hurst Mill Bridge
Choughey Hill Farm
Hesnall Cl
Hurst Mill La
Geo. Hampson's Bldgs
Waltham Ave
Bedford Moss
Acreville Gr
Carr Brook
Lowfield Gdns
Sandfield Cres
Glazebury
Whalley Ave
Meadowbank Gdns
Queen's Ave
Duke Ave
Windy Bank Farm
Glazebury CE (VA) Prim Sch
Coronation Ave
Hurst La
Windy Bank Wood
PO
Hurst Hall Farm
Light Oaks Hall
Old Moss La
Light Oaks Moss Farm
Light Oaks Rd
George and Dragon Inn (PH)
Light Oaks Bridge
Knowles Wood
Hitchfield Wood
Glaze Brook
Warrington Rd
Old Woods
Fowley Common
Wood End Farm
Moss Side Farm
Raven Bridge
White Gate Farm
Moss La
Fowley Common La
Heyshoot La
Hebden Ave
Hawthorne Ave
Moss House Farm
Chapelhouse Farm
Red House Farm
Platt House Farm
Bevin Ave
Eden Ave
Sewage Works
Holmleigh Farm
Moss Lodge Farm
Beaverbrook Ave
Churchill Ave
Attlee Ave
Allen Ave
Clarke Ave
Withington Ave
B5212
Culcheth Cty Prim Sch
Cawley Farm
Beech Ave
Culcheth High Sch
Holcroft Hall
Shaw St
Ribchester Gdns
Holcroft La
Walton Rd
Church La
Sawley Cl
Culcheth
Bent La
Avon Rd
Bollin Cl
Crow Wood
Thames Rd
Weaver Rd
Medway Rd
Ratcliffe House Farm
Pigeon Wood
Derwent Cl
Severn Rd
New Hall La
Bentham Rd
Howard Rd
Holcroft Cottage
New Hall
Frank's Farm
Hanging Birch Farm
Little Woolden Hall
Willow Brook
Boundary Drain

91

A   B   C   D   E   F

8

7

97

6

Moss
Bank

Shooter's
Grove

RINDLE RD

Astley Moss

LC

Four Winds
Farm

Birch
Farm

Chat Moss

Olive Mount
Farm

Railway View
Farm

5

Moss
Farm

96

OUTLOOK LA

RASPBERRY LA

New
Farm

Mosslands
Farm

TWELVE YARDS RD

Woodbarn
Farm

4

Birch View
Farm

Oakfield

Irlam
Moss

ASTLEY RD

Ebenezer
Farm

Larkhill
House

M62

Hope Cottage
Farm

Hephzibah
Farm

3

Little Woolden
Moss

95

SUNNINGDALE DR

CRANFORD DR

BALSHAW CT

NEWLANDS AVE

THE LOCKS

PARRS CT

BROOKLANDS CL

Woodstock
Farm

2

Boundary Drain

Ringing Pits
Farm

MOSS RD

Plant Cottage
Farm

Springfield

BALSHAW AVE

DITCHFIELD WAY

SPRINGFIELD LA

SPRINGFIELD RD

STUART AVE

LEE CT

LONDON RD

CALDER AVE

Birch
Court

Little
Haven

ELSINORE
AVE

GREENSIDE DR

VICTORIA RD

Worsley View
Farm

1

Birch Tree
Farm

LEADER WILLIAMS RD

HOWARTH DR

PALATINE

Great Molden
Moss

ROSE AVE

SSF CRES

BAINES AVE

FRANCIS RD

B5320

Prospect
Grange

ROSCOE RD

WALKER RD

94

9   A   B   70   C   D   71   E   F

93
78

A
B
C
D
E
F
8
7
97
6
5
96
4
3
95
2
1
94
72
73
74
LC
BARTON MOSS RD
M62
Brighton Grange
Moulder's Farm
Manor Farm
Nursery Farm
Birch Farm
Tunnel Farm
TWELVE YARDS RD
Brookhouse Sports Ctr
Barton Moss Prim Sch
Crem
Cemy
Barton Aerodrome
Black Wood
Bartonmoss Farm
Barton Moss
Univ of Manchester (Lab)
Football Gd
Salteye Brook
Barton Locks
Parkhall
Barton Grange
RASPBERRY LA
Gladwyn Farm
Ferry P
Sewage Works
Recn Gd
Fallows Farm
LIVERPOOL RD
Manchester Ship Canal
Woods End
Calder Bank
CH
Davyhulme Park Golf Course
Moorfield Prim Sch
St Joseph's RC Prim Sch
Fiddlers Lane Prim Sch
Liby
PO
P
B5320
Woodsend Prim Sch
CADISHEAD WAY
Woodsend Park
Wellacre Jun Sch
Wellacre Inf Sch
Flixton
Flixton Inf Sch
Flixton Jun Sch
IRLAM RD
Delamere Sch
Wellacre High Sch
St Monica's RC Prim Sch
Towns Gate
Woodlands
Grave Yard
Boat House (PH)
Irlam Prim Sch
Irlam Locks
Sewage Works
FLIXTON RD
B5158
Flixton Sta
St Michael's CE (VA) Prim Sch
The Village
B5213
A57
1 ROSLYN AVE
2 ALEXANDRA CT
3 PARSONAGE RD
4 HAMPSTEAD AVE
5 GRASMERE AVE
6 READE HOUSE
7 BRENTWOOD
1 HOLLY CT
2 ST CLEMENT'S CT
1 WESTON RD
2 ETHERLEY CL
BRADWELL WLK 1
WOODSEND CIRC 2
MARBURY CL 3
QUEENS CT 1
ASHWORTH AVE 2
BRIDLE CL 3
AMBUSCADE CT 4
MAYFIELD IND EST
BOUNDARY TRAD PK

93
106

79
96

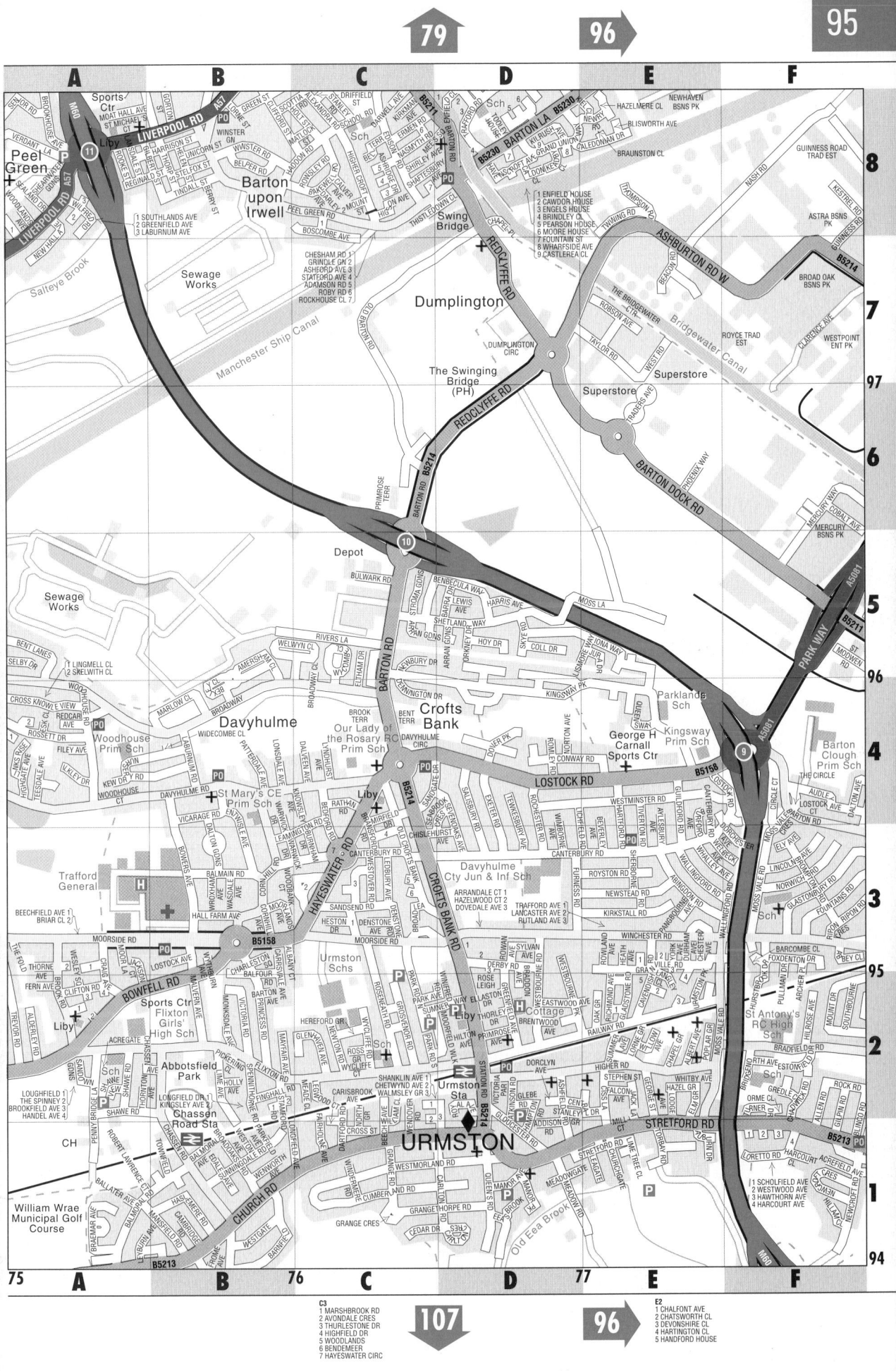

C3
1 MARSHBROOK RD
2 AVONDALE CRES
3 THURLESTONE DR
4 HIGHFIELD DR
5 WOODLANDS
6 BENDEMEER
7 HAYESWATER CIRC

E2
1 CHALFONT AVE
2 CHATSWORTH CL
3 DEVONSHIRE CL
4 HARTINGTON CL
5 HANDFORD HOUSE

107
96

95
80

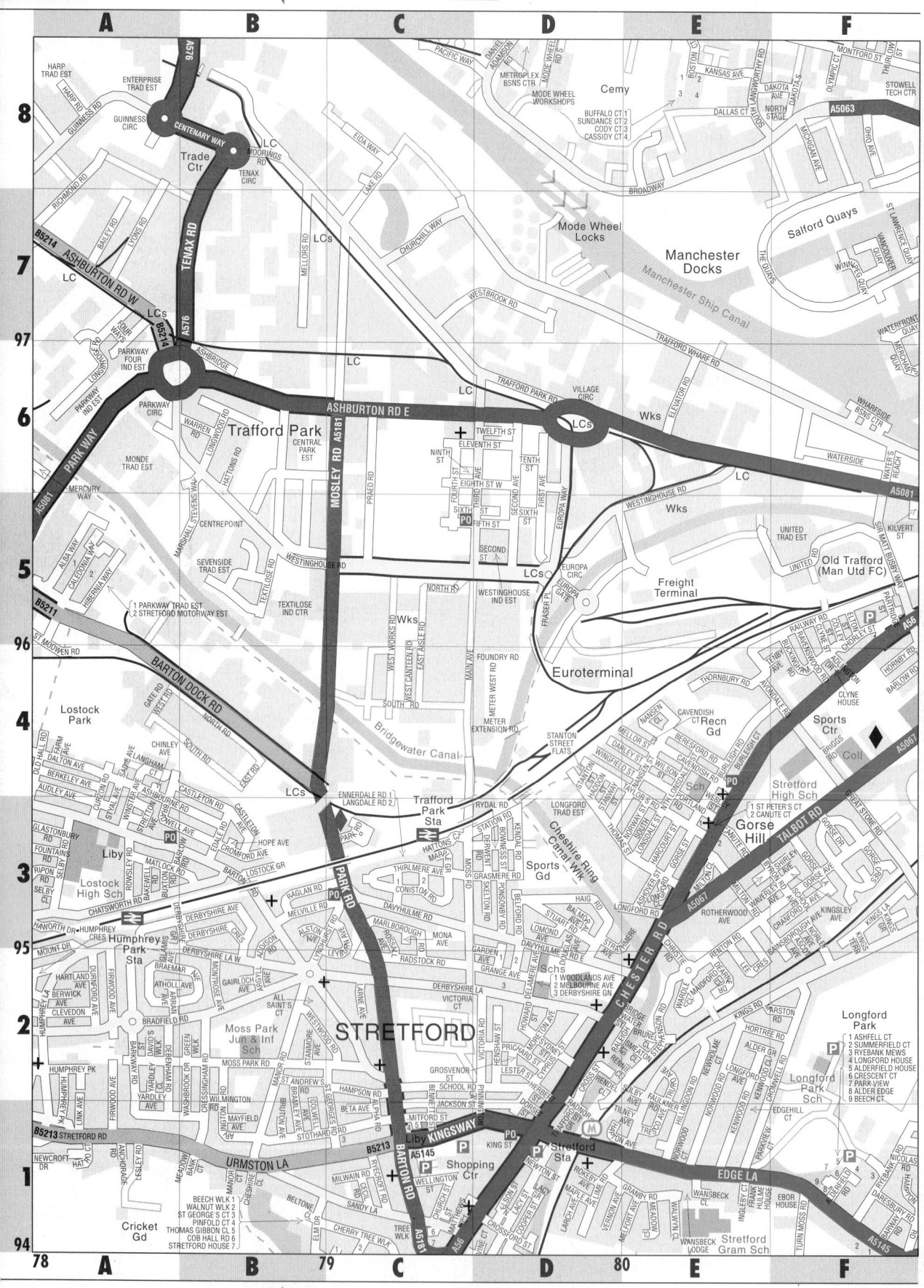
A
B
C
D
E
F
8
7
97
6
5
96
4
3
95
2
1
94
78
79
80
HARP TRAD EST
HARP RD
GUINNESS RD
ENTERPRISE TRAD EST
GUINNESS CIRC
CENTENARY WAY
A576
Trade Ctr
TENAX CIRC
MOORINGS
LC
TENAX RD
RICHMOND RD
BAILEY RD
LYONS RD
B5214
ASHBURTON RD W
LCs
FOUR WAYS
PARKWAY FOUR IND EST
LONGBRIDGE RD
PARKWAY IND EST
PARKWAY CIRC
ASHBRIDGE
MELLORS RD
EIDA WAY
LAKE RD
CHURCHILL WAY
PACIFIC WAY
DANIEL ADAMSON RD
METROPLEX BSNS CTR
MODE WHEEL RD S
MODE WHEEL WORKSHOPS
Cemy
BUFFALO CT 1
SUNDANCE CT 2
CODY CT 3
CASSIDY CT 4
BOSTON CT
KANSAS AVE
DALLAS CT
SOUTH LANGWORTHY RD
DAKOTA AVE
DAKOTA S
NORTH STAGE
OLYMPIC CT
MONTFORD ST
THURLOW ST
STOWELL TECH CTR
A5063
MICHIGAN AVE
OHIO AVE
BROADWAY
Mode Wheel Locks
Manchester Docks
Manchester Ship Canal
Salford Quays
THE QUAYS
ST LAWRENCE QUAY
VANCOUVER QUAY
WINNIPEG QUAY
WATERFRONT QUAY
MERCHANTS QUAY
WESTBROOK RD
TRAFFORD WHARF RD
TRAFFORD PARK RD
VILLAGE CIRC
ELEVATOR RD
WHARFSIDE BSNS CTR
WATERSIDE
WATER'S REACH
A5081
ASHBURTON RD E
Trafford Park
WARREN RD
LONGWOOD RD
HATTONS RD
CENTRAL PARK EST
MOSLEY RD
A5181
PRAED RD
TWELFTH ST
ELEVENTH ST
NINTH ST
FOURTH ST
THIRD AVE
EIGHTH ST W
SIXTH ST
FIFTH ST
PO
SECOND AVE
TENTH ST
FIRST AVE
SIXTH ST
EUROPA WAY
SECOND ST
Wks
WESTINGHOUSE RD
LC
MONDE TRAD EST
PARK WAY
MERCURY WAY
A5081
MARSHALL STEVENS WAY
CENTREPOINT
SEVENSIDE TRAD EST
TEXTILOSE RD
WESTINGHOUSE RD
ALBA WAY
CALEDONIA WAY
HIBERNIA WAY
1 PARKWAY TRAD EST
2 STRETFORD MOTORWAY EST
TEXTILOSE IND CTR
B5211
ST MODWEN RD
BARTON DOCK RD
NORTH RD
WEST WORKS RD
WEST CANTEEN RD
EAST AISLE RD
MAIN AVE
FOUNDRY RD
METER WEST RD
NORTH RD
WESTINGHOUSE IND EST
LCs
EUROPA CIRC
EUROPA GATE
FRASER PL
Freight Terminal
Euroterminal
UNITED TRAD EST
UNITED RD
Old Trafford (Man Utd FC)
SIR MATT BUSBY WAY
KILVERT ST
Lostock Park
GATE RD
WEST RD
SOUTH RD
EAST RD
CHINLEY AVE
SOUTH RD
METER EXTENSION RD
Bridgewater Canal
STANTON STREET FLATS
OLD HALL RD
FARM AVE
DALTON AVE
BERKELEY AVE
AUDLEY AVE
LANGHAM CT
ASHBOURNE RD
CASTLETON RD
LCs
ENNERDALE RD 1
LANGDALE RD 2
Trafford Park Sta
RYDAL RD
LONGFORD TRAD EST
Cheshire Ring Canal Wlk
GLASTONBURY RD
FOUNTAINS RD
RIPON RD
SELBY RD
Liby
Lostock High Sch
PO
HOPE AVE
CROMFORD AVE
LOSTOCK GR
BARTON RD
MATLOCK RD
BAKEWELL RD
BUXTON RD
BASLOW RD
EDALE RD
PARK RD
HATTONS CT
THIRLMERE AVE
CONISTON RD
STATION RD
DERWENT RD
BOWNESS ST
KENDAL RD
GRASMERE RD
SKELTON RD
PONSONBY RD
BELFORD RD
MOSS RD
Sports Gd
CHATSWORTH RD
HAWORTH DR
HUMPHREY CRES
Humphrey Park Sta
MOUNT DR
DERBYSHIRE AVE
DERBYSHIRE CRES
RAGLAN RD
MELVILLE RD
DAVYHULME RD
MARLBOROUGH RD
MONA AVE
DERBYSHIRE LA W
RADSTOCK RD
GARDEN AVE
GRANGE AVE
DAVYHULME RD E
Schs
1 WOODLANDS AVE
2 MELBOURNE AVE
3 DERBYSHIRE GN
HARTLAND CL
BERWICK AVE
CLEVEDON AVE
BRAEMAR AVE
ATHOLL AVE
GAIRLOCH AVE
ARGYLL AVE
ALL SAINT'S CT
DERBYSHIRE LA
VICTORIA CT
BRADFIELD RD
Moss Park Jun & Inf Sch
MOSS PARK RD
STRETFORD
HUMPHREY PK
FIRWOOD AVE
DURNFORD AVE
LINK AVE
YARDLEY AVE
WILMINGTON RD
MAYFIELD AVE
ST ANDREW'S
HAMPSON RD
BETA AVE
STOTHARD RD
GROSVENOR ST
SCHOOL RD
JACKSON ST
MITFORD ST
KINGSWAY
Liby
A5145
P
Shopping Ctr
WELLINGTON ST
B5213 STRETFORD RD
B5213
URMSTON LA
NEWCROFT DR
ANCHORAGE RD
LESLEY RD
MEADOW BANK CT
BELTONE CL
MILWAIN RD
CECIL RD
RYECROFT RD
SANDY LA
CHERRY TREE WLK
TREE WLK
BARTON RD
A5181
A56
Cricket Gd
BEECH WLK 1
WALNUT WLK 2
ST GEORGE'S CT 3
PINFOLD CT 4
THOMAS GIBBON CL 5
COB HALL RD 6
STRETFORD HOUSE 7
KING ST
NEWTON ST
Stretford Sta
ROKEBY AVE
LIME RD
MAPLE AVE
LARCH AVE
VERNON AVE
MELFORT AVE
GRANBY RD
MEADOW CL
WALWYN CL
WANSBECK CL
WANSBECK LODGE
Stretford Gram Sch
EDGE LA
EBOR HOUSE
TURN MOSS RD
A5145
CHESTER RD
A5067
TALBOT RD
Gorse Hill
Stretford High Sch
Coll
Sports Ctr
CLYNE HOUSE
A5067
Recn Gd
CAVENDISH CT
NANSEN CL
MELLOR ST
DARLEY ST
WINGFIELD ST
BERESFORD RD
CAVENDISH RD
WILSON ST
PORTLAND RD
BURLEIGH RD
BURLEIGH CT
Sch
1 ST PETER'S CT
2 CANUTE CT
THORNBURY RD
AVONDALE RD
TENBY AVE
RAILWAY RD
PARTRIDGE
HORNBY RD
BARLOW RD
LONGFORD RD
ROTHERWOOD AVE
KINGSLEY AVE
RENTON RD
LEE CRES
KINGS RD
HORTREE RD
ALDER GR
NORWOOD RD
HILLINGDON RD
LONGFORD AVE
KENWOOD RD
CROMWELL RD
EDGEHILL CT
PARKVIEW CT
Longford Park Sch
Longford Park
1 ASHFELL CT
2 SUMMERFIELD CT
3 RYEBANK MEWS
4 LONGFORD HOUSE
5 ALDERFIELD HOUSE
6 CRESCENT CT
7 PARK VIEW
8 ALDER EDGE
9 BEECH CT
RYEBANK RD
NICOLAS RD
HAMPTON RD
DARESBURY RD
BARWAY RD
ALDERFIELD RD

95
108

For full street detail of the highlighted area see pages 161 and 162.

97

81   98

A B C D E F

109   98

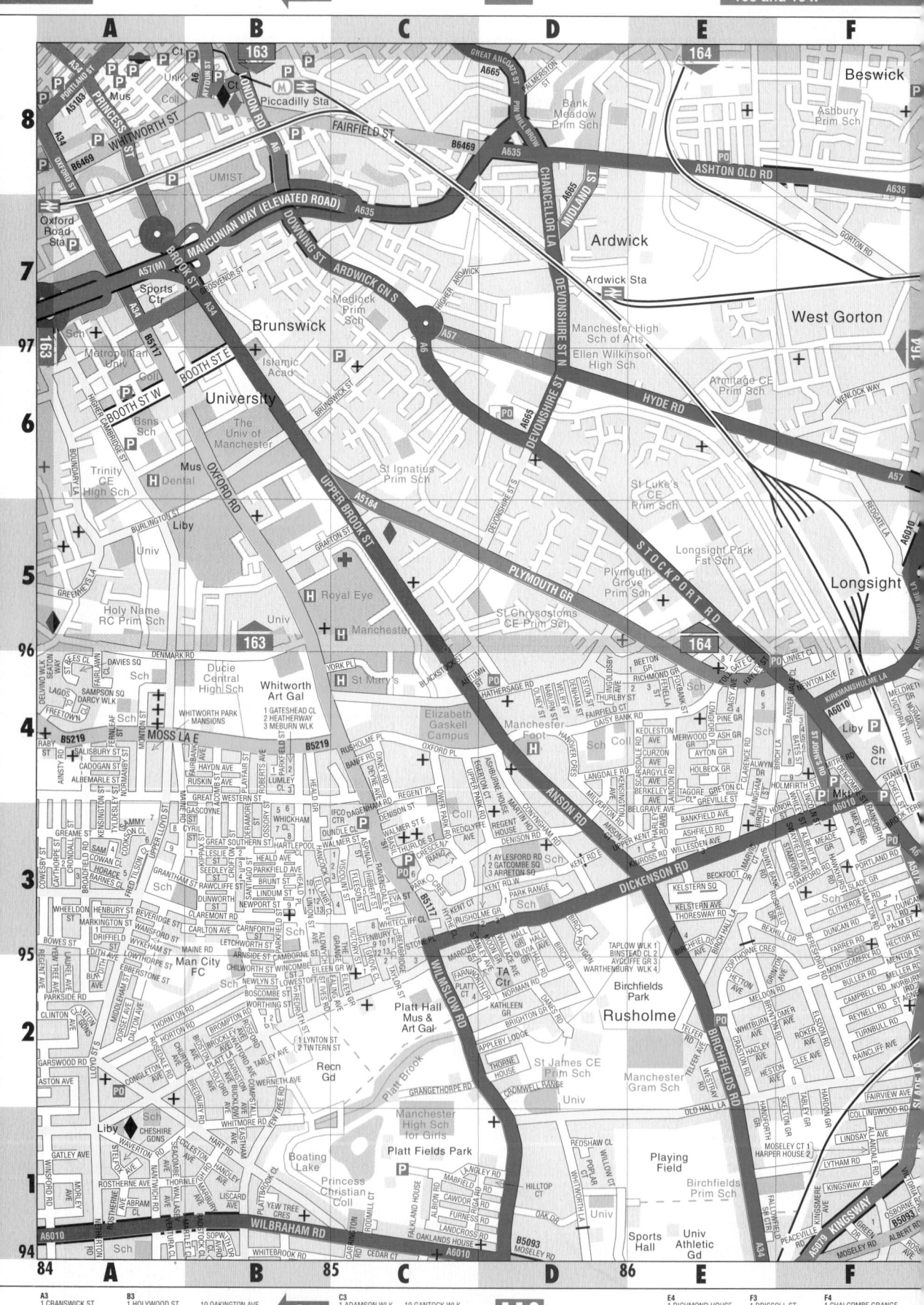

98

← 97

↑ 82

For full street detail of the highlighted area see pages 163 and 164.

99
For full street detail of the highlighted area see page 165.
E7
1 EDISON ST
2 TUNSTALL ST
3 OLD HALL ST
4 BROUGH ST
5 BARBER ST
6 SWINDELL'S ST
7 TINNINGHAM CL
8 RICHARDSON ST
9 MINTRIDGE CL
10 BARN WLK
11 PLUMBLEY ST
12 ALVAN SQ
83
100
F6
1 PETERBOROUGH ST
2 SWANHILL CL
3 ATHERFIELD CL
4 HORATIO ST
5 ALDCROFT ST
6 MARCHIONESS ST
F7
1 SOUTH CLIFFE ST
2 REGINALD ST
3 CLEMENT CT
4 FAIRSTEAD WLK
A
B
C
D
E
F
Openshaw
Clayton Brook Prim Sch
St Brigid's RC Prim Sch (Jun & Inf)
Openshaw CE Prim Sch
Ashton Canal
Tameside Trail
Fairfield Road Prim Sch
St Gregory's High Sch
ASHTON OLD RD
Ashbury's Sta
Manchester Coll of Arts & Tech Openshaw Ctr
New Smithfield Mkt
Gorton Sta
St Francis' RC Prim Sch
All Saints Prim Sch
Gorton Brook Fst Sch
TA Ctr
Car Auction
Abbey Hey
Wright Robinson High Sch
Abbey Hey Inf & Jun Schs
E6
1 EVENLEY CL
2 MONMOUTH ST
3 FRESHWATER ST
4 RUTLAND ST
5 ERNOCROFT GR
6 RUMBOLD ST
7 COMPSTALL GR
8 WENTWORTH AVE
1 HAVERS RD
2 BRAMHALL ST
3 PLANTATION ST
4 CROWTHER ST
Belle Vue
Belle Vue Sta
HYDE RD
Gorton
Gorton Lower Resr
Debdale Park
Recn Gd
Debdale
ALBERT AVE 1
BEATRICE AVE 2
HAROLD AVE 3
QUARMBY RD 4
HIGHFIELD RANGE 5
CARLTON RANGE 6
CLAREMONT RANGE 7
GODFREY RANGE 8
Sports Ctr
1 BOUGAINVILLEA GDNS
2 ANTILLES CL
3 CHIPPING SQ
4 HETHERINGTON WLK
5 HOWTON CL
Sacred Heart RC Jun Sch
Ryder Brow Sta
Cemy
Aspinal Prim Sch
BROADACRE RD 1
COLBORNE AVE 2
LONSDALE AVE 3
BIRTLES AVE 4
ELIZABETH CT 5
BROOK GREEN LA 6
LANDOR CT 7
ARRAS GR 8
1 MACFARREN ST
2 HOLLINS GR
3 TALLIS ST
4 SHERRINGTON ST
Gorton Mount Jun & Inf Sch
Spurley Hey High Sch
Crowcroft Park Prim Sch
NETHERBURY CL
FERNWOOD AVE 1
RUTH ST 2
SOUTHCROSS RD 3
Melland Field
B3
1 BICKERDIKE CT
2 NEWSHAM WLK
3 CULLERCOATS WLK
4 WYLAM WLK
5 SPECTON WLK
6 METHUEN ST
7 LOCKWOOD ST
8 WILPSHIRE AVE
Sports Gd
St Albans RC High Sch
Melland Sch
LYNHURST RD 1
SANDBACH RD 2
FARNDON RD 3
Reddish North Sta
Fir Tree Prim Sch
ASHBROOK LA 3
SPEY HOUSE 4
1 ASHFORD AVE
2 RYDAL MOUNT
MOUNT RD
STOCKPORT RD
REDDISH LA
GORTON RD
LEVENSHULME TRAD EST
Levenshulme
North Reddish
WELLAND ST 1
THE DENES 2
CAMPBELL ST 3
Liby
Cty Prim Sch
1 CUNDIFF CT
2 REDGRAVE WLK
Golf Course
ALBERT RD
8
97
7
6
96
5
4
3
95
2
1
94
87
88
89
A1
1 PARK LODGE
2 MOTHERWELL AVE
3 MONTROSE CRES
4 THE CRESCENT
5 FIRSBY ST
6 CRESCENT GR
7 YEW TREE AVE
8 LEVENSHULME TERR
9 CHINWELL VIEW
10 FARM SIDE PL
11 STATION VIEW
12 BK CHAPEL ST
13 DRURY ST
14 ALEXANDRA TERR
15 BEECH RANGE
A2
1 RUSHFORD CT
2 WARWICK HOUSE
3 ARK ST
4 PRINCE ALBERT AVE
5 LEABANK ST
6 ELTHAM ST
7 LAMSHOLME CL
8 HORSTEAD WLK
B1
1 HARWICH CL
2 DERBY GR
3 MONTREAL ST
4 KING EDWARD ST
5 WESTMINSTER ST
6 ROSTRON ST
7 BUFFOLINE TRAD EST
8 LOSTOCK AVE
9 RAWDON CL
10 GREENWAY AVE
D4
1 MILTON MOUNT
2 MILKWOOD GR
3 ENGLEFIELD GR
D4
4 MILLARD WLK
D5
1 CHEDDAR ST
2 WALNUT ST
3 ACHESON ST
4 ASHKIRK ST
5 ROXBURGH ST
6 DEERFOLD CL
7 BURTINSHAW ST
111
D5
8 BROXWOOD CL
9 BROGAN ST
D6
1 ANNESLEY GDNS
2 CORNWALL CT
3 SANDFORD AVE
4 THOMAS REGAN CT
5 ROBE WLK
100
D7
1 STENSON SQ
2 BRUCE WLK
3 LILY THOMAS CT
4 BOTHA CL
5 WEAVER WLK
6 DORMAN ST
7 KELMARSH CL

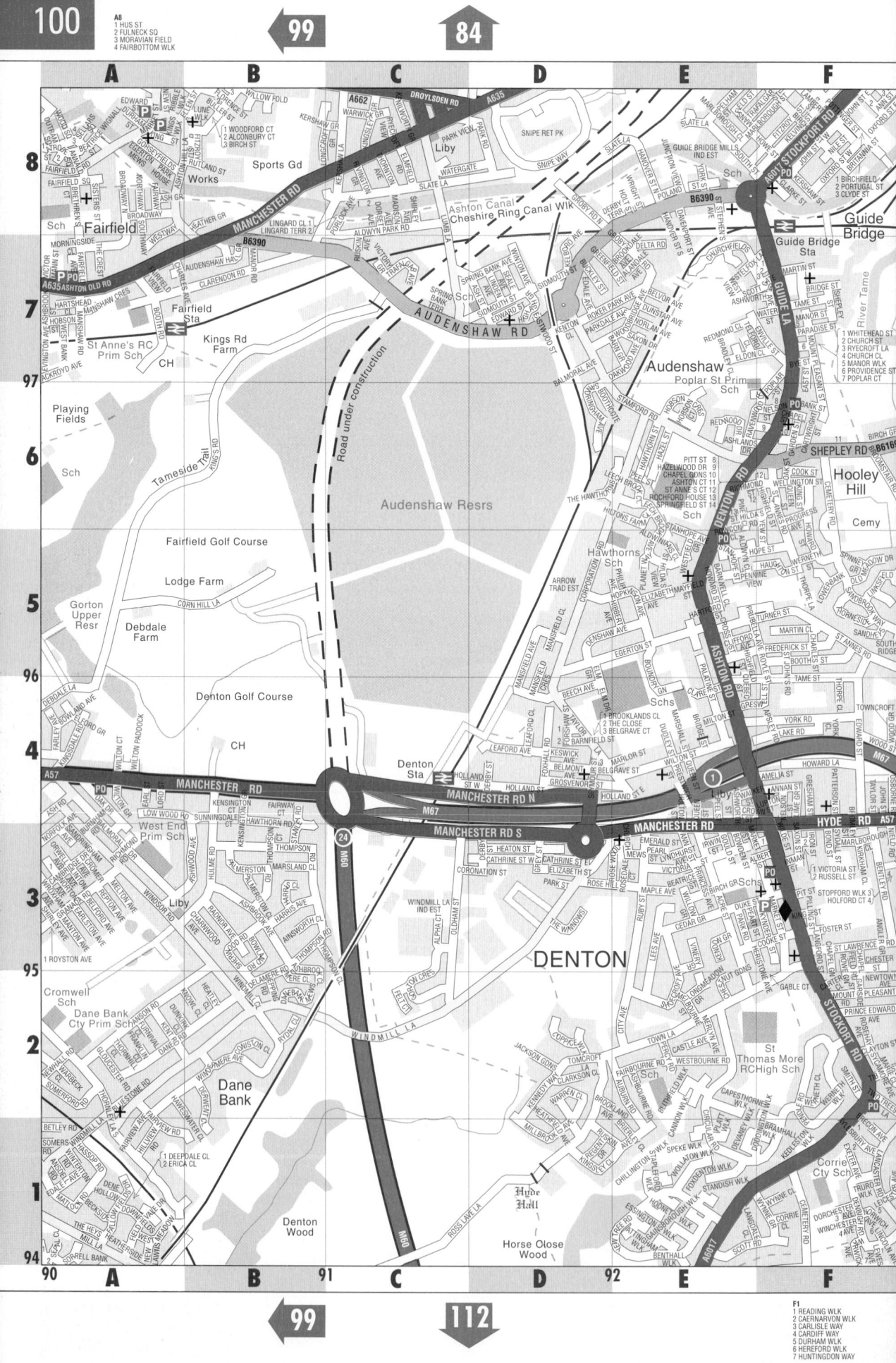

100

A8
1 HUS ST
2 FULNECK SQ
3 MORAVIAN FIELD
4 FAIRBOTTOM WLK

99   84

F1
1 READING WLK
2 CAERNARVON WLK
3 CARLISLE WAY
4 CARDIFF WAY
5 DURHAM WLK
6 HEREFORD WLK
7 HUNTINGDON WAY

85

C6
1 VICTORIA MEWS
2 CONSORT CL

D5
1 SPENCER AVE
2 GLENWOOD AVE
3 BENNET MEWS
4 SACK ST

102

D8
1 CONCORD WAY
2 SHEPLEY CL
3 JACKSON AVE
4 REECE CT
5 CLAYTON ST
6 PLOUGH ST

F5
1 GAINSBOROUGH WLK
2 WENTWORTH WLK

F8
1 CLARENCE HOUSE
2 THE ARCADE

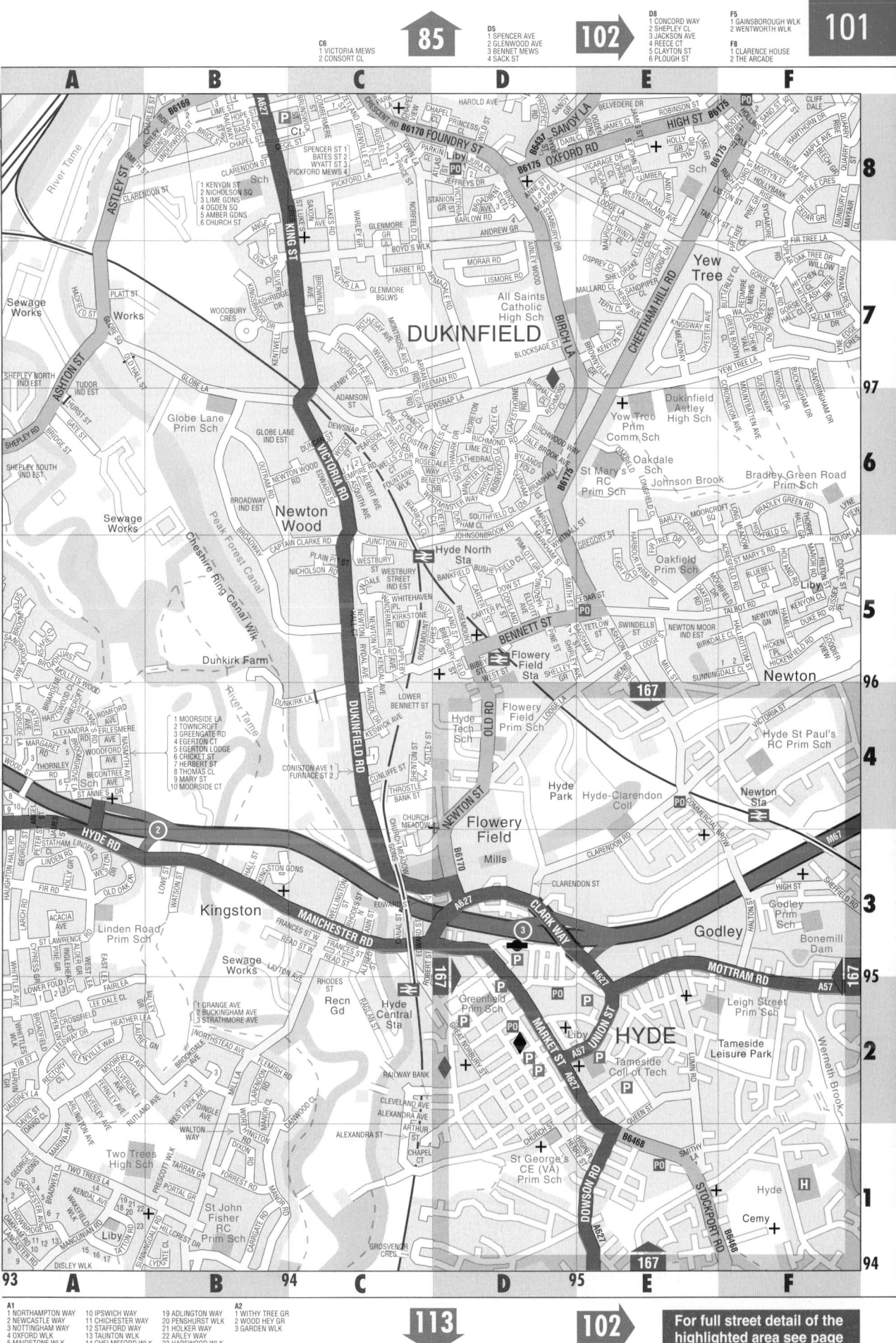

A1
1 NORTHAMPTON WAY
2 NEWCASTLE WAY
3 NOTTINGHAM WAY
4 OXFORD WLK
5 MAIDSTONE WLK
6 PEMBROKE WAY
7 SHREWSBURY WAY
8 BOSTON WLK
9 WELSHPOOL WAY
10 IPSWICH WAY
11 CHICHESTER WAY
12 STAFFORD WAY
13 TAUNTON WLK
14 CHELMSFORD WLK
15 GAWSWORTH WAY
16 THORSBY WAY
17 HADDON WAY
18 MORTON TERR
19 ADLINGTON WAY
20 PENSHURST WLK
21 HOLKER WAY
22 ARLEY WAY
23 HAREWOOD WLK

A2
1 WITHY TREE GR
2 WOOD HEY GR
3 GARDEN WLK

113

102

For full street detail of the highlighted area see page 167.

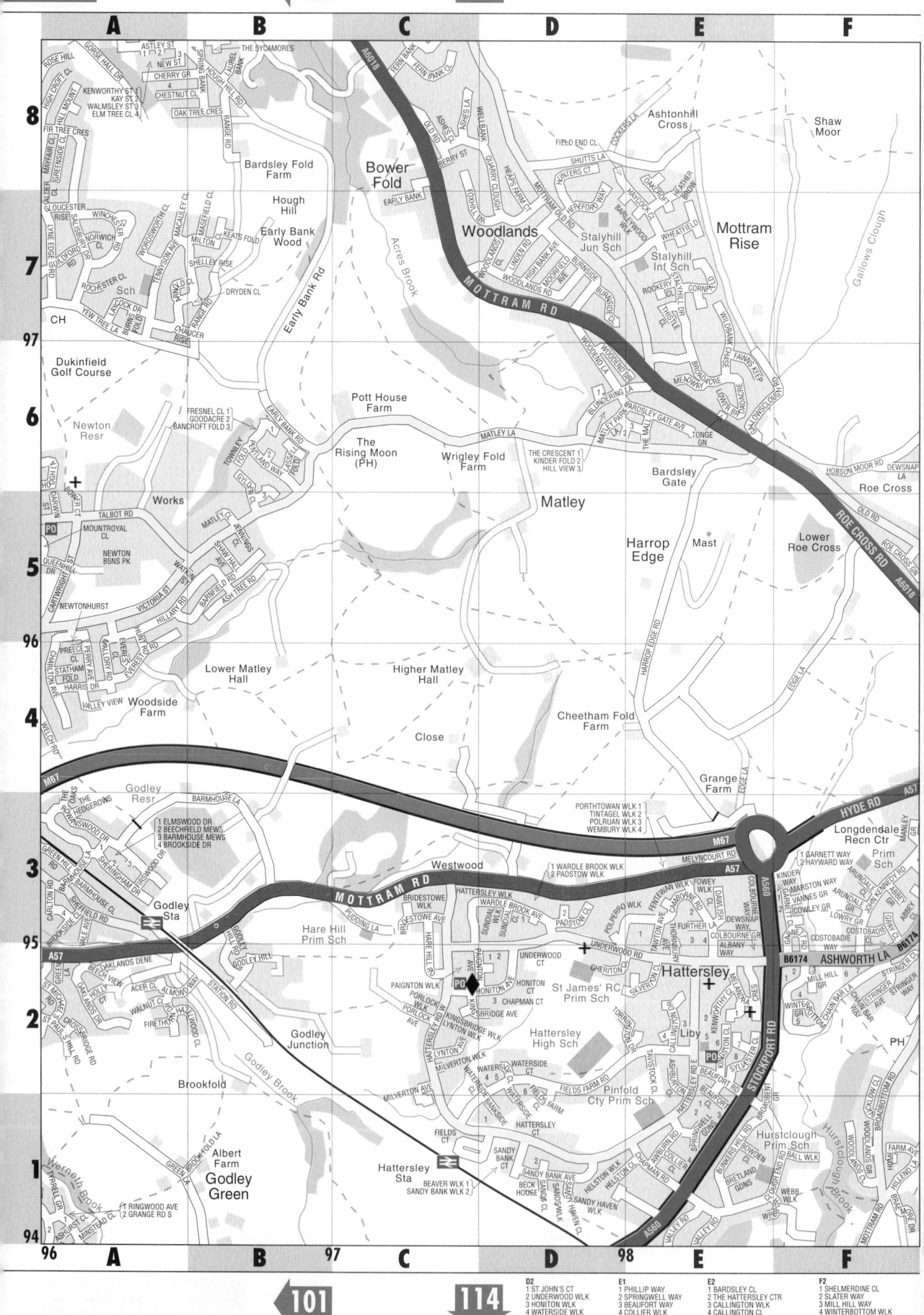

ASTLEY ST
ROSE HILL
GORSE HALL DR
1 2
3 NEW ST
THE SYCAMORES
SPRINGBOUGH HILL WAY
LAUREL BANK
FERN BANK
FERN BANK CL
SHUTTS LA
ASHTONHILL Cross
Shaw Moor
HIGH CROFT CL
FIR TREE CRES
KENWORTHY ST
KAY ST 2
WALMSLEY ST 3
ELM TREE CL 4
CHERRY GR
CHESTNUT CL
OAK TREE CRES
RANGE RD
Bardsley Fold Farm
Bower Fold
ASHES LA
BERRY ST
FIELD END CL
HUNTERS CT
HAYCOCK LA
Gallows Clough

GLOUCESTER RISE
NORWICH CL
ROCHESTER CL
Sch
CH
Hough Hill
Early Bank Wood
SHELLEY RISE
DRYDEN CL
Early Bank
Woodlands
Stalyhill Jun Sch
Stalyhill Int Sch
Mottram Rise

Dukinfield Golf Course
Newton Resr
FRESNEL CL 1
GOODACRE 2
BANCROFT FOLD 3
Pott House Farm
The Rising Moon (PH)
Wrigley Fold Farm
MATLEY LA
THE CRESCENT 1
KINDER FOLD 2
HILL VIEW 3
Bardsley Gate
Roe Cross
Lower Roe Cross

Works
TALBOT RD
MOUNTROYAL CL
PO
NEWTON BSNS PK
Matley
Harrop Edge
Mast
ROE CROSS RD
A6018

QUEEN HILL DR
CARTWRIGHT
VICTORIA ST
HILLARY RD
ASH TREE RD
EDGE LA

Newtonhurst
Lower Matley Hall
Higher Matley Hall

PREECE CL
PERRY AVE
STATHAM FOLD
HARRIS DR
VALLEY VIEW
Woodside Farm
Close
Cheetham Fold Farm
Grange Farm

M67
THE OAKS
THE HEDGEROWS
Godley Resr
BARMHOUSE LA
1 ELMSWOOD DR
2 BEECHFIELD MEWS
3 BARMHOUSE MEWS
4 BROOKSIDE DR
Westwood
PORTHTOWAN WLK 1
TINTAGEL WLK 2
POLRUAN WLK 3
WEMBURY WLK 4
M67
HYDE RD A57
Longdendale Recn Ctr
Prim Sch

GREENHILL RD
CARLTON RD
BROOKSIDE RD
Godley Sta
MOTTRAM RD
Hare Hill Prim Sch
BRIDESTOWE WLK
WARDLE BROOK AVE
1 WARDLE BROOK WLK
2 PADSTOW WLK
MELYNCOURT RD
A57
KINDER WAY
1 GARNETT WAY
2 HAYWARD WAY
ARUNDALE

A57
OAKLANDS DENE
BIRCH VIEW
ACER AVE
STATION RD
Godley Hill
HARE HILL RD
PAIGNTON WLK
UNDERWOOD CT
PO
Hattersley
B6174 ASHWORTH LA

WALNUT CL
FIRETHORN
Godley Junction
PORLOCK WLK
HONITON AVE
HONITON CT
CHAPMAN CT
St James' RC Prim Sch
Liby

Brookfold
Godley Brook
MILVERTON WLK
KINGSBRIDGE AVE
KING ST
Hattersley High Sch
PO

Werneth Brook
Albert Farm
Godley Green
1 RINGWOOD AVE
2 GRANGE RD S
FIELDS CT
Hattersley Sta
BEAVER WLK 1
SANDY BANK WLK 2
SANDY BANK CT
BECK HOUSE
Pinfold Cty Prim Sch
Hurstclough Prim Sch
A560
PH

D2
1 ST JOHN'S CT
2 UNDERWOOD WLK
3 HONITON WLK
4 WATERSIDE WLK
5 BANKSIDE WLK
6 FIELDS FARM WLK

E1
1 PHILLIP WAY
2 SPRINGWELL WAY
3 BEAUFORT WAY
4 COLLIER WLK

E2
1 BARDSLEY CL
2 THE HATTERSLEY CTR
3 CALLINGTON WLK
4 CALLINGTON CL
5 TAMESIDE CT
6 KINGSTON ARC
7 WORTHINGTON CL
8 SYLVESTER WAY

F2
1 SHELMERDINE CL
2 SLATER WAY
3 MILL HILL WAY
4 WINTERBOTTOM WLK
5 KNOWLE WAY
6 GREEN WAY
7 GREEN WLK

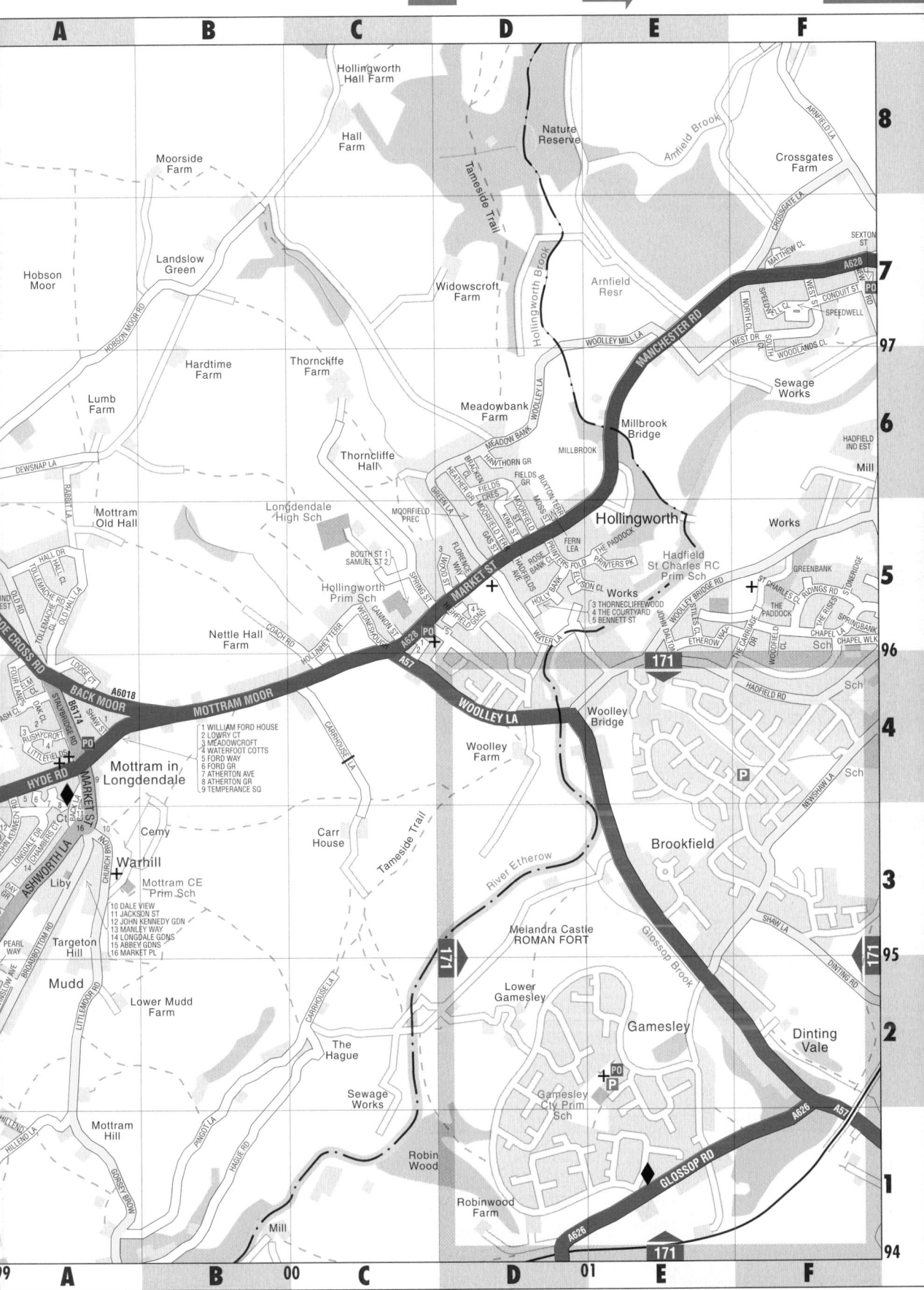

115 104

For full street detail of the
highlighted area see page
171.

A   B   C   D   E   F

8

A628

Townhead Farm

Valehouse Wood

Valehouse Resr

Deepclough

Higher Deepclough

B6105

LOWER SQ

Cockerhill

WOODHEAD RD

Valehouse Farm

Longdendale Trail

Nell's Pike

ARNFIELD LA RD

OLD RD

MANCHESTER RD

THE STOCKS

CHAPEL

7

CHURCH ST   A628

BANK LA

Tintwistle CE (VA) Sch

Tintwistle

Devil's Elbow

Ogden Clough

NEW ROW

97

River Etherow

Bottoms Resr

Resr

Resrs

Peak Naze

Tintwistle Bridge

WATERSIDE

THE LODGE

LAKESIDE

THE CROFT

LODGE

BANK

GREENFIELD ST

GODDARD LA

PETER ST

BROSSCROFT VILLAGE

BROSSCROFT

WOODSEAT

6

MASONS GR

CHEW WOOD

WILMANS

RHODESWOOD DR

Padfield Cty Prim Sch

JACKSON

PADFIELD MAIN RD

Upper Swineshaw Resr

Blackshaw

BANKBOTTOM

DALE HOUSE DR

TOPSHOME WAY

VICTORIA

RICHMOND

ELLINGTON AVE

A5
1 NEW BANK ST
2 OLD HALL SQ
3 THE CROSS
4 EVESHAM AVE
5 PINGOTT LA
6 BLENHEIM CL

WESLEY ST

ALBERT ST

OSBORNE

LAMBGATES

GARTSIDE

GAMSFIELD

5

PARADISE

HILL LA

CLUB ST

BURY ST

PO

LANGFIELD WAY

CT

QUEEN

Liby

Hadfield

RHODES ST

BARBER ST

POST ST

REGENT ST

TEMPLE ST

TEMPLE AVE

Padfield

Little Padfield Farm

CHAPEL

SPRING

WALTERS

GUNS

HADFIELD RD

SALISBURY

STANYFORTH

PLATT ST

BRICKFIELD ST

LEES ROW

96

SOUTH

CHURCH

CHRIST ST

MARLON

Railway

Hadfield Sta

HOLLINS IND PK

REDGATE

MARSDEN ST

NEWSHAW LA

CASTLE ST

LONE ST

QUEEN ST

THE AVENUE

MARLON BROW

PARK RD

Cemy

WOODHEAD RD

Swineshaw Resr

4

BLOOMSOMS DR

LITTLEBROOK CL

GODDARD RD

Banks Wood

Castlehill Wood

Bettenhill

CEMETERY RD

Cat Wood

Glossopdale Comm Coll

Mouselow

Mast

Broom Hill

Shire Hill

Laneside Farm

3

Mouselow Quarry

Hilltop

Wimberryhill

H

Moorside

SHIRE WAY

BUTE ST

CASTLE HILL

THORPE ST

DUNNE LA

HAWKSHEAD

CHARLES LA

HOPE ST

WATER ST

Shaw

HILLTOP RD

Wood's H

NORTH RD

BOWDEN RD

KINGSMOOR FIELDS

BLACKSHAW RD

SHEPLEY ST

95

PARK CRES

HAYWARDS CL

HEATH RD

All Saints' RC Prim Sch

WELL GATE ST

WESLEY ST

Howard Park

PARTINGTON CT

PARK DENE DR

FERNHILL CL

FERNHILL CT

CHURCH CL

Shire Hill

Shelf Brook

Dinting Junc

Higher Dinting

ASHES LA

HOWARD RD

Talbot House Sch

HALL MEADOW

CHURCH ST

Duke of Norfolk's CE Prim Sch

PO

Old Glossop

2

Dinting Sta

ASHES LA

DINTING RD

BIRCHSIDE AVE

EBM GR

TEN FOOT CL

CEDAR

GLENBROOK DR

MERE FOLD

MILL

Glossopdale Comm Coll

TALBOT RD

KERSHAW RD

PARK CL

Manor Park

MANOR RD

WOODCOCK AVE

PEGROVE RD

LC

St Luke's CE Prim Sch

Liby

H

DROVERS WLK

Duke of Norfolk's CE Prim Sch

QUEEN'S DR

DINTING LA TRAD EST

Works

GLOSSOP

WREN NEST RD

SURREY ST

HOWARD ST

LORD ST

TALBOT ST

CHARLES ST

FITZALAN

NORFOLK ST

KENT RD

RYLE AVE

KINGED

HURSTBROOK CL

1

A57

Dinting CE (VA) Prim Sch

Glossop Brook

SHREWSBURY ST

EDWARDS

WREN NEST TERR

SUMMERS PL

BERNARD ST

RAILWAY ST

HENRY ST

SMITHY CL

DROVERS WLK

RIVERSIDE CL

CORN ST

JORDAN ST

SHEFFIELD RD

MILLERSDALE CT 1
HILLWOOD DR 2
PARTINGTON CT 3
DOVEDALE CT 4
HATHERSAGE DR 5

COWBROOK AVE

A5

PAMBERLY

A6016

HIGH ST W

A624

B6105

P P i

HIGH ST E

REGENT ST

MILL ST

CROFT MANOR

SILK ST

BIRCH LA

SWITH CL

94

02   A   B   03   C   D   04   E   F

C1
1 ST MARY'S RD
2 BROOK ST
3 HALL'S CT
4 CROSS ST
5 CENTRAL STORE
6 MARKET ST

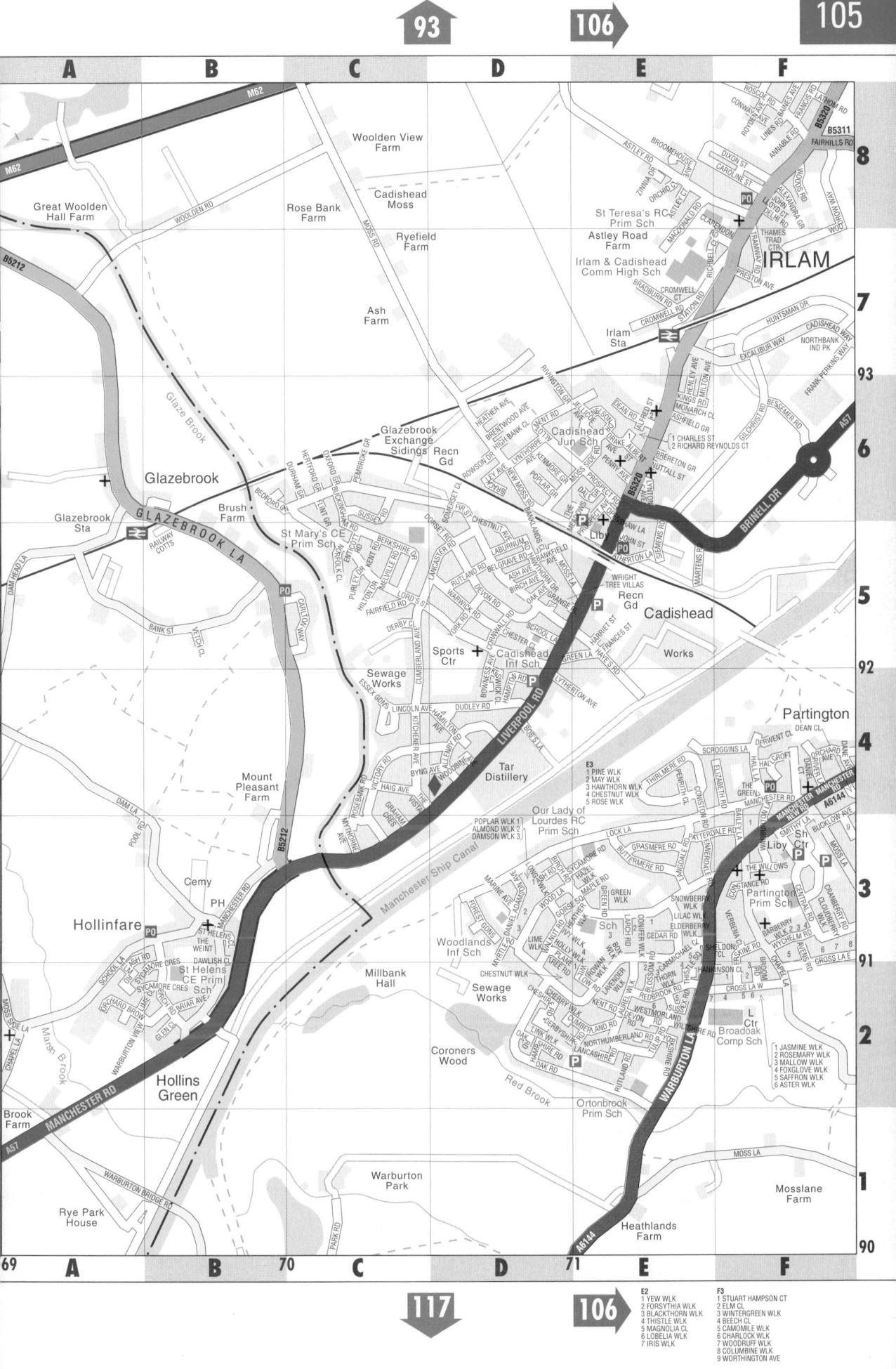

A B C D E F

8

7

93

6

5

92

4

3

91

2

1

90

M62
M62
Woolden View Farm
Great Woolden Hall Farm
Rose Bank Farm
Cadishead Moss
Ryefield Farm
WOOLDEN RD
MOSS RD
B5212
Ash Farm
Glaze Brook
Glazebrook
Glazebrook Exchange Sidings Recn Gd
Brush Farm
Glazebrook Sta
GLAZEBROOK LA
Railway Cotts
DAM HEAD LA
St Mary's CE Prim Sch
BANK ST
VETCH CL
CARLTON WAY
P
Sewage Works
Essex Gdns
Mount Pleasant Farm
POOL RD
DAM LA
B5212
Hollinfare
Cemy
PH
PO
MANCHESTER RD
St Helens CE Prim Sch
THE WEINT
DAWLISH CL
Marsh Brook
MOSS SIDE LA
CHAPEL LA
Hollins Green
Brook Farm
A57
Rye Park House
WARBURTON BRIDGE RD
PARK RD
Warburton Park
Sports Ctr
Cadishead Inf Sch
LIVERPOOL RD
Tar Distillery
Our Lady of Lourdes RC Prim Sch
POPLAR WLK 1
ALMOND WLK 2
DAMSON WLK 3
Manchester Ship Canal
Millbank Hall
Woodlands Inf Sch
Sewage Works
Coroners Wood
Red Brook
Ortonbrook Prim Sch
Heathlands Farm
A6144
Cadishead
WRIGHT TREE VILLAS
Recn Gd
Works
St Teresa's RC Prim Sch
Astley Road Farm
Irlam & Cadishead Comm High Sch
IRLAM
B5320
B5311
FAIRHILLS RD
Irlam Sta
Cadishead Jun Sch
Liby
PO
P
BRINELL DR
A57
Partington
Partington Prim Sch
Liby
Sh Ctr
P
A6144
MANCHESTER RD
WARBURTON LA
Broadoak Comp Sch
E3
1 PINE WLK
2 MAY WLK
3 HAWTHORN WLK
4 CHESTNUT WLK
5 ROSE WLK
1 JASMINE WLK
2 ROSEMARY WLK
3 MALLOW WLK
4 FOXGLOVE WLK
5 SAFFRON WLK
6 ASTER WLK
Mosslane Farm

E2
1 YEW WLK
2 FORSYTHIA WLK
3 BLACKTHORN WLK
4 THISTLE WLK
5 MAGNOLIA CL
6 LOBELIA WLK
7 IRIS WLK
F3
1 STUART HAMPSON CT
2 ELM CL
3 WINTERGREEN WLK
4 BEECH CL
5 CAMOMILE WLK
6 CHARLOCK WLK
7 WOODRUFF WLK
8 COLUMBINE WLK
9 WORTHINGTON AVE

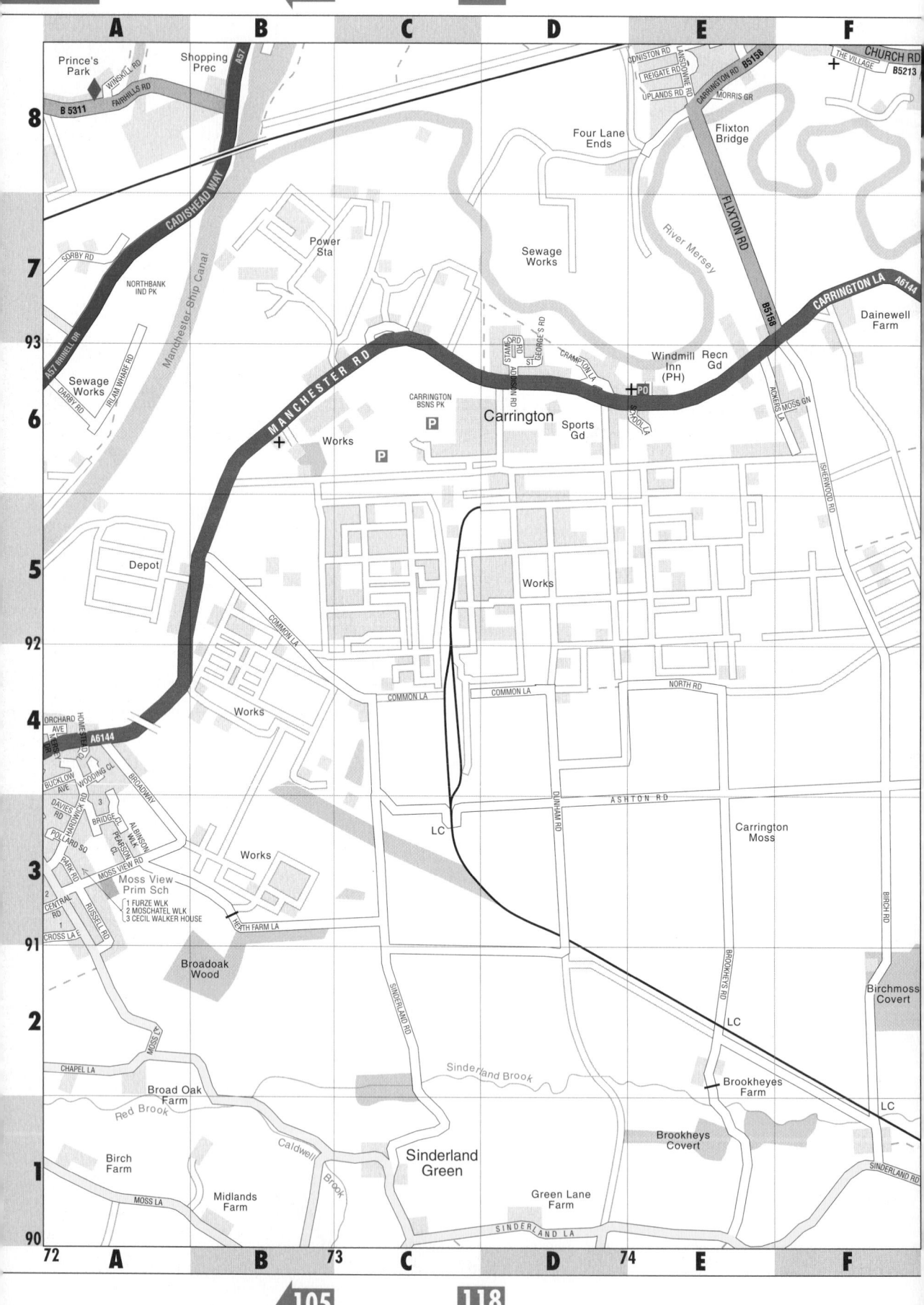
A
B
C
D
E
F
Prince's Park
Shopping Prec
WINSKILL RD
FAIRHILLS RD
B 5311
A57
CONISTON RD
REIGATE RD
LANSDOWNE RD
UPLANDS RD
CARRINGTON RD B5158
MORRIS GR
CHURCH RD
THE VILLAGE
B5213
Four Lane Ends
Flixton Bridge
CADISHEAD WAY
Power Sta
Sewage Works
River Mersey
FLIXTON RD
B5158
SORBY RD
NORTHBANK IND PK
Manchester Ship Canal
CARRINGTON LA
A6144
Dainewell Farm
A57 BRINELL DR
IRLAM WHARF RD
Sewage Works
DARBY RD
MANCHESTER RD
ST GEORGE'S RD
STAMFORD RD
CRAMPTON LA
Windmill Inn (PH)
Recn Gd
PO
ADDISON RD
CARRINGTON BSNS PK
Carrington
Sports Gd
SCHOOL LA
ACKERS LA
MOSS GN
Works
ISHERWOOD RD
Depot
Works
COMMON LA
COMMON LA
COMMON LA
NORTH RD
Works
ORCHARD AVE
HOMESTEAD
A6144
BUCKLOW AVE
WOODING CL
BROADWAY
DAVIES RD
HARDWICK RD
BRIDGE CL
ALBINSON WLK
PEARSON CL
POLLARD SQ
PARK RD
MOSS VIEW RD
ASHTON RD
DUNHAM RD
LC
Carrington Moss
Works
Moss View Prim Sch
1 FURZE WLK
2 MOSCHATEL WLK
3 CECIL WALKER HOUSE
CENTRAL RD
RUSSELL RD
CROSS LA E
HEATH FARM LA
BIRCH RD
Broadoak Wood
SINDERLAND RD
BROOKHEYS RD
Birchmoss Covert
LC
MOSS LA
CHAPEL LA
Sinderland Brook
Broad Oak Farm
Brookheyes Farm
Red Brook
LC
Caldwell Brook
Brookheys Covert
Birch Farm
Sinderland Green
SINDERLAND RD
Midlands Farm
Green Lane Farm
MOSS LA
SINDERLAND LA
72
73
74
8
7
93
6
5
92
4
3
91
2
1
90

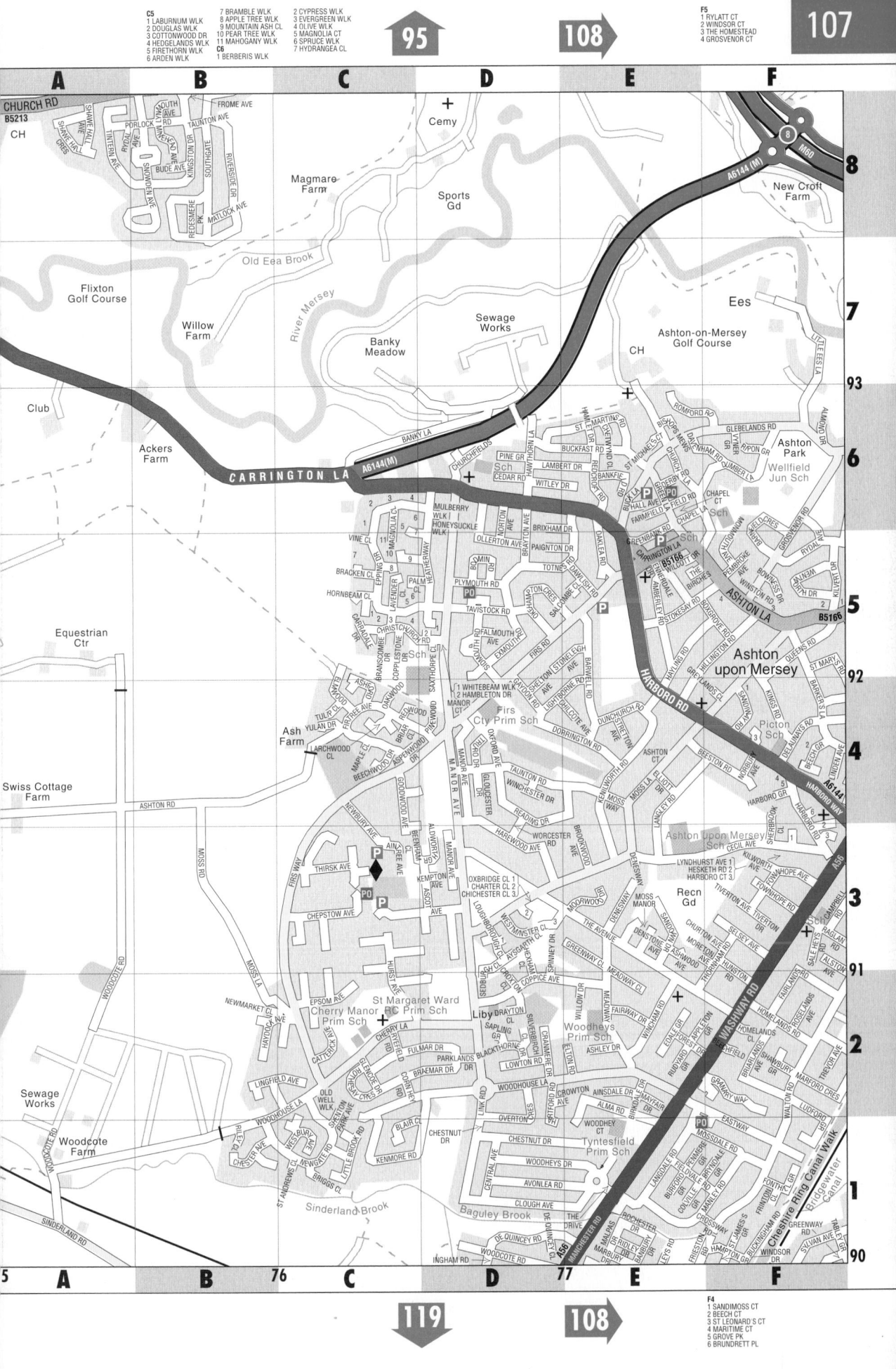
C5
1 LABURNUM WLK
2 DOUGLAS WLK
3 COTTONWOOD DR
4 HEDGELANDS WLK
5 FIRETHORN WLK
6 ARDEN WLK
7 BRAMBLE WLK
8 APPLE TREE WLK
9 MOUNTAIN ASH CL
10 PEAR TREE WLK
11 MAHOGANY WLK
C6
1 BERBERIS WLK
2 CYPRESS WLK
3 EVERGREEN WLK
4 OLIVE WLK
5 MAGNOLIA CT
6 SPRUCE WLK
7 HYDRANGEA CL
95
108
F5
1 RYLATT CT
2 WINDSOR CT
3 THE HOMESTEAD
4 GROSVENOR CT
A
B
C
D
E
F
8
7
93
6
5
92
4
3
91
2
1
90
CHURCH RD
B5213
CH
Cemy
Magmare Farm
Sports Gd
New Croft Farm
A6144 (M)
M60
Old Eea Brook
Flixton Golf Course
Willow Farm
River Mersey
Banky Meadow
Sewage Works
Ees
Ashton-on-Mersey Golf Course
Club
Ackers Farm
CARRINGTON LA
BANKY LA
Ashton Park
Wellfield Jun Sch
ASHTON LA
B5166
Equestrian Ctr
Ashton upon Mersey
HARBORO RD
Picton Sch
Ash Farm
Swiss Cottage Farm
ASHTON RD
MOSS RD
Firs Cty Prim Sch
MANOR AVE
Ashton upon Mersey Sch
Recn Gd
A56
WASHWAY RD
MOSS LA
WOODCOTE RD
St Margaret Ward RC Prim Sch
Cherry Manor Prim Sch
Liby
Woodheys Prim Sch
Tyntesfield Prim Sch
Sewage Works
Woodcote Farm
WOODHOUSE LA
Sinderland Brook
Baguley Brook
SINDERLAND RD
MANCHESTER RD
Cheshire Ring Canal Walk
Bridgewater Canal
5
A
B
76
C
D
77
E
F
119
108
F4
1 SANDIMOSS CT
2 BEECH CT
3 ST LEONARD'S CT
4 MARITIME CT
5 GROVE PK
6 BRUNDRETT PL

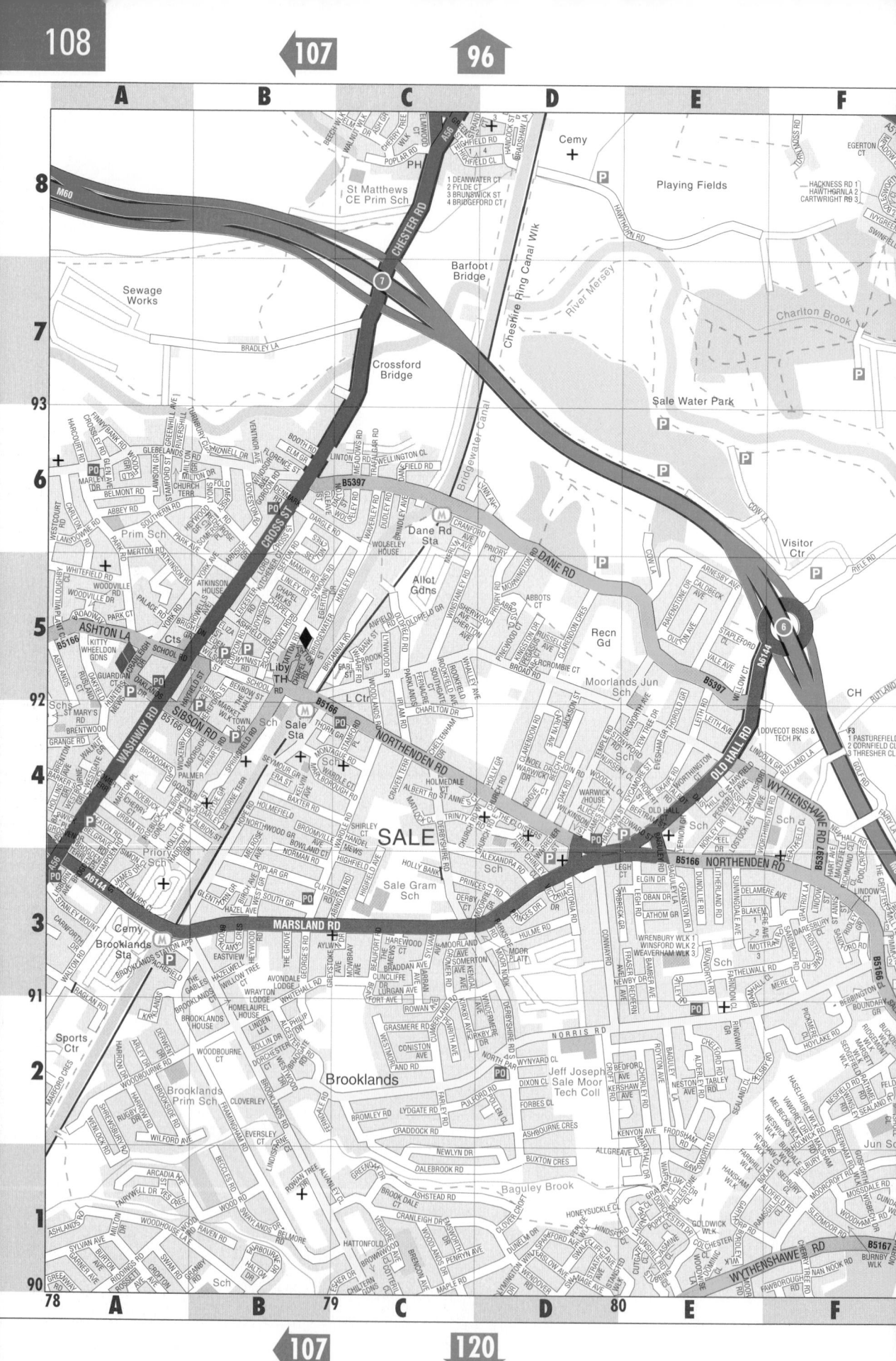

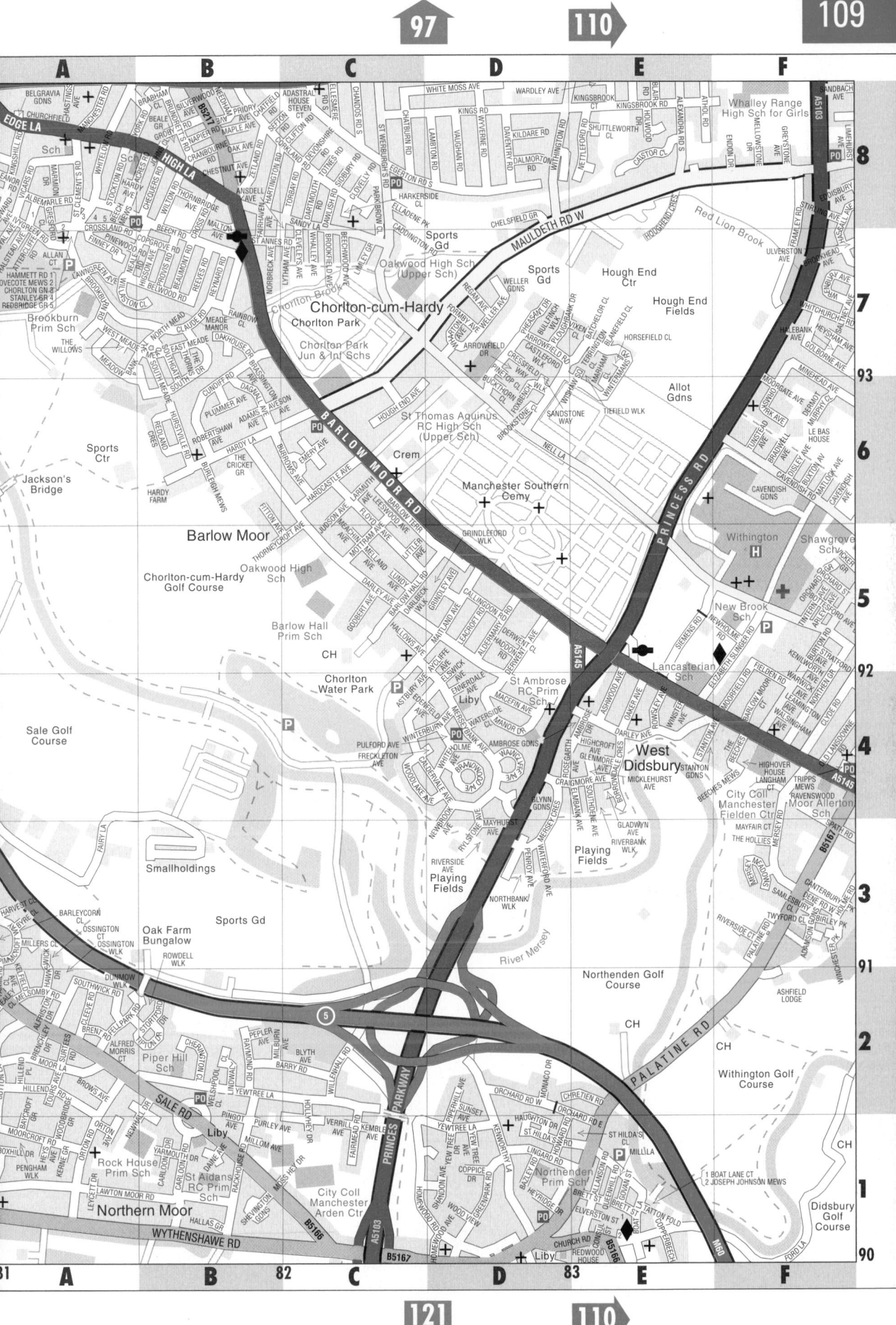

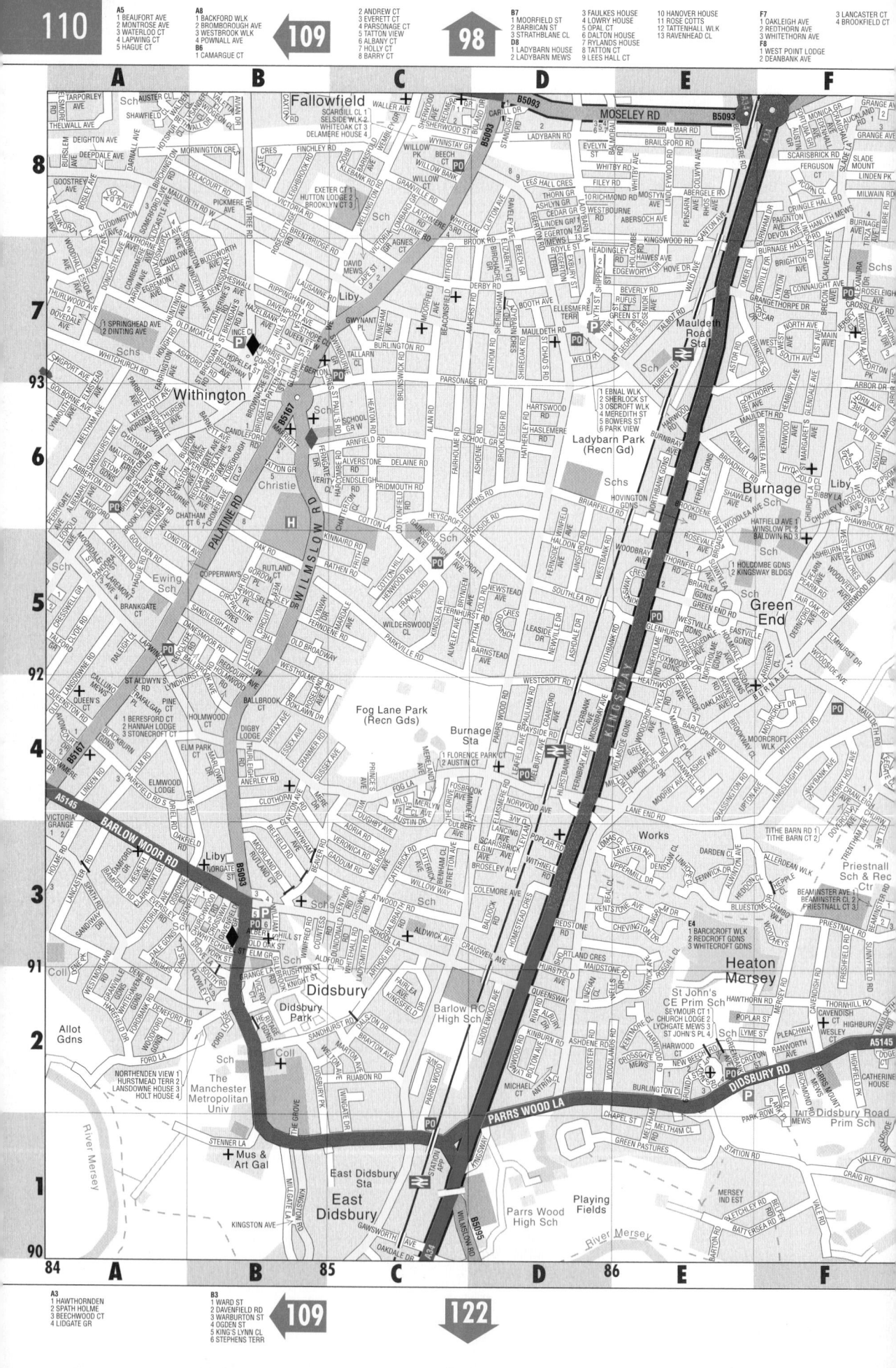

110
A5
1 BEAUFORT AVE
2 MONTROSE AVE
3 WATERLOO CT
4 LAPWING CT
5 HAGUE CT
A8
1 BACKFORD WLK
2 BROMBOROUGH AVE
3 WESTBROOK WLK
4 POWNALL AVE
B6
1 CAMARGUE CT
109
2 ANDREW CT
3 EVERETT CT
4 PARSONAGE CT
5 TATTON VIEW
6 ALBANY CT
7 HOLLY CT
8 BARRY CT
98
B7
1 MOORFIELD ST
2 BARBICAN ST
3 STRATHBLANE CL
D8
1 LADYBARN HOUSE
2 LADYBARN MEWS
3 FAULKES HOUSE
4 LOWRY HOUSE
5 OPAL CT
6 DALTON HOUSE
7 RYLANDS HOUSE
8 TATTON CT
9 LEES HALL CT
10 HANOVER HOUSE
11 ROSE COTTS
12 TATTENHALL WLK
13 RAVENHEAD CL
F7
1 OAKLEIGH AVE
2 REDTHORN AVE
3 WHITETHORN AVE
F8
1 WEST POINT LODGE
2 DEANBANK AVE
3 LANCASTER CT
4 BROOKFIELD CT
A B C D E F
8 7 93 6 5 92 4 3 91 2 1 90
84 85 86
Fallowfield
Withington
Christie
Ewing Sch
Ladybarn Park (Recn Gd)
Mauldeth Road Sta
Burnage
Green End
Fog Lane Park (Recn Gds)
Burnage Sta
Heaton Mersey
Priestnall Sch & Rec Ctr
Didsbury
Didsbury Park
The Manchester Metropolitan Univ
Mus & Art Gal
Barlow RC High Sch
St John's CE Prim Sch
Dídsbury Road Prim Sch
East Didsbury Sta
East Didsbury
Parrs Wood High Sch
Playing Fields
River Mersey
Allot Gdns
Works
MOSELEY RD
WILMSLOW RD
PALATINE RD
KINGSWAY
BARLOW MOOR RD
PARRS WOOD LA
DIDSBURY RD
1 SPRINGHEAD AVE
2 DINTING AVE
1 EBNAL WLK
2 SHERLOCK ST
3 OSCROFT WLK
4 MEREDITH ST
5 BOWERS ST
6 PARK VIEW
1 HOLCOMBE GDNS
2 KINGSWAY BLDGS
1 BERESFORD CT
2 HANNAH LODGE
3 STONECROFT CT
1 FLORENCE PARK CT
2 AUSTIN CT
E4
1 BARCICROFT WLK
2 REDCROFT GDNS
3 WHITECROFT GDNS
1 TITHE BARN RD
2 TITHE BARN CT
1 BEAMINSTER AVE
2 BEAMINSTER CL
3 PRIESTNALL CT
1 SEYMOUR CT
2 CHURCH LODGE
3 LYCHGATE MEWS
4 ST JOHN'S PL
1 NORTHENDEN VIEW
2 HURSTMEAD TERR
3 LANSDOWNE HOUSE
4 HOLT HOUSE
1 EXETER CT
2 HUTTON LODGE
3 BROOKLYN CT
1 SCARGILL CL
2 SELSIDE WLK
3 WHITEOAK CT
4 DELAMERE HOUSE
1 HATFIELD AVE
2 WINSLOW PL
3 BALDWIN RD
A3
1 HAWTHORNDEN
2 SPATH HOLME
3 BEECHWOOD CT
4 LIDGATE GR
B3
1 WARD ST
2 DAVENFIELD RD
3 WARBURTON ST
4 OGDEN ST
5 KING'S LYNN CL
6 STEPHENS TERR
109
122

For full street detail of the
highlighted area see pages
68 and 169.

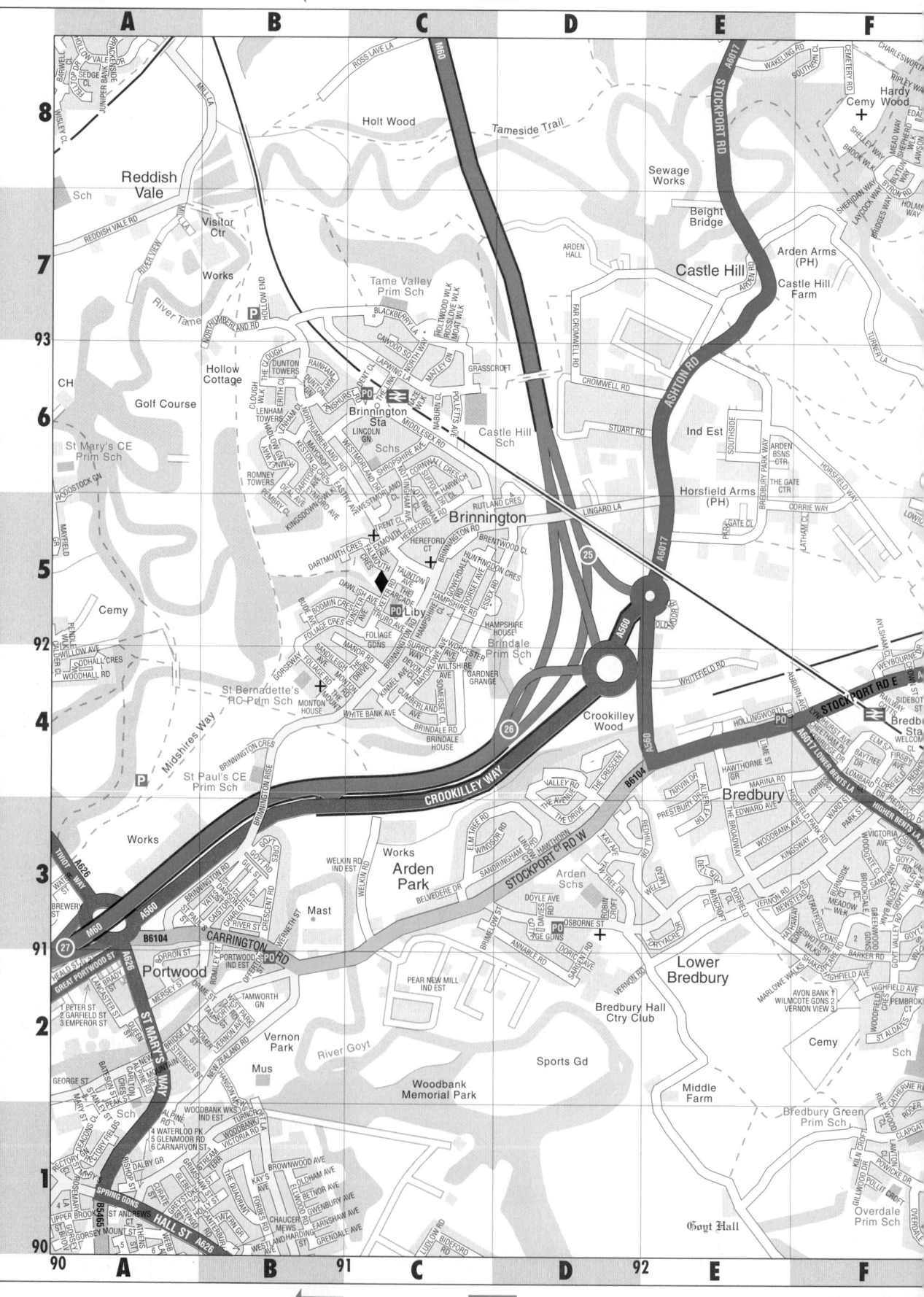

SYLVESTER WAY
ROSSETTI WLK
HOAD WLK
HARDYWOOD RD
LONGFELLOW WLK
SOUTHEY WLK

7 MAYFIELD AVE
8 GOLDSMITH WAY
9 ARNOLD WLK
10 MOORE WLK
11 LAMB WLK
12 SWINBURNE WAY
13 CONSTABLE WLK

14 BRACKENHILL TERR
15 MARLOWE WLK
A8
1 HAYFIELD WLK
2 CHISWORTH WLK
3 BUXTON WAY
4 CHESTERFIELD WAY

5 ILKESTON WLK
6 HATHERSAGE WAY
7 MACAULAY WAY
8 CAMPION WAY
9 POPE WAY
10 DRYDEN WAY
11 FITZGERALD CT

12 SOUTHEY CT
13 CASTLETON CT
14 CASTLETON WAY

101
114

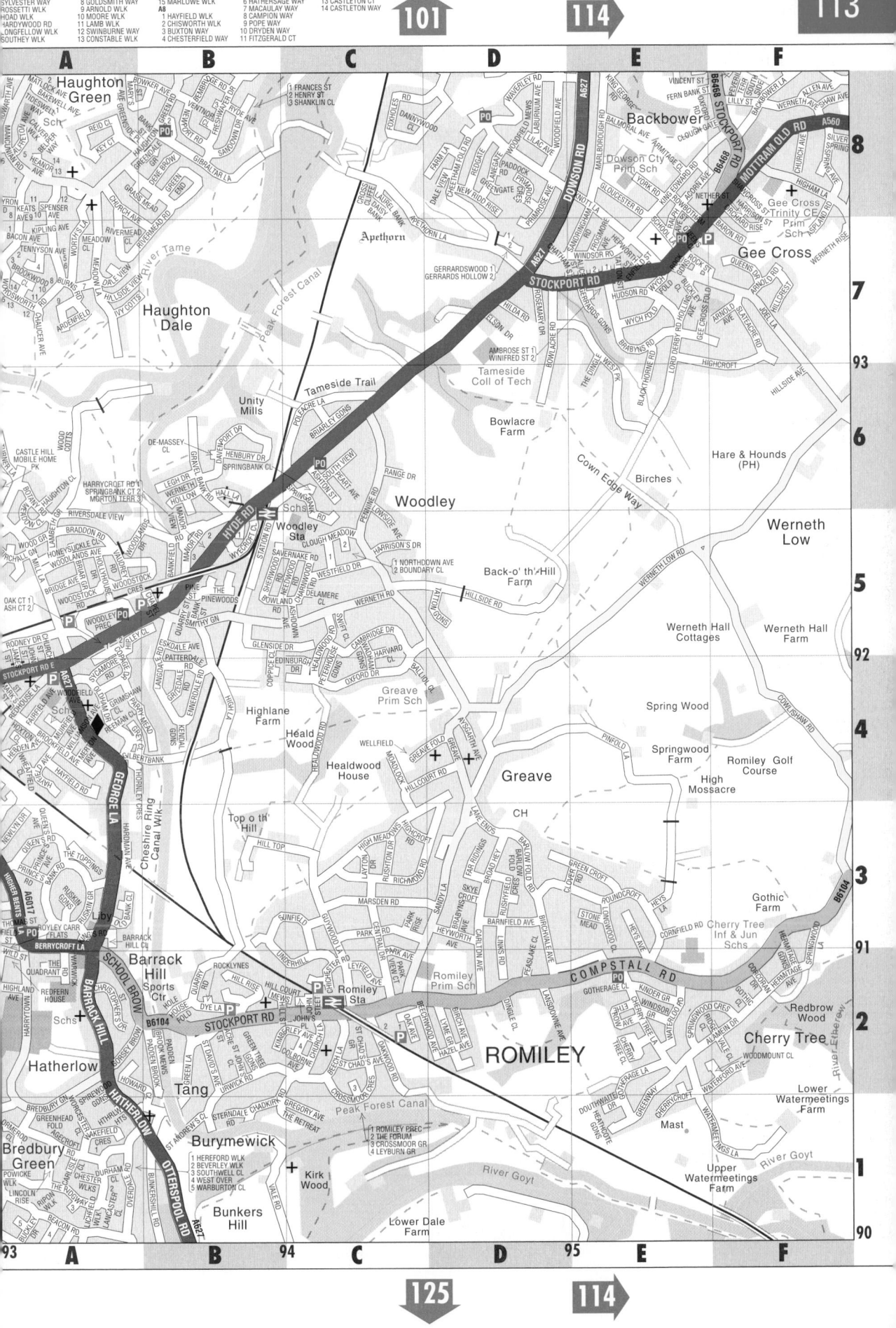

125
114

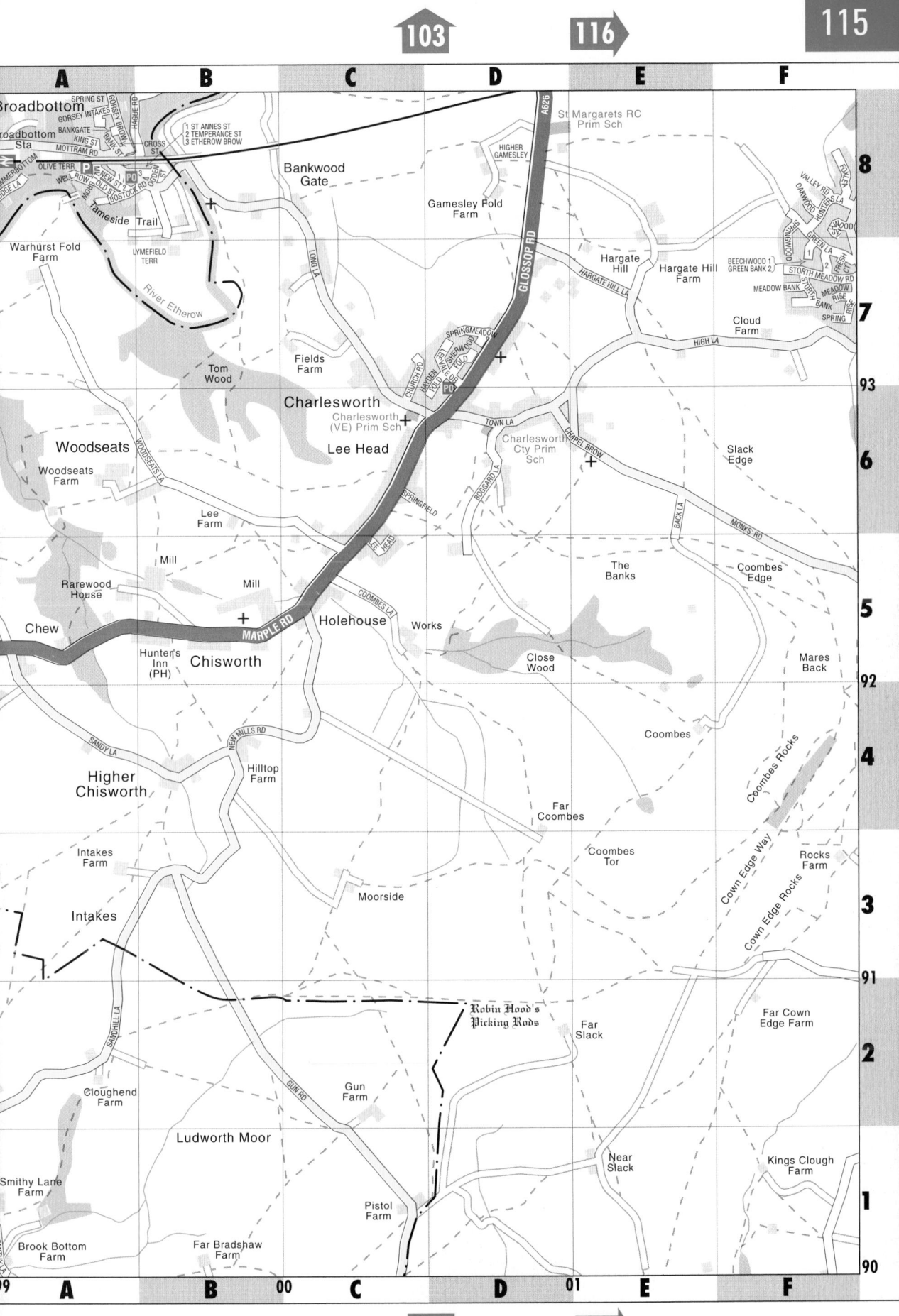
A
B
C
D
E
F
Broadbottom
Broadbottom Sta
Bankwood Gate
St Margarets RC Prim Sch
Higher Gamesley
Gamesley Fold Farm
Tameside Trail
Warhurst Fold Farm
Lymefield Terr
River Etherow
Hargate Hill
Hargate Hill Farm
Glossop Rd
A626
Long La
Hargate Hill La
Cloud Farm
High La
Fields Farm
Tom Wood
Charlesworth
Charlesworth (VE) Prim Sch
Town La
Charlesworth Cty Prim Sch
Chapel Brow
Woodseats
Woodseats Farm
Woodseats La
Lee Head
Slack Edge
Springfield
Boggard La
Back La
Monks Rd
Lee Farm
Mill
The Banks
Coombes Edge
Rarewood House
Coombes La
Chew
Marple Rd
Holehouse
Works
Hunter's Inn (PH)
Chisworth
Close Wood
Mares Back
Coombes
Sandy La
New Mills Rd
Higher Chisworth
Hilltop Farm
Coombes Rocks
Far Coombes
Intakes Farm
Coombes Tor
Rocks Farm
Cown Edge Way
Moorside
Intakes
Cown Edge Rocks
Robin Hood's Picking Rods
Far Cown Edge Farm
Far Slack
Sandhill La
Cloughend Farm
Gun Rd
Gun Farm
Ludworth Moor
Near Slack
Kings Clough Farm
Smithy Lane Farm
Pistol Farm
Brook Bottom Farm
Far Bradshaw Farm
8
7
93
6
5
92
4
3
91
2
1
90
99
00
01

115
104

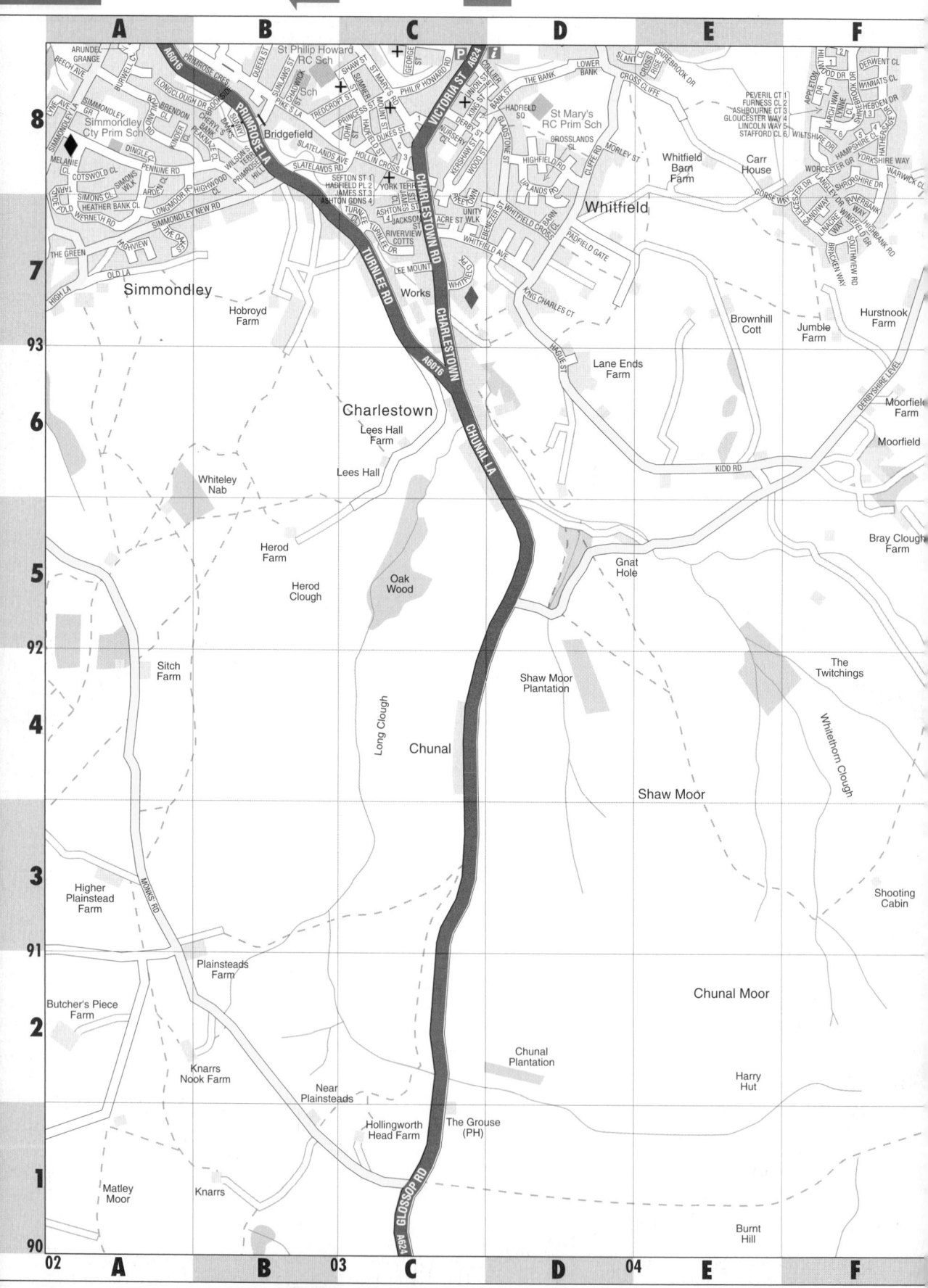
A
B
C
D
E
F
8
7
93
6
5
92
4
3
91
2
1
90
02
03
04
St Philip Howard RC Sch
Sch
St Mary's RC Prim Sch
Simmondley Cty Prim Sch
Bridgefield
Whitfield
Whitfield Barn Farm
Carr House
Simmondley
Hobroyd Farm
Works
Charlestown
Lees Hall Farm
Lees Hall
Brownhill Cott
Jumble Farm
Hurstnook Farm
Lane Ends Farm
Moorfield Farm
Moorfield
Whiteley Nab
Herod Farm
Herod Clough
Oak Wood
Gnat Hole
Bray Clough Farm
Sitch Farm
Shaw Moor Plantation
The Twitchings
Long Clough
Chunal
Shaw Moor
Whitethorn Clough
Higher Plainstead Farm
Shooting Cabin
Plainsteads Farm
Chunal Moor
Butcher's Piece Farm
Knarrs Nook Farm
Chunal Plantation
Harry Hut
Near Plainsteads
Hollingworth Head Farm
The Grouse (PH)
Matley Moor
Knarrs
Burnt Hill
A6016
A624
PRIMROSE LA
VICTORIA ST
CHARLESTOWN RD
TURNLEE RD
CHARLESTOWN
CHUNAL LA
GLOSSOP RD
MONKS RD
KIDD RD
DERBYSHIRE LEVEL
SIMMONDLEY NEW RD
OLD LA
HIGH LA
THE GREEN
KING CHARLES CT
HAGUE ST
PEVERIL CT 1
FURNESS CL 2
ASHBOURNE CT 3
GLOUCESTER WAY 4
LINCOLN WAY 5
STAFFORD CL 6
SEFTON ST 1
HADFIELD PL 2
JAMES ST 3
ASHTON GDNS 4

115

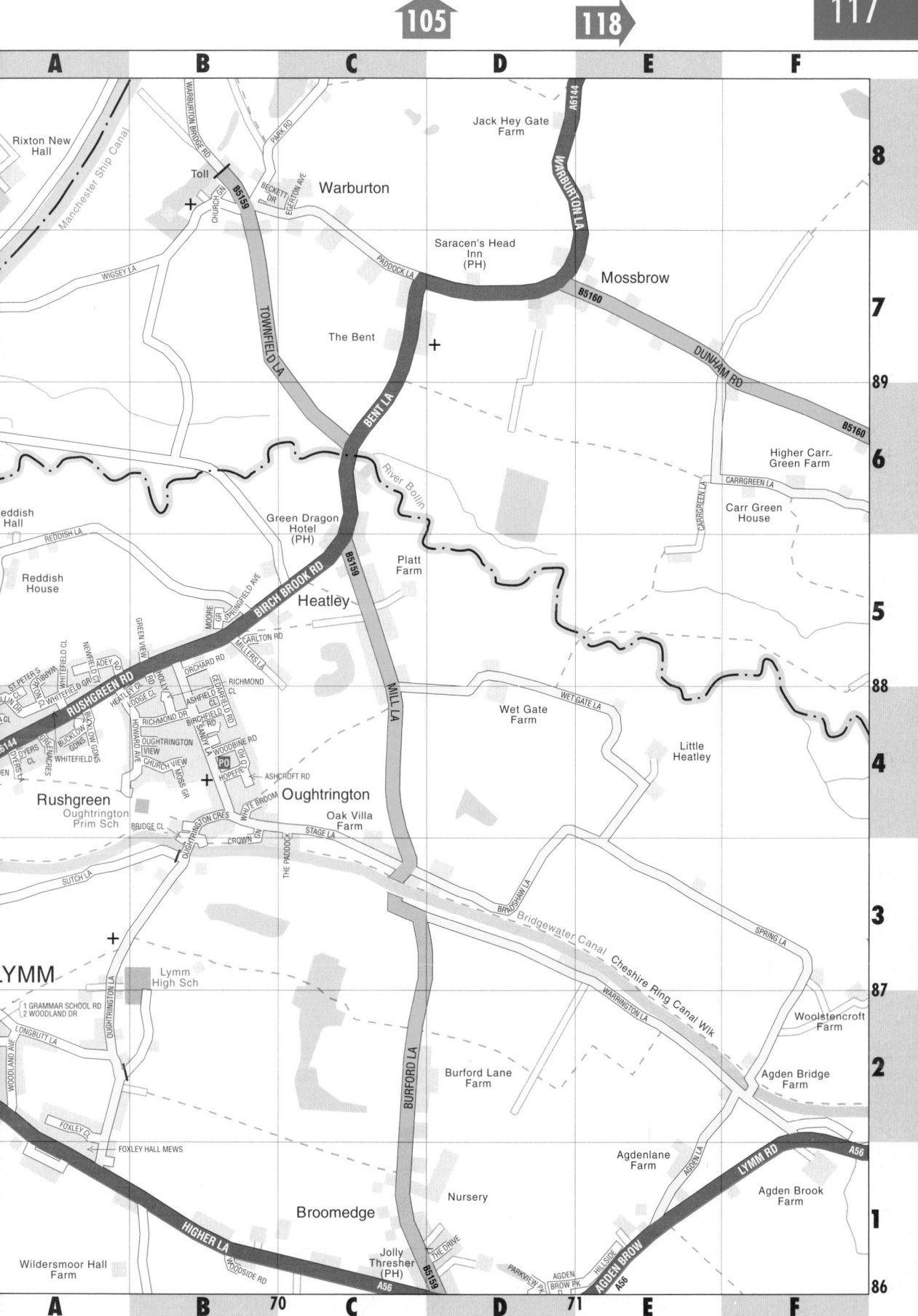
A
B
C
D
E
F
Rixton New Hall
Manchester Ship Canal
Toll
Warburton
Jack Hey Gate Farm
Saracen's Head Inn (PH)
Mossbrow
The Bent
Higher Carr Green Farm
Carr Green House
River Bollin
Reddish Hall
Reddish House
Green Dragon Hotel (PH)
Platt Farm
Heatley
Wet Gate Farm
Little Heatley
Rushgreen
Oughtrington Prim Sch
Oughtrington
Oak Villa Farm
Bridgewater Canal
Cheshire Ring Canal Wlk
LYMM
Lymm High Sch
Woolstencroft Farm
Agden Bridge Farm
Burford Lane Farm
Agdenlane Farm
Agden Brook Farm
Nursery
Broomedge
Jolly Thresher (PH)
Wildersmoor Hall Farm
WARBURTON BRIDGE RD
PARK RD
BECKETT DR
EGERTON AVE
CHURCH GN
B5159
WARBURTON LA
A6144
PADDOCK LA
WIGSEY LA
TOWNFIELD LA
B5160
DUNHAM RD
BENT LA
CARRGREEN LA
REDDISH LA
BIRCH BROOK RD
SPRINGFIELD AVE
MOORE GR
CARLTON RD
MILLERS LA
RUSHGREEN RD
ORCHARD RD
RICHMOND CL
CEDARFIELD RD
ASHFIELD CL
BIRCHFIELD RD
SANDY LA
WOODBINE RD
HOPEFIELD RD
ASHCROFT RD
MILL LA
WET GATE LA
OUGHTRINGTON VIEW
CHURCH VIEW
MOSS GR
WHITEFIELD GDNS
DYERS CL
BRIDGE CL
OUGHTRINGTON CRES
CROWN GN
WHITE BROOM
STAGE LA
THE PADDOCK
SUTCH LA
BRADSHAW LA
SPRING LA
WARRINGTON LA
1 GRAMMAR SCHOOL RD
2 WOODLAND DR
LONGBUTT LA
OUGHTRINGTON LA
WOODLAND AVE
FOXLEY CL
FOXLEY HALL MEWS
BURFORD LA
HIGHER LA
WOODSIDE RD
A56
THE DRIVE
PARKVIEW PK
AGDEN BROW PK
HILLSIDE
AGDEN BROW
AGDEN LA
LYMM RD
8
7
89
6
5
88
4
3
87
2
1
86
70
71

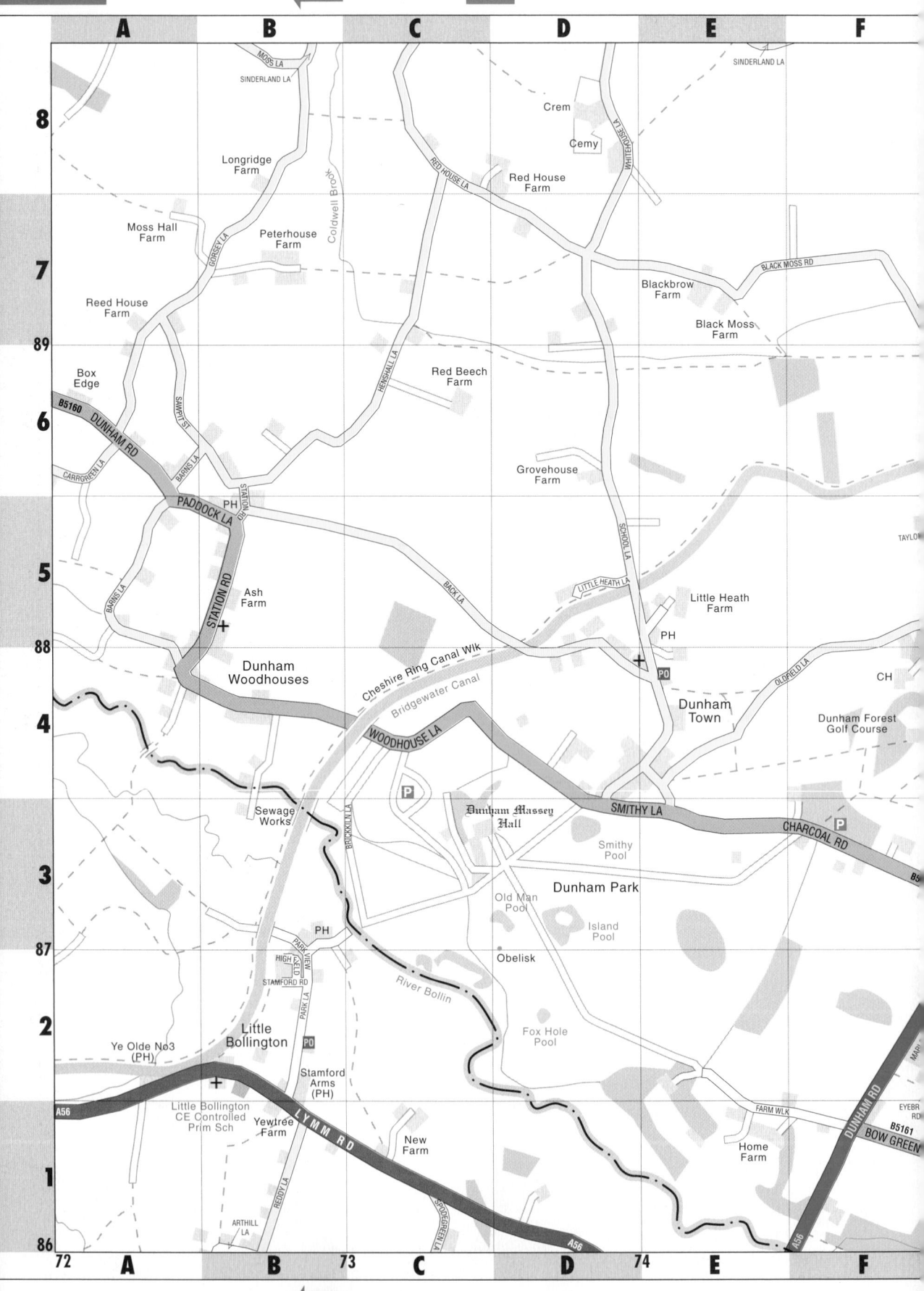
117

106

A
B
C
D
E
F
8
7
89
6
5
88
4
3
87
2
1
86
72
73
74
MOSS LA
SINDERLAND LA
Crem
Cemy
WHITEHOUSE LA
Longridge Farm
Coldwell Brook
RED HOUSE LA
Red House Farm
Moss Hall Farm
Peterhouse Farm
GORSEY LA
BLACK MOSS RD
Blackbrow Farm
Reed House Farm
Black Moss Farm
Box Edge
HENSHALL LA
Red Beech Farm
B5160
DUNHAM RD
SAWPIT ST
CARRGREEN LA
BARNS LA
Grovehouse Farm
PADDOCK LA
PH
STATION RD
SCHOOL LA
TAYLOR
BACK LA
LITTLE HEATH LA
Little Heath Farm
Ash Farm
BARNS LA
PH
Dunham Woodhouses
Cheshire Ring Canal Wlk
PO
OLDFIELD LA
CH
Bridgewater Canal
Dunham Town
Dunham Forest Golf Course
WOODHOUSE LA
P
Dunham Massey Hall
SMITHY LA
Sewage Works
BRICKKILN LA
CHARCOAL RD
P
Smithy Pool
B5
Dunham Park
Old Man Pool
Island Pool
PH
PARK VIEW
HIGH FIELD
Obelisk
STAMFORD RD
River Bollin
PARK LA
Little Bollington
Fox Hole Pool
Ye Olde No3 (PH)
PO
Stamford Arms (PH)
A56
Little Bollington CE Controlled Prim Sch
Yewtree Farm
LYMM RD
FARM WLK
DUNHAM RD
EYEBR RD
B5161
BOW GREEN
New Farm
Home Farm
REDDY LA
ARTHILL LA
SPODEGREEN LA
A56
A56

117

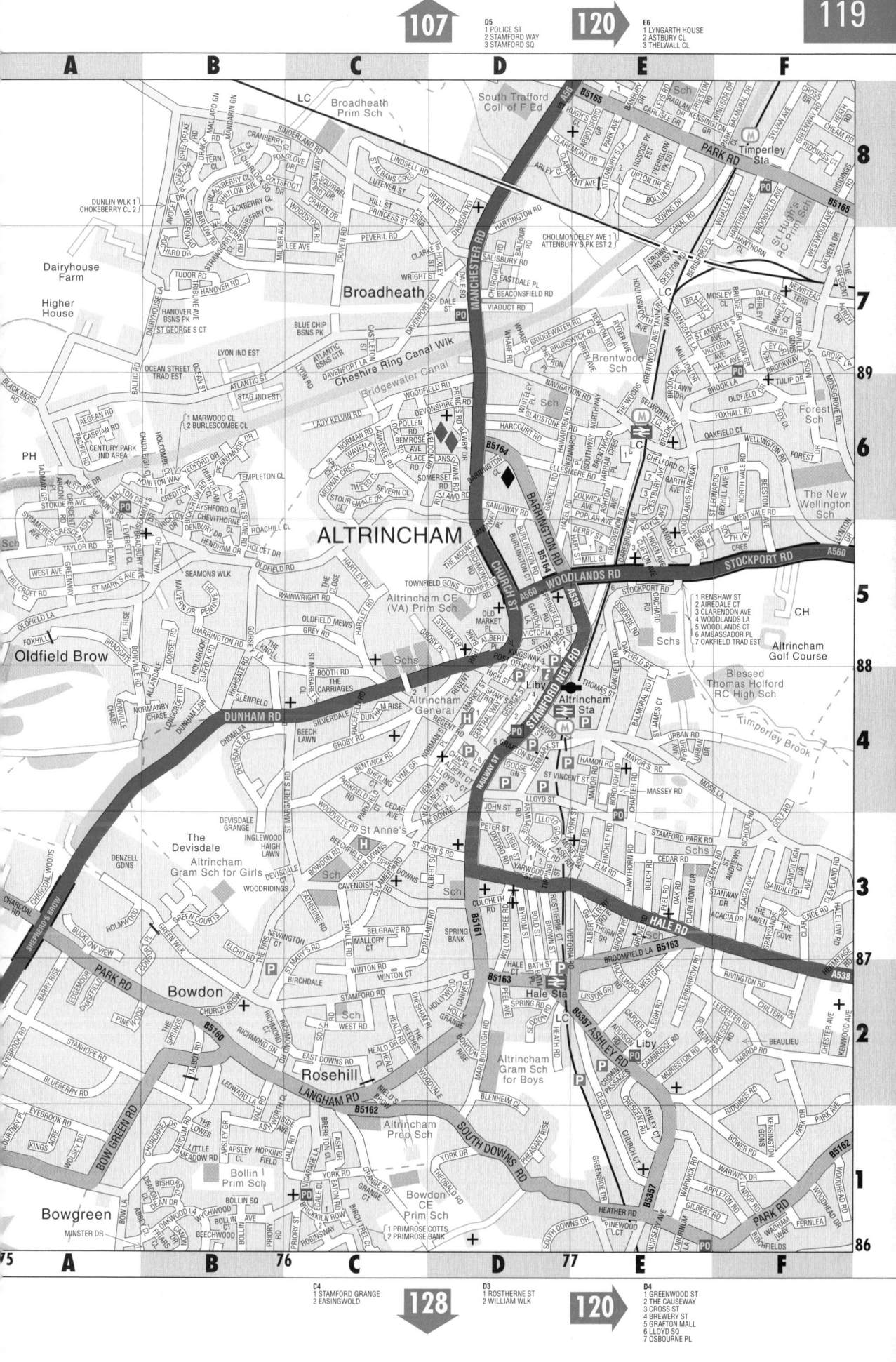
107
D5
1 POLICE ST
2 STAMFORD WAY
3 STAMFORD SQ
120
E6
1 LYNGARTH HOUSE
2 ASTBURY CL
3 THELWALL CL
A
B
C
D
E
F
Broadheath Prim Sch
South Trafford Coll of F Ed
Timperley Sta
St Hugh's RC Prim Sch
DUNLIN WLK 1
CHOKEBERRY CL 2
Dairyhouse Farm
Higher House
Broadheath
CHOLMONDELEY AVE 1
ATTENBURY'S PK EST 2
Cheshire Ring Canal Wlk
Bridgewater Canal
Brentwood Sch
Forest Sch
1 MARWOOD CL
2 BURLESCOMBE CL
The New Wellington Sch
ALTRINCHAM
Altrincham CE (VA) Prim Sch
1 RENSHAW ST
2 AIREDALE CT
3 CLARENDON AVE
4 WOODLANDS LA
5 WOODLANDS CT
6 AMBASSADOR PL
7 OAKFIELD TRAD EST
Altrincham Golf Course
Oldfield Brow
Schs
Blessed Thomas Holford RC High Sch
Altrincham General
Altrincham Sta
Timperley Brook
St Anne's
The Devisdale
Altrincham Gram Sch for Girls
Bowdon
Rosehill
Hale Sta
Altrincham Gram Sch for Boys
Altrincham Prep Sch
Bollin Prim Sch
Bowdon CE Prim Sch
Bowgreen
1 PRIMROSE COTTS
2 PRIMROSE BANK
DUNHAM RD
MANCHESTER RD
WOODLANDS RD
STOCKPORT RD
HALE RD
PARK RD
LANGHAM RD
SOUTH DOWNS RD
ASHLEY RD
BOW GREEN RD
STAMFORD NEW RD
CHURCH ST
BARRINGTON RD
8
7
89
6
5
88
4
3
87
2
1
86
75
76
77
C4
1 STAMFORD GRANGE
2 EASINGWOLD
128
D3
1 ROSTHERNE ST
2 WILLIAM WLK
120
D4
1 GREENWOOD ST
2 THE CAUSEWAY
3 CROSS ST
4 BREWERY ST
5 GRAFTON MALL
6 LLOYD SQ
7 OSBOURNE PL

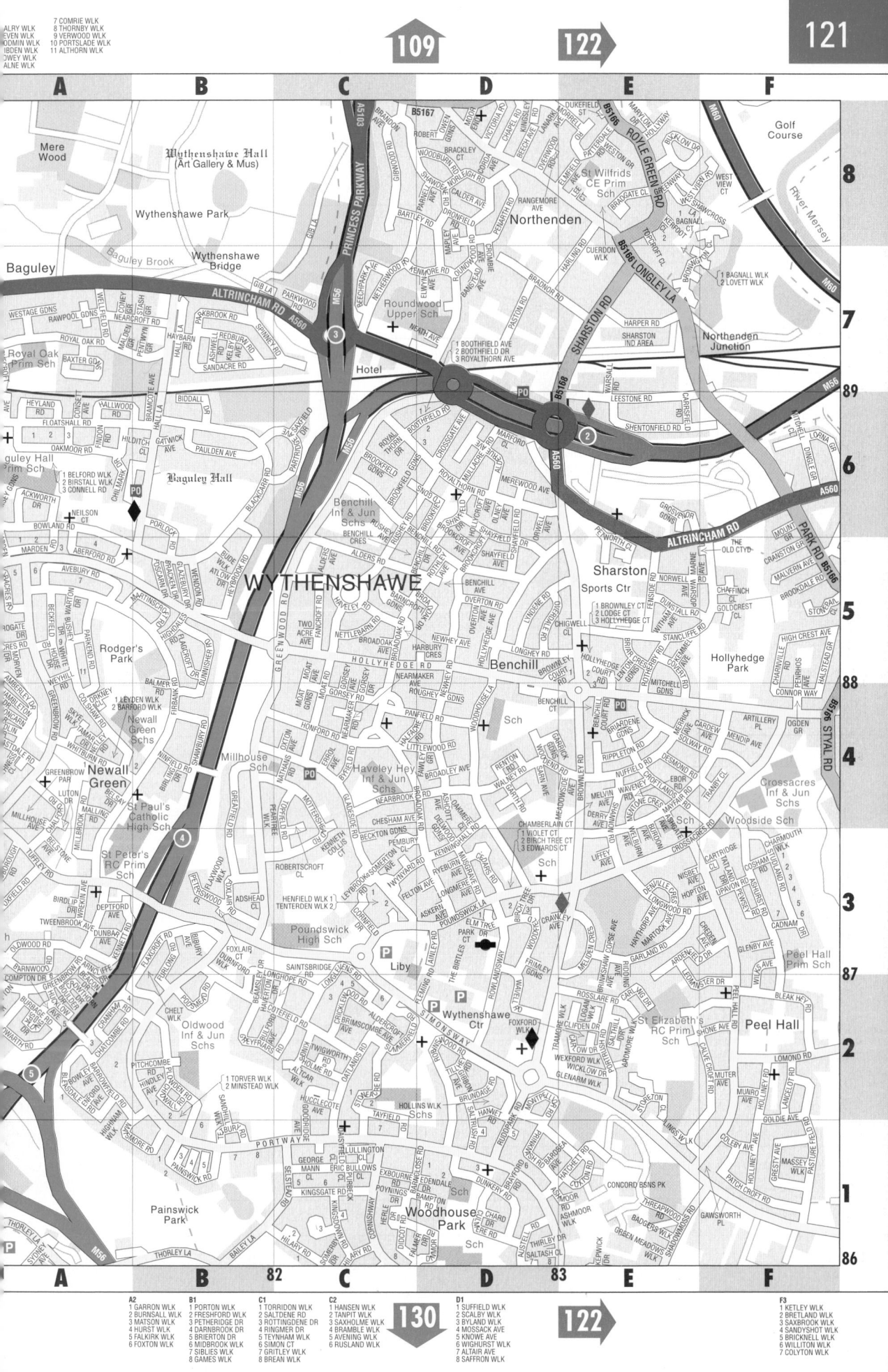

121
109
122
130
122
ALRY WLK
EVEN WLK
ODMIN WLK
IBDEN WLK
OWEY WLK
ALNE WLK
7 COMRIE WLK
8 THORNBY WLK
9 VERWOOD WLK
10 PORTSLADE WLK
11 ALTHORN WLK
A
B
C
D
E
F
8
7
89
6
5
88
4
3
87
2
1
86
82
83
Mere Wood
Wythenshawe Hall (Art Gallery & Mus)
Wythenshawe Park
Baguley
Baguley Brook
Wythenshawe Bridge
ALTRINCHAM RD
PRINCESS PARKWAY
Northenden
St Wilfrids CE Prim Sch
Golf Course
River Mersey
ROYLE GREEN RD
LONGLEY LA
SHARSTON RD
Roundwood Upper Sch
Northenden Junction
Hotel
Royal Oak Prim Sch
Baguley Hall
Baguley Hall Prim Sch
Benchill Inf & Jun Schs
WYTHENSHAWE
Sharston
Sports Ctr
Hollyhedge Park
Benchill
Rodger's Park
Newall Green
Newall Green Schs
Millhouse Sch
Haveley Hey Inf & Jun Schs
St Paul's Catholic High Sch
St Peter's RC Prim Sch
Crossacres Inf & Jun Schs
Woodside Sch
Poundswick High Sch
Liby
Wythenshawe Ctr
Peel Hall Prim Sch
Peel Hall
St Elizabeth's RC Prim Sch
Oldwood Inf & Jun Schs
Hollins Schs
Woodhouse Park
Painswick Park
CONCORD BSNS PK
PORTWAY
SIMONSWAY
STYAL RD
PARK RD
A2
1 GARRON WLK
2 BURNSALL WLK
3 MATSON WLK
4 HURST WLK
5 FALKIRK WLK
6 FOXTON WLK
B1
1 PORTON WLK
2 FRESHFORD WLK
3 PETHERIDGE DR
4 DARNBROOK DR
5 BRIERTON DR
6 MIDBROOK WLK
7 SIBLIES WLK
8 GAMES WLK
C1
1 TORRIDON WLK
2 SALTDENE RD
3 ROTTINGDENE DR
4 RINGMER DR
5 TEYNHAM WLK
6 SIMON CT
7 GRITLEY WLK
8 BREAN WLK
C2
1 HANSEN WLK
2 TANPIT WLK
3 SAXHOLME WLK
4 BRAMBLE WLK
5 AVENING WLK
6 RUSLAND WLK
D1
1 SUFFIELD WLK
2 SCALBY WLK
3 BYLAND WLK
4 MOSSACK AVE
5 KNOWE AVE
6 WIGHURST WLK
7 ALTAIR AVE
8 SAFFRON WLK
F3
1 KETLEY WLK
2 BRETLAND WLK
3 SAXBROOK WLK
4 SANDYSHOT WLK
5 BRICKNELL WLK
6 WILLITON WLK
7 COLYTON WLK

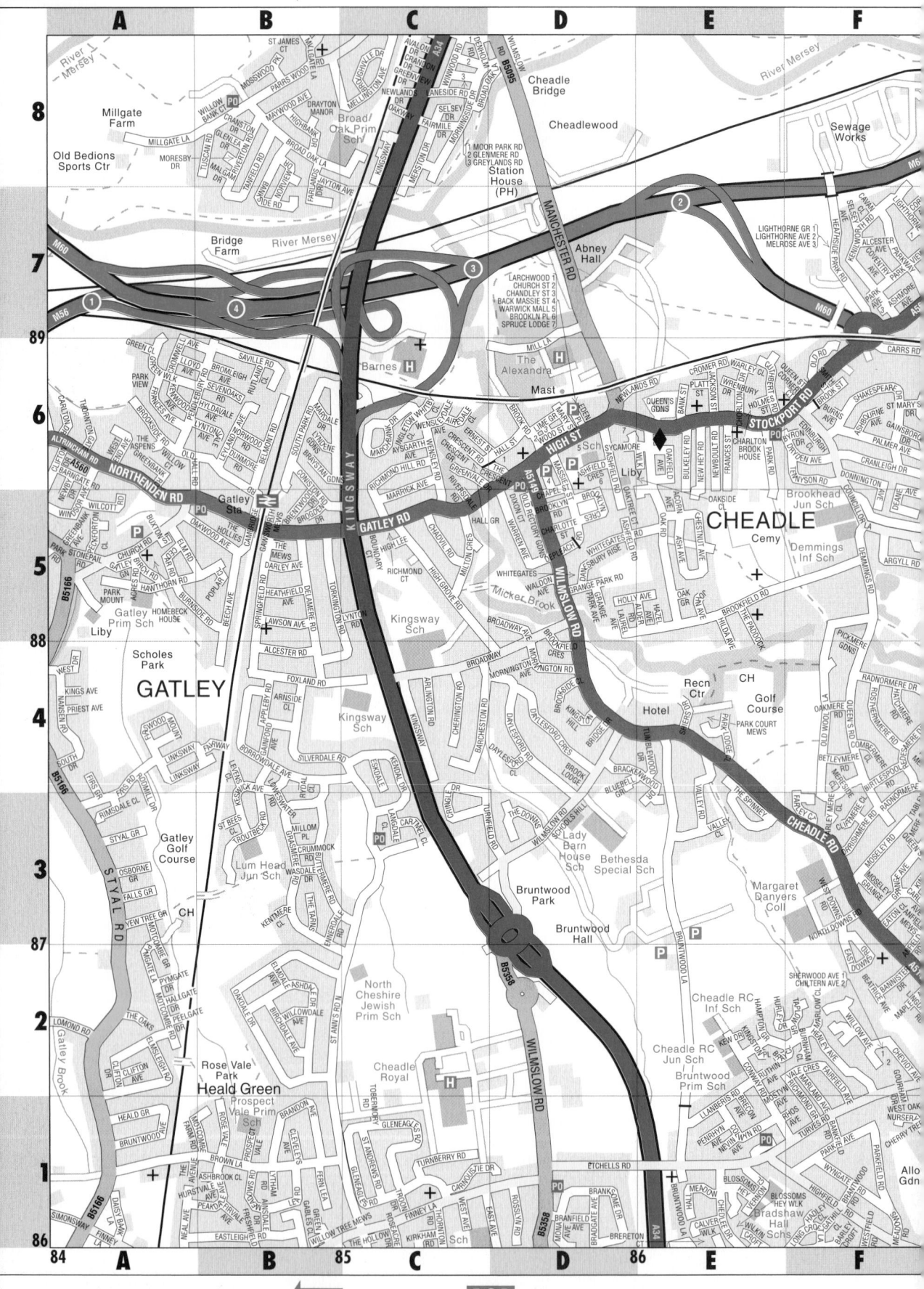

B8
1 TRANMERE RD
2 EGREMONT GR
3 ST JOHNS WLK
4 STOCKTON AVE
5 MERTON RD

C8
1 BRINKSWAY TRAD EST
2 HIGHFIELD ST
3 BENNETT ST
4 BENNETT CL
5 BONAR CL
6 CONGHAM RD
7 LLANFAIR RD
8 LAINTON CT

F4
1 HAWTHORN LODGE
2 OAKLEIGH
3 RAVENSWOOD CT
4 FIRCROFT CT

For full street detail of the highlighted area see page 170.

123 112

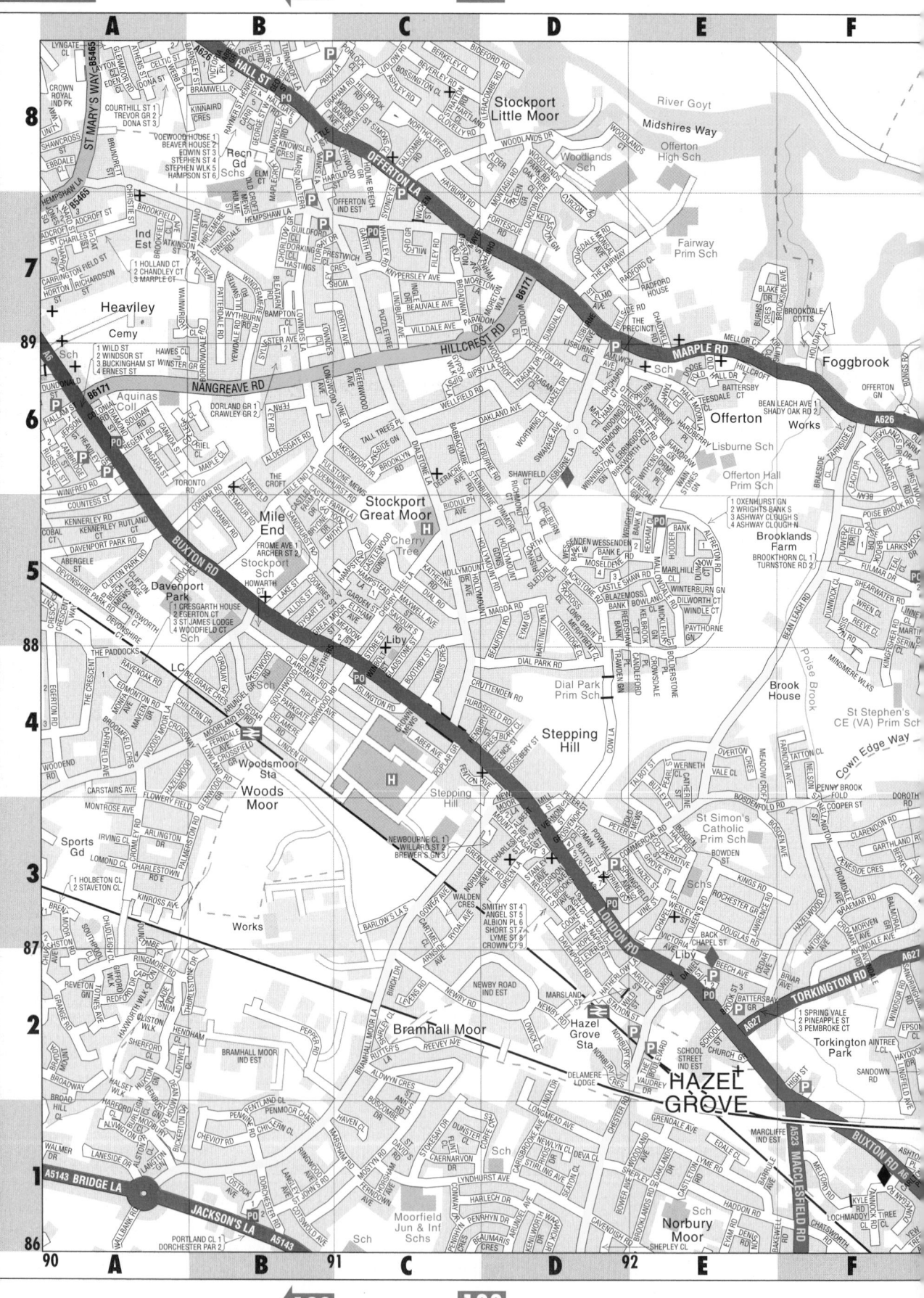

123 133

F5
1 CHAPEL FIELDS
2 EMPRESS AVE
3 RECTORY CT
4 PARK BGLWS
5 WATERSIDE AVE
6 STIRLING AVE

F5
7 COTEFIELD CL
F6
1 OVERDALE
2 HOLLINS TERR
3 RIDGEDALE CTR
4 THE HOLLINS

5 CHURCH ST
6 WALMERSLEY CT
7 DERBY WAY
8 DERBY ST
9 SPRINGFIELD AVE
10 HIGHFIELD RD
11 LYCHWOOD

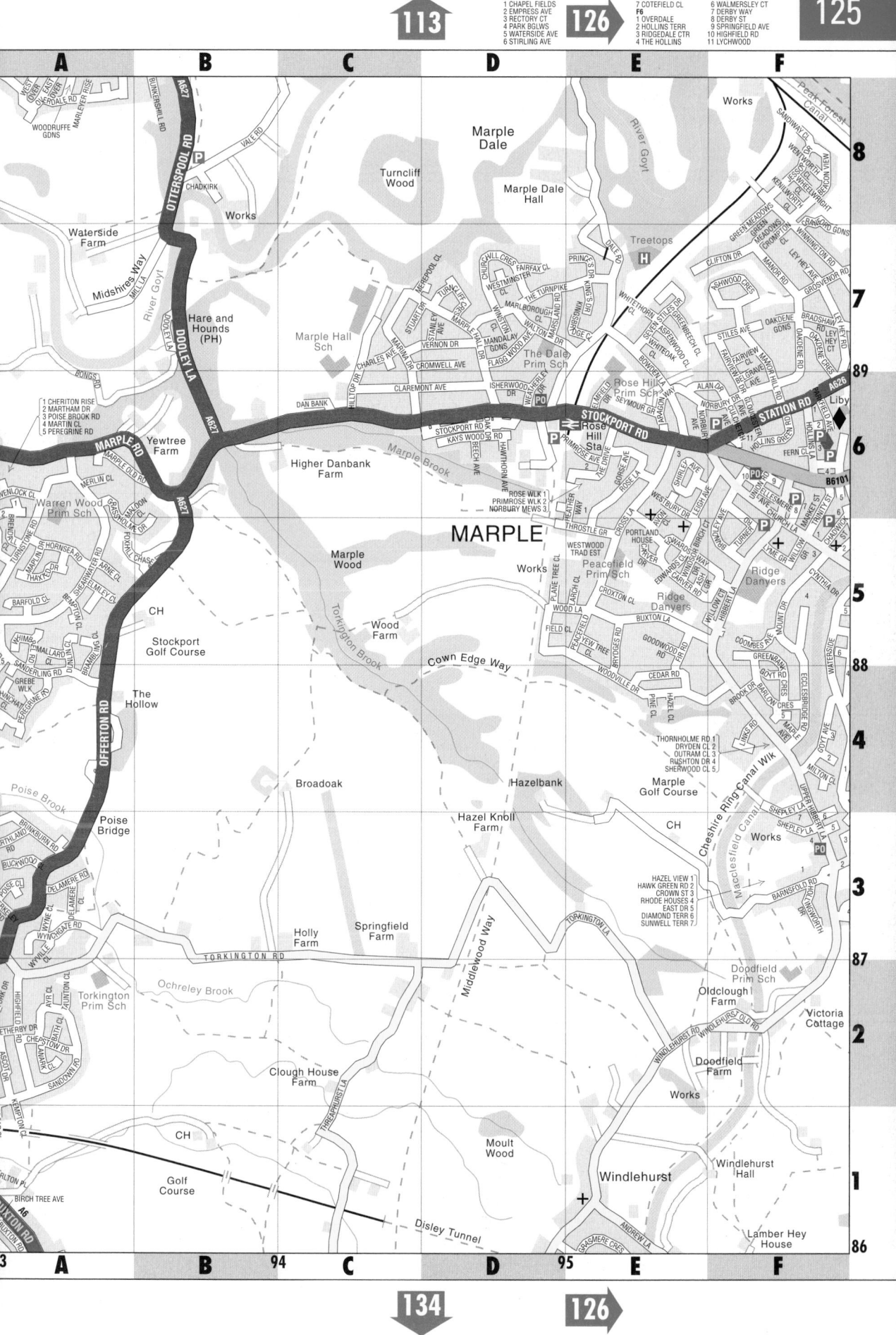

125
114

125
135

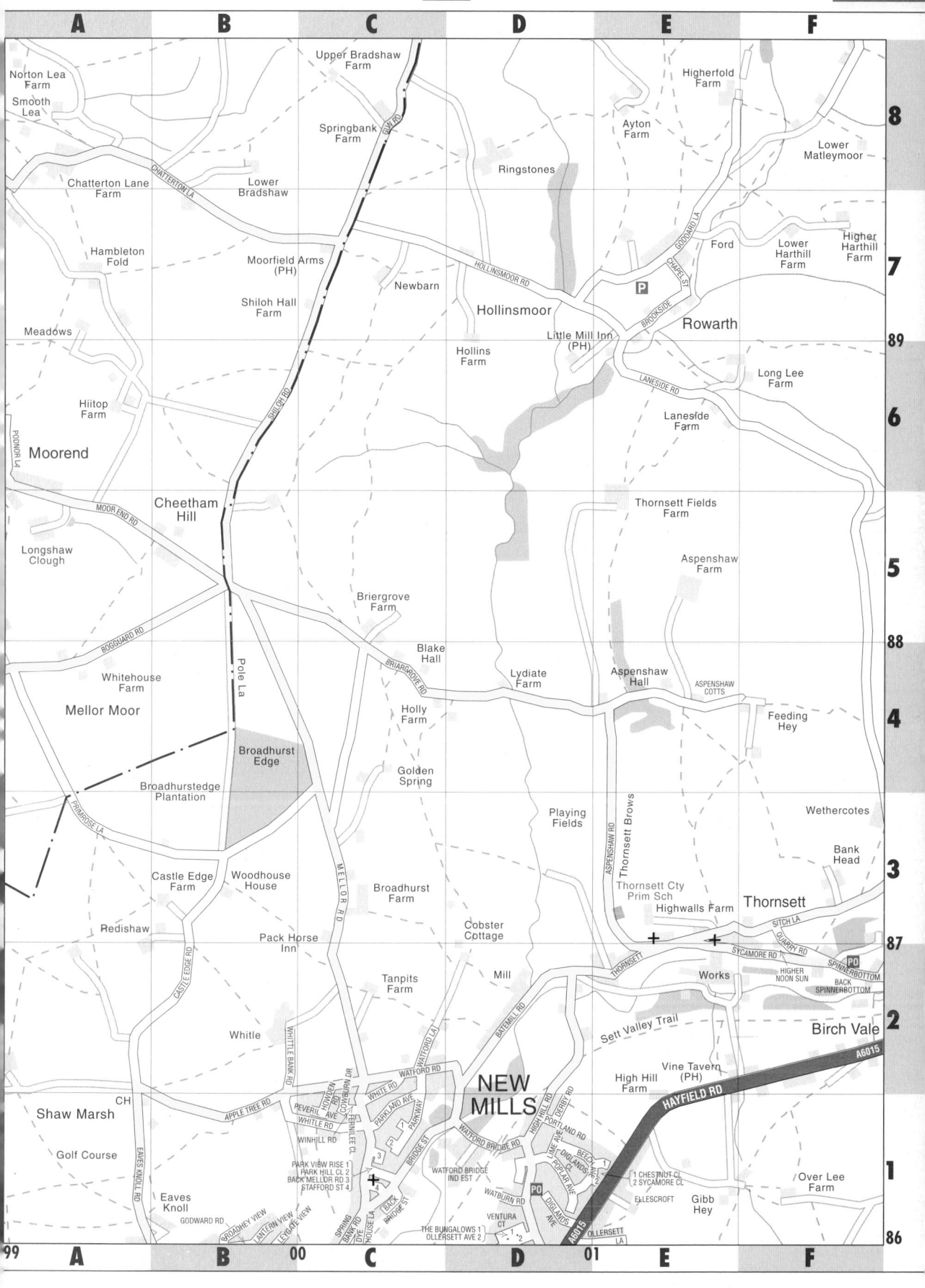

A B C D E F

8

7

89

6

5

88

4

3

87

2

Birch Vale

1

86

99 A B 00 C D 01 E F

Norton Lea Farm
Smooth Lea
Chatterton Lane Farm
CHATTERTON LA
Hambleton Fold
Meadows
Hiltop Farm
Moorend
PODNOR LA
MOOR END RD
Longshaw Clough
Whitehouse Farm
Mellor Moor
PRIMROSE LA
BOGGUARD RD
Castle Edge Farm
Redishaw
CASTLE EDGE RD
Whitle
Shaw Marsh
CH
Golf Course
EAVES KNOLL RD
Eaves Knoll
GODWARD RD
BROADMEY VIEW
LANTERN VIEW
LEYGATE VIEW

Upper Bradshaw Farm
Springbank Farm
Lower Bradshaw
Moorfield Arms (PH)
Shiloh Hall Farm
SHILOH RD
Cheetham Hill
Pole La
Broadhurst Edge
Broadhurstedge Plantation
Woodhouse House
Pack Horse Inn
MELLOR RD
Tanpits Farm
WHITLE BANK RD
NURWELL
FERNILEE CL
Peveril Ave
WHITLE RD
WINHILL RD
APPLE TREE RD
Newbarn
HOLLINSMOOR RD
Hollinsmoor
Hollins Farm
Briergrove Farm
Blake Hall
BRIARGROVE RD
Lydiate Farm
Holly Farm
Golden Spring
Broadhurst Farm
Cobster Cottage
Mill
Playing Fields
Park View Rise 1
Park Hill Cl 2
Back Mellor Rd 3
Stafford St 4
WHITE RD
PARKLAND AVE
PARKWAY
HOWDEN
BRIDGE ST
WATFORD RD
WATFORD LA
SPRING BANK RD
DYE HOUSE LA
BACK BRIDGE ST
NEW MILLS
WATFORD BRIDGE RD
WATFORD BRIDGE IND EST
WATBURN RD
VENTURA CT
THE BUNGALOWS 1
OLLERSETT AVE 2
BATEMILL RD
Ringstones
Ayton Farm
Higherfold Farm
Lower Matleymoor
GODDARD LA
Ford
Lower Harthill Farm
Higher Harthill Farm
CHAPEL ST
P
BROOKSIDE
Rowarth
Little Mill Inn (PH)
LANESIDE RD
Long Lee Farm
Laneside Farm
Thornsett Fields Farm
Aspenshaw Farm
Aspenshaw Hall
ASPENSHAW COTTS
Feeding Hey
Wethercotes
Bank Head
ASPENSHAW RD
THORNSETT BROWS
Thornsett Cty Prim Sch
Highwalls Farm
Thornsett
SITCH LA
QUARRY RD
SYCAMORE RD
+
+
Works
HIGHER NOON SUN
PO
SPINNERBOTTOM
BACK SPINNERBOTTOM
THORNSETT
Sett Valley Trail
Vine Tavern (PH)
High Hill Farm
HAYFIELD RD
A6015
HIGH LANE
DERBY RD
PORTLAND RD
BEECH AVE
DIGLANDS AVE
POPLAR AVE
PO
1 Chestnut Cl
2 Sycamore Cl
ELLESCROFT
Gibb Hey
A6015
OLLERSETT LA
Over Lee Farm

119

A
B
C
D
E
F
MINSTER DR
CUMBERLAND DR
OAKWOOD LA
BOLLIN AVE
PRIORY RD
PRIORY ST
BAILEY WLK
SUNNY BANK RD
THE GORSE
BOW LA
1 ASHWOOD
2 WESTMORELAND CL
3 OAKWOOD CT
SOUTH DOWNS DR
SOUTH RD
ASHLEY MILL LA N
MADELEY CL
NURSERY AVE
LABURNUM LA
AVON RD
TOLLAND LA
ARTHOG DR
ARTHOG RD
WYNGATE RD
WESTFIELDS
THE AVENUE
BANKHALL LA
BELGRAVIA GDNS
Ashley Heath
Pool Bank Farm
Bow Green Farm
The Priory
River Bollin
Coppice Farm
ASHLEY MILL LA
ASHLEY RD
Sewage Works
Dairy House Farm
Ryecroft Farm
Ashley Hall
M56
CASTLE MILL LA
Ashley Sta
GOW LA
EGERTON MOSS
Birkin House
Blackburn's Brook
DIRTY LA
Briddon Weir Farm
Ashley
PO
BACK LA
TANYARD LA
Ashley CE (VC) Prim Sch
Birkin Farm
Stock Farm
LAMB LA
BIRKINHEATH LA
Hough Green Farm
Shaw Green Farm
MARSH LA
Birkinheath Covert
ASHLEY RD
Arden House
Twiss's Wood
Lower House Farm
MOBBERLEY RD
Ward's Plantation
Birtles Farm
Sugar Brook Farm
Sugar Brook
Birkin Brook
Primrose Hill Farm
Rabbit Warren
Deer Enclosure
BREACH HOUSE LA
Tatton Park
Mobberley Brook
Kell House Farm
PEPPER ST
SMITH LA
8
7
85
6
5
84
4
3
83
2
1
82
75
76
77

120
130
A
B
C
D
E
F
8
7
85
6
5
84
4
3
83
2
1
82
79
80
St Ambrose Coll
THE SQUARE
Halebarns
HALE RD
A538
M56
Elmridge Prim Sch
CH
Altrincham Priory
Hale Golf Course
Flaxhigh Covert
Cricket Gd
Hotel
Cargo Ctr
Mast
Oak Farm
The Romper (PH)
Warburton Green
Keepers Cottage
Halebank Farm
Tanyard Farm
WILMSLOW RD
River Bollin
Thorns Green
Back Lane Farm
CASTLE MILL LA
BACK LA
Chapel House Farm
Cotteril Clough
Castle Mill Farm
MILL LA
Castle Hill Farm
Castle Hill
BRICKHILL LA
Middle House
Higherhouse Farm
Meadowlands
CASTLE MILL LA
Blackshaw Heys Farm
BREACH HOUSE LA
Breach House Farm
Stock-in-Hey Farm
Beehive Farm
Bollinhouse Farm
Woodend
Woodend Farm
WOODEND LA
Yarwood House Farm
Cherry Tree Farm
WOOD LA
WOOD LA

130

129
121
129
136

A   B   C   D   E   F

8

7

85

6

5

84

4

3

83

2

1

82

81   A   82   B   C   D   83   E   F

Sports Field

Works

Woodhouse Park Prim Sch

Cornishway

Nursery

Ringway Trad Est

D8
1 ROSSETT AVE
2 WHITEFRIARS WLK
3 CORNISHWAY IND EST

1 DUFTON WLK
2 LISMORE WLK
3 FOLEY WLK
4 BRADING WLK
5 BEAGLE WLK
6 LYNSIDE WLK
COPGROVE WLK

EMERALD RD

Moss Nook

Terminal 2

Hotel

Hotel

Manchester Airport Sta

Manchester Airport

Exit Rd W

Terminal 1

Terminal 1 Domestic

PH

Boundary Terr

Oak Tree Farm

Beech Farm

Moss La

Moss Lane Farm

Holly Farm

Cloughbank Farm

Moss Farm

Holly La

Lode Hill Farm

Styal Cross

Norcliffe Farm

Lode Hill

Oak Brow Cotts

Styal

Birch Farm

Oversley Lodge Farm

Altrincham Rd

River Bollin

The Mews

Norcliffe Hall

Styal Cty Prim Sch

Farmfold

Styal Gn

Cross Farm

Oversley Farm

Aviation Viewing Park

Styal Country Park

Shaws Fold

Quarry Bank Rd

Wilmslow Rd   A538

Hotel

Altrincham Rd

Bank House Farm

Quarry Bank Mill

Morley

Hooksbank Wood

Dooley's La

Morley Gn

Oak Farm

Stamford Lodge

Mast

Transmitting Station

Worms Hill

Wood Farm

Mossbrow

Mobberley Rd

Morley Green

A538

Woodlands Rd

Vale Rd

Kings Rd

Carwood Rd

131
D5
1 TARVIN WAY
2 OVERTON WAY
3 STRETTON WAY
4 BIRTLES WAY
5 PEACOCK WAY
6 KELSALL WAY
122
7 CUDDINGTON WAY
8 WILLASTOR WAY
9 NORBURY WAY
10 PICKMERE CT
11 EASTHAM WAY
12 UPTON WAY
13 ASTON WAY
132
14 HOOTON WAY
15 CHRISTLETON WAY
E5
1 SUTTON WAY
2 CHELFORD CT
3 SOMERFORD WAY
4 TATTON CT
5 MARTON WAY
6 NANTWICH WAY
7 HASSALL WAY
8 MARTHALL WAY
A
B
C
D
E
F
Heald Green Sta
Heald Green
Recn Gd
GREENCOURTS BSNS PK
Liby
Sch
Cheadle Prep Sch
Outwood Prim Sch
Bolshaw Cty Prim Sch
Wood Farm
Outwood Farm
Yew Tree Farm
Griffin Farm
Outwood House
1 DAME HOLLOW
2 BRIDGEWATER CL
Stanley Green
Gill Bent Farm
Gillbent
St James RC High Sch
LEAFIELD DR 1
ST JAMES CT 2
The Royal School for the Deaf
Bolshaw Farm
Waggon & Horses Hotel (PH)
Hotel
WILMSLOW RD
STANLEY RD
B5094
A555
A34
B5358
B5166
HATHAWAY CL 1
STRATFORD SQ 2
BRISTOL CL 3
Bollinhey Farm
The Grange
Playing Field
STANLEY GREEN IND EST
STANLEY GREEN RET PK
Beech Farm
Parkfield
Handforth
Styal Sta
Deandale Farm
Highfield
Knowle House
SOUTHFIELD CL 1
KNOWLE GN 2
HUNTER'S VIEW 3
SPINNEY CL 4
Brooke Farm
1 TOFT WAY
2 GAWSWORTH WAY
3 WEAVERHAM WAY
4 FRODSHAM WAY
St Benedict's RC Prim Sch
Langley House
Styal Green
Linney's Bridge
River Dean
Handforth Sta
Handforth Bridge
DEANWAY TRAD EST
STATION RD
DEAN RD
Bollin Cross Sch
Finney Green
Hall Wood
1 BRINDLEY GR
2 TARPORLEY WLK
HM Prison & Young Offenders Inst
Works
Lacey Green Cty Prim Sch
Lacey Green
Cemy
Colshaw Cty Prim Sch
SUMMERFIELDS CTR
Schs
HANDFORTH RD
STYAL RD
8
7
85
6
5
84
4
3
83
2
1
82
85
86
D1
1 MILLBROOK GR
2 REDBROOK GR
3 SHELBROOK GR
4 WADEBROOK GR
5 DINGLEBROOK GR
6 LIME WLK
7 CROWBROOK GR
137
D2
1 TARBROOK GR
2 CLIFFBROOK GR
3 BENSON WLK
4 CARDENBROOK GR
5 TIMBERSBROOK GR
6 LADYBROOK GR
7 FODEN WLK
8 TAME WLK
132
D4
1 HILLBRE WAY
2 SEALAND WAY
3 ECCLESTON WAY
4 HELSBY WAY
5 HEATLEY WAY
6 ELWORTH WAY
7 PARKGATE WAY
E1
1 BUDWORTH WLK
2 EDLESTONE GR
3 WOODCOTT GR
4 KETTLESHULME WLK
5 TILSTON WLK
6 SNAPEBROOK GR
7 DAIRYBROOK GR
8 APPLETON WLK
9 MOORSBROOK GR
10 RAINOW WAY
11 PEAKFORTON WLK
12 SALTERSBROOK GR
13 PINWOOD CT

131
123

A
B
C
D
E
F
8
7
85
6
5
84
4
3
83
2
1
82
87
88
89
CHEADLE HULME
BRAMHALL
Smithy Green
Cheadle Hulme Sch
Hulme Hall Jun Sch
Schs
Cheadle Hulme High Sch
Sports Ctr
Thorn Grove Prim Sch
Hursthead Cty Jun Sch
Hursthead Inf Sch
Bramall Park Golf Course
Carr Wood Park
Pownall Green Cty Prim Sch
Pownall Green
Bramhall Sta
Liby
Bramhall High Sch
Ladybrook Prim Sch
Lady Brook
Kitt's Moss
Moss Hey Prim Sch
Valley Sch
Syddal Park Prep Sch
Queensgate Prim Sch
Recn Gd
Lower Bent Farm
Sports Gd
Chester's Croft Park
Hall Moss
Hawthorn Farm
Sports Ctr
Riding School
Moorend Farm
Walnut-Tree Farm
Moor Farm
Threeways Farm
Nursery
Barr Green Farm
Blossoms Turkey Farm
Grove-end Farm
Community Centre
Factory
Hilltop Farm
Woodford
Pump Farm
Back Lane Farm
PH
Moss Wood
River Dean
Kingstreet
Woodford Aerodrome
Dean Farm
Old Fold Farm
DAIRY HOUSE SMALL HOLDINGS
RAVENOAK RD A5149
ACK LA W
ACK LA E
CHURCH RD
B5095
HULME HALL RD
GROVE LA
B5094
MEADOW LA
MOSS LA
BRAMHALL LA S
A5102
A5149
WOODFORD RD
A555
SPATH LA
SPATH LA E
DAIRY HOUSE RD
DAIRY HOUSE LA
HALL MOSS LA
JENNY LA
MOOR LA
FODEN LA
WOODHALL CL
BLOSSOMS LA
CHURCH LA
CHESTER RD
WILMSLOW RD
OLD HALL LA
BRIDLE CT
BRIDLE RD
QUEENSGATE
MEADWAY
CROSSWAY
MOUNTFIELD RD
SYDDAL RD
THE BRAMHALL CTR
FORBES PK
GRASMERE CRES
CARR WOOD AVE
RAMSDALE RD
HILLBROOK RD
GLENHOLME RD
CONVAMORE RD
BIRCHWAY
THORNWAY
LARCHWAY
BRAMWAY
DENEWAY
WOODS LA
VICARAGE AVE
WOODSTOCK AVE
PINGATE LA
CH

124
134

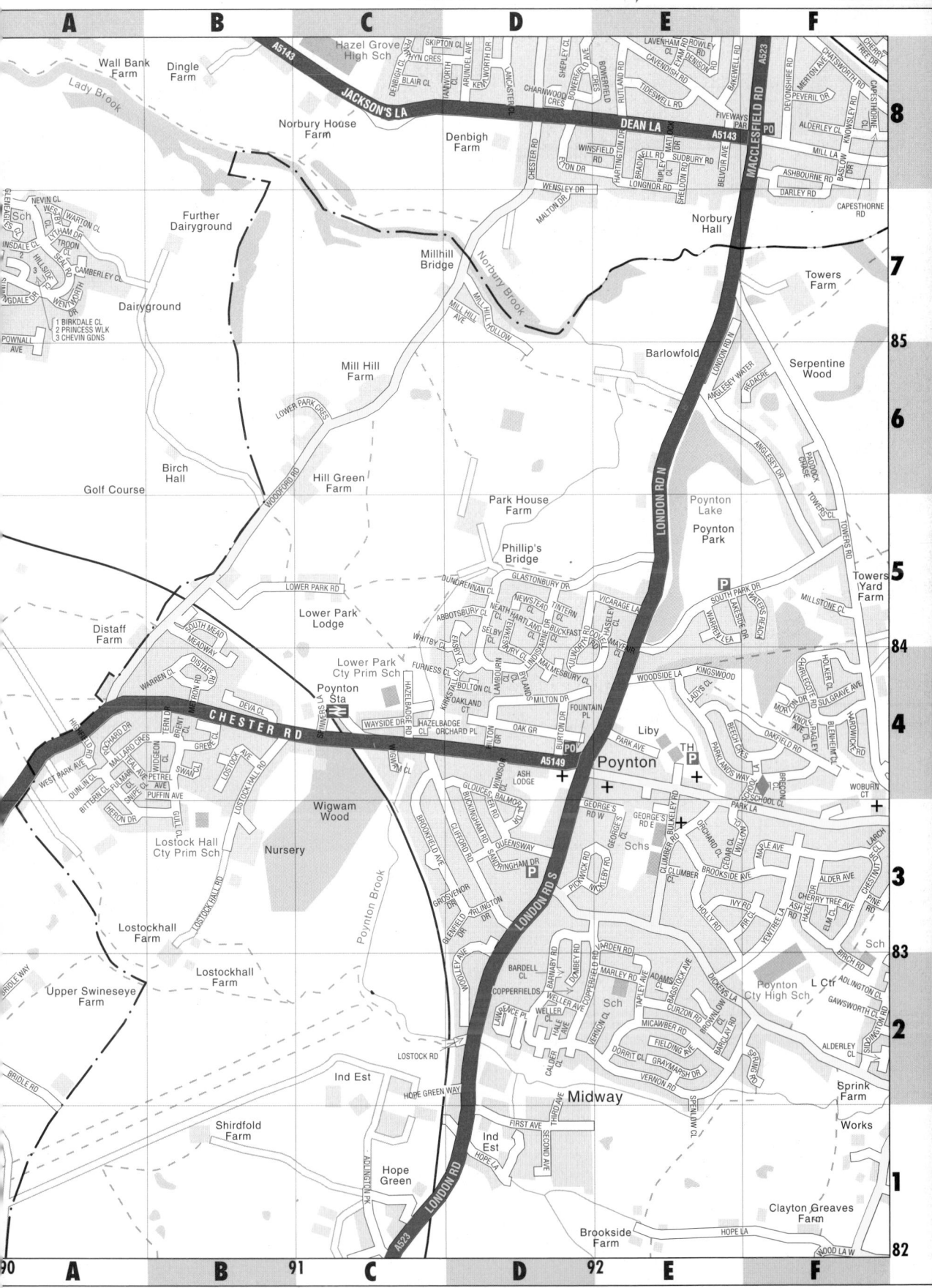
A
B
C
D
E
F
8
7
85
6
5
84
4
3
83
2
1
82
90
91
92
Wall Bank Farm
Dingle Farm
Lady Brook
Hazel Grove High Sch
JACKSON'S LA
A5143
Norbury House Farm
Denbigh Farm
DEAN LA
MACCLESFIELD RD
A523
Norbury Hall
Further Dairyground
Dairyground
Millhill Bridge
Norbury Brook
Towers Farm
Barlowfold
Serpentine Wood
Mill Hill Farm
LOWER PARK CRES
WOODFORD RD
Birch Hall
Golf Course
Hill Green Farm
Park House Farm
LONDON RD N
Poynton Lake
Poynton Park
Phillip's Bridge
Towers Yard Farm
LOWER PARK RD
Lower Park Lodge
Distaff Farm
Lower Park Cty Prim Sch
Poynton Sta
CHESTER RD
A5149
Poynton
Liby
TH
Wigwam Wood
Nursery
Lostock Hall Cty Prim Sch
LOSTOCK HALL RD
Schs
LONDON RD S
Poynton Brook
Lostockhall Farm
Lostockhall Farm
Upper Swineseye Farm
Sch
Poynton Cty High Sch
L Ctr
LOSTOCK RD
Ind Est
HOPE GREEN WAY
Midway
Shirdfold Farm
Ind Est
Hope Green
LONDON RD
Sprink Farm
Works
Clayton Greaves Farm
Brookside Farm
HOPE LA
BRIDLE RD
1 BIRKDALE CL
2 PRINCESS WLK
3 CHEVIN GDNS

134

133

125

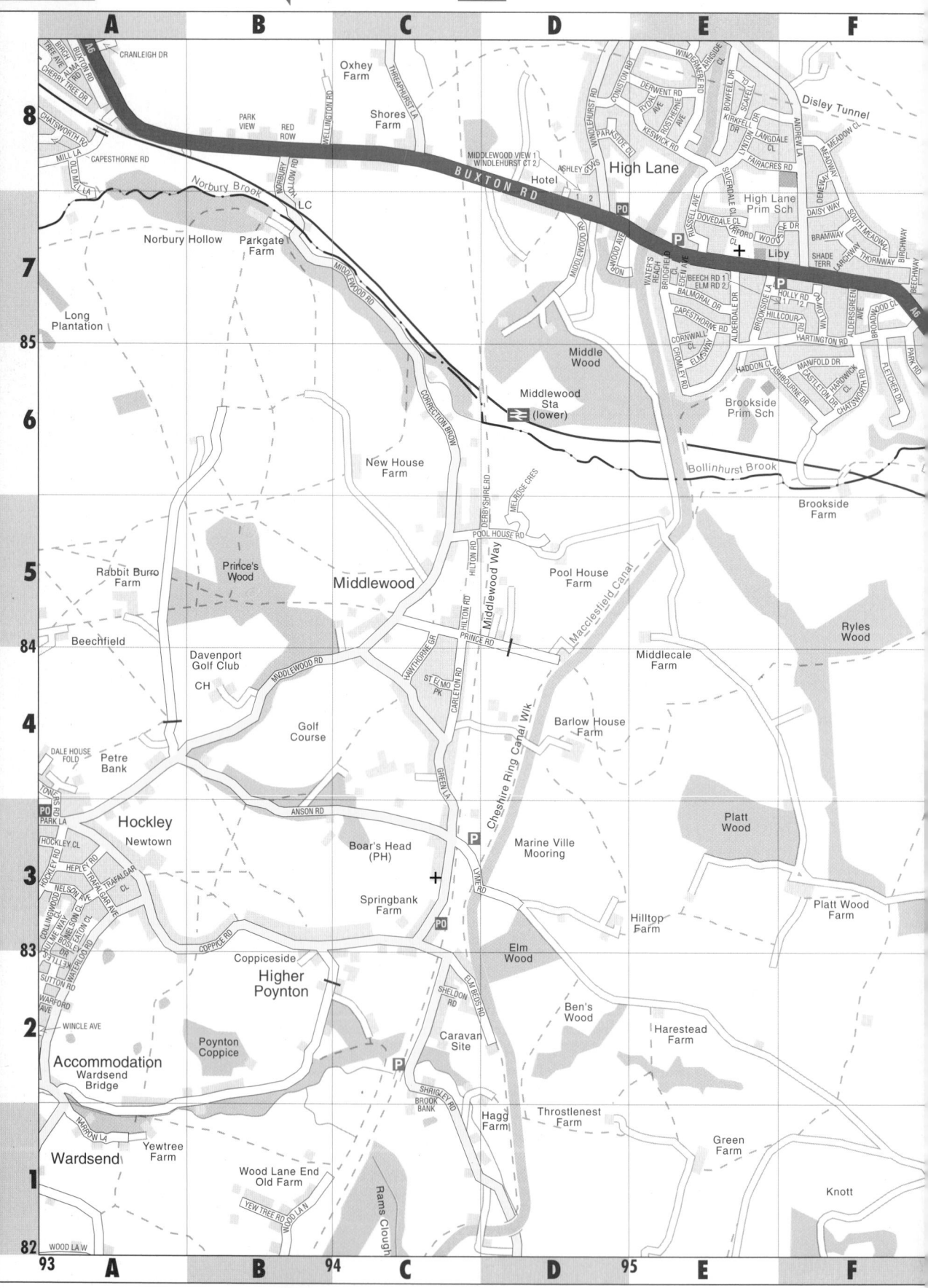

A
B
C
D
E
F
8
7
85
6
5
84
4
3
83
2
1
82
93
94
95
Oxhey Farm
Shores Farm
Disley Tunnel
High Lane
BUXTON RD
Hotel
High Lane Prim Sch
Liby
Norbury Brook
LC
Norbury Hollow
Parkgate Farm
Long Plantation
Middle Wood
Middlewood Sta (lower)
Brookside Prim Sch
New House Farm
Bollinhurst Brook
Brookside Farm
Rabbit Burro Farm
Prince's Wood
Middlewood
Pool House Farm
Middlewood Way
Macclesfield Canal
Ryles Wood
Beechfield
Davenport Golf Club
CH
Middlecale Farm
Golf Course
Barlow House Farm
Petre Bank
Cheshire Ring Canal Wlk
Hockley
Newtown
Boar's Head (PH)
Marine Ville Mooring
Platt Wood
Springbank Farm
Hilltop Farm
Platt Wood Farm
Coppiceside
Higher Poynton
Elm Wood
Ben's Wood
Harestead Farm
Poynton Coppice
Caravan Site
Accommodation
Wardsend Bridge
Hagg Farm
Throstlenest Farm
Green Farm
Wardsend
Yewtree Farm
Wood Lane End Old Farm
Rams Clough
Knott

133

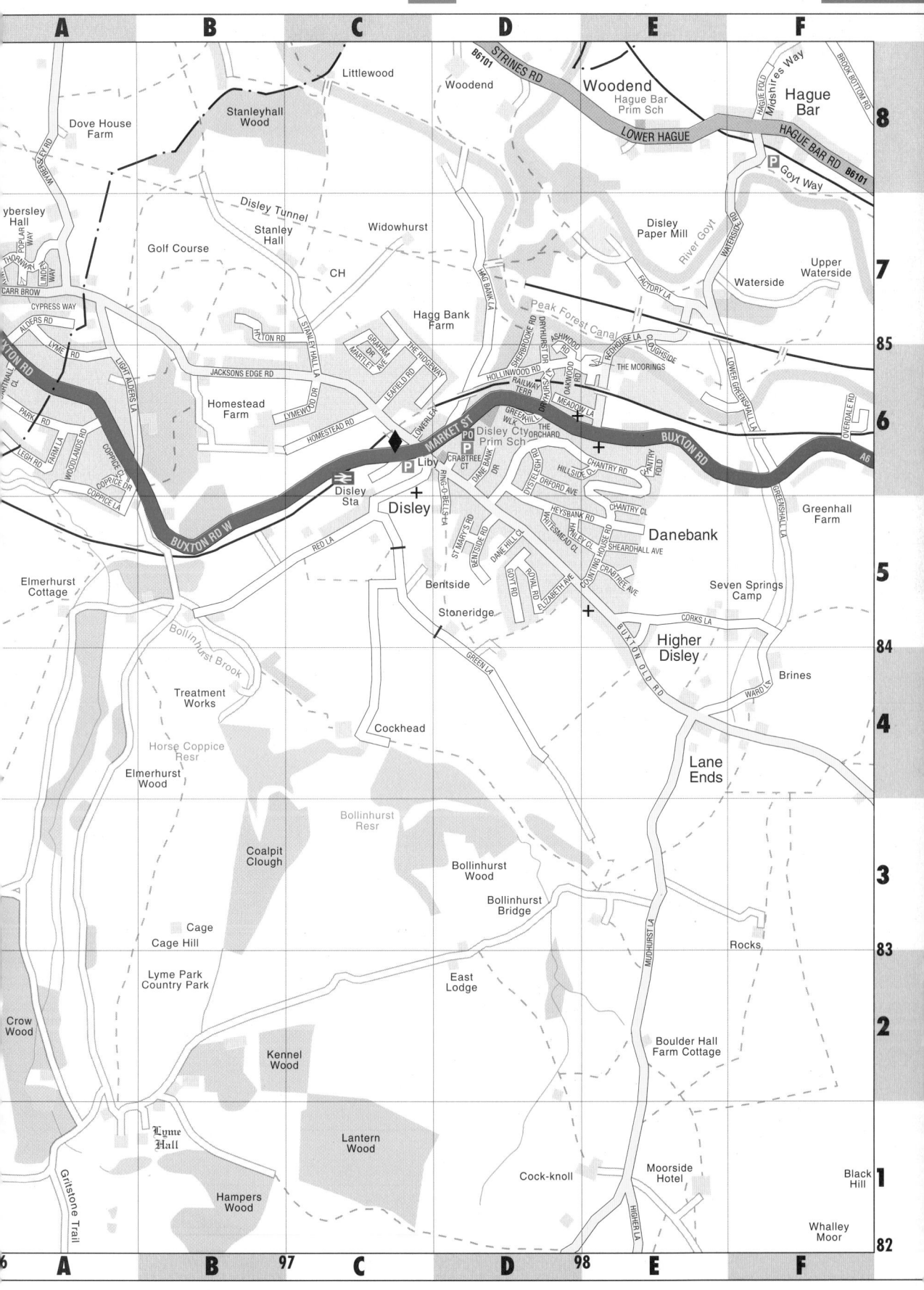
A
B
C
D
E
F
Littlewood
Woodend
STRINES RD
B6101
Woodend
Hague Bar Prim Sch
LOWER HAGUE
Hague Bar
HAGUE BAR RD
B6101
Midshires Way
BROOK BOTTOM RD
HAGUE FOLD
Goyt Way
Stanleyhall Wood
Dove House Farm
WYBERSLEY RD
ybersley Hall
POPLAR WAY
THORNWAY
LINDEN WAY
CARR BROW
CYPRESS WAY
ALDERS RD
LYME RD
Disley Tunnel
Stanley Hall
Golf Course
Widowhurst
CH
Disley Paper Mill
River Goyt
WATERSIDE RD
Waterside
Upper Waterside
FACTORY LA
HAG BANK LA
Hagg Bank Farm
Peak Forest Canal
HILTON RD
STANLEY HALL LA
GRAHAM DR
MARTLET AVE
THE RIDGEWAY
LEAFIELD RD
SHERBROOKE RD
DRYHURST DR
ASHWOOD RD
OAKWOOD RD
REDHOUSE LA
CLOUGHSIDE
THE MOORINGS
LOWER GREENSHALL LA
HOLLINWOOD RD
RAILWAY TERR
MEADOW LA
JACKSONS EDGE RD
LIGHT ALDERS LA
BUXTON RD
Homestead Farm
LYMEWOOD DR
HOMESTEAD RD
LOWERLEA
MARKET ST
GREEN WLK
THE ORCHARD
Disley Cty Prim Sch
PO
P
BUXTON RD
OVERDALE RD
A6
PARK RD
WOODLANDS RD
FARM LA
LEGH RD
COPPICE CL
COPPICE DR
COPPICE LA
Liby
CRABTREE CT
DANE BANK DR
DYSTELEGH RD
HILLSIDE CL
CHANTRY RD
CHANTRY FOLD
ORFORD AVE
Disley Sta
Disley
RING-O-BELLS LA
HEYSBANK RD
CHANTRY CL
GREENSHALL LA
Greenhall Farm
BUXTON RD W
RED LA
ST MARY'S RD
BENTSIDE RD
DANE HILL CL
WHITESMEAD CL
HANLEY CL
COUNTING HOUSE RD
SHEARDHALL AVE
Danebank
CRABTREE AVE
Elmerhurst Cottage
Bentside
GOYT RD
ROYAL RD
ELIZABETH AVE
Seven Springs Camp
Stoneridge
CORKS LA
Bollinhurst Brook
BUXTON OLD RD
Higher Disley
GREEN LA
Brines
WARD LA
Treatment Works
Cockhead
Horse Coppice Resr
Lane Ends
Elmerhurst Wood
Bollinhurst Resr
Coalpit Clough
Bollinhurst Wood
Bollinhurst Bridge
Cage
Cage Hill
MUDHURST LA
Rocks
Lyme Park Country Park
East Lodge
Crow Wood
Boulder Hall Farm Cottage
Kennel Wood
Lyme Hall
Lantern Wood
Gritstone Trail
Cock-knoll
Moorside Hotel
HIGHER LA
Black Hill
Hampers Wood
Whalley Moor
8
7
85
6
5
84
4
3
83
2
1
82
97
98

130

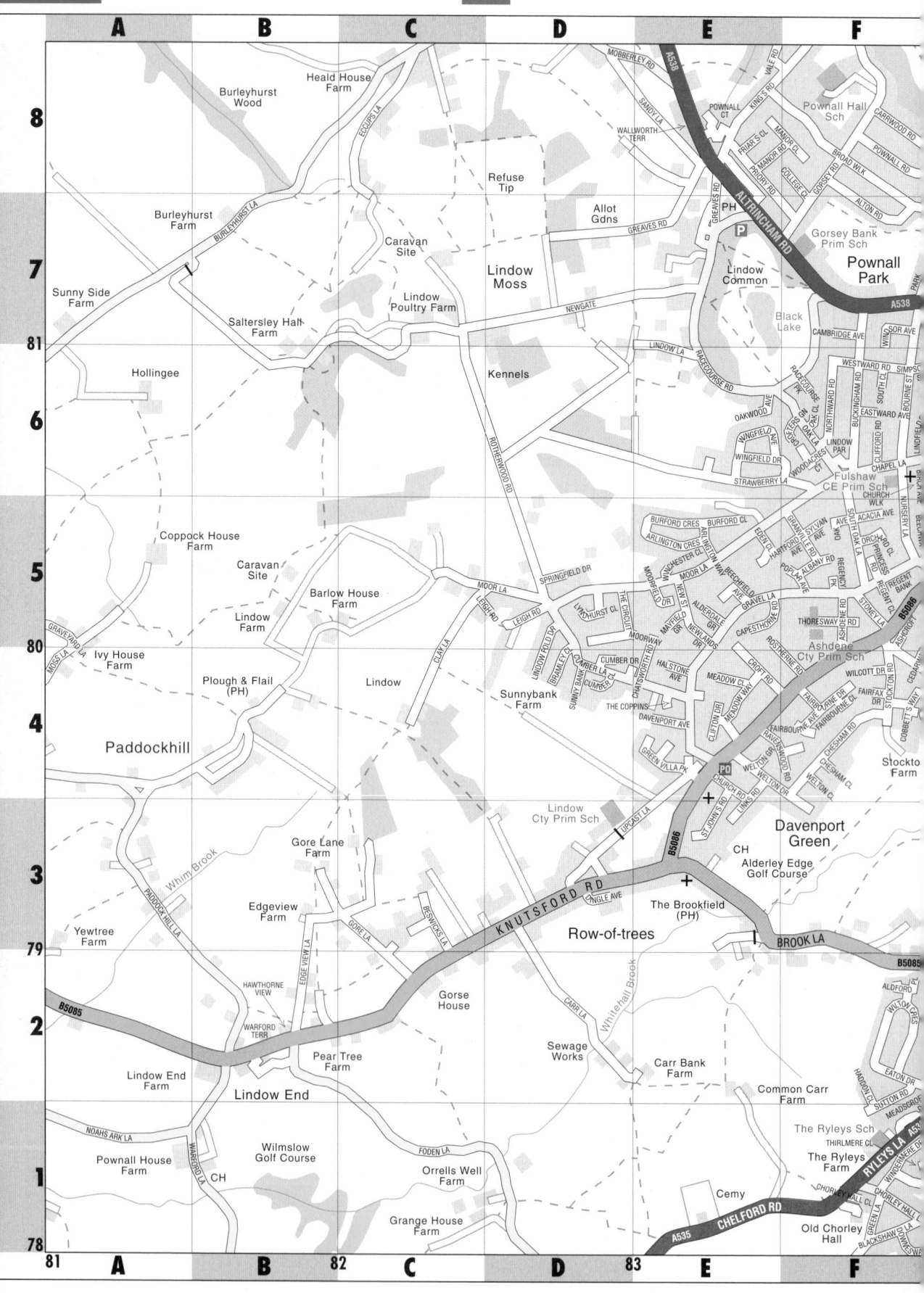

A
B
C
D
E
F
8
7
81
6
5
80
4
3
79
2
1
78
81
82
83
Burleyhurst Wood
Heald House Farm
Pownall Hall Sch
Refuse Tip
Burleyhurst Farm
Allot Gdns
Caravan Site
Gorsey Bank Prim Sch
Lindow Moss
Lindow Common
Pownall Park
Sunny Side Farm
Lindow Poultry Farm
Saltersley Hall Farm
Black Lake
Hollingee
Kennels
Fulshaw CE Prim Sch
Coppock House Farm
Caravan Site
Barlow House Farm
Lindow Farm
Ivy House Farm
Ashdene Cty Prim Sch
Plough & Flail (PH)
Lindow
Sunnybank Farm
Paddockhill
Stockto Farm
Lindow Cty Prim Sch
Davenport Green
Gore Lane Farm
Alderley Edge Golf Course
Edgeview Farm
The Brookfield (PH)
Yewtree Farm
Row-of-trees
Gorse House
Sewage Works
Lindow End Farm
Pear Tree Farm
Carr Bank Farm
Lindow End
Common Carr Farm
The Ryleys Sch
Wilmslow Golf Course
Pownall House Farm
Orrells Well Farm
The Ryleys Farm
Cemy
Grange House Farm
Old Chorley Hall
KNUTSFORD RD
ALTRINCHAM RD
BROOK LA
CHELFORD RD
RYLEYS LA
NEWGATE
MOOR LA
BURLEYHURST LA
ROTHERWOOD RD
CLAY LA
PADDOCK HILL LA
CARR LA
FODEN LA
NOAHS ARK LA
WARFORD LA
GORE LA
EDGE VIEW LA
BESWICKS LA
UPCAST LA
GRAVEYARD LA
MOSS LA
ECCUPS LA
STRAWBERRY LA
LINDOW LA
RACECOURSE RD
GREAVES RD
MOBBERLEY RD
SANDY LA
WALLWORTH TERR
POWNALL CT
HAWTHORNE VIEW
WARFORD TERR
Whim Brook
Whitehall Brook
A538
B5086
B5085
A535
PH
CH

131

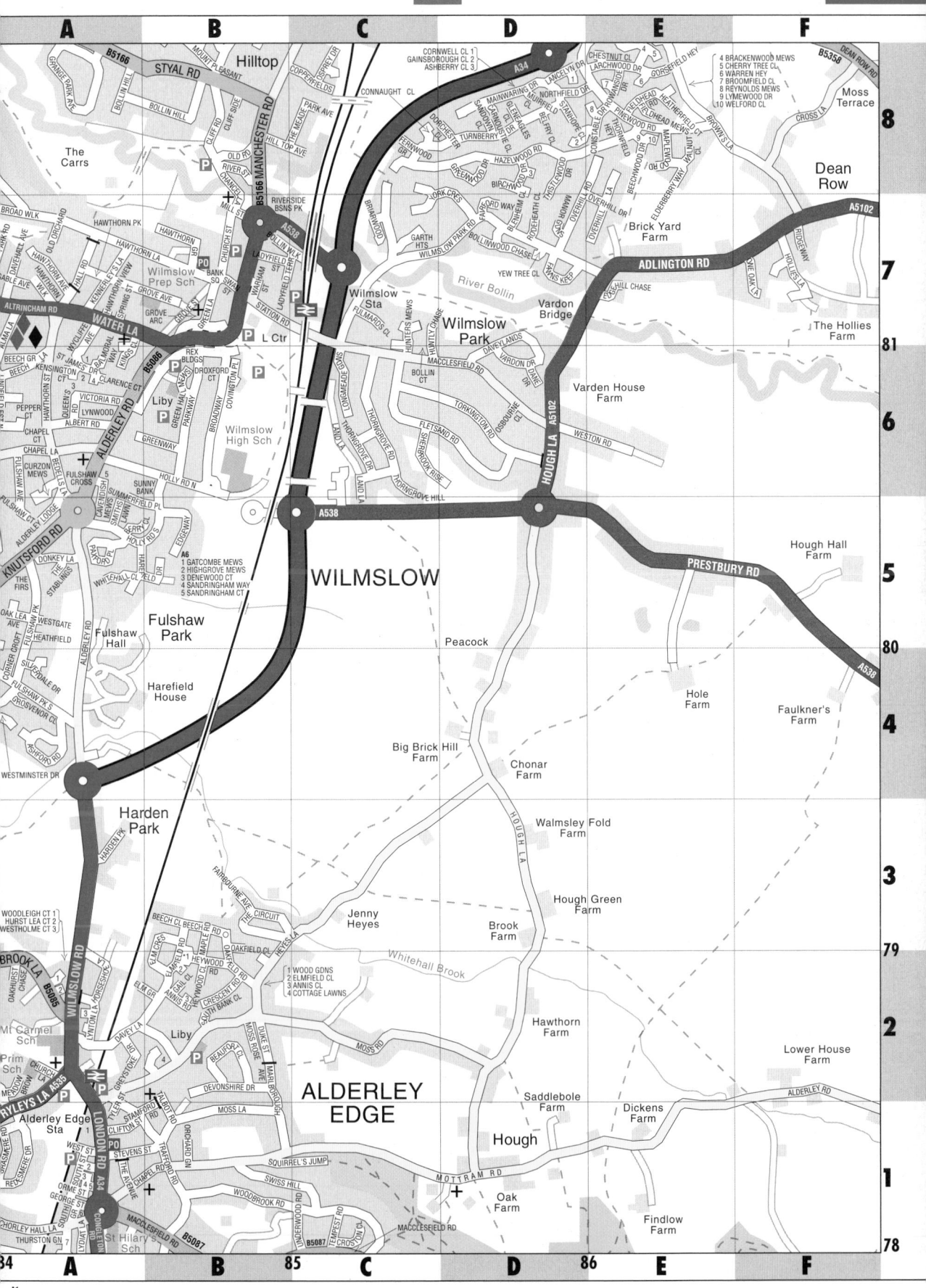

A1
1 THE PARADE
2 BROWN ST
3 GREEN ST
4 MASSEY ST
5 CHAPEL ST
6 HUBERT WORTHINGTON HOUSE
7 CARLISLE ST

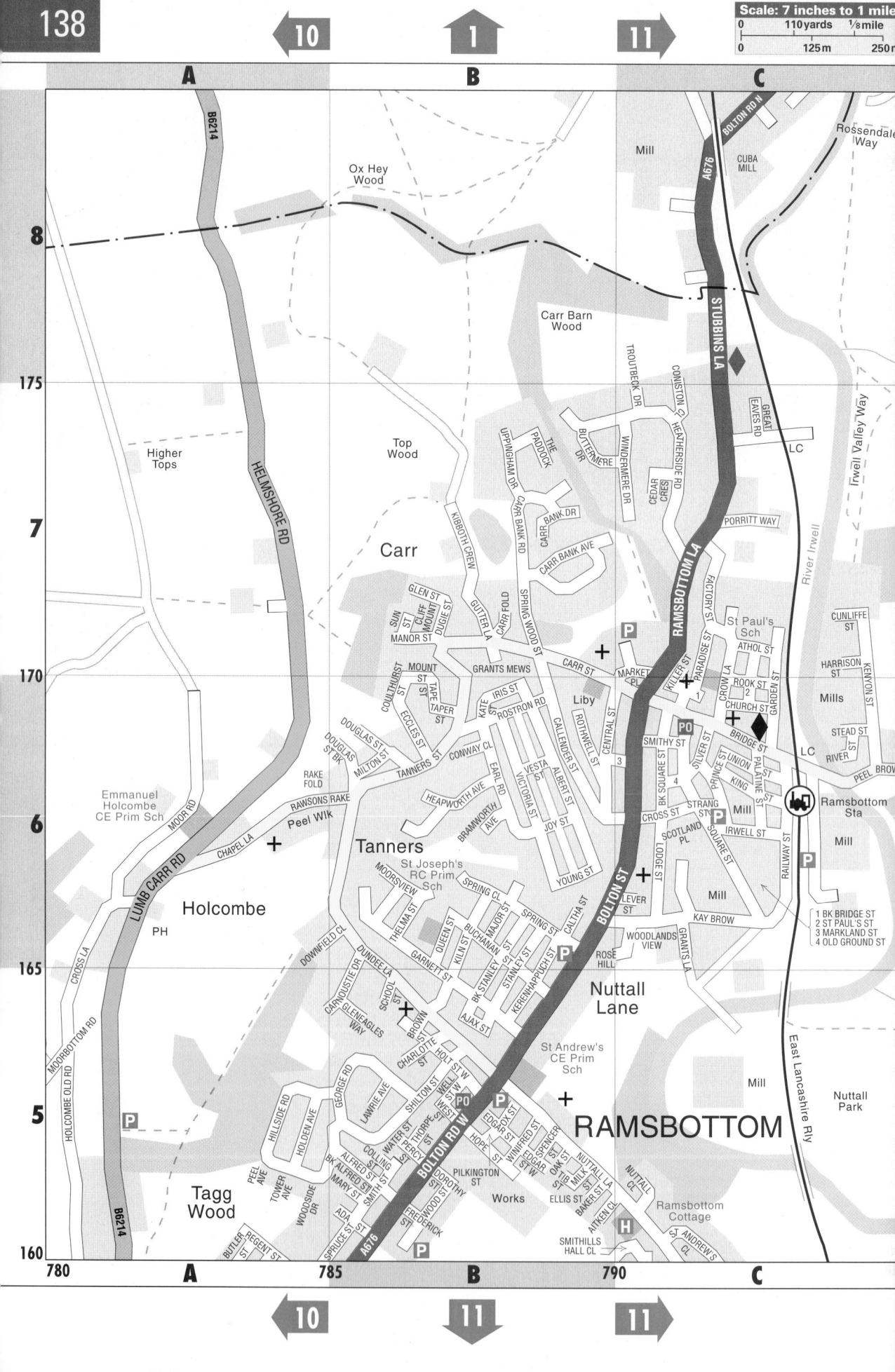
10
1
11
Scale: 7 inches to 1 mile
0
110 yards
⅛ mile
0
125 m
250 m
A
B
C
8
175
7
170
6
165
5
160
780
785
790
B6214
Ox Hey Wood
Mill
CUBA MILL
BOLTON RD N
Rossendale Way
A676
STUBBINS LA
Carr Barn Wood
TROUTBECK DR
CONISTON CL
GREAT EAVES RD
Irwell Valley Way
LC
Higher Tops
HELMSHORE RD
Top Wood
UPPINGHAM DR
THE PADDOCK
BUTTERMERE DR
WINDERMERE DR
HEATHERSIDE RD
CEDAR CRES
PORRITT WAY
River Irwell
CARR BANK DR
CARR BANK RD
CARR BANK AVE
KIBBOTH CREW
Carr
RAMSBOTTOM LA
FACTORY ST
St Paul's Sch
GLEN ST
CLIFF MOUNT
DUGIE ST
SUN ST
MANOR ST
GUTTER LA
CARR FOLD
SPRING WOOD ST
ATHOL ST
CUNLIFFE ST
HARRISON ST
KENYON ST
MOUNT ST
GRANTS MEWS
CARR ST
MARKET PL
KILLER ST
PARADISE ST
CROW LA
ROOK ST
GARDEN ST
CHURCH ST
Mills
COULTHURST ST
TAPE ST
TAPER ST
IRIS ST
KATE ST
ROSTRON RD
CALLENDER ST
Liby
ROTHWELL ST
CENTRAL ST
PO
SMITHY ST
SILVER ST
BRIDGE ST
STEAD ST
RIVER ST
PEEL BROW
DOUGLAS ST
DOUGLAS ST BK
MILTON ST
ECCLES ST
TANNERS ST
CONWAY CL
EARL RD
VESTA ST
ALBERT ST
VICTORIA ST
BK SQUARE ST
PRINCE ST
UNION ST
KING ST
PALATINE ST
Ramsbottom Sta
RAKE FOLD
RAWSONS RAKE
Emmanuel Holcombe CE Prim Sch
MOOR RD
Peel Wlk
CHAPEL LA
HEAPWORTH AVE
BRAMWORTH AVE
JOY ST
CROSS ST
STRANG ST
SCOTLAND PL
SQUARE ST
IRWELL ST
Mill
RAILWAY ST
Tanners
St Joseph's RC Prim Sch
MOORSVIEW
SPRING CL
YOUNG ST
LODGE ST
LEVER ST
BOLTON ST
CALTHA ST
LUMB CARR RD
Holcombe
PH
THELMA ST
QUEEN ST
BUCHANAN ST
MAJOR ST
SPRING ST
KAY BROW
1 BK BRIDGE ST
2 ST PAUL'S ST
3 MARKLAND ST
4 OLD GROUND ST
DOWNFIELD CL
KILN ST
GARNETT ST
WOODLANDS VIEW
GRANTS LA
CROSS LA
DUNDEE LA
BK STANLEY ST
STANLEY ST
KERENHAPPUCH ST
ROSE HILL
Nuttall Lane
CARNOUSTIE DR
GLENEAGLES WAY
SCHOOL ST
BROWN ST
AJAX ST
MOORBOTTOM RD
CHARLOTTE ST
HOLT ST W
St Andrew's CE Prim Sch
East Lancashire Rly
HOLCOMBE OLD RD
HILLSIDE RD
HOLDEN AVE
GEORGE RD
LAWRIE AVE
SHILTON ST
WELL ST W
WEST ST
Mill
Nuttall Park
EDGAR ST
WINIFRED ST
SPENCER ST
RAMSBOTTOM
WATER ST
THORPE ST
PERCY ST
COLLING ST
HOPE ST
EDGAR ST W
OAK ST
NUTTALL LA
MILK ST
TIB ST
NUTTALL CL
BOLTON RD W
ALFRED ST
BK ALFRED ST
MARY ST
SMITH ST
DOROTHY ST
PILKINGTON ST
Tagg Wood
PEEL AVE
TOWER AVE
WOODSIDE DR
Works
ELLIS ST
BAKER ST
AITKEN CL
Ramsbottom Cottage
ADA ST
SPRUCE ST
WOOD ST
FREDERICK ST
BUTLER ST
REGENT ST
SMITHILLS HALL CL
ST ANDREW'S CL
11

cale: 7 inches to 1 mile
110 yards
1/8 mile
125 m
250 m
30
E6
1 KENILWORTH
2 PENDENNIS
3 GOODRICH
4 FARINGDON
5 EDLINGHAM
14
E6
6 DONNINGTON
7 BEVERSTON
8 SHIRBURN
9 THORNBURY
31
F8
1 HOPE CT
2 KERSHAW ST
3 THE BANK
4 NEW BUILDINGS PL
5 FREISTON
6 CARTMEL
7 EDINGTON
8 BROMFIELD
9 DUNSTABLE
10 ATHERSTONE
139
D
E
F
Spotland Prim Sch
HASLAM ST
EDMUND ST
PILLING ST
MOLYNEUX ST
CINNAMON CL
SPOTLAND RD
Spotland Bridge
FALINGE RD
SHERIFF ST
Town Head
WHITWORTH RD
A58
A671
A680
A6060
ST MARY'S GATE
HOLLAND ST
CLOVER ST
MARKET WAY
STATIONERS ENTRY 1
THE BUTTS AVE 2
THE WHEATSHEAF CTR
UNDERWOOD
COLLEGE RD
DUNKIRK RISE 1
TENTERCROFT 2
TOWN MILL BROW 3
Hopwood Hall Coll
River Spodden
River Roch
MELLOR ST
ROCHDALE
Mitchell Hey
Ct
Pol HQ
Liby
Art Gal
TH
TOWN HALL SQ
THE ESPLANADE
SOUTH PAR
SMITH ST
B6266
B6223
Mus
1 BEATRICE ST
2 MALVERN ST E
BURY RD
B6222
Oakenrod Prim Sch
DANE ST
MACMILLAN ST
Sparrow Hill Comm Prim Sch
SPARROW HILL
Glebe House Sch
MILNROW RD
A640
DRAKE ST
CORPORATION RD
BRIDGEFIELD ST
ROCHDALE IND CTR
SPARTH BOTTOMS RD
ST ALBAN'S CT
ST ALBAN'S TERR
CASTLE AVE
CASTLE HILL
MANCHESTER RD
Beech House Sch
Mandale Park
St John's Prim Sch
Rochdale Sta
STATION RD
TWEEDALE ST
B6224
DURHAM ST
Beechwood Convent Prim Sch
Highfield
Brimrod Prim Sch
B6452
Stoneyfield
120
125
130
135
7
6
5
8
885
890
895
30
E8
1 GREEN LA
2 THORNTREE PL
3 BROOKS PL
4 DAISY ST
5 HALLIWELL ST
6 WHITELEY'S PL
7 HOLLAND RISE
8 PERSHORE
9 ROMSEY
10 QUINTON
11 STAVORDALE
12 THETFORD
13 ULLESTHORPE
14 NEWSTEAD
15 VAYNOR
30
E8
16 OLLERTON
17 LINDISFARNE
18 MELROSE
19 HINTON
20 IBSLEY
21 JOHNSTON
22 ZEDBURGH
E8
23 WAVERLEY
24 EXBURY
25 YARWELL
26 ABBEYDALE
27 KIRKSTALL
28 GLASTONBURY
31

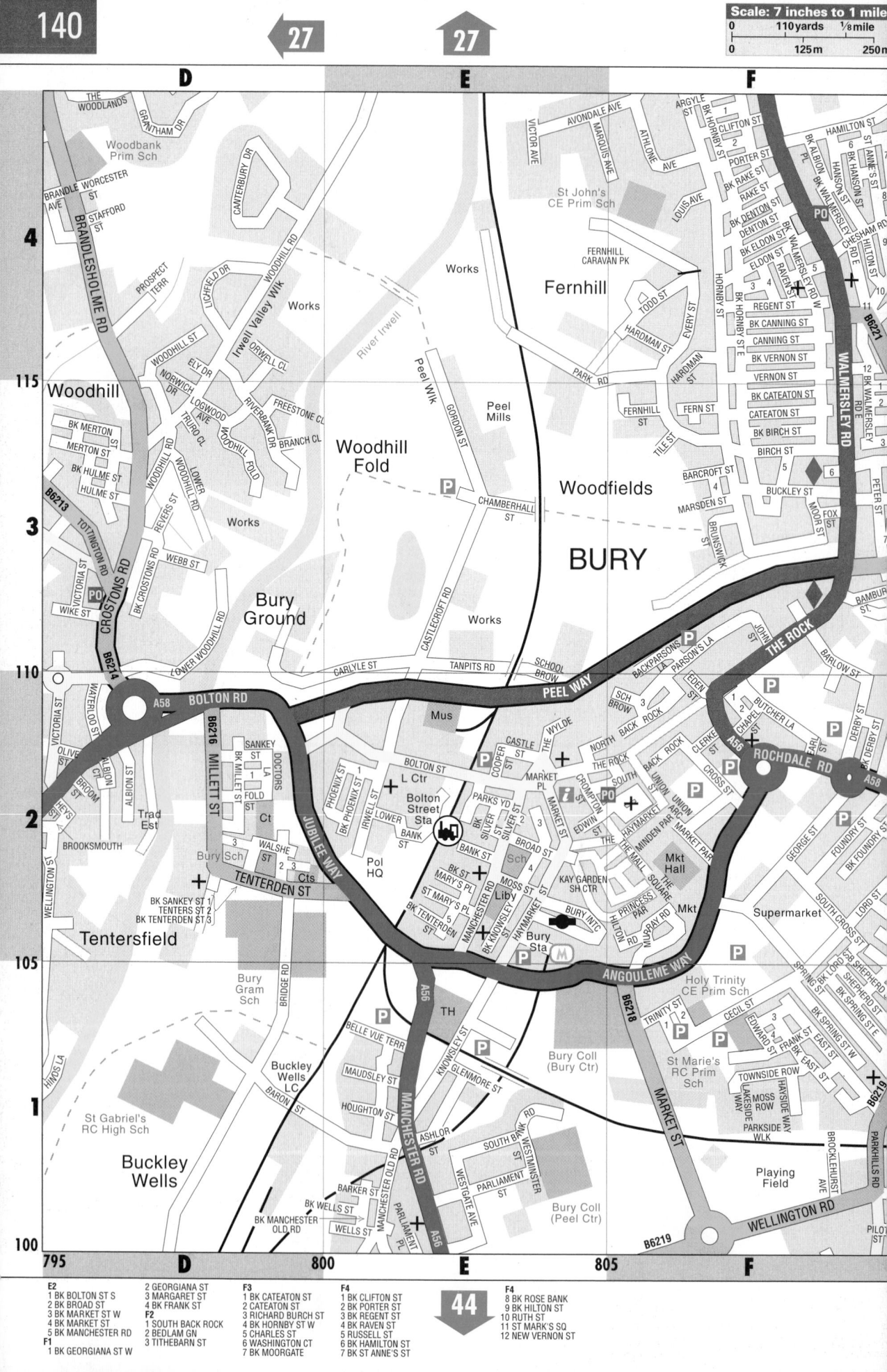

Scale: 7 inches to 1 mile
0   110 yards   ⅛ mile
0   125m   250m

D   E   F

THE WOODLANDS
Woodbank Prim Sch
GRANTHAM DR
BRANDLE WORCESTER AVE
STAFFORD ST
BRANDLESHOLME RD
PROSPECT TERR
CANTERBURY DR
WOODHILL RD
LICHFIELD DR
WOODHILL ST
IRWELL VALLEY WLK
ORWELL CL
River Irwell
Peel Wlk
Works
Works
Works
Fernhill
St John's CE Prim Sch
AVONDALE AVE
MARQUIS AVE
VICTOR AVE
ATHLONE AVE
ARGYLE ST
BK HORNBY ST
CLIFTON ST
PORTER ST
BK RAKE ST
RAKE ST
HAMILTON ST
BK ANNE'S ST
HANSON ST
BK HANSON ST
BK ALBION PL
BK WALMERSLEY RD
PO
CHESHAM RD E
10
B6221
11
WALMERSLEY RD
BK WALMERSLEY RD W
12
BK WALMERSLEY RD E

4

Woodhill
BK MERTON ST
MERTON ST
BK HULME ST
HULME ST
NORWICH DR
LOGWOOD AVE
TRURO CL
REVERS ST
RIVERBANK DR
FREESTONE CL
BRANCH CL
WOODHILL FOLD
LOWER WOODHILL RD
Woodhill Fold
Works
Works
P
CHAMBERHALL ST
Peel Mills
Woodfields
GORDON ST
PARK RD
FERNHILL CARAVAN PK
TODD ST
HARDMAN ST
EVERY ST
FERNHILL ST
HARDMAN ST
FERN ST
TILE ST
REGENT ST
BK CANNING ST
CANNING ST
BK VERNON ST
VERNON ST
BK CATEATON ST
CATEATON ST
BK BIRCH ST
BIRCH ST
BARCROFT ST
MARSDEN ST
BRUNSWICK
BUCKLEY ST
5
6
MOOR ST
FOX ST
PETER ST
BAMBUR

115
B6213
TOTTINGTON RD
CROSTONS RD
VICTORIA ST
WIKE ST
PO
BK CROSTONS RD
WEBB ST
LOWER WOODHILL RD
CASTLECROFT RD
Bury Ground
Works
CARLYLE ST
TANPITS RD
SCHOOL BROW
PEEL WAY
BURY
THE ROCK
JOHN ST
BARLOW ST

3
B6214

110
WATERLOO RD
VICTORIA ST
A58 BOLTON RD
Mus
BACKPARSONS LA
PARSON'S LA
P
BACK ROCK
SCH BROW
EDEN ST
P
BUTCHER LA
DERBY ST
DERBY ST
A56
A58

2
OLIVE ST
ALBION CT
BROOM ST
SELBY ST
BROOKSMOUTH
Trad Est
B6216
MILLETT ST
BK MILLETT ST
FOLD
SANKEY ST
LA
DOCTORS LA
Ct
Bury Sch
WALSHE ST
3
2
Cts
PHOENIX ST
BK PHOENIX ST
IRWELL ST
LOWER BANK ST
BOLTON ST
L Ctr
Bolton Street Sta
BK SILVER ST
SILVER ST
PARKS YD
BROAD ST
BK ST
BANK ST
MARKET PL
COOPER ST
CASTLE ST
THE WYLDE
NORTH BACK ROCK
THE ROCK
SOUTH
BACK ROCK
CLERKE ST
UNION ST
UNION ARC
CROSS ST
ROCHDALE RD
GEORGE ST
FOUNDRY ST
BK FOUNDRY ST
A56

Tentersfield
BK SANKEY ST 1
TENTERS ST 2
BK TENTERDEN ST 3
TENTERDEN ST
Pol HQ
MARY'S PL
BK MARY'S PL
ST MARY'S PL
BK TENTERDEN
MANCHESTER ST
BK KNOWSLEY ST
HAYMARKET
MOSS ST
RUSSELL ST
Liby
KAY GARDEN
SH CTR
BURY INTC
EDWIN ST
EDWARD ST
THE MALL
MINDEN PAR
HAYMARKET
MARKET PAR
Mkt Hall
THE SQUARE
PRINCESS PAR
MURRAY RD
HILTON ST
Mkt
Supermarket
SOUTH CROSS ST
LORD ST
SHEPHERD ST
BK SHEPHERD ST
SPRING ST

105
WELLINGTON ST
HINDS LA
Bury Gram Sch
BRIDGE RD
BELLE VUE TERR
A56
TH
KNOWSLEY ST
Bury Sta
M
ANGOULEME WAY
P
B6218
TRINITY ST
Holy Trinity CE Prim Sch
CECIL ST
SPRING ST EAST
BK SPRING ST E
FRANK ST EAST
BK LORD ST
BK SHEPHERD ST E

1
St Gabriel's RC High Sch
Buckley Wells LC
MAUDSLEY ST
BARON ST
HOUGHTON ST
MANCHESTER RD
ASHLOR
GLENMORE ST
SOUTH BANK RD
Bury Coll (Bury Ctr)
WESTMINSTER AVE
St Marie's RC Prim Sch
MARKET ST
TOWNSIDE ROW
HAYSIDE ROW
LAKESIDE WAY
MOSS ROW
PARKSIDE WLK
Playing Field
B6219

Buckley Wells
BK WELLS ST
BK MANCHESTER OLD RD
WELLS ST
BARKER ST
MANCHESTER OLD RD
PARLIAMENT PL
A56
BARKER ST
SOUTH BANK RD
PARLIAMENT ST
WESTGATE AVE
Bury Coll (Peel Ctr)
WELLINGTON RD
BROCKLEHURST AVE
PARKHILLS RD
PILO ST

100
795   D   800   E   805   F

E2
1 BK BOLTON ST S
2 BK BROAD ST
3 BK MARKET ST W
4 BK MARKET ST
5 BK MANCHESTER RD
F1
1 BK GEORGIANA ST W
2 GEORGIANA ST
3 MARGARET ST
4 BK FRANK ST
F2
1 SOUTH BACK ROCK
2 BEDLAM GN
3 TITHEBARN ST
F3
1 BK CATEATON ST
2 CATEATON ST
3 RICHARD BURCH ST
4 BK HORNBY ST W
5 CHARLES ST
6 WASHINGTON CT
7 BK MOORGATE
F4
1 BK CLIFTON ST
2 BK PORTER ST
3 BK REGENT ST
4 BK RAVEN ST
5 RUSSELL ST
6 BK HAMILTON ST
7 BK ST ANNE'S ST
F4
8 BK ROSE BANK
9 BK HILTON ST
10 RUTH ST
11 ST MARK'S SQ
12 NEW VERNON ST
44

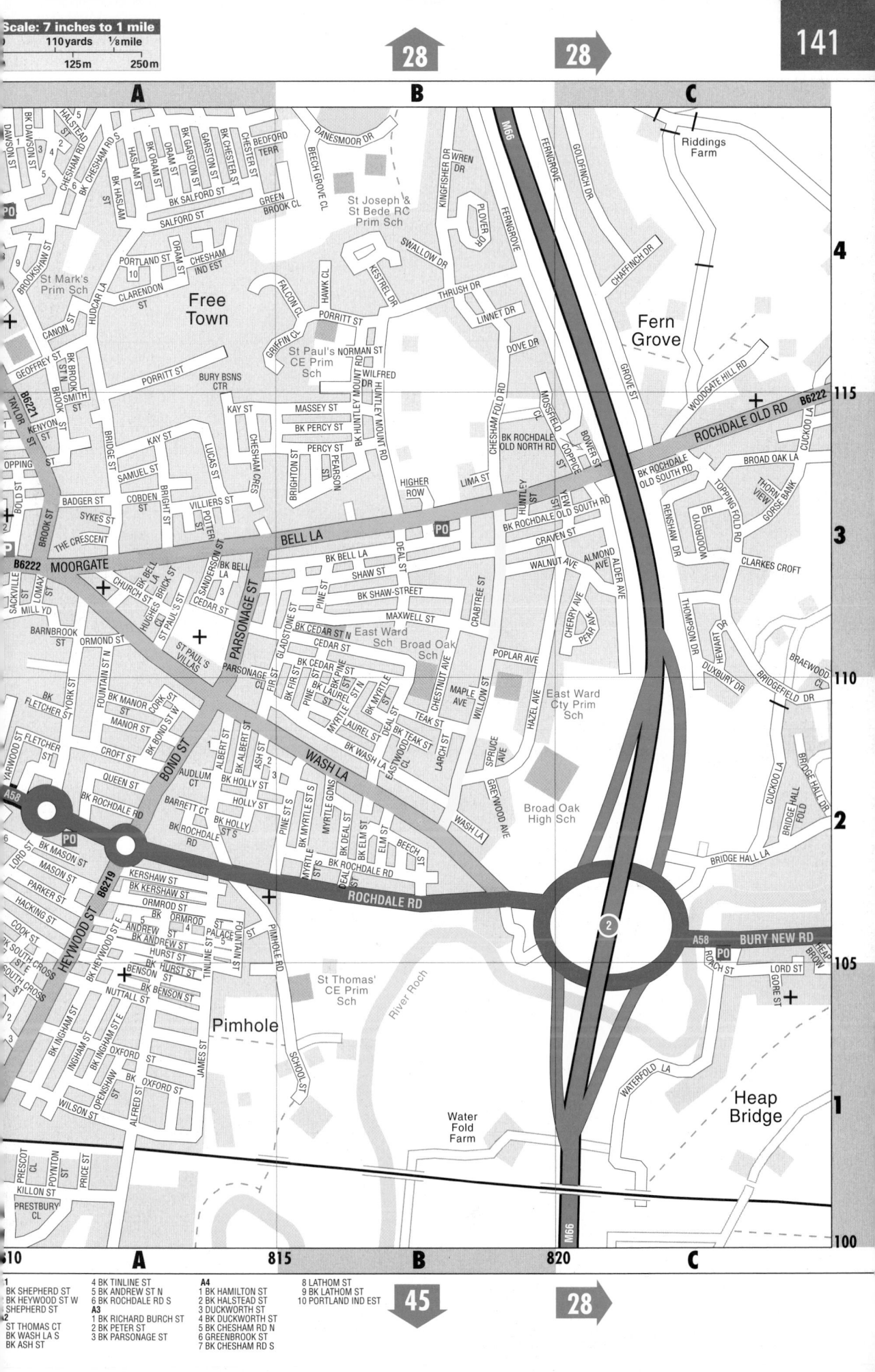

Scale: 7 inches to 1 mile

110 yards   1/8 mile

125m   250m

28 **28**

A   **B**   **C**

4

115

3

110

2

105

1

100

810   **A**   815   **B**   820   **C**

45   **28**

Free Town

St Mark's Prim Sch

BK DAWSON ST
DAWSON ST
HALSTEAD ST
CHESHAM RD S
BK CHESHAM RD S
HASLAM ST
BK HASLAM ST
OWEN ST
ORAM ST
BK GARSTON ST
GARSTON ST
CHESTER ST
BEDFORD TERR
BROOK CL
GREEN
BK SALFORD ST
SALFORD ST
CHESHAM IND EST
PORTLAND ST
HUDCAR LA
CLARENDON ST
BROOKSHAW ST
GEOFFREY ST
CANON ST
BK BROOK ST
BROOK ST
SMITH ST
PORRITT ST
BURY BSNS CTR
KAY ST
B6221
TAYLOR ST
KENYON ST
OPPING
BOLD ST
BRIDGE ST
SAMUEL ST
BADGER ST
SYKES ST
COBDEN ST
THE CRESCENT
B6222
MOORGATE
SACKVILLE
OMAX ST
MILL YD
BARNBROOK ST
ORMOND ST
FOUNTAIN ST N
CHURCH ST
BK BELL LA
HUGHES
ST PAUL'S
CEDAR ST
BRICK ST
SANDERSON ST
PARSONAGE ST
ST PAUL'S VILLAS
PARSONAGE
FIR ST
GLADSTONE ST
PINE ST
BK CEDAR ST N
CEDAR ST
BK CEDAR ST
PINE ST N
FIR ST S
BK FIR ST
LARKPINE
BK LAUREL ST
MYRTLE ST
LAUREL ST
DEAL ST
TEAK ST
BK TEAK ST
BK WASH LA
EASTWOOD CL
WASH LA
BK FLETCHER ST
BK MANOR CT
CORK ST
MANOR ST
BK BOND ST W
BOND ST
CROFT ST
QUEEN ST
AUDLUM CT
ALBERT ST
BK ALBERT ST
ASH ST
HOLLY ST
BK HOLLY ST
BARRETT CT
BK ROCHDALE RD
YARWOOD ST
FLETCHER ST
A58
BK MASON ST
BK HOLLY ST S
PINE ST S
MYRTLE ST S
MYRTLE GDNS
BK DEAL ST
ELM ST
BK ELM ST
BEECH ST
BK ROCHDALE RD
GREYWOOD AVE
ROCHDALE RD
HEYWOOD ST
B6219
KERSHAW ST
BK KERSHAW ST
ORMROD ST
BK ORMROD
ST PALACE
FOUNTAIN ST
PIMHOLE RD
LORD ST
MASON ST
PARKER ST
HACKING ST
COOK ST
BK SOUTH CROSS
SOUTH CROSS ST E
BK HEYWOOD ST E
BK ANDREW ST
ANDREW ST
HURST ST
BK HURST ST
BENSON ST
BK BENSON ST
NUTTALL ST
INGHAM ST
JAMES ST
TINLINE ST
SCHOOL ST
BK INGHAM ST
OXFORD ST
OPENSHAW ST
BK OXFORD ST
WILSON ST
ALFRED ST
PRESCOT CL
POYNTON ST
PRICE ST
KILLON ST
PRESTBURY CL
Pimhole
St Thomas' CE Prim Sch
River Roch
Water Fold Farm

St Joseph & St Bede RC Prim Sch
DANESMOOR DR
BEECH GROVE CL
SWALLOW DR
FALCON CL
HAWK CL
KESTREL DR
PORRITT ST
GRIFFIN CL
St Paul's CE Prim Sch
NORMAN ST
WILFRED ST
HUNTLEY MOUNT RD
BK HUNTLEY MOUNT RD
MASSEY ST
BK PERCY ST
PERCY ST
BRIGHTON ST
PEARSON
HIGHER ROW
BELL LA
SHAW ST
BK SHAW-STREET
MAXWELL ST
CRABTREE ST
East Ward Sch
Broad Oak Sch
CHESTNUT AVE
MAPLE AVE
WILLOW ST
POPLAR AVE
SPRUCE AVE
Broad Oak High Sch
HAZEL AVE
KINGFISHER DR
WREN DR
PLOVER DR
THRUSH DR
LINNET DR
DOVE DR
CHESHAM FOLD RD
BK ROCHDALE OLD NORTH RD
LIMA ST
HUNTLEY ST
BK ROCHDALE OLD SOUTH RD
ROCHDALE OLD SOUTH RD
WALNUT AVE
CRAVEN ST
MOSSFIELD
COPPICE
BOWER ST
CHERRY AVE
PEAR AVE
ALMOND AVE
ALDER AVE
PO
M66
FERNGROVE
GROVE ST
Fern Grove
GOLDFINCH DR
CHAFFINCH DR
Riddings Farm
WOODGATE HILL RD
ROCHDALE OLD RD
B6222
115
BROAD OAK LA
THORN VIEW
GORSE BANK
TOPPING FOLD RD
RENSHAW DR
DUXBURY DR
THOMPSON DR
HEWART ST
BRIDGEFIELD DR
CLARKES CROFT
BRAEWOOD CL
CUCKOO ST
CUCKOO LA
BRIDGE HALL FOLD
BRIDGE HALL DR
BRIDGE HALL LA
ROCH ST
A58
BURY NEW RD
East Ward Cty Prim Sch
PO
LORD ST
GORE ST
HEAP BRGH
WATERFOLD LA
Heap Bridge

1
BK SHEPHERD ST
BK HEYWOOD ST W
SHEPHERD ST
2
ST THOMAS CT
BK WASH LA S
BK ASH ST

4 BK TINLINE ST
5 BK ANDREW ST N
6 BK ROCHDALE RD S
A3
1 BK RICHARD BURCH ST
2 BK PETER ST
3 BK PARSONAGE ST

A4
1 BK HAMILTON ST
2 BK HALSTEAD ST
3 DUCKWORTH ST
4 BK DUCKWORTH ST
5 BK CHESHAM RD N
6 GREENBROOK ST
7 BK CHESHAM RD S

8 LATHOM ST
9 BK LATHOM ST
10 PORTLAND IND EST

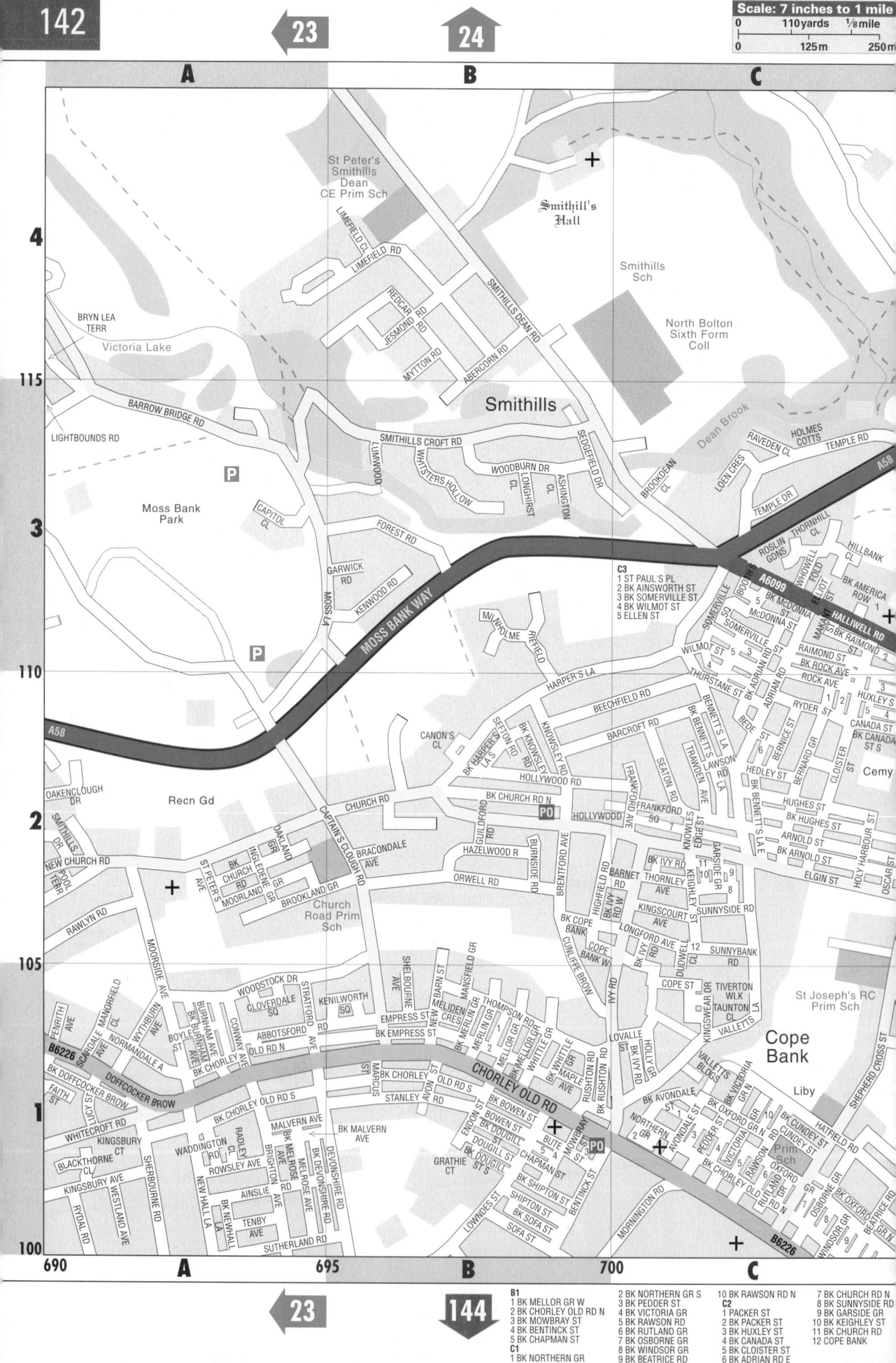
23
24
Scale: 7 inches to 1 mile
0 110 yards 1/8 mile
0 125m 250m
A
B
C
St Peter's Smithills Dean CE Prim Sch
Smithill's Hall
Smithills Sch
North Bolton Sixth Form Coll
Smithills
Victoria Lake
BRYN LEA TERR
LIGHTBOUNDS RD
BARROW BRIDGE RD
Moss Bank Park
CAPITOL CL
Dean Brook
RAVEDEN CL
HOLMES COTTS
TEMPLE RD
A58
LOEN CRES
TEMPLE DR
BROOKDEAN CL
SEDGEFIELD DR
ASHINGTON CL
LONGHIRST CL
WOODBURN DR
WHITSTERS HOLLOW
SMITHILLS CROFT RD
LUMWOOD
LIMEFIELD CL
LIMEFIELD RD
REDCAR RD
JESMOND RD
MYTTON RD
ABERCORN RD
SMITHILLS DEAN RD
FOREST RD
GARWICK RD
KENWOOD RD
MOSS LA
MOSS BANK WAY
MILNHOLME
RIEFIELD
C3
1 ST PAUL'S PL
2 BK AINSWORTH ST
3 BK SOMERVILLE ST
4 BK WILMOT ST
5 ELLEN ST
A6099
HALLIWELL RD
THORNHILL CL
ROSLIN GDNS
HILLBANK CL
BK AMERICA ROW
WHOWELL FOLD
ELLIOT ST
MAKANT ST
BOOTH ST
SOMERVILLE SQ
SOMERVILLE ST
BK McDONNA ST
McDONNA ST
BK RAIMOND ST
RAIMOND ST
BK ROCK AVE
ROCK AVE
HUXLEY ST
RYDER ST
CANADA ST
BK CANADA ST S
WILMOT ST
THURSTANE ST
ADRIAN RD
BEDE ST
BERNICE ST
BERNARD GR
CLOISTER ST
Cemy
HARPER'S LA
BEECHFIELD RD
BARCROFT RD
BK BENNETT'S LA
BENNETT'S LA
TRAWDEN AVE
LAWSON RD
HEDLEY ST
HUGHES ST
BK HUGHES ST
ARNOLD ST
BK ARNOLD ST
HOLY HARBOUR ST
ELGIN ST
OSCAR ST
CANON'S CL
SEFTON RD
BK KNOWSLEY RD
KNOWSLEY RD
BK HARPER'S LA S
HOLLYWOOD RD
SEATON RD
FRANKFORD AVE
FRANKFORD SQ
HOLLYWOOD
KNOWLES ST
EDGE ST
GARSIDE GR
BK IVY RD
THORNLEY AVE
BARNET RD
KINGSCOURT AVE
KEIGHLEY ST
SUNNYSIDE RD
A58
Recn Gd
OAKENCLOUGH DR
SMITHILLS DR
NEW CHURCH RD
POOL TERR
CHURCH RD
CAPTAIN'S CLOUGH RD
BK CHURCH RD N
PO
GUILDFORD RD
HAZELWOOD R
BURNSIDE RD
BRENTFORD AVE
ORWELL RD
HIGHFIELD RD
BK IVY RD W
OAKLAND GR
INGLEDENE GR
BK CHURCH RD
MOORLAND GR
ST PETER'S AVE
BRACONDALE AVE
BROOKLAND GR
Church Road Prim Sch
RAWLYN RD
BK COPE BANK
COPE BANK W
CUNLIFFE BROW
LONGFORD AVE
BK IVY RD
DUDWELL CL
SUNNYBANK RD
COPE ST
TIVERTON WLK
TAUNTON CL
KINGSWEAR DR
VALLETTS LA
St Joseph's RC Prim Sch
Cope Bank
IVY RD
LOVALLE ST
BK IVY RD
HOLLY GR
MOORSIDE AVE
WOODSTOCK DR
CLOVERDALE SQ
STRATFORD AVE
KENILWORTH SQ
SHELBOURNE AVE
NEW BARN ST
MANSFIELD GR
MELIDEN CRES
THOMPSON RD
BK MERLIN GR
MERLIN GR
MELLOR GR
BK MELLOR GR
WHITTLE GR
BK WHITTLE GR
MAPLE AVE
RUSHTON RD
BK RUSHTON RD
EMPRESS ST
BK EMPRESS ST
ABBOTSFORD RD
OLD RD N
CONWAY AVE
BURNHAM AVE
BK BURNHAM AVE
BOYLE ST
WYTHBURN AVE
NORMANDALE A
MANORFIELD CL
SCARDALE AVE
PENRITH AVE
B6226
DOFFCOCKER BROW
BK DOFFCOCKER BROW
FAITH ST
LUCY ST
BK CHORLEY OLD RD
CHORLEY OLD RD
BK CHORLEY OLD RD S
MARCUS ST
BK CHORLEY OLD RD S
STANLEY RD
AVON ST
WHITECROFT RD
KINGSBURY CT
BLACKTHORNE CL
KINGSBURY AVE
WESTLAND AVE
RYDAL RD
SHERBOURNE RD
WADDINGTON RD
RADLEY CL
ROWSLEY AVE
NEW HALL LA
BK NEWHALL LA
AINSLIE RD
TENBY AVE
SUTHERLAND RD
BRIGHTON AVE
BK MELROSE AVE
MELROSE AVE
MALVERN AVE
BK DEVONSHIRE RD
DEVONSHIRE RD
BK MALVERN AVE
GRATHIE CT
ENDON ST
BK BOWEN ST
BOWEN ST
BK DOUGILL ST
DOUGILL ST
BK DOUGILL ST S
BUTE ST
CHAPMAN ST
MOWBRAY ST
PO
BK SHIPTON ST
SHIPTON ST
BK SOFA ST
SOFA ST
LOWNDES ST
BENTINCK ST
MORNINGTON RD
VALLETTS BLDGS
BK AVONDALE ST
AVONDALE ST
NORTHERN GR
BK VICTORIA GR N
BK OXFORD GR
PEDDER ST
VICTORIA GR
BK CHORLEY OLD RD N
RAWSON RD
OXFORD GR
RUTLAND GR
Prim Sch
Liby
BK CUNDEY ST
CUNDEY ST
HATFIELD RD
SHEPHERD CROSS ST
OSBORNE GR
BK OXFORD GR
WINDSOR GR
BEATRICE RD
GR N
B6226
690
695
700
100
105
110
115
1
2
3
4
23
144
B1
1 BK MELLOR GR W
2 BK CHORLEY OLD RD N
3 BK MOWBRAY ST
4 BK BENTINCK ST
5 BK CHAPMAN ST
C1
1 BK NORTHERN GR
2 BK NORTHERN GR S
3 BK PEDDER ST
4 BK VICTORIA GR
5 BK RAWSON RD
6 BK RUTLAND GR
7 BK OSBORNE GR
8 BK WINDSOR GR
9 BK BEATRICE RD
10 BK RAWSON RD N
C2
1 PACKER ST
2 BK PACKER ST
3 BK HUXLEY ST
4 BK CANADA ST
5 BK CLOISTER ST
6 BK ADRIAN RD E
7 BK CHURCH RD N
8 BK SUNNYSIDE RD
9 BK GARSIDE GR
10 BK KEIGHLEY ST
11 BK CHURCH RD
12 COPE BANK

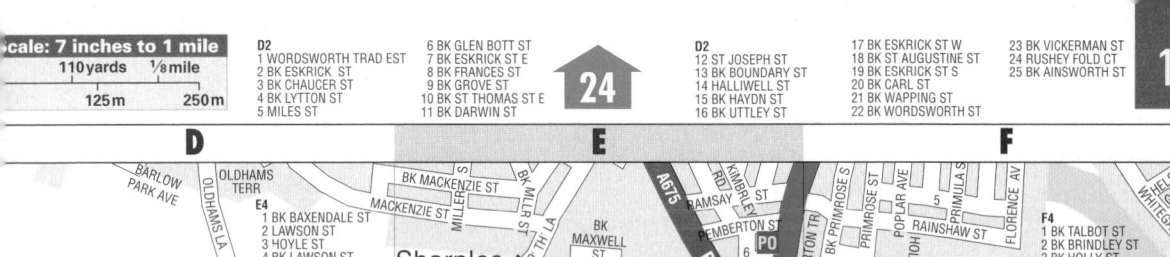

Scale: 7 inches to 1 mile
110 yards | 1/8 mile
125 m | 250 m

D2
1 WORDSWORTH TRAD EST
2 BK ESKRICK ST
3 BK CHAUCER ST
4 BK LYTTON ST
5 MILES ST

6 BK GLEN BOTT ST
7 BK ESKRICK ST E
8 BK FRANCES ST
9 BK GROVE ST
10 BK ST THOMAS ST E
11 BK DARWIN ST

24

D2
12 ST JOSEPH ST
13 BK BOUNDARY ST
14 BK HALLIWELL ST
15 BK HAYDN ST
16 BK UTTLEY ST

17 BK ESKRICK ST W
18 BK ST AUGUSTINE ST
19 BK ESKRICK ST S
20 BK CARL ST
21 BK WAPPING ST
22 BK WORDSWORTH ST

23 BK VICKERMAN ST
24 RUSHEY FOLD CT
25 BK AINSWORTH ST

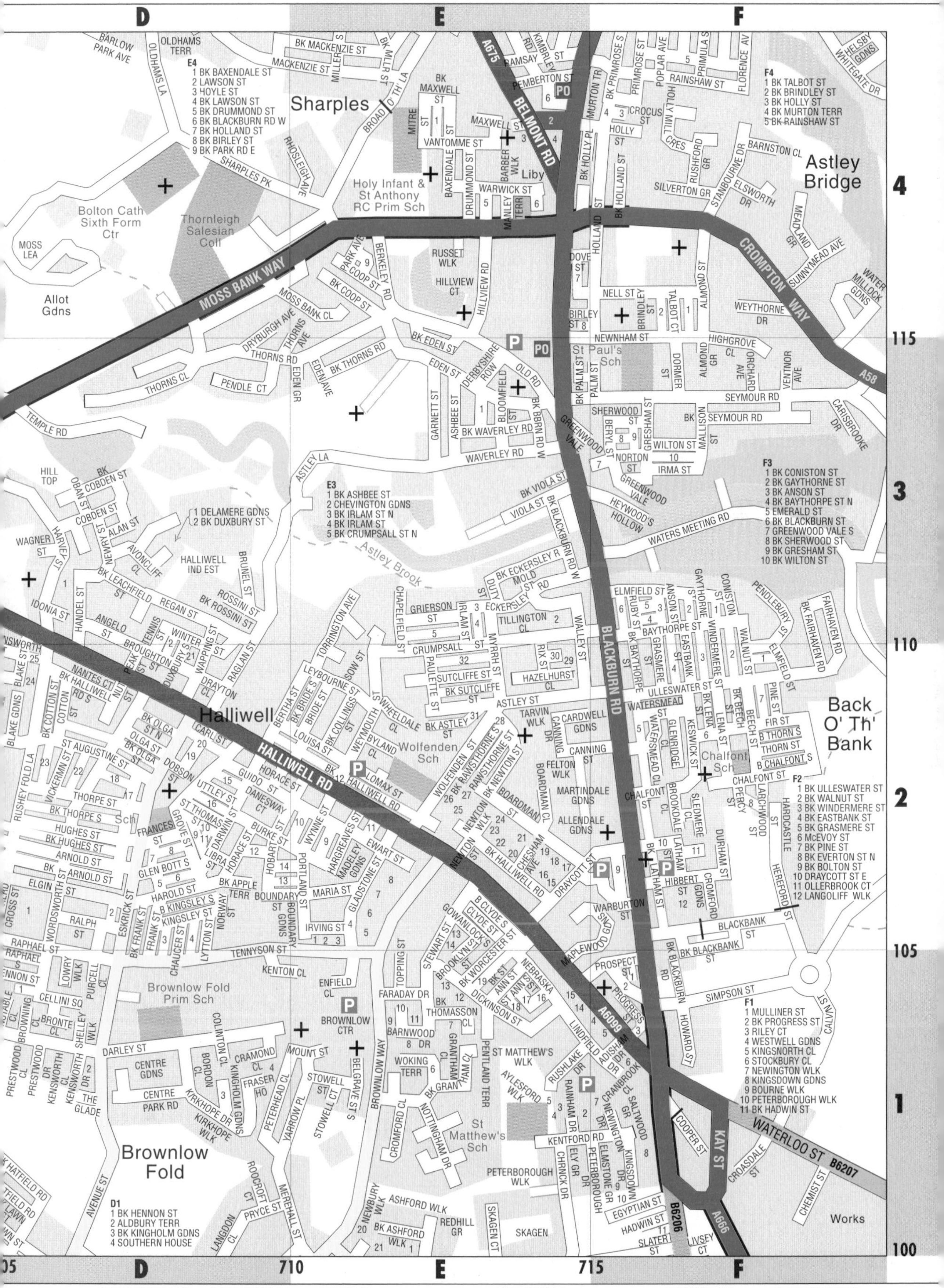

E4
1 BK BAXENDALE ST
2 LAWSON ST
3 HOYLE ST
4 BK LAWSON ST
5 BK DRUMMOND ST
6 BK BLACKBURN RD W
7 BK HOLLAND ST
8 BK BIRLEY ST
9 BK PARK RD E

F4
1 BK TALBOT ST
2 BK BRINDLEY ST
3 BK HOLLY ST
4 BK MURTON TERR
5 BK RAINSHAW ST

E3
1 BK ASHBEE ST
2 CHEVINGTON GDNS
3 BK IRLAM ST N
4 BK IRLAM ST
5 BK CRUMPSALL ST N

1 DELAMERE GDNS
2 BK DUXBURY ST

F3
1 BK CONISTON ST
2 BK GAYTHORNE ST
3 BK ANSON ST
4 BK BAYTHORPE ST N
5 EMERALD ST
6 BK BLACKBURN ST
7 GREENWOOD VALE S
8 BK SHERWOOD ST
9 BK GRESHAM ST
10 BK WILTON ST

F2
1 BK ULLESWATER ST
2 BK WALNUT ST
3 BK WINDERMERE ST
4 BK EASTBANK ST
5 BK GRASMERE ST
6 MCEVOY ST
7 BK PINE ST
8 BK EVERTON ST N
9 BK BOLTON ST
10 DRAYCOTT ST E
11 OLLERBROOK CT
12 LANGOLIFF WLK

F1
1 MULLINER ST
2 BK PROGRESS ST
3 RILEY CT
4 WESTWELL GDNS
5 KINGSNORTH CL
6 STOCKBURY CL
7 NEWINGTON WLK
8 KINGSDOWN GDNS
9 BOURNE WLK
10 PETERBOROUGH WLK
11 BK HADWIN ST

D1
1 BK HENNON ST
2 ALDBURY TERR
3 BK KINGHOLM GDNS
4 SOUTHERN HOUSE

IDHURST CL
AINHAM GR
WOODCHURCH CL
WESTMARSH CL
OUNTFIELD WLK
K WOKING GDNS
HOMASSON CL

8 ST MATTHEW'S TERR
9 FOSTER TERR
10 BARNWOOD TERR
11 BARNWOOD CL
12 DICKINSON TERR
13 DICKINSON CL
14 HIGHBROOK GR
15 FERNHURST GR

16 GLENTHORNE ST
17 BK NEVADA ST
18 NEVADA ST
19 WORCESTER ST
20 SHAFTSBURY CL
21 FARNHAM CL
E2
1 IRVING HOUSE

2 KEATS WLK
3 TENNYSON WLK
4 BELGRAVE ST
5 BELGRAVE GDNS
6 GLADSTONE CL
7 LONGTOWN GDNS
8 WHITCHURCH GDNS
9 BK HARGREAVES ST

10 BK WYNNE ST
11 BK EWART ST
12 MARSH ST
13 BK STEWART ST
14 BOSTON ST
15 WITNEY CL
16 WATFORD ST
17 WESTWICH TERR

18 BENWICK TERR
19 YORK TERR
20 CHESTER WLK
21 HUNTINGDON WLK
22 LANCASTER WLK
23 NEWTON TERR
24 LANCASTER TERR
25 KEMPSTON GDNS

26 WOLFENDEN TERR
27 TANWORTH WLK
28 CHARLOTTE ST
29 HOLYHURST WLK
30 PINEWOOD CL
31 BK WOLFENDEN ST
32 BK CRUMPSALL ST

Scale: 7 inches to 1 mile
0 110 yards 1/8 mile
0 125m 250

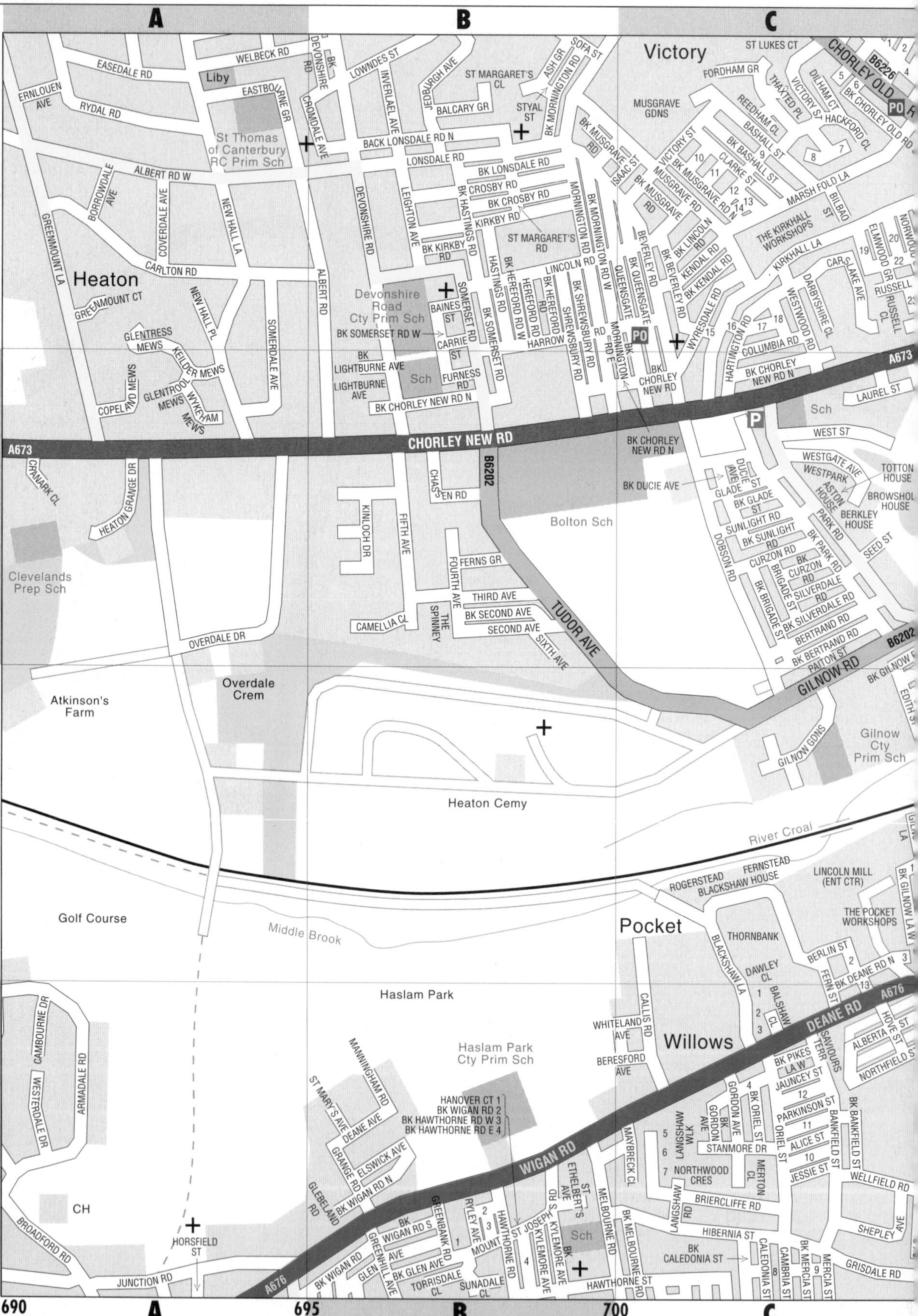

A **B** **C**

Victory

Heaton

Devonshire Road Cty Prim Sch

St Thomas of Canterbury RC Prim Sch

CHORLEY NEW RD

A673

Bolton Sch

Clevelands Prep Sch

Atkinson's Farm

Overdale Crem

Heaton Cemy

River Croal

Golf Course

Middle Brook

Haslam Park

Haslam Park Cty Prim Sch

Pocket

Willows

Gilnow Cty Prim Sch

GILNOW RD

TUDOR AVE

DEANE RD

WIGAN RD

A676

CH

8 095 7 090 6 085 5 080

690 695 700

C5
1 TORBAY CL
2 BLACKSHAW ROW
3 LANGLEY DR
4 BK DEANE RD
5 HEARLESDEN CRES
6 NEASDEN GR
7 COLINDALE CL
8 CAMBRIA SQ
9 NORTHUMBRIA ST
10 BK ALICE ST
11 BK PARKINSON ST
12 BK JAUNCEY ST
13 HOVE ST N

C6
1 BK VINE ST
2 BK FERN ST E
3 WASHINGTON ST
4 RYLEY ST
5 BK GILNOW LA

C8
1 BK BATTENBERG RD
2 BATTENBERG RD
3 BK WALDECK ST
4 BK CHORLEY OLD RD N
5 MOORE'S CT
6 TURK ST
7 CAVENHAM GR
8 METFIELD PL
9 MABEL ST
10 BK VICTORY ST E
11 LONGDEN ST
12 BK LONGDEN ST
13 BK CLARKE ST
14 BK MARSH FOLD LA
15 SCORTON ST
16 BK HARTINGTON RD
17 BK COLUMBIA RD
18 BK WESTWOOD RD
19 BK ELMWOOD GR W
20 BK ELMWOOD GR
21 BK NORWOOD GR
22 BK RUSSELL ST
23 BK RUSSELL CL

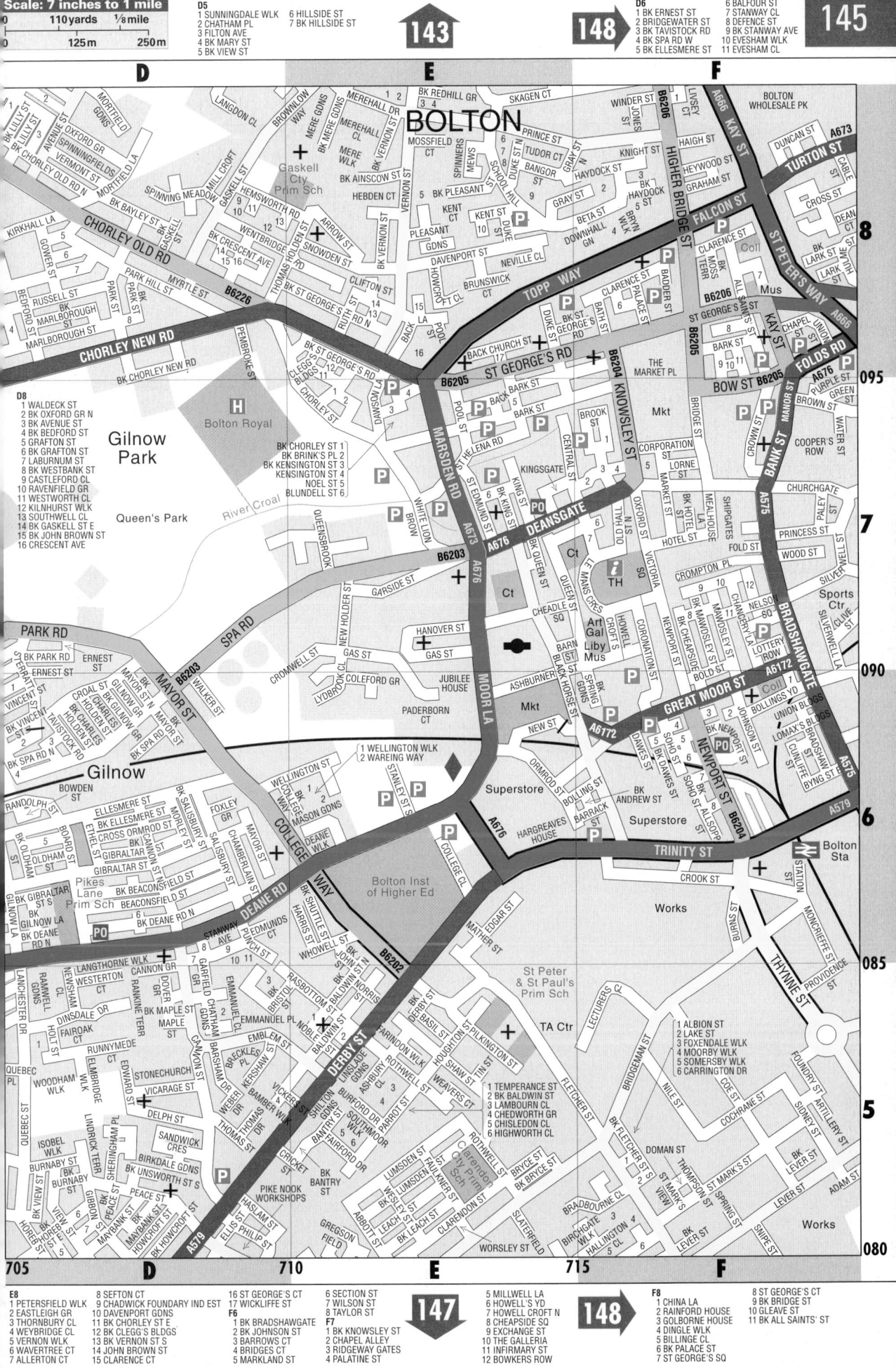

Scale: 7 inches to 1 mile
0 110 yards 1/8 mile
0 125 m 250 m
D5
1 SUNNINGDALE WLK
2 CHATHAM PL
3 FILTON AVE
4 BK MARY ST
5 BK VIEW ST
6 HILLSIDE ST
7 BK HILLSIDE ST
143
148
D6
1 BK ERNEST ST
2 BRIDGEWATER ST
3 BK TAVISTOCK RD
4 BK SPA RD W
5 BK ELLESMERE ST
6 BALFOUR ST
7 STANWAY CL
8 DEFENCE ST
9 BK STANWAY AVE
10 EVESHAM WLK
11 EVESHAM CL
145
D
E
F
BOLTON
BOLTON WHOLESALE PK
Gaskell Cty Prim Sch
CHORLEY OLD RD
CHORLEY NEW RD
TOPP WAY
FALCON ST
HIGHER BRIDGE ST
KAY ST
ST PETER'S WAY
TURTON ST
ST GEORGE'S RD
KNOWSLEY ST
THE MARKET PL
BOW ST
FOLDS RD
Bolton Royal
Gilnow Park
Queen's Park
River Croal
D8
1 WALDECK ST
2 BK OXFORD GR N
3 BK AVENUE ST
4 BK BEDFORD ST
5 GRAFTON ST
6 BK GRAFTON ST
7 LABURNUM ST
8 BK WESTBANK ST
9 CASTLEFORD CL
10 RAVENFIELD GR
11 WESTWORTH CL
12 KILNHURST WLK
13 SOUTHWELL CL
14 BK GASKELL ST E
15 BK JOHN BROWN ST
16 CRESCENT AVE
BK CHORLEY ST 1
BK BRINK'S PL 2
BK KENSINGTON ST 3
KENSINGTON ST 4
NOEL ST 5
BLUNDELL ST 6
MARSDEN RD
DEANSGATE
Mkt
TH
Ct
Art Gal Liby Mus
BANK ST
BRADSHAWGATE
CHURCHGATE
Sports Ctr
SPA RD
PARK RD
MAYOR ST
MOOR LA
GREAT MOOR ST
NEWPORT ST
JUBILEE HOUSE
PADERBORN CT
Gilnow
1 WELLINGTON WLK
2 WAREING WAY
Superstore
HARGREAVES HOUSE
TRINITY ST
Bolton Sta
COLLEGE WAY
DEANE RD
Pikes Lane Prim Sch
Bolton Inst of Higher Ed
Works
St Peter & St Paul's Prim Sch
TA Ctr
DERBY ST
THYNNE ST
1 ALBION ST
2 LAKE ST
3 FOXENDALE WLK
4 MOORBY WLK
5 SOMERSBY WLK
6 CARRINGTON DR
1 TEMPERANCE ST
2 BK BALDWIN ST
3 LAMBOURN CL
4 CHEDWORTH GR
5 CHISLEDON CL
6 HIGHWORTH CL
Clarendon Cty Prim Sch
PIKE NOOK WORKSHOPS
FLETCHER ST
095
090
085
080
8
7
6
5
705
710
715
E8
1 PETERSFIELD WLK
2 EASTLEIGH GR
3 THORNBURY CL
4 WEYBRIDGE CL
5 VERNON WLK
6 WAVERTREE CT
7 ALLERTON CT
8 SEFTON CT
9 CHADWICK FOUNDARY IND EST
10 DAVENPORT GDNS
11 BK CHORLEY ST E
12 BK CLEGG'S BLDGS
13 BK VERNON ST S
14 JOHN BROWN ST
15 CLARENCE CT
16 ST GEORGE'S CT
17 WICKLIFFE ST
F6
1 BK BRADSHAWGATE
2 BK JOHNSON ST
3 BARROWS CT
4 BRIDGES CT
5 MARKLAND ST
6 SECTION ST
7 WILSON ST
8 TAYLOR ST
F7
1 BK KNOWSLEY ST
2 CHAPEL ALLEY
3 RIDGEWAY GATES
4 PALATINE ST
147
5 MILLWELL LA
6 HOWELL'S YD
7 HOWELL CROFT N
8 CHEAPSIDE SQ
9 EXCHANGE ST
10 THE GALLERIA
11 INFIRMARY ST
12 BOWKERS ROW
148
F8
1 CHINA LA
2 RAINFORD HOUSE
3 GOLBORNE HOUSE
4 DINGLE WLK
5 BILLINGE CL
6 BK PALACE ST
7 ST GEORGE'S SQ
8 ST GEORGE'S CT
9 BK BRIDGE ST
10 GLEAVE ST
11 BK ALL SAINTS' ST

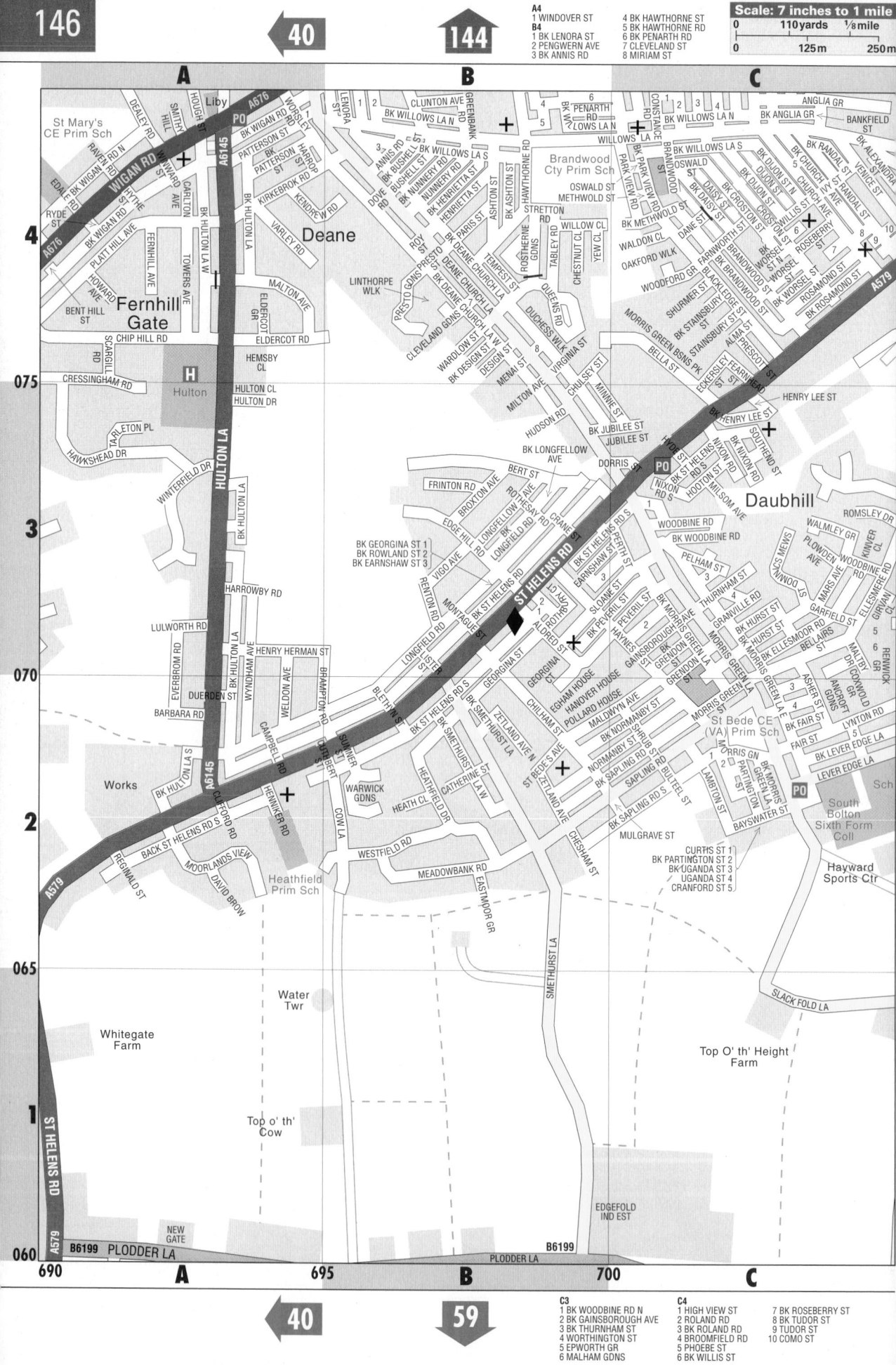

◄ 40

▲ 144

A4
1 WINDOVER ST
B4
1 BK LENORA ST
2 PENGWERN AVE
3 BK ANNIS RD
4 BK HAWTHORNE ST
5 BK HAWTHORNE RD
6 BK PENARTH RD
7 CLEVELAND ST
8 MIRIAM ST

St Mary's CE Prim Sch

Fernhill Gate

Deane

Hulton

Daubhill

Brandwood City Prim Sch

St Bede CE (VA) Prim Sch

South Bolton Sixth Form Coll

Hayward Sports Ctr

Heathfield Prim Sch

Whitegate Farm

Water Twr

Top o' th' Cow

Top O' th' Height Farm

Edgefold Ind Est

New Gate

Works

BK GEORGINA ST 1
BK ROWLAND ST 2
BK EARNSHAW ST 3

CURTIS ST 1
BK PARTINGTON ST 2
BK UGANDA ST 3
UGANDA ST 4
CRANFORD ST 5

075

070

065

060

4

3

2

1

690   A   695   B   700   C

C3
1 BK WOODBINE RD N
2 BK GAINSBOROUGH AVE
3 BK THURNHAM ST
4 WORTHINGTON ST
5 EPWORTH GR
6 MALHAM GDNS

C4
1 HIGH VIEW ST
2 ROLAND RD
3 BK ROLAND RD
4 BROOMFIELD RD
5 PHOEBE ST
6 BK WILLIS ST

7 BK ROSEBERRY ST
8 BK TUDOR ST
9 TUDOR ST
10 COMO ST

D4
1 BROADHURST CT
2 BRANDON ST
3 BROADHURST ST
4 BK BRANDON ST W
5 BK BRANDON ST

6 BK WILLOWS LA
7 MELTHAM PL
8 MARTHA ST
9 ALEXANDRA ST
10 BK ST HELENS RD
11 BK SANDON ST W

D4
12 BK SUNNING HILL ST
13 SUNNING HILL ST
14 BK AUBURN ST
15 SWAN LA
16 BK RIBBLESDALE RD

E4
1 BK FLORA ST
2 BK HIGH ST W
3 JOHN CROSS ST
4 SPRING MILL CL
5 BK ROXALINA ST

145 ◀

42 ▶

59 ▼

42 ▶

Grid references: D E F — 4 075 3 070 2 065 1 060

Bottom grid: 705 D 710 E 715 F

1 CARRINGTON DR
2 BK LEVER ST
3 BINBROOK WLK
4 SANDHAM WLK
5 SANDHAM ST
6 BK RISHTON LA
7 MARLBROOK WLK

WETHERAL DR 1
GREENHEAD WLK 2
LANGDALE ST 3
BK MILFORD RD 4

F3
1 BK CESTRIAN ST
2 BK RUDOLPH ST
3 NIGHTINGALES WLK
4 BK ALDER ST
5 BK BEECHWOOD ST
6 BK MEREDITH ST
7 WADE ST

8 BK CALVERT RD

Map labels:
Works, Liby, Sch, DERBY ST, A579, London St, Bishop Bridgeman CE Prim Sch, St Williams' RC Prim Sch, Lever Edge Prim Sch, Hayward Sch, Great Lever & Farnworth Golf Course, Lever Edge, Will Hill, Holme Fold Farm, Scot Meadow Farm, Townleys Farm, Bolton District General, Haywood Park View, Recreation Field, Minerva Rd

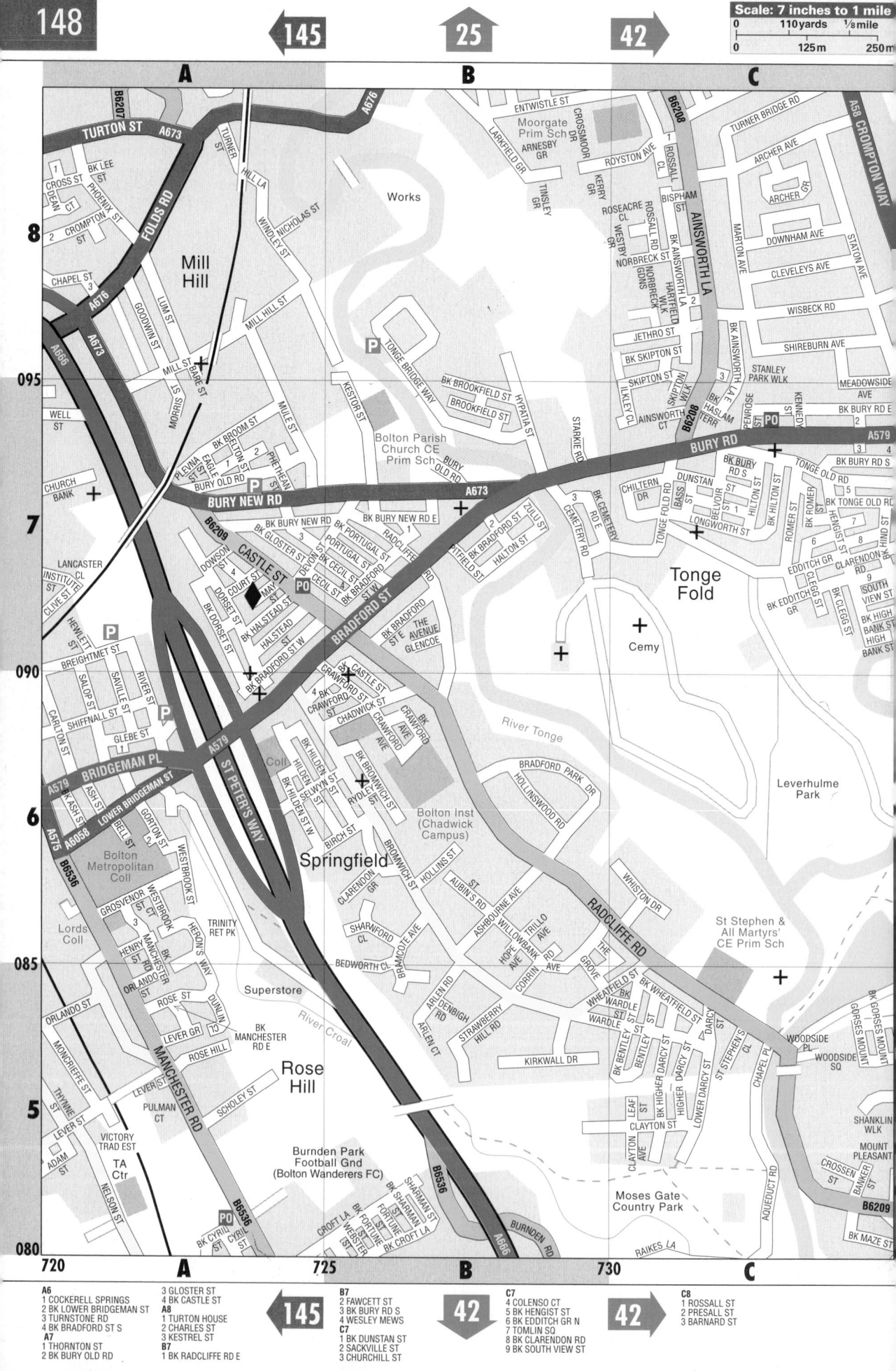

145 25 42

Scale: 7 inches to 1 mile
0 110 yards ⅛ mile
0 125m 250m

A B C

8

095

7

090

085

6

5

080

720 A 725 B 730 C

A6
1 COCKERELL SPRINGS
2 BK LOWER BRIDGEMAN ST
3 TURNSTONE RD
4 BK BRADFORD ST S
A7
1 THORNTON ST
2 BK BURY OLD RD

3 GLOSTER ST
4 BK CASTLE ST
A8
1 TURTON HOUSE
2 CHARLES ST
3 KESTREL ST
B7
1 BK RADCLIFFE RD E

B7
2 FAWCETT ST
3 BK BURY RD S
4 WESLEY MEWS
C7
1 BK DUNSTAN ST
2 SACKVILLE ST
3 CHURCHILL ST

C7
4 COLENSO CT
5 BK HENGIST ST
6 BK EDDITCH GR N
7 TOMLIN SQ
8 BK CLARENDON RD
9 BK SOUTH VIEW ST

C8
1 ROSSALL ST
2 PRESALL ST
3 BARNARD ST

145 42 42

Key map places (on map image):

Mill Hill, Works, Moorgate Prim Sch, Bolton Parish Church CE Prim Sch, Tonge Fold, Cemy, River Tonge, Leverhulme Park, Lancaster Institute, Bolton Inst (Chadwick Campus), Springfield, Bolton Metropolitan Coll, Lords Coll, St Stephen & All Martyrs' CE Prim Sch, Superstore, Rose Hill, Burden Park Football Gnd (Bolton Wanderers FC), Moses Gate Country Park, Woodside Sq, Shanklin Wlk, Mount Pleasant

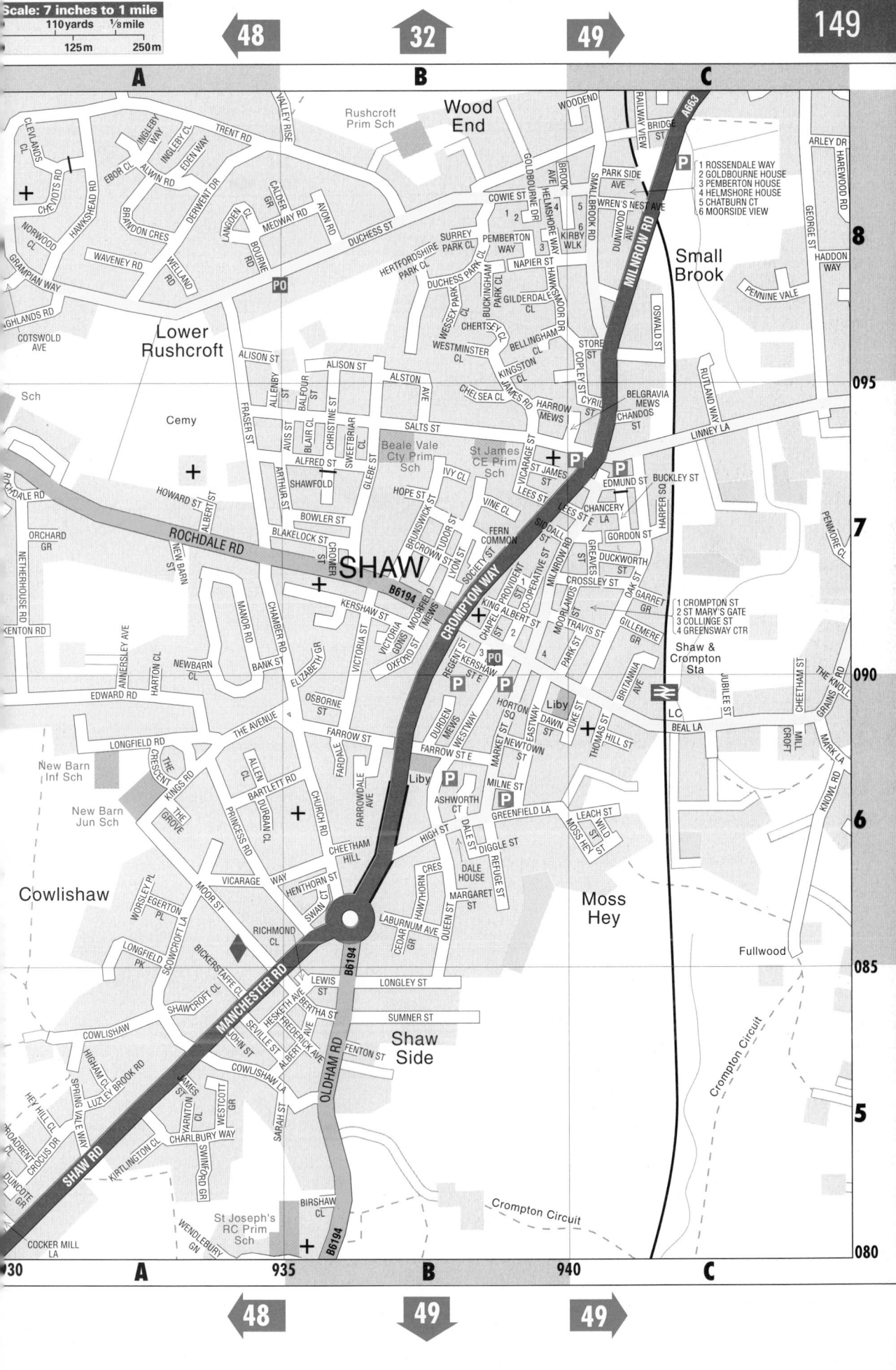

Scale: 7 inches to 1 mile
110 yards
1/8 mile
125 m
250 m
48
32
49
A
B
C
Wood End
Rushcroft Prim Sch
Lower Rushcroft
Small Brook
SHAW
Cowlishaw
Moss Hey
Shaw Side
Fullwood
Shaw & Crompton Sta
Beale Vale Cty Prim Sch
St James CE Prim Sch
New Barn Inf Sch
New Barn Jun Sch
St Joseph's RC Prim Sch
Cemy
Sch
Liby
PO
LC
FERN COMMON
DALE HOUSE
Crompton Circuit
1 ROSSENDALE WAY
2 GOLDBOURNE HOUSE
3 PEMBERTON HOUSE
4 HELMSHORE HOUSE
5 CHATBURN CT
6 MOORSIDE VIEW
1 CROMPTON ST
2 ST MARY'S GATE
3 COLLINGE ST
4 GREENSWAY CTR
ROCHDALE RD
CROMPTON WAY
MILNROW RD
MANCHESTER RD
SHAW RD
OLDHAM RD
A663
B6194
DUCHESS ST
LINNEY LA
BEAL LA
SALTS ST
EDWARD RD
8
095
7
090
6
085
5
080
930
935
940

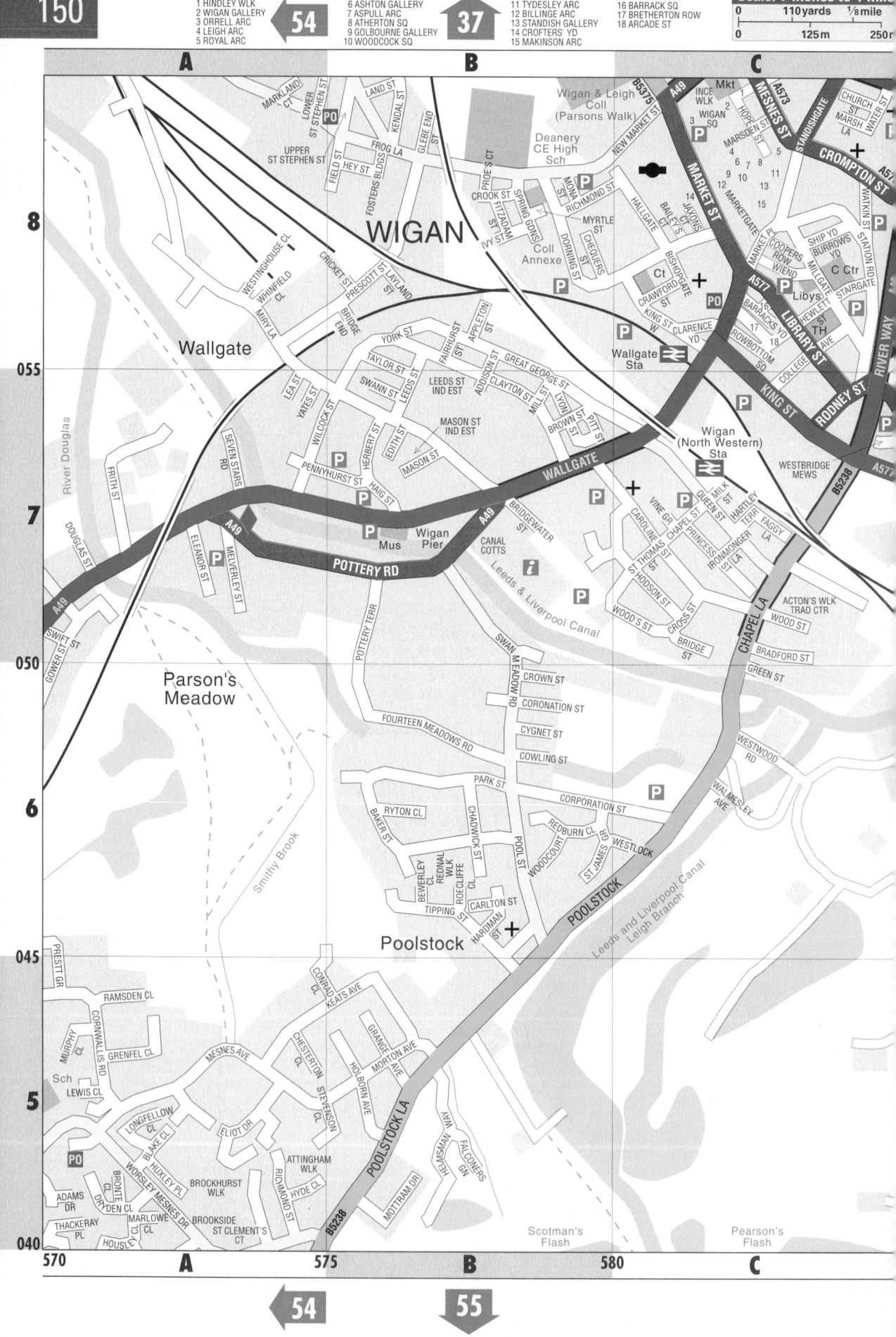
C8
1 HINDLEY WLK
2 WIGAN GALLERY
3 ORRELL ARC
4 LEIGH ARC
5 ROYAL ARC
6 ASHTON GALLERY
7 ASPULL ARC
8 ATHERTON SQ
9 GOLBOURNE GALLERY
10 WOODCOCK SQ
11 TYDESLEY ARC
12 BILLINGE ARC
13 STANDISH GALLERY
14 CROFTERS' YD
15 MAKINSON ARC
16 BARRACK SQ
17 BRETHERTON ROW
18 ARCADE ST
54
37
Scale: 7 inches to 1 mile
0
110 yards
1/8 mile
0
125 m
250 m
A
B
C
8
055
7
050
6
045
5
040
570
575
580
WIGAN
Wallgate
Wigan & Leigh Coll (Parsons Walk)
Deanery CE High Sch
Coll Annexe
Mkt
INCE WLK
WIGAN SQ
MESNES ST
A573
STANDISHGATE
CHURCH ST
MARSH LA
WATER ST
CROMPTON ST
MARKET ST
MARSDEN ST
HOPE ST
MARKETGATE
MARKET PL
COOPERS ROW
WIEND
SHIP YD
BURROWS YD
MILLGATE
C Ctr
STATION RD
WATKIN ST
STAIRGATE
Libys
HEWLETT ST
TH
AVE
LIBRARY ST
A577
BARRACKS YD
ROWBOTTOM SQ
COLLEGE
KING ST
RODNEY ST
RIVER WAY
A49
B5375
NEW MARKET ST
HALLGATE
BAILEY'S CT
JAXONS CT
BISHOPGATE
Ct
CRAWFORD ST
PO
KING ST W
CLARENCE YD
Wallgate Sta
Wigan (North Western) Sta
WESTBRIDGE MEWS
B5238
MARKLAND CT
LOWER ST STEPHEN ST
UPPER ST STEPHEN ST
LAND ST
KENDAL ST
GLEBE END ST
FROG LA
FIELD ST
HEY ST
FOSTERS BLDGS
PROE'S CT
CROOK ST
FITZADAM ST
IVY ST
SPRING GDNS
MONA ST
RICHMOND ST
MYRTLE ST
CHEQUERS
DORNING ST
WESTINGHOUSE CL
WHINFIELD CL
CRICKET ST
PRESCOTT ST
LAYLAND ST
BRIDGE END
MIRY LA
YORK ST
FAIRHURST ST
APPLETON ST
TAYLOR ST
SWANN ST
LEEDS ST
LEEDS ST IND EST
ADDISON ST
GREAT GEORGE ST
CLAYTON ST
MILL ST
LYON ST
BROWN ST
PITT ST
MASON ST IND EST
MASON ST
LEA ST
YATES ST
WILCOCK ST
HERBERT ST
EDITH ST
PENNYHURST ST
HAIG ST
SEVEN STARS RD
WALLGATE
River Douglas
FRITH ST
DOUGLAS ST
ELEANOR ST
MELVERLEY ST
POTTERY RD
Mus
Wigan Pier
BRIDGEWATER ST
CANAL COTTS
Leeds & Liverpool Canal
VINE GR
CAROLINE ST
CHAPEL ST
QUEEN ST
MILK ST
HARTLEY TERR
FAGGY LA
PRINCESS ST
IRONMONGER LA
ST THOMAS ST
HODSON ST
CROSS ST
WOOD'S ST
BRIDGE ST
ACTON'S WLK TRAD CTR
WOOD ST
BRADFORD ST
GREEN ST
CHAPEL LA
SWIFT ST
GOWER ST
Parson's Meadow
POTTERY TERR
SWAN MEADOW RD
CROWN ST
CORONATION ST
CYGNET ST
COWLING ST
FOURTEEN MEADOWS RD
PARK ST
CORPORATION ST
WESTWOOD RD
WALMESLEY AVE
RYTON CL
BAKER ST
CHADWICK ST
POOL ST
REDBURN CL
WOODCOURT
ST JAMES GR
WESTLOCK
BEWERLEY CL
REDNAL WLK
ROECLIFFE CL
CARLTON ST
TIPPING ST
HARDMAN ST
POOLSTOCK
Leeds and Liverpool Canal Leigh Branch
Smithy Brook
Poolstock
PRESTT GR
RAMSDEN CL
CORNWALLIS RD
MURPHY CL
GRENFEL CL
Sch
LEWIS CL
CONRAD CL
KEATS AVE
MESNES AVE
CHESTERTON CL
GRANGE AVE
MORTON AVE
HOLBORN AVE
STEVENSON CL
LONGFELLOW CL
BLAKE CL
ELIOT DR
HUXLEY PL
WORSLEY MESNES DR
BRONTE CL
DRYDEN CL
ADAMS DR
THACKERAY PL
MARLOWE CL
HOUSLEY CL
BROCKHURST WLK
BROOKSIDE
ST CLEMENT'S CT
RICHMOND ST
HYDE CL
ATTINGHAM WLK
POOLSTOCK LA
MOTTRAM DR
HELMSMAN WAY
FALCONERS GN
Scotman's Flash
Pearson's Flash
55

Scale: 7 inches to 1 mile
0 110 yards 1/8 mile
0 125 m 250 m

D8
1 LIMEFIELD
2 RUSSELL HOUSE
3 WITHALL HOUSE
4 CROMPTON HOUSE
5 ALLIANCE ST

37 56

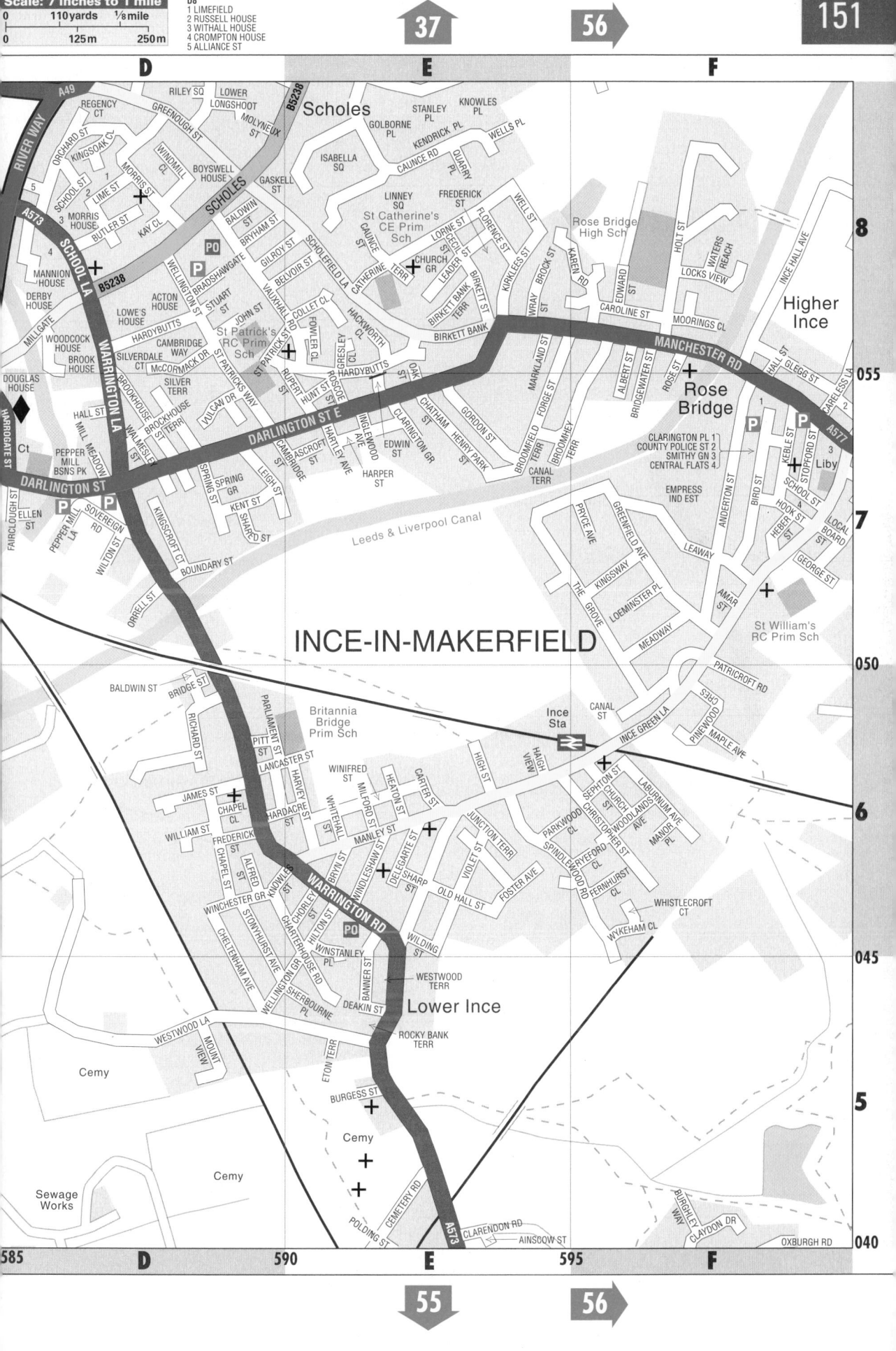

55 56

65 48

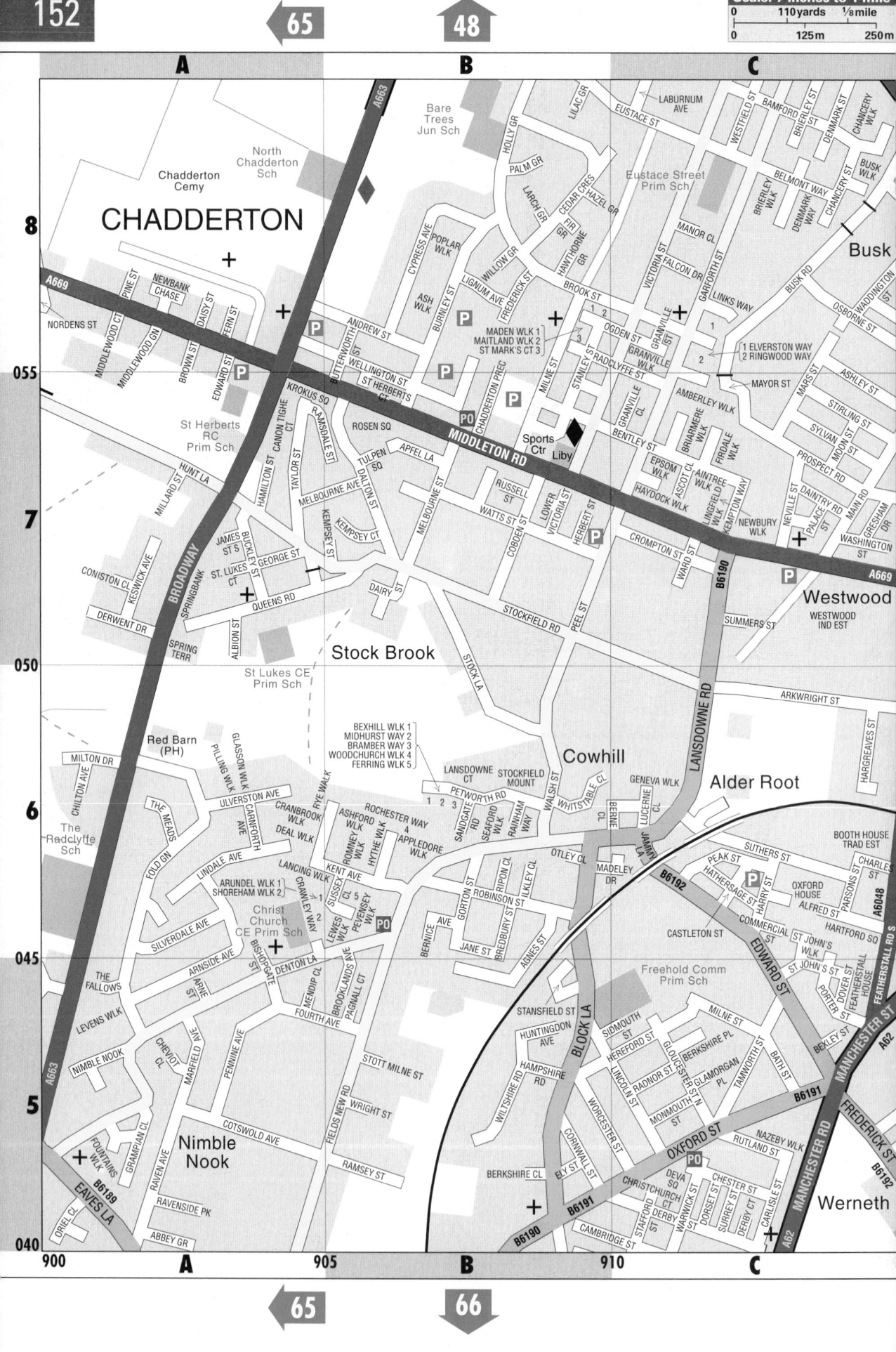
Scale: 7 inches to 1 mile
0 110 yards 1/8 mile
0 125m 250m
A B C
8 055 7 050 6 045 5 040
900 905 910
CHADDERTON
Chadderton Cemy
North Chadderton Sch
Bare Trees Jun Sch
Eustace Street Prim Sch
Busk
Westwood
WESTWOOD IND EST
Stock Brook
St Herberts RC Prim Sch
St Lukes CE Prim Sch
Cowhill
Alder Root
Red Barn (PH)
The Radclyffe Sch
Christ Church CE Prim Sch
Freehold Comm Prim Sch
Nimble Nook
Werneth
Sports Ctr
Liby
BOOTH HOUSE TRAD EST
OXFORD HOUSE
MIDDLETON RD
BROADWAY
LANSDOWNE RD
BLOCK LA
OXFORD ST
MANCHESTER RD
MANCHESTER ST
EDWARD ST
FREDERICK ST
FEATHERSTALL RD S
EAVES LA
A663 A669 A6048 A62 B6190 B6191 B6192 B6189
MADEN WLK 1
MAITLAND WLK 2
ST MARK'S CT 3
1 ELVERSTON WAY
2 RINGWOOD WAY
BEXHILL WLK 1
MIDHURST WAY 2
BRAMBER WAY 3
WOODCHURCH WLK 4
FERRING WLK 5
ARUNDEL WLK 1
SHOREHAM WLK 2

65 66

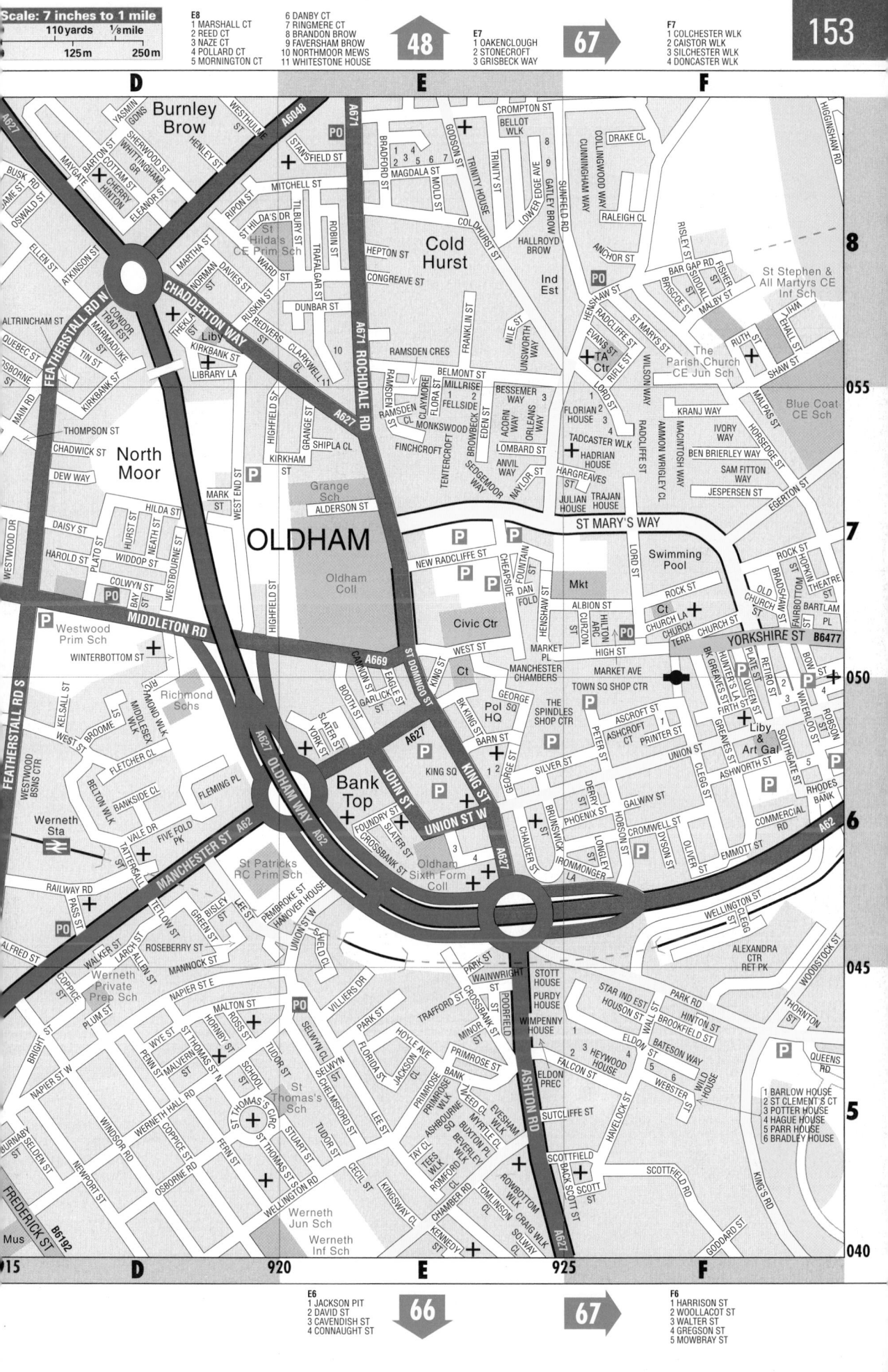

Scale: 7 inches to 1 mile
110 yards
1/8 mile
125 m
250 m
E8
1 MARSHALL CT
2 REED CT
3 NAZE CT
4 POLLARD CT
5 MORNINGTON CT
6 DANBY CT
7 RINGMERE CT
8 BRANDON BROW
9 FAVERSHAM BROW
10 NORTHMOOR MEWS
11 WHITESTONE HOUSE
48
E7
1 OAKENCLOUGH
2 STONECROFT
3 GRISBECK WAY
67
F7
1 COLCHESTER WLK
2 CAISTOR WLK
3 SILCHESTER WLK
4 DONCASTER WLK
D
E
F
8
055
7
050
6
045
5
040
915
920
925
Burnley Brow
Cold Hurst
North Moor
OLDHAM
Bank Top
Oldham Coll
Grange Sch
St Hilda's CE Prim Sch
Civic Ctr
Mkt
Swimming Pool
Ind Est
St Stephen & All Martyrs CE Inf Sch
The Parish Church CE Jun Sch
Blue Coat CE Sch
Westwood Prim Sch
Richmond Schs
Werneth Sta
St Patricks RC Prim Sch
Oldham Sixth Form Coll
Werneth Private Prep Sch
St Thomas's Sch
Werneth Jun Sch
Werneth Inf Sch
Liby & Art Gal
Pol HQ
THE SPINDLES SHOP CTR
TOWN SQ SHOP CTR
MANCHESTER CHAMBERS
ALEXANDRA CTR RET PK
Mus
A627
A6048
A671
A671 ROCHDALE RD
A669
A62
B6477
B6192
CHADDERTON WAY
MIDDLETON RD
FEATHERSTALL RD N
FEATHERSTALL RD S
OLDHAM WAY
MANCHESTER ST
ST MARY'S WAY
YORKSHIRE ST
UNION ST W
KING ST
JOHN ST
ASHTON RD
FREDERICK ST
1 BARLOW HOUSE
2 ST CLEMENT'S CT
3 POTTER HOUSE
4 HAGUE HOUSE
5 PARR HOUSE
6 BRADLEY HOUSE
E6
1 JACKSON PIT
2 DAVID ST
3 CAVENDISH ST
4 CONNAUGHT ST
66
67
F6
1 HARRISON ST
2 WOOLLACOT ST
3 WALTER ST
4 GREGSON ST
5 MOWBRAY ST

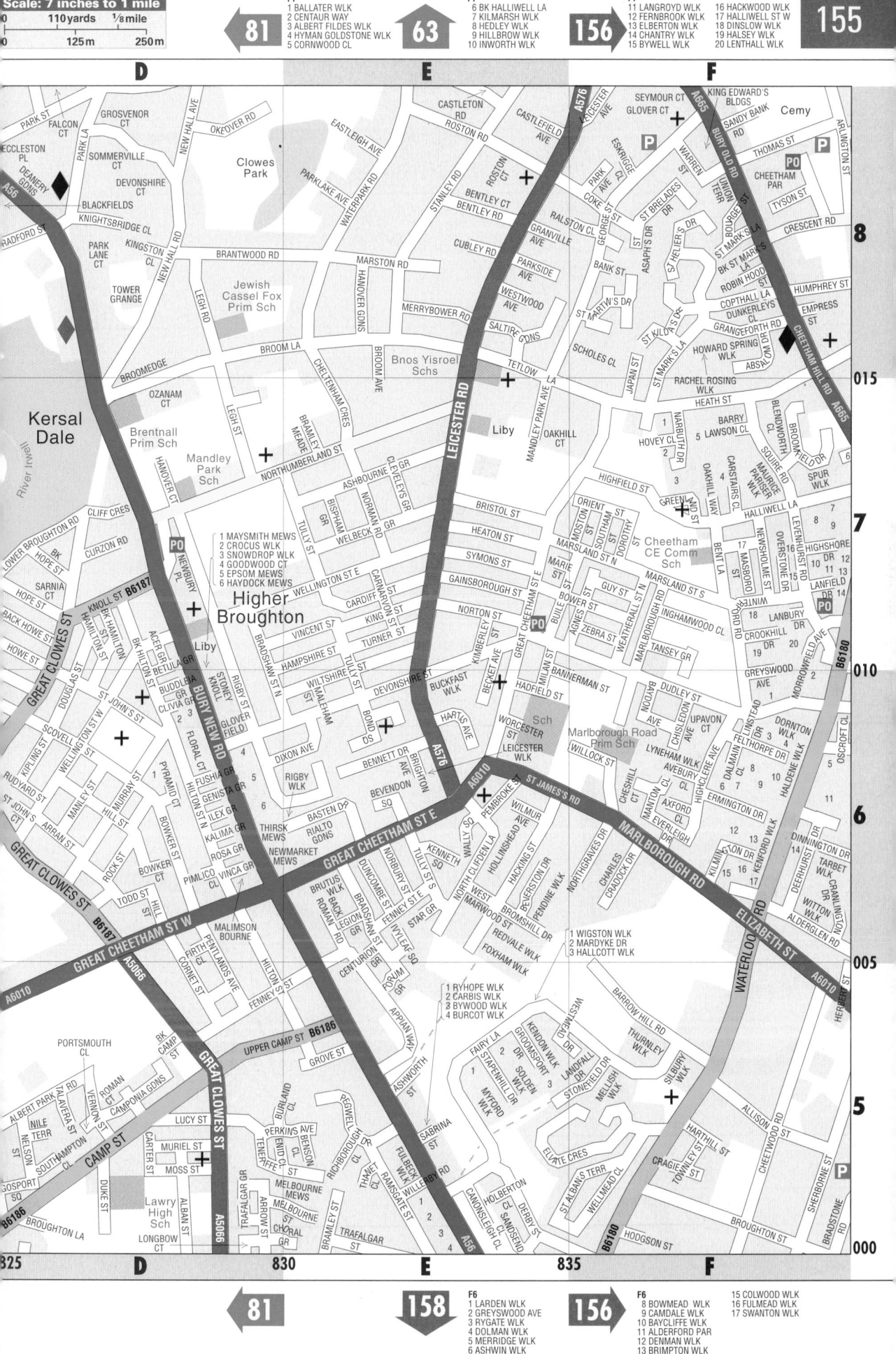
Scale: 7 inches to 1 mile
0
110 yards
1/8 mile
0
125 m
250 m
81
F7
1 BALLATER WLK
2 CENTAUR WAY
3 ALBERT FILDES WLK
4 HYMAN GOLDSTONE WLK
5 CORNWOOD CL
63
F7
6 BK HALLIWELL LA
7 KILMARSH WLK
8 HEDLEY WLK
9 HILLBROW WLK
10 INWORTH WLK
156
F7
11 LANGROYD WLK
12 FERNBROOK WLK
13 ELBERTON WLK
14 CHANTRY WLK
15 BYWELL WLK
16 HACKWOOD WLK
17 HALLIWELL ST W
18 DINSLOW WLK
19 HALSEY WLK
20 LENTHALL WLK
155
D
E
F
8
015
7
010
6
005
5
000
825
830
835
Clowes Park
Kersal Dale
River Irwell
Jewish Cassel Fox Prim Sch
Bnos Yisroel Schs
Brentnall Prim Sch
Mandley Park Sch
Higher Broughton
Cheetham CE Comm Sch
Marlborough Road Prim Sch
Lawry High Sch
Cemy
Liby
Sch
1 MAYSMITH MEWS
2 CROCUS WLK
3 SNOWDROP WLK
4 GOODWOOD CT
5 EPSOM MEWS
6 HAYDOCK MEWS
1 WIGSTON WLK
2 MARDYKE DR
3 HALLCOTT WLK
1 RYHOPE WLK
2 CARBIS WLK
3 BYWOOD WLK
4 BURCOT WLK
BURY NEW RD
LEICESTER RD
GREAT CHEETHAM ST E
GREAT CHEETHAM ST W
GREAT CLOWES ST
MARLBOROUGH RD
ELIZABETH ST
WATERLOO RD
CHEETHAM HILL RD
BURY OLD RD
ST JAMES'S RD
NORTHUMBERLAND ST
BROOM LA
TETLOW LA
BRANTWOOD RD
MARSTON RD
UPPER CAMP ST
CAMP ST
BROUGHTON LA
BROUGHTON ST
A56
A576
A665
A6010
A5066
B6187
B6186
B6180
81
158
F6
1 LARDEN WLK
2 GREYSWOOD AVE
3 RYGATE WLK
4 DOLMAN WLK
5 MERRIDGE WLK
6 ASHWIN WLK
7 ALDERWOOD WLK
156
F6
8 BOWMEAD WLK
9 CAMDALE WLK
10 BAYCLIFFE WLK
11 ALDERFORD PAR
12 DENMAN WLK
13 BRIMPTON WLK
14 CARGATE WLK
15 COLWOOD WLK
16 FULMEAD WLK
17 SWANTON WLK

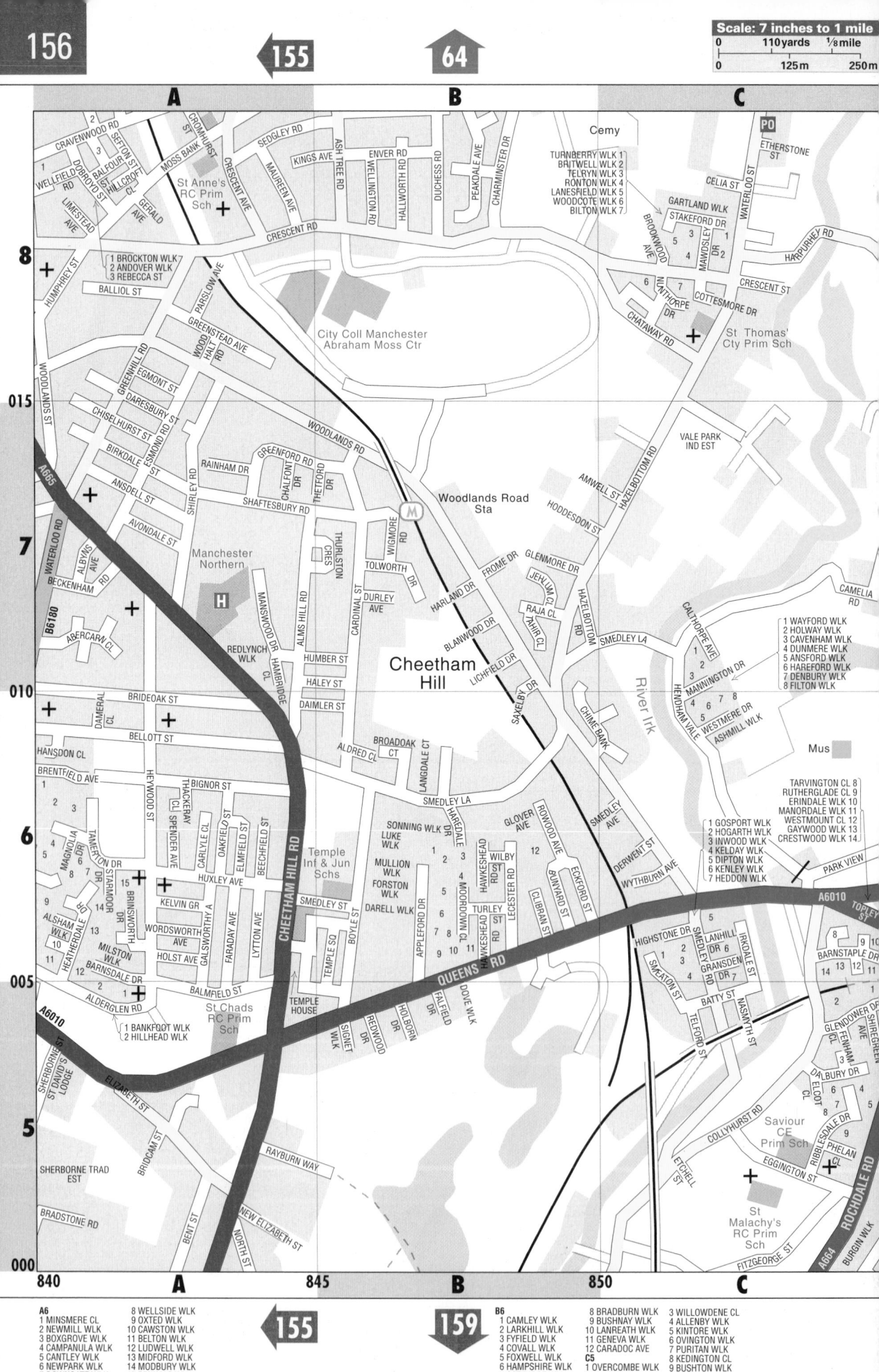

156

155

64

Scale: 7 inches to 1 mile
0   110 yards   ⅛ mile
0   125m   250m

PO

Cemy

St Anne's RC Prim Sch

1 BROCKTON WLK
2 ANDOVER WLK
3 REBECCA ST

City Coll Manchester
Abraham Moss Ctr

TURNBERRY WLK 1
BRITWELL WLK 2
TELRYN WLK 3
RONTON WLK 4
LANESFIELD WLK 5
WOODCOTE WLK 6
BILTON WLK 7

GARTLAND WLK

St Thomas' Cty Prim Sch

Woodlands Road Sta

Manchester Northern

H

Cheetham Hill

River Irk

1 WAYFORD WLK
2 HOLWAY WLK
3 CAVENHAM WLK
4 DUNMERE WLK
5 ANSFORD WLK
6 HAREFORD WLK
7 DENBURY WLK
8 FILTON WLK

Mus

TARVINGTON CL 8
RUTHERGLADE CL 9
ERINDALE WLK 10
MANORDALE WLK 11
WESTMOUNT CL 12
GAYWOOD WLK 13
CRESTWOOD WLK 14

1 GOSPORT WLK
2 HOGARTH WLK
3 INWOOD WLK
4 KELDAY WLK
5 DIPTON WLK
6 KENLEY WLK
7 HEDDON WLK

PARK VIEW

Temple Inf & Jun Schs

1 BANKFOOT WLK
2 HILLHEAD WLK

St Chads RC Prim Sch

TEMPLE HOUSE

St David's Lodge

Saviour CE Prim Sch

SHERBORNE TRAD EST

St Malachy's RC Prim Sch

840   A   845   B   850   C

A6
1 MINSMERE CL
2 NEWMILL WLK
3 BOXGROVE WLK
4 CAMPANULA WLK
5 CANTLEY WLK
6 NEWPARK WLK
7 DOWNGATE WLK
8 WELLSIDE WLK
9 OXTED WLK
10 CAWSTON WLK
11 BELTON WLK
12 LUDWELL WLK
13 MIDFORD WLK
14 MODBURY WLK
15 BENHALE WLK

B6
1 CAMLEY WLK
2 LARKHILL WLK
3 FYFIELD WLK
4 COVALL WLK
5 FOXWELL WLK
6 HAMPSHIRE WLK
7 CORRIDGE WLK
8 BRADBURN WLK
9 BUSHNAY WLK
10 LANREATH WLK
11 GENEVA WLK
12 CARADOC AVE
C5
1 OVERCOMBE WLK
2 TYNWELL WLK
3 WILLOWDENE CL
4 ALLENBY WLK
5 KINTORE WLK
6 OVINGTON WLK
7 PURITAN WLK
8 KEDINGTON CL
9 BUSHTON WLK

BROMWICH DR
CLATFORD WLK
OAKRIDGE WLK
BINDON WLK
WATFIELD WLK
HOLMFOOT WLK

7 LINSLADE WLK
8 SELWOOD WLK
9 PORTWOOD WLK
10 TREMAIN WLK
11 CALDERBROOK WLK
D8
1 MILLPOOL WLK

2 PATHFIELD WLK
3 MURROW WLK
4 DERVILLE WLK
5 SHAPWICK CL
6 HARROWDENE WLK
7 BRENLEY WLK
8 ROXWELL WLK

9 PORTAL WLK
10 HAYGROVE WLK
11 MAYBROOK WLK
E7
1 WILLOW BANK
2 ORPINGTON RD
3 OSBORNE RD

4 ASHGILL WLK
5 GLENPARK WLK
6 DRYGATE WLK
7 BELSYDE WLK
8 NORBET WLK
9 PURTON WLK
10 BANKHALL WLK

64

83

11 LOWREY WLK
12 DURHAM ST
13 EVANTON ST
14 MERTON WLK
15 TRONGATE WLK
16 VIEWFIELD WLK
17 FIRDON WLK

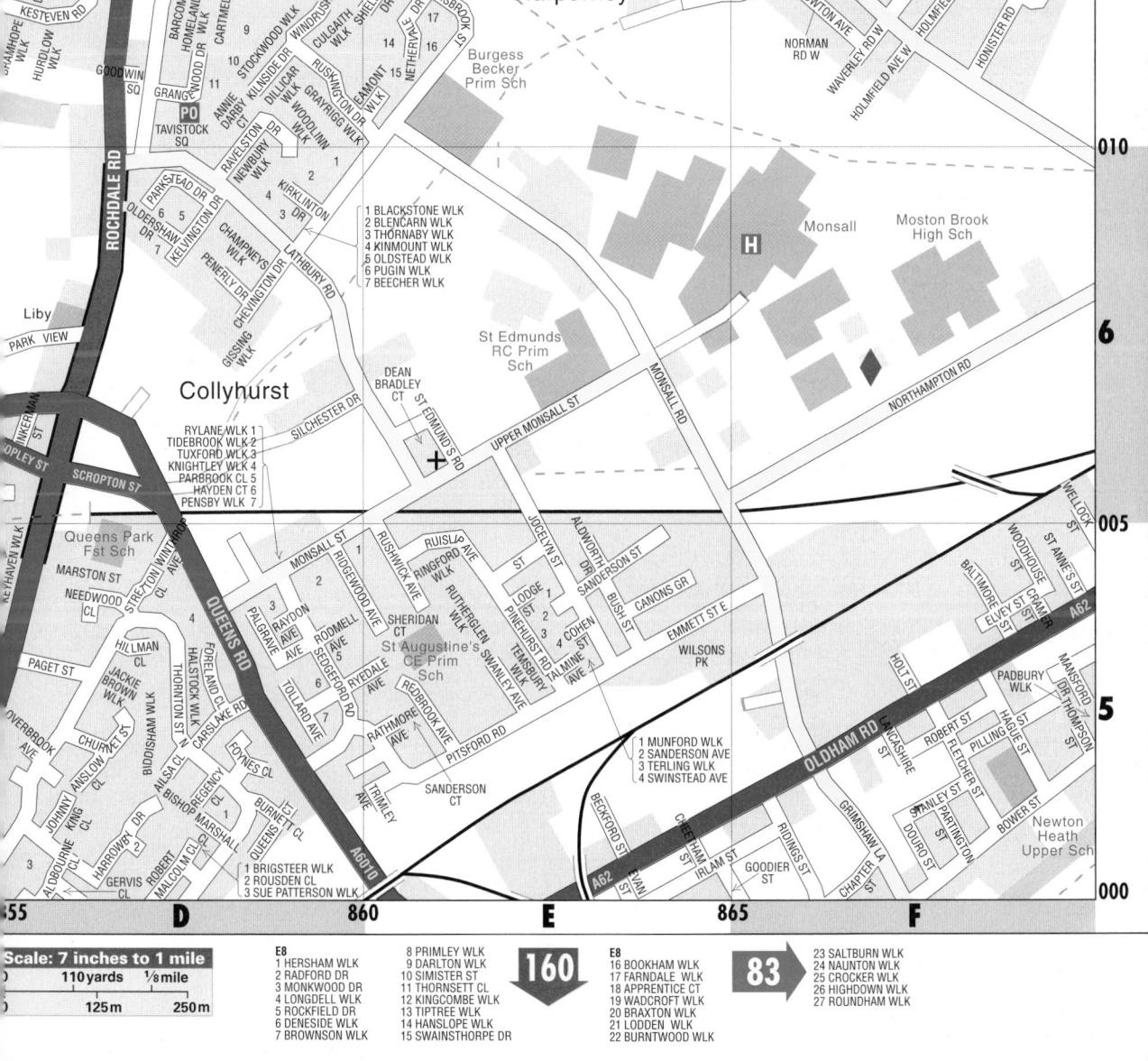

Scale: 7 inches to 1 mile
110 yards   1/8 mile
125m   250m

E8
1 HERSHAM WLK
2 RADFORD DR
3 MONKWOOD DR
4 LONGDELL WLK
5 ROCKFIELD DR
6 DENESIDE WLK
7 BROWNSON WLK

8 PRIMLEY WLK
9 DARLTON WLK
10 SIMISTER ST
11 THORNSETT CL
12 KINGCOMBE WLK
13 TIPTREE WLK
14 HANSLOPE WLK
15 SWAINSTHORPE DR

160

E8
16 BOOKHAM WLK
17 FARNDALE WLK
18 APPRENTICE CT
19 WADCROFT WLK
20 BRAXTON WLK
21 LODDEN WLK
22 BURNTWOOD WLK

83

23 SALTBURN WLK
24 NAUNTON WLK
25 CROCKER WLK
26 HIGHDOWN WLK
27 ROUNDHAM WLK

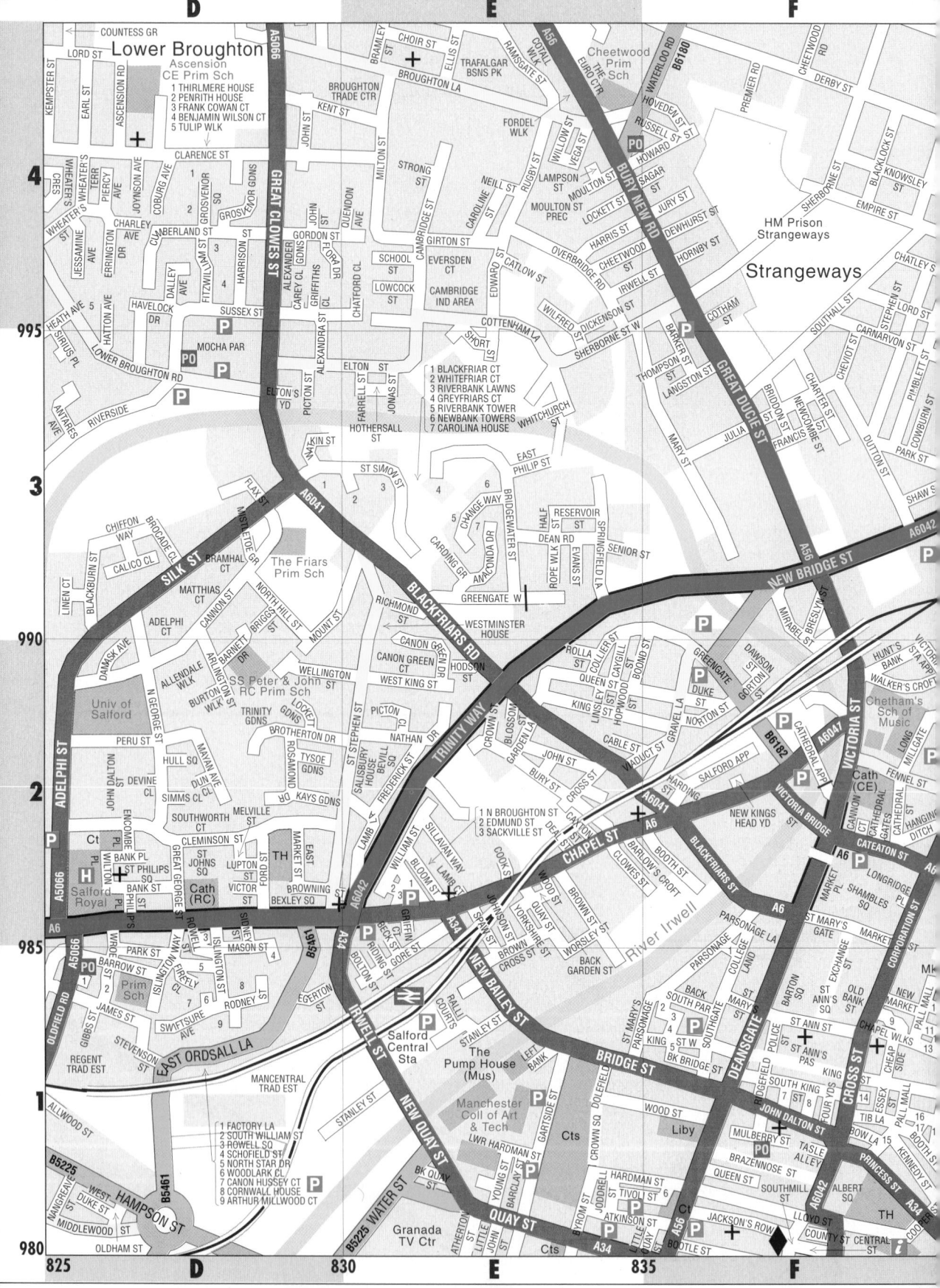

Scale: 7 inches to 1 mile
0 · 110 yards · 1/8 mile
0 · 125 m · 250 m

D · E · F

COUNTESS GR
Lower Broughton
Ascension CE Prim Sch
1 THIRLMERE HOUSE
2 PENRITH HOUSE
3 FRANK COWAN CT
4 BENJAMIN WILSON CT
5 TULIP WLK

KEMPSTER ST
LORD ST
EARL ST
ASCENSION RD
WHEATER'S CRES
WHEATER'S TERR
PIERCY AVE
JOYNSON AVE
COBURG AVE
GROSVENOR SQ
GROSVENOR GDNS
GREAT CLOWES ST
BROUGHTON TRADE CTR
BRAMLEY CHOIR ST
ELLIS ST
TRAFALGAR ST
RAMSGATE ST
BROUGHTON LA
COTAL WLK
A56 THE EURO CTR
Cheetwood Prim Sch
CHEETWOOD RD
DERBY ST
WATERLOO RD
B6180

HEATH AVE
SIRIUS PL
ANTARES AVE
JESSAMINE
CHARLEY AVE
ERRINGTON DR
CUMBERLAND ST
HATTON AVE
DALLEY AVE
FITZWILLIAM ST
HAVELOCK DR
HARRISON ST
SUSSEX ST
LOWER BROUGHTON RD
MOCHA PAR
PO
ALEXANDRA ST
CAREY CL
GRIFFITHS CL
GORDON ST
FLORA DR
CHATFORD CL
SCHOOL ST
LOWCOCK ST
EVERSDEN CT
CAMBRIDGE IND AREA
EDWARD ST
CATLOW ST
WILFRED ST
DICKENSON ST
SHERBORNE ST W
OVERBRIDGE RD
CHEETWOOD
IRWELL ST
BARKER ST
COTHAM ST
GREAT DUCIE ST
A56
FORDEL WLK
WILLOW ST
VEGA ST
LAMPSON ST
MOULTON ST
LOCKETT ST
MOULTON ST PREC
HARRIS ST
SAGAR ST
JURY ST
HOWARD ST
RUSSELL ST
HOVEDEN ST
PREMIER RD
CHEETWOOD RD
SHERBORNE ST
BLACKLOCK ST
KNOWSLEY ST
EMPIRE ST
CHATLEY S
HM Prison Strangeways
Strangeways
STEPHEN ST
LORD ST
CARNARVON ST
CHEVIOT ST
SHERBORNE ST
NEWCOMBE ST
CHAPTER ST
BRIDDON ST
FRANCIS ST
PIMBLETT ST
COBURN ST
PARK ST
SHAW S
A6642
A6042

MISTLETOE GR
FLAX ST
A6041
CHIFFON WAY
BROCADE CL
CALICO CL
BLACKBURN ST
LINEN CT
SILK ST
BRAMHAL CT
CANNON ST
NORTH HILL ST
BRIGGS ST
MOUNT ST
The Friars Prim Sch
MATTHIAS CT
ADELPHI CT
RICHMOND ST
CANON GREEN DR
CANON GREEN CT
WEST KING ST
HODSON ST
BLACKFRIARS RD
WESTMINSTER HOUSE
NEW BRIDGE ST
A56
A6642
P

1 BLACKFRIAR CT
2 WHITEFRIAR CT
3 RIVERBANK LAWNS
4 GREYFRIARS CT
5 RIVERBANK TOWER
6 NEWBANK TOWERS
7 CAROLINA HOUSE

WAT KIN ST
ST SIMON ST
CHANGE WAY
CARDING GR
ANACONDA DR
GREENGATE W
BRIDGEWATER ST
EAST PHILIP ST
DEAN RD
ROPE WLK
EVANS ST
HALF ST
RESERVOIR ST
SPRINGFIELD LA
SENIOR ST

Univ of Salford
ADELPHI ST
A5066
DAMASK AVE
N GEORGE ST
PERU ST
JOHN DALTON ST
DEVINE CL
HULL SQ
MAYAN AVE
DUN LN
SIMMS CL
ALLENDALE WLK
BURTON WLK
TRINITY GDNS
BROTHERTON DR
ROSAMOND DR
TYSOE GDNS
KAYS GDNS
SS Peter & John RC Prim Sch
WELLINGTON ST
LOCKET ST
PICTON ST
NATHAN DR
SALISBURY HOUSE
ST STEPHEN ST
BEVILL ST
FREDERICK ST
SOUTHWORTH CT
MELVILLE ST
CLEMINSON ST
MARKET ST
EAST ST
LAMB LN
WILLIAM ST
SILLAVAN WAY
BLOOM ST
TRINITY WAY
CROWN ST
BLOSSOM ST
GARDEN LA
JOHN ST
BURY ST
CROSS ST
ROLLA ST
QUEEN ST
KING ST
LINSLEY ST
COLLIER ST
HOPWOOD ST
CAYGILL ST
BOOND ST
GORTON ST
NORTON ST
GRAVEL LA
CABLE ST
VIADUCT ST
GREENGATE
DAWSON ST
MIRABEL ST
BRESLYN ST
HUNT'S BANK
Chetham's Sch of Music
WALKER'S CROFT
VICTORIA STA APPT
A6047
CATHEDRAL APP
B6182
VICTORIA BRIDGE
Cath (CE)
CATHEDRAL GATES
HANGING DITCH
FENNEL ST
LONG MILLGATE
A6
P

1 N BROUGHTON ST
2 EDMUND ST
3 SACKVILLE ST

PERU ST
DUN LN
ENCOMBE PL
WILLIAM ST
BANK PL
GREAT GEORGE ST
ST PHILIPS SQ
BANK ST
Ct PL
Salford Royal
H
Cath (RC)
ST JOHNS SQ
LUPTON ST
FORD ST
VICTOR ST
BROWNING ST
BEXLEY SQ
GRIFFIN ST
A6042
BECK ST
GORE ST
RIDING ST
BOLTON ST
A34
JOHNSON ST
SPAW ST
BROWN ST
CROSS ST W
BACK GARDEN ST
YORKSHIRE ST
QUAY ST
WOOD ST
BROWN ST
WORSLEY ST
CHAPEL ST
A6041
A6
HARDING ST
SALFORD APP
NEW KINGS HEAD YD
VICTORIA BRIDGE ST
BLACKFRIARS ST
BOOTH ST
BARLOW'S CROFT
CLOWES ST
River Irwell
PARSONAGE LA
MARKET PL
SHAMBLES SQ
ST MARY'S GATE
CATEATON ST
LONGRIDGE PL
CORPORATION ST
A6
P

A6
A5066
A6
PO
BARROW ST
Prim Sch
PARK ST
ISLINGTON WAY
FIREFLY CL
JAMES ST
GIBBS ST
STEVENSON ST
SWIFTSURE AVE
RODNEY ST
MASON ST
EGERTON ST
EAST ORDSALL LA
MANCENTRAL TRAD EST
STANLEY ST
A6165
IRWELL ST
Salford Central Sta
RALLI COURTS
A34
NEW BAILEY ST
STANLEY ST
The Pump House (Mus)
LEFT BANK
BRIDGE ST
ST MARY'S PARSONAGE
ST MARY'S ST
PARSONAGE
BACK SOUTH PAR
SOUTHGATE
BACK PARADE
ST ANN'S SQ
ST ANN ST
OLD BANK ST
EXCHANGE ST
KING ST
POLICE
ST ANN'S PAS
NEW MARKET
PALL MALL
CHAPEL WLKS
OLD MILLGATE
CROSS ST
CHEAPSIDE
DEANSFIELD
DEANSGATE
RIDGEFIELD
14
NEW MARKET
ESSEX ST
PALL MALL
BOOTH ST
TIB LA
KENNEDY ST

REGENT TRAD EST
ALLWOOD ST
OLDFIELD RD
1 FACTORY LA
2 SOUTH WILLIAM ST
3 ROWELL SQ
4 SCHOFIELD ST
5 NORTH STAR DR
6 WOODLARK CL
7 CANON HUSSEY CT
8 CORNWALL HOUSE
9 ARTHUR MILLWOOD CT
HAMPSON ST
B5225
B5461
WEST DUKE ST
MANGREAVE ST
MIDDLEWOOD ST
OLDHAM ST
STANLEY ST
NEW QUAY ST
WATER ST
B5225
BK QUAY ST
Granada TV Ctr
QUAY ST
ATHERTON ST
LITTLE JOHN ST
YOUNG ST
BARCLAY ST
LWR HARDMAN ST
GARTSIDE ST
Cts
CROWN SQ
DOLEFIELD
GARTSIDE ST
HARDMAN ST
Manchester Coll of Art & Tech
WOOD ST
Liby
JOHN DALTON ST
TASLE ALLEY
MULBERRY ST
PO
BRAZENNOSE ST
QUEEN ST
SOUTHMILL ST
BYROM ST
JODDRELL ST
TIVOLI ST
ATKINSON ST
A34
A56
BOOTLE ST
JACKSON'S ROW
COUNTY ST
LLOYD ST
TH
ALBERT SQ
A6042
A34
PRINCESS ST
CROSS ST
JOHN DALTON ST
BOW LA
BROWN ST
MARSDEN ST
CHANCERY LA
CHANCERY PL
COOPER ST
CENTRAL ST
i

F1
1 BK COLLEGE LAND
2 DUNLOP ST
3 GARDEN LA
4 SMITHY LA
5 BUTTER LA
6 SIDNEY ST
7 BOW ST
8 ST JAMES'S SQ
9 BK POOL FOLD
10 NORFOLK ST
11 KENT ST
12 SUSSEX ST
13 MARSDEN ST
14 TOWN HALL LA
15 CLARENCE ST
16 CHANCERY LA
17 CHANCERY PL
18 BROWN ST

4
995
3
990
2
985
1
980

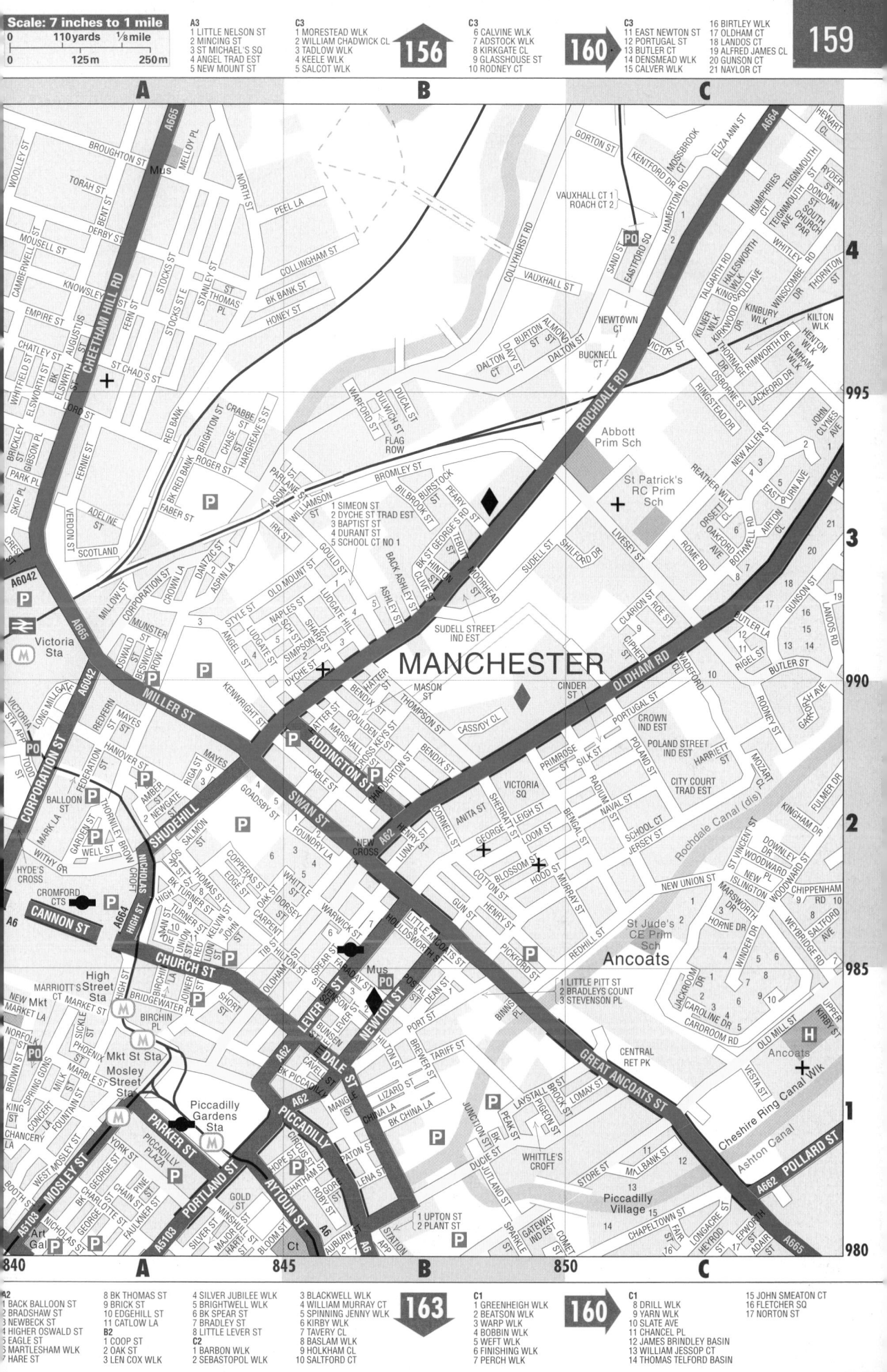

A3
1 LITTLE NELSON ST
2 MINCING ST
3 ST MICHAEL'S SQ
4 ANGEL TRAD EST
5 NEW MOUNT ST

C3
1 MORESTEAD WLK
2 WILLIAM CHADWICK CL
3 TADLOW WLK
4 KEELE WLK
5 SALCOT WLK

156

C3
6 CALVINE WLK
7 ADSTOCK WLK
8 KIRKGATE CL
9 GLASSHOUSE ST
10 RODNEY CT

160

C3
11 EAST NEWTON ST
12 PORTUGAL ST
13 BUTLER ST
14 DENSMEAD WLK
15 CALVER WLK

16 BIRTLEY WLK
17 OLDHAM CT
18 LANDOS CT
19 ALFRED JAMES CL
20 GUNSON CT
21 NAYLOR CT

A2
1 BACK BALLOON ST
2 BRADSHAW ST
3 NEWBECK ST
4 HIGHER OSWALD ST
5 EAGLE ST
6 MARTLESHAM WLK
7 HARE ST

8 BK THOMAS ST
9 BRICK ST
10 EDGEHILL ST
11 CATLOW LA
B2
1 COOP ST
2 OAK ST
3 LEN COX WLK

4 SILVER JUBILEE WLK
5 BRIGHTWELL WLK
6 BK SPEAR ST
7 BRADLEY ST
8 LITTLE LEVER ST
C2
1 BARBON WLK
2 SEBASTOPOL WLK

3 BLACKWELL WLK
4 WILLIAM MURRAY CT
5 SPINNING JENNY WLK
6 KIRBY WLK
7 TAVERY CL
8 BASLAM WLK
9 HOLKHAM CL
10 SALTFORD CT

163

C1
1 GREENHEIGH WLK
2 BEATSON WLK
3 WARP WLK
4 BOBBIN WLK
5 WEFT WLK
6 FINISHING WLK
7 PERCH WLK

160

C1
8 DRILL WLK
9 YARN WLK
10 SLATE AVE
11 CHAPEL PL
12 JAMES BRINDLEY BASIN
13 WILLIAM JESSOP CT
14 THOMAS TELFORD BASIN

15 JOHN SMEATON CT
16 FLETCHER SQ
17 NORTON ST

159
157
83

Scale: 7 inches to 1 mile
0   110 yards   1/8 mile
0   125 m   250 m

D   **E**   **F**

4

995

3

990

2

985

1

980

855   **D**   860   **E**   865   **F**

159
164
83

OLDHAM RD
A6010
A62
A6010
A662
ALAN TURING WAY
ASHTON NEW RD
MERRILL ST
POLLARD ST

Miles Platting

Bradford

Corpus Christi RC Prim Sch
Miles Platting Prim Sch
St Mark's CE Prim Sch
St Anne's RC Prim Sch
St Gregorys RC High Sch
CE Sch of the Resurrection
Grange Sch
Leacroft Sch

Sports Gd

Rochdale Canal (dis)
Ashton Canal
River Medlock

1 KEYWORTH WLK
2 ALBURN CT
3 NORBURY CL
4 EDINBURGH SQ
5 LOXLEY WLK

1 BLACKFORD WLK
2 STANBURY WLK

1 BEECHCROFT CL
2 MICKLEBY WLK

BOLNEY WLK
LASHBROOK CL
WTOLLESBURY ST
THORNTON ST N
RYDER ST
COLLYHURST ST
THORNTON ST
WILMCOTE RD
HAMPSON ST
HELGA ST
BK HMPSN
FERDINAND
JOHNSON SQ
COLCHESTER ST
NELSON CT
DROITWICH RD
THORNDEN
SHARDLOW CL
FIR ST
SHETLAND RD
FARNBOROUGH RD
SHENFIELD
STALHAM
WHITFORD WLK
TILBURY WLK
NUNEATON DR
WINSTANLEY RD
KINGSLAND
DENVER AVE
LOWER VICKERS ST
ANSCOMBE CL
BERKSHIRE RD
REGINALD LATHAM CT
LIME ST
LEWIS ST
BROADHAVEN RD
Liby

BACKTON PL
GILBROOK AVE
ROSEWELL CL
FALKLAND AVE
REEDHAM WLK
KILSBY WLK
BEDNAL AVE
ASHBURY PL
SAWLEY RD
LIFTON AVE
HAVEN SQ
NILBY WLK
ASHBURY AVE
NELSON ST
JAMES ST
VARLEY ST
VICKERS ST
POCHIN ST

PRINCESS ST
RHODES ST
NEW ST
CANADA ST
DREWETT ST
NORTON ST
GODIER ST
CHAPTER ST
LORD NORTH ST
WEDGEWOOD ST
HELSTON ST
FALMOUTH ST
CORELLI ST
CLIFTON ST
GRIMSHAW LA
BRISCOE LA

COLESHILL ST
IRON ST
SANDAL ST
KENWYN ST
PADSTOW ST
PENZANCE ST
BROOKHILL ST
HOOTON ST
SYCAMORE CT
THE MEWS
BROXTON ST
ROYDALE ST
SAXON ST
BARKING ST
STRACEY ST
GLEDEN ST

EASTLEIGH DR
MEDWAY WLK
CRINAN WLK
SLEAFORD CL
EXFORD CL
TIDESWELL AVE
BOURDON ST
ALKER RD
OULTON WLK
WINFELL DR
HOLLAND ST
QUEENSBURY CT
WARDLE ST
TEWKESBURY RD
DARTON AVE
EASTHELL
NAIRN WLK
BARBECK CL
CHARNLEY CL
DINSDALE
CRANFIELD CL
TINSLEY CL
BRADFORD RD
SABDEN CL
SANDAL CT
HADLOW WLK
STRACEY ST

GRANSHAW ST
DANSON ST
LANCHESTER

BURNELL CL
DARFIELD WLK
OLDBURY
MELLOR ST
SMALLRIDGE CL
SAMOUTH
NAYLOR ST
KEITH WLK
LOSTOCK ST
CHALE CL
CROOM WLK
WHALLEY
MARCER
WELWYN WLK
SOLLINGTON RD
AXBRIDGE WLK
RIDGEWAY ST
AUDLEM CL
LATTON ST
LANSTEAD DR
MANSTEAD WLK
SHAWHILL WLK
GLEDEN ST
MILLHEAD AVE
CYRUS ST
UPPER HELENA ST
UPPER CAMBRIAN ST
ADSWOOD
HOLTOWN IND EST

WOODWARD ST
BUTLER ST
ROLLESTON AVE
FIRBECK DR
WOODWARD CT
HALMORE RD
CHIPPENHAM CT
CHIPPENHAM RD
TROUTBECK AVE
TIDWORTH AVE
OLD MILL ST
PIERCY ST
SPECTATOR ST
BESWICK ST
WANSFELL WLK
CROSSLEY CT
LITTLE HOLME ST
PRESSHYRE AVE
FROST ST
COWAN ST E
POLLARD ST E
BRANSON ST
CAVALIERS ST
CYRUS ST
LIND ST
WESTON ST
PUMP ST
HOLT TOWN
KEYMER ST
ALLAMS ST
PHILIPS PARK RD
HAILSHAM ST
BROMING ST
FAIRBAIRN
BASLOW ST
ROWSLEY ST
STOTT ST
PARCEL ST
CLASS ST
TOPAZ ST
STUART ST
NEW VIADUCT ST
Ind Est
FORGE LA

HACKLETON CL
THE VICTORIA IND EST
MUNDAY ST
BOND ST
PROVIDENCE ST
MALTA ST
HARRISON ST
MAYES GDNS
SNELL ST
TAME ST
OSWALD ST
ANCOATS GRN N
BADBY CL
MAIDFORD CL
ADSTONE CL
BLISWORTH CL
PATTISHALL CL
HARDING ST
EVERY ST
CATERHAM ST
TUTBURY ST
GRACE WLK
FAIRHAM WLK
PRICE ST
TOWCESTER CL
TAUNTON ST
GURNEY ST
SIDWELL WLK
PALMERSTON ST
VIADUCT ST
BEVAN CL
ATTLEE WAY
GAITSKELL CL
RIMMER CL
PURSLOW CL
RAMAGE WLK
BLAKEMORE WLK
BELLIS CL
COUNCILLOR ST
HASSOP CL
ORME CL
DARLEY ST
CROSTON WLK
STEDMAN WLK
EUCLID CL
RYLANCE CL
SILFIELD
LONGHAM CL
BURBRIDGE CL
BLACKROCK ST
ISCA ST
ELLINGHAM CL
ALBERT ST
PILGRIM DR
YEOMAN CL
REDFIELD CL
TURNPIKE WLK
LIMETREE WLK
RAGLAN CL
ROUSE CL
ROUSE CL
HOPEDALE CL
NEWCOMBE CL
SWALLOW ST
BISAY CL
CROMARTY WLK
FAIRISLE CL
ROCKALL WLK
VIKING ST
HAVANA CL
KEY WEST
FREDA WLK
DORIC CL
VALLEY WLK
BURNS CL
ABERNANT CL
SARAH ANN ST
EDWAN ST
HILLKIRK ST
CARRUTHERS ST

F1
1 MANILLA WLK
2 CASTLETON WLK
3 ALDERSHOT WLK
4 COWPER WLK
5 JENKYN WLK
6 LIGHTFOOT WLK
7 ASHCOMBE WLK

F1
8 MAGPIE WLK
9 WARNER WLK
10 SUNBEAM WLK
11 MOUNTFIELD WLK
12 SEABRIGHT WLK
13 ATLANTIC WLK
14 LEGHORN WLK

15 CAIRN WLK
16 ARROWSMITH WLK
17 QUARRY WLK
18 WOODVALE WLK
19 BANNER WLK
20 DIGBY WLK
21 PRATT WLK
22 RANDALL WLK

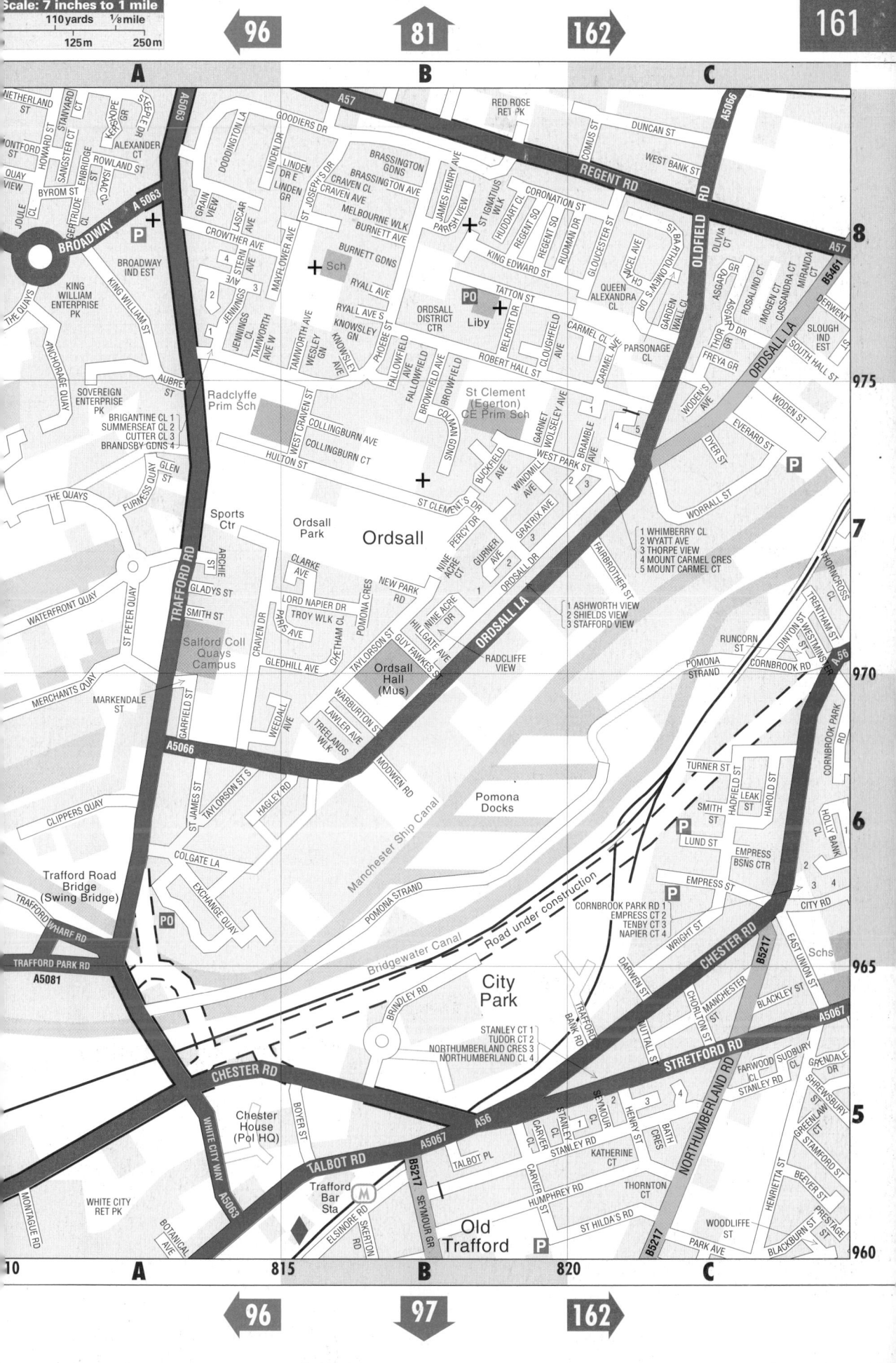

Scale: 7 inches to 1 mile
110 yards
⅛ mile
125 m
250 m
96
81
162
161
A
B
C
NETHERLAND ST
STANYARD CT
KELSOPE GR
STEEPLE DR
ALEXANDER CT
MONTFORD ST
HOWARD ST
SANGSTER CT
EMBRIDGE ST
ROWLAND ST
ISAAC CL
QUAY VIEW
BYROM ST
GERTRUDE CL
JOULE CL
BROADWAY
A 5063
A5063
BROADWAY IND EST
KING WILLIAM ENTERPRISE PK
KING WILLIAM ST
THE QUAYS
ANCHORAGE QUAY
AUBREY ST
SOVEREIGN ENTERPRISE PK
BRIGANTINE CL 1
SUMMERSEAT CL 2
CUTTER CL 3
BRANDSBY GDNS 4
GLEN ST
FURNESS QUAY
WATERFRONT QUAY
ST PETER QUAY
MERCHANTS QUAY
MARKENDALE ST
CLIPPERS QUAY
Trafford Road Bridge (Swing Bridge)
TRAFFORD WHARF RD
TRAFFORD PARK RD
A5081
A57
GOODIERS DR
DODDINGTON LA
LINDEN DR
LINDEN DR E
LINDEN GR
ST JOSEPH'S DR
GRAIN VIEW
LASCAR AVE
CROWTHER AVE
STERN AVE
JENNINGS AVE
JENNINGS CL
TAMWORTH AVE W
TAMWORTH AVE
MAYFLOWER AVE
WESLEY GN
KNOWSLEY GN
KNOWSLEY AVE
BRASSINGTON GDNS
BRASSINGTON AVE
CRAVEN CL
CRAVEN AVE
MELBOURNE WLK
BURNETT AVE
BURNETT GDNS
Sch
RYALL AVE
RYALL AVE S
PHOEBE ST
FALLOWFIELD AVE
BROWFIELD AVE
BROWFIELD
JAMES HENRY AVE
PARISH VIEW
ST IGNATIUS WLK
HUDDART CL
REGENT SQ
RUDMAN DR
CORONATION ST
KING EDWARD ST
GLOUCESTER ST
TATTON ST
PO
Liby
ORDSALL DISTRICT CTR
BELFORT DR
CLOUGHFIELD AVE
ROBERT HALL ST
CARMEL CL
CARMEL AVE
QUEEN ALEXANDRA CL
CHANCEL AVE
ST BARTHOLOMEW'S DR
GARDEN WALL CL
PARSONAGE CL
RED ROSE RET PK
COMUS ST
DUNCAN ST
WEST BANK ST
REGENT RD
A5066
OLDFIELD RD
OLIVIA CT
ASGARD GR
ASGARD DR
THOR GR
ROSALIND CT
IMOGEN CT
CASSANDRA CT
MIRANDA CT
B5461
DERWENT
SLOUGH IND EST
ORDSALL LA
SOUTH HALL ST
FREYA GR
WODEN'S AVE
WODEN ST
EVERARD ST
DYER ST
WORRALL ST
Radclyffe Prim Sch
WEST CRAVEN ST
COLLINGBURN AVE
COLLINGBURN CT
HULTON ST
COLMAN GDNS
St Clement (Egerton) CE Prim Sch
GARNET WOLSELEY AVE
BRAMBLE AVE
WEST PARK ST
BUCKFIELD AVE
WINDMILL AVE
GRATRIX AVE
ST CLEMENT'S DR
Sports Ctr
Ordsall Park
Ordsall
PERCY DR
NINE ACRE CT
GURNER AVE
ORDSALL DR
FAIRBROTHER ST
1 WHIMBERRY CL
2 WYATT AVE
3 THORPE VIEW
4 MOUNT CARMEL CRES
5 MOUNT CARMEL CT
TRAFFORD RD
ARCHIE ST
CLARKE AVE
NEW PARK RD
GLADYS ST
SMITH ST
LORD NAPIER DR
TROY WLK
PARIS AVE
POMONA CRES
CRAVEN DR
CHETHAM CL
Salford Coll Quays Campus
GLEDHILL AVE
TAYLORSON ST
GUY FAWKES ST
HILLGATE AVE
NINE ACRE DR
1 ASHWORTH VIEW
2 SHIELDS VIEW
3 STAFFORD VIEW
RADCLIFFE VIEW
Ordsall Hall (Mus)
GARFIELD ST
WEEDALL AVE
WARBURTON ST
LAWLER AVE
TREELANDS WLK
A5066
MODWEN RD
ST JAMES ST
TAYLORSON ST S
HAGLEY RD
Pomona Docks
Manchester Ship Canal
COLGATE LA
EXCHANGE QUAY
POMONA STRAND
Bridgewater Canal
Road under construction
City Park
BRINDLEY RD
STANLEY CT 1
TUDOR CT 2
NORTHUMBERLAND CRES 3
NORTHUMBERLAND CL 4
TRAFFORD BANK RD
RUNCORN ST
POMONA STRAND
CORNBROOK RD
DINTON ST
WESTMINSTER ST
TRENTHAM ST
THORNCROSS CL
A56
CORNBROOK PARK RD
TURNER ST
HADFIELD ST
LEAK ST
HAROLD ST
SMITH ST
LUND ST
EMPRESS BSNS CTR
EMPRESS ST
HOLLY BANK CL
CORNBROOK PARK RD 1
EMPRESS CT 2
TENBY CT 3
NAPIER CT 4
WRIGHT ST
CITY RD
Schs
CHESTER RD
B5217
EAST UNION ST
DARWEN ST
CHORLTON ST
MANCHESTER ST
BLACKLEY ST
NUTTALL ST
A5067
STRETFORD RD
FARWOOD CL
SUDBURY CL
GRENDALE DR
STANLEY RD
SHREWSBURY ST
GREENLAW CT
STAMFORD ST
CHESTER RD
Chester House (Pol HQ)
BOYER ST
WHITE CITY WAY
A5063
A56
A5067
TALBOT RD
TALBOT PL
CARVER CL
STANLEY CL
SEYMOUR CL
HENRY ST
BATH CRES
STANLEY RD
KATHERINE CT
NORTHUMBERLAND RD
CARVER ST
HUMPHREY RD
THORNTON CT
ST HILDA'S RD
Trafford Bar Sta
ELSINORE RD
SKERTON RD
SEYMOUR GR
Old Trafford
WHITE CITY RET PK
MONTAGUE RD
BOTANICAL AVE
HENRIETTA ST
BEEVER ST
WOODLIFFE ST
BLACKBURN ST
PRESTAGE ST
PARK AVE
8
975
7
970
6
965
5
960
810
815
820
97

D6
1 MALVERN ROW
2 THAMES CT
3 AVON CT
4 WELLAND CT
5 TAMAR CT
6 BOLLIN CT
7 TRAFFORD CT
8 RYLANDS CT
9 MILLINGTON WLK
10 TOWNFIELD WLK
11 BOWGREEN WLK
12 MERESIDE WLK
13 WARDSEND WLK
14 HEYROSE WLK
15 NORCOT WLK

D6
16 PLATTWOOD WLK
17 OLDGATE WLK
18 TOWNCLIFFE WLK
19 DILLMASS WLK
20 STOCKLEY WLK
21 WINCHAM CL
22 ROYCE CT

D6
23 SPRINGSIDE WLK
24 DUDLOW WLK
25 HILLFOOT WLK
26 ROSSHILL WLK

F6
1 KNOWLES PL
2 HORNCHURCH CT
3 ELSTON WLK
4 DODWORTH CL
5 DARNETH CL
6 MORAN WLK
7 PINDER WLK
8 RAGLAN WLK

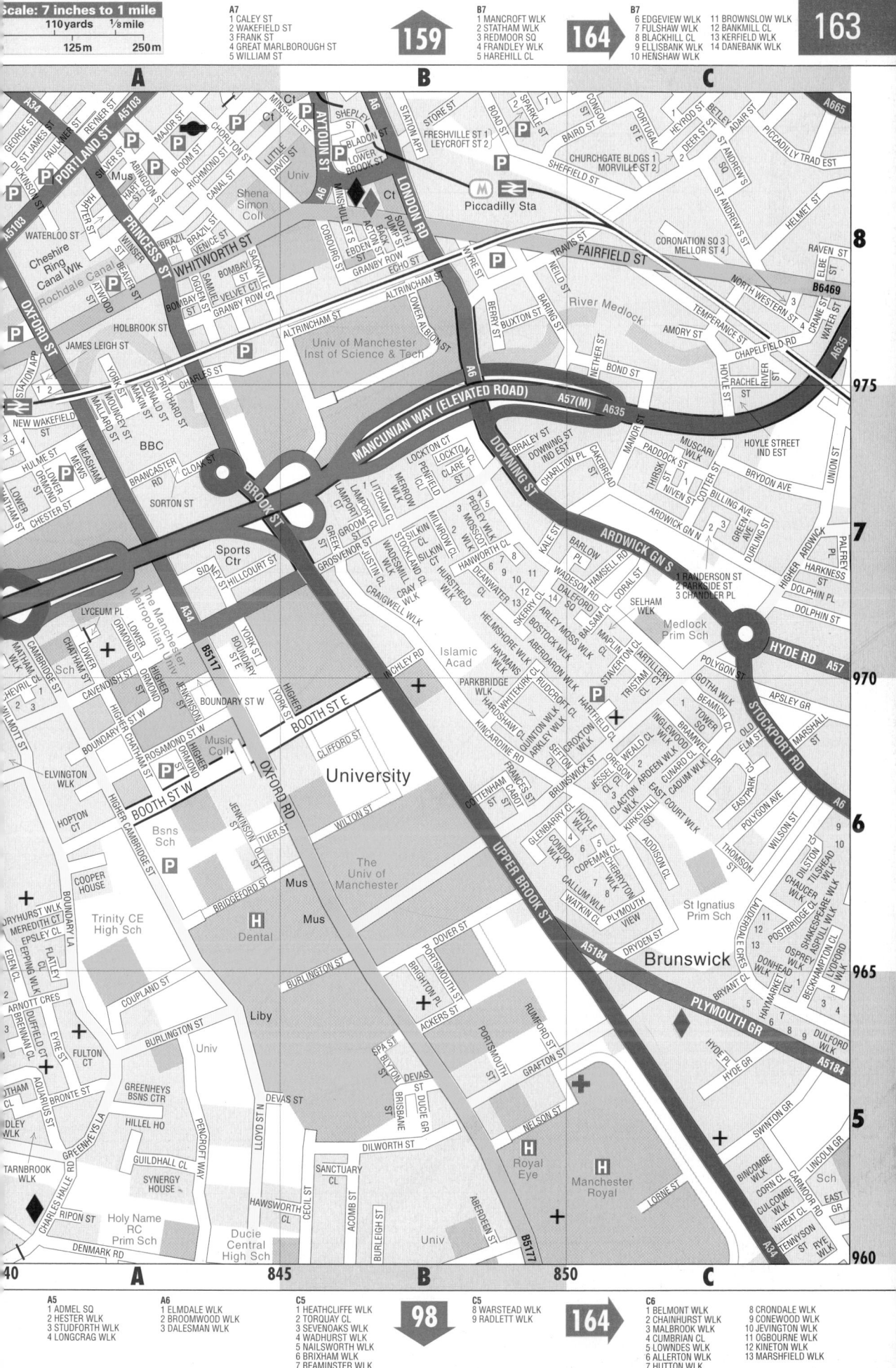

Scale: 7 inches to 1 mile					

110 yards   1/8 mile
125m   250m

A7
1 CALEY ST
2 WAKEFIELD ST
3 FRANK ST
4 GREAT MARLBOROUGH ST
5 WILLIAM ST

159

B7
1 MANCROFT WLK
2 STATHAM WLK
3 REDMOOR SQ
4 FRANDLEY WLK
5 HAREHILL CL

164

B7
6 EDGEVIEW WLK   11 BROWNSLOW WLK
7 FULSHAW WLK   12 BANKMILL CL
8 BLACKILL CL   13 KERFIELD WLK
9 ELLISBANK WLK   14 DANEBANK WLK
10 HENSHAW WLK

163

A5
1 ADMEL SQ
2 HESTER WLK
3 STUDFORTH WLK
4 LONGCRAG WLK

A6
1 ELMDALE WLK
2 BROOMWOOD WLK
3 DALESMAN WLK

C5
1 HEATHCLIFFE WLK
2 TORQUAY CL
3 SEVENOAKS WLK
4 WADHURST WLK
5 NAILSWORTH WLK
6 BRIXHAM WLK
7 BEAMINSTER WLK

98

C5
8 WARSTEAD WLK
9 RADLETT WLK

164

C6
1 BELMONT WLK   8 CRONDALE WLK
2 CHAINHURST WLK   9 CONEWOOD WLK
3 MALBROOK WLK   10 JEVINGTON WLK
4 CUMBRIAN CL   11 OGBOURNE WLK
5 LOWNDES WLK   12 KINETON WLK
6 ALLERTON WLK   13 MARSHFIELD WLK
7 HUTTON WLK

Scale: 7 inches to 1 mile
0   110 yards   ⅛ mile
0   125 m   250 m

D   **E**   **F**

A665
GREAT ANCOATS ST
RIPLEY CL
LINTON CL
ANCOATS GR
PALMERSTON ST
CORK ST
ANCOATS
SPIRE WLK
LACY WLK
ALDERMAN SQ
ASHLAR DR
HELSBY WLK
MARKHAM CL
ADEN CL
MORNA WLK
River Medlock
COALBROOK WLK
RIMMER CL
CYCLONE ST 1
NEWCHURCH ST 2
TOWNLEY ST
JOBLING ST
GILLINGHAM SQ
GLYNEATH
BLACKROCK ST
HINCKLEY ST
SIAM ST
BARMOUTH ST
BORDAN ST
SARAH ST

HELMET ST
Bank Meadow Prim Sch
LIMEKILN LA
LIME BANK ST
BYRCLAND CL
VIADUCT ST
HOLT ST
HARRY THORNEYCROFT WLK
FERRY ST
RYLANCE ST
TED JACKSON WLK
BALDWIN WRIGHT ROBINSON
MYRTLE ST
HANNAH CL
BINGLEY CL
MANIPUR ST
Beswick
CHARLESWORTH ST
Ashbury Prim Sch
SHEFFORD CL
BRENNOCK CL
LUCAS WLK
CAMPION ST
P

8
ADLOW IND PK
A635
PIN MILL BROW
MAYO ST
NORWAY ST
NANSEN ST
POPLAR ST
HUGHES ST
CLARIBEL ST
BELLEW ST
REDVERS ST
BADEN ST
WISELEY ST
WILL GRIFFITH WLK
OLIVER ST
WYNNE CL
HART WELL CL
HEYBURY CL
PENDLEGREEN CL
TYROL WLK
ALDRIDGE CL

MILL GREEN ST
WILLIAM ST
A635 FAIRFIELD ST
DARK LA
CRESBURY ST
ADLINGTON ST
GLENBARRY ST
HOOPER ST
P0
ASHTON OLD RD
BELL CRES

975
NORTH WESTERN ST
MIDLAND ST
A665
HANDSWORTH ST
PITTBROOK ST
RONDIN RD
RONDIN CL
GABLE ST
STAINFORTH ST
TULEY ST
KAY ST
MITCHELL ST
A635
WOLVETON ST

TEMPERANCE ST
CHANCELLOR LA
DAINTON ST
Ardwick
TONGE ST
GORTON RD

THAMES IND EST
HIGHER ARDWICK
BLIND LA

7
HARKNESS ST
DEVONSHIRE ST N
Ardwick Sta
VAUGHAN IND EST

DALBERG ST
FORD ST
NICHOLLS ST
BLUCHER ST
ANTHONY CL
WIGLEY ST
MATTHEW ST
West Gorton
Works
VAUGHAN ST

970
A57
Manchester High Sch of Arts
Ellen Wilkinson High Sch
BENNETT ST
TROWTREE AVE
ST BENEDICT'S SQ
GREGORY ST
MARRYAT CT
BASECHURCH WLK 1
SOMERWOOD WLK 2
WROXETER WLK 3
WOOLFALL CL 4
BAYSTON WLK 5
WOODROW WLK 6
WITTERAGE
KEMPLEY CL

CARIOCCA ENT PK
WHIXHALL AVE
CLIVEWOOD WLK
ERCALL AVE
SUNDERTON WLK
REABROOK AVE
BENEDICT CT
KNIVETON RD
WENLOCK WAY
PENFOLD WLK
LLOYD CL
SKARRATT CL
GORTONVILLA WLK
BEGONIA WLK
BEAUMARIS CL

SYNDALL CL
SYNDALL AVE
P0
DEVONSHIRE ST
A665
OLEBROOK CL
ROCKINGHAM CL
COVERDALE CRES
STANSBY GDNS
WARMINGTON DR
ROSTRON AVE
SHROPSHIRE SQ
ASHOVER AVE
ARMITAGE CT
DENEHURST ST
BRUNET WLK
KINLEY CL
CLOWES ST

6
A6
TARLETON WLK
MARCHMONT CL
KERSHAW WLK
NAKED CL
DARTFORD CL
Armitage CE Prim Sch
TOLL BAR CL
GREY ST
CULAND ST
HAVERFORD ST
BALHAM WLK
POLLITT CL
FAIRHAVEN ST
AINSDALE ST
DONNISON ST

CAVANAGH CL
PEMBROKE CL
GUIDE POST SQ
BAINBRIDGE CL
COTTINGHAM RD
MORBOURNE CL
PATCHETT ST
COPPING ST
DEEPDENE ST
PENRHYN
A57
A6010

INSTOW CL
DEVONSHIRE ST S
HITCHIN WLK
HUNTSWORTH WLK
ST STEPHEN'S CL
PORTGATE WLK
STOCKPORT RD
CASHMOR WLK
LANGPORT AVE
HALSBURY CL
SANDRIDGE WLK
MILNTHORPE WAY
LIDBROOK WLK
MARTINDALE CRES
IPSWICH WLK
BURDETT WAY
HOLDNESS CL
CHIPSTEAD WLK
EDLIN CL
NEW BANK ST
REDGATE LA

965
TALLAND WLK
DANECROFT CL
BRATTON WLK
DOBSON CL
DENEWELL CL
BLETCHLEY CL
FLUXTON WLK
FERNBROOK CL
ROYDS CL
MARKFIELD AVE
Sports Hall
St Luke's CE Prim Sch
Longsight Park Fst Sch
CULFORD CL
COCHRANE AVE
KNOWLDALE WAY
DILLON DR
SAXTHORPE WLK
Longsight

A5184
WHITESTONE WLK
BUSH MOOR WLK
HILLFIELD CL
WINTERFORD AVE
BASILDON CL
FROBISHER CL
ETRURIA CL
LUCIEN CL
SOUTH ST
BRITNALL AVE
CURLEW WLK
RIVINGTON WLK

5
St Chrysostoms CE Prim Sch
ELMSCOTT WLK
CROSSBANK CL
IVYBRIDGE CL
WALCOTT CL
DRYBROOK CL
CAMROSE WLK
PLYMOUTH GR
BLAKEDOWN WLK 1
LAWNSWOOD WLK 2
MORPETH WLK 3
BERIGAN CL
RICHMOND GR E
KINGFISHER CL
RONA WLK
CRINGLEFORD WLK
MULL AVE
EARL WLK
LAMB CL
BELLE VUE AVE

EAST GR
SOUTH GR
CHELFORD CL
HOLKER CL
KESWICK CL
BRANDISH CL
Plymouth Grove Prim Sch
PLYMOUTH AVE
GRINDLOW ST
A6
PORTLAND CRES
WEST GR
NORTH GR
UPPER WEST GR
EDBROOK WLK
HATHERSAGE RD
PLYMOUTH GR W
A5184
A6010

960
855   **D**   **860**   **E**   **865**   **F**

Scale: 7 inches to 1 mile
110 yards
1/8 mile
125 m
250 m
83
99
A
B
C
Openshaw
Works
Works
Works
St Brigid's RC Prim Schs (Jun & Inf)
Liby
PO
Mkt
Openshaw CE Prim Sch
Ashbury's Sta
Manchester Coll of Arts & Tech Openshaw Ctr
New Smithfield Mkt
Corn Brook
St Francis' RC Prim Sch
All Saints Prim Sch
Gorton Brook Fst Sch
TA Ctr
Car Auction
Gorton Parks
Gorton Ind Est
Victoria House
City Course Trad Est
Belle Vue
Belle Vue Sta
ALAN TURING WAY
A6010
ASHTON OLD RD
A635
POTTERY LA
GORTON RD
GORTON LA
HYDE RD
B6178
MOUNT RD
A57
KIRKMANSHULME LA
CLAYTON LA
CLAYTON LA S
CYCLE ST
STAINBURN RD
KELBROOK RD
PARKHOUSE ST
SOUTH ST
WHITWORTH ST
WHITWORTH ST E
BESSEMER ST
PRESTON ST
RAILWAY ST
HAMMERSTONE RD
GATEWAY RD
FROXMER ST
BOND ST
MARK RD
JARMAIN ST
AMBROSE ST
TEXTILE ST
ELLENBROOK CL
GALSTON ST
HERNE ST
WESLEY ST
DYER ST
BOSWORTH ST
GRAHAM ST
BEVERDALE CL
CABLESTEAD WLK
BROWNHILL ST
BUTTERWORTH ST
MILL ST
LARNE ST
HOLROYD ST
WILSON ST
GOOLE ST
STOPLEY WLK
OUTRINGTON WLK
WINDERMERE CL
WINSLOW ST
SELBY ST
COLLIERY ST
RIDINGS ST
DULGAR ST
REFORM WLK
THAMES CL
FLAVION WLK
NEDEN CL
ST BARNABAS SQ
ABBEYFIELD SQ
TRAFALGAR WLK
NEWTOWN CL
MAYTON ST
BEEDE ST
FASTNET ST
KERWIN WLK
SPARTA WLK
CHURCHFIELD WLK
PITMAN CL
WADE WLK
DAWNAY ST
ODELL ST
FERN ST
REDBY ST
WOOD ST
STORE ST
BARTLETT ST
VINCENT ST
CRAYDON ST
WELCOMB ST
BERTHA ST
COMPASS ST
TRAM ST
NUTTALL ST
BILL WILLIAMS CL
APPLECROSS WLK
STAN JOLLY WLK
MALLAIG WLK
JINNAH CL
AVIEMORE WLK
READING CL
KIRKTOWN WLK
GREENSIDE ST
DUNSTON ST
CONNIE ST
STATON ST
BRIGHAM ST
VICTORIA CT
TIMPERLEY ST
NICHOLAS OWEN CL
ALDERMOOR CL
CORONATION ST
GREER ST
MEECH ST
RANGE ST
GATE ST
HOVIS ST
ELYSIAN ST
VICTORIA ST
BRADE CL
FREELAND WLK
PETERCHURCH WLK
ECCLES CL
GODLEY CL
DERBYSHIRE ST
DAKLEY ST
SILKSTONE ST
WESTLAKE ST
WIDNES ST
BEULAH ST
MILES ST
AINES ST
BOYD ST
WHEATLEY WLK
WENLOCK WAY
LILFORD CL
CLOWES ST
BENFLEET CL
BOULEY WLK
CONQUEST CL
DASHWOOD WLK
RADBOURNE CL
ABBOTSBURY CL
NEENTON SQ
KIMBOLTON CL
DIDLEY SQ
ROMSLEY CL
WESTBROOK SQ
GARDINER ST
BRINSOP SQ
BURTREE ST
KESTREL WLK
FLAMINGO CL
CORMORANT WLK
POLESWORTH CL
CHALLENOR SQ
VALANCE CL
DANETT CL
DOUGALL WLK
BRIDGEND CL
SHARNFORD SQ
APOLLO WLK
ELLISTON SQ
BLACKWIN ST
LAURENCE CL
RITSON CL
ENDCOTT CL
BONCHURCH WLK
STONEHURST CL
REANEY WLK
GRENDON WLK
BIRCH ST
CORBY ST
RUNHALL CL
BELLE VUE ST
SUTTON ST
GREAT JONES ST
DONNISON ST
BERTRAM ST
FARNLEY ST
MALPAS ST
BOUNDARY ST
MILNE CL
GREAT NELSON ST
COALBURN ST
FENTON ST
COMO WLK
JENNISON CL
MARJORIE CL
HILLCOTE WLK
DEEROAK CL
DALKEITH ST
CROSSLEY ST
LEACH ST
BEALEY CL
TRANMERE CL
WOODLAND ST
NORMAN ST
QUEENSLAND RD
QUEENS AVE
STRADBROKE CL
FURNIVAL RD
TAYLOR ST
PINETREE ST
PIPEWELL AVE
BRIGSTOCK AVE
SEATHWAITE WLK
HAMPDEN CRES
KETTLEWELL WLK
HINCASTER WLK 1
LITTLEHAM WLK 2
LANGCLIFFE WLK 3
HEPTONSTALL WLK 4
CAMBERT LA
THORNBURY WAY
GARRATT WAY
WHITWELL WAY
KELD WLK
KILNSLEY WLK
ROSGILL WLK
PATRICK RODDY CT
BRYSON WLK
BEYER CL
DUNNERDALE WLK
HEVERSHAM WLK
GRIZEBECK CL
BELPER WLK
EMBLETON WLK
MIDDLEWICH WLK
PEACOCK CL
BUTTRESS ST
FRANCESCA WLK
BURSTON ST
ANCHORAGE WLK
EARLSWOOD WLK
GLENCASTLE RD
WILLIAMS RD
CHATSWORTH RD
SUNNY BROW RD
WILLIAMS ST
BRAGENHAM ST
AGNEW RD
BECKETT ST
PARKDALE AVE
MOUNTBATTEN ST
BRACEWELL CL
SCARCROFT RD
FOXLEY WLK
LOCKHART CL
ELLEN WILKINSON CRES
HOSKINS CL
IQBAL CL
TARRINGTON CL
DUNLEY CL
PENCOMBE CL
RIGTON CL
COLLINGTON CL
TINSHILL CL
THORALBY CL
REDGATE LA
8
975
7
970
6
965
5
960
870
875
880

166
C3
1 FLETCHER ST
2 MULBERRY ST
3 CROSS GLEBE ST
4 ARLINGTON ST
5 SLOANE ST
6 ST MICHAEL'S SQ
7 STAMFORD ARC
8 OLD SQ
84
85
85
Scale: 7 inches to 1 mile
0
110 yards
1/8 mile
0
125m
250m
A
B
C
4
995
3
990
2
985
1
980
930
935
940
ASHTON-UNDER-LYNE
Charlestown
Hurst Brook
Hurst Knoll CE (VC) Prim Sch
Playing Fields
Canon Johnson CE Prim Sch
Holy Trinity CE Prim Sch
St Ann's RC Prim Sch
St James' CE Prim Sch
St Peter's CE Prim Sch
Ashton Sta
TH & Mus
Mkt
THE ARCHADE
LADYSMITH SH CTR
Liby
Coll
Superstore
CAVENDISH MILL
Mus
River Tame
Ashton Canal
Peak Forest Canal
Cemy
PLANTATION IND EST
WHITELANDS TERR
WELLINGTON CTR
CHARLESTOWN IND EST
MOUNT PLEASANT TRAD EST
PARK PARADE IND EST
BURLINGTON HOUSE
ELLISON HOUSE
OLDHAM RD
CAVENDISH ST
WELLINGTON RD
PENNY MEADOW
PARK PAR
MANCHESTER RD
STOCKPORT RD
KING ST
ASTLEY ST
CRESCENT RD
WHITELANDS
PARK RD
MOSSLEY RD
SCOTLAND ST
A627
A670
A635
A6017
B6194
B6170
B6445
B6169
A1
1 GROSVENOR HOUSE
2 RYECROFT HOUSE
3 BOLLINGTON CL
4 MOUNT CL
5 VICTORIA CT
6 GROSVENOR PL
7 CECIL WLK
8 REDBRICK CT
9 GROSVENOR CT
10 UPTON WLK
11 SOUTHGATE WAY
A2
1 BENTINCK TERR
2 BENTINCK HOUSE
3 PORTLAND HOUSE
84
4 WELBECK HOUSE
5 MARGARET HOUSE
6 ST PETER'S ST
7 BRADGATE ST
B1
1 LYME TERR
2 PICKMERE TERR
3 WOOLLEY TERR
101
4 BUDE TERR
5 TATTON TERR
6 BROMPTON TERR
7 QUEEN'S TERR
8 ALDERLEY TERR
9 CHAMPAGNOLE CT
10 GEORGE CT
11 DEAN CT
12 CRESCENT VIEW
13 WELLINGTON TERR
14 KING'S TERR
15 WARWICK TERR
16 EARL TERR
17 DUKE'S TERR
18 TAYLOR TERR
19 PEEL TERR
20 NEWTON TERR
21 COOK TERR
22 DENYER TERR
23 JOHNSON TERR
24 HATTON TERR
25 DANTY ST
26 GASKELL ST
C1
1 RAVEN TERR
2 PENNINE TERR
3 FRANCIS TERR
4 KENDAL TERR
5 SHAW TERR
6 PLEASANT TERR
7 ASTLEY TERR

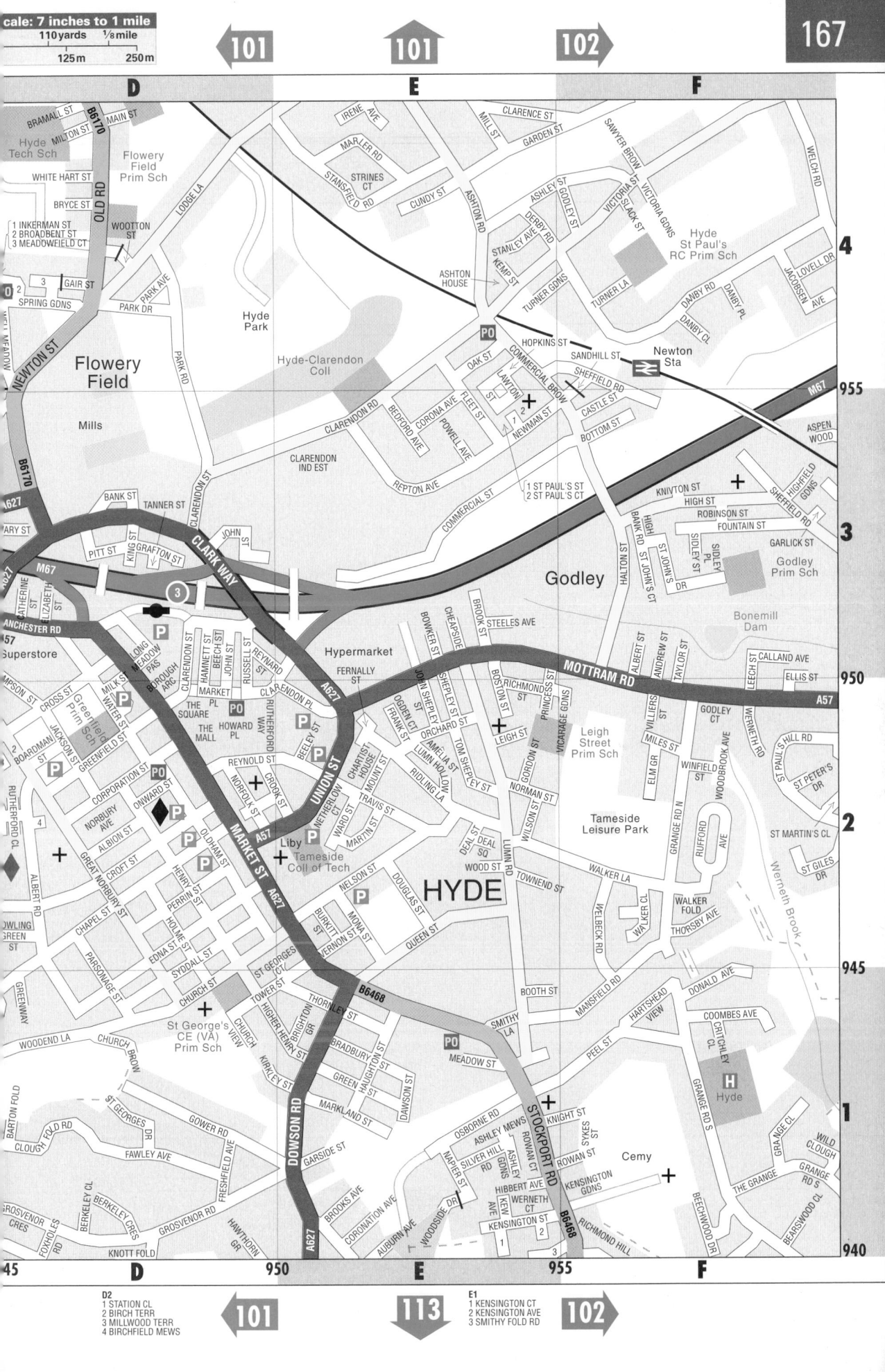

cale: 7 inches to 1 mile
110 yards
1/8 mile
125 m
250 m
101
101
102
D
E
F
Hyde Tech Sch
Flowery Field Prim Sch
Hyde Park
Hyde-Clarendon Coll
Flowery Field
Mills
CLARENDON IND EST
Hyde St Paul's RC Prim Sch
Newton Sta
ASHTON HOUSE
Godley
Godley Prim Sch
Bonemill Dam
Hypermarket
Superstore
Greenfield Prim Sch
Leigh Street Prim Sch
Tameside Leisure Park
Liby
Tameside Coll of Tech
HYDE
St George's CE (VA) Prim Sch
Hyde
Cemy
MOTTRAM RD
M67
A57
A627
B6170
B6468
Wernerth Brook
4
3
2
1
955
950
945
940
45
950
955
D2
1 STATION CL
2 BIRCH TERR
3 MILLWOOD TERR
4 BIRCHFIELD MEWS
E1
1 KENSINGTON CT
2 KENSINGTON AVE
3 SMITHY FOLD RD
101
113
102

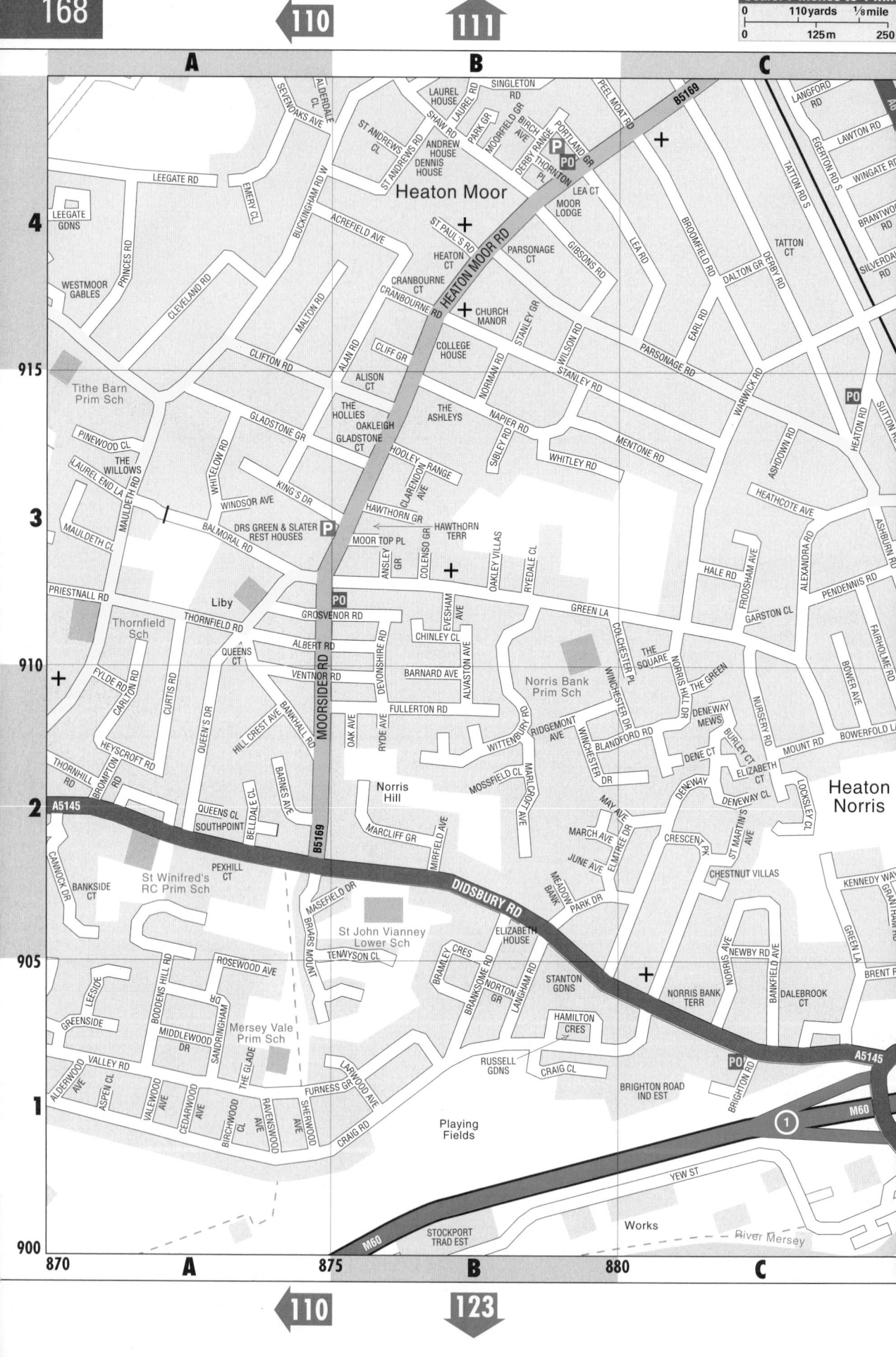

Scale: 7 inches to 1 mile
110yards
1/8mile
125m
250m
111
112
169
D
E
F
WHITEHILL IND EST
WHITEHILL ST
WHITEHILL ST W
HAIGH AVE
Whitehill Prim Sch
Recn Gd
WENSLEY RD
DYSERTH GR
GLASWEN GR
PENSARN GR
GAIR RD
B6167
BOLLIN WLK
DANE WLK
WILLOW AVE
BEECHWOOD AVE
GR
ACACIA
WOODHALL RD
ROSEDALE RD
ST LEONARD'S RD
DENBY LA
A626
EMPRESS DR
GOWER RD
MARLBOROUGH DR
GLENFIELD RD
WARWICK RD
WARWICK CT
WARWICK CL
St Annes RC High Sch
HOLMFIELD CL
SPATHFIELD CT
WHITEFIELD
All Saints CE Prim Sch
SELBY ST
KINGSLEY AVE
BOURNVILLE AVE
HORACE GR
THE PARKLANDS
REUBEN ST
MORTON ST
STANBANK ST
MANCHESTER RD
BOURNE ST
COLIN RD
ALL SAINTS' RD
SHARPLES ST
BARDSLEY ST
BURTON ST
LLOYD ST
GRAFTON ST
SAMUEL ST
FARMER ST
CHURCHILL ST
EDMUND CL
BURTON WLK
GRESHAM WLK
HESKETH ST
ALBION CL
LOWER MOAT CL
MEAL ST
CONWAY ST
ANN ST
HAWKINS ST
WESTON ST
RALEIGH ST
DRAKE CT
FROBISHER PL
CABOT PL
CORONATION ST
BANKFIELD TRAD EST
BANKFIELD ST
HALSTON CL
GREG ST
BANGOR ST
SCOTT CL
REDDISH RD
MORGAN PL
HILDA ST
CLARE RD
MELTON ST
NORWAY GR
HILDA GR
BROUGHTON RD
JOWETT ST
JERSEY RD
SANDY LA
PEARSON ST
BURY ST
ROSE ST
CLARENDON ST
WALMSLEY ST
MANVERS ST
TIVIOT WAY
915
4
HEATON RD
VAUGHAN RD
SPARTHFIELD RD
ASHBURN GR
RENA CT
SPARTH CT
SPARTH LA
SPARTH HALL
FAIRLAWN
RENA CL
YEALAND AVE
ASHBURN RD
GAIL AVE
HILARY CL
DUNBLANE AVE
BOWERFOLD LA
WELLINGTON RD N
ELLEN ST
DENBIGH ST
CROMWELL ST
BELMONT ST
CHEVIOT CL
LLOYD ST
ATHOL ST
HARWOOD ST
CHURCH ST
OXFORD WAY
COTSWOLD RD
MALVERN CL
STITCH LA
BASIL ST
CLEMENT ST
BELMONT WAY
BELMONT CL
INCE ST
HESKETH ST
BELMONT ST
BAKER ST
INCE CL
HAPTON PL
SHORT ST
MENDIP CT
MENDIP CL
HAMILTON SQ
BELMONT SH CTR
OLD RD
SHEFFIELD ST
SHORT ST E
CLARKETHORN TERR
Lancashire Hill
WHARF ST
GLADSTONE MEWS
WHERNSIDE CL
GORDON ST
TUNSTALL ST
ORPHANAGE ST
NICHOLSON ST
CYMBAL CT
THE LONGSONS
KINGS CT
THE BENTLEYS
STONEMILL TERR
PENNY LA
LANCASHIRE HILL
PENDLEBURY TOWERS
HANOVER TOWERS
MEADOW IND EST
River Tame
3
WATER ST
BREWERY ST
MARSLAND ST
RICHARD ST
PORTWOOD PL
910
QUANTOCK CL
LOVE LA
SOUTHDOWN CL
HEATON TOWERS
WILKINSON RD
CANNING ST
FLORENCE ST
GREENHALGH ST
DODGE HILL
MULBERRY MEWS
CHURCH RD
PARSONAGE ST
NORRIS TOWERS
ROMAN RD
Recn Gd
St Mary's RC Prim Sch
STANBRIDGE CT
WYATT ST
M60
RICHARD ST
BACK WATER ST
AVENUE ST
BREWERY ST
HOWARD ST
GREAT PORTWOOD ST
A560
KNIGHTSBRIDGE
B6167
Superstore
KING ST E
THE PEEL CTR
2
HIGHER BURY ST
LONGSIGHT ST
WYCLIFFE ST
ANDREW ST
GEORGE'S RD
FIR ST
LAUREL ST
GREEN LANE IND EST
ROOTH ST
GREEN LA
LOWER BURY ST
BRENT RD
RAILWAY ST
GREAT EGERTON ST
LITTLE EGERTON ST
DANIEL'S LA
TIVIOT DALE
PERCY ST
BRIDGE ST
WARREN ST
CORPORATION ST
River Goyt
HATTON ST
PRINCE'S ST
WOODMAN ST
BRIDGEFIELD ST
CASTLE YARD
VERNON ST
SHAWCROSS FOLD
MILLGATE
PARK ST
Superstore
BROWN ST
PRINCE'S ST
MERSEYWAY
DEANERY WAY
ADLINGTON WLK
GREAT UNDERBANK
LITTLE UNDERBANK
MARKET PL
MEALHOUSE BROW
NEW BRIDGE LA
905
PORT ST
LEYLAND ST
ARDEN WLK
VERNON WLK
ROYAL OAK YD
UNDERBANK
HARVEY ST
NORTH HARVEY ST
WALKER ST
PICKFORD'S BROW
HIGH BANK SIDE
St Joseph's RC Sch
TRAVIS BROW
A5145
HOPE ST
A560
GAS ST
HEATON LA
ASTLEY ST
COTTON TREE ST
MERSEY SQ
CHESTERGATE
NORTH PL
ST PETERSGATE
ETCHELLS ST
TATTON ST
HIGH ST
LOWER HILLGATE
CHURCHGATE
APSLEY ST
LAVENDERS BROW
ACORN BSNS CTR
HEATON LA
STOCKPORT
TALBOT ST
HOOPER ST
ST PETER'S SQ
FLETCHER ST
LOWER CARRS
ORCHARD ST
1
No 2 PASSAGE
CHESTER ST
River Mersey
KING ST W
CHESTERGATE
SWAINE ST
WELLINGTON MILL
DAW BANK
WELLINGTON RD S
LAWRENCE ST
DUKE ST
LORD ST
Ct
Liby
WELLINGTON ST
BANBURY ST
GARNETT ST
WESLEY ST
HOPES CARR
COVENT GARDEN
CHESTERGATE
HOLLYWOOD WAY
FORD ST
BRINKSWAY
ALBERT ST
OWEN ST
GOUGH ST
KINGSTON ST
HARDMAN ST
COOK ST
VIADUCT ST
EXCHANGE ST
LOTTERY ST
WEST ST
WOOD ST
A5145
A560
STATION RD
LORD ST
NORBURY ST
PICCADILLY
LONDON SQ
LONDON PL
HOLBORN ST
LOWE ST
MASSEY ST
JOHN ST
LEE ST
Ct
Pol HQ
MIDDLE HILLGATE
WATSON SQ
WATERLOO RD
MOUNT ST
GORSEY
JOULES CT
CANAL ST
A6
900
885
890
895
170
112

123

E8
1 CHATHAM HOUSE
2 BOWDON HOUSE
3 PEMBROKE HOUSE
4 PALATINE HOUSE

169

E8
5 LANCASTER HOUSE
6 DURHAM HOUSE
7 SIMPSON ST
8 FRANCES ST

124

F8
1 LOONIES CT
2 JOULES CT
3 OLD GARDENS ST
4 HOLLINGWORTH CL
5 MOTTRAM ST
6 RATCLIFFE ST
7 GROSVENOR ST

123
123
124

Scale: 7 inches to 1 mile
0 110yards 1/8 mile
0 125m 250m

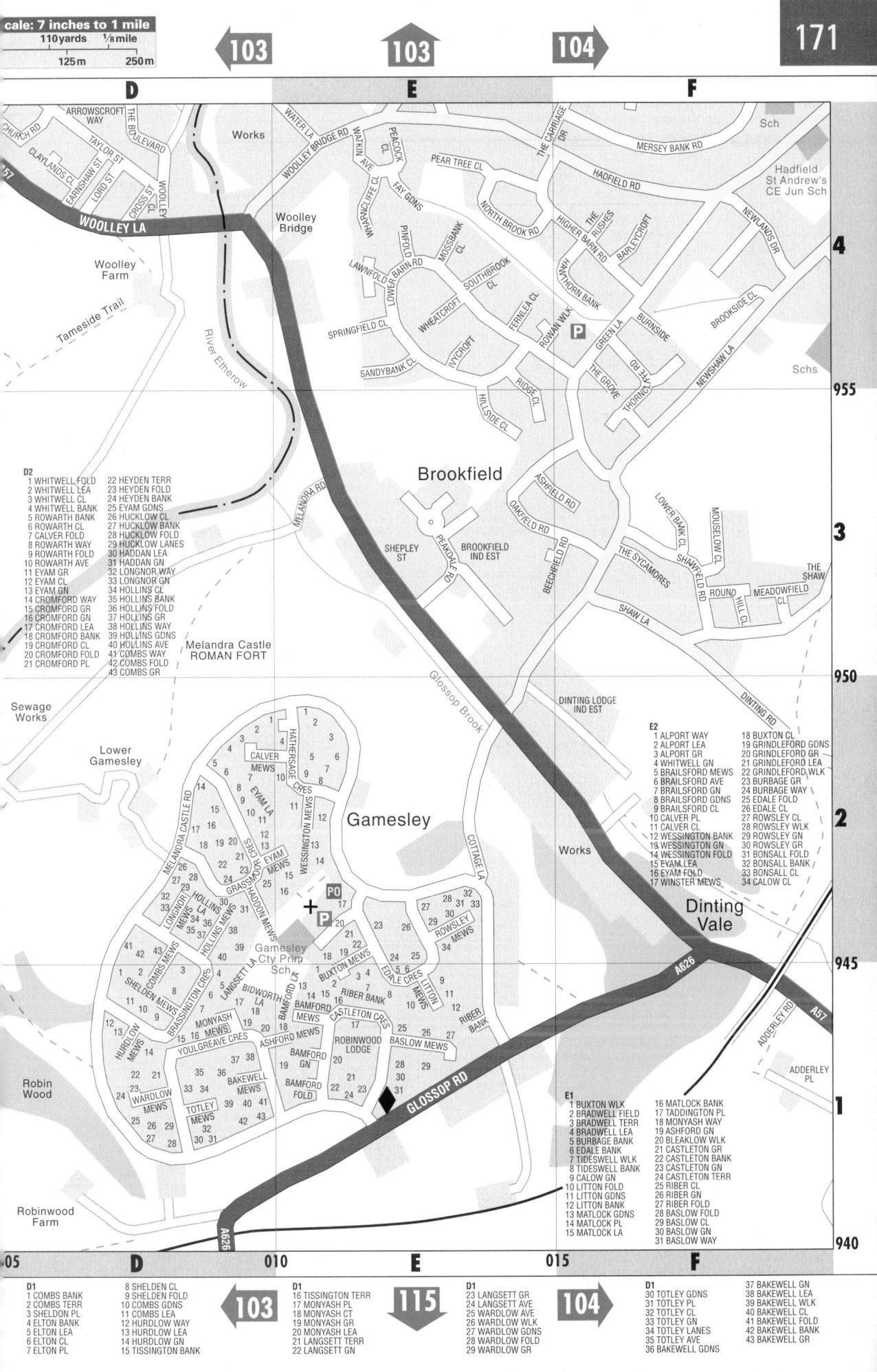

D E F

4

WOOLLEY LA

Brookfield

955

3

950

Gamesley

Dinting Vale

945

2

Works

1

940

05   D   010   E   015   F

Church Rd, Arrowscroft Way, The Boulevard, Taylor St, Claylands Cl, Earnshaw St, Lord St, Cross St, Woolley, Woolley Bridge Rd, Water La, Watkin Ave, Wharncliffe Cl, Peacock Cl, Fay Gdns, Pear Tree Cl, North Brook Rd, Higher Barn Rd, Hadfield Rd, Mersey Bank Rd, Hadfield St Andrew's CE Jun Sch, Newlands Dr, Sch, Works, Woolley Bridge, Woolley Farm, Tameside Trail, River Etherow, Springfield Cl, Lawnfold, Lower Barn Rd, Pinfold, Mossbank Cl, Wheatcroft, Southbrook Cl, Fernlea Cl, Hawthorn Bank, Rowan Wlk, The Rushes, Barleycroft, Green La, Burnside, Brookside Cl, Newshaw La, Schs, The Shaw, Ivycroft, Sandybank Cl, Hillside Cl, Ridge Cl, The Grove, Thorncliffe, Gate Rd, Lower Bank Cl, Mouselow Cl, Shawfield Rd, The Sycamores, The Shaw, Meadowfield Cl, Round Hill Cl, Melandra Rd, Ashfield Rd, Oakfield Rd, Beechfield Rd, Shepley St, Peakdale Rd, Brookfield Ind Est, Shaw La, Melandra Castle ROMAN FORT, Glossop Brook, Dinting Lodge Ind Est, Dinting Rd, Sewage Works, Lower Gamesley, Calver Mews, Hathersage Cres, Eyam La, Wessington Mews, Cottage La, A626, Adderley Rd, A57, Melandra Castle Rd, Grassmoor Cres, Haddon Mews, Eyam Mews, PO, P, Rowsley Mews, Longnor Mews, Hollins La, Hollins Mews, Combs Mews, Shelden Mews, Brassington Cres, Langsett La, Bidworth La, Bamford La, Buxton Mews, Riber Bank, Edale Cres, Litton Mews, Riber Bank, Adderley Pl, Gamesley Cty Prim Sch, Monyash Mews, Ashford Mews, Castleton Cres, Baslow Mews, Robin Wood, Hurdlow Mews, Youlgreave Cres, Bamford Gn, Robinwood Lodge, Wardlow Mews, Totley Mews, Bakewell Mews, Bamford Fold, GLOSSOP RD, Robinwood Farm, A626

D2
1 WHITWELL FOLD
2 WHITWELL LEA
3 WHITWELL CL
4 WHITWELL BANK
5 ROWARTH BANK
6 ROWARTH CL
7 CALVER FOLD
8 ROWARTH WAY
9 ROWARTH FOLD
10 ROWARTH AVE
11 EYAM GR
12 EYAM CL
13 EYAM GN
14 CROMFORD WAY
15 CROMFORD GR
16 CROMFORD GN
17 CROMFORD LEA
18 CROMFORD BANK
19 CROMFORD CL
20 CROMFORD FOLD
21 CROMFORD PL
22 HEYDEN TERR
23 HEYDEN FOLD
24 HEYDEN BANK
25 EYAM GDNS
26 HUCKLOW CL
27 HUCKLOW BANK
28 HUCKLOW FOLD
29 HUCKLOW LANES
30 HADDAN LEA
31 HADDAN GN
32 LONGNOR WAY
33 LONGNOR GN
34 HOLLINS CL
35 HOLLINS BANK
36 HOLLINS FOLD
37 HOLLINS GR
38 HOLLINS WAY
39 HOLLINS GDNS
40 HOLLINS AVE
41 COMBS WAY
42 COMBS FOLD
43 COMBS GR

E2
1 ALPORT WAY
2 ALPORT LEA
3 ALPORT GR
4 WHITWELL GN
5 BRAILSFORD MEWS
6 BRAILSFORD AVE
7 BRAILSFORD GN
8 BRAILSFORD GDNS
9 BRAILSFORD CL
10 CALVER PL
11 CALVER CL
12 WESSINGTON BANK
13 WESSINGTON GN
14 WESSINGTON FOLD
15 EYAM LEA
16 EYAM FOLD
17 WINSTER MEWS
18 BUXTON CL
19 GRINDLEFORD GDNS
20 GRINDLEFORD GR
21 GRINDLEFORD LEA
22 GRINDLEFORD WLK
23 BURBAGE GR
24 BURBAGE WAY
25 EDALE FOLD
26 EDALE CL
27 ROWSLEY CL
28 ROWSLEY WLK
29 ROWSLEY GN
30 ROWSLEY GR
31 BONSALL FOLD
32 BONSALL BANK
33 BONSALL CL
34 CALOW CL

E1
1 BUXTON WLK
2 BRADWELL FIELD
3 BRADWELL TERR
4 BRADWELL LEA
5 BURBAGE BANK
6 EDALE BANK
7 TIDESWELL WLK
8 TIDESWELL BANK
9 CALOW GN
10 LITTON FOLD
11 LITTON GDNS
12 LITTON BANK
13 MATLOCK GDNS
14 MATLOCK PL
15 MATLOCK LA
16 MATLOCK BANK
17 TADDINGTON PL
18 MONYASH WAY
19 ASHFORD GN
20 BLEAKLOW WLK
21 CASTLETON GR
22 CASTLETON BANK
23 CASTLETON GN
24 CASTLETON TERR
25 RIBER CL
26 RIBER GN
27 RIBER FOLD
28 BASLOW FOLD
29 BASLOW CL
30 BASLOW GN
31 BASLOW WAY

D1
1 COMBS BANK
2 COMBS TERR
3 SHELDON PL
4 ELTON BANK
5 ELTON LEA
6 ELTON CL
7 ELTON PL
8 SHELDEN CL
9 SHELDEN FOLD
10 COMBS GDNS
11 COMBS LEA
12 HURDLOW WAY
13 HURDLOW LEA
14 HURDLOW GN
15 TISSINGTON BANK

D1
16 TISSINGTON TERR
17 MONYASH PL
18 MONYASH CT
19 MONYASH GR
20 MONYASH LEA
21 LANGSETT TERR
22 LANGSETT GN

D1
23 LANGSETT GR
24 LANGSETT AVE
25 WARDLOW AVE
26 WARDLOW PL
27 WARDLOW GDNS
28 WARDLOW FOLD
29 WARDLOW GR

D1
30 TOTLEY GDNS
31 TOTLEY PL
32 TOTLEY CL
33 TOTLEY GN
34 TOTLEY LANES
35 TOTLEY AVE
36 BAKEWELL GDNS

37 BAKEWELL GN
38 BAKEWELL LEA
39 BAKEWELL WLK
40 BAKEWELL CL
41 BAKEWELL FOLD
42 BAKEWELL BANK
43 BAKEWELL GR

Index

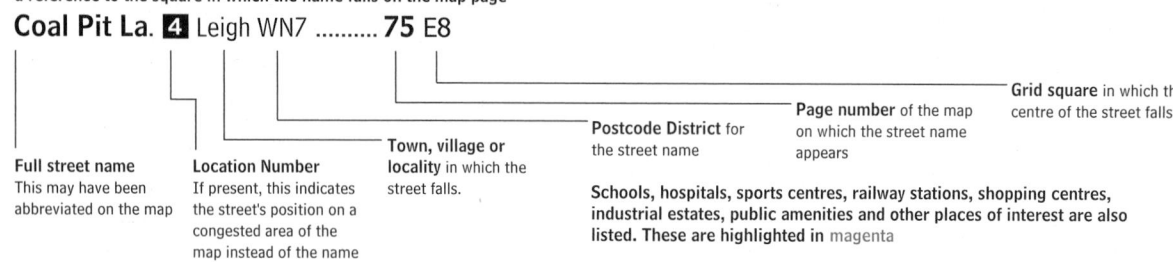

Street names are listed alphabetically and show the locality, the Postcode District, the page number and a reference to the square in which the name falls on the map page

Coal Pit La. ▣ Leigh WN7 .... **75** E8

Full street name
This may have been abbreviated on the map

Location Number
If present, this indicates the street's position on a congested area of the map instead of the name

Town, village or locality in which the street falls.

Postcode District for the street name

Page number of the map on which the street name appears

Grid square in which the centre of the street falls

Schools, hospitals, sports centres, railway stations, shopping centres, industrial estates, public amenities and other places of interest are also listed. These are highlighted in magenta

Abbreviations used in the index

Alt'ham **Altrincham**	Ctr **Centre**	Dr **Drive**	Ind Est **Industrial Estate**	Pas **Passage**
App **Approach**	Cir **Circus**	Dro **Drove**	Intc **Interchange**	Pl **Place**
Arc **Arcade**	Cl **Close**	E **East**	Junc **Junction**	Prec **Precinct**
Ave **Avenue**	Comm **Common**	Espl **Esplanade**	La **Lane**	Prom **Promenade**
Bvd **Boulevard**	Cnr **Corner**	Est **Estate**	M'ster **Manchester**	Ret Pk **Retail Park**
Bldgs **Buildings**	Cotts **Cottages**	Gdns **Gardens**	N **North**	Rd **Road**
Bsns Pk **Business Park**	Ct **Court**	Gn **Green**	Orch **Orchard**	R'dale **Rochdale**
Bsns Ctr **Business Centre**	Ctyd **Courtyard**	Gr **Grove**	Par **Parade**	Rdbt **Roundabout**
Bglws **Bungalow**	Cres **Crescent**	Hts **Heights**	Pk **Park**	S **South**

Sq **Square**	
Strs **Stairs**	
Stps **Steps**	
St **Street, Saint**	
Terr **Terrace**	
Trad Est **Trading Estate**	
Wlk **Walk**	
W **West**	
Yd **Yard**	

Andrew St.
Droylsden M35 & M43 ... 84 C4
Andrew St. Failsworth M35 ... 83 E8
Andrew St. Hyde SK14 ... 167 F3
Andrew St. Middleton M24 ... 65 C7
Andrew St. Mossley OL5 ... 86 C8
Andrew St. Stockport SK4 ... 169 D2
Andrew's Terr. 3 BL5 ... 39 E1
Andrews Ave. M41 ... 94 E3
Andy Nicholson Wlk. M9 ... 157 F8
Anemone Dr. BB4 ... 1 A8
Anerley Rd. M20 ... 110 B4
Anfield Cl. BL9 ... 45 B3
Anfield Mews. SK8 ... 122 F3
Anfield Rd. Bolton BL3 ... 147 F2
Anfield Rd. Cheadle SK8 ... 122 F3
Anfield Rd. Failsworth M40 ... 65 D1
Anfield Rd. Sale M33 ... 108 C5
Angel Cl. SK16 ... 101 B8
Angel St. Dukinfield M34 ... 101 A4
Angel St. Hazel Grove SK7 ... 124 D3
Angel St. M'ster M4 ... 159 A3
Angel Trad Est. 4 M4 ... 159 A3
Angela Ave. OL1 & OL2 ... 48 E2
Angela St. M15 ... 162 D7
Angelko Rise. OL1 ... 49 D3
Angelo St. BL1 ... 143 D2
Angle St. 23 BL2 ... 25 B1
Angler Gr. M34 ... 100 F3
Anglesea Ave. SK2 ... 170 F6
Anglesey Cl. OL7 ... 85 A6
Anglesey Dr. SK12 ... 133 F6
Anglesey Gr. SK8 ... 123 A6
Anglesey Rd. OL7 ... 84 F6
Anglesey Water. SK12 ... 133 E6
Angleside Ave. M19 ... 110 E4
Anglezarke Rd. PR6 ... 21 A7
Anglia Gr. BL3 ... 146 C4
Angouleme Way. BL9 ... 140 F1
Angus Ave. Heywood OL10 ... 29 A1
Angus Ave. Leigh WN7 ... 75 C7
Angus St. OL13 ... 3 C8
Aniline St. M11 ... 83 B1
Anita St. M4 ... 159 B2
Anjou Bvd. WN5 ... 54 F8
Ann La. M29 ... 77 C5
Ann Sq. OL4 ... 67 D8
Ann St. Denton M34 ... 100 E3
Ann St. Dukinfield OL7 ... 100 F8
Ann St. Dukinfield SK14 ... 101 C3
Ann St. Farnworth BL4 ... 60 E7
Ann St. Heywood OL10 ... 29 D3
Ann St. Leigh WN7 ... 75 E8
Ann St. R'dale OL11 ... 139 F6
Ann St. Reddish SK5 ... 169 E4
Annable Rd. Bredbury SK6 ... 112 D3
Annable Rd. Droylsden M43 ... 84 B1
Annable Rd. Irlam M44 ... 105 F8
Annable Rd. M'ster M18 ... 99 E6
Annald Sq. M43 ... 100 A8
Annan Gr. WN4 ... 73 E5
Annan St. M34 ... 100 F4
Annandale Gdns. WN8 ... 53 A7
Anne Cl. 6 OL7 ... 85 A6
Anne Line Cl. 3 OL11 ... 31 A5
Anne St. SK16 ... 101 D8
Annecy Cl. BL8 ... 27 B4
Annersley Ave. OL2 ... 149 A6
Annesley Cres. WN3 ... 54 F3
Annesley Gdns. 1 M18 ... 99 D6
Annesley Rd. M40 ... 65 E1
Annette Ave. WA12 ... 89 A5
Annie Darby Ct. M9 ... 157 D7
Annie St. Ramsbottom BL0 ... 11 A4
Annie St. Salford M5 & M6 ... 154 E2
Annis Cl. SK9 ... 137 B2
Annis Rd. Alderley Edge SK9 137 B2
Annis Rd. Bolton BL3 ... 146 B4
Annis St. M9 ... 157 E7
Annisdale Cl. M30 ... 79 B2
Annisfield Ave. OL3 ... 69 C5
Anscombe Cl. M10 & M40 ... 160 D3
Ansdell Ave. M21 ... 109 C8
Ansdell Dr. M43 ... 83 E2
Ansdell Rd. Horwich BL6 ... 22 C4
Ansdell Rd. R'dale OL16 ... 31 B4
Ansdell Rd. Reddish SK5 ... 100 A1
Ansdell Rd. Wigan WN5 ... 54 D5
Ansdell St. M8 ... 156 A7
Ansell Cl. M18 ... 99 D6
Anselms Ct. OL8 ... 66 C4
Ansford Wlk. M9 ... 156 C6
Ansleigh Ave. M8 ... 64 A1
Ansley Gr. SK4 ... 168 B3
Anslow Cl. M40 ... 157 D5
Anson Ave. M27 ... 79 E6
Anson Cl. SK7 ... 132 F5
Anson Ct. M14 ... 98 D3
Anson Pl. WN5 ... 54 C8
Anson Rd. Handforth SK9 ... 131 E1
Anson Rd. M'ster M14 ... 98 D3
Anson Rd. Poynton SK12 ... 134 B3
Anson Rd.
Reddish M34 & SK5 ... 100 A2
Anson Rd. Swinton M27 ... 79 E6
Anson St. Bolton BL1 ... 143 F3
Anson St. Swinton M28 ... 79 B4
Anson St. Wigan WN5 ... 54 F7
Answell Ave. M8 ... 64 A2
Antares Ave. M7 ... 158 D3
Anthistle Ct. M5 ... 154 D2
Anthony Cl. M12 ... 164 E7
Anthony St. OL5 ... 68 B1
Anthorn Rd. WN3 ... 54 E3
Antilles Cl. M12 ... 99 A4
Antler Ct. WN4 ... 73 B6
Anton Wlk. M9 ... 157 D7
Antrim Cl. M'ster M19 ... 110 D2
Antrim Cl. Wigan WN3 ... 54 C2
Anvil Cl. WN5 ... 53 D5
Anvil St. OL13 ... 3 E8
Anvil Way. OL1 ... 153 E7
Apethorn La. SK14 ... 113 D7
Apfel La. OL9 ... 152 B7
Apollo Ave. BL9 ... 44 F3
Apollo Wlk. M12 ... 165 A6
Apperley Grange. M30 ... 79 E4
Appian Way. M7 & M8 ... 155 E5
Apple Cl. OL8 ... 67 C3
Apple Dell Ave. WA3 ... 74 C1
Apple St. SK14 ... 114 D7
Apple Tree Ct. M5 ... 81 A2
Apple Tree Rd. SK12 ... 127 B1
Apple Tree Wlk. 8 M33 ... 107 C5
Appleby Ave. Alt'ham WA15 120 C5
Appleby Ave.
Dukinfield SK14 ... 101 C5
Appleby Ave. M'ster M12 ... 99 A3
Appleby Cl. Bury BL8 ... 26 F2
Appleby Cl. Stockport SK3 ... 170 D5
Appleby Gdns. 1 Bolton BL2 25 B1
Appleby Gdns. Whitefield M45 44 F3
Appleby Lodge. M14 ... 98 D2
Appleby Rd. SK8 ... 122 B4
Appleby Wlk. 4 OL2 ... 48 E4
Applecross Wlk. M11 ... 165 C8
Appledore Dr. Alt'ham M23 120 D7
Appledore Dr. Bolton BL2 ... 25 F3
Appledore Wlk. OL9 ... 152 B6
Appleford Dr. M8 ... 156 B6
Applethwaite. WN2 ... 56 B8
Appleton Dr. SK13 ... 116 F8
Appleton Gr. M33 ... 107 E2
Appleton Rd. Alt'ham WA15 119 F1
Appleton Rd. Reddish SK4 ... 111 D6
Appleton St. WN3 ... 150 B8
Appleton Wlk. 8 SK9 ... 131 E1
Applewood. M24 ... 65 E7
Appley Bridge Sta. WN6 ... 35 C7
Appley Cl. WN6 ... 18 C2
Appley La N.
Appley Bridge WN6 ... 18 C1
Appley La S. WN6 & WN8 ... 35 C6
Apprentice Ct. 18 M9 ... 157 E8
April Cl. OL8 ... 67 C4
Apsley Cl. WA14 ... 119 B1
Apsley Gr. Alt'ham WA14 ... 119 B1
Apsley Gr. M'ster M12 ... 163 C6
Apsley Pl. OL7 ... 166 A2
Apsley Rd. M34 ... 100 F4
Apsley Side. OL5 ... 86 C8
Apsley St. SK1 ... 169 F1
Aquarius St. M15 ... 163 A5
Aqueduct Rd. BL3 ... 148 C5
Aquinas Coll. SK2 ... 124 A6
Aragon Dr. OL10 ... 29 C2
Aragon Way. SK6 ... 125 E6
Arbor Ave. M'ster M19 ... 110 F6
Arbor Dr. M19 ... 110 F7
Arbor Gr. Droylsden M43 ... 83 F3
Arbor Gr. Walkden M38 ... 59 E4
Arbory Ave. M40 ... 83 B7
Arbory Cl. WN7 ... 76 C5
Arbour Cl. Bury BL9 ... 27 E6
Arbour Cl. Salford M6 ... 154 F3
Arbour La. WN6 ... 19 B1
Arbour Rd. OL4 ... 67 E4
Arbroath St. M43 ... 83 E1
Arbury Ave. Cheadle SK3 ... 123 A7
Arbury Ave. R'dale OL11 ... 139 E5
Arcade St. 18 WN1 ... 150 C8
Arcade The. Brinnington SK5 112 C5
Arcade The. 2
Stalybridge SK15 ... 101 F8
Arcadia Ave. M33 ... 108 A1
Arch La. WN4 ... 72 B3
Arch St. Bolton BL1 ... 25 A1
Arch St. Bolton BL1 ... 148 A8
Archade The. OL6 ... 166 B3
Archer Ave. BL2 ... 148 C8
Archer Gr. BL2 ... 148 C8
Archer Pk. M24 ... 64 E8
Archer Pl. M32 ... 95 F3
Archer St. Boothstown M28 ... 77 E7
Archer St. Leigh WN7 ... 76 B2
Archer St. M'ster M11 ... 83 A2
Archer St. Mossley OL5 ... 68 C2
Archer St. Stockport SK2 ... 124 C5
Archie St. M5 ... 161 A7
Arclid Cl. SK9 ... 131 E1
Arcon Cl. OL16 ... 31 E6
Arcon Dr. M16 ... 97 E3
Arcon Pl. WA14 ... 119 A6
Ardale Ave. M40 ... 65 C2
Ardcombe Ave. M9 ... 64 C5
Ardeen Wlk. M13 ... 163 C6
Arden Ave. M24 ... 65 B5
Arden Bsns Ctr. SK6 ... 112 E6
Arden Cl. Ashton-u-L OL6 ... 85 F6
Arden Cl. Bury BL9 ... 44 E8
Arden Cl. Gatley SK8 ... 131 C7
Arden Cl. Glossop SK13 ... 116 A8
Arden Ct. SK7 ... 123 D1
Arden Gr. M40 ... 65 C1
Arden Hall. SK6 ... 112 D7
Arden House. OL2 ... 48 E4
Arden Jun Sch. SK6 ... 112 D3
Arden Lodge Rd. M23 ... 120 E7
Arden Prim Sch. SK6 ... 112 D3
Arden Rd. SK6 ... 112 E7
Arden St. OL9 ... 66 A3
Arden Wlk. 6 Sale M33 ... 107 C5
Arden Wlk. Stockport SK1 ... 169 E1
Ardenfield. M34 ... 113 A7
Ardenfield Dr. M22 ... 121 E3
Ardens Cl. M27 ... 61 D2
Ardent Way. M25 ... 63 B1
Ardern Gr. SK1 ... 170 F8
Ardern Rd. M8 ... 63 F2
Arderne Rd. WA15 ... 120 A8
Ardingly Wlk. M23 ... 120 D8
Ardley Rd. BL6 ... 22 C4
Ardmore Wlk. M22 ... 121 E2
Ardwick Gn N. M12 ... 163 C7
Ardwick Gn S. M13 ... 163 C7
Ardwick Sta. M12 ... 164 D7
Argo St. BL3 ... 147 D4
Argosy Dr.
Alt'ham M90 & WA15 ... 129 F7
Argosy Dr. Eccles M30 ... 94 F7
Argus St. OL8 ... 66 C2
Argyle Ave. M'ster M14 ... 98 E4
Argyle Ave. Walkden M28 ... 60 C5
Argyle Ave. Whitefield M45 ... 63 A8
Argyle Cres. OL10 ... 29 B1
Argyle Par. OL10 ... 29 A1
Argyle St. Atherton M46 ... 58 C2
Argyle St. Bury BL9 ... 140 F4
Argyle St. Droylsden M43 ... 84 A1
Argyle St. Hazel Grove SK7 ... 124 E2
Argyle St. Heywood OL10 ... 29 A1
Argyle St. Hindley WN2 ... 56 E5
Argyle St. M'ster M18 ... 99 D5
Argyle St. Oldham OL1 ... 67 B8
Argyle St. 14
R'dale OL11 & OL16 ... 31 A4
Argyle St. 3 Swinton M27 ... 79 E7
Argyle St. Wigan WN5 ... 54 F6
Argyll Ave. M32 ... 96 B2
Argyll Cl. Failsworth M35 ... 84 B7
Argyll Cl. Garswood WN4 ... 72 C4
Argyll Park Rd. M35 ... 84 B7
Argyll Rd. Cheadle SK8 ... 122 F5
Argyll Rd. Oldham OL9 ... 65 F4
Argyll St. Ashton-u-L OL6 ... 85 E3
Argyll St. Mossley OL5 ... 68 C1
Ariel Wlk. WA3 ... 90 E8
Ark St. 8 M19 ... 99 A2
Arkendale Cl. M35 ... 84 C7
Arkholme. M28 ... 78 A8
Arkholme Wlk. M40 ... 83 B7
Arkle Ave. SK8 & SK9 ... 131 E4
Arkley Wlk. M13 ... 163 B6
Arkwright Dr. SK6 ... 126 A6
Arkwright Rd. SK6 ... 126 A6
Arkwright St. Horwich BL6 ... 22 C2
Arkwright St. Oldham OL9 ... 152 C6
Arkwright Way. OL11 ... 31 A2
Arlen Ct. BL2 ... 148 B5
Arlen Rd. BL2 ... 148 B5
Arlen Way. OL10 ... 29 B2
Arley Ave. Bury BL9 ... 27 F6
Arley Ave. M'ster M20 ... 109 F5
Arley Cl. Alt'ham WA14 ... 119 D8
Arley Cl. Dukinfield SK16 ... 101 D6
Arley Cl. Wigan WN2 ... 38 B2
Arley Dr. Sale M33 ... 108 A2
Arley Dr. Shaw OL2 ... 49 D8
Arley Gr. SK3 ... 123 D4
Arley La. WN1 & WN2 ... 20 D2
Arley Mere Cl. SK8 ... 122 F3
Arley Moss Wlk. M13 ... 163 B7
Arley St. Ince-i-M WN2 ... 55 F4
Arley St. Radcliffe M26 ... 44 B1
Arley Way. Atherton M46 ... 58 E2
Arley Way. 22 Denton M34 ... 101 A1
Arlies Cl. SK15 ... 86 A4
Arlies La. SK15 ... 86 B4
Arlies Prim Sch. SK15 ... 86 A4
Arlies St. OL6 ... 85 D4
Arlington Ave. Denton M34 101 A2
Arlington Ave. M'ster M25 ... 63 B2
Arlington Ave. Swinton M27 ... 79 D6
Arlington Cl. BL9 ... 11 C2
Arlington Cres. SK9 ... 136 E5
Arlington Dr.
Golborne WA3 & WN7 ... 91 C8
Arlington Dr. Poynton SK12 133 D3
Arlington Dr. Stockport SK2 124 A3
Arlington Rd. Cheadle SK8 ... 122 C4
Arlington Rd. Stretford M32 ... 96 B1
Arlington St. 4
Ashton-u-L OL6 ... 166 C3
Arlington St. Bolton BL3 ... 147 F3
Arlington St. M'ster M8 ... 155 F8
Arlington St. M'ster M3 ... 158 D2
Arlington Way. SK9 ... 136 E5
Arliss Ave. M19 ... 111 A8
Arm Rd. OL15 ... 15 E4
Armadale Ave. M9 ... 65 A4
Armadale Cl. SK3 ... 170 F5
Armadale Rd. Bolton BL3 ... 40 E5
Armadale Rd.
Dukinfield SK16 ... 101 D7
Armdale Rise. OL4 ... 49 E1
Armentieres. SK15 ... 86 A1
Armit Rd. OL4 ... 68 E5
Armitage Ave. Walkden M38 ... 59 F4
Armitage CE Prim Sch.
M12 ... 164 E6
Armitage Cl. Hyde SK14 ... 113 E8
Armitage Cl. Middleton M24 ... 64 D7
Armitage Cl. Oldham OL8 ... 66 C3
Armitage Ct. M12 ... 164 F6
Armitage Gr. M38 ... 59 F4
Armitage House. M6 ... 80 C3
Armitage Owen Wlk. 4
M40 ... 83 A7
Armitage Rd. WA14 ... 119 D3
Armitage St. M30 ... 79 D1
Armitstead St. 5 WN2 ... 56 D4
Armour Pl. M9 ... 64 C2
Armoury Bank. WN4 ... 73 B3
Armoury St. SK3 ... 170 E8
Armstrong Hurst Cl. OL12 ... 15 B2
Armstrong St. Horwich BL6 ... 22 C2
Armstrong St. Wigan WN2 ... 38 A3
Arncliffe Cl. 5 BL4 ... 42 D1
Arncliffe Dr. M23 ... 121 A3
Arncliffe Rise. OL4 ... 50 A4
Arncot Rd. BL1 ... 24 F5
Arncott Cl. OL2 ... 49 A4
Arne Cl. SK2 ... 125 A5
Arne St. OL9 ... 152 A5
Arnesby Ave. M33 ... 108 E5
Arnesby Gr. BL2 ... 148 B8
Arnfield Dr. M28 ... 78 B6
Arnfield La.
Hollingworth SK14 ... 103 F8
Arnfield Rd. M'ster M20 ... 110 C6
Arnfield Rd. Stockport SK3 ... 170 D5
Arnold Ave. Heywood OL10 ... 46 E7
Arnold Ave. Hyde SK14 ... 113 F7
Arnold Cl. SK16 ... 102 A7
Arnold Ct. M16 ... 97 E1
Arnold Dr. Droylsden M43 ... 84 A1
Arnold Dr. Middleton M24 ... 47 C3
Arnold Rd. Bolton BL7 ... 24 F8
Arnold Rd. Hyde SK14 ... 113 F7
Arnold Rd. M'ster M16 ... 97 E1
Arnold St. Ashton-u-L OL6 ... 166 C3
Arnold St. Bolton BL1 ... 142 C2
Arnold St. Oldham OL1 ... 67 A8
Arnold St. Stockport SK3 ... 170 E7
Arnold Wlk. 9 M34 ... 113 A7
Arnott Cres. M15 ... 162 F5
Arnside Ave.
Hazel Grove SK7 ... 124 C2
Arnside Ave. Ince-i-M WN2 ... 56 A7
Arnside Ave. Oldham OL9 ... 152 A5
Arnside Ave. Reddish SK4 ... 111 E6
Arnside Cl. Gatley SK8 ... 122 B4
Arnside Cl. High Lane SK6 ... 134 E8
Arnside Cl. Shaw OL2 ... 49 D7
Arnside Dr. Dukinfield SK14 101 C4
Arnside Dr. R'dale OL11 ... 29 E5
Arnside Dr. Salford M6 ... 80 B3
Arnside Gr. Bolton BL2 ... 42 E8
Arnside Gr. Sale M33 ... 108 B6
Arnside Rd. Hindley WN2 ... 57 A5
Arnside Rd. Wigan WN5 ... 54 B8
Arnside St. M14 ... 98 B2
Arran Ave. Oldham OL8 ... 66 F3
Arran Ave. Sale M33 ... 108 C3
Arran Ave. Stretford M32 ... 96 A2
Arran Cl. BL3 ... 40 E6
Arran Gdns. M41 ... 95 C5
Arran Gr. M26 ... 43 E5
Arran Rd. SK16 ... 101 C7
Arran St. 12 M'ster M40 ... 64 F1
Arran St. M'ster M7 ... 155 D6
Arran Wlk. OL10 ... 29 A1
Arrandale Ct. M41 ... 95 D3
Arras Gr. M34 ... 99 F3
Arreton Sq. M14 ... 98 D3
Arrivals Way. M90 ... 130 B7
Arrow St. Bolton BL1 ... 145 E8
Arrow St. Leigh WN7 ... 76 B3
Arrow St. M'ster M7 ... 155 D5
Arrow Trad Est. M34 ... 100 D5
Arrowfield Dr. M21 ... 109 D7
Arrowfield Rd. M21 ... 109 D7
Arrowhill Rd. BL8 ... 43 F8
Arrowscroft Way. SK14 ... 171 D4
Arrowsmith Ct. 7 BL6 ... 22 E1
Arrowsmith Wlk. 16 M11 ... 160 F1
Arthill La. WA14 ... 118 B1
Arthington St. OL16 ... 31 B8
Arthog Dr. WA15 ... 128 F8
Arthog Rd. Alt'ham WA15 ... 128 F8
Arthog Rd. M'ster M20 ... 110 C3
Arthur Ave. M28 ... 60 C5
Arthur La. BL2 ... 26 B2
Arthur Millwood Ct. M3 ... 158 D1
Arthur Rd. M16 ... 97 C3
Arthur St. Bury BL8 ... 27 C2
Arthur St. Eccles M30 ... 79 C1
Arthur St. Farnworth BL4 ... 60 D8
Arthur St. Heywood OL10 ... 29 D2
Arthur St. Hindley WN2 ... 56 E5
Arthur St. Hyde SK14 ... 101 C1
Arthur St. Leigh WN7 ... 75 E4
Arthur St. Little Lever BL3 ... 43 B3
Arthur St. Prestwich M25 ... 62 F4
Arthur St. R'dale OL12 ... 139 D8
Arthur St. Reddish SK5 ... 111 E7
Arthur St. Shaw OL2 ... 149 B7
Arthur St. Swinton M27 ... 79 D7
Arthur St. Walkden M28 ... 60 E1
Arthur St. Walkden M28 ... 60 F2
Arthur Terr. 4 SK5 ... 111 E7
Arthurs La. OL3 ... 69 B6
Artillery Ct. M13 ... 163 C7
Artillery Pl. M22 ... 121 F4
Artillery St. Bolton BL3 ... 145 F5
Artillery St. M'ster M3 ... 162 E8
Arundale. BL5 ... 39 F2
Arundale Ave. M16 & M21 ... 97 E1
Arundale Cl. SK14 ... 102 F3
Arundale Ct. M16 ... 97 E1
Arundale Gr. SK14 ... 102 F3
Arundale Prim Sch. SK14 ... 102 F3
Arundel Ave.
Hazel Grove SK7 ... 133 D8
Arundel Ave. Prestwich M45 ... 63 B7
Arundel Ave. R'dale OL11 ... 30 E4
Arundel Ave. Urmston M41 ... 94 C1
Arundel Cl. Alt'ham WA15 ... 120 C1
Arundel Cl. Bury BL8 ... 27 C6
Arundel Cl. Mossley SK15 ... 86 F6
Arundel Dr. WN7 ... 75 F6
Arundel Gr. SK2 ... 124 B4
Arundel Grange.
Glossop SK13 ... 104 A1
Arundel Rd. SK8 ... 132 A6
Arundel St. Ashton-u-L OL6 ... 85 E3
Arundel St. Bolton BL1 ... 24 E5
Arundel St. Glossop SK13 ... 104 C1
Arundel St. Hindley WN2 ... 56 E5
Arundel St. M'ster M15 ... 162 D7
Arundel St. Mossley OL5 ... 68 B1
Arundel St. Oldham OL4 ... 67 C7
Arundel St. R'dale OL11 ... 30 E4
Arundel St. Swinton M27 ... 61 C1
Arundel St. Wigan WN5 ... 54 F6
Arundel Wlk. OL9 ... 152 A6
Asby Cl. M24 ... 46 D2
Ascension CE Prim Sch.
M7 ... 158 D4
Ascension Rd. M7 ... 158 D4
Ascot Ave. Sale M33 ... 107 D3
Ascot Ave. Stretford M32 ... 96 F3
Ascot Cl. Oldham OL9 ... 152 C7
Ascot Cl. R'dale OL11 ... 29 E8
Ascot Dr. Atherton M46 ... 58 E4
Ascot Dr. Hazel Grove SK7 ... 125 A2
Ascot Dr. Urmston M41 ... 94 C2
Ascot Meadows. BL9 ... 44 E8
Ascot Par. M19 ... 110 F6
Ascot Rd. Failsworth M40 ... 83 B4
Ascot Rd. Little Lever BL3 ... 42 F3
Ascot Wlk. M6 ... 81 A5
Ascroft Ave. WN6 ... 36 F3
Ascroft St. Oldham OL1 ... 153 F6
Ascroft St. Wigan WN1 ... 151 E7
Asgard Dr. M5 ... 161 C8
Asgard Gr. M5 ... 161 C8
Ash Ave. Alt'ham WA14 ... 119 A5
Ash Ave. Cheadle SK8 ... 122 E5
Ash Ave. Irlam M44 ... 105 D5
Ash Ave. Newton-l-W WA12 ... 89 C2
Ash Cl. Appley Bridge WN6 ... 35 D7
Ash Cl. Ashton-u-L OL6 ... 85 D5
Ash Cl. Littleborough OL12 ... 15 C4
Ash Cl. Mottram-i-L SK14 ... 103 A4
Ash Ct. SK6 ... 113 A5
Ash Dr. M27 ... 61 C2
Ash Field Sch. M28 ... 60 E1
Ash Gr. Alt'ham WA14 ... 119 C1
Ash Gr. Alt'ham WA15 ... 119 F7
Ash Gr. Bolton BL2 ... 25 F3
Ash Gr. Bolton BL1 ... 144 B8
Ash Gr. Bury BL8 ... 27 A5
Ash Gr. Droylsden M34 ... 100 A8
Ash Gr. Gatley SK8 ... 131 B8
Ash Gr. 8 Horwich BL6 ... 22 E1
Ash Gr. Littleborough OL15 ... 15 F5
Ash Gr. M'ster M13 ... 98 E4
Ash Gr. Marple SK6 ... 125 E5
Ash Gr. Newhey OL16 ... 32 A3
Ash Gr. Oldham OL4 ... 68 A7
Ash Gr. Orrell WN5 ... 53 F6
Ash Gr. Prestwich M25 ... 63 A6
Ash Gr. Ramsbottom BL8 ... 10 F3
Ash Gr. Reddish SK4 ... 111 D5
Ash Gr. Royton OL2 ... 48 D6
Ash Gr. Stalybridge SK15 ... 85 F3
Ash Gr. Standish WN6 ... 36 F8
Ash Gr. Stretford M32 ... 108 C8
Ash Gr. Swinton M27 ... 79 D5
Ash Gr. Walkden M28 ... 60 E1
Ash Gr. Westhoughton BL5 ... 57 E7
Ash Grove Cres. WN5 ... 71 E6
Ash Hill Dr. OL5 ... 86 E8
Ash House. M16 ... 97 E2
Ash La. Alt'ham WA15 ... 120 C2
Ash La. Wigan WN2 ... 38 A2
Ash Lea Sch. M30 ... 79 E3
Ash Leigh Dr. BL1 ... 40 E8
Ash Lodge. SK12 ... 133 D4
Ash Rd. Coppull PR7 ... 19 E8
Ash Rd. Droylsden M43 ... 83 F2
Ash Rd. Hollinfare WA3 ... 105 A2
Ash Rd. Kearsley BL4 ... 60 F5
Ash Rd. Partington M31 ... 105 D3
Ash Rd. Poynton SK12 ... 133 F3
Ash Rd. Reddish M34 ... 99 F3
Ash Sq. OL4 ... 67 D8
Ash St. Bolton BL2 ... 148 A6
Ash St. Bury BL9 ... 141 A2
Ash St. Denton M34 ... 100 D7
Ash St. Failsworth M35 ... 83 E8
Ash St. Golborne WA3 ... 74 B2
Ash St. Hazel Grove SK7 ... 124 D3
Ash St. Heywood OL10 ... 29 B3
Ash St. M'ster M8 & M9 ... 157 D7
Ash St. Middleton M24 ... 65 C8
Ash St. Oldham OL4 ... 67 B6
Ash St. R'dale OL11 ... 30 C2
Ash St. Salford M6 ... 154 F2
Ash St. Stockport SK3 ... 123 B8
Ash St. 2 Tyldesley M29 ... 59 A1
Ash Tree Ave. M43 ... 83 F2
Ash Tree Dr. SK16 ... 101 F7
Ash Tree Rd. Hyde SK14 ... 102 B5
Ash Tree Rd. M'ster M8 ... 64 A1
Ash Wlk. Chadderton OL9 ... 152 B8
Ash Wlk. Middleton M24 ... 64 F6
Ashawe Cl. M38 ... 59 E3
Ashawe Gr. M38 ... 59 F3
Ashawe Terr. M38 ... 59 E3
Ashbank Ave. BL3 ... 40 E6
Ashbee St. BL1 ... 143 E3
Ashberry Cl. SK9 ... 137 D8
Ashborne Dr. BL9 ... 11 D2
Ashbourne Ave. Bolton BL2 148 B6
Ashbourne Ave.
Cheadle SK8 ... 122 F6
Ashbourne Ave. Hindley WN2 56 F5
Ashbourne Ave.
Middleton M24 ... 47 C3
Ashbourne Ave. Urmston M41 94 E2
Ashbourne Ave. Wigan WN2 ... 38 A2
Ashbourne Cl. Leigh WN7 ... 57 D1
Ashbourne Cl.
Littleborough OL12 ... 15 D6
Ashbourne Cres. M33 ... 108 D2
Ashbourne Ct. SK13 ... 116 F8
Ashbourne Dr. Ashton-u-L OL6 85 F6
Ashbourne Dr.
High Lane SK6 ... 134 F6
Ashbourne Gdns. WN2 ... 56 F5
Ashbourne Gr. M'ster M7 ... 155 E7
Ashbourne Gr.
Whitefield M45 ... 44 D1
Ashbourne Gr. Worsley M28 ... 78 E8
Ashbourne Rd. Denton M34 100 E2
Ashbourne Rd. Eccles M30 ... 79 E1
Ashbourne Rd.
Hazel Grove SK7 ... 133 F8
Ashbourne Rd. Pendlebury M6 80 C5
Ashbourne Rd. Stretford M32 96 A3
Ashbourne Sq. OL8 ... 153 E5
Ashbourne St. OL11 ... 13 E1
Ashbridge. M17 ... 96 B6
Ashbridge Rd. M35 ... 84 B6
Ashbrook Ave. M34 ... 100 B3
Ashbrook Cl. Gatley SK8 ... 122 B1
Ashbrook Cl. Reddish M34 ... 100 B3
Ashbrook Cl. Whitefield M45 ... 63 B8
Ashbrook Cres. OL12 ... 15 C4
Ashbrook Farm Cl. SK5 ... 99 F2
Ashbrook Hey La.
OL12 & OL16 ... 15 C4
Ashbrook La. SK5 ... 99 F2
Ashbrook St. M11 ... 100 A7
Ashburn Ave. M19 ... 110 F5
Ashburn Gr. SK4 ... 169 D3
Ashburn Rd. SK4 ... 169 D3
Ashburne House. M14 ... 98 D4
Ashburner St. BL1 ... 145 E6
Ashburton Cl. SK14 ... 102 E2
Ashburton Rd. SK3 ... 170 E5
Ashburton Rd E. M17 ... 96 C6
Ashburton Rd W. M17, M41 ... 95 E7
Ashbury Cl. BL3 ... 145 E5
Ashbury Pl. M40 ... 160 E4
Ashbury Prim Sch. M11 ... 164 F8
Ashbury's Sta. M12 ... 165 A7
Ashby Ave. M19 ... 110 E4
Ashby Cl. BL3 ... 42 C2
Ashby Gr. Leigh WN7 ... 75 C8
Ashby Gr. Whitefield M45 ... 63 B7
Ashby Rd. WN3 ... 55 B3
Ashcombe Dr. Bolton BL2 ... 43 A6
Ashcombe Dr. Radcliffe M26 ... 43 D5
Ashcombe Wlk. 7 M11 ... 160 F1
Ashcott Ave. M22 ... 121 D4
Ashcott Cl. BL6 ... 40 E5
Ashcroft. Littleborough OL12 ... 15 D4
Ashcroft. Wilmslow SK9 ... 136 F5
Ashcroft Ave. M6 ... 154 E4
Ashcroft Ct. OL1 ... 153 F6
Ashcroft Rd. WA13 ... 117 B4
Ashcroft St. WN2 ... 56 E4
Ashdale Ave. BL3 ... 40 E5
Ashdale Cl. SK5 ... 111 F5
Ashdale Cres. M43 ... 83 F1
Ashdale Dr. Gatley SK8 ... 122 B2
Ashdale Dr. M'ster M20 ... 110 D5
Ashdale Rd. Hindley WN2 ... 57 A5
Ashdale Rd. Wigan WN3 ... 55 A2
Ashdene. OL12 ... 14 D4
Ashdene Cl.
Oldham OL1 & OL9 ... 48 C1
Ashdene Cl. Oldham OL4 ... 67 F7
Ashdene Cres. BL2 ... 25 D4
Ashdene Cty Prim Sch.
SK9 ... 136 F5
Ashdene Rd. M'ster SK4 ... 110 D2
Ashdene Rd. M'ster M20 ... 110 D6
Ashdene Rd. Wilmslow SK9 ... 136 F5
Ashdene Rise. OL1 ... 49 D4
Ashdown Ave. M'ster M9 ... 64 D4
Ashdown Ave. Romiley SK6 113 C5
Ashdown Dr. Bolton BL2 ... 25 C3
Ashdown Dr. Boothstown M28 78 A7
Ashdown Dr. Pendlebury M27 80 A6
Ashdown Gr. M9 ... 64 D4
Ashdown Rd. SK4 ... 168 C3
Ashdown Terr. M9 ... 64 D4
Ashdown Way. OL2 ... 48 E8
Asher St. BL3 ... 146 C2
Ashes Cl. SK15 ... 102 C8
Ashes Dr. BL2 ... 42 F8
Ashes La. Glossop SK13 ... 104 B2
Ashes La. Milnrow OL16 ... 31 F7
Ashes La. Oldham OL4 ... 67 F6
Ashes La. Stalybridge SK15 ... 102 C8
Ashfell Ct. M21 ... 96 F1
Ashfield. M34 ... 101 A5
Ashfield Ave. Atherton M46 ... 58 C4
Ashfield Ave. Hindley WN2 ... 56 F4
Ashfield Ave. R'dale OL11 ... 139 F5
Ashfield Cl. Lymm WA13 ... 117 B4
Ashfield Cl. Salford M6 ... 154 E3
Ashfield Cres. Billinge WN5 ... 71 E4
Ashfield Cres. Cheadle SK8 122 D6
Ashfield Cres. Oldham OL4 ... 67 F6
Ashfield Dr. Aspull WN2 ... 38 C5
Ashfield Dr. Failsworth M40 ... 83 D4
Ashfield Gr. Bolton BL1 ... 25 A6
Ashfield Gr. Irlam M44 ... 105 E6
Ashfield Gr.
Reddish M18 & M34 ... 99 F4
Ashfield Gr. Romiley SK6 ... 114 B1
Ashfield Gr. Stockport SK3 ... 123 F4
Ashfield House. OL11 ... 139 F5
Ashfield La. OL16 ... 31 F4
Ashfield Lodge. M20 ... 109 F2
Ashfield Park Dr. WN6 ... 36 F8
Ashfield Rd. Adlington PR6 ... 21 B8
Ashfield Rd. Alt'ham WA15 ... 119 E3
Ashfield Rd. Cheadle SK8 ... 122 D5
Ashfield Rd. Cheadle SK8 ... 122 D6
Ashfield Rd. Hadfield SK13 ... 171 E3
Ashfield Rd. M'ster M13 ... 98 E3
Ashfield Rd. R'dale OL11 ... 139 F5
Ashfield Rd. Sale M33 ... 108 B5
Ashfield Rd. Stockport SK3 ... 123 F4
Ashfield Rd. Urmston M41 ... 95 D2
Ashfield Sq. M43 ... 83 F2
Ashfield St. M'ster M11 ... 160 F2
Ashfield St. Oldham OL8 ... 66 C3
Ashfield Terr. WN6 ... 35 C8
Ashfield Valley Prim Sch.
OL11 ... 30 E4
Ashford. M33 ... 107 C4
Ashford Ave. Boothstown M28 77 F6
Ashford Ave. Eccles M30 ... 95 C8
Ashford Ave. Reddish SK5 ... 99 F2
Ashford Ave. Swinton M27 ... 79 C7
Ashford Cl. Bolton BL2 ... 25 E4
Ashford Cl. Bury BL8 ... 27 B1
Ashford Cl. Handforth SK9 ... 131 C4
Ashford Ct. 1 OL4 ... 49 D1
Ashford Gn. 19 SK13 ... 171 E1
Ashford Mews. SK13 ... 171 E1
Ashford Rd. M'ster M20 ... 110 B7
Ashford Rd. Reddish SK4 ... 111 D6
Ashford Rd. Wilmslow SK9 ... 137 A4
Ashford Rise. WN1 ... 37 B4
Ashford St. Heywood OL10 ... 28 F2
Ashford Wlk. Bolton BL1 ... 143 E1
Ashford Wlk. Oldham OL9 ... 152 B6
Ashgate Ave. M22 ... 121 E4
Ashgill Wlk. 4 M9 ... 157 E7
Ashgrove. OL16 ... 31 B1
Ashia Cl. OL16 ... 31 B6
Ashill Wlk. M3 ... 162 E8
Ashington Cl. BL1 ... 142 B3
Ashington Dr. BL8 ... 26 F2
Ashkirk St. 4 M18 ... 99 D5
Ashland Ave.
Ashton-i-M WN4 ... 73 A4
Ashland Ave. 5 Wigan WN1 37 C2
Ashlands. M33 ... 108 A5
Ashlands Ave.
Boothstown M28 ... 78 A7
Ashlands Ave. Failsworth M40 65 C1
Ashlands Ave. Swinton M27 ... 79 D6
Ashlands Cl. BL0 ... 1 D2
Ashlands Dr. M34 ... 100 E6
Ashlands Rd. WA15 ... 108 A1
Ashlar Dr. M12 ... 164 E8
Ashlea Gr. OL4 ... 68 B6
Ashleigh Ave. SK13 ... 104 B2
Ashleigh Cl. OL2 ... 48 E2
Ashleigh Rd. WA15 ... 120 B8
Ashley Ave. Bolton BL2 ... 42 D8
Ashley Ave. M'ster M16 ... 97 D4

Bishop's Cl. Bolton BL3 42 A2
Bishop's Cl. Cheadle SK8 123 A5
Bishop's Rd. BL3 42 A2
Bishopbridge Cl. BL3 147 F4
Bishopdale Cl. OL2 48 D5
Bishopgate. WN1 150 C8
Bishopgate St. OL9 152 A5
Bishops Cl. Alt'ham WA14 119 B1
Bishops Cl. Ashton-u-L OL7 85 A5
Bishops Gate. M1 162 F8
Bishops Mews. M33 107 E6
Bishops Rd. M25 63 C2
Bishops Wlk. OL7 166 A1
Bishopton Cl. M19 99 C1
Bisley Ave. M23 120 F6
Bisley St. OL8 153 D6
Bismarck St. OL4 & OL8 67 A5
Bispham Ave. Bolton BL2 42 F7
Bispham Ave. Reddish SK5 99 F3
Bispham Cl. BL8 26 F1
Bispham Dr. WN4 72 F5
Bispham Gr. M7 155 E7
Bispham Hall Bsns Pk. WN5 53 C2
Bispham St. BL2 148 C8
Bittern Cl. Poynton SK12 133 A4
Bittern Cl. R'dale OL11 29 F7
Bittern Dr. M43 84 C3
Bk Adcroft St. SK1 170 F7
Bk Alfred St. BL0 138 B5
Bk Andrew St. OL5 86 C8
Bk Cecil St. OL5 86 C8
Bk Chapel St. 12 M19 99 A1
Bk Grosvenor St. 2 SK15 86 A1
Bk Knowl St. SK15 86 B2
Bk Melbourne St. 1 SK15 86 A1
Bk Stayley Rd. OL5 86 D8
Bk Water St. OL6 166 C4
Black Brock Rd. SK4 111 D7
Black Horse St. Blackrod BL6 21 C3
Black Horse St. Bolton BL1 145 E6
Black Horse St.
Farnworth BL4 60 E7
Black La. BL0 12 B7
Black Moss Cl. M26 43 D3
Black Moss Rd. WA14 118 F7
Blackbank St. BL1 143 F2
Blackberry Cl. WA14 119 B8
Blackberry La. SK5 112 C7
Blackburn Cl. WA3 90 E8
Blackburn Gdns. M20 110 A4
Blackburn Old Rd. BL7 8 C4
Blackburn Pl. M5 81 C1
Blackburn Rd. Bolton BL7, BL1 8 C4
Blackburn Rd. Bolton BL1 143 F2
Blackburn Rd. Edenfield BL0 1 D5
Blackburn St. M'ster M3 158 D3
Blackburn St. M'ster M16 161 C5
Blackburn St. Prestwich M25 63 C4
Blackburn St. Radcliffe M26 44 A3
Blackburn St. Radcliffe M26 44 B2
Blackcap Cl. M28 78 B7
Blackcarr Rd. M23 121 B6
Blackcroft Cl. M27 79 E8
Blackfield La. M7 81 C8
Blackfields. M7 155 D8
Blackford Ave. BL9 44 F4
Blackford Rd. SK4 111 B7
Blackford Wlk. M40 160 D3
Blackfriar Ct. M3 158 D3
Blackfriars Rd. M3 158 E2
Blackfriars St. M3 158 F2
Blackhill Cl. 8 M13 163 B7
Blackhorse Ave. BL6 21 C2
Blackhorse Cl. BL6 21 C3
Blackleach Dr. M28 60 D5
Blackledge St. BL3 146 C4
Blackley Cl. BL9 45 A2
Blackley Golf Course. M24 65 B4
Blackley New Rd. M9 & M25 64 B3
Blackley Park Rd. M9 64 D1
Blackley St. M'ster M16 161 C5
Blackley St. Middleton M24 64 B7
Blackleyhurst Ave. WN5 71 E5
Blacklock St. M8 158 F4
Blackmoor Ave. M29 77 B5
Blackpits Rd. OL11 13 D1
Blackpool St. 19 M11 83 C2
Blackrock. SK15 86 C6
Blackrock St. M'ster M11 164 F8
Blackrod Brow. BL6 21 B4
Blackrod By-Pass Rd. BL6 21 D2
Blackrod Cty Prim Sch.
WN2 38 E8
Blackrod Dr. BL8 26 F1
Blackrod Sta. BL6 21 E2
Blacksail Wlk. 3 OL1 49 A1
Blackshaw House. BL3 144 C6
Blackshaw La.
Alderley Edge SK9 136 F1
Blackshaw La. Bolton BL3 144 C6
Blackshaw La. Royton OL2 49 A4
Blackshaw Lane Prim Sch.
OL2 49 A4
Blackshaw Prim Sch. BL2 43 A6
Blackshaw Rd. SK13 104 E2
Blackshaw Row. 2 BL3 144 C5
Blackshaw St. SK3 170 E8
Blacksmith La. OL11 30 B4
Blackstock St. M13 98 C4
Blackstone Ave. OL16 31 C8
Blackstone Edge Old Rd.
OL15 16 E6
Blackstone Edge Rd. HX6 7 F5
Blackstone Rd. SK2 124 D5
Blackstone Wlk. M9 157 D6
Blackthorn Ave. M'ster M19 111 A7
Blackthorn Ave. Wigan WN6 36 F3
Blackthorn Cl. OL12 14 E2
Blackthorn Rd. OL8 84 C8
Blackthorn Wlk. 3 M31 105 E2
Blackthorne Cl. BL1 142 A1
Blackthorne Dr. M33 107 D2
Blackthorne Rd. SK14 113 E7
Blackwell Wlk. 3 M4 159 C2
Blackwin St. M12 & M18 165 A6
Blackwood Dr. M23 120 D8
Blackwood Rd. OL13 3 B7
Blackwood St. BL3 42 A4
Bladen Cl. SK8 123 A4
Bladon St. M1 163 B8
Blainscough Rd. PR7 19 E8
Blair Ave. Hindley WN2 57 B3
Blair Ave. Urmston M41 94 E2
Blair Ave. Walkden M38 60 B4
Blair Cl. Hazel Grove SK7 133 C8
Blair Cl. Sale M33 107 C1
Blair Cl. Shaw OL2 149 B7
Blair La. BL2 25 D1
Blair Rd. M16 97 E1
Blair St. Bolton BL7 25 A8
Blair St. Kearsley BL4 61 B6
Blair St. M'ster M16 162 D5
Blair St. R'dale OL12 14 D1
Blairhall Ave. M40 83 A7
Blairmore Dr. BL3 40 E5
Blake Ave. M46 58 D5
Blake Cl. WN3 150 A5
Blake Dr. SK2 124 E7
Blake Gdns. BL1 143 D2
Blake St. Bolton BL7 25 A7
Blake St. Bolton BL1 143 D2
Blake St. R'dale OL16 31 A8
Blakeborough House. 7
M46 58 D3
Blakedown Wlk. M12 164 E5
Blakefield Dr. M28 60 E1
Blakelock St. OL2 149 B7
Blakemere Ave. M33 108 E3
Blakemore Wlk. M11 160 E1
Blakeswell Cl. M41 94 D3
Blakey Cl. BL3 40 F4
Blakey St. M12 & M18 99 A4
Blanche St. OL12 15 A2
Blanche Wlk. 10 OL1 67 A8
Bland Cl. M35 83 E7
Bland Rd. M25 63 B2
Bland Wlk. 10 M15 97 E4
Blandford Ave. M28 79 A8
Blandford Cl. Bury BL8 27 D5
Blandford Cl. Tyldesley M29 59 A1
Blandford Ct. SK15 86 A2
Blandford Dr. Failsworth M40 65 D2
Blandford House. 7 SK15 86 A2
Blandford Rd. Eccles M30 79 B2
Blandford Rd. Salford M6 81 B4
Blandford Rd.
Stockport SK4 168 C2
Blandford Rise. Horwich BL6 22 F1
Blandford St.
Ashton-u-L OL6 & OL7 166 A3
Blandford St.
Stalybridge SK15 86 A2
Blanefield Cl. M21 109 E7
Blantyre Ave. M28 60 E2
Blantyre Rd. M27 80 B6
Blantyre St. Hindley WN2 56 E6
Blantyre St. M'ster M15 162 D7
Blantyre St. Swinton M27 61 D1
Blantyre St. Worsley M28 79 A3
Blanwood Dr. M8 156 B7
Blaven Cl. SK3 170 F5
Blaydon Cl. WN2 38 D5
Blazemoss Bank. SK2 124 D5
Bleach St. WN2 56 C4
Bleackley St. BL8 27 C4
Bleak Hey Rd. M22 121 F2
Bleak St. BL2 25 B2
Bleakholt Rd. BL0 1 F1
Bleakledge Gr. WN2 56 F7
Bleakley St. 1 M45 44 E1
Bleaklow Cl. WN3 55 B2
Bleaklow Wlk. 20 SK13 171 E1
Bleasby St. OL4 67 C7
Bleasdale Cl. Horwich BL6 39 F8
Bleasdale Cl. Whitefield BL9 45 A3
Bleasdale Rd. Bolton BL1 23 F2
Bleasdale Rd.
Wythenshawe M22 121 A2
Bleasdale St. OL2 48 E5
Bleasedale Rd. WN2 57 A5
Bleasefell Chase. M28 78 A5
Bleatarn Rd. SK1 124 B7
Bledlow Cl. M30 79 E3
Blencarn Wlk. M9 157 D6
Blendworth Cl. M8 155 F7
Blenheim Ave. M16 97 D2
Blenheim Cl. Alt'ham WA14 119 D2
Blenheim Cl. 6
Hadfield SK14 104 A5
Blenheim Cl. Heywood OL10 29 E2
Blenheim Cl. Poynton SK12 133 F4
Blenheim Cl. Whitefield BL9 45 A5
Blenheim Cl. Wilmslow SK9 137 D7
Blenheim Dr. WN7 76 E7
Blenheim Rd.
Ashton-i-M WN4 73 D2
Blenheim Rd. Bolton BL2 42 E6
Blenheim Rd. Bramhall SK8 123 B2
Blenheim Rd. M'ster M16 97 A3
Blenheim Rd. Wigan WN5 54 C8
Blenheim St. 13 R'dale OL12 14 C1
Blenheim St. Tyldesley M29 76 F8
Blenhiem Ave. OL1 49 D3
Blenmore Cl. M26 44 C5
Blantyre Ave. WN2 42 A7
Bleriot St. BL3 147 D3
Blessed Thomas Holford
RC High Sch. WA15 119 E4
Bletchley Cl. M13 164 D5
Bletchley Rd. SK4 110 E1
Blethyn St. BL3 146 B2
Blewberry Cl. WN7 75 F7
Bligh Rd. 15 BL5 39 E1
Blinco Rd. M41 95 F2
Blind La. M12 164 D7
Blindsill Rd. BL4 60 B7
Blissford Cl. WN2 56 D4
Blisworth Ave. M30 95 E8
Blisworth Cl. M4 160 D1
Blithfield Wlk. M34 100 E2
Block La. OL9 152 B5
Blockage St. SK16 101 D7
Blodwell St. M5 & M6 154 F2
Blofield Ct. BL4 60 D7
Blomley St. OL11 30 C2
Bloom St. M'ster M3 158 E2
Bloom St. M'ster M1 163 A8
Bloom St. Ramsbottom BL0 11 A4
Bloom St. Stockport SK3 170 D8
Bloomfield Dr.
Boothstown M28 78 A7
Bloomfield Dr. Whitefield BL9 45 B3
Bloomfield Rd. BL4 60 D6
Bloomfield St. BL1 143 E3
Bloomsbury Gr. WA15 120 A6
Bloomsbury La. WA15 120 A6
Blossom Pl. OL16 139 F8
Blossom Rd. M31 105 E2
Blossom St. M'ster M3 158 E2
Blossom St. M'ster M4 159 B2
Blossom St. 11
Tyldesley M29 59 A1
Blossoms Hey. SK8 122 E1
Blossoms Hey Wlk. SK8 122 E1
Blossoms La. SK7 132 B2
Blossoms St. SK2 170 F7
Bloxham Wlk. M9 64 F3
Blucher St. Ashton-u-L OL7 85 A6
Blucher St. M'ster M5 81 C1
Blucher St. M'ster M12 164 E6
Blue Bell Ave. M'ster M40 65 A1
Blue Bell Ave. Wigan WN6 36 F4
Blue Chip Bsns Pk. WA14 119 C7
Blue Coat CE Sch. OL1 153 F7
Bluebell Ave. BB4 1 A8
Bluebell Cl. SK14 101 F5
Bluebell Dr. OL11 30 B3
Bluebell Gr. SK8 122 D4
Blueberry Dr. OL2 49 D7
Blueberry Rd. WA14 119 A2
Bluefields. OL2 49 D8
Bluestone Dr. SK4 110 E3
Bluestone Rd. M'ster M40 83 A8
Bluestone Rd.
Reddish M34 & SK5 100 A2
Blundell Cl. BL9 45 B3
Blundell La. BL6 21 A2
Blundell Mews. WN3 54 D4
Blundell St. BL1 145 D7
Blundering La. SK15 102 D6
Blunn St. OL8 66 F4
Blyborough Cl. M6 154 E4
Blyth Ave. Littleborough OL15 15 F3
Blyth Ave. Wythenshawe M23 109 C2
Blyth Cl. WA15 120 D6
Blythe Ave. SK7 132 C6
Blyton St. M15 163 B5
Blyton Way. M34 112 F8
Bnos Yisroel Schs. M7 155 E8
Boad St. M1 163 B8
Boar Green Cl. M40 83 C7
Board St. Ashton-u-L OL6 85 D4
Board St. Bolton BL3 145 D6
Boardale Dr. M24 46 E1
Boardman Cl. BL1 143 E2
Boardman Fold Cl. M24 65 A5
Boardman Fold Rd. M24 65 A5
Boardman La. M24 64 C8
Boardman Rd. M8 63 F2
Boardman St.
Blackrod BL6 & PR7 21 D2
Boardman St. Bolton BL1 143 E2
Boardman St. Eccles M30 79 E1
Boardman St. Hyde SK14 167 D2
Boars Head Ave. WN6 37 A7
Boarsgreave La. BB4 2 F6
Boarshaw Clough. M24 47 B2
Boarshaw Cres. M24 47 C3
Boarshaw Cty Prim Sch.
M24 47 B3
Boarshaw Ind Est. M24 47 B2
Boarshaw La. M24 47 D3
Boarshaw Rd. M24 47 B2
Boarshurst La. OL3 69 C5
Boat La. Diggle OL3 51 E5
Boat La. Irlam M44 94 B2
Boat La. Wythenshawe M22 109 E1
Boat Lane Ct. M22 109 E1
Boatmans Row. M29 77 C4
Bob Brook Cl. M35 & M40 83 C6
Bob Massey Cl. M11 83 C1
Bob's La. M44 105 D4
Bobbin Wlk. 4 M'ster M4 159 C1
Bobbin Wlk. 7 Oldham OL4 67 A6
Bodden St. WA3 75 A1
Boddens Hill Rd. SK4 168 A1
Boddington Rd. Eccles M30 79 A1
Bodiam Rd. BL8 10 F2
Bodley St. M11 83 C2
Bodmin Cl. OL2 49 A3
Bodmin Cres. SK5 112 B5
Bodmin Dr. Bramhall SK7 132 E7
Bodmin Dr. Platt Bridge WN2 56 A1
Bodmin Rd. Sale M33 107 D5
Bodmin Rd. Tyldesley M29 77 C8
Bodmin Wlk. 3 M23 121 A5
Bodney Wlk. M9 64 B3
Bogburn La. PR7 19 D6
Boggard La. SK14 115 D6
Bogguard Rd. SK12 & SK6 127 A5
Bognor Rd. SK3 123 E4
Bolam Cl. M23 108 F1
Boland Dr. M14 110 D8
Bold St. Alt'ham WA14 119 D3
Bold St. Bolton BL1 145 F6
Bold St. Bury BL9 141 A3
Bold St. Leigh WN7 75 F5
Bold St. Leigh WN7 75 F6
Bold St. M'ster M16 97 E4
Bold St. M'ster M15 162 E5
Bold St. Swinton M27 61 F2
Bold St. Wigan WN5 54 E5
Bolderod Pl. 4 OL1 67 A8
Bolderstone Pl. SK2 124 E4
Bolderwood Dr. WN2 56 D4
Bolesworth Cl. M21 108 F8
Boleyn Ct. Handforth SK9 131 B1
Boleyn Ct. Heywood OL10 29 C1
Bolholt Terr. BL8 27 B4
Bolivia St. M5 80 C2
Bollin Ave. WA14 119 B1
Bollin Cl. Culcheth WA3 92 A2
Bollin Cl. Kearsley BL4 61 B6
Bollin Cl. Lymm WA13 117 A4
Bollin Cross Sch. SK9 131 A2
Bollin Ct. Alt'ham WA14 119 B1
Bollin Ct. 6 M'ster M15 162 D6
Bollin Ct. Wilmslow SK9 137 C6
Bollin Dr. Alt'ham WA14 119 E8
Bollin Dr. Lymm WA13 117 A4
Bollin Dr. Sale M33 108 B2
Bollin Hill. SK9 137 B8
Bollin House. M7 81 C5
Bollin Prim Sch. WA14 119 B1
Bollin Sq. WA14 119 B1
Bollin Way. M45 45 C2
Bollin Wlk. Reddish SK5 169 F4
Bollin Wlk. Whitefield M45 45 C2
Bollin Wlk. Wilmslow SK9 137 C7
Bolling St. BL3 145 F6
Bollings Yd. BL1 145 F6
Bollington Cl. 3 OL7 166 A1
Bollington Rd.
M'ster M10 & M40 160 D2
Bollington Rd. Reddish SK4 111 D5
Bollington St. OL7 166 A1
Bollinway. WA15 129 A8
Bollinwood Chase. SK9 137 D7
Bolney St. WN2 38 A3
Bolney Wlk. M40 160 D4
Bolshaw Cty Prim Sch.
SK8 131 B7
Bolshaw Farm La. SK8 131 C6
Bolshaw Rd. SK8 131 C6
Bolton Ave. Bramhall SK8 132 B6
Bolton Ave. M'ster M19 110 D2
Bolton Cath Sixth
Form Ctr. BL1 143 D4
Bolton Cl. Golborne WA3 91 B8
Bolton Cl. Poynton SK12 133 D4
Bolton Cl. Prestwich M25 62 F2
Bolton Coll. BL2 148 A6
Bolton District Gen Hospl.
BL4 147 F1
Bolton Golf Course. BL6 40 A8
Bolton House Rd. WN2 74 F8
Bolton Inst (Chadwick
Campus). BL2 148 B6
Bolton Inst of H Ed. BL3 145 E6
Bolton Metropolitan Coll.
Bolton BL1 145 F8
Bolton Metropolitan Coll.
Bolton BL2 148 A6
Bolton Muslim Girls Sch.
BL3 147 D4
Bolton Old Rd. M46 58 E3
Bolton Parish Church
CE Prim Sch. BL2 148 B7
Bolton Rd.
Adlington BL6 & PR6 21 D6
Bolton Rd.
Ashton-i-M WN2 & WN4 73 D5
Bolton Rd. Aspull WN2 38 D4
Bolton Rd. Atherton M46 58 E4
Bolton Rd. Bolton BL7 9 D5
Bolton Rd. Bolton BL2 25 C5
Bolton Rd. Bolton BL3 40 D2
Bolton Rd. Bury BL8 27 C1
Bolton Rd. Bury BL8 140 D2
Bolton Rd. Farnworth BL4 42 D2
Bolton Rd. Kearsley BL4 60 F7
Bolton Rd. Pendlebury M27 80 C7
Bolton Rd. R'dale OL11 30 B4
Bolton Rd. Radcliffe M26 43 E3
Bolton Rd. Ramsbottom BL8 10 D2
Bolton Rd. Salford M6 80 E5
Bolton Rd. Swinton M27 & BL8 62 A1
Bolton Rd. Walkden M28 60 D4
Bolton Rd. Westhoughton BL5 39 F1
Bolton Rd N. BL0 1 D2
Bolton Rd W. Ramsbottom BL8 10 F3
Bolton Rd W.
Ramsbottom BL0 & BL8 11 A4
Bolton Royal Infmy. BL1 145 D7
Bolton Sch. BL1 144 B7
Bolton Sq. WN1 37 E1
Bolton St. Bury BL9 140 E2
Bolton St. Garswood WN4 72 D5
Bolton St. M'ster M3 158 E1
Bolton St. Oldham OL4 67 B6
Bolton St. Radcliffe M26 43 F3
Bolton St. Ramsbottom BL0 138 B6
Bolton St. Reddish SK5 111 E7
Bolton Sta. BL3 145 F6
Bolton Street Sta. BL9 140 E2
Bolton Wholesale Pk. BL1 145 F8
Boltons Yd. OL3 69 B8
Bombay Rd. Shevington WN5 36 C1
Bombay Rd. Stockport SK3 123 C7
Bombay St. 5
Ashton-u-L OL6 85 D4
Bombay St. M'ster M1 163 A8
Bonar Cl. SK3 123 C8
Bonar Rd. 5 SK3 123 C8
Boncarn Dr. M23 121 A4
Bonchurch Wlk. M12 165 B6
Bond Cl. BL6 22 C3
Bond Sq. M7 155 E6
Bond St. Bury BL9 141 A2
Bond St. Denton M34 100 F3
Bond St. Edenfield BL0 1 E2
Bond St. Leigh WN7 75 F5
Bond St. M'ster M12 163 C8
Bond St. R'dale OL12 15 A2
Bond St. Stalybridge SK15 86 A3
Bond St. Tyldesley M46 58 F1
Bond's La. PR7 20 F7
Bondmark Rd. M18 165 C6
Bongs Rd. SK2 & SK6 125 A6
Bonhill Wlk. M11 83 B2
Bonholt Ind Est. 11 BL8 27 B4
Bonington Rise. SK6 126 B8
Bonis Cres. SK2 124 C4
Bonny Brow St. M24 64 B7
Bonnywell Rd. WN7 75 F3
Bonsall Bank. 32 SK13 171 E2
Bonsall Cl. 33 SK13 171 E2
Bonsall Fold. 31 SK13 171 E2
Bonsall St. M15 162 F6
Bonscale Cres. M24 46 E3
Bonville Chase. WA14 119 A4
Bonville Rd. WA14 119 A4
Boodle St. OL6 166 B4
Bookham Wlk. 16 M9 157 E8
Boond St. M'ster M3 158 E2
Boond St. M'ster M4 160 D1
Boonfields. BL7 25 A8
Boot La. BL1 23 E1
Booth Ave. M14 110 D7
Booth Bridge Cl. M24 64 C7
Booth Cl. 4 SK15 85 F1
Booth Ct. BL4 60 D8
Booth Dr. M41 94 F5
Booth Hall Dr. BL8 26 F5
Booth Hall Hospl. M9 64 F3
Booth Hall Rd. M9 65 A3
Booth Hill La. OL1 48 E1
Booth House Trad Est.
OL9 152 C6
Booth Rd. Alt'ham WA14 119 C4
Booth Rd. Bacup OL13 3 B8
Booth Rd.
Droylsden M34 & M43 100 A7
Booth Rd. Handforth SK9 131 A1
Booth Rd. Little Lever BL3 43 B2
Booth Rd. M'ster M16 97 C3
Booth Rd. Sale M33 108 B6
Booth St. Ashton-u-L OL6 166 B2
Booth St. Bolton BL1 142 C3
Booth St. Bury BL8 26 F5
Booth St. Denton M34 100 F5
Booth St. Failsworth M35 83 E7
Booth St. Hollingworth SK14 103 C5
Booth St. Hyde SK14 167 E1
Booth St. M'ster M2 158 F1
Booth St. M'ster M3 158 F2
Booth St. Middleton M24 65 D6
Booth St. Newton-l-W WA12 89 A3
Booth St. 2 Oldham OL4 67 E6
Booth St. Oldham OL9 153 E6
Booth St. Rawtenstall BB4 2 E8
Booth St. Stalybridge SK15 101 F8
Booth St. Stockport SK3 170 E7
Booth St E. M13 163 B6
Booth St W. M15 163 A6
Booth Way. BL8 26 F5
Booth's Brow Rd. WN4 72 D6
Booth's Hall. M28 78 B5
Booth's Hall Gr. M28 78 B6
Booth's Hall Rd. M28 78 B6
Booth's Hall Way. M28 78 B6
Boothby Rd. M27 61 E1
Boothby St. SK2 124 C4
Boothcote. M34 100 D6
Boothfield. 11 Bury BL8 27 C3
Boothfield. Worsley M28 79 A3
Boothfield Ave. M22 121 D6
Boothfield Dr. M22 121 D6
Boothfield Rd. M22 121 D6
Boothroyden Cl. M24 64 C7
Boothroyden Rd. M24 & M9 64 C6
Boothroyden Terr. M9 64 C6
Boothsbank Ave. M28 78 B6
Boothshall Paddock. M28 78 B5
Boothshall Way. M28 78 A5
Boothstown Dr. M28 78 A5
Boothway. 8 M30 79 F2
Bootle St. M2 162 F8
Bor Ave. WN3 55 B4
Bordale Ave. M9 157 F7
Bordan St. M11 164 F8
Borden Cl. 5 WN2 37 F2
Borden Way. BL9 45 A6
Border Brook La. M28 78 A6
Bordesley Ave. M38 60 A6
Bordley Wlk. M23 108 E1
Bordon Cl. BL1 143 D1
Bordon Rd. SK3 123 B7
Bores Hill. WN1 20 C4
Boringdon Cl. M40 83 B6
Borland Ave. M40 65 D1
Borough Arc. SK14 167 D2
Borough Ave. Radcliffe BL9 44 D5
Borough Ave. Swinton M27 62 A1
Borough Rd. Alt'ham WA15 119 E4
Borough Rd. Salford M5 154 D1
Borough St. 5 SK15 86 A1
Borrans The. M28 77 F5
Borron Rd. WA12 89 B5
Borron St. SK1 112 A2
Borrowdale Ave. Bolton BL1 144 A8
Borrowdale Ave. Gatley SK8 122 B4
Borrowdale Cl. OL2 48 D6
Borrowdale Cres.
Ashton-u-L OL7 84 F4
Borrowdale Cres.
M'ster M20 109 E4
Borrowdale Dr. R'dale OL11 30 C4
Borrowdale Dr.
Whitefield BL9 45 A3
Borrowdale Rd.
Middleton M24 46 E2
Borrowdale Rd.
Stockport SK2 124 B6
Borrowdale Rd. Wigan WN5 54 B7
Borrowdale Terr. SK15 86 A4
Borsdane Ave. WN2 38 E3
Borsdane Brook Sch. WN2 56 C5
Borsden St. M27 61 D2
Borth Ave. SK2 124 C7
Borwell St. M18 99 D5
Boscobel Rd. BL3 42 B2
Boscombe Ave. M30 95 C8
Boscombe Dr. SK7 124 C1
Boscombe St. M'ster M14 98 B2
Boscombe St.
Reddish M34 & SK5 99 F2
Boscow Rd. BL3 43 A2
Bosden Ave. SK7 124 F3
Bosden Cl. Handforth SK9 131 D5
Bosden Cl. Stockport SK1 170 F8
Bosden Fold. SK1 170 F8
Bosden Hall Rd. SK7 124 E3
Bosdenfold Rd. SK7 124 E3
Bosdin Rd E. M41 94 E1
Bosdin Rd W. M41 94 E1
Bosley Ave. M20 110 A8
Bosley Cl. SK9 131 D2
Bosley Dr. SK12 134 A3
Bosley Rd. SK3 123 A8
Bossall Ave. M9 64 E4
Bossington Cl. SK2 124 C8
Bostock Rd. SK14 115 A8
Bostock Wlk. M13 163 B7
Boston Cl. Bramhall SK7 132 D7
Boston Cl. Culcheth WA3 91 F4
Boston Cl. Failsworth M35 83 F8
Boston Ct. M5 96 E8
Boston Gr. WN7 75 E8
Boston St. 14 Bolton BL1 143 E2
Boston St. Hyde SK14 167 E2
Boston St. Oldham OL8 66 F4
Boston Wlk. 8 M34 101 A1
Boswell Ave. M34 84 D1
Boswell Pl. WN3 54 F3
Boswell Way. M24 47 E4
Bosworth Cl. M45 63 C8
Bosworth Sq. OL11 30 D4
Bosworth St. Horwich BL6 22 B4
Bosworth St. M'ster M11 165 A8
Bosworth St. R'dale OL11 30 D4
Botanical Ave. M16 161 A5
Botany Cl. Heywood OL10 29 B2
Botany Cl. Wigan WN2 38 B2
Botany La. OL6 166 C3
Botany Rd. Romiley SK6 113 A6
Botany Rd. Worsley M28 79 A4
Botha Cl. 4 M11 99 D7
Botham Cl. M'ster M15 162 F5
Bothwell Rd. M10 & M40 159 C3
Botley St. OL5 68 B1
Bottesford Ave. M20 109 F5
Bottom o' th' Knotts Brow.
BL7 9 E3
Bottom o' th' Moor.
Horwich BL6 23 A3
Bottom o' th' Moor.
Oldham OL1 & OL4 67 B7
Bottom o'th Moor. BL2 25 D2
Bottom St. SK14 167 F3
Bottomfield Cl. OL1 49 A1
Bottomley Rd. OL14 6 C6
Bottomley Side. M9 64 C2
Bougainvillea Gdns. M12 99 A4
Boughey St. WN7 75 E5
Boulden Dr. BL8 27 C5
Boulder Dr. M23 121 A2
Boulderstone Rd. SK15 86 A4
Boulevard The.
Hazel Grove SK7 124 E2
Boulevard The.
Hollingworth SK14 171 D4
Bouley Wlk. M12 165 A6
Boundary Cl. Mossley SK15 86 C6
Boundary Cl. Romiley SK6 113 C5
Boundary Cotts. OL5 86 E7
Boundary Ct. SK8 122 C5
Boundary Dr. BL2 & BL3 43 A5
Boundary Gdns. Bolton BL1 143 E2
Boundary Gdns. Oldham OL1 48 E1
Boundary Gr. M33 108 F2
Boundary La. M'ster M15 163 A6
Boundary La.
Shevington Moor WN6 19 A3
Boundary Park Football Gd
(Oldham Ath FC). OL1 48 D2
Boundary Park Rd. OL1 48 C1
Boundary Rd. Cheadle SK8 123 A6
Boundary Rd. Irlam M44 94 C3
Boundary Rd. Swinton M27 61 F1
Boundary St. Bolton BL1 143 D2
Boundary St. Leigh WN7 76 B4
Boundary St.
Littleborough OL15 16 B6
Boundary St. M'ster M12 165 A6
Boundary St. R'dale OL11 139 F5
Boundary St. Tyldesley M29 59 A1
Boundary St. Wigan WN1 151 D7
Boundary St E. M13 163 A7
Boundary St W. M15 163 A6
Boundary Terr. SK9 130 F6
Boundary The. M27 61 E4
Boundary Trad Pk. M44 94 C3
Boundary Wlk. OL11 139 E5
Boundry Gn. M34 100 E4
Bourdon St. M10 & M40 160 D3
Bourget St. M7 & M8 155 F8
Bournbrook Ave. M38 60 A6
Bourne Ave. Golborne WA3 90 D8
Bourne Ave. Swinton M27 79 F7
Bourne Dr. M40 65 B1
Bourne House. 1 M6 154 F2
Bourne Rd. OL2 149 A8
Bourne St. Oldham OL9 66 B2
Bourne St. Reddish SK4 169 E4
Bourne St. Wilmslow SK9 136 F6
Bourne Wlk. 9 BL1 143 F1
Bournelea Ave. M19 110 F6
Bourneville Dr. BL8 27 A2
Bournville Ave. SK4 169 E4
Bournville Gr. M19 99 C1
Bourton Cl. BL8 27 B3
Bourton Ct. M29 59 D1
Bourton Dr. M18 99 B4
Bow Green Rd. WA14 119 A1
Bow La. Alt'ham WA14 128 B8
Bow La. Heywood OL10 29 D2
Bow La. M'ster M2 158 F1
Bow Rd. WN7 76 B3
Bow St. Ashton-u-L OL6 166 B3
Bow St. Bolton BL1 145 F7
Bow St. Dukinfield SK16 166 C2
Bow St. 7 M'ster M2 158 F1
Bow St. Oldham OL1 153 F7
Bow St. R'dale OL11 30 D3
Bow St. Stockport SK3 123 C8
Bowden Cl. Culcheth WA3 91 F4
Bowden Cl. Leigh WN7 76 C2
Bowden Cl. Middleton OL11 47 D8
Bowden Cl.
Mottram-i-L SK14 102 E1
Bowden La. SK6 125 E6
Bowden Rd. Glossop SK13 104 C3
Bowden Rd. Pendlebury M27 80 A7
Bowden St. Bolton BL3 145 D6
Bowden St. Denton M34 100 E3
Bowden St. Hazel Grove SK7 124 D2
Bowdon Ave. M14 97 F1
Bowdon CE Aided Prim
Sch. WA14 119 C1
Bowdon House. 2 SK3 170 E8
Bowdon Prep Sch. WA14 119 C2

Bowdon Rd. WA14 119 C3
Bowdon Rise. WA14 119 D2
Bowdon St. SK3 170 E8
Bowen Cl. SK7 132 F5
Bowen St. BL1 142 B1
Bower Ave. Hazel Grove SK7 124 D1
Bower Ave. Littleborough OL12 15 D4
Bower Ave. Stockport SK4 168 C2
Bower Ct. SK14 102 A5
Bower Gr. SK15 86 C2
Bower La. OL9 66 A2
Bower Rd. WA15 119 F1
Bower St. Bury BL9 141 C3
Bower St. M'ster M40 83 A5
Bower St. M'ster M7 155 F7
Bower St. Oldham OL1 67 B8
Bower St. Reddish SK5 99 F2
Bower Terr. M43 84 C3
Bowerfield Ave. SK7 133 D8
Bowerfield Cres. SK7 133 E8
Bowerfold La. SK4 169 D2
Bowers Ave. M41 95 B3
Bowers St. M14 110 E7
Bowery Ave. SK8 131 F6
Bowes Cl. BL8 27 B5
Bowes St. M14 97 F3
Bowfell Dr. SK6 134 E8
Bowfell Gr. M9 64 B4
Bowfell Rd. M41 95 B2
Bowfield Wlk. 18 M40 83 C5
Bowgreave Ave. BL2 42 F7
Bowgreen Wlk. 11 M15 162 D6
Bowker Ave. M34 113 B8
Bowker Bank Ave. M8 63 F2
Bowker Cl. OL11 13 E1
Bowker Ct. M7 155 D6
Bowker St. Haslingden BB4 1 C5
Bowker St. Hyde SK14 167 E3
Bowker St. M'ster M7 155 D6
Bowker St. Radcliffe M26 44 A3
Bowker St. Walkden M28 60 B3
Bowker Vale Gdns. M9 63 F3
Bowker Vale Prim Sch. M8 63 F4
Bowker Vale Sta. M8 63 F3
Bowkers Row. 12 BL1 145 F7
Bowlacre Rd. SK14 113 D7
Bowland Ave. Ashton-i-M WN4 73 B4
Bowland Ave. Golborne WA3 74 C1
Bowland Ave. Reddish M18 100 A4
Bowland Cl. Ashton-u-L OL6 85 C7
Bowland Cl. Bury BL8 26 F3
Bowland Cl. Shaw OL2 48 E7
Bowland Cl. Stockport SK2 124 E5
Bowland Ct. M33 108 B4
Bowland Dr. BL1 23 E2
Bowland Gr. OL16 31 F4
Bowland Rd. Glossop SK13 116 A8
Bowland Rd. Reddish M34 100 B3
Bowland Rd. Romiley SK6 113 B5
Bowland Rd. Wythenshawe M23 121 A6
Bowlee Cl. BL9 45 A2
Bowler St. M'ster M19 111 B8
Bowler St. Shaw OL2 149 B7
Bowlers Wlk. OL12 14 F2
Bowley Ave. M22 121 A2
Bowling Green Row. M46 58 B2
Bowling Green St. Heywood OL10 29 D2
Bowling Green St. Hyde SK14 167 D2
Bowling Green Way. OL11 29 F7
Bowling Rd. M18 99 E3
Bowling St. OL9 66 B2
Bowlings The. WN6 37 A2
Bowman Cres. OL6 85 D3
Bowmead Wlk. 8 M8 155 F6
Bowmeadow Grange. 2 M12 98 F4
Bowmont Cl. SK8 123 A4
Bowness Ave. Cheadle SK8 123 B1
Bowness Ave. Irlam M44 105 D4
Bowness Ave. R'dale OL12 14 C1
Bowness Ave. Reddish SK4 111 E6
Bowness Ct. 5 M24 46 D2
Bowness Cty Prim Sch. BL3 42 F3
Bowness Dr. M33 107 F5
Bowness Pl. WN2 56 B8
Bowness Rd. Alt'ham WA15 120 D5
Bowness Rd. Ashton-u-L OL7 84 F4
Bowness Rd. Bolton BL3 147 D4
Bowness Rd. Little Lever BL3 42 F4
Bowness Rd. Middleton M24 46 D1
Bowness St. Droylsden M11 & M43 99 F7
Bowness St. Stretford M32 96 D3
Bowness Wlk. 7 OL2 48 E4
Bowring St. M7 81 C5
Bowscale Cl. 3 M13 98 F4
Bowstone Hill Rd. BL2 & BL8 26 B5
Box St. Littleborough OL15 16 A5
Box St. Ramsbottom BL0 11 D6
Box Wlk. M31 105 E3
Boxgrove Rd. M33 107 F5
Boxgrove Wlk. 3 M8 156 A6
Boxhill Dr. M23 109 A1
Boxtree Ave. M18 99 D4
Boyd Cl. Standish WN6 19 F1
Boyd St. M12 165 A7
Boyd's Wlk. SK16 101 C7
Boydell St. WN7 75 F6
Boydell's Houses. WN2 75 B8
Boyer St. M15 & M16 161 B5
Boyle St. Bolton BL1 142 A1
Boyle St. M'ster M8 156 B6
Boysnope Cres. M30 94 C4
Boyswell House. WN1 151 D8
Brabant Rd. SK8 123 B2
Brabazon Pl. WN5 54 C8
Brabham Cl. M'ster M21 109 B8
Brabyns Ave. SK6 113 D3
Brabyns Brow. SK6 126 A7
Brabyns Rd. SK14 113 E7
Brabyns Sch. SK6 126 B7
Bracadale Dr. SK3 170 F5
Bracewell Cl. M12 165 B5
Bracken Ave. M28 60 E3
Bracken Cl. Bolton BL1 24 D6
Bracken Cl. Droylsden OL7 84 D2
Bracken Cl. Heywood OL10 46 D8
Bracken Cl. Hollingworth SK14 103 D6
Bracken Cl. Marple SK6 126 C7
Bracken Cl. Oldham OL4 67 F6
Bracken Cl. Sale M33 107 C5
Bracken Dr. M23 121 B5
Bracken Gr. BB4 1 A8
Bracken Lea. BL5 57 F5
Bracken Lea Fold. OL12 14 B2
Bracken Rd. Atherton M46 58 D2
Bracken Rd. Leigh WN7 75 B5
Bracken Way. SK13 116 F7
Brackenfield Wlk. WA15 120 D6
Brackenhill Terr. 14 M34 113 A7
Brackenhurst Ave. OL5 68 E1
Brackenlea Pl. SK3 170 D5
Brackenside. SK5 112 A8
Brackenwood Dr. SK8 122 E4
Brackenwood Mews. SK9 137 E8
Brackley Ave. Irlam M44 105 D6
Brackley Ave. M'ster M15 162 D7
Brackley Ct. M22 121 D8
Brackley Dr. M24 65 A5
Brackley Lodge. M30 79 F3
Brackley Rd. Atherton BL5 59 A8
Brackley Rd. Eccles M27 & M30 79 D4
Brackley Rd. Reddish SK4 111 D5
Brackley Sq. 5 OL1 67 A8
Brackley St. Farnworth BL4 60 D8
Brackley St. 9 Oldham OL1 67 A8
Brackley St. Walkden M28 60 C4
Bracondale Ave. BL1 142 B2
Bradbourne Cl. BL3 145 F5
Bradburn Ave. 4 M30 79 D1
Bradburn Cl. 2 M30 79 D1
Bradburn Gr. 5 M30 79 D1
Bradburn Rd. M44 105 E7
Bradburn St. M30 79 D1
Bradburn Wlk. 8 M8 156 B6
Bradbury Ave. WA14 119 A5
Bradbury St. Ashton-u-L OL7 166 A4
Bradbury St. Hyde SK14 167 E1
Bradbury St. Radcliffe M26 44 A2
Bradbury Wlk. 10 OL2 48 E4
Bradbury's La. OL3 69 D3
Bradda Mount. SK7 124 A2
Braddan Ave. M33 108 C3
Bradden Cl. M5 81 A1
Braddocks Cl. OL12 & OL16 15 D4
Braddon Ave. M41 95 D2
Braddon Rd. SK6 113 A5
Braddon St. 1 M11 83 C1
Bradyll Rd. BL5 58 F8
Brade Cl. M11 165 C8
Bradfield Ave. M5 & M6 80 C2
Bradfield Cl. SK5 99 E2
Bradfield Rd. M32 & M41 96 A2
Bradford Ave. BL3 42 B3
Bradford Cres. 17 BL3 42 A4
Bradford Ct. M40 65 C1
Bradford Park Dr. BL2 148 B6
Bradford Rd. Bolton BL3, BL4 42 A2
Bradford Rd. Eccles M30 79 E4
Bradford Rd. M'ster M10 & M11 & M40 160 E2
Bradford St. Bolton BL2 148 B7
Bradford St. Farnworth BL4 60 D7
Bradford St. Oldham OL1 153 E8
Bradford St. Wigan WN3 150 C7
Bradgate Ave. SK8 122 D1
Bradgate Cl. M22 121 E8
Bradgate Rd. Alt'ham WA14 119 A5
Bradgate Rd. Sale M33 108 B2
Bradgate St. Ashton-u-L OL7 166 A1
Bradgate St. 7 Ashton-u-L OL7 166 A2
Bradgreen Rd. M28 79 C3
Brading Wlk. M22 130 E8
Bradlegh Rd. WA12 89 B1
Bradley Ave. M7 81 B7
Bradley Cl. Alt'ham WA15 119 E7
Bradley Cl. Denton M34 100 E7
Bradley Dr. BL9 45 B2
Bradley Fold. SK15 86 B2
Bradley Fold Cotts. BL2 43 B6
Bradley Fold Rd. BL2 & BL3 & BL8 & M26 43 C7
Bradley Fold Trad Est. BL3 43 C6
Bradley Green Rd. SK14 101 F6
Bradley Green Road Prim Sch. SK14 101 F6
Bradley Hill Trad Est. WN6 20 A2
Bradley House. OL8 153 F5
Bradley La. Little Lever BL3 43 B5
Bradley La. Newhey OL16 32 B4
Bradley La. Newton-l-W WA5 & WA12 89 A1
Bradley La. Sale M32 & M33 108 B7
Bradley La. Standish WN6 19 F2
Bradley St. 7 M'ster M1 & M60 159 B2
Bradley St. Newhey OL16 32 B4
Bradleys Count. M1 159 B1
Bradney Cl. M9 64 B4
Bradnor Rd. M22 121 D7
Bradshaw Ave. Failsworth M35 83 E5
Bradshaw Ave. M'ster M20 110 B7
Bradshaw Ave. Whitefield M45 44 E2
Bradshaw Brow. BL2 25 C4
Bradshaw Cres. SK6 126 A7
Bradshaw Fold Ave. M40 65 D3
Bradshaw Hall Dr. BL2 25 C6
Bradshaw Hall Inf Sch. SK8 122 E1
Bradshaw Hall Jun Sch. SK8 122 E1
Bradshaw Hall La. Cheadle SK8 131 E8
Bradshaw Hall La. Gatley SK8 131 D8
Bradshaw La. Lymm WA13 117 D3
Bradshaw La. Stretford M32 108 D8
Bradshaw Meadows. BL2 25 D6
Bradshaw Rd. Bolton BL2 & BL7 25 D7
Bradshaw Rd. Bury BL8 26 D5
Bradshaw Rd. Marple SK6 125 F7
Bradshaw St. Atherton M46 58 D3
Bradshaw St. Bolton BL2 145 F6
Bradshaw St. Farnworth BL4 60 D7
Bradshaw St. Heywood OL10 29 E2
Bradshaw St. M'ster M7 155 E6
Bradshaw St. 2 M'ster M4 & M60 159 A2
Bradshaw St. Middleton M24 65 C7
Bradshaw St. Oldham OL1 153 F7
Bradshaw St. 9 R'dale OL16 31 A8
Bradshaw St. Radcliffe M26 43 F3
Bradshaw St. Wigan WN1 37 E2
Bradshaw St. Wigan WN5 54 A6
Bradshaw St N. M7 155 D7
Bradshawgate. Bolton BL1 & BL3 145 F7
Bradshawgate. Leigh WN7 75 F5
Bradshawgate. Wigan WN1 151 D8
Bradshawgate Sh Arc. 7 WN7 75 F5
Bradstone Rd. M8 156 A5
Bradwell Ave. M'ster M20 109 F6
Bradwell Ave. Stretford M32 96 A3
Bradwell Dr. SK8 131 C7
Bradwell Field. 2 SK13 171 E1
Bradwell Lea. 4 SK13 171 E1
Bradwell Pl. 7 BL2 25 B1
Bradwell Rd. Golborne WA3 90 E7
Bradwell Rd. Hazel Grove SK7 133 E8
Bradwell Terr. 3 SK13 171 E1
Bradwell Wlk. M41 94 D3
Bradwen Ave. M8 64 A1
Bradwen Cl. M34 101 A1
Brady St. Horwich BL6 22 A4
Brady St. Stockport SK1 112 A2
Brae Side. OL8 66 E2
Braeburn Ct. WN7 75 D5
Braemar Ave. Stretford M32 96 A2
Braemar Ave. Urmston M41 95 A1
Braemar Dr. M33 107 C2
Braemar Gdns. BL3 40 E5
Braemar Gr. OL10 29 A1
Braemar La. M28 78 B6
Braemar Rd. Hazel Grove SK7 124 F3
Braemar Rd. M'ster M14 110 E8
Braemar Wlk. WN2 38 D5
Braemore Cl. Shaw OL2 48 E8
Braemore Cl. Wigan WN3 54 D2
Braemore Dr. Bury BL9 28 D2
Braemore Dr. Mottram-i-L SK14 102 F1
Braeside Cl. SK2 124 F6
Braeside Cres. WN5 71 D5
Braeside Gr. BL3 40 F5
Braewood Cl. BL9 28 D2
Bragenham St. M18 165 C5
Braidhaven. WN6 35 E7
Brailsford Ave. 6 SK13 171 E2
Brailsford Cl. 9 SK13 171 E2
Brailsford Gdns. 8 SK13 171 E2
Brailsford Gn. 7 SK13 171 E2
Brailsford Mews. 5 SK13 171 E2
Brailsford Rd. Bolton BL2 25 C3
Brailsford Rd. M'ster M14 110 E8
Braintree Rd. M22 130 E8
Braithwaite. WN6 36 A6
Braithwaite Rd. Golborne WA3 90 D8
Braithwaite Rd. Middleton M24 46 D4
Brakehouse Cl. OL16 31 E6
Brakesmere Gr. M28 60 A4
Braley St. M12 163 B7
Bramall Cl. BL9 45 B2
Bramall Hall (Mus). SK7 123 E1
Bramall Mount. SK3 170 F5
Bramall Park Golf Course. SK7 132 D8
Bramall St. SK14 167 D4
Bramber Way. OL9 152 B6
Bramble Ave. Oldham OL4 49 D1
Bramble Ave. Salford M5 161 C7
Bramble Cl. OL15 15 F5
Bramble Gr. WN5 54 E7
Bramble Wlk. 7 Sale M33 107 C5
Bramble Wlk. 4 Wythenshawe M22 121 C2
Bramblewood. M24 65 E8
Brambling Cl. Droylsden M43 84 C2
Brambling Cl. Hazel Grove SK2 125 A5
Brambling Dr. BL5 57 D6
Bramcote Ave. Bolton BL2 148 B6
Bramcote Ave. Wythenshawe M23 121 B6
Bramdean Ave. BL2 25 E5
Bramfield Wlk. M15 162 D7
Bramhall Ave. BL2 26 A4
Bramhall Cl. Alt'ham WA15 120 D6
Bramhall Cl. Dukinfield SK16 101 D6
Bramhall Cl. Milnrow OL16 31 E5
Bramhall Cl. Sale M33 108 E3
Bramhall Ct. M3 158 D3
Bramhall Ctr The. SK7 132 E6
Bramhall High Sch. SK7 132 F8
Bramhall La. SK2 & SK3 170 F5
Bramhall La S. Bramhall SK7 132 E7
Bramhall La S. Stockport SK3 & SK7 123 E2
Bramhall Moor Ind Est. SK7 124 B2
Bramhall Moor La. SK2 & SK7 124 C2
Bramhall Park Rd. SK7 & SK8 123 D1
Bramhall St. Bolton BL3 42 B3
Bramhall St. M'ster M18 99 E5
Bramhall Sta. SK7 132 E6
Bramhall Wlk. M34 100 F1
Bramham Rd. SK6 126 A4
Bramhope Wlk. M9 157 D7
Bramley Ave. M'ster M19 111 A8
Bramley Ave. Stretford M32 96 B1
Bramley Cl. Bramhall SK7 132 E6
Bramley Cl. Swinton M27 & M28 79 C6
Bramley Cl. Wilmslow SK9 136 D4
Bramley Cres. SK4 168 B1
Bramley Dr. Bramhall SK7 132 E6
Bramley Dr. Bury BL8 27 C6
Bramley Meade. M7 155 E7
Bramley Rd. 6 Bolton BL7 24 F6
Bramley Rd. Bolton BL1 & BL7 25 A6
Bramley Rd. Bramhall SK7 132 E6
Bramley Rd. R'dale OL11 29 E8
Bramley St. M7 155 E5
Brammay Dr. BL8 26 E6
Brampton Cl. WN2 55 F1
Brampton Rd. Bolton BL3 146 A2
Brampton Rd. Stockport SK7 123 F2
Brampton St. 9 M46 58 D3
Bramway. Bramhall SK7 132 C7
Bramway. High Lane SK6 134 F7
Bramwell Dr. M13 163 C6
Bramwell St. SK1 124 B8
Bramworth Ave. BL0 138 B6
Brancaster Rd. M1 163 A7
Branch Cl. BL8 140 D3
Branch Rd. OL15 15 F1
Branch St. Bacup OL13 3 D8
Branch St. Ince-i-M WN2 56 A7
Brancker St. BL5 40 C1
Brandish Cl. M13 164 D5
Brandle Ave. BL8 27 C4
Brandlehow Dr. M24 46 C2
Brandlesholme Prim Sch. BL8 27 C6
Brandlesholme Rd. Bury BL8 27 C6
Brandon Ave. Eccles M30 80 A5
Brandon Ave. Gatley SK8 122 B1
Brandon Ave. Reddish M34 99 F3
Brandon Ave. Wythenshawe M22 121 C8
Brandon Brow. 8 OL1 153 E8
Brandon Cl. Bury BL8 27 D5
Brandon Cl. Orrell WN8 53 A7
Brandon Cres. OL2 149 A8
Brandon Rd. M6 80 B5
Brandon St. 2 Bolton BL3 147 D4
Brandon St. Milnrow OL16 31 D6
Brandram Rd. M25 63 C4
Brandreth Pl. WN6 19 F1
Brandsby Gdns. M5 161 A8
Brandwood. OL1 47 E1
Brandwood Ave. M21 109 D4
Brandwood Cl. M28 78 A8
Brandwood Cty Prim Sch. BL3 146 C4
Brandwood Fold. BL7 9 E5
Brandwood Pk. OL13 3 B8
Brandwood Rd. OL13 3 B8
Brandwood St. BL3 146 C4
Branfield Ave. SK8 122 D1
Brankgate Ct. M20 110 A5
Branksome Ave. M25 63 B4
Branksome Dr. Cheadle SK8 122 D1
Branksome Dr. M'ster M9 64 B6
Branksome Dr. Pendlebury M6 80 B5
Branksome Rd. SK4 168 B1
Bransby Ave. M9 64 E4
Branscombe Dr. M33 107 C5
Branscombe Gdns. BL3 42 D5
Bransdale Ave. OL2 48 C4
Bransdale Cl. BL3 40 F4
Bransford Cl. WN4 73 C2
Bransford Rd. Droylsden M11 99 E8
Bransford Rd. Urmston M41 95 C3
Branson St. M10 & M40 160 D2
Branson Wlk. WA15 120 C6
Branston Rd. M40 65 D2
Brantfell Gr. BL2 42 F8
Branthwaite. Ince-i-M WN2 38 B1
Brantingham Ct. M16 97 E1
Brantingham Rd. M16 & M21 97 D1
Brantwood Cl. OL2 48 C4
Brantwood Dr. BL2 42 F8
Brantwood Rd. Cheadle SK8 122 F1
Brantwood Rd. M'ster M7 155 D8
Brantwood Rd. M'ster SK4 168 C4
Brantwood Terr. M9 157 F7
Branwood Prep Sch. M30 79 E3
Brassey St. Ashton-u-L OL6 166 B4
Brassey St. Middleton M24 47 A1
Brassington Ave. M'ster M21 109 B7
Brassington Ave. Salford M5 161 B8
Brassington Cres. SK13 171 D1
Brassington Gdns. M5 161 B8
Brassington Rd. M19 & SK4 110 E4
Brathay Cl. BL2 25 F2
Bratton Cl. WN3 54 C2
Bratton Wlk. M13 164 D6
Brattray Dr. M24 46 E3
Braunston Cl. M30 95 E8
Braxton Wlk. 20 M9 157 E8
Bray Ave. M30 79 B3
Bray Cl. SK8 122 E2
Braybrook Dr. BL1 40 D7
Brayford Rd. M22 121 D1
Brayshaw Cl. OL10 29 C1
Brayside Rd. M19 & M20 110 D4
Braystan Gdns. SK8 122 B6
Brayton Ave. M'ster M20 110 C2
Brayton Ave. Sale M33 107 D5
Brayton Ct. WN2 56 D6
Brazennose St. M2 158 F1
Brazil Pl. M1 163 A8
Brazil St. M1 163 A8
Brazley Ave. Bolton BL3 42 B3
Brazley Ave. Horwich BL6 22 E1
Breach House La. WA15 129 B8
Bread St. M18 99 E6
Breaktemper. BL5 39 E1
Brean Wlk. 8 M22 121 C1
Brearley St. OL13 3 D8
Breaston Ave. WN7 76 C3
Brechin Way. OL10 29 A1
Brechin Wlk. 16 M11 83 C1
Breck Rd. M30 79 B2
Breckland Cl. SK15 86 D2
Breckland Dr. BL1 40 D8
Breckles Pl. BL3 145 D5
Brecon Ave. Cheadle SK8 122 E1
Brecon Ave. Denton M34 100 F1
Brecon Ave. M'ster M19 110 F7
Brecon Ave. Urmston M41 94 D3
Brecon Cl. Platt Bridge WN2 56 B2
Brecon Cl. Poynton SK12 133 F4
Brecon Cl. Royton OL2 48 C6
Brecon Cres. OL6 85 B6
Brecon Dr. Bury BL9 44 E7
Brecon Dr. Hindley WN2 57 A3
Brecon Wlk. 6 OL8 66 B2
Bredbury Dr. BL4 60 E8
Bredbury Gn. SK6 113 A1
Bredbury Green Prim Sch. SK6 112 F1
Bredbury Hall Ctry Club. SK6 112 D2
Bredbury Park Way. SK6 112 E6
Bredbury Rd. M14 98 B2
Bredbury St. Dukinfield SK14 101 D5
Bredbury St. Oldham OL9 152 B6
Bredbury Sta. SK6 112 F4
Brede Wlk. M23 120 D8
Breeze Hill. WN6 37 B7
Breeze Hill Rd. Atherton M46 58 F5
Breeze Hill Rd. Oldham OL4 67 D5
Breeze Hill Sch. OL4 67 D5
Breeze Mount. M25 63 C3
Breightmet Dr. BL2 42 E7
Breightmet Fold La. BL2 42 F8
Breightmet Golf Course. BL2 26 A1
Breightmet St. BL2 & BL1 148 A7
Brellafield Dr. OL2 48 F8
Brenbar Cres. OL12 4 D1
Brenchley Dr. M23 109 A2
Brencon Ave. M23 108 C1
Brendall Cl. SK2 125 A5
Brendon Ave. M'ster M40 83 A7
Brendon Ave. Reddish SK5 111 F6
Brendon Cl. SK13 116 A8
Brendon Dr. M34 84 D1
Brendon Hills. OL2 48 D3
Brenley Wlk. 7 M9 157 D8
Brennan Cl. M15 163 A5
Brennan Ct. OL8 66 C2
Brennock Cl. M11 164 F8
Brent Cl. Little Lever BL3 43 B5
Brent Cl. Poynton SK12 133 B4
Brent Moor Rd. SK7 124 A3
Brent Rd. Stockport SK4 168 C1
Brent Rd. Wythenshawe M23 109 A2
Brentbridge Rd. M14 110 B8
Brentfield Ave. M7 & M8 156 A6
Brentford Ave. BL1 142 B2
Brentford Rd. SK5 111 F6
Brentford St. M9 157 E7
Brentnall Prim Sch. M7 155 D7
Brentnall St. SK1 170 F7
Brentnor Rd. M40 65 C3
Brenton Ave. Sale M33 108 A4
Brentwood. Sale M33 108 A4
Brentwood. Salford M6 154 E3
Brentwood. Urmston M41 94 F1
Brentwood. Wigan WN5 54 D5
Brentwood Ave. Alt'ham WA14 119 E7
Brentwood Ave. Irlam M44 105 D6
Brentwood Ave. Swinton M28 79 B6
Brentwood Ave. Urmston M41 95 D2
Brentwood Cl. Brinnington SK5 112 D5
Brentwood Cl. Littleborough OL15 15 F3
Brentwood Cl. M'ster M16 97 F3
Brentwood Cl. Stalybridge SK15 86 C2
Brentwood Cres. WA14 119 E6
Brentwood Ct. M25 62 F3
Brentwood Dr. Eccles M30 79 D4
Brentwood Dr. Farnworth BL3 & BL4 42 C2
Brentwood Dr. Gatley SK8 122 B5
Brentwood Rd. Adlington PR6 21 B8
Brentwood Rd. Swinton M27 79 D6
Brentwood Sch. WA14 119 E7
Brereton Cl. WA14 119 C1
Brereton Ct. SK8 122 E1
Brereton Dr. M28 78 F7
Brereton Gr. M44 105 E6
Brereton Rd. Eccles M30 78 F1
Brereton Rd. Handforth SK9 131 E3
Breslyn St. M3 158 F3
Bretherton Row. 17 WN1 150 C8
Bretherton St. WN2 56 C6
Brethren's Cl. M43 100 A8
Bretland Gdns. SK14 102 E1
Bretland Wlk. 2 M22 121 F3
Brett Rd. Boothstown M28 77 F6
Brett St. M22 109 E1
Brettargh St. M6 81 A4
Bretton Wlk. M22 130 D8
Brewer St. M1 159 B1
Brewer's Gn. SK7 124 D3
Brewerton Rd. OL4 67 C6
Brewery La. WN7 76 A5
Brewery St. 4 Alt'ham WA14 119 D4
Brewery St. Stockport SK1 169 F3
Brewster St. M'ster M9 157 D8
Brewster St. 4 Middleton M24 47 A2
Brian Ave. M43 84 C3
Brian Rd. BL4 60 A8
Brian St. OL11 30 B2
Briar Ave. Hazel Grove SK7 124 F2
Briar Ave. Hollinfare WA3 105 D2
Briar Ave. Oldham OL4 49 D1
Briar Cl. Ashton-i-M WN4 73 A4
Briar Cl. Hindley WN2 57 B4
Briar Cl. R'dale OL12 14 A1
Briar Cl. Sale M33 107 C4
Briar Cl. Urmston M41 95 A3
Briar Cres. M22 121 E5
Briar Gr. Leigh WN7 75 E8
Briar Gr. Oldham OL9 48 B1
Briar Gr. Romiley SK6 113 A5
Briar Hill Ave. M38 59 E4
Briar Hill Cl. M38 59 E4
Briar Hill Gr. M38 59 E4
Briar Hill Way. 6 M6 81 A3
Briar Lea Cl. BL3 147 E4
Briar Rd. Golborne WA3 90 B8
Briar Rd. Wigan WN5 54 E7
Briar St. Bolton BL2 42 D7
Briar St. R'dale OL11 139 D6
Briarcroft Dr. M46 58 A1
Briardene. M34 101 A4
Briardene Gdns. M22 121 E4
Briarfield. BL7 8 D2
Briarfield Rd. Alt'ham WA15 120 C6
Briarfield Rd. Cheadle SK8 123 B3
Briarfield Rd. Farnworth BL4 42 A1
Briarfield Rd. M'ster M19 & M20 110 D6
Briarfield Rd. Reddish SK4 111 E6
Briarfield Rd. Worsley M28 78 F7
Briarfields Rd. OL3 51 A2
Briargrove Rd. SK12 127 C4
Briarlands Ave. M33 107 F2
Briarlands Cl. SK7 132 D6
Briarlea Gdns. M19 110 E5
Briarley Gdns. SK6 113 C6
Briarly. WN6 37 A7
Briarmere Wlk. OL9 152 C7
Briars Mount. SK4 168 A2
Briarstead Cl. SK7 132 D7
Briarwood. SK9 137 C7
Briarwood Ave. Droylsden M43 83 F3
Briarwood Ave. Sale M33 120 E8
Briarwood Chase. SK8 123 B1
Briarwood Cres. SK6 126 A3
Briary Dr. M29 77 B8
Brice St. SK16 101 B8
Brick Ground. OL12 13 C2
Brick Kiln La. 7 WN1 37 C1
Brick St. Bury BL9 141 A3
Brick St. 9 M'ster M4 159 A2
Brick St. Newton-l-W WA12 89 A3
Brickbridge Rd. SK6 126 A5
Brickfield St. Hadfield SK14 104 B5
Brickfield St. R'dale OL16 15 B2
Brickhill La. WA15 129 B4
Brickkiln La. WA14 118 C3
Brickkiln Row. WA14 119 C1
Brickley St. M3 159 A3
Bricknell Wlk. 5 M22 121 F3
Bridcam St. M8 156 A5
Briddon St. M3 158 F3
Bride St. BL1 143 E2
Brideoak St. M7 & M8 156 A6
Brideoake St. Leigh WN7 76 B4
Brideoake St. Oldham OL4 67 E8
Bridestowe Ave. SK14 102 C3
Bridestowe Wlk. SK14 102 C3
Bridge Ave. SK6 113 A5
Bridge Bank Rd. OL15 16 A3
Bridge Cl. Lymm WA13 117 B4
Bridge Cl. Partington M31 106 A3
Bridge Cl. 6 Radcliffe M26 44 B2
Bridge Dr. Cheadle SK8 122 D4
Bridge Dr. Handforth SK9 131 D3
Bridge End. Delph OL3 50 F4
Bridge End. Wigan WN6 150 B8
Bridge End Cl. BB4 1 A7
Bridge Gr. WA15 119 F7
Bridge Hall Dr. BL9 141 C2
Bridge Hall Fold. BL9 141 C2
Bridge Hall La. BL9 28 D2
Bridge Hall Prim Sch. SK3 170 D6
Bridge La. SK7 123 F1
Bridge Mills Bsns Pk. M6 80 F5
Bridge Rd. Bury BL9 140 D1
Bridge Rd. Sale M23 120 C7
Bridge St. Bolton BL1 145 F7
Bridge St. Bury BL9 141 A3
Bridge St. Denton M34 100 E4
Bridge St. Droylsden M43 99 E8
Bridge St. Dukinfield M34 100 F7
Bridge St. Dukinfield SK16 101 A6
Bridge St. Farnworth BL4 42 E1
Bridge St. Golborne WA12 & WA3 90 A7
Bridge St. Haslingden BB4 1 C6
Bridge St. Heywood OL10 29 C2
Bridge St. Hindley WN2 56 E6
Bridge St. Horwich BL6 22 C4
Bridge St. Ince-i-M WN3 151 D6
Bridge St. Kearsley M26 61 B8
Bridge St. Littleborough OL12 15 C3
Bridge St. M'ster M3 158 E1
Bridge St. Middleton M24 65 A8
Bridge St. Milnrow OL16 31 F6
Bridge St. New Mills SK12 127 C1
Bridge St. Newton-l-W WA12 89 B3
Bridge St. 1 Oldham OL1 67 A6
Bridge St. Oldham OL4 67 F6
Bridge St. R'dale OL11 30 C1
Bridge St. Ramsbottom BL0 138 C6
Bridge St. Rawtenstall BB4 2 E7
Bridge St. Shaw OL2 149 C8
Bridge St. Stalybridge SK15 85 F1
Bridge St. Stockport SK1 169 F2
Bridge St. Swinton M27 80 A8
Bridge St. Uppermill OL3 69 B7
Bridge St. Whitworth OL12 4 C1
Bridge St. Wigan WN2 38 A3
Bridge St. Wigan WN3 150 C7
Bridge's St. M46 58 B2
Bridgecrest Ct. SK8 123 A2
Bridgecroft St. WN2 56 E6
Bridgefield Ave. SK9 131 C1
Bridgefield Cres. 4 OL4 67 F6
Bridgefield Dr. BL9 28 D2
Bridgefield St. R'dale OL11 139 D7
Bridgefield St. Radcliffe M26 44 B3
Bridgefield St. Stockport SK1 169 E2
Bridgefield Wlk. 7 M26 44 B3
Bridgefold Rd. OL11, OL12 139 D8
Bridgefoot Cl. M28 78 A5
Bridgeford Ct. M32 108 D8
Bridgeford St. M'ster M15 163 A6

Carnforth Rd. Cheadle SK8 . 123 C4
Carnforth Rd. Reddish SK4 & SK5 .... 111 D7
Carnforth Sq. OL11 .... 47 D7
Carnforth St. M14 .... 98 B3
Carnoustie Cl. Failsworth M40 83 C7
Carnoustie Cl. Wilmslow SK9 .... 137 D8
Carnoustie Dr. Gatley SK8 . 122 C1
Carnoustie Dr. Ramsbottom BL0 .... 138 B5
Carnwood Cl. M40 .... 83 D4
Carolina House. M3 .... 158 E3
Caroline Dr. M4 .... 159 C1
Caroline St. Ashton-u-L OL6 166 C3
Caroline St. Bolton BL3 .... 147 D4
Caroline St. Irlam M44 .... 105 F8
Caroline St. M'ster M7 .... 158 E4
Caroline St. Stalybridge SK15 86 A1
Caroline St. Stockport SK3 .. 170 D7
Caroline St. Wigan WN3 .... 150 C7
Caroline St. Wigan WN1 .... 151 F8
Carpenters La. M4 .... 159 A2
Carpenters Way. OL16 .... 31 B4
Carpenters Wlk. M43 .... 83 F1
Carr Ave. M25 .... 62 F2
Carr Bank Ave. M'ster M9 ..... 63 F3
Carr Bank Ave. Ramsbottom BL0 .... 138 B7
Carr Bank Dr. BL0 .... 138 B7
Carr Bank Rd. BL0 .... 138 B7
Carr Brook Dr. M46 .... 58 E4
Carr Brow. SK6 .... 135 A7
Carr Cl. SK1 .... 124 B8
Carr Common Rd. WN2 .... 57 D3
Carr Fold. BL0 .... 138 B7
Carr Gr. OL16 .... 32 A6
Carr House La. WN6 .... 18 F8
Carr House Rd. OL4 .... 67 F6
Carr La. Alderley Edge SK9 ... 136 D2
Carr La. Diggle OL3 .... 51 C5
Carr La. Golborne WA3 .... 91 A7
Carr La. Leigh WA3 & WN7 .... 91 E8
Carr La. Mossley SK15 .... 86 F7
Carr La. Newhey OL16 .... 32 C6
Carr La. Rawtenstall BB4 .... 2 F7
Carr La. Uppermill OL3 .... 69 B7
Carr La. Wigan WN3 .... 55 B3
Carr Mill Cres. WN5 .... 71 E4
Carr Mill Jun Sch. WA11 ...... 71 C1
Carr Mill Rd. WA11 & WN5 ... 71 D3
Carr Rd. Alt'ham WA15 .... 120 B2
Carr Rd. Horwich BL6 .... 22 B5
Carr Rd. Irlam M44 .... 94 B2
Carr Rise. SK15 .... 86 F7
Carr St. Ashton-u-L OL6 .... 85 D5
Carr St. Hindley WN2 .... 56 D6
Carr St. Leigh WN7 .... 75 C5
Carr St. Ramsbottom BL0 ..... 138 B7
Carr St. Swinton M27 .... 79 D7
Carr Wood Ave. SK7 .... 132 E8
Carr Wood Rd. SK7 .... 123 E1
Carradale Dr. M33 .... 107 C5
Carradale Wlk. 5 M40 .... 83 A6
Carradon Dr. WN6 .... 19 E1
Carrbrook Cl. SK15 .... 86 E6
Carrbrook Cres. SK15 .... 86 F6
Carrbrook Dr. OL1 .... 48 E1
Carrbrook Ind Est. SK15 .... 87 A6
Carrbrook Rd. SK15 .... 86 F7
Carrbrook Terr. 6 M26 .... 44 C4
Carrfield Ave. Alt'ham WA15 120 D6
Carrfield Ave. Stockport SK3 124 A4
Carrfield Ave. Walkden M38 .. 59 E4
Carrfield Cl. M38 .... 59 E4
Carrfield Gr. M38 .... 59 E4
Carrgate Rd. M34 .... 101 B1
Carrgreen Cl. M19 .... 110 F5
Carrgreen La. WA13 .... 117 F6
Carrhill Quarry Cl. OL5 .... 68 C2
Carrhill Rd. OL5 .... 68 C2
Carrhouse La. Gamesley SK14 .... 103 C2
Carrhouse La. Hollingworth SK14 .... 103 C4
Carriage Dr The. SK14 .... 103 F5
Carriage St. M15 .... 162 D5
Carriages The. WA14 .... 119 C4
Carrick Gdns. M24 .... 46 F4
Carrie St. BL1 .... 144 B8
Carrigart. M25 .... 63 B3
Carrill Gr. M19 .... 99 A1
Carrill Gr E. M19 .... 99 A1
Carrington Bsns Pk. M31 . 106 C6
Carrington Cl. OL16 .... 15 D3
Carrington Dr. BL3 .... 145 F5
Carrington Field St. SK1 & SK2 .... 124 A7
Carrington Gr. WN7 .... 75 F7
Carrington House. M6 .... 80 C4
Carrington La. Sale M41 & M33 .... 107 C6
Carrington La. Sale M33 ..... 107 E5
Carrington Rd. Adlington PR7 20 F7
Carrington Rd. Flixton M31 & M41 .... 106 E8
Carrington Rd. M'ster M14 ... 98 C1
Carrington Rd. Stockport SK1 .... 112 B3
Carrington St. Leigh WN7 ..... 75 F7
Carrington St. Oldham OL9 ... 66 B3
Carrington St. Swinton M27 ... 62 B1
Carrmel Ct. OL3 .... 50 F3
Carrock Wlk. M24 .... 46 B1
Carron Ave. M9 .... 64 F1
Carron Gr. BL2 .... 42 F7
Carrs Ave. SK3 & SK8 .... 123 A6
Carrs Rd. SK8 .... 122 F6
Carrsfield Rd. M22 .... 121 E6
Carrslea Cl. M26 .... 43 E5
Carrsvale Ave. M41 .... 95 B3
Carrswood Rd. M23 .... 120 D8
Carruthers Cl. OL10 .... 29 F3
Carruthers St. M4 .... 160 D1
Carrwood. WA15 .... 129 B7
Carrwood Hey. BL0 .... 11 A4
Carrwood Rd. SK9 .... 136 F8
Carsdale Rd. M22 .... 130 E8
Carslake Ave. BL1 .... 144 C8
Carslake Rd. M40 .... 157 D5
Carson Rd. M19 .... 111 A8
Carstairs Ave. SK2 .... 124 A4
Carstairs Cl. M7 & M8 .... 155 F7
Carswell Cl. M29 .... 59 C1
Carter Cl. M34 .... 100 F2
Carter Pl. SK14 .... 101 D5
Carter St. Bolton BL3 .... 42 A4
Carter St. Dukinfield SK14 .... 101 D5
Carter St. Farnworth BL4 .... 60 E7
Carter St. Ince-i-M WN3 .... 151 E6
Carter St. M'ster M7 .... 155 D5
Carter St. Mossley OL5 .... 86 C8
Carter St. Salford M5 .... 80 C1
Carter St. Stalybridge SK15 .... 86 B2
Carthage St. OL8 .... 66 F4
Carthorpe Arch. M5 .... 154 F1
Cartleach Gr. Walkden M28 .. 60 A2
Cartleach La. M28 .... 60 A2
Cartmel. 6 OL12 .... 139 F8
Cartmel Ave. Milnrow OL16 .... 31 F4
Cartmel Ave. Reddish SK4 ... 111 E6
Cartmel Ave. Wigan WN1 .... 37 B3
Cartmel Cl. Bolton BL3 .... 40 D2
Cartmel Cl. Gatley SK8 .... 122 C3
Cartmel Cl. Hazel Grove SK7 124 C3
Cartmel Cl. Oldham OL8 .... 66 D3
Cartmel Cl. Whitefield BL9 ..... 45 A3
Cartmel Cres. Bolton BL2 .... 25 C2
Cartmel Cres. Failsworth OL9 65 F2
Cartmel Ct. M9 .... 65 A4
Cartmel Dr. WA15 .... 120 D6
Cartmel Gr. M28 .... 79 B7
Cartmel Wlk. M'ster M9 .... 157 D7
Cartmel Wlk. Middleton M24 . 46 F2
Cartridge Cl. M22 .... 121 F3
Cartridge St. OL10 .... 29 C2
Cartwright Gr. WN7 .... 57 D1
Cartwright Rd. M21 .... 108 F8
Cartwright St. Denton M34 . 100 F6
Cartwright St. Dukinfield SK14 .... 102 A5
Carver Ave. M25 .... 63 C5
Carver Cl. M16 .... 161 B5
Carver Dr. SK6 .... 125 E5
Carver Rd. Alt'ham WA15 .... 119 E2
Carver Rd. Marple SK6 .... 125 E5
Carver St. M16 .... 161 B5
Carver Wlk. M15 .... 162 F5
Carwood Gr. BL6 .... 22 D1
Cashmere Rd. SK3 .... 123 C7
Cashmore Dr. WN2 .... 56 D4
Cashmore Wlk. M12 .... 164 E6
Caspian Rd. WA14 .... 119 A6
Cassandra Ct. M5 .... 161 C8
Cassidy Cl. M4 .... 159 B2
Cassidy Ct. M5 .... 96 E8
Cassidy Gdns. M24 .... 46 D4
Casson Gate. OL12 .... 14 E1
Casson St. M35 .... 83 F7
Casterton Way. M28 .... 78 A5
Castle Ave. Denton M34 ...... 100 E2
Castle Ave. R'dale OL11 ...... 139 E6
Castle Cl. M43 .... 84 B2
Castle Cres. BL6 .... 22 C5
Castle Croft. BL2 .... 25 E3
Castle Ct. OL6 .... 85 B7
Castle Dr. PR7 .... 20 E6
Castle Edge Rd. SK12 .... 127 B2
Castle Farm Dr. SK2 .... 124 B5
Castle Farm La. SK2 .... 124 C5
Castle Gr. Leigh WN7 .... 76 D6
Castle Gr. Ramsbottom BL0 .... 11 A2
Castle Hall Cl. SK15 .... 86 B1
Castle Hall Ct. 11 SK15 .... 86 A1
Castle Hall View. 10 SK15 .... 86 A1
Castle Hill. Glossop SK13 .... 104 E2
Castle Hill. Newton-l-W WA12 89 E4
Castle Hill. R'dale OL11 ...... 139 E6
Castle Hill Cres. OL11 .... 139 E6
Castle Hill Cty Prim Sch. BL2 .... 25 B2
Castle Hill Mobile Home Pk. SK6 .... 113 A6
Castle Hill Pk. WN2 .... 56 F7
Castle Hill Rd. Bury BL9 .... 28 D5
Castle Hill Rd. Hindley WN2 .. 56 E6
Castle Hill Rd. M'ster M25 .... 63 D2
Castle Hill Sch. SK5 .... 112 C6
Castle Hill St. Bolton BL2 ...... 25 B2
Castle Hill St. Bolton BL2 ...... 25 B3
Castle House La. PR7 .... 20 E6
Castle Irwell Student Village. M6 & M7 .. 81 B5
Castle L Ctr. BL9 .... 140 E2
Castle La. OL5 & SK15 .... 86 F8
Castle Mews. BL4 .... 60 D7
Castle Mill La. Alt'ham WA15 129 B5
Castle Rd. BL9 .... 45 C4
Castle Rise. 4 WN2 .... 56 E5
Castle Shaw Rd. SK2 .... 124 E5
Castle St. Bolton BL2 .... 148 A7
Castle St. Bury BL9 .... 140 E2
Castle St. Eccles M30 .... 79 F2
Castle St. Farnworth BL4 .... 60 D7
Castle St. Hadfield SK14 ...... 104 A4
Castle St. Hindley WN2 .... 56 E6
Castle St. Hyde SK14 .... 167 F3
Castle St. M'ster M3 .... 162 E8
Castle St. Middleton M24 .... 65 D7
Castle St. Ramsbottom BL9 .... 11 C2
Castle St. Stalybridge SK15 ... 86 A1
Castle St. Stockport SK3 ...... 170 D7
Castle St. Stockport SK3 ...... 170 E8
Castle St. Tyldesley M29 .... 58 F1
Castle Terr. SK15 .... 110 F6
Castle Way. M27 .... 62 A3
Castle Wlk. OL6 .... 85 B7
Castle Yard. SK1 .... 169 F2
Castlebrook Cl. BL9 .... 45 B4
Castlebrook High Sch. BL9 .. 45 C3
Castlecroft Ave. BL6 .... 21 D2
Castlecroft Rd. BL9 .... 140 E3
Castledene Ave. M6 .... 154 E3
Castlefield Ave. M7 .... 155 E8
Castlefield Ctr. M3 .... 162 E8
Castleford Cl. 9 BL1 .... 145 D8
Castleford St. OL1 .... 48 C1
Castleford Wlk. M21 .... 109 D7
Castlehawk Golf Course. OL11 .... 30 A1
Castlemere Dr. OL2 .... 49 D8
Castlemere Rd. M9 .... 64 C3
Castlemere St. OL11 & OL16 139 E6
Castlemere Terr. OL11 .... 139 F6
Castlemill St. OL1 .... 67 B7
Castlemoor Ave. M7 .... 81 B8
Castlerea Cl. M30 .... 95 D8
Castlerigg Dr. Middleton M24 46 C2
Castlerigg Dr. Royton OL2 ..... 48 C6
Castleton Ave. M32 .... 96 B3
Castleton Bank. 22 SK13 ..... 171 E1
Castleton Cres. SK13 .... 171 E1
Castleton Ct. 13 Denton M34 .... 113 A8
Castleton Ct. 13 Tyldesley M29 .... 58 F1
Castleton Dr. SK6 .... 134 F6
Castleton Gn. 23 SK13 .... 171 E1
Castleton Gr. Ashton-u-L OL6 85 F6
Castleton Gr. 21 Gamesley SK13 .... 171 E1
Castleton Prim Sch. OL11 ... 30 D2
Castleton Rd. Hazel Grove SK7 .... 124 E1
Castleton Rd. 11 M'ster M7 .. 63 E1
Castleton Rd. M'ster M7 ...... 155 E8
Castleton Rd. Royton OL16 & OL2 .... 48 D8
Castleton Rd. Stretford M32 . 96 B4
Castleton Rd S. OL11 .... 30 D3
Castleton St. Alt'ham WA14 119 C7
Castleton St. Bolton BL2 .... 25 B2
Castleton St. Oldham OL9 ... 152 C6
Castleton Sta. OL11 .... 30 C2
Castleton Terr. 24 SK13 ...... 171 E1
Castleton Way. 14 Denton M34 .... 113 A8
Castleton Way. Wigan WN3 .. 54 C2
Castleton Wlk. 2 M11 .... 160 F1
Castleway. Alt'ham WA15 .... 129 C7
Castleway. Hindley WN2 .... 57 A5
Castleway. R'dale OL11 .... 30 B1
Castleway. Salford M6 .... 154 E4
Castlewood Gdns. SK2 .... 124 C5
Castlewood Rd. M7 .... 81 A8
Castlewood Sq. 3 BL2 .... 25 C1
Caston Cl. M16 .... 97 E4
Catchdale Cl. M9 .... 64 C5
Catches Cl. OL11 .... 30 B8
Catches La. OL11 .... 14 B1
Cateaton St. 2 Bury BL9 ..... 140 F3
Cateaton St. M'ster M3, M4 . 158 F2
Caterham St. M4 .... 160 D1
Catesby Rd. M16 .... 97 D3
Catfield Wlk. M15 .... 162 D7
Catford Rd. M23 .... 120 F5
Cathedral App. M3 .... 158 F2
Cathedral Cl. SK16 .... 101 D6
Cathedral Gates. M4 .... 158 F2
Cathedral Rd. OL9 .... 48 A1
Cathedral St. M4 .... 158 F2
Catherine House. SK4 .... 110 F2
Catherine Rd. Alt'ham WA14 119 C3
Catherine Rd. Bredbury SK6 112 F2
Catherine Rd. M'ster M8 .... 63 E1
Catherine Rd. Swinton M27 ... 79 C7
Catherine St. Bolton BL3 ...... 146 B2
Catherine St. Bury BL9 .... 44 E6
Catherine St. Hazel Grove SK7 .... 124 E3
Catherine St. Hyde SK14 ..... 167 D3
Catherine St. Leigh WN7 .... 75 F6
Catherine St. M'ster M11 & M18 .... 99 E7
Catherine St. 8 Oldham OL4 67 E6
Catherine St. Worsley M28 ... 79 B3
Catherine St E. BL6 .... 22 B4
Catherine St W. BL6 .... 22 B5
Catherine Terr. WN1 .... 151 E8
Catherine Way. WA12 .... 89 B2
Catherston Cl. 7 M16 .... 97 E3
Cathrine St E. M34 .... 100 D3
Cathrine St W. M34 .... 100 D3
Catlow La. 11 M4 & M60 ...... 159 A2
Catlow St. M7 .... 158 E4
Cato St. BL0 .... 11 A4
Caton Cl. BL9 .... 44 E8
Caton St. OL11 & OL16 .... 139 F6
Catterall Cres. BL2 .... 25 E6
Catterick Ave. M'ster M20 .. 110 C3
Catterick Ave. Sale M33 ...... 107 C2
Catterick Dr. BL3 .... 43 A3
Catterick Rd. M20 .... 110 C3
Catterwood Dr. SK6 .... 114 B2
Cattlin Way. OL8 .... 66 C2
Caunce Ave. WA3 .... 90 A7
Caunce Rd. WN1 .... 151 E8
Caunce St. WN1 .... 151 E8
Causeway Head. BB4 .... 1 A8
Causeway The. 2 Alt'ham WA14 .... 119 D4
Causeway The. Oldham OL9 .. 65 E5
Causewood Cl. OL4 .... 49 E4
Causey Dr. M24 .... 46 D3
Cavalier St. M10 & M40 .... 160 D2
Cavan Cl. SK3 .... 122 F7
Cavanagh Cl. M13 .... 164 D6
Cavannah Ct. OL1 .... 49 E3
Cavell St. M1 & M60 .... 159 B1
Cavell Way. M5 .... 81 A1
Cavendish Ave. M'ster M20 . 109 F6
Cavendish Ave. Swinton M27 62 C3
Cavendish Ct. M'ster M7 .... 63 D1
Cavendish Ct. M'ster SK4 .... 110 F2
Cavendish Ct. Stretford M32 . 96 E4
Cavendish Dr. WN3 .... 54 D2
Cavendish Gdns. M20 .... 109 F6
Cavendish Gr. M30 .... 79 E3
Cavendish Mews. SK9 .... 137 A6
Cavendish Mill. OL7 .... 166 B2
Cavendish Pl. M'ster M11 ...... 83 A2
Cavendish Pl. Swinton M27 ... 80 A8
Cavendish Rd. Alt'ham WA14 .... 119 C3
Cavendish Rd. Eccles M30 .... 79 E4
Cavendish Rd. Hazel Grove SK7 .... 133 E8
Cavendish Rd. M'ster M25 & M7 .... 63 D1
Cavendish Rd. M'ster M20 .. 109 F6
Cavendish Rd. M'ster SK4 ... 110 F2
Cavendish Rd. Stretford M32 96 E4
Cavendish Rd. Swinton M28 .. 79 B6
Cavendish Rd. Urmston M41 . 95 E2
Cavendish Road Prim Sch. M20 .... 110 A5
Cavendish St. Ashton-u-L OL6 .... 166 A2
Cavendish St. Leigh WN7 ...... 75 F7
Cavendish St. M'ster M15 .. 163 A6
Cavendish St. 3 Oldham OL9 .... 153 E6
Cavenham Gr. 7 BL1 .... 144 C8
Cavenham Wlk. M9 .... 156 C7
Caversham Dr. M9 .... 157 E8
Cawdor Ave. BL4 .... 42 B2
Cawdor Ct. BL4 .... 42 C2
Cawdor House. M30 .... 95 D8
Cawdor Pl. WA15 .... 120 C6
Cawdor Rd. M'ster M14 .... 98 C1
Cawdor Rd. Radcliffe M26 ..... 44 B2
Cawdor St. Eccles M30 .... 79 C1
Cawdor St. Farnworth BL4 ..... 42 C1
Cawdor St. Hindley WN2 .... 56 E5
Cawdor St. Leigh WN7 .... 75 F4
Cawdor St. M'ster M15 .... 162 D7
Cawdor St. Swinton M27 .... 79 D8
Cawdor St. Walkden M28 ...... 60 E2
Cawdor St. 2 Wigan WN5 ...... 54 F6
Cawdor Wlk. 6 BL4 .... 42 C2
Cawley Ave. Culcheth WA3 .... 91 E4
Cawley Ave. Prestwich M25 ... 62 F2
Cawood Sq. SK5 .... 112 C6
Cawston Wlk. 10 M8 .... 156 A6
Caxton Cl. WN3 .... 54 F2
Caxton Rd. M14 .... 110 B8
Caxton St. Heywood OL10 ..... 29 D2
Caxton St. M'ster M3 .... 158 E2
Caxton St. R'dale OL11 .... 30 C1
Caxton Way. M5 & M6 .... 81 B1
Caygill St. M3 .... 158 E2
Cayley St. OL16 .... 31 B7
Caythorpe St. M14 .... 98 A3
Cayton St. M12 & M13 .... 99 A3
CE Sch of the Resurrection. M11 .... 160 F1
Ceal The. SK6 .... 114 B2
Cecil Ave. Sale M33 .... 107 F3
Cecil Ave. Wigan WN6 .... 37 A2
Cecil Ct. SK3 .... 170 E7
Cecil Dr. M41 .... 94 E2
Cecil Gr. M18 .... 99 D5
Cecil Rd. Alt'ham WA15 .... 119 E2
Cecil Rd. Eccles M30 .... 79 E1
Cecil Rd. M'ster M9 .... 64 D5
Cecil Rd. Stretford M32 .... 96 C1
Cecil St. Ashton-u-L OL7 .... 84 F1
Cecil St. Ashton-u-L OL7 ..... 166 A1
Cecil St. Bolton BL2 .... 148 B7
Cecil St. Bury BL9 .... 140 F1
Cecil St. Dukinfield SK16 ..... 101 C8
Cecil St. Ince-i-M WN2 .... 55 E4
Cecil St. Leigh WN7 .... 76 A4
Cecil St. Littleborough OL15 .. 15 F5
Cecil St. M'ster M15 .... 163 B5
Cecil St. Mossley OL5 .... 86 C8
Cecil St. Oldham OL8 .... 153 E5
Cecil St. R'dale OL11 .... 139 F5
Cecil St. Royton OL2 .... 48 C4
Cecil St. Stalybridge SK15 .... 86 A1
Cecil St. Walkden M28 .... 60 D1
Cecil St. Walkden M28 .... 60 D3
Cecil St. Wigan WN1 .... 151 E8
Cecil Walker House. M31 . 106 A3
Cecil Wlk. 7 OL7 .... 166 A1
Cecilia St. BL3 .... 42 A4
Cedar Ave. Alt'ham WA14 .... 119 C4
Cedar Ave. Ashton-u-L OL6 ... 85 D5
Cedar Ave. Atherton M46 .... 58 B4
Cedar Ave. Golborne WA3 ..... 91 A7
Cedar Ave. Hazel Grove SK7 124 E2
Cedar Ave. Heywood OL10 .... 29 C3
Cedar Ave. Hindley WN2 .... 56 F3
Cedar Ave. Horwich BL6 .... 22 E1
Cedar Ave. Little Lever BL3 ... 43 B2
Cedar Ave. Standish WN6 ...... 36 F8
Cedar Ave. Whitefield M45 .... 62 F6
Cedar Cl. Glossop SK13 ...... 104 B2
Cedar Cl. Poynton SK12 .... 133 E3
Cedar Cres. Newton-l-W WA12 89 D2
Cedar Cres. Oldham OL9 ..... 152 B5
Cedar Cres. Ramsbottom BL0 138 C7
Cedar Ct. Culcheth WA3 .... 91 F1
Cedar Ct. M'ster M14 .... 98 C1
Cedar Dr. Droylsden M43 ...... 84 C2
Cedar Dr. Kearsley M27 .... 61 D4
Cedar Dr. Urmston M41 .... 95 C1
Cedar Dr. Wigan WN1 .... 37 D2
Cedar Gr. Denton M34 .... 100 E3
Cedar Gr. Farnworth BL4 .... 60 B8
Cedar Gr. Garswood WN4 ...... 72 D5
Cedar Gr. M'ster M14 .... 110 D8
Cedar Gr. M'ster SK4 .... 111 C5
Cedar Gr. Orrell WN5 .... 53 F6
Cedar Gr. Prestwich M25 .... 63 A6
Cedar Gr. Royton OL2 .... 48 D6
Cedar Gr. Shaw OL2 .... 149 B6
Cedar Gr. Stalybridge SK16 . 101 F8
Cedar Gr. Westhoughton BL5 . 57 E7
Cedar La. Newhey OL16 .... 32 A3
Cedar La. Uppermill OL4 .... 68 D6
Cedar Lodge. SK7 .... 132 F7
Cedar Mews. OL7 .... 85 B5
Cedar Pl. M7 .... 81 C4
Cedar Rd. Alt'ham WA15 ..... 119 E3
Cedar Rd. Failsworth M35 ..... 83 F6
Cedar Rd. Gatley SK8 .... 122 A5
Cedar Rd. Leigh WN7 .... 75 E8
Cedar Rd. Marple SK6 .... 125 E4
Cedar Rd. Middleton M24 ...... 65 C8
Cedar Rd. Partington M31 ... 105 E3
Cedar Rd. Sale M33 .... 107 D6
Cedar Rd. Stockport SK2 ..... 124 B4
Cedar St. Ashton-u-L OL6 ...... 85 D4
Cedar St. Bury BL9 .... 141 A3
Cedar St. Bury BL9 .... 141 B3
Cedar St. Dukinfield SK14 ... 101 E5
Cedar St. Newton-l-W WA12 .. 89 C2
Cedar St. 4 Oldham OL4 .... 67 C7
Cedar St. R'dale OL12 .... 14 F1
Cedar St. Walsden OL14 .... 6 A8
Cedarfield Rd. WA13 .... 117 B4
Cedars Rd. M22 .... 121 D3
Cedarway. SK9 .... 136 F5
Cedarwood Ave. SK4 .... 168 A1
Cedric Rd. M'ster M8 .... 63 E2
Cedric Rd. Oldham OL4 .... 67 C7
Cedric St. M5 & M6 .... 154 E2
Celandine Cl. OL15 .... 15 F6
Celandine Wlk. WN3 .... 54 B4
Celia St. M8 .... 156 C8
Cellini Sq. BL1 .... 143 D1
Celtic St. SK1 .... 124 A8
Cemetery La. BL9 .... 45 A7
Cemetery Rd. Bolton BL3 & BL4 .... 42 F1
Cemetery Rd. Bolton BL2 .... 148 B7
Cemetery Rd. Denton M34 .. 100 F1
Cemetery Rd. Denton M34 .. 100 F6
Cemetery Rd. Droylsden M43 83 F1
Cemetery Rd. Failsworth M35 83 F6
Cemetery Rd. Glossop SK13 104 C4
Cemetery Rd. Ince-i-M WN3 151 E5
Cemetery Rd. Mossley OL5 ... 86 E8
Cemetery Rd. Radcliffe M26 .. 43 F4
Cemetery Rd. Ramsbottom BL0 .... 11 A4
Cemetery Rd. Royton OL2 ...... 48 C5
Cemetery Rd. Salford M5 .... 154 E1
Cemetery Rd. Swinton M27 ... 61 E1
Cemetery St. Middleton M24 . 47 A1
Cemetery St. 2 Westhoughton BL5 .... 39 E1
Cemetery View. PR7 .... 21 A6
Cennick Cl. OL4 .... 67 D6
Centaur Cl. M27 .... 61 F2
Centaur Way. 2 M8 .... 155 F7
Centenary Circ. M5 .... 80 B1
Centenary Ct. BL3 .... 147 F4
Centenary Way. Eccles M5 ... 80 A1
Centenary Way. Eccles M17 . 96 B8
Central Ave. Atherton M46 .... 58 E4
Central Ave. Bury BL9 .... 44 D7
Central Ave. Eccles M41 .... 95 E6
Central Ave. Edenfield BL0 .... 1 D2
Central Ave. Farnworth BL4 ... 60 B8
Central Ave. Leigh WN7 .... 76 C3
Central Ave. Littleborough OL15 .... 16 B6
Central Ave. M'ster M19 .... 99 A1
Central Ave. Sale M33 .... 107 D1
Central Ave. Salford M6 .... 80 E6
Central Ave. Swinton M27 ..... 62 D2
Central Ave. Uppermill OL3 ... 69 B5
Central Ave. Walkden M28 .... 60 C2
Central CE Prim Sch. M29 .. 59 A1
Central Dr. Bury BL9 .... 27 F8
Central Dr. Gatley SK8 .... 131 D8
Central Dr. Pendlebury M27 ... 80 B7
Central Dr. Reddish SK5 ...... 111 F5
Central Dr. Romiley SK6 ...... 113 C3
Central Dr. Shevington WN6 .. 36 B6
Central Dr. Stockport SK7 ..... 123 D2
Central Dr. Urmston M41 .... 95 E2
Central Dr. Westhoughton BL5 39 F1
Central Flats. WN2 .... 151 F7
Central House. 17 M9 .... 64 E5
Central Park Est. M17 .... 96 B6
Central Park Way. WN1 .... 37 D1
Central Pk. WN1 .... 37 D2
Central Prim Sch. Denton M34 .... 100 E3
Central Prim Sch. Leigh WN7 75 F5
Central Rd. M'ster M20 .... 110 A5
Central Rd. Partington M31 . 105 F3
Central Rd. Wythenshawe M90 .... 130 C6
Central Ret Pk. M4 .... 159 C1
Central St. Bolton BL1 .... 145 E7
Central St. M'ster M2 .... 158 F1
Central St. Ramsbottom BL0 138 C6
Central Store. 5 SK13 .... 104 C1
Central Way. Alt'ham WA14 119 D4
Central Way. Newton-l-W WA12 .... 89 E2
Centre Ct. WN7 .... 75 B1
Centre Gdns. BL1 .... 143 D1
Centre Park Rd. BL1 .... 143 D1
Centre The. WN7 .... 76 E6
Centre Vale. OL15 .... 16 C7
Centre Vale Cl. OL15 .... 16 C7
Centrepoint. M17 .... 96 B5
Centurion Gr. M7 .... 155 E6
Century Lodge. BL4 .... 60 C8
Century Park Ind Area. WA14 .... 119 A6
Century St. M1 .... 162 E8
Cestrian St. BL3 .... 147 F3
Ceylon St. Failsworth M40 .... 83 A6
Ceylon St. Oldham OL4 .... 67 D5
Chadderton Dr. BL9 .... 45 A2
Chadderton Hall Jun Sch. OL9 .... 48 A2
Chadderton Hall Rd. OL1 & OL9 .... 47 F1
Chadderton Ind Est. M24 ..... 65 C5
Chadderton Park Rd. OL9 .... 47 F1
Chadderton Prec. OL9 .... 152 B7
Chadderton St. M4 .... 159 B2
Chadderton Way. Oldham OL1 & OL9 .... 48 C1
Chadderton Way. Oldham OL9 .... 153 D8
Chaddesley Wlk. M11 .... 165 A8
Chaddock La. Boothstown M28 .... 77 F6
Chaddock La. Tyldesley M28 & M29 .... 77 D6
Chaddock Level The. M28 ... 78 A5
Chadkirk. SK6 .... 125 B8
Chadkirk Rd. SK6 .... 113 B1
Chadvil Rd. SK8 .... 122 C5
Chadwell Rd. SK2 .... 124 E7
Chadwick Cl. 12 M'ster M14 . 98 B3
Chadwick Cl. Milnrow OL16 ... 32 A5
Chadwick Fold. Bury BL9 ...... 27 F7
Chadwick Fold. Heywood OL10 .... 29 F2
Chadwick Foundary Ind Est. 9 BL1 .... 145 E8
Chadwick Hall Rd. OL11 .... 30 B6
Chadwick La. R'dale OL10 & OL11 .... 30 A2
Chadwick La. R'dale OL16 .... 31 C2
Chadwick Rd. Eccles M30 ..... 79 E2
Chadwick Rd. Urmston M41 .. 95 F2
Chadwick St. Ashton-u-L OL6 85 E2
Chadwick St. Bolton BL2 ..... 148 B6
Chadwick St. Bury BL9 .... 28 E4
Chadwick St. Glossop SK13 116 B8
Chadwick St. 2 Hindley WN2 56 E6
Chadwick St. Leigh WN7 .... 75 F6
Chadwick St. Little Lever BL3 43 B3
Chadwick St. Marple SK6 .... 125 F5
Chadwick St. Milnrow OL16 ... 31 D7
Chadwick St. Oldham OL9 .. 153 D7
Chadwick St. R'dale OL11 ... 139 D7
Chadwick St. Stockport SK1 170 F8
Chadwick St. Swinton M27 .... 79 F8
Chadwick St. Wigan WN3 .... 150 B6
Chadwick Terr. OL12 .... 14 D4
Chaffinch Cl. Droylsden M43 . 84 C3
Chaffinch Cl. Oldham OL4 ..... 67 D4
Chaffinch Cl. Wythenshawe M22 .... 121 F5
Chaffinch Dr. BL9 .... 141 C4
Chain Bar La. SK14 .... 102 F2
Chain Bar Way. SK14 .... 102 F2
Chain Rd. M9 .... 64 D5
Chain St. M60 .... 159 A1
Chain Wlk. 16 M9 .... 64 E5
Chainhurst Wlk. 2 M13 .... 163 C6
Chalbury Cl. 6 WN2 .... 56 D4
Chalcombe Grange. 1 M12 98 F4
Chale Cl. M40 .... 160 D3
Chale Dr. M24 .... 65 C6
Chale Gn. BL2 .... 25 E3
Chalfont Ave. 1 M41 .... 95 E2
Chalfont Dr. M'ster M8 .... 156 A7
Chalfont Dr. Tyldesley M29 ... 77 A8
Chalfont Dr. Walkden M28 ..... 78 E8
Chalfont House. 2 M6 .... 154 F2
Chalfont Prim Sch. BL1 .... 143 F2
Chalfont St. BL1 .... 143 F2
Chalford Rd. M23 .... 121 A4
Challenge Way. WN5 .... 36 D1
Challenor Sq. M12 .... 165 A6
Chamber Hall Cl. OL8 .... 66 D4
Chamber House Dr. OL11 ..... 30 B3
Chamber Rd. Oldham OL8 ..... 66 D4
Chamber Rd. Shaw OL2 ...... 149 A7
Chamberhall St. BL9 .... 140 E3
Chamberlain Ct. M22 .... 121 E4
Chamberlain Rd. SK15 .... 86 C5
Chamberlain St. BL3 .... 145 D6
Chambers Ct. SK14 .... 103 A3
Chambers Field Ct. 8 Salford M5 .... 81 A1
Chambers Field Ct. Salford M5 .... 161 A8
Champagnole Ct. 9 SK16 ... 166 B1
Champneys Wlk. M9 .... 157 D6
Chancel Ave. M5 .... 161 C8
Chancel Cl. SK16 .... 101 C6
Chancel La. SK9 .... 137 B8
Chancel Pl. 11 M'ster M1 ... 159 C1
Chancel Pl. R'dale OL16 ..... 139 F7
Chancellor La. M12 .... 164 D7
Chancery Cl. M29 .... 77 B8
Chancery La. Bolton BL1 ..... 145 F7
Chancery La. 16 M'ster M3 . 158 F1
Chancery La. Shaw OL2 ...... 149 C7
Chancery La. Uppermill OL3 .. 51 A2
Chancery Pl. 17 M'ster M3 . 158 F1
Chancery Pl. M'ster M60 ..... 159 A1
Chancery St. Oldham OL4 ..... 67 C6
Chancery St. Oldham OL9 ... 152 C8
Chancery Wlk. OL9 .... 152 C8
Chandler Pl. M12 .... 163 C7
Chandley Ct. SK1 .... 124 A7
Chandley St. SK8 .... 122 D6
Chandos Gr. M5 & M6 .... 154 D2
Chandos Rd. M'ster M25 .... 63 B2
Chandos Rd. M'ster M21 .... 97 C1
Chandos Rd. M'ster SK4 ..... 111 C6
Chandos Rd S. M21 .... 109 C8
Chandos St. OL2 .... 149 C7
Change Way. M3 .... 158 E3
Channing Ct. 18 OL16 .... 31 B6
Channing Sq. 25 OL16 .... 31 B6
Channing St. OL16 .... 31 B6
Chanters Ave. M46 .... 58 E3
Chanters The. M28 .... 78 C7
Chantlers Ave. BL8 .... 27 A1
Chantlers Prim Sch. BL8 ...... 27 A2
Chantry Cl. Disley SK12 ...... 135 E5
Chantry Cl. Reddish SK5 ..... 111 E7
Chantry Cl. Westhoughton BL5 .... 57 F5
Chantry Fold. SK12 .... 135 E6
Chantry Rd. SK12 .... 135 E6
Chantry Wlk. Ashton-i-M WN4 72 F5
Chantry Wlk. 14 M'ster M8 . 155 F7
Chapel Alley. 2 BL1 .... 145 F7
Chapel Brow. Charlesworth SK14 .... 115 E6
Chapel Brow. Tintwistle SK14 .... 104 A7
Chapel Cl. Dukinfield SK16 .. 101 D8
Chapel Cl. Ince-i-M WN3 ..... 151 D6
Chapel Cl. Whitefield BL9 ..... 45 B4
Chapel Croft. OL2 .... 48 D4
Chapel Ct. Alt'ham WA14 ..... 119 D4
Chapel Ct. Hyde SK14 .... 101 C1
Chapel Ct. 5 Mossley OL5 ..... 68 C1
Chapel Ct. Sale M33 .... 107 E6
Chapel Ct. Wilmslow SK9 .... 137 A6
Chapel Dr. WA15 .... 129 C7
Chapel Field Rd. M34 .... 100 F3
Chapel Fields. Edgworth BL7 .. 9 C4

Chapel Fields. 1
Marple SK6 125 F5
Chapel Fields La. WN2 56 E5
Chapel Gate. OL16 31 F6
Chapel Gdns. M34 100 F6
Chapel Gn. M34 100 F3
Chapel Gr. M41 95 E2
Chapel Grange. BL7 9 C4
Chapel Green Rd. WN2 56 E5
Chapel Hill. OL15 16 B5
Chapel La. Alt'ham WA15 129 C7
Chapel La. Coppull PR7 19 F8
Chapel La. Hollinfare WA3 105 A2
Chapel La. Hollingworth SK14 103 F5
Chapel La. M'ster M9 64 C3
Chapel La. Partington M31 105 F2
Chapel La. R'dale OL11 29 C8
Chapel La. Ramsbottom BL8 138 A6
Chapel La. Royton OL2 48 D4
Chapel La. Sale M33 107 E6
Chapel La.
Wigan WN1 & WN3 150 C7
Chapel La. Wilmslow SK9 137 A6
Chapel Meadow. M28 78 B7
Chapel Pl. Ashton-i-M WN4 73 B3
Chapel Pl. Bolton BL2 & BL3 148 C5
Chapel Pl. Eccles M41 95 D8
Chapel Rd.
Alderley Edge SK9 137 A1
Chapel Rd. Irlam M44 94 A2
Chapel Rd. M'ster M25 63 A1
Chapel Rd. Oldham OL8 66 C2
Chapel Rd. Sale M33 108 B5
Chapel Rd.
Swinton M27 & M28 79 C7
Chapel Rd. Uppermill OL3 69 A6
Chapel Rd.
Wythenshawe M22 121 D8
Chapel St. Adlington PR7 20 F6
Chapel St. Alderley Edge SK9 137 A1
Chapel St. Ashton-i-M WN4 73 B3
Chapel St. Ashton-u-L OL6 166 C3
Chapel St. Atherton M46 58 D3
Chapel St. 14 Bacup OL13 3 C8
Chapel St. Blackrod BL6 21 D2
Chapel St. Bolton BL7 8 D3
Chapel St. Bolton BL1 145 F8
Chapel St. Boothstown M28 77 F6
Chapel St. Bury BL8 26 F7
Chapel St. Bury BL9 140 F2
Chapel St. Cheadle SK8 122 D5
Chapel St. Denton M34 100 F6
Chapel St. Droylsden M43 84 B1
Chapel St. Dukinfield SK16 101 B8
Chapel St. 3 Eccles M30 79 C1
Chapel St. Farnworth BL4 60 E8
Chapel St. Glossop SK13 104 C1
Chapel St. Hazel Grove SK7 124 E3
Chapel St. Heywood OL10 29 D2
Chapel St. Hindley WN2 56 D5
Chapel St. Horwich BL6 22 C3
Chapel St. Hyde SK14 167 D2
Chapel St. Ince-i-M WN3 151 D6
Chapel St. Kearsley M26 61 B8
Chapel St. Leigh WN2 56 E1
Chapel St. Leigh WN7 76 B4
Chapel St. Little Lever BL3 43 B3
Chapel St. Littleborough OL15 6 D2
Chapel St. Littleborough OL12 15 C7
Chapel St. M'ster M19 99 B1
Chapel St. M'ster SK4 110 D2
Chapel St. M'ster M3 158 E2
Chapel St. 7 Middleton M24 46 F1
Chapel St. 6 Mossley OL5 68 C1
Chapel St. Newton-l-W WA12 89 B3
Chapel St. Oldham OL4 67 E6
Chapel St. Platt Bridge WN2 56 B2
Chapel St. Prestwich M25 63 A4
Chapel St. 10 R'dale OL11 31 A4
Chapel St. Romiley SK6 113 B5
Chapel St. Rowarth SK12 127 E7
Chapel St. Royton OL2 48 D4
Chapel St. Shaw OL2 149 B7
Chapel St. Stalybridge SK15 86 A2
Chapel St. Swinton M27 62 A1
Chapel St. Tyldesley M29 77 A8
Chapel St. Uppermill OL3 69 B8
Chapel St. Whitworth OL12 14 C8
Chapel St. Wigan WN2 38 A2
Chapel St. Wigan WN5 54 B5
Chapel St. Wigan WN5 54 B6
Chapel St. Wigan WN3 150 C7
Chapel Street Cty
Prim Sch. M19 99 B1
Chapel Terr. WA3 91 B8
Chapel View. SK16 101 C8
Chapel Way. PR7 19 F8
Chapel Wlk. 1 Eccles M30 79 F2
Chapel Wlk. Golborne WN7 75 B1
Chapel Wlk.
Hollingworth SK14 103 F5
Chapel Wlk. M'ster M25 62 F1
Chapel Wlk. Middleton M24 64 C7
Chapel Wlk. Whitefield M45 45 B1
Chapel Wlks. Bramhall SK8 132 B6
Chapel Wlks. M'ster M2 158 F1
Chapel Wlks. Sale M33 108 B5
Chapelfield. M26 44 C1
Chapelfield Cl. SK15 86 D4
Chapelfield Dr. M28 60 B3
Chapelfield Prim Sch. M26 44 C1
Chapelfield Rd. M12 163 C8
Chapelfield St. BL1 143 E3
Chapelhill Dr. M9 64 C3
Chapelstead. BL5 57 F5
Chapeltown Rd. Edgworth BL7 9 C2
Chapeltown Rd.
Radcliffe M26 62 A8
Chapeltown St. M1 159 C1
Chapelway Gdns. OL2 48 D6
Chaplin Cl. M6 154 E4
Chapman Ct. SK14 102 D2
Chapman Mews. M18 99 D5
Chapman Rd. SK14 102 E1
Chapman St. Bolton BL1 142 B1
Chapman St. M'ster M18 99 D5
Chappell Rd. M43 84 A2
Chapter St. M10 & M40 160 F4
Charcoal Rd. WA14 118 F3
Charcoal Woods. WA14 119 A3
Charcon Wlk. 3 OL2 48 E4
Chard Dr. M22 121 D1
Chard St. M26 44 A3
Chardin Ave. SK6 126 C8
Charges St. OL7 84 F1
Chariot St. M11 99 D8
Charity St. WN7 75 C5
Charlbury Ave. M'ster M25 63 E3
Charlbury Ave. Reddish SK5 111 F6
Charlbury Way. OL2 149 A5
Charlecote Rd. SK12 133 F4
Charles Ave.
Droylsden M34 & M43 100 A7
Charles Ave. Marple SK6 125 C7
Charles Barry Cres. M15 162 E6
Charles Cradock Dr. M7 155 F6
Charles Ct. WA15 120 B6
Charles Halle Rd. M15 163 A5
Charles Holden St. BL1 145 D6
Charles La. Glossop SK13 104 E3
Charles La. Milnrow OL16 32 A5
Charles Mews. OL16 32 A5
Charles Morris Cl. M35 84 B8
Charles Morris House. M35 84 A7
Charles St. Ashton-u-L OL7 166 B2
Charles St. Bolton BL7 8 D2
Charles St. 2 Bolton BL1 148 A8
Charles St. 5 Bury BL9 140 F3
Charles St. Denton M34 100 F5
Charles St. Droylsden M43 83 E1
Charles St. Dukinfield SK16 166 B1
Charles St. 3 Farnworth BL4 42 E1
Charles St. Farnworth BL4 60 E7
Charles St. Glossop SK13 104 C1
Charles St. Golborne WA3 74 A1
Charles St. Hazel Grove SK7 124 D3
Charles St. Heywood OL10 46 E8
Charles St. Hindley WN2 56 E7
Charles St. Ince-i-M WN2 56 A7
Charles St. Irlam M44 105 E6
Charles St. Leigh WN7 76 A5
Charles St. Leigh WN7 76 A6
Charles St. Littleborough OL15 16 A5
Charles St. M'ster M1 163 A8
Charles St. Oldham OL9 152 C6
Charles St. Royton OL2 48 D4
Charles St. Salford M6 154 F4
Charles St. Stockport SK1 124 A7
Charles St. Swinton M27 61 D2
Charles St. Tyldesley M29 58 F1
Charles St. Whitefield M45 62 F7
Charles St. 2 Wigan WN1 37 C1
Charles Whitaker St. OL12 13 F1
Charles Wlk. M45 62 F7
Charleston Ct. M29 76 F8
Charleston Prim Sch. M6 81 B4
Charleston Sq. M41 95 B3
Charleston St. OL8 66 F4
Charlestown. SK13 116 C7
Charlestown Cl. OL6 166 B3
Charlestown Ind Est. OL6 166 B4
Charlestown Prim Sch. M9 65 B3
Charlestown Rd.
Glossop SK13 116 C7
Charlestown Rd. M'ster M9 64 E2
Charlestown Rd E. SK2 124 A3
Charlestown Rd W. SK3 123 F3
Charlesworth Ave.Bolton BL3 42 B3
Charlesworth Ave.
Denton M34 112 F8
Charlesworth Cty Prim Sch.
SK14 115 D6
Charlesworth St.
M'ster M11 164 F8
Charlesworth St.
Stockport SK1 170 F7
Charlesworth (VE)
Prim Sch. SK14 115 C6
Charley Ave. M7 158 D4
Charlock Ave. BL5 57 E6
Charlock Sq. WA14 119 B8
Charlock Wlk. 6 M31 105 F3
Charlotte La. OL4 68 E5
Charlotte St. 28 Bolton BL1 143 E2
Charlotte St. Cheadle SK8 122 D5
Charlotte St Edgworth BL7 9 C4
Charlotte St.M'ster M1, M60 159 A1
Charlotte St.
R'dale OL11 & OL16 31 B3
Charlotte St.
Ramsbottom BL0 138 B5
Charlotte St. Stockport SK1 112 B3
Charlton Ave. Eccles M30 79 D1
Charlton Ave. Hyde SK14 102 A4
Charlton Ave. Prestwich M25 63 B3
Charlton Ct. 2 M16 97 C3
Charlton Dr. Sale M33 108 C4
Charlton Dr. Swinton M27 61 D2
Charlton Pl. M12 163 B7
Charlton Rd. M19 99 B1
Charlton Sh Ctr. M21 97 B1
Charminster Dr. M8 156 B8
Charmouth Wlk. M22 121 F3
Charnley Cl. M10 & M40 160 E3
Charnley St. M45 62 F8
Charnock Dr. BL1 143 E1
Charnock Rd. WA3 91 F3
Charnock St. Abram WN2 56 B1
Charnock's Yd. 2 WN5 54 F5
Charnville Rd. M22 121 F5
Charnwood Ave. M34 100 B3
Charnwood Cl.
Ashton-u-L OL6 85 C7
Charnwood Cl. Shaw OL2 48 E8
Charnwood Cl. Tyldesley M29 77 B8
Charnwood Cl. Walkden M28 60 C2
Charnwood Cres. SK7 133 D8
Charnwood Rd.M'ster M9 64 D5
Charnwood Rd.Romiley SK6 113 C5
Charter. M30 79 F1
Charter Ave. M26 44 C2
Charter Cl. M33 107 D3
Charter Rd. WA15 119 E2
Charter St. M'ster M3 158 F3
Charter St. Oldham OL1 67 A8
Charter St. R'dale OL11, OL16 31 B4
Charterhouse Rd. WN3 151 E6
Chartist House. SK14 167 E2
Chartwell Cl. M5 & M6 154 F2
Chartwell Dr. M23 120 E7
Chase St. M3 159 A3
Chase The. M28 79 A5
Chasefield. WA14 119 A2
Chaseley Rd. R'dale OL12 139 E8
Chaseley Rd. Salford M6 154 E4
Chasetown Cl. M23 120 D6
Chassen Ave. M41 95 B2
Chassen Rd. Bolton BL1 144 B7
Chassen Rd. Urmston M41 95 B1
Chassen Road Sta. M41 95 B1
Chataway Rd. M8 156 C8
Chatburn Ave.Golborne WA3 74 C1
Chatburn Ave.
Middleton OL11 47 D8
Chatburn Ct. Culcheth WA3 91 F2
Chatburn Ct. Shaw OL2 149 C8
Chatburn Gdns.
Heywood OL10 28 F2
Chatburn Rd. Bolton BL1 23 F3
Chatburn Rd. M'ster M21 109 C8
Chatburn Sq. OL11 47 D8
Chatcombe Rd. M22 121 A2
Chatfield Rd. M21 109 B8
Chatford Cl. M7 158 E4
Chatham Ct. M20 110 A6
Chatham Gdns. BL3 145 D5
Chatham Gr. M20 110 A6
Chatham House. 1 SK3 170 E8
Chatham Pl. 2 BL3 145 D5
Chatham Rd. M'ster M16 97 C3
Chatham Rd. Reddish M18 99 E3
Chatham St. Hyde SK14 113 E7
Chatham St. Ince-i-M WN2 56 A8
Chatham St. Leigh WN7 75 F7
Chatham St.
M'ster M1 & M60 159 B1
Chatham St. Stockport SK3 170 D8
Chatham St. Wigan WN1 151 E7
Chatley Rd. M30 78 F1
Chatley St. M8 159 A4
Chatswood Ave. SK2 170 F6
Chatsworth Ave.
Culcheth WA3 91 F4
Chatsworth Ave.
Ince-i-M WN2 55 F4
Chatsworth Ave.
Prestwich M25 63 B4
Chatsworth Cl.
Alt'ham WA15 120 C5
Chatsworth Cl.
Ashton-i-M WN4 72 F4
Chatsworth Cl.Droylsden M43 83 E3
Chatsworth Cl.Shaw OL2 49 D8
Chatsworth Cl. 2
Urmston M41 95 E2
Chatsworth Cl. Whitefield BL9 45 A5
Chatsworth Ct. Adlington PR7 20 F8
Chatsworth Ct.
Stockport SK2 124 A5
Chatsworth Dr. Leigh WN7 76 D7
Chatsworth Dr. Leigh WN7 76 E7
Chatsworth Gr.
Little Lever BL3 43 A4
Chatsworth Gr. M'ster M16 97 D2
Chatsworth Rd.
Droylsden M43 83 E2
Chatsworth Rd. Eccles M30 79 F4
Chatsworth Rd.
Hazel Grove SK7 133 F8
Chatsworth Rd.
High Lane SK6 134 F6
Chatsworth Rd.M'ster M18 165 C5
Chatsworth Rd.Radcliffe M26 43 D5
Chatsworth Rd.Stretford M32 96 A3
Chatsworth Rd.Swinton M28 79 C5
Chatsworth Rd.
Wilmslow SK9 136 E4
Chatsworth St. Oldham OL4 67 C5
Chatsworth St. R'dale OL12 14 E3
Chatsworth St. Wigan WN5 54 C5
Chatteris Cl. WN2 56 E4
Chatterton. BL0 1 C2
Chatterton Cl. M20 110 C6
Chatterton La. SK12 & SK6 127 B8
Chatterton Old La. BL0 1 C2
Chatterton Rd. BL0 1 C1
Chattock Cl. M16 97 E3
Chatton Cl. BL8 26 F2
Chatwell Ct. OL16 32 C4
Chatwood Rd. M40 65 D2
Chaucer Ave. Denton M34 113 A7
Chaucer Ave. Droylsden M43 84 A1
Chaucer Ave. Radcliffe M26 43 E4
Chaucer Ave. Reddish SK5 99 D1
Chaucer Gr. Atherton M46 58 D5
Chaucer Gr. Leigh WN7 75 D8
Chaucer Mews. SK1 112 B1
Chaucer Pl. Abram WN2 56 B1
Chaucer Pl. Wigan WN1 37 C3
Chaucer Rd. M24 47 B2
Chaucer Rise. SK16 102 A7
Chaucer St. Bolton BL1 143 D2
Chaucer St. Oldham OL1 153 E6
Chaucer St. R'dale OL11 30 C2
Chaucer St. Royton OL2 48 E5
Chaucer Wlk. M13 163 C6
Chaumont Way. OL6 166 B3
Chauncy Rd. M35 & M40 83 E8
Chaytor Ave. M40 83 B7
Cheadle Ave. M7 81 A7
Cheadle Heath
Jun & Inf Sch.SK3 123 A7
Cheadle Hulme High Sch.
SK8 132 B7
Cheadle Hulme Sch. SK8 132 A8
Cheadle Hulme Sta. SK8 123 B2
Cheadle Old Rd. SK3 123 C7
Cheadle Prep Sch. SK8 131 C7
Cheadle Prim Sch. SK8 122 D6
Cheadle RC Inf Sch. SK8 122 E2
Cheadle Rc Jun Sch. SK8 122 E2
Cheadle Rd. Cheadle SK8 122 F3
Cheadle Royal Hospl. SK8 122 C2
Cheadle Sq. BL1 145 E7
Cheadle St. M11 99 D8
Cheam Rd. WA15 119 F8
Cheap Side. M24 47 A2
Cheapside. Hyde SK14 167 E3
Cheapside. M'ster M2 158 F1
Cheapside. Oldham OL1 153 E7
Cheapside Sq. 8 BL1 145 F7
Cheddar St. 1 M18 99 D5
Chedlee Dr. SK8 131 E8
Chedlin Dr. M23 121 A4
Chedworth Cres. M38 60 A6
Chedworth Gr. BL3 145 E5
Cheerybble St. M11 & M43 99 F7
Cheesden Wlk. M45 45 C1
Cheetham Ave. M24 47 B1
Cheetham CE Comm Sch.
M8 155 F7
Cheetham Fold Rd. SK14 113 D8
Cheetham Gdns. 6 SK15 86 B1
Cheetham Gr. WN3 54 F5
Cheetham Hill. Shaw OL2 149 B6
Cheetham Hill.
Whitworth OL12 4 D3
Cheetham Hill Rd.
Dukinfield SK14, SK15, SK16 101 E7
Cheetham Hill Rd.
M'ster M3 & M7 & M8 156 A5
Cheetham Hill Rd.
M'ster M3 & M4 159 A3
Cheetham Par. M8 155 F8
Cheetham Pl. SK6 112 F4
Cheetham Rd. M27 80 A7
Cheetham St. Failsworth M35 84 A8
Cheetham St.
M'ster M10 & M40 157 E5
Cheetham St. Middleton M24 64 F8
Cheetham St. Oldham OL1 67 B7
Cheetham St.
R'dale OL12 & OL16 139 F8
Cheetham St. Radcliffe M26 44 C4
Cheetham St. Shaw OL2 149 C6
Cheetham's Cres. OL2 49 A4
Cheethams The. BL6 38 E7
Cheetwood Prim Sch. M8 158 E4
Cheetwood Rd. M7 & M8 155 F5
Cheetwood St. M7 & M8 158 E4
Chelbourne Dr. 3 OL8 66 B2
Chelburn Cl. Leigh WN2 56 E1
Chelburn Cl. Stockport SK2 124 D5
Chelburn View. OL15 6 C1
Cheldon Wlk. 8 M40 83 C6
Chelford Ave. Bolton BL1 24 E5
Chelford Ave. Golborne WA3 90 D8
Chelford Cl. Alt'ham WA15 119 E6
Chelford Cl. M'ster M13 164 D5
Chelford Cl. Middleton M24 47 C2
Chelford Cl. Wigan WN3 54 F2
Chelford Ct. 2 SK9 131 E5
Chelford Dr. Swinton M27 61 E2
Chelford Dr. Tyldesley M29 77 C6
Chelford Gr. SK3 170 D5
Chelford Rd.
Alderley Edge SK9 136 E1
Chelford Rd. Handforth SK9 131 D5
Chelford Rd. M'ster M16 97 C3
Chelford Rd. Sale M33 108 E2
Chell St. M12 98 F4
Chellow Dene. OL5 68 B1
Chelmarsh Ave. WN4 73 C3
Chelmer Cl.
Westhoughton BL5 40 A1
Chelmer Gr. OL10 29 A3
Chelmorton Gr. WN3 54 C2
Chelmsford Ave. M40 83 B4
Chelmsford Dr. WN3 55 A4
Chelmsford Mews. WN1 37 C2
Chelmsford Rd. SK3 123 C8
Chelmsford St. OL8 153 E5
Chelmsford Wlk. 11 M34 101 A1
Chelsea Ave. M26 43 D4
Chelsea Cl. OL2 149 B7
Chelsea Rd. Bolton BL3 147 D3
Chelsea Rd. Failsworth M40 83 C5
Chelsea Rd. Urmston M41 94 C1
Chelsea St. Bury BL9 44 F4
Chelsea St. R'dale OL11 139 D5
Chelsfield Gr. M21 109 D8
Chelston Ave. M40 65 D2
Chelston Dr. Gatley SK8 131 C6
Chelston Dr. Haslingden BB4 1 A7
Chelt Wlk. M22 121 B2
Cheltenham Ave. WN3 151 D5
Cheltenham Cres. M7 155 E7
Cheltenham Dr.
Newton-l-W WA12 89 C5
Cheltenham Dr. Orrell WN5 53 D2
Cheltenham Dr. Sale M33 108 C4
Cheltenham Gn. M24 65 A6
Cheltenham Rd.
Cheadle SK3 123 A7
Cheltenham Rd. M'ster M21 97 B2
Cheltenham Rd.
Middleton M24 65 A6
Cheltenham St. Oldham OL1 49 B1
Cheltenham St. R'dale OL11 30 D4
Cheltenham St. Salford M6 81 A4
Cheltenham St. 3
Wigan WN2 37 F2
Chelwood Cl. BL1 24 D7
Chelworth Manor. SK8 123 C1
Chemical St. WA12 89 B3
Chemist St. BL1 143 F1
Cheney Cl. M18 99 D7
Chepstow Ave. M33 107 C3
Chepstow Cl. OL11 29 F8
Chepstow Dr. SK7 125 A2
Chepstow Gr. WN7 76 E7
Chepstow Rd. M'ster M21 97 A1
Chepstow Rd. Swinton M27 62 A2
Chepstow St. M1 162 F8
Chepstow St S. M1 162 F8
Chequers Rd. M21 109 B8
Chequers St. WN1 150 B8
Cherington Cl.
Handforth SK9 131 F3
Cherington Cl.
Wythenshawe M23 109 B2
Cherington Dr. M29 59 C1
Cherington Rd. SK8 122 C4
Cheriton Ave. M33 108 C5
Cheriton Cl. SK14 102 D2
Cheriton Dr. BL2 42 E6
Cheriton Gdns. BL6 22 B5
Cheriton Rd. M41 94 D3
Cheriton Rise. SK2 125 A6
Cherrington Dr. OL11 30 A8
Cherry Ave. Ashton-u-L OL6 85 B6
Cherry Ave. Bury BL9 141 C3
Cherry Ave. Oldham OL8 67 C3
Cherry Cres. BB4 1 F8
Cherry Ct. M33 108 A4
Cherry Dr. M27 80 A8
Cherry Gr. Leigh WN7 75 F8
Cherry Gr. R'dale OL11 30 A8
Cherry Gr. Royton OL2 48 C6
Cherry Gr. Stalybridge SK15 102 A8
Cherry Gr. Wigan WN6 36 F3
Cherry Hall Dr. OL2 48 E7
Cherry Hinton. OL11 153 D8
Cherry Holt Ave. SK4 110 F4
Cherry La.
Denshaw OL15 & OL3 33 B3
Cherry La. Sale M33 107 C2
Cherry Manor Prim Sch.
M33 107 C2
Cherry Orchard Cl. SK7 123 D1
Cherry St. M25 63 C5
Cherry Tree Ave.
Farnworth BL4 60 A8
Cherry Tree Ave.
Poynton SK12 133 F3
Cherry Tree Cl. Romiley SK6 113 E2
Cherry Tree Cl.
Wilmslow SK9 137 E8
Cherry Tree Ct. 3 Salford M6 81 A2
Cherry Tree Ct.Standish WN6 19 D2
Cherry Tree Dr. SK7 134 A8
Cherry Tree Gr. Atherton M46 58 C4
Cherry Tree Gr. Leigh WN7 75 D6
Cherry Tree Hospl. SK2 124 C5
Cherry Tree Inf Sch. SK6 113 E3
Cherry Tree Jun Sch. SK6 113 E2
Cherry Tree La
Billinge WA11 71 A2
Cherry Tree La. Bury BL8 27 C1
Cherry Tree La.
Rawtenstall BB4 1 F8
Cherry Tree La.Romiley SK6 113 E2
Cherry Tree La.
Stockport SK2 124 C5
Cherry Tree Prim Sch. BL4 59 E8
Cherry Tree Rd.
Cheadle SK8 123 A1
Cherry Tree Rd.
Golborne WA3 90 F8
Cherry Tree Rd.
Wythenshawe M23 108 F1
Cherry Tree Way. Bolton BL2 25 C5
Cherry Tree Way.
Haslingden BB4 1 B7
Cherry Tree Way. 5
Horwich BL6 22 E1
Cherry Tree Wlk.
Mossley OL5 68 B1
Cherry Tree Wlk.
Stretford M32 96 C1
Cherry Wlk. Cheadle SK8 132 C8
Cherry Wlk. Partington M31 105 D2
Cherrycroft. SK6 113 E1
Cherryton Wlk. M13 163 C6
Cherrywood. M24 65 D7
Cherrywood Ave. BL5 57 A7
Cherrywood Cl.Walkden M28 60 B1
Chertsey Cl. Droylsden M18 99 E5
Chertsey Cl. Shaw OL2 149 B8
Chervil Wlk. WN3 54 C4
Cherwell Ave. OL10 29 B3
Cherwell Cl. Aspull WN2 38 C6
Cherwell Cl. Cheadle SK8 132 A7
Cherwell Cl. Oldham OL8 66 C1
Cherwell Cl. Whitefield M45 63 A8
Cherwell Rd. BL5 39 F2
Cheryl's Bank. SK13 116 B8
Chesham Ave.Bolton BL1 143 E2
Chesham Ave.Middleton OL11 47 D7
Chesham Ave. Urmston M41 94 E3
Chesham Ave.
Wythenshawe M22 121 C4
Chesham Cl. Hadfield SK14 104 B5
Chesham Cl. Wilmslow SK9 136 F4
Chesham Cres. BL9 141 A3
Chesham Cty
Prim Sch. BL9 28 A5
Chesham Fold Rd. BL9 141 B4
Chesham House. 2 M6 154 F1
Chesham Ind Est. BL9 141 A4
Chesham Pl. WA14 119 C2
Chesham Rd. Bury BL9 28 A5
Chesham Rd. Eccles M30 95 C8
Chesham Rd. 3 Oldham OL4 67 C6
Chesham Rd. Wilmslow SK9 136 F4
Chesham St. BL3 146 B2
Cheshill Ct. M7 155 F6
Cheshire Cl.
Newton-l-W WA12 89 E3
Cheshire Cl. Stretford M32 96 B1
Cheshire Ct. BL0 11 D6
Cheshire Gdns. M14 98 A1
Cheshire Rd.Mossley SK15 86 E5
Cheshire Rd.Partington M31 105 D2
Cheshire Sq. SK15 86 E5
Cheshire St. OL5 86 D8
Cheshires The. OL5 68 D1
Chesney Ave. OL9 65 E2
Chesshyre Ave. M40 160 D1
Chessington Rise. M27 62 A3
Chester Ave. Alt'ham WA15 119 F2
Chester Ave. Dukinfield SK16 101 E7
Chester Ave. Golborne WA3 90 D8
Chester Ave. Little Lever BL3 43 B4
Chester Ave. R'dale OL11 30 A6
Chester Ave. Sale M33 107 B1
Chester Ave.
Stalybridge SK15 86 D3
Chester Ave. Urmston M41 95 E3
Chester Ave. Whitefield M45 63 A7
Chester Cl. Handforth SK9 131 E2
Chester Cl. Irlam M44 105 D5
Chester Cl. Little Lever BL3 43 B4
Chester Cres. BB4 1 B8
Chester Dr. Ashton-i-M WN4 73 D2
Chester Dr. Ramsbottom BL0 11 A4
Chester House (Pol HQ).
M16 161 A5
Chester Pl. Adlington PR6 21 A8
Chester Pl. 7 Royton OL2 48 D4
Chester Rd.
Hazel Grove SK7 & SK12 124 D1
Chester Rd.M'ster M15, M17 161 A5
Chester Rd.M'ster M15, M16 161 C6
Chester Rd.
Poynton SK12 & SK7 133 B4
Chester Rd.
Stretford M16 & M32 96 E3
Chester Rd. Tyldesley M29 77 D8
Chester Rd. Woodford SK7 132 E2
Chester Sq. OL7 166 A2
Chester St. Bury BL9 141 A4
Chester St. Denton M34 100 F2
Chester St. Leigh WN7 75 F5
Chester St. M'ster M1 163 A7
Chester St. Oldham OL9 152 C5
Chester St. Prestwich M25 63 A5
Chester St. Stockport SK3 169 D1
Chester St. Swinton M27 79 F7
Chester St. Tyldesley M46 58 E1
Chester Walks. SK6 113 A1
Chester Wlk. 20 BL1 143 E2
Chesterfield Gr. OL6 85 D3
Chesterfield St. OL4 67 B6
Chesterfield Way. 4 M34 113 A8
Chestergate. SK3 169 E1
Chesterton Cl. WN3 150 A5
Chesterton Dr. BL3 40 E5
Chesterton Gr. M43 84 A2
Chesterton Rd. Oldham OL1 49 B2
Chesterton Rd. Sale M23 120 D8
Chestnut Ave. Atherton M46 58 C4
Chestnut Ave. Bury BL8 27 A5
Chestnut Ave. Bury BL9 141 B2
Chestnut Ave. Cheadle SK8 122 E5
Chestnut Ave. Droylsden M43 83 E3
Chestnut Ave. Irlam M44 105 D5
Chestnut Ave. Leigh WN7 75 F3
Chestnut Ave. M'ster M21 109 B8
Chestnut Ave. Walkden M28 60 D2
Chestnut Ave. Whitefield M45 62 F7
Chestnut Cl. Bolton BL3 146 B4
Chestnut Cl. New Mills SK12 127 E1
Chestnut Cl. Oldham OL4 67 D8
Chestnut Cl.
Stalybridge SK15 102 A8
Chestnut Cl. Wilmslow SK9 137 E8
Chestnut Cres. OL8 67 A2
Chestnut Ct. SK7 123 D2
Chestnut Dr. Leigh WN7 75 F2
Chestnut Dr. Poynton SK12 133 F3
Chestnut Dr. Rawtenstall BB4 1 F8
Chestnut Dr. Sale M33 107 D1
Chestnut Dr.
Westhoughton BL5 57 F7
Chestnut Dr S. WN7 75 F1
Chestnut Gdns. M34 100 E2
Chestnut Gr. Ashton-i-M WN4 73 D4
Chestnut Gr. Failsworth M35 83 F6
Chestnut Gr. Golborne WA3 90 F8
Chestnut Gr. Hindley WN2 57 A4
Chestnut Gr. Radcliffe M26 62 A8
Chestnut La. WN7 75 F2
Chestnut Rd. Wigan WN1 37 E2
Chestnut Rd. Worsley M28 79 A4
Chestnut St. OL9 66 A3
Chestnut Villas. SK4 168 C2
Chestnut Way. OL15 15 F6
Chestnut Wlk.
Partington M31 105 D2
Chestnut Wlk. 4
Partington M31 105 E3
Chesworth Cl. SK1 170 F8
Chesworth Ct. M43 83 F1
Chesworth Fold. SK1 170 F8
Chesworth Wlk. M15 162 D7
Chetham Cl. M5 161 B7
Chetham's Sch of Music.
M4 158 F2
Chetwode Ave. WN4 73 B1
Chetwyn Ave. Bolton BL7 25 A7
Chetwyn Ave. Royton OL2 48 C4
Chetwynd Ave. M41 95 C2
Chetwynd Cl. M33 107 E6
Chevassut Prim Sch. M15 162 E7
Chevassut St. M15 162 E6
Chevin Gdns. SK7 133 A7
Chevington Dr. M'ster SK4 110 E3
Chevington Dr.
M'ster M40 & M9 157 D6
Chevington Gdns. 2 BL1 143 E3
Cheviot Ave. Cheadle SK8 122 F2
Cheviot Ave. Oldham OL8 66 E3
Cheviot Ave. Royton OL2 48 C3
Cheviot Cl. Bolton BL1 24 D5
Cheviot Cl. Bury BL8 27 A3
Cheviot Cl. Horwich BL6 22 C5
Cheviot Cl. Middleton M24 65 D8
Cheviot Cl. Milnrow OL16 32 A7
Cheviot Cl. Oldham OL9 152 A5
Cheviot Cl. Ramsbottom BL0 11 C4
Cheviot Cl. Salford M6 154 E3
Cheviot Cl. Stockport SK4 169 D3
Cheviot Cl. Wigan WN3 54 C2
Cheviot Ct. OL8 66 E4
Cheviot Rd. SK7 124 B1
Cheviot St. M3 158 F3
Cheviots Rd. OL2 149 A8
Chevithorne Cl. WA14 119 B5
Chevril Cl. M15 163 A6
Chevron Cl. R'dale OL11 30 B3
Chevron Cl. 3
Salford M5 & M6 81 B2
Chevron Pl. WA14 119 D7
Chew Brook Dr. OL3 69 B5
Chew Moor La. BL5 & BL6 40 A2
Chew Rd. Uppermill OL3 70 A2
Chew Vale. Dukinfield SK16 101 F7
Chew Vale. Uppermill OL3 69 B5
Chew Valley Rd. OL3 69 B5
Chicago Ave. M90 130 B7

Chichester Ave. M46 58 A2
Chichester Bsns Ctr. OL16 31 A7
Chichester Cl.
Littleborough OL15 15 F3
Chichester Cl. Sale M33 107 D3
Chichester Cres. OL9 48 A1
Chichester Rd. M'ster M15 162 E5
Chichester Rd. M'ster M15 162 F5
Chichester Rd. Romiley SK6 113 C2
Chichester St. OL16 31 B7
Chichester Way. 11 M34 101 A1
Chidlow Ave. M20 110 A7
Chidwall Rd. M22 121 B2
Chief St. OL4 67 A6
Chiffon Way. M3 158 D3
Chigwell Cl. M22 121 E5
Chilcombe Wlk. 5 M9 64 E5
Chilcote Ave. M33 107 E4
Childwall Cl. BL3 147 E2
Chilgrove Ave. BL6 21 D1
Chilham Rd. Eccles M30 79 F4
Chilham Rd. Walkden M28 60 E2
Chilham St. Bolton BL3 146 B2
Chilham St. Swinton M27 79 E6
Chilham St. Wigan WN5 54 B6
Chillingham Dr. WN7 76 C4
Chillington Wlk. M34 100 E1
Chilmark Dr. M23 121 A6
Chiltern Ave. Atherton M46 58 F5
Chiltern Ave. Cheadle SK8 122 F2
Chiltern Ave. Urmston M41 94 F3
Chiltern Cl. Ashton-i-M WN4 73 C2
Chiltern Cl. Horwich BL6 22 C5
Chiltern Cl. Ramsbottom BL0 11 C4
Chiltern Cl. Shaw OL2 48 F8
Chiltern Cl. Stockport SK7 124 B1
Chiltern Cl. Walkden M28 78 E8
Chiltern Dr. Alt'ham WA15 119 F2
Chiltern Dr. Bolton BL2 148 C7
Chiltern Dr. Bury BL8 27 B4
Chiltern Dr. Royton OL2 48 C4
Chiltern Dr. Stockport SK2 124 B4
Chiltern Dr. Swinton M27 79 F6
Chiltern Dr. Wigan WN3 54 D2
Chiltern Gdns. Sale M33 108 C1
Chiltern Rd. Culcheth WA3 91 E4
Chiltern Rd. Ramsbottom BL0 11 C4
Chiltern Way. M29 77 B8
Chilton Ave. OL9 152 A6
Chilton Cl. WN7 75 F7
Chilton Dr. M24 65 C7
Chilworth St. M14 98 B2
Chime Bank. M8 & M9 156 B6
Chimes Rd. WN4 72 F6
China La. 1 Bolton BL1 145 F8
China La. M'ster M1 & M60 159 B1
Chingford Wlk. 5 M13 98 F4
Chinley Ave. M'ster M40 83 A8
Chinley Ave. Stretford M32 96 A4
Chinley Cl. M'ster SK4 168 B3
Chinley Cl. Sale M33 108 D3
Chinley Cl. Stockport SK7 123 E3
Chinley St. M6 81 B5
Chinnor Cl. WN7 75 F7
Chinwell View. 9 M19 99 A1
Chip Hill Rd. BL3 146 A4
Chippendale Pl. OL6 85 E5
Chippenham Ave. SK2 124 D7
Chippenham Ct. M40 160 D2
Chippenham Rd. M4 160 D2
Chipping Fold. OL16 31 F5
Chipping Rd. BL1 23 F2
Chipping Sq. M12 99 A4
Chipstead Wlk. M12 164 E5
Chirmside St. 4 BL8 27 B1
Chirton Wlk. 9 M40 83 A7
Chisacre Dr. WN6 35 D7
Chiselhurst St. M8 156 A7
Chisholm Cl. WN6 19 B2
Chisholm Ct. 10 M24 46 F1
Chisholm St. M11 & M18 99 D7
Chisholme Cl. BL8 10 F2
Chisledon Ave. M7 & M8 155 F6
Chisledon Cl. BL3 145 E5
Chislehurst Ave. M41 95 D3
Chislehurst Cl. BL8 27 B1
Chisnall Ave. WN6 18 F6
Chisnall La. Coppull PR7 19 C6
Chisnall La.
Wrightington Bar PR7 19 A5
Chiswell St. WN5 54 C5
Chiswick Dr. BL3 43 B5
Chiswick Rd. M20 110 C3
Chisworth Cl. Leigh WN7 75 E7
Chisworth Cl. Stockport SK7 123 E3
Chisworth St. BL2 25 B3
Chisworth Wlk. 2 M34 113 A8
Choir St. M7 158 E4
Chokeberry Cl. WA14 119 B8
Cholmondeley Ave. WA14 119 E8
Cholmondeley Rd. M6 80 C4
Chomlea. WA14 119 B4
Chomlea Manor. M6 80 C4
Choral Gr. M7 155 D5
Chorley Cl. BL8 26 F1
Chorley Hall Cl. SK9 136 F1
Chorley Hall La. SK9 137 A1
Chorley New Rd.
Bolton BL1 & BL6 40 C7
Chorley New Rd.
Horwich BL6 22 C2
Chorley New Rd Inf Sch.
BL6 22 D2
Chorley New Rd Prim Sch.
BL6 22 D2
Chorley Old Rd.
Bolton BL1 & BL6 23 C3
Chorley Old Rd. Bolton BL1 142 B1
Chorley Rd. Adlington PR6 21 A8
Chorley Rd.
Adlington BL6 & PR6 21 B5
Chorley Rd. Sale M33 108 E2
Chorley Rd. Standish WN1 20 C3
Chorley Rd. Swinton M27 79 F8
Chorley Rd.
Westhoughton BL5 & BL6 39 C4
Chorley St. Adlington PR6 21 B8
Chorley St. Bolton BL1 145 E7
Chorley St. Ince-i-M WN3 151 E6
Chorley St.
Stretford M16 & M32 96 F5
Chorley Wood Ave. M19 110 F6
Chorlton Dr. SK8 122 E6
Chorlton Fold. M27 & M30 79 D4
Chorlton Gn. M21 109 A8
Chorlton Gr. SK1 124 B7
Chorlton Park Jun & Inf Schs.
M21 109 C6
Chorlton Rd. M15 & M16 162 D6
Chorlton St. M'ster M16 161 C5
Chorlton St. M'ster M1 163 A8
Chorlton Water Park.
M21 109 C4
Chorlton-cum-Hardy
CE Prim Sch. M21 109 A8
Chorlton-cum-Hardy
Golf Course. M21 109 B5
Chowbent Cl. M46 58 E3
Chowbent Prim Sch. M46 58 D3
Chretien Rd. M20 & M22 109 E2
Christ Church Ainsworth
CE Prim Sch. BL2 26 C1
Christ Church CE Prim Sch.
Denshaw OL3 33 D1
Christ Church CE Prim Sch.
Leigh WN7 75 F4
Christ Church CE Prim Sch.
Oldham OL9 152 A6
Christ Church Cl. BL2 25 F2
Christ Church La. BL2 25 F3
Christ Church (Patricroft)
CE Prim Sch. M30 79 D2
Christ Church (VA)
Prim Sch. BL8 26 F4
Christ the King RC
Prim Sch. Failsworth M40 83 C5
Christ the King RC
Prim Sch. Walkden M28 60 E2
Christ's Church CE
Prim Sch. BL2 25 F2
Christchurch Ave. M5 81 B2
Christchurch Ct. OL9 152 C5
Christchurch Rd. M33 107 C5
Christie Hospl &
Holt Radium Inst. M20 110 B6
Christie Rd. M32 96 E2
Christie St. SK1 124 A7
Christine St. OL2 149 B7
Christleton. WN6 36 B6
Christleton Ave. SK4 111 D5
Christleton Way. 15 SK9 131 D5
Christopher Acre. OL11 13 E1
Christopher St.
Failsworth M40 83 D4
Christopher St.
Ince-i-M WN3 151 F6
Christopher St. Salford M5 81 B1
Chronnell Dr. BL2 42 E8
Chudleigh Cl. Alt'ham WA14 119 B6
Chudleigh Cl. Stockport SK7 124 A3
Chudleigh Rd. M8 64 A2
Chulsey Gate La. BL6 40 A4
Chulsey St. BL3 146 B4
Chunal La. SK13 116 C6
Church Ave. Bolton BL3 145 D7
Church Ave. Denton M34 113 A8
Church Ave. 7
Failsworth M40 83 C5
Church Ave. Handforth SK9 131 A2
Church Ave. Hyde SK14 113 F8
Church Ave. Leigh WN2 75 A8
Church Ave. Middleton OL11 47 D6
Church Ave.
Salford M5 & M6 154 D2
Church Bank. BL1 148 A7
Church Brow. Alt'ham WA14 119 B4
Church Brow. Hyde SK14 167 D1
Church Brow.
Mottram-i-L SK14 103 A3
Church Cl. Dukinfield M34 100 F7
Church Cl. Glossop SK13 104 E2
Church Cl. Handforth SK9 131 D3
Church Cl. Kearsley M26 61 B6
Church Croft. BL9 45 C4
Church Ct. Alt'ham WA15 119 E1
Church Ct. Dukinfield SK16 166 B1
Church Ct. Edenfield BL0 1 D4
Church Dr. Newton-l-W WA12 89 C1
Church Dr. Orrell WN5 53 D5
Church Dr. Prestwich M25 63 A4
Church Fields. OL3 51 A2
Church Fold. PR7 19 F8
Church Gn. Lymm WA13 117 B8
Church Gn. Radcliffe M26 44 D4
Church Gn. Salford M6 154 F3
Church Gr. SK7 124 E2
Church La.
Alderley Edge SK9 137 A2
Church La. Culcheth WA3 91 F3
Church La. Edenfield BL0 1 D4
Church La. Golborne WA3 90 D7
Church La. M'ster M25 & M7 63 C1
Church La. M'ster M19 110 F6
Church La. M'ster M9 157 E8
Church La. M'ster M40 & M9 157 F5
Church La. Marple SK6 125 F5
Church La. Mossley OL5 68 D1
Church La. Oldham OL1 153 F7
Church La. Prestwich M25 63 A4
Church La. R'dale OL16 139 F7
Church La. Romiley SK6 113 C2
Church La. Sale M33 107 E6
Church La. Shevington WN6 36 A6
Church La. Uppermill OL3 51 D1
Church La.
Westhoughton BL5 39 E3
Church La. Whitefield M45 44 E1
Church La. Woodford SK7 132 C2
Church La.
Wrightington Bar WN6 18 D8
Church Lodge. SK4 110 E6
Church Manor. SK4 168 B4
Church Meadow.
Dukinfield SK14 101 C3
Church Meadow.
Uppermill OL4 68 E5
Church Meadow.
Whitefield BL9 45 C4
Church Meadow Gdns.
SK14 101 C3
Church Meadows. BL2 25 F3
Church Mews. Denton M34 100 E3
Church Mews. 1
Radcliffe M26 44 C1
Church Pl. OL10 29 D2
Church Rd. Bolton BL1 142 B2
Church Rd.
Charlesworth SK14 115 C7
Church Rd. Cheadle SK8 132 B8
Church Rd. Eccles M30 79 F2
Church Rd. Farnworth BL4 60 E8
Church Rd.
Gatley M22 & SK8 122 A5
Church Rd. Handforth SK9 131 D3
Church Rd.
Hollingworth SK14 171 D4
Church Rd. Kearsley M26 61 A8
Church Rd. Middleton M24 65 D7
Church Rd. Moorend SK6 126 E6
Church Rd. Platt Bridge WN2 56 B3
Church Rd. R'dale OL16 31 B6
Church Rd. Ramsbottom BL0 11 E8
Church Rd. Sale M33 108 D4
Church Rd. Shaw OL2 149 B6
Church Rd. Stockport SK4 169 E2
Church Rd. Tyldesley M29 77 C6
Church Rd.
Uppermill OL3 & OL4 68 E5
Church Rd. Uppermill OL3 69 C8
Church Rd. Urmston M41 95 D1
Church Rd. Walkden M28 60 D3
Church Rd. Wilmslow SK9 136 E4
Church Rd.
Wythenshawe M22 109 E1
Church Rd E. M33 108 D4
Church Rd W. M33 108 D4
Church Road Prim Sch.
BL1 142 B2
Church St. Adlington PR6 21 A7
Church St. Ainsworth BL2 26 D1
Church St. Alt'ham WA14 119 D5
Church St. Ashton-u-L OL6 166 B2
Church St. Aspull WN2 38 B6
Church St. Atherton M46 58 D3
Church St. Bacup OL13 3 C8
Church St. Blackrod BL6 21 C2
Church St. Bolton BL2 25 D5
Church St. Bury BL8 26 F5
Church St. Bury BL9 141 A3
Church St. Cheadle SK8 122 D6
Church St. Delph OL3 50 E4
Church St. Droylsden M43 84 B1
Church St. Dukinfield M34 100 F7
Church St. Dukinfield SK16 166 B1
Church St. Eccles M30 79 F2
Church St. Failsworth M35 83 F8
Church St. Farnworth BL4 60 E7
Church St. Farnworth BL4 60 E8
Church St. Glossop SK13 104 D2
Church St. Golborne WA3 74 B1
Church St. Hadfield SK14 104 A4
Church St. Heywood OL10 29 D2
Church St. Hindley WN2 56 D5
Church St. Horwich BL6 22 C3
Church St. Hyde SK14 167 D1
Church St. Ince-i-M WN3 151 F6
Church St. Leigh WN7 75 F5
Church St. Little Lever BL3 42 F3
Church St. Littleborough OL16 15 D3
Church St. Littleborough OL15 16 B5
Church St. M'ster M4 & M60 159 A2
Church St. M'ster SK4 169 E3
Church St. 5 Marple SK6 125 F6
Church St. Marple SK6 126 A5
Church St. Middleton M24 47 A2
Church St. Newhey OL16 32 B4
Church St. Newton-l-W WA12 89 E4
Church St. Oldham OL4 67 E5
Church St. Oldham OL1 153 F7
Church St. Orrell WN8 53 C7
Church St. Orrell WN5 53 E5
Church St. Pendlebury M27 80 B8
Church St. R'dale OL11 139 E6
Church St. Radcliffe M26 44 B2
Church St. Rawtenstall BB4 2 E8
Church St. Romiley SK6 113 A5
Church St. Royton OL2 48 D4
Church St. Stalybridge SK15 86 A2
Church St. Standish WN6 19 E1
Church St. Stretford M32 96 C1
Church St. Swinton M27 79 E8
Church St. Tintwistle SK14 104 A7
Church St. Westhoughton BL5 39 E2
Church St. Whitworth OL12 14 C8
Church St. Wigan WN1 37 C1
Church St. Wigan WN5 54 B6
Church St. Wigan WN1 150 C8
Church St. Wilmslow SK9 137 B7
Church St E. Oldham OL4 67 E8
Church St E. Radcliffe M26 44 C3
Church St S. SK13 104 E2
Church St W. M26 44 B3
Church Stile. OL11 & OL16 139 F7
Church Street Ind Est.
3 M24 47 A2
Church Terr. Handforth SK9 131 D4
Church Terr. Milnrow OL16 32 A5
Church Terr. Oldham OL1 153 F7
Church Terr. Sale M33 108 A6
Church View. Handforth SK9 131 A2
Church View. Hyde SK14 167 D1
Church View. Irlam M44 94 A2
Church View. Lymm WA13 117 B4
Church View.
R'dale OL11 & OL12 13 E2
Church Wlk. Farnworth BL4 60 C8
Church Wlk. Kearsley M27 61 F4
Church Wlk. 5 Royton OL2 48 D4
Church Wlk. Stalybridge SK15 86 A3
Church Wlk. Wilmslow SK9 136 F6
Churchbank. SK15 86 D2
Churchdale Rd. M9 64 B4
Churchfield. M'ster M21 109 A8
Churchfield. Shevington WN6 36 A5
Churchfield Cl. M26 43 F1
Churchfield Rd. 5 M6 80 D5
Churchfield Wlk. M11 165 A8
Churchfields. Alt'ham WA14 119 B1
Churchfields. Denton M34 100 F4
Churchfields. Sale M33 107 D6
Churchgate. Bolton BL1 145 F7
Churchgate. Stockport SK1 169 F1
Churchgate. Urmston M41 95 E1
Churchgate Bldgs. M1 163 C8
Churchill Ave. Ainsworth BL2 26 D1
Churchill Ave.
Fowley Common WA3 92 B4
Churchill Ave. M'ster M16 97 D2
Churchill Cl. OL10 46 E8
Churchill Cres. Marple SK6 125 D7
Churchill Cres. Reddish SK5 99 E1
Churchill Ct. M6 154 F2
Churchill Dr. BL3 & M26 43 C3
Churchill Rd. WA14 119 D7
Churchill St. 3 Bolton BL1 148 C7
Churchill St. Oldham OL4 67 A6
Churchill St.
R'dale OL11 & OL12 14 C1
Churchill St. Stockport SK4 169 D3
Churchill St E. OL4 67 A6
Churchill Way.
Salford M5 & M6 81 A2
Churchill Way. Stretford M17 96 C7
Churchlands La. WN6 19 F1
Churchley Cl. SK3 123 A6
Churchley Rd. SK3 123 A7
Churchside Cl. M9 64 D2
Churchstoke Wlk. M23 120 E7
Churchston Ave. SK7 124 A2
Churchtown Ave. BL2 42 F7
Churchward Sq. BL6 22 C2
Churchwood Rd. M20 110 B3
Churnet St. M40 157 D5
Churnett Cl. BL5 39 F2
Churston Ave. M9 64 E4
Churton Ave. M'ster M14 98 B2
Churton Ave. Sale M33 107 F3
Churton Gr. WN6 19 B2
Churton Rd. M18 99 C3
Churwell Ave. SK4 110 F4
Cicero St. M'ster M9 157 F8
Cicero St. Oldham OL1 49 A1
Cinder Hill La.
M24 & OL1 & OL2 48 A3
Cinder St. M4 159 C2
Cinnabar Dr. M24 46 F2
Cinnamon Ave. WN2 57 A4
Cinnamon Brow. WN8 53 C6
Cinnamon Cl. OL12 139 D8
Cinnamon St. OL12 139 D8
Cipher St. M4 159 C3
Circle Ct. M41 95 F4
Circle The. M32 95 F4
Circuit The.
Alderley Edge SK9 137 B3
Circuit The. Bramhall SK8 132 A7
Circuit The. M'ster M20 110 B5
Circuit The. Stockport SK3 123 C6
Circuit The. Wilmslow SK9 136 D5
Circular Rd. Denton M34 100 E1
Circular Rd. M'ster M25 63 B2
Circular Rd. M'ster M20 110 B5
Circus St. M1 & M60 159 B1
Cirencester Cl. M38 60 A6
Ciss La. M41 95 E2
Citrus Way. M6 81 A2
City Ave. M34 100 E2
City Coll. M23 120 F8
City Coll Manchester
Abraham Moss Ctr. M8 156 B8
City Coll Manchester
Arden Ctr. M23 109 C1
City Coll Manchester
Fielden Ctr. M20 109 F4
City Course Trad Est. M11 165 A7
City Court Trad Est. M4 159 C2
City Rd. Boothstown M28 78 A8
City Rd. M'ster M15 & M16 162 D6
City Rd. Wigan WN5 54 B7
City Rd E. M15 162 F7
City Wlk. M27 80 B8
Civic Wlk. 1 OL10 29 D2
Clacton Wlk. M13 163 C6
Clague St. M11 83 A2
Claife Ave. M40 65 B2
Clammerclough Rd. BL4 60 F8
Clandon Ave. M30 79 B1
Clanwood Cl. WN3 54 E2
Clap Gate La. WN3 54 E3
Clapgate. SK6 112 F1
Clapgate Rd. OL11 13 E1
Clapham St. M40 83 C8
Clara Gorton Ct. 12 OL16 31 B6
Clara St. Oldham OL9 66 C4
Clara St. R'dale OL11 139 F5
Clara St. Whitworth OL12 4 D1
Clare Ave. SK9 131 C3
Clare Cl. BL8 27 D5
Clare Ct. BL4 147 F1
Clare Rd. M'ster M19 111 A8
Clare Rd. Reddish SK5 169 F4
Clare St. Denton M34 100 E4
Clare St. M'ster M5 81 C1
Clare St. M'ster M1 163 B7
Clarebank. BL1 40 F7
Claremont Ave.
Alt'ham WA14 119 E8
Claremont Ave. Hindley WN2 56 F5
Claremont Ave. M'ster M20 110 A5
Claremont Ave. Marple SK6 111 C5
Claremont Ave. Marple SK6 125 C6
Claremont Dr.Alt'ham WA14 119 E8
Claremont Dr.Walkden M38 60 B5
Claremont Gr. Alt'ham WA15 119 E3
Claremont Gr. M'ster M20 110 A3
Claremont Jun & Inf Sch.
M14 98 A3
Claremont Range.
M18 & M34 99 F4
Claremont Rd. Billinge WN5 71 E5
Claremont Rd. Cheadle SK8 132 A8
Claremont Rd. Culcheth WA3 91 D4
Claremont Rd. M'ster M16 97 F3
Claremont Rd. M'ster M14 98 B3
Claremont Rd. Milnrow OL16 31 F5
Claremont Rd. R'dale OL11 30 C7
Claremont Rd. Sale M33 108 B5
Claremont Rd.
Stockport SK2 124 B4
Claremont St. Ashton-u-L OL6 85 E4
Claremont St. Failsworth M35 83 F8
Claremont St. Oldham OL9 48 C1
Claremont St. Oldham OL8 66 F2
Claremont Terr. OL14 6 F5
Clarence Arc. OL6 166 B2
Clarence Ave. Eccles M17 95 F7
Clarence Ave. Oldham OL8 66 D4
Clarence Ave.
Whitefield M45 63 A7
Clarence Ct. 15 Bolton BL1 145 E8
Clarence Ct. Wilmslow SK9 137 A6
Clarence House. 1 SK15 101 F8
Clarence Rd. Alt'ham WA15 119 F3
Clarence Rd. Ashton-u-L OL6 166 C4
Clarence Rd. M'ster M13 98 E4
Clarence Rd. M'ster SK4 111 C5
Clarence Rd. Swinton M27 79 C7
Clarence St. 6
Ashton-i-M WN4 72 F5
Clarence St. Bolton BL1 145 F8
Clarence St. Farnworth BL4 42 E1
Clarence St. Golborne WA3 74 A1
Clarence St. Hyde SK14 167 E4
Clarence St. Ince-i-M WN2 56 A7
Clarence St. Leigh WN7 76 B4
Clarence St. M'ster M7 158 D4
Clarence St. 15 M'ster M3 158 F1
Clarence St.
Newton-l-W WA12 89 A4
Clarence St. R'dale OL12 14 D2
Clarence St. Royton OL2 49 A3
Clarence St.
Stalybridge OL6 & SK15 & SK16 85 E1
Clarence St. Tyldesley M46 58 E2
Clarence Yd. WN1 150 C8
Clarendon Ave.
Alt'ham WA15 119 E5
Clarendon Ave. M'ster SK4 168 B3
Clarendon Cres. Eccles M30 79 F3
Clarendon Cres. Sale M33 108 D5
Clarendon Cty Prim Sch.
BL3 145 E5
Clarendon Fields Prim Sch.
SK16 101 B8
Clarendon Gr. BL2 148 B6
Clarendon Ind Est. SK14 167 E3
Clarendon Pl. SK14 167 E2
Clarendon Rd. Bolton BL2 148 C7
Clarendon Rd. Denton M34 101 B2
Clarendon Rd.
Droylsden M34 100 B7
Clarendon Rd. Eccles M30 79 F3
Clarendon Rd.
Hazel Grove SK7 124 F3
Clarendon Rd. Hyde SK14 167 E3
Clarendon Rd.
Ince-i-M WN2 & WN3 151 E5
Clarendon Rd. Irlam M44 105 F7
Clarendon Rd. M'ster M16 97 D2
Clarendon Rd. Sale M33 108 D4
Clarendon Rd. Swinton M27 79 F8
Clarendon Rd. Urmston M41 94 E3
Clarendon Rd W. M16 & M21 97 B2
Clarendon Recn Ctr. M5 81 A2
Clarendon Road Prim Sch.
M30 79 F3
Clarendon St. Bolton BL3 145 E5
Clarendon St. Bury BL9 141 A4
Clarendon St.
Dukinfield SK16 101 A8
Clarendon St.
Dukinfield SK16 101 B8
Clarendon St. Hyde SK14 167 D3
Clarendon St. M'ster M15 162 F6
Clarendon St. M'ster M15 162 F7
Clarendon St. Mossley OL5 86 D8
Clarendon St. R'dale OL16 31 B4
Clarendon St. Stockport SK5 169 F3
Clarendon St. Whitefield M45 62 F8
Claribel St. M11 164 E8
Claridge Rd. M21 97 A1
Clarington Gr. WN1 151 E7
Clarington Pl. WN2 151 F7
Clarion St. M4 159 C3
Clark Ave. M18 99 E5
Clark Way. SK14 167 D3
Clark's Cross. M25 63 D8
Clark's Hill. M25 63 A4
Clarke Ave. Culcheth WA3 92 A4
Clarke Ave. Salford M5 161 B7
Clarke Brow. M24 47 A1
Clarke Cres. Alt'ham WA15 120 B3
Clarke Cres. Walkden M38 59 E6
Clarke St. Alt'ham WA14 119 D7
Clarke St. Bolton BL1 144 C8
Clarke St. Dukinfield OL7 100 F8
Clarke St. Farnworth BL4 60 E7
Clarke St. Heywood OL10 29 D2
Clarke St. Leigh WN7 75 E4
Clarke St. R'dale OL12 & OL16 15 B2
Clarke's La. OL12 139 D8
Clarkes Croft. BL9 141 C3
Clarkethorn Terr. SK4 169 E3
Clarksfield Jun & Inf Sch.
OL4 67 C6
Clarksfield Rd. OL4 67 C6
Clarksfield St. OL4 67 C6
Clarkson Cl. Denton M34 100 D2
Clarkson Cl. Middleton M24 64 C7
Clarkwell Cl. OL1 153 E8
Class St. M11 160 F1
Clatford Wlk. 2 M9 157 D7
Claude Ave. M27 79 D8
Claude Rd. M21 109 B7
Claude St. M'ster M8 64 A1
Claude St. Swinton M27 79 D8
Claude St. Wigan WN5 54 D6
Claude St. Worsley M28 79 B3
Claudia Sq. SK15 86 E5
Claughton Ave. Bolton BL2 42 F7
Claughton Ave. Walkden M28 78 C8
Claughton Rd. BL8 26 F5
Claverham Wlk. 4 M23 120 E7
Claverton Rd. M23 120 E5
Claxton Ave. M9 64 D3
Clay Bank. M43 83 F1
Clay Bank St. OL10 29 C3
Clay Cotts. OL5 68 E4
Clay Hall. M6 154 F1
Clay La. Alt'ham WA15 120 D4
Clay La. Handforth SK9 131 C5
Clay La. R'dale OL11 29 E8
Clay La. Wilmslow SK9 136 C4
Clay La. Wythenshawe M23 120 F4
Clay St. Bolton BL7 25 A7
Clay St. Littleborough OL15 15 F5
Clay St. Oldham OL8 66 E4
Claybank Dr. Bury BL8 26 D7
Claybank Dr. Bury BL8 26 E7
Claybar Dr. M30 79 E3
Claybrook Wlk. M11 83 A1
Clayburn Rd. M15 162 E6
Claycourt Ave. M28 79 B4
Claydon Dr. Ince-i-M WN2 151 F5
Claydon Dr.
Little Lever BL3 & M26 43 C5
Clayfield Dr. OL11 29 F8
Claygate Dr. M9 64 D5
Clayhill Wlk. M9 64 E1
Claylands Cl. SK14 171 D4
Claymore. OL1 153 E7
Claymore St. Bolton BL3 147 F3
Claymore St. Droylsden M18 99 E6
Claypool Prim Sch. BL6 22 F1
Claypool Rd. BL6 22 E1
Claythorpe Wlk. 2 M8 63 E2
Clayton Ave. Bolton BL3 148 C5
Clayton Ave. Golborne WA3 90 E8
Clayton Ave. M'ster M20 110 B4
Clayton Ave. Rawtenstall BB4 1 E8
Clayton Brook Prim Sch.
M11 99 D8
Clayton Cl. Bury BL8 26 F1
Clayton Cl. M'ster M15 162 E5
Clayton Hall Rd. M11 83 C2
Clayton House. WN7 75 C5
Clayton La. M11 83 B1
Clayton La S. M11 & M12 165 A7
Clayton St. Bolton BL3 148 C5
Clayton St. Denton M34 100 F2
Clayton St. Droylsden M11 83 B2
Clayton St. 5
Dukinfield SK16 101 D8
Clayton St. 5 Failsworth M35 83 F7
Clayton St. Oldham OL9 66 A3
Clayton St. R'dale OL12 15 B2
Clayton St. Wigan WN3 150 B7
Claytonbrook Rd. M11 83 D1
Claytons Cl. OL4 67 F7
Cleabarrow Dr. M28 78 A5
Cleadon Ave. M18 99 C4
Cleadon Dr S. BL8 27 C5
Cleavley St. M30 79 B2
Clee Ave. M13 98 F2
Cleethorpes Ave. M9 64 B3
Cleeve Rd. 2 Oldham OL4 67 C6
Cleeve Rd.
Wythenshawe M23 109 A2
Cleeve Way. SK8 132 B6
Clegg Hall Rd. OL15 & OL16 15 E1
Clegg Pl. 2 OL6 85 D4
Clegg St. 6 Bacup OL13 3 C8
Clegg St. Bolton BL2 148 C7
Clegg St. Bredbury SK6 112 F3
Clegg St. Droylsden M43 83 F1
Clegg St. Littleborough OL15 15 F7
Clegg St. Milnrow OL16 32 A5
Clegg St. Oldham OL4 68 A6
Clegg St. Oldham OL1 153 F6
Clegg St. Shaw OL2 48 F8
Clegg St. Tyldesley M29 77 A5
Clegg St. Whitefield M45 62 F7
Clegg St. Whitworth OL12 4 C2
Clegg's Bldgs. BL1 145 E8
Clegg's Ct. OL12 4 C2
Clegg's La. M38 60 A5
Cleggswood Ave. OL15 16 A3
Clelland St. BL4 60 E7
Clematis Wlk. M27 61 E2
Clement Ave. M46 58 A2
Clement Ct. 3 Droylsden M11 99 F7
Clement Ct. 13 R'dale OL16 31 B6
Clement Rd. SK6 126 C7
Clement Royds St. OL12 139 E8
Clement Scott Cl. M9 64 F4
Clement St. SK4 169 E3
Clementina St. OL12 14 F1
Cleminson St. M3 158 D2
Clemshaw Cl. OL10 29 C1
Clerewood Ave. SK8 131 B7
Clerke St. BL9 140 F2
Clerks Ct. M5 80 B2
Clevedon Ave. M41 96 A2
Clevedon Dr. WN3 54 D4
Clevedon Rd. OL9 48 B1
Clevedon St. M9 157 E7
Cleveland Ave. Hyde SK14 101 C2
Cleveland Ave. M'ster M19 99 B2
Cleveland Ave. Salford M6 80 C3
Cleveland Ave. Wigan WN3 54 C3
Cleveland Cl. Ramsbottom BL0 11 C3
Cleveland Cl. Swinton M27 62 A2
Cleveland Dr.Ashton-i-M WN4 73 C4
Cleveland Dr.Golborne WA3 74 D1
Cleveland Dr.Milnrow OL16 32 A6
Cleveland Gdns. BL3 146 B4
Cleveland Gr. OL2 48 C3
Cleveland Rd. Alt'ham WA15 119 F3
Cleveland Rd. M'ster M8 64 B2
Cleveland Rd. M'ster SK4 168 A4
Cleveland St. 7 BL3 146 B4
Clevelands Prep Sch. BL1 144 A7
Cleveleys Ave. Bolton BL2 148 C8
Cleveleys Ave. Bury BL9 44 E7
Cleveleys Ave. Gatley SK8 122 B1
Cleveleys Ave. M'ster M21 109 C7
Cleveleys Ave. R'dale OL16 31 B3
Cleveleys Gr. M7 155 E7
Cleves Ct. OL10 29 C1
Clevlands Cl. OL2 149 A8
Cleworth Cl. M29 77 C4

Cooper St. Bury BL9 140 E2
Cooper St. Dukinfield SK16 166 B1
Cooper St. Glossop SK13 104 B1
Cooper St. Hazel Grove SK7 124 F3
Cooper St. Horwich BL6 22 B4
Cooper St. Littleborough OL16 15 D4
Cooper St. M'ster M2 158 F1
Cooper St. Oldham OL4 68 A7
Cooper St. Stockport SK1 170 F7
Cooper St. Stretford M32 96 D1
Cooper Terr. OL16 31 B8
Cooper's La. PR7 18 B8
Cooper's Row. BL1 145 F7
Cooperative St. OL14 6 A7
Coopers Glen. WN2 56 A8
Coopers Row. WN1 150 C8
Cop Rd. OL1 & OL2 49 C4
Copage Dr. SK6 113 A4
Cope Bank. 12 BL1 142 C2
Cope Bank W. BL1 142 B2
Cope Cl. M12 99 E7
Cope St. BL1 142 C1
Copeland Ave. M27 62 C1
Copeland Cl. M24 46 C1
Copeland Dr. WN6 19 F1
Copeland Mews. BL1 144 A7
Copeland St. SK14 101 D5
Copeman Cl. M13 163 C6
Copenhagen Sq. 20 OL16 31 A8
Copenhagen St. Failsworth M40 83 A6
Copenhagen St. R'dale OL16 31 A8
Copesthorne Cl. WN2 38 C6
Copgrove Rd. M21 109 B7
Copgrove Wlk. M22 130 E7
Copley Ave. SK15 86 C2
Copley High Sch. SK15 86 D2
Copley Park Mews. SK15 86 C2
Copley Rd. M21 97 A2
Copley St. OL2 149 C8
Copper La. M45 62 B7
Copperas Cl. WN6 36 F7
Copperas La. Aspull WN2 38 A6
Copperas La. Blackrod BL6 21 B1
Copperas La. Droylsden M43 99 E8
Copperas St. M4 159 A2
Copperbeech. M22 109 E1
Copperbeech Dr. WN6 37 B7
Copperfield. WN1 37 C2
Copperfield Rd. Bramhall SK8 132 B5
Copperfield Rd. Poynton SK12 133 D2
Copperfields. Bolton BL6 40 B3
Copperfields. Poynton SK12 133 D2
Copperfields. Wilmslow SK9 137 C8
Copperways. M20 110 B5
Coppice Ave. M33 107 D2
Coppice Cl. High Lane SK12 135 A6
Coppice Cl. Romiley SK6 113 B4
Coppice Dr. High Lane SK12 135 A6
Coppice Dr. Orrell WN5 53 D2
Coppice Dr. Whitworth OL12 14 D7
Coppice Dr. Wigan WN3 54 F2
Coppice Dr. Wythenshawe M22 109 D1
Coppice Inf Sch. OL8 66 E4
Coppice Jun Sch. OL8 66 E4
Coppice La. SK12 135 A5
Coppice Rd. SK12 134 B3
Coppice St. Bury BL9 141 C3
Coppice St. Oldham OL8 153 D5
Coppice The. Alt'ham WA15 129 B8
Coppice The. Bolton BL2 25 D5
Coppice The. Middleton M24 65 B5
Coppice The. Ramsbottom BL0 11 A4
Coppice The. Swinton M28 79 C5
Coppice The. Worsley M28 78 F8
Coppice Vale. BL0 11 C3
Coppice Way. SK9 131 E3
Coppice Wlk. M34 100 D2
Copping St. M12 164 F6
Coppingford Cl. OL12 14 A2
Coppins The. SK9 136 E4
Coppleridge Dr. M8 64 A2
Copplestone Ct. M27 61 C1
Copplestone Dr. M33 107 C5
Coppull Cross Rds. PR7 19 F7
Coppull Hall La. PR7 20 B8
Coppull La. WN1 37 D2
Coppull Moor La. PR7 19 E6
Copse Ave. M22 121 E3
Copse Dr. BL9 27 F6
Copse The. Alt'ham WA15 129 D7
Copse The. Edgworth BL7 9 C2
Copse The. Marple SK6 126 C8
Copse The. Newton-l-W WA12 89 B4
Copse Wlk. OL15 15 F5
Copson St. M20 110 B7
Copster Ave. OL8 66 E3
Copster Hill Rd. OL8 66 E4
Copster Pl. OL8 66 E3
Copthall La. M7 & M8 155 F8
Copthorn Wlk. BL8 26 F5
Copthorne Cl. OL10 46 D8
Copthorne Cres. M13 98 E3
Copthorne Dr. BL2 42 E6
Coptrod Head Cl. OL12 14 E4
Coral Ave. Cheadle SK8 123 A1
Coral Ave. Platt Bridge WN2 56 A2
Coral Gr. WN7 75 E4
Coral Rd. SK8 123 A1
Coral St. M'ster M13 163 C7
Coral St. Wigan WN6 37 A3
Coralin Way. WN4 72 F7
Coram St. M18 99 F6
Corbar Rd. SK2 124 B5
Corbett St. M'ster M11 83 A1
Corbett St. R'dale OL16 31 B8
Corby St. M12 165 A6
Corcoran Cl. OL10 29 C3
Corcoran Dr. SK6 113 F2
Corda Ave. M22 121 D8
Corday La. M25 63 D8
Cordingley Ave. M43 99 F8
Cordova Ave. M34 99 F3
Corelli St. M10 & M40 160 F4
Corfe Cl. Aspull WN2 38 D5
Corfe Cl. Urmston M41 94 C1
Corfe Cres. SK7 124 D1
Corhampton Cres. M46 58 E5
Corinth Wlk. M28 60 D2
Corinthian Ave. M7 81 C5
Cork St. Ashton-u-L OL6 166 C3
Cork St. Bury BL9 141 A2
Cork St. M'ster M12 164 D8
Corkland Cl. OL6 85 E2
Corkland Rd. M'ster M21 109 C8
Corkland St. OL6 85 E2
Corks La. SK12 135 E5
Corley Ave. SK3 122 F7
Cormallen Gr. M35 84 A7
Cormorant Cl. M28 60 C3
Cormorant Wlk. M12 165 A6
Corn Cl. M13 163 C5
Corn Hey Rd. M33 107 C2
Corn Hill La. M34 100 B5
Corn Mill Cl. OL12 15 C4
Corn St. Failsworth M35 83 C6
Corn St. Glossop SK13 104 D1
Corn St. Leigh WN7 75 D5
Corn St. Oldham OL4 67 A7
Cornall St. BL8 27 C3
Cornbrook Cl. OL12 15 C6
Cornbrook Ct. M15 162 D6
Cornbrook Gr. M16 162 D5
Cornbrook Park Rd. M15 161 C6
Cornbrook Rd. M15 161 C7
Cornbrook St. M16 162 D5
Cornbrook Wlk. M16 162 D5
Cornelian Gr. WN4 72 F5
Cornell St. M4 159 B2
Corner Croft. SK9 137 A4
Corner Ct. SK8 122 F6
Corner La. WN2 & WN7 57 D3
Corner St. OL6 166 C2
Cornergate. BL5 57 E5
Cornet St. M7 155 D5
Cornfield. SK15 102 E7
Cornfield Cl. Bury BL9 27 F7
Cornfield Cl. 2 Sale M33 108 F3
Cornfield Dr. M22 121 C3
Cornfield Rd. SK6 113 E3
Cornfield St. OL16 32 A5
Cornford Ave. M18 99 B3
Cornhill Ave. M41 95 B3
Cornhill Rd. M41 95 B3
Cornhill St. OL1 & OL4 49 D2
Cornish Way. OL2 49 A4
Cornishway. M22 130 D8
Cornishway Ind Est. 3 M22 130 D8
Cornlea Dr. M28 78 C7
Cornwall Ave. Atherton BL5 58 F8
Cornwall Ave. M'ster M19 111 B8
Cornwall Ave. Tyldesley M29 59 A3
Cornwall Cl. SK6 134 E7
Cornwall Cres. Brinnington SK5 112 C6
Cornwall Cres. Diggle OL3 51 B4
Cornwall Cres. Standish WN1 20 B1
Cornwall Ct. 2 M18 99 D6
Cornwall Dr. Bury BL9 45 A8
Cornwall Dr. Hindley WN2 56 F6
Cornwall House. M3 158 D1
Cornwall Pl. WN5 54 C6
Cornwall Rd. Droylsden M43 84 A3
Cornwall Rd. Gatley SK8 131 B8
Cornwall Rd. Irlam M44 105 D5
Cornwall St. 2 Eccles M30 79 C1
Cornwall St. M'ster M11, M18 99 D7
Cornwall St. Oldham OL9 152 B5
Cornwallis Rd. WN3 150 A5
Cornwell Cl. SK9 137 D8
Cornwood Cl. 5 M8 155 F7
Corona Ave. Hyde SK14 167 E3
Corona Ave. Oldham OL8 66 E3
Coronation Ave. Atherton M46 58 C5
Coronation Ave. Dukinfield SK16 101 F6
Coronation Ave. Glazebury WA3 92 C7
Coronation Ave. Heywood OL10 46 E8
Coronation Ave. Hyde SK14 167 E1
Coronation Dr. Leigh WN7 76 E6
Coronation Dr. Newton-l-W WA11 89 A7
Coronation Dr. Newton-l-W WA12 89 E1
Coronation Gdns. M26 43 E4
Coronation Rd. Ashton-u-L OL6 85 C6
Coronation Rd. Droylsden M43 83 F3
Coronation Rd. Failsworth M35 83 E6
Coronation Rd. Radcliffe M26 43 E4
Coronation Rd. Wigan WN6 36 D3
Coronation Sq. Little Lever BL3 43 B3
Coronation Sq. M'ster M12 163 C8
Coronation St. Bolton BL1 145 F7
Coronation St. Denton M34 100 D3
Coronation St. Garswood WN4 72 D6
Coronation St. Ince-i-M WN2 55 F3
Coronation St. M'ster M3 162 E8
Coronation St. M'ster M11 165 C8
Coronation St. Reddish SK5 169 E4
Coronation St. Salford M5 161 B8
Coronation St. Swinton M27 62 A1
Coronation St. Wigan WN3 150 B6
Coronation Wlk.Billinge WN5 71 D4
Coronation Wlk. Radcliffe M26 43 E5
Corporation Rd. Denton M34 100 D5
Corporation Rd. Eccles M30 79 F1
Corporation Rd. R'dale OL11 139 D6
Corporation Rd. R'dale OL11 139 D7
Corporation St. Bolton BL1 145 F7
Corporation St. Hyde SK14 167 D2
Corporation St. M'ster M4 & M60 159 A2
Corporation St. Middleton M24 65 A8
Corporation St. Stalybridge SK15 86 A1
Corporation St. Stockport SK1 169 F2
Corporation St. Wigan WN3 150 B6
Corpus Christ RC Inf & Jun Sch. OL9 66 B4
Corpus Christi RC Prim Sch. M40 160 D4
Corran Cl. M30 79 B2
Correction Brow. SK12 134 C6
Corridge Wlk. 7 M8 156 B6
Corrie Cl. M34 100 F1
Corrie Cres. M26 & M27 61 D4
Corrie Cty Sch. M34 100 F1
Corrie Dr. M26 61 D5
Corrie Rd. M27 62 A3
Corrie St. M38 60 A4
Corrie Way. SK6 112 F5
Corrigan St. M18 99 E6
Corrin Rd. BL2 148 B5
Corring Way. BL1 25 B4
Corringham Rd. M19 111 C7
Corriss Ave. M9 64 A5
Corry St. OL10 29 E2
Corsey Rd. WN2 56 E4
Corsock Dr. WN1 37 E1
Corson St. BL4 42 D2
Corston Gr. BL6 21 D1
Corston Wlk. M40 83 B6
Corwen Ave. M9 157 E8
Corwen Cl. OL8 66 B2
Cosgrove Cres. M35 83 E5
Cosgrove Rd. M35 83 E5
Cosham Rd. M22 121 F3
Costabeck Wlk. M40 83 D4
Costessey Way. WN3 54 C3
Costobadie Cl. SK14 102 F3
Costobadie Way. SK14 102 F3
Cosworth Cl. WN7 76 B4
Cotaline Cl. OL11 30 B3
Cotall Wlk. M8 158 E4
Cote Green La. SK6 114 B1
Cote Green Rd. SK6 114 C1
Cote La. Delph OL3 51 B7
Cote La. Littleborough OL15 15 F6
Cote La. Uppermill OL5 68 E3
Cotefield Ave. BL3 147 F3
Cotefield Cl. 7 SK6 125 F5
Cotefield Rd. M22 121 C2
Cotford Rd. BL1 24 F5
Cotham St. M3 158 F4
Cotman Dr. SK6 126 C8
Cotswold Ave. Golborne WA3 90 D6
Cotswold Ave. Hazel Grove SK7 124 B1
Cotswold Ave. Oldham OL9 152 A5
Cotswold Ave. Shaw OL2 48 F8
Cotswold Ave. Shaw OL2 149 A8
Cotswold Ave. Urmston M41 94 F3
Cotswold Ave. Wigan WN5 54 B5
Cotswold Cl. Glossop SK13 116 A8
Cotswold Cl. Prestwich M25 63 C5
Cotswold Cl. Ramsbottom BL0 11 C4
Cotswold Cres. Bury BL8 27 B3
Cotswold Cres. Milnrow OL16 32 A7
Cotswold Dr. Horwich BL6 22 C5
Cotswold Dr. Royton OL2 48 B3
Cotswold Dr. Salford M6 154 F3
Cotswold Rd. SK4 169 D3
Cottage Croft. BL2 25 D5
Cottage Gdns. SK6 112 D3
Cottage Hospl. M41 95 D2
Cottage La. SK13 171 E2
Cottage Lawns. SK9 137 B2
Cottage Wlk. Droylsden M43 83 F3
Cottage Wlk. R'dale OL12 14 C4
Cottam Cres. SK6 126 B7
Cottam Gr. M27 80 A7
Cottam St. Bury BL8 27 C3
Cottam St. Oldham OL1 153 D8
Cottenham La. M3 & M7 158 E4
Cottenham St. M13 163 B6
Cotter St. M12 163 C7
Cotterdale Cl. M16 97 D2
Cotteril Cl. Sale M23 120 C8
Cotterill St. M5 & M6 81 B2
Cottesmore Dr. M8 156 C8
Cottesmore Gdns. WA15 129 C8
Cottesmore Way. WA3 74 B1
Cottingham Dr. OL6 166 C4
Cottingham Rd. M12 164 E6
Cotton Fold. OL16 31 C6
Cotton Hill. M20 110 C5
Cotton La. M20 110 C6
Cotton St. Bolton BL1 143 D2
Cotton St. Leigh WN7 75 D5
Cotton St. M'ster M4 159 B2
Cotton St E. OL6 & OL7 166 B2
Cotton St W. OL7 166 A2
Cotton Tree Cl. OL4 67 E8
Cotton Tree St. SK3 & SK4 169 E1
Cottonfield Rd. M20 110 C6
Cottonwood Dr. 3 M33 107 C5
Cottrell Rd. WA15 129 D7
Cotts The. OL4 50 B1
Coucill Sq. BL4 60 E8
Coulsden Dr. M9 64 D3
Coulthart St. OL6 166 B3
Coulthurst St. BL0 138 B6
Coultshead Ave. WN5 71 E6
Counce Ave. WA12 89 B1
Council Ave. WN4 73 B3
Councillor La. SK8 123 A4
Councillor St. M11 160 E1
Count St. OL16 31 A4
Countess Ave. SK8 131 E5
Countess Gr. M5 & M7 158 D4
Countess La. M26 43 D4
Countess Pl. M25 63 C4
Countess Rd. M20 110 B3
Countess St. Ashton-u-L OL6 85 D2
Countess St. Stockport SK2 124 A5
Counthill Dr. M8 63 E2
Counthill Rd. OL4 49 D1
Counthill Sch. OL4 49 D2
Counting House Rd. SK12 135 E5
County Ave. OL6 85 E4
County Police St. WN2 151 F7
County Rd. M28 60 A4
County St. M'ster M2 158 F1
County St. Oldham OL8 66 C2
Coupes Gn. BL5 57 F6
Coupland Cl. OL4 49 F4
Coupland Rd. WN2 57 C4
Coupland St. M'ster M15 163 A5
Coupland St. Whitworth OL12 14 C8
Courage Low La. WN6 18 D5
Courier Pl. WN5 36 E1
Courier St. M18 99 F6
Course View. OL4 67 E3
Court Dr. M40 83 E4
Court House Way. 4 OL10 29 D2
Court St. Bolton BL2 148 A7
Court St. Uppermill OL3 69 B8
Courtfield Ave. M9 64 D4
Courthill St. SK1 124 A8
Courtney Gn. SK9 131 D2
Courtney Pl. WA14 119 A1
Courtyard Dr. M28 60 A3
Courtyard The. SK14 103 D5
Cousin Fields. BL2 25 C7
Covall Wlk. 4 M8 156 B6
Cove The. WA15 119 F3
Covell Rd. SK12 133 D5
Covent Garden. SK1 169 F1
Coventry Ave. SK3 122 F7
Coventry Gr. OL9 48 A1
Coventry Rd. M26 43 F5
Coventry St. OL11 139 F6
Coverdale Ave. Bolton BL1 144 A8
Coverdale Ave. Royton OL2 48 C5
Coverdale Cl. OL10 29 C1
Coverdale Cres. M12 164 E6
Coverdale Rd. BL5 57 D8
Coverham Ave. OL4 67 D4
Coverhill Rd. OL4 68 B5
Covert Rd. Oldham OL4 67 D3
Covert Rd. Wythenshawe M22 121 E5
Coverts The. WN6 36 F2
Covington Pl. SK9 137 B6
Cow La. Alt'ham WA15 128 F6
Cow La. Bolton BL3 146 B2
Cow La. Failsworth M35 83 E7
Cow La. M'ster M5 81 C1
Cow La. Oldham OL4 67 C7
Cow La. Sale M33 108 E5
Cow La. Stockport SK2 & SK7 124 D4
Cow Lees. BL5 40 A1
Cowan St. M10 & M40 160 D2
Cowbrook Ave. SK13 104 F1
Cowburn Dr. SK12 127 C1
Cowburn St. Heywood OL10 29 E1
Cowburn St. Hindley WN2 56 F6
Cowburn St. 1 Leigh WN7 75 D5
Cowburn St. M'ster M3 158 F3
Cowdals Rd. BL6 40 B4
Cowesby St. M'ster M14 98 A3
Cowhill La. OL6 166 C3
Cowie St. OL2 149 B8
Cowley Gr. SK14 102 F3
Cowley Rd. BL1 24 F5
Cowley St. 9 M40 83 C6
Cowley Terr. M9 64 A5
Cowling St. M'ster M25 & M7 80 F8
Cowling St. Oldham OL8 66 F4
Cowling St. Wigan WN3 150 B6
Cowlishaw. OL2 149 A5
Cowlishaw La. OL2 149 A5
Cowlishaw Rd. SK14 & SK6 113 F4
Cowm Park Way N. OL12 4 D2
Cowm Park Way S. OL12 4 C1
Cowm St. OL12 4 E5
Cowm Top La. OL11 30 E2
Cowpe Rd. BB4 2 F7
Cowper Ave. M46 58 D5
Cowper St. Ashton-u-L OL6 166 C3
Cowper St. Leigh WN7 75 D5
Cowper St. Middleton M24 65 D8
Cowper Wlk. 4 M11 160 F1
Cox Green Cl. BL7 8 D3
Cox Green Rd. Bolton BL7 8 E2
Cox Green Rd. 2 Bolton BL7 24 F8
Coxfield. WN6 35 D7
Coxton Rd. M22 121 E1
Coxwold Gr. BL3 146 C2
Crab Brow. M46 58 B3
Crab La. M9 64 B4
Crab Lane Prim Sch. M9 64 B4
Crab Tree La. M46 58 D2
Crabbe St. M3 159 A3
Crabtree Ave. Alt'ham WA15 129 D7
Crabtree Ave. Disley SK12 135 E5
Crabtree Ct. SK12 135 D6
Crabtree La. M11 83 D1
Crabtree Rd. Oldham OL1 67 B8
Crabtree Rd. Wigan WN5 54 D7
Crabtree St. BL9 141 B3
Craddock Rd. M33 108 C2
Craddock St. 4 OL5 68 C1
Cradley Ave. M11 99 D8
Crag Ave. BL9 11 D2
Crag Gr. WA11 71 B1
Crag La. BL9 11 D2
Cragg Rd. OL1 48 A2
Cragie St. M7 & M8 155 F5
Craig Ave. Bury BL8 27 B1
Craig Ave. Urmston M41 95 A3
Craig Cl. SK4 168 B1
Craig Rd. M'ster M18 99 C4
Craig Rd. Stockport SK4 168 B1
Craig Wlk. OL8 153 E5
Craigend Dr. M9 157 E7
Craighall Ave. M19 110 F8
Craighall Rd. BL1 24 E6
Craiglands. OL11 & OL16 31 B2
Craigmore Ave. M20 109 E4
Craignair Ct. M27 80 C7
Craigslands Ave. M40 83 A6
Craigweil Ave. M20 110 D3
Craigwell Rd. M25 63 E2
Craigwell Wlk. M13 163 B7
Crail Pl. OL10 28 F1
Cramer St. M10 & M40 157 F5
Crammond Cl. M35 & M40 83 D6
Cramond Cl. BL1 143 D1
Crampton Dr. WA15 129 C8
Crampton La. M31 106 D6
Cranage Rd. M19 111 B8
Cranark Cl. BL1 144 A7
Cranberry Ave. Walsden OL14 6 B7
Cranberry Ave. Wigan WN6 36 F3
Cranberry Cl. WA14 119 B8
Cranberry Rd. M31 105 F3
Cranberry St. OL4 67 B6
Cranborne Cl. Horwich BL6 22 F1
Cranborne Cl. Standish WN6 19 D1
Cranbourne Ave. SK8 123 B2
Cranbourne Cl. OL7 166 A4
Cranbourne Ct. SK4 168 B4
Cranbourne Rd. Ashton-u-L OL6 & OL7 166 B4
Cranbourne Rd. M'ster M16 97 C4
Cranbourne Rd. M'ster M21 109 B8
Cranbourne Rd. M'ster SK4 168 B4
Cranbourne Rd. R'dale OL11 29 E6
Cranbourne St. M5 81 C1
Cranbourne Terr. OL6 85 B5
Cranbrook Ave. WN4 73 A4
Cranbrook Cl. BL1 143 F1
Cranbrook Dr. M25 63 C2
Cranbrook Gdns. OL7 166 B4
Cranbrook Rd. Reddish M34 99 F3
Cranbrook Rd. Swinton M28 79 B4
Cranbrook St. Ashton-u-L OL7 166 B4
Cranbrook St. Oldham OL4 67 C6
Cranbrook St. Radcliffe M26 44 C5
Cranbrook Way. WN1 37 B4
Cranbrook Wlk. OL9 152 A6
Cranby St. 6 WN2 56 D5
Crandon Ct. M27 62 A1
Crandon Dr. M20 122 C8
Crane St. Bolton BL3 146 B3
Crane St. Coppull PR7 19 D6
Crane St. M'ster M12 163 C8
Cranefield Wlk. 9 M16 97 F4
Cranfield Cl. M10 & M40 160 D2
Cranfield Rd. Horwich BL6 39 E7
Cranfield Rd. Wigan WN3 55 A3
Cranford Ave. M'ster M20 110 D4
Cranford Ave. Sale M33 108 C6
Cranford Ave. Stretford M32 96 F3
Cranford Ave. Whitefield M45 44 E2
Cranford Cl. Pendlebury M6 80 B6
Cranford Cl. Whitefield M45 44 E2
Cranford Dr. M44 93 F3
Cranford Gdns. Marple SK6 125 F8
Cranford Gdns. Urmston M41 94 E3
Cranford House. M30 79 F3
Cranford Rd. Handforth SK9 131 A1
Cranford Rd. Urmston M41 94 E3
Cranford St. BL3 146 C2
Cranham Ave. WA3 90 E7
Cranham Cl. Bury BL8 27 B3
Cranham Cl. Walkden M38 60 A6
Cranham Rd. M22 121 A2
Crank Rd. WA11 & WN5 71 B8
Crankwood Rd. WN2 & WN7 74 D5
Cranleigh. WN6 37 A8
Cranleigh Ave. SK4 110 F4
Cranleigh Cl. Blackrod BL6 21 D1
Cranleigh Cl. Oldham OL4 49 E1
Cranleigh Dr. Cheadle SK8 122 F6
Cranleigh Dr. Hazel Grove SK7 134 A8
Cranleigh Dr. Sale M33 108 A5
Cranleigh Dr. Sale M23 & M33 108 C1
Cranleigh Dr. Tyldesley M29 77 B8
Cranleigh Dr. Walkden M38 78 E8
Cranlington Dr. M7 & M8 155 F6
Cranmer Ct. OL10 29 C1
Cranmer Rd. M20 110 B4
Cranmere Ave. M18 & M19 99 C2
Cranmere Dr. M33 107 D2
Cranshaw St. M29 77 D8
Cranstal Dr. WN2 57 A5
Cranston Dr. M'ster M20 122 B8
Cranston Dr. Sale M33 108 E3
Cranston Gr. M22 121 F5
Cranswick St. 1 M14 98 A3
Crantock Dr.Gatley SK8 131 C8
Crantock Dr.Stalybridge SK15 86 D3
Crantock St. M18 99 B3
Cranwell Ave. WA3 91 F4
Cranwell Dr. M19 110 E4
Cranworth Ave. M29 77 A8
Cranworth St. SK15 86 B1
Craston Rd. M13 98 E2
Craunton. 13 M30 79 F2
Craven Ave. Golborne WA3 90 E7
Craven Ave. Salford M5 161 B8
Craven Cl. M5 161 B8
Craven Ct. BL6 22 D2
Craven Dr. Alt'ham WA14 119 C8
Craven Dr. Salford M5 161 A7
Craven Gdns. OL11 139 E5
Craven House. OL14 6 A8
Craven Pl. Bolton BL1 23 E2
Craven Pl. 3 Droylsden M11 83 C2
Craven Rd. Alt'ham WA14 119 C7
Craven Rd. 1 Reddish SK5 111 F6
Craven St. Ashton-u-L OL6 85 D5
Craven St. Bury BL9 141 C3
Craven St. M'ster M5 81 C1
Craven St. Oldham OL1 48 E1
Craven St E. BL6 22 D2
Craven Terr. M33 108 C4
Cravenhurst Ave. M40 83 B4
Cravenwood Prim Sch. M8 64 A1
Cravenwood Rd. M8 156 A8
Crawford Ave. Adlington PR7 20 E5
Crawford Ave. Aspull WN2 38 C5
Crawford Ave. Bolton BL2 148 B6
Crawford Ave. Tyldesley M29 58 E2
Crawford Ave. Worsley M28 79 A8
Crawford Cl. WN2 38 C5
Crawford Sq. OL10 29 A1
Crawford St. Ashton-u-L OL6 85 D2
Crawford St. Aspull WN2 38 C4
Crawford St. Bolton BL2 148 B6
Crawford St. Eccles M30 79 D3
Crawford St. 24 Failsworth M40 83 C5
Crawford St. R'dale OL11 & OL16 31 B6
Crawford St. Walsden OL14 6 B8
Crawford St. Wigan WN1 150 C8
Crawley Ave. Eccles M30 80 A3
Crawley Ave. Wythenshawe M22 121 E3
Crawley Cl. M29 59 C1
Crawley Gr. SK2 124 B6
Crawley Way. OL9 152 A6
Cray The. OL16 31 E6
Cray Wlk. M13 163 B7
Craydon St. M11 165 C8
Crayfield Rd. M19 111 B8
Crayford Rd. M40 83 B4
Creaton Way. M24 46 D4
Creden Ave. M22 121 F3
Crediton Cl. Alt'ham WA14 119 B6
Crediton Cl. M'ster M15 162 F5
Crediton Dr.Bolton BL2 43 A7
Crediton Dr.Platt Bridge WN2 56 A1
Crediton House. M6 80 A3
Creel Cl. M9 64 B4
Cremer. M30 80 A2
Cresbury St. M12 164 D8
Crescent. M5 81 C2
Crescent Ave. Ashton-i-M WN4 73 A4
Crescent Ave. Atherton BL5 59 A8
Crescent Ave. 16 Bolton BL1 145 D8
Crescent Ave. Farnworth BL4 60 C6
Crescent Ave. M'ster M25 63 B2
Crescent Ave.M'ster M8 156 A8
Crescent Ave.Pendlebury M27 80 B8
Crescent Cl. Dukinfield SK16 166 C1
Crescent Cl. Stockport SK3 124 A5
Crescent Ct. M21 96 F1
Crescent Dr. M38 60 B5
Crescent Gr. Cheadle SK8 122 C6
Crescent Gr. M'ster M25 63 B2
Crescent Gr. 6 M'ster M19 99 A1
Crescent Pk. SK4 168 C2
Crescent Range. M14 98 C3
Crescent Rd. Alderley Edge SK9 137 B2
Crescent Rd. Alt'ham WA14 119 A6
Crescent Rd. Alt'ham WA15 119 E1
Crescent Rd. Bolton BL3 42 B3
Crescent Rd. Cheadle SK8 122 C6
Crescent Rd. Dukinfield SK16 166 C1
Crescent Rd. Failsworth OL9 65 E2
Crescent Rd. Horwich BL6 39 F8
Crescent Rd. Kearsley BL4 60 F6
Crescent Rd. M'ster M8 & M7 156 A8
Crescent Rd. R'dale OL11 30 B4
Crescent Rd. Stockport SK1 112 B3
Crescent St. M8 156 C8
Crescent The. Alt'ham WA14 119 A5
Crescent The. Alt'ham WA15 119 F7
Crescent The. Bolton BL7 25 A7
Crescent The. Bolton BL2 25 F4
Crescent The. Bredbury SK6 112 D4
Crescent The. Bury BL9 141 A3
Crescent The. Cheadle SK8 122 D6
Crescent The. Droylsden M43 83 F1
Crescent The. Horwich BL6 22 E1
Crescent The. Ince-i-M WN2 56 B7
Crescent The. Irlam M44 94 B3
Crescent The. Little Lever BL3 43 B2
Crescent The. 4 M'ster M19 99 A1
Crescent The. Middleton M24 64 E8
Crescent The. Mossley OL5 68 B1
Crescent The. Prestwich M25 63 B4
Crescent The. Radcliffe M26 43 D5
Crescent The. Shaw OL2 149 A6
Crescent The. Stalybridge SK15 102 D6
Crescent The. Stockport SK3 124 A4
Crescent The. Urmston M41 94 F3
Crescent The. Westhoughton BL5 57 E7
Crescent The. Whitworth OL12 14 C8
Crescent The. Wigan WN5 54 D6
Crescent The. Worsley M28 79 A5
Crescent View. 12 SK16 166 B1
Crescent Way. SK3 124 A5
Cresgarth House. SK3 124 A4
Cressell Pk. WN6 19 B1
Cressfield Way. M21 109 D7
Cressingham Rd.Bolton BL3 146 A4
Cressingham Rd. Stretford M32 96 B2
Cressington Cl. 4 M5 & M6 154 E2
Cresswell Gr. M20 110 A5
Crest Lodge. SK7 123 F2
Crest St. M3 159 A3
Crest The. M34 & M43 100 A7
Crestfold. M28 60 A4
Crestwood Ave. WN3 54 F3
Crestwood Wlk. M40 156 C6
Crete St. OL8 66 F4
Crewe Rd. M23 120 E8
Crib Fold. OL3 51 A2
Crib La. OL3 51 A2
Criccieth Ave. WN2 38 D5
Criccieth Rd. SK3 123 A7
Criccieth Way. 2 M21 97 F4
Cricket Gr The. M21 109 B6
Cricket St. Bolton BL3 145 D5
Cricket St. Dukinfield M34 101 A4
Cricket St. Wigan WN6 150 B8
Cricket View. OL16 31 F5
Cricket's La. OL6 85 D3
Cricketers Way. BL5 57 F8
Cricketfield La. M28 60 C3
Cricklewood Rd. M22 121 C2
Crimble La. OL10 &OL11 29 F3
Crimble St. OL12 139 D8
Crimbles St. OL4 67 E8
Crime La. M35 & OL8 84 D7

Crimsworth Ave. M16 ... 97 B2
Crinan Sq. OL10 ... 28 F1
Crinan Way. BL2 ... 42 F6
Crinan Wlk. M40 ... 160 D3
Cringle Cl. BL3 ... 40 F4
Cringle Dr. SK8 ... 122 C3
Cringle Hall Rd. M19 ... 110 F8
Cringle Rd. M19 ... 111 C7
Cringleford Wlk. M12 ... 164 F5
Crippen St. M46 ... 58 A1
Cripple Gate. WN6 ... 19 A2
Cripple Gate La. OL11 ... 30 E1
Crispin Rd. M22 ... 130 E8
Critchley Cl. SK14 ... 167 F1
Criterion St. SK5 ... 99 F2
Croal St. BL1 ... 145 D6
Croal Wlk. M45 ... 45 B1
Croasdale Dr. OL2 ... 48 E5
Croasdale St. BL1 ... 143 F1
Crocker Wlk. 25 M9 ... 157 E8
Crocus Dr. OL2 ... 149 A5
Crocus St. BL1 ... 143 F4
Crocus Wlk. M3 ... 155 D6
Croft Acres. BL0 ... 1 D2
Croft Ave. Atherton M46 ... 58 D2
Croft Ave. Golborne WA3 ... 73 F2
Croft Ave. Middleton M25 ... 63 F8
Croft Ave. Orrell WN5 ... 53 D5
Croft Bank. 4 M'ster M7 ... 81 C5
Croft Bank. M'ster M18 ... 99 E5
Croft Bank. Stalybridge SK15 ... 86 D4
Croft Brow. OL8 ... 66 E2
Croft Cl. WA15 ... 129 C6
Croft Dr. BL8 ... 26 E6
Croft Gate. BL2 ... 25 E4
Croft Gates Rd. M24 ... 64 D7
Croft Gr. M38 ... 59 F5
Croft Head. OL2 ... 48 D4
Croft Head Dr. OL16 ... 31 F7
Croft Hill Rd. M40 ... 65 A1
Croft Ind Est. BL9 ... 45 A5
Croft La. Bolton BL3 ... 148 B5
Croft La. Radcliffe M26 ... 44 C4
Croft La. Whitefield BL9 ... 45 A5
Croft Manor. SK13 ... 104 E1
Croft Pl. M29 ... 76 F8
Croft Rd. Cheadle SK8 ... 123 B2
Croft Rd. Sale M33 ... 108 D2
Croft Rd. Wilmslow SK9 ... 136 E4
Croft Side. BL3 ... 42 E5
Croft Sq. OL12 ... 15 C3
Croft St. Bolton BL3 ... 42 B4
Croft St. Bury BL9 ... 141 A2
Croft St. Droylsden M11 ... 83 B1
Croft St. 4 Failsworth M35 ... 66 A1
Croft St. Golborne WA3 ... 90 A8
Croft St. Hyde SK14 ... 167 D2
Croft St. Littleborough OL12 ... 15 C3
Croft St. M'ster M5 & M7 ... 81 C5
Croft St. Stalybridge SK15 ... 86 B2
Croft St. Walkden M38 ... 59 F5
Croft St. Westhoughton BL5 ... 39 E3
Croft The. Hadfield SK14 ... 104 A6
Croft The. Oldham OL8 ... 66 E2
Croft The. Orrell WN5 ... 53 D3
Croft The. Stockport SK2 ... 124 B6
Croft The. Westhoughton BL5 ... 39 E3
Croft The. Whitefield BL9 ... 45 A6
Crofters Brook. M26 ... 44 C4
Crofters Gn. SK9 ... 136 F6
Crofters Hall Wlk. M40 ... 83 B7
Crofters The. M33 ... 108 F3
Crofters Wlk. BL2 ... 25 C6
Crofters' Yd. 14 WN1 ... 150 C8
Crofthill Ct. OL12 ... 15 D4
Croftlands. Orrell WN5 ... 155 D7
Croftlands. Ramsbottom BL0 ... 11 A3
Croftlands Rd. M22 ... 121 E4
Croftleigh Cl. M45 ... 44 E2
Crofton Ave. Sale WA15 ... 120 A8
Crofton Gdns. WA3 ... 91 E3
Crofton St. M'ster M16 ... 97 D4
Crofton St. M'ster M14 ... 98 B3
Crofton St. Oldham OL8 ... 66 F3
Crofts Bank Rd. M41 ... 95 D3
Croftside Ave. M28 ... 60 E3
Croftside Cl. M28 ... 60 E3
Croftside Gr. M28 ... 60 E3
Croftwood Sq. WN5 ... 36 C2
Croichley Fold. BL8 ... 10 D2
Cromar Rd. SK7 ... 124 F3
Cromarty Ave. OL9 ... 65 F3
Cromarty Sq. OL10 ... 28 F1
Cromarty Wlk. M11 ... 160 F1
Crombie Ave. M22 ... 121 D7
Crombouke Dr. WN7 ... 57 E1
Crombouke Fold. M28 ... 78 B7
Cromdale Ave. Bolton BL1 ... 144 B8
Cromdale Ave.
Hazel Grove SK7 ... 124 F3
Cromedale Cres. WN6 ... 37 A7
Cromer Ave. Bolton BL2 ... 25 C1
Cromer Ave. M'ster M20 ... 110 B6
Cromer Ave. Reddish M34 ... 100 A3
Cromer Dr. M46 ... 58 A2
Cromer Ind Est. M24 ... 47 B1
Cromer Rd. Bury BL8 ... 27 D5
Cromer Rd. Cheadle SK8 ... 122 E6
Cromer Rd. Sale M33 ... 108 C3
Cromer Rd. Wigan WN3 ... 54 E3
Cromer St. Droylsden M11 ... 83 D1
Cromer St. Middleton M24 ... 47 B1
Cromer St. R'dale OL12 ... 139 E8
Cromer St. Shaw OL2 ... 149 B7
Cromer St. Stockport SK1 ... 112 A2
Cromford Ave. M32 ... 96 B3
Cromford Bank. 18 SK13 ... 171 D2
Cromford Cl. Bolton BL1 ... 143 E1
Cromford Cl. 19
Gamesley SK13 ... 171 D2
Cromford Cts. M4 ... 159 A2
Cromford Dr. WN5 ... 54 B5
Cromford Fold. 20 SK13 ... 171 D2
Cromford Gdns. BL1 ... 143 F2
Cromford Gn. 16 SK13 ... 171 D2
Cromford Gr. 15 SK13 ... 171 D2
Cromford Lea. 17 SK13 ... 171 D2
Cromford Pl. 21 SK13 ... 171 D2
Cromford St. OL1 ... 67 A8
Cromford Way. 14 SK13 ... 171 D2
Cromhurst St. M8 ... 156 A8
Cromley Rd. High Lane SK6 ... 134 E6
Cromley Rd. Stockport SK2 ... 124 A3
Crompton Ave. Bolton BL2 ... 42 E8
Crompton Ave.
R'dale OL11 & OL16 ... 31 B3
Crompton Cl. Bolton BL1 ... 25 A4
Crompton Cl. Marple SK6 ... 125 F7
Crompton Cl. Radcliffe M26 ... 62 B8
Crompton Ct. BL3 ... 43 C3
Crompton Fold Prim Sch.
BL2 ... 42 E7
Crompton House. 4 WN1 ... 151 D8
Crompton House Sch. OL2 ... 48 F7
Crompton Pl. Bolton BL1 ... 145 F7
Crompton Pl. Radcliffe M26 ... 44 B3
Crompton Rd. Horwich BL6 ... 39 F8
Crompton Rd. Kearsley M26 ... 61 A8
Crompton Rd. M'ster M19 ... 111 A7
Crompton St. Ashton-u-L OL6 ... 85 E4
Crompton St. Bolton BL1 ... 148 A8
Crompton St. Bury BL9 ... 140 E2
Crompton St. Farnworth BL4 ... 60 E7
Crompton St. Ince-i-M WN2 ... 55 F3
Crompton St. Oldham OL9 ... 152 C7
Crompton St. Oldham OL1 ... 153 E8
Crompton St.
Platt Bridge WN2 ... 56 B3
Crompton St. Royton OL2 ... 48 D3
Crompton St. Royton OL2 ... 48 E3
Crompton St. Shaw OL2 ... 149 B7
Crompton St. Swinton M27 ... 79 E8
Crompton St. Walkden M38 ... 59 D5
Crompton St. Walkden M28 ... 60 F2
Crompton St. Wigan WN1 ... 150 C8
Crompton Vale. BL2 ... 42 D8
Crompton Way. Bolton BL2 ... 25 C2
Crompton Way. Shaw OL2 ... 149 B7
Cromwell Ave. Gatley SK8 ... 122 A6
Cromwell Ave. M'ster M16 ... 97 C2
Cromwell Ave. Marple SK6 ... 125 D7
Cromwell Ct. M44 ... 105 E7
Cromwell Gr. 9 M'ster M7 ... 81 C5
Cromwell Gr. M'ster M19 ... 99 B1
Cromwell Range. M14 ... 98 D2
Cromwell Rd. Bramhall SK7 ... 132 D6
Cromwell Rd. Denton SK6 ... 112 D6
Cromwell Rd. Eccles M30 ... 79 D2
Cromwell Rd. Irlam M44 ... 105 E7
Cromwell Rd. Prestwich M25 ... 63 C4
Cromwell Rd. Royton OL2 ... 48 C6
Cromwell Rd. Salford M6 ... 81 B5
Cromwell Rd. Stretford M32 ... 96 F2
Cromwell Rd. Swinton M27 ... 61 E1
Cromwell Rd. Whitefield M45 ... 44 D2
Cromwell Sch. M34 ... 100 A2
Cromwell St. Bolton BL1 ... 145 E7
Cromwell St. Heywood OL10 ... 29 D1
Cromwell St. Oldham OL1 ... 153 F6
Cromwell St. Stockport SK4 ... 169 D3
Crondale Wlk. 8 M13 ... 163 C6
Crondall St. M14 ... 98 A3
Cronfield Wlk. M21 ... 97 F4
Cronkeyshaw Rd. OL12 ... 14 F1
Cronshaw St. M19 ... 111 B8
Crook St. Adlington PR7 ... 20 F7
Crook St. Bolton BL3 ... 145 F6
Crook St. Hindley WN2 ... 56 D4
Crook St. Hyde SK14 ... 167 E2
Crook St. 10 R'dale OL16 ... 31 A8
Crook St. 5 Radcliffe M26 ... 44 B3
Crook St. Wigan WN1 ... 150 B8
Crookall St. WN4 ... 73 C4
Crooke Rd. WN6 ... 36 C3
Crookhill Dr. M7 & M8 ... 155 F7
Crookhurst Ave. WN5 ... 71 D6
Crookilley Way. SK1 & SK6 ... 112 C4
Croom Wlk. M40 ... 160 D2
Cropton Way. WN2 ... 56 F3
Crosby Ave. M28 ... 60 F2
Crosby Gr. M46 ... 58 E4
Crosby Meadow Sch. M9 ... 64 F4
Crosby Rd. Bolton BL1 ... 144 B8
Crosby Rd. Failsworth M40 ... 83 D5
Crosby Rd. Radcliffe BL8 ... 43 E7
Crosby Rd. 3 Salford M6 ... 80 D5
Crosby St. Atherton M46 ... 58 E4
Crosby St. R'dale OL12 ... 15 A2
Crosby St. Stockport SK2 ... 170 F7
Crosfield Ave. BL9 ... 11 C2
Crosfield Gr. M18 ... 99 D4
Cross Ave. M25 ... 63 A6
Cross Cliffe. Glossop SK13 ... 116 E8
Cross Cliffe. Hyde SK14 ... 113 C8
Cross Field Cl. OL2 ... 32 C1
Cross Glebe St. 3 OL6 ... 166 C3
Cross Gr. WA15 ... 119 F8
Cross Keys St. M4 ... 159 B2
Cross Knowle View. M41 ... 95 A4
Cross La.
Droylsden M35 & M43 ... 84 D4
Cross La. M'ster M18 ... 99 D5
Cross La. Marple SK6 ... 125 E5
Cross La. Newton-l-W WA12 ... 89 B4
Cross La. Orrell WN5 ... 53 D3
Cross La. Radcliffe M26 ... 44 C4
Cross La. Ramsbottom BL8 ... 138 A6
Cross La. Salford M5 & M6 ... 81 B2
Cross La. Wilmslow SK9 ... 137 F8
Cross La E. M31 ... 105 F3
Cross La W. M31 ... 105 F2
Cross Lees. OL12 ... 15 A3
Cross Ormrod St. BL3 ... 145 D6
Cross Rd. Gatley SK8 ... 131 B7
Cross Rd. M'ster M21 ... 109 B8
Cross Rise. SK13 ... 116 E8
Cross St. 3 Alt'ham WA14 ... 119 D4
Cross St. Ashton-u-L OL6,OL7 ... 166 A2
Cross St. Aspull WN2 ... 38 B6
Cross St. Atherton M46 ... 58 E3
Cross St. Bolton BL7 ... 25 A7
Cross St. Bolton BL1 ... 145 F8
Cross St. Bury BL9 ... 140 F2
Cross St. Denton M34 ... 100 E5
Cross St. Farnworth BL4 ... 60 D8
Cross St. Glossop SK13 ... 104 C1
Cross St. Golborne WA3 ... 90 A7
Cross St. Hadfield SK14 ... 104 A4
Cross St. Heywood OL10 ... 29 E1
Cross St. Hindley WN2 ... 56 E5
Cross St. Hollingworth SK14 ... 171 D4
Cross St. Hyde SK14 ... 167 D2
Cross St. Ince-i-M WN2 ... 55 E4
Cross St. Kearsley BL4 ... 61 B6
Cross St. Leigh WN7 ... 76 A4
Cross St. Little Lever BL3 ... 43 B3
Cross St. M'ster M3 ... 158 E2
Cross St. M'ster M1, M2, M4 ... 158 F1
Cross St. M'ster M16 ... 162 D5
Cross St. 9 Middleton M24 ... 46 F1
Cross St. Milnrow OL16 ... 31 D7
Cross St. 4 Mossley OL5 ... 68 C2
Cross St. Mottram-i-L SK14 ... 115 B8
Cross St. Oldham OL1 & OL4 ... 67 B7
Cross St. 3 Oldham OL4 ... 67 E6
Cross St. Oldham OL4 ... 68 A6
Cross St. R'dale OL11 ... 30 C2
Cross St. Radcliffe M26 ... 44 B3
Cross St. Ramsbottom BL0 ... 138 C6
Cross St. Sale M32 & M33 ... 108 B6
Cross St. Stalybridge SK15 ... 86 D4
Cross St. Standish WN6 ... 19 E1
Cross St. Stretford M32 ... 96 D2
Cross St. Swinton M27 ... 62 D2
Cross St. Swinton M28 ... 79 C7
Cross St. Tyldesley M29 ... 76 F8
Cross St. Urmston M41 ... 95 C1
Cross St. Whitefield M45 ... 44 E1
Cross St. 9 Wigan WN5 ... 54 B6
Cross St. Wigan WN3 ... 150 C7
Cross The. 3 SK14 ... 104 A5
Crossacres Cty
Prim Sch. M22 ... 121 E4
Crossacres Inf Sch. M22 ... 121 F4
Crossacres Jun Sch. M22 ... 121 F4
Crossacres Rd. M22 ... 121 E3
Crossbank Ave. OL4 ... 67 F7
Crossbank Cl. M13 ... 164 D5
Crossbank St. Oldham OL8 ... 153 E5
Crossbank St. Oldham OL8 ... 153 E6
Crossbank Way. M24 ... 46 F1
Crossbridge Rd. SK14 ... 102 A2
Crossby Cl. M9 ... 64 F5
Crosscliffe Cl. 4 M16 ... 97 F4
Crossdale Rd. Bolton BL2 ... 42 F8
Crossdale Rd. Hindley WN2 ... 57 A5
Crossdale Rd. M'ster M9 ... 64 F4
Crossdale Way. WA11 ... 71 B1
Crossefield Rd. SK8 ... 123 A3
Crossen St. BL3 ... 148 C5
Crossfell Ave. M9 ... 64 B5
Crossfield Ave. WA3 ... 91 F2
Crossfield Cl. Denton M34 ... 101 A2
Crossfield Cl.
Littleborough OL12 ... 15 C6
Crossfield Cl.
Stalybridge SK15 ... 86 A1
Crossfield Dr. Radcliffe M26 ... 43 E3
Crossfield Dr. Swinton M27 ... 61 E1
Crossfield Dr. Worsley M28 ... 78 F7
Crossfield Gr. Romiley SK6 ... 114 B1
Crossfield Gr. Stockport SK2 ... 124 B4
Crossfield Pl. OL11 ... 31 A5
Crossfield Rd. Alt'ham WA15 ... 120 B2
Crossfield Rd.
Handforth SK9 ... 131 D4
Crossfield Rd.
Irlam M30 & M44 ... 94 C4
Crossfield Rd.
Littleborough OL12 ... 15 C6
Crossfield St. BL9 ... 44 F4
Crossford Dr. BL3 ... 40 E4
Crossford St. M32 ... 96 D1
Crossgate Ave. M22 ... 121 D6
Crossgate La. SK14 ... 103 F7
Crossgate Mews. SK4 ... 110 E2
Crossgates Prim Sch. OL16 ... 32 A7
Crossgates Rd. OL16 ... 32 A7
Crossgill. M29 ... 77 B5
Crosshill Cl. 6 M16 ... 97 F4
Crosshill Wlk. BL3 ... 40 E5
Crossings The. WA12 ... 89 C3
Crossland Rd. Droylsden M43 ... 84 B2
Crossland Rd. M'ster M21 ... 109 A8
Crosslands. M25 ... 63 A3
Crosslands Cl. SK13 ... 116 D8
Crosslands Rd. M28 ... 77 F6
Crosslee Cty Prim Sch. M9 ... 64 F4
Crossley Cres. OL6 ... 85 E6
Crossley Rd.
M'ster M19 & SK4 ... 111 A7
Crossley Rd. Sale M33 ... 108 A6
Crossley St. Little Lever BL3 ... 43 A3
Crossley St. M'ster M18 ... 165 B6
Crossley St. Milnrow OL16 ... 31 E6
Crossley St. Oldham OL2 ... 48 E2
Crossley St. Shaw OL2 ... 149 C7
Crossley St. 8
Stalybridge SK15 ... 85 F2
Crossmead Dr. 3 M9 ... 64 E5
Crossmoor Cres. SK6 ... 113 C1
Crossmoor Dr. BL2 ... 148 B8
Crossmoor Gr. SK6 ... 113 C2
Crosswaite Rd. SK2 ... 124 E6
Crossway. Bramhall SK7 ... 132 E5
Crossway. M'ster M20 ... 110 B3
Crossway. Stockport SK2 ... 124 A4
Crossway Cl. WN4 ... 73 E5
Crossway Rd. M33 ... 107 F1
Crossways. OL8 ... 67 A1
Croston Ave. PR6 ... 21 A8
Croston Cl. SK9 ... 137 C1
Croston Close Rd. BL0 & BL9 ... 12 C4
Croston St. Bolton BL3 ... 146 C4
Croston St. Hindley WN2 ... 56 C6
Croston Wlk. M11 ... 160 E1
Crostons Rd. BL8 ... 140 D3
Croton St. SK4 ... 110 E2
Croughton Cl. M18 ... 99 D7
Crow Hill. SK15 ... 86 E5
Crow Hill N. M24 ... 64 F7
Crow Hill S. M24 ... 64 F6
Crow Hill View. OL4 ... 67 F5
Crow La. BL0 ... 138 C6
Crow La E. WA12 ... 89 C4
Crow La W. WA12 ... 89 A4
Crow Orchard Rd.
Shevington Moor WN6 ... 19 A1
Crow Tree Ave. 5 OL13 ... 3 B8
Crow Trees La. BL7 ... 9 C7
Crow Wood Rd. Edenfield BL0 ... 1 D6
Crow Wood Rd.
Golborne WA3 ... 74 D1
Crow's Nest. BL3 ... 42 F5
Crow's Nest Cotts. BL3 ... 42 F5
Crowbank Wlk. M40 ... 83 A5
Crowborough Cl. BL6 ... 22 F1
Crowborough Wlk. M15 ... 162 F5
Crowbrook Gr. 7 SK9 ... 131 D1
Crowcombe Wlk. 14 M16 ... 97 E4
Crowcroft Park Prim Sch.
M12 ... 99 A3
Crowcroft Rd. M12 & M13 ... 99 A3
Crowden Rd. M40 ... 65 B2
Crowhill Rd. OL7 ... 84 F4
Crowhurst Dr. WN1 ... 37 B3
Crowhurst Wlk. 2 M23 ... 120 E7
Crowland Gdns. SK8 ... 132 B6
Crowland Rd. Bolton BL2 ... 25 C2
Crowland Rd.
Wythenshawe M23 ... 120 F3
Crowley La. OL4 ... 49 D1
Crowley Rd. Alt'ham WA15 ... 120 B6
Crowley Rd. M'ster M9 ... 157 F8
Crown Bsns Ctr. M35 ... 83 F8
Crown Ct. SK7 ... 124 D3
Crown Fields Cl. WA12 ... 89 B5
Crown Gdns. Edgworth BL7 ... 9 D6
Crown Gdns.
Newton-l-W WA12 ... 89 B4
Crown Gdns. 13 R'dale OL16 ... 31 A5
Crown Gn. WA13 ... 117 B4
Crown Gr. WN7 ... 76 D6
Crown Hill. OL5 ... 86 D8
Crown Ind Est.
Alt'ham WA14 ... 119 E7
Crown Ind Est. M'ster M4 ... 159 C2
Crown La. Horwich BL6 ... 22 A4
Crown La. M'ster M4 ... 159 A3
Crown Mews. SK2 ... 124 C4
Crown Park Dr. WA12 ... 89 B5
Crown Passages. WA15 ... 119 E2
Crown Point. BL7 ... 9 D6
Crown Point Ave. M40 ... 83 C5
Crown Rd. OL10 ... 29 B2
Crown Royal Ind Pk. SK1 ... 124 A8
Crown Sq. M3 ... 158 E1
Crown St. Ashton-u-L OL6 ... 166 B2
Crown St. Atherton M46 ... 58 B3
Crown St. Bolton BL1 ... 145 F7
Crown St. Bredbury SK6 ... 112 F4
Crown St. Denton M34 ... 100 E4
Crown St. 20 Failsworth M40 ... 83 C5
Crown St. Failsworth M35 ... 83 F8
Crown St. Hindley WN2 ... 56 C6
Crown St. M'ster M3 ... 158 E2
Crown St. M'ster M15 ... 162 E7
Crown St. Marple SK6 ... 125 F3
Crown St. Newton-l-W WA12 ... 89 A3
Crown St. R'dale OL16 ... 31 B5
Crown St. Shaw OL2 ... 149 B7
Crown St. Wigan WN3 ... 150 B6
Crowndale. BL7 ... 9 D7
Crowneast St. OL11 ... 30 C7
Crowsdale Pl. SK2 ... 124 E4
Crowshaw Dr. OL12 ... 14 E3
Crowswood Dr. SK15 ... 86 D6
Crowther Ave. M5 ... 161 A8
Crowther Ct. OL15 ... 15 E4
Crowther St.
Littleborough OL15 ... 15 E4
Crowther St. M'ster M18 ... 99 E5
Crowther St. R'dale OL16 ... 31 B3
Crowthorn Dr. M23 ... 121 A2
Crowthorn Rd.
Ashton-u-L OL7 ... 84 F1
Crowthorn Rd. Edgworth BL7 ... 10 B8
Crowthorn Rd. Reddish SK4 ... 111 D7
Croxdale Cl. OL7 ... 84 E5
Croxdale Wlk. M9 ... 64 D5
Croxton Ave. R'dale OL16 ... 31 B8
Croxton Cl. Marple SK6 ... 125 E5
Croxton Cl. Sale M33 ... 107 D2
Croxton Wlk. 8 Horwich BL6 ... 22 B4
Croxton Wlk. M'ster M13 ... 163 C6
Croyde Cl. Bolton BL2 ... 25 F3
Croyde Cl.
Wythenshawe M22 ... 130 F7
Croydon Ave. Leigh WN7 ... 75 F8
Croydon Ave. Middleton OL11 ... 47 D8
Croydon Ave. Royton OL2 ... 48 C6
Croydon Dr. M40 ... 83 C4
Croydon Sq. OL11 ... 47 D8
Crummock Cl. BL3 ... 42 F3
Crummock Dr. Middleton M24 ... 46 E3
Crummock Dr. Wigan WN3 ... 54 F3
Crummock Rd. Farnworth BL4 ... 59 E7
Crummock Rd. Gatley SK8 ... 122 B3
Crumpsall La. M8 ... 64 A1
Crumpsall Lane Prim Sch.
M8 ... 64 A1
Crumpsall St. BL1 ... 143 E3
Crumpsall Sta. M8 ... 64 A1
Crumpsall Vale. M9 ... 64 C2
Crundale Rd. 7
Bolton BL1 & BL7 ... 24 F6
Cruttenden Rd. SK2 ... 124 D4
Cryer St. M35 & M43 ... 84 C4
Cuba Mill. BL0 ... 138 C8
Cuba St. M24 ... 65 C8
Cubley Rd. M7 ... 155 E8
Cuckoo Gr. M25 ... 63 B6
Cuckoo La. Bury BL9 ... 141 C2
Cuckoo La. Bury BL9 ... 141 C3
Cuckoo La. Prestwich M25 ... 63 B6
Cuddington Ave. M20 ... 110 A8
Cuddington Cres. SK3 ... 170 D6
Cuddington Way. 7 SK9 ... 131 D5
Cudworth Rd. M9 ... 64 A5
Cuerdon Wlk. M22 ... 121 E8
Culand St. M12 ... 164 E6
Culbert Ave. M20 ... 110 C3
Culcheth Ave. SK6 ... 125 F6
Culcheth Ave. Abram WN2 ... 56 B1
Culcheth Cty Prim Sch.
WA3 ... 92 A3
Culcheth Hall Dr. WA3 ... 91 F4
Culcheth Hall Prep Sch.
WA14 ... 119 D3
Culcheth High Sch. WA3 ... 92 A3
Culcheth La. M40 ... 83 C4
Culcheth Rd. WA14 ... 119 D3
Culcombe Wlk. M13 ... 163 C5
Culcross Ave. WN3 ... 54 C4
Culford Cl. M12 ... 164 E5
Culgaith Wlk. M9 ... 157 D7
Cullen Cl. WN2 ... 56 A8
Cullen Gr. M9 ... 64 F3
Cullercoats Wlk. 3 M18 ... 99 B3
Culmere Rd. M22 ... 121 D1
Culmington Cl. M15 ... 162 E5
Culross Ave. Bolton BL3 ... 40 E6
Culross Ave. Failsworth M40 ... 65 E1
Culver Rd. SK3 ... 170 D5
Culvercliffe Wlk. M3 ... 162 E8
Culverdon Wlk. M6 ... 80 F6
Culvert St. Oldham OL4 ... 67 E8
Culvert St. R'dale OL16 ... 31 B2
Culvert St. Wigan WN6 ... 37 A3
Culverwell Dr. M5 & M6 ... 81 B2
Culzean Cl. WN7 ... 76 C4
Cumber Cl. SK9 ... 136 D4
Cumber Dr. SK9 ... 136 D4
Cumber La. SK9 ... 136 D4
Cumberbatch Pl. WN2 ... 55 F4
Cumberland Ave.
Brinnington SK5 ... 112 C4
Cumberland Ave.
Dukinfield SK16 ... 101 E8
Cumberland Ave.
Heywood OL10 ... 29 A2
Cumberland Ave. Irlam M44 ... 105 C5
Cumberland Ave.
Swinton M27 ... 61 F2
Cumberland Ave.
Tyldesley M29 ... 58 F2
Cumberland Cl. BL9 ... 44 E6
Cumberland Dr.
Alt'ham WA14 ... 128 B8
Cumberland Dr.
Oldham OL1 & OL2 ... 48 D2
Cumberland Gr. OL6 & OL7 ... 166 B4
Cumberland Rd.
Atherton M46 ... 58 F4
Cumberland Rd. M'ster M9 ... 64 D1
Cumberland Rd.
Partington M31 ... 105 E2
Cumberland Rd. R'dale OL11 ... 30 F2
Cumberland Rd. Sale M33 ... 108 C2
Cumberland Rd.
Urmston M41 ... 95 C1
Cumberland St. M'ster M7 ... 158 D4
Cumberland St. 3
Stalybridge SK15 ... 85 F2
Cumberland St. 2
Wigan WN1 ... 37 E1
Cumbermere La. M29 ... 59 B2
Cumbrae Gdns. M5 ... 154 E1
Cumbrae Rd. M19 ... 99 C1
Cumbria Ct. M25 ... 62 F1
Cumbria Wlk. M6 ... 81 B4
Cumbrian Cl. 4 M'ster M13 ... 163 C6
Cumbrian Cl.
Platt Bridge WN2 ... 56 B2
Cumbrian Cl. Shaw OL2 ... 48 F8
Cummings St. OL8 ... 66 C2
Cunard Cl. M13 ... 163 C6
Cuncliffe Dr. Sale M33 ... 108 C3
Cuncliffe Dr. Shaw OL2 ... 49 D7
Cundall Wlk. M23 ... 108 F1
Cundey St. BL1 ... 142 C1
Cundiff Ct. M19 ... 99 C1
Cundiff Rd. M21 ... 109 B6
Cundy St. SK14 ... 167 E4
Cunliffe Ave.
Newton-l-W WA12 ... 89 B5
Cunliffe Ave. Ramsbottom BL0 ... 11 A4
Cunliffe Brow. BL1 ... 142 B1
Cunliffe Ct. WN7 ... 75 A4
Cunliffe St. Bolton BL2 ... 145 F6
Cunliffe St. Dukinfield SK14 ... 101 C4
Cunliffe St. Leigh WN7 ... 75 C5
Cunliffe St. Radcliffe M26 ... 44 C3
Cunliffe St. Ramsbottom BL0 ... 138 C7
Cunliffe St. Stockport SK3 ... 123 C8
Cunningham Dr. Gatley M22 ... 131 A8
Cunningham Dr.
Whitefield M45 ... 45 B2
Cunningham Rd. BL5 ... 57 D7
Cunningham Way. OL1 ... 153 F8
Curate St. SK1 ... 112 A1
Curlew Cl. OL11 ... 29 F7
Curlew Dr. M44 ... 94 A4
Curlew Rd. OL4 ... 67 E4
Curlew Wlk. M12 ... 164 E5
Currier La. OL6 ... 85 D2
Curteis St. BL6 ... 22 B4
Curtels Cl. M28 ... 79 C7
Curtis Gr. SK14 ... 104 A5
Curtis Rd. M'ster SK4 ... 168 A2
Curtis Rd. Reddish M19 ... 99 C1
Curtis St. Bolton BL3 ... 146 C2
Curtis St. Wigan WN5 ... 54 D6
Curven Edge. BB4 ... 1 A7
Curzon Ave. M14 ... 98 E4
Curzon Dr. WA15 ... 120 B6
Curzon Gn. SK2 ... 124 D7
Curzon Mews. SK9 ... 137 A5
Curzon Rd. Ashton-u-L OL6 ... 85 D4
Curzon Rd. Bolton BL1 ... 144 C7
Curzon Rd. Gatley SK8 ... 131 B7
Curzon Rd. M'ster M7 ... 155 D7
Curzon Rd. Poynton SK12 ... 133 E2
Curzon Rd. R'dale OL11 ... 30 F2
Curzon Rd. Sale M33 ... 108 B5
Curzon Rd. Stockport SK2 ... 124 D7
Curzon Rd. Stretford M32 ... 96 A4
Curzon St. Mossley OL5 ... 68 C1
Curzon St. Oldham OL1 ... 153 F7
Cut La. OL12 ... 13 F1
Cutgate Cl. M23 ... 108 E1
Cutgate Rd. OL12 ... 14 B1
Cuthbert Ave. M12, M18, M19 ... 99 B2
Cuthbert Mayne Ct. OL16 ... 139 E6
Cuthbert Rd. SK8 ... 122 E6
Cuthbert St. Bolton BL3 ... 146 B2
Cuthbert St. Wigan WN5 ... 54 D6
Cuthill Wlk. M40 ... 83 D4
Cutland St. 18 M40 ... 83 A6
Cutler Cres. OL13 ... 3 D7
Cutler Hill Rd. M35 ... 84 C7
Cutler La. OL13 ... 3 D7
Cutnook La. Irlam M44 ... 94 A3
Cutter Cl. M5 ... 161 A8
Cycle St. M11 ... 165 B8
Cyclone St. M11 ... 164 F8
Cygnet St. WN3 ... 150 B6
Cygnus Ave. M7 ... 81 C3
Cymbal Ct. SK5 ... 169 F3
Cynthia Dr. SK6 ... 125 F5
Cypress Ave. OL9 ... 152 B8
Cypress Cl. SK3 ... 123 C8
Cypress Gr. Denton M34 ... 101 A3
Cypress Gr. Kearsley BL4 ... 60 F7
Cypress Rd. Droylsden M43 ... 84 A3
Cypress Rd. Oldham OL4 ... 67 D8
Cypress Rd. Wigan WN5 ... 54 E6
Cypress Rd. Worsley M28 ... 79 A4
Cypress St. M'ster M8 & M9 ... 157 D7
Cypress St. Middleton M24 ... 65 C8
Cypress Way. SK6 ... 135 A7
Cypress Wlk. 2 M33 ... 107 C6
Cyprus Cl. Oldham OL4 ... 67 D6
Cyprus Cl. Salford M5 & M6 ... 154 F1
Cyprus St. M32 ... 96 D2
Cyril St. Bolton BL3 ... 148 A5
Cyril St. M'ster M14 ... 98 B3
Cyril St. Shaw OL2 ... 149 C7
Cyrus St. M10 & M40 ... 160 E2
D'Olivera Ct. 7 M24 ... 46 E2
Daccamill Dr. M27 ... 79 F6
Dacre Ave. M16 ... 97 B2
Dacre Cl. M24 ... 46 B1
Dacre Rd. OL11 ... 30 F4
Dacres Ave. OL3 ... 68 F4
Dacres Dr. Uppermill OL3 ... 68 F4
Dacres Rd. OL3 ... 68 F4
Daffodil Cl. Haslingden BB4 ... 1 A8
Daffodil Cl. R'dale OL12 ... 14 E3
Daffodil Rd. BL4 ... 42 A1
Daffodil St. BL1 ... 24 F5
Dagenham Rd. M14 ... 98 C4
Dagmar St. M28 ... 60 C4
Dagnall Ave. M21 ... 109 B6
Dahlia Cl. OL12 ... 14 D3
Dailton Rd. WN8 ... 53 A7
Daimler St. M8 ... 156 B6
Dain Cl. SK16 ... 101 D8
Daine Ave. M23 ... 109 B1
Dainton St. M12 ... 164 D7
Daintry Cl. M15 ... 162 F6
Daintry Rd. OL9 ... 152 C7
Dairy House La. SK7 ... 132 B4
Dairy House Rd. SK7 ... 132 B5
Dairy House
Small Holdings. SK7 ... 132 B4
Dairy St. OL9 ... 152 B7
Dairyground Rd. SK7 ... 132 F7
Dairyhouse La. WA14 ... 119 B7
Daisy Ave. Farnworth BL4 ... 42 A1
Daisy Ave. M'ster M13 ... 98 E4
Daisy Ave. Newton-l-W WA12 ... 89 C2
Daisy Bank. Culcheth WA3 ... 91 E3
Daisy Bank. Failsworth M40 ... 83 D5
Daisy Bank. Hyde SK14 ... 113 C8
Daisy Bank Ave. M6 ... 80 C6
Daisy Bank La. SK8 ... 122 A1
Daisy Bank Rd. M14 ... 98 D4
Daisy Hall Dr. BL5 ... 57 E5
Daisy Hall CE
(St James) Sch. BL5 ... 57 F5
Daisy Hill Ct. OL4 ... 67 E8
Daisy Hill Dr. PR6 ... 21 A8
Daisy Hill Rd. OL5 ... 68 D1
Daisy Hill Sta. BL5 ... 57 F6
Daisy Mews. SK3 ... 123 D4
Daisy Nook Ctry Pk. OL8 ... 84 E6
Daisy Rd. WN5 ... 54 E6
Daisy St. Bolton BL3 ... 146 C4
Daisy St. 6 Bury BL8 ... 27 C2
Daisy St. Oldham OL9 ... 152 A8
Daisy St. Oldham OL9 ... 153 D7
Daisy St. 4 R'dale OL12 ... 139 E8
Daisy St. Stockport SK1 & SK2 ... 170 F7
Daisy Way. SK6 ... 134 F7
Daisybank Cl. WN2 ... 56 D5
Daisyfield Cl. M22 ... 121 C1
Daisyfield Ct. BL8 ... 27 C1
Daisyfield Wlk. M28 ... 60 D3
Daisyhill Cl. M33 ... 108 E4
Daisyhill Ct. BL5 ... 57 F5
Dakerwood Cl. 3 M40 ... 83 C5
Dakins Rd. WN7 ... 76 B3
Dakley St. M11 ... 165 C7
Dakota Ave. M5 ... 96 F8
Dakota S. M5 ... 96 F8
Dalbeatie Rise. WN1 ... 37 F1
Dalbeattie St. M9 ... 64 E1
Dalberg St. M12 ... 164 D7
Dalbury Dr. M40 ... 156 C5
Dalby Ave. M27 ... 79 E7
Dalby Gr. SK1 ... 112 A1
Dalby Rd. WN2 ... 57 B5
Dale Ave. Bramhall SK7 ... 132 F8
Dale Ave. Eccles M30 ... 79 C3
Dale Ave. Uppermill OL5 ... 68 E3
Dale Brook Ave. SK16 ... 101 D6
Dale Fields. OL3 ... 50 F4
Dale Gr. Alt'ham WA15 ... 119 F7
Dale Gr. Ashton-u-L OL7 ... 85 A5
Dale Gr. Irlam M44 ... 105 E6
Dale Gr. Leigh WN7 ... 75 C4
Dale Grove Sch. OL7 ... 85 A5
Dale House. OL2 ... 149 B6
Dale House Fold. SK12 ... 134 A4
Dale Ind Est. M26 ... 44 A2
Dale La. OL3 ... 50 F5
Dale Lee. BL5 ... 58 A8
Dale Prim Sch The. SK6 ... 125 D7

Dale Rd. Golborne WA3 ... 90 A7
Dale Rd. Marple SK6 ... 125 E7
Dale Rd. Middleton M24 ... 47 B2
Dale Sq. Alt'ham WA14 ... 119 D7
Dale Sq. Royton OL2 ... 48 F4
Dale St. Alt'ham WA14 ... 119 D7
Dale St. Ashton-u-L OL6 ... 86 A6
Dale St. 8 Bacup OL13 ... 3 C8
Dale St. Bury BL8 ... 27 C4
Dale St. Farnworth BL4 ... 42 E1
Dale St. Ince-i-M WN2 ... 55 F3
Dale St. Leigh WN7 ... 75 C5
Dale St. M'ster M1, M4, M60 159 B1
Dale St. Middleton M24 ... 65 B7
Dale St. Milnrow OL16 ... 31 F6
Dale St. R'dale OL16 ... 31 C7
Dale St. Ramsbottom BL0 ... 1 C1
Dale St. Shaw OL2 ... 149 B6
Dale St. Stalybridge SK15 ... 85 F1
Dale St. Stockport SK3 ... 170 D7
Dale St. Swinton M27 ... 79 E6
Dale St. Westhoughton BL5 ... 57 F5
Dale St. Whitefield M45 ... 44 E1
Dale St E. Ashton-u-L OL7 ... 166 A2
Dale St E. Horwich BL6 ... 22 D2
Dale St W. Ashton-u-L OL7 .. 166 A2
Dale St W. Horwich BL6 ... 22 D2
Dale View. Denton M34 ... 113 A7
Dale View. Hyde SK14 ... 113 D8
Dale View. Littleborough OL15 15 F2
Dale View. Mottram-i-L SK14 103 A3
Dale View. Newton-l-W WA12 89 E4
Dalebank. M46 ... 58 C5
Dalebank Mews. M27 ... 61 D5
Dalebeck Cl. M45 ... 63 C8
Dalebeck Wlk. M45 ... 63 C8
Dalebrook Ct. SK4 ... 168 C1
Dalebrook Rd. M33 ... 108 C1
Dalecrest. WN5 ... 53 D1
Daleford Sq. M13 ... 163 C7
Dalegarth Ave. BL1 & BL6 ... 40 C7
Dalehead Cl. M18 ... 99 F6
Dalehead Dr. OL2 ... 49 D7
Dalehead Gr. WN7 ... 75 C4
Dalehead Pl. WA11 ... 71 B1
Dales Ave. M'ster M8 ... 63 F2
Dales Ave. Whitefield M45 ... 44 D1
Dales Brow. Bolton BL7 ... 24 F6
Dales Brow. Swinton M27 ... 79 E6
Dales Brow Ave. OL7 ... 85 A5
Dales Gr. M28 ... 60 F1
Dales La. M45 ... 44 E1
Dales Park Dr. M27 ... 79 D6
Dalesbrook Cl. BL3 ... 43 A4
Dalesfield Cres. OL5 ... 68 E1
Dalesford Cl. WN7 ... 91 C8
Daleside Ave. WN4 ... 73 A8
Dalesman Wlk. 3 M15 ... 163 A6
Daleswood Ave. M45 ... 44 D1
Dalham Ave. M9 ... 65 A2
Dalkeith Ave. SK5 ... 111 F7
Dalkeith Gr. BL3 ... 40 F5
Dalkeith Rd. Hindley WN2 ... 57 A5
Dalkeith Rd. Reddish SK5 ... 111 F7
Dalkeith Sq. OL10 ... 29 A1
Dalkeith St. M18 ... 165 B6
Dallas Ct. M5 ... 96 E8
Dalley Ave. M7 ... 158 D4
Dallimore Rd. M23 ... 120 E6
Dalmahoy Cl. M40 ... 83 C8
Dalmain Cl. M7 & M8 ... 155 F6
Dalmeny Terr. OL11 ... 30 F4
Dalmorton Rd. M21 ... 109 D8
Dalny St. M19 ... 99 B1
Dalry Wlk. 1 M23 ... 121 A5
Dalrybrook Gr. 7 SK9 ... 131 E1
Dalston Ave. M35 ... 84 B8
Dalston Dr. Billinge WA11 ... 71 B1
Dalston Dr. Bramhall SK7 ... 132 C5
Dalston Dr. M'ster M20 ... 110 C2
Dalston Gr. WN3 ... 54 D3
Dalton Ave. M'ster M14 ... 98 A2
Dalton Ave. Milnrow OL16 ... 31 D7
Dalton Ave. Stretford M32 ... 96 A4
Dalton Ave. Swinton M27 ... 62 C3
Dalton Ave. Whitefield M45 ... 63 A7
Dalton Cl. Milnrow OL16 ... 31 D7
Dalton Cl. Ramsbottom BL0 ... 11 A4
Dalton Cl. Wigan WN5 ... 54 B7
Dalton Ct. M40 ... 159 B4
Dalton Dr. Pendlebury M27 ... 80 D7
Dalton Dr. Wigan WN3 ... 54 E2
Dalton Fold. BL5 ... 57 F8
Dalton Gdns. M41 ... 95 B3
Dalton Gr. Ashton-i-M WN4 ... 73 A4
Dalton Gr. M'ster SK4 ... 168 C4
Dalton House. 6 M14 ... 110 D8
Dalton Rd. M'ster M9 ... 64 D5
Dalton Rd. Middleton M24 ... 64 B7
Dalton St. Bury BL8 ... 27 B2
Dalton St. Chadderton OL9 ... 152 B7
Dalton St. Eccles M30 ... 79 D3
Dalton St. Failsworth M35 ... 83 E8
Dalton St. M'ster M40 ... 159 B4
Dalton St. Oldham OL1 & OL4 . 67 B7
Dalton St. Sale M33 ... 108 C6
Daltry St. OL1 ... 67 A8
Dalveen Ave. M41 ... 95 C4
Dalveen Dr. WA15 ... 119 F7
Dalwood Cl. WN2 ... 56 F4
Dalymount Cl. BL2 ... 25 B2
Dam Head Dr. M9 ... 64 E3
Dam Head La. WA3 ... 105 A5
Dam La. Ashton-i-M WA3 ... 73 F3
Dam La. Hollinfare WA3 ... 105 A4
Damask Ave. M3 ... 158 D2
Dame Hollow. SK8 ... 131 D7
Dame St. OL9 ... 153 D8
Dameny Ct. SK7 ... 132 E8
Dameral Cl. M7 & M8 ... 156 A6
Damery Rd. SK7 ... 132 E8
Damian Dr. WA12 ... 89 A5
Damien St. M12 ... 99 B2
Dams Head Fold. BL5 ... 39 F1
Damson Wlk. M31 ... 105 D3
Dan Bank. SK6 ... 125 C6
Dan Fold. OL1 ... 153 E7
Danbury Wlk. M23 ... 120 D8
Danby Cl. SK14 ... 167 F4
Danby Ct. 6 OL1 ... 153 E8
Danby Pl. SK14 ... 167 F4
Danby Rd. Bolton BL3 ... 147 E3
Danby Rd. Hyde SK14 ... 167 F4
Danby Wlk. M9 ... 64 E1
Dane Ave. Cheadle SK3 ... 123 A8
Dane Ave. Partington M31 ... 105 F4
Dane Bank Cty Prim Sch.
M34 ... 100 A2
Dane Bank Dr. SK12 ... 135 D6
Dane Cl. SK7 ... 123 D3
Dane Dr. SK9 ... 137 D6
Dane Hill Cl. SK12 ... 135 D5
Dane Rd. Reddish M34 ... 100 A2
Dane Rd. Sale M33 ... 108 D5
Dane Road Sta. M33 ... 108 C6
Dane St. Bolton BL3 ... 146 C4
Dane St. M'ster M18 ... 99 E7
Dane St. Mossley OL5 ... 68 D3
Dane St. 7 Oldham OL4 ... 67 C7
Dane St. R'dale OL11 ... 139 E7
Dane Wlk. SK5 ... 169 F4
Danebank Mews. M34 ... 100 B2
Danebank Wlk. 14 M13 ... 163 B7
Danebridge Cl. BL4 ... 60 E8
Danebury Cl. WN2 ... 56 D4
Danecroft Cl. M13 ... 164 D5
Danefield Ct. SK8 ... 131 D8
Danefield Rd. M33 ... 108 C6
Daneholme Rd. M19 ... 110 E5
Danes Ave. WN2 ... 56 E6
Danes Brook Cl. WN2 ... 56 E6
Danes Gn. WN2 ... 56 E7
Danes Rd. M14 ... 98 D2
Danesbury Cl. WN5 ... 71 E4
Danesbury Rd. BL1 & BL2 ... 25 B4
Danesbury Rise. SK8 ... 122 D5
Daneshill. M25 ... 63 B6
Danesmoor Dr. BL9 ... 141 B4
Danesmoor Rd. M20 ... 110 B5
Danesway. M'ster M25 ... 63 D2
Danesway. Pendlebury M27 ... 80 C6
Danesway. Wigan WN1 ... 37 B3
Danesway Ct. BL1 ... 143 D2
Daneswood Ave. M'ster M9 . 64 F4
Daneswood Ave.
Whitworth OL12 ... 14 C8
Daneswood Cl. OL12 ... 14 C8
Danett Cl. M12 ... 165 B6
Danforth Gr. M19 ... 111 B8
Daniel Adamson Ave. M31 105 D3
Daniel Adamson Rd. M5 ... 154 D1
Daniel Ct. M31 ... 105 F4
Daniel Fold. OL12 ... 14 B2
Daniel St. Hazel Grove SK7 .. 124 E2
Daniel St. Heywood OL10 ... 29 B2
Daniel St. Oldham OL1 ... 67 C8
Daniel St. Royton OL2 ... 49 A3
Daniel St. Whitworth OL12 ... 4 D2
Daniel's La. SK1 ... 169 E2
Danisher La. OL8 ... 84 F8
Dannywood Cl. SK14 ... 113 C8
Danson St. M10 & M40 ... 160 E3
Dantall Ave. M9 ... 65 A3
Dante Cl. M6 ... 80 A4
Danty St. 25 SK16 ... 166 B1
Dantzic St. M4 & M60 & M8 159 A3
Danwood Cl. M34 ... 101 B1
Dapple Gr. M11 ... 165 A8
Darbishire St. BL1 ... 25 A1
Darby La. WN2 ... 56 D6
Darby Rd. M44 ... 106 A6
Darbyshire Cl. BL1 ... 144 C8
Darbyshire House. WA15 .. 120 C7
Darbyshire St. M26 ... 44 A3
Darbyshire Wlk. 1 M26 ... 44 B3
Darcy St. BL2 ... 148 C5
Darcy Wlk. M14 ... 98 A4
Darden Cl. SK4 ... 110 E3
Darell Wlk. M8 ... 156 B6
Darenth Cl. 5 M15 ... 162 F6
Daresbury Ave.
Alt'ham WA15 ... 119 E5
Daresbury Ave. Urmston M41 94 E4
Daresbury Cl. Sale M33 ... 108 F3
Daresbury Cl. Stockport SK3 170 D5
Daresbury Rd. M21 ... 96 F1
Daresbury St. M'ster M8 ... 156 A7
Daresham Wlk. 5 M16 ... 97 E4
Darfield Wlk. M40 ... 160 D3
Dargai St. M11 ... 83 D1
Dargle Rd. M33 ... 108 B6
Darian Ave. M22 ... 130 D8
Daric Cl. WN7 ... 75 C1
Dark La. Blackrod BL6 ... 21 B3
Dark La. Delph OL3 ... 50 E6
Dark La. M'ster M12 ... 164 D8
Dark La. Mossley OL5 ... 68 D2
Dark La. Uppermill OL3 ... 69 A8
Darlbeck Wlk. M21 ... 109 C5
Darley Ave. Eccles M30 ... 95 C8
Darley Ave. Farnworth BL4 ... 42 E1
Darley Ave. Gatley SK8 ... 122 B5
Darley Ave. M'ster M21 ... 109 C5
Darley Gr. BL4 ... 42 E1
Darley House. 5 M6 ... 154 E1
Darley Rd. Hazel Grove SK7 . 133 F7
Darley Rd. M'ster M16 ... 97 C3
Darley Rd. R'dale OL11 ... 30 F4
Darley Rd. Wigan WN3 ... 55 B3
Darley St. Bolton BL1 ... 143 D1
Darley St. Farnworth BL4 ... 60 E8
Darley St. Horwich BL6 ... 22 B5
Darley St. M'ster M11 ... 160 F1
Darley St. Sale M33 ... 108 B4
Darley St. Stretford M32 ... 96 E4
Darlington Cl. BL8 ... 27 B5
Darlington Rd. M'ster M20 110 A6
Darlington Rd. R'dale OL11 ... 30 F3
Darlington St. Ince-i-M WN2 56 A7
Darlington St. Tyldesley M29 59 A1
Darlington St. Wigan WN1 . 151 D7
Darlington St E.
Tyldesley M29 ... 59 B1
Darlington St E.Wigan WN1 151 E7
Darliston Ave. M9 ... 64 A5
Darlton Wlk. 9 M9 ... 157 E8
Darnall Ave. M14 ... 110 A8
Darnbrook Dr. 4 M22 ... 121 B1
Darncombe Cl. M16 ... 97 F4
Darnhall St. WN2 ... 55 F4
Darnhill Cty Prim Sch.
OL10 ... 28 F1
Darnley Ave. M28 ... 60 C1
Darnley St. M16 ... 97 D4
Darnton Rd. OL6 & SK15 ... 85 E3
Darran Ave. WN3 ... 54 F3
Darras Rd. M18 ... 99 C3
Dart Cl. OL9 ... 65 F8
Dartford Ave.
Brinnington SK5 ... 112 B6
Dartford Ave. Eccles M30 ... 79 B2
Dartford Cl. M12 ... 164 D6
Dartford Rd. M41 ... 95 C1
Dartington Cl. Alt'ham M23 120 D6
Dartington Cl. Stockport SK7 123 F2
Dartmouth Cl. 4 OL8 ... 66 F4
Dartmouth Cres. SK5 ... 112 C5
Dartmouth Rd. M'ster M21 109 C8
Dartmouth Rd.
Whitefield M45 ... 63 A7
Dartnall Cl. SK12 ... 135 A6
Darton Ave. M10 & M40 ... 160 E3
Darul-uloom Islamic Coll.
BL8 ... 10 F4
Darvel Ave. WN4 ... 72 C4
Darvel Cl. BL2 ... 42 F6
Darwell Ave. M30 ... 95 C8
Darwen Rd. Bolton BL7 ... 25 A7
Darwen St. M16 ... 161 C5
Darwin Gr. SK7 ... 132 E6
Darwin St. Bolton BL1 ... 143 D2
Darwin St. Dukinfield SK14 .. 102 A5
Darwin St. Oldham OL4 ... 67 C5
Dashwood Rd. M25 ... 62 F5
Dashwood Wlk. M12 ... 165 A6
Datchett Terr. OL11 ... 30 F4
Dauntesy Ave. M27 ... 80 D7
Davehall Ave. SK9 ... 137 A7
Davenfield Gr. M20 ... 110 B3
Davenfield Rd. 2 M20 ... 110 B3
Davenham Rd.
Handforth SK9 ... 131 D4
Davenham Rd. Reddish SK5 .. 99 F2
Davenham Rd. Sale M33 ... 107 F6
Davenhill Rd. M19 ... 111 A8
Davenport Ave. M'ster M20 110 B7
Davenport Ave. Radcliffe M26 43 F6
Davenport Ave.
Wilmslow SK9 ... 136 E4
Davenport Dr. SK6 ... 113 B6
Davenport Fold. BL2 ... 26 A3
Davenport Fold Rd. BL2 ... 26 A4
Davenport Gdns. 10 BL1 ... 145 E8
Davenport La. WA14 ... 119 C7
Davenport Lodge. SK3 ... 170 F5
Davenport Park Rd. SK2 ... 124 A5
Davenport Rd.
Alt'ham WA14 ... 119 C7
Davenport Rd.
Hazel Grove SK7 ... 124 D2
Davenport Sch. SK3 ... 123 F4
Davenport St. Bolton BL1 ... 145 E8
Davenport St. Denton M34 . 100 E8
Davenport St. Droylsden M43 83 E1
Davenport Sta. SK3 ... 170 F5
Daventry Rd. M'ster M21 ... 109 D8
Daventry Rd. R'dale OL11 ... 30 F3
Davey La. SK9 ... 137 B2
Daveyhulme St. OL12 ... 15 B1
Daveylands. Urmston M41 ... 94 F5
Daveylands. Wilmslow SK9 . 137 D7
David Brow. BL3 ... 146 A2
David Cl. M34 ... 101 A1
David Lewis Cl. OL16 ... 31 C6
David Mews. M14 ... 110 C7
David Pegg Wlk. M40 ... 83 B5
David St. Bacup OL13 ... 3 D8
David St. Bury BL8 ... 27 C4
David St. Denton M34 ... 101 A2
David St. 2 Oldham OL1 ... 153 E6
David St. 16 R'dale OL12 ... 14 F1
David St. Reddish SK5 ... 111 E8
David St N. 15 OL12 ... 14 F1
David's Farm Cl. M24 ... 65 C7
David's Rd. M43 ... 83 E2
Davids La. OL4 ... 67 F7
Davidson Dr. M24 ... 65 B6
Davidson Wlk. WN5 ... 54 E7
Davies Ave.Gatley SK8 ... 131 B6
Davies Ave Newton-l-W WA12 89 C4
Davies Rd. Bredbury SK6 ... 112 D3
Davies Rd. Partington M31 ... 106 A3
Davies Sq. M14 ... 98 A4
Davies St. Ashton-u-L OL7 ... 84 F1
Davies St. Kearsley BL4 ... 61 A7
Davies St. Oldham OL1 ... 153 D8
Davies St. Platt Bridge WN2 ... 56 A2
Davis St. M30 ... 79 F1
Davy Ave. M27 ... 62 D2
Davy St. M40 ... 159 B4
Davyhulme Circ. M41 ... 95 C4
Davyhulme Cty
Jun & Inf Sch.M41 ... 95 D3
Davyhulme Park
Golf Course.M41 ... 94 F3
Davyhulme Rd. Stretford M32 96 C3
Davyhulme Rd. Urmston M41 94 F4
Davyhulme Rd. Urmston M41 95 B4
Davyhulme Rd E. M32 ... 96 D3
Daw Bank. SK3 ... 169 E1
Dawber St. WN4 ... 73 D4
Dawes St. BL3 ... 145 F6
Dawley Cl. Ashton-i-M WN4 ... 73 A3
Dawley Cl. Bolton BL3 ... 144 C6
Dawlish Ave.
Brinnington SK5 ... 112 C5
Dawlish Ave. Chadderton OL9 47 F1
Dawlish Ave. Cheadle SK8 ... 131 F7
Dawlish Ave. Droylsden M43 . 83 E1
Dawlish Cl. Bramhall SK7 ... 132 E7
Dawlish Cl. Hattersley SK14 102 E3
Dawlish Cl. Hollinfare WA3 . 105 B3
Dawlish Rd. M'ster M21 ... 109 C8
Dawlish Rd. Sale M33 ... 107 E5
Dawn St. OL2 ... 149 B6
Dawnay St. M11 ... 165 B7
Dawnwood Sq. WN5 ... 36 C2
Dawson Ave. WN6 ... 37 A3
Dawson La. BL1 ... 145 E7
Dawson Rd. Alt'ham WA14 . 119 D8
Dawson Rd. Gatley SK8 ... 131 D8
Dawson St. Atherton M46 ... 58 C3
Dawson St. Bury BL9 ... 141 A4
Dawson St. Heywood OL10 ... 29 C2
Dawson St. Hyde SK14 ... 167 E1
Dawson St. M'ster M3 ... 158 F2
Dawson St. M'ster M15 ... 162 D8
Dawson St. 5 Oldham OL4 .. 67 D6
Dawson St. Oldham OL4 ... 67 E5
Dawson St. R'dale OL12 ... 139 F8
Dawson St. Stockport SK1 ... 112 B3
Dawson St. Swinton M27 ... 80 A8
Day Dr. M35 ... 83 F6
Day Gr. SK14 ... 103 A3
Dayfield. WN8 ... 53 B7
Daylesford Cl. SK8 ... 122 D4
Daylesford Cres. SK8 ... 122 D4
Daylesford Rd. SK8 ... 122 D4
De La Salle Coll. M6 ... 80 C3
De Lacy Dr. BL2 ... 25 B1
De Quincey Cl. WA14 ... 107 D1
De Quincey Rd. WA14 ... 107 D1
De Trafford Dr. WN2 ... 56 B8
De Trafford Ho. 13 M30 ... 79 D1
De Traffords The. M44 ... 94 B3
De-Massey Cl. SK6 ... 113 B6
Deacon Ave. Swinton M27 ... 61 E1
Deacon Cl. WA14 ... 119 B1
Deacon St. OL16 ... 15 B1
Deacon Trad Est. WA12 ... 89 A2
Deacons Cl. SK1 ... 112 A1
Deacons Cres. BL8 ... 27 A5
Deacons Dr. M6 ... 80 D6
Deakin St. WN3 ... 151 E5
Deakins Bsns Pk. BL7 ... 8 D2
Deal Ave. SK5 ... 112 B6
Deal Cl. M40 ... 83 D5
Deal Sq. SK14 ... 167 E2
Deal St. Bolton BL3 ... 147 F3
Deal St. Bury BL9 ... 141 B2
Deal St. Hyde SK14 ... 167 E2
Deal St. M'ster M3 ... 158 E2
Deal Wlk. OL9 ... 152 A6
Dealey Rd. BL3 ... 146 A4
Dean Ave. Failsworth M40 ... 83 B6
Dean Ave. M'ster M16 ... 97 B3
Dean Bank Dr. OL16 ... 31 B1
Dean Bradley Ct. M40 ... 157 E6
Dean Brook Cl. M40 ... 83 B7
Dean Cl. Billinge WN5 ... 71 D3
Dean Cl. Edenfield BL0 ... 1 D3
Dean Cl. Farnworth BL4 ... 59 F8
Dean Cl. Handforth SK9 ... 131 C1
Dean Cl. Orrell WN8 ... 53 C7
Dean Cl. Partington M31 ... 105 F4
Dean Cl. Whitefield M45 ... 62 D7
Dean Cres. WN5 ... 54 B8
Dean Ct. Bolton BL1 ... 148 A8
Dean Ct. 11 Dukinfield SK16 166 B1
Dean Ct. Golborne WA3 ... 90 A7
Dean Ct. M'ster M15 ... 162 D6
Dean Ct. R'dale OL11 ... 30 F4
Dean Dr. Alt'ham WA14 ... 119 B1
Dean Dr. Handforth SK9 ... 131 D2
Dean La. Failsworth M40 ... 83 B6
Dean La. Hazel Grove SK7 ... 133 E8
Dean Lane Sta. M40 ... 83 B6
Dean Meadow. WA12 ... 89 C4
Dean Moor Rd. SK7 ... 124 A1
Dean Rd. Golborne WA3 ... 90 A7
Dean Rd. Handforth SK9 ... 131 E3
Dean Rd. Irlam M44 ... 105 E6
Dean Rd. M'ster M3 ... 158 E3
Dean Rd. Reddish M18 ... 99 E4
Dean Row Cty Jun Sch.
SK9 ... 131 E1
Dean Row Rd.Wilmslow SK9 137 F8
Dean St.
Ashton-u-L OL6 & OL7 ... 166 A3
Dean St. Failsworth M35 ... 83 E7
Dean St. M'ster M1 & M60 ... 159 B1
Dean St. Mossley OL5 ... 68 B1
Dean St. R'dale OL16 ... 15 B1
Dean St. Radcliffe M26 ... 43 F3
Dean St. Stalybridge SK15 ... 86 A1
Dean Villas. OL14 ... 6 B7
Dean Wlk. M24 ... 46 D2
Dean Wood Ave. WN5 ... 53 E8
Dean Wood Golf Crse. WN8 53 D8
Deanbank Ave. 2 M19 ... 110 F8
Deane Ave. Alt'ham WA15 ... 120 A5
Deane Ave. Bolton BL3 ... 144 B5
Deane Ave. Cheadle SK8 ... 122 F5
Deane Church La. BL3 ... 146 B4
Deane Rd. BL3 ... 145 D6
Deane Sch The. BL3 ... 40 F4
Deane Wlk. BL3 ... 145 E6
Deanery CE High Sch.
WN1 ... 150 B8
Deanery Gdns. M7 ... 155 D8
Deanery Way. SK1 ... 169 F2
Deanroyd Rd. OL14 ... 6 B7
Deans Prim Sch The. M27 .. 79 E8
Deans Rd. M27 ... 79 E7
Deanscourt Ave. M27 ... 79 E8
Deansgate. Bolton BL1 ... 145 E7
Deansgate. Hindley WN2 ... 56 E6
Deansgate.M'ster M1,M2,M3 158 F1
Deansgate.M'ster M15 ... 162 E7
Deansgate. Radcliffe M26 ... 44 B3
Deansgate La. WA14, WA15 119 E7
Deansgate Sta. M1 ... 162 E7
Deansgreave Rd. OL13 ... 4 B7
Deanshut Rd. OL8 ... 67 A2
Deansway. M27 ... 79 E8
Deanswood Dr. M9 ... 64 A5
Deanwater Cl. M13 ... 163 B7
Deanwater Ct.Gatley SK8 ... 131 C8
Deanwater Ct.Stretford M32 108 C8
Deanway. Handforth SK9 ... 131 C1
Deanway. M'ster M40 ... 83 A8
Deanway. Urmston M41 ... 94 D2
Deanway Trad Est. SK9 ... 131 D3
Dearden Ave. M38 ... 60 A5
Dearden Clough. BL0 ... 1 E2
Dearden Fold. BL0 ... 1 E2
Dearden St. Little Lever BL3 .. 43 A4
Dearden St.
Littleborough OL15 ... 16 B6
Dearden St. 12
Stalybridge SK15 ... 86 A2
Deardens Fold. BL8 ... 27 C1
Deardens St. BL8 ... 27 C1
Dearne Dr. M32 ... 96 E2
Dearnley CE Prim Sch.
OL12 ... 15 E4
Dearnley Cl. OL15 ... 15 E4
Debdale La.
Reddish M18 & M34 ... 99 F4
Debdale La. Tyldesley M29 ... 76 F4
Deben Cl. WN6 ... 19 D1
Debenham Ave. M40 ... 83 C4
Debenham Ct. BL4 ... 60 D7
Debenham Rd. M32 ... 96 A2
Dee Ave. WA15 ... 120 D5
Dee Dr. BL4 ... 61 B5
Dee Rd. M29 ... 77 C7
Deep La. Littleborough OL15 ... 16 C1
Deep La. Milnrow OL15 & OL16 32 B8
Deepcar St. M12 & M19 ... 99 A2
Deepdale. Leigh WN7 ... 76 C3
Deepdale. Oldham OL4 ... 67 D6
Deepdale Ave. Billinge WA11 71 C1
Deepdale Ave. M'ster M14 . 110 A8
Deepdale Ave. R'dale OL16 ... 31 C6
Deepdale Ave. Royton OL2 ... 48 C8
Deepdale Cl. SK5 ... 100 A1
Deepdale Cl. M9 ... 65 B3
Deepdale Dr. M27 ... 80 D7
Deepdale Rd. BL2 ... 25 F1
Deepdene St. M12 ... 164 F6
Deeping Ave. M16 ... 97 D2
Deeplish Prim Sch. OL11 ... 31 A5
Deeplish Rd. OL11 ... 139 F5
Deeplish St. OL11 ... 139 F5
Deeply Vale La. BL9 ... 12 C2
Deer St. M1 ... 163 C8
Deeracre Ave. SK2 ... 124 C6
Deerfold Cl. 6 M18 ... 99 D5
Deerhurst Dr. M7 & M8 ... 155 F6
Deeroak Cl. M18 ... 165 B6
Deerpark Rd. M16 ... 97 E3
Defence St. 8 BL3 ... 145 D6
Defiance St. M46 ... 58 C3
Deganwy Gr. SK5 ... 111 F5
Deighton Ave. M14 ... 110 A8
Delacourt Rd. M14 ... 110 B8
Delafield Ave. M12 ... 99 A2
Delaford Ave. M28 ... 78 E7
Delaford Cl. SK3 ... 123 E4
Delaford Wlk. M40 ... 83 D4
Delahays Lodge. WA15 ... 120 B5
Delahays Dr. WA15 ... 120 B2
Delahays Range. M18 & M34 99 F4
Delahays Rd. WA15 ... 120 B2
Delaine Rd. M20 ... 110 C6
Delamer Rd. WA14 ... 119 C3
Delamere Ave.Golborne WA3 90 E6
Delamere Ave.Pendlebury M6 80 C6
Delamere Ave. Sale M33 ... 108 E3
Delamere Ave. Shaw OL2 ... 30 F8
Delamere Ave. Stretford M32 96 D2
Delamere Ave. Swinton M27 . 62 B2
Delamere Ave.Whitefield M45 62 E8
Delamere Cl.
Hazel Grove SK7 ... 125 A3
Delamere Cl. Mossley SK15 .. 86 E6
Delamere Cl. Romiley SK6 .. 113 C5
Delamere Gdns. BL1 ... 143 D3
Delamere House. M14 ... 110 C8
Delamere Lodge. SK7 ... 124 D2
Delamere Rd. Gatley SK8 ... 122 B5
Delamere Rd. Handforth SK9 131 E4
Delamere Rd.
Hazel Grove SK7 ... 125 A3
Delamere Rd. M'ster M19 ... 99 B1
Delamere Rd. R'dale OL16 ... 31 C4
Delamere Rd. Reddish M34 100 B2
Delamere Rd. Stockport SK2 124 B4
Delamere Rd. Urmston M41 .. 94 F2
Delamere Sch. M41 ... 94 D2
Delamere St. Ashton-u-L OL6 166 B2
Delamere St. Bury BL9 ... 28 A5
Delamere St.
Droylsden M11 & M18 ... 99 F7
Delamere St. 6 Oldham OL8 67 B5
Delamere Way. WN8 ... 53 A7
Delaunays Rd. M'ster M8 ... 64 B2
Delaunays Rd. Sale M33 ... 107 F4
Delaware Wlk. M9 ... 157 D7
Delbooth Ave. M41 ... 94 E4
Delegarte St. WN3 ... 151 E6
Delfhaven Ct. WN6 ... 37 A7
Delft Wlk. M6 ... 81 A5
Delfur Rd. SK7 ... 132 F7
Delhi Rd. M44 ... 105 F8
Dell Ave. Pendlebury M27 ... 80 D7
Dell Ave. Wigan WN6 ... 36 E3
Dell Cl. OL4 ... 67 F5
Dell Gdns. OL12 ... 14 B2
Dell Meadow. OL12 ... 14 C5
Dell Rd. OL12 ... 14 B3
Dell Side. SK6 ... 112 E3
Dell Side Way. OL12 ... 14 C2
Dell St. BL2 ... 25 C5
Dell The. Appley Bridge WN6 . 35 D7
Dell The. Orrell WN8 ... 53 B7
Dellar St. OL12 ... 14 C1
Dellcot Cl. M'ster M25 ... 63 D2
Dellcot Cl. Pendlebury M6 ... 80 B5
Dellcot La. M28 ... 78 F5
Dellhide Cl. OL4 ... 68 A6
Dellside Cl. WN4 ... 72 D5
Dellside Gr. M28 ... 60 E3
Delph Ave. BL7 ... 8 D3
Delph Brook Way. BL7 ... 8 D2
Delph Gr. WN7 ... 57 D1
Delph Hill Cl. BL1 ... 23 E2
Delph La. Ainsworth BL2 ... 26 C1
Delph La. Delph OL3 ... 50 F5
Delph Lodge. OL3 ... 50 F3
Delph New Rd. OL3 ... 50 E2
Delph Prim Sch. OL3 ... 50 E5
Delph Rd. OL3 ... 50 C8
Delph St. Bolton BL3 ... 145 D5
Delph St. Milnrow OL16 ... 31 F6
Delph St. Wigan WN6 ... 37 B1
Delphi Ave. M28 ... 60 D2
Delphside Cl. WN5 ... 53 D5
Delphside Rd. WN5 ... 53 D5
Delside Ave. M40 ... 83 A8
Delta Cl. OL2 ... 48 D2
Delta Rd. M34 ... 100 E7
Delta Wlk. M40 ... 83 A7
Delvino Wlk. M14 ... 98 A4
Delwood Gdns. M22 ... 121 D3
Demesne Cl. SK15 ... 86 C1
Demesne Cres. SK15 ... 86 C1
Demesne Dr. SK15 ... 86 C1
Demesne Rd. M16 ... 97 E2
Demmings Inf Sch. SK8 ... 122 F5
Demmings Rd. SK8 ... 122 F5
Dempsey Dr. M45 ... 45 B2
Den Hill Dr. OL4 ... 67 F6
Den La. Oldham OL4 ... 67 F7
Den La. Uppermill OL3 ... 69 B8
Denbigh Cl. SK7 ... 133 C8
Denbigh Dr. OL2 ... 48 F6
Denbigh Gr. M46 ... 58 C5
Denbigh Pl. M5 ... 81 A2
Denbigh Rd. Bolton BL2 ... 148 B5
Denbigh Rd. Denton M34 ... 100 F1
Denbigh Rd. Swinton M27 ... 62 B2
Denbigh St. Mossley OL5 ... 86 D8
Denbigh St. Oldham OL8 ... 66 F3
Denbigh St. Stockport SK4 .. 169 D3
Denbigh Wlk. M15 ... 162 E5
Denbury Dr. WA14 ... 119 B5
Denbury Gn. SK7 ... 124 A1
Denbury Wlk. M9 ... 156 C6
Denby La. SK4 ... 169 D4
Denby Rd. SK16 ... 101 C7
Denbydale Way. OL2 ... 48 C4
Dencombe St. M13 ... 98 F4
Dene Bank. BL2 ... 25 C5
Dene Brow. M34 ... 113 B8
Dene Ct. SK4 ... 168 C2
Dene Dr. M24 ... 64 F7
Dene Gr. WN7 ... 75 B4
Dene Hollow. SK5 ... 100 A1
Dene Pk. M20 ... 110 A3
Dene Rd. M20 ... 110 A2
Dene Rd W. M20 ... 109 F3
Dene St. Bolton BL2 ... 25 C5
Dene St. Leigh WN7 ... 75 B4
Denefield Cl. SK6 ... 114 B1
Deneford Rd. M20 ... 110 A2
Denehurst Rd. OL11 ... 30 C8
Denehurst St. M12 ... 164 F6
Denes The. SK5 ... 99 F1
Deneside Cres. SK7 ... 124 F3
Deneside Wlk. 6 M9 ... 157 E8
Denesway. M33 ... 107 E3
Deneway. Bramhall SK7 ... 132 D7
Deneway. High Lane SK6 ... 134 F8
Deneway. Stockport SK4 ... 168 C2
Deneway Cl. SK4 ... 168 C2
Deneway Mews. SK4 ... 168 C2
Denewell Cl. M13 ... 164 D6
Denewood Ct. SK9 ... 137 A6
Denford Cl. WN3 ... 54 F3
Denham Cl. BL1 ... 25 A5
Denham Dr. Bramhall SK7 .. 132 D7
Denham Dr. Irlam M44 ... 94 A1
Denham Dr. Wigan WN3 ... 55 A3
Denham St. M'ster M13 ... 98 D4
Denham St. Radcliffe M26 ... 43 F6
Denhill Rd. M15 ... 162 F5
Denhill Road Ind Est. M15 162 F5
Denholm Rd. M20 ... 122 C8
Denholme. WN8 ... 53 A7
Denholme Rd. OL11 ... 30 F4
Denhurst Rd. OL15 ... 16 B6
Denis Ave. M16 ... 97 E2
Denison Ct. 7 M14 ... 98 C3
Denison Rd. Hazel Grove SK7 133 E8
Denison Rd. M'ster M14 ... 98 D3
Denison St. M14 ... 98 C3
Deniston Rd. SK4 ... 111 B5
Denman Wlk. 12 M7 ... 155 F6
Denmark Rd. M'ster M15 ... 98 A4
Denmark Rd. Sale M33 ... 108 B6
Denmark St. Alt'ham WA14 119 D4
Denmark St. Oldham OL4 ... 67 B7
Denmark St. Oldham OL9 ... 152 C8
Denmark St. R'dale OL16 ... 31 A8
Denmark Way. OL9 ... 152 C8
Denmore Rd. M40 ... 65 D3
Dennington Dr. M41 ... 95 C4
Dennis House. SK4 ... 168 B4
Dennison Ave. M20 ... 110 B7
Dennison Rd. SK8 ... 132 B8
Denshaw. WN8 ... 53 A7
Denshaw Ave. M34 ... 100 D5
Denshaw Cl. M19 ... 110 E3
Denshaw Rd. OL3 ... 50 D5
Densmead Wlk. 14 M40 ... 159 C3
Densmore St. 6 M35 ... 83 F7
Denson Rd. WA15 ... 120 B8
Denstone Ave. Eccles M30 ... 79 E3
Denstone Ave. Sale M33 ... 107 E3
Denstone Ave. Urmston M41 95 C3
Denstone Cres. BL2 ... 25 D2
Denstone Rd. Reddish SK5 ... 99 F1
Denstone Rd. Salford M6 ... 80 D5
Denstone Rd. Urmston M41 .. 95 C3
Denstone Wlk. 15 M9 ... 64 E3
Dent Cl. SK5 ... 112 C6
Dental Hospl. M15 ... 163 A6
Dentdale Cl. BL1 ... 40 D6
Dentdale Wlk. M22 ... 130 C8
Denton Golf Course. M34 . 100 B4
Denton Gr. WN5 ... 54 B8
Denton La. OL9 ... 152 A5
Denton Rd. Denton M34 ... 100 E6
Denton Rd. Little Lever BL3 ... 43 B6
Denton St. Bury BL9 ... 140 F4
Denton St. Heywood OL10 ... 29 C2
Denton St. 7 R'dale OL12 ... 14 F1
Denton Sta. M34 ... 100 C4
Denver Ave. M10 & M40 ... 160 D3

Drummond Way. WN7 76 B5
Drury La. OL9 66 B3
Drury St. 13 M19 99 A1
Dryad Cl. M27 61 F2
Drybrook Cl. M13 164 E5
Dryburgh Ave. BL1 143 D4
Dryclough Wlk. OL2 48 E3
Dryden Ave. Ashton-i-M WN4 72 F6
Dryden Ave. Cheadle SK8 122 F6
Dryden Ave. Swinton M27 79 D7
Dryden Cl. Dukinfield SK16 102 B7
Dryden Cl. Marple SK6 125 F4
Dryden Cl. Wigan WN3 150 A5
Dryden Rd. 4 M16 97 C3
Dryden St. M13 163 C6
Dryden Way. 10 M34 113 A8
Dryfield La. BL6 22 A5
Drygate Wlk. 6 M9 157 E7
Dryhurst Dr. SK12 135 D6
Dryhurst La. SK12 135 D6
Dryhurst Wlk. M15 163 A6
Drymoss. Oldham OL8 67 A1
Dryton Wlk. WN2 38 A2
Drywood Ave. M28 79 A5
Ducal St. M40 159 B3
Duchess Park Cl. OL2 149 B8
Duchess Rd. M8 156 B8
Duchess St. OL2 149 B8
Duchess Wlk. BL3 146 B4
Duchy Ave. Atherton BL5 59 A8
Duchy Ave. Walkden M28 78 D8
Duchy Bank. M6 80 D6
Duchy Rd. M6 80 E5
Duchy St. Salford M6 154 F3
Duchy St. Stockport SK3 170 D7
Ducie Ave. BL1 144 C7
Ducie Central High Sch. M14 98 B4
Ducie Central High Sch for Boys. M14 98 D4
Ducie Gr. M15 163 B5
Ducie St. M'ster M1 & M60 159 B1
Ducie St. Oldham OL8 66 F2
Ducie St. Radcliffe M26 43 F5
Ducie St. Whitefield M45 62 F8
Duckshaw La. BL4 60 D8
Duckworth La. BB4 1 E8
Duckworth Rd. M25 62 F3
Duckworth St. 3 Bury BL9 141 A4
Duckworth St. Shaw OL2 149 C7
Duddon Ave. BL2 25 F1
Duddon Cl. Standish WN6 36 F7
Duddon Cl. Whitefield M45 63 C8
Duddon Wlk. 24 M24 46 E2
Dudley Ave. Bolton BL2 25 C1
Dudley Ave. Whitefield M45 62 F8
Dudley Cl. M15 162 E5
Dudley Ct. 10 M16 97 D3
Dudley Rd. Irlam M44 105 D4
Dudley Rd. M'ster M16 97 D3
Dudley Rd. Sale M33 108 C6
Dudley Rd. Sale WA15 120 B7
Dudley Rd. Swinton M27 61 F1
Dudley St. Ashton-i-M WN4 73 A5
Dudley St. Denton M34 100 E4
Dudley St. Eccles M30 79 C1
Dudley St. M'ster M7 & M8 155 F6
Dudley St. 6 Oldham OL4 67 D6
Dudlow Wlk. 24 M15 162 D6
Dudwell Cl. BL1 142 C2
Duerden St. BL3 146 A2
Duffield Ct. M15 163 A5
Duffield Gdns. M9 64 F5
Duffield Rd. Middleton M9 64 F5
Duffield Rd. Salford M6 80 D5
Duffins Cl. OL12 14 D3
Dufton Wlk. 1 Middleton M24 46 E2
Dufton Wlk. Wythenshawe M22 130 E8
Dugdale Ave. M9 64 E4
Dugie St. BL0 138 B7
Duice Pl. M5 81 C1
Duke Ave. Cheadle SK8 131 F6
Duke Ave. Glazebury WA3 92 C7
Duke Ct. M16 162 D5
Duke of Norfolk's CE Prim Sch. Glossop SK13 104 D1
Duke of Norfolk's CE Prim Sch. Glossop SK13 104 E2
Duke Pl. M3 162 E8
Duke Rd. Ainsworth BL2 26 C1
Duke Rd. Dukinfield SK14 101 F5
Duke St. Alderley Edge SK9 137 B2
Duke St. Ashton-i-M WN4 73 C3
Duke St. Ashton-u-L OL6 166 B3
Duke St. Bolton BL1 145 E8
Duke St. Denton M34 100 E3
Duke St. Failsworth M35 84 A8
Duke St. Golborne WA3 74 A1
Duke St. Heywood OL10 29 B2
Duke St. Leigh WN7 76 A4
Duke St. Littleborough OL15 16 A5
Duke St. M'ster M7 155 D5
Duke St. M'ster M3 158 F2
Duke St. M'ster M3 162 E8
Duke St. Mossley OL5 68 E1
Duke St. Newton-l-W WA12 89 B3
Duke St. Platt Bridge WN2 56 A3
Duke St. R'dale OL12 14 F1
Duke St. Radcliffe M26 44 B2
Duke St. Ramsbottom BL0 11 A4
Duke St. Rawtenstall BB4 2 E8
Duke St. Shaw OL2 149 C6
Duke St. Stalybridge SK15 85 F1
Duke St. Stockport SK1 169 F1
Duke St. Swinton M28 79 C4
Duke St. Tyldesley M29 77 C6
Duke St. Walkden M38 60 A5
Duke St. Walkden M27 & M28 61 A2
Duke St. Wigan WN1 37 C2
Duke St. Wigan WN3 54 F4
Duke St N. BL1 145 E8
Duke's Terr. 17 SK16 166 B1
Dukefield St. M22 121 E8
Dukes Ave. BL3 43 A4
Dukes Platting. OL6 85 F5
Dukes St. SK13 116 C8
Dukesgate Cty Prim Sch. M38 60 A5
Dukinfield Astley High Sch. SK16 101 E6
Dukinfield Golf Course. SK16 102 A6
Dukinfield Rd. SK14 101 C4
Dukinfield St. 6 WN7 76 A5
Dulford Wlk. M13 163 C5
Dulgar St. M11 165 B8
Dulverton St. M40 83 B6
Dulwich St. M40 159 B3
Dumbarton Cl. SK5 111 F6
Dumbarton Dr. OL10 46 A8
Dumbarton Gn. WN6 36 E2
Dumbarton Rd. Heywood OL10 29 A1
Dumbarton Rd. Reddish SK5 111 F6
Dumbell St. M27 61 F2
Dumber La. M33 107 F6
Dumers Cl. M26 44 D4
Dumers La. BL9 & M26 44 E5
Dumfries Ave. OL3 33 C2
Dumfries Dr. OL3 33 C2
Dumfries Wlk. OL10 29 A1
Dumplington Circ. M41 95 D7
Dun Cl. M3 158 D2
Dunbar Ave. M23 121 A3
Dunbar Gr. OL10 45 F8
Dunbar St. OL1 153 E8
Dunblane Ave. Bolton BL3 40 E5
Dunblane Ave. Stockport SK4 169 D2
Dunblane Cl. WN4 72 C4
Dunblane Gr. OL10 46 A8
Duncan Ave. WA12 89 C5
Duncan Edwards House. 13 M6 154 F3
Duncan Pl. WN5 54 E7
Duncan Rd. M13 98 F3
Duncan St. Bolton BL1 145 F8
Duncan St. Dukinfield SK16 101 C6
Duncan St. Horwich BL6 22 C3
Duncan St. M'ster M7 81 C6
Duncan St. Salford M5 161 C8
Dunchurch Cl. BL6 40 D6
Dunchurch Rd. M33 107 E4
Duncombe Cl. SK7 124 A3
Duncombe Dr. M40 83 B7
Duncombe Rd. BL3 147 E2
Duncombe St. M7 155 E6
Duncote Gr. OL2 149 A5
Dundee Cl. OL10 28 F1
Dundee La. BL0 138 B6
Dundonald Rd. Cheadle SK8 132 A7
Dundonald Rd. M'ster M20 110 C3
Dundonald St. SK2 170 F6
Dundraw Cl. M24 46 B1
Dundrennan Cl. SK12 133 D5
Dunecroft. M34 101 A4
Dunedin Dr. M6 80 F6
Dunedin Rd. BL8 10 F2
Dunelm Dr. M23 108 D1
Dunford Wlk. M40 65 C3
Dunham Ave. WA3 73 F1
Dunham Cl. BL5 57 D5
Dunham Forest Golf Course. WA14 118 F4
Dunham Gr. WA3 & WN7 76 C2
Dunham Lawn. WA14 119 B4
Dunham Pk. WA14 118 D3
Dunham Rd. Alt'ham WA14 118 F1
Dunham Rd. Alt'ham WA14 119 B4
Dunham Rd. Dukinfield SK16 101 D6
Dunham Rd. Partington M31 106 D3
Dunham Rd. Partington WA13 117 E7
Dunham Rise. WA14 119 C4
Dunham St. OL4 67 E8
Dunkeld Gdns. 2 M23 120 F6
Dunkeld Rd. M23 120 F6
Dunkerley Ave. M35 83 F7
Dunkerley St. Ashton-u-L OL7 85 A5
Dunkerley St. Oldham OL4 67 C7
Dunkerley St. Royton OL2 48 D4
Dunkerleys Cl. M8 155 F8
Dunkery Rd. M22 121 D1
Dunkirk Cl. M34 100 A2
Dunkirk La. SK14 101 B4
Dunkirk Rd. M45 44 F1
Dunkirk Rise. OL12 139 E7
Dunkirk St. M43 84 B1
Dunley Cl. M12 165 A5
Dunlin Ave. WA12 89 C4
Dunlin Cl. Bolton BL2 148 A5
Dunlin Cl. Hazel Grove SK7 125 A5
Dunlin Cl. Poynton SK12 133 A4
Dunlin Cl. R'dale OL11 29 F7
Dunlin Dr. M44 94 A3
Dunlin Wlk. WA14 119 B8
Dunlop Ave. OL11 30 E4
Dunlop St. 2 M3 158 F1
Dunmail Ave. WA11 71 C1
Dunmail Cl. M29 77 C6
Dunmail Dr. M24 46 E3
Dunmere Wlk. M9 156 C6
Dunmore Rd. SK8 122 B6
Dunmow Ct. SK2 124 E5
Dunmow Wlk. M23 109 A2
Dunne La. SK13 104 E2
Dunnerdale Wlk. M18 165 C5
Dunnisher Rd. M23 121 B5
Dunnock Cl. SK2 124 F5
Dunollie Rd. M33 108 E3
Dunoon Cl. OL10 29 A1
Dunoon Dr. BL1 24 C5
Dunoon Rd. Aspull WN2 38 D5
Dunoon Rd. Reddish SK5 111 F7
Dunoon Wlk. M9 157 D7
Dunrobin Cl. OL10 46 A8
Dunscar Cl. M45 62 D7
Dunscar Golf Course. BL7 8 C1
Dunscar Ind Est. BL7 24 E7
Dunscar Sq. BL7 24 F8
Dunscore Rd. WN3 54 E3
Dunsdale Dr. WN4 73 C3
Dunsfold Dr. M23 120 D8
Dunsford Ct. OL4 67 F5
Dunsley Ave. M40 65 D2
Dunsmore Cl. M16 97 E4
Dunsop Dr. BL1 23 F3
Dunstable. 9 OL12 139 F8
Dunstable St. M19 99 B1
Dunstall Rd. M22 121 E5
Dunstan Cl. M40 83 A8
Dunstan St. BL2 148 C7
Dunstar Ave. M34 100 E7
Dunster Ave. Brinnington SK5 112 C5
Dunster Ave. M'ster M9 64 E4
Dunster Ave. R'dale OL11 139 E5
Dunster Ave. Swinton M27 62 B2
Dunster Cl. Hazel Grove SK7 124 C1
Dunster Cl. Platt Bridge WN2 56 A1
Dunster Dr. M41 94 C1
Dunster Pl. M28 77 F7
Dunster Rd. M28 77 F7
Dunsters Ave. BL8 27 C5
Dunsterville Terr. OL11 139 E5
Dunston St. M11 165 C8
Dunton Gn. SK5 112 B6
Dunton Towers. SK5 112 B6
Dunvegan Ct. OL10 28 F1
Dunvegan Rd. SK7 124 F1
Dunwood Ave. OL2 149 C8
Dunwoods Park Cts. OL2 32 C1
Dunworth St. M14 98 B3
Durant St. M4 159 B3
Durban Cl. OL2 149 A6
Durban Rd. BL1 24 E5
Durban St. Ashton-u-L OL7 84 E1
Durban St. Atherton M46 58 C2
Durban St. Leigh WN2 & WN7 74 E4
Durban St. Oldham OL8 66 C3
Durban St. R'dale OL11 30 C2
Durden Mews. OL2 149 B6
Durham Ave. M41 95 E3
Durham Cl. Dukinfield SK16 101 D6
Durham Cl. Little Lever BL3 43 B4
Durham Cl. Romiley SK6 113 A1
Durham Cl. Swinton M27 61 F2
Durham Cl. Tyldesley M29 59 A3
Durham Cres. M35 84 A6
Durham Dr. Ashton-u-L OL6 85 D8
Durham Dr. Bury BL9 45 A8
Durham Dr. Ramsbottom BL0 11 B3
Durham Gr. M44 105 C6
Durham House. 6 SK3 170 E8
Durham Rd. Handforth SK9 131 D5
Durham Rd. 3 Hindley WN2 56 E5
Durham Rd. Pendlebury M6 80 C4
Durham St. Bolton BL1 143 F2
Durham St. Droylsden M43 100 A8
Durham St. 12 M'ster M9 157 E7
Durham St. Oldham OL9 66 C4
Durham St. R'dale OL11 31 A5
Durham St. Radcliffe M26 44 C5
Durham St. Reddish SK5 99 E2
Durham St. Wigan WN1 37 E1
Durham Wlk. 5 Denton M34 100 F1
Durham Wlk. Heywood OL10 29 A2
Durley Ave. M'ster M8 156 B7
Durley Ave. Sale WA15 120 B7
Durling St. M12 163 C7
Durn St. OL15 16 C6
Durnford Ave. M41 96 A2
Durnford Cl. OL12 13 D2
Durnford St. M24 46 F1
Durnford Wlk. M22 121 B3
Durrell Way. WA3 90 E8
Durrington Wlk. M40 65 C3
Dursley Dr. WN4 73 D4
Dutton Gr. WN7 76 C2
Dutton St. M3 158 F3
Duty St. BL1 143 E3
Duxbury Ave. Bolton BL2 25 E5
Duxbury Ave. Little Lever BL3 43 A5
Duxbury Dr. BL9 141 C2
Duxbury St. BL1 143 D2
Duxford Lodge. M8 63 F2
Dyche St. M4 159 B3
Dyche Street Trad Est. M4 159 B3
Dye House La. New Mills SK12 127 C1
Dye House La. R'dale OL12 & OL16 15 C3
Dye La. SK6 113 B2
Dyer St. Golborne WA3 73 F1
Dyer St. M'ster M11 165 A8
Dyer St. Salford M5 161 C7
Dyers Cl. WA13 117 A4
Dyers Ct. OL15 16 A6
Dyers La. WA13 117 A4
Dymchurch Ave. M26 61 C7
Dymchurch St. M40 83 C4
Dysart St. 4 Ashton-u-L OL6 85 D2
Dysart St. Stockport SK2 124 B5
Dysarts Cl. OL5 68 E3
Dyserth Gr. SK5 169 F4
Dyson Cl. BL4 60 D8
Dyson Gr. OL4 67 F8
Dyson St. Farnworth BL4 60 D7
Dyson St. Mossley OL5 68 B2
Dyson St. Oldham OL1 153 F6
Dystelegh Rd. SK12 135 D6

Eades St. M6 81 A3
Eadington St. M8 64 A1
Eafield Ave. OL16 31 F7
Eafield Cl. OL16 31 F7
Eafield Rd. Littleborough OL15 & OL16 15 E3
Eafield Rd. R'dale OL16 15 C1
Eagar St. M35 83 C6
Eagle Ct. M16 162 E5
Eagle Dr. M6 81 A5
Eagle Mill Ct. OL3 50 F5
Eagle St. Bolton BL2 148 A7
Eagle St. 5 M'ster M4 159 A2
Eagle St. Oldham OL9 153 E6
Eagle St. R'dale OL11 & OL16 31 A6
Eagle Tech Pk. OL11 31 A4
Eagles Nest. M25 63 A3
Eagley Bank. OL12 4 E6
Eagley Brow. BL7 24 F7
Eagley Dr. BL8 27 A1
Eagley Ind Est. BL7 24 F7
Eagley Inf Sch. BL7 25 A8
Eagley Jun Sch. BL7 25 B8
Eagley Way. BL1 & BL7 24 F7
Ealees. OL15 16 C5
Ealees Rd. OL15 16 C5
Ealing Ave. M14 98 C2
Ealing Pl. M19 111 A6
Eames Ave. M26 61 A8
Eamont Wlk. M9 157 D7
Earby Gr. M9 64 F3
Earl Rd. Handforth SK8 & SK9 131 E5
Earl Rd. M'ster SK4 168 C4
Earl Rd. Ramsbottom BL0 138 B6
Earl St. Atherton M46 58 B2
Earl St. Bury BL9 140 F2
Earl St. 6 Heywood OL10 29 C2
Earl St. Ince-i-M WN2 56 A7
Earl St. Leigh WN7 76 A4
Earl St. M'ster M7 158 D4
Earl St. Middleton OL11 47 D8
Earl St. Mossley OL5 68 B1
Earl St. Prestwich M25 63 C4
Earl St. Ramsbottom BL0 11 D6
Earl St. Reddish M34 100 A4
Earl St. Sale M33 108 C5
Earl St. Stockport SK3 170 D8
Earl St. Wigan WN1 37 C1
Earl Terr. 16 SK16 166 B1
Earl Wlk. M12 164 F5
Earl's Lodge. M35 83 D6
Earle Rd. SK7 123 E3
Earle St. Ashton-u-L OL7 84 F2
Earle St. Newton-l-W WA12 89 A3
Earlesdon Cres. M38 60 A5
Earlestown Dist CE Jun Sch. WA12 89 A3
Earlestown Sta. WA12 89 B3
Earls Way. M35 83 D6
Earlston Ave. M34 100 A3
Earlswood Wlk. Bolton BL1 147 F4
Earlswood Wlk. M'ster M18 165 C6
Early Bank. SK15 102 C7
Early Bank Rd. SK14 & SK16 102 B6
Earnshaw Ave. R'dale OL12 14 E3
Earnshaw Ave. Stockport SK1 112 B1
Earnshaw Cl. OL7 84 F5
Earnshaw St. Bolton BL3 146 B3
Earnshaw St. Hollingworth SK14 171 D4
Easby Cl. Bramhall SK8 132 B6
Easby Cl. Poynton SK12 133 D4
Easby Rd. M24 46 F3
Easedale Cl. M41 94 F3
Easedale Rd. BL1 144 A8
Easington Wlk. 10 M40 83 A6
Easingwold. 2 WA14 119 C4
East Aisle Rd. M17 & M32 96 C5
East Ave. Gatley SK8 131 D8
East Ave. Golborne WA3 74 C1
East Ave. Leigh WN7 76 C3
East Ave. M'ster M19 110 F7
East Ave. Stalybridge SK15 86 A3
East Ave. Whitefield M45 44 E2
East Bond St. WN7 76 A5
East Bridgewater St. 4 WN7 76 A4
East Central Dr. M27 80 B7
East Court Wlk. M13 163 C6
East Cres. M24 64 F7
East Didsbury Sta. M20 110 C1
East Downs Rd. Alt'ham WA14 119 C2
East Downs Rd. Cheadle SK8 122 F2
East Dr. Marple SK6 125 F3
East Dr. Pendlebury M27 80 B7
East Dr. Salford M6 80 E5
East Dr. Whitefield BL9 45 B4
East Gate St. OL12 & OL16 139 F8
East Gr. M13 164 D5
East Grange. M11 83 C3
East Hill St. 8 OL4 67 A6
East Lancashire Rly. BL0 138 C5
East Lancashire Rd. Ashton-i-M WA11,WA12,WA3 89 C7
East Lancashire Rd. Leigh WA3 76 B1
East Lancashire Rd. Pendlebury M27 80 B6
East Lancashire Rd. Swinton M27 & M28 79 D7
East Lancashire Rd. Tyldesley M28 & M29 & WA3 77 C5
East Lancashire Rd. Worsley M28 & M26 & M27 78 D7
East Lea. M34 101 A2
East Lynn Dr. M28 61 A3
East Market St. M3 158 D2
East Meade. Bolton BL3 147 E2
East Meade. M'ster M25 63 D2
East Meade. M'ster M21 109 B7
East Meade. Swinton M26 & M27 79 E6
East Moor. M28 78 A7
East Mount. WN5 53 F6
East Newton St. 11 M10 & M40 159 C3
East Ordsall La. M3 & M5 158 D1
East Over. SK6 125 A8
East Park Cl. M13 163 C6
East Philip St. M3 158 E3
East Rd. Eccles M41 95 F6
East Rd. M'ster M12 & M18 99 A3
East Rd. M'ster M18 99 B4
East Rd. Mossley SK15 86 E6
East Rd. Stretford M32 96 B4
East Rd. Wythenshawe M90 130 C7
East St. Ashton-i-M WN4 73 D4
East St. 3 Ashton-u-L OL6 85 D4
East St. Bury BL9 140 F1
East St. Dukinfield M34 100 F7
East St. Edenfield BL0 1 D4
East St. Haslingden BB4 1 A7
East St. Hindley WN2 57 B3
East St. Littleborough OL12 15 C6
East St. Littleborough OL15 16 C5
East St. Milnrow OL16 31 D7
East St. R'dale OL16 31 A8
East St. Radcliffe M26 44 B3
East St. Tyldesley M46 58 F1
East Union St. M16 161 C6
East Vale. SK6 126 A5
East View. 5 Middleton M24 64 F8
East View. Ramsbottom BL0 1 C1
East View. Ramsbottom BL0 11 C3
East Ward Cty Prim Sch. BL9 141 B2
East Ward Cty Prim Sch (Annexe). BL9 141 B3
East Way. BL1 25 B3
East Wlk. BL7 8 D2
Eastbank St. BL1 143 F2
Eastbourne Gr. BL1 144 A8
Eastbourne St. Oldham OL8 67 B4
Eastbourne St. R'dale OL11 139 F5
Eastbrook Ave. 2 M26 44 C4
Eastburn Ave. M10 & M40 159 C3
Eastchurch Cl. BL4 60 D7
Eastcombe Ave. M7 81 B7
Eastcote Rd. SK5 111 F5
Eastcote Wlk. 5 BL4 42 E1
Eastdale Pl. WA14 119 D7
Easterdale. OL4 67 C6
Eastern Ave. M27 62 D3
Eastern By-Pass. Droylsden M11 83 C2
Eastern By-Pass. M'ster M11 99 D8
Eastern Circ. M19 111 A6
Eastfield. M6 154 E4
Eastfield Ave. M'ster M10 & M40 160 E3
Eastfield Ave. Middleton M24 65 A7
Eastfields. M26 43 E5
Eastford Sq. M40 159 C4
Eastgarth. WN2 56 B2
Eastgarth Wlk. 21 M9 64 E3
Eastgate. OL12 14 C7
Eastgate St. OL7 166 A1
Eastgrove Ave. BL1 24 E6
Eastham Ave. Bury BL9 27 F6
Eastham Ave. M'ster M14 98 B1
Eastham Way. 11 Handforth SK9 131 D5
Eastham Way. Walkden M38 60 B5
Easthaven Ave. 4 M11 83 C2
Eastholme Dr. M19 111 B7
Easthope Cl. M20 110 B7
Eastlands Rd. M9 64 E5
Eastleigh Ave. M7 155 E8
Eastleigh Cres. WN7 76 B3
Eastleigh Dr. M10 & M40 160 D3
Eastleigh Gr. 2 BL1 145 E8
Eastleigh Rd. Gatley SK8 122 B1
Eastleigh Rd. M'ster M25 63 E3
Eastmoor Dr. M40 83 D4
Eastmoor Gr. BL3 146 B2
Eastnor Cl. M15 162 D6
Easton Cl. Middleton M24 65 C7
Easton Cl. Wigan WN3 55 A2
Easton Dr. SK8 123 A5
Easton Rd. M43 83 E1
Eastpark Cl. M13 163 C6
Eastry Ave. SK5 112 B6
Eastview. M33 108 B3
Eastville Gdns. M19 110 E5
Eastward Ave. SK9 136 F6
Eastway. Middleton M24 46 F1
Eastway. Sale M33 107 F1
Eastway. Shaw OL2 149 B6
Eastway. Urmston M41 95 A3
Eastwell Rd. Ashton-i-M WN4 73 A3
Eastwell Rd. Wigan WN6 36 F3
Eastwood Ave. Droylsden M43 83 E1
Eastwood Ave. Failsworth M40 65 F1
Eastwood Ave. Newton-l-W WA12 89 F3
Eastwood Ave. Urmston M41 95 D2
Eastwood Ave. Walkden M28 60 A2
Eastwood Cl. BL9 141 B2
Eastwood Gr. WN7 75 D5
Eastwood Rd. M40 65 E1
Eastwood St. Denton M34 100 D7
Eastwood St. 11 Littleborough OL15 16 B5
Eastwood Terr. BL1 40 E8
Eatock Cty Prim Sch. BL5 57 E6
Eatock St. WN2 56 B3
Eatock Way. BL5 57 D6
Eaton Cl. Cheadle SK8 122 F3
Eaton Cl. Poynton SK12 134 A3
Eaton Cl. Swinton M27 61 F2
Eaton Dr. Alderley Edge SK9 136 F2
Eaton Dr. Ashton-u-L OL7 84 F4
Eaton Dr. Sale WA15 120 A8
Eaton Rd. Alt'ham WA14 119 C1
Eaton Rd. M'ster M8 63 F1
Eaton Rd. Sale M33 108 A4
Eaton St. WN2 56 E6
Eaves Knoll Rd. SK12 127 A1
Eaves La. OL9 152 A5
Ebbdale Cl. SK1 124 A8
Ebberstone St. M14 98 A2
Ebden St. M1 163 B8
Ebenezer St. Glossop SK13 116 D7
Ebenezer St. 2 M'ster M15 162 F7
Ebnal Wlk. M14 110 D7
Ebor Cl. OL2 149 A8
Ebor House. M21 96 F1
Ebor Rd. M22 121 E4
Ebor St. OL15 16 B5
Ebsworth St. M'ster M40 83 A8
Ebsworth St. M'ster M40 157 F8
Ebury St. M26 43 F3
Eccles CE High Sch. M30 78 F1
Eccles Cl. M11 165 C8
Eccles Coll. M30 79 F4
Eccles New Rd. M30 & M5 & M6 80 C2
Eccles Old Rd. M30 & M6 80 C3
Eccles Rd. Swinton M27 79 F6
Eccles Rd. Wigan WN5 36 B1
Eccles St. BL0 138 B6
Eccles Sta. M30 79 F2
Ecclesbridge Rd. SK6 125 F4
Eccleshall St. M11 83 C1
Eccleston Ave. 28 Bolton BL2 25 B1
Eccleston Ave. M'ster M14 98 B1
Eccleston Ave. Swinton M27 79 D7
Eccleston Cl. BL8 27 A1
Eccleston Pl. M7 155 D8
Eccleston Rd. SK3 123 E4
Eccleston St. Failsworth M35 84 A8
Eccleston St. Wigan WN1 37 C1
Eccleston Way. 3 SK9 131 D4
Eccups La. SK9 136 C8
Echo St. M1 163 B8
Eckersley Ave. WN2 56 D3
Eckersley Cl. 1 M23 120 F6
Eckersley Fold La. M46 58 A1
Eckersley Rd. BL1 143 E3
Eckersley St. Bolton BL3 146 C4
Eckersley St. Wigan WN1 37 E1
Eckford St. M8 156 B6
Eclipse Cl. OL16 31 C7
Edale Ave. Denton M34 100 D7
Edale Ave. Denton M34 112 F8
Edale Ave. M'ster M40 83 A8
Edale Ave. Reddish SK5 100 A1
Edale Ave. Urmston M41 95 B1
Edale Bank. 6 SK13 171 E1
Edale Cl. Alt'ham WA14 119 C1
Edale Cl. Atherton M46 58 C3
Edale Cl. 26 Gamesley SK13 171 E2
Edale Cl. Gatley SK8 131 D7
Edale Cl. Hazel Grove SK7 124 E1
Edale Cl. Irlam M44 94 A1
Edale Cres. SK13 171 E1
Edale Dr. WN6 19 E2
Edale Fold. 25 SK13 171 E2
Edale Gr. Ashton-u-L OL6 86 A6
Edale Gr. Sale M33 107 E2
Edale Rd. Bolton BL3 146 A4
Edale Rd. Farnworth BL4 60 C7
Edale Rd. Leigh WN7 76 C4
Edale Rd. Stretford M32 96 B3
Edale St. M6 81 B5
Edbrook Wlk. M13 164 D5
Eddie Colman Cl. M40 83 B5
Eddisbury Ave. M'ster M20 109 F8
Eddisbury Ave. Urmston M41 94 D4
Edditch Gr. BL2 148 C7
Eddleston St. WN4 72 F6
Eddystone Cl. 6 M5 81 A1
Eden Ave. Bolton BL1 143 E3
Eden Ave. Edenfield BL0 1 D3
Eden Ave. Fowley Common WA3 92 C4
Eden Ave. High Lane SK6 134 E7
Eden Bank. WN7 76 B6
Eden Cl. Heywood OL10 29 A3
Eden Cl. M'ster M15 163 A6
Eden Cl. 3 Platt Bridge WN2 56 A2
Eden Cl. Stockport SK1 124 A8
Eden Cl. Wilmslow SK9 136 E5
Eden Ct. Edenfield BL0 1 D2
Eden Ct. M'ster M19 111 A8
Eden Gr. Bolton BL1 143 E3
Eden Gr. Leigh WN7 75 C5
Eden Pl. Cheadle SK8 122 D6
Eden Pl. Sale M33 108 B5
Eden St. Bolton BL1 143 E3
Eden St. Bury BL9 140 F2
Eden St. Edenfield BL0 1 D1
Eden St. Oldham OL1 153 E7
Eden St. R'dale OL12 139 D8
Eden Way. OL2 149 A8
Edenbridge Dr. M26 61 B7
Edenbridge Rd. Cheadle SK8 123 B4
Edenbridge Rd. Failsworth M40 83 B4
Edendale Dr. M22 121 D1
Edenfield Ave. M21 109 D4
Edenfield CE Prim Sch. BL0 1 D4
Edenfield La. M28 78 F4
Edenfield Rd. M'ster M25 & M8 63 E2
Edenfield Rd. R'dale OL11 & OL12 13 D2
Edenfield St. OL11 & OL12 14 C1
Edenhall Ave. M19 110 F8
Edenhall Gr. WN2 56 F3
Edenham Wlk. 1 M40 65 D2
Edenhurst Dr. WA15 120 B5
Edenhurst Rd. SK2 124 B6
Edensor Dr. WA15 120 C3
Edenvale. M28 78 A7
Edgar St. Bolton BL3 145 E6
Edgar St. R'dale OL16 15 C2
Edgar St. Ramsbottom BL0 138 B5
Edgar St W. BL0 138 B5
Edgbaston Dr. M16 97 A3
Edge Fold Cres. M28 78 D8
Edge Fold Rd. M28 60 D1
Edge Gn. M28 78 C8
Edge Green La. WA3 73 F2
Edge Green Rd. WA3 & WN4 73 F4
Edge Green St. WN4 73 D4
Edge Hall Rd. WN5 53 E5
Edge Hill Ave. OL2 48 E3
Edge Hill Rd. Bolton BL3 146 B3
Edge Hill Rd. Oldham OL2 48 E3
Edge La. Bacup OL13 4 C8
Edge La. Bolton BL1 23 C5
Edge La. Droylsden M43 & M11 83 D2
Edge La. Edgworth BL7 9 A8
Edge La. Stalybridge SK14 102 F4
Edge La. Stretford M21 & M32 96 E1
Edge Lane Rd. OL1 67 A8
Edge Lane St. OL2 48 E4
Edge St. M4 159 A2
Edge View. OL1 47 E1
Edge View La. WA16 136 B2
Edge Ware Gr. WN3 54 D3
Edgedale Ave. M19 110 E5
Edgefield Ave. M9 64 E4
Edgefold Ind Est. BL4 146 B1
Edgehill Chase. SK9 137 E7
Edgehill Cl. M5 & M6 154 F2
Edgehill Ct. M32 96 E1
Edgehill Rd. M6 80 C3
Edgehill St. 10 M4 159 A2
Edgeley Fold. SK3 123 C7

194 Edg – Ent

Edgeley Park(Stockport County FC). SK3 ... 170 E7
Edgeley Rd. Flixton M31 & M41 ... 106 F8
Edgeley Rd. Stockport SK3 .. 123 B7
Edgeley Rd. Urmston M41 .. 107 A8
Edgemoor. WA14 ... 119 A2
Edgemoor Cl. Oldham OL4 ... 49 D1
Edgemoor Cl. Radcliffe M26 .. 43 E5
Edgemoor Cl. Whitworth OL12 4 E5
Edgemoor Dr. OL11 ... 29 F5
Edgerley Pl. WN4 ... 73 A3
Edgerton Rd. WA3 ... 90 F8
Edgerton Wlk. M28 ... 60 D3
Edgeview Wlk. 6 M13 ... 163 B7
Edgeware Ave. M25 & M8 ... 63 F4
Edgeware Rd. Failsworth OL9 65 E3
Edgeware Rd. Worsley M28 .. 79 A4
Edgeway. SK9 ... 137 B5
Edgeway Rd. WN3 ... 55 A1
Edgewood. WN6 ... 36 A5
Edgeworth Ave. BL2 ... 26 D1
Edgeworth Dr. Bury BL8 ... 27 A1
Edgeworth Dr. M'ster M14 110 E7
Edgeworth Rd. Golborne WA3 73 F1
Edgeworth Rd. Hindley WN2 57 A3
Edgmont Ave. BL3 ... 147 D4
Edgware Rd. M40 ... 83 B4
Edgworth CE/Meth Prim Sch. BL7 ... 9 D5
Edgworth Cl. OL10 ... 29 A2
Edilom Rd. M8 ... 63 E2
Edinburgh Cl. Cheadle SK8 . 122 F6
Edinburgh Cl. Ince-i-M WN2 . 56 A8
Edinburgh Dr. Hindley WN2 .. 57 B3
Edinburgh Dr. Romiley SK6 113 C4
Edinburgh Dr. Wigan WN5 ... 54 D5
Edinburgh Rd. BL3 ... 43 A2
Edinburgh Sq. M40 ... 160 E4
Edinburgh Way. OL11 ... 30 D4
Edinburgh Wlk. WN2 ... 38 D5
Edington. 7 OL12 ... 139 F8
Edison Rd. M30 ... 95 C8
Edison St. 1 M11 ... 99 E7
Edith Ave. M14 ... 98 A3
Edith Cavell Cl. M11 ... 83 C1
Edith Cliff Wlk. M40 ... 65 F1
Edith St. Bolton BL1 ... 144 C6
Edith St. Farnworth BL4 ... 60 D7
Edith St. Oldham OL8 ... 66 F3
Edith St. Ramsbottom BL0 ... 11 E8
Edith St. Wigan WN3 ... 150 B7
Edlestone Gr. 2 SK9 ... 131 E1
Edlin Cl. M12 ... 164 E5
Edlingham. 5 OL11 ... 139 E6
Edlington Wlk. 12 M40 ... 83 C6
Edmonds St. M24 ... 47 B1
Edmonton Rd.Failsworth M40 83 A4
Edmonton Rd. Stockport SK2 & SK3 ... 124 A4
Edmund Cl. SK4 ... 169 E4
Edmund Dr. WN7 ... 75 C5
Edmund Potter Hospl. BL1 . 40 F7
Edmund St. Droylsden M43 ... 84 A1
Edmund St. Failsworth M35 .. 83 F8
Edmund St. M'ster M3 ... 158 E2
Edmund St. Milnrow OL16 ... 31 F6
Edmund St. R'dale OL12 ... 139 D8
Edmund St. 8 Radcliffe M26 44 C4
Edmund St. Salford M6 ... 154 E3
Edmund St. Shaw OL2 ... 149 C7
Edmund St. Walsden OL14 ... 6 A8
Edmunds Ct. BL3 ... 145 D6
Edmunds Fold. OL15 ... 15 F6
Edna Rd. WN7 ... 75 C7
Edna St. SK14 ... 167 D2
Edson Rd. M9 ... 63 F3
Edward Ave. Bredbury SK6 . 112 E3
Edward Ave. Littleborough OL15 ... 15 F3
Edward Ave. M'ster M21 ... 109 A8
Edward Ave. Salford M5 & M6 80 C3
Edward Charlton Rd. M16 & M21 ... 97 A2
Edward Dr. WN4 ... 73 B4
Edward Onyon Ct. M5 ... 154 E2
Edward Rd. M'ster M9 ... 64 D5
Edward Rd. Shaw OL2 ... 149 A6
Edward St. Ashton-u-L OL6 ... 85 E2
Edward St. Bolton BL3 ... 145 D5
Edward St. Bury BL9 ... 140 F1
Edward St. Chadderton OL9 152 A8
Edward St. Denton M34 ... 100 D7
Edward St. Denton M34 ... 100 F4
Edward St. Droylsden M43 .. 100 A8
Edward St. Dukinfield SK14 . 101 C3
Edward St. Dukinfield SK16 . 101 C6
Edward St. Farnworth BL4 ... 42 B2
Edward St. Glossop SK13 ... 104 C1
Edward St. Horwich BL6 ... 22 A3
Edward St. Kearsley M26 ... 61 B8
Edward St. Leigh WN7 ... 76 A4
Edward St. Littleborough OL12 15 D4
Edward St. M'ster M9 ... 157 E8
Edward St. M'ster M7 ... 158 E4
Edward St. Middleton M24 ... 47 A1
Edward St. Oldham OL9 ... 152 C5
Edward St. Prestwich M25 ... 63 A5
Edward St. R'dale OL16 ... 31 A8
Edward St. Radcliffe M26 ... 44 B2
Edward St. Romiley SK6 ... 114 B1
Edward St. Sale M33 ... 108 E4
Edward St. Stockport SK1 ... 170 F8
Edward St. Westhoughton BL5 57 E8
Edward St. Whitworth OL12 ... 4 D2
Edward St. Wigan WN1 ... 37 C2
Edward St. Wigan WN1 ... 151 F8
Edwards Cl. SK6 ... 125 E5
Edwards Ct. M22 ... 121 D3
Edwards Way. SK6 ... 125 E5
Edwin Rd. M11 ... 160 E1
Edwin St. Bury BL9 ... 140 E2
Edwin St. Stockport SK1 ... 124 B8
Edwin St. Wigan WN1 ... 151 E7
Edwin Waugh Gdns. OL12 ... 14 D3
Edzell Wlk. 18 M11 ... 83 C1
Easebrook. M41 ... 95 D1
Egbert St. 18 M40 ... 83 A7
Egerton Ave. WA13 ... 117 C8
Egerton Cl. OL10 ... 29 D1
Egerton Cres. M20 ... 110 B7
Egerton Ct. Dukinfield M34 . 101 A4
Egerton Ct. M'ster M13 ... 98 C4
Egerton Ct. Stockport SK3 ... 124 A4
Egerton Ct. Stretford M21 ... 108 F8
Egerton Dr. Alt'ham WA15 .. 120 A3
Egerton Dr. Sale M33 ... 108 B5
Egerton Gr. M28 ... 60 D3
Egerton Lodge. M34 ... 101 A4
Egerton Mews. Droylsden M43 ... 100 A8
Egerton Mews. M'ster M14 110 D8
Egerton Moss. WA15 ... 128 E5
Egerton Park Comm High Sch. M34 ... 100 E4
Egerton Pk. M28 ... 79 B7
Egerton Pl. OL2 ... 149 A6
Egerton Prim Sch. BL7 ... 8 D3
Egerton Rd. Alt'ham WA15 . 120 A2
Egerton Rd.Eccles M27 & M30 79 D4
Egerton Rd. Handforth SK9 . 131 B1
Egerton Rd. M'ster M14 ... 110 D8
Egerton Rd. Stockport SK3 .. 124 A4
Egerton Rd. Walkden M28 ... 60 D3
Egerton Rd. Whitefield M45 ... 62 F7
Egerton Rd N. M'ster M16 & M21 ... 97 C1
Egerton Rd N. M'ster SK4 .. 111 C5
Egerton Rd S. M'ster M21 .. 109 C8
Egerton Rd S. M'ster SK4 ... 168 C4
Egerton St. Abram WN2 ... 74 B7
Egerton St. Ashton-u-L OL6 . 166 C3
Egerton St. Denton M34 ... 100 E5
Egerton St. Droylsden M43 ... 84 B1
Egerton St. Eccles M30 ... 79 B2
Egerton St. Farnworth BL4 ... 42 C1
Egerton St. Heywood OL10 ... 29 C1
Egerton St. Littleborough OL15 16 C5
Egerton St. M'ster M3 ... 158 D1
Egerton St. M'ster M15 ... 162 D7
Egerton St. Middleton M24 ... 64 C7
Egerton St. Mossley OL5 ... 68 C2
Egerton St. Oldham OL1 ... 67 A8
Egerton St. Prestwich M25 ... 63 C4
Egerton Terr. M14 ... 110 D7
Eggington St. M40 ... 156 C5
Egham Ct. 18 BL2 ... 25 B1
Egham House. BL3 ... 146 B2
Egmont St. M'ster M8 ... 156 A8
Egmont St. Mossley OL5 ... 86 D8
Egmont St. Salford M6 ... 80 E6
Egremont Ave. M20 ... 110 A7
Egremont Cl. BL9 & M45 ... 45 A1
Egremont Ct. M7 ... 81 C8
Egremont Gr. 2 SK3 ... 123 B8
Egremont Rd. OL16 ... 31 F4
Egret Dr. M44 ... 94 A3
Egypt La. M45 ... 45 D1
Egyptian St. BL1 ... 143 F1
Ehlinger Ave. SK14 ... 104 A5
Eida Way. M17 ... 96 C8
Eight Acre. M45 ... 62 C7
Eighth Ave. OL8 ... 66 D1
Eighth St W. M17 ... 96 D6
Eileen Gr. M14 ... 98 C2
Eileen Gr W. M14 ... 98 B2
Elaine Ave. M9 ... 65 B2
Elaine Cl. WN4 ... 73 D5
Elbain Wlk. M40 ... 83 C5
Elbe St. M12 ... 163 C8
Elberton Wlk. 13 M8 ... 155 F7
Elbow La. OL11 ... 31 A6
Elbow St. M19 ... 99 A1
Elbut La. BL9 ... 28 F5
Elcho Rd. WA14 ... 119 B3
Elcombe Ave. WA3 ... 90 E7
Elcot Cl. M40 ... 156 C5
Elder Cl. SK2 ... 124 D8
Elder Gr. M40 ... 65 F2
Elder Rd. OL4 ... 67 E6
Elder St. OL16 ... 31 B5
Elderberry Cl. WN1 ... 37 B4
Elderberry Way. SK9 ... 137 E8
Elderberry Wlk. M31 ... 105 E3
Eldercot Gr. BL3 ... 146 A4
Eldercot Rd. BL3 ... 146 A4
Eldercroft Rd. WA15 ... 120 D5
Elderfield Dr. SK6 ... 112 F4
Eldermount Rd. M9 ... 64 D2
Elderwood. M24 ... 65 E7
Eldon Cl. M34 ... 100 E7
Eldon Gdns. WN4 ... 73 A6
Eldon Pl. M30 ... 79 C1
Eldon Prec. OL8 ... 153 E5
Eldon Rd. Irlam M44 ... 94 A2
Eldon Rd. Stockport SK3 ... 123 C7
Eldon St. Bolton BL2 ... 25 B2
Eldon St. Bury BL9 ... 140 F4
Eldon St. Leigh WN7 ... 75 D6
Eldon St. Oldham OL8 ... 153 F5
Eldridge Dr. M40 ... 83 A5
Eleanor Rd. M'ster M21 ... 109 A8
Eleanor Rd. Oldham OL8 ... 48 E3
Eleanor St. Bolton BL1 ... 25 A5
Eleanor St. Oldham OL1 ... 153 D8
Eleanor St. Wigan WN3 ... 150 A7
Electo St. M18 ... 99 E7
Elevator Rd. M17 ... 96 E6
Eleventh St. M17 ... 96 D6
Elf Mill Cl. SK3 ... 170 E6
Elford Gr. M18 & M34 ... 100 A4
Elgar St. M12 & M18 ... 99 A4
Elgin Ave. Garswood WN4 ... 72 D4
Elgin Ave. M'ster M20 ... 110 D3
Elgin Cl. WN2 ... 56 A8
Elgin Dr. M33 ... 108 E3
Elgin Rd. Dukinfield SK16 ... 101 C6
Elgin Rd. Oldham OL4 ... 67 C5
Elgin St. Ashton-u-L OL7 ... 166 A4
Elgin St. Bolton BL1 ... 142 C2
Elgin St. R'dale OL11 ... 31 A5
Elgin St. Stalybridge SK15 ... 86 B1
Elgol Cl. SK3 ... 170 F5
Elgol Ct. OL10 ... 29 A1
Elgol Dr. BL3 ... 40 E6
Elham Cl. M26 ... 61 C7
Eli St. OL9 ... 66 A3
Elim St. OL15 ... 16 C7
Elim Terr. OL15 ... 16 C7
Eliot Dr. WN3 ... 150 A5
Eliot Rd. M30 ... 79 D1
Elishaw Row. M6 ... 154 F1
Eliza Ann St. 4 Eccles M30 .. 79 C1
Eliza Ann St. M'ster M40 ... 159 C4
Eliza St. M'ster M15 ... 162 E6
Eliza St. Ramsbottom BL0 ... 11 D6
Eliza St. Sale M33 ... 108 B5
Elizabeth Ave. Denton M34 100 E5
Elizabeth Ave. Disley SK12 . 135 D5
Elizabeth Ave. Leigh WN2 ... 56 E1
Elizabeth Ave. Oldham OL9 ... 66 A3
Elizabeth Ave. Royton OL2 ... 48 D3
Elizabeth Ave. 1 Stalybridge SK15 ... 86 A2
Elizabeth Ave. Stockport SK1 170 F8
Elizabeth Ct. M'ster M14 ... 110 D7
Elizabeth Ct. Reddish M34 ... 99 F3
Elizabeth Ct. Stockport SK4 168 C2
Elizabeth Dr. BB4 ... 1 A8
Elizabeth Gaskell Campus. M'ster M13 ... 98 C4
Elizabeth Gr. OL2 ... 149 B7
Elizabeth House. SK4 ... 168 B2
Elizabeth Rd. M31 ... 105 F4
Elizabeth Slinger Rd. M20 109 F5
Elizabeth St. Ashton-u-L OL6 166 B4
Elizabeth St. Atherton M46 ... 58 D3
Elizabeth St. Denton M34 ... 100 D3
Elizabeth St. Edenfield BL0 ... 1 D3
Elizabeth St. 2 Heywood OL10 ... 29 C2
Elizabeth St. Hyde SK14 ... 167 D3
Elizabeth St. Ince-i-M WN2 ... 56 B8
Elizabeth St. Leigh WN7 ... 76 B3
Elizabeth St.M'ster M7 & M8 155 F6
Elizabeth St. M'ster M8 ... 156 A5
Elizabeth St. Prestwich M25 .. 63 C4
Elizabeth St. R'dale OL11 ... 30 C3
Elizabeth St. 3 Radcliffe M26 44 A3
Elizabeth St. 1 Swinton M27 61 F1
Elizabeth St. Whitefield M45 . 62 F7
Elizabethan Ct. 10 M29 ... 58 F1
Elizabethan Dr. WN2 ... 55 E4
Elizabethan Way. Milnrow OL16 ... 31 F5
Elizabethan Wlk. 1 WN2 ... 56 A2
Elkstone Ave. M38 ... 60 A6
Elkstone Cl. WN3 ... 54 C2
Elkwood Cl. WN1 ... 37 B4
Elladene Pk. M21 ... 109 C8
Ellan Wlk. 10 M11 ... 83 C1
Ellanby Cl. M14 ... 98 B3
Elland Cl. BL9 ... 45 B2
Ellaston Dr. M41 ... 95 D2
Ellastone Rd. M6 ... 80 C4
Ellbourne Rd. M9 ... 64 A3
Ellen Brook Rd. M22 ... 130 D8
Ellen Gr. M26 ... 61 C5
Ellen St. 5 Bolton BL1 ... 142 C3
Ellen St. Droylsden M34 ... 100 B8
Ellen St. Ince-i-M WN2 ... 56 A7
Ellen St. Oldham OL9 ... 153 D8
Ellen St. Stockport SK4 ... 169 D3
Ellen St. Wigan WN1 ... 151 D7
Ellen Wilkinson Cres. M12 165 A5
Ellen Wilkinson High Sch. M12 ... 164 D6
Ellenbrook Cl. M12 ... 165 B6
Ellenbrook Prim Sch. M28 .. 78 C8
Ellenbrook Rd. M28 ... 78 B7
Ellendale Grange. M28 ... 78 B8
Ellenhall Cl. M9 ... 157 D8
Ellenor Dr. M29 ... 77 C7
Ellenroad St. OL16 ... 32 A4
Ellenrod Dr. OL12 ... 14 A2
Ellenrod La. OL12 ... 14 A2
Elleray Cl. BL3 ... 43 C3
Elleray Rd. Middleton M9 ... 64 F5
Elleray Rd. Salford M6 ... 80 D5
Ellerbeck Cl. WN6 ... 36 F7
Ellerbeck Cres. M28 ... 78 C8
Ellerby Ave. M27 ... 62 A3
Ellescroft. SK12 ... 127 E1
Ellesmere Ave. Ashton-u-L OL6 ... 85 C7
Ellesmere Ave. Eccles M30 ... 79 E2
Ellesmere Ave. Marple SK6 . 125 F6
Ellesmere Ave. Walkden M28 60 C3
Ellesmere Cl. SK16 ... 101 E8
Ellesmere Dr. SK8 ... 123 A5
Ellesmere Gdns. BL3 ... 147 D3
Ellesmere Golf Course. M28 60 F1
Ellesmere Rd.Alt'ham WA14 119 E6
Ellesmere Rd. Ashton-i-M WN4 ... 72 F4
Ellesmere Rd. Bolton BL3 ... 146 C3
Ellesmere Rd. Cheadle SK3 123 A7
Ellesmere Rd. Culcheth WA3 91 E3
Ellesmere Rd. Eccles M30 ... 79 E3
Ellesmere Rd. M'ster M21 ... 97 C1
Ellesmere Rd. Wigan WN5 ... 54 D6
Ellesmere Rd N. SK4 ... 111 C5
Ellesmere Rd S. M21 ... 109 C8
Ellesmere Ret Pk. M28 ... 60 D4
Ellesmere Sh Ctr. M28 ... 60 D3
Ellesmere St. Bolton BL3 ... 145 D6
Ellesmere St. 14 Eccles M30 . 79 D1
Ellesmere St. Failsworth M35 83 F8
Ellesmere St. Farnworth BL4 . 60 D8
Ellesmere St. Leigh WN7 ... 75 F4
Ellesmere St. M'ster M15 ... 162 D7
Ellesmere St. R'dale OL11 ... 139 F5
Ellesmere St. Swinton M27 ... 62 A1
Ellesmere St. Swinton M27 ... 79 D7
Ellesmere St. Tyldesley M29 . 59 A1
Ellesmere St. Tyldesley M29 . 77 C5
Ellesmere St. Walkden M38 .. 60 C4
Ellesmere Terr. M14 ... 110 D7
Ellesmere Wlk. 3 BL4 ... 60 D8
Ellingham Cl. M11 ... 160 F1
Elliot Sq. 11 OL1 ... 67 A8
Elliot St. Bolton BL1 ... 142 C3
Elliot St. Oldham OL4 ... 67 E6
Elliot Wlk. M24 ... 47 C3
Elliott Ave. Dukinfield SK14 . 101 D5
Elliott Ave. Golborne WA3 ... 74 B1
Elliott Dr. Hindley WN2 ... 56 E7
Elliott Dr. Sale M33 ... 107 E4
Elliott St. Farnworth BL4 ... 60 C7
Elliott St. R'dale OL12 & OL16 31 A8
Elliott St. Tyldesley M29 ... 76 F8
Ellis Cres. M28 ... 60 B3
Ellis Fold. OL12 ... 13 E2
Ellis La. M24 ... 64 B8
Ellis Rd. WN5 ... 71 D4
Ellis St. Bolton BL3 ... 145 D5
Ellis St. Bury BL8 ... 27 B2
Ellis St. Hyde SK14 ... 167 F2
Ellis St. M'ster M7 ... 158 E4
Ellis St. Ramsbottom BL0 ... 138 B5
Ellis St. Wigan WN1 ... 37 E1
Ellisbank Wlk. 9 M13 ... 163 B7
Ellisland Wlk. 1 M40 ... 83 A6
Ellison Cl. SK14 ... 103 D5
Ellison House. OL7 ... 166 A1
Ellison St. SK13 ... 104 D1
Elliston Sq. M12 ... 165 A6
Ellor St. M6 ... 154 F3
Ellwood Rd. SK1 ... 112 B1
Elm Ave. Garswood WN4 ... 72 D5
Elm Ave. Golborne WA3 ... 74 A1
Elm Ave. Newton-l-W WA12 ... 89 C2
Elm Ave. Radcliffe M26 ... 61 F8
Elm Ave. Standish WN6 ... 36 F8
Elm Ave. Wigan WN5 ... 54 E6
Elm Beds Rd. SK12 ... 134 C2
Elm Cl. Mottram-i-L SK14 ... 103 A4
Elm Cl. 2 Partington M31 ... 105 F3
Elm Cl. Poynton SK12 ... 133 F3
Elm Cres. Alderley Edge SK9 137 B3
Elm Cres. Swinton M28 ... 79 A7
Elm Croft. WN1 ... 37 B4
Elm Ct. SK1 ... 124 B8
Elm Dr. Billinge WN5 ... 71 D5
Elm Dr. Denton M34 ... 100 D4
Elm Dr. Stretford M32 ... 108 C8
Elm Gr. Alderley Edge SK9 ... 137 B2
Elm Gr. Ashton-u-L OL6 ... 85 C5
Elm Gr. Bolton BL7 ... 25 A8
Elm Gr. Denton M34 ... 100 D5
Elm Gr. Droylsden M43 ... 83 D2
Elm Gr. Farnworth BL4 ... 60 B8
Elm Gr. Glossop SK13 ... 104 C2
Elm Gr. 6 Horwich BL6 ... 22 E1
Elm Gr. Hyde SK14 ... 167 F2
Elm Gr. Littleborough OL12 ... 15 C6
Elm Gr. M'ster M20 ... 110 B3
Elm Gr. Newhey OL16 ... 32 A3
Elm Gr. Oldham OL4 ... 68 B6
Elm Gr. Prestwich M25 ... 63 A6
Elm Gr. R'dale OL11 ... 139 E5
Elm Gr. Sale M33 ... 108 B6
Elm Gr. Swinton M27 ... 61 B2
Elm Gr. Urmston M41 ... 95 E2
Elm Park Ct. M20 ... 110 B4
Elm Rd. Abram WN2 ... 74 C7
Elm Rd. Alt'ham WA15 ... 119 E3
Elm Rd. Gatley SK8 ... 122 A5
Elm Rd. High Lane SK6 ... 134 F7
Elm Rd. Hollinfare WA3 ... 105 A2
Elm Rd. Kearsley BL4 ... 60 F5
Elm Rd. Little Lever BL3 ... 43 B2
Elm Rd. M'ster M20 ... 110 A4
Elm Rd. Oldham OL8 ... 66 D2
Elm Rd. Westhoughton BL5 ... 57 F7
Elm Rd S. SK3 ... 123 A7
Elm St. Bredbury SK6 ... 112 F4
Elm St. Bury BL9 ... 141 B2
Elm St. Eccles M30 ... 79 D1
Elm St. Edenfield BL0 ... 1 E3
Elm St. Failsworth M35 ... 83 F8
Elm St. Farnworth BL4 ... 42 E1
Elm St. Heywood OL10 ... 29 D2
Elm St. Leigh WN7 ... 75 F3
Elm St. Middleton M24 ... 65 C8
Elm St. Platt Bridge WN2 ... 56 A2
Elm St. R'dale OL12 ... 14 F1
Elm St. Ramsbottom BL0 ... 11 D6
Elm St. Swinton M27 ... 61 E1
Elm St. 4 Tyldesley M29 ... 59 A1
Elm St. Whitworth OL12 ... 4 D2
Elm Tree Cl. Failsworth M35 . 84 B7
Elm Tree Cl. Stalybridge SK15 ... 102 A8
Elm Tree Dr. Dukinfield SK16 101 F7
Elm Tree Dr. Wythenshawe M22 ... 121 D3
Elm Tree Rd. Bredbury SK6 112 C3
Elm Tree Rd. Golborne WA3 .. 90 F8
Elm Wood Prim Sch. M24 ... 65 C8
Elmbank Ave. M20 ... 109 E4
Elmbank Rd. M24 ... 65 C8
Elmbridge Wlk. Bolton BL3 145 D5
Elmbridge Wlk. 2 Failsworth M40 ... 83 A6
Elmdale Ave. SK8 ... 122 B2
Elmdale Wlk. 1 M15 ... 163 A6
Elmfield. WN6 ... 36 B6
Elmfield Ave. Atherton M46 .. 58 C4
Elmfield Ave. Wythenshawe M22 ... 121 E8
Elmfield Cl. SK9 ... 137 B2
Elmfield Dr. SK6 ... 125 E6
Elmfield House. SK3 ... 170 F5
Elmfield Rd. Alderley Edge SK9 ... 137 B2
Elmfield Rd. Droylsden M34 100 C8
Elmfield Rd. Stockport SK3 .. 170 F5
Elmfield Rd. Wigan WN1 ... 37 B5
Elmfield St. Bolton BL1 ... 143 F2
Elmfield St. M'ster M7 & M8 156 A6
Elmgate Gr. M19 ... 99 A1
Elmham Wlk. M40 ... 159 C4
Elmhow Gr. WN3 ... 55 A2
Elmhurst Dr. M19 ... 110 F5
Elmin Wlk. M15 ... 162 E7
Elmley Cl. SK2 ... 125 A5
Elmore Wood. OL15 ... 15 E6
Elmpark Gate. OL12 ... 14 B3
Elmpark Gr. OL12 ... 14 B3
Elmpark Vale. OL12 ... 14 B3
Elmpark View. OL12 ... 14 B3
Elmpark Way. OL12 ... 14 B3
Elmridge. WN7 ... 76 B6
Elmridge Dr. WA15 ... 129 C8
Elmridge Prim Sch. WA15 129 C8
Elms Bank High Sch. M45 ... 44 F2
Elms Cl. M45 ... 44 F2
Elms Farm. 3 M45 ... 44 F2
Elms Rd. M'ster SK4 ... 111 B5
Elms Rd. Stalybridge SK15 ... 86 D3
Elms Rd. Whitefield M45 ... 44 F1
Elms St. M45 ... 44 F1
Elms The. Golborne WA3 ... 90 F7
Elms The. Littleborough OL15 15 E4
Elms The. Mossley OL5 ... 68 B1
Elms The. 4 Whitefield M45 . 44 F2
Elmsbury St. 1 WN4 ... 72 F5
Elmscott Wlk. M13 ... 164 D5
Elmsdale Ave. M9 ... 64 D5
Elmsfield Ave. OL11 ... 13 E1
Elmsleigh Ct. M30 ... 79 F3
Elmsleigh Rd. SK8 ... 122 A2
Elmsmere Rd. M20 ... 110 D4
Elmstead Ave. M20 ... 110 A6
Elmsted Cl. SK8 ... 123 B3
Elmstone Gr. BL1 ... 143 F1
Elmsway. Alt'ham WA15 ... 129 B8
Elmsway. Bramhall SK7 ... 132 C7
Elmsway. High Lane SK6 ... 134 E6
Elmswood Ave. M14 ... 97 F2
Elmswood Dr. SK14 ... 102 A3
Elmsworth Ave. M19 ... 99 B1
Elmton Rd. M9 ... 64 E3
Elmtree Dr. SK4 ... 168 C2
Elmwood. M33 ... 107 C4
Elmwood Ave. WN4 ... 73 A2
Elmwood Cl. BL5 ... 59 A6
Elmwood Ct. M32 ... 108 C8
Elmwood Dr. OL2 ... 48 C5
Elmwood Gr. Bolton BL1 ... 144 C8
Elmwood Gr. Farnworth BL4 . 60 C6
Elmwood Gr. M'ster M9 ... 157 F7
Elmwood Lodge. M20 ... 110 A4
Elnup Ave. WN6 ... 36 B6
Elsa Rd. M19 ... 99 C1
Elsdon Dr. Atherton M46 ... 58 E4
Elsdon Dr. M'ster M18 ... 99 D6
Elsdon Gdns. 8 BL2 ... 25 B1
Elsdon Rd. M13 ... 98 F2
Elsham Dr. M28 ... 60 B3
Elsham Gdns. M18 ... 99 B4
Elsie St. Farnworth BL4 ... 60 C7
Elsie St. M'ster M9 ... 157 E8
Elsie St. Ramsbottom BL0 ... 11 A4
Elsinore Ave. M44 ... 94 A1
Elsinore Cl. M35 ... 84 B7
Elsinore Rd. M16 ... 97 A4
Elsinore St. BL2 ... 25 B3
Elsma Rd. M40 ... 83 E4
Elsmore Rd. M14 ... 110 A8
Elson Dr. SK14 ... 113 D7
Elson St. BL8 ... 27 B4
Elstead Gr. WN4 ... 72 D4
Elstead Wlk. M9 ... 64 A3
Elsted Rd. OL4 ... 68 E5
Elston Ave. WA12 ... 89 C5
Elston Wlk. 3 M15 ... 162 F6
Elstree Ave. M40 ... 83 B4
Elstree Gr. SK3 ... 170 D8
Elswick Ave. Bolton BL3 ... 144 B5
Elswick Ave. Bramhall SK7 . 132 E7
Elswick Ave. M'ster M21 ... 109 D4
Elsworth Dr. BL1 ... 143 F4
Elsworth St. M3 ... 159 A4
Elterwater Cl. BL8 ... 27 B4
Eltham Ave. SK2 ... 124 C5
Eltham Dr. M41 ... 95 C5
Eltham St. 6 M19 ... 99 A2
Elton Ave. Farnworth BL4 ... 59 F8
Elton Ave. M'ster M19 ... 111 A8
Elton Bank. 4 SK13 ... 171 D1
Elton Brook Cl. BL8 ... 27 C3
Elton Cl. 6 Gamesley SK13 171 D1
Elton Cl. Golborne WA3 ... 90 E7
Elton Cl. Handforth SK9 ... 131 E1
Elton Cl. Whitefield M45 ... 63 A8
Elton Cty Prim Sch. BL8 ... 27 C4
Elton Dr. SK7 ... 133 D8
Elton High Sch. BL8 ... 27 A4
Elton House. WN5 ... 54 C7
Elton Lea. 5 SK13 ... 171 D1
Elton Pl. 7 SK13 ... 171 D1
Elton Rd. M33 ... 107 E2
Elton St. Bolton BL2 ... 148 A7
Elton St. M'ster M7 ... 158 E3
Elton St. R'dale OL11 ... 30 C1
Elton St. Stretford M17 & M32 96 F5
Elton Vale Rd. BL8 ... 27 B2
Elton's Yd. M7 ... 158 D3
Elvate Cres. M7 & M8 ... 155 F5
Elverdon Cl. M15 ... 162 E5
Elverston St. M22 ... 109 E1
Elverston Way. OL9 ... 152 C8
Elvey St. M10 & M40 ... 157 F5
Elvington Cres. M28 ... 78 C8
Elvington Wlk. M15 ... 163 A6
Elvira Cl. M35 ... 84 B7
Elway Rd. WN4 ... 73 C4
Elwick Cl. 8 M16 ... 97 F3
Elworth Way. 6 SK9 ... 131 D4
Elworthy Gr. WN1 ... 37 E2
Elwyn Ave. M22 ... 121 D7
Ely Ave. M32 ... 95 F3
Ely Cl. M28 ... 78 B8
Ely Cres. M35 ... 83 F5
Ely Dr. Bury BL8 ... 140 D4
Ely Dr. Tyldesley M29 ... 77 C7
Ely Gr. BL1 ... 143 E1
Ely St. OL9 ... 152 B5
Elysian St. M11 ... 165 C8
Embankment Rd. BL7 ... 9 C5
Embassy Wlk. M18 ... 99 D4
Ember St. M11 ... 83 D2
Emblem St. BL3 ... 145 D5
Embleton Wlk. M18 ... 165 C6
Emerald Ave. WN7 ... 75 E4
Emerald Cotts. BL8 ... 10 F3
Emerald Rd. M22 ... 130 F7
Emerald St. 5 Bolton BL1 ... 143 F3
Emerald St. Denton M34 ... 100 E3
Emerald St. Wigan WN6 ... 37 A3
Emerson Ave. M30 ... 80 A3
Emerson Dr. M24 ... 46 F1
Emerson St. Salford M5 ... 154 D2
Emerson St. Swinton M27 ... 61 F1
Emery Ave. M21 ... 109 C6
Emery Cl. SK4 ... 168 A4
Emily Beavan Cl. M11 ... 83 B1
Emily Pl. M43 ... 83 F1
Emley St. M19 ... 99 B1
Emlyn Gr. SK8 ... 123 A6
Emlyn St. Farnworth BL4 ... 42 C1
Emlyn St. 2 Hindley WN2 ... 56 D5
Emlyn St. Swinton M27 ... 79 D8
Emlyn St. Walkden M28 ... 60 D3
Emma St. Oldham OL8 ... 66 F3
Emma St. R'dale OL12 ... 139 E8
Emmanuel Cl. BL3 ... 145 D5
Emmanuel Ct. OL6 ... 166 B4
Emmanuel Holcombe CE Prim Sch. BL8 ... 138 A6
Emmanuel Pl. BL3 ... 145 D5
Emmeline Grange. M6 ... 154 E2
Emmett St. BL6 ... 22 B3
Emmett St E. M10 & M40 ... 157 E5
Emmott St. OL1 ... 153 F6
Emmous Wlk. M6 ... 154 F3
Emperor St. SK1 ... 112 A2
Empire Rd. Bolton BL2 ... 42 E7
Empire Rd. Dukinfield SK16 101 C6
Empire St. M8 ... 158 F4
Empress Ave. 2 SK6 ... 125 F5
Empress Bsns Ctr. M16 ... 161 C6
Empress Ct. M16 ... 161 C6
Empress Dr. Leigh WN7 ... 76 E6
Empress Dr. Reddish SK4 ... 169 D4
Empress Ind Est. WN2 ... 151 F7
Empress St. Bolton BL1 ... 142 B1
Empress St. M'ster M8 ... 155 F8
Empress St. M'ster M16 ... 161 C6
Emsworth Cl. 6 BL2 ... 25 B1
Emsworth Dr. M33 ... 108 C1
Ena Cres. WN7 ... 75 C7
Ena St. Bolton BL3 ... 42 A3
Ena St. Oldham OL1 ... 49 C1
Enbridge St. M5 ... 161 A8
Encombe Pl. M3 ... 158 D2
Endcott Cl. M18 ... 165 B6
Enderby Rd. M40 ... 65 C1
Ending Rake. OL12 ... 14 C4
Endon Dr. M21 ... 109 F8
Endon St. BL1 ... 142 B1
Endsleigh Gdns. 1 WN7 ... 75 F5
Endsleigh Rd. M20 ... 110 C6
Endsley Ave. M28 ... 60 C1
Endsor Cl. M16 ... 97 F3
Energy St. M10 & M40 ... 160 E3
Enfield Ave. M'ster M19 ... 111 A6
Enfield Ave. Oldham OL8 ... 66 E3
Enfield Cl. Bolton BL1 ... 143 E1
Enfield Cl. Bury BL9 ... 44 F5
Enfield Cl. Eccles M30 ... 95 D8
Enfield Cl. R'dale OL11 ... 29 E8
Enfield Dr. 7 M11 ... 83 C2
Enfield Gr. WN7 ... 76 B6
Enfield House. M30 ... 95 D8
Enfield Rd. Eccles M27 ... 79 D4
Enfield Rd. Swinton M27 & M28 ... 79 E6
Enfield St. Hyde SK14 ... 113 E7
Enfield St. Walkden M28 ... 60 D5
Enfield St. Wigan WN5 ... 54 C5
Enford Ave. M22 ... 121 A2
Engell Cl. M18 ... 99 D5
Engels House. M30 ... 95 D8
Engine Fold Rd. M28 ... 60 A3
Engine La. M29 ... 59 B4
Engine St. OL9 ... 66 B4
Engineer St. WN2 ... 56 A7
Engledene. BL1 ... 24 D6
Englefield Gr. 3 M18 ... 99 D4
English Martyrs Sch. M41 ... 95 C2
English Matyrs' RC Prim Sch. M16 ... 97 E1
English St. WN7 ... 76 A4
Enid Cl. M7 ... 155 D5
Enid Pl. WN2 ... 73 F8
Ennerdale Ave. Ashton-i-M WN4 ... 73 B5
Ennerdale Ave. Billinge WA11 71 B1
Ennerdale Ave. 4 Bolton BL2 25 F1
Ennerdale Ave. M'ster M21 109 D4
Ennerdale Ave. Royton OL2 ... 48 C7
Ennerdale Ave. Swinton M27 79 F6
Ennerdale Cl. BL3 ... 42 F3
Ennerdale Dr. Sale M33 ... 107 E5
Ennerdale Dr. Sale WA15 ... 120 A8
Ennerdale Dr. Whitefield BL9 45 A2
Ennerdale Gdns. BL2 ... 25 E1
Ennerdale Gr. Ashton-u-L OL7 84 F5
Ennerdale Gr. Farnworth BL4 59 E8
Ennerdale Pl. WN2 ... 56 B8
Ennerdale Rd. Gatley SK8 ... 122 B3
Ennerdale Rd. Hindley WN2 .. 56 E5
Ennerdale Rd. Leigh WN7 ... 76 C4
Ennerdale Rd. Middleton M24 46 F2
Ennerdale Rd. Partington M31 ... 105 E3
Ennerdale Rd. R'dale OL11 ... 30 B4
Ennerdale Rd. Romiley SK6 113 B4
Ennerdale Rd. Stockport SK1 124 B7
Ennerdale Rd. Stretford M32 96 C3
Ennerdale Rd. Tyldesley M29 77 B7
Ennerdale Terr. SK15 ... 86 A3
Ennis Cl. M23 ... 120 E5
Ennismore Ave. M30 ... 80 A2
Enstone Dr. M40 ... 65 D1
Enstone Way. M29 ... 59 C1
Enterprise Ct. M27 ... 80 E7
Enterprise Trad Est. M31 ... 96 A8
Enticott Rd. M44 ... 105 C5
Entwisle Ave. M41 ... 95 B4
Entwisle Rd. OL16 ... 31 A8
Entwisle Row. BL4 ... 60 D8
Entwisle St. 1 Farnworth BL4 42 E1
Entwisle St. Milnrow OL16 ... 31 E6
Entwisle St. Swinton M27 ... 61 D1
Entwistle Gr. WN7 ... 76 C3
Entwistle Hall La. BL7 ... 9 B8
Entwistle St. M26 ... 44 B2

Entwistle Sta. BL7 9 B8
Enver Rd. M8 156 B8
Enville Rd. Alt'ham WA14 119 C3
Enville Rd. M'ster M40 65 B1
Enville Rd. Salford M6 80 E6
Enville St. Ashton-u-L OL6 166 C3
Enville St. Denton M34 100 F7
Enville St. M'ster M9 64 D3
Envoy Cl. WN5 36 E1
Enys Wlk. M6 81 A5
Ephraim's Fold. WN2 38 D6
Epping Cl. Ashton-u-L OL6 85 C7
Epping Cl. Chadderton OL9 65 E8
Epping Dr. M33 107 C5
Epping Rd. M34 100 B2
Epping Wlk. M15 163 A5
Eppleworth Rise. M27 62 A3
Epsley Cl. M15 163 A6
Epsom Ave.
Handforth SK8 & SK9 131 E4
Epsom Ave. M'ster M19 110 F6
Epsom Ave. Sale M33 107 C2
Epsom Cl. SK7 124 F2
Epsom Croft. PR6 21 B7
Epsom Dr. WN2 73 F7
Epsom Mews. M7 155 D6
Epsom Wlk. OL9 152 C7
Epson Cl. OL11 29 F8
Epworth Gr. 5 BL3 146 C3
Epworth St. M60 159 C1
Equitable St. Milnrow OL16 31 F5
Equitable St. Oldham OL4 67 D8
Equitable St. 3 R'dale OL11 31 A6
Era St. Bolton BL2 42 E7
Era St. Sale M33 108 B4
Ercall Ave. M12 164 E6
Eric Brook Cl. 8 M14 98 A3
Eric Bullows Cl. M22 121 C1
Eric St. Littleborough OL15 16 A6
Eric St. Oldham OL4 67 C6
Erica Ave. OL4 49 F4
Erica Cl. SK5 100 A1
Erica Dr. M19 110 E4
Erica Wlk. WN7 75 B5
Erin St. M11 99 E7
Erindale Wlk. M40 156 C6
Erith Cl. SK5 112 B6
Erith Rd. OL4 67 C6
Erlesmere Ave. M34 101 A4
Erlesmere Cl. OL4 49 F4
Erlington Ave. M16 97 B2
Ermen Rd. M30 95 C8
Ermington Dr. M7 & M8 155 F6
Erneley Cl. M12 & M18 99 B3
Ernest St. Bacup OL13 4 C8
Ernest St. Bolton BL1 145 D7
Ernest St. Cheadle SK8 122 C6
Ernest St. Prestwich M25 62 F4
Ernest St. Stockport SK2 124 A6
Ernest Terr. OL12 15 B1
Ernlouen Ave. BL1 144 A8
Ernocroft Gr. 5 M18 99 E6
Ernocroft La. SK14 & SK6 114 E3
Ernocroft Rd. SK6 114 B1
Erradale Cres. WN3 54 D2
Erringdon Cl. SK2 124 E6
Errington Cl. BL3 40 F5
Errington Dr. M7 158 D4
Errol Ave. M'ster M9 64 A5
Errol Ave. Wythenshawe M22 121 C4
Errwood Cres. M19 111 A8
Errwood Rd. M'ster M19 111 A7
Erskine Cl. BL3 40 E5
Erskine Pl. Abram WN2 56 B1
Erskine Rd. M'ster M9 64 E5
Erskine Rd. Partington M31 105 F3
Erskine St. M'ster M15 162 D6
Erskine St. Romiley SK6 114 B3
Erwin St. M40 83 B6
Eryngo St. SK1 112 A1
Escott Wlk. 4 M16 97 F3
Esher Dr. M23 & M33 108 C1
Esk Ave. BL0 1 D5
Esk Cl. M41 95 A4
Eskdale. SK8 122 C4
Eskdale Ave. Blackrod BL6 38 E7
Eskdale Ave. Bolton BL2 25 F2
Eskdale Ave. Bramhall SK7 132 C5
Eskdale Ave. M'ster M20 110 A7
Eskdale Ave. Oldham OL8 66 D4
Eskdale Ave. R'dale OL11 30 B4
Eskdale Ave. Romiley SK6 113 B5
Eskdale Ave. Royton OL2 48 D7
Eskdale Ave. Uppermill OL3 69 B5
Eskdale Ave. Wigan WN1 37 B3
Eskdale Cl. BL9 45 A3
Eskdale Dr.
Alt'ham M23 & WA15 120 C7
Eskdale Dr. Middleton M24 46 F3
Eskdale Gr. BL4 59 F8
Eskdale House. 3 M13 98 E4
Eskdale Mews. OL3 69 B5
Eskdale Rd. Ashton-i-M WN4 73 B4
Eskdale Rd. Hindley WN2 56 E5
Eskdale Terr. SK15 86 A4
Eskrick St. BL1 143 D2
Eskrigge Cl. M7 155 F8
Esmond Rd. M7 & M8 156 A7
Esmont Dr. M24 46 E3
Esplanade The.
OL11 & OL16 139 E7
Essex Ave. Droylsden M43 84 A3
Essex Ave. Heywood OL10 28 E1
Essex Ave. M'ster M20 110 B4
Essex Ave. Stockport SK3 123 B8
Essex Cl. Failsworth M35 83 F5
Essex Cl. Shaw OL2 48 F7
Essex Dr. BL9 45 A8
Essex Gdns. M44 105 C4
Essex Pl. Swinton M27 61 F2
Essex Pl. Tyldesley M29 58 F3
Essex Rd. Brinnington SK5 112 C5
Essex Rd. Reddish M18 99 F4
Essex Rd. Standish WN1 37 B8
Essex St. Horwich BL6 22 D1
Essex St. M'ster M2 158 F1
Essex St. R'dale OL11 139 F6
Essex St. Wigan WN1 37 E1
Essex Way. M16 162 D5
Essingdon St. BL3 147 D4
Essington Wlk. M34 100 E1
Est Bank Rd. BL0 11 A3
Estate St. OL8 66 F4
Estate St S. 3 OL8 66 F4
Esther Fold. BL5 57 E8
Esther St. OL4 67 D7
Esthwaite Dr. M29 77 A7
Eston St. M13 98 D4
Estonfield Dr. M41 95 F2
Eswick St. M11 83 C1
Etchell St. M40 156 C5
Etchells Prim Sch. SK8 122 C1
Etchells Rd. SK8 122 D1
Etchells St. SK1 169 F1
Ethel Ave. M'ster M9 64 D5
Ethel Ave. Pendlebury M27 80 B8
Ethel Cl. OL16 31 B6
Ethel St. Bolton BL3 145 D6
Ethel St. Oldham OL8 66 F3
Ethel St. R'dale OL16 31 B6
Ethel St. Whitworth OL12 4 D2
Ethel Terr. M19 99 A1
Etherley Cl. M44 94 A2
Etherow Ave. Failsworth M40 65 F2
Etherow Ave. Romiley SK6 113 E2
Etherow Brow. SK14 115 B8
Etherow Ctry Pk. SK6 114 C4
Etherow Way. SK14 103 E5
Etherstone St. Leigh WN7 75 E4
Etherstone St. M'ster M9 156 C8
Eton Ave. OL8 66 E3
Eton Cl. OL11 30 B6
Eton Ct. M16 162 D5
Eton Hill Ind Est. M26 44 C5
Eton Hill Rd. M26 44 C5
Eton St. WN7 75 F3
Eton Terr. WN3 151 E5
Eton Way. WN5 53 F8
Eton Way N. M26 44 C5
Eton Way S. M26 44 D5
Etruria Cl. M13 164 E5
Ettington Cl. BL8 27 A3
Ettrick Cl. M11 99 D7
Euclid Cl. M11 160 E1
Euro Ctr The. M8 158 E4
Europa Bsns Pk. SK3 123 B6
Europa Circ. M17 96 D5
Europa Gate. M17 96 D5
Europa Trad Est. M26 61 B7
Europa Way. Cheadle SK3 123 B6
Europa Way. Kearsley M26 61 B7
Europa Way. Stretford M17 96 D5
Euroterminal. M17 & M32 96 D4
Eustace St. Bolton BL3 42 A3
Eustace St. Oldham OL9 152 C8
Eustace Street Prim Sch.
OL9 152 C8
Euston Ave. M9 65 A3
Euxton Cl. BL8 27 A1
Eva Rd. SK3 123 A7
Eva St. Leigh WN7 75 C7
Eva St. M'ster M14 98 C3
Eva St. R'dale OL12 15 A2
Evan Cl. WN6 36 D4
Evan St. M10 & M40 157 E5
Evans Cl. M20 110 A3
Evans Rd. M30 79 A1
Evans St. Ashton-u-L OL6 85 D4
Evans St. Horwich BL6 22 D4
Evans St. Leigh WN7 75 F5
Evans St. M'ster M3 158 E3
Evans St. Middleton M24 65 B8
Evans St. Oldham OL1 153 F8
Evanton Wlk. 13 M9 157 E7
Eve St. OL8 66 F2
Evelyn St. M'ster M14 110 D8
Evelyn St. Oldham OL1 49 B1
Evening St. M35 83 F8
Evenley Cl. 1 M18 99 E6
Everard Cl. M28 78 C8
Everard St. M5 161 C7
Everbrom Rd. BL3 146 A3
Everdingen Wlk. OL1 49 D3
Everest Ave. OL6 & OL7 85 B5
Everest Cl. SK14 102 A4
Everest Pl. 4 WN1 37 C2
Everest Rd. Atherton M46 58 C5
Everest Rd. Hyde SK14 102 A4
Everest St. OL11 31 A2
Everett Ct. 3 M20 110 B6
Everett Rd. M20 110 B6
Everglade. OL8 67 A1
Evergreen Wlk. 3 M33 107 C6
Everleigh Cl. BL2 25 E5
Everleigh Dr. M7 & M8 155 F6
Eversden Ct. M7 158 E4
Eversley Ct. M33 108 B2
Eversley Rd. M20 110 A3
Everton Rd. Oldham OL8 66 D3
Everton Rd. Reddish SK5 99 F2
Everton St. Garswood WN4 72 D5
Everton St. Swinton M27 79 E8
Every St. Bury BL9 140 F4
Every St. M'ster M11 & M40 160 D1
Every St. Ramsbottom BL0 11 D6
Evesham Ave. Alt'ham M23 120 D7
Evesham Ave. 4
Hadfield SK14 104 A5
Evesham Ave. M'ster SK4 168 B3
Evesham Cl. 11 Bolton BL3 145 D6
Evesham Cl. Middleton M24 65 B5
Evesham Dr. BL3 & BL4 42 B2
Evesham Gdns. M24 65 A5
Evesham Gr. Ashton-u-L OL6 85 C7
Evesham Gr. Sale M33 108 E4
Evesham Rd. Cheadle SK8 123 A4
Evesham Rd. M'ster M9 65 A2
Evesham Rd. Middleton M24 65 B5
Evesham Wlk. 10
Bolton BL3 145 D6
Evesham Wlk. Middleton M24 65 B5
Evesham Wlk. Oldham OL8 153 E5
Eveside Cl. SK8 123 B4
Evington Ave. M11 100 A7
Ewan St. M18 99 D6
Ewart Ave. M5 81 A1
Ewart St. BL1 143 E2
Ewhurst Ave. M27 79 D6
Ewing Cl. M8 64 A1
Ewing Sch. M20 110 A5
Ewood. 12 Eccles M30 79 F2
Ewood. Oldham OL8 85 A8
Ewood Dr. BL8 44 A8
Ewood La. BB4 1 C7
Exbourne Rd. M22 121 C1
Exbridge Wlk. M40 83 D4
Exbury. 24 OL12 139 E8
Exbury St. M14 110 D7
Excalibur Way. M44 105 F7
Excelsior Terr. OL16 15 F3
Exchange Quay. M5 161 A6
Exchange St. 9 Bolton BL1 145 F7
Exchange St. Edenfield BL0 1 D3
Exchange St. M'ster M2 158 F1
Exchange St. 5 Oldham OL4 67 B7
Exchange St. Stockport SK3 169 E1
Exeter Ave. Bolton BL2 25 B2
Exeter Ave. Denton M34 100 F1
Exeter Ave. Eccles M30 80 A4
Exeter Ave. Farnworth BL4 59 F8
Exeter Ave. Radcliffe M26 44 A5
Exeter Cl. Cheadle SK8 131 F8
Exeter Cl. Dukinfield SK16 101 D6
Exeter Cl. M'ster M14 110 E8
Exeter Ct. 3 Middleton M24 46 F1
Exeter Dr. Ashton-u-L OL6 85 D7
Exeter Dr. Aspull WN2 38 D5
Exeter Dr. Irlam M44 94 B2
Exeter Gr. OL11 139 F5
Exeter Rd. Brinnington SK5 112 C5
Exeter Rd. Hindley WN2 56 E5
Exeter Rd. Urmston M41 95 D4
Exeter St. R'dale OL11 139 F5
Exeter St. Salford M6 154 E2
Exeter Wlk. SK7 132 F7
Exford Ave. WN3 55 B4
Exford Cl.
M'ster M10 & M40 160 D3
Exford Cl. Reddish SK5 111 F6
Exford Dr. BL2 43 A6
Exhall Cl. M38 60 A6
Exit Rd W. M90 130 B7
Exmoor Cl. OL6 85 C7
Exmouth Ave. SK5 112 C5
Exmouth Pl. OL11 31 A4
Exmouth Rd. M33 107 D5
Exmouth Sq. OL11 31 A3
Exmouth St. OL11 31 A3
Exmouth Wlk. 7 M16 97 F3
Exton Wlk. 18 M16 97 E4
Eyam Cl. 12 SK13 171 D2
Eyam Fold. 16 SK13 171 E2
Eyam Gdns. 25 SK13 171 D2
Eyam Gn. 13 SK13 171 D2
Eyam Gr. 11 Gamesley SK13 171 D2
Eyam Gr. Stockport SK2 124 D5
Eyam La. SK13 171 D2
Eyam Lea. 15 SK13 171 E2
Eyam Mews. SK13 171 D2
Eyam Rd. SK7 124 E1
Eyebrook Rd. Alt'ham WA14 119 A2
Eyet St. WN7 75 E5
Eynford Ave. SK5 112 B6
Eyre St. M15 163 A5

Faber St. M4 159 A3
Factory Brow. Blackrod BL6 21 D3
Factory Brow. Middleton M24 64 C7
Factory Fold. WN2 56 A7
Factory Hill. BL6 22 D4
Factory La. Adlington PR6 21 B8
Factory La. Disley SK12 135 E7
Factory La. M'ster M9 64 D1
Factory La. M'ster M3 158 D1
Factory St. Middleton M24 64 F8
Factory St. Radcliffe M26 44 B3
Factory St. Ramsbottom BL0 138 C7
Factory St. Tyldesley M29 58 F1
Factory St E. M46 58 C3
Factory St W. M46 58 C3
Faggy La. WN3 150 C7
Failsworth Ind Est. 2 M35 83 C6
Failsworth Rd. M35 84 C7
Failsworth Sch. M35 84 A7
Failsworth Sch (Lwr). M35 83 F7
Failsworth Sh Ctr. 1 M35 83 F7
Failsworth Sta. M35 83 E8
Fair Acres. BL2 25 E3
Fair Hill. BB4 1 A7
Fair Oak Rd. M19 110 F5
Fair St. Bolton BL3 146 C2
Fair St. M'ster M1 & M60 159 C1
Fair St. Swinton M27 62 A1
Fair View. Bacup OL13 4 C8
Fair View. Billinge WN5 71 D5
Fair View. Littleborough OL15 16 C7
Fair View Ave. WN5 71 D5
Fair Way. OL11 30 B1
Fairacres. WN6 19 B1
Fairacres Rd. SK6 134 E8
Fairbairn St. Horwich BL6 22 B3
Fairbairn St. M'ster M11 160 F2
Fairbank. M43 99 F8
Fairbank Ave. M14 98 B4
Fairbank Dr. M24 46 D2
Fairbottom St. OL1 153 E7
Fairbottom Wlk. 4 M35 100 A8
Fairbourne Ave. Wigan WN3 55 A4
Fairbourne Ave.
Wilmslow SK9 136 F4
Fairbourne Ave.
Wilmslow SK9 137 B3
Fairbourne Cl. SK9 136 F4
Fairbourne Dr.
Sale M33,WA15 108 B1
Fairbourne Dr.
Wilmslow SK9 136 F4
Fairbourne Rd. Denton M34 100 E2
Fairbourne Rd. Reddish M19 99 C1
Fairbrook Dr. M6 154 E2
Fairbrother St. M5 161 C7
Fairclough St. Bolton BL3 42 A4
Fairclough St. Hindley WN2 56 D6
Fairclough St. M'ster M11 83 A2
Fairclough St.
Newton-l-W WA12 89 B3
Fairclough St. Wigan WN1 151 D7
Fairfax Ave. Alt'ham WA15 120 A6
Fairfax Ave. M'ster M20 110 B4
Fairfax Cl. SK6 125 D7
Fairfax Dr.
Littleborough OL15 15 F3
Fairfax Dr. Wilmslow SK9 136 F4
Fairfax Rd. M25 63 A5
Fairfield. OL6 85 C8
Fairfield Ave. Cheadle SK8 122 F2
Fairfield Ave.
Droylsden M34 & M35 & M43 100 A7
Fairfield Ave.
Platt Bridge WN2 56 A3
Fairfield Ave. Romiley SK6 113 A4
Fairfield Ave. Wigan WN5 54 D5
Fairfield Ct. M14 98 D4
Fairfield Dr. BL9 28 D3
Fairfield General Hospl.
BL9 28 E4
Fairfield Golf Course. M34 100 B5
Fairfield High Sch
for Girls. M43 100 A8
Fairfield House. M43 84 A1
Fairfield Prim Sch. BL9 28 D3
Fairfield Rd. Alt'ham WA15 120 C5
Fairfield Rd.
Droylsden M11 & M43 99 F8
Fairfield Rd. Farnworth BL4 60 C7
Fairfield Rd. Irlam M44 105 C5
Fairfield Rd. Middleton M24 46 E1
Fairfield Road Prim Sch.
M43 99 F8
Fairfield Sq. M43 100 A8
Fairfield St.
M'ster M1 & M12 163 C8
Fairfield St. Salford M6 80 E5
Fairfield St. Wigan WN5 54 D5
Fairfield Sta. M34 100 A7
Fairfield View. M34 100 A7
Fairfields. Bolton BL7 24 F8
Fairfields. Oldham OL8 66 E2
Fairford Cl. SK5 111 F5
Fairford Dr. BL3 145 E5
Fairford Way. Reddish SK5 111 F5
Fairford Way. Wilmslow SK9 137 D7
Fairham Wlk. M4 160 D1
Fairhaven Ave. M'ster M21 109 B8
Fairhaven Ave.
Westhoughton BL5 58 B8
Fairhaven Ave.
Whitefield M45 62 D7
Fairhaven Cl. SK7 132 F8
Fairhaven Rd. BL1 143 F3
Fairhaven St. M12 164 F6
Fairhill Terr. BB4 1 A7
Fairhills Rd. M44 106 A8
Fairholme Ave.
Ashton-i-M WN4 73 B4
Fairholme Ave. Urmston M41 95 C1
Fairholme Rd. M'ster M20 110 C6
Fairholme Rd. M'ster SK4 168 C3
Fairhope Ave. M6 80 C3
Fairhurst Ave. WN6 19 D3
Fairhurst Dr. M28 59 F2
Fairhurst St. Leigh WN7 75 E5
Fairhurst St. Wigan WN3 150 B8
Fairisle Cl. M11 160 F1
Fairlands Pl. OL11 31 B2
Fairlands Rd. Bury BL9 27 F6
Fairlands Rd. Sale M33 107 F2
Fairlands St. OL11 31 B2
Fairlands View. OL11 31 B2
Fairlawn. SK4 169 D3
Fairlawn Cl. M14 98 A4
Fairlea. M34 101 A2
Fairlea Ave. M20 110 C2
Fairlee Ave. M34 84 C1
Fairleigh Ave. M6 80 C3
Fairless Rd. M30 79 D1
Fairlie Ave. BL3 40 F5
Fairlie Dr. WA15 120 B8
Fairlyn Cl. BL5 59 A7
Fairlyn Dr. BL5 59 A7
Fairman Cl. M16 97 F3
Fairmead Rd. M23 109 C1
Fairmile Dr. M20 122 C8
Fairmount Ave. BL2 42 E8
Fairmount Rd. M27 & M28 79 C6
Fairoak Ct. BL3 145 D5
Fairstead Wlk. 4 M11 99 F7
Fairthorne Grange. OL7 84 F1
Fairview Ave. M'ster M19 98 F2
Fairview Ave. Reddish M34 100 A1
Fairview Cl. Ashton-i-M WN4 73 B4
Fairview Cl. Chadderton OL9 65 F8
Fairview Cl. Marple SK6 125 F7
Fairview Cl.
R'dale OL11 & OL12 13 C2
Fairview Dr. SK6 125 F7
Fairview Rd. Alt'ham WA15 120 C5
Fairview Rd. Reddish M34 100 A1
Fairway. Bramhall SK7 132 D6
Fairway. Droylsden M34 100 A8
Fairway. Gatley SK8 122 B4
Fairway. M'ster M25 63 D2
Fairway. Milnrow OL16 32 A6
Fairway. Pendlebury M27 80 C7
Fairway. Whitworth OL12 14 C7
Fairway Ave. Bolton BL2 26 A4
Fairway Ave. Sale M23 120 D7
Fairway Cres. OL2 48 D6
Fairway Ct. M34 100 B4
Fairway Dr. M33 107 E2
Fairway Prim Sch. SK2 124 E7
Fairway Rd. Oldham OL4 67 E4
Fairway Rd. Whitefield BL9 45 A3
Fairway The. Failsworth M40 83 C8
Fairway The. Stockport SK2 124 D7
Fairways. BL6 22 C3
Fairways Cl. SK13 104 F1
Fairways The.
Garswood WN4 72 D2
Fairways The.
Westhoughton BL5 57 E8
Fairways The. Whitefield M45 62 F6
Fairwood Rd. M23 120 D7
Fairy La. M'ster M7 & M8 155 E5
Fairy La.
Wythenshawe M23 & M33 109 A3
Fairy St. BL8 27 C2
Fairywell Cl. SK9 131 D1
Fairywell Dr. M33 108 A1
Fairywell Rd. WA15 120 C7
Faith St. Bolton BL1 142 A1
Faith St. Leigh WN7 75 C5
Falcon Ave. M41 95 E2
Falcon Cl. Bury BL9 141 B4
Falcon Cl. R'dale OL12 13 E2
Falcon Cres. M27 62 C2
Falcon Ct. M'ster M7 155 D8
Falcon Ct. M'ster M16 162 E5
Falcon Dr. Irlam M44 94 B4
Falcon Dr. Middleton M24 46 E3
Falcon Dr. Oldham OL9 152 C8
Falcon Dr. Walkden M38 60 A5
Falcon St. Bolton BL1 145 F8
Falcon St. Oldham OL8 153 F5
Falconers Gn. WN3 150 B5
Falconwood Chase. M28 78 C6
Falconwood Cl. 11 WN6 37 A1
Falfield Dr. M8 156 B5
Falinge Fold. OL12 14 D1
Falinge Mews. OL12 139 E8
Falinge Park High Sch.
OL12 14 D1
Falinge Rd. OL12 14 E1
Falkirk Dr. Bolton BL2 42 F6
Falkirk Dr. Ince-i-M WN2 56 A8
Falkirk Gr. WN5 54 C8
Falkirk St. 5 OL4 67 C7
Falkirk Wlk. 5 M23 121 A2
Falkland Ave. M'ster M10 160 D4
Falkland Ave. R'dale OL11 30 C8
Falkland Cl. OL4 49 E4
Falkland Dr. WN4 72 C4
Falkland House. M14 98 C1
Falkland Rd. BL2 43 A7
Fall Bank. SK4 111 D6
Fall Birch Hospl. BL6 23 A1
Fall Birch Rd. BL6 39 F8
Fallons Rd. M27 & M28 61 C1
Fallow Cl. BL5 39 E2
Fallow Fields Dr. SK5 100 A1
Fallowfield. M5 161 B8
Fallowfield Ave. M5 161 B7
Fallowfield Dr. OL12 14 D2
Fallowfield Sh Ctr. M14 98 E1
Fallows The. OL9 152 A5
Falls Gr. SK8 122 A3
Falmer Cl. BL8 27 C6
Falmer Dr. M22 121 D1
Falmer St. M18 99 F6
Falmouth Ave. Sale M33 107 D5
Falmouth Ave. Urmston M41 94 E3
Falmouth Cres. SK5 112 C5
Falmouth Rd. M44 94 B2
Falmouth St.
M'ster M10 & M40 160 F4
Falmouth St. Oldham OL8 66 F4
Falmouth St. 20 R'dale OL11 31 A5
Falsgrave Cl. M40 83 A5
Falshaw Dr. BL9 11 E1
Falside Wlk. 17 M40 83 C5
Falston Ave. M40 65 D2
Falstone Ave. BL0 11 C4
Falstone Cl. WN3 54 E2
Falterley Rd. M23 120 F8
Fancroft Rd. M22 121 C5
Fane Wlk. M9 64 B3
Far Cromwell Rd. SK6 112 D7
Far Hey Cl. M26 43 E3
Far La. M18 99 D4
Far Ridings. SK6 113 D3
Far Woodseats La. SK14 114 F5
Faraday Ave.
M'ster M7 & M8 156 A6
Faraday Ave. Swinton M27 62 D2
Faraday Dr. BL1 143 E1
Faraday St. M1 & M60 159 B1
Farcroft Ave. M26 44 C6
Farcroft Cl. M23 120 F8
Fardale. OL2 149 B6
Farden Dr. M23 120 D8
Fardon Cl. WN3 54 F3
Farefield Ave. WA3 73 F2
Fareham Cl. M16 162 D5
Farewell Cl. 1 OL11 30 C2
Farholme. OL1 48 C2
Farholme La. OL13 3 D8
Faringdon. 4 OL11 139 E6
Faringdon Wlk. BL3 145 E5
Farland Pl. BL3 40 F5
Farlands Dr. M20 122 B7
Farley Ave. M18 & M34 100 A4
Farley Ct. SK8 122 F3
Farley La. WN8 35 A3
Farley Rd. M33 108 C2
Farley Way. SK5 99 E1
Farm Ave. Adlington PR6 21 A8
Farm Ave. Stretford M32 96 A4
Farm Cl. Bury BL8 26 F6
Farm Cl. Reddish SK4 111 C6
Farm La. High Lane SK12 135 A6
Farm La. Hyde SK14 113 D8
Farm La. Middleton M25 63 E8
Farm La. Wigan WN2 38 A2
Farm La. Worsley M28 78 F5
Farm Meadow Rd. WN5 53 E5
Farm Rd. OL8 84 C8
Farm Side Pl. 10 M19 99 A1
Farm St. Failsworth M35 83 E6
Farm St. Heywood OL10 46 E8
Farm St. Oldham OL1 & OL9 48 B1
Farm Way. WA12 89 E1
Farm Wlk. Alt'ham WA14 118 E1
Farm Wlk. Littleborough OL15 15 F5
Farm Wlk. R'dale OL16 15 C1
Farm Yd. M19 99 A1
Farman St. BL3 147 D3
Farmer St. SK4 169 E3
Farmers Cl. M33 109 A3
Farmfield. M33 107 E6
Farmfold. SK9 130 F3
Farmside Ave. M44 94 A3
Farmstead Cl. M35 84 C6
Farmway. M24 65 A7
Farn Ave. SK5 99 F2
Farnborough Rd. Bolton BL1 24 E6
Farnborough Rd.
M'ster M10 & M40 160 D3
Farncombe Cl. 2 M23 120 D7
Farndale Gr. WN4 73 C2
Farndale Sq. M38 60 C3
Farndale Wlk. 17 M9 157 E8
Farndon Ave. SK7 124 F4
Farndon Cl. M33 108 E3
Farndon Dr. WA15 120 A6
Farndon Rd. SK5 99 E2
Farnham Ave. M9 64 D5
Farnham Cl. 21 Bolton BL1 143 E1
Farnham Cl. Cheadle SK8 132 A7
Farnham Cl. Leigh WN7 75 F6
Farnham Dr. M44 94 B1
Farnhill Wlk. M23 108 E1
Farnley Cl. OL12 13 F2
Farnley St. M12 165 A6
Farnsfield. WN1 37 F1
Farnsworth Ave. OL7 85 B5
Farnsworth Cl. OL7 85 B5
Farnworth Dr. M14 98 C2
Farnworth St. Bolton BL3 146 C4
Farnworth St. 7
Heywood OL10 29 C2
Farnworth St. 6 Leigh WN7 76 B4
Farnworth Sta. BL4 42 E1
Farr Cl. WN3 54 F5
Farr St. SK3 170 D8
Farrand Rd. OL8 66 B2
Farrant Rd. M12 & M18 99 A4
Farrar Rd. M43 99 F8
Farrell St. M'ster M7 158 E3
Farrell St. Wigan WN5 54 C5
Farrer Rd. M13 98 F3
Farrier's Croft. WN6 36 E3
Farriers La. OL11 30 B4
Farringdon Dr. M26 43 E4
Farringdon St. M6 154 E3
Farrington Ave. M20 110 A7
Farrow St. OL2 149 B6
Farrow St E. OL2 149 B6
Farrowdale Ave. OL2 149 B6
Farwood Cl. M16 161 C5
Fastnet St. M11 165 A8
Fatherford Cl. OL3 51 D5
Faulkenhurst Mews. OL1 48 C1
Faulkenhurst St. OL1 & OL9 48 C1
Faulkes House. 3 M14 110 D8
Faulkner Dr. WA15 120 B5
Faulkner Rd. M32 96 E2
Faulkner St. Bolton BL3 145 E5
Faulkner St. M'ster M1 163 A8
Faulkner St. R'dale OL16 139 F7
Fauvel Pl. SK13 104 C1
Fauvel Rd. SK13 104 C2
Faversham Brow. 9 OL1 153 E8
Faversham St. M40 83 B7
Fawborough Rd. M23 108 F1
Fawcett St. 2 BL2 148 B7
Fawcetts Fold. BL5 39 E4
Fawley Ave. SK14 167 D1
Fawley Gr. M22 121 D4
Fawns Keep.
Stalybridge SK15 102 E6
Fawns Keep. Wilmslow SK9 137 D7
Fay Ave. M9 65 B2
Fay Gdns. SK14 171 E4
Faywood Dr. SK6 126 A6
Fearn St. OL10 29 C2
Fearney Side. BL3 42 F3
Fearnham Cl. WN7 75 E1
Fearnhead Ave. BL6 22 B5
Fearnhead Cl. BL4 60 E8
Fearnhead St. BL3 146 C4
Fearnley Way. WA12 89 B1
Fearns Moss. OL13 3 A8
Featherstall House. OL9 152 C5
Featherstall Rd. OL15 16 A5
Featherstall Rd N.
OL1 & OL9 153 D8
Featherstall Rd S. OL9 153 D6
Fecit La. BL0 & OL12 12 C8
Federation St.
M'ster M4 & M60 159 A2
Federation St. Prestwich M25 62 F5
Feldom Rd. M23 108 F2
Fell St. Bury BL8 27 C2
Fell St. Leigh WN7 75 B5
Fellbridge Cl. BL5 40 B1
Fellbrigg Cl. M18 99 C3
Fellfoot Cl. M28 77 F5
Felling Wlk. 6 M14 98 B3
Fellpark Rd. M23 109 A2
Fells Gr. M28 60 F1
Fellside. Bolton BL2 26 A3
Fellside. Oldham OL1 153 E7
Fellside. Wigan WN1 37 D2
Fellside Cl. BL8 10 F1
Fellside Gn. SK15 86 A3
Felltop Dr. SK5 112 A8
Felskirk Rd. M22 130 C8
Felsted. BL1 40 E8
Felt Ct. M34 100 C2
Felthorpe Dr. M7 & M8 155 F6
Felton Ave. M22 121 D3
Felton Cl. BL9 45 A5
Felton Wlk. BL1 143 E2
Fence St. SK2 124 D4
Fencegate Ave. SK4 111 D5
Fenchurch Ave. M40 83 C4
Fencot Dr. M18 99 A4
Fenella St. M13 98 E4
Fenham Cl. M40 156 C5
Fenmore Ave. M18 99 B3
Fenn St. M15 162 E6
Fennel St. M3 & M4 158 F2
Fenners Cl. BL3 147 D3
Fenney St. M7 155 D5
Fenney St E. M7 155 E6
Fenside Rd. M22 121 E5
Fenstock Wlk. M40 83 D4
Fentewan Wlk. SK14 102 E3
Fenton Ave. SK2 & SK7 124 D4
Fenton Mews. OL11 139 F5
Fenton St. Bury BL8 27 C3

Foxley Cl. Droylsden M43 99 E8
Foxley Cl. Lymm WA13 117 A2
Foxley Gr. BL3 145 D6
Foxley Hall Mews. WA13 117 A1
Foxley Wlk. M12 165 A5
Foxton St. M24 64 C7
Foxton Wlk. 6 M23 121 A2
Foxwell Wlk. 5 M8 156 B6
Foxwood Dr. OL5 68 D2
Foxwood Gdns. M19 110 E5
Foy St. WN4 73 B3
Foynes Cl. M40 157 D5
Fram St. M'ster M9 157 F8
Fram St. Salford M6 154 E2
Framingham Rd. M33 108 B2
Framley Rd. M20 & M21 109 F7
Frampton Cl. M24 65 B7
France St. Hindley WN2 56 D6
France St. Westhoughton BL5 57 E6
France St. Wigan WN5 54 F7
Frances Ave. SK8 122 A6
Frances Pl. M46 58 A2
Frances St. Bolton BL1 143 D2
Frances St. Cheadle SK8 122 E6
Frances St. Denton M34 113 B8
Frances St. Dukinfield SK14 101 C3
Frances St. Irlam M44 105 E5
Frances St. Littleborough OL16 15 D4
Frances St. M'ster M13 163 B6
Frances St. Oldham OL1 49 B1
Frances St. 8
Stockport SK1 & SK3 170 E8
Frances St W. SK14 101 C3
Francesca Wlk. M18 165 C6
Francis Ave. Eccles M30 79 E2
Francis Ave. Walkden M28 60 F2
Francis Rd. Irlam M44 93 F1
Francis Rd. M'ster M20 110 C5
Francis St. Eccles M30 79 D3
Francis St. Failsworth M35 83 F7
Francis St. Farnworth BL4 42 D1
Francis St. Hindley WN2 56 E5
Francis St. Leigh WN7 75 E7
Francis St. M'ster M3 158 F3
Francis St. Tyldesley M29 77 D8
Francis Terr. 3 SK16 166 C1
Frandley Wlk. 4 M13 163 B7
Frank Cowan Ct. M7 158 D4
Frank Hulme House. M32 96 E1
Frank Perkins Way. M44 105 F7
Frank St. Bolton BL1 143 D2
Frank St. Bury BL9 140 F1
Frank St. Failsworth M35 83 E7
Frank St. Hyde SK14 167 E2
Frank St. 3 M'ster M1 163 A7
Frank St. Salford M6 81 A4
Frank Swift Wlk. 5 M14 98 A3
Frankby Cl. M27 80 C7
Frankford Ave. BL1 142 C2
Frankford Sq. BL1 142 C2
Frankland Cl. M11 83 B2
Franklin Cl. M34 100 A2
Franklin Rd. M43 84 A1
Franklin St. Eccles M30 79 D2
Franklin St. Oldham OL1 153 E8
Franklin St. R'dale OL16 31 B5
Franklyn Ave. M41 94 E2
Franklyn Rd. M18 99 E6
Frankton Rd. M45 62 F7
Franton Rd. M11 83 B2
Fraser Ave. M33 108 E3
Fraser House. BL1 143 D1
Fraser Pl. M17 96 D5
Fraser Rd. M'ster M8 63 F1
Fraser Rd. Wigan WN5 54 E7
Fraser St. Ashton-u-L OL6 166 C3
Fraser St. R'dale OL11 & OL16 31 B4
Fraser St. Shaw OL2 149 A7
Fraser St. Swinton M27 62 A1
Fraternitas Terr. M43 83 E3
Frawley Ave. WA12 89 C5
Freckleton Ave. M21 109 C4
Freckleton Dr. BL8 43 F8
Freckleton St. WN1 37 C2
Fred Longworth High Sch.
M29 58 E1
Fred Tilson Cl. M14 98 A3
Freda Wlk. M11 160 F1
Frederica Gdns. WN2 56 A3
Frederick Ave. OL2 149 B5
Frederick Ct. BL4 60 E8
Frederick Rd. M6 & M7 81 B4
Frederick St. Ashton-i-M WN4 73 A5
Frederick St.
Ashton-u-L OL6 & SK15 85 E2
Frederick St. Denton M34 100 F5
Frederick St. Farnworth BL4 60 D8
Frederick St. Hindley WN2 56 D5
Frederick St. Ince-i-M WN3 151 D6
Frederick St.
Littleborough OL15 16 A6
Frederick St. M'ster M3 158 E2
Frederick St. Oldham OL8 66 D4
Frederick St. Oldham OL9 152 B8
Frederick St.
Ramsbottom BL0 138 B5
Frederick St. Wigan WN1 151 E8
Free La. BB4 1 A6
Freehold Comm Prim Sch.
OL9 152 C5
Freehold St. OL11 139 E5
Freeholds Rd. OL12 4 E6
Freeholds Terr. OL12 4 E6
Freeland Wlk. M11 165 C8
Freelands. M29 59 C1
Freeman Ave. OL6 85 D3
Freeman Rd. SK16 101 C7
Freemantle St. SK3 170 D8
Freesia Ave. 9 M28 59 F3
Freestone Cl. BL8 140 D3
Freetown. SK13 116 C7
Freetown Cl. M14 98 A4
Freetrade St. OL11 139 E6
Freiston. 5 OL12 139 F8
Fremantle Ave. M18 99 D3
French Ave. 5 Oldham OL1 49 C1
French Ave. Stalybridge SK15 86 C1
French Barn La. M9 64 C3
French Gr. BL3 42 D5
French St. Ashton-u-L OL6 85 D4
French St. Stalybridge SK15 86 C1
Frensham Wlk. M23 120 F4
Fresca Rd. OL1 49 D4
Fresh Ct. SK13 115 F7
Freshfield. SK8 131 B8
Freshfield Ave. Atherton M46 58 C4
Freshfield Ave. Bolton BL3 147 D2
Freshfield Ave. Bolton BL3 147 F2
Freshfield Ave. Hyde SK14 167 D1
Freshfield Ave.
Prestwich M25 63 C6
Freshfield Cl. Failsworth M35 84 A6
Freshfield Cl. Romiley SK6 114 B1
Freshfield Gr. BL3 147 F2
Freshfield Rd. Hindley WN2 56 F5
Freshfield Rd. M'ster SK4 110 F3
Freshfield Rd. Wigan WN3 54 E3
Freshfield Wlk. 11 M11 83 C2
Freshfields. M26 43 D5
Freshford Wlk. 2 M22 121 B1
Freshville St. M'ster M1 163 B8
Freshwater Dr. M34 113 B8
Freshwater St. 3 M18 99 E6
Freshwinds Ct. OL4 67 D4
Fresnel Cl. SK14 102 B6
Frew Cl. M9 65 B2
Frewland Ave. SK3 123 F4
Freya Gr. M5 161 C8
Friar's Cl. SK9 136 E8
Friar's Rd. M33 108 B4
Friarmere Rd. OL3 50 E5
Friars Cl. Alt'ham WA14 119 B1
Friars Cl. Tyldesley M29 59 D1
Friars Cres. OL11 30 F2
Friars Ct. M5 60 F2
Friars Prim Sch The. M3 158 D3
Friendship Ave. M18 99 E4
Frieston Rd. WA14 119 E8
Friezland Cl. SK15 86 E6
Friezland La. OL3 69 A4
Friezland Prim Sch. OL4 68 E5
Frimley Gdns. M22 121 D3
Frinton Ave. M40 65 E1
Frinton Cl. M33 107 F1
Frinton Rd. BL3 146 B3
Frith Rd. M20 110 C5
Frith St. WN5 & WN6 150 A7
Frobisher Cl. M13 164 D5
Frobisher Pl. SK5 169 E4
Frobisher Rd. OL15 6 C1
Frodsham Ave. SK4 168 C3
Frodsham Cl. WN6 36 D3
Frodsham Rd. M33 108 E2
Frodsham St. 8 M14 98 B3
Frodsham Way. SK9 131 E4
Frog La. Wigan WN6 37 A1
Frog La. Wigan WN1 & WN6 150 B8
Frogley St. BL2 25 B3
Frogmore Ave. SK14 113 E7
Frome Ave. Stockport SK2 124 C5
Frome Ave. Urmston M41 95 B1
Frome Cl. M29 77 C6
Frome Dr. M8 156 B7
Frome St. OL4 67 C6
Frost St. M'ster M10 & M40 160 D1
Frost St. Oldham OL8 66 E4
Frostlands Rd. 24 M16 97 E4
Frowde Wlk. 7 M16 97 E4
Froxmer St. M18 165 C6
Fryent Cl. BL6 21 D2
Fulbeck Ave. WN3 55 A2
Fulbeck Wlk. M8 155 E5
Fulbrook Dr. SK8 132 A6
Fulbrook Way. M29 59 C1
Fulham Ave. M40 83 B5
Fulham St. OL4 67 C6
Full Pot La. OL11 29 E8
Fullerton Rd. SK4 168 B2
Fulmar Cl. Poynton SK12 133 A4
Fulmar Cl. Westhoughton BL5 57 D6
Fulmar Dr. Hazel Grove SK2 124 F5
Fulmar Dr. Sale M33 107 C2
Fulmar Gdns. OL11 29 F7
Fulmards Cl. SK9 137 C7
Fulmead Wlk. 16 M7 155 F6
Fulmer Dr. M40 160 D2
Fulmere Ct. M27 79 D6
Fulneck Sq. 2 M43 100 A8
Fulshaw Ave. SK9 137 A6
Fulshaw CE Prim Sch. SK9 136 F6
Fulshaw Cross. SK9 137 A5
Fulshaw Ct. SK9 137 A5
Fulshaw Pk. SK9 137 A5
Fulshaw Pk S. SK9 137 A4
Fulshaw Wlk. 7 M13 163 B7
Fulstone Mews. SK2 124 B6
Fulthorpe Wlk. 13 M9 64 E5
Fulton Ct. M15 163 A5
Fulwell Ave. M46 76 E8
Fulwood Ave. M9 64 F4
Fulwood Cl. BL8 26 F1
Fulwood Rd. WA3 90 E7
Furbarn La. OL11 29 D8
Furbarn Rd. OL11 29 D8
Furlong Cl. WN2 73 F7
Furlong Rd. M22 121 B3
Furnace St. Ashton-u-L SK16 166 B2
Furnace St. Dukinfield SK14 101 C4
Furness Ave. Ashton-u-L OL7 84 F5
Furness Ave. Bolton BL2 25 B2
Furness Ave. Heywood OL10 29 C3
Furness Ave.
Littleborough OL15 16 A6
Furness Ave. Oldham OL8 67 C3
Furness Ave. Whitefield M45 63 A8
Furness Cl. Glossop SK13 116 F8
Furness Cl. Milnrow OL16 31 E6
Furness Cl. Poynton SK12 133 D4
Furness Cres. WN7 57 D1
Furness Gr. SK4 168 A1
Furness Quay. M5 161 A7
Furness Rd. Bolton BL1 144 B7
Furness Rd. Bramhall SK8 132 C6
Furness Rd. M'ster M14 98 C1
Furness Rd. Middleton M24 47 A3
Furness Rd. Urmston M41 95 D3
Furness Sq. BL2 25 B2
Furnival Cl. M34 100 A2
Furnival Rd. M18 165 C5
Furnival St. Leigh WN7 75 F7
Furnival St. Reddish SK5 99 F2
Furrow Comm Prim Sch.
M24 46 D2
Further Field. OL11 13 D1
Further Heights Rd. 1 OL12 14 F1
Further Hey Cl. OL4 67 E7
Further La. SK14 102 E3
Further Pits. OL11 30 C7
Furtherwood Rd. OL1 48 C1
Furze Ave. BL5 57 F7
Furze La. OL4 49 D1
Furze Wlk. M31 106 A3
Fushia Gr. M7 155 D6
Fyfield Wlk. 3 M8 156 B6
Fylde Ave. Bolton BL2 42 E7
Fylde Ave. Gatley SK8 131 C8
Fylde Ct. M32 108 C8
Fylde Rd. SK4 168 A2
Fylde St. BL4 42 D2
Fylde St E. BL4 42 D2

Gabbot St. PR6 21 A7
Gable Ave. SK9 137 A7
Gable Ct. M34 100 F2
Gable Dr. M24 46 E1
Gable St. Bolton BL2 25 D5
Gable St. M'ster M12 164 F8
Gable St. Newton-l-W WA12 89 B3
Gables The. M33 108 B3
Gabriel Wlk. 11 M16 97 F3
Gabriels The. OL2 48 F7
Gadbury Ave. M46 58 B3
Gaddum Rd. Alt'ham WA14 119 B1
Gaddum Rd. M'ster M20 110 C3
Gail Ave. SK4 169 D2
Gail Cl. Alderley Edge SK9 137 B2
Gail Cl. Failsworth M35 83 E5
Gainford Ave. SK8 122 B4
Gainford Gdns. M40 65 B1
Gainford Rd. SK5 99 F1
Gainford Wlk. BL3 147 E4
Gainsborough Ave.
Bolton BL3 146 C3
Gainsborough Ave.
M'ster M20 110 C5
Gainsborough Ave.
Marple SK6 126 B8
Gainsborough Ave.
Oldham OL8 66 E4
Gainsborough Ave.
Stretford M32 96 F3
Gainsborough Cl.
Wigan WN3 54 D3
Gainsborough Cl.
Wilmslow SK9 137 D8
Gainsborough Dr.
Cheadle SK8 122 F6
Gainsborough Dr.
R'dale OL11 30 E3
Gainsborough Rd.
Chadderton OL9 47 E1
Gainsborough Rd.
Droylsden M34 84 D1
Gainsborough Rd.
Ramsbottom BL0 11 B1
Gainsborough St. M7 155 E7
Gainsborough Wlk.
Denton M34 100 E1
Gainsborough Wlk. 1
Dukinfield SK14 101 F5
Gair Rd. SK5 169 F4
Gair St. SK14 167 D4
Gairloch Ave. M32 96 B2
Gaitskell Cl. M11 160 E1
Galbraith Rd. M20 110 C3
Gale Dr. M24 46 D2
Gale Rd. M25 62 F3
Gale St. Heywood OL10 29 B2
Gale St. R'dale OL12 14 F3
Galena St. OL11 30 E4
Gales Terr. OL11 139 E5
Galgate Cl. Bury BL8 26 F1
Galgate Cl. M'ster M15 162 E7
Galindo St. BL2 25 C4
Galland St. OL4 67 D7
Galleria The. 10 BL1 145 F7
Galloway Cl. Bolton BL3 40 E5
Galloway Cl. Heywood OL10 45 F8
Galloway Dr. M27 61 F4
Galloway Rd. M27 79 D6
Gallowsclough Rd. SK15 102 E6
Galston St. M11 165 A8
Galsworthy Ave. M7 & M8 156 A6
Galvin Rd. M9 64 B3
Galway St. OL1 153 F6
Galway Wlk. WA15 120 F2
Galwey Gr. WN1 37 C4
Gamble St. WN7 76 A5
Gambleside Cl. M28 78 B8
Gambrel Bank Rd. OL6 85 B6
Gambrel Gr. OL6 85 B6
Game St. OL4 67 C5
Games Wlk. 8 M22 121 B1
Gamesley Cty Prim Sch.
SK13 171 E2
Gamma Wlk. M11 83 B2
Gan Eden. 13 M7 63 E1
Gandy La. OL12 14 D4
Gantley Ave. WN5 53 D3
Gantley Cres. WN5 53 D3
Gantley Rd. WN5 53 D4
Gantock Wlk. 10 M14 98 C3
Ganton Ave. M45 62 D7
Garbrook Ave. M9 64 C5
Garden Ave. Droylsden M43 84 B2
Garden Ave. Stretford M32 96 D3
Garden City. BL0 11 A2
Garden Cl. OL15 15 F2
Garden La. Alt'ham WA14 119 D5
Garden La. Boothstown M28 78 A6
Garden La. M'ster M3 158 E2
Garden La. 3 M'ster M3 158 F1
Garden La. 17 R'dale OL16 31 A8
Garden Row. Heywood OL10 29 C4
Garden Row. R'dale OL12 14 D2
Garden St. Denton M34 100 F6
Garden St. Eccles M30 79 E1
Garden St. Farnworth BL4 60 E8
Garden St. Heywood OL10 29 C2
Garden St. Hyde SK14 167 E4
Garden St. M'ster M4 & M60 159 A2
Garden St. Newhey OL16 32 B4
Garden St. Oldham OL1 67 A7
Garden St. Oldham OL4 67 F5
Garden St. Ramsbottom BL0 11 C3
Garden St. Ramsbottom BL0 138 C6
Garden St. Stockport SK2 124 C5
Garden St. Tyldesley M29 77 A8
Garden Terr. OL2 48 C7
Garden Wall Cl. M5 161 C8
Garden Way. OL15 15 F2
Garden Wlk. Ashton-u-L OL6 166 C4
Garden Wlk. 3 Denton M34 101 A2
Gardens The. Bolton BL1, BL7 24 F6
Gardens The. Eccles M30 80 A4
Gardner. M30 79 E2
Gardner Grange. SK5 112 C4
Gardner Rd. M25 62 F4
Gardner St. M'ster M12 165 B6
Gardner St. Salford M6 81 A3
Garfield Ave. M19 99 B1
Garfield Cl. OL11 13 E1
Garfield Gr. BL3 145 D5
Garfield St. Bolton BL3 146 C3
Garfield St. Salford M5 161 A6
Garfield St. Stockport SK1 112 A2
Garforth Ave. M10 & M40 159 C2
Garforth St. OL9 152 C8
Gargrave Ave. BL1 23 F2
Gargrave St. M'ster M7 80 F8
Gargrave St. 2 Oldham OL4 67 B6
Garland Rd. M22 121 E3
Garlick St. Hyde SK14 167 F3
Garlick St. M'ster M18 99 D5
Garlick St. Oldham OL9 153 E6
Garnant Cl. M9 157 F8
Garner Ave. WA15 108 A1
Garner Cl. WA14 119 D2
Garner Dr. Salford M5 & M6 154 D3
Garner Dr. Tyldesley M29 77 B5
Garner Dr. Worsley M28 79 C3
Garner's La. SK3 170 E5
Garnet St. OL1 67 B8
Garnet Wolseley Ave. M5 161 B7
Garnett Cl. SK14 102 F3
Garnett Rd. SK14 102 F3
Garnett St. Bolton BL1 143 E3
Garnett St. Ramsbottom BL0 138 B5
Garnett St. Stockport SK1 169 F1
Garnett Way. SK14 102 F3
Garnham Wlk. 14 M9 64 E5
Garratt Way. M18 165 C5
Garret Gr. OL2 149 C7
Garrett Hall Prim Sch. M29 77 D7
Garrett Hall Rd. M28 77 E7
Garrett La. M28 & M29 77 D7
Garrett Wlk. SK3 123 C8
Garrick Gdns. M22 121 D4
Garron Wlk. 1 M22 121 A2
Garrowmore Wlk. 22 M9 64 E3
Garsdale La. BL1 & BL6 40 D7
Garside Ave. WA3 90 D7
Garside Gr. Bolton BL1 142 C2
Garside Gr. Wigan WN3 54 E2
Garside Hey Rd. BL8 27 B6
Garside St. Bolton BL1 145 E7
Garside St. Denton M34 100 F2
Garside St. Hyde SK14 167 E1
Garstang Ave. BL2 42 F7
Garstang Dr. BL8 26 F1
Garston Ave. M46 58 B5
Garston Cl. Leigh WN7 57 E1
Garston Cl. M'ster SK4 168 C3
Garston St. BL9 141 A4
Garswood Cres. WN5 71 E4
Garswood Cty Prim Sch.
WN4 72 C4
Garswood Dr. BL8 27 B6
Garswood Old Rd.
WA11, WN4 71 E1
Garswood Rd. Billinge WN5 71 F4
Garswood Rd. Bolton BL3 147 E2
Garswood Rd.
Garswood WA11 72 C3
Garswood Rd. M'ster M14 98 A2
Garswood St. WN4 73 B3
Garth Ave. WA15 119 E6
Garth Hts. SK9 137 C7
Garth Rd. Marple SK6 126 A6
Garth Rd. Stockport SK2 124 C7
Garth Rd. Wythenshawe M22 121 D4
Garth The. M5 154 D2
Garthland Rd. SK7 124 F3
Garthmere Rd. M46 58 F5
Garthorne Cl. M16 97 D4
Garthorp Rd. M23 108 E1
Garthwaite Ave. OL8 66 E4
Gartland Wlk. M8 156 C8
Garton Dr. WA3 74 E1
Garton Wlk. 12 M9 64 E5
Gartside St. Ashton-u-L OL7 84 E1
Gartside St. Delph OL3 50 E4
Gartside St. M'ster M3 158 E1
Gartside St. Oldham OL4 67 B5
Garwick Rd. BL1 142 B3
Garwood Sta. WN4 72 D3
Garwood St. M15 162 F7
Gas St. Adlington PR7 21 A6
Gas St. Ashton-u-L OL6 166 B3
Gas St. Bolton BL1 145 E7
Gas St. Farnworth BL4 60 D8
Gas St. 6 Heywood OL10 29 D2
Gas St. Hollingworth SK14 103 D5
Gas St. Leigh WN7 75 F5
Gas St. Platt Bridge WN2 56 B2
Gas St. R'dale OL11 139 E7
Gas St. Stockport SK4 169 E1
Gascoyne St. M14 98 B3
Gaskell Cl. OL15 16 A6
Gaskell Cty Prim Sch. BL1 145 E8
Gaskell Rd. Alt'ham WA14 119 D6
Gaskell Rd. Eccles M30 79 E1
Gaskell Rise. OL1 49 E1
Gaskell St. Bolton BL1 145 D8
Gaskell St. 26
Dukinfield SK16 166 B1
Gaskell St. Failsworth M40 83 D6
Gaskell St. Hindley WN2 56 E7
Gaskell St. Swinton M27 61 F2
Gaskell St. Wigan WN1 151 D8
Gaskell's Brow. WN4 72 E5
Gaskill St. OL10 29 A2
Gaskin Wlk. M9 64 D5
Gatcombe Mews. SK9 137 A6
Gatcombe Sq. M14 98 D3
Gate Ctr The. SK6 112 E6
Gate Field Cl. M26 43 E3
Gate Keeper Fold. OL7 85 A7
Gate Rd. M32 96 A4
Gate St. Dukinfield SK16 101 A6
Gate St. M'ster M11 165 C8
Gate St. R'dale OL11 139 F5
Gate Stirrup. M28 79 A5
Gateacre Wlk. M23 120 E8
Gategill Gr. WN5 53 D3
Gatehead Croft. OL3 50 F3
Gatehead Mews. OL3 50 F3
Gatehead Rd. OL3 50 F3
Gatehouse Rd. M28 60 A4
Gatesgarth Rd. M24 46 C2
Gateshead Cl. M14 98 B4
Gateside Wlk. 6 M9 64 E5
Gateway Cres. OL9 65 E4
Gateway Ind Est. M1 159 B1
Gateway Rd. M18 165 C6
Gateways The. M27 61 F1
Gathill Cl. SK8 122 F1
Gathurst Golf Course. WN6 35 F5
Gathurst La. WN5 & WN6 36 A4
Gathurst Rd. WN5 35 F2
Gathurst St. M18 99 E6
Gathurst Sta. WN5 36 A3
Gatley Ave. M14 98 A1
Gatley Brow. OL1 153 E8
Gatley Gn. SK8 122 A5
Gatley Golf Course. SK8 122 A3
Gatley Prim Sch. SK8 122 A5
Gatley Rd. Cheadle SK8 122 C5
Gatley Rd. Sale M33 108 E3
Gatley Sta. SK8 122 B5
Gatling Ave. M12 99 B2
Gatwick Ave. M23 121 B6
Gavel Wlk. M24 46 E1
Gavin Ave. M5 81 A1
Gawsworth Ave. M20 110 C1
Gawsworth Cl.
Alt'ham M23 & WA15 120 D6
Gawsworth Cl. Bramhall SK7 132 E6
Gawsworth Cl.
Hadfield SK14 104 A5
Gawsworth Cl.Poynton SK12 133 F2
Gawsworth Cl.Shaw OL2 48 F7
Gawsworth Cl.
Stockport SK3 170 D5
Gawsworth Mews. SK8 122 B5
Gawsworth Pl. M22 121 F1
Gawsworth Rd. Golborne WA3 73 F1
Gawsworth Rd. Sale M33 108 E1
Gawsworth Way. 15
Denton M34 101 A1
Gawsworth Way.
Handforth SK9 131 E4
Gawthorpe Cl. BL9 45 A5
Gaydon Rd. M33 107 D4
Gayford Wlk. 9 M9 64 E5
Gaythorn St. M3 & M5 81 C1
Gaythorne St. BL1 143 F3
Gayton Cl. WN3 54 D3
Gayton Wlk. 7 M40 65 D2
Gaywood Wlk. M40 156 C6
Gee Cross Fold. SK14 113 E7
Gee Cross Trinity CE
Prim Sch. SK14 113 F8
Gee La. Eccles M30 79 B3
Gee La. 7 Oldham OL8 66 B2
Gee St. Oldham OL8 66 B2
Gee St. Stockport SK3 170 D7
Geinsbury Cl. OL8 67 B4
Gelder Clough Res Cvan Pk.
OL10 29 C5
Gellert Pl. BL5 57 E6
Gellert Rd. BL5 57 E6
Gellfield La. OL3 51 D1
Gencoyne Dr. BL1 24 D6
Gendre Rd. BL7 24 E8
Geneva Rd. SK7 123 E3
Geneva Terr. OL11 30 C8
Geneva Wlk. 11 M'ster M8 156 B6
Geneva Wlk. Oldham OL9 152 C6
Genista Gr. M7 155 D6
Geo. Hampson's Bldgs.
WA3 92 C8
Geoff Bent Wlk. M40 83 B5
Geoffrey St. Atherton BL5 58 F8
Geoffrey St. Bury BL9 141 A4
Geoffrey St. Ramsbottom BL0 11 A4
George Barton St. 24 BL2 25 B1
George Ct. 10 SK16 166 B1
George H Carnall
Sports Ctr. M41 95 E4
George La. SK6 113 A4
George Leigh St. M4 159 B2
George Mann Cl. M22 121 C1
George Rd. BL0 138 B5
George Sq. OL1 153 E6
George St.Alderley Edge SK9 137 A1
George St. Alt'ham WA14 119 D4
George St. Ashton-i-M WN4 73 C4
George St. Ashton-u-L OL6 166 C3
George St. 3 Atherton M46 58 D3
George St. 4 Bacup OL13 3 C8
George St. Bury BL9 140 F2
George St. Chadderton OL9 152 A7
George St. Denton M34 101 A3
George St. Eccles M30 79 C1
George St. Failsworth M35 83 F8
George St. Farnworth BL4 60 B7
George St. Farnworth BL4 60 E7
George St. Glossop SK13 116 C8
George St. Heywood OL10 29 B3
George St. Hindley WN2 56 E5
George St. Horwich BL6 22 C3
George St. Ince-i-M WN2 151 F7
George St. Irlam M44 94 B3
George St. Littleborough OL16 15 D3
George St. 8
Littleborough OL15 16 B5
George St. M'ster M25 63 B1
George St. M'ster M7 & M8 155 F8
George St. M'ster M1 163 A8
George St. Milnrow OL16 31 E7
George St. Mossley OL5 68 C1
George St. Newton-l-W WA12 89 A4
George St. Oldham OL1 153 E6
George St. R'dale OL12, OL16 31 A8
George St. Radcliffe M26 43 F3
George St. Romiley SK6 114 B2
George St. Shaw OL2 149 C8
George St. 5
Stalybridge SK15 86 A2
George St. Stockport SK1 112 A2
George St. Urmston M41 95 E2
George St. Westhoughton BL5 57 F8
George St. Whitefield M45 44 E1
George St. Whitworth OL12 14 C8
George St E. SK1 124 B8
George St W. SK1 124 B8
George Thomas Ct. M9 157 D8
George Tomlinson Sch. BL4 60 E6
George's Cl. SK12 133 E3
George's La. Horwich BL6 22 E5
George's Rd. Sale M33 108 B3
George's Rd. Stockport SK4 169 D2
George's Rd E. SK12 133 E3
George's Rd W. SK12 133 E3
George's Row. 2 BB4 2 F8
George's Terr. WN5 53 D5
Georgian Ct. 5 Leigh WN7 76 B4
Georgian Ct. 12
Tyldesley M29 58 F1
Georgian Sq. 2 WN2 56 A2
Georgiana St. 2 Bury BL9 140 F1
Georgiana St. 3
Farnworth BL4 42 B2
Georgina Ct. BL3 146 B3
Georgina St. BL3 146 B3
Gerald Ave. M8 156 A8
Gerald Rd. M6 & M7 81 B5
Gerard St. WN4 73 B3
Germain Cl. M9 64 C5
Gerrard Ave. WA15 120 A8
Gerrard Cl. WN2 38 D2
Gerrard Rd. WN5 71 E5
Gerrard St. Farnworth BL4 60 E8
Gerrard St. Leigh WN7 75 F5
Gerrard St. R'dale OL11 31 A2
Gerrard St. 2 Salford M6 81 A3
Gerrard St. Stalybridge SK15 86 B1
Gerrard St. 5
Westhoughton BL5 39 E1
Gerrards Cl. M44 94 A2
Gerrards Gdns. SK14 113 E7
Gerrards Hollow. SK14 113 D7
Gerrardswood. SK14 113 D7
Gertrude Cl. M5 161 A8
Gertrude St. OL12 4 E6
Gervis Cl. M40 157 D5
Ghyll Gr. Billinge WA11 71 B1
Ghyll Gr. Walkden M28 60 E2
Giants Hall Rd. WN6 36 E3
Gib Fold. M46 58 D4
Gib La. M23 121 C8
Gibb La. SK6 126 E5
Gibb Rd. M28 79 B7
Gibbon Ave. M22 121 D2
Gibbon St. Bolton BL3 145 D5
Gibbon St. M'ster M11 83 A2
Gibbons Rd. WN4 72 D3
Gibbs St. M3 158 D1
Gibraltar La. M34 113 B8
Gibraltar St. Bolton BL3 145 D6
Gibraltar St. Oldham OL4 67 D5
Gibsmere Cl. M23 120 D6
Gibson Ave. M18 99 F6
Gibson Gr. M28 60 A3
Gibson La. M28 60 A3
Gibson Pl. M3 159 A3
Gibson St. Bolton BL2 25 C1
Gibson St. Leigh WN2 56 D1
Gibson St. Oldham OL4 67 C6
Gibson St. R'dale OL16 31 C8
Gibson Terr. OL7 166 A1
Gibson Way. WA14 119 C8
Gibsons Rd. SK4 168 B4
Gibwood Rd. M22 121 C8
Giden Wlk. 11 M9 64 E5
Gidlow Ave. Adlington PR6 21 A7
Gidlow Ave. Wigan WN6 37 A2
Gidlow La. WN6 37 A2
Gidlow New Houses. WN6 37 A4
Gidlow St. 1 Hindley WN2 56 D6
Gidlow St. M'ster M18 99 E6
Gifford Pl. WN2 56 F4
Gifford Wlk. SK7 124 A2
Gigg La. BL9 44 F8
Gilbert Rd. WA15 119 E1
Gilbert St. Eccles M30 95 B8
Gilbert St. Hindley WN2 56 D5
Gilbert St. M'ster M15 162 E7
Gilbert St. Ramsbottom BL0 1 C1
Gilbert St. Salford M6 154 F1
Gilbert St. Walkden M28 60 D1
Gilbertbank. SK6 113 B4
Gilchrist Rd. M44 105 F6
Gilda Brook Rd. M30 & M5 80 A2
Gilda Cres. M30 80 A3
Gilda Rd. M28 77 F7
Gilded Hollins Prim Sch.
WN7 75 C1
Gildenhall. M35 84 A7
Gilderdale Cl. OL2 149 B8
Gilderdale St. 7 BL3 42 A4
Gildersdale Dr. M9 64 C6
Gildridge Rd. M16 97 E1
Giles St. M12 & M18 99 A4
Gilesgate. 3 M14 98 C3
Gill Ave. WN6 36 B6
Gill Bent Rd. SK8 132 A7
Gill St. M'ster M9 64 F1
Gill St. Stockport SK1 112 B3
Gillan Rd. WN6 37 B3

Gillbrook Rd. M20 110 B2
Gillbrow Cres. WN1 37 F1
Gillemere Gr. OL2 149 C7
Gillers Gn. M28 60 C3
Gillford Ave. M'ster M9 64 F1
Gillford Ave. M'ster M9 157 F8
Gilliburns Wlk. BL5 57 F5
Gillingham Rd. M30 79 B2
Gillingham Sq. M11 164 F8
Gillwood Dr. SK6 112 F1
Gilman Cl. M9 64 C2
Gilman St. M9 64 C2
Gilmerton Dr. 22 M40 83 C5
Gilmore Dr. M25 63 B5
Gilmore St. SK3 170 E7
Gilmour St. M24 65 A8
Gilmour Terr. M9 64 F1
Gilnow Cty Prim Sch. BL1 144 C6
Gilnow Gdns. BL1 144 C6
Gilnow Gr. BL1 145 D6
Gilnow La. BL3 145 D6
Gilnow Rd. BL1 144 C6
Gilpin Pl. WN2 55 F2
Gilpin Rd. M41 95 F2
Gilpin Wlk. M24 46 E1
Gilroy St. WN1 151 D8
Giltbrook Ave. M10 & M40 160 D4
Gilwell Dr. M23 120 F4
Gin Croft La. BL0 1 E4
Gingham Brow. BL6 22 E4
Gingham Ct. 7 M26 44 C4
Gingham Pk. M26 43 E5
Gipsy La. Stockport SK2 124 C6
Gipsy La. Stockport SK2 124 D6
Girton Ave. WN4 72 F4
Girton St. Bolton BL2 42 D7
Girton St. M'ster M7 158 E4
Girton Wlk. M40 65 D1
Girvan Ave. M40 65 D2
Girvan Cl. BL3 146 C3
Girvan Cres. WN4 72 D4
Girvan Wlk. OL10 28 F1
Gisborn Dr. M6 81 A5
Gisburn Ave. Bolton BL1 23 E2
Gisburn Ave. Golborne WA3 73 F2
Gisburn Dr. BL8 26 E3
Gisburn Rd. OL11 31 A3
Gisburne Ave. M40 65 D2
Gissing Wlk. M40 157 D6
Givendale Dr. M8 64 A2
Glabyn Ave. BL6 39 F8
Glade Brow. OL4 68 A6
Glade St. BL1 144 C7
Glade The. Bolton BL1 143 D1
Glade The. Shevington WN6 36 B6
Glade The. Stockport SK4 168 A1
Gladeside Rd. M22 121 C4
Gladstone Cl. 6 BL1 143 E2
Gladstone Cres. OL11 31 A3
Gladstone Ct. Farnworth BL4 42 C1
Gladstone Ct. M'ster M15 & M16 97 E4
Gladstone Ct. M'ster SK4 168 B3
Gladstone Gr. SK4 168 A3
Gladstone Mews. SK4 169 E3
Gladstone Pl. BL4 42 C1
Gladstone Rd. Alt'ham WA14 119 D6
Gladstone Rd. Eccles M30 79 E2
Gladstone Rd. Farnworth BL4 42 D1
Gladstone Rd. Urmston M41 95 E2
Gladstone St. Bolton BL1 143 E2
Gladstone St. Bury BL9 141 B3
Gladstone St. Glossop SK13 116 D8
Gladstone St. Hadfield SK14 104 A4
Gladstone St. Oldham OL4 67 B6
Gladstone St. Stockport SK2 124 C4
Gladstone St. Swinton M27 80 A8
Gladstone St. Westhoughton BL5 39 E1
Gladstone Terrace Rd. OL3 69 A4
Gladville Dr. SK8 123 A6
Gladwyn Ave. M20 109 E4
Gladys St. 3 Farnworth BL4 42 D2
Gladys St. M'ster M16 97 C4
Gladys St. Salford M5 161 A7
Glaisdale. OL4 67 D6
Glaisdale Cl. Ashton-i-M WN4 73 C3
Glaisdale Cl. Bolton BL2 25 B2
Glaisdale St. BL2 25 B2
Glaister La. BL2 25 D1
Glamis Ave. Droylsden M11 83 B3
Glamis Ave. Heywood OL10 46 F8
Glamis Ave. Stretford M32 96 A2
Glamis Cl. WN7 76 D6
Glamorgan Pl. OL9 152 C5
Glandon Dr. SK8 132 C8
Glanford Ave. M9 64 A3
Glanton Wlk. M40 65 D1
Glanvor Rd. SK3 123 C8
Glass St. BL4 60 E7
Glassbrook St. WN6 37 A1
Glasscroft Cl. M14 97 F2
Glasshouse St. 9 M4 159 C3
Glasson Wlk. OL9 152 A6
Glastonbury. 28 OL12 139 E8
Glastonbury Ave. Alt'ham WA15 120 B2
Glastonbury Ave. Bramhall SK8 132 C6
Glastonbury Ave. Golborne WA3 91 C8
Glastonbury Dr. SK12 133 D5
Glastonbury Gdns. M26 43 E5
Glastonbury Rd. Tyldesley M29 7[illegible] B7
Glastonbury Rd. Urmston M32 95 F3
Glaswen Gr. SK5 169 F4
Glaze Wlk. M45 45 C2
Glazebrook Cl. OL10 29 C1
Glazebrook La. WA3 105 B5
Glazebrook Sta. WA3 105 B5
Glazebury CE (VA) Prim Sch. WA3 92 C7
Glazebury Dr. M23 121 B5
Glazedale Ave. OL2 48 C5
Glaziers La. WA3 91 D2
Gleave St. 10 Bolton BL1 145 F8
Gleave St. Sale M33 108 B6
Gleaves Ave. BL2 26 A4
Gleaves Rd. M30 79 E1
Glebe Ave. WN4 73 C2
Glebe Cl. WN6 19 F1
Glebe End St. WN6 150 B8
Glebe House. M24 47 A2
Glebe House Sch. OL11 139 E6
Glebe La. OL1 49 E4
Glebe Rd. Standish WN6 19 F1
Glebe Rd. Urmston M41 95 D2
Glebe St. Ashton-u-L OL6 166 C3
Glebe St. Bolton BL2 148 A6
Glebe St. Hindley WN2 57 C2
Glebe St. Leigh WN7 75 F6
Glebe St. Oldham OL9 66 A3
Glebe St. Radcliffe M26 44 B3
Glebe St. Shaw OL2 149 B7
Glebe St. Stockport SK1 112 A1
Glebe St. Westhoughton BL5 39 E1
Glebeland. WA3 91 E2
Glebeland Rd. BL3 144 B5
Glebelands Rd. Prestwich M25 63 B5
Glebelands Rd. Sale M33 108 A6
Glebelands Rd. Wythenshawe M23 120 F6
Gleden St. M'ster M10, M40 160 E2
Gleden St. M'ster M10, M40 160 E3
Gledhall St. SK15 86 A2
Gledhill Ave. M5 161 B7
Gledhill Cl. OL2 32 A1
Gledhill St. M20 110 B7
Gledhill Way. BL7 9 A1
Glegg St. WN2 151 F8
Glemsford Cl. Failsworth M40 83 B6
Glemsford Cl. Wigan WN3 55 B3
Glen Ave. Bolton BL3 144 B5
Glen Ave. Kearsley BL4 61 B6
Glen Ave. M'ster M9 64 F1
Glen Ave. Sale M33 108 A6
Glen Ave. Swinton M27 79 D8
Glen Ave. Worsley M28 79 A8
Glen Bott St. BL1 143 D2
Glen Cl. WA3 105 B2
Glen Cres. OL13 3 A8
Glen Dr. WN6 35 E8
Glen Gdns. OL12 14 F2
Glen Gr. Middleton M24 65 C7
Glen Gr. Royton OL2 48 D5
Glen Rd. Oldham OL4 67 C6
Glen Rd. Rawtenstall BB4 2 F8
Glen Rise. WA15 120 A5
Glen Royd. 1 OL12 14 C1
Glen St. Bacup OL13 3 E8
Glen St. Ramsbottom BL0 138 B7
Glen St. Salford M5 161 A7
Glen The. Bolton BL1 40 E7
Glen The. Middleton M24 65 B6
Glen View. Littleborough OL15 16 C7
Glen View. Royton OL2 48 D5
Glenarm Wlk. M22 121 E2
Glenart. M30 79 E3
Glenavon Dr. R'dale OL12 14 D3
Glenavon Dr. Shaw OL2 48 F8
Glenbarry Cl. M13 163 B6
Glenbarry St. M12 164 D8
Glenbeck Rd. M45 44 E1
Glenboro Ave. BL8 27 C2
Glenborough Ave. OL13 3 C8
Glenbourne Pk. SK7 132 D5
Glenbranter Ave. WN2 56 A8
Glenbrook Gdns. BL4 42 D2
Glenbrook Hill. SK13 104 C2
Glenbrook Rd. M9 64 A5
Glenburn St. BL3 147 D3
Glenby Ave. M22 121 F3
Glencar. BL5 57 D7
Glencar Dr. 8 M40 65 D2
Glencastle Rd. M18 99 C4
Glencoe. BL2 148 B7
Glencoe Cl. OL10 28 F1
Glencoe Dr. Bolton BL2 42 F6
Glencoe Dr. Sale M33 107 C2
Glencoe Pl. OL11 139 D7
Glencoe St. 3 OL8 66 C2
Glencross Ave. M16 & M21 97 A2
Glendale. M27 62 B2
Glendale Ave. Ashton-i-M WN4 73 C4
Glendale Ave. M'ster M19 110 F6
Glendale Ave. Whitefield BL9 44 F3
Glendale Cl. Boothstown M28 77 F7
Glendale Cl. 8 Heywood OL10 29 D2
Glendale Ct. OL8 66 F4
Glendale Dr. BL3 40 F6
Glendale Rd. Boothstown M28 77 F7
Glendale Rd. Eccles M30 80 A3
Glenden Foot. OL12 14 D2
Glendene Ave Bramhall SK7 132 D5
Glendene Ave. Droylsden M43 84 C3
Glendevon Cl. Bolton BL3 40 F5
Glendevon Cl. Ince-i-M WN2 56 A8
Glendevon Pl. M45 63 B7
Glendinning St. M6 154 E2
Glendon Cres. OL6 85 B7
Glendon Ct. OL1 49 E4
Glendore. M5 80 C2
Glendower Dr. M40 156 C5
Gleneagles. BL3 40 F3
Gleneagles Ave. 10 Droylsden M11 83 C2
Gleneagles Ave. Heywood OL10 46 D8
Gleneagles Cl. Bramhall SK7 133 A7
Gleneagles Cl. Wilmslow SK9 137 D8
Gleneagles Rd. Gatley SK8 122 C1
Gleneagles Rd. Urmston M41 94 F3
Gleneagles Way. BL0 138 B5
Glenfield. WA14 119 B4
Glenfield Dr. SK12 133 D3
Glenfield Rd. SK4 169 D4
Glenfield Sq. 2 BL4 42 B2
Glenfyne Rd. M6 80 D5
Glengarth. OL3 69 B7
Glengarth Dr. BL1 & BL6 40 C6
Glenham Ct. 1 M15 97 E4
Glenhaven Ave. M41 95 C2
Glenholme Rd. SK7 132 D7
Glenhurst Rd. M19 110 E5
Glenilla Ave. M28 78 E7
Glenlea Dr. M20 122 B8
Glenluce Wlk. BL3 40 E5
Glenmaye Gr. WN2 57 A5
Glenmere Rd. M20 122 C8
Glenmoor Rd. SK1 112 A1
Glenmore Ave. Farnworth BL3 & BL4 42 A2
Glenmore Ave. M'ster M20 109 E4
Glenmore Bglws. SK16 101 C7
Glenmore Cl. Bolton BL3 40 E5
Glenmore Cl. R'dale OL11 29 E5
Glenmore Dr. Failsworth M35 84 B8
Glenmore Dr. M'ster M8 156 B7
Glenmore Gr. SK16 101 C8
Glenmore Rd. BL8 10 F2
Glenmore St. BL9 140 E1
Glenolden St. M11 83 D2
Glenpark. WN7 76 B6
Glenpark Wlk. 5 M9 157 E7
Glenridding Cl. OL1 49 A1
Glenridge Cl. BL1 143 F2
Glenroy Wlk. 15 M9 64 E5
Glensdale Dr. M40 65 E1
Glenshee Dr. BL3 40 F5
Glenside. WN6 18 B2
Glenside Ave. M18 99 D3
Glenside Dr. Bolton BL3 147 F2
Glenside Dr. Romiley SK6 113 B5
Glenside Gdns. M35 84 B7
Glenside Gr. M28 60 E3
Glent View. SK15 86 A4
Glenthorn Gr. M33 108 B3
Glenthorn Rd. M9 64 D6
Glenthorne Dr. OL7 166 A4
Glenthorne St. 18 BL1 143 E1
Glentress Mews. BL1 144 A8
Glentrool Mews. BL1 144 A7
Glenville Way. M34 101 A2
Glenville Wlk. 13 SK15 86 A1
Glenwood Ave. 2 SK14 101 D5
Glenwood Dr. M'ster M9 157 E7
Glenwood Dr. Middleton M24 47 C1
Glenwood Gr. SK2 124 B4
Glenwyn Ave. M9 64 E4
Globe Ind Est. M26 44 B3
Globe La. Bolton BL7 8 D3
Globe La. Dukinfield SK16 101 B7
Globe Lane Ind Est. SK16 101 B6
Globe Lane Prim Sch. SK16 101 B6
Globe Sq. SK16 101 A7
Glodwick. OL4 67 B5
Glodwick Inf Sch. OL4 67 B5
Glodwick Rd. OL4 & OL8 67 B6
Glossop Brook Rd. SK13 104 B1
Glossop Central Sta. SK13 104 C1
Glossop Rd. Charlesworth SK13 & SK14 115 D7
Glossop Rd. Romiley SK14 & SK6 114 D3
Glossop Rd. Rowarth SK12 & SK13 116 C1
Glossopdale Comm Coll. Glossop SK13 104 C2
Glossopdale Comm Coll. Hadfield SK14 104 A4
Gloster St. 3 BL2 148 A7
Gloucester Ave. 2 Golborne WA3 90 B8
Gloucester Ave. Heywood OL10 46 C8
Gloucester Ave. Horwich BL6 22 D2
Gloucester Ave. Littleborough OL12 15 D4
Gloucester Ave. M'ster M19 111 B8
Gloucester Ave. Marple SK6 125 F6
Gloucester Ave. Whitefield M45 63 A8
Gloucester Cl. OL6 85 D8
Gloucester Cres. WN2 56 E6
Gloucester Ct. BL6 22 D2
Gloucester Dr. Diggle OL3 51 C4
Gloucester Dr. Sale M33 107 D4
Gloucester Pl. Atherton M46 58 D4
Gloucester Pl. 1 Salford M6 81 A3
Gloucester Rd. Droylsden M43 84 A3
Gloucester Rd. Gatley SK8 131 C7
Gloucester Rd. Hyde SK14 113 E8
Gloucester Rd. Middleton M24 65 B6
Gloucester Rd. Poynton SK12 133 D4
Gloucester Rd. Reddish M34 100 A2
Gloucester Rd. Salford M6 80 C4
Gloucester Rd. Urmston M41 95 D1
Gloucester Rd. Wigan WN5 54 C6
Gloucester Rise. SK16 102 A7
Gloucester St. Atherton M46 58 D3
Gloucester St. 1 M'ster M15 162 F7
Gloucester St. Salford M6 81 A4
Gloucester St. Salford M5 161 C8
Gloucester St. Stockport SK3 170 D7
Gloucester St N. OL9 152 C5
Gloucester Way. SK13 116 F8
Glover Ave. M8 156 B6
Glover Ct. M7 155 F8
Glover Field. M7 155 D6
Glover St. Horwich BL6 22 B4
Glover St. Leigh WN7 75 C8
Glover St. Newton-l-W WA12 89 C3
Glyn Ave. WA15 120 A2
Glyneath Cl. M11 164 F8
Glynn Gdns. M20 109 D4
Glynne St. BL4 60 C8
Glynrene Dr. M27 61 C1
Glynwood Pk. BL4 42 C1
GM & BM Nat Coll The. M16 97 D2
GMex. M2 162 F8
GMex Sta. M1 162 F8
Goadsby St. M4 159 A2
Goats Gate Terr. M45 44 D2
Godbert Ave. M21 109 C5
Goddard La. Hadfield SK14 104 A6
Goddard La. Rowarth SK12 127 E7
Goddard Rd. SK14 104 A4
Goddard St. OL8 66 F4
Godfrey Ave. M43 83 D3
Godfrey Ermen Meml CE Prim Sch. M30 95 C8
Godfrey Range. M18 & M34 99 F4
Godfrey Rd. M6 80 C5
Godlee Dr. M27 79 D7
Godley Cl. M11 165 C8
Godley Ct. SK14 167 F2
Godley Hill. SK14 102 B2
Godley Hill Rd. SK14 102 B3
Godley Prim Sch. SK14 167 F3
Godley St. SK14 167 F4
Godley Sta. SK14 102 A3
Godmond Hall Dr. M28 77 F5
Godson St. OL1 48 E1
Godward Rd. SK12 127 B1
Godwin St. M18 99 E6
Goit Pl. OL16 139 F7
Golborne (All Saints) RC Prim Sch. WA3 90 B8
Golborne Ave. M20 109 F7
Golborne Cty Prim Sch. WA3 90 A8
Golborne Dale Rd. WA12 90 A5
Golborne Ent Pk. WA3 74 A1
Golborne Gallery. 9 WN1 150 C8
Golborne House. 3 BL1 145 F8
Golborne Pl. WN1 151 E8
Golborne Rd. Ashton-i-M WA3 & WN4 73 E4
Golborne Rd. Golborne WA3 90 C8
Golborne St. WA12 89 E4
Golbourne High Sch. WA3 74 C1
Golbourne St Thomas' CE Jun & Inf Sch. WA3 74 B1
Gold St. M60 159 A1
Goldborne House. OL2 149 B8
Goldbourne Dr. OL2 149 B8
Goldbrook Cl. 2 OL10 29 E1
Goldcraft Cl. 4 OL10 29 E1
Goldcrest Cl. Boothstown M28 78 B7
Goldcrest Cl. Wythenshawe M22 121 F5
Golden St. Eccles M30 79 D1
Golden St. Shaw OL2 49 E8
Goldenhill Ave. M11 83 C3
Goldenways. WN1 37 C2
Goldfinch Dr. BL9 141 C4
Goldfinch Way. M43 84 C3
Goldie Ave. M22 121 F2
Goldrill Ave. BL2 42 F8
Goldrill Gdns. BL2 42 F8
Goldsmith Ave. Oldham OL1 49 E4
Goldsmith Ave. Salford M5 154 D2
Goldsmith Pl. WN3 55 A4
Goldsmith Rd. SK5 99 E1
Goldsmith St. BL3 147 D4
Goldsmith Way. 8 M34 113 A7
Goldstein Rd. BL6 40 B4
Goldswcrthy Rd. M41 94 E2
Goldwick Wlk. M23 108 E1
Golf Rd. Alt'ham WA15 119 F3
Golf Rd. Sale M33 108 F4
Gooch Cl. M16 97 E3
Gooch Dr. WA12 89 D2
Gooch St. BL6 22 C2
Goodacre. SK14 102 B6
Gooden St. OL10 29 E1
Goodier St. M'ster M10, M40 160 F4
Goodier St. Sale M33 108 A4
Goodier View. SK14 101 F5
Goodiers Dr. M5 161 B8
Goodison Cl. BL9 45 B3
Goodlad St. BL8 27 B4
Goodman St. M9 64 E1
Goodrich. 3 OL11 139 E6
Goodridge Ave. M22 121 C1
Goodrington Rd. SK9 131 E3
Goodshaw Rd. M28 78 C8
Goodwill Cl. M27 79 F7
Goodwin Sq. M8 & M9 157 D7
Goodwin St. BL1 148 A8
Goodwood Ave. Sale M33 107 C4
Goodwood Ave. Sale M23 120 D7
Goodwood Cl. BL3 42 F3
Goodwood Cres. WA15 120 C6
Goodwood Ct. M7 155 D6
Goodwood Dr. Oldham OL1 49 B1
Goodwood Dr. Pendlebury M27 80 B7
Goodwood Rd. SK6 125 E5
Goodworth Wlk. M40 83 B7
Goole St. M11 165 A8
Goose Cote Hill. BL7 8 E1
Goose Gn. WA14 119 D4
Goose La. OL12 139 F8
Goosetrey Cl. SK9 131 E1
Goostrey Ave. M'ster M20 110 A8
Gorden St. 11 OL13 3 C8
Gordon Ave. Bolton BL3 144 C5
Gordon Ave. Garswood WN4 72 E4
Gordon Ave. Hazel Grove SK7 124 D3
Gordon Ave. M'ster M19 111 B8
Gordon Ave. Oldham OL9 66 A3
Gordon Ave. Oldham OL4 67 C6
Gordon Cl. WN5 54 E8
Gordon Pl. M20 110 B5
Gordon Rd. Eccles M30 79 D3
Gordon Rd. Sale M33 108 B6
Gordon Rd. Swinton M27 79 C6
Gordon St. 14 Ashton-u-L OL6 85 D4
Gordon St. Bury BL9 140 E3
Gordon St. Droylsden M18 99 E6
Gordon St. Hyde SK14 167 E2
Gordon St. Leigh WN7 75 F6
Gordon St. M'ster M7 158 D4
Gordon St. M'ster M16 162 D5
Gordon St. Newhey OL16 32 B3
Gordon St. Oldham OL9 65 F4
Gordon St. Oldham OL4 68 A6
Gordon St. 9 R'dale OL11 31 A5
Gordon St. Shaw OL2 149 C7
Gordon St. 3 Stalybridge SK15 86 B1
Gordon St. Stockport SK4 & SK5 169 E3
Gordon St. Wigan WN1 151 E7
Gordon Terr. 2 SK15 86 A2
Gordon Way. OL10 28 F1
Gordonstoun Cres. WN5 53 F7
Gore Ave. Failsworth M35 84 B7
Gore Ave. Salford M5 & M6 154 D2
Gore Cres. M5 154 D3
Gore Dr. M5 154 D3
Gore La. SK9 & WA16 136 C3
Gore St. Bury BL9 141 C1
Gore St. M'ster M3 158 E1
Gore St. M'ster M1 159 B1
Gore St. Salford M6 81 A3
Gore St. Wigan WN5 54 B6
Gore's La. WA11 71 A5
Gorebrook Ct. M18 99 A4
Goredale Ave. M18 99 E4
Gorelan Rd. M18 99 D5
Goring Ave. M18 99 D6
Gorman St. 9 WN6 37 A1
Gorman Wlk. WN3 54 F5
Gorrel St. 4 OL11 31 A5
Gorrells Way. OL11 30 D3
Gorrels Cl. OL11 30 D3
Gorrels Way. OL11 30 E3
Gorse Ave. Droylsden M43 84 C2
Gorse Ave. Marple SK6 125 E6
Gorse Ave. Mossley OL5 68 E1
Gorse Ave. Oldham OL8 67 C3
Gorse Ave. Stretford M32 96 F3
Gorse Bank. BL9 141 C3
Gorse Bank Rd. WA15 129 C7
Gorse Bank Sch. OL9 65 F5
Gorse Cres. M32 96 F3
Gorse Dr. Stretford M32 96 F3
Gorse Dr. Walkden M38 59 F6
Gorse Gr. BB4 1 A8
Gorse Hall Cl. SK16 101 F7
Gorse Hall Cty Prim Sch. SK15 86 A1
Gorse Hall Dr. SK15 85 F1
Gorse Hall Rd. SK16 101 F7
Gorse Hill Prim Sch. M32 96 E4
Gorse La. M32 96 F3
Gorse Rd. Milnrow OL16 32 A6
Gorse Rd. Swinton M27 79 E6
Gorse Rd. Walkden M28 60 E2
Gorse Sq. M31 105 D3
Gorse St. Oldham OL9 65 F4
Gorse St. Stretford M32 96 E3
Gorse The. WA14 128 B8
Gorse Way. SK13 116 F7
Gorse Wlk. WN7 75 B5
Gorsefield Cl. M26 44 A4
Gorsefield Dr. 1 M27 79 F7
Gorsefield Hey. SK9 137 E8
Gorsefield Prim Sch. M26 44 A4
Gorselands. SK8 132 B5
Gorses Dr. WN2 38 C6
Gorses Mount. BL2 & BL3 148 C5
Gorses Rd. BL2 & BL3 42 D5
Gorseway. SK5 112 B4
Gorsey Ave. M22 121 C4
Gorsey Bank Prim Sch. SK9 136 F7
Gorsey Bank Rd. SK3 123 B8
Gorsey Brow. Billinge WN5 71 E5
Gorsey Brow. Mottram-i-L SK14 103 A1
Gorsey Brow. Romiley SK6 113 A2
Gorsey Brow. Stockport SK1 112 A1
Gorsey Brow Cl. WN5 71 D5
Gorsey Clough Wlk. BL8 26 F5
Gorsey Dr. M22 121 C4
Gorsey Hey. BL5 57 E7
Gorsey Hill St. OL10 29 D1
Gorsey Intakes. SK14 115 A8
Gorsey La. Alt'ham WA14 119 B5
Gorsey La. Ashton-u-L OL6 85 F6
Gorsey La. Partington WA13 118 B7
Gorsey Mount St. SK1 112 A1
Gorsey Rd. Wilmslow SK9 136 F8
Gorsey Rd. Wythenshawe M22 121 C4
Gorsey Way. OL6 85 E6
Gorseyfields. M43 100 A8
Gorsly Bank. OL15 16 C7
Gorston Wlk. M22 130 C8
Gort Cl. M45 45 A1
Gorton Brook Fst Sch. M12 165 A6
Gorton Cres. M34 100 C2
Gorton Cross Ctr. M18 99 D5
Gorton Fold. BL6 22 C3
Gorton Gr. M28 60 C5
Gorton Ind Est. M18 165 C6
Gorton La. M12 & M18 165 B6
Gorton Mount Inf Sch. M18 99 C3
Gorton Mount Jun Sch. M18 99 C3
Gorton Parks. M18 165 C6
Gorton Rd.M'ster M12 164 F7
Gorton Rd. Reddish M34 & SK5 99 F2
Gorton St. Ashton-u-L OL7 84 F1
Gorton St. Bolton BL2 148 A6
Gorton St. Eccles M30 79 B1
Gorton St. Farnworth BL4 60 B7
Gorton St. Heywood OL10 29 E2
Gorton St. M'ster M3 158 F2
Gorton St. M'ster M40 159 C4
Gorton St. Oldham OL9 152 B6
Gorton Sta. M12 99 D6
Gortonvilla Wlk. M12 164 F6
Gosforth Cl. Bury BL8 27 C5
Gosforth Cl. Oldham OL1 49 A1
Gosforth Wlk. M23 108 F1
Goshen La. BL9 44 F6
Goshen Sports Ctr. BL9 45 A6
Gosling Cl. 3 M16 97 F3
Gosport Sq. M7 155 D5
Gosport Wlk. M8 156 C6
Goss Hall St. OL4 67 C6
Gotha Wlk. M13 163 C6
Gotherage Cl. SK6 113 E2
Gotherage La. SK6 113 E2
Gothic Cl. SK6 113 F2
Gough St. Heywood OL10 29 E2
Gough St. Stockport SK3 169 D1
Gould St. Denton M34 100 E3
Gould St. M'ster M4 159 B3
Gould St. Oldham OL1 67 B8
Goulden Rd. M20 110 A5
Goulden St. M'ster M4 159 B2
Goulden St. Salford M6 154 E2
Goulder Rd. M18 99 E3
Gourham Dr. SK8 122 F2
Govan St. M22 109 E1
Gowan Dr. M24 46 D1
Gowan Rd. M16 97 E1
Gowanlock's St. BL1 143 E2
Gower Ave. SK7 124 C3
Gower Rd. Hyde SK14 167 D1
Gower Rd. Reddish SK4 169 D4
Gower St. Ashton-u-L OL6 166 C3
Gower St. Bolton BL1 145 D8
Gower St. Farnworth BL4 42 C1
Gower St. Leigh WN7 75 E4
Gower St. Oldham OL1 67 A7
Gower St. Swinton M27 62 A1
Gower St. Wigan WN5 150 A7
Gowerdale Rd. SK5 112 C5
Gowers St. OL16 31 B8
Gowran Pk. 3 OL4 67 D6
Gowy Cl. SK9 131 E1
Goya Rise. OL1 49 D4
Goyt Ave. SK6 125 F4
Goyt Cres. Bredbury SK6 112 F3
Goyt Cres. Stockport SK1 112 B3
Goyt Hey Ave. WN5 71 E5
Goyt Rd. Disley SK12 135 D5
Goyt Rd. Marple SK6 125 F4
Goyt Rd. Stockport SK1 112 B3
Goyt Valley Rd. SK6 112 F3
Goyt Valley Wlk. SK6 112 F3
Goyt Wlk. M45 45 B2
Grace St. Horwich BL6 22 B3
Grace St. Leigh WN7 75 C5
Grace St. R'dale OL12 15 A2
Grace Wlk. M4 160 D1
Gracie Ave. 2 Oldham OL1 67 B8
Gradwell St. SK3 170 D8
Grafton Ave. M30 80 A4
Grafton Ct. M'ster M16 162 E5
Grafton Ct. 14 R'dale OL16 31 B6
Grafton Mall. 5 WA14 119 D4
Grafton St. Adlington PR7 20 F6
Grafton St. Alt'ham WA14 119 D4
Grafton St. Ashton-u-L OL6 85 D2
Grafton St. Atherton M46 58 A1
Grafton St. 5 Bolton BL1 145 D8
Grafton St. Bury BL9 44 F8
Grafton St. Failsworth M35 84 A8
Grafton St. Hyde SK14 167 D3
Grafton St. M'ster M13 163 B5
Grafton St. M'ster SK4 169 E3
Grafton St. Newton-l-W WA12 89 B3
Grafton St. Oldham OL1 49 E4
Grafton St. R'dale OL16 31 B6
Grafton St. Stalybridge SK15 86 D3
Graham Ave. WN6 18 C2
Graham Cres. M44 105 C3
Graham Dr. SK12 135 C6
Graham Rd. Salford M6 80 C4
Graham Rd. Stockport SK1 124 C8
Graham St. Abram WN2 56 A1
Graham St. Ashton-u-L OL7 84 F1
Graham St. Bolton BL1 145 F8
Graham St. M'ster M11 165 A8
Grain View. M5 161 A8
Grainger Ave. M12 99 A3
Grains Rd. Delph OL3 50 C4
Grains Rd. Shaw OL1 & OL2 49 D7
Gralam Cl. M33 108 E1
Grammar School Rd. Lymm WA13 117 A2
Grammar School Rd. Oldham OL8 66 B2
Grampian Cl. OL9 152 A5
Grampian Way. Golborne WA3 74 D1
Grampian Way. Shaw OL2 149 A8
Granada Rd. M34 100 A3
Granada TV Ctr. M3 158 E1
Granary La. Worsley M28 78 F5
Granary Way. M33 107 F2
Granby Rd. Cheadle SK8 132 B8
Granby Rd. Sale WA15 108 A1
Granby Rd. Stockport SK2 124 B5
Granby Rd. Stretford M32 96 E1
Granby Rd. Swinton M27 79 C7
Granby Row. M1 163 A8
Granby St. Bury BL8 26 F4
Granby St. Oldham OL9 66 A3
Grand Union Way. M30 95 D8
Grandale St. 5 M14 98 C3
Grandidge St. OL11 139 E5
Grange Ave. Alt'ham WA15 120 A2
Grange Ave. Cheadle SK8 & M19 122 F3
Grange Ave. Denton M34 101 B2
Grange Ave. Eccles M30 79 D4
Grange Ave. Little Lever BL3 43 C3
Grange Ave. Milnrow OL16 31 F4
Grange Ave. Oldham OL8 66 C4
Grange Ave. Reddish SK4 111 D5
Grange Ave. Sale WA15 120 B7
Grange Ave. Stretford M32 96 D2
Grange Ave. Swinton M27 61 D2
Grange Ave. Urmston M41 94 E2
Grange Ave. Wigan WN5 54 B7
Grange Ave. Wigan WN3 150 B5
Grange Cl. Golborne WA3 90 C6
Grange Cl. Hyde SK14 167 F1
Grange Cres. M41 95 C1
Grange Ct. Alt'ham WA14 119 C1
Grange Ct. Oldham OL8 66 D4
Grange Dr. Eccles M30 79 D4
Grange Dr. M'ster M9 64 F3
Grange Gr. M45 62 F8
Grange La. Delph OL3 50 F6
Grange La. M'ster M20 110 B2
Grange Mill Wlk. M40 83 B7
Grange Park Ave. Ashton-u-L OL6 85 F6
Grange Park Ave. Cheadle SK8 122 D5

Greville St. M13 98 E4
Grey Cl. SK6 113 A4
Grey Knotts. M28 78 A5
Grey Mare La. M11 83 A1
Grey Rd. Alt'ham WA14 119 C5
Grey Rd. Ashton-i-M WN4 73 A4
Grey St. Ashton-u-L OL6 166 C2
Grey St. Denton M34 100 D3
Grey St. M'ster M12 164 E6
Grey St. Middleton M24 46 F1
Grey St. Prestwich M25 63 C4
Grey St. Radcliffe M26 44 B3
Grey St. Stalybridge SK15 86 C1
Greyfriars. WN4 72 F4
Greyfriars Ct. M3 158 E3
Greyfriars Rd. M22 121 B2
Greyhound Dr. M6 81 C5
Greylands Cl. M33 107 F4
Greylands Rd. M20 122 C8
Greymont Rd. Bury BL9 27 F6
Greysham Ct. M16 97 E2
Greystoke Ave. Alt'ham WA15 120 D5
Greystoke Ave. Reddish M19 99 C1
Greystoke Ave. Sale M33 108 B3
Greystoke Cres. M45 44 E2
Greystoke Dr. Alderley Edge SK9 137 A2
Greystoke Dr. Bolton BL1 24 E6
Greystoke Dr. Middleton M24 46 D2
Greystoke La. M35 83 D6
Greystoke St. SK1 112 A1
Greystone Ave. Aspull WN2 38 C5
Greystone Ave. M'ster M21 109 F8
Greystone Wlk. SK4 111 D7
Greyswood Ave. 2 M7, M8 155 F6
Greytown Cl. M6 80 F5
Greywood Ave. BL9 141 B2
Grid La. SK6 114 F1
Grierson St. BL1 143 E3
Grierson Wlk. 20 M16 97 E4
Griffe La. BL9 45 D4
Griffin Cl. BL9 141 B4
Griffin Ct. M3 158 E2
Griffin Gr. M19 111 A8
Griffin Rd. M35 83 D6
Griffin St. M7 81 C6
Griffiths Cl. M7 158 D4
Griffiths St. 10 M40 83 C5
Grime St. BL0 11 A4
Grimeford La. BL6 & PR6 21 C5
Grimes Cotts. OL11 13 F1
Grimes St. OL11 & OL12 13 F1
Grimscott Cl. 7 M9 64 F1
Grimshaw Ave. M35 84 A8
Grimshaw Cl. SK6 113 A4
Grimshaw La. M'ster M10 & M40 160 F4
Grimshaw La. Middleton M24 65 C7
Grimshaw St. Failsworth M35 83 E8
Grimshaw St. Golborne WA3 74 A1
Grimshaw St. Stockport SK1 112 A1
Grimstead Cl. M23 120 E6
Grindall Ave. M40 65 B2
Grindle Gn. M30 95 C8
Grindleford Gdns. 19 SK13 171 E2
Grindleford Gr. 20 SK13 171 E2
Grindleford Lea. 21 SK13 171 E2
Grindleford Wlk. 22 Gamesley SK13 171 E2
Grindleford Wlk. M'ster M21 109 D5
Grindley Ave. M21 109 D5
Grindlow St. M13 164 E5
Grindlow Wlk. WN3 54 C2
Grindon Ave. M7 81 A7
Grindrod St. 1 M26 44 A4
Grindsbrook Rd. BL8 & M26 43 F7
Grinton Ave. M13 98 F2
Grisbeck Way. 3 OL1 153 E7
Grisdale Dr. M24 46 E2
Grisdale Rd. BL3 144 C5
Grisedale Ave. OL2 48 C8
Grisedale Ct. M9 65 A4
Grisedale Rd. OL11 30 B4
Gristlehurst La. BL9 & OL10 29 A5
Gritley Wlk. 7 M22 121 C1
Grizebeck Cl. M18 165 C6
Grizedale Cl. Bolton BL1 23 F2
Grizedale Cl. Mossley SK15 86 F7
Grizedale Dr. WN2 56 A7
Grizedale Rd. SK6 113 B4
Groby Pl. WA14 119 D5
Groby Rd. Alt'ham WA14 119 C4
Groby Rd. Denton M34 100 E7
Groby Rd. M'ster M21 109 B8
Groby Rd N. M34 100 D8
Groby St. Oldham OL8 67 A3
Groby St. Stalybridge SK15 86 C1
Groom St. M1 163 B7
Groomsport Dr. M7 & M8 155 E5
Grosvenor Ave. Golborne WA3 90 D8
Grosvenor Ave. 5 Whitefield M45 44 E1
Grosvenor Cl. Walkden M28 60 C5
Grosvenor Cl. Wilmslow SK9 137 A4
Grosvenor Cres. SK14 101 C1
Grosvenor Ct. 9 Ashton-u-L OL7 166 A1
Grosvenor Ct. 9 M'ster M21 97 E3
Grosvenor Ct. M'ster M7 155 D8
Grosvenor Ct. Sale M33 107 F5
Grosvenor Dr. Poynton SK12 133 D3
Grosvenor Dr. Walkden M28 60 C5
Grosvenor Gdns. M'ster M7 158 D4
Grosvenor Gdns. Newton-l-W WA12 89 C2
Grosvenor Gdns. 9 Stalybridge SK15 86 A1
Grosvenor Gdns. Wythenshawe M22 121 E6
Grosvenor House. 1 Ashton-u-L OL7 166 A1
Grosvenor House. M'ster M16 97 E1
Grosvenor House. 8 Stalybridge SK15 86 A1
Grosvenor House Mews. M8 63 F2
Grosvenor Pl. 6 OL7 166 A1
Grosvenor Rd. Alt'ham WA14 119 E5
Grosvenor Rd. Cheadle SK8 123 C4
Grosvenor Rd. Eccles M28 79 A3
Grosvenor Rd. Hyde SK14 167 D1
Grosvenor Rd. Leigh WN7 75 D6
Grosvenor Rd. M'ster M16 97 D2
Grosvenor Rd. M'ster SK4 168 B3
Grosvenor Rd. Marple SK6 125 F7
Grosvenor Rd. Pendlebury M27 80 B7
Grosvenor Rd. Sale M33 107 F6
Grosvenor Rd. Urmston M41 95 C2
Grosvenor Rd. Walkden M28 60 C5
Grosvenor Rd. 4 Whitefield M45 44 E1
Grosvenor Rd Cty Prim Sch. M27 80 B7
Grosvenor Sq. M'ster M7 158 D4
Grosvenor Sq. Sale M33 108 A4
Grosvenor St. Ashton-u-L OL7 84 F1
Grosvenor St. Ashton-u-L OL7 166 A1
Grosvenor St. Bolton BL2 & BL3 148 A6
Grosvenor St. Bury BL9 44 F8
Grosvenor St. Denton M34 100 D4
Grosvenor St. Hazel Grove SK7 124 D3
Grosvenor St. Heywood OL10 29 C1
Grosvenor St. Hindley WN2 56 D5
Grosvenor St. Kearsley BL4 60 F7
Grosvenor St. Little Lever BL3 43 B4
Grosvenor St. M'ster M1 163 B7
Grosvenor St. Prestwich M25 63 C4
Grosvenor St. R'dale OL11 30 C1
Grosvenor St. Radcliffe M26 43 F4
Grosvenor St. 6 Stalybridge SK15 86 A1
Grosvenor St. 7 Stockport SK1 170 F8
Grosvenor St. Stretford M32 96 D2
Grosvenor St. Swinton M27 61 F2
Grosvenor St. 3 Wigan WN5 54 F6
Grosvenor Way. Horwich BL6 22 C3
Grosvenor Way. Oldham OL1 & OL2 48 D2
Grotton Hollow. OL4 68 A6
Grotton Meadows. OL4 68 B5
Grouse St. OL12 14 F1
Grove. OL15 16 C8
Grove Arc. SK9 137 A2
Grove Ave. Adlington PR6 21 A7
Grove Ave. Failsworth M35 83 E5
Grove Ave. Wilmslow SK9 137 B7
Grove Cl. M14 98 C2
Grove Cotts. OL3 51 D6
Grove Cres. PR6 21 A7
Grove Ct. M33 108 D4
Grove Hill. M28 77 F6
Grove La. Alt'ham WA15 120 A6
Grove La. Alt'ham WA15 120 B3
Grove La. Bramhall SK7 & SK8 132 A6
Grove La. M'ster M20 110 B3
Grove La. Standish WN6 36 F8
Grove Pk. 5 M33 107 F4
Grove Pl. WN6 36 F8
Grove Rd. Alt'ham WA15 119 E3
Grove Rd. Middleton M24 47 B2
Grove Rd. Orrell WN8 53 C8
Grove Rd. Stalybridge SK15 86 D4
Grove Rd. Uppermill OL3 69 B7
Grove Sch The. WA15 120 A6
Grove Spring. M45 44 E2
Grove St. Ashton-i-M WN4 73 A4
Grove St. Ashton-u-L OL7 84 E5
Grove St. Bolton BL1 143 D2
Grove St. Bury BL9 141 C3
Grove St. Droylsden M43 99 F8
Grove St. Farnworth BL4 60 E8
Grove St. Hazel Grove SK7 124 E3
Grove St. Heywood OL10 29 E2
Grove St. Leigh WN7 76 B4
Grove St. M'ster M7 155 E5
Grove St. Oldham OL1 67 B7
Grove St. R'dale OL11 139 E5
Grove St. Stalybridge SK16 85 D1
Grove St. Uppermill OL3 69 B5
Grove St. Wilmslow SK9 137 B7
Grove Terr. OL4 67 E8
Grove The. Appley Bridge WN6 18 C2
Grove The. Bolton BL2 148 B5
Grove The. Bramhall SK8 132 A6
Grove The. Eccles M30 79 F1
Grove The. Golborne WA3 74 D1
Grove The. Hadfield SK14 171 F4
Grove The. Ince-i-M WN2 151 F7
Grove The. Little Lever BL3 43 B3
Grove The. M'ster M20 110 B1
Grove The. Sale M33 108 B3
Grove The. Shaw OL2 149 A6
Grove The. Stockport SK3 170 E7
Grove The. Uppermill OL3 50 F1
Grove The. Urmston M41 94 F1
Grovehurst. M27 & M28 79 C6
Grovewood Cl. OL7 84 E5
Grovewood Dr. WN6 35 E8
Grundey St. SK7 124 E2
Grundy Ave. M25 62 F2
Grundy Rd. BL4 60 E7
Grundy St. Bolton BL3 147 D4
Grundy St. Golborne WA3 90 A7
Grundy St. Heywood OL10 46 E8
Grundy St. M'ster SK4 110 E2
Grundy St. Walkden M28 60 F2
Grundy St. Westhoughton BL5 39 E1
Grundy's Cl. M29 77 C5
Guardian Angel's RC Prim Sch. BL8 27 B3
Guardian Ct. M33 108 A5
Guernsey Cl. M19 111 A6
Guest Rd. M25 63 A6
Guest St. WN7 76 B5
Guide Bridge Mills Ind Est. M34 100 E8
Guide Bridge Sta. M34 100 F8
Guide La. M34 100 F7
Guide Post Sq. M13 164 D6
Guide St. M5 80 C1
Guido St. Bolton BL1 143 E2
Guido St. Failsworth M35 83 E7
Guild Ave. M28 60 D2
Guild St. BL7 25 B7
Guildford Ave. SK8 132 A6
Guildford Cl. SK1 124 B7
Guildford Cres. WN6 36 F3
Guildford Dr. OL6 85 C7
Guildford Gr. M24 47 C3
Guildford Rd. Bolton BL1 142 B2
Guildford Rd. Dukinfield SK16 102 A7
Guildford Rd. M'ster M19 99 B2
Guildford Rd. Salford M6 80 B4
Guildford Rd. Urmston M41 95 E4
Guildford St. OL16 31 A7
Guildhall Cl. M15 163 A5
Guilford Rd. M30 79 B1
Guinness Circ. M17 96 A8
Guinness House. 2 OL16 31 B6
Guinness Rd. M17 96 A8
Guinness Road Trad Est. M17 95 F8
Guiseley Cl. BL9 27 E8
Gull Cl. SK12 133 B3
Gullane Cl. M40 83 C7
Gun Rd. SK12 & SK6 115 C2
Gun St. M4 159 B2
Gunson Ct. 20 M40 159 C3
Gunson St. M10 & M40 159 C3
Gunters Ave. BL5 57 F6
Gurner Ave. M5 161 B7
Gurney St. M4 160 D1
Gutter La. BL0 138 B7
Guy Fawkes St. M5 161 B7
Guy St. M7 155 F7
Guywood La. SK6 113 C3
Gwelo St. M11 83 A2
Gwenbury Ave. SK1 112 B1
Gwendor Ave. M8 & M9 63 F2
Gwladys St. SK15 86 E6
Gwynant Pl. M20 110 C7
Gylden Cl. SK14 102 B5
Gypsy La. OL11 30 C3
Gypsy Wlk. SK2 124 C6
Gyte's La. M19 99 C2

Habergham Cl. M28 78 C7
Hackberry Cl. WA14 119 B8
Hacken Bridge Rd. BL3 42 D4
Hacken La. BL3 42 C4
Hackford Cl. Bolton BL1 144 C8
Hackford Cl. Bury BL8 27 D5
Hacking St. Bury BL9 141 A2
Hacking St. M'ster M7 155 E6
Hacking St. Prestwich M25 63 A4
Hackle St. M11 83 C2
Hackleton Cl. M4 160 D1
Hackness Rd. M21 108 F8
Hackney Ave. M40 83 C4
Hackney Cl. M26 44 A5
Hackwood Wlk. 16 M8 155 F7
Hackworth Cl. WN1 151 E8
Hadbutt La. M29 76 F4
Haddan Gn. 31 SK13 171 D2
Haddan Lea. 30 SK13 171 D2
Haddington Dr. M9 64 E3
Haddon Ave. M40 65 F1
Haddon Cl. Alderley Edge SK9 136 F2
Haddon Cl. High Lane SK6 134 E6
Haddon Cl. Whitefield BL9 45 A5
Haddon Gr. Alt'ham WA15 119 F7
Haddon Gr. Reddish SK5 111 E7
Haddon Gr. Sale M33 108 A4
Haddon Hall Rd. M43 83 E2
Haddon House. M5 154 D3
Haddon Mews. SK13 171 D2
Haddon Rd. Eccles M30 95 C8
Haddon Rd. Gatley SK8 131 C7
Haddon Rd. Golborne WA3 74 D2
Haddon Rd. Hazel Grove SK7 124 E1
Haddon Rd. M'ster M21 109 D5
Haddon Rd. Swinton M27,M28 79 C6
Haddon Rd. Wigan WN3 54 E3
Haddon St. 5 Ashton-i-M WN4 72 F5
Haddon St. R'dale OL11 30 E4
Haddon St. Salford M6 81 B5
Haddon St. Stretford M32 96 D4
Haddon Way. 17 Denton M34 101 A1
Haddon Way. Shaw OL2 149 C8
Hadfield Ave. OL9 66 B4
Hadfield Cres. OL6 85 E5
Hadfield Cty Inf Sch. SK14 103 F5
Hadfield Ind Est. SK14 103 F6
Hadfield Pl. SK13 116 C8
Hadfield Rd. SK14 171 F4
Hadfield Sq. SK13 116 C8
Hadfield St. Dukinfield SK16 101 A7
Hadfield St. Glossop SK13 116 C8
Hadfield St. M'ster M7 155 E6
Hadfield St. M'ster M15 161 C6
Hadfield St. Oldham OL8 66 F3
Hadfield St Andrew's CE Jun Sch. SK14 171 F4
Hadfield St Charles RC Prim Sch. SK14 103 E5
Hadfield Sta. SK14 104 A5
Hadfields Ave. SK14 103 D5
Hadleigh Cl. BL1 25 A6
Hadley Ave. M13 98 E2
Hadley Cl. SK8 122 F1
Hadley St. M6 81 B5
Hadlow Gn. SK5 112 B6
Hadlow Wlk. M40 160 E3
Hadrian House. OL1 153 F7
Hadwin St. BL1 143 F1
Hafton Rd. M7 81 B6
Hag Bank La. SK12 135 D7
Hag Fold Sta. M46 58 C5
Haggate. OL2 48 C3
Haggate Cres. OL2 48 C3
Hagley Rd. M5 161 A6
Hags The. BL9 45 A5
Hague Bar Prim Sch. SK12 135 E8
Hague Bar Rd. SK12 135 F8
Hague Bush Cl. WA3 74 E1
Hague Ct. 5 M20 110 A5
Hague Fold. SK12 135 F8
Hague House. OL8 153 F5
Hague Pl. 3 SK15 86 A2
Hague Rd. M'ster M20 110 A5
Hague Rd. Mottram-i-L SK14 103 B1
Hague St. Ashton-u-L OL6 85 D4
Hague St. Glossop SK13 116 D6
Hague St. M'ster M10 & M40 157 F5
Hague St. Oldham OL4 67 E8
Haig Ave. M44 105 C4
Haig Ct. BL8 27 B1
Haig Rd. Aspull WN2 38 B7
Haig Rd. Bury BL8 27 B1
Haig Rd. Stretford M32 96 D3
Haig St. WN3 150 B7
Haigh & Aspull (St David's) CE Prim Sch. WN2 38 B7
Haigh Ave. SK4 111 E5
Haigh Country Park. WN2 37 F5
Haigh Hall Cl. BL0 11 B4
Haigh La. M24 & OL9 47 E1
Haigh Lawn. WA14 119 B3
Haigh Pk. SK4 111 E5
Haigh Rd. WN2 38 C6
Haigh St. Bolton BL1 145 F8
Haigh St. R'dale OL11 31 A6
Haigh View. Ince-i-M WN3 151 E6
Haigh View. Wigan WN1 37 D2
Hail St. BL0 11 A4
Haile Dr. M28 77 F6
Hailsham Cl. BL8 27 C7
Hailsham St. M11 160 F2
Hailwood St. OL11 30 E4
Hainworth Cl. M40 65 C1
Haldon Rd. M20 110 D5
Hale Ave. SK12 133 D2
Hale Cl. WN7 76 B2
Hale Ct. WA14 119 D2
Hale Golf Course. WA15 129 A7
Hale Gr. WN4 72 F5
Hale Green Ct. WA15 120 A3
Hale La. M35 & M40 83 E8
Hale Low Rd. WA15 119 F3
Hale Prep Sch. WA15 119 E3
Hale Rd. Alt'ham WA15 & WA14 120 B1
Hale Rd. M'ster SK4 168 C3
Hale Sta. WA14 119 D2
Hale Wlk. SK8 123 A5
Halebank Ave. M20 109 F7
Hales Cl. M43 83 F3
Halesden Rd. SK4 111 D5
Halesfield. WN2 57 B2
Halesworth Wlk. M40 159 C4
Halewood Ave. WA3 73 F1
Haley Cl. 5 SK5 111 F8
Haley St. M8 156 B7
Half Acre. M26 43 F6
Half Acre Dr. OL11 30 C6
Half Acre La. Blackrod BL6 21 C2
Half Acre La. R'dale OL11 30 B6
Half Acre Mews. OL11 30 B6
Half Acre Rd. OL11 30 B6
Half Edge La. M30 79 F3
Half Moon La. SK2 124 E6
Half St. M'ster M3 158 E3
Half St. Middleton M24 46 F1
Halfacre Rd. M22 121 C4
Halford Dr. M40 83 C8
Halfpenny Bridge Ind Est. 1 OL11 31 A6
Halifax Rd. Littleborough OL12 15 C3
Halifax Rd. Littleborough OL15 16 D7
Halifax St. OL6 166 B4
Haliwell St. OL15 16 C5
Hall Ave. Alt'ham WA15 119 F7
Hall Ave. M'ster M14 98 D3
Hall Ave. Sale M33 107 E6
Hall Ave. Stalybridge SK15 86 C5
Hall Bank. M30 79 C2
Hall Cl. Mottram-i-L SK14 103 A5
Hall Cl. Shevington WN6 36 B6
Hall Coppice The. BL7 8 E1
Hall Dr. Middleton M24 64 F7
Hall Dr. Mottram-i-L SK14 103 A5
Hall Farm Ave. M41 95 B3
Hall Fold. OL12 14 C8
Hall Gdns. OL12 14 C2
Hall Gn. WN8 53 B7
Hall Gr. Cheadle SK8 122 C6
Hall Gr. M'ster M14 98 D3
Hall Green Cl. Dukinfield SK16 166 C1
Hall Green Cl. Orrell WN8 53 B7
Hall Green Rd. SK16 166 C1
Hall House La. WN7 76 C4
Hall i' th' Wood La. Bolton BL1 25 A4
Hall i' th' Wood La. Bolton BL1 & BL2 25 B3
Hall i' th' Wood Sta. BL2 25 B3
Hall La. Appley Bridge WN6 18 D2
Hall La. Bolton BL3 & BL4 42 E3
Hall La. Farnworth BL4 42 D2
Hall La. Horwich BL6 39 E7
Hall La. Partington M31 105 F4
Hall La. Pennington Green WN2 38 D2
Hall La. Romiley SK6 113 B6
Hall La. Wigan WN1 37 D4
Hall La. Wigan WN3 & WN5 54 A4
Hall La. Wythenshawe M23 121 B6
Hall Lane Gr. WN2 56 D8
Hall Lee Dr. BL5 40 A1
Hall Meadow. SK8 122 E1
Hall Meadow Rd. SK13 104 D2
Hall Moss La. SK7 132 C4
Hall Moss Rd. M9 65 A3
Hall Rd. Alt'ham WA14 119 C1
Hall Rd. Ashton-u-L OL6 85 C5
Hall Rd. Bramhall SK7 123 D1
Hall Rd. Handforth SK9 131 E3
Hall Rd. M'ster M14 98 D3
Hall Rd. Wilmslow SK9 137 A7
Hall St. Ashton-i-M WN2 73 E7
Hall St. Ashton-u-L OL6 85 E2
Hall St. Bury BL8 26 E4
Hall St. Bury BL8 27 C4
Hall St. Cheadle SK8 122 D6
Hall St. Denton SK14 101 B3
Hall St. Failsworth M35 83 D6
Hall St. 1 Farnworth BL4 42 D2
Hall St. Heywood OL10 29 E1
Hall St. Ince-i-M WN2 151 F8
Hall St. Middleton M24 65 A8
Hall St. M'ster M1 162 F8
Hall St. 3 Oldham OL4 67 B7
Hall St. Radcliffe M26 43 F6
Hall St. Ramsbottom BL0 11 C2
Hall St. Royton OL2 48 D4
Hall St. Stockport SK1 112 A1
Hall St. Swinton M27 61 F2
Hall St. Whitworth OL12 14 B8
Hall St. Whitworth OL12 14 C8
Hall St. Wigan WN1 151 D7
Hall Wood Rd. SK9 131 D2
Hall's Ct. 3 SK13 104 C1
Hallam Rd. M40 83 B5
Hallam St. Radcliffe M26 44 D4
Hallam St. Stockport SK2 124 A6
Hallam Wlk. 19 M16 97 E4
Hallas Gr. M23 109 B1
Hallbottom St. SK14 101 F5
Hallbridge Gdns. WN8 53 B8
Hallcott Wlk. M8 155 E5
Hallcroft. M31 105 F4
Hallcroft Gdns. OL16 31 E6
Hallgate. Westhoughton BL5 57 E5
Hallgate. Wigan WN1 150 C8
Hallgate Dr. SK8 122 A2
Hallgate Rd. SK1 124 B8
Halliday Ct. OL15 15 E4
Halliday Rd. M40 83 B4
Halliford Rd. M40 83 A6
Hallington Cl. BL3 145 F5
Halliwell Ave. OL8 66 E3
Halliwell Ind Est. BL1 143 D3
Halliwell La. M7 & M8 155 F7
Halliwell Rd. Bolton BL1 143 D2
Halliwell Rd. M'ster M25 62 F1
Halliwell St. 14 Bolton BL1 143 D2
Halliwell St. Milnrow OL16 31 E7
Halliwell St. Oldham OL9 66 A2
Halliwell St. 5 R'dale OL12 139 E8
Halliwell St W. 17 M7, M8 155 F7
Halliwell Wlk. M25 62 F1
Hallkirk Wlk. 4 M40 65 D2
Hallman La. M22 & M90 130 D7
Hallows Ave. M21 109 C5
Hallows Farm Ave. OL12 14 D2
Hallroyd Brow. OL1 153 E8
Hallstead Ave. M38 59 E4
Hallstead Gr. M38 59 E4
Hallsville Rd. M19 99 C1
Hallsworth Rd. M30 79 A1
Hallwood Ave. M6 80 C5
Hallwood Rd. M23 121 A6
Hallworth Ave. M34 84 C1
Hallworth Rd. M8 156 B8
Hallworthy Cl. WN7 75 B1
Halmore Rd. M10 & M40 160 D2
Halsall Cl. BL9 27 F6
Halsall Dr. BL3 147 E2
Halsbury Cl. M12 164 E6
Halset Wlk. SK7 124 A2
Halsey Cl. OL9 65 E2
Halsey Wlk. 19 M8 155 F7
Halshaw La. BL4 60 F7
Halsmere Dr. M9 64 E3
Halstead Ave. M'ster M21 109 A7
Halstead Ave. Salford M6 80 E5
Halstead Dr. M44 94 B1
Halstead Gr. M22 121 F5
Halstead St. Bolton BL2 148 A7
Halstead St. Bury BL9 141 A4
Halstead Wlk. BL9 28 A5
Halstock Wlk. M40 157 D5
Halston Cl. SK5 169 F4
Halstone Ave. SK9 136 E4
Halter Cl. M26 44 A5
Halton Bank. M27 & M6 154 F4
Halton Dr. WA15 108 B1
Halton House. 4 M6 154 F1
Halton Rd. M11 83 C2
Halton St. Bolton BL2 148 B7
Halton St. Hyde SK14 167 F3
Halvard Ave. BL9 27 F6
Halvard Ct. BL9 27 F6
Halvis Gr. M16 97 B3
Hambleden Cl. BL3 40 F5
Hambledon Cl. M46 58 E5
Hambleton Cl. BL8 26 F1
Hambleton Dr. Sale M33 107 D5
Hambleton Dr. Wythenshawe M23 121 A4
Hambleton Rd. SK8 131 C8
Hamblett St. WN7 75 B5
Hambridge Cl. M8 156 A7
Hamel St. Bolton BL3 147 E3
Hamel St. Dukinfield SK14 101 F5
Hamer Cl. OL7 166 A1
Hamer Cty Prim Sch. OL16 15 B2
Hamer Dr. M16 162 D5
Hamer Hall Cres. OL12 15 B1
Hamer Hill. M9 64 C3
Hamer La. OL16 15 B1
Hamer St. Bolton BL2 25 B1
Hamer St. Heywood OL10 29 B2
Hamer St. Radcliffe M26 44 C4
Hamer St. Ramsbottom BL0 11 B2
Hamer's Bldg. OL10 29 B2
Hamerton Rd. M40 159 C4
Hamilcar Ave. M30 79 E2
Hamilton Ave. Eccles M30 79 E1
Hamilton Ave. Irlam M44 105 D4
Hamilton Ave. Royton OL2 48 B3
Hamilton Cl. Bury BL8 27 B3
Hamilton Cl. Prestwich M25 63 A3
Hamilton Cres. SK4 168 B1
Hamilton Ct. Little Lever BL3 43 B3
Hamilton Ct. Wigan WN5 54 E8
Hamilton Gr. M16 162 D5
Hamilton Lodge. 6 M14 98 C3
Hamilton Rd. Garswood WN4 72 D4
Hamilton Rd. Hindley WN2 56 F4
Hamilton Rd. M'ster M13 98 F3
Hamilton Rd. Prestwich M25 63 A3
Hamilton Rd. Tyldesley M29 77 D6
Hamilton Rd. Whitefield M45 62 E8
Hamilton Sq. Stockport SK4 169 E3
Hamilton Sq. Wigan WN5 54 E8
Hamilton St. Ashton-u-L OL7 84 F1
Hamilton St. Atherton M46 58 C2
Hamilton St. Bolton BL1 24 E5
Hamilton St. Bury BL9 140 F4
Hamilton St. Chadderton OL9 152 A7
Hamilton St. Leigh WN7 75 D6
Hamilton St. M'ster M7 155 D7
Hamilton St. M'ster M16 162 D5
Hamilton St. Oldham OL4 67 B7
Hamilton St. Stalybridge SK15 85 F2
Hamilton St. Swinton M27 61 D1
Hamilton St. Worsley M28 79 B3
Hamilton Way. OL10 28 E1
Hamlet Dr. M33 107 E6
Hamlet The. BL6 40 B8
Hammer Terr. BL0 11 C3
Hammerstone Rd. M18 165 C6
Hammett Rd. M21 109 A8
Hammond Ave. Bacup OL13 3 D8
Hammond Ave. Reddish SK4 111 E5
Hamnet Cl. BL1 25 A5
Hamnett St. Droylsden M11 & M43 83 D1
Hamnett St. Hyde SK14 167 D3
Hamon Rd. WA15 119 E4
Hampden Cres. M18 165 C5
Hampden Gr. M30 79 D2
Hampden Pl. WN5 36 D1
Hampden Rd. Prestwich M25 63 C4
Hampden Rd. Sale M33 108 A3
Hampden Rd. Shaw OL2 49 D6
Hampden St. Heywood OL10 29 D1
Hampden St. R'dale OL11 139 F6
Hampshire Cl. Brinnington SK5 112 C5
Hampshire Cl. Bury BL9 45 A8
Hampshire Cl. Glossop SK13 116 F8
Hampshire House. SK5 112 C5
Hampshire Rd. Brinnington SK5 112 C5
Hampshire Rd. Droylsden M43 84 A3
Hampshire Rd. Oldham OL9 152 B5
Hampshire Rd. Partington M31 105 D2
Hampshire St. M7 155 E7
Hampshire Wlk. 6 M8 156 B6
Hampson Ave. WA3 91 F3
Hampson Cl. Ashton-i-M WN4 73 B2
Hampson Cl. 5 Eccles M30 79 B1
Hampson Cres. SK9 131 C4
Hampson Fold. M26 43 F4
Hampson Mill La. BL9 44 F5
Hampson Pl. OL6 85 E6
Hampson Rd. Ashton-u-L OL6 85 E6
Hampson Rd. Stretford M32 96 C2
Hampson Sq. 5 M26 44 A4
Hampson St. Atherton M46 58 C3
Hampson St. Droylsden M43 84 A2
Hampson St. Eccles M30 79 B1
Hampson St. Horwich BL6 22 B4
Hampson St. M'ster M3, M5 158 D1
Hampson St. M'ster M10 & M40 160 D4
Hampson St. Radcliffe M26 44 A3
Hampson St. Sale M33 108 D4
Hampson St. Stockport SK1 124 B8
Hampson St. Swinton M27 62 A1
Hampstead Ave. M41 94 E1
Hampstead Dr. SK2 124 C5
Hampstead La. SK2 124 C5
Hampstead Rd. WN6 19 D1
Hampton Gr. Bury BL9 27 F6
Hampton Gr. Cheadle SK8 122 E2
Hampton Gr. Leigh WN7 76 E7
Hampton Gr. Sale WA14 107 F1
Hampton Rd. Bolton BL3 42 A3
Hampton Rd. Failsworth M35 84 B8
Hampton Rd. Irlam M44 105 D4
Hampton Rd. Stretford M21 96 F1
Hampton Rd. Urmston M41 95 D2
Hampton St. OL8 66 D4
Hamsell Rd. M13 163 C7
Hanborough Ct. M29 76 F8
Hancock Cl. M14 98 B3
Hancock St. M32 108 D8
Hand La. Leigh WN7 75 E2
Handel Ave. M41 95 A2
Handel Mews. M33 108 C4
Handel St. BL1 143 D3
Handford House. 5 M41 95 E2
Handforth Gr. M13 98 E2
Handforth Hall Cty Prim Sch. SK9 131 D4
Handforth Rd. Handforth SK9 131 E1
Handforth Rd. Reddish SK5 111 F5
Handforth Sta. SK9 131 D3
Handley Ave. M14 98 B1
Handley Cl. SK3 123 C5
Handley Rd. SK7 123 E3
Handley St. Bury BL9 44 F8
Handley St. R'dale OL12 139 D8
Hands La. OL11 30 A7
Handsworth St. M12 164 D7
Hanging Birch. M24 64 B7
Hanging Chadder La. OL2 48 C7
Hanging Ditch. M4 158 F2
Hanging Lees Cl. OL16 32 C4
Hani Ct. M8 63 F1
Hankinson Cl. M31 105 E2
Hankinson Way. M6 81 A3
Hanley Cl. Disley SK12 135 D5
Hanley Cl. Middleton M24 65 A5
Hanlith Mews. M19 110 F8
Hanlon St. M'ster M8 63 F1
Hanlon St. M'ster M8 156 A8
Hanmer St. WN2 56 D5
Hannah Baldwin Cl. M11 164 F8

Hannah Lodge. M20 110 A4
Hannah St. M12 99 A2
Hannerton Rd. OL2 49 D7
Hannesburg Gdns. M23 120 F4
Hannet Rd. M22 121 D2
Hanover Bsns Pk. WA14 119 B7
Hanover Cres. M14 98 D4
Hanover Ct. Bolton BL3 144 B5
Hanover Ct. M'ster M7 155 D7
Hanover Ct. Swinton M28 79 B6
Hanover Gdns. M7 155 E8
Hanover House. Bolton BL3 146 B2
Hanover House. 10 M'ster M14 110 D8
Hanover House.Oldham OL8 153 D6
Hanover Rd. Alt'ham WA14 119 B7
Hanover Rd. Hindley WN2 56 C6
Hanover St. Bolton BL1 145 E7
Hanover St. Leigh WN7 76 A6
Hanover St. Littleborough OL15 16 A5
Hanover St. M'ster M4 & M60 159 A2
Hanover St. Mossley OL5 68 C1
Hanover St. R'dale OL11 30 C2
Hanover St. Stalybridge SK15 85 F2
Hanover St N. M34 100 E8
Hanover St S. M34 100 E8
Hanover Towers. SK5 169 F3
Hansdon Cl. M8 156 A6
Hansen Wlk. 1 M22 121 C2
Hansham Wlk. M23 108 E1
Hanslope Wlk. 14 M9 157 E8
Hanson Cl. M24 47 A1
Hanson Mews. SK1 112 B2
Hanson Rd. M40 83 B7
Hanson St. Bury BL9 140 F4
Hanson St. Middleton M24 47 A1
Hanson St. Oldham OL4 67 C7
Hanworth Cl. M13 163 B7
Hapsford Wlk. M40 83 A5
Hapton Ave. M32 96 D1
Hapton Pl. SK4 169 E3
Hapton St. M19 99 A1
Harbern Cl. M30 79 D4
Harbern Dr. WN7 57 D2
Harbord St. M24 65 A8
Harboro Ct. M33 107 F3
Harboro Gr. M33 107 F4
Harboro Rd. M33 107 E4
Harboro Way. M33 107 F4
Harbour Farm Rd. SK14 101 E5
Harbour La. Edgworth BL7 9 D5
Harbour La. Milnrow OL16 31 F5
Harbour La N. OL16 31 F6
Harbourne Ave. M28 78 C8
Harbourne Cl. M28 78 C8
Harburn Wlk. M22 130 E8
Harbury Cl. WN6 36 F2
Harbury Cres. M22 121 C5
Harbury Wlk. WN6 36 F2
Harcles Dr. BL0 11 B2
Harcombe Rd. M20 110 C6
Harcourt Ave. M41 95 F1
Harcourt Cl. M41 95 F1
Harcourt Ind Ctr. M28 60 D5
Harcourt Mews. 10 BL6 22 B4
Harcourt Rd. Alt'ham WA14 119 D6
Harcourt Rd. Sale M33 108 A6
Harcourt St. Oldham OL1 67 B8
Harcourt St. Reddish SK5 111 F8
Harcourt St. Stretford M32 96 E3
Harcourt St. Walkden M28 60 D5
Hard La. OL12 15 A8
Hardacre St. WN3 151 D6
Hardberry Pl. SK2 124 E6
Hardcastle Ave. M21 109 C6
Hardcastle Rd. SK3 170 D7
Hardcastle St. Bolton BL1 143 F2
Hardcastle St. 7 Oldham OL1 67 A7
Hardcastle St. Oldham OL1 153 F7
Harden Dr. BL2 25 D2
Harden Hills. OL2 49 D8
Harden Pk. SK9 137 A3
Hardfield Rd. M24 65 B5
Hardfield St. OL10 29 D2
Hardicker St. M19 111 B7
Hardie Ave. BL4 60 B7
Harding St. Adlington PR6 21 B8
Harding St. Dukinfield SK14 101 D5
Harding St. M'ster M3 158 F2
Harding St. M'ster M4 160 D1
Harding St. Salford M6 81 A4
Harding St. Stockport SK1 112 B1
Hardman Ave. M'ster M25 63 D2
Hardman Ave. Rawtenstall BB4 2 A8
Hardman Ave. Romiley SK6 113 A3
Hardman Cl. Radcliffe M26 43 F6
Hardman Cl. Rawtenstall BB4 2 F7
Hardman Dr. BB4 2 F7
Hardman Fold. BL3 42 B2
Hardman Fold Sch. M35 83 D7
Hardman La. M35 83 E8
Hardman Rd. SK5 111 F8
Hardman St. Bury BL9 140 F4
Hardman St. Failsworth M35 83 D7
Hardman St. Farnworth BL4 60 E7
Hardman St. Heywood OL10 29 D2
Hardman St. M'ster M3 158 E1
Hardman St. Milnrow OL16 32 A5
Hardman St. Oldham OL9 66 B3
Hardman St. Radcliffe M26 43 F6
Hardman St. Stockport SK3 170 D8
Hardman St. Wigan WN3 150 B6
Hardman Terr. OL13 3 D8
Hardman's La. BL7 24 F8
Hardman's Mews. M45 62 F6
Hardman's Rd. M45 62 F6
Hardmans. BL7 24 F7
Hardon Gr. M13 98 F2
Hardrow Cl. WN3 55 B2
Hardrush Fold. M35 84 A6
Hardshaw Cl. M13 163 B6
Hardsough La. BL0 1 D5
Hardwick Cl. High Lane SK6 134 F6
Hardwick Cl. Little Lever BL3 43 B5
Hardwick Rd.Ashton-i-M WN4 73 A5
Hardwick Rd. Partington M31 106 A3
Hardwick St. OL7 84 F2
Hardwicke Rd. SK12 133 F4
Hardwicke St. OL11 30 E4
Hardy Ave. M21 109 A8
Hardy Cl. BL5 39 E3
Hardy Dr. Alt'ham WA15 119 F7
Hardy Dr. Bramhall SK7 132 D7
Hardy Farm. M21 109 B6
Hardy Gr. Swinton M27 79 D5
Hardy Gr. Worsley M28 78 F8
Hardy La. M21 109 B6
Hardy Mill Cty Prim Sch. BL2 25 F4
Hardy Mill Rd. Bolton BL2 25 F4
Hardy Mill Rd. Bolton BL2 26 A3
Hardy St. Ashton-u-L OL6 85 E6
Hardy St. Eccles M30 79 B1
Hardy St. Oldham OL4 & OL8 67 A6
Hardy St. Wigan WN6 37 A1
Hardybutts. Wigan WN1 151 D8
Hardybutts. Wigan WN1 151 E8
Hardywood Rd. 4 M34 113 A7
Hare Dr. BL9 45 B4
Hare Hill Prim Sch. SK14 102 C3
Hare Hill Rd. Hattersley SK14 102 C2
Hare Hill Rd. Littleborough OL15 16 B6
Hare St. 7 M'ster M4 159 A2
Hare St. R'dale OL11 31 A6
Hare St. R'dale OL11 139 F5
Harebell Ave. 10 M28 59 F3
Harebell Cl. OL12 14 D3
Haredale Dr. M8 156 B6
Harefield Ave. OL11 139 F5
Harefield Dr. Heywood OL10 29 F2
Harefield Dr. M'ster M20 110 A2
Harefield Dr. Wilmslow SK9 137 B5
Harefield Rd. SK9 131 E4
Hareford Wlk. M9 156 C6
Harehill Cl. 5 M13 163 B7
Hareshill Rd. OL10 46 C7
Harewood Ave. R'dale OL11 13 D2
Harewood Ave. Sale M33 107 D3
Harewood Cl. OL11 13 D2
Harewood Ct. M33 108 C3
Harewood Dr. R'dale OL11 13 C2
Harewood Dr. Royton OL2 48 C5
Harewood Gr. SK5 111 E8
Harewood Rd. Hindley WN2 56 C5
Harewood Rd. Irlam M44 94 B2
Harewood Rd. R'dale OL11 13 D2
Harewood Rd. Shaw OL2 49 D8
Harewood Way. R'dale OL11 13 C2
Harewood Way. Swinton M27 61 F2
Harewood Wlk. 23 M34 101 A1
Harford Cl. SK7 124 A1
Hargate Ave. OL12 14 A2
Hargate Cl. BL9 11 C2
Hargate Dr. Alt'ham WA15 120 A1
Hargate Dr. Irlam M44 94 A3
Hargate Hill La. SK13 115 E7
Hargrave Cl. M9 64 C6
Hargreave's St. M8 159 A3
Hargreaves House. BL3 145 E6
Hargreaves Rd. WA15 120 C6
Hargreaves St. Bolton BL1 143 E2
Hargreaves St. Oldham OL9 152 C6
Hargreaves St. Oldham OL1 153 F7
Hargreaves St. R'dale OL11 30 C4
Harkerside Cl. M21 109 C8
Harkness St. M12 164 D7
Harland Dr. Ashton-i-M WN4 73 C3
Harland Dr. M'ster M8 156 B7
Harland Way. OL12 14 B2
Harlea Ave. WN2 57 A3
Harlech Ave. Hindley WN2 57 B4
Harlech Ave. Prestwich M25 & M45 63 B7
Harlech Dr. SK7 124 D1
Harlech St. WN4 72 F5
Harleen Gr. SK2 124 D7
Harley Ave. Ainsworth BL2 26 D1
Harley Ave. Bolton BL2 25 E3
Harley Ave. M'ster M14 98 E3
Harley Ct. M24 46 F1
Harley Hall Royal Northern Coll of Music. M16 97 E1
Harley Rd. Middleton M24 46 F1
Harley Rd. Sale M33 108 C5
Harley St. Ashton-u-L OL6 166 B3
Harley St. M'ster M11 99 D8
Harling Rd. M22 121 E7
Harlington Cl. 3 M23 120 D7
Harlock Ct. M6 81 B3
Harlow Dr. M18 99 D3
Harlyn Ave. SK7 132 F7
Harmer Cl. M40 83 B5
Harmol Gr. OL7 84 F6
Harmony St. OL4 67 A6
Harmsworth Dr. SK4 111 B5
Harmsworth St. M6 154 E2
Harmuir Cl. WN6 36 E4
Harold Ave. Ashton-i-M WN4 73 A5
Harold Ave. Dukinfield SK16 101 D8
Harold Ave. Reddish M18 99 F4
Harold Lees. OL10 29 F3
Harold Priestnall Cl. M40 83 B6
Harold St. Aspull WN2 38 D5
Harold St. Bolton BL1 143 D2
Harold St. Failsworth M35 83 F7
Harold St. M'ster M15, M16 161 C6
Harold St. Middleton M24 46 E1
Harold St. Oldham OL9 153 D7
Harold St. Prestwich M25 62 F4
Harold St. R'dale OL16 15 C2
Harold St. Stockport SK ,SK2 124 B8
Haroldene St. BL2 25 B2
Harp Ind Est. OL11 30 D2
Harp Rd. M17 96 A8
Harp St. M11 99 E7
Harp Trad Est. M17 96 A8
Harper Fold Rd. M26 43 E3
Harper Green Rd. BL3 & BL4 42 B1
Harper Green Sch. BL4 42 B1
Harper House. M19 98 F1
Harper Pl. OL6 166 C3
Harper Rd. M22 121 E7
Harper Sq. OL2 149 C7
Harper St. Farnworth BL4 42 B2
Harper St. Hindley WN2 56 C4
Harper St. Oldham OL8 66 E4
Harper St. R'dale OL11 139 E5
Harper St. Stockport SK3 170 E7
Harper St. Wigan WN1 151 E7
Harper's La. BL1 142 B2
Harpford Cl. BL2 43 A5
Harpford Dr. BL2 43 A5
Harptree Gr. WN7 75 D7
Harpur Mount Prim Sch. M9 157 D8
Harpurhey Rd. M8 & M9 157 D8
Harridge Ave. R'dale OL12 14 C3
Harridge Ave. Stalybridge SK15 86 D2
Harridge St. OL12 14 C3
Harridge The. OL12 14 C3
Harriet St. Irlam M44 105 E5
Harriet St. Walkden M28 60 D3
Harriett St. M'ster M4 159 C2
Harriett St. R'dale OL16 31 A7
Harringay Rd. M40 83 B5
Harrington Rd. WA14 119 B5
Harrington St. M18 99 E5
Harris Ave. Reddish M34 100 B3
Harris Ave. Urmston M41 95 D5
Harris Cl. Heywood OL10 28 E1
Harris Cl. Reddish M34 100 B3
Harris Dr. Hyde SK14 102 A4
Harris Dr. Whitefield BL9 & M45 45 B2
Harris Rd. WN6 19 B3
Harris St. Bolton BL3 145 E6
Harris St. M'ster M7 & M8 158 E4
Harrison Ave. M19 99 B2
Harrison Cl. OL12 15 A6
Harrison Cres. BL6 21 C3
Harrison Rd. PR7 21 A6
Harrison St. Bacup OL13 4 A8
Harrison St. Eccles M30 95 B8
Harrison St. Hindley WN2 57 B3
Harrison St. Horwich BL6 22 B4
Harrison St. Hyde SK14 113 F8
Harrison St. M'ster M4 158 D4
Harrison St. M'ster M4 160 D1
Harrison St. 1 Oldham OL1 153 F6
Harrison St. Ramsbottom BL0 138 C7
Harrison St. Stalybridge SK15 86 A2
Harrison St. Stockport SK1 & SK2 170 F7
Harrison St. Walkden M38 60 A4
Harrison St. 4 Wigan WN5 54 F6
Harrison Way. WA12 89 C4
Harrison's Dr. SK6 113 C5
Harrock La. WN6 18 A5
Harrogate Ave. M25 63 D2
Harrogate Cl. M18 99 E7
Harrogate Dr. SK5 111 E8
Harrogate Rd. SK5 99 E1
Harrogate Sq. BL8 26 F1
Harrogate St. WN1 151 D7
Harrop Court Rd. OL3 51 D5
Harrop Edge La. OL3 51 B5
Harrop Edge Rd. SK14 & SK15 102 E4
Harrop Green. OL3 51 D5
Harrop Green La. OL3 51 D5
Harrop Rd. WA15 119 F2
Harrop St. Bolton BL3 146 A4
Harrop St. Droylsden M18 99 F6
Harrop St. 10 Stalybridge SK15 86 A2
Harrop St. Stockport SK1 124 A7
Harrop St. Walkden M28 60 B3
Harrow Ave. M'ster M19 111 A6
Harrow Ave. Oldham OL8 66 E3
Harrow Ave. R'dale OL11 30 A6
Harrow Cl. Bury BL9 44 F5
Harrow Cl. Orrell WN5 53 F8
Harrow Cres. WN7 75 F3
Harrow Dr. M33 108 A2
Harrow Mews. OL2 149 B7
Harrow Pl. WN2 55 F4
Harrow Rd. Bolton BL1 144 B8
Harrow Rd. Sale M33 108 A2
Harrow Rd. Shevington WN5 36 D1
Harrow St. M'ster M8 64 B1
Harrow St. R'dale OL11 31 B2
Harrowby Ct. BL4 60 B8
Harrowby Dr. M40 157 D5
Harrowby Fold. BL4 60 C8
Harrowby La. BL4 60 C8
Harrowby Rd. Bolton BL1 23 F2
Harrowby Rd. Bolton BL3 146 A3
Harrowby Rd. Swinton M27 79 E7
Harrowby St. Farnworth BL4 60 C8
Harrowby St. Wigan WN5 54 E6
Harrowdene Wlk. 6 M9 157 D8
Harry Hall Gdns. M7 81 C3
Harry Pigott Ave. M40 83 A7
Harry Rd. SK5 111 F8
Harry St. Oldham OL2 48 E2
Harry St. Oldham OL9 152 C6
Harry St. R'dale OL11 30 B3
Harry Thorneycroft Wlk. M11 164 E8
Harry's Ct. 3 WN7 75 D5
Harrycroft Rd. SK6 113 B5
Harrytown. SK6 113 A2
Harrytown RC High Sch. SK6 113 A2
Hart Ave. Droylsden M43 84 B1
Hart Ave. Sale M33 108 F3
Hart Common CE Prim Sch. BL5 57 B7
Hart Ct. OL5 68 B2
Hart Dr. BL9 45 B4
Hart Hill Dr. M5 154 D3
Hart Mill Cl. OL5 68 B2
Hart Rd. M14 98 E1
Hart St. Alt'ham WA14 119 E5
Hart St. Droylsden M43 84 B1
Hart St. M'ster M60 159 A1
Hart St. Tyldesley M29 77 C8
Hart St. Westhoughton BL5 57 B7
Hart's Houses. BL6 22 D5
Harter St. M1 163 A8
Hartfield Cl. M13 163 C6
Hartfield Wlk. BL2 148 C8
Hartford Ave. Heywood OL10 29 B3
Hartford Ave. Reddish SK4 111 D6
Hartford Ave. Wilmslow SK9 136 F5
Hartford Cl. OL10 29 B3
Hartford Gdns. WA15 120 D5
Hartford Rd. Sale M33 107 D2
Hartford Rd. Urmston M41 95 E4
Hartford Sq. OL9 152 C6
Hartford St. M34 100 E5
Harthill St. M7 & M8 155 F5
Hartington Cl. 4 M41 95 E2
Hartington Ct. OL2 48 E4
Hartington Dr.Droylsden M11 83 B3
Hartington Dr. Hazel Grove SK7 133 E8
Hartington Dr. Standish WN6 36 F7
Hartington Rd. Alt'ham WA14 119 D8
Hartington Rd.Bolton BL1 144 C8
Hartington Rd.Bramhall SK7 132 E6
Hartington Rd.Gatley SK8 131 D8
Hartington Rd. High Lane SK12 & SK6 134 F7
Hartington Rd. M'ster M21 109 B8
Hartington Rd. Stockport SK2 124 D5
Hartington Rd. Worsley M28 79 A3
Hartington St. M14 97 F3
Hartis Ave. M7 155 E6
Hartland Ave. M41 96 A2
Hartland Cl. Poynton SK12 133 D5
Hartland Cl. Stockport SK2 124 C8
Hartland Cl. Tyldesley M29 77 B8
Hartland St. OL10 29 D2
Hartlebury. OL11 139 E6
Hartlepool Cl. M14 98 B3
Hartley Ave. M'ster M25 63 D3
Hartley Ave. Wigan WN1 151 E7
Hartley Gr. Irlam M44 94 B4
Hartley Gr. Wigan WN5 54 B7
Hartley La. OL11 30 E3
Hartley Rd. Alt'ham WA14 119 C5
Hartley Rd. M'ster M21 97 A1
Hartley St. Heywood OL10 29 D2
Hartley St. Horwich BL6 22 B3
Hartley St. Littleborough OL12 15 C6
Hartley St. Littleborough OL15 16 A5
Hartley St. M'ster M40 & M9 157 F8
Hartley St. Milnrow OL16 31 D7
Hartley St. R'dale OL12 14 B1
Hartley St. Stalybridge SK15 86 D3
Hartley St. Stockport SK3 170 D8
Hartley St. 13 Wigan WN5 54 B6
Hartley Terr. WN3 150 C7
Harton Ave. M18 99 C3
Harton Cl. OL2 149 A6
Harts Farm Mews. WN7 75 F7
Harts La. WN8 53 A8
Hartshead Ave. Ashton-u-L OL6 85 C6
Hartshead Ave. Stalybridge SK15 86 A3
Hartshead Cl. M11 100 A7
Hartshead Cres. M35 84 C6
Hartshead High Sch. OL6 85 E7
Hartshead Rd. OL6 85 C6
Hartshead St. OL4 67 F5
Hartshead View. SK14 167 F1
Hartsop Dr. M24 46 C2
Hartswell Cl. WA3 74 A2
Hartswood Cl. M34 101 A4
Hartswood Rd. M20 110 D6
Hartwell Cl. Bolton BL2 25 C3
Hartwell Cl. M'ster M11 164 F8
Harty. M30 79 E2
Harvard Cl. SK6 113 C5
Harvard St. 13 OL11 31 A4
Harvest Cl. Salford M6 80 E5
Harvest Cl. Wythenshawe M33 109 A3
Harvey Cl. M11 165 A8
Harvey Ct. WN7 75 B1
Harvey La. WA3 73 F1
Harvey St. Bolton BL1 143 D3
Harvey St. Bury BL8 27 C3
Harvey St. Ince-i-M WN3 151 E6
Harvey St. Oldham OL9 66 A2
Harvey St. R'dale OL12 15 B2
Harvey St. Stockport SK1 169 F1
Harvin Gr. M34 101 A2
Harwich Cl. Brinnington SK5 112 C6
Harwich Cl. 1 M'ster M19 99 B1
Harwin Cl. OL12 14 D3
Harwood Cres. BL8 26 E7
Harwood Ct. M'ster SK4 110 E2
Harwood Ct. Salford M6 81 B4
Harwood Dr. BL8 27 A1
Harwood Gdns. OL10 29 D1
Harwood Golf Course. BL2 26 A4
Harwood Gr. 27 BL2 25 B1
Harwood Meadow. BL2 25 F3
Harwood Meadows Cty Prim Sch.BL2 25 F3
Harwood Park Prim Sch. OL10 29 D1
Harwood Rd. Bury BL2 & BL8 26 C6
Harwood Rd. M'ster SK4 110 E2
Harwood Rd. M'ster M19 110 E6
Harwood St. Littleborough OL15 15 F5
Harwood St. M'ster SK4 169 E3
Harwood Vale. BL2 25 E3
Harwood Vale Ct. BL2 25 E3
Harwood Wlk. BL8 26 E7
Haseldine St. WN4 72 F6
Haseley Cl. Little Lever BL3 43 B5
Haseley Cl. Poynton SK12 133 E5
Haselhurst Wlk. M23 108 F2
Hasguard Cl. BL1 40 F8
Haskoll St. BL6 22 D1
Haslam Brow. BL9 44 E8
Haslam Hey Cl.Ainsworth BL2 26 C1
Haslam Hey Cl.Bury BL8 26 F2
Haslam Park Cty Prim Sch. BL3 144 B5
Haslam Rd. SK3 170 E6
Haslam St. Bolton BL3 145 D5
Haslam St. Bury BL9 141 A4
Haslam St. Middleton M24 65 C7
Haslam St. R'dale OL12 139 D8
Haslemere Ave. WA15 129 C6
Haslemere Dr. SK8 123 A1
Haslemere Ind Est. WN4 72 F8
Haslemere Rd. M'ster M20 110 D6
Haslemere Rd. Urmston M41 95 B1
Haslingden Cty High Sch. BB4 1 B8
Hassal St. BL9 44 E5
Hassall Ave. M20 109 F7
Hassall St. 4 SK15 86 B1
Hassall Way. 7 SK9 131 E5
Hassnes Cl. WN3 55 B2
Hassop Ave. M7 81 A7
Hassop Cl. M11 160 E1
Hassop Rd. SK5 100 A1
Hastings Ave. M'ster M21 109 A8
Hastings Ave. Prestwich M45 63 B7
Hastings Cl. Bramhall SK8 123 C2
Hastings Cl. Prestwich M45 63 B7
Hastings Cl. Stockport SK1 & SK2 124 B7
Hastings Dr. M41 94 E3
Hastings Rd. Bolton BL1 144 B8
Hastings Rd. Prestwich M25 63 C5
Hastings Rd. Worsley M28 79 A4
Hastings St. OL11 139 F5
Hasty La. Alt'ham WA15 129 E8
Hasty La. Alt'ham M90, WA15 129 F8
Hasty La. Wythenshawe M90 130 A8
Hatchett Rd. M22 121 E1
Hatchmere Cl. M23 & WA15 120 D6
Hatchmere Rd. SK8 122 F4
Hatfield Ave. M19 110 F6
Hatfield Cl. WN2 55 F4
Hatfield Rd. BL1 142 C1
Hatford Cl. M29 59 C1
Hathaway Cl. SK8 131 B7
Hathaway Ct. WN7 76 B6
Hathaway Dr. BL1 25 A5
Hathaway Gdns. SK6 112 F3
Hathaway Rd. BL9 45 A3
Hathaway Wlk. WN2 55 F4
Hatherleigh Wlk. BL2 42 F6
Hatherley Rd. M20 110 D6
Hatherlow. SK6 113 A1
Hatherlow Hts. SK6 113 A1
Hatherlow La. SK7 124 D2
Hatherop Cl. M30 79 B1
Hathersage Ave. M5 & M6 154 D3
Hathersage Cres. SK13 171 E2
Hathersage Dr. Glossop SK13 116 F8
Hathersage Rd. M13 98 D4
Hathersage St. OL9 152 C6
Hathersage Way. 6 M34 113 A8
Hathershaw La. OL8 66 F3
Hathershaw Sch. OL8 66 F2
Hatro Ct. M41 96 A1
Hatter St. M4 159 B2
Hattersley Ct. SK14 102 D1
Hattersley Ctr The. 2 SK14 102 E2
Hattersley High Sch. SK14 102 D2
Hattersley Rd E. SK14 102 E2
Hattersley Rd W. SK14 102 C2
Hattersley Sta. SK14 102 C1
Hattersley Wlk. SK14 102 C3
Hatton Ave. Atherton M46 58 D5
Hatton Ave. M'ster M7 158 D3
Hatton Gr. BL1 25 A5
Hatton St. Adlington PR7 20 F6
Hatton St. M'ster M12 99 A3
Hatton St. Stockport SK1 169 E2
Hatton Terr. 24 SK16 166 B1
Hattonfold. M33 108 C1
Hattons Ct. M32 96 C3
Hattons Rd. M17 96 B6
Haugh Farm. OL16 32 C4
Haugh Fold. OL16 32 C4
Haugh Hill Rd. OL4 49 E3
Haugh La. OL16 32 C4
Haugh Sq. OL16 32 C4
Haughton Cl. SK6 113 A6
Haughton Dr. M22 109 D1
Haughton Green Rd. M34 113 B8
Haughton Hall Rd. M34 101 A3
Haughton St. Denton M34 100 F5
Haughton St. Hyde SK14 167 E1
Havana Cl. M11 160 F1
Haveley Hey Inf Sch. M22 121 C4
Haveley Hey Jun Sch. M22 121 C4
Haveley Rd. M22 121 C5
Havelock Dr. M7 158 D4
Havelock St. OL8 153 F5
Haven Cl. Hazel Grove SK7 124 C1
Haven Cl. Radcliffe M26 43 D5
Haven Cl. Uppermill OL4 68 D6
Haven Dr. M43 83 E2
Haven La. OL4 49 E3
Haven St. M6 154 D3
Haven The. Alt'ham WA15 119 F3
Haven The. Little Lever BL3 43 B3
Havenbrook Gr. BL0 11 A3
Havenscroft Ave. M30 95 D8
Havenwood Rd. WN1 37 B4
Havercroft Cl. WN3 54 E3
Haverfield Rd. M9 64 E3
Haverford St. M12 164 F6
Haverhill Gr. BL2 25 B2
Havers Rd. M18 99 E5
Haversham Rd. M8 63 E2
Haverton Dr. M22 121 B2
Havisham Cl. BL6 40 B4
Haw Clough La. OL3 69 C6
Hawarden Ave. M16 97 C2
Hawarden Rd. WA14 119 D6
Hawarden St. BL1 24 E5
Hawdraw Gn. SK2 124 E6
Hawes Ave. Farnworth BL4 59 E8
Hawes Ave. M'ster M14 110 E7
Hawes Ave. Swinton M27 79 E6
Hawes Cl. Bury BL8 27 B5
Hawes Cl. Stockport SK2 124 A6
Hawes Cres. WN4 73 B5
Haweswater Ave. Ince-i-M WN2 56 B7
Haweswater Ave. Tyldesley M29 77 B7
Haweswater Cl. M34 100 A2
Haweswater Cres. BL9 45 B5
Haweswater Dr. M24 46 E2
Haweswater Mews. 5 M24 46 E2
Hawick Gr. OL10 28 E1
Hawk Cl. BL9 141 B4
Hawk Green Rd. SK6 126 A3
Hawk Rd. M44 94 A3
Hawk Yard La. OL3 69 D5
Hawke St. SK15 86 C1
Hawker Ave. BL3 147 D3
Hawkeshead Rd. M8 156 B6
Hawkhurst Rd. M13 98 F3
Hawkhurst St. Leigh WN7 76 B4
Hawkhurst St. Leigh WN7 76 C5
Hawkins St. SK5 169 E4
Hawkins Way. Littleborough OL15 6 C1
Hawkley Ave. WN3 54 F2
Hawkley Hall High Sch. WN3 55 B3
Hawkrigg Cl. WN6 36 F7
Hawkshaw Cl. WN2 38 A3
Hawkshaw Ct. 9 Salford M5 81 A1
Hawkshaw Ct. Salford M5 161 A8
Hawkshaw La. BL8 10 B5
Hawkshaw St. BL6 22 B3
Hawkshead Dr. Bolton BL3 146 A3
Hawkshead Dr. Middleton M24 46 E1
Hawkshead Dr. Royton OL2 48 D6
Hawkshead Rd. Glossop SK13 104 E3
Hawkshead Rd. Shaw OL2 149 A8
Hawksheath Cl. BL7 8 E1
Hawksley St. Horwich BL6 22 D2
Hawksley St. Oldham OL8 66 C3
Hawksmoor Dr. OL2 149 B8
Hawkstone Ave. Droylsden M43 83 E3
Hawkstone Ave. Whitefield M45 62 D7
Hawkstone Cl. BL2 25 E3
Hawkswick Dr. M23 109 A2
Hawkworth. M29 77 B5
Hawkyard Farm. OL3 69 D5
Hawley Dr. WA15 129 B8
Hawley Gn. OL12 14 D2
Hawley La. WA15 129 B8
Hawley St. M19 111 B8
Haworth Ave. BL0 11 A2
Haworth Cl. BL9 44 F6
Haworth Dr. Bacup OL13 3 C8
Haworth Dr. Stretford M32 96 A3
Haworth Rd. M18 99 D4
Haworth St. Bury BL8 26 F4
Haworth St. Edgworth BL7 9 D5
Haworth St. Hindley WN2 56 D6
Haworth St. Oldham OL1 48 E1
Haworth St. Radcliffe M26 44 B3
Hawsworth Cl. M15 163 B5
Hawthorn Ave. Alt'ham WA15 119 F8
Hawthorn Ave. Bury BL8 27 C4
Hawthorn Ave. Eccles M30 79 D3
Hawthorn Ave. Edenfield BL0 1 D2
Hawthorn Ave. Garswood WN4 72 D5
Hawthorn Ave. Hindley WN2 57 A4
Hawthorn Ave. Marple SK6 125 D6
Hawthorn Ave. Newton-l-W WA12 89 D3
Hawthorn Ave. Orrell WN5 53 F6
Hawthorn Ave. Radcliffe M26 44 B1
Hawthorn Ave. Ramsbottom BL0 11 A2
Hawthorn Ave. Standish WN1 37 B6
Hawthorn Ave. Urmston M41 95 F1
Hawthorn Ave. Walkden M28 60 E1
Hawthorn Ave. Wigan WN5 54 D6
Hawthorn Ave. Wilmslow SK9 137 A7
Hawthorn Bank. Bolton BL2 25 E4
Hawthorn Bank. Hadfield SK14 171 F4
Hawthorn Cl. Alt'ham WA15 119 F7
Hawthorn Cl. Billinge WN5 71 D5
Hawthorn Cl. Tyldesley M29 59 D1
Hawthorn Cres. Bury BL8 26 F7
Hawthorn Cres. Shaw OL2 149 B6
Hawthorn Ct. SK6 112 D3
Hawthorn Dr. Eccles M6 80 B4
Hawthorn Dr. Irlam M44 105 D5
Hawthorn Dr. M'ster M19 110 F7
Hawthorn Dr.Pendlebury M27 80 C7
Hawthorn Dr. Stalybridge SK15 101 F8
Hawthorn Gr. Bramhall SK7 132 C6
Hawthorn Gr. Hollingworth SK14 103 D6
Hawthorn Gr. Hyde SK14 167 D1
Hawthorn Gr. M'ster SK4 168 B3
Hawthorn Gr. Wilmslow SK9 137 B7
Hawthorn La. Sale M33 107 D6
Hawthorn La. Stretford M21 108 F8
Hawthorn La. Wilmslow SK9 137 A7
Hawthorn Lodge. 1 SK3 123 F4
Hawthorn Pk. SK9 137 A7
Hawthorn Rd. Alt'ham WA15 119 E3
Hawthorn Rd. Droylsden M43 84 C2
Hawthorn Rd. Failsworth M40 65 F1
Hawthorn Rd. Gatley SK8 122 A5
Hawthorn Rd. Kearsley BL4 61 B5
Hawthorn Rd. M'ster SK4 110 E1
Hawthorn Rd. Oldham OL8 66 B1
Hawthorn Rd. R'dale OL11 29 E6
Hawthorn Rd. Reddish M34 100 B4
Hawthorn Rd. Stretford M32 108 E8
Hawthorn Rd. Westhoughton BL5 57 F7
Hawthorn Rd S. M43 84 C2
Hawthorn St. Denton M34 100 E6
Hawthorn St. M'ster M18 99 E5
Hawthorn St. Wilmslow SK9 137 A6

Heyrose Wlk. 14 M15 162 D6
Heys Ave. Romiley SK6 113 E3
Heys Ave. Swinton M27 61 D2
Heys Ave. Wythenshawe M23 109 A1
Heys Cl N. M27 61 C2
Heys La. Heywood OL10 29 A1
Heys La. Romiley SK6 113 E3
Heys Prim Sch The. OL6 85 D3
Heys Rd. Ashton-u-L OL6 85 D3
Heys Rd. Prestwich M25 63 B5
Heys St. Bury BL8 140 D2
Heys St. Hindley WN2 56 C6
Heys The. Prestwich M25 63 B5
Heys The. Reddish SK5 100 A1
Heys View. M25 63 B4
Heysbank Rd. SK12 135 D5
Heyscroft Rd. M'ster M20 110 C6
Heyscroft Rd. M'ster SK4 168 A2
Heysham Ave. M20 109 F7
Heysham Rd. WN5 54 B7
Heyshaw Wlk. M23 108 F1
Heyside. OL2 49 A3
Heyside Ave. OL2 49 A3
Heyside Cl. SK15 86 E6
Heywood Ave. Golborne WA3 74 B1
Heywood Ave. Oldham OL4 68 A8
Heywood Ave. Swinton M27 62 B2
Heywood Cl. SK9 137 B2
Heywood Comm High Sch. OL10 28 E1
Heywood Ct. M25 64 A7
Heywood Distribution Pk. OL10 46 A8
Heywood Fold Rd. OL4 67 F7
Heywood Gdns. Golborne WA3 74 B1
Heywood Gdns. Prestwich M25 63 B4
Heywood Gr. M33 108 B6
Heywood Hall Rd. OL10 29 D3
Heywood House. Atherton M46 58 C3
Heywood House. Oldham OL8 153 F5
Heywood House. Salford M6 80 C3
Heywood Ind Est. OL10 45 F7
Heywood Ind Pk. OL10 45 F8
Heywood La. OL4 68 A7
Heywood Old Rd. M24 & M25 & OL10 46 B3
Heywood Rd. Alderley Edge SK9 137 B2
Heywood Rd. Prestwich M25 63 C7
Heywood Rd. R'dale OL11 30 C1
Heywood Rd. Sale M33 108 B3
Heywood St. Bolton BL1 145 F8
Heywood St. Bury BL9 141 A2
Heywood St. Failsworth M35 83 D7
Heywood St. Little Lever BL3 43 B3
Heywood St. M'ster M7 & M8 156 A6
Heywood St. Oldham OL4 67 E8
Heywood St. Swinton M27 79 E8
Heywood Way. M6 154 F3
Heywood's Hollow. BL1 143 F3
Heyworth Ave. SK6 113 D3
Heyworth St. 4 M5 & M6 154 E1
Hibbert Ave. Denton M34 100 E5
Hibbert Ave. Hyde SK14 167 E1
Hibbert Cres. M35 84 A6
Hibbert La. SK6 125 F5
Hibbert St. Bolton BL1 143 F2
Hibbert St. M'ster M14 98 C3
Hibbert St. Oldham OL4 67 E7
Hibbert St. Reddish SK4 & SK5 111 E5
Hibernia St. BL3 144 C5
Hibernia Way. M32 96 A5
Hibson Ave. OL12 13 E2
Hibson Cl. OL12 15 C6
Hic Bibi La. PR7 19 E6
Hicken Pl. SK14 101 F5
Hickenfield Rd. SK14 101 F5
Hickton Dr. WA14 119 B6
Hieland Rd. WN1 37 E2
Higginshaw La. OL1 & OL2 49 A2
Higginshaw Rd. OL1 67 A8
Higginson Rd. SK5 111 E8
Higginson St. WN7 76 A5
Higgs Cl. OL4 67 D7
High Ash Gr. M34 100 D7
High Ave. BL2 42 E7
High Bank. Alt'ham WA14 119 D5
High Bank. Atherton BL5 59 A6
High Bank. Bolton BL7 24 F7
High Bank. M'ster M18 99 E5
High Bank Ave. SK15 102 D7
High Bank Cl. M44 105 D6
High Bank Cres. M25 63 C3
High Bank Gr. M25 63 C3
High Bank La. BL6 40 B8
High Bank Rd. Droylsden M43 99 F8
High Bank Rd. Hyde SK14 167 F3
High Bank Rd. Pendlebury M27 80 B7
High Bank Side. SK1 169 F1
High Bank St. BL2 148 C7
High Barn Cl. OL11 139 E5
High Barn Jun Sch. OL2 48 E4
High Barn La. OL12 4 C3
High Barn Rd. Middleton M24 65 A7
High Barn Rd. Royton OL2 48 F4
High Barn St. OL2 48 E4
High Beeches. BL3 43 B5
High Beeches Cres. WN4 73 A6
High Bent Ave. SK8 132 A6
High Birch Spec Sch. OL11 30 B4
High Brindle. M6 154 F4
High Crest Ave. M22 121 F5
High Croft Cl. SK15 102 A8
High Elm Dr. WA15 129 C8
High Elm Rd. WA15 129 D7
High Elms. SK8 132 B5
High Field. WA14 118 B2
High Grove Rd. Cheadle SK8 122 C5
High Grove Rd. Uppermill OL4 68 E5
High Hill Rd. SK12 127 D1
High Hurst Cl. M24 64 C7
High Knowls. OL4 68 A4
High La. Charlesworth SK13 & SK14 115 E7
High La. M'ster M21 109 B8
High La. Romiley SK6 113 B4
High Lane Prim Sch. SK6 134 F8
High Lawn Cty Prim Sch. BL1 24 E6
High Lee. SK8 122 C5
High Lee La. OL4 50 B4
High Legh Rd. M11 99 D8
High Level Rd. OL11 31 A6
High Meadow. SK8 131 E8
High Meadows. Bolton BL7 25 B8
High Meadows. Romiley SK6 113 C3
High Moor Cres. OL4 49 E1
High Moor La. WN6 18 B4
High Moor View. OL4 49 E1
High Mount. BL2 25 E3
High Peak. OL15 16 F5
High Peak Rd. Ashton-u-L OL6 86 A6
High Peak Rd. Whitworth OL12 14 C6
High Peak St. M40 83 B6
High Pk. WN6 36 C6
High Rid La. Horwich BL6 23 B1
High St. Alt'ham WA14 119 D4
High St. Atherton M46 58 D3
High St. Bolton BL3 147 E4
High St. Bury BL8 26 F4
High St. Cheadle SK8 122 D6
High St. Delph OL3 50 F5
High St. Droylsden M43 84 B1
High St. Edgworth BL7 9 C4
High St. Golborne WA3 90 A8
High St. Hazel Grove SK7 124 F2
High St. Heywood OL10 29 B2
High St. Horwich BL6 22 B4
High St. Hyde SK14 167 F3
High St. Ince-i-M WN3 151 E6
High St. Leigh WN7 76 A5
High St. Little Lever BL3 43 B3
High St. Littleborough OL15 15 F5
High St. M'ster M4 & M60 159 A1
High St. M'ster M4 159 A2
High St. Middleton M24 47 A1
High St. Middleton M24 47 A2
High St. Mossley OL5 68 D2
High St. Newton-l-W WA12 89 D4
High St. Oldham OL4 67 E6
High St. Oldham OL1 153 F7
High St. R'dale OL12 139 F8
High St. Royton OL2 48 D4
High St. Shaw OL2 149 B6
High St. Stalybridge SK15 & SK16 85 F1
High St. Stalybridge SK15 86 A1
High St. Standish WN6 19 E1
High St. Stockport SK1 169 F1
High St. Tyldesley M29 58 F1
High St. Tyldesley M29 77 B5
High St. Uppermill OL3 69 B8
High St. Walkden M28 60 D3
High St. Wigan WN1 37 D2
High St. Wigan WN2 38 B3
High St E. SK13 104 D1
High St W. SK13 104 B1
High Stile La. OL3 51 D2
High Stile St. BL4 60 E7
High Street Sta. M1 159 A1
High View St. Bolton BL1 24 E6
High View St. 1 Bolton BL3 146 C4
High Wood Fold. SK6 126 C8
Higham Cl. OL2 149 A5
Higham La. SK14 114 A7
Higham St. SK8 123 A1
Higham View. M6 81 A3
Highbank Cres. OL4 68 E5
Highbank Dr. M20 122 B8
Highbank Private Hospl. BL8 26 F4
Highbank Rd. Glossop SK13 116 F7
Highbank Rd. Newhey OL16 32 C4
Highbank Rd. Whitefield BL9 44 F3
Highbridge Cl. BL2 43 A6
Highbrook Gr. 10 BL1 143 E1
Highbury. SK4 110 F2
Highbury Ave. Irlam M44 94 A1
Highbury Ave. Urmston M41 94 E2
Highbury Rd. M'ster M16 97 C3
Highbury Rd. Reddish SK4 111 C6
Highbury Way. OL2 48 D6
Highclere Ave. M7 & M8 155 F6
Highclere Rd. M8 63 F2
Highcliffe Ct. WN6 36 F7
Highcliffe Rd. M9 64 A3
Highclove La. M28 77 F5
Highcroft. SK14 113 F6
Highcroft Ave. M20 109 E4
Highcroft Rd. SK6 113 C3
Highcroft Way. OL12 14 F4
Highdales Rd. M23 121 B5
Highdown Wlk. 26 M9 157 E8
Higher Ainsworth Rd. BL8 & M26 43 E7
Higher Ardwick. M12 163 C7
Higher Arthurs. OL3 69 B6
Higher Bank Rd. OL15 16 A3
Higher Barlow Row. SK1 170 F8
Higher Barn. BL6 22 F3
Higher Barn Rd. SK14 171 F4
Higher Bents La. SK6 113 A3
Higher Blue Bell Cotts. BL5 39 C4
Higher Bridge St. BL1 145 F8
Higher Bury St. SK4 169 D2
Higher Calderbrook Rd. OL15 6 C2
Higher Cambridge St. M15 163 A6
Higher Carr La. OL3 69 B7
Higher Chatham St. M15 163 A6
Higher Cleggswood Ave. OL15 16 A3
Higher Count Hill. OL4 49 E2
Higher Croft. Eccles M30 95 C8
Higher Croft. Whitefield M45 62 C6
Higher Cross La. OL3 69 C8
Higher Crossbank. OL4 67 F8
Higher Damshead. BL5 57 F8
Higher Darcy St. BL2 148 C5
Higher Dean St. M26 43 E3
Higher Downs. WA14 119 C3
Higher Drake Meadow. BL5 57 E5
Higher Dunscar. BL7 8 E1
Higher Fold La. BL0 11 E7
Higher Folds Prim Sch. WN7 76 D7
Higher Fullwood. OL1 49 D4
Higher Gamesley. SK14 115 D8
Higher Gn. Ashton-u-L OL6 166 C4
Higher Gn. Salford M6 154 F4
Higher Green La. M29 77 C6
Higher Henry St. SK14 167 E1
Higher Hillgate. SK1 & SK2 170 F8
Higher House Cl. OL9 66 A4
Higher La. Aspull WN2 38 A4
Higher La. Disley SK12 135 E1
Higher La. Lymm WA13 117 B1
Higher La. Orrell WN8 53 C7
Higher La. Whitefield M45 62 E8
Higher Lane Cty Jun & Inf Sch. M45 62 F7
Higher Lime Rd. OL8 84 C8
Higher Lodge. OL12 13 D2
Higher Lomax La. OL10 29 A3
Higher Lydgate Pk. OL4 68 C6
Higher Market St. BL4 60 E8
Higher Moulding. BL9 28 E5
Higher Newtons. OL5 68 D2
Higher Noon Sun. SK12 127 F2
Higher Ormond St. M15 163 A6
Higher Oswald St. 4 M4 159 A2
Higher Park. OL2 32 C2
Higher Pit La. BL8 43 E8
Higher Rd. M41 95 E2
Higher Ridings. BL7 24 F7
Higher Rise. OL2 32 A1
Higher Row. BL9 141 B3
Higher Shady La. BL7 25 C7
Higher Shore Rd. OL12, OL15 15 E7
Higher Southfield. BL5 57 E7
Higher Summerseat. BL0 11 B2
Higher Swan La. BL3 147 D3
Higher Tame St. SK15 86 B2
Higher Turf La. OL4 50 B1
Higher Turf Pk. OL2 48 E3
Higher Wharf St. OL6 & OL7 166 B2
Higher Wheat La. OL16 31 C8
Higher Wood St. M24 46 F1
Higher York St. M13 163 B6
Highfield. Sale M33 108 C3
Highfield. Wigan WN3 54 D4
Highfield Ave. Atherton M46 58 E5
Highfield Ave. Bolton BL2 26 A3
Highfield Ave. Boothstown M28 & M29 77 F7
Highfield Ave. Bredbury SK6 112 F2
Highfield Ave. Golborne WA3 89 F8
Highfield Ave. Heywood OL10 29 A2
Highfield Ave. Leigh WN7 76 C3
Highfield Ave. Radcliffe M26 44 C1
Highfield Ave. Shevington WN6 36 A6
Highfield Ave. Wigan WN1 37 E1
Highfield CE Prim Sch. WN3 54 D4
Highfield Cl. Adlington PR6 21 A7
Highfield Cl. Dukinfield SK14 101 F6
Highfield Cl. Stockport SK3 123 F4
Highfield Cl. Stretford M32 108 C8
Highfield Cres. SK9 131 C1
Highfield Ct. BL4 60 B7
Highfield Dr. Eccles M30 79 D3
Highfield Dr. Farnworth BL4 60 A7
Highfield Dr. Middleton M24 64 F7
Highfield Dr. Mossley OL5 86 C8
Highfield Dr. Oldham OL2 48 E2
Highfield Dr. Pendlebury M27 80 C7
Highfield Dr. Standish WN6 36 F7
Highfield Dr. 4 Urmston M41 95 C3
Highfield Est. SK9 131 C1
Highfield Gdns. Hollingworth SK14 103 D5
Highfield Gdns. Hyde SK14 167 F3
Highfield Gr. WN2 38 C5
Highfield Grange Ave. WN3 54 E2
Highfield House. SK3 170 F5
Highfield La. Golborne WA3 90 C5
Highfield La. Whitefield M45 44 F3
Highfield Park Rd. SK6 112 F3
Highfield Parkway. SK7 132 D4
Highfield Pk. SK4 110 F2
Highfield Pl. Prestwich M25 63 A5
Highfield Pl. Reddish M18 99 F4
Highfield Prim Sch. M41 95 F2
Highfield Private Hospl. OL11 139 E5
Highfield Range. M18 99 F4
Highfield Rd. Adlington PR6 21 A7
Highfield Rd. Alt'ham WA15 120 A3
Highfield Rd. Alt'ham WA15 120 B5
Highfield Rd. Blackrod BL6 21 E1
Highfield Rd. Bolton BL1 142 B2
Highfield Rd. Cheadle SK8 122 F1
Highfield Rd. Eccles M30 79 D4
Highfield Rd. Edenfield BL0 1 D3
Highfield Rd. Farnworth BL4 60 A8
Highfield Rd. Glossop SK13 116 D8
Highfield Rd. Hazel Grove SK7 125 A2
Highfield Rd. Hindley WN2 56 D7
Highfield Rd. Marple SK6 125 F6
Highfield Rd. Marple SK6 126 B6
Highfield Rd. Milnrow OL16 32 A6
Highfield Rd. Poynton SK12 133 A4
Highfield Rd. Prestwich M25 63 A5
Highfield Rd. R'dale OL11 31 A6
Highfield Rd. Reddish M19 99 C1
Highfield Rd. Salford M5 & M6 154 F2
Highfield Rd. Stockport SK7 123 F3
Highfield Rd. Stretford M32 108 C8
Highfield Rd. Walkden M38 59 F5
Highfield Rd N. PR6 21 A8
Highfield St. Denton M34 100 E5
Highfield St. Denton M34 100 F6
Highfield St. Dukinfield SK16 166 B1
Highfield St. Kearsley BL4 61 A6
Highfield St. M'ster M7, M8 155 F7
Highfield St. Middleton M24 65 B8
Highfield St. Oldham OL9 153 D7
Highfield St. 2 Stockport SK3 123 C8
Highfield St W. SK16 166 B1
Highfield Terr. Ashton-u-L OL7 85 A7
Highfield Terr. M'ster M9 157 D8
Highfield Terr. Oldham OL1 & OL4 49 D2
Highfields Cty Prim Sch. BL4 60 A8
Highgate. BL3 40 C2
Highgate Ave. M41 95 A4
Highgate Cres. Appley Bridge WN6 35 E7
Highgate Cres. M'ster M18 99 D3
Highgate Dr. Royton OL2 48 C7
Highgate Dr. Walkden M38 59 E5
Highgate House. 6 OL8 66 D2
Highgate La. Walkden M38 59 E5
Highgate La. Whitworth OL12 14 C5
Highgate Rd. Alt'ham WA14 119 B4
Highgate Rd. Orrell WN8 53 B7
Highgrove Cl. BL1 143 F3
Highgrove La. M28 78 A5
Highgrove Mews. SK9 137 A6
Highgrove The. BL1 23 D1
Highland Ave. SK6 113 A2
Highland Rd. Bolton BL7 25 C8
Highland Rd. Horwich BL6 22 E1
Highland View. 1 OL5 68 C2
Highland Wlk. M35 83 D6
Highlands. Littleborough OL15 16 A3
Highlands. Royton OL2 48 C3
Highlands Dr. SK2 124 F6
Highlands Rd. Hazel Grove SK2 124 F6
Highlands Rd. R'dale OL10 29 E5
Highlands Rd. Royton OL2 48 C3
Highlands Rd. Shaw OL2 149 A8
Highlands The. 3 OL5 68 C1
Highmead St. M18 99 D5
Highmead Wlk. M16 162 D5
Highmeadow. M26 43 F1
Highmore Dr. M9 64 E3
Highnam Wlk. M22 121 A1
Highover House. M20 109 F4
Highshore Dr. M7 & M8 155 F7
Highstone Dr. M8 156 C6
Highthorne Gn. OL2 48 C8
Highview. SK13 116 A7
Highview Wlk. M9 157 E6
Highwood. OL11 13 E1
Highwood Cl. 3 Bolton BL2 25 F1
Highwood Cl. Glossop SK13 116 B8
Highwoods Cl. WN4 73 B5
Highworth Cl. BL3 145 E5
Highworth Dr. M40 65 D2
Higifield Ave. M33 108 C3
Higson Ave. Bredbury SK6 112 F2
Higson Ave. Eccles M30 95 C8
Higson Ave. M'ster M21 109 B7
Hilary Ave. Atherton M46 58 C5
Hilary Ave. Gatley SK8 131 D8
Hilary Ave. Golborne WA3 74 D1
Hilary Ave. Oldham OL8 84 F8
Hilary Cl. SK4 169 D2
Hilary Gr. BL4 60 D7
Hilary Rd. M22 121 C1
Hilary St. OL11 30 D1
Hilbre Ave. OL1 48 D2
Hilbre Rd. M19 110 F8
Hilbury Ave. M9 64 D1
Hilda Ave. Bury BL8 26 F6
Hilda Ave. Cheadle SK8 122 E5
Hilda Gr. SK5 169 F4
Hilda Rd. SK14 113 D7
Hilda St. 6 Bolton BL3 42 A4
Hilda St. Heywood OL10 29 D3
Hilda St. Leigh WN7 75 D6
Hilda St. Oldham OL9 153 D7
Hilda St. Reddish SK5 169 F4
Hilden Ct. M16 97 D4
Hilden St. Bolton BL2 148 A6
Hilden St. 4 Leigh WN7 75 F5
Hilditch Cl. M23 121 B6
Hildyard St. WN5 54 F6
Hiley Rd. Eccles M30 79 A1
Hilgay Cl. WN3 54 D3
Hill Cl. WN6 35 E8
Hill Cot Rd. BL1 24 F5
Hill Court Mews. SK6 113 B2
Hill Cres. Leigh WN7 75 C8
Hill Cres. M'ster M9 64 A3
Hill Crest. M46 58 F5
Hill Crest Ave. Leigh WN7 75 C8
Hill Crest Ave. M'ster SK4 168 A2
Hill Dr. SK9 131 E3
Hill End Rd. OL3 50 F4
Hill Farm Cl. OL8 67 B3
Hill House Fold La. WN6 18 C5
Hill House La. WN6 18 C5
Hill La. Blackrod BL6 21 C2
Hill La. Bolton BL2 148 A8
Hill La. M'ster M9 64 D4
Hill Mount. SK15 102 A8
Hill Rise. Alt'ham WA14 119 A5
Hill Rise. Ramsbottom BL0 11 A4
Hill Rise. Romiley SK6 113 B2
Hill Side. BL1 40 F7
Hill St. Alt'ham WA14 119 C8
Hill St. Ashton-u-L OL6 & OL7 166 B2
Hill St. Bury BL8 26 F4
Hill St. Dukinfield SK16 166 B1
Hill St. Heywood OL10 29 C2
Hill St. Hindley WN2 56 D6
Hill St. Leigh WN7 75 E5
Hill St. M'ster M20 110 B7
Hill St. M'ster M7 155 D6
Hill St. Middleton M24 47 A3
Hill St. Oldham OL4 67 B7
Hill St. R'dale OL16 31 A7
Hill St. Radcliffe M26 43 F4
Hill St. Ramsbottom BL9 11 C3
Hill St. Romiley SK6 113 B2
Hill St. Shaw OL2 149 C6
Hill St. Wigan WN6 37 B1
Hill St. Wigan WN2 38 B2
Hill Top. Alt'ham WA15 120 A1
Hill Top. Atherton M46 58 F5
Hill Top. Bolton BL1 143 D3
Hill Top. Little Lever BL3 43 A4
Hill Top. Romiley SK6 113 B3
Hill Top Ave. Cheadle SK8 132 B8
Hill Top Ave. Prestwich M25 63 B4
Hill Top Ave. Wilmslow SK9 137 B8
Hill Top Ct. SK8 123 B1
Hill Top Cty Prim Sch. OL11 31 A1
Hill Top Dr. Alt'ham WA15 120 A1
Hill Top Dr. R'dale OL11 30 F2
Hill Top Fold. 1 WN2 56 E6
Hill Top La. OL3 & OL4 50 C4
Hill Top Rd. M28 60 D4
Hill View. Delph OL3 50 F4
Hill View. Stalybridge SK15 102 E6
Hill View Dr. PR7 19 D8
Hill's Ct. 3 BL8 27 B4
Hillam Cl. M41 95 F1
Hillary Ave. Ashton-u-L OL6 & OL7 85 B5
Hillary Ave. Wigan WN5 54 D5
Hillary Rd. SK14 102 A5
Hillbank. WN6 37 A7
Hillbank Cl. BL1 142 C3
Hillbank St. OL11 47 D6
Hillbeck Cres. WN4 72 D4
Hillbrae Ave. WA11 71 A1
Hillbre Way. 1 SK9 131 D4
Hillbrook Ave. M40 65 B2
Hillbrook Rd. Bramhall SK7 132 D6
Hillbrook Rd. Stockport SK1 & SK2 124 C8
Hillbrow Wlk. 9 M8 155 F7
Hillbury Rd. SK7 123 F1
Hillcote Wlk. M18 165 B6
Hillcourt Rd. High Lane SK6 134 F7
Hillcourt Rd. Romiley SK6 113 C4
Hillcourt St. M1 163 A7
Hillcrest. Eccles M6 80 A3
Hillcrest. Hyde SK14 113 F7
Hillcrest. Middleton M24 65 A7
Hillcrest. Platt Bridge WN2 56 B2
Hillcrest Ave. OL10 29 A3
Hillcrest Cres. OL10 29 A3
Hillcrest Dr. Denton M34 101 B1
Hillcrest Dr. Reddish M19 111 B8
Hillcrest Gram Sch. SK3 170 F6
Hillcrest Rd. Prestwich M25 62 F2
Hillcrest Rd. R'dale OL11 30 D1
Hillcrest Rd. Stockport SK7 123 F1
Hillcrest Rd. Stockport SK2 124 C7
Hillcrest Rd. Tyldesley M29 77 D8
Hillcroft. Oldham OL8 67 A1
Hillcroft. Stockport SK2 124 E6
Hillcroft Cl. M8 156 A8
Hillcroft House. 6 M6 154 F3
Hillcroft Rd. WA14 119 A5
Hilldale Ave. M9 64 E4
Hilldean. WN8 53 C8
Hillel House. M15 163 A5
Hillend. SK14 103 A1
Hillend La. SK14 103 A1
Hillend Pl. M23 109 A2
Hillend Rd. M23 & M33 109 A2
Hillfield. M5 154 D2
Hillfield Cl. M13 164 D5
Hillfield Dr. Bolton BL2 25 B1
Hillfield Dr. Boothstown M28 78 A7
Hillfield Wlk. 10 BL2 25 B1
Hillfoot Wlk. 25 M15 162 D6
Hillgate Ave. M5 161 B7
Hillgate St. OL6 166 C4
Hillhead Wlk. M8 156 A5
Hillhouse Ct. OL12 30 B3
Hillier St. M9 157 E8
Hillier St N. M9 157 E8
Hillingdon Cl. M35 84 B8
Hillingdon Dr. M9 65 B2
Hillingdon Rd. Stretford M32 96 E2
Hillingdon Rd. Whitefield M45 62 D7
Hillington Rd. Sale M33 107 F5
Hillington Rd. Stockport SK3 123 C8
Hillkirk St. M11 160 E1
Hillman Cl. M40 157 D5
Hillock The. Bolton BL2 25 D5
Hillock The. Tyldesley M29 77 B5
Hillreed. WN6 36 F1
Hills La. BL9 45 C2
Hillsborough Dr. BL9 45 B2
Hillsdale Gr. BL2 25 E3
Hillside. WA13 117 E1
Hillside Ave. Ashton-i-M WN4 72 F8
Hillside Ave. Atherton M46 58 E4
Hillside Ave. Blackrod BL6 21 E1
Hillside Ave. Bolton BL7 25 C8
Hillside Ave. Diggle OL3 51 C3
Hillside Ave. Farnworth BL4 60 C7
Hillside Ave. Horwich BL6 22 C4
Hillside Ave. M'ster M7 81 A8
Hillside Ave. Mossley SK15 86 F6
Hillside Ave. Oldham OL4 67 C7
Hillside Ave. Oldham OL4 68 B5
Hillside Ave. Romiley SK14 113 F6
Hillside Ave. Royton OL2 48 E5
Hillside Ave. Shaw OL2 49 D8
Hillside Ave. Walkden M28 60 C4
Hillside Ave. Whitefield M45 44 F3
Hillside Cl. Billinge WN5 71 D5
Hillside Cl. Bolton BL2 25 E5
Hillside Cl. Bolton BL3 40 D2
Hillside Cl. Bramhall SK7 133 A7
Hillside Cl. Disley SK12 135 E6
Hillside Cl. Hadfield SK14 171 E3
Hillside Cl. M'ster M40 65 A1
Hillside Cl. Wigan WN3 54 D3
Hillside Cres. Ashton-u-L OL6 85 F5
Hillside Cres. Bury BL9 27 F6
Hillside Cres. Horwich BL6 22 C4
Hillside Ct. BL1 40 F7
Hillside Dr. Middleton M24 47 C2
Hillside Dr. Salford M27 80 D6
Hillside Gr. SK6 114 B1
Hillside Rd. Alt'ham WA15 120 A3
Hillside Rd. Ramsbottom BL0 138 A5
Hillside Rd. Romiley SK14 & SK6 113 D5
Hillside Rd. Stockport SK2 124 D7
Hillside St. 6 BL3 145 D5
Hillside View. Denton M34 113 A7
Hillside View. Milnrow OL16 32 A6
Hillside Way. OL12 4 C1
Hillside Wlk. OL12 14 D4
Hillspring Rd. OL4 68 A6
Hillstone Ave. OL12 14 D4
Hillstone Cl. BL8 10 F2
Hilltop. OL12 14 C5
Hilltop Ave. M'ster M9 64 D3
Hilltop Ave. Whitefield M45 63 B8
Hilltop Ct. M'ster M8 63 F2
Hilltop Ct. M'ster M14 98 D1
Hilltop Dr. Bury BL8 26 E6
Hilltop Dr. Haslingden BB4 1 C7
Hilltop Dr. Marple SK6 125 F7
Hilltop Gr. M45 63 B8
Hilltop Rd. SK13 104 B2
Hillview Ct. BL1 143 E4
Hillview Rd. Bolton BL1 143 E4
Hillview Rd. Reddish M34 & SK5 100 A1
Hillwood Ave. M8 63 F3
Hillwood Dr. Glossop SK13 116 F8
Hilly Croft. BL7 24 F8
Hillyard St. 7 BL8 27 C3
Hilmarton Cl. BL2 25 E5
Hilrose Ave. M41 95 F2
Hilson Ct. M43 84 A1
Hilton Arc. OL1 153 F7
Hilton Ave. Horwich BL6 22 A3
Hilton Ave. Urmston M41 95 D2
Hilton Bank. M28 60 B3
Hilton Cl. WN7 76 A5
Hilton Cres. Ashton-u-L OL6 85 C5
Hilton Cres. Boothstown M28 78 B6
Hilton Ct. SK3 170 E8
Hilton Dr. Irlam M44 105 C5
Hilton Dr. M'ster M25 63 B2
Hilton Fold La. M24 47 B1
Hilton Gr. Poynton SK12 133 D4
Hilton Gr. Walkden M28 60 B3
Hilton La. Prestwich M25 63 A2
Hilton La. Walkden M28 60 B2
Hilton Lodge. M25 63 B2
Hilton Pl. WN2 38 C6
Hilton Rd. Bury BL9 140 F2
Hilton Rd. Disley SK12 135 B7
Hilton Rd. High Lane SK12 134 C5
Hilton Rd. Stockport SK7 123 F1
Hilton Sq. M27 62 A1
Hilton St. Ashton-i-M WN4 73 C3
Hilton St. Bolton BL2 148 C7
Hilton St. Bury BL9 140 F4
Hilton St. Dukinfield SK14 101 F5
Hilton St. M'ster M7 155 D5
Hilton St. M'ster M1 159 B1
Hilton St. M'ster M4 & M60 159 B2
Hilton St. Stockport SK3 170 D8
Hilton St. Walkden M38 60 A4
Hilton St. Wigan WN1 37 D1
Hilton St N. M7 155 D6
Hilton Wlk. M24 64 C8
Hiltons Farm Cl. M34 100 E6
Himley Rd. M11 83 C3
Hincaster Wlk. M18 165 C5
Hinchcliffe Wlk. 13 M16 97 E4
Hinchcombe Cl. M38 60 A6
Hinckley St. M11 164 F8
Hind Hill St. OL10 29 D1
Hind Rd. WN5 54 D8
Hind St. BL2 148 C7
Hind's Head Ave. WN6 18 F6
Hindburn Cl. M45 45 B1
Hindburn Dr. M28 78 A8
Hindburn Wlk. M45 45 B1
Hinde St. M40 83 A8
Hindell Terr. OL3 50 F4
Hindhead Wlk. M40 83 D4
Hindle Dr. OL2 48 C3
Hindle St. Bacup OL13 3 D8
Hindle St. Radcliffe M26 44 A3
Hindles Cl. M46 58 A1
Hindley (All Saints) CE Prim Sch. WN2 56 E5
Hindley Ave. M22 121 B2
Hindley Castle Hill St Philips CE Sch. WN2 56 F6
Hindley Cl. OL7 84 F1
Hindley Cty Prim Sch. WN2 56 E5
Hindley Green Cty Prim Sch. WN2 57 B3
Hindley Hall Golf Course. Hindley WN2 56 D8
Hindley Mill La. WN2 56 F7
Hindley Rd. BL5 & WN2 57 D5
Hindley St. Ashton-u-L OL7 84 F1
Hindley St. Stockport SK1 170 F8
Hindley Sta. WN2 56 D7
Hindley Wlk. 1 WN1 150 C8
Hinds La. Bury BL8 27 C1
Hinds La. Bury BL8 & BL9 44 C7
Hindsford CE Prim Sch. M46 58 E1
Hindsford Cl. M23 & M33 108 E1
Hindsford St. M46 58 F1
Hinkler Ave. BL3 147 E3
Hinstock Cres. M18 99 D5
Hinton. 19 OL12 139 E8
Hinton Cl. OL11 29 E6
Hinton Gr. Hyde SK14 114 A8
Hinton St. M'ster M4 159 B3
Hinton St. Oldham OL8 153 F5
Hipley Cl. SK6 113 A5
Hirons La. OL4 68 A5
Hirst Ave. M28 60 C5
Hitchen Cl. SK16 101 F7
Hitchen Dr. SK16 101 F7
Hitchin Wlk. M13 164 D5
Hive St. OL8 66 B2
HM Prison Strangeways. M3 158 F4
Hoad Wlk. 3 M34 113 A7
Hoade St. WN2 56 E7
Hob Hey La. WA3 91 D3

Houghton Rd. M8 64 A1
Houghton St. Bolton BL3 145 E5
Houghton St. Bury BL9 140 E1
Houghton St. Leigh WN7 75 F6
Houghton St. Newton-l-W WA12 89 B3
Houghton St. Oldham OL2 48 E2
Houghton St. Salford M27 80 D6
Houghwood Grange. WN4 72 F3
Houldsworth Ave. WA14 119 E7
Houldsworth Golf Course. SK5 111 D8
Houldsworth Mill Ind Est. SK5 111 E7
Houldsworth Sq. 2 SK5 111 E7
Houldsworth St. M'ster M1 & M60 159 B2
Houldsworth St. 2 Radcliffe M26 43 F5
Houldsworth St. Reddish SK5 111 E7
Houseley Ave. OL9 66 A3
Housley Cl. WN3 150 A5
Houson St. OL8 153 F5
Houston Pk. M5 154 F1
Hove Cl. BL8 10 F1
Hove Dr. M14 110 E7
Hove St. BL3 144 C5
Hove St N. 13 BL3 144 C5
Hoveden St. M8 158 F4
Hoverty Prec. WA12 89 B1
Hovey Cl. M7 & M8 155 F7
Hovingham St. OL16 31 B8
Hovington Gdns. M19 110 E6
Hovis St. M11 165 C8
How Clough Cl. M28 60 F2
How Clough Dr. M28 60 F2
How Lea Dr. BL9 27 F6
Howard Ave. Bolton BL3 146 A4
Howard Ave. Cheadle SK8 123 A1
Howard Ave. Eccles M30 79 D3
Howard Ave. Kearsley BL4 60 F7
Howard Ave. Lymm WA13 117 B4
Howard Ave. Reddish SK4 111 C6
Howard Cl. Glossop SK13 104 B2
Howard Cl. Romiley SK6 113 A2
Howard Ct. OL6 166 C3
Howard Dr. WA15 120 A1
Howard Hill. BL9 45 A5
Howard La. M34 100 F4
Howard Pl. Hyde SK14 167 D2
Howard Pl. R'dale OL12 & OL16 139 F8
Howard Rd. Culcheth WA3 92 A2
Howard Rd. Wythenshawe M22 109 D1
Howard Spring Wlk. M8 155 F8
Howard St. Ashton-u-L OL7 166 A4
Howard St. Denton M34 100 E5
Howard St. Glossop SK13 104 C1
Howard St. M'ster M8 158 F4
Howard St. Oldham OL4 49 E1
Howard St. R'dale OL12 139 F8
Howard St. Radcliffe M26 44 B3
Howard St. Salford M5 161 A8
Howard St. Shaw OL2 149 A7
Howard St. Stalybridge SK15 86 D4
Howard St. Stockport SK1 169 F2
Howard St. Stretford M32 96 D2
Howard St. Wigan WN5 54 C5
Howard Way. OL15 6 C1
Howard's La. OL5 68 F1
Howards La. WN5 53 F7
Howarth Ave. M28 79 C7
Howarth Cl. M11 83 A1
Howarth Cross St. OL16 15 B2
Howarth Ct. 8 Radcliffe M26 44 B3
Howarth Ct. Stockport SK2 124 B5
Howarth Dr. M44 93 F1
Howarth Farm Way. OL12 15 C3
Howarth Gn. OL12 15 C3
Howarth Sq. OL16 31 A8
Howarth St. Farnworth BL4 60 D7
Howarth St. Leigh WN7 76 B4
Howarth St. Littleborough OL15 16 B6
Howarth St. M'ster M16 97 C4
Howarth St. Westhoughton BL5 57 F8
Howarth Wlk. 3 M26 44 B3
Howbridge Cl. M28 78 C8
Howbro Dr. OL7 84 E5
Howcroft Cl. BL1 145 E8
Howcroft St. BL3 145 D5
Howden Cl. SK5 99 E2
Howden Dr. WN3 55 B4
Howden Rd. M'ster M9 64 C5
Howden Rd. New Mills SK12 127 C1
Howe Bridge CE Prim Sch. M46 58 B2
Howe Bridge Cl. WN7 58 A1
Howe Dr. BL0 11 B2
Howe St. Ashton-u-L OL7 100 F8
Howe St. M'ster M7 155 D7
Howell Croft N. 7 BL1 145 F7
Howell Croft S. BL1 145 F7
Howell's Yd. 6 BL1 145 F7
Howells Ave. M33 108 B5
Howgill St. M11 & M43 83 D1
Howsin Ave. BL2 25 B4
Howton Cl. M12 99 A4
Howty Cl. SK9 131 D1
Hoxton Cl. SK6 113 A4
Hoy Dr. M41 95 D5
Hoylake Cl. Failsworth M40 83 D8
Hoylake Cl. Leigh WN7 75 D2
Hoylake Rd. Stockport SK3 123 B8
Hoylake Rd. Wythenshawe M33 108 F2
Hoyland Cl. M12 164 F6
Hoyle Ave. OL8 153 E5
Hoyle St. Bacup OL13 3 E8
Hoyle St. 3 Bolton BL1 143 E4
Hoyle St. M'ster M12 163 C8
Hoyle St. Radcliffe M26 44 C1
Hoyle St. Whitworth OL12 4 D2
Hoyle Street Ind Est. M12 163 C7
Hoyle Wlk. M13 163 C6
Hoyle's Terr. OL16 31 E6
Hqward St. BL1 143 F1
Hubert Worthington House. SK9 137 A1
Hucclecote Ave. M22 121 C2
Hucklow Ave. M23 121 A2
Hucklow Bank. 27 SK13 171 D2
Hucklow Cl. 26 SK13 171 D2
Hucklow Fold. 28 SK13 171 D2
Hucklow Lanes. 29 SK13 171 D2
Hudcar La. BL9 141 A4
Huddart Cl. M5 161 B8
Huddersfield Rd. Diggle OL3 51 C7
Huddersfield Rd. Diggle OL3 51 D5
Huddersfield Rd. Newhey OL16 & OL2 & OL3 32 D5
Huddersfield Rd. Oldham OL1 & OL4 67 D8
Huddersfield Rd. Stalybridge OL5 & SK15 86 E4
Hudson Rd. Bolton BL3 146 B3
Hudson Rd. Hyde SK14 113 E7
Hudson St. OL9 66 A2
Hudsons Pas. OL15 16 C7
Hudsons Wlk. OL11 30 C7
Hudswell Cl. M45 62 E8
Hugh Lupus St. BL1 25 A5
Hugh Oldham Dr. M7 81 C6
Hugh St. OL16 31 A8
Hughes Ave. BL6 22 A4
Hughes Cl. BL9 141 A3
Hughes St. Bolton BL1 142 C2
Hughes St. Bolton BL1 143 D2
Hughes St. M'ster M11 164 E8
Hughes Way. M30 79 A1
Hughley Cl. Royton OL2 49 A4
Hughtrede St. OL11 31 B3
Hugo St. Failsworth M40 83 A7
Hugo St. Farnworth BL4 42 B2
Hugo St. R'dale OL11 30 D2
Hulbert St. Bury BL8 27 C1
Hulbert St. Middleton M24 47 B1
Hull Mill La. OL3 50 F5
Hull Sq. M3 158 D2
Hullet Cl. WN6 35 E8
Hully St. 7 SK15 85 F2
Hulme Ct. M15 162 E7
Hulme Gr. WN7 75 C6
Hulme Gram Sch for Girls The. OL8 66 D4
Hulme Gram Sch The. OL8 66 D4
Hulme Hall Ave. SK8 132 B8
Hulme Hall Cl. SK8 123 A1
Hulme Hall Cres. SK8 132 A8
Hulme Hall Jun Sch. SK8 132 B8
Hulme Hall Rd.Cheadle SK8 123 A1
Hulme Hall Rd. M'ster M15 162 D7
Hulme Hall Schs. SK8 123 A1
Hulme Pl. M5 81 C1
Hulme Rd. Bolton BL2 25 E5
Hulme Rd.Kearsley BL4 & M26 61 C7
Hulme Rd. Leigh WN7 75 C6
Hulme Rd. Reddish M34 100 B3
Hulme Rd. Reddish SK4 111 D6
Hulme Rd. Sale M33 108 D3
Hulme St. Ashton-u-L OL6 85 D5
Hulme St. Bolton BL1 145 F8
Hulme St. Bury BL8 140 D3
Hulme St. M'ster M3 & M5 81 C1
Hulme St. M'ster M15 162 D7
Hulme St. M'ster M15 162 E7
Hulme St. Oldham OL8 66 E4
Hulme St. Stockport SK1 124 B7
Hulme Wlk. M15 162 F6
Hulme's Terr. BL2 43 C8
Hulmes Rd. M35 & M40 83 E5
Hulton Ave. M28 60 B3
Hulton Cl. BL3 146 A3
Hulton District Ctr. M28 60 A4
Hulton Dr. Bolton BL3 146 A3
Hulton Dr. M'ster M16 97 E4
Hulton Hospl. BL3 146 A3
Hulton La. BL3 146 A3
Hulton St. Denton M34 100 E4
Hulton St. Failsworth M35 83 E7
Hulton St. Salford M5 161 A7
Humber Dr. BL9 27 F7
Humber Pl. WN5 54 C7
Humber Rd. Milnrow OL16 32 A6
Humber Rd. Tyldesley M29 77 C7
Humber St. M'ster M8 156 B7
Humber St. Salford M5 154 D1
Humberstone Ave. M15 162 F6
Hume St. M'ster M19 111 B8
Hume St. R'dale OL16 31 A5
Humphrey Booth Gdns. M6 154 E3
Humphrey Cres. M41 96 A2
Humphrey La. M32 & M41 96 A2
Humphrey Park Sta. M32 96 A3
Humphrey Pk. M41 96 A2
Humphrey Rd. M16 161 B5
Humphrey St. Ince-i-M WN2 56 A7
Humphrey St. M'ster M7 & M8 155 F8
Humphries Ct. M40 159 C4
Huncoat Ave. SK4 111 D5
Huncote Dr. M9 64 E1
Hunger Hill Ave. BL3 40 E2
Hungerford Wlk. 5 M23 120 D7
Hunmanby Ave. M15 162 F7
Hunstanton Dr. BL8 27 D5
Hunston Rd. M33 107 F2
Hunt Ave. OL6 & OL7 85 B5
Hunt Fold Dr. BL8 10 F1
Hunt La. OL9 152 A7
Hunt Rd. SK14 102 A5
Hunt St. Atherton M46 58 D3
Hunt St. M'ster M9 64 D1
Hunt St. Wigan WN1 151 E7
Hunt's Bank. M'ster M3 158 F2
Hunt's Bank. Westhoughton BL5 57 F6
Hunter Dr. M26 44 A5
Hunter Rd. WN5 36 E1
Hunter's La. Oldham OL1 153 F7
Hunter's La. R'dale OL12 & OL16 139 F8
Hunter's View. SK9 131 C3
Hunters Cl. SK9 131 F1
Hunters Ct. SK15 102 D8
Hunters Gn. BL8 10 F3
Hunters Hill. BL9 45 B4
Hunters Hill La. OL3 51 C6
Hunters La. Glossop SK13 115 F8
Hunters La. R'dale OL16 139 F8
Hunters Mews. Sale M33 108 A5
Hunters Mews. Wilmslow SK9 137 C7
Hunterston Ave. M30 80 A2
Huntingdon Ave. OL9 152 B5
Huntingdon Cres. SK5 112 C5
Huntingdon Way. 7 M34 100 F1
Huntingdon Wlk. 21 BL1 143 E2
Huntington Ave. M20 110 A7
Huntley Mount Rd. BL9 141 B3
Huntley Rd. Cheadle SK3 123 B7
Huntley Rd. M'ster M8 63 E2
Huntley St. BL9 141 B3
Huntly Chase. SK9 137 C7
Huntly Way. OL10 28 E1
Huntroyde Ave. 26 BL2 25 C1
Hunts Rd. 2 M6 80 D5
Huntsham Cl. WA14 119 B6
Huntsman Dr. M44 105 F7
Huntsworth Wlk. M13 164 D5
Hurdlow Ave. M7 81 A7
Hurdlow Gn. 14 SK13 171 D1
Hurdlow Lea. 13 SK13 171 D1
Hurdlow Mews. SK13 171 D1
Hurdlow Way. 12 SK13 171 D1
Hurdlow Wlk. M9 157 D7
Hurdsfield Rd. SK2 124 D4
Hurford Ave. M18 99 D6
Hurlbote Cl. SK9 131 D5
Hurley Dr. SK8 122 E2
Hurlston Rd. BL3 147 D2
Hurst Ave. Bramhall SK8 132 C6
Hurst Ave. Sale M33 107 C2
Hurst Bank Rd. OL6 85 E4
Hurst Brook Cl. OL6 166 C4
Hurst Cl. BL5 58 F7
Hurst Cross. OL6 85 D5
Hurst Ct. Ashton-u-L OL6 85 E5
Hurst Ct. Wythenshawe M23 120 F4
Hurst Gr. OL6 85 E5
Hurst Green Cl. BL8 43 F8
Hurst Hall Dr. OL6 85 E5
Hurst Inf Sch. OL6 85 D5
Hurst Knoll CE (VC) Prim Sch. OL6 166 C4
Hurst La. WA3 92 C7
Hurst Lea Ct. SK9 137 A2
Hurst Meadow. OL16 31 C3
Hurst Methodist Jun Sch. OL6 85 D7
Hurst Mill La. WA3 92 C8
Hurst Rd. SK13 104 F1
Hurst St. Bolton BL3 146 C3
Hurst St. Bury BL9 141 A2
Hurst St. Dukinfield SK16 101 A6
Hurst St. Hindley WN2 56 C6
Hurst St. Leigh WN7 76 B3
Hurst St. Oldham OL9 153 D7
Hurst St. R'dale OL11 31 A5
Hurst St. Reddish SK5 111 E7
Hurst St. Walkden M28 60 D6
Hurst Wlk. 4 M22 121 A2
Hurstbank Ave. M19 110 D4
Hurstbourne Ave. M11 83 B2
Hurstbrook Cl. SK13 104 F1
Hurstbrook Dr. M32 95 F2
Hurstclough Prim Sch. SK14 102 E1
Hurstead. OL12 15 D4
Hurstead Gn. OL16 15 D4
Hurstead Rd. OL16 31 F6
Hursted Rd. OL16 31 F6
Hurstfield Rd. M28 78 B8
Hurstfold Ave. M19 110 D3
Hursthead Cty Jun Sch. SK8 132 C7
Hursthead Inf Sch. SK8 132 C6
Hursthead Rd. SK8 132 B7
Hursthead Wlk. M13 163 B7
Hurstmead Terr. M20 110 B2
Hurstvale Ave. SK8 122 B1
Hurstville Rd. M21 109 B6
Hurstway Dr. 33 M9 64 E3
Hurstwood Rd. SK2 124 F6
Hus St. 1 Droylsden M43 100 A8
Husteads. OL3 50 E1
Husteads La. OL3 50 F1
Hutchinson Rd. OL11 & OL12 13 D2
Hutchinson St. R'dale OL11 30 C6
Hutchinson St. 4 Radcliffe M26 44 C4
Hutchinson Way. M26 44 A3
Huttock End La. OL13 3 D8
Hutton Ave. Ashton-u-L OL6 85 E3
Hutton Ave. Boothstown M28 77 F6
Hutton Cl. WA3 91 E5
Hutton Lodge. M14 110 C7
Hutton St. WN1 20 A3
Hutton Wlk. 7 M13 163 C6
Huxley Ave. M7 & M8 156 A6
Huxley Cl. SK7 132 E7
Huxley Dr. SK7 132 E7
Huxley Pl. WN3 150 A5
Huxley St. Alt'ham WA14 119 D7
Huxley St. Bolton BL1 142 C2
Huxley St. 6 Oldham OL4 67 C6
Huxton Gn. SK7 124 A2
Huyton Rd. PR6 21 A6
Huyton Terr. PR6 21 B6
Hyacinth Cl. SK3 170 D5
Hyatt Cres. WN6 19 C3
Hyde Central Sta. SK14 101 C2
Hyde Cl. WN3 150 A5
Hyde Dr. M28 60 C2
Hyde Fold Cl. M19 110 F6
Hyde Gr. M'ster M13 163 C5
Hyde Gr. Sale M33 108 B4
Hyde Gr. Walkden M28 60 C2
Hyde Hospl. SK14 167 F1
Hyde North Sta. SK14 101 C5
Hyde Pl. M13 163 C5
Hyde Rd.Denton M34 & SK14 101 A3
Hyde Rd. M'ster M12 & M18 & M34 99 D4
Hyde Rd. M'ster M12 164 E6
Hyde Rd. Oldham M24 65 E6
Hyde Rd.Romiley SK14 & SK6 113 B5
Hyde Rd. Walkden M28 60 C2
Hyde Sq. M24 46 E1
Hyde St. Bolton BL3 146 C3
Hyde St.Droylsden M35 & M43 84 C4
Hyde St. Dukinfield SK16 101 D8
Hyde St. M'ster M15 162 D5
Hyde St Paul's RC Prim Sch. SK14 167 F4
Hyde Tech Sch. SK14 167 D4
Hyde's Cross. M4 159 A2
Hyde-Clarendon Coll. SK14 167 E4
Hydes Terr. SK15 86 B2
Hydon Brook Wlk. OL11 30 C4
Hydrangea Cl. 7 M33 107 C6
Hyldavale Ave. SK8 122 B6
Hylton Dr. Ashton-u-L OL7 84 F5
Hylton Dr. Cheadle SK8 132 C8
Hyman Goldstone Wlk. 4 M8 155 F7
Hyndman Ct. M5 154 D2
Hypatia St. BL2 148 B7
Hythe Cl. M14 98 C3
Hythe Rd. SK3 123 B8
Hythe St. BL3 146 A4
Hythe Wlk. OL9 152 B6

Ibberton Wlk. 8 M9 64 F1
Ibsley. 20 OL12 139 E8
Ice House Cl. 5 M28 59 F3
Iceland St. M6 154 F2
Idonia St. BL1 143 D3
Ifco Ctr. M14 98 C3
Ilex Gr. M7 155 D6
Ilford St. M11 83 B2
Ilfracombe Rd. SK2 124 D8
Ilfracombe St. M40 83 D6
Ilk St. M11 83 B2
Ilkeston Dr. WN2 38 F3
Ilkeston Wlk. 5 Denton M34 113 A8
Ilkeston Wlk. 4 Failsworth M40 83 A6
Ilkley Cl. Bolton BL2 148 C7
Ilkley Cl. Oldham OL9 152 B6
Ilkley Cres. SK5 111 E8
Ilkley Dr. M41 95 A4
Ilkley St. M'ster M40 83 A8
Illingworth Ave. SK15 86 C2
Illona Dr. M7 81 A8
Ilminster. OL11 139 E6
Ilminster Wlk. 2 M9 64 E5
Ilthorpe Wlk. 7 M40 83 A6
Imex Bsns Pk. M13 98 F3
Imogen Ct. M5 161 C8
Imperial Dr. WN7 76 D6
Ina Ave. BL1 23 F1
Ince Cl. M'ster M20 110 B7
Ince Cl. M'ster SK4 169 E3
Ince Green La. Ince-i-M WN2 & WN3 151 F6
Ince Hall Ave. Ince-i-M WN2 & WN3 56 A8
Ince Hall Ave. Wigan WN2 151 F8
Ince St. SK4 169 E3
Ince Sta. WN2 151 F6
Ince Wlk. WN1 150 C8
Ince-in-Makerfield CE Prim Sch. WN2 56 A7
Inchcape Dr. M9 64 B4
Inchfield Cl. OL11 29 E8
Inchfield Rd. M'ster M40 65 B1
Inchfield Rd. Walsden OL14 6 A8
Inchley Rd. M13 163 B7
Inchwood Mews. OL4 49 E4
Incline Rd. OL8 66 C2
Independent St. BL3 43 A3
India St. BL0 11 C3
Indigo St. M6 80 F5
Indigo Wlk. M6 80 F5
Industrial Cotts. 10 BB4 2 F8
Industrial St. Ramsbottom BL0 1 C1
Industrial St. Westhoughton BL5 57 F7
Industry Rd. 8 OL12 14 F1
Industry St. 14 Littleborough OL15 16 B5
Industry St. Oldham OL9 66 A4
Industry St. R'dale OL11 13 E1
Industry St. Whitworth OL12 4 D2
Infant St. M25 63 C4
Infirmary St. 11 BL1 145 F7
Ingersol Rd. BL6 22 E1
Ingham Ave. WA12 89 B1
Ingham Brow. BL6 22 F4
Ingham Rd. Sale WA14 107 D1
Ingham St. Bury BL9 141 A1
Ingham St. Failsworth M40 83 E4
Ingham St. Leigh WN7 75 E8
Ingham St. 5 Oldham OL1 67 A7
Inghams La. OL15 16 B5
Inghamwood Cl. M7 & M8 155 F7
Ingle Dr. SK2 124 C7
Ingle Rd. SK8 123 A6
Ingleby Ave. M9 64 F4
Ingleby Cl. Shaw OL2 149 A8
Ingleby Cl. Standish WN6 19 D2
Ingleby Ct. M32 96 E1
Ingleby Way. OL2 149 A8
Ingledene Ave. M7 63 E1
Ingledene Ct. 8 M7 63 E1
Ingledene Gr. BL1 142 A2
Inglefield. OL11 13 F1
Inglehead Cl. M34 101 A2
Ingles Fold. M28 78 B7
Inglesham Cl. WN7 75 E1
Ingleton Ave. M8 64 B2
Ingleton Cl. Bolton BL2 25 D4
Ingleton Cl. Cheadle SK8 122 C6
Ingleton Cl. Royton OL2 48 D5
Ingleton Dr. WA11 71 B1
Ingleton Mews. BL8 27 B4
Ingleton Rd. SK3 123 C7
Inglewhite Ave. WN1 37 C2
Inglewhite Cl. BL9 44 D7
Inglewhite Cres. 1 WN1 37 C2
Inglewhite Pl. 2 WN1 37 C2
Inglewood. WA14 119 B3
Inglewood Ave. WN1 151 E7
Inglewood Cl. OL7 84 F5
Inglewood Rd. M24 47 E1
Inglewood Wlk. M13 163 C6
Inglis St. OL15 16 B6
Ingoe Cl. OL10 29 F3
Ingoldsby Ave. M13 98 D4
Ingram Dr. SK4 110 E3
Ingram St. Platt Bridge WN2 56 A3
Ingram St. Shevington WN6 36 F2
Ings Ave. OL12 14 B2
Ings La. OL12 14 C2
Ink St. OL16 139 F7
Inkerman St. Hyde SK14 167 D4
Inkerman St. M'ster M40 157 D6
Inkerman St. 12 R'dale OL12 14 F1
Inman St. Bury BL9 44 E8
Inman St. Denton M34 100 F3
Innes Sch. OL12 14 C1
Innes St. M18 99 B3
Innis Ave. M40 83 C5
Inst of Islamic H Ed. BL7 25 A8
Institute St. BL1 & BL2 148 A7
Instow Cl. Chadderton OL9 47 F1
Instow Cl. M'ster M13 164 D6
Intake Rd. OL3 69 B3
International App. M90 130 C7
Invar Rd. M27 61 D1
Inver Wlk. 10 M40 65 D2
Inverbeg Dr. Bolton BL2 43 A7
Invergarry Wlk. 19 M11 83 C1
Inverlael Ave. BL1 144 B8
Inverness Ave. M9 65 A4
Inverness Cl. WN2 38 D5
Inverness Rd. SK16 101 C7
Inward Dr. WN6 36 A5
Inwood Wlk. M8 156 C6
Inworth Wlk. 10 M8 155 F7
Iona Pl. BL2 25 C2
Iona Way. M41 95 E5
Ionian Gdns. 2 M7 81 C5
Ipswich St. OL11 139 F5
Ipswich Way. 10 M34 101 A1
Ipswich Wlk. M12 164 E5
Iqbal Cl. M12 165 A5
Irby Wlk. SK8 123 A4
Ireby Cl. M24 46 C2
Iredale Cres. WN6 36 F7
Iredine St. 6 M11 83 C1
Irene Ave. SK14 101 E5
Iris Ave. Farnworth BL4 42 A1
Iris Ave. Kearsley BL4 60 F5
Iris St. Oldham OL8 66 F3
Iris St. Ramsbottom BL0 138 B6
Iris Wlk. 7 M31 105 E2
Irk St. M4 159 A3
Irk Vale Dr. OL1 & OL9 47 E1
Irk Wlk. M45 45 B2
Irkdale St. M40 & M8 156 C6
Irlam Ave. M30 79 D1
Irlam & Cadishead Comm High Sch. M44 105 E7
Irlam Endowed Prim Sch. M44 94 A2
Irlam Prim Sch. M44 94 A1
Irlam Rd. Sale M33 108 C4
Irlam Rd. Urmston M41 94 D2
Irlam Sq. M6 80 D5
Irlam St. Bolton BL1 143 E3
Irlam St. M'ster M10 & M40 157 E5
Irlam Sta. M44 105 E7
Irlam Wharf Rd. M44 106 A6
Irma St. BL1 143 F3
Iron St. Denton M34 100 F3
Iron St. Horwich BL6 22 C2
Iron St. M'ster M10 & M40 160 E3
Ironmonger La. Oldham OL1 153 F6
Ironmonger La. Wigan WN3 150 C7
Irvin Dr. M22 & SK8 131 A8
Irvin St. M35 83 C6
Irvine Ave. M28 78 A6
Irvine St. WN7 75 F6
Irving Cl. SK2 124 A3
Irving House. 1 BL1 143 E2
Irving St. Bolton BL1 143 E2
Irving St. Oldham OL8 66 B2
Irwell Ave. Eccles M30 79 F1
Irwell Ave. Walkden M38 60 B4
Irwell Cl. 4 M26 44 B2
Irwell Gr. M30 79 F1
Irwell Pl. Eccles M30 79 F1
Irwell Pl. Salford M5 81 C2
Irwell Pl. Wigan WN5 54 C6
Irwell Rd. WN5 53 F7
Irwell St. Bury BL9 140 E2
Irwell St. Kearsley M26 61 A8
Irwell St. M'ster M3 158 E1
Irwell St. M'ster M7 & M8 158 E4
Irwell St. Radcliffe M26 44 B2
Irwell St. Ramsbottom BL0 138 C6
Irwell St. Salford M6 81 A6
Irwell Vale Rd. BB4 1 C6
Irwell Vale Sta. BL0 1 C5
Irwell Wlk. OL8 66 C3
Irwin Dr. SK9 131 C5
Irwin Rd. WA14 119 D8
Irwin St. M34 100 E3
Isa St. BL0 11 A4
Isaac Cl. M5 161 A8
Isaac St. BL1 144 C8
Isabella Cl. M16 97 C4
Isabella Sq. WN1 151 E8
Isabella St. OL12 15 A2
Isaiah St. OL8 66 F4
Isca St. M11 160 F1
Isel Wlk. M24 46 D2
Isherwood Dr. SK6 125 D6
Isherwood Fold. BL7 9 D7
Isherwood Rd. M31 106 F6
Isherwood St. Heywood OL10 29 E1
Isherwood St. Leigh WN7 75 E8
Isherwood St. R'dale OL11 31 A6
Isis Cl. M7 81 A8
Islamic Acad. M13 163 B6
Islamic High Sch for Girls. M21 109 A8
Island Cotts. BL9 11 C2
Island Row. WN2 56 B7
Islington Rd. SK2 124 C4
Islington St. M3 158 D2
Islington Way. M3 158 D1
Isobel Cl. M30 79 B1
Isobel Wlk. Bolton BL1 145 D5
Isobel Wlk. M'ster M16 97 F4
Ivanhoe Ave. WA3 74 D1
Ivanhoe Ct. BL3 & BL4 42 C2
Ivanhoe St. Farnworth BL3 & BL4 42 C2
Ivanhoe St. Oldham OL1 49 C1
Iveagh Ct. 19 OL16 31 B6
Ivor St. OL11 30 B3
Ivory Way. OL1 153 F7
Ivy Ave. WA12 89 C2
Ivy Bank Cl. BL1 24 E5
Ivy Bank Rd. BL1 24 E5
Ivy Cl. Droylsden M43 83 F3
Ivy Cl. Shaw OL2 149 B7
Ivy Cotts. Denton M34 113 A7
Ivy Cotts. Rawtenstall BB4 2 F8
Ivy Dr. M24 64 F6
Ivy Gr. Farnworth BL4 60 B8
Ivy Gr. Kearsley BL4 60 F7
Ivy Gr. Walkden M38 59 F4
Ivy House Rd. WA3 74 D1
Ivy Rd. Bolton BL1 142 B1
Ivy Rd. Bury BL8 27 B2
Ivy Rd. Golborne WA3 90 B8
Ivy Rd. Poynton SK12 133 E3
Ivy Rd. Westhoughton BL5 57 F7
Ivy St. Ashton-i-M WN4 73 B3
Ivy St. Bolton BL3 146 C4
Ivy St. Eccles M30 79 D1
Ivy St. M'ster M40 83 A8
Ivy St. 1 Rawtenstall BB4 2 F8
Ivy St. Wigan WN1 & WN6 150 B8
Ivy Wlk. M31 105 D3
Ivybridge Cl. M13 164 D5
Ivycroft. SK14 171 E4
Ivydale Dr. WN7 76 C5
Ivygreen Dr. OL4 67 F6
Ivygreen Rd. M'ster M21 109 A8
Ivylea Rd. M19 110 E4
Ivyleaf Sq. M7 155 E6

Jack La. Droylsden M43 84 C2
Jack La. Urmston M41 95 E2
Jack McCann Ct. 10 OL16 31 A8
Jack St. 7 BL2 25 C1
Jack Taylor Ct. OL12 15 B1
Jack's La. BL5 57 A8
Jackdaw Rd. BL8 10 F2
Jackie Brown Wlk. M40 157 D5
Jackman Ave. OL10 46 D7
Jackroom Dr. M4 159 C1
Jackson Ave. Culcheth WA3 91 E3
Jackson Ave. 3 Dukinfield SK16 101 D8
Jackson Cl. OL8 153 E5
Jackson Cres. M15 162 E7
Jackson Ct. M41 95 A3
Jackson Gdns. M34 100 D2
Jackson Pit. 1 OL1 153 E6
Jackson Pl. OL16 31 B8
Jackson St. Cheadle SK8 122 E6
Jackson St. Failsworth M35 83 D6
Jackson St. Farnworth BL4 60 D8
Jackson St. Glossop SK14 104 C5
Jackson St. Glossop SK13 116 C7
Jackson St. Hyde SK14 167 D2
Jackson St. Ince-i-M WN2 56 A7
Jackson St. Kearsley BL4 60 F7
Jackson St. Littleborough OL12 15 C6
Jackson St. Middleton M24 65 B8
Jackson St. Mottram-i-L SK14 103 A3
Jackson St. Oldham OL4 67 B7
Jackson St. Oldham OL4 67 F6
Jackson St. R'dale OL16 31 B6
Jackson St. Radcliffe M26 44 B2
Jackson St. Sale M33 108 D5
Jackson St. Stretford M32 96 C1
Jackson St. Walkden M28 60 C4
Jackson St. Whitefield M45 62 F7
Jackson's La. Hazel Grove SK7 133 C8
Jackson's Row. M2 158 F1
Jacksons Edge Rd. SK12 & SK6 135 B6
Jacob St. WN2 56 D6
Jacobsen Ave. SK14 167 F4
Jaffrey St. WN7 75 E5
James Andrew St. M24 47 B1
James Bentley Wlk. 4 M40 83 C5
James Brindley Basin. 12 M1 159 C1
James Brindley Prim Sch. M28 60 C1
James Butterworth Ct. 6 OL16 31 B6
James Butterworth St. 9 OL16 31 B6
James Cl. SK16 101 E8
James Corbett Rd. M5 154 D1
James Henry Ave. M5 161 B8
James Hill St. 13 OL15 16 B5
James Leech St. SK1 & SK3 170 E8
James Leigh St. M1 163 A8
James Pl. Coppull PR7 19 E8
James Pl. Standish WN6 19 D2
James Rd. OL2 149 B7
James Sq. WN6 19 D2
James St. Ashton-i-M WN2 73 E7
James St. Bacup OL13 3 B7
James St. Bolton BL7 8 D3
James St. Bury BL9 141 A1
James St. Droylsden M43 84 B2
James St. Dukinfield M34 101 A4
James St. Dukinfield SK16 101 E8
James St. Failsworth M35 84 A7
James St. Glossop SK13 116 C8
James St. Heywood OL10 29 D3
James St. Horwich BL6 21 F3
James St. Ince-i-M WN3 151 D6

James St. Kearsley BL4 .... 60 F8
James St. Little Lever BL3 ...... 43 B3
James St. Littleborough OL15 . 15 E4
James St. M'ster M3 .... 158 D1
James St. M'ster M10 & M40 160 D3
James St. Prestwich M25 .... 63 A5
James St. R'dale OL12 .... 15 C4
James St. 5
R'dale OL12 & OL16 .... 31 A8
James St. Radcliffe M26 .... 44 B2
James St. Romiley SK6 .... 113 A5
James St. Sale M33 .... 108 D4
James St. Shaw OL2 .... 149 A5
James St. Stockport SK3 .... 170 E7
James St. Tyldesley M46 .... 58 E1
James St. Tyldesley M29 .... 76 F8
James St. Whitworth OL12 .... 4 D2
James St S. OL9 .... 152 A7
James's St. OL4 .... 49 D1
Jameson St. OL11 .... 30 B2
Jammy La. OL9 .... 152 C6
Jane Barter House. 1 BL4 . 60 D8
Jane St. Oldham OL9 .... 152 B6
Jane St. R'dale OL12 .... 139 E8
Jane St. Whitworth OL12 .... 4 E6
Japan St. M7 & M8 .... 155 F7
Jarmain St. M12 .... 165 A7
Jarvis St. 11 Oldham OL4 .... 67 A6
Jarvis St. R'dale OL12 .... 14 F1
Jasmine Ave. M43 .... 84 C2
Jasmine Cl. M23 .... 108 E1
Jasmine Rd. WN5 .... 54 D7
Jasmine Wlk. M31 .... 105 F2
Jason St. M4 .... 159 B3
Jasper Wlk. 21 M16 .... 97 E4
Jauncey St. BL3 .... 144 C5
Jaxons Ct. WN1 .... 150 C8
Jayton Ave. M20 .... 122 B8
Jean Ave. WN7 .... 75 E2
Jean Cl. M12 & M19 .... 99 A2
Jedburgh Ave. BL1 .... 144 B8
Jeff Joseph Sale Moor
Tech Coll. M33 .... 108 D2
Jefferson Way. OL12 .... 14 F3
Jeffrey St. WN2 .... 56 A8
Jeffrey Wlk. OL10 .... 29 A2
Jeffreys Dr. SK16 .... 101 D8
Jehlum Cl. M8 .... 156 B7
Jellicoe Ave. M44 .... 105 E6
Jenkinson St. Hindley WN2 .... 56 D6
Jenkinson St. M'ster M15 .. 163 A6
Jenkyn Wlk. 5 M11 .... 160 F1
Jenner Cl. M15 .... 162 D7
Jennet Hey. WN4 .... 72 F6
Jennet's La. Glazebury WA3 .. 76 C1
Jennings Ave. M5 .... 161 A8
Jennings Cl. Hyde SK14 .... 102 B5
Jennings Cl. Salford M5 .... 161 A8
Jennings St. SK3 .... 170 D7
Jennison Cl. M18 .... 165 B6
Jenny Beck Gr. BL3 .... 147 E4
Jenny La. SK7 .... 132 E4
Jenny St. OL8 .... 66 C2
Jepheys Pl. 17 OL12 .... 14 F1
Jepheys St. OL12 .... 14 F1
Jepson St. SK2 .... 124 A6
Jericho Rd. BL9 .... 28 E4
Jermyn St. OL12 .... 31 A8
Jerrold St. 5 OL15 .... 16 B5
Jersey Cl. M19 .... 110 F7
Jersey Rd. SK5 .... 169 F4
Jersey St. Ashton-u-L OL6 .... 166 B4
Jersey St. M'ster M20 & M4 159 C2
Jerusalem Pl. M2 .... 162 F8
Jesmond Ave. M25 .... 63 B2
Jesmond Dr. BL8 .... 27 C5
Jesmond Gr. SK8 .... 132 B8
Jesmond Rd. BL1 .... 142 B4
Jesmond Wlk. M9 .... 64 D5
Jespersen St. OL1 .... 153 F7
Jessamine Ave. M7 .... 158 D4
Jessel Cl. M13 .... 163 C6
Jessica Way. WN7 .... 75 B4
Jessie St. Bolton BL3 .... 144 C5
Jessie St. Failsworth M40 .... 83 A6
Jessop Dr. SK6 .... 125 F8
Jessop St. M18 .... 99 D5
Jethro St. Bolton BL2 .... 25 C4
Jethro St. Bolton BL2 .... 148 C8
Jetson St. M18 .... 99 F6
Jevington Wlk. 10 M13 .... 163 C6
Jewish Cassel Fox
Prim Sch.M7 .... 155 D8
Jewish Day Prim Sch. M25 . 63 B2
Jimmy McMullen Wlk. 6
M14 .... 98 A3
Jinnah Cl. M11 .... 165 C8
Jo St. M5 .... 81 A1
Joan St. M40 .... 83 A7
Jobling St. M11 .... 164 F8
Jocelyn St. M10 & M40 & M9 157 E5
Joddrell St. M3 .... 158 E1
Joe Connolly Way. BB4 .... 2 E8
Joel La. Hyde SK14 .... 113 F7
Johannesburg Gdns. M23 . 120 F4
John Ashworth St. OL12 .... 15 B1
John Atkinson Ct. M5 .... 154 D2
John Ave. SK8 .... 122 E5
John Booth St. OL4 .... 67 F5
John Brown St. 14 BL1 .... 145 E8
John Clynes Ave.
M10 & M40 .... 159 C3
John Cross St. BL3 .... 147 E4
John Dalton St.
Hollingworth SK14 .... 103 E5
John Dalton St. M'ster M3 158 D2
John Dalton St. M'ster M2 . 158 F1
John Foran Cl. M40 .... 83 B6
John Henry St. OL12 .... 4 D4
John Heywood St. M11 .... 83 B2
John Kemble Ct. OL11 .... 30 D4
John Kennedy Gdn. SK14 . 103 A3
John Kennedy Rd. SK14 ..... 102 F3
John Knott St. OL4 .... 67 F6
John Lee Fold. M24 .... 47 A1
John Lloyd Ct. M44 .... 105 F8
John Nash Cres. M15 .... 162 E6
John Roberts Cl. OL11 .... 139 E5
John Robinson Wlk. 8 M40 83 A7
John Shepley St. SK14 .... 167 E2
John Smeaton Ct. 18 M1 .. 159 C1
John St. Alt'ham WA14 .... 119 D4
John St. Ashton-i-M WN4 .... 73 D5
John St. Bolton BL7 .... 25 A7
John St. Bury BL9 .... 140 F3
John St. Denton M34 .... 100 F4
John St. Droylsden M43 .... 83 F1
John St. Eccles M30 .... 79 B1
John St. Failsworth M35 .... 65 F1
John St. Farnworth BL4 .... 60 E8
John St. Glossop SK13 .... 116 C8
John St. Golborne WA3 .... 90 A8
John St. Hazel Grove SK7 .... 124 D3
John St. Heywood OL10 .... 29 D2
John St. Heywood OL10 .... 29 D3
John St. Hindley WN2 .... 57 B3
John St. Hyde SK14 .... 167 D3
John St. Irlam M44 .... 105 E5
John St. Leigh WN7 .... 75 F5
John St. Little Lever BL3 .... 43 B3
John St. Littleborough OL16 .... 15 C3
John St. Littleborough OL15 .... 16 A5
John St. M'ster M7 .... 158 D4
John St. M'ster M3 .... 158 E2
John St. M'ster M4 .... 159 A2
John St. Marple SK6 .... 126 A5
John St. Middleton M25 .... 63 E8
John St. Oldham OL4 .... 68 A6
John St. Oldham OL9 .... 153 E6
John St. R'dale OL16 & OL12 .. 31 A8
John St. Romiley SK6 .... 113 A4
John St. Romiley SK6 .... 114 B3
John St. Royton OL2 .... 48 D4
John St. Sale M33 .... 108 B5
John St. Shaw OL2 .... 149 A5
John St. Stalybridge SK15 ...... 86 C5
John St. Stockport SK1 .... 169 F1
John St. Swinton M27 .... 80 A8
John St. 7 Tyldesley M29 ...... 59 A1
John St. Walkden M28 .... 60 D4
John St. Whitworth OL12 .... 4 D2
John St. 4 Wigan WN5 .... 54 D5
John St. Wigan WN1 .... 151 D8
John St E. OL7 .... 84 F1
John St W. OL7 .... 100 F8
John Steet. SK6 .... 113 C2
John William St.
Droylsden M11 .... 83 C1
John William St. Eccles M30 79 F2
John's Pl. SK6 .... 113 C2
Johnny King Cl. M40 .... 157 D5
Johns Cl. M21 .... 109 B8
Johnson Ave. Leigh WN2 ...... 56 E1
Johnson Ave.
Newton-l-W WA12 .... 89 B5
Johnson Ave. Oldham OL1 ..... 49 E5
Johnson Cl. WN7 .... 75 B4
Johnson Fold Ave. BL1 .... 23 E2
Johnson Fold Cty Prim Sch.
BL1 .... 23 F3
Johnson Gr. M24 .... 64 E8
Johnson St. Atherton WN7 ..... 58 A1
Johnson St. Bolton BL1 .... 145 F6
Johnson St. M'ster M3 .... 158 E3
Johnson St. M'ster M15 .... 162 D6
Johnson St. Radcliffe M26 ..... 44 B1
Johnson St. Salford M27 .... 80 D6
Johnson St. Tyldesley M29 .... 59 A1
Johnson St. 11 Wigan WN5 .. 54 B6
Johnson Terr. 23 SK16 .... 166 B1
Johnson's Sq. M10 & M40 . 160 D4
Johnsonbrook Rd. SK14 ..... 101 D5
Johnston. 21 OL12 .... 139 E8
Johnston Ave. OL15 .... 15 F3
Join Rd. M33 .... 108 D4
Joiner St. M'ster M5 .... 81 C1
Joiner St.
M'ster M1 & M4 & M60 .... 159 A1
Jolly Brows. BL2 .... 25 D3
Jolly Tar La. PR7 .... 20 B7
Jonas St. M'ster M9 .... 157 E8
Jonas St. M'ster M7 .... 158 E3
Jonathan Cl. BB4 .... 1 A8
Jones Sq. SK1 .... 170 F7
Jones St. Bolton BL1 .... 145 F8
Jones St. Hadfield SK14 .... 104 A5
Jones St. Horwich BL6 .... 22 B4
Jones St. Oldham OL2 .... 48 E2
Jones St. Oldham OL1 .... 67 A8
Jones St. R'dale OL16 .... 31 A6
Jones St. Radcliffe M26 .... 44 B4
Jones St. Salford M6 .... 154 F2
Jonquil Dr. M28 .... 59 F3
Jopson St. M24 .... 47 B1
Jordan Ave. OL2 .... 49 D8
Jordan St. Glossop SK13 ...... 104 E1
Jordan St. M'ster M15 .... 162 E7
Joseph Eastham High Sch.
M28 .... 60 B3
Joseph Jennings Ct. OL7 .... 85 A6
Joseph Johnson Mews.
Wythenshawe M22 .... 109 E1
Joseph St. Eccles M30 .... 79 B1
Joseph St. Failsworth M35 ...... 83 F8
Joseph St. 1 Farnworth BL4 42 D1
Joseph St. Littleborough OL15 16 B6
Joseph St. Marple SK6 .... 126 A6
Joseph St. Middleton M24 ...... 46 F1
Joseph St. R'dale OL12 .... 14 D2
Joseph St. Radcliffe M26 .... 44 B2
Josephine Dr. M27 .... 80 A7
Joshua La. M24 .... 65 D7
Josslyn Rd. M5 .... 154 D3
Joule Cl. M5 .... 161 A8
Joule St. M9 .... 64 E1
Joules Ct. 2 SK1 .... 170 F8
Jowett St. Oldham OL1 .... 49 C1
Jowett St. Reddish SK5 .... 169 F4
Jowett's Wlk. OL7 .... 84 F2
Jowkin La. OL11 .... 29 D6
Joy Pl. OL12 .... 14 F2
Joy St. R'dale OL12 .... 14 F2
Joy St. Ramsbottom BL0 ...... 138 B6
Joyce St. M40 .... 83 B7
Joynson Ave. M7 .... 158 D4
Joynson St. M33 .... 108 B5
Jubilee. OL16 .... 32 C2
Jubilee Ave. Orrell WN5 .... 53 D4
Jubilee Ave. Radcliffe M26 ..... 44 C1
Jubilee Ave. Stalybridge SK16 85 E1
Jubilee Cl. M30 .... 79 D3
Jubilee Cotts. M28 .... 60 C3
Jubilee Ct. M'ster M16 .... 97 B4
Jubilee Ct. Reddish SK5 .... 99 F2
Jubilee House. BL1 .... 145 E6
Jubilee Rd. M24 .... 47 B1
Jubilee St. Bolton BL3 .... 146 C3
Jubilee St. Salford M6 .... 154 F2
Jubilee St. Shaw OL2 .... 149 C6
Jubilee Terr. M24 .... 47 B2
Jubilee Way. BL9 .... 140 D2
Judith St. OL12 .... 14 C3
Judson Ave. M21 .... 109 C6
Judy St. M9 .... 157 F8
Julia Mews. 4 BL6 .... 22 B4
Julia St. Horwich BL6 .... 22 B4
Julia St. M'ster M3 .... 158 F3
Julia St. R'dale OL12 .... 139 E8
Julian House. OL1 .... 153 F7
Julius St. M19 .... 111 B8
Jumbles Ctry Park. BL7 .... 9 D2
Junction Alley. OL16 .... 139 F7
Junction La. WA12 .... 89 B3
Junction Rd. Bolton BL3 .... 40 F5
Junction Rd. Bolton BL3 .... 144 A5
Junction Rd.Dukinfield SK14 101 C5
Junction Rd.
Stockport SK1 & SK2 .... 170 F7
Junction Rd W. BL3 & BL6 .... 40 D5
Junction St. Middleton M24 .... 65 D6
Junction St. Oldham OL8 .... 66 E4
Junction Terr. WN3 .... 151 E6
Junction View. M34 .... 100 E8
June Ave. Leigh WN7 .... 75 C6
June Ave. Stockport SK4 ...... 168 B2
June St. OL7 .... 166 A2
Juniper Bank. SK5 .... 112 A8
Juniper Cl. OL4 .... 49 F4
Juniper Dr. Hindley WN2 .... 57 A3
Juniper Dr. Milnrow OL16 .... 31 D7
Jupiter Gr. WN3 .... 54 E2
Jupiter Wlk. M40 .... 83 A5
Jura Cl. SK16 .... 101 D8
Jura Dr. M41 .... 95 E5
Jurby Ave. M9 .... 64 D4
Jury St. Leigh WN7 .... 75 E7
Jury St. M'ster M8 .... 158 F4
Justin Cl. M13 .... 163 B7
Jutland Ave. OL11 .... 30 C8
Jutland Gr. BL5 .... 39 F1
Jutland St. M1 .... 159 B1

Kale St. M13 .... 163 B7
Kalima Gr. M7 .... 155 D6
Kane Ct. WA3 .... 75 A1
Kansas Ave. M5 .... 96 E8
Kara St. M6 .... 154 E2
Karen Rd. WN1 .... 151 F8
Kaskenmoor Sch. OL8 .... 66 B1
Kate St. BL0 .... 138 B6
Kathan Cl. OL16 .... 31 B7
Katherine Ct. M16 .... 161 C5
Katherine Rd. SK2 .... 124 C5
Katherine St. OL6 & OL7 ..... 166 A2
Kathkin Ave. M8 .... 64 B2
Kathleen Gr. M14 .... 98 D2
Kathleen St. OL12 .... 139 D7
Kay Ave. SK6 .... 112 D3
Kay Brow. Heywood OL10 ...... 29 B2
Kay Brow. Ramsbottom BL0 . 138 C6
Kay Cl. WN1 .... 151 D8
Kay Garden Sh Ctr. BL9 ..... 140 E2
Kay St. Atherton M46 .... 58 D2
Kay St. Bolton BL1 .... 145 F8
Kay St. Bury BL9 .... 141 A3
Kay St. Edgworth BL7 .... 9 C4
Kay St. Heywood OL10 .... 29 C2
Kay St. Little Lever BL3 .... 43 A3
Kay St. M'ster M12 .... 164 F7
Kay St. R'dale OL11 .... 139 E5
Kay St. Ramsbottom BL0 & BL9 11 C3
Kay St. Salford M6 .... 80 F6
Kay St. 16 Stalybridge SK15 .... 86 A1
Kay St. Stalybridge SK15 ...... 102 A8
Kay's Ave. SK1 .... 112 B1
Kaye Ave. WA3 .... 91 F3
Kayfields. BL2 .... 25 E4
Kayley Ind Est. OL7 .... 84 F3
Kays Gdns. M3 .... 158 D2
Kays Wood Rd. SK6 .... 125 D6
Keadby Cl. M30 .... 95 D8
Keal Dr. M44 .... 94 B4
Kean Pl. M30 .... 79 D1
Keane Cl. M29 .... 58 F1
Keane St. OL7 .... 166 A3
Kearsley Dr. BL3 .... 42 B3
Kearsley Hall Rd. M26 .... 61 C7
Kearsley Mount Sh Prec.
BL4 .... 61 B6
Kearsley Rd. Kearsley M26 .... 61 D8
Kearsley Rd. M'ster M8 .... 64 A2
Kearsley St. Eccles M30 .... 79 B2
Kearsley St. Leigh WN7 .... 75 D5
Kearsley St. Wigan WN6 .... 37 B1
Kearsley Sta. BL4 .... 61 A7
Kearsley Vale. M26 .... 61 B8
Kearsley West Cty Prim Sch.
BL4 .... 60 E7
Kearton Dr. M30 & M5 .... 80 A1
Keary Cl. M18 .... 99 D6
Keaton Cl. M6 .... 154 E4
Keats Ave. Denton M34 .... 113 A8
Keats Ave. Droylsden M43 ..... 84 A2
Keats Ave. Orrell WN5 .... 53 D1
Keats Ave. R'dale OL12 .... 14 A1
Keats Ave. Wigan WN6 .... 36 E3
Keats Ave. Wigan WN3 .... 150 B5
Keats Cl. M46 .... 58 E5
Keats Cres. M26 .... 43 E4
Keats Fold. SK16 .... 102 B7
Keats Rd. Eccles M30 .... 79 D1
Keats Rd. Oldham OL1 .... 49 B1
Keats Rd. Ramsbottom BL8 ..... 10 F2
Keats St. WN7 .... 75 D7
Keats Way. 7 Abram WN2 ..... 56 B1
Keats Wlk. 2 BL1 .... 143 E2
Keb La. OL8 .... 85 A8
Keble Ave. OL8 .... 66 E3
Keble Gr. WN7 .... 75 C8
Keble St. WN2 .... 151 F7
Kedington Cl. 8 M40 .... 156 C5
Kedleston Ave. M14 .... 98 E4
Kedleston Gn. SK2 .... 124 D7
Kedleston Wlk. M34 .... 100 F1
Keele Wlk. 4 M10 & M40 .. 159 C3
Keeley Cl. M40 .... 83 C4
Keepers Dr. OL12 .... 13 E2
Keighley Ave. M43 .... 84 A3
Keighley Cl. BL8 .... 26 F2
Keighley St. BL1 .... 142 C2
Keilder Mews. BL1 .... 144 A7
Keilder Sq. M6 .... 154 F1
Keith Dr. SK3 .... 123 B7
Keith Wlk. M40 .... 160 D3
Kelboro Ave. M34 .... 100 D7
Kelbrook Ct. SK2 .... 124 E5
Kelbrook Rd. M11 & M40 .... 165 B8
Kelby Ave. M23 .... 121 B7
Keld Cl. BL8 .... 27 B5
Keld Wlk. M18 .... 165 C5
Kelday Wlk. M8 .... 156 C6
Kelfield Ave. M23 .... 109 A2
Kellbank Rd. WN3 .... 54 E3
Kellbrook Cres. M'ster M7 ..... 63 B1
Kellbrook Cres. M'ster M7 ..... 81 A8
Kellet Wlk. M11 .... 83 B2
Kellett Cl. WN5 .... 36 D1
Kellett St. 4 Bolton BL7 .... 24 F6
Kellett St. R'dale OL16 .... 31 B8
Kelling Wlk. M15 .... 162 D7
Kelmarsh Cl. 7 M11 .... 99 D7
Kelsall Cres. SK3 .... 170 D6
Kelsall Dr. Alt'ham WA15 ..... 120 C6
Kelsall Dr. Droylsden M43 ..... 83 F3
Kelsall Rd. SK8 .... 123 A5
Kelsall St. M'ster M12 .... 164 F6
Kelsall St. Oldham OL9 .... 153 D6
Kelsall St. R'dale OL16 .... 139 F8
Kelsall St. Sale M33 .... 108 B4
Kelsall Way. 6 SK9 .... 131 D5
Kelsey Wlk. M9 .... 64 B5
Kelso Cl. OL8 .... 66 F1
Kelson Ave. OL7 .... 166 A4
Kelstern Ave. M13 .... 98 E3
Kelstern Sq. M13 .... 98 E3
Kelverlow St. OL4 .... 67 C6
Kelvin Ave. Middleton M24 ..... 64 B6
Kelvin Ave. Sale M33 .... 108 B4
Kelvin Cl. WN4 .... 72 D4
Kelvin Gr. M'ster M7 & M8 .. 156 A6
Kelvin Gr. Wigan WN3 .... 54 F4
Kelvin St. Ashton-u-L OL7 .... 100 F8
Kelvin St. M'ster M4 .... 159 A2
Kelvindale Dr. WA15 .... 120 C7
Kelvington Dr. M9 .... 157 D6
Kelway Terr. WN1 .... 37 D1
Kelwood Ave. BL9 .... 28 D5
Kemball. 3 M30 .... 79 F2
Kemble Ave. M23 .... 109 C1
Kemble Cl. BL6 .... 22 B5
Kemmel Ave. M22 .... 121 E5
Kemnay Wlk. 11 M11 .... 83 C1
Kemp Rd. SK6 .... 126 C7
Kemp St. Hyde SK14 .... 167 E4
Kemp St. Middleton M24 .... 64 F8
Kempley Cl. M12 .... 164 F6
Kempnough Hall Rd. M28 ..... 78 F7
Kempsey Ct. OL9 .... 152 B7
Kempsey St. OL9 .... 152 B7
Kempsey Wlk. M40 .... 65 D1
Kempster St. M5 & M7 .... 158 D4
Kempston Gdns. 25 BL1 ...... 143 E2
Kempton Ave. Little Lever BL3 43 A2
Kempton Ave. Sale M33 .... 107 D3
Kempton Cl. Droylsden M43 .. 84 C2
Kempton Cl.
Hazel Grove SK7 .... 125 A1
Kempton Cl.
Newton-l-W WA12 .... 89 D5
Kempton Rd. M19 .... 111 A8
Kempton Way. OL9 .... 152 C7
Kemsing Wlk. 1 M5 .... 81 A1
Kenchester Ave. M11 .... 99 D8
Kendal Ave. Ashton-u-L OL7 .. 84 F4
Kendal Ave. Denton M34 ...... 101 A1
Kendal Ave. Dukinfield SK14 101 C5
Kendal Ave. R'dale OL12 .... 13 E2
Kendal Ave. Sale M33 .... 108 C3
Kendal Ave. Urmston M41 ...... 94 E4
Kendal Cl. Alt'ham WA15 ...... 120 D5
Kendal Cl. Heywood OL10 ...... 46 E8
Kendal Dr. Bramhall SK7 ..... 132 C5
Kendal Dr. Bury BL9 .... 44 D7
Kendal Dr. Gatley SK8 .... 122 C4
Kendal Dr. Shaw OL2 .... 49 D7
Kendal Gdns. SK6 .... 113 B4
Kendal Gr. Ashton-i-M WN4 ... 73 B4
Kendal Gr. Leigh WN7 .... 75 D5
Kendal Gr. Walkden M28 .... 60 F2
Kendal Gr. Whitefield M45 ...... 62 F8
Kendal Rd. Bolton BL1 .... 144 C8
Kendal Rd. Boothstown M28 .. 77 E7
Kendal Rd. Hindley WN2 .... 56 E5
Kendal Rd. Ince-i-M WN2 .... 56 A7
Kendal Rd. Pendlebury M6 ..... 80 C5
Kendal Rd. Ramsbottom BL0 ... 11 A2
Kendal Rd. Stretford M32 .... 96 D3
Kendal Rd W.
Ramsbottom BL0 .... 10 F2
Kendal St. WN6 .... 150 B8
Kendal Terr. 4 SK16 .... 166 C1
Kendal Wlk. M24 .... 46 E1
Kendall Rd. M9 .... 63 F3
Kendon Gr. M34 .... 100 E3
Kendon Wlk. M8 .... 155 E5
Kendrew Rd. BL3 .... 146 A4
Kendrew Wlk. M9 .... 64 E1
Kendrick Pl. WN1 .... 151 E8
Kenford Wlk. M7 .... 155 F6
Kenhall Rd. WN7 .... 76 C4
Kenilworth. 1 OL11 .... 139 E6
Kenilworth Ave.
Chadderton OL9 .... 47 E1
Kenilworth Ave.
Cheadle SK8 .... 123 A3
Kenilworth Ave.
Handforth SK9 .... 131 D3
Kenilworth Ave. M'ster M20 109 F5
Kenilworth Ave. Swinton M27 62 B3
Kenilworth Ave.
Whitefield M45 .... 63 A7
Kenilworth Cl. Marple SK6 .. 125 F8
Kenilworth Cl. Oldham OL4 ... 67 F5
Kenilworth Cl. Radcliffe M26 43 F6
Kenilworth Dr.
Hazel Grove SK7 .... 133 D8
Kenilworth Dr. Hindley WN2 . 56 F4
Kenilworth Dr. Leigh WN7 .... 76 E7
Kenilworth Gdns. WA12 .... 89 C1
Kenilworth Gr. M34 .... 100 C8
Kenilworth Rd. Cheadle SK3 122 F7
Kenilworth Rd. Golborne WA3 90 E7
Kenilworth Rd.
Royton OL11 & OL16 .... 48 C8
Kenilworth Rd. Sale M33 .... 107 E4
Kenilworth Rd. Urmston M41 94 C2
Kenilworth Sq. BL1 .... 142 B1
Kenion Rd. OL11 .... 30 B6
Kenion St. OL16 .... 139 F7
Kenley Wlk. M8 .... 156 C6
Kenmay Ave. BL3 .... 40 F6
Kenmere Gr. M40 .... 65 B1
Kenmor Ave. BL8 .... 27 A1
Kenmore Cl. M45 .... 63 B8
Kenmore Dr. WA15 .... 120 B3
Kenmore Gr. Garswood WN4 72 D4
Kenmore Gr. Irlam M44 .... 105 D6
Kenmore Rd. Sale M33 .... 107 C1
Kenmore Rd. Whitefield M45 63 B8
Kenmore Rd.
Wythenshawe M22 .... 121 D7
Kenmore Way. M45 .... 63 B8
Kennard Cl. M9 .... 64 F1
Kennard Pl. WA14 .... 119 E6
Kennedy Cl. Standish WN6 .... 36 F8
Kennedy Dr. Little Lever BL3 . 43 C3
Kennedy Dr.
Whitefield BL9 & M45 .... 45 B2
Kennedy Rd. Salford M5 .... 80 C2
Kennedy Rd. Tyldesley M29 .... 77 D6
Kennedy St. Bolton BL2 .... 148 C7
Kennedy St. M'ster M2 .... 158 F1
Kennedy St. Oldham OL8 ..... 153 E5
Kennedy Way. Denton M34 100 D2
Kennedy Way. Stockport SK4168 C2
Kennerley Ct. SK2 .... 124 A5
Kennerley Lodge. SK3 .... 170 F5
Kennerley Rd. SK2 .... 124 A5
Kennerley's La. SK9 .... 137 A7
Kennet Cl. BL5 .... 39 E1
Kennet Way. WN7 .... 75 F7
Kenneth Ave. WN7 .... 75 D6
Kenneth Collis Ct. M22 .... 121 C3
Kenneth Gr. WN7 .... 75 D6
Kenneth Sq. M7 .... 155 E6
Kennett Rd. M22 & M23 ...... 121 A3
Kenninghall Rd. M22 .... 121 D3
Kennington Ave. M40 .... 83 B4
Kennington Fold. BL3 .... 147 D3
Kenside Wlk. 2 M16 .... 97 F3
Kensington Ave.
Ashton-u-L OL6 .... 85 E4
Kensington Ave.
Chadderton OL9 .... 65 E8
Kensington Ave. 2
Hyde SK14 .... 167 E1
Kensington Ave. M'ster M14 98 D4
Kensington Ave.
Radcliffe M26 .... 43 D4
Kensington Ave. Royton OL2 48 C6
Kensington Cl. Milnrow OL16 32 A6
Kensington Cl.
Ramsbottom BL8 .... 11 A1
Kensington Ct. 1
Hyde SK14 .... 167 E1
Kensington Ct. M'ster M7 ..... 81 C8
Kensington Ct. Reddish M34 100 B4
Kensington Ct.
Wilmslow SK9 .... 137 A6
Kensington Dr. Bury BL8 ...... 44 A8
Kensington Dr. Horwich BL6 . 22 D3
Kensington Dr. Leigh WN7 ..... 76 E7
Kensington Dr. Salford M5 .. 154 D3
Kensington Gdns.
Alt'ham WA15 .... 119 F1
Kensington Gdns.
Hyde SK14 .... 167 F1
Kensington Gr. Reddish M34 100 B4
Kensington Gr. Sale WA14 .. 119 E8
Kensington Gr. 14
Stalybridge SK15 .... 86 A1
Kensington Rd.
Failsworth M35 .... 84 B8
Kensington Rd. M'ster M21 .. 97 B2
Kensington Rd. Oldham OL8 . 66 D4
Kensington Rd.
Stockport SK3 .... 123 B7
Kensington Rd. 3
Wigan WN5 .... 54 D5
Kensington St. Bolton BL1 . 145 E7
Kensington St. Hyde SK14 .. 167 E1
Kensington St. M'ster M14 ... 98 A3
Kensington St. R'dale OL11 .. 30 E5
Kenslow Ave. M8 .... 63 F2
Kensworth Cl. Alt'ham M23 120 D6
Kensworth Cl. Bolton BL1 .... 143 D1
Kensworth Dr. BL1 .... 143 D1
Kent Ave. Cheadle SK8 .... 123 C5
Kent Ave. Droylsden M43 ...... 83 E1
Kent Ave. Oldham OL9 .... 152 B6
Kent Ave. Platt Bridge WN2 ... 56 A2
Kent Cl. Diggle OL3 .... 51 C4
Kent Cl. Walkden M28 .... 60 B2
Kent Ct. Bolton BL1 .... 145 E8
Kent Ct. M'ster M14 .... 98 C3
Kent Dr. Bury BL9 .... 45 A8
Kent Dr. Kearsley BL4 .... 61 B6
Kent Rd. Atherton M46 .... 58 C4
Kent Rd. Failsworth M35 .... 83 E8
Kent Rd. Glossop SK13 .... 104 D1
Kent Rd. Irlam M44 .... 105 C5
Kent Rd. Partington M31 ...... 105 E2
Kent Rd. Reddish M34 .... 100 A2
Kent Rd. Stockport SK3 .... 123 B8
Kent Rd. Tyldesley M29 .... 59 A2
Kent Rd E. M14 .... 98 D3
Kent Rd W. M14 .... 98 D3
Kent St. Bolton BL1 .... 145 E8
Kent St. Leigh WN7 .... 76 E4
Kent St. M'ster M7 .... 158 D4
Kent St. 11 M'ster M2 .... 158 F1
Kent St. M'ster M1 .... 159 A1
Kent St. Oldham OL8 .... 66 F4
Kent St. R'dale OL11 .... 139 F6
Kent St. Swinton M27 .... 61 F2
Kent St. Wigan WN1 .... 151 D7
Kent Way. WA12 .... 89 B1
Kent Wlk. Haslingden BB4 .... 1 A8
Kent Wlk. Heywood OL10 .... 29 A1
Kentford Dr. M40 .... 159 C4
Kentford Gr. 6 BL4 .... 60 C8
Kentford Rd. BL1 .... 143 F1
Kentmere Ave. Billinge WA11 71 C1
Kentmere Ave. R'dale OL12 .. 15 B3
Kentmere Cl. SK8 .... 122 B3
Kentmere Ct. M9 .... 65 B4
Kentmere Dr. Middleton M24 46 E3
Kentmere Dr. Tyldesley M29 . 77 B7
Kentmere Gr. BL4 .... 59 F7
Kentmere Rd.
Alt'ham M23 & WA15 .... 120 D6
Kentmere Rd. Bolton BL2 ...... 25 F1
Kentmere Cl. SK4 .... 110 E2
Kenton Ave. M18 .... 99 C3
Kenton Cl. Bolton BL1 .... 143 D1
Kenton Cl. Denton M34 .... 100 D7
Kenton Rd. Shaw OL2 .... 48 F7
Kenton Rd. Shaw OL2 .... 149 A7
Kenton St. OL8 .... 67 B5
Kentsford Dr. BL3 .... 43 B5
Kentstone Ave. M19 & SK4 .. 110 E3
Kentucky St. OL4 .... 67 C6
Kentwell Cl. SK16 .... 101 B7
Kenwick Dr.M40 .... 65 E2
Kenwood Ave.Alt'ham WA15 119 F2
Kenwood Ave. Bramhall SK7 132 D5
Kenwood Ave. Gatley SK8 .. 122 A6
Kenwood Ave. Leigh WN7 ...... 76 C5
Kenwood Ave. M'ster M19 .. 110 F6
Kenwood Cl. Leigh WN7 .... 76 C4
Kenwood Cl. Stretford M32 .... 96 E2
Kenwood La. M28 .... 78 F5
Kenwood Rd. Bolton BL1 ..... 142 B3
Kenwood Rd. Oldham OL1 ...... 48 C1
Kenwood Rd. Reddish SK5 ..... 99 E2
Kenwood Rd. Stretford M32 .. 96 E1
Kenworthy Ave. OL6 .... 85 E5
Kenworthy Cl. SK14 .... 102 E2
Kenworthy La. M22 .... 109 D1
Kenworthy St. R'dale OL16 .... 31 C7
Kenworthy St. 3
Stalybridge SK15 .... 86 A1
Kenworthy St.
Stalybridge SK15 .... 102 A8
Kenworthy Terr. OL16 .... 31 C7
Kenwright St. M4 .... 159 A2
Kenwyn St. M10 & M40 .... 160 E3
Kenyon Ave. Dukinfield SK16 101 E7
Kenyon Ave. Oldham OL8 ...... 66 F3
Kenyon Ave. Sale M33 .... 108 E2
Kenyon Cl. SK14 .... 101 F5
Kenyon Fold. OL10 & OL11 ... 29 E5
Kenyon Gr. M38 .... 59 E4
Kenyon La. Culcheth WA3 ...... 91 A4
Kenyon La. M'ster M40 .... 83 A8
Kenyon La. Middleton M24 ..... 65 C8
Kenyon La. Prestwich M25 .... 63 C4
Kenyon Rd. Little Lever BL3 ... 43 B5
Kenyon Rd. Standish WN6 ...... 19 D2
Kenyon Rd. Wigan WN1 .... 37 C2
Kenyon St. Bacup OL13 .... 4 B8
Kenyon St. Bury BL9 .... 141 A3
Kenyon St. Droylsden M18 ..... 99 F6
Kenyon St. Dukinfield SK16 . 101 B8
Kenyon St. Heywood OL10 ..... 29 C2
Kenyon St. Leigh WN7 .... 75 D8
Kenyon St. Radcliffe M26 .... 44 B3
Kenyon St. Ramsbottom BL0 138 C6
Kenyon Terr. M38 .... 59 E3
Kenyon Way. Bury BL8 .... 26 F5
Kenyon Way. Walkden M38 .... 59 E4
Keppel Rd. M21 .... 97 B1
Keppel St. OL6 .... 166 C3
Kepwick Dr.
Wythenshawe M22 .... 121 E1
Kerans Dr. BL5 .... 39 E1
Kerenhappuch St. BL0 .... 138 B6
Kerfield Wlk. 13 M13 .... 163 B7
Kerfoot Cl. M22 .... 121 E8
Kerfoot St. WN7 .... 76 C4
Kermishaw Nook. M29 .... 77 B6
Kermoor Ave. BL1 .... 24 E6
Kerne Gr. M23 .... 109 A1
Kerr St. M9 .... 64 D3
Kerrera Dr. M5 & M6 .... 154 D1
Kerridge Dr. SK6 .... 112 F4
Kerridge Wlk. 1 M16 .... 97 F3
Kerrier Cl. M30 .... 80 A2
Kerry Gr. BL2 .... 148 B8
Kerry Wlk. M23 .... 120 F3
Kersal Ave. Pendlebury M27 .. 80 C8
Kersal Ave. Walkden M38 ...... 60 B4
Kersal Bank. M7 .... 81 C8
Kersal Bar. M7 .... 63 C1
Kersal Cl. M25 .... 63 A1
Kersal Crag. M25 & M7 .... 63 C1
Kersal Dr. WA15 .... 120 C7
Kersal Hall Ave. M7 .... 81 A8
Kersal High Sch. M7 .... 81 A8
Kersal Rd. M25 & M7 .... 63 A1
Kersal Vale Ct. M7 .... 81 A8
Kersal Vale Rd. M25 & M7 ..... 80 F8
Kersal Way. M7 .... 81 B7
Kersh Ave. M19 .... 111 B8
Kershaw Ave. Little Lever BL3 43 A4
Kershaw Ave. Prestwich M25 62 F2
Kershaw Ave. Sale M33 .... 108 E2
Kershaw Dr. OL9 .... 65 D3
Kershaw Gr. M34 .... 100 C8
Kershaw La. M34 .... 100 C8
Kershaw Rd. M35 .... 83 F7

Kershaw St. Bolton BL2 25 C5
Kershaw St. Bolton BL3 145 D5
Kershaw St. Bury BL9 141 A2
Kershaw St. Droylsden M43 83 F1
Kershaw St. Dukinfield OL7 100 F8
Kershaw St. Glossop SK13 116 C8
Kershaw St. Heywood OL10 29 B2
Kershaw St. 2 R'dale OL12 139 F8
Kershaw St. Royton OL2 48 D5
Kershaw St. Shaw OL2 149 B7
Kershaw St. Tyldesley M29 59 A1
Kershaw St. Wigan WN5 54 B6
Kershaw St E. OL2 149 B7
Kershaw Way. WA12 89 C5
Kershaw Wlk. M12 164 D6
Kershope Gr. M5 161 A8
Kersley St. OL4 67 B6
Kerswell Wlk. M40 83 A6
Kerwin Wlk. M11 165 A8
Kerwood Dr. OL2 48 E3
Kesteven Rd. M8 & M9 155 F7
Keston Ave. Droylsden M43 83 E1
Keston Ave. M'ster M9 65 A3
Keston Cres. SK5 112 B6
Keston Rd. 4 OL1 49 C1
Kestor St. BL2 148 D5
Kestrel Ave. Droylsden M34 84 C1
Kestrel Ave. Farnworth BL4 59 F7
Kestrel Ave. Oldham OL4 67 C5
Kestrel Ave. Swinton M27 62 B2
Kestrel Ave. Walkden M38 60 A5
Kestrel Cl. Marple SK6 126 A3
Kestrel Cl. Prestwich M25 63 B6
Kestrel Dr. Ashton-i-M WN4 73 C6
Kestrel Dr. Bury BL9 141 B4
Kestrel Dr. Irlam M44 94 A3
Kestrel Rd. M17 95 F8
Kestrel St. 3 BL1 148 A8
Kestrel Wlk. M12 165 A6
Keswick Ave. Ashton-u-L OL7 84 F5
Keswick Ave.
Chadderton OL9 152 A7
Keswick Ave. Denton M34 100 D4
Keswick Ave.
Dukinfield SK14 101 C4
Keswick Ave. Gatley SK8 122 B4
Keswick Ave. Oldham OL8 67 A3
Keswick Ave. Urmston M41 94 E1
Keswick Cl. Irlam M44 105 D4
Keswick Cl. M'ster M13 164 D5
Keswick Cl. Middleton M24 46 D2
Keswick Cl. Stalybridge SK15 86 A4
Keswick Ct. 3 M24 46 D2
Keswick Dr. Bramhall SK7 132 C5
Keswick Dr. Bury BL9 44 D7
Keswick Gr. M6 154 F2
Keswick Pl. WN2 56 A7
Keswick Rd. Alt'ham WA15 120 D6
Keswick Rd. High Lane SK6 134 E8
Keswick Rd. Reddish SK4 111 D7
Keswick Rd. Walkden M28 60 F2
Keswick St. Bolton BL1 143 F2
Keswick St. R'dale OL11 30 C2
Ketley Wlk. 1 M22 121 F3
Kettering Rd. M19 99 B2
Kettleshulme Way. SK12 134 A3
Kettleshulme Wlk. 4 SK9 131 E1
Kettlewell Wlk. M18 165 C5
Ketton Cl. M11 99 E7
Kevin Ave. OL2 48 E2
Kevin St. M19 111 B8
Kew Ave. SK14 167 E1
Kew Dr. Cheadle SK8 122 E2
Kew Dr. Urmston M41 95 A4
Kew Gdns. M40 65 A1
Kew Rd. Failsworth M35 84 A8
Kew Rd. Oldham OL4 67 C6
Kew Rd. R'dale OL11 31 A3
Key Ct. M34 113 A8
Key West Cl. M11 160 F1
Keyhaven Wlk. M40 157 D6
Keymer St. M11 160 E2
Keynsham Rd. M11 83 B3
Keystone Cl. M6 154 E4
Keyworth Wlk. M40 160 E4
Khartoum St. Droylsden M11 83 D2
Khartoum St. M'ster M16 97 D4
Kibbles Brow. BL7 25 B8
Kibboth Crew. BL0 138 B7
Kibworth Cl. M45 62 D8
Kibworth Wlk. 7 M9 64 E5
Kid St. 4 M24 46 F1
Kidacre Wlk. 2 M40 83 A7
Kidd Rd. SK13 116 E6
Kidderminster Way. OL9 47 F1
Kidwall Wlk. 9 M9 64 F1
Kiel Cl. M30 95 E8
Kilbride Ave. BL2 42 F6
Kilbuck La. WA11 89 A8
Kilburn Ave. Ashton-i-M WN4 73 D4
Kilburn Ave. M'ster M9 64 D5
Kilburn Cl. SK8 131 B7
Kilburn Cl. WN7 57 D1
Kilburn Dr. WN6 36 A7
Kilburn Gr. WN3 54 D3
Kilburn Rd.Orrell WN5 & WN8 53 C5
Kilburn Rd. Radcliffe M26 43 E4
Kilburn Rd. Stockport SK3 123 C7
Kilburn St. 5 OL1 & OL4 49 D1
Kildale Cl. BL3 40 E4
Kildare Cres. OL11 30 F2
Kildare Grange. WN2 56 C5
Kildare Rd. M'ster M21 109 D8
Kildare Rd. Swinton M27 79 E6
Kildare St. Farnworth BL4 60 C7
Kildare St. Hindley WN2 56 C5
Kildare St. Wigan WN5 54 F6
Kildonan Dr. BL3 40 F6
Killer St. BL0 138 C6
Killington Cl. WN3 55 B2
Killingworth Mews. BL6 22 D1
Killon St. BL9 141 A1
Kilmaine Dr. BL3 40 E5
Kilmarsh Wlk. 7 M8 155 F7
Kilmington Dr. M7 & M8 155 F6
Kilmory Dr. BL2 42 F6
Kiln Bank. OL12 4 C2
Kiln Bank La. OL12 4 C2
Kiln Brow. BL7 25 C8
Kiln Croft. SK6 112 F1
Kiln Croft La. SK9 131 E4
Kiln Field. BL7 24 F8
Kiln Hill Cl. OL1 47 F2
Kiln Hill La. OL1 47 F2
Kiln La. Hadfield SK14 104 A5
Kiln La. Milnrow OL16 31 F6
Kiln St. Little Lever BL3 43 A3
Kiln St. Ramsbottom BL0 138 B5
Kiln Terr. 5 OL13 3 D8
Kilner Cl. BL9 45 B4
Kilner Wlk. M40 159 C4
Kilnerdeyne Terr. OL16 139 E6
Kilnhurst Wlk. 12 BL1 145 D8
Kilnside Dr. M9 157 D7
Kilnsley Wlk. M18 165 C5
Kilnwick Cl. M18 99 B3
Kilphin The. BL6 40 B8
Kilrush Ave. M30 95 D8
Kilsby Cl. Bolton BL6 40 D6
Kilsby Cl. Farnworth BL4 42 C2
Kilsby Wlk. M40 160 D4
Kilshaw St. WN5 54 C5
Kilton Wlk. M40 159 C4
Kilvert Dr. M33 107 F5
Kilvert St. Stretford M17 96 F5
Kilworth Ave. M33 107 F3
Kilworth Dr. BL6 40 D6
Kilworth St. OL11 139 D5
Kimberley Ave. SK6 113 C2
Kimberley Pl. WN4 73 B3
Kimberley Rd. BL1 24 E5
Kimberley St. Bacup OL13 3 A7
Kimberley St. M'ster M7 155 E7
Kimberley St. Oldham OL8 66 C3
Kimberley St. Stockport SK3 170 E7
Kimberley Wlk. M15 162 D7
Kimberly St. WN6 37 A1
Kimble Cl. BL8 10 F2
Kimbolton Cl. M12 165 A6
Kinburn Rd. M19 & SK4 110 D2
Kinbury Wlk. M40 159 C4
Kincardine Rd. M13 163 B6
Kincraig Cl. Bolton BL3 40 E4
Kincraig Cl. M'ster M11 83 C1
Kinder Ave. Ashton-u-L OL6 86 A6
Kinder Ave. Oldham OL4 67 D5
Kinder Cl. SK13 116 A8
Kinder Ct. SK3 170 E7
Kinder Dr. SK6 126 A6
Kinder Fold. SK15 102 D6
Kinder Gr. Ashton-i-M WN4 72 F6
Kinder Gr. Romiley SK6 113 E2
Kinder House. M5 154 D3
Kinder Mews. OL3 69 B5
Kinder St. Stalybridge SK15 86 A2
Kinder St. Stockport SK3 170 E7
Kinder Way. Middleton M24 46 F2
Kinder Way.
Mottram-i-L SK14 102 F3
Kinders Cres. OL3 69 B5
Kinders La. OL3 69 B6
Kinderton Ave. M20 110 B7
Kineton Wlk. 12 M13 163 C6
King Albert St. OL2 149 B7
King Charles Ct. SK13 116 D7
King David High Sch. M8 63 F1
King David Jun & Inf Schs.
M8 63 F1
King Edward Ave. SK13 104 D1
King Edward Rd. SK14 113 E8
King Edward St. Eccles M30 79 C2
King Edward St. 4
M'ster M19 99 B1
King Edward St. Salford M5 161 B8
King Edward's Bldgs. M7 155 F8
King George Cl. WN4 73 B3
King George Rd. Hyde SK14 113 E8
King George Rd.
Newton-l-W WA11 89 A7
King La. Oldham OL1 49 E4
King La. Oldham OL1 49 E5
King Sq. OL9 153 E6
King St. 5 Bolton BL7 24 F8
King St. Bolton BL2 25 D5
King St. Bolton BL1 145 E7
King St. Delph OL3 50 F4
King St. Denton M34 100 F3
King St. Denton M34 100 F6
King St. Droylsden M43 100 A8
King St. Dukinfield SK16 101 C7
King St. Eccles M30 79 F1
King St. Failsworth M35 83 D6
King St. Farnworth BL4 60 D8
King St. Glossop SK13 116 C8
King St. Heywood OL10 29 D1
King St. Hindley WN2 56 D6
King St. Hollingworth SK14 103 D5
King St. Horwich BL6 22 A4
King St. Hyde SK14 167 D3
King St. Ince-i-M WN2 56 A7
King St. Leigh WN7 75 F4
King St. M'ster M7 155 E7
King St. M'ster M8 158 E2
King St. M'ster M2 158 F1
King St. Middleton M24 47 A1
King St. Mossley OL5 68 D1
King St. Mottram-i-L SK14 115 A8
King St. Newton-l-W WA12 89 B3
King St. Oldham OL9 153 E6
King St. R'dale OL16 139 F7
King St. Radcliffe M26 44 B2
King St. Ramsbottom BL0 138 C6
King St. Rawtenstall BB4 2 E8
King St. Salford M6 80 D5
King St. 8 Stalybridge SK15 86 A2
King St. Stretford M32 96 D1
King St. Westhoughton BL5 39 F1
King St. Whitworth OL12 4 D3
King St. Wigan WN1 150 C7
King St E. R'dale OL11 139 F6
King St E. Stockport SK1 169 F2
King St S. OL11 139 E5
King St W. M'ster M3 158 F1
King St W. Wigan WN1 150 C8
King William Ent Pk. M5 161 A8
King William St. Salford M5 161 A8
King William St.
Tyldesley M29 76 F8
King William St.Worsley M28 79 A3
King's Ave. WA3 90 F7
King's Cl. Droylsden M18 99 F6
King's Cl. Stockport SK7 123 F2
King's Cres. M46 76 E8
King's Dr. M'ster SK4 168 A3
King's Dr. Marple SK6 125 E7
King's Dr. Middleton M24 64 D8
King's Gdns. WN7 76 C5
King's Lynn Cl. 5 M20 110 B3
King's Rd. Ashton-i-M WN4 73 A5
King's Rd. Ashton-u-L OL6 85 E5
King's Rd. M'ster M25 63 C2
King's Rd. Oldham OL8 153 F5
King's Rd. R'dale OL16 31 B5
King's Rd. Reddish M34 100 B6
King's Rd. Romiley SK6 113 A3
King's Rd. Wilmslow SK9 136 E3
King's Terr. 14 SK16 166 B1
King's Wlk. OL6 85 D5
Kingcombe Wlk. 12 M9 157 E7
Kingfisher Ave. M34 84 C1
Kingfisher Cl. M12 164 E5
Kingfisher Ct.
Ashton-i-M WN4 73 B6
Kingfisher Ct. R'dale OL12 15 C4
Kingfisher Dr. Bury BL9 141 B4
Kingfisher Dr. Farnworth BL4 59 F7
Kingfisher Mews. SK6 126 A6
Kingfisher Rd. SK2 124 F5
Kingham Dr. M4 159 C2
Kingholm Gdns. BL1 143 D1
Kingmoor Ave. M26 44 B4
Kings Acre. WA14 119 A1
Kings Ave. Gatley SK8 122 A4
Kings Ave. M'ster M8 156 B8
Kings Ave. Whitefield M45 44 E2
Kings Cl. Prestwich M25 63 C5
Kings Cl. Wilmslow SK9 137 A6
Kings Cres. M16 97 B3
Kings Ct. Stockport SK5 169 F3
Kings Ct. 11 Tyldesley M29 58 F1
Kings Dr. SK8 123 A3
Kings Gr. R'dale OL12 15 C4
Kings Gr. Stretford M32 96 F3
Kings La. M16 & M32 96 F3
Kings Rd. Cheadle SK8 123 A3
Kings Rd. Failsworth OL9 65 E3
Kings Rd. Golborne WA3 90 A7
Kings Rd. Hazel Grove SK7 124 E3
Kings Rd. Irlam M44 105 E6
Kings Rd. M'ster M16 & M32 97 B3
Kings Rd. M'ster M16 & M21 109 D8
Kings Rd. Sale M33 107 F4
Kings Rd. Shaw OL2 149 A6
Kings Rd. Stretford M32 96 E2
Kings Road Prim Sch. M16 97 A3
Kings Terr. M32 96 F3
Kings Wlk. M43 100 A8
Kingsbridge Ave.
Ainsworth BL2 26 D1
Kingsbridge Ave.
Hattersley SK14 102 C2
Kingsbridge Cl. SK6 125 E7
Kingsbridge Ct. M9 157 D7
Kingsbridge Dr. SK16 101 B7
Kingsbridge Rd.
M'ster M8 & M9 157 D7
Kingsbridge Rd. 5
Oldham OL8 67 B5
Kingsbridge Wlk. SK14 102 C2
Kingsbrook Ct. M21 109 E8
Kingsbrook Rd. M16 & M21 109 E8
Kingsbury Ave. BL1 142 A1
Kingsbury Ct. BL1 142 A1
Kingsbury Rd. M11 83 C2
Kingscliffe St. M9 157 E8
Kingscourt Ave. BL1 142 C2
Kingscroft Ct. WN1 151 D7
Kingsdale Rd. M18 & M34 100 A4
Kingsdown Cres. WN1 37 C4
Kingsdown Dr. BL1 143 F1
Kingsdown Gdns. 8 BL1 143 F1
Kingsdown Rd. Abram WN2 74 B7
Kingsdown Rd.
Wythenshawe M22 121 C1
Kingsdown Wlk. SK5 112 B5
Kingsfield Dr. M20 110 C2
Kingsfield Way. M29 77 B8
Kingsfold Ave. M40 159 C4
Kingsfold Cl. BL2 42 E6
Kingsford St. M5 154 D2
Kingsgate. BL1 145 E7
Kingsgate Rd. M22 121 C1
Kingshill Ct. WN6 36 F7
Kingshill Rd. M21 109 A8
Kingsholme Rd. M22 121 C2
Kingsland Cl. M10 & M40 160 D3
Kingsland Rd. Cheadle SK3 123 A7
Kingsland Rd. Farnworth BL4 42 A1
Kingsland Rd. R'dale OL11 30 B3
Kingslea. PR7 20 F8
Kingslea Rd. M20 110 C5
Kingsleigh Rd. SK4 110 F4
Kingsley Ave. Handforth SK9 131 C2
Kingsley Ave. M'ster M7 81 B7
Kingsley Ave. M'ster M9 157 F7
Kingsley Ave. Reddish SK4 169 E4
Kingsley Ave. Stretford M32 96 F3
Kingsley Ave. Urmston M41 95 B2
Kingsley Ave. Whitefield M45 63 B8
Kingsley Ave. Wigan WN3 54 F3
Kingsley Cl. Ashton-u-L OL6 86 A5
Kingsley Cl. Denton M34 100 D1
Kingsley Dr. Cheadle SK8 123 A3
Kingsley Dr. Oldham OL4 67 E7
Kingsley Gr. M34 100 C8
Kingsley Rd. Alt'ham WA15 120 B7
Kingsley Rd. Hindley WN2 56 F5
Kingsley Rd. Middleton M24 47 B2
Kingsley Rd. Oldham OL4 67 C6
Kingsley Rd. Swinton M27 61 D1
Kingsley Rd. Walkden M28 60 C4
Kingsley Rd.
Wythenshawe M22 121 D8
Kingsley St. Bolton BL1 143 D2
Kingsley St. Bury BL8 27 B2
Kingsley St. Leigh WN7 75 C7
Kingsmead Mews. M9 64 C5
Kingsmede. WN1 37 D3
Kingsmere Ave. M19 98 F1
Kingsmill Ave. M19 111 B8
Kingsmoor Fields. SK13 104 D3
Kingsmoor Rd. SK13 104 D2
Kingsneath Ave. M11 83 B3
Kingsnorth Cl. 5 BL1 143 F1
Kingsnorth Rd. M41 94 E4
Kingsoak Cl. WN1 151 D8
Kingston Arc. 6 SK14 102 E2
Kingston Ave. Bolton BL2 25 C1
Kingston Ave. M'ster M20 110 B1
Kingston Ave. 5 Oldham OL1 49 B1
Kingston Ave. Oldham OL9 66 A4
Kingston Cl. Hattersley SK14 102 E2
Kingston Cl. M'ster M7 155 D8
Kingston Cl. Shaw OL2 149 B8
Kingston Cl. Wigan WN3 55 B3
Kingston Cres. BB4 1 A7
Kingston Dr. Royton OL2 48 C6
Kingston Dr. Sale M33 108 D5
Kingston Dr. Urmston M41 107 B8
Kingston Gdns. SK14 101 B3
Kingston Gr. M9 64 F4
Kingston Hill. SK8 122 D4
Kingston Pl. SK8 122 E2
Kingston Rd. Failsworth M35 84 B7
Kingston Rd. Handforth SK9 131 D5
Kingston Rd. M'ster M20 110 B1
Kingston Rd. Radcliffe BL9 44 C6
Kingston St. SK3 169 D1
Kingsway. Alt'ham WA14 119 D5
Kingsway. Bredbury SK6 112 E3
Kingsway.
Cheadle M20 & SK8 122 C6
Kingsway. Dukinfield SK16 101 E7
Kingsway. Ince-i-M WN2 151 F7
Kingsway. Kearsley BL4 60 F6
Kingsway. M'ster M19 98 F1
Kingsway. M'ster M19 110 D4
Kingsway. Middleton M24 65 B6
Kingsway. Newton-l-W WA12 89 C2
Kingsway. Pendlebury M27 80 C6
Kingsway. R'dale OL11 & OL16 31 C5
Kingsway. Stockport SK7 123 F2
Kingsway. Stretford M32 96 C1
Kingsway. Walkden M28 78 D8
Kingsway. Wigan WN1 37 D2
Kingsway Ave. M19 98 F1
Kingsway Bldgs. M19 110 E5
Kingsway Cl. OL8 153 E5
Kingsway Cres. M19 110 E5
Kingsway Pk. M41 95 D4
Kingsway Prim Sch. M41 95 E4
Kingsway Sch. SK8 122 C4
Kingswear Dr. BL1 142 C1
Kingswood. SK12 133 E4
Kingswood Gr. SK5 99 F1
Kingswood Rd.
M'ster M14 & M19 110 E8
Kingswood Rd.Middleton M24 46 F3
Kingswood Rd.
Prestwich M25 62 F5
Kingswood Rd. Swinton M28 79 B4
Kingthorpe Gdns. BL1 147 F4
Kingwood Ave. BL1 40 F8
Kingwood Cres. WN5 54 D6
Kinlet Rd. WN3 54 C4
Kinlett Wlk. 11 M40 65 D2
Kinley Cl. M12 164 F6
Kinloch Dr. BL1 144 B7
Kinloch St. M'ster M11 83 A2
Kinloch St. Oldham OL8 67 A4
Kinmel Ave. SK5 112 C4
Kinmel Wlk. 4 M23 120 F6
Kinmount Wlk. M9 157 D6
Kinnaird Cres. SK1 124 B8
Kinnaird Rd. M20 110 C5
Kinnerly Gr. M28 60 A1
Kinniside Cl. WN3 55 A2
Kinross Ave. Garswood WN4 72 C4
Kinross Ave.
Stockport SK2 & SK7 124 A3
Kinross Dr. BL3 40 F5
Kinross Rd. M14 98 E3
Kinsale Wlk. M23 120 F3
Kinsey Ave. M23 120 F7
Kinsley Dr. M28 60 C2
Kintbury St. WN2 73 F7
Kintore Ave. SK7 124 F3
Kintore Wlk. 5 M40 156 C5
Kintyre Ave. M5 154 E1
Kintyre Cl. 5 M11 83 C1
Kintyre Dr. BL3 40 E5
Kinver Cl. BL3 146 C3
Kinver Rd. M40 65 C2
Kipling Ave. Denton M34 113 A7
Kipling Ave. Droylsden M43 84 A3
Kipling Ave. Wigan WN3 55 A4
Kipling Cl. SK2 124 E7
Kipling Gr. WN7 75 D7
Kipling Rd. OL1 49 B2
Kipling St. M7 155 D6
Kippax St. M14 98 B3
Kirby Ave. Atherton M46 58 C5
Kirby Ave. Failsworth OL9 65 D3
Kirby Ave. Swinton M27 79 D5
Kirby Rd. WN7 75 E5
Kirby Wlk. 6 M'ster M4 159 C2
Kirby Wlk. Shaw OL2 149 B8
Kirk Rd. M19 111 B7
Kirk St. M18 99 D5
Kirkbank St. Oldham OL9 153 D7
Kirkbank St. Oldham OL9 153 D8
Kirkbeck. WN7 76 C3
Kirkburn View. BL8 27 C5
Kirkby Ave. Failsworth M40 83 B7
Kirkby Ave. Sale M33 108 C2
Kirkby Cl. BL9 44 E7
Kirkby Dr. M33 108 D2
Kirkby Rd. Bolton BL1 144 B8
Kirkby Rd. Culcheth WA3 91 F3
Kirkdale Ave. M40 65 D2
Kirkdale Dr. OL2 48 C5
Kirkdale Gdns. WN8 53 A7
Kirkebrok Rd. BL3 146 A4
Kirkfell Dr. High Lane SK6 134 E8
Kirkfell Dr. Tyldesley M29 77 B7
Kirkfell Wlk. OL1 48 F1
Kirkgate Cl. 8 M10 & M40 159 C3
Kirkhall La. Bolton BL1 144 C8
Kirkhall La. Leigh WN7 75 F6
Kirkhall Wkshp The. BL1 144 C8
Kirkham Ave. Golborne WA3 90 E6
Kirkham Ave. M'ster M18 99 D6
Kirkham Cl. M34 100 F3
Kirkham Rd. Gatley SK8 131 C8
Kirkham Rd. Leigh WN7 75 D2
Kirkham St. Abram WN2 74 B8
Kirkham St. Bolton BL2 25 C1
Kirkham St. Oldham OL9 153 E7
Kirkham St. Salford M5 154 E1
Kirkham St. Walkden M38 60 A5
Kirkhaven Sq. M10 & M40 160 E4
Kirkhill Wlk. 12 M40 65 D2
Kirkholt Wlk. 11 M9 64 E3
Kirkhope Dr. BL1 143 D1
Kirkhope Wlk. BL1 143 D1
Kirklands. Bolton BL2 25 D2
Kirklands. Sale M33 108 A2
Kirklee Ave. OL9 48 A1
Kirklee Rd. OL11 30 D2
Kirklees St. Bury BL8 26 F7
Kirklees St. Wigan WN1 151 E8
Kirklees Wlk. M45 63 B8
Kirkless La. WN2 38 B1
Kirkless St. WN2 38 A3
Kirkless Villas. WN2 38 A2
Kirkley St. SK14 167 E1
Kirklinton Dr. M9 157 D6
Kirkman Ave. M30 95 C8
Kirkman Cl. M18 99 D4
Kirkman St. BL9 44 F3
Kirkmanshulme La.
M'ster M12 164 F4
Kirkmanshulme La.
M'ster M12 & M18 165 B5
Kirkpatrick St. WN2 57 B3
Kirkstall. 27 OL12 139 E8
Kirkstall Ave. Heywood OL10 29 C3
Kirkstall Ave.
Littleborough OL15 16 A7
Kirkstall Cl. SK12 133 D4
Kirkstall Gdns. M26 43 E5
Kirkstall Rd. Middleton M24 46 F3
Kirkstall Rd. Urmston M41 95 E3
Kirkstall Sq. M13 163 C6
Kirkstead Cl. M11 165 A8
Kirkstead Rd. SK8 132 C6
Kirkstile Cres. WN3 54 E2
Kirkstile Pl. M27 61 E4
Kirkstone. WN5 54 C7
Kirkstone Ave. M28 60 F1
Kirkstone Cl. OL1 48 F1
Kirkstone Dr. Middleton M24 46 E2
Kirkstone Dr. Royton OL2 48 D6
Kirkstone Rd.
Dukinfield SK14 101 C5
Kirkstone Rd. Failsworth M40 65 C2
Kirktown Wlk. M11 165 C8
Kirkwall Dr. BL2 148 B5
Kirkway. M'ster M9 65 A4
Kirkway. Middleton M24 65 A7
Kirkway. R'dale OL11 30 F2
Kirkwood Dr. M40 159 C4
Kirtley Ave. M30 79 D3
Kirtlington Cl. OL2 149 A5
Kirton Lodge. M25 63 C4
Kirton Wlk. M9 64 C5
Kitchen St. 14 OL16 31 A8
Kitchener Ave. M44 105 C4
Kitchener St. Bolton BL3 42 B3
Kitchener St. Bury BL8 27 B1
Kitepool St. M28 79 A4
Kitt Green Rd. WN5 54 C8
Kitt's Moss La. SK7 132 D6
Kitter St. OL12 15 C3
Kittiwake Cl. M29 77 A7
Kitty Wheeldon Gdns. M33 108 A5
Kiveton Cl. M28 60 C2
Kiveton Dr. WN4 73 C2
Knacks La. OL12 14 A5
Knaresborough Cl. SK5 99 E1
Knaresborough Rd. WN2 56 E4
Knarr Barn La. OL3 50 D3
Knarr La. OL3 50 E2
Kneller Wlk. OL1 49 D4
Knight Cres. M24 46 D4
Knight St. Ashton-u-L OL7 84 F2
Knight St. Bolton BL1 145 F8
Knight St. Bury BL8 27 C2
Knight St. Hyde SK14 167 E1
Knight St. M'ster M20 110 B2
Knight's Cl. M25 63 B5
Knightley Wlk. M40 157 D5
Knights Ct. M30 80 A2
Knightsbridge. SK1 169 F2
Knightsbridge Cl. M7 155 D8
Knightscliffe Cres. WN6 35 D6
Knightshill Cres. WN6 37 A1
Kniveton Rd. M12 164 F6
Knivton St. SK14 167 F3
Knob Hall Gdns. M23 120 F3
Knole Ave. SK12 133 F4
Knoll St. M'ster M7 155 D7
Knoll St. R'dale OL11 30 C2
Knoll The. Alt'ham WA14 119 B5
Knoll The. Mossley OL5 68 B1
Knoll The. Shaw OL2 149 C6
Knott Fold. SK14 167 D1
Knott Hill La. OL3 50 E3
Knott Hill St. OL12 4 E6
Knott La. Bolton BL1 23 F2
Knott La. Hyde SK14 113 E8
Knott Lanes. OL8 84 F8
Knott St. M5 154 D1
Knott's Houses. WN7 91 C8
Knotts Brow. BL7 9 F4
Knowe Ave. 5 M22 121 D1
Knowl Cl. Ramsbottom BL0 11 C4
Knowl Cl. Reddish M34 100 B2
Knowl Hill Dr. OL12 13 E2
Knowl La. OL12 13 B5
Knowl Meadow. BB4 1 A6
Knowl Rd. Milnrow OL16 31 D6
Knowl Rd. Shaw OL2 149 C6
Knowl St. Oldham OL8 66 C2
Knowl St. Stalybridge SK15 86 B2
Knowl Syke St. OL12 15 C7
Knowl Top La. OL3 69 D7
Knowl View. Bury BL8 27 A6
Knowl View.
Littleborough OL15 15 F2
Knowl View Res Sch. OL11 29 E7
Knowldale Way. M12 164 E5
Knowle Ave. OL7 166 A4
Knowle Dr. M25 63 A2
Knowle Gn. SK9 131 C3
Knowle Pk. SK9 131 C3
Knowle Rd. SK6 126 D6
Knowle Way. 5 SK14 102 F2
Knowles Ave. WN3 54 F4
Knowles Ct. M6 80 B3
Knowles Edge St. BL1 142 C2
Knowles Pl. 1 M'ster M15 162 F6
Knowles Pl. Wigan WN1 151 E8
Knowles St. Bolton BL1 25 A1
Knowles St. Ince-i-M WN3 151 D6
Knowles St. Radcliffe M26 44 A4
Knowles The. OL8 66 C1
Knowls La. OL4 67 F5
Knowlsley Grange. BL1 40 D7
Knowsley. OL4 68 A7
Knowsley Ave. Atherton M46 58 C4
Knowsley Ave. Golborne WA3 74 B1
Knowsley Ave. Oldham OL4 68 A7
Knowsley Ave. Salford M5 161 B8
Knowsley Ave. Urmston M41 95 C4
Knowsley Cres.
Stockport SK1 124 B8
Knowsley Cres.
Whitworth OL12 4 E6
Knowsley Dr. Leigh WN7 75 E2
Knowsley Dr. Oldham OL4 68 A7
Knowsley Dr. Swinton M27 79 D5
Knowsley Gn. Oldham OL4 68 A7
Knowsley Gn. Salford M5 161 B8
Knowsley Gr. BL6 22 D1
Knowsley Jun Sch. OL4 68 A7
Knowsley Park Way. BB4 1 B8
Knowsley Rd. Ainsworth BL2 26 C1
Knowsley Rd. Bolton BL1 142 B2
Knowsley Rd. Haslingden BB4 1 B8
Knowsley Rd.
Hazel Grove SK7 133 F8
Knowsley Rd. Stockport SK1 124 B8
Knowsley Rd. Whitefield M45 62 F8
Knowsley Rd. Wigan WN6 37 A3
Knowsley Rd Ind Est. BB4 1 B8
Knowsley St. Bolton BL1 145 F7
Knowsley St. Bury BL9 140 E1
Knowsley St. Leigh WN7 75 D5
Knowsley St. M'ster M8 159 A4
Knowsley St. R'dale OL12 139 E8
Knowsley Terr. OL4 68 A7
Knutsford Ave. M'ster M16 97 D3
Knutsford Ave. Reddish SK4 111 D7
Knutsford Ave. Sale M33 108 E4
Knutsford Rd. M'ster M18 99 C4
Knutsford Rd.
Wilmslow SK9 & WA16 136 D3
Knutsford St. M6 154 E2
Knutsford View. WA15 129 C8
Knutshaw Cres. BL3 40 E2
Knypersley Ave. SK2 124 C7
Kranj Way. OL1 153 F7
Krokus Sq. OL9 152 A7
Kyle Rd. SK7 124 F1
Kylemore Ave. BL3 144 B5
Kynder St. M34 100 F3

Labtec St. M27 62 B1
Laburnum Ave.
Ashton-u-L OL6 85 C6
Laburnum Ave. Atherton M46 58 E3
Laburnum Ave. Bury BL8 26 F7
Laburnum Ave.
Droylsden M34 84 C1
Laburnum Ave. Eccles M30 95 A8
Laburnum Ave.
Failsworth M35 83 F6
Laburnum Ave. Hyde SK14 113 D8
Laburnum Ave.
Ince-i-M WN3 151 F6
Laburnum Ave. Leigh WN7 75 E8
Laburnum Ave. Oldham OL9 48 C1
Laburnum Ave. Shaw OL2 149 B6
Laburnum Ave.
Stalybridge SK15 101 F8
Laburnum Ave. Swinton M27 79 E6
Laburnum Ave.
Whitefield M45 62 F7
Laburnum Ct. BL8 26 F7
Laburnum Dr.
Whitefield M45 & BL9 45 A1
Laburnum Dr. Wigan WN6 37 A4
Laburnum Gr. Horwich BL6 22 E1
Laburnum Gr. Prestwich M25 63 A5
Laburnum Gr. Tyldesley M29 59 D1
Laburnum La. Alt'ham WA15 128 E8
Laburnum La. Newhey OL16 32 A3
Laburnum Pk. BL2 25 B5
Laburnum Rd. Farnworth BL4 60 B8
Laburnum Rd. Golborne WA3 90 F7
Laburnum Rd. Haslingden BB4 1 A7
Laburnum Rd. Irlam M44 105 D5
Laburnum Rd. M'ster M18 99 D4
Laburnum Rd. Middleton M24 65 C8
Laburnum Rd. Oldham OL8 84 C8
Laburnum Rd. Reddish M34 99 F3
Laburnum Rd. Urmston M41 95 B4
Laburnum Rd. Walkden M28 60 E1
Laburnum St.Ashton-i-M WN4 73 B2
Laburnum St. Atherton M46 58 E3
Laburnum St. 7 Bolton BL1 145 D8
Laburnum St. Salford M6 154 F2
Laburnum Terr. OL11 30 E4
Laburnum Villas. OL8 67 A1
Laburnum Way.
Littleborough OL15 15 F5
Laburnum Way.
Stockport SK3 123 B8
Laburnum Wlk. 1 M33 107 C5
Lacey Ave. SK9 131 B1

Moorfield Hts. OL5 86 E7
Moorfield Inf Sch. SK7 124 C1
Moorfield Jun Sch. SK7 124 C1
Moorfield Mews. OL2 149 B7
Moorfield Par. M44 94 B3
Moorfield Pl. 3 OL12 14 F1
Moorfield Prec. SK14 103 D5
Moorfield Prim Sch. M44 94 A3
Moorfield Rd. Irlam M44 94 B3
Moorfield Rd. M'ster M20 109 F4
Moorfield Rd. 1 Oldham OL8 66 B2
Moorfield Rd. Salford M6 80 D5
Moorfield Rd. Swinton M27 79 C6
Moorfield St. Hollingworth SK14 103 D5
Moorfield St. 1 M'ster M20 110 B7
Moorfield St. Platt Bridge WN2 56 B3
Moorfield Terr. Hollingworth SK14 103 D5
Moorfield Terr. Mossley OL5 86 E7
Moorfield Wlk. M41 95 D2
Moorgate. BL9 141 A3
Moorgate Ave. M'ster M20 109 F6
Moorgate Ave. R'dale OL11 30 A7
Moorgate Ct. BL2 25 B1
Moorgate Dr. Mossley SK15 86 E6
Moorgate Dr. Tyldesley M29 77 C5
Moorgate Mews. OL5 86 E7
Moorgate Prim Sch. BL2 148 B8
Moorgate Rd. Bury BL8 43 F8
Moorgate Rd. Mossley SK15 86 E7
Moorgate St. OL3 69 B8
Moorhead St. M4 159 B3
Moorhey Rd. M38 59 F6
Moorhey St. OL4 67 B6
Moorhouse Prim Sch. OL16 31 E6
Moorings Cl. WN1 151 F8
Moorings Rd. M17 96 B8
Moorings The. Disley SK12 135 E6
Moorings The. Uppermill OL5 68 E3
Moorings The. Worsley M28 79 A5
Moorland Ave. Droylsden M43 83 E1
Moorland Ave. M'ster M8 63 F2
Moorland Ave. Milnrow OL16 32 A6
Moorland Ave. R'dale OL11 29 F8
Moorland Ave. Sale M33 108 C3
Moorland Ave. Uppermill OL3 50 F2
Moorland Ave. Whitworth OL12 14 C7
Moorland Cres. OL12 14 C7
Moorland Dr. Cheadle SK8 131 F8
Moorland Dr. Horwich BL6 22 F3
Moorland Dr. Walkden M38 60 A6
Moorland Gr. BL1 142 A2
Moorland Rd. Ashton-i-M WN4 73 E5
Moorland Rd. Hindley WN2 56 C5
Moorland Rd. M'ster M20 110 B3
Moorland Rd. Mossley SK15 86 E5
Moorland Rd. Stockport SK2 124 B4
Moorland St. Littleborough OL15 16 C7
Moorland St. R'dale OL12 14 E1
Moorland Terr. OL12 14 A1
Moorlands Ave. Leigh WN7 75 F3
Moorlands Ave. Urmston M41 95 B3
Moorlands Cres. OL5 68 D1
Moorlands Dr. OL5 68 E3
Moorlands Jun Sch. M33 108 E5
Moorlands St. OL2 149 C7
Moorlands View. Bolton BL3 146 A2
Moorlands View. Edenfield BL0 1 D5
Moorlea. M35 83 F8
Moorsbrook Gr. 9 SK9 131 E1
Moorsholme Ave. 8 M40 83 A7
Moorside. OL11 30 F3
Moorside Ave. Ainsworth BL2 26 D1
Moorside Ave. Bolton BL1 142 A1
Moorside Ave. Droylsden M43 84 C2
Moorside Ave. Farnworth BL4 60 B7
Moorside Ave. Horwich BL6 22 C4
Moorside Ave. Oldham OL4 49 F4
Moorside Cres. M43 84 C2
Moorside Ct. Dukinfield M34 101 A4
Moorside Ct. Sale M33 108 B4
Moorside High Sch. M27 79 D7
Moorside House. WA15 120 C7
Moorside La. M34 101 A4
Moorside Lodge. M27 79 D8
Moorside Prim Sch. Droylsden M43 84 B1
Moorside Prim Sch. Swinton M27 79 D7
Moorside Rd. Bury BL8 26 E5
Moorside Rd. M'ster M8 64 A1
Moorside Rd. M'ster M25, M7 81 C8
Moorside Rd. M'ster SK4 168 A2
Moorside Rd. Mossley OL5 68 E1
Moorside Rd. Swinton M27 79 D8
Moorside Rd. Urmston M41 94 E3
Moorside Rd. Urmston M41 95 B3
Moorside St. M43 84 C2
Moorside View. OL2 149 C8
Moorside & Wardley Sta. M27 61 D1
Moorside Wlk. WN5 54 B8
Moorsview. BL0 138 B6
Moorton Ave. M19 110 F7
Moorton Pk. M19 110 F7
Moortop Cl. M9 64 A5
Moorville Rd. M6 80 C5
Moorway. SK9 136 D5
Moorway Dr. M9 65 A4
Moorwood Dr. M33 107 E3
Mora Ave. OL9 48 B1
Mora St. M9 157 F8
Moran Cl. SK9 131 E2
Moran Wlk. 6 M15 162 A6
Morar Dr. BL2 43 A7
Morar Rd. SK16 101 D7
Moravian Cl. SK16 101 C7
Moravian Field. 3 M43 100 A8
Moray Cl. BL0 11 A4
Moray Rd. OL9 66 A4
Morbourne Cl. M12 164 E6
Morden Ave. Ashton-i-M WN4 73 B3
Morden Ave. 17 Droylsden M11 83 C2
Morecambe Cl. M40 83 B6
Morely St. OL4 49 E1
Moresby Cl. WN7 75 D5
Moresby Dr. M20 122 B8
Morestead Wlk. 1 M40 159 C3
Moreton Ave. Bramhall SK7 132 E5
Moreton Ave. Sale M33 107 F3
Moreton Ave. Stretford M32 96 D2
Moreton Ave. Whitefield M45 44 F1
Moreton Cl. Dukinfield SK16 101 D6
Moreton Cl. Golborne WA3 73 F1
Moreton Dr. Bury BL8 27 B3
Moreton Dr. Handforth SK9 131 E3
Moreton Dr. Leigh WN7 75 E1
Moreton La. SK2 124 C7
Moreton St. OL9 65 F8
Moreton Wlk. SK2 124 D7
Morgan Pl. SK5 169 F4
Morgan St. OL15 16 B5
Morillon Rd. M44 94 A4
Morland Rd. M16 97 C4
Morley Ave. M'ster M14 98 A1
Morley Ave. Swinton M27 79 E6
Morley Gn. SK9 130 C1
Morley Rd. M26 43 D4
Morley St. Atherton M46 58 C2
Morley St. Bolton BL3 145 D6
Morley St. Bury BL9 44 F8
Morley St. Glossop SK13 116 D8
Morley St. R'dale OL16 15 B1
Morley St. Whitefield M45 62 F8
Morley Way. OL3 69 B5
Morley's La. Leigh M29 76 F3
Morna Wlk. M12 164 D8
Morningside Cl. Droylsden M35 & M43 100 A7
Morningside Cl. 23 R'dale OL16 31 B6
Morningside Dr. M20 122 C8
Mornington Ave. SK8 122 D4
Mornington Cres. M14 110 B8
Mornington Ct. 5 OL1 153 E8
Mornington High Sch. WN2 56 F5
Mornington Rd. Adlington PR6 21 B8
Mornington Rd. Atherton M46 58 F6
Mornington Rd. Bolton BL1 144 B8
Mornington Rd. Cheadle SK8 122 D4
Mornington Rd. Hindley WN2 56 F5
Mornington Rd. R'dale OL11 31 A3
Mornington Rd. Sale M33 108 D5
Morpeth Cl. OL7 84 E4
Morpeth St. M27 79 E6
Morpeth Wlk. M12 164 E5
Morrell Rd. M22 121 E8
Morris Fold Dr. BL6 40 C6
Morris Gn. BL3 146 C2
Morris Gn Bsns Pk. BL3 146 C4
Morris Gr. M31 106 E8
Morris Green La. BL3 146 C3
Morris Green St. BL3 146 C2
Morris House. WN1 151 D8
Morris Rd. WN8 53 A7
Morris St. Bolton BL1 148 A7
Morris St. 1 Hindley WN2 56 D5
Morris St. Ince-i-M WN2 55 E4
Morris St. M'ster M20 110 B7
Morris St. Oldham OL4 67 A5
Morris St. Radcliffe BL9 44 E5
Morris St. Tyldesley M29 58 F1
Morris St. Wigan WN1 151 D8
Morrison St. BL3 147 E3
Morrison Wlk. M40 83 A5
Morrowfield Ave. M7 & M8 155 F7
Morse Rd. M40 83 B5
Mort Fold. M38 60 A5
Mort La. M28 & M29 & M38 59 E2
Mort St. Farnworth BL4 60 B8
Mort St. Hindley WN2 57 A5
Mort St. Horwich BL6 22 B4
Mort St. Leigh WN7 75 B5
Mort St. 8 Tyldesley M29 58 F1
Mort St. Wigan WN6 37 A1
Mortar St. Oldham OL4 67 C7
Mortar St. Oldham OL4 67 C8
Mortfield Gdns. BL1 145 D8
Mortfield La. BL1 145 D8
Mortimer Ave. M9 64 E4
Mortimer St. OL1 67 A8
Mortlake Cl. M28 59 F3
Mortlake Dr. M40 83 B5
Morton Ave. WN3 150 B5
Morton Cl. WN3 54 C2
Morton Dr. SK12 133 F4
Morton St. Failsworth M35 83 C6
Morton St. Middleton M24 47 A1
Morton St. Radcliffe M26 44 B2
Morton St. Reddish SK4 169 E4
Morton Terr. 18 Denton M34 101 A1
Morton Terr. Romiley SK6 113 B5
Mortons The. BL5 39 E2
Morven Ave. SK7 124 F3
Morven Dr. M23 121 A5
Morven Gr. BL2 42 F7
Morville Dr. WN3 55 B4
Morville Rd. M16 & M21 97 D1
Morville St. M1 163 C8
Moschatel Wlk. M31 106 A3
Moscow Rd. SK3 170 D7
Moscow Rd E. SK3 170 D7
Mosedale Ave. WA11 71 B1
Mosedale Cl. Alt'ham M23 120 E6
Mosedale Cl. Tyldesley M29 77 C6
Mosedale Rd. M24 46 E2
Moseldene Rd. SK2 124 D5
Moseley Ct. M19 98 F1
Moseley Grange. SK8 122 F3
Moseley Rd. Cheadle SK8 122 F3
Moseley Rd. M'ster M14 110 E8
Moseley St. SK3 170 E8
Moses Gate Ctry Pk. BL3 42 D4
Moses Gate Sta. BL4 42 C2
Moses Gate Wkshp. 2 BL4 42 D2
Mosley Ave. Bury BL9 27 F5
Mosley Ave. Ramsbottom BL0 11 B2
Mosley Cl. WA15 119 F7
Mosley Common Rd. Boothstown M28 & M29 77 F7
Mosley Common Rd. Boothstown M28 78 A7
Mosley Rd. Alt'ham WA15 120 B6
Mosley Rd. Stretford M17 96 C6
Mosley St. M'ster M1 & M60 159 A1
Mosley St. Radcliffe M26 43 F4
Mosley Street Sta. M1 159 A1
Moss Ave. Leigh WN7 76 B5
Moss Ave. Orrell WN5 53 D3
Moss Ave. R'dale OL16 31 C6
Moss Bank. Bramhall SK7 & SK8 132 C5
Moss Bank. M'ster M8 156 A8
Moss Bank Ave. M43 84 C2
Moss Bank Cl. BL1 143 E4
Moss Bank Ct. M43 84 C2
Moss Bank Gr. M27 61 D2
Moss Bank Rd. Billinge WA11 71 B2
Moss Bank Rd. Swinton M27 61 D2
Moss Bank Way. Bolton BL1 23 E1
Moss Bank Way. Bolton BL1 142 B3
Moss Bridge Rd. OL16 31 C5
Moss Brook Rd. M9 157 E7
Moss Cl. Haslingden BB4 1 A8
Moss Cl. Radcliffe M26 43 D5
Moss Colliery Rd. M27 61 E4
Moss Croft Cl. M41 94 E3
Moss Cty Prim Sch The. BL3 42 F6
Moss Dr. BL6 22 F3
Moss Fold. M29 77 C8
Moss Gate Rd. OL16 & OL2 32 A1
Moss Gn. M31 106 F6
Moss Gr. Lymm WA13 117 B4
Moss Gr. Shaw OL2 31 E1
Moss Gr. Standish WN6 36 E8
Moss Grange Ave. M16 97 D4
Moss Grove Ct. 2 M15 97 E4
Moss Hall Rd. BL9 & OL10 45 F7
Moss Hey Dr. M23 109 B1
Moss Hey Prim Sch. SK7 132 C5
Moss Hey St. OL2 149 C6
Moss House La. M28 78 A5
Moss House Terr. M9 64 C1
Moss Ind Est. Golborne WN7 75 B1
Moss Ind Est. R'dale OL16 31 B5
Moss La. Alderley Edge SK9 137 B1
Moss La. Alt'ham WA14, WA15 119 E4
Moss La. Alt'ham WA15 119 F7
Moss La. Alt'ham WA15 120 A5
Moss La. Appley Bridge WN6 18 E3
Moss La. Ashton-u-L OL7 84 E2
Moss La. Blackrod BL6 21 F2
Moss La. Bolton BL1 142 B3
Moss La. Bramhall SK7 132 D5
Moss La. Fowley Common WA3 92 D5
Moss La. Golborne WA3 90 B5
Moss La. Irlam M44 105 D5
Moss La. Kearsley BL4 61 B5
Moss La. Middleton M9 64 F5
Moss La. Mottram-i-L SK14 114 F8
Moss La. Partington M31 105 F3
Moss La. Partington M31, WA13, WA14 106 A2
Moss La. Platt Bridge WN2 56 A3
Moss La. R'dale OL16 31 A6
Moss La. Royton OL2 49 A3
Moss La. Sale M33 107 B3
Moss La. Sale M33 107 E4
Moss La. Swinton M27 61 D2
Moss La. Tyldesley M29 77 A1
Moss La. Urmston M41 95 E5
Moss La. Walkden BL4 & M28 60 E4
Moss La. Whitefield M45 62 F8
Moss La. Wilmslow WA16 136 A4
Moss La. Wythenshawe SK9 130 E6
Moss La E. M14 & M16 98 A4
Moss La W. M15 & M16 97 F4
Moss Lea. BL1 143 D4
Moss Lodge La. OL7 84 E1
Moss Manor. M33 107 E3
Moss Meadow. BL5 39 E2
Moss Meadow Rd. M6 80 C4
Moss Mill St. OL16 31 B5
Moss Park Jun & Inf Sch. M32 96 B2
Moss Park Rd. M32 & M41 96 B2
Moss Pl. 5 BL9 44 E8
Moss Rd. Alderley Edge SK9 137 C2
Moss Rd. Irlam M44 93 B1
Moss Rd. Irlam M44 105 C7
Moss Rd. Kearsley BL4 60 E5
Moss Rd. Orrell WN5 53 D3
Moss Rd. Sale M33 107 B3
Moss Rd. Stretford M17 & M32 96 C3
Moss Rose. SK9 137 B2
Moss Row. Bury BL9 140 F1
Moss Row. R'dale OL11 13 D1
Moss Shaw Way. M26 43 E5
Moss Side Ent Est. M15 162 F5
Moss Side La. Hollinfare WA3 105 A2
Moss Side La. R'dale OL16 31 C5
Moss Side Rd. M44 105 E6
Moss Side St. OL12 4 E5
Moss St. Bury BL9 140 E2
Moss St. Droylsden M34 84 B1
Moss St. Droylsden M43 84 B2
Moss St. 2 Farnworth BL4 42 E1
Moss St. 5 Heywood OL10 29 C2
Moss St. Hollingworth SK14 103 D5
Moss St. Ince-i-M WN2 55 F3
Moss St. M'ster M7 155 D5
Moss St. Oldham OL4 67 E8
Moss St. Platt Bridge WN2 56 A3
Moss St. R'dale OL16 31 B6
Moss St. Ramsbottom BL9 11 D2
Moss St. Wigan WN6 37 A1
Moss St. 10 Wigan WN5 54 B6
Moss St E. OL6 166 B3
Moss St W. OL7 84 F2
Moss Terr. Ashton-u-L OL7 166 A2
Moss Terr. R'dale OL16 31 B6
Moss Terr. 3 Wigan WN5 54 B5
Moss The. M24 65 B6
Moss Vale Cres. M32 95 F3
Moss Vale Rd. M41 95 E2
Moss View Prim Sch. M31 106 A3
Moss View Rd. Bolton BL2 42 E8
Moss View Rd. Partington M31 106 A3
Moss Way. M33 107 E4
Mossack Ave. 4 M22 121 D1
Mossbank Cl. SK14 171 E4
Mossbank Gr. OL10 29 C3
Mossbray Ave. M19 110 D4
Mossbrook Ct. M40 159 C4
Mossbrook Dr. M38 59 E6
Mossclough Ct. M9 157 E7
Mosscot Wlk. M13 163 B7
Mossdale Ave. BL1 40 D7
Mossdale Rd. Ashton-i-M WN4 73 A8
Mossdale Rd. Sale M33 107 F1
Mossdale Rd. Wythenshawe M23 108 F1
Mossdown Rd. OL2 49 A3
Mossfield Cl. Bury BL9 141 B4
Mossfield Cl. Stockport SK4 168 B2
Mossfield Ct. BL1 145 E8
Mossfield Dr. M9 65 A4
Mossfield Gn. M30 94 C4
Mossfield Prim Sch. Heywood OL10 29 C3
Mossfield Prim Sch. Swinton M27 61 F1
Mossfield Rd. Alt'ham WA15 120 D6
Mossfield Rd. Farnworth BL4 60 B8
Mossfield Rd. Kearsley BL4 60 F5
Mossfield Rd. Swinton M27 61 F2
Mossgrove Rd. WA15 119 F6
Mossgrove St. 7 OL8 66 D2
Mosshall Cl. M15 162 D6
Mossland Cl. OL10 46 D8
Mossland Gr. BL3 40 D2
Mosslee Ave. M8 63 F3
Mossley CE Prim Sch. OL5 68 B1
Mossley Rd. Ashton-u-L OL6 85 E4
Mossley Rd. Ashton-u-L OL5 & OL6 86 A7
Mossley Rd. Ashton-u-L OL6 166 C3
Mossley Rd. Uppermill OL4 68 D5
Mossley Sta. OL5 68 C1
Mossmere Rd. SK8 123 A4
Mossway. M24 & M9 64 F5
Mosswood Pk. M20 122 B8
Mosswood Rd. SK9 131 E1
Mossy Lea Cty Prim Sch. WN6 18 F6
Mossy Lea Fold. WN6 19 A3
Mossy Lea Rd. WN6 18 F5
Moston Bank Ave. M9 157 F7
Moston Brook High Sch. M40 157 F6
Moston Fields Prim Sch. M40 65 A1
Moston La. M'ster M40 65 B2
Moston La. M'ster M9 & M40 157 F8
Moston La E. OL9 & M40 65 E1
Moston Lane Prim Sch. M40 157 F8
Moston Rd. M24 65 D5
Moston St. M'ster M7 155 F7
Moston St. Reddish SK5 111 F8
Moston Sta. M40 65 D2
Mostyn Ave. Bury BL9 27 F5
Mostyn Ave. Cheadle SK8 122 E1
Mostyn Ave. M'ster M14 110 E8
Mostyn Rd. SK7 124 C1
Mostyn St. SK15 & SK16 101 F8
Motcombe Farm Rd. SK8 122 B1
Motcombe Gr. SK8 122 A3
Motcombe Rd. SK8 122 A2
Mother Street Prim Sch. M35 83 D7
Motherwell Ave. 2 M19 99 A1
Mottershead Ave. BL3 43 A4
Mottershead Rd. M22 121 C4
Mottram Ave. M21 109 C5
Mottram CE Prim Sch. SK14 103 A3
Mottram Cl. SK8 123 A5
Mottram Dr. Alt'ham WA15 120 A5
Mottram Dr. Wigan WN3 150 B5
Mottram Fold. SK1 170 F8
Mottram Mews. 6 BL6 22 B4
Mottram Moor. SK14 103 B4
Mottram Old Rd. Hyde SK14 114 B8
Mottram Old Rd. Stalybridge SK15 102 D7
Mottram Rd. Alderley Edge SK9 137 D1
Mottram Rd. Hattersley SK14 102 C3
Mottram Rd. Mottram-i-L SK14 115 A8
Mottram Rd. Sale M33 108 F3
Mottram Rd. Stalybridge SK14 & SK15 102 D7
Mottram St. Horwich BL6 22 B4
Mottram St. 5 Stockport SK1 170 F8
Mough La. OL9 65 E3
Mouldsworth Ave. M'ster M20 110 A7
Mouldsworth Ave. Reddish SK4 111 D6
Moulton St. M7 & M8 158 E4
Moulton St Prec. M8 158 E4
Mouncey St. M1 163 A7
Mount Ave. Littleborough OL12 & OL16 15 E4
Mount Ave. Littleborough OL15 16 A7
Mount Ave. Rawtenstall BB4 2 F8
Mount Carmel Cres. M5 161 C7
Mount Carmel Ct. M5 161 C7
Mount Carmel Sch. SK9 137 A2
Mount Cl. 4 OL7 166 A1
Mount Cres. WN5 53 F6
Mount Dr. Marple SK6 125 F5
Mount Dr. Urmston M41 95 F2
Mount Fold. M24 65 B7
Mount Gr. M22 121 F6
Mount La. OL3 50 E1
Mount Pleasant. Adlington PR6 21 A8
Mount Pleasant. 16 Bacup OL13 3 C8
Mount Pleasant. Bolton BL3 148 C5
Mount Pleasant. Edgworth BL7 9 D5
Mount Pleasant. Hazel Grove SK7 124 D3
Mount Pleasant. Middleton M25 63 F8
Mount Pleasant. Middleton M24 64 C8
Mount Pleasant. Ramsbottom BL9 11 F3
Mount Pleasant. Wilmslow SK9 137 B8
Mount Pleasant Rd. Denton M34 100 F2
Mount Pleasant Rd. Farnworth BL4 59 F8
Mount Pleasant St. Ashton-u-L OL6 166 C3
Mount Pleasant St. Dukinfield M34 100 F7
Mount Pleasant St. Horwich BL6 22 D1
Mount Pleasant St. Oldham OL4 67 B7
Mount Pleasant Trad Est. OL6 166 C4
Mount Pleasant Wlk. M26 44 A4
Mount Rd. M'ster M18 & M19 99 C3
Mount Rd. Middleton M24 65 A7
Mount Rd. Prestwich M25 63 C6
Mount Rd. Romiley SK14 114 A6
Mount Rd. Stockport SK4 168 C2
Mount Sion Rd. M26 43 E2
Mount Skip La. M38 60 A4
Mount St. Bolton BL1 143 E1
Mount St. Eccles M30 95 C8
Mount St. Glossop SK13 116 C8
Mount St. Heywood OL10 29 D1
Mount St. Horwich BL6 22 D2
Mount St. Hyde SK14 167 E2
Mount St. Leigh WN7 75 C4
Mount St. M'ster M3 158 D3
Mount St. M'ster M2 162 F8
Mount St. Oldham OL2 48 E3
Mount St. R'dale OL11 30 C1
Mount St. R'dale OL12 139 E8
Mount St. Ramsbottom BL0 138 B6
Mount St. Stalybridge SK15 86 A2
Mount St. Swinton M27 79 F7
Mount St Joseph Sch. BL4 42 A2
Mount St Joseph's Rd. BL3 144 B5
Mount Terr. M43 83 E3
Mount The. Alt'ham WA14 119 D5
Mount The. Alt'ham WA15 129 C8
Mount The. Ashton-u-L OL6 85 D3
Mount The. Brinnington SK5 112 B4
Mount View. Ince-i-M WN3 151 D5
Mount View. Uppermill OL3 69 B8
Mount View Rd. OL2 49 D6
Mount Zion Rd. BL9 44 F5
Mountain Ash. OL12 14 B3
Mountain Ash Cl. R'dale OL12 14 B3
Mountain Ash Cl. 9 Sale M33 107 C5
Mountain Ash Cotts. OL3 33 D1
Mountain Gr. M28 60 C4
Mountain Rd. PR7 19 E8
Mountain St. Failsworth M40 83 D4
Mountain St. Mossley OL5 68 C1
Mountain St. Stockport SK1 112 A2
Mountain St. Walkden M28 60 C4
Mountbatten Ave. SK16 101 F6
Mountbatten Cl. BL9 45 C2
Mountbatten St. M18 165 C5
Mountfield. M25 63 B4
Mountfield Ct. WN5 53 F7
Mountfield Rd. Bramhall SK7 132 E5
Mountfield Rd. Stockport SK3 123 C7
Mountfield Wlk. 5 Bolton BL1 143 E1
Mountfield Wlk. 11 M'ster M11 160 F1
Mountford Ave. M8 63 F2
Mountheath Ind Pk. M25 63 B1
Mountmorres Cl. BL5 59 A7
Mountroyal Cl. SK14 102 A5
Mountside Cl. OL12 14 F2
Mountside Cres. M25 62 F4
Mousell St. M8 159 A4
Mouselow Cl. SK13 171 F3
Mow Halls La. OL3 51 A1
Mowbray Ave. M'ster M25 63 C1
Mowbray Ave. Sale M33 108 C3
Mowbray St. Ashton-u-L OL7 166 A2
Mowbray St. Bolton BL1 142 B1
Mowbray St. 5 Oldham OL1 153 F6
Mowbray St. R'dale OL11 30 B3
Mowbray St. Stockport SK1 170 F8
Mowbray Wlk. 4 M24 46 E2
Moxley Rd. M8 63 F1
Moyse Ave. BL8 26 F5
Mozart Cl. M4 159 C2
Mudhurst La. SK12 135 E3
Muirfield Ave. SK6 113 A4
Muirfield Cl. Bolton BL3 40 F3
Muirfield Cl. Failsworth M40 83 C7
Muirfield Cl. Heywood OL10 29 D1
Muirfield Cl. Prestwich M25 63 B5
Muirfield Cl. Wilmslow SK9 137 D8
Muirfield Dr. M29 77 C7
Muirhead Ct. M6 81 A5
Mulberry Ave. WA3 90 F7
Mulberry Cl. Gatley SK8 131 C7
Mulberry Cl. R'dale OL11 139 E5
Mulberry Cl. Wigan WN5 54 D6
Mulberry Ct. 7 M6 81 A3
Mulberry Mews. SK4 169 E2
Mulberry Mount St. SK3 170 E8
Mulberry Rd. M6 81 A3
Mulberry St. 2 Ashton-u-L OL6 166 C3
Mulberry St. M'ster M2 158 F1
Mulberry Wlk. Droylsden M43 99 E8
Mulberry Wlk. Sale M33 107 D6
Mule St. BL2 148 A7
Mulgrave Rd. M28 79 A8
Mulgrave St. Bolton BL3 146 C2
Mulgrave St. Swinton M27 61 D1
Mulgrove Wlk. 29 M9 64 E3
Mull Ave. M12 164 F5
Mullacre Rd. M22 121 D6
Mulliner St. 1 BL1 143 F1
Mullineux St. M28 60 D2
Mullins Ave. WA12 89 C5
Mullion Cl. SK5 99 D2
Mullion Dr. WA15 119 E6
Mullion Wlk. M8 156 B6
Mulmount Cl. OL8 66 C3
Mumps. OL1 67 A7
Mumps Sta. OL4 67 A6
Munday St. M4 160 D1
Munford Wlk. M40 157 E5
Municipal Cl. 2 OL10 29 D2
Munn Rd. M9 64 C5
Munro Ave. Orrell WN5 53 E6
Munro Ave. Wythenshawe M22 121 F2
Munslow Wlk. M9 64 F3
Munster St. M4 159 A3
Muriel St. Heywood OL10 29 E2
Muriel St. M'ster M7 155 D5
Muriel St. R'dale OL16 31 B5
Murieston Rd. WA15 119 E2
Murphy Cl. WN3 150 A5
Murray Rd. BL9 140 F2
Murray St. Atherton M46 58 B2
Murray St. M'ster M7 155 D6
Murray St. M'ster M4 159 C2
Murrayfield. OL11 29 E6
Murrow Wlk. 3 M9 157 D8
Murton Terr. BL1 143 F4
Mus of Science & Ind. M3 162 E8
Mus of Science & Ind (Air & Space Gal). M3 162 E8
Musbury Ave. SK8 123 B2
Muscari Wlk. M12 163 C7
Musden Ave. BB4 1 A7
Musden Wlk. SK4 111 D7
Museum St. M1 162 F8
Musgrave Gdns. BL1 144 C8
Musgrave Rd. Bolton BL1 144 C8
Musgrave Rd. Wythenshawe M22 121 D3
Muslin St. M5 81 C1
Mustard La. WA3 91 B1
Muter Ave. M22 121 F2
Mutual St. OL10 29 E3
My St. M5 & M6 154 E1
Mycroft Cl. WN7 75 E8
Myerscroft Cl. M40 65 E1
Myford Wlk. M8 155 E5
Myrrh St. BL1 143 E2
Myrtle Ave. Ashton-i-M WN4 72 F6
Myrtle Ave. Leigh WN7 75 F7
Myrtle Ave. Newton-l-W WA12 89 C2
Myrtle Bank. M25 63 A1
Myrtle Cl. OL8 153 E5
Myrtle Gdns. BL9 141 B2
Myrtle Gr. Billinge WN5 71 D4
Myrtle Gr. Droylsden M43 84 C2
Myrtle Gr. M'ster M25 63 B2
Myrtle Gr. Reddish M34 99 F3
Myrtle Gr. Whitefield M45 44 D2
Myrtle Pl. M7 81 C4
Myrtle Rd. Middleton M24 47 C2
Myrtle Rd. Partington M31 105 D3
Myrtle St. Bolton BL1 145 D8
Myrtle St. M'ster M16 97 C4
Myrtle St. M'ster M11 164 F8
Myrtle St. Stockport SK3 123 B8
Myrtle St. Wigan WN1 150 B8
Myrtle St N. BL9 141 B2
Myrtle St S. BL9 141 B2
Myrtleleaf Gr. M5 154 D2
Mytham Cty Prim Sch. BL3 43 B3
Mytham Gdns. BL3 43 B2
Mytham Rd. BL3 43 B2
Mythorn Wlk. M40 83 B5
Mythorne Ave. M44 105 C3
Mytton Rd. BL1 142 B4

Nabbs Fold. BL8 10 F3
Nabbs Way. BL8 11 A1
Naburn Cl. SK5 112 C6
Naburn St. M13 98 D4
Nada Lodge. M8 63 F1
Nada Rd. M8 63 F1
Naden Wlk. M45 63 A8
Nadin St. OL8 66 E3
Nadine St. M6 154 E3
Nailsworth Wlk. 5 M13 163 C5
Nairn Cl. WN6 19 D1
Nairn Wlk. M40 160 E3
Nall St. M'ster M19 111 B7
Nall St. Milnrow OL16 31 E6
Nallgate. OL16 31 C2
Nameplate Cl. M30 79 B2
Nan Nook Rd. M23 108 F1
Nancy St. M15 162 D6
Nandywell. BL3 43 B3
Nangreave Rd. SK1 & SK2 124 B6
Nangreave St. M5 158 D1
Nangreaves St. WN7 75 C5
Nansen Ave. M30 79 C3
Nansen Cl. M32 96 E4
Nansen Rd. SK8 122 A4
Nansen St. M'ster M11 164 E8
Nansen St. Salford M6 154 E2
Nansen St. Stretford M32 96 E4
Nansmoss La. SK9 130 D1
Nantes Ct. BL1 143 D2
Nantwich Ave. OL12 14 F3
Nantwich Cl. SK8 123 A5
Nantwich Rd. M14 98 A1
Nantwich Way. 6 SK9 131 E5
Nantwich Wlk. BL3 147 E4
Napier Ct. M16 161 C6
Napier House. OL14 6 A8
Napier Rd. M'ster M21 109 B8
Napier Rd. M'ster SK4 168 B3
Napier Rd. Worsley M28 79 C3
Napier St. Hazel Grove SK7 124 D3
Napier St. Hyde SK14 167 E1
Napier St. Shaw OL2 149 B8
Napier St. Swinton M27 79 D7

Napier St E. OL8 153 D5
Napier St W. OL8 153 D5
Naples Rd. SK3 123 B7
Naples St. M4 159 A3
Narbonne Ave. M30 80 A4
Narbuth Dr. M7 & M8 155 F7
Narcissus Ave. BB4 1 A8
Narcissus Wlk. 6 M28 59 F3
Narrow La. SK10 134 A1
Naseby Ave. M9 64 F4
Naseby Ct. M25 63 C5
Naseby Pl. M25 63 C5
Naseby Rd. SK5 99 F1
Naseby Wlk. M45 63 C8
Nash Rd. M17 95 F8
Nasmyth Ave. M34 101 A4
Nasmyth Bsns Ctr. M30 79 C2
Nasmyth Rd. M30 95 C8
Nasmyth St. Horwich BL6 22 C3
Nasmyth St. M'ster M40 & M8 156 C5
Nately Rd. M16 97 A2
Nathan Dr. M3 158 E2
Nathaniel Ct. WN2 56 B3
Nathans Rd. M22 121 C4
National Cycling Ctr. M11 83 A2
Naunton Ave. WN7 75 C5
Naunton Rd. M24 65 B7
Naunton Wlk. 24 M9 157 E8
Naval St. M4 159 C2
Navenby Ave. M16 97 C4
Navenby Rd. WN3 55 A2
Navigation Cl. WN7 75 E4
Navigation Prim Sch. WA14 119 D6
Navigation Rd. WA14, WA15 119 D6
Navigation Road Sta. WA14 119 E6
Naylor Ave. WA3 90 B8
Naylor Ct. 21 M40 159 C3
Naylor St. Atherton M46 58 C2
Naylor St. M'ster M10 & M40 160 D3
Naylor St. Oldham OL1 153 E7
Naylorfarm Ave. WN6 35 F5
Nazarene Theological Coll The. M20 110 A3
Naze Ct. 3 OL1 153 E8
Naze Wlk. SK5 112 C6
Nazeby Wlk. OL9 152 C5
Neal Ave. Ashton-u-L OL6 85 D3
Neal Ave. Gatley SK8 122 A1
Neale Ave. OL3 69 B5
Neale Rd. M21 109 B7
Near Birches Par. OL4 67 E4
Near Hey Cl. M26 43 E3
Nearbrook Rd. M22 121 C4
Nearcroft Rd. M23 121 B7
Nearmaker Ave. M22 121 C4
Nearmaker Rd. M22 121 C4
Neasden Gr. 6 BL3 144 C5
Neath Ave. M22 121 D7
Neath Cl. Poynton SK12 133 D5
Neath Cl. Prestwich M45 63 C7
Neath Fold. BL3 147 D3
Neath St. OL9 153 D7
Nebo St. BL3 147 D4
Nebraska St. BL1 143 E1
Neden Cl. M11 165 B8
Needham Ave. M21 109 B8
Needwood Cl. M40 157 D5
Needwood Rd. SK6 113 C5
Neenton Sq. M12 165 A7
Neild Gdns. WN7 75 E4
Neild St. M'ster M1 163 B8
Neild St. Oldham OL8 66 F4
Neill St. M7 158 E4
Neilson Cl. M24 65 C7
Neilson Ct. M23 121 A6
Neilston Ave. M40 83 B7
Nel Pan La. WN7 75 D8
Nell Carrs. BL0 11 E8
Nell La. M20 & M21 109 D6
Nell St. BL1 143 F4
Nellie St. OL10 29 B2
Nelson Ave. Eccles M30 79 D3
Nelson Ave. Poynton SK12 134 A3
Nelson Cl. SK12 134 A3
Nelson Cl. M'ster M15 97 E4
Nelson Ct. M'ster M40 160 D4
Nelson Dr. Droylsden M43 83 E2
Nelson Dr. Ince-i-M WN2 56 A8
Nelson Dr. Irlam M44 105 E6
Nelson Fold. M27 62 A1
Nelson Mandela Ct. 11 M16 97 E3
Nelson Rd. M9 64 D5
Nelson Sq. BL1 145 F7
Nelson St. Atherton M46 58 B3
Nelson St. Atherton M46 58 B4
Nelson St. Bacup OL13 4 C8
Nelson St. Bolton BL3 148 A5
Nelson St. 6 Bury BL9 44 F8
Nelson St. Denton M34 100 F4
Nelson St. Denton M34 100 F6
Nelson St. Eccles M30 79 D2
Nelson St. Farnworth BL4 60 E8
Nelson St. Hazel Grove SK7 124 F4
Nelson St. Heywood OL10 29 D1
Nelson St. 5 Hindley WN2 56 D6
Nelson St. Horwich BL6 22 D3
Nelson St. Hyde SK14 167 E2
Nelson St. Little Lever BL3 43 B3
Nelson St. 7 Littleborough OL15 16 B5
Nelson St. M'ster M7 155 D5
Nelson St. M'ster M10, M40 160 E4
Nelson St. M'ster M13 163 B5
Nelson St. Middleton M24 65 C7
Nelson St. Newton-l-W WA12 89 A3
Nelson St. Oldham OL4 67 E5
Nelson St. R'dale OL16 139 F7
Nelson St. Salford M5 154 E1
Nelson St. Stretford M32 96 D1
Nelson St. Tyldesley M29 77 B8
Nelson St. Walsden OL14 6 A8
Nelson Way. OL9 66 B4
Nelstrop Cres. SK4 111 D6
Nelstrop Rd. SK4 111 D6
Nelstrop Rd N. M19,SK4,SK5 111 C8
Nelstrop Wlk. SK4 111 C6
Nepaul Rd. M9 64 E1
Neptune Gdns. 11 M7 81 C5
Nesbit St. BL2 25 B3
Nesfield Rd. M23 108 F2
Neston Ave. Bolton BL1 24 F5
Neston Ave. M'ster M20 110 A6
Neston Ave. Sale M33 108 E2
Neston Cl. OL2 49 D7
Neston Gr. SK3 170 D5
Neston Rd. Bury BL8 26 F5
Neston Rd. R'dale OL16 31 C4
Neston St. M18 99 F7
Neston Way. SK9 131 D3
Neswick Wlk. M23 108 F2
Nether Hey St. OL8 67 B4
Nether St. Hyde SK14 113 F8
Nether St. M'ster M12 163 C8
Netherbury Cl. M18 99 C3
Netherby Rd. WN6 37 A3
Nethercroft Rd. WA15 120 C5
Netherfield Cl. OL8 66 C4
Netherfield Rd. BL3 147 E2
Netherfields. WN7 75 D7
Netherhey La. OL1 48 C2
Netherhouse Rd. OL2 149 A7
Netherland St. M5 161 A8
Netherlees. OL4 67 D5
Netherley Rd. PR7 19 E8
Netherlow Ct. SK14 167 E2
Netherton Gr. BL4 42 B2
Netherton Rd. M14 98 A1
Nethervale Dr. M9 157 E7
Netherwood Rd. M22 121 C7
Netley Ave. OL12 14 F3
Netley Gdns. M26 43 E5
Netley Gr. OL8 67 C4
Netley Rd. M23 121 A4
Nettlebarn Rd. M22 121 C5
Nettleford Rd. M16 & M21 109 E8
Nettleton Gr. M9 64 F1
Nevada St. 18 BL1 143 E1
Nevendon Dr. M23 120 F4
Nevile Ct. M7 81 B8
Nevile Rd. M7 81 B8
Nevill Rd. SK7 123 E2
Nevill Road Inf Sch. SK7 123 E2
Nevill Road Jun Sch. SK7 123 E2
Neville Cardus Wlk. 12 M14 98 C3
Neville Cl. BL1 145 E8
Neville Dr. M44 94 A4
Neville St. Hazel Grove SK7 124 D3
Neville St. Newton-l-W WA12 89 A3
Neville St. Oldham OL9 152 C7
Neville St. Platt Bridge WN2 56 A3
Nevin Ave. SK8 122 E1
Nevin Cl. Bramhall SK7 133 A7
Nevin Cl. 5 Oldham OL8 66 B2
Nevin Rd. M40 65 D1
Nevis Gr. BL1 24 D5
Nevis St. OL11 31 A2
Nevy Fold Ave. BL6 22 F3
New Allen St. M10 & M40 159 C3
New Bailey St. M3 158 E1
New Bank St. Hadfield SK14 104 A5
New Bank St. M'ster M12 165 A8
New Bank St. Tyldesley M29 77 A8
New Barn. BB4 1 B6
New Barn Ave. WN4 73 C3
New Barn Inf Sch. OL2 149 A6
New Barn Jun Sch. OL2 149 A6
New Barn La. Leigh WN7 75 E2
New Barn La. R'dale OL11 30 E4
New Barn La. Rawtenstall BB4 2 A8
New Barn Rd. OL8 67 A2
New Barn St. Bolton BL1 142 B1
New Barn St. 11 R'dale OL11 31 A5
New Barn St. Shaw OL2 149 A7
New Barton St. M6 80 C5
New Beech Rd. SK4 110 E2
New Bridge La. SK1 112 A2
New Bridge St. M3 158 F3
New Briggs Fold. BL7 8 E2
New Broad La. OL16 31 C3
New Broadcasting House (BBC). M1 163 A7
New Brook Sch. M20 109 F5
New Brunswick St. BL6 22 B3
New Buildings Pl. 4 OL16 139 F8
New Chapel La. BL6 22 F2
New Church Coll. M26 44 C2
New Church Ct. M45 62 F7
New Church Rd. BL1 23 F2
New Church St. M26 44 B3
New City Rd. M28 78 A8
New Collier's Row. BL1 23 E6
New Court Dr. BL7 8 E3
New Croft High Sch. M6 154 F3
New Cross. M4 159 B2
New Cross St. Salford M5, M6 80 C2
New Cross St. Swinton M27 80 A7
New Drake Gn. BL5 57 E5
New Earth St. Mossley OL5 68 D2
New Earth St. Oldham OL4 67 C5
New Elizabeth St. M8 156 A5
New Ellesmere App. M28 60 D4
New Elm Rd. M3 162 D8
New Field Cl. R'dale OL16 31 B8
New Field Cl. Radcliffe M26 43 E3
New Fold. WN5 53 C4
New Forest Rd. M23 120 C8
New Gate. BL5 146 A1
New George St. 8 BL8 27 C3
New Green. BL2 25 E6
New Hall Ave. Eccles M30 95 A8
New Hall Ave. Gatley SK8 131 B7
New Hall Ave. M'ster M7 155 D8
New Hall La. Bolton BL1 144 A8
New Hall La. Culcheth WA3 91 E1
New Hall La. Culcheth WA3 92 A2
New Hall Mews. BL6 23 D1
New Hall Pl. BL1 144 A8
New Hall Rd. Bury BL9 28 E4
New Hall Rd. M'ster M7 155 D8
New Hall Rd. Sale M33 108 F4
New Herbert St. M6 80 C5
New Hey Rd. Cheadle SK8 122 E6
New Hey Rd. Denshaw HD3 34 F8
New Heys Way. BL2 25 D6
New Holder St. BL1 145 E7
New Houses. OL4 68 C8
New Islington. M20 & M4 159 C2
New Kings Head Yd. M3 158 F2
New La. Bolton BL2 25 E2
New La. Eccles M30 79 B1
New La. Middleton M24 47 A1
New La. Royton OL2 48 D4
New Lane Ct. BL2 25 E2
New Lawns. SK5 100 A1
New Lees St. OL6 85 D5
New Line. OL13 4 B8
New Lodge. WN1 37 D2
New Market. M2 158 F1
New Market La. M1 159 A1
New Market St. WN1 150 C8
New Meadow. BL6 40 C7
New Miles La. WN6 35 F5
New Mill St. OL15 16 A5
New Mills Rd. SK14 & SK6 115 B4
New Moor La. SK7 124 D3
New Moss Rd. M44 105 D6
New Moston Inf Sch. M40 65 E2
New Moston Jun Sch. M40 65 E2
New Mount St. 5 M4 159 A3
New Park Rd. M5 161 B7
New Quay St. M3 158 E1
New Radcliffe St. OL1 153 E7
New Raven Ct. BL3 43 A3
New Rd. Adlington PR6 21 D8
New Rd. Aspull WN2 38 A5
New Rd. Littleborough OL15 15 F5
New Rd. Oldham OL8 66 E4
New Rd. Radcliffe M26 44 B4
New Rd. Tintwistle SK14 104 A7
New Rd. Whitworth OL12 4 B1
New Ridd Rise. SK14 113 D8
New Rock. BL5 57 F5
New Royd Ave. OL4 67 F8
New Smithfield Mkt. M18 165 C7
New St. Alt'ham WA14 119 D4
New St. Ashton-i-M WN4 73 C4
New St. Blackrod BL6 21 D2
New St. Bolton BL1 145 E6
New St. Bury BL8 26 F6
New St. Droylsden M43 100 A8
New St. Eccles M30 79 C1
New St. Littleborough OL15 15 F4
New St. M'ster M10 & M40 160 E4
New St. Milnrow OL16 32 A5
New St. Mottram-i-L SK14 115 A8
New St. Oldham OL4 67 E6
New St. Platt Bridge WN2 56 A2
New St. R'dale OL12 14 E2
New St. Radcliffe M26 44 B2
New St. Stalybridge SK15 102 A8
New St. Swinton M27 62 A1
New St. Uppermill OL3 69 B8
New St. Wigan WN5 54 B5
New St. Wilmslow SK9 136 E5
New Tame. OL3 50 C7
New Tempest Rd. BL6 40 C4
New Thomas St. M6 81 A4
New Tong Field. BL7 24 F7
New Union St. M20 & M4 159 C2
New Vernon St. 12 BL9 140 F4
New Viaduct St. M12 160 E2
New Wakefield St. M1 163 A7
New Way. OL12 4 C1
New Wellington Sch The. WA15 119 F6
New York. BL3 40 F5
New York Ave. M90 130 B7
New York St. OL10 29 B2
New Zealand Rd. SK1 112 B2
Newall Gr. WN7 75 F6
Newall Green High Sch. M23 120 F3
Newall Green Inf Sch. M22 121 B4
Newall Green Jun Sch. M22 121 A4
Newall Rd. M23 120 F3
Newall St. Littleborough OL15 16 B6
Newall St. Walsden OL14 6 A8
Newark Ave. Little Lever M26 43 C5
Newark Ave. 3 M'ster M14 98 B3
Newark Park Way. OL2 48 C6
Newark Rd. Hindley WN2 56 C4
Newark Rd. R'dale OL12 14 F3
Newark Rd. Reddish SK5 111 F5
Newark Rd. Swinton M27 62 B2
Newark Sq. OL12 14 F3
Newark St. WN6 36 F1
Newbank Chase. OL9 152 A8
Newbank Towers. M3 158 E3
Newbarn Cl. OL2 149 A7
Newbeck St. 3 M4 159 A2
Newberry Gr. SK3 170 D5
Newbold Cl. M15 162 F6
Newbold Moss. OL16 31 B8
Newbold St. Bury BL8 27 C2
Newbold St. R'dale OL16 31 C7
Newboult Rd. SK8 122 E6
Newbourne Cl. SK7 124 D3
Newbreak Cl. 2 OL4 67 D8
Newbreak St. 3 OL4 67 D8
Newbridge. OL5 86 D8
Newbridge Cl. WN4 72 D3
Newbridge Gdns. BL2 25 E4
Newbrook Ave. M21 109 D4
Newbrook Rd. BL5 & M46 58 F6
Newburn Ave. M9 64 F4
Newburn Cl. WN3 54 E4
Newbury Ave. M33 107 C4
Newbury Cl. SK8 122 A6
Newbury Dr. Eccles M30 79 B3
Newbury Dr. Urmston M41 95 C5
Newbury Gr. OL10 46 C8
Newbury Pl. M7 155 D7
Newbury Rd. Gatley SK8 131 C7
Newbury Rd. Little Lever BL3 42 F3
Newbury Wlk. Bolton BL1 143 E1
Newbury Wlk. M'ster M9 157 E8
Newbury Wlk. Oldham OL9 152 C7
Newby Dr. Alt'ham WA14 119 D6
Newby Dr. Gatley M22 122 A6
Newby Dr. Middleton M24 46 F3
Newby Dr. Sale M33 108 E3
Newby Rd. Bolton BL2 25 F2
Newby Rd. Hazel Grove SK7 124 D2
Newby Rd. Stockport SK4 168 C2
Newby Road Ind Est. SK7 124 D2
Newby Sq. WN5 54 B5
Newcastle St. M15 162 F7
Newcastle St. 3 M15 162 F7
Newcastle Way. 2 M34 101 A1
Newchurch. OL8 85 A8
Newchurch Cl. 6 M26 44 B3
Newchurch Cty Prim Sch. WA3 91 E2
Newchurch La. WA3 91 F2
Newchurch Rd. OL13 3 C8
Newchurch St. M'ster M11 164 F8
Newchurch St. R'dale OL11 30 D1
Newchurch Wlk. 5 M26 44 B3
Newcliffe Rd. M9 64 F4
Newcombe Cl. M11 160 F1
Newcombe Dr. M38 59 F6
Newcombe Rd. BL0 11 B2
Newcombe St. M3 158 F3
Newcroft. M35 84 B6
Newcroft Cres. M41 95 F1
Newcroft Dr. Stockport SK3 170 D6
Newcroft Dr. Stretford M41 96 A1
Newcroft Rd. M41 95 F1
Newdale Rd. M18 99 B2
Newearth Rd. M28 78 B8
Newenden Rd. WN1 37 B4
Newfield Ct. WA13 117 A5
Newfield Head La. OL16 32 B5
Newfield View. OL16 32 A6
Newgate. R'dale OL12, OL16 139 F7
Newgate. Wilmslow SK9 136 D7
Newgate Ave. WN6 35 E8
Newgate Dr. M38 60 A6
Newgate Rd. M33 107 C1
Newgate St. M4 & M60 159 A2
Newhall Ave. BL3 43 B6
Newhall Dr. M23 109 B2
Newhall Rd. SK5 100 A2
Newham Ave. M11 83 B2
Newhaven Ave. Droylsden M18 99 F7
Newhaven Ave. Leigh WN7 75 F8
Newhaven Bsns Pk. M30 79 E1
Newhaven Cl. BL8 27 C7
Newhaven Wlk. 4 BL2 25 B1
Newhey Ave. M22 121 D5
Newhey Cty Prim Sch. OL16 32 A4
Newhey Rd. Milnrow OL16 32 A5
Newhey Rd. Wythenshawe M22 121 D5
Newholme Ct. M32 96 E2
Newholme Gdns. M38 60 C3
Newholme Rd. M20 109 F5
Newhouse Cl. OL12 15 C6
Newhouse Cres. OL11 29 E8
Newhouse Rd. OL10 46 D8
Newhouse St. OL12 15 C6
Newick Wlk. 6 M9 64 E3
Newington Ave. M8 63 F3
Newington Ct. WA14 119 B3
Newington Dr. Bolton BL1 143 F1
Newington Dr. Bury BL8 27 A1
Newington Wlk. 7 BL1 143 F1
Newland Ave. WN5 54 D5
Newland Dr. BL5 58 F8
Newland St. M8 64 B1
Newlands. M35 83 E4
Newlands Ave. Bolton BL2 25 F1
Newlands Ave. Bramhall SK7 132 F8
Newlands Ave. Cheadle SK8 132 A7
Newlands Ave. Eccles M30 94 F7
Newlands Ave. Irlam M44 94 A2
Newlands Ave. R'dale OL12 14 F3
Newlands Ave. Tyldesley M29 77 A6
Newlands Ave. Whitefield M45 44 E1
Newlands Cl. Cheadle SK8 132 A7
Newlands Cl. R'dale OL12 14 F3
Newlands Dr. Blackrod BL6 38 E7
Newlands Dr. Golborne WA3 90 D8
Newlands Dr. Hadfield SK14 171 F4
Newlands Dr. M'ster M20 122 C8
Newlands Dr. Pendlebury M27 80 C6
Newlands Dr. Prestwich M25 63 A5
Newlands Dr. Wilmslow SK9 136 E5
Newlands Rd. Cheadle SK8 122 D6
Newlands Rd. Leigh WN7 75 F3
Newlands Rd. Wythenshawe M23 120 F8
Newlands Wlk. M24 46 E3
Newlyn Ave. SK15 86 D3
Newlyn Cl. SK7 124 D1
Newlyn Dr. Ashton-i-M WN4 73 B1
Newlyn Dr. Romiley SK6 113 A3
Newlyn Dr. Sale M33 108 C1
Newlyn St. M14 98 B2
Newman Ave. WN6 37 A2
Newman Cl. WN2 56 C6
Newman St. Ashton-u-L OL6 166 A3
Newman St. Hyde SK14 167 E3
Newman St. R'dale OL16 15 C3
Newman St. Wigan WN1 37 E2
Newmarket Cl. M33 107 B2
Newmarket Gr. OL7 84 E5
Newmarket Mews. M7 155 D6
Newmarket Rd. Ashton-u-L OL7 84 F5
Newmarket Rd. Little Lever BL3 43 A2
Newmill Wlk. 2 M8 156 A6
Newnham St. BL1 143 F4
Newpark Wlk. 6 M8 156 A6
Newport Ave. SK5 111 E7
Newport Mews. BL4 60 D7
Newport Rd. Bolton BL3 42 A3
Newport Rd. Denton M34 113 B8
Newport Rd. M'ster M21 97 A1
Newport St. Bolton BL1, BL3 145 F6
Newport St. Bury BL8 27 A5
Newport St. Farnworth BL4 60 D7
Newport St. M'ster M14 98 B3
Newport St. Middleton M24 47 C1
Newport St. Oldham OL8 153 D5
Newport St. Salford M6 154 E2
Newquay Ave. BL2 26 D1
Newquay Dr. SK7 132 F7
Newry Rd. M30 95 E8
Newry St. BL1 143 D3
Newsham Cl. BL3 145 D5
Newsham Wlk. 2 M'ster M18 99 B3
Newsham Wlk. Shevington WN6 36 F1
Newshaw La. SK13 171 F4
Newsholme Cl. WA3 91 F3
Newsholme St. M7 & M8 155 F7
Newstead. 14 OL12 139 E8
Newstead Ave. Ashton-u-L OL6 85 C7
Newstead Ave. M'ster M20 110 D5
Newstead Cl. SK12 133 D5
Newstead Gr. SK6 112 F3
Newstead Rd. Urmston M41 95 E3
Newstead Rd. Wigan WN3 54 F3
Newstead Terr. WA15 119 F7
Newton Ave. M'ster M12 98 F4
Newton Ave. M'ster M20 110 A6
Newton Bank Sch. WA12 89 E4
Newton Bsns Pk. SK14 102 A5
Newton Cl. WN1 37 D2
Newton Comm Hospl. WA12 89 B2
Newton Cres. M24 46 D3
Newton Cty Prim Sch. WA12 89 D3
Newton Dr. BL8 11 A1
Newton Gn. SK14 101 F5
Newton Hall Ct. SK14 101 C5
Newton Hall Rd. SK14 101 C5
Newton Heath Upper Sch. M40 157 F5
Newton La. WA12 89 E6
Newton Moor Ind Est. SK14 101 E5
Newton Park Dr. WA12 89 F3
Newton Rd. Alt'ham WA14 119 E7
Newton Rd. Billinge WN5, WA9, WN4 71 F6
Newton Rd. Failsworth M35 83 F5
Newton Rd. Golborne WA12 90 D5
Newton Rd. Golborne WA3 & WN7 91 A8
Newton Rd. Handforth SK9 131 A1
Newton Rd. M'ster M24 64 B6
Newton Rd. Newton-l-W WA12 89 F1
Newton Rd. Urmston M41 95 C2
Newton St. Ashton-u-L OL6 166 C3
Newton St. Bolton BL1 143 E2
Newton St. Bury BL9 27 F6
Newton St. Droylsden M43 84 C3
Newton St. Failsworth M40 83 C6
Newton St. Hyde SK14 167 D4
Newton St. Leigh WN7 75 F5
Newton St. M'ster M1, M4, M60 159 B1
Newton St. R'dale OL16 31 A5
Newton St. 4 Stalybridge SK15 85 F2
Newton St. Stockport SK3 170 E8
Newton St. Stretford M32 96 D1
Newton Sta. SK14 167 F4
Newton Terr. 23 Bolton BL1 143 E2
Newton Terr. 20 Dukinfield SK16 166 B1
Newton Westpark Prim Sch. WN7 75 C8
Newton Wlk. BL1 143 E2
Newton Wood Rd. SK16 101 B6
Newton-le-Willows Comm Sch. WA12 89 D5
Newton-le-Willows Sta. WA12 89 E3
Newtondale Ave. OL2 48 C4
Newtonhurst. SK14 102 A5
Newtonmore Wlk. M11 83 B1
Newtown Ave. M34 100 F2
Newtown Cl. M'ster M11 165 B8
Newtown Cl. Swinton M27 61 F2
Newtown Ct. M'ster M40 159 C4
Newtown Ct. Prestwich M25 63 C4
Newtown St. Prestwich M25 63 C4
Newtown St. Shaw OL2 149 B6
Newville Dr. M20 110 D5
Ney St. OL7 84 F6
Neyland Cl. BL1 40 F7
Niagara St. SK2 124 A6
Nicholas Croft. M4 159 A2
Nicholas Owen Cl. M11 165 C8
Nicholas Rd. OL8 66 E4
Nicholas St. Bolton BL2 148 A8
Nicholas St. M'ster M1 & M60 159 A1
Nicholls St. M12 164 D7
Nichols St. M6 81 B3
Nicholson Rd. SK14 101 C5
Nicholson Sq. SK16 101 B8
Nicholson St. Oldham OL4 67 E6
Nicholson St. R'dale OL11 139 F5
Nicholson St. Stockport SK4 & SK5 169 E2
Nickleby Rd. SK12 133 E3
Nicol Mere Cty Prim Sch. WN4 73 B5
Nicol Mere Dr. WN4 73 A5
Nicol Rd. WN4 73 B5
Nicola St. BL7 24 E8
Nicolas Rd. M21 97 A1
Nield Rd. M34 100 F3
Nield St. OL5 68 B2
Nield's Brow. WA14 119 C2
Nields Way. SK6 126 D4
Nigel Rd. M9 157 F7
Nigher Moss Ave. OL16 31 C6
Nightingale Cl. SK9 131 B1
Nightingale Ct. 10 WN1 37 A1
Nightingale Dr. M34 & M43 84 C1
Nightingale Rd. BL6 21 C3
Nightingale St. PR6 21 A8
Nightingales Wlk. 3 BL3 147 F3
Nile St. Bolton BL3 145 F5
Nile St. Dukinfield OL7 100 F8
Nile St. Oldham OL1 153 E8
Nile St. R'dale OL16 31 A8
Nile Terr. M7 155 D5
Nimble Nook. OL9 152 A5
Nina Dr. M40 65 C3
Nine Acre Ct. M5 161 B7
Nine Acre Dr. M5 161 B7
Ninehouse La. BL1 147 F4
Ninfield Rd. M22 & M23 121 B4
Ninian Ct. 2 M24 46 F1
Ninian Gdns. M28 60 D3
Ninth Ave. OL8 66 D1
Ninth St. M17 96 C6
Nipper La. M45 44 E2
Nisbet Ave. M22 121 E3
Niven St. M12 163 C7
Nixon Rd. BL3 146 C3
Nixon Rd S. BL3 146 C3
Nixon St. Failsworth M35 83 E7
Nixon St. R'dale OL11 30 B3
Nixon St. Stockport SK3 170 E8
No 2 Passage. SK3 169 D1
Noahs Ark La. WA16 136 A1
Noble Meadow. OL12 15 D4
Noble St. Bolton BL3 145 E5
Noble St. 7 Leigh WN7 76 A5
Noble St. Oldham OL8 66 F4
Noel Dr. M33 108 D4
Noel St. BL1 145 E7
Nolan St. M9 157 E8
Nona St. M6 154 E3
Nook Farm Ave. OL12 14 F3
Nook Fields. BL2 25 E3
Nook La. Ashton-u-L OL6 85 E6
Nook La. Golborne WA3 90 B8
Nook La. Tyldesley M29 77 D2
Nook Terr. OL12 14 F3
Nook The. Appley Bridge WN6 35 E7
Nook The. Bramhall SK7 132 D5
Nook The. Worsley M28 79 A4
Noon Ct. WA12 89 B1
Noon Sun Cl. OL3 69 A4
Noon Sun St. OL12 14 F1
Norbet Wlk. 8 M9 157 E7
Norbreck Ave. Cheadle SK8 123 A6
Norbreck Ave. M'ster M21 109 B7
Norbreck Cres. WN6 37 A2
Norbreck Gdns. BL2 148 C8
Norbreck St. BL2 148 C8
Norburn Rd. M13 98 F2
Norbury Ave. Billinge WN5 71 D6
Norbury Ave. Hyde SK14 167 D2
Norbury Ave. Marple SK6 125 F6
Norbury Ave. Sale M33 107 E5
Norbury Ave. 7 Salford M6 80 D5
Norbury Ave. Uppermill OL4 68 C6
Norbury Cl. M40 160 E4
Norbury Cres. SK7 124 D2
Norbury Dr. SK6 125 F6
Norbury Gr. Bolton BL1 25 A4
Norbury Gr. Hazel Grove SK7 124 E2
Norbury Gr. Swinton M27 61 F1
Norbury Hall Prim Sch. SK7 124 E1
Norbury Hollow Rd. SK7 134 B8
Norbury House. 4 OL4 67 B5
Norbury La. OL8 67 D3
Norbury Mews. SK6 125 E6
Norbury St. Leigh WN7 75 D5
Norbury St. M'ster M7 155 E6
Norbury St. R'dale OL16 31 B4
Norbury St. Stockport SK1 169 F1
Norbury Way. 9 SK9 131 D5
Norcot Wlk. 15 M15 162 D6
Norcross Cl. SK2 124 D5
Nordale Pk. OL12 13 D2
Nordek Cl. OL2 48 D5
Nordek Dr. OL2 48 D5
Norden Ave. M20 110 A6
Norden Cl. OL11 13 C2
Norden Comm Prim Sch. OL12 13 F2
Norden Ct. BL3 147 E4
Norden Rd. OL10 & OL11 29 E6
Norden Way. OL11 13 C2
Nordens Dr. OL9 47 F1
Nordens Rd. OL9 65 F8
Nordens St. OL9 152 A8
Noreen Ave. M25 63 C5
Norfield Cl. SK16 101 C8
Norfolk Ave. Droylsden M43 83 F3
Norfolk Ave. Heywood OL10 29 A2
Norfolk Ave. M'ster M18 99 C4
Norfolk Ave. Reddish M34 99 F3
Norfolk Ave. Reddish SK4 111 C6
Norfolk Ave. Whitefield M45 63 A8
Norfolk Cl. Hindley WN2 57 A6
Norfolk Cl. Irlam M44 105 C5
Norfolk Cl. Little Lever BL3 43 B4
Norfolk Cl. Littleborough OL15 6 C1
Norfolk Cl. Shaw OL2 48 F7
Norfolk Cres. M35 83 E6
Norfolk Dr. BL4 42 D1
Norfolk Gdns. M41 94 D3
Norfolk House. 8 M7 63 E1
Norfolk Rd. Atherton M46 58 C4
Norfolk Rd. M'ster M18 99 C4
Norfolk Rd. Orrell WN5 53 E1
Norfolk St. Glossop SK13 104 D1
Norfolk St. Hyde SK14 167 D2
Norfolk St. 10 M'ster M2 158 F1
Norfolk St. M'ster M1 159 A1
Norfolk St. Oldham OL9 66 C4
Norfolk St. R'dale OL11 139 F6
Norfolk St. Salford M6 81 A5
Norfolk St. Walkden M28 60 D6
Norfolk St. Wigan WN6 37 A2
Norfolk St. 9 Wigan WN5 54 F6
Norfolk Way. OL2 48 D2
Norford Way. OL11 29 E7
Norgate St. M20 110 B3
Norlan Ave. M34 100 E7
Norland Wlk. M40 83 A5
Norleigh Rd. M22 121 D8
Norley Ave. M32 96 F3
Norley Cl. OL1 48 B2
Norley Dr. M'ster M19 99 C2
Norley Dr. Sale M33 108 E4
Norley Hall Ave. WN5 54 C6
Norley Rd. Leigh WN7 75 B4
Norley Rd. Wigan WN5 54 C7
Norman Ave. Hazel Grove SK7 124 C3

Norman Ave. Newton-l-W WA11 89 A7
Norman Ave. Newton-l-W WA12 89 E3
Norman Cl. M24 47 C1
Norman Gr. M'ster M12 98 F4
Norman Gr. M'ster M12, M18 99 A4
Norman Gr. Reddish SK5 111 E7
Norman House Prep Sch. M40 65 D3
Norman Rd. Alt'ham WA14 119 C6
Norman Rd. Ashton-u-L OL6 85 C6
Norman Rd. M'ster M14 98 D2
Norman Rd. M'ster M7 155 E7
Norman Rd. M'ster SK4 168 B3
Norman Rd. R'dale OL11 139 D6
Norman Rd. Sale M33 108 B3
Norman Rd. Stalybridge SK15 85 F7
Norman Rd W. M9 157 F7
Norman St. Bury BL9 141 B4
Norman St. Failsworth M35 66 A1
Norman St. Hyde SK14 167 E2
Norman St. M'ster M12 165 B5
Norman St. Middleton M24 47 B1
Norman St. Oldham OL1 153 D8
Norman St. Radcliffe M26 44 D4
Norman Weall Ct. 5 M24 47 A2
Norman's Pl. WA14 119 D4
Normanby Chase. WA14 119 B4
Normanby Gr. M27 61 E1
Normanby Rd. M28 60 C1
Normanby St. Bolton BL3 146 C2
Normanby St. M'ster M14 98 A4
Normanby St. Swinton M27 61 E1
Normanby St. Wigan WN5 54 B6
Normandale Ave. BL1 142 A1
Normandy Cres. M26 43 F3
Normanton Ave. M6 80 C3
Normanton Cl. WN6 36 E4
Normanton Dr. M9 64 E4
Normanton Rd. SK3 & SK8 123 A6
Normington St. 1 OL4 67 C7
Norreys Ave. M41 94 E3
Norreys St. OL16 31 A8
Norris Ave. SK4 168 C2
Norris Bank Prim Sch. SK4 168 B3
Norris Bank Terr. SK4 168 C1
Norris Hill Dr. SK4 168 D1
Norris Rd. M33 108 D2
Norris St. Bolton BL3 145 E5
Norris St. Farnworth BL4 60 D7
Norris St. Little Lever BL3 43 A3
Norris St. Tyldesley M29 77 A8
Norris Towers. SK4 168 C2
North Area Coll. SK4 111 B5
North Ave. Eccles M41 95 E6
North Ave. Farnworth BL4 60 B8
North Ave. Leigh WN7 74 F4
North Ave. Leigh WN7 76 C3
North Ave. M'ster M19 110 F7
North Ave. Ramsbottom BL8 10 F1
North Ave. Stalybridge SK15 86 A3
North Ave. Uppermill OL3 69 B5
North Ave. Whitefield BL9 45 B4
North Back Rock. Bury BL9 140 F2
North Blackfield La. M7 81 C8
North Bolton Sixth Form Coll. BL1 142 C4
North Brook Rd. SK14 171 E4
North Broughton St. M3 158 E2
North Butts St. WN7 76 B3
North Cestrian Gram Sch. WA14 119 C5
North Chadderton Sch. Chadderton OL9 48 A2
North Chadderton Sch. Chadderton OL9 152 A8
North Cheshire Jewish Prim Sch. SK8 122 C2
North Circ. M45 63 A6
North Cl. SK14 103 F7
North Clifden La. M7 155 E6
North Cres. Droylsden M11 & M43 83 D3
North Cres. Failsworth M40 65 D3
North Croft. OL8 67 A3
North Dean St. M27 62 A1
North Downs Rd. SK8 122 F3
North Dr. Appley Bridge WN6 18 C2
North Dr. Droylsden M34 84 C1
North Dr. Pendlebury M27 80 B7
North Edge. WN7 76 B6
North Gate. OL8 66 E2
North George St. M3 158 D2
North Gr. M'ster M13 164 D5
North Gr. Urmston M41 95 C2
North Gr. Walkden M28 60 C3
North Harvey St. SK1 169 F1
North Heaton Prim Sch. SK4 111 C6
North Hill St. M3 158 D3
North La. R'dale OL12 139 F8
North La. Tyldesley M29 77 A6
North Lonsdale St. M32 96 E4
North Manchester General Hospl. M8 64 B1
North Manchester Golf Course. M24 64 D8
North Manchester High Sch for Boys. M9 65 B3
North Manchester High Sch for Girls. M40 65 A1
North Mead. M21 109 B7
North Nook. OL4 67 F8
North Par. Newhey OL16 32 C4
North Par. Sale M33 108 D2
North Park Rd. SK7 123 E3
North Phoebe St. M5 161 B8
North Pl. SK1 169 F1
North Rd. Alt'ham WA15 129 A8
North Rd. Atherton M46 58 B5
North Rd. Carrington M31 106 E4
North Rd. Droylsden M11, M43 83 C2
North Rd. Droylsden M34 84 D1
North Rd. Glossop SK13 104 C3
North Rd. Prestwich M25 62 F5
North Rd. Stretford M32 96 B4
North Rd. Stretford M17 96 C5
North Rd. Wythenshawe M90 130 C6
North Reddish Inf Sch. SK5 99 F1
North Reddish Jun Sch. SK5 99 F1
North Rise. OL3 69 B5
North St. Ashton-i-M WN4 73 D5
North St. Ashton-u-L OL6 166 A2
North St. Atherton M46 58 E3
North St. Heywood OL10 29 B2
North St. Leigh WN7 76 B4
North St. M'ster M8 159 A4
North St. Middleton M24 47 A2
North St. R'dale OL16 31 A8
North St. Radcliffe M26 44 C4
North St. Ramsbottom BL0 1 C2
North St. Royton OL2 48 D3
North St. 1 Royton OL2 48 D4
North St. Whitworth OL12 4 C1
North Stage. M5 96 F8
North Star Dr. M3 158 D1
North Trafford Coll of F Ed. M32 96 F4
North Vale Rd. WA15 119 F6
North Veiw. M45 44 E2
North View. Mossley OL5 68 E1
North View. Ramsbottom BL0 1 C2
North View. Ramsbottom BL0 11 B2
North View Cl. OL4 68 C5
North Walkden Prim Sch. M28 60 C5
North Way. Bolton BL1 25 B4
North Way. Brinnington SK5 112 C6
North Western St. M'ster M19 111 A8
North Western St. M'ster M1 & M2 163 C8
North Western St. M'ster M12 164 D7
North Woodley. 6 M26 44 C1
Northallerton Rd. M7 81 B6
Northampton Rd. M10 & M40 & M9 157 F6
Northampton Way. 1 M34 101 A1
Northavon Cl. M30 80 A1
Northbank Gdns. M19 110 E6
Northbank Ind Pk. M44 105 F7
Northbank Wlk. M20 109 D3
Northbourne St. M6 154 E2
Northbrook Ave. M9 63 F4
Northcliffe Rd. SK2 124 C8
Northcombe Rd. SK3 170 E5
Northcote Rd. SK7 132 F7
Northcroft. WN1 37 F1
Northdale Rd. M9 64 B5
Northdene Dr. OL11 29 F6
Northdown Ave. M'ster M15 162 D6
Northdown Av. Romiley SK6 113 C5
Northdowns Rd. OL2 48 F8
Northen Gr. M20 109 F4
Northend Rd. SK15 86 B2
Northenden Golf Cse. M22 109 E2
Northenden Prim Sch. M22 109 D1
Northenden Rd. Gatley M22 & SK8 122 A6
Northenden Rd. Sale M33 108 C4
Northenden Rd. Sale M33 108 E3
Northenden View. M20 110 B2
Northern Ave. M27 62 C3
Northern Gr. BL1 142 C1
Northfield Ave. M40 & OL9 65 F2
Northfield Ct. WN3 74 C1
Northfield Dr. SK9 137 D8
Northfield Rd. Bury BL9 27 F6
Northfield Rd. Failsworth M40 65 F2
Northfield St. BL3 144 C5
Northfleet Rd. Eccles M30 94 F8
Northgate. OL12 14 C7
Northgate La. OL1 49 E3
Northgate Rd. SK3 123 C8
Northgraves Dr. M7 155 F6
Northland Rd. Bolton BL1 24 F6
Northland Rd. M'ster M9 65 A3
Northlands. M26 43 E5
Northleach Cl. BL8 27 B3
Northleigh Dr. M25 63 D3
Northleigh House. 1 M16 97 B2
Northleigh Rd. M16 97 B3
Northmoor Mews. 10 OL1 153 E8
Northmoor Rd. M12 & M18 99 A3
Northolme Gdns. M19 110 E5
Northolt Ave. WN7 75 F8
Northolt Ct. M11 83 D2
Northolt Dr. BL3 147 F4
Northolt Rd. Wythenshawe M23 108 F1
Northridge Rd. M9 64 D6
Northside Ave. M41 94 F1
Northstead Ave. M34 101 B2
Northumberland Ave. OL6 & OL7 166 B4
Northumberland Cl. M16 161 C5
Northumberland Cres. M16 161 C5
Northumberland Rd. Brinnington SK5 112 B6
Northumberland Rd. M'ster M16 161 C5
Northumberland Rd. Partington M31 105 E2
Northumberland St. M'ster M7 155 E7
Northumberland St. Wigan WN1 37 E1
Northumbria St. 9 BL3 144 C5
Northurst Dr. M8 63 F3
Northward Rd. SK9 136 F6
Northway. Alt'ham WA14 119 E6
Northway. Droylsden M43 100 A8
Northway. 4 Eccles M30 79 F2
Northway. Wigan WN1 37 C1
Northways. WN6 19 D2
Northwell St. 2 WN7 75 E8
Northwold Cl. WN3 54 D3
Northwold Dr. Bolton BL1 40 E8
Northwold Dr. M'ster M9 65 B3
Northwood. BL2 25 D4
Northwood Ave. Cheadle SK8 123 A3
Northwood Ave. Newton-l-W WA12 89 F3
Northwood Cres. BL3 144 C5
Northwood Gr. M33 108 B4
Norton Ave. M'ster M12 99 B3
Norton Ave. Reddish M34 100 A3
Norton Ave. Sale M33 107 D6
Norton Ave. Urmston M41 95 D4
Norton Gr. SK4 168 B1
Norton Grange. M25 63 D3
Norton Rd. Boothstown M28 77 E7
Norton Rd. R'dale OL12 14 F3
Norton St. Bolton BL1 143 F3
Norton St. M'ster M16 97 D4
Norton St. M'ster M7 155 E7
Norton St. M'ster M3 158 F2
Norton St. 17 M'ster M60 159 C1
Norton St. M'ster M10, M40 160 E4
Norview Dr. M20 122 B8
Norville Ave. M40 & M9 65 D3
Norway Gr. SK5 169 F4
Norway St. Bolton BL1 143 D2
Norway St. M'ster M11 164 E8
Norway St. Salford M6 154 E2
Norway St. Stretford M32 96 E3
Norweb Way. WN7 76 B3
Norwell Rd. M22 121 E5
Norwich Ave. Ashton-i-M WN4 73 D3
Norwich Ave. Chadderton OL9 48 A1
Norwich Ave. Denton M34 100 F1
Norwich Ave. Golborne WA3 90 D8
Norwich Ave. R'dale OL11 30 B7
Norwich Cl. Ashton-u-L OL6 85 D8
Norwich Cl. Dukinfield SK16 102 A7
Norwich Dr. BL8 140 D3
Norwich Rd. M32 95 F3
Norwich St. OL11 31 A5
Norwick Cl. BL3 40 E4
Norwood. M25 63 B2
Norwood Ave. Ashton-i-M WN4 72 F6
Norwood Ave. Bramhall SK7 132 D5
Norwood Ave. Golborne WA3 90 F7
Norwood Ave. High Lane SK6 134 D7
Norwood Ave. M'ster M7 81 B8
Norwood Ave. M'ster M20 110 D4
Norwood Ave. Tyldesley M29 77 B6
Norwood Ave. Wigan WN6 37 A3
Norwood Cl. Adlington PR6 21 A8
Norwood Cl. Shaw OL2 149 A8
Norwood Cl. Walkden M28 78 E8
Norwood Cres. OL2 48 E2
Norwood Ct. M32 96 E1
Norwood Dr. Alt'ham WA15 120 D5
Norwood Dr. Swinton M27 79 D7
Norwood Gr. Bolton BL1 144 C8
Norwood Gr. Oldham OL2 48 E2
Norwood Lodge. M7 81 B8
Norwood Rd. Gatley SK8 122 B6
Norwood Rd. Stockport SK2 124 B4
Norwood Rd. Stretford M32 96 E2
Noseby Ct. M25 63 C5
Nostell Rd. WN4 73 A5
Nottingham Ave. SK5 112 C5
Nottingham Cl. SK5 112 C6
Nottingham Dr. Ashton-u-L OL6 85 B7
Nottingham Dr. Bolton BL1 143 E1
Nottingham Dr. Brinnington SK5 112 C6
Nottingham Dr. Failsworth M35 84 A6
Nottingham Pl. WN1 37 E1
Nottingham Way. 3 M34 101 A1
Nowell Ct. M24 47 A3
Nowell House. M24 47 A3
Nowell Rd. M24 47 A3
Nudger Cl. OL3 50 F2
Nudger Gn. OL3 51 A2
Nuffield Rd. M22 121 E4
Nugent House Sch. WN5 71 D4
Nugent Rd. BL3 147 E3
Nugget St. OL4 67 B6
Nuneaton Dr. M10 & M40 160 D3
Nuneham Ave. M20 110 C7
Nunfield Cl. M40 65 B2
Nunnery Rd. BL3 146 B4
Nunthorpe Dr. M8 156 C8
Nursery Ave. WA15 128 E8
Nursery Cl. Glossop SK13 116 C8
Nursery Cl. Sale M33 108 D4
Nursery La. Cheadle SK3 123 A7
Nursery La. Wilmslow SK9 136 F5
Nursery Rd. Cheadle SK8 123 A1
Nursery Rd. Failsworth M35 84 A7
Nursery Rd. Prestwich M25 63 A4
Nursery Rd. Stockport SK4 168 C2
Nursery Rd. Urmston M41 95 A4
Nursery St. M'ster M16 97 C3
Nursery St. Salford M6 154 F3
Nuthurst Rd. M40 65 D1
Nutsford Vale. M18 99 B4
Nutt La. M25 63 E8
Nutt St. WN1 37 E2
Nuttal Ave. M45 62 F8
Nuttal Mews. M45 62 F8
Nuttall Ave. Horwich BL6 22 A3
Nuttall Ave. Little Lever BL3 43 C3
Nuttall Ave. Whitefield M45 62 F8
Nuttall Cl. BL0 138 C5
Nuttall Hall Cott s. BL0 11 D5
Nuttall Hall Rd. BL0 11 D5
Nuttall La. BL0 138 B5
Nuttall Mews. M45 62 F8
Nuttall Rd. BL0 11 D4
Nuttall Sq. BL9 44 F5
Nuttall St. Atherton M46 58 E3
Nuttall St. Bury BL9 141 A1
Nuttall St. Irlam M44 105 E6
Nuttall St. M'ster M16 161 C5
Nuttall St. M'ster M11 165 A7
Nuttall St. Oldham OL8 67 B4

O'Kane House. 10 M30 79 D1
Oadby Cl. M12 99 A4
Oak Ave. Abram WN2 74 C7
Oak Ave. Cheadle SK8 123 A2
Oak Ave. Golborne WA3 90 B8
Oak Ave. Hindley WN2 57 A3
Oak Ave. 9 Horwich BL6 22 E1
Oak Ave. Irlam M44 105 D5
Oak Ave. Little Lever BL3 43 B3
Oak Ave. M'ster M21 109 B8
Oak Ave. M'ster SK4 168 B2
Oak Ave. Middleton M24 65 A7
Oak Ave. Newton-l-W WA12 89 D3
Oak Ave. Ramsbottom BL0 11 A2
Oak Ave. Reddish M18 99 F4
Oak Ave. Romiley SK6 113 C2
Oak Ave. Royton OL2 48 D6
Oak Ave. Standish WN6 36 F8
Oak Ave. Whitefield M45 62 F7
Oak Ave. Wilmslow SK9 136 F5
Oak Bank. M'ster M9 157 D8
Oak Bank. Prestwich M25 62 F1
Oak Bank. Prestwich M25 63 C5
Oak Bank Ave. M9 64 F1
Oak Bank Cl. M45 63 B8
Oak Brow Cotts. SK9 130 E4
Oak Cl. Mottram-i-L SK14 103 A4
Oak Cl. Whitworth OL12 4 D4
Oak Cl. Wilmslow SK9 136 F6
Oak Cotts. SK9 130 E4
Oak Ct. SK6 113 A5
Oak Dr. Bramhall SK7 132 C7
Oak Dr. M'ster M14 98 D1
Oak Dr. Marple SK6 125 D6
Oak Dr. Reddish M34 100 A4
Oak Gates. BL7 8 E1
Oak Gr. Ashton-u-L OL6 85 D6
Oak Gr. Cheadle SK8 122 E5
Oak Gr. Eccles M30 79 B1
Oak Gr. Poynton SK12 133 D4
Oak Gr. Urmston M41 95 E2
Oak Hill. OL15 15 F5
Oak Hill Cl. WN1 37 B4
Oak La. Whitefield M45 63 B8
Oak La. Wilmslow SK9 136 F6
Oak Lea Ave. SK9 137 A5
Oak Lodge. SK7 132 F7
Oak Mews. SK9 131 C1
Oak Rd. Alt'ham WA15 119 E3
Oak Rd. Cheadle SK8 122 E5
Oak Rd. Failsworth M35 83 F6
Oak Rd. M'ster M7 81 C5
Oak Rd. M'ster M20 110 B5
Oak Rd. Oldham OL8 66 D2
Oak Rd. Partington M31 105 D2
Oak Rd. Sale M33 108 D4
Oak St. Atherton WN7 58 A1
Oak St. Denton M34 100 F6
Oak St. Eccles M30 79 D1
Oak St. Glossop SK13 104 C1
Oak St. Hazel Grove SK7 124 D3
Oak St. Heywood OL10 29 B3
Oak St. Hyde SK14 167 E4
Oak St. Leigh WN7 75 F3
Oak St. Littleborough OL15 16 C5
Oak St. M'ster M4 159 A2
Oak St. 2 M'ster M4 159 B2
Oak St. Middleton M24 65 D7
Oak St. Newhey OL16 32 B4
Oak St. R'dale OL16 139 F7
Oak St. 2 Radcliffe M26 44 C1
Oak St. Ramsbottom BL0 138 B5
Oak St. Shaw OL2 149 C7
Oak St. Stockport SK3 123 B8
Oak St. Swinton M27 62 A1
Oak St. Tyldesley M29 59 A1
Oak St. Whitworth OL12 4 D5
Oak St. Wigan WN1 151 E7
Oak Terr. OL15 6 D2
Oak Tree Cl. Atherton WN7 58 A1
Oak Tree Cl. Stockport SK2 124 D8
Oak Tree Cres. SK15 102 B8
Oak Tree Dr. SK16 101 F7
Oak View. OL12 4 D4
Oak View Rd. OL3 69 B5
Oak Wood View. SK15 86 C6
Oakbank. WN2 56 B3
Oakbank Ave. OL9 65 F8
Oakbank Dr. BL1 24 D6
Oakcliffe Rd. OL12 & OL16 15 D4
Oakcroft. SK15 102 E8
Oakdale. BL2 25 E4
Oakdale Cl. M45 62 D8
Oakdale Ct. Delph OL3 50 E3
Oakdale Ct. Stalybridge SK15 86 B2
Oakdale Dr. Gatley SK8 122 B2
Oakdale Dr. M'ster M20 110 C1
Oakdale Dr. Tyldesley M29 77 C6
Oakdale Sch. SK16 101 E6
Oakdene. M27 & M28 79 B6
Oakdene Ave. Gatley SK8 131 C7
Oakdene Ave. Reddish SK4 111 D5
Oakdene Cres. SK6 125 F7
Oakdene Gdns. SK6 125 F7
Oakdene Rd. Marple SK6 125 F7
Oakdene Rd. Middleton M24 65 C8
Oakdene Rd. Sale WA15 120 B8
Oakdene St. M9 157 F8
Oaken Bank Rd. OL10 47 A5
Oaken Clough. 3 OL7 85 A6
Oaken Clough Dr. 1 OL7 85 A6
Oaken Clough Terr. OL7 84 F6
Oaken St. OL7 85 A6
Oakenbottom Rd. BL2 42 D7
Oakenclough. 1 OL1 153 E7
Oakenclough Cl. SK9 131 D2
Oakenclough Dr. BL1 23 F2
Oakenden Cl. WN4 73 A6
Oakengates. WN6 19 F1
Oakenrod Hill. OL11 30 C6
Oakenrod Prim Sch. OL11 139 D7
Oakenshaw Ave. OL12 14 C6
Oakenshaw View. OL12 14 C6
Oaker Ave. M20 109 E4
Oakes St. BL4 60 F7
Oakes The. SK13 116 A7
Oakfield. Dukinfield SK16 101 E6
Oakfield. M'ster M25 63 D3
Oakfield. Sale M33 108 A5
Oakfield Ave. Atherton M46 58 C4
Oakfield Ave. Cheadle SK8 122 E6
Oakfield Ave. Droylsden M43 83 F1
Oakfield Ave. Golborne WA3 73 F1
Oakfield Ave. M'ster M16 97 A3
Oakfield Ave. M'ster M16 97 D3
Oakfield Ave. Mossley SK15 86 E6
Oakfield Cl. Alderley Edge SK9 137 B3
Oakfield Cl. Horwich BL6 22 F2
Oakfield Cres. WN2 38 C5
Oakfield Ct. WA15 119 F6
Oakfield Dr. M38 59 E5
Oakfield Gr. Farnworth BL4 60 C6
Oakfield Gr. M'ster M18 99 D4
Oakfield Prim Sch. SK14 101 E5
Oakfield Rd. Alderley Edge SK9 137 B2
Oakfield Rd. Alt'ham WA15 119 E4
Oakfield Rd. Dukinfield SK14 101 E5
Oakfield Rd. Hadfield SK13 171 E3
Oakfield Rd. M'ster M20 110 A3
Oakfield Rd. Poynton SK12 133 B4
Oakfield Rd. Stockport SK3 170 F5
Oakfield St. Alt'ham WA15 119 E5
Oakfield St. M'ster M7 & M8 156 A6
Oakfield Terr. OL11 30 C8
Oakfield Trad Est. WA15 119 E5
Oakfold Ave. OL6 85 D6
Oakford Ave. M10 & M40 159 C3
Oakford Wlk. BL3 146 C4
Oakham Cl. BL8 27 D5
Oakham Mews. M7 63 D1
Oakham Rd. M34 101 A1
Oakhead. WN7 76 C3
Oakhill Cl. BL2 43 A7
Oakhill Ct. M7 155 E7
Oakhill Trad Est. M28 60 C6
Oakhill Way. M8 155 F7
Oakhouse Dr. M21 109 B7
Oakhurst Chase. SK9 137 A2
Oakhurst Dr. SK3 & SK8 123 B5
Oakhurst Gr. BL5 57 C7
Oakington Ave. 10 M14 98 B3
Oakland Ave. Eccles M6 80 B4
Oakland Ave. M'ster M19 110 E4
Oakland Ave. Stockport SK2 124 D6
Oakland Ct. SK12 133 D4
Oakland Gr. BL1 142 A2
Oakland Terr. OL11 30 C1
Oaklands. BL1 40 F7
Oaklands Ave. Cheadle SK8 123 A2
Oaklands Ave. Marple SK6 126 C8
Oaklands Cl. SK9 131 E1
Oaklands Cty Inf Sch. SK9 131 E1
Oaklands Dene. SK14 102 A2
Oaklands Dr. Hazel Grove SK7 124 E1
Oaklands Dr. Hyde SK14 102 A2
Oaklands Dr. Prestwich M25 63 B4
Oaklands Dr. Sale M33 108 A5
Oaklands Hospl The. M6 80 B4
Oaklands House. M14 98 C1
Oaklands Pk. OL4 68 F5
Oaklands Rd. Edenfield BL0 1 D2
Oaklands Rd. Golborne WA3 90 F7
Oaklands Rd. M'ster M7 81 A8
Oaklands Rd. Oldham OL2 48 E2
Oaklands Rd. Swinton M27 79 D6
Oaklands Rd. Uppermill OL4 68 F5
Oaklea. 1 M'ster M16 97 C3
Oaklea. Shevington Moor WN6 19 A2
Oaklea Rd. M33 107 E5
Oakleigh. M'ster SK4 168 B3
Oakleigh. 2 Stockport SK3 123 F4
Oakleigh Ave. Alt'ham WA15 120 A7
Oakleigh Ave. Bolton BL3 42 A2
Oakleigh Ave. 1 M'ster M19 110 F7
Oakleigh Cl. OL10 46 E7
Oakley Ave. WN5 71 E6
Oakley Cl. Failsworth M40 83 A5
Oakley Cl. Radcliffe M26 62 A8
Oakley Pk. BL1 40 F7
Oakley St. Littleborough OL15 15 E4
Oakley St. Salford M5 154 D1
Oakley Villas. SK4 168 B3
Oaklings The. WN2 57 A3
Oakmere Ave. M28 79 C4
Oakmere Cl. M22 121 D4
Oakmere Rd. Cheadle SK8 122 F4
Oakmere Rd. Handforth SK9 131 D5
Oakmoor Dr. M7 81 B8
Oakmoor Rd. M23 121 A6
Oakridge Wlk. 3 M9 157 D7
Oaks Ave. BL2 25 C5
Oaks La. BL1 & BL2 25 B5
Oaks Prim Sch The. BL1 24 F6
Oaks The. Gatley SK8 122 A5
Oaks The. Hyde SK14 102 A3
Oakshaw Dr. OL12 14 A1
Oakside Cl. SK8 122 E6
Oaktree Ct. SK8 122 D5
Oakville Dr. M30 80 A4
Oakville Terr. 11 M40 64 F1
Oakway. M20 122 C8
Oakwell Dr. M'ster M7 & M8 63 E1
Oakwell Dr. Whitefield BL9 45 B3
Oakwell Mansions. M7 63 E1
Oakwood. Chadderton M24 65 E7
Oakwood. Glossop SK13 115 F8
Oakwood. Sale M33 107 C4
Oakwood Ave. Ashton-i-M WN4 73 A2
Oakwood Ave. Denton M34 100 E7
Oakwood Ave. Failsworth M40 65 D1
Oakwood Ave. Gatley SK8 122 B5
Oakwood Ave. Kearsley M27 61 E4
Oakwood Ave. Shevington WN6 35 F5
Oakwood Ave. Walkden M28 60 F2
Oakwood Ave. Wilmslow SK9 136 E8
Oakwood Cl. BL8 27 B3
Oakwood Ct. WA14 128 B8
Oakwood Dr. Bolton BL1 40 F8
Oakwood Dr. Leigh WN7 75 E1
Oakwood Dr. Pendlebury M6 80 B5
Oakwood Dr. Walkden M28 60 F2
Oakwood Est. M5 154 D1
Oakwood High Sch. M'ster M21 109 C5
Oakwood High Sch. Pendlebury M6 80 C5
Oakwood High Sch (Upper Sch). M21 109 C7
Oakwood La. WA14 119 B1
Oakwood Rd. Disley SK12 135 D6
Oakwood Rd. Romiley SK6 113 C2
Oakworth Croft. OL4 49 F4
Oakworth St. M9 64 C3
Oat St. SK1 124 A7
Oatlands Rd. M22 121 C2
Oban Ave. OL1 49 B1
Oban Cres. SK3 123 D4
Oban Dr. Garswood WN4 72 C4
Oban Dr. Sale M33 108 E3
Oban Gr. BL1 24 E5
Oban St. BL1 143 D3
Oban Way. WN2 38 D5
Oberlin St. Oldham OL4 67 D7
Oberlin St. R'dale OL11 139 D5
Oberon Cl. M30 79 D2
Occlestone Cl. M33 108 E1
Ocean St. WA14 119 B6
Ocean Street Trad Est. WA14 119 B7
Ocean Wlk. M15 162 F5
Ockendon Dr. M9 157 E7
Octavia Dr. M40 83 C4
Octavia House. 7 M6 154 F3
Odell St. M11 165 B7
Odessa Ave. M6 80 B4
Odette St. M18 99 C4
Off Grove Rd. SK15 86 D4
Off Ridge Hill La. 2 SK15 85 F2
Off Stamford St. SK15 86 D4
Offerton Dr. SK2 124 D6
Offerton Fold. SK2 124 C7
Offerton Gn. SK2 124 F6
Offerton Hall Prim Sch. SK2 124 E6
Offerton High Sch. SK2 124 E8
Offerton Ind Est. SK2 124 C7
Offerton La. SK1 & SK2 124 C8
Offerton Rd. SK2 & SK7 125 A4
Offerton St. Horwich BL6 22 A3
Offerton St. Stockport SK1 112 B2
Ogbourne Wlk. 11 M13 163 C6
Ogden Cl. Heywood OL10 29 A2
Ogden Cl. Whitefield M45 45 A1
Ogden Ct. SK14 167 E2
Ogden Gdns. SK16 101 E8
Ogden Gr. M22 121 F4
Ogden La. M'ster M11 & M18 99 D7
Ogden La. Newhey OL16 32 D5
Ogden Rd. Bramhall SK7 132 D5
Ogden Rd. Failsworth M35 83 F6
Ogden Sq. SK16 101 B8
Ogden St. 4 M'ster M20 110 B3
Ogden St. Middleton M24 65 A8
Ogden St. Mottram-i-L SK14 115 B8
Ogden St. 9 Oldham OL4 67 D6
Ogden St. Oldham OL9 152 C8
Ogden St. Prestwich M25 63 C4
Ogden St. R'dale OL11 30 C2
Ogden St. Swinton M27 79 F7
Ogden Wlk. M45 63 A8
Ogmore Wlk. M40 65 C2
Ogwen Dr. M25 63 B5
Ohio Ave. M5 96 F8
Okehampton Cl. M26 43 C5
Okehampton Cres. M33 107 D5
Okell Gr. WN7 75 D6
Okeover Rd. M7 155 D8
Olaf St. 13 BL2 25 B1
Old Bank Cl. SK6 113 A3
Old Bank St. M2 158 F1
Old Barn Pl. BL7 25 A8
Old Barton Rd. M41 95 C7
Old Bedions Spts Ctr. M20 122 A8
Old Bent La. OL12 15 A7
Old Birley St. M15 162 F5
Old Boston. WA11 89 A7
Old Boston Trad Est. WA11 89 B8
Old Broadway. M20 110 B5
Old Brook Cl. OL2 49 D8
Old Brow. Mossley OL5 68 C1
Old Brow La. OL16 15 C3
Old Brown Ct. OL5 86 C8
Old Chapel St. SK3 170 D7
Old Church St. Failsworth M40 83 C6
Old Church St. Oldham OL1 153 F7
Old Clay Dr. OL12 15 D4
Old Clough La. Walkden M28 60 F1
Old Clough La. Worsley M28 78 F8
Old Colliery Yd. WN4 72 C3
Old Croft Mews. SK1 124 B7
Old Crofts Bank. M41 95 C3
Old Cross St. OL6 166 C3
Old Ctyd The. M22 121 F5
Old Delph Rd. OL11 13 F1
Old Doctors St. BL8 26 F7
Old Eagley Mews. BL1 24 F6
Old Edge La. OL2 48 E2
Old Elm St. M13 163 C6
Old Engine La. BL0 11 D6
Old Farm Cres. M43 99 F8
Old Farm Dr. SK2 124 F6
Old Fold. Swinton M30 79 C4
Old Fold. 7 Wigan WN5 54 B6
Old Fold Rd. Aspull WN2 38 D5
Old Fold Rd. Westhoughton BL5 57 C7
Old Garden The. WA15 120 B7
Old Gardens St. 3 SK1 170 F8
Old Gn. BL2 25 E6
Old Green. BL8 10 F1
Old Greenwood La. BL6 22 D1
Old Ground St. BL0 138 C6
Old Hall Cl. SK13 104 D2
Old Hall Clough. BL6 40 C7
Old Hall Cres. SK9 131 E3
Old Hall Ct. Sale M33 108 E4
Old Hall Ct. Whitefield M45 62 C7
Old Hall Cty Prim Sch. BL8 27 B7
Old Hall Dr. Ashton-i-M WN4 73 A2
Old Hall Dr. M'ster M18 99 D4
Old Hall Dr. Stockport SK2 124 E6

Pemberton St. M'ster M16 ... 97 C4
Pemberton St. 3 R'dale OL11 30 C2
Pemberton St. Walkden M38 60 B4
Pemberton Sta. WN3 ... 54 D4
Pemberton Way. OL2 ... 149 B8
Pembridge Fold. M24 ... 65 C8
Pembridge Rd. M9 ... 64 F4
Pembroke Ave. Eccles M30 .. 79 D2
Pembroke Ave. Sale M33 ... 107 F5
Pembroke Cl. Horwich BL6 ... 22 A4
Pembroke Cl. M'ster M13 .. 164 D6
Pembroke Ct. Bredbury SK6 112 F2
Pembroke Ct. Hazel Grove SK7 ... 124 E2
Pembroke Ct. Pendlebury M27 80 B8
Pembroke Ct. 14 R'dale OL12 14 F1
Pembroke Dr. Bury BL9 ... 44 E7
Pembroke Dr. Oldham OL4 ... 49 E4
Pembroke Gr. M44 ... 105 C6
Pembroke House. 3 SK3 . 170 E8
Pembroke Rd. Hindley WN2 .. 57 C3
Pembroke Rd. Shevington WN5 ... 36 D1
Pembroke St. Bolton BL1 ... 145 D8
Pembroke St. Littleborough OL15 ... 16 B6
Pembroke St. M'ster M7 ... 155 E6
Pembroke St. Oldham OL8 . 153 D6
Pembroke St. 3 Salford M6 154 E1
Pembroke Way. 6 M34 ... 101 A1
Pembry Cl. SK5 ... 112 B5
Pembury Cl. M22 ... 121 C3
Penarth Rd. Bolton BL3 ... 146 B4
Penarth Rd. Wythenshawe M22 ... 121 D8
Penbury Rd. WN1 ... 37 B5
Pencombe Cl. M12 ... 165 A5
Pencroft Way. M15 ... 163 A5
Pendeen Cl. M29 ... 77 A7
Pendennis. 2 OL11 ... 139 E6
Pendennis Ave. BL6 ... 40 D5
Pendennis Cl. M26 ... 43 C5
Pendennis Cres. WN2 ... 57 A3
Pendennis Rd. SK4 ... 168 C3
Pendine Wlk. M7 ... 155 E6
Pendle Cl. Bury BL8 ... 27 B3
Pendle Cl. Oldham OL4 ... 67 D5
Pendle Cl. Wigan WN5 ... 54 D5
Pendle Ct. BL1 ... 143 D3
Pendle Dr. BL6 ... 22 C5
Pendle Gdns. WA3 ... 91 E2
Pendle Gr. OL2 ... 48 C3
Pendle Rd. Denton M34 ... 100 F2
Pendle Rd. Golborne WA3 ... 74 C1
Pendle Wlk. SK5 ... 112 A4
Pendlebury Cl. M25 ... 62 F2
Pendlebury Fold. BL3 ... 40 D2
Pendlebury La. WN1 & WN2 . 37 D6
Pendlebury Rd. Gatley SK8 122 B6
Pendlebury Rd. Swinton M27 79 F8
Pendlebury St. BL1 ... 143 F3
Pendlebury Towers. SK5 .. 169 F3
Pendlecroft Ave. M27 ... 80 C7
Pendlegreen Cl. M11 ... 164 F8
Pendleton Coll. M6 ... 154 D4
Pendleton Gn. 14 M6 ... 154 F3
Pendleton Sta. M6 ... 81 A4
Pendleton Way. M6 ... 154 F3
Pendleway. M27 ... 62 A1
Pendragon Pl. M35 ... 84 A7
Pendrell Wlk. 32 M9 ... 64 E3
Penelope Rd. 4 M6 ... 80 D5
Penerly Dr. M40 & M9 ... 157 D6
Penfair Cl. M11 ... 83 A1
Penfield Cl. M1 ... 163 B7
Penfold Wlk. M12 ... 164 F6
Pengarth Rd. BL6 ... 22 C4
Pengham Wlk. M23 ... 109 A1
Pengwern Ave. 2 BL3 ... 146 B4
Penhale Mews. SK7 ... 132 F7
Penhall Wlk. M40 ... 83 A5
Peninsula. M7 ... 81 B7
Penistone Ave. M'ster M9 ... 65 A3
Penistone Ave. R'dale OL16 .. 31 C6
Penistone Ave. Salford M6 ... 80 C3
Penketh Ave. M'ster M18 ... 99 B4
Penketh Ave. Tyldesley M29 . 77 B6
Penketh St. WN6 ... 37 B2
Penleach Ave. WN7 ... 76 B5
Penmere Gr. M33 ... 107 E1
Penmoor Chase. SK7 ... 124 B1
Penmore Cl. OL2 ... 49 D7
Penn Gn. SK8 ... 123 B1
Penn House Cl. SK7 ... 132 E8
Penn St. Farnworth BL4 ... 60 C8
Penn St. Heywood OL10 ... 29 D1
Penn St. Horwich BL6 ... 22 C3
Penn St. M'ster M40 ... 157 F8
Penn St. Oldham OL8 ... 153 D5
Penn St. R'dale OL16 ... 139 F8
Pennant Dr. M25 ... 63 A5
Pennant St. OL1 ... 67 B8
Pennant St Ind Est. 9 OL1 . 67 B8
Pennell Dr. WN3 ... 54 F5
Pennell St. M11 ... 83 D1
Pennine Ave. Oldham OL9 .. 152 A5
Pennine Ave. Wigan WN3 ... 54 C2
Pennine Cl. Bury BL8 ... 27 B3
Pennine Cl. Horwich BL6 ... 22 C5
Pennine Cl. M'ster M9 ... 64 F4
Pennine Ct. 3 Oldham OL4 .. 67 A6
Pennine Ct. Stalybridge SK15 86 D3
Pennine Ct. Swinton M27 ... 62 A1
Pennine Dr. Alt'ham WA14 . 119 B5
Pennine Dr. Ashton-u-L OL6 .. 85 E4
Pennine Dr. Littleborough OL12 ... 15 C6
Pennine Dr. Milnrow OL16 ... 32 A6
Pennine Gr. Ashton-u-L OL6 .. 85 E6
Pennine Gr. Leigh WN7 ... 75 C8
Pennine La. WA3 ... 74 C1
Pennine Prec. OL16 ... 31 F5
Pennine Rd. Glossop SK13 .. 116 A8
Pennine Rd. Horwich BL6 ... 22 C5
Pennine Rd. Romiley SK6 ... 113 C6
Pennine Rd. Stockport SK7 . 124 B1
Pennine Terr. 2 SK16 ... 166 C1
Pennine Vale. OL2 ... 149 C8
Pennine View. Denton M34 100 E5
Pennine View. Littleborough OL15 ... 6 D2
Pennine View. Mossley OL5 .. 68 D1
Pennine View. Royton OL2 ... 48 E4
Pennine View. Stalybridge SK15 ... 86 C4
Pennine Wlk. WN2 ... 56 B2
Pennington Ave. WN7 ... 75 E3
Pennington Cl. Pennington Green WN2 ... 38 E2
Pennington Cl. Walkden M38 59 E4
Pennington Ct. WN7 ... 75 B1
Pennington Flash Ctry Pk. WN7 ... 75 B3
Pennington Gdns. WN7 ... 75 E3
Pennington Green La. WN2 38 E2
Pennington La. Ince-i-M WN2 56 A8
Pennington La. Standish WN2 37 E8
Pennington Mews. WN7 ... 75 E3
Pennington Rd. Bolton BL3 . 147 F3
Pennington Rd. Leigh WN7 .. 75 F3
Pennington St. Bury BL8 ... 26 F4
Pennington St. 4 Hindley WN2 ... 56 D6
Pennington St. M'ster M12 & M19 ... 99 A2
Pennington St. Oldham OL9 .. 66 B3
Pennington St. 1 Walkden M28 ... 60 E2
Penny Bridge La. M41 ... 95 A2
Penny Brook Fold. SK7 ... 124 F3
Penny La. Newton-l-W WA11 & WA12 ... 89 A7
Penny La. Stockport SK5 ... 169 F3
Penny Meadow. OL6 ... 166 C3
Pennygate Cl. WN2 ... 56 D6
Pennyhurst St. WN3 ... 150 B7
Pennymoor Dr. WA14 ... 119 B6
Penrhos Ave. M22 ... 121 F4
Penrhyn Ave. Cheadle SK8 . 122 E1
Penrhyn Ave. Middleton M24 65 A7
Penrhyn Cres. SK7 ... 133 C8
Penrhyn Dr. Hazel Grove SK7 124 D1
Penrhyn Dr. Prestwich M25 ... 63 B4
Penrhyn Gr. M46 ... 58 C5
Penrhyn Rd. SK3 ... 123 C8
Penrice Cl. M26 ... 43 D5
Penrice Fold. M28 ... 78 B7
Penrith Ave. Ashton-u-L OL7 .. 84 F5
Penrith Ave. Bolton BL1 ... 142 A1
Penrith Ave. Droylsden M11 .. 83 B3
Penrith Ave. Oldham OL8 ... 66 C4
Penrith Ave. Prestwich M45 ... 63 A8
Penrith Ave. Reddish SK5 ... 99 F1
Penrith Ave. Sale M33 ... 108 C2
Penrith Ave. Walkden M28 ... 60 F2
Penrith Cl. M44 ... 105 E4
Penrith Cres. WN4 ... 73 B4
Penrith House. M7 ... 158 D4
Penrith St. OL11 ... 139 F5
Penrod Pl. M6 ... 81 B4
Penrose Gdns. M24 ... 47 B1
Penrose St. BL2 ... 148 C7
Penroy Ave. M20 ... 109 D3
Penroyson Cl. M12 ... 164 F6
Penruddock Wlk. 4 M13 ... 98 F4
Penry Ave. M44 ... 105 E6
Penryn Ave. Royton OL2 ... 48 F3
Penryn Ave. Sale M33 ... 108 C1
Penryn Ct. M7 ... 63 D1
Pensarn Ave. M14 ... 110 E8
Pensarn Gr. SK5 ... 169 F4
Pensby Cl. M27 ... 80 C7
Pensby Wlk. M40 ... 157 D5
Pensford Ct. BL2 ... 25 E6
Pensford Rd. M23 ... 120 F3
Penshaw Ave. WN3 ... 55 B3
Penshurst Rd. SK5 ... 112 B6
Penshurst Wlk. 20 M34 ... 101 A1
Penson St. WN1 ... 37 D2
Penthorpe Dr. OL2 ... 48 F3
Pentland Ave. M40 ... 65 C2
Pentland Cl. SK7 ... 124 B1
Pentland Terr. BL1 ... 143 E1
Pentland Way. SK14 ... 102 B6
Pentlands Ave. M7 ... 155 D5
Penton Wlk. 5 M16 ... 97 F3
Pentwyn Gr. M23 ... 121 B7
Penzance St. M10 & M40 ... 160 E3
Peover Ave. M33 ... 108 E4
Peover Rd. SK9 ... 131 E5
Peover Wlk. SK8 ... 123 A5
Pepler Ave. M23 ... 109 B2
Peploe Wlk. M23 ... 108 D1
Pepper Ct. SK9 ... 137 A6
Pepper La. WN6 ... 19 B3
Pepper Mill Bsns Pk. WN1 151 D7
Pepper Mill La. WN1 ... 151 D7
Pepper Rd. SK7 ... 124 B2
Pepper St. WA16 ... 128 F1
Pepperhill Wlk. 1 M21 ... 97 F4
Peppermint Cl. OL16 ... 32 C4
Pepys Pl. WN3 ... 55 A4
Perch St. 4 WN1 ... 37 E1
Perch Wlk. 7 M4 ... 159 C1
Percival Rd. M43 ... 84 B1
Percival Wlk. OL2 ... 48 E3
Percy Dr. M5 ... 161 B7
Percy Rd. M34 ... 100 E3
Percy St. Bolton BL1 ... 143 F2
Percy St. Bury BL9 ... 140 F3
Percy St. Farnworth BL4 ... 60 E7
Percy St. M'ster M15 ... 162 D6
Percy St. Oldham OL4 ... 67 C7
Percy St. R'dale OL16 ... 31 B5
Percy St. Ramsbottom BL0 .. 138 B5
Percy St. Stalybridge SK15 ... 86 B2
Percy St. Stockport SK1 ... 169 F2
Percy St. Whitworth OL12 ... 4 C4
Peregrine Cres. M43 ... 84 C3
Peregrine Dr. M44 ... 94 A3
Peregrine Rd. SK2 ... 125 A4
Periton Wlk. 8 M9 ... 64 E3
Perivale Dr. OL8 ... 67 B4
Perkins Ave. M7 ... 155 E5
Pernham St. OL4 ... 67 C7
Perrin St. SK14 ... 167 D2
Perry Ave. SK14 ... 102 A4
Perry Brook Comm Prim Sch. WN4 ... 73 A7
Perry Rd. WA15 ... 120 B6
Perrybrook Wlk. WN4 ... 73 D4
Perrygate Ave. M20 ... 110 A6
Perrymead. M25 ... 63 C6
Perryn Pl. WN6 ... 19 F1
Pershore. 6 OL12 ... 139 E8
Pershore Rd. M24 ... 47 A3
Perth Ave. Ince-i-M WN2 ... 56 A8
Perth Ave. Oldham OL9 ... 66 A4
Perth Cl. SK7 ... 132 F5
Perth Rd. OL11 ... 31 B2
Perth St. Bolton BL3 ... 146 C3
Perth St. Royton OL2 ... 49 A4
Perth St. Swinton M27 ... 79 D7
Peru St. M3 ... 158 D2
Peter Martin St. 2 BL6 ... 22 B4
Peter Moss Way. M19 ... 99 C1
Peter St. Alt'ham WA14 ... 119 D3
Peter St. Ashton-i-M WN4 ... 73 C3
Peter St. Bury BL9 ... 140 F3
Peter St. Denton M34 ... 101 A3
Peter St. Eccles M30 ... 79 D1
Peter St. Golborne WA3 ... 90 A8
Peter St. Hadfield SK14 ... 104 A6
Peter St. Hazel Grove SK7 ... 124 D3
Peter St. Hindley WN2 ... 56 D5
Peter St. Leigh WN7 ... 76 B4
Peter St. M'ster M2 ... 162 F8
Peter St. Oldham OL1 ... 153 F6
Peter St. Stockport SK1 ... 112 A2
Peter St. 14 Tyldesley M29 ... 58 F1
Peter St. Westhoughton BL5 ... 57 A7
Peter St. Wigan WN5 ... 54 B8
Peterborough Cl. OL6 ... 85 B6
Peterborough Dr. 10 BL1 ... 143 F1
Peterborough St. 1 M18 ... 99 F6
Peterborough Wlk. BL1 ... 143 E1
Peterchurch Wlk. M11 ... 165 C8
Peterhead Cl. BL1 ... 143 D1
Peterhead Wlk. 4 M5 ... 81 A1
Peterhouse Gdns. SK6 ... 113 C4
Peterhouse Wlk. WN4 ... 72 F3
Peterloo Ct. 5 M5 ... 154 E2
Peterloo Terr. 8 M24 ... 47 A2
Peters Ct. WA15 ... 120 D5
Petersburg Rd. SK3 ... 170 D6
Petersfield Dr. M23 ... 120 D7
Petersfield Gdns. WA3 ... 91 E4
Petersfield Wlk. 1 BL1 ... 145 E8
Peterswood Cl. M22 ... 121 B3
Petheridge Dr. 3 M22 ... 121 B1
Petrel Ave. SK12 ... 133 B4
Petrel Cl. Droylsden M43 ... 84 C3
Petrel Cl. R'dale OL11 ... 29 F7
Petrel Cl. Tyldesley M29 ... 77 A8
Petrie Ct. M6 ... 81 B4
Petrie St. OL12 ... 139 F8
Petrock Wlk. 5 M40 ... 83 C5
Petticoat La. WN2 ... 56 B7
Petts Cres. OL15 ... 16 A6
Petunia Wlk. 8 M28 ... 59 F3
Petworth Ave. WN3 ... 54 D2
Petworth Cl. M22 ... 121 E5
Petworth Rd. OL9 ... 152 B6
Pevensey Ct. M9 ... 65 A2
Pevensey Rd. M6 ... 80 E5
Pevensey Wlk. OL9 ... 152 B6
Peveril Ave. SK12 ... 127 C1
Peveril Cl. M25 & M45 ... 63 C7
Peveril Cres. M21 ... 97 A2
Peveril Ct. SK13 ... 116 F8
Peveril Dr. SK7 ... 133 F8
Peveril Rd. Alt'ham WA14 ... 119 C7
Peveril Rd. Oldham OL1 ... 49 C1
Peveril Rd. Salford M5 ... 154 D2
Peveril St. BL3 ... 146 C3
Peveril Terr. SK14 ... 113 F8
Pewfist Gn. BL5 ... 57 E6
Pewfist Spinney The. BL5 ... 57 D7
Pewfist The. BL5 ... 57 E7
Pewsey Rd. M22 ... 121 F3
Pexhill Ct. SK4 ... 168 A2
Pexwood. OL1 ... 47 E1
Pheasant Cl. M28 ... 78 B6
Pheasant Dr. M21 ... 109 D7
Pheasant Rise. WA14 ... 119 D1
Phelan Cl. M40 ... 156 C5
Phethean St. Bolton BL2 ... 148 A7
Phethean St. Farnworth BL4 . 42 C2
Philip Arnold Ct. 2 BL4 ... 60 C8
Philip Ave. M34 ... 100 E5
Philip Cl. 6 WN5 ... 54 D5
Philip Dr. M33 ... 108 B2
Philip Howard Rd. SK13 ... 116 C8
Philip St. Bolton BL3 ... 145 D5
Philip St. Eccles M30 ... 79 D1
Philip St. Oldham OL4 ... 67 C8
Philip St. R'dale OL11 ... 139 F5
Philips Ave. BL4 ... 60 D7
Philips Dr. M45 ... 62 D6
Philips High Sch. M45 ... 62 E8
Philips Park Rd. M'ster M11 160 F2
Philips Park Rd. Whitefield M45 ... 62 D6
Phillimore St. OL4 ... 67 E5
Phillip Way. 1 SK14 ... 102 E1
Phillips Pl. M45 ... 62 F7
Phillips St. WN7 ... 75 E8
Phipps St. M28 ... 60 C4
Phoebe St. 5 Bolton BL3 ... 146 C4
Phoebe St. Salford M5 ... 161 B8
Phoenix Cl. OL10 ... 29 F1
Phoenix Park Ind Est. OL10 29 F1
Phoenix Pl. OL4 ... 67 F7
Phoenix St. Bolton BL1 ... 148 A8
Phoenix St. Bury BL9 ... 140 E2
Phoenix St. Farnworth BL4 ... 60 D7
Phoenix St. Littleborough OL15 16 B6
Phoenix St. M'ster M60 ... 159 A1
Phoenix St. Oldham OL4 ... 67 F7
Phoenix St. Oldham OL1 ... 153 F6
Phoenix St. R'dale OL12 ... 14 C1
Phoenix Way. Eccles M41 ... 95 E6
Phoenix Way. Radcliffe M26 .. 44 A2
Phyllis St. Middleton M24 ... 65 C7
Phyllis St. R'dale OL11 & OL12 14 B1
Picadilly. WN5 ... 71 E5
Piccadilly. M'ster M1 & M4 & M60 ... 159 B1
Piccadilly. Stockport SK1 ... 169 F1
Piccadilly Gdns Sta. M1 ... 159 A1
Piccadilly Plaza. M1 ... 159 A1
Piccadilly Sta. M1 ... 163 B8
Piccadilly Trad Est. M1 ... 163 C8
Piccadilly Village. M1 ... 159 C1
Pickering Cl. Alt'ham WA15 120 A7
Pickering Cl. Bury BL8 ... 27 B5
Pickering Cl. Kearsley M26 ... 61 A8
Pickering Cl. Urmston M41 ... 95 B2
Pickford Ave. BL3 ... 43 C3
Pickford Ct. M16 ... 162 E5
Pickford La. SK16 ... 101 C8
Pickford Mews. SK16 ... 101 C8
Pickford St. M4 ... 159 B2
Pickford Wlk. OL2 ... 48 E3
Pickford's Brow. SK1 ... 169 F1
Pickhill La. OL3 ... 69 B8
Pickhill Mews. OL3 ... 69 B8
Pickley Gn. WN7 ... 57 E1
Pickmere Ave. M20 ... 110 B8
Pickmere Cl. 4 Droylsden M43 ... 84 B1
Pickmere Cl. Stockport SK3 123 C6
Pickmere Cl. Wythenshawe M33 ... 108 F2
Pickmere Ct. 10 SK9 ... 131 D5
Pickmere Gdns. SK8 ... 122 F4
Pickmere Rd. SK9 ... 131 D5
Pickmere Terr. 2 SK16 ... 166 B1
Picksley St. WN7 ... 76 B4
Pickthorn Cl. WN2 ... 56 B3
Pickup St. Ince-i-M WN2 ... 151 F7
Pickup St. R'dale OL16 ... 31 A7
Pickwick Rd. SK12 ... 133 D3
Picton Cl. M3 ... 158 E2
Picton Dr. SK9 ... 131 E2
Picton Sch. M33 ... 107 F4
Picton Sq. 4 OL4 ... 67 A6
Picton St. Ashton-u-L OL7 ... 85 A6
Picton St. M'ster M7 ... 158 D3
Picton Wlk. 9 M16 ... 97 F3
Pierce St. OL1 ... 49 C1
Piercy Ave. M7 ... 158 D4
Piercy St. Failsworth M35 ... 83 E7
Piercy St. M'ster M40 ... 160 D2
Pierpoint St. WA12 ... 90 A7
Piethorne Cl. OL16 ... 32 C4
Pigeon St. M1 & M60 ... 159 B1
Piggott St. BL4 ... 60 C7
Pigot St. 2 WN5 ... 54 B6
Pike Ave. Atherton M46 ... 58 A2
Pike Ave. Failsworth M35 ... 84 C6
Pike Fold Golf Course. M9 . 64 D6
Pike Fold La. M9 ... 64 C3
Pike Fold Prim Sch. M9 ... 64 C3
Pike Nook Wkshp. BL3 ... 145 D5
Pike Rd. BL3 ... 147 D4
Pike St. OL11 ... 139 F5
Pike View. BL6 ... 22 D4
Pike View Cl. OL4 ... 67 B5
Pike's La. SK13 ... 116 B8
Pikehouse Cotts. OL15 ... 16 D7
Pikes Lane Prim Sch. BL3 145 D6
Pilgrim Dr. M11 ... 160 F1
Pilgrims Way. WN6 ... 37 A7
Pilkington Dr. M45 ... 45 B2
Pilkington Rd. Kearsley BL4 . 60 F6
Pilkington Rd. M'ster M9 ... 65 A3
Pilkington Rd. Radcliffe M26 43 F4
Pilkington St. Bolton BL3 ... 145 E5
Pilkington St. Hindley WN2 ... 56 D6
Pilkington St. Middleton M24 47 C1
Pilkington St. Ramsbottom BL0 ... 138 B5
Pilkington Way. M26 ... 44 A2
Pilling Field. BL7 ... 8 E1
Pilling St. Bury BL8 ... 27 C3
Pilling St. Denton M34 ... 100 F3
Pilling St. Leigh WN7 ... 75 D5
Pilling St. M'ster M10 & M40 157 F5
Pilling St. R'dale OL12 ... 139 D8
Pilling St. 3 Rawtenstall BB4 .. 2 F8
Pilling Wlk. OL9 ... 152 A6
Pilning St. BL3 ... 42 A4
Pilot Ind Est. BL3 ... 42 B4
Pilot St. BL9 ... 140 F1
Pilsley Cl. WN5 ... 36 A1
Pilsworth Cotts. BL9 ... 45 C5
Pilsworth Rd. Heywood BL9 & OL10 ... 45 C7
Pilsworth Rd. Heywood OL10 46 A8
Pilsworth Way. BL9 ... 45 A6
Pimblett St. Golborne WA3 ... 90 A7
Pimblett St. M'ster M3 ... 158 F3
Pimbo La. WN8 ... 53 A4
Pimhole Rd. BL9 ... 141 A2
Pimlico Cl. M7 ... 155 D6
Pimlott Gr. Dukinfield SK14 . 101 D5
Pimlott Gr. Prestwich M25 ... 62 F3
Pimlott Rd. BL1 ... 25 B3
Pimmcroft Way. M23, M33 109 A3
Pin Mill Brow. M12 ... 164 D8
Pincher Wlk. 14 M11 ... 83 C1
Pinder Wlk. 7 M15 ... 162 F6
Pine Ave. Newton-l-W WA12 .. 89 D2
Pine Ave. Whitefield M45 ... 62 F6
Pine Cl. Denton M34 ... 100 E6
Pine Cl. Marple SK6 ... 125 E4
Pine Ct. M'ster M20 ... 110 A4
Pine Ct. Stockport SK7 ... 123 D2
Pine Gr. Denton M34 ... 101 A3
Pine Gr. Eccles M30 ... 79 E4
Pine Gr. Farnworth BL4 ... 60 B8
Pine Gr. Golborne WA3 ... 90 C8
Pine Gr. M'ster M13 ... 98 E4
Pine Gr. Prestwich M45 ... 63 A6
Pine Gr. Royton OL2 ... 48 D6
Pine Gr. Sale M33 ... 107 D6
Pine Gr. Stalybridge SK16 ... 101 F8
Pine Gr. Swinton M27 ... 79 D7
Pine Gr. Westhoughton BL5 ... 57 E7
Pine Gr. Worsley M28 ... 78 E8
Pine Lodge. SK7 ... 132 F7
Pine Meadow. M26 ... 61 C6
Pine Rd. Bramhall SK7 ... 132 F8
Pine Rd. Dukinfield SK15 ... 101 E8
Pine Rd. M'ster M20 ... 110 B4
Pine Rd. Poynton SK12 ... 133 F3
Pine Rd. Wigan WN5 ... 54 E6
Pine St. Ashton-u-L OL6 ... 166 B4
Pine St. Bolton BL1 ... 143 F2
Pine St. Bury BL9 ... 141 B2
Pine St. Chadderton OL9 ... 152 A8
Pine St. Dukinfield SK14 ... 101 D5
Pine St. Heywood OL10 ... 29 D2
Pine St. Littleborough OL15 ... 16 B6
Pine St. M'ster M60 ... 159 A1
Pine St. Middleton M24 ... 65 C7
Pine St. Newhey OL16 ... 32 B4
Pine St. R'dale OL16 ... 31 B7
Pine St. Radcliffe M26 ... 44 B4
Pine St. Romiley SK6 ... 113 B5
Pine St. Stockport SK3 ... 170 D8
Pine St. 5 Tyldesley M29 ... 59 A1
Pine St S. BL9 ... 141 B3
Pine Tree Rd. OL8 ... 66 D1
Pine View. WN3 ... 54 B1
Pine Wlk. 1 M31 ... 105 E3
Pineapple St. SK7 ... 124 E2
Pinehurst Rd. M10 & M40 .. 157 E5
Pines The. WN7 ... 75 F3
Pinetop Cl. M21 ... 109 D7
Pinetree St. M18 ... 165 C5
Pinevale. WN6 ... 37 A7
Pineway. OL4 ... 67 F6
Pinewood. Alt'ham WA14 ... 119 A2
Pinewood. Ashton-i-M WN4 ... 73 A2
Pinewood. Chadderton M24 ... 65 E7
Pinewood. Sale M33 ... 107 D4
Pinewood Cl. Abram WN2 ... 74 C7
Pinewood Cl. 30 Bolton BL1 143 E2
Pinewood Cl. Dukinfield SK16 ... 166 C1
Pinewood Cl. M'ster SK4 ... 168 A3
Pinewood Cres. Ince-i-M WN2 ... 151 F6
Pinewood Cres. Orrell WN5 . 53 E6
Pinewood Cres. Ramsbottom BL0 ... 11 B2
Pinewood Ct. Alt'ham WA14 & WA15 ... 119 E1
Pinewood Ct. Sale M33 ... 108 D5
Pinewood Rd. M'ster M21 .. 109 A7
Pinewood Rd. Wilmslow SK9 137 E8
Pinewoods The. SK6 ... 113 B5
Pinfold. Hadfield SK14 ... 171 E4
Pinfold. R'dale OL11 ... 139 E6
Pinfold Ave. M9 ... 65 A2
Pinfold Cl. Alt'ham WA15 ... 129 D7
Pinfold Cl. Westhoughton BL5 57 D5
Pinfold Ct. M32 ... 96 C1
Pinfold Cty Prim Sch. SK14 102 E1
Pinfold Dr. Cheadle SK8 ... 123 A1
Pinfold Dr. Prestwich M25 ... 62 F5
Pinfold La. Alt'ham M90 & WA15 ... 129 F6
Pinfold La. Romiley SK6 ... 113 E4
Pinfold La. Whitefield M45 ... 62 F8
Pinfold Rd. M28 ... 60 C1
Pinfold St. WN2 ... 56 A7
Pingate Dr. SK8 ... 132 A6
Pingate La. SK8 ... 132 A6
Pingate La S. SK8 ... 132 A6
Pingle La. OL3 ... 50 E5
Pingot. OL2 ... 32 D1
Pingot Ave. M23 ... 109 B1
Pingot Ct. 6 WN7 ... 75 D5
Pingot La. SK14 ... 103 B1
Pingot Rd. WN5 ... 71 E5
Pingot The. Irlam M44 ... 94 B3
Pingot The. Leigh WN7 ... 75 D5
Pingott La. 5 SK14 ... 104 A5
Pink Bank La. M12 & M18 ... 99 A4
Pinnacle Dr. BL7 ... 8 E2
Pinner Pl. M19 ... 111 A6
Pinnington La. M32 ... 96 D2
Pinnington Rd. M18 ... 99 D6
Pinwood Ct. 13 SK9 ... 131 E1
Pioneer Rd. M27 ... 62 D2
Pioneer St. Droylsden M11 ... 83 B2
Pioneer St. Horwich BL6 ... 22 C4
Pioneer St. 4 Littleborough OL15 ... 16 B5
Pioneer St. Walsden OL14 ... 6 A7
Pioneers St. 4 OL11 ... 31 A6
Pioneers Villa. OL16 ... 32 E4
Piper Hill Sch. M23 ... 109 B2
Piperhill Ave. M22 ... 109 D2
Pipers The. WA3 ... 90 F8
Pipewell Ave. M18 ... 165 C5
Pipit Ave. WA12 ... 89 C3
Pipit Cl. M43 ... 84 C2
Pirie Wlk. 4 M40 ... 83 C6
Pit La. OL16 & OL2 ... 31 D1
Pit St. Denton M34 ... 100 F3
Pit St. Oldham OL9 ... 66 B4
Pitcairn House. 12 M30 ... 79 D1
Pitchcombe Rd. M22 ... 121 B2
Pitcombe Cl. BL1 ... 24 D7
Pitfield Gdns. M23 ... 120 F7
Pitfield La. BL2 ... 25 F4
Pitfield St. BL2 ... 148 B7
Pitman Cl. M11 ... 165 A8
Pitmore Wlk. 3 M40 ... 65 D2
Pits Farm Ave. OL11 ... 30 C7
Pitsford Rd. M10 & M40 ... 157 E5
Pitshouse. OL12 ... 13 E2
Pitshouse La. OL11 & OL12 .. 13 E2
Pitt St. Denton M34 ... 100 F6
Pitt St. Heywood OL10 ... 29 C2
Pitt St. Hyde SK14 ... 167 D3
Pitt St. Ince-i-M WN3 ... 151 D6
Pitt St. Oldham OL4 ... 67 A5
Pitt St. R'dale OL12 ... 139 F8
Pitt St. Radcliffe M26 ... 43 E3
Pitt St. Stockport SK3 ... 170 D8
Pitt St. Wigan WN3 ... 150 B7
Pitt St E. OL4 ... 67 B5
Pittbrook St. M12 ... 164 D7
Pixmore Ave. BL1 ... 25 B4
Place Rd. WA14 ... 119 C6
Plain Pit St. SK14 ... 101 C5
Plainsfield Cl. M16 ... 97 F4
Plane Ave. WN5 ... 54 E7
Plane Ct. 4 M6 ... 81 A2
Plane Rd. M35 ... 83 F5
Plane St. OL4 ... 67 C7
Plane Tree Cl. SK6 ... 125 D5
Plane Tree Gr. WA11 ... 89 A7
Plane Tree Rd. M31 ... 105 D3
Planet Way. M34 ... 100 E5
Planetree Rd. WA15 ... 120 A2
Planetree Wlk. M23 ... 120 C8
Plank La. WN7 ... 75 B4
Plant Cl. M33 ... 108 A5
Plant Hill High Sch. M9 ... 64 C4
Plant Hill Rd. M9 ... 64 D4
Plant St. M60 ... 159 B1
Plantation Ave. M28 ... 60 C4
Plantation Gates. WN1 ... 37 E2
Plantation Ind Est. OL6 ... 166 C2
Plantation Rd. BL7 ... 9 F7
Plantation St. Ashton-u-L OL6 & SK16 ... 85 D2
Plantation St. Bacup OL13 ... 3 C8
Plantation St. M'ster M18 ... 99 E5
Plantation View. BL0 ... 11 C3
Plate St. OL1 ... 153 F7
Plato St. OL9 ... 153 D7
Platt Ave. OL6 ... 85 C6
Platt Croft. WN7 ... 76 C4
Platt Ct. M14 ... 98 C2
Platt Fold Rd. WN7 ... 76 A6
Platt Fold St. WN7 ... 76 A5
Platt Hall Art Gal & Mus. M14 ... 98 C2
Platt Hill Ave. BL3 ... 146 A4
Platt La. Atherton BL5 ... 58 B7
Platt La. Hindley WN2 ... 56 D5
Platt La. M'ster M14 ... 98 B2
Platt La. Standish WN1 ... 20 B3
Platt La. Uppermill OL3 ... 50 F2
Platt La. Wigan WN1 ... 37 E1
Platt St. Cheadle SK8 ... 122 E6
Platt St. Dukinfield SK16 ... 101 A7
Platt St. Hadfield SK14 ... 104 B5
Platt St. Leigh WN7 ... 75 F6
Platt St. 8 Oldham OL4 ... 67 F6
Platt St. Platt Bridge WN2 ... 56 A2
Platt Wlk. M34 ... 100 E1
Plattbrook Cl. M14 ... 98 B1
Platting Gr. Ashton-u-L OL7 ... 84 F5
Platting La. OL11 ... 31 A4
Platting Rd. OL4 ... 68 C7
Platts Dr. M44 ... 94 A2
Plattwood Wlk. 16 M15 ... 162 D6
Play St. SK1 ... 170 F8
Playfair Cl. OL10 ... 46 E7
Playfair St. Bolton BL2 ... 24 F6
Playfair St. M'ster M14 ... 98 B4
Pleachway. SK4 ... 110 F2
Pleasance Way. WA12 ... 89 D4
Pleasant Ct. 5 OL11 ... 30 C2
Pleasant Gdns. BL1 ... 145 E8
Pleasant Rd. M30 ... 79 E1
Pleasant St. Bury BL8 ... 26 F4
Pleasant St. Heywood OL10 ... 29 C4
Pleasant St. M'ster M8, M9 157 D7
Pleasant St. R'dale OL11 ... 30 C2
Pleasant Terr. 6 SK16 ... 166 C1
Pleasant View. Bacup OL13 ... 3 C7
Pleasant View. Radcliffe M26 62 B8
Pleasant Way. SK7 & SK8 ... 132 C6
Pleasington Dr. Bury BL8 ... 26 E2
Pleasington Dr. Failsworth M40 ... 65 C2
Plevna St. BL2 ... 148 A7
Plodder La. BL4 & BL5 ... 59 D8
Plodder La Prim Sch. BL4 ... 60 B8
Plough Cl. M41 ... 94 C1
Plough St. 6 SK16 ... 101 D8
Ploughbank Dr. M21 ... 109 D7
Ploughfields. BL5 ... 39 E3
Plover Cl. Newton-l-W WA12 . 89 C3
Plover Cl. R'dale OL11 ... 29 F7
Plover Dr. Alt'ham WA14 ... 119 B8
Plover Dr. Bury BL9 ... 141 B4
Plover Dr. Irlam M44 ... 94 A4
Plowden Ave. BL3 ... 146 C3
Plowden Rd. M22 ... 121 B2
Plowley Cl. M20 ... 110 B2
Plucksbridge Rd. SK6 ... 126 B3
Plum St. OL8 ... 153 D5
Plum Tree Ct. 2 M5 ... 81 A2
Plumbley Dr. M16 ... 97 C3
Plumbley St. 11 M18 ... 99 E7
Plumley Cl. SK3 ... 170 F5
Plumley Rd. SK9 ... 131 D5
Plummer Ave. M21 ... 109 B6
Plumpton Cl. OL1 & OL2 ... 48 E1
Plumpton Dr. BL9 ... 27 E6
Plumpton Rd. OL11 ... 48 C8
Plumpton Wlk. 6 M13 ... 98 F4
Plunge Rd. BL0 ... 1 E3
Plymouth Ave. M13 ... 164 E5
Plymouth Cl. OL6 ... 85 C7
Plymouth Dr. Bramhall SK7 . 132 F7
Plymouth Dr. 1 Farnworth BL4 ... 59 F8
Plymouth Gr. M'ster M13 ... 164 D5
Plymouth Gr. Radcliffe M26 .. 43 D5
Plymouth Gr. Standish WN6 .. 37 A7
Plymouth Gr. Stockport SK3 123 B7
Plymouth Gr W. M13 ... 164 E5
Plymouth Grove Prim Sch. M13 ... 164 E5
Plymouth Rd. M33 ... 107 D5
Plymouth St. OL8 ... 66 F4
Plymouth View. M13 ... 163 C6
Plymtree Cl. M8 ... 63 E2
Pobgreen La. OL3 ... 51 D1
Pochard Dr. Alt'ham WA14 . 119 B7
Pochard Dr. Poynton SK12 .. 133 A4
Pochin St. M10 & M40 ... 160 E3
Pocket Nook La. WA3 ... 91 B7
Pocket Nook Rd. BL6 ... 40 B3
Pocket Wkshp The. BL3 ... 144 C6
Pocklington Dr. M23 ... 120 F7
Podnor La. SK6 ... 127 A6
Podsmead Rd. M22 ... 121 B2
Poet's Nook. WN7 ... 75 E4
Poise Brook Dr. SK2 ... 124 F5

Regent Ct. Alt'ham WA14 119 D4
Regent Ct. M'ster M7 63 D1
Regent Ct. M'ster SK4 111 C5
Regent Dr. Bolton BL6 40 B7
Regent Dr. Denton M34 100 D1
Regent Dr. Leigh WN7 76 D7
Regent House. M14 98 D3
Regent Pl. M14 98 C4
Regent Rd. Alt'ham WA14 119 D4
Regent Rd. Bolton BL6 40 B6
Regent Rd. Platt Bridge WN2 56 A3
Regent Rd. Salford M5 81 A1
Regent Rd. Salford M15, M5 161 C8
Regent Rd. Stockport SK2 124 A6
Regent Road Ind Est. M5 162 D8
Regent Sq. M16 161 B8
Regent St. Bury BL9 140 F4
Regent St. Eccles M30 79 F2
Regent St. Failsworth M40 83 D5
Regent St. Glossop SK13 104 D1
Regent St. Hadfield SK14 104 B5
Regent St. Heywood OL10 29 B2
Regent St. 3 Hindley WN2 56 D5
Regent St. Littleborough OL15 16 B5
Regent St. Middleton M24 46 F2
Regent St. Newton-l-W WA12 89 D3
Regent St. Oldham OL1 67 A7
Regent St. R'dale OL12, OL16 15 A1
Regent St. 2 R'dale OL16 31 A8
Regent St. Ramsbottom BL0 11 A4
Regent St. Shaw OL2 149 B7
Regent St. Tyldesley M46 58 E2
Regent Trad Est. M3 158 D1
Regent Wlk. BL4 60 D8
Regents Dr. OL5 86 D8
Regina Ave. SK15 86 A2
Regina Cres. WN7 76 E6
Regina Ct. M6 80 A3
Reginald Latham Ct. M40 160 D3
Reginald St. Bolton BL3 146 A2
Reginald St. 2 Droylsden M11 99 F7
Reginald St. Eccles M30 95 A8
Reginald St. Swinton M27 61 D1
Reid Cl. M34 113 A8
Reigate Cl. BL8 27 B1
Reigate Rd. M31 & M41 106 E8
Reins Lee Ave. OL8 67 A2
Reins Lee Rd. OL7 85 A6
Reliance St. M40 83 C6
Reliance Street Ent Pk. 1
M40 83 C6
Reliance Street Trad Est.
M35 & M40 83 C6
Rembrandt Wlk. OL1 49 D4
Rena Cl. SK4 169 D3
Rena Ct. SK4 169 D3
Rendel Cl. Newton-l-W WA12 89 D2
Rendel Cl. Stretford M32 96 D2
Renfrew Cl. WN3 55 A3
Renfrew Dr. BL3 40 F3
Renfrew Rd. WN2 38 D5
Rennie Cl. M32 96 E2
Renshaw Ave. M30 79 D1
Renshaw Dr. BL9 141 C3
Renshaw St. Alt'ham WA14 119 E5
Renshaw St. Eccles M30 79 D1
Renton Rd. Bolton BL3 146 B3
Renton Rd. Stretford M32 96 E3
Renton Rd.
Wythenshawe M22 121 D4
Renwick Gr. BL3 146 C3
Renwick Sq. WN4 72 F3
Repton Ave. Droylsden M43 83 D3
Repton Ave. Failsworth M40 65 E1
Repton Ave. Hyde SK14 167 E3
Repton Ave. Ince-i-M WN2 55 F4
Repton Ave. Oldham OL8 66 D3
Repton Ave. Reddish M34 100 A3
Repton Ave. Urmston M41 94 D2
Reservoir Rd. SK3 170 D7
Reservoir St. Aspull WN2 38 F3
Reservoir St. Ince-i-M WN2 56 A8
Reservoir St. M'ster M3 158 E3
Reservoir St. R'dale OL16 15 C1
Reservoir St. Salford M6 154 F2
Restormel Ave. WN2 38 D5
Retford Ave. OL16 31 B4
Retford Cl. BL8 27 E5
Retford St. OL4 & OL8 67 B5
Retiro St. OL1 153 F6
Retreat The. SK6 113 C1
Reuben St. SK4 169 E4
Revers St. BL8 140 D3
Reveton Gn. SK7 124 A2
Rex Bldgs. SK9 137 B6
Reynard Rd. M21 109 B7
Reynard St. SK14 167 D3
Reynell Rd. M13 98 F2
Reyner St. Ashton-u-L OL6 85 E2
Reyner St. M'ster M1 163 A8
Reynold St. SK14 167 D2
Reynolds Cl. Atherton BL5 58 F6
Reynolds Dr. Atherton BL5 58 F7
Reynolds Dr. M'ster M18 99 D6
Reynolds Dr. Marple SK6 126 B8
Reynolds Mews. SK9 137 E8
Reynolds Rd. M16 97 C4
Rhine Cl. BL8 26 F7
Rhiwlas Dr. BL9 44 F8
Rhode Houses. SK6 125 F3
Rhode St. BL8 26 F6
Rhodes Ave. Haslingden BB4 1 A7
Rhodes Ave. Oldham OL4 67 F5
Rhodes Ave. Uppermill OL3 51 C1
Rhodes Bank. OL1 67 A6
Rhodes Cres. OL11 30 F3
Rhodes Dr. BL9 45 A2
Rhodes Hill. OL4 67 F5
Rhodes St. Dukinfield SK14 101 C3
Rhodes St. Glossop SK14 104 B5
Rhodes St. M'ster M10, M40 160 E4
Rhodes St. Oldham OL1 67 A7
Rhodes St. Oldham OL4 67 F7
Rhodes St. R'dale OL12 15 B3
Rhodes St. Royton OL2 49 A3
Rhodes St N. SK14 101 C3
Rhodeswood Dr. SK14 104 A6
Rhos Ave. Cheadle SK8 122 E1
Rhos Ave. M'ster M14 110 E8
Rhos Ave. Middleton M24 65 A7
Rhos Dr. SK7 124 D1
Rhosleigh Ave. BL1 143 E4
Rialto Gdns. M7 155 E6
Ribbesford Rd. WN3 54 C4
Ribble Ave. Bolton BL2 42 E7
Ribble Ave. Chadderton OL9 47 F1
Ribble Ave. Littleborough OL15 15 F6
Ribble Cl. Culcheth WA3 91 F2
Ribble Cres. WN5 71 C3
Ribble Dr. Boothstown M28 77 F6
Ribble Dr. Bury BL9 27 F8
Ribble Dr. Kearsley BL4 61 B5
Ribble Dr. Whitefield M45 45 A1
Ribble Dr. Wigan WN5 54 C7
Ribble Drive Cty Prim Sch.
M45 45 A1
Ribble Gr. Heywood OL10 29 A3
Ribble Gr. Leigh WN7 75 C5
Ribble Rd. Oldham OL8 66 C3
Ribble Rd. Platt Bridge WN2 56 A2
Ribble Rd.
Shevington Moor WN6 19 B2
Ribble St. Bacup OL13 4 A8
Ribble St. R'dale OL11 30 E4
Ribble Wlk. M43 100 A8
Ribblesdale Cl. OL10 46 E7
Ribblesdale Dr. M40 156 C5
Ribblesdale Rd. BL3 147 D4
Ribbleton Cl. BL8 26 F1
Ribchester Dr. BL9 44 D7
Ribchester Gdns. WA3 92 A3
Ribchester Gr. BL2 25 E1
Ribchester Wlk. M15 162 F6
Riber Bank. SK13 171 E1
Riber Cl. 25 SK13 171 E1
Riber Fold. 27 SK13 171 E1
Riber Gn. 26 SK13 171 E1
Rice St. M3 162 E8
Richard Burch St. 3 BL9 140 F3
Richard Gwyn Cl. BL5 57 D6
Richard Reynolds Ct. M44 105 E6
Richard St. Failsworth M35 83 F7
Richard St. Ince-i-M WN3 151 D6
Richard St. R'dale OL11 139 F6
Richard St. Radcliffe M26 43 F3
Richard St. Ramsbottom BL0 11 E7
Richard St. Stockport SK1 169 F2
Richards Rd. WN6 19 B3
Richardson Cl. M45 44 F1
Richardson Rd. M30 79 E2
Richardson St. 8 M'ster M18 99 E7
Richardson St.
Stockport SK1 124 A7
Richbell Cl. M44 105 F7
Richborough Cl. M7 & M8 155 E5
Richelieu St. BL3 42 A4
Richmond Ave.
Handforth SK9 131 D4
Richmond Ave. M'ster M25 63 C1
Richmond Ave. Oldham OL9 66 A4
Richmond Ave. Royton OL2 48 D4
Richmond Ave. Urmston M41 95 E2
Richmond Cl. Bury BL8 26 F6
Richmond Cl. Culcheth WA3 91 D4
Richmond Cl.
Dukinfield SK16 101 D6
Richmond Cl. Hadfield SK14 104 A5
Richmond Cl. Lymm WA13 117 B4
Richmond Cl. Mossley OL5 86 E8
Richmond Cl. Sale M33 108 F3
Richmond Cl. Shaw OL2 149 B5
Richmond Cl.
Stalybridge SK15 86 A1
Richmond Cl. Standish WN1 37 B7
Richmond Cl. Whitefield M45 62 D7
Richmond Cres. OL5 86 E8
Richmond Ct. Alt'ham WA14 119 B2
Richmond Ct. Cheadle SK8 122 C5
Richmond Ct. Stockport SK2 124 D5
Richmond Cty Inf Sch.
OL9 153 D6
Richmond Cty Jun Sch.
OL9 153 D6
Richmond Dr. Leigh WN7 76 D7
Richmond Dr. Lymm WA13 117 B4
Richmond Dr. Swinton M28 79 C8
Richmond Gdns. Bolton BL3 42 B3
Richmond Gdns.
Newton-l-W WA12 89 C2
Richmond Gn. WA14 119 B2
Richmond Gr. Cheadle SK8 122 F1
Richmond Gr. Eccles M30 79 E3
Richmond Gr. Farnworth BL4 42 A1
Richmond Gr. Leigh WN7 76 E6
Richmond Gr. M'ster M13 98 E4
Richmond Gr E. M12 164 E5
Richmond Hill. Hyde SK14 167 F1
Richmond Hill. Wigan WN5 54 C6
Richmond Hill Rd. SK8 122 C6
Richmond House. 1
M'ster M13 98 E4
Richmond House. 7
Stalybridge SK15 86 A1
Richmond Rd.
Alt'ham WA14 119 C2
Richmond Rd.
Alt'ham WA14 119 D5
Richmond Rd.
Ashton-i-M WN4 72 F5
Richmond Rd.
Boothstown M28 77 E7
Richmond Rd.
Dukinfield SK16 101 D6
Richmond Rd. Eccles M17 96 A7
Richmond Rd. Failsworth M35 84 B8
Richmond Rd. Hindley WN2 57 A3
Richmond Rd. M'ster M14 110 D8
Richmond Rd. M'ster SK4 110 F2
Richmond Rd. Reddish M34 100 A3
Richmond Rd. Romiley SK6 113 C3
Richmond St. Ashton-u-L OL7 84 F3
Richmond St. Atherton M46 58 C2
Richmond St. Bury BL9 44 E8
Richmond St. Denton M34 100 F6
Richmond St. Droylsden M43 84 C2
Richmond St. Horwich BL6 22 B3
Richmond St. Hyde SK14 167 E2
Richmond St. M'ster M3 158 E3
Richmond St. M'ster M1 163 A8
Richmond St.
Stalybridge SK15 86 C2
Richmond St. Wigan WN3 150 A5
Richmond St. Wigan WN1 150 B8
Richmond Terr. SK6 126 B1
Richmond Wlk. Oldham OL9 153 D6
Richmond Wlk. Radcliffe M26 43 E6
Ricroft Rd. SK6 114 B3
Ridding Ave. M22 121 E3
Ridding Cl. SK2 124 D6
Riddings Ct. WA15 119 F8
Riddings Rd. Alt'ham WA15 119 F2
Riddings Rd. Sale M33, WA15 108 A1
Riddings Rd. Sale WA15 120 A8
Riddle Ct. M5 80 C2
Ridge Ave. Alt'ham WA15 129 D6
Ridge Ave. Marple SK6 126 A4
Ridge Ave. Standish WN1 37 B7
Ridge Cl. Hadfield SK14 171 E3
Ridge Cl. Romiley SK6 113 F2
Ridge Cres. Marple SK6 126 A3
Ridge Cres. Whitefield M45 63 B8
Ridge Danyers. Marple SK6 125 E5
Ridge Danyers. Marple SK6 125 F5
Ridge End Fold. SK6 126 A2
Ridge Gr. M45 63 B8
Ridge Hill La.
Stalybridge SK15 86 A3
Ridge La. OL3 51 D5
Ridge Pk. SK7 132 D6
Ridge Rd. SK6 126 A3
Ridge The. SK6 126 A3
Ridge Wlk. M9 64 D3
Ridgecroft. OL6 & OL7 85 B6
Ridgedale Ctr. 3 SK6 125 F6
Ridgefield. M2 158 F1
Ridgefield St. M35 83 E6
Ridgemont Ave. SK4 168 B2
Ridgemont Wlk. M23 108 F2
Ridgeway. Golborne WA3 90 E7
Ridgeway. Swinton M27 62 B2
Ridgeway. Wilmslow SK9 137 F7
Ridgeway Gates. 3 BL1 145 F7
Ridgeway Rd. WA15 120 C5
Ridgeway St. M10 & M40 160 D2
Ridgeway The. SK12 135 C6
Ridgewell Ave. WA3 90 D8
Ridgewood. OL9 65 E8
Ridgewood Ave.
M10, M40, M9 157 D5
Ridgmont Cl. BL6 22 F3
Ridgmont Dr. Boothstown M28 77 F6
Ridgmont Dr. Horwich BL6 22 F3
Ridgmont Rd. SK7 132 E5
Ridgway. BL6 21 C2
Ridgway The. SK6 113 A1
Riding Cl. M29 77 D7
Riding Fold La. M28 79 A5
Riding Gate. BL2 25 E6
Riding Gate Mews. BL2 25 E6
Riding Head La. BL0 11 F8
Riding La. WN4 73 F5
Riding St. M3 158 E1
Ridings Ct. OL3 51 A2
Ridings Rd. SK14 103 F5
Ridings St. M'ster M10, M40 157 F5
Ridings St. M'ster M11 165 B8
Ridley Dr. WA14 107 E1
Ridley Gr. M33 108 F3
Ridley St. OL4 67 A6
Ridley Wlk. M15 163 A5
Ridling La. SK14 167 E2
Ridsdale Ave. M20 110 A6
Ridsdale Way. M6 81 A5
Ridyard St. Platt Bridge WN2 56 B3
Ridyard St. Walkden M28, M38 60 C4
Ridyard St. Wigan WN5 54 E7
Riefield. BL1 142 B3
Rifle Rd. M21 & M33 108 F5
Rifle St. OL1 153 F8
Riga Rd. M14 98 C1
Riga St. M4 & M60 159 A2
Rigby Ave. Blackrod BL6 21 C2
Rigby Ave. Radcliffe M26 44 C5
Rigby Ct. Bolton BL3 147 F4
Rigby Ct. R'dale OL12 13 E2
Rigby Gr. M38 59 E4
Rigby La. Bolton BL2 25 C5
Rigby St. Alt'ham WA14 119 D3
Rigby St. Ashton-i-M WN4 73 A3
Rigby St. Bolton BL3 147 F4
Rigby St. Golborne WA3 90 A8
Rigby St. Hindley WN2 56 E6
Rigby St. M'ster M7 155 D6
Rigby Wlk. M7 155 E6
Rigby's Yd. 6 WN5 54 B6
Rigel Pl. M7 81 C3
Rigel St. M10 & M40 159 C3
Rigton Cl. M12 165 A5
Riley Cl. M33 107 B1
Riley Ct. 3 BL1 143 F1
Riley La. WN2 38 B7
Riley Sq. Wigan WN1 37 D1
Riley Sq. Wigan WN1 151 D8
Riley St. M46 58 A1
Riley Wood Cl. SK6 112 F1
Rilston Ave. WA3 91 D3
Rimington Ave. WA3 74 C1
Rimington Cl. WA3 91 E3
Rimmer Cl. M11 160 E1
Rimmington Cl. M9 65 A2
Rimsdale Cl. SK8 122 A3
Rimsdale Wlk. BL3 40 E5
Rimworth Dr. M10 & M40 159 C4
Rindle Rd. M29 93 C8
Ring Lows La. OL12 15 A4
Ring-o-Bells La. SK12 135 D6
Ringcroft Gdns. M40 65 B1
Ringfield Cl. M16 97 E4
Ringford Wlk. M40 157 E5
Ringley Ave. WA3 73 F1
Ringley Chase. M45 62 E8
Ringley Cl. M45 62 D8
Ringley Dr. M45 62 D7
Ringley Gr. BL1 24 E5
Ringley Hey. M45 62 D8
Ringley Meadows. M26 61 C7
Ringley Old Brow. M26 61 C7
Ringley Pk. M45 62 D8
Ringley Rd. Kearsley M26 61 C8
Ringley Rd. Kearsley M26 61 D8
Ringley Rd.
Whitefield M45 & M26 62 C7
Ringley Rd W. M26 61 E8
Ringley St. M9 157 D8
Ringlow Ave. M27 79 C7
Ringlow Park Rd. M27, M28 79 C7
Ringmer Dr. 4 M22 121 C1
Ringmere Ct. 7 OL1 153 E8
Ringmore Rd. SK7 124 A2
Rings Cl. M35 83 F6
Ringstead Cl. SK9 131 D1
Ringstead Dr. M10 & M40 159 C3
Ringstone. M25 63 A3
Ringway Ave. WN7 75 F8
Ringway Golf Cse. WA15 120 C1
Ringway Gr. M33 108 E2
Ringway Rd. M22 & M90 130 D7
Ringway Rd W. M22 & M90 130 D8
Ringway Trad Est. M22 130 E8
Ringwood Ave.
Droylsden M34 84 C1
Ringwood Ave.
Hazel Grove SK7 124 B1
Ringwood Ave. Hyde SK14 102 A1
Ringwood Ave.
M'ster M12 & M18 99 B3
Ringwood Ave. Radcliffe M26 44 B1
Ringwood Ave.
Ramsbottom BL0 11 A4
Ringwood Way. OL9 152 C8
Rink St. M14 & M20 110 D7
Ripley Ave. Bramhall SK8 132 B5
Ripley Ave. Stockport SK2 124 B4
Ripley Cl. Hazel Grove SK7 133 E8
Ripley Cl. M'ster M4 164 D8
Ripley Cres. M41 94 F5
Ripley Dr. Leigh WN7 75 F6
Ripley Dr. Wigan WN3 & WN5 54 C4
Ripley St. BL1 & BL2 25 B4
Ripley Way. M34 112 F8
Ripon Ave. Bolton BL1 23 F1
Ripon Ave. Golborne WA3 90 D8
Ripon Ave. 1 Wigan WN6 37 B3
Ripon Cl. Alt'ham WA15 120 C1
Ripon Cl. Little Lever BL3 42 F3
Ripon Cl. Newton-l-W WA12 89 C5
Ripon Cl. Oldham OL9 152 B6
Ripon Cl. Radcliffe BL9 44 D5
Ripon Cl. 5 Whitefield M45 44 F2
Ripon Cres. M32 95 F3
Ripon Dr. Ashton-i-M WN4 73 D2
Ripon Dr. Bolton BL1 23 F1
Ripon Gr. M33 107 F6
Ripon Hall Ave. BL0 11 B4
Ripon Rd. M32 95 F3
Ripon St. Ashton-u-L OL6 166 C3
Ripon St. M'ster M15 163 A5
Ripon St. Oldham OL1 153 D8
Ripon Wlk. SK6 113 A1
Rippenden Ave. M21 97 A2
Rippingham Rd. M20 110 B7
Rippleton Rd. M22 121 E4
Ripponden Rd. Denshaw OL3 33 D3
Ripponden Rd.
Oldham OL1 & OL4 49 E3
Ripponden St. 11
OL1 & OL4 49 C1
Ripton Wlk. M9 64 B4
Risbury Wlk. 5 M40 83 C6
Rise The. Oldham OL4 67 F7
Rise The. Wigan WN6 36 C3
Rises The. SK14 103 F5
Rishton Ave. BL3 147 F2
Rishton La. BL3 147 F3
Rishworth Cl. SK2 124 D5
Rishworth Dr. M40 83 E8
Rishworth Rise. OL2 32 A1
Rising La. OL8 66 E2
Rising Lane Cl. OL8 66 E2
Risley Ave. M9 64 D1
Risley St. OL1 153 F8
Rita Ave. 4 M14 98 B3
Ritson Cl. M18 165 B6
Riva Rd. M19 110 D2
River La. M31 105 F4
River Pl. Milnrow OL16 31 F6
River Pl. M'ster M15 162 E7
River St. Bolton BL2 148 A6
River St. Heywood OL10 29 D3
River St. M'ster M12 162 F7
River St. M'ster M12 163 C8
River St. R'dale OL16 139 F7
River St. Radcliffe M26 44 B2
River St. Ramsbottom BL0 138 C6
River St. Stockport SK1 112 B3
River St. Wilmslow SK9 137 B8
River View. SK5 112 A7
River View Cl. M25 62 F2
River Way. WN1 150 C8
Riverbank Dr. BL8 140 D3
Riverbank Lawns. M3 158 E3
Riverbank The. M26 61 A8
Riverbank Tower. M3 158 E3
Riverbank Way. SK13 116 F7
Riverbank Wlk. M20 109 E4
Riverdale Cl. WN6 36 D4
Riverdale Rd. M9 64 B3
Rivermead. OL16 32 B3
Rivermead Ave. WA15 129 C7
Rivermead Cl. M34 113 A7
Rivermead Rd. M34 113 B7
Riverpark Rd. M11 & M40 83 A3
Rivers La. M41 95 C5
Rivers St. WN5 53 E6
Riversdale Dr. OL8 67 A1
Riversdale Rd. SK8 122 C5
Riversdale View. SK6 113 A5
Riversdale Ct. M25 63 A3
Rivershill. M33 108 A6
Rivershill Dr. OL10 29 B1
Rivershill Gdns. WA15 129 D6
Riverside. Bolton BL1 25 A2
Riverside. Chadderton OL1 47 E1
Riverside. Dukinfield SK16 166 C1
Riverside. M'ster M7 158 D3
Riverside Ave. Irlam M44 94 B1
Riverside Ave. M'ster M21 109 D3
Riverside Ave. Wigan WN1 37 D1
Riverside Bsns Pk. SK9 137 B7
Riverside Cl. SK13 104 D1
Riverside Ct. M'ster M20 109 F3
Riverside Ct. Whitworth OL12 4 D4
Riverside Dr. Kearsley M26 61 B8
Riverside Dr. Ramsbottom BL0 11 B2
Riverside Dr. Urmston M41 107 B8
Riverside Rd. M26 44 D4
Riversleigh Cl. BL1 23 F3
Riversmeade. Bolton BL2 25 C7
Riversmeade. Leigh WN7 76 A6
Riverstone Dr. M23 120 D7
Riverton Rd. M20 122 B8
Riverview Cotts. SK13 116 C7
Riverview Ct. M7 81 C8
Riviera Ct. OL11 13 C2
Rivington. M6 80 C4
Rivington Ave. Adlington PR6 21 B7
Rivington Ave. Golborne WA3 74 C1
Rivington Ave.
Pendlebury M27 80 C8
Rivington Ave.
Platt Bridge WN2 56 B3
Rivington Ave. Wigan WN1 37 B2
Rivington & Blackrod
High Sch. BL6 22 B6
Rivington & Blackrod High
Sch (Annexe). BL6 22 B4
Rivington Cres. M27 80 C7
Rivington Ct. M45 62 C7
Rivington Dr. Bury BL8 27 A1
Rivington Dr. Leigh WN2 74 F8
Rivington Dr. Orrell WN8 53 C7
Rivington Dr. Shaw OL2 49 D7
Rivington Gr.
Droylsden M34 100 C8
Rivington Gr. Irlam M44 105 D6
Rivington La. Adlington PR6 21 D6
Rivington La. Horwich BL6 22 A7
Rivington Pl. PR7 19 D6
Rivington Rd. Alt'ham WA15 119 F2
Rivington Rd. Oldham OL4 68 A7
Rivington Rd. Salford M6 80 C4
Rivington Service Area.
PR6 21 E4
Rivington St. Atherton M46 58 B2
Rivington St. Blackrod BL6 21 D2
Rivington St. Oldham OL1 48 F1
Rivington St. R'dale OL12 14 F1
Rivington Way. WN6 36 F8
Rivington Wlk. M12 164 F5
Rix St. BL1 143 E2
Rixson St. OL4 49 D2
Rixton Ct. M16 97 B3
Rixton Dr. M29 77 B8
RL Hughes Prim Sch. WN4 73 A3
Roach Ct. M40 159 C4
Roach Gn. WN1 37 E1
Roach Pl. OL16 31 A8
Roach St. Bury BL9 44 F4
Roach St. Bury BL9 141 C2
Roaches Mews. OL5 68 D3
Roaches Way. OL5 68 E3
Roachill Cl. WA14 119 B5
Roachwood Cl. OL9 65 E7
Road La. OL12 14 D4
Roading Brook Rd. BL2 26 B3
Roads Ford Ave. OL16 31 F7
Roadside Ct. WA3 90 C8
Roaring Gate La. WA15 120 E2
Rob La. WA12 89 E5
Robe Wlk. 5 M18 99 D6
Robert Hall St. M5 161 B8
Robert Lawrence Ct. M41 95 A1
Robert Malcolm Cl. M40 157 D5
Robert Owen Gdns. M22 121 D8
Robert Owen St. M43 84 C2
Robert Saville Ct. OL11 30 C6
Robert St. Bolton BL2 25 E5
Robert St. Bury BL8 27 C3
Robert St. Dukinfield SK16 101 B8
Robert St. Dukinfield SK14 101 C3
Robert St. 6 Failsworth M35 66 A1
Robert St. Heywood OL10 46 E8
Robert St. M'ster M10, M40 157 F5
Robert St. M'ster M3 158 F3
Robert St. Oldham OL8 66 B3
Robert St. Platt Bridge WN2 56 A3
Robert St. Prestwich M25 63 C4
Robert St. 15 R'dale OL16 31 A8
Robert St. Radcliffe M26 44 A4
Robert St. Ramsbottom BL0 1 C1
Robert St. Sale M33 108 E4
Robert St. Tyldesley M46 58 E1
Roberts Ave. M14 98 B4
Roberts St. M30 79 D1
Robertscroft Cl. M22 121 C3
Robertshaw Ave. M21 109 B6
Robertshaw St. WN7 75 E7
Robertson St. M26 44 A4
Robin Cl. BL4 59 F7
Robin Croft. SK6 112 D3
Robin Dr. M44 94 A3
Robin Hill Dr. WN6 19 B2
Robin Hill La. WN6 19 C3
Robin Hood La. WN6 18 B3
Robin Hood St. M7 155 F8
Robin Park Rd. Wigan WN5 54 F7
Robin Park Rd. Wigan WN5 150 A4
Robin Rd. BL0 11 B2
Robin St. OL1 153 E8
Robin's La. Billinge WA11 71 A8
Robin's La. Bramhall SK7 132 D7
Robinia Cl. M30 94 F8
Robins Cl. Bramhall SK7 132 E7
Robins Cl. Droylsden M43 84 C3
Robins La. WA3 91 D2
Robinsbay Rd. M22 130 E8
Robinson La. OL7 84 F3
Robinson St. Ashton-u-L OL6 166 B4
Robinson St. Dukinfield SK15 101 E8
Robinson St. 15 Horwich BL6 22 B4
Robinson St. Hyde SK14 167 F3
Robinson St. Leigh WN7 76 A4
Robinson St. Oldham OL9 152 B6
Robinson St. R'dale OL16 31 A7
Robinson St. Stockport SK3 170 D7
Robinson St. 14
Tyldesley M29 59 A1
Robinsway. WA14 119 C1
Robinswood Rd. M22 121 D2
Robinwood Lodge. SK13 171 E1
Robson Ave. M41 95 E7
Robson Pl. Abram WN2 74 B8
Robson St. Oldham OL1 67 A6
Robson St. Oldham OL1 153 F6
Roby Mill. WN8 35 B3
Roby Mill CE Prim Sch. WN8 35 B3
Roby Rd. M30 95 C8
Roby St. M1 159 B1
Roby Well Way. WN5 71 D5
Roch Ave. OL10 29 A2
Roch Cl. M45 45 B1
Roch Cres. M45 45 C1
Roch Mills Cres. OL11 30 C5
Roch Mills Gdns. OL11 139 D5
Roch Pl. WN2 55 F2
Roch St. OL16 15 B1
Roch Valley Way. OL11 30 C5
Roch Way. M45 45 B1
Roch Wlk. M45 45 B1
Rochbury Cl. OL11 29 F6
Rochdale Golf Cse. OL11 30 A8
Rochdale Ind Ctr. OL11 139 D6
Rochdale Infmy. OL12 14 F1
Rochdale La. Heywood OL10 29 D2
Rochdale La. Royton OL2 48 D5
Rochdale Old Rd. BL9 28 D4
Rochdale Rd. Bacup OL13 4 B8
Rochdale Rd. Bury BL9 141 B2
Rochdale Rd.
Denshaw OL2 & OL3 33 C3
Rochdale Rd. Edenfield BL0 1 F2
Rochdale Rd. Heywood OL10 29 D2
Rochdale Rd.
Littleborough HX6 & OL15 7 E1
Rochdale Rd. M'ster M9 64 D3
Rochdale Rd.
M'ster M40, M8, M9 157 D6
Rochdale Rd.
Middleton M24 & OL11 47 C4
Rochdale Rd. Milnrow OL16 31 E7
Rochdale Rd. Oldham OL1 48 E1
Rochdale Rd.
Oldham OL1 & OL9 153 E8
Rochdale Rd.
Ramsbottom BL0 & BL9 12 B7
Rochdale Rd. Royton OL2 48 D6
Rochdale Rd.
Shaw OL2 & OL16 48 F8
Rochdale Rd. Shaw OL2 149 B7
Rochdale Rd.
Walsden OL14 & OL15 6 B6
Rochdale Rd E. OL10 & OL11 29 F3
Rochdale Sta. OL11 139 F6
Roche Gdns. SK8 132 B6
Roche Rd. OL3 50 E5
Rochester Ave. Bolton BL2 25 E1
Rochester Ave. M'ster M25 63 C2
Rochester Ave. Walkden M28 60 C1
Rochester Cl. Ashton-u-L OL6 85 C7
Rochester Cl.
Dukinfield SK16 102 A7
Rochester Cl. Golborne WA3 90 A8
Rochester Dr. WA14 107 E1
Rochester Gr. SK7 124 E3
Rochester Rd. M41 95 D4
Rochester Way. OL9 152 B6
Rochford Ave. Whitefield M45 62 D7
Rochford Ave.
Wythenshawe M22 130 D8
Rochford Cl. M45 62 D7
Rochford House. M34 100 E6
Rochford Rd. M30 94 F8
Rock Ave. BL1 142 C2
Rock Fold. BL7 8 F1
Rock Gdns. SK14 113 E7
Rock House Prim Sch.
M23 109 A1
Rock Nook. OL15 6 D1
Rock Rd. Boothstown M28 78 B2
Rock Rd. Urmston M41 95 F2
Rock St. Ashton-u-L OL7 85 A5
Rock St. Droylsden M11 99 E8
Rock St. Golborne WA3 74 A2
Rock St. 3 Heywood OL10 29 E1
Rock St. Horwich BL6 22 B3
Rock St. Hyde SK14 113 E7
Rock St. M'ster M7 155 D6
Rock St. Oldham OL1 153 F7
Rock St. Radcliffe M26 44 B2
Rock St. Ramsbottom BL0 11 E7
Rock Terr. Bolton BL7 8 F1
Rock Terr. Mossley OL5 68 D3
Rock The. Bury BL9 140 E2
Rock The. Bury BL9 140 F3
Rockall Wlk. M11 160 F1
Rockbourne Cl. WN2 56 D4
Rockcliffe Villas. OL13 3 E8
Rockdove Ave. M15 162 F7
Rockfield Dr. 5 M9 157 E8
Rockhampton St. M18 99 E5
Rockhaven Ave. BL6 22 C4
Rockhouse Cl. M30 95 C8
Rockingham Cl. M'ster M12 164 D6
Rockingham Cl. Shaw OL2 48 E8
Rockland Wlk. 6 M40 65 C2
Rockley Gdns. M6 81 B4
Rocklyn Ave. M40 65 C2
Rocklynes. SK6 113 B2
Rockmead Dr. M9 64 E3
Rocky Bank Terr. WN3 151 E5
Rocky La. M27 & M30 79 D4
Roda St. M9 157 F7
Rodborough Rd. M23 121 A3
Rodeheath Cl. SK9 137 D7
Rodenhurst Dr. 14 M40 83 A7
Rodepool Cl. SK9 131 D2
Rodgers Cl. BL5 57 E6
Rodgers Way. BL5 57 E6
Rodmell Ave. M10 & M40 157 D5
Rodmell Cl. BL7 24 F7
Rodmill Ct. M14 98 C1

Ruskington Dr. M9 157 D7
Rusland Ct. M'ster M9 65 A3
Rusland Ct. Sale M33 108 A5
Rusland Dr. BL2 25 E2
Rusland Wlk. [6] M22 121 C2
Russel St. OL11 139 E5
Russeldene Rd. WN3 54 E3
Russell Ave. High Lane SK6 134 E7
Russell Ave. M'ster M16 97 D2
Russell Ave. Sale M33 108 D5
Russell Cl. BL1 144 C8
Russell Ct. Farnworth BL4 60 E7
Russell Ct. M'ster M16 97 C3
Russell Ct. Walkden M38 60 C3
Russell Dr. M44 94 A2
Russell Gdns. SK4 168 B1
Russell House. [2] WN1 151 D8
Russell Rd. M'ster M16 97 D3
Russell Rd. Partington M31 106 A3
Russell Rd. Pendlebury M6 80 B5
Russell Scott Prim Sch. M34 100 E4
Russell St. [6] Ashton-u-L OL6 85 D4
Russell St. Atherton M46 58 C3
Russell St. Bolton BL1 145 D8
Russell St. [5] Bury BL9 140 F4
Russell St. Denton M34 100 F3
Russell St. Dukinfield SK16 101 C8
Russell St. Eccles M30 79 F2
Russell St. Farnworth BL4 60 E8
Russell St. Heywood OL10 29 E1
Russell St. Hindley WN2 57 C2
Russell St. Hyde SK14 167 D3
Russell St. Ince-i-M WN2 56 A8
Russell St. M'ster M16 97 F3
Russell St. M'ster M8 158 F4
Russell St. Mossley OL5 68 C1
Russell St. Oldham OL9 152 B7
Russell St. Prestwich M25 63 C4
Russell St. Stockport SK2 124 A6
Russell St. Walkden M38 60 C3
Russet Rd. M9 64 D1
Russet Wlk. BL1 143 E4
Rustons Wlk. [2] M40 65 E1
Ruth Ave. M40 65 E1
Ruth St. Bolton BL1 145 E8
Ruth St. [10] Bury BL9 140 F4
Ruth St. Edenfield BL0 1 D2
Ruth St. M'ster M18 99 D3
Ruth St. Oldham OL1 153 F8
Ruth St. Whitworth OL12 4 D1
Ruthen La. M16 97 B4
Rutherford Ave. [2] M14 98 B3
Rutherford Cl. SK14 167 D2
Rutherford Dr. BL5 58 F7
Rutherford Way. SK14 167 D2
Rutherglade Cl. M40 156 C6
Rutherglen Dr. BL3 40 F6
Rutherglen Wlk. M40 157 E5
Ruthin Ave. Cheadle SK8 122 E2
Ruthin Ave. M'ster M9 64 C5
Ruthin Ave. Middleton M24 65 A6
Ruthin Cl. Oldham OL8 66 B2
Ruthin Cl. Salford M6 81 A2
Ruthin Ct. M6 81 A2
Rutland. OL11 139 E6
Rutland Ave. Atherton M46 58 F5
Rutland Ave. Denton M34 101 B2
Rutland Ave. Golborne WA3 90 D7
Rutland Ave. M'ster M16 97 A3
Rutland Ave. M'ster M20 110 A6
Rutland Ave. Swinton M27 61 F2
Rutland Ave. Urmston M41 95 E3
Rutland Cl. [5] Ashton-u-L OL6 85 D2
Rutland Cl. Gatley SK8 122 B6
Rutland Cl. Little Lever BL3 43 B4
Rutland Cres. SK5 112 D6
Rutland Ct. M'ster M20 110 B3
Rutland Ct. Stockport SK2 124 A5
Rutland Dr. Ashton-i-M WN4 73 C4
Rutland Dr. Bury BL9 45 A8
Rutland Dr. M'ster M7 63 D1
Rutland Gr. Bolton BL1 142 C1
Rutland Gr. Farnworth BL4 60 C7
Rutland La. M33 108 F4
Rutland Rd. Alt'ham WA14 119 D6
Rutland Rd. Droylsden M43 83 E2
Rutland Rd. Eccles M30 79 F3
Rutland Rd. Hazel Grove SK7 133 E8
Rutland Rd. Hindley WN2 56 F6
Rutland Rd. Irlam M44 105 D5
Rutland Rd. Partington M31 105 E2
Rutland Rd. Tyldesley M29 58 F1
Rutland Rd. Walkden M28 60 D1
Rutland St. Ashton-u-L OL6 85 D2
Rutland St. Bolton BL3 147 D4
Rutland St. Droylsden M34 100 B8
Rutland St. Dukinfield SK14 101 D5
Rutland St. Failsworth M35 83 F8
Rutland St. Heywood OL10 29 D3
Rutland St. Leigh M46 & WN7 76 E4
Rutland St. [4] M'ster M18 99 E6
Rutland St. Oldham OL9 152 C5
Rutland St. Swinton M27 61 E1
Rutland Way. OL2 149 C7
Rutland Wlk. BB4 1 A8
Rutter's La. SK7 124 C2
Ryall Ave. M5 161 B8
Ryall Ave S. M5 161 B8
Ryan St. M11 99 E7
Ryburn Sq. OL11 29 E6
Rydal Ave. Chadderton OL9 47 F1
Rydal Ave. Droylsden M43 83 E1
Rydal Ave. Dukinfield SK14 101 C5
Rydal Ave. Hazel Grove SK7 124 C3
Rydal Ave. High Lane SK6 134 E8
Rydal Ave. Hindley WN2 56 E5
Rydal Ave. Middleton M24 64 F6
Rydal Ave. Orrell WN5 53 F7
Rydal Ave. Royton OL2 48 C8
Rydal Ave. Sale M33 107 F5
Rydal Ave. Swinton M28 79 B4
Rydal Ave. Urmston M41 107 A8
Rydal Cl. Ashton-i-M WN4 73 C4
Rydal Cl. Blackrod BL6 21 C3
Rydal Cl. Bury BL9 44 E7
Rydal Cl. Gatley SK8 122 B4
Rydal Cl. Reddish M34 100 B2
Rydal Cl. Tyldesley M29 77 A7
Rydal Cres. Swinton M27 79 F7
Rydal Cres. Walkden M28 60 E1
Rydal Dr. WA15 129 D8
Rydal Gr. Ashton-u-L OL7 166 A4
Rydal Gr. Farnworth BL4 59 F7
Rydal Gr. Heywood OL10 46 D8
Rydal Gr. Whitefield M45 63 A8
Rydal House. [4] M28 60 E2
Rydal Mount. SK5 99 F2
Rydal Pl. Abram WN2 74 B8
Rydal Pl. Ince-i-M WN2 56 B8
Rydal Rd. Bolton BL1 144 A8
Rydal Rd. Haslingden BB4 1 C8
Rydal Rd. Little Lever BL3 43 A3
Rydal Rd. Stretford M32 96 D3
Rydal St. Leigh WN7 75 E5
Rydal St. Newton-l-W WA12 89 C3
Rydal Wlk. Stalybridge SK15 86 A3
Rydal Wlk. Wigan WN5 54 C7
Ryde Ave. Denton M34 113 B8
Ryde Ave. M'ster SK4 168 B2
Ryde St. Bolton BL3 146 A4
Ryde St. Wigan WN5 54 E6
Ryder Ave. WA14 119 E7
Ryder Brow. M18 99 D4
Ryder Brow Sta. M18 99 D4
Ryder Gr. WN7 76 C2
Ryder St. Bolton BL1 142 C2
Ryder St. Heywood OL10 29 D2
Ryder St. M'ster M10 & M40 160 D4
Ryderbrow Rd. M18 99 D4
Rydings La. OL12 15 A5
Rydings Rd. OL12 15 B4
Rydings Sch. OL12 15 B4
Rydley St. BL2 148 B6
Rye Bank Rd. M16 97 B3
Rye Croft. M45 62 C7
Rye Croft Ave. M6 80 C3
Rye Hill. BL5 57 F8
Rye St. OL10 29 E3
Rye Walk. OL9 152 A6
Rye Wlk. M13 163 C5
Ryebank Gr. OL6 85 D5
Ryebank Mews. M21 96 F1
Ryebank Rd. M21 96 F1
Ryeburn Ave. M22 121 D3
Ryeburn Dr. BL2 25 B5
Ryeburn Wlk. M41 94 F4
Ryeburne St. OL4 67 C7
Ryecroft Ave. Bury BL8 26 F6
Ryecroft Ave. Golborne WA3 74 E1
Ryecroft Ave. Heywood OL10 29 E2
Ryecroft Cl. OL9 65 F3
Ryecroft Dr. BL5 39 D3
Ryecroft Gr. M23 121 A7
Ryecroft House. [2] OL7 166 A1
Ryecroft La. Dukinfield M34 100 F7
Ryecroft La. Worsley M28 78 F4
Ryecroft Rd. M32 96 C1
Ryecroft St. OL7 84 F1
Ryecroft View. M34 100 C8
Ryedale Ave. M10 & M40 157 D5
Ryedale Cl. SK4 168 B3
Ryefield. M6 80 D6
Ryefield Cl. WA15 120 C5
Ryefield Rd. M33 107 C2
Ryefield St. BL1 25 A1
Ryefields. OL12 15 D4
Ryefields Dr. OL3 51 B1
Ryeford Cl. WN3 151 F6
Ryeland Cl. OL16 31 B4
Rylands. BL5 57 F8
Rylands Ct. BL5 57 F8
Rygate Wlk. [3] M8 155 F6
Ryhope Wlk. M8 155 E6
Rylance St. M11 164 E8
Ryland Cl. SK5 99 F1
Rylands Ave. WN6 37 A2
Rylands Ct. [8] M15 162 D6
Rylands House. [7] M14 110 D8
Rylands St. M18 99 E6
Rylane Wlk. M40 157 D5
Rylatt Ct. M33 107 F5
Ryley Ave. BL3 144 B5
Ryley St. [4] BL3 144 C6
Ryleys La. SK9 136 F1
Ryleys Sch The. SK9 136 F1
Rylstone Ave. M21 109 D3
Ryther Gr. M9 64 B5
Ryton Ave. M18 99 C3
Ryton Cl. WN3 150 B6

Sabden Cl. Bury BL9 27 F7
Sabden Cl. Heywood OL10 29 A2
Sabden Cl. M'ster M10, M40 160 E3
Sabden Rd. BL1 23 E2
Sabrina St. M7 81 C8
Sack St. [4] SK14 101 D5
Sackville Cl. OL2 32 A1
Sackville St. Ashton-u-L OL6 166 B3
Sackville St. [2] Bolton BL2 148 C7
Sackville St. Bury BL9 141 A3
Sackville St. M'ster M3 158 E2
Sackville St. M'ster M1 163 A8
Sackville St. [6] R'dale OL11 30 C2
Sacred Heart RC Inf Sch. M18 99 D4
Sacred Heart RC Jun Sch. M18 99 C4
Sacred Heart RC Prim Sch. Hindley WN2 57 B3
Sacred Heart RC Prim Sch. Leigh WN7 75 E5
Sacred Heart RC Prim Sch. Oldham OL1 49 C2
Sacred Heart RC Prim Sch. R'dale OL16 31 C6
Sacred Heart RC Prim Sch. Tyldesley M46 58 E1
Sacred Heart RC Prim Sch. Westhoughton BL5 39 F1
Sacred Heart RC Prim Sch. Wythenshawe M23 120 F6
Saddle Ct. [6] WN5 54 F6
Saddle Gr. M43 84 D3
Saddle St. BL2 25 B2
Saddleback Cl. M28 78 B6
Saddleback Cres. WN5 54 B6
Saddleback Rd. WN5 54 B7
Saddlewood Ave. M19, M20 110 D2
Saddleworth Prep Sch. OL4 68 C8
Saddleworth Sch. OL3 51 B1
Sadie Ave. M32 96 A4
Sadler St. Bolton BL3 42 A4
Sadler St. Middleton M24 46 F1
Sadler St. [2] Middleton M24 47 A1
Saffron Dr. OL4 49 D2
Saffron Wlk. Partington M31 105 F2
Saffron Wlk. [8] Wythenshawe M22 121 D1
Sagar St. M8 158 F4
Sagars Rd. SK9 131 C3
SS Aidan & Oswald's RC Prim Sch. OL2 48 E3
SS Peter & John RC Prim Sch. M3 158 D2
SS Simon & Jude's CE Prim Sch. BL3 42 A3
St Aelred's RC High Sch. WA12 89 D4
St Agnes CE Prim Sch. M13 98 F3
St Agnes Rd. M13 98 F2
St Agnes St. M34 99 F3
St Agnes's CE Prim Sch. OL4 68 A4
St Aidan's Cl. Billinge WN5 71 E6
St Aidan's Cl. R'dale OL11 139 D5
St Aidan's Gr. M7 81 B6
St Aidan's Rc Prim Sch. WN3 54 D2
St Aidans RC Prim Sch. M23 109 B1
St Aiden's Cl. Radcliffe M26 44 A1
St Alban's Ave. SK4 111 C5
St Alban's Ct. OL11 139 E6
St Alban's St. OL16 139 E6
St Alban's Terr. M'ster M7 & M8 155 F5
St Alban's Terr. R'dale OL11 139 E6
St Albans Ave. Ashton-u-L OL6 85 C7
St Albans Ave. Failsworth M40 83 B5
St Albans Cl. Newton-l-W WA11 89 A7
St Albans Cl. Oldham OL8 66 F4
St Albans Cres. WA14 119 C8
St Albans RC High Sch. M18 99 D2
St Aldates. SK6 112 F2
St Aldwyn's Rd. M20 110 B5
St Alphonsus RC Prim Sch. M16 162 D5
St Ambrose Barlow RC High Sch. M27 79 F7
St Ambrose Barlow RC Prim Sch. M29 77 A5
St Ambrose Coll. WA15 129 B8
St Ambrose Gdns. M6 154 F2
St Ambrose RC Prim Sch. M'ster M21 109 D4
St Ambrose RC Prim Sch. Stockport SK3 170 E5
St Ambrose Rd. Oldham OL1 49 C1
St Ambrose Rd. Tyldesley M29 77 A5
St Andrew's Ave. Alt'ham WA15 119 F7
St Andrew's Ave. Droylsden M43 83 E1
St Andrew's (Boothstown) CE Prim Sch. M28 78 A6
St Andrew's C E Prim Sch. BL0 138 B5
St Andrew's CE Prim Sch. Eccles M30 79 E1
St Andrew's CE Prim Sch. M'ster M19 111 B8
St Andrew's CE Prim Sch. Radcliffe M26 43 F6
St Andrew's CE Prim Sch. Shevington WN6 36 F2
St Andrew's Cl. Ramsbottom BL0 138 C5
St Andrew's Cl. Romiley SK6 113 B1
St Andrew's Cres. WN2 56 D5
St Andrew's Dr. Heywood OL10 29 D1
St Andrew's Dr. Shevington WN6 36 F2
St Andrew's RC Prim Sch. BL2 42 E8
St Andrew's Rd. Radcliffe M26 43 F6
St Andrew's Rd. Stretford M32 96 B2
St Andrew's Sq. M1 163 C8
St Andrew's St. M'ster M1 163 C8
St Andrew's St. Radcliffe M26 43 F6
St Andrew's View. M26 43 F6
St Andrews Ave. M30 79 E1
St Andrews Cl. M'ster SK4 168 B4
St Andrews Cl. Sale M33 107 C1
St Andrews Ct. Alt'ham WA15 119 F3
St Andrews Ct. Stockport SK1 112 A1
St Andrews Dr. Heywood OL10 46 D8
St Andrews Dr. Leigh WN7 76 C5
St Andrews Meth Prim Sch. M28 60 B3
St Andrews Over Hulton CE Prim Sch. BL5 59 A8
St Andrews Rd. Bolton BL6 40 B7
St Andrews Rd. Gatley SK8 122 C1
St Andrews Rd. M'ster SK4 168 B4
St Ann St. Bolton BL1 143 E1
St Ann St. M'ster M2 158 F1
St Ann's Pas. M2 158 F1
St Ann's RC Inf Sch. M32 96 D2
St Ann's RC Jun Sch. M32 96 D2
St Ann's RC Prim Sch. OL6 166 A3
St Ann's Rd. Hazel Grove SK7 124 C1
St Ann's Rd. Prestwich M25 63 A3
St Ann's Rd. R'dale OL16 31 D8
St Ann's Rd N. SK8 122 B2
St Ann's Rd S. SK8 131 C8
St Ann's Sq. Gatley SK8 131 C8
St Ann's Sq. M'ster M2 158 F1
St Ann's St. M27 79 E8
St Anne's Ave. Oldham OL2 48 E3
St Anne's Ave. Salford M6 154 E3
St Anne's Ave. Tyldesley M46 58 E1
St Anne's CE Prim Sch. Oldham OL2 48 E3
St Anne's CE Prim Sch. Sale M33 108 D4
St Anne's CE Prim Sch. Wigan WN6 36 D3
St Anne's Cres. OL4 68 D5
St Anne's Ct. Denton M34 100 E6
St Anne's Ct. Sale M33 108 C4
St Anne's Ct. Shevington WN6 35 F5
St Anne's Cty Prim Sch. M34 101 A4
St Anne's Dr. Dukinfield M34 101 A4
St Anne's Dr. Shevington WN6 36 A5
St Anne's Gdns. OL10 29 F2
St Anne's Hospl. WA14 119 C3
St Anne's RC Prim Sch. Droylsden M34 100 A7
St Anne's RC Prim Sch. M'ster M8 156 A8
St Anne's RC Prim Sch. M'ster M4 160 D1
St Anne's RC Prim Sch. Oldham OL4 67 C7
St Anne's Rd. M34 101 A4
St Anne's St. Bury BL9 140 F4
St Anne's St. M'ster M10 & M40 157 F5
St Annes RC High Sch. SK4 169 D4
St Annes Rd. Denton M34 100 F6
St Annes Rd. Horwich BL6 22 C4
St Annes Rd. M'ster M21 109 B7
St Annes Sq. OL3 50 F4
St Annes St. SK14 115 A8
St Anns Cl. M25 63 A3
St Anns St. M33 108 F3
St Anselm's RC Prim Sch. OL12 4 D2
St Anthony's RC Prim Sch. M22 121 D1
St Antony's RC High Sch. M41 95 F2
St Asaph's Dr. M7 155 F8
St Asaphs Dr. OL6 85 B6
St Aubin's Rd. BL2 148 B6
St Aubyn's Rd. WN1 37 C4
St Augustine of Canterbury RC Sch. OL8 66 D3
St Augustine St. Bolton BL1 143 D2
St Augustine St. M'ster M10 & M40 157 E5
St Augustine's CE Prim Sch. M'ster M40 157 E5
St Augustine's CE Prim Sch. Pendlebury M27 80 B8
St Augustine's Rd. SK3 123 B8
St Augustine's Sch. M15 163 A7
St Austell Ave. M29 77 C8
St Austell Dr. Gatley SK8 131 B8
St Austell Dr. Ramsbottom BL8 10 F2
St Austell House. M21 97 E1
St Austell Rd. M21 97 E1
St Austell's Dr. M27 80 C7
St Austells Dr. M25 63 B5
St Barnabas Sq. M11 165 B8
St Barnabas's Dr. OL15 16 A6
St Bartholomew St. [4] BL3 42 A4
St Bartholomew's CE Prim Sch. OL12 14 C8
St Bartholomew's Dr. M5 161 C8
St Bede CE (VA) Prim Sch. BL3 146 C2
St Bede's Ave. BL3 146 B2
St Bede's Coll. M16 97 E3
St Bees Cl. Gatley SK8 122 B3
St Bees Cl. M'ster M14 98 A4
St Bees Rd. BL2 25 C2
St Bees Wlk. [9] M24 46 E2
St Benedict's RC Prim Sch. SK9 131 E3
St Benedict's Sq. M12 164 F6
St Benedicts RC Prim Sch. WN2 56 C6
St Bernadett's RC Prim Sch. WN6 36 A6
St Bernadette's RC Prim Sch. Brinnington SK5 112 B4
St Bernadette's RC Prim Sch. Whitefield M45 44 F2
St Bernard's Ave. [1] M6, M7 81 C5
St Bernard's Cl. M6 81 B5
St Bernard's RC Prim Sch. Bolton BL3 40 E5
St Bernard's RC Prim Sch. M'ster M19 110 F6
St Boniface RC Prim Sch. M7 81 C6
St Boniface Rd. M7 81 C4
St Brannock's Rd. M21 97 C1
St Brannocks Rd. SK8 132 B7
St Brelades Dr. M7 155 F8
St Brendan's RC Prim Sch. BL2 25 F4
St Brendan's Rd. M20 110 B7
St Brendan's Rd N. M20 110 B7
St Bride St. M16 162 D5
St Brides Cl. BL6 22 A4
St Brides Way. M16 162 D5
St Brigid's RC Prim Sch (Jun & Inf). M11 165 A8
St Catherine's CE Prim Sch. Horwich BL6 22 B3
St Catherine's CE Prim Sch. Wigan WN1 151 E8
St Catherine's RC Prim Sch. Golborne WA3 90 E7
St Catherine's RC Prim Sch. M'ster M20 110 C3
St Catherine's Rd. M20 110 B7
St Catherines Prep Sch. SK6 126 B7
St Chad's Ave. SK6 113 C2
St Chad's CE Prim Sch. OL3 51 C1
St Chad's Cl. OL16 139 F7
St Chad's Ct. OL16 139 F7
St Chad's Gr. SK6 113 C2
St Chad's Jun Sch. BL9 44 F8
St Chad's Rd. M14 & M20 110 D7
St Chad's St. M8 159 A4
St Chads Cres. Oldham OL8 66 D1
St Chads Cres. Uppermill OL3 69 C8
St Chads RC Prim Sch. M8 156 A5
St Charles Cl. SK14 103 F5
St Charles's RC Prim Sch. M27 79 D8
St Christopher's Ave. OL6 85 E6
St Christopher's Dr. SK6 113 A2
St Christopher's RC Prim Sch. Ashton-u-L OL6 85 E6
St Christopher's RC Prim Sch. Romiley SK6 113 A2
St Christopher's Rd. OL6 85 E6
St Chrysostoms CE Prim Sch. M13 164 D5
St Clair Rd. BL8 10 F3
St Clare Terr. BL6 39 F8
St Clare's RC Inf Sch. M9 64 C5
St Clare's RC Jun Sch. M9 64 C5
St Clement (Egerton) CE Prim Sch. M5 161 B7
St Clement's CE Prim Sch. M18 99 E7
St Clement's Ct. Irlam M44 94 B3
St Clement's Ct. Oldham OL8 153 F5
St Clement's Ct. Prestwich M25 63 C4
St Clement's Ct. Wigan WN3 150 A5
St Clement's Dr. M5 161 B7
St Clement's Rd. M'ster M21 109 A8
St Clement's Rd. Wigan WN1 37 C4
St Clement's St. WN2 55 F4
St Columbo's RC Prim Sch. BL2 25 B4
St Cuthbert's RC High Sch. OL16 31 B1
St Cuthbert's RC Inf Sch. WN5 54 D6
St Cuthbert's RC Jun Sch. WN5 54 D6
St Cuthbert's RC Prim Sch. M20 110 C6
St Damian's RC High Sch. OL6 85 E7
St David's Ave. SK6 113 B2
St David's Cl. OL6 85 D7
St David's Cres. WN2 38 B5
St David's Lodge. M8 156 A5
St David's Rd. SK7 124 C1
St David's Wlk. M32 96 A2
St Davids Cl. M33 108 A3
St Domingo St. OL9 153 E6
St Dominics Mews. BL3 146 C3
St Dominics Way. M24 65 A7
St Dunstan's RC Prim Sch. M40 83 A8
St Dunston Wlk. [14] M40 83 A6
St Edmund Arrowsmith RC High Sch. WN4 73 A2
St Edmund Hall Cl. BL0 11 C4
St Edmund St. BL1 145 E7
St Edmund's RC Sch. M38 60 B4
St Edmund's Rd. M40 & M9 157 E6
St Edmunds RC Prim Sch. M40 157 E6
St Edward's RC Prim Sch. Oldham OL4 67 E7
St Edward's RC Prim Sch. Wigan WN5 54 F7
St Edward's RC Sch. M14 98 B2
St Edwards CE Prim Sch. OL11 30 C2
St Elisabeth's CE Prim Sch. SK5 111 E8
St Elisabeth's Way. SK5 111 E8
St Elizabeth's RC Prim Sch. M22 121 E2
St Elizabeth's Rd. WN2 38 B5
St Elmo Ave. SK2 124 D7
St Elmo Pk. SK12 134 C4
St Ethelbert's Ave. BL3 144 B5
St Ethelbert's RC Prim Sch. BL3 144 B5
St Francis' RC Prim Sch. M12 165 B6
St Gabriel Cl. WN8 35 C3
St Gabriel's CE Prim Sch. M24 65 D7
St Gabriel's Cl. OL11 30 D1
St Gabriel's RC High Sch. BL9 140 D1
St Gabriel's RC Prim Sch. Leigh WN7 76 E7
St Gabriel's RC Prim Sch. R'dale OL11 30 D1
St George's Ave. M'ster M15 162 D7
St George's Ave. Sale WA15 120 A8
St George's Ave. Westhoughton BL5 57 E6
St George's CE Inf Sch. Atherton M46 58 B4
St George's CE Inf Sch. Stockport SK2 170 F6
St George's CE Jun Sch. SK2 170 F6
St George's CE Prim Sch. Salford M6 81 A5
St George's CE Prim Sch. Tyldesley M29 76 F8
St George's CE (VA) Prim Sch. SK14 167 D1
St George's Cres. Eccles M6 80 A3
St George's Cres. Sale WA15 120 B8
St George's Cres. Walkden M28 60 D2
St George's Ct. Alt'ham WA14 119 B7
St George's Ct. [16] Bolton BL1 145 E8
St George's Ct. [8] Bolton BL1 145 F8
St George's Ct. Eccles M30 79 F1
St George's Ct. Stretford M32 96 C1
St George's Ct. Whitefield BL9 45 C3
St George's Dr. M40 83 B7
St George's Gdns. M34 101 A1
St George's Pl. Atherton M46 58 B4
St George's Pl. Salford M6 81 A5
St George's Prim Sch. OL2 49 D7
St George's RC High Sch. M28 60 C2
St George's Rd. Bolton BL1 145 E8
St George's Rd. Carrington M31 106 D6
St George's Rd. Droylsden M43 83 F3
St George's Rd. M'ster M14 110 E7
St George's Rd. R'dale OL11 29 F8
St George's Sq. [7] Bolton BL1 145 F8
St George's Sq. Failsworth OL9 65 E3
St George's St. Bolton BL1 145 F8
St George's St. Stalybridge SK15 86 A3
St George's St. Tyldesley M29 76 F8
St George's Terr. BB4 3 A6
St George's Way. M6 81 A4
St Georges CE Prim Sch. BL5 57 D7
St Georges Ct. Hyde SK14 167 E2
St Georges Ct. M'ster M15 162 D7
St Georges Dr. SK14 167 D1
St Georges Rd. Stretford M32 96 C1
St Georges Rd. Whitefield BL9 45 C4
St Germain St. BL4 60 C8
St Gilbert's RC Prim Sch. M30 79 B2
St Giles Dr. SK14 167 F2
St Gregory's High Sch. M11 99 E8
St Gregory's RC Prim Sch. BL4 60 E8
St Gregorys Cl. BL4 60 C8
St Gregorys RC High Sch. M11 160 E1
St Helen's Coll Newton Campus. WA12 89 B4
St Helena Rd. BL1 145 E7
St Helens CE Prim Sch. WA3 105 B2
St Helens Cl. WA3 105 B3
St Helens Rd. Bolton BL3 & BL5 146 B3
St Helens Rd. Golborne WN7 75 C1
St Helens Rd. Leigh WN7 75 E2
St Helier's Dr. M7 & M8 155 F8
St Heliers St. BL3 147 D4
St Herberts Ct. OL9 152 B7
St Herberts RC Prim Sch. OL9 152 A7
St Hilary's Sch. SK9 137 A1
St Hilda's CE Prim Sch. M'ster M16 97 B2
St Hilda's CE Prim Sch. Oldham OL1 153 D8
St Hilda's CE Prim Sch. Prestwich M25 63 C4
St Hilda's Cl. M22 109 E1
St Hilda's Dr. OL1 153 D8
St Hilda's Rd. Denton M34 100 F6
St Hilda's Rd. M'ster M16 161 C5
St Hilda's Rd. Wythenshawe M22 109 D1
St Hilda's View. M34 100 E5
St Hugh of Lincoln RC Prim Sch. M32 95 F3
St Hugh's CE Prim Sch. OL4 67 E3
St Hugh's Cl. WA14 119 E8
St Hugh's RC Prim Sch. WA15 119 F8
St Ignatius Prim Sch. M13 163 C6
St Ignatius Wlk. M5 161 B8
St Ives Ave. SK8 123 A6
St Ives Cres. M33 108 A1
St Ives Rd. M14 98 B2
St Jame's Cl. OL16 & OL2 48 C8
St James Ave. Bolton BL2 42 E7
St James' Ave. Bury BL8 27 B4
St James' CE Prim Sch. Ashton-u-L OL6 166 C3
St James CE Prim Sch. Farnworth BL4 60 C7
St James CE Prim Sch. Littleborough OL12 15 C6
St James CE Prim Sch. M'ster M14 98 D2
St James' CE Prim Sch. M'ster M18 99 D5
St James CE Prim Sch. Shaw OL2 149 B7
St James' CE Prim Sch. Wigan WN3 54 F5
St James Cl. Glossop SK13 116 C7
St James Cl. Salford M6 80 B3
St James Cres. Leigh WN2 74 F8
St James Ct. Alt'ham WA15 119 E4
St James Ct. Cheadle SK8 131 F6
St James' Ct. Eccles M6 80 B3
St James Ct. M'ster M20 122 B8
St James Ct. [4] Oldham OL4 67 C8
St James Dr. Sale M33 108 A3
St James' Dr. Wilmslow SK9 137 A6
St James' Gr. [8] Heywood OL10 29 C2
St James Gr. Wigan WN3 150 B6
St James Lodge. SK3 124 A4
St James' RC High Sch. SK8 131 F6
St James' RC Prim Sch. Hattersley SK14 102 D2
St James' RC Prim Sch. Orrell WN5 53 D4
St James Rd. M'ster SK4 111 B5

St James' Rd. Orrell WN5 ..... 53 D4
St James St. Ashton-u-L OL6 . 85 D2
St James St. Eccles M30 .... 79 E2
St James St. Farnworth BL4 ... 60 B7
St James St. Heywood OL10 ... 29 C2
St James St. M'ster M1 .... 163 A8
St James St. Milnrow OL16 ..... 31 F6
St James' St. Rawtenstall BB4 . 2 E8
St James St. Salford M5 ...... 161 A6
St James St. Shaw OL2 .... 149 B7
St James St. Westhoughton BL5 .... 57 F5
St James' Way. SK8 .... 131 F6
St James's CE Sch. BL4 .... 60 A8
St James's Gr. WA14 .... 107 F1
St James's RC Prim Sch. M6 .... 154 F3
St James's Rd. M7 .... 155 E6
St James's Sq. 8 M2 .... 158 F1
St James's St. OL1 .... 67 B7
St James's Terr. OL10 .... 29 C2
St John Bosco RC Prim Sch. M9 .... 65 A3
St John Fisher RC High Sch. WN6 .... 36 F2
St John Fisher RC Prim Sch. Denton M34 .... 101 B1
St John Fisher RC Prim Sch. Middleton M24 .... 47 B3
St John Fisher & St Thomas More RC Prim Sch. M22 121 D4
St John Rigby RC Coll. WN5 35 F2
St John Southworth RC Prim Sch. WN4 .... 73 D4
St John St. Atherton M46 .... 58 D3
St John St. Dukinfield SK16 .. 101 E8
St John St. 1 Eccles M30 ..... 79 D1
St John St. Horwich BL6 .... 22 B3
St John St. Irlam M44 .... 94 A2
St John St. M'ster M3 .... 162 E8
St John St. Newton-l-W WA12 89 A3
St John St. 6 Oldham OL4 ..... 67 E6
St John St. Oldham OL4 .... 67 F6
St John St. Salford M27 .... 80 D6
St John St. Walkden M28 .... 60 D4
St John St. Wigan WN5 .... 54 B6
St John the Baptist CE Sch. WN2 .... 37 F3
St John the Evangelist RC Prim Sch. BL7 .... 24 F8
St John Vianney Lower Sch. SK4 .... 168 B2
St John Vianney Upper Sch. M16 .... 97 B2
St John with St Michael CE Prim Sch. OL12 .... 4 E5
St John's Ave. Droylsden M43 84 B2
St John's Ave. Westhoughton BL5 .... 39 D3
St John's CE Inf Sch. Failsworth M35 .... 83 F8
St John's CE Inf Sch. Leigh WN7 .... 75 F6
St John's CE Jun Sch. M35 . 84 A7
St John's CE Prim Sch. Bury BL9 .... 140 F4
St John's CE Prim Sch. Coppull PR7 .... 19 D6
St John's CE Prim Sch. Farnworth BL4 .... 60 E8
St John's CE Prim Sch. Hindley WN2 .... 57 B3
St John's CE Prim Sch. M'ster M13 .... 98 E4
St John's CE Prim Sch. M'ster SK4 .... 110 E2
St John's CE Prim Sch. Middleton M24 .... 47 E6
St John's CE Prim Sch. Radcliffe M26 .... 44 B1
St John's CE Prim Sch. Wigan WN5 .... 54 B6
St John's Cl. Dukinfield SK16 101 E8
St John's Cl. Romiley SK6 .... 113 B2
St John's Ct. 5 Abram WN2 . 56 B1
St John's Ct. 1 Hattersley SK14 .... 102 D2
St John's Ct. Hyde SK14 .... 167 F3
St John's Ct. M'ster M7 .... 155 D6
St John's Ct. 4 R'dale OL16 . 31 B6
St John's Ct. Radcliffe M26 .... 44 C2
St John's Dr. Hyde SK14 .... 167 F3
St John's Dr. 3 R'dale OL16 . 31 B6
St John's Gdns. OL5 .... 68 D2
St John's Ind Est. OL4 .... 67 E6
St John's Mosley Common CE Prim Sch. M28 .... 77 F7
St John's Pl. SK4 .... 110 E2
St John's RC Prim Sch. M'ster M21 .... 97 A1
St John's RC Prim Sch. R'dale OL11 .... 139 F6
St John's Rd. Alt'ham WA14 119 D3
St John's Rd. Aspull WN2 .... 38 B5
St John's Rd. Bolton BL6 .... 40 B4
St John's Rd. Boothstown M28 & M29 .... 77 E7
St John's Rd. Denton M34 .... 100 F5
St John's Rd. Hazel Grove SK7 .... 124 B1
St John's Rd. M'ster M16 .... 97 C4
St John's Rd. M'ster M13 .... 98 F4
St John's Rd. M'ster SK4 ..... 110 E2
St John's Rd. Wilmslow SK9 136 E3
St John's St. Abram WN2 .... 74 B8
St John's St. Farnworth BL4 ... 60 E8
St John's St. M'ster M7 .... 155 D6
St John's St. Oldham OL9 .... 152 C5
St John's St. Radcliffe M26 ..... 44 B2
St John's St. Rawtenstall BB4 .... 2 F8
St John's (VC) Prim Sch. SK16 .... 101 E8
St John's Wlk. OL9 .... 152 C6
St Johns CE Prim Sch. Pendlebury M6 .... 80 C6
St Johns CE Prim Sch. R'dale OL12 .... 15 B4
St Johns Ct. OL4 .... 67 F7
St Johns Sq. M3 .... 158 D2
St Johns Wlk. 3 SK3 .... 123 B8
St Johns Wood. BL6 .... 40 B4
St Joseph St. 12 BL1 .... 143 D2
St Joseph & St Bede RC Prim Sch. BL9 .... 141 B4
St Joseph's Con Ctr. WN8 ... 35 B2
St Joseph's Dr. R'dale OL16 .. 31 B4
St Joseph's Dr. Salford M5 . 161 B8
St Joseph's Prim Sch. M44 . 94 A3
St Joseph's RC High Sch. OL10 .... 29 C1
St Joseph's RC Inf Sch. SK5 .... 111 E8
St Joseph's RC Jun Sch. SK5 .... 111 E8
St Joseph's RC Prim Sch. Adlington PR6 .... 21 B8
St Joseph's RC Prim Sch. Bacup OL13 .... 3 D8
St Joseph's RC Prim Sch. Bolton BL1 .... 142 C1
St Joseph's RC Prim Sch. Heywood OL10 .... 29 C1
St Joseph's RC Prim Sch. Leigh WN7 .... 76 A4
St Joseph's RC Prim Sch. M'ster M13 .... 98 E4
St Joseph's RC Prim Sch. Mossley OL5 .... 68 C1
St Joseph's RC Prim Sch. Ramsbottom BL0 .... 138 B6
St Joseph's RC Prim Sch. Sale M33 .... 108 B4
St Joseph's RC Prim Sch. Salford M5 .... 161 B8
St Joseph's RC Prim Sch. Shaw OL2 .... 149 B5
St Joseph's RC Prim Sch. Shevington Moor WN6 .... 19 A3
St Joseph's RC Prim Sch. Walkden M38 .... 60 A5
St Joseph's RC Sch. Horwich BL6 .... 22 E1
St Joseph's RC Sch. Stockport SK1 .... 169 F1
St Josephs Ave. M45 .... 63 C7
St Jude's CE Prim Sch. M4 .... 159 C2
St Jude's Jun Sch. WN3 ...... 54 F5
St Jude's RC Inf Sch. WN3 . 54 F5
St Katherines Dr. BL6 .... 21 C3
St Kentigern's RC Prim Sch. M14 .... 98 A1
St Kilda Ave. BL4 .... 60 F6
St Kilda's Ave. M43 .... 83 F3
St Kilda's Dr. M7 .... 155 F8
St Lawrence Quay. M5 .... 96 F7
St Lawrence Rd. M34, M16 101 A3
St Leonard's Ave. BL6 .... 22 F1
St Leonard's Ct. 3 M33 ...... 107 F4
St Leonard's Rd. SK4 .... 111 D5
St Leonard's Sq. 3 M24 .... 47 A1
St Leonard's St. M24 .... 47 A1
St Leonards Dr. WA15 .... 119 F6
St Lesmo Ct. SK3 .... 123 C7
St Lesmo Rd. SK3 .... 123 C7
St Lewis RC Prim Sch. WA3 .... 91 B1
St Luke St. OL11 .... 139 F5
St Luke with All Saints CE Prim Sch. M5 .... 154 D1
St Luke's Ave. WA3 .... 90 D8
St Luke's CE Prim Sch. Glossop SK13 .... 104 C1
St Luke's CE Prim Sch. Golborne WA3 .... 90 E7
St Luke's CE Prim Sch. Heywood OL10 .... 29 D3
St Luke's CE Prim Sch. M'ster M12 .... 164 E5
St Luke's Cres. SK16 .... 101 C8
St Luke's Dr. WN5 .... 53 E4
St Luke's RC Prim Sch. M6 . 80 C5
St Luke's Rd. M5 & M6 .... 154 E2
St Lukes CE Prim Sch. OL9 152 A7
St Lukes Ct. Bolton BL1 .... 144 C8
St. Lukes Ct. Chadderton OL9 .... 152 A7
St Lukes Wlk. 15 M40 .... 83 A6
St Malachy's RC Prim Sch. M40 .... 156 C5
St Malo Rd. WN1 .... 37 C4
St Margaret Mary RC Prim Sch. WN2 .... 57 A4
St Margaret Mary's RC Prim Sch. M40 .... 65 D3
St Margaret Ward RC Prim Sch. M33 .... 107 C2
St Margaret's Ave. M19 ...... 110 F6
St Margaret's CE Prim Sch. M'ster M16 .... 97 D2
St Margaret's CE Prim Sch. Oldham OL8 .... 66 B2
St Margaret's CE Prim Sch. Prestwich M25 .... 63 D7
St Margaret's Cl. Alt'ham WA14 .... 119 C4
St Margaret's Cl. Bolton BL1 144 B8
St Margaret's Cl. Prestwich M25 .... 63 C6
St Margaret's Gdns. OL8 ...... 66 C3
St Margaret's Prim Sch. OL10 .... 29 A1
St Margaret's Rd. Alt'ham WA14 .... 119 C4
St Margaret's Rd. Bolton BL1 .... 144 B8
St Margaret's Rd. Cheadle SK8 .... 123 A6
St Margaret's Rd. Failsworth M24 & M40 .... 65 D3
St Margaret's Rd. Prestwich M25 .... 63 C6
St Margarets RC Prim Sch. SK13 .... 115 D8
St Marie's RC Prim Sch. BL9 .... 140 F1
St Maries RC Prim Sch. WN6 .... 19 E2
St Mark St. SK16 .... 166 B1
St Mark's Ave. Alt'ham WA14 .... 119 A5
St Mark's Ave. Royton OL2 ..... 49 A4
St Mark's Ave. Wigan WN5 .... 54 F7
St Mark's CE Prim Sch. Bury BL9 .... 141 A4
St Mark's CE Prim Sch. M'ster M40 .... 160 D3
St Mark's CE Prim Sch. Romiley SK6 .... 113 A4
St Mark's CE Prim Sch. Worsley M28 .... 78 F6
St Mark's Cl. OL2 .... 49 A4
St Mark's Cres. M28 .... 60 D1
St Mark's Ct. OL9 .... 152 B8
St Mark's La. M7 & M8 .... 155 F8
St Mark's RC Prim Sch. M27 .... 62 A2
St Mark's Sq. 11 BL9 .... 140 F4
St Mark's St. Bolton BL3 .... 145 F5
St Mark's St. Reddish M19 ..... 99 C1
St Mark's St. Romiley SK6 ... 113 A4
St Mark's View. BL3 .... 145 F5
St Mark's Wlk. BL3 .... 147 E4
St Marks CE Prim Sch. WN5 54 F6
St Martin's Ave. SK4 .... 168 C2
St Martin's CE Prim Sch. OL8 .... 67 B2
St Martin's Cl. Droylsden M43 83 F3
St Martin's Cl. Hyde SK14 .... 167 F2
St Martin's Dr. M7 & M8 ...... 155 F8
St Martin's Rd. Marple SK6 . 126 A6
St Martin's Rd. Oldham OL8 ... 67 B2
St Martin's Sch. M33 .... 107 E5
St Martin's St. OL11 .... 30 D1
St Martins Rd. M33 .... 107 E6
St Mary & St John RC Prim Sch. WN1 .... 37 D1
St Mary's Ave. Billinge WN5 ... 71 C4
St Mary's Ave. Bolton BL3 ... 144 B5
St Mary's Ave. Denton M34 . 113 A8
St Mary's CE Prim Sch. Bolton BL3 .... 146 A4
St Mary's CE Prim Sch. Droylsden M43 .... 84 B1
St Mary's CE Prim Sch. Failsworth M40 .... 65 C1
St Mary's CE Prim Sch. Golborne WA3 .... 91 A8
St Mary's CE Prim Sch. Ince-i-M WN2 .... 55 F4
St Mary's CE Prim Sch. Irlam M44 .... 105 C5
St Mary's CE Prim Sch. M'ster M16 .... 97 E4
St Mary's CE Prim Sch. Prestwich M25 .... 63 A4
St Mary's CE Prim Sch. R'dale OL11 .... 31 A4
St Mary's CE Prim Sch. Ramsbottom BL8 .... 10 C2
St Mary's CE Prim Sch. Reddish SK5 .... 112 A6
St Mary's CE Prim Sch. Sale M33 .... 108 A4
St Mary's CE Prim Sch. Shaw OL2 .... 48 F8
St Mary's CE Prim Sch. Uppermill OL3 .... 69 C4
St Mary's CE Prim Sch. Urmston M41 .... 95 B4
St Mary's Cl. Aspull WN2 .... 38 B5
St Mary's Cl. Atherton M46 ..... 58 E2
St Mary's Cl. R'dale OL16 .... 31 B4
St Mary's Cl. Stockport SK1 . 112 A1
St Mary's Crest. OL3 .... 69 C5
St Mary's Ct. Failsworth M40 . 83 B8
St Mary's Ct. M'ster M8 .... 63 F1
St Mary's Ct. Prestwich M25 .. 63 A4
St Mary's Dr. Cheadle SK8 .... 122 F6
St Mary's Dr. Reddish SK5 .... 111 F6
St Mary's Dr. Uppermill OL3 ... 69 C5
St Mary's Gate. M'ster M3 ... 158 F2
St Mary's Gate. R'dale OL11, OL12, OL16 .... 139 E8
St Mary's Gate. Shaw OL2 ... 149 B7
St Mary's Gate. Uppermill OL3 .... 69 B8
St Mary's Hall Rd. M8 .... 63 F1
St Mary's Hospl. M13 .... 98 C4
St Mary's Parsonage. M3 ... 158 F1
St Mary's Pl. BL9 .... 140 E2
St Mary's Prim Sch. M35 ...... 83 E6
St Mary's RC High Sch. M29 .... 77 A4
St Mary's RC Inf Sch. WA12 . 89 C4
St Mary's RC Jun Sch. WA12 .... 89 B3
St Mary's RC Prim Sch. Ashton-u-L OL6 .... 85 D4
St Mary's RC Prim Sch. Denton M34 .... 100 E3
St Mary's RC Prim Sch. Dukinfield SK16 .... 101 E6
St Mary's RC Prim Sch. Glossop SK13 .... 116 D8
St Mary's RC Prim Sch. Horwich BL6 .... 22 B4
St Mary's RC Prim Sch. Horwich BL6 .... 22 D2
St Mary's RC Prim Sch. M'ster M19 .... 111 A8
St Mary's RC Prim Sch. Marple SK6 .... 126 B7
St Mary's RC Prim Sch. Radcliffe M26 .... 44 A4
St Mary's RC Prim Sch. Stockport SK4 .... 169 E2
St Mary's RC Prim Sch. Swinton M27 .... 79 F8
St Mary's RC Sch. Eccles M30 79 E1
St Mary's RC Sch. Middleton M24 .... 46 E2
St Mary's Rd. Alt'ham WA14 119 C3
St Mary's Rd. Aspull WN2 .... 38 C5
St Mary's Rd. Disley SK12 ... 135 D5
St Mary's Rd. Dukinfield SK14 .... 101 F5
St Mary's Rd. Failsworth M40 83 B7
St Mary's Rd. 1 Glossop SK13 .... 104 C1
St Mary's Rd. Glossop SK13 116 C8
St Mary's Rd. Prestwich M25 . 63 B4
St Mary's Rd. Sale M33 .... 107 F5
St Mary's Rd. Walkden M28 ... 60 C5
St Mary's St. M'ster M3 .... 158 F1
St Mary's St. M'ster M15 ..... 162 E5
St Mary's Way. 2 Leigh WN7 75 F5
St Mary's Way. Oldham OL1 . 153 F7
St Mary's Way. Stockport SK1 .... 112 A2
St Marys St. OL1 .... 153 F8
St Mathews CE Prim Sch Highfield. WN3 .... 54 C4
St Matthew's CE Inf Sch. M24 .... 47 F2
St Matthew's CE Prim Sch. Bolton BL1 .... 143 E1
St Matthew's CE Prim Sch. Little Lever BL3 .... 43 A3
St Matthew's CE Prim Sch. Stockport SK3 .... 170 E8
St Matthew's Cl. WN3 .... 54 C4
St Matthew's Dr. OL1 .... 48 A2
St Matthew's RC High Sch. Failsworth M40 .... 65 C2
St Matthew's RC High Sch. M'ster M9 .... 64 F1
St Matthew's Rd. SK3 .... 170 D8
St Matthew's Terr. 8 Bolton BL1 .... 143 E1
St Matthew's Terr. Stockport SK3 .... 170 D8
St Matthew's Wlk. BL1 ...... 143 E1
St Matthews CE Prim Sch. M32 .... 108 C8
St Matthews Ct. M32 .... 96 C1
St Mawes Ct. M26 .... 43 C5
St Maxentious CE Prim Sch. BL2 .... 25 D5
St Michael's Ave. Atherton M46 .... 58 A1
St Michael's Ave. Bolton BL3 42 B2
St Michael's Ave. Bramhall SK7 .... 132 E8
St Michael's Bamford CE Prim Sch. OL10 .... 29 D5
St Michael's CE Prim Sch. Bolton BL3 .... 42 C3
St Michael's CE Prim Sch. Middleton M24 .... 65 A5
St Michael's CE (VA) Prim Sch. M41 .... 94 F1
St Michael's Ct. Eccles M30 .. 95 A8
St Michael's Ct. 7 Wigan WN1 .... 37 C2
St Michael's RC Prim Sch. M45 .... 45 B1
St Michael's Rd. SK14 .... 102 A2
St Michael's Sq. 6 Ashton-u-L OL6 .... 166 C3
St Michael's Sq. 3 M'ster M4 .... 159 A3
St Michaels Cl. Bury BL8 .... 43 F8
St Michaels Ct. M33 .... 107 E6
St Modwen Rd. Stretford M32 96 A5
St Monica's RC High Sch. M25 .... 63 C3
St Monica's RC Sch. M41 ..... 94 E2
St Nathaniel's CE Prim Sch. WN2 .... 56 B3
St Nicholas Rd. WA3 .... 75 A1
St Osmund's Dr. BL2 .... 42 E7
St Osmund's Gr. BL2 .... 42 E7
St Osmund's RC Prim Sch. BL2 .... 42 E7
St Oswald's RC Prim Sch. Ashton-i-M WN4 .... 73 B3
St Oswald's RC Prim Sch. Coppull PR7 .... 19 D8
St Oswald's Rd. M18 & M19 .. 99 B2
St Oswalds Rd. WN4 .... 73 A2
St Ouen Ctr. M28 .... 60 D3
St Patrick St. WN1 .... 151 D8
St Patrick's RC High Sch. M30 .... 79 B2
St Patrick's RC Prim Sch. M'ster M40 .... 159 C3
St Patrick's RC Prim Sch. R'dale OL12 .... 14 F1
St Patrick's RC Prim Sch. Wigan WN1 .... 151 D8
St Patricks RC Prim Sch. OL9 .... 153 D6
St Patricks Way. WN1 .... 151 D7
St Paul's Ave. WN3 .... 54 F4
St Paul's C E Prim Sch. BL0 .... 138 C6
St Paul's Catholic High Sch. M22 .... 121 B4
St Paul's CE Inf Sch. OL2 .... 48 D4
St Paul's CE Jun Sch. OL2 ... 48 C3
St Paul's CE Prim Sch. Adlington PR6 .... 21 A7
St Paul's CE Prim Sch. Bolton BL1 .... 143 F3
St Paul's CE Prim Sch. Brinnington SK5 .... 112 B4
St Paul's CE Prim Sch. Bury BL9 .... 141 B4
St Paul's CE Prim Sch. M'ster M20 .... 110 B6
St Paul's CE Prim Sch. Walkden M28 .... 60 F2
St Paul's CE Prim Sch. Wigan WN3 .... 54 F3
St Paul's Cl. PR6 .... 21 A8
St Paul's Ct. Hyde SK14 .... 167 E3
St Paul's Ct. Radcliffe M26 ..... 44 A1
St Paul's Hill. SK14 .... 102 A2
St Paul's Hill Rd. SK14 .... 167 F2
St Paul's Pl. 1 BL1 .... 142 C3
St Paul's Prim Sch. SK15 ...... 86 C2
St Paul's Rd. M'ster M25 .... 63 C1
St Paul's Rd. M'ster M20 ..... 110 C6
St Paul's Rd. M'ster SK4 ...... 168 B4
St Paul's St. Bury BL9 .... 141 A3
St Paul's St. Hyde SK14 .... 167 E3
St Paul's St. Ramsbottom BL0 .... 138 C6
St Paul's St. Reddish SK1 ..... 112 A3
St Paul's St. Stalybridge SK15 86 C2
St Paul's Villas. BL9 .... 141 A3
St Pauls CE Prim Sch. Salford M5 .... 81 B1
St Pauls CE Prim Sch. Walkden M28 .... 60 E3
St Pauls Cl. SK15 .... 86 C2
St Pauls Ct. M7 .... 63 C1
St Pauls Peel CE Prim Sch. M38 .... 59 F5
St Pauls RC Prim Sch. SK12 .... 133 E2
St Pauls Rd. M28 .... 60 E2
St Pauls Trad Est. SK15 .... 86 C2
St Peter Quay. M5 .... 161 A7
St Peter & St Paul's Prim Sch. BL3 .... 145 E5
St Peter's Ave. BL1 .... 142 A2
St Peter's CE Prim Sch. Ashton-i-M WN4 .... 72 F6
St Peter's CE Prim Sch. Ashton-u-L OL7 .... 166 A1
St Peter's CE Prim Sch. Bury BL9 .... 44 E6
St Peter's CE Prim Sch. Farnworth BL4 .... 60 D7
St Peter's CE Prim Sch. Hindley WN2 .... 56 C5
St Peter's CE Prim Sch. Newton-l-W WA12 .... 89 E4
St Peter's CE Prim Sch. R'dale OL16 .... 31 B5
St Peter's CE Prim Sch. Swinton M27 .... 79 E8
St Peter's Cl. WA13 .... 117 A4
St Peter's Ct. M32 .... 96 E3
St Peter's Dr. SK14 .... 167 F2
St Peter's Gate. OL14 .... 6 B8
St Peter's RC High Sch. WN5 .... 53 F7
St Peter's RC Prim Sch. Hazel Grove SK7 .... 124 D1
St Peter's RC Prim Sch. Middleton M24 .... 65 A7
St Peter's RC Prim Sch. Stalybridge SK15 .... 86 A1
St Peter's RC Prim Sch. Wythenshawe M22 .... 121 A3
St Peter's Rd. Bury BL9 .... 44 F6
St Peter's Rd. Swinton M27 .... 79 E8
St Peter's Smithills Dean CE Prim Sch. BL1 .... 142 B4
St Peter's Sq. M'ster M1 ...... 162 F8
St Peter's Sq. Stockport SK1 169 F1
St Peter's Sq Sta. M2 .... 162 F8
St Peter's St. 6 Ashton-u-L OL7 .... 166 A2
St Peter's St. R'dale OL16 ...... 31 B6
St Peter's Terr. BL4 .... 60 D7
St Peter's Way. Bolton BL1, BL2, BL3, BL4 .... 42 B4
St Peter's Way. Bolton BL1 .. 145 F8
St Peters CE Jun Sch. WN7 . 75 C5
St Petersgate. SK1 & SK3 ..... 169 F1
St Philip Howard RC Sch. SK13 .... 116 B8
St Philip's Ave. BL3 .... 147 D4
St Philip's CE Prim Sch. M46 .... 58 E3
St Philip's Pl. M3 .... 158 D2
St Philip's RC Prim Sch. M'ster M7 .... 63 C1
St Philip's RC Prim Sch. Stockport SK2 .... 124 E6
St Philip's Rd. M18 .... 99 D4
St Philips CE Prim Sch. M'ster M3 .... 158 D1
St Philips CE Prim Sch. M'ster M15 .... 162 F6
St Philips Sq. M3 .... 158 D2
St Phillip's Dr. OL1 & OL2 ...... 48 E1
St Raphael's RC Prim Sch. SK15 .... 86 E4
St Richard's RC Prim Sch. Atherton M46 .... 58 C4
St Richard's RC Prim Sch. M'ster M12 .... 99 B3
St Robert's RC Prim Sch. M13 .... 98 F3
St Saviour's Cty Prim Sch. OL13 .... 3 F8
St Saviour's Rd. SK2 .... 124 C5
St Saviours CE Prim Sch. M26 .... 61 C7
St Sebastian's RC Prim Sch. M6 .... 81 A5
St Simon St. M3 .... 158 E3
St Simon's Catholic Prim Sch. SK7 .... 124 E3
St Simons Cl. SK2 .... 124 C8
St Stephen & All Martyrs CE Inf Sch. OL1 .... 153 F8
St Stephen & All Martyrs' CE Prim Sch. BL2 .... 148 C5
St Stephen CE Prim Sch. BL4 .... 61 A6
St Stephen St. M'ster M3 .... 158 E2
St Stephen St. 6 Oldham OL1 .... 67 A8
St Stephen's Ave. Denton M34 .... 100 E8
St Stephen's Ave. Wigan WN1 .... 37 E2
St Stephen's CE Prim Sch. Bury BL8 .... 27 B1
St Stephen's CE Prim Sch. Tyldesley M29 .... 77 B6
St Stephen's CE Prim Sch. Wigan WN1 .... 37 E2
St Stephen's CE (VA) Prim Sch. SK2 .... 124 F4
St Stephen's Cl. Bolton BL2 148 C5
St Stephen's Cl. M'ster M13 164 D5
St Stephen's Gdns. Kearsley BL4 .... 61 A6
St Stephen's Gdns. 10 Middleton M24 .... 47 A2
St Stephen's RC Prim Sch. M43 .... 84 A2
St Stephen's Rd. WN6 .... 19 C1
St Stephens Cl. M29 .... 77 A5
St Teresa's RC Prim Sch. Irlam M44 .... 105 E8
St Teresa's RC Prim Sch. Little Lever BL3 .... 43 A3
St Teresa's RC Prim Sch. M'ster M16 .... 97 A3
St Teresa's RC Prim Sch. Orrell WN8 .... 35 B1
St Teresa's Rd. M16 .... 97 A3
St Thomas Aquinas RC High Sch. M16 .... 97 E1
St Thomas Aquinus RC High Sch (Upper Sch). M21 .... 109 D7
St Thomas' CE Parochial Sch. SK4 .... 111 C6
St Thomas CE Prim Sch. Ashton-i-M WN4 .... 73 C3
St Thomas' CE Prim Sch. Bury BL9 .... 141 B1
St Thomas CE Prim Sch. Leigh WN7 .... 76 B4
St Thomas CE Prim Sch. Newhey OL16 .... 32 B4
St Thomas CE Prim Sch. Oldham OL4 .... 67 E5
St Thomas' CE Prim Sch. Stockport SK1 .... 170 F8
St Thomas CE Prim Sch. Westhoughton BL5 .... 40 B1
St Thomas CE (VA) Prim Sch. OL1 .... 49 E4
St Thomas Cl. Haslingden BB4 . 1 A7
St Thomas' Cl. Radcliffe M26 . 44 A3
St Thomas Ct. 1 BL9 .... 141 A2
St Thomas' Cty Prim Sch. M8 .... 156 C8
St Thomas Hospl. SK3 .... 170 E8
St Thomas More RC High Sch. Denton M34 .... 100 F2
St Thomas More RC High Sch. Wigan WN5 .... 54 F7
St Thomas More RC Prim Sch. M24 .... 65 A5
St Thomas of Canterbury RC Prim Sch. Bolton BL1 . 144 A8
St Thomas of Canterbury RC Prim Sch. M'ster M7 .. 155 E6
St Thomas' Pl. M8 .... 159 A4
St Thomas St. Bolton BL1 .... 143 D2
St Thomas St. Wigan WN3 .. 150 C7
St Thomas St N. OL8 .... 153 D5
St Thomas St S. OL8 .... 153 E5
St Thomas the Martyr CE Prim Sch. WN8 .... 53 B7
St Thomas's CE Prim Sch. Bolton BL1 .... 143 D2
St Thomas's CE Prim Sch. Oldham OL8 .... 153 D5
St Thomas's Circ. OL8 .... 153 D5
St Thomas's Ct. WN8 .... 53 C7
St Thomas's Pl. SK1 .... 170 F8
St Veronica's RC Prim Sch. BB4 .... 1 B7
St Vincent de Paul RC High Sch. M14 .... 98 D3
St Vincent RC Prim Sch. OL12 .... 14 A1
St Vincent St. Alt'ham WA15 119 E4
St Vincent St. M'ster M20 & M4 .... 159 C2
St Vincent's RC Inf Sch. WA15 .... 119 E5
St Vincent's RC Jun Sch. WA15 .... 119 E5
St Werburgh's Rd. M21 & M16 .... 109 C8
St Wilfred's CE Jun & Inf Schs. WN6 .... 19 F1
St Wilfred's CE Prim Sch. M40 .... 83 D5
St Wilfred's Dr. OL12 .... 14 D4
St Wilfrid's RC Prim Sch. M15 .... 162 E6
St Wilfrid's Rd. WN6 .... 19 F1
St Wilfrid's Way. WN6 .... 19 E1
St Wilfrids CE Prim Sch. M22 .... 121 E8
St Wilfrids St. M15 .... 162 E6
St William's RC Prim Sch. WN2 .... 151 F7
St Williams Ave. BL3 .... 147 E3
St Williams' RC Prim Sch. BL3 .... 147 E3
St Willibrord's RC Prim Sch. M11 .... 83 C3
St Winifred's RC Prim Sch. SK4 .... 168 A2
Saintsbridge Rd. M22 .... 121 C2
Salcombe Ave. BL2 .... 26 D1
Salcombe Cl. Sale M33 .... 107 E5
Salcombe Cl. Wigan WN1 ...... 37 E2
Salcombe Gr. Bolton BL2 .... 42 F6
Salcombe Rd. Droylsden M11 & M43 .... 99 D8
Salcombe Rd. Stockport SK2 124 C8
Salcot Wlk. 5 M40 .... 159 C3
Sale Golf Course. M33 .... 109 A4
Sale Gram Sch. M33 .... 108 C3
Sale Heys Rd. M33 .... 107 F3
Sale La. M29 .... 77 D8
Sale Rd. M23 & M33 .... 109 B2
Sale St. OL15 .... 16 B6
Sale Sta. M33 .... 108 B4
Sale Water Pk. M33 .... 108 E7
Sale West Cty Sec Sch. M33 .... 107 D5
Salem Gr. OL4 .... 67 D6
Sales's La. BL9 .... 12 B3
Salesbury Way. WN3 .... 55 A3

Salford App. M3 158 F2
Salford Central Sta. M3 158 E1
Salford Coll (Quays Campus). M5 161 A7
Salford Coll (Wardley Campus). M27 61 C2
Salford Coll (Worsley Campus). M28 60 D1
Salford Crescent Sta. M6 81 B2
Salford Foyer. M6 154 F3
Salford Rd. BL5, M28, M38 59 C7
Salford Royal Hospl. M3 158 D2
Salford St. Bury BL9 141 A4
Salford St. Oldham OL4 67 C5
Salik Gdns. OL11 139 F5
Salisbury Ave. Heywood OL10 46 C8
Salisbury Ave. Hindley WN2 56 E6
Salisbury Cres. OL6 85 D7
Salisbury Dr. Dukinfield SK15 & SK16 102 A7
Salisbury Dr. M'ster M25 63 C2
Salisbury House. M3 158 E2
Salisbury Rd. Alt'ham WA14 119 D7
Salisbury Rd. 1 Ashton-i-M WN4 73 A5
Salisbury Rd. Eccles M30 80 A4
Salisbury Rd. Horwich BL6 22 F1
Salisbury Rd. M'ster M21 97 C1
Salisbury Rd. Oldham OL4 67 B6
Salisbury Rd. Radcliffe M26 43 E5
Salisbury Rd. Swinton M27 79 E7
Salisbury Rd. Urmston M41 95 D4
Salisbury Rd. Whitefield M45 62 F8
Salisbury St. Bolton BL3 145 D6
Salisbury St. Golborne WA3 90 A8
Salisbury St. Hadfield SK14 104 A5
Salisbury St. M'ster M14 98 A4
Salisbury St. Middleton M24 47 B1
Salisbury St. Reddish SK5 111 F8
Salisbury St. Shaw OL2 48 F8
Salisbury Terr. BL3 43 C3
Salisbury Way. M29 77 B8
Salix Ct. M6 81 A3
Salkeld Ave. WN4 72 F3
Salkeld St. OL11 139 F5
Salley St. OL15 6 C2
Sallowfields. WN5 53 D5
Salmon Fields. OL2 48 F3
Salmon St. M'ster M4 159 A2
Salmon St. 1 Wigan WN1 37 E1
Salmsbury Hall Cl. BL0 11 C4
Salop St. Bolton BL2 148 A6
Salop St. Salford M6 81 A4
Saltash Cl. M22 121 D1
Saltburn Wlk. 23 M9 157 E8
Saltdene Rd. 2 M22 121 C1
Salter Rake Gate. OL14 6 B8
Saltergate. BL3 40 F4
Saltergate Mews. M5 81 A1
Saltersbrook Gr. 12 SK9 131 E1
Salterton Wlk. 17 M40 83 A7
Salteye Rd. M30 79 A1
Saltford Ave. M4 159 C2
Saltford Ct. 10 M4 159 C2
Salthill Ave. OL10 46 E7
Salthill Dr. M22 121 E2
Saltire Gdns. M7 155 E8
Saltney Ave. M20 109 F7
Saltram Cl. BL3 & M26 43 C5
Saltram Rd. WN3 54 C4
Saltrush Rd. M22 121 D1
Salts Dr. OL15 16 A6
Salts St. OL2 149 B7
Saltwood Gr. BL1 143 F1
Salvin Wlk. 27 M9 64 E3
Sam Cowan Cl. M14 98 A3
Sam Fitton Way. OL1 153 F7
Sam Rd. OL3 51 C5
Sam Reid Wlk. 9 M16 97 E4
Sam Swire St. M15 162 F5
Samian Gdns. M7 81 C5
Samlesbury Cl. M'ster M20 109 F3
Samlesbury Cl. Shaw OL2 48 E7
Sammy Cookson Cl. M14 98 A3
Samouth Cl. M10 & M40 160 D3
Sampson Sq. M14 98 A4
Samson St. OL16 31 C8
Samuel La. OL2 48 E8
Samuel Laycock Spec Sch. SK15 85 F4
Samuel Ogden St. M1 163 A8
Samuel St. Bury BL9 141 A3
Samuel St. Failsworth M35 & M40 83 F8
Samuel St. Hollingworth SK14 103 C4
Samuel St. M'ster M19 111 B8
Samuel St. Middleton M24 47 A2
Samuel St. R'dale OL11 30 C2
Samuel St. Stockport SK4 169 D3
Samuel St. Tyldesley M46 58 F1
Sanby Ave. M18 99 C4
Sanby Rd. M18 99 C4
Sanctuary Cl. M15 163 B5
Sand Banks. BL1 24 F6
Sand Beds La. BL0 & OL12 2 B5
Sand Hole La. R'dale OL11 29 E5
Sand Hole La. R'dale OL11 30 F1
Sand Hole Rd. BL4 61 A6
Sand St. M'ster M40 159 C4
Sand St. Stalybridge SK15 101 F8
Sandacre Rd. M23 121 B7
Sandal Ct. M40 160 E3
Sandal St. M10 & M40 160 E3
Sandalwood. BL5 57 D6
Sandalwood Dr. WN6 36 F3
Sandbach Ave. M14 & M20 109 F8
Sandbach Rd. Reddish SK5 99 E2
Sandbach Rd. Sale M33 108 F3
Sandbach Wlk. SK8 123 A4
Sandbank Gdns. OL12 4 C2
Sandbed La. Delph OL3 51 A5
Sandbed La. Mossley OL5 68 C2
Sandbrook Gdns. WN5 53 D5
Sandbrook Rd. WN5 53 C5
Sandbrook Way. M34 101 A5
Sandby Dr. SK6 126 B8
Sanderling Cl. BL5 57 D6
Sanderling Dr. WN7 76 A6
Sanderling Rd. SK2 125 A4
Sanderson Ave. M40 157 E5
Sanderson Cl. M28 79 B7
Sanderson Ct. M40 157 E5
Sanderson La. PR7 18 A8
Sanderson St. Bury BL9 141 A3
Sanderson St. Leigh WN7 75 E5
Sanderson St. M'ster M10 & M40 157 E5
Sanderson's Croft. WN7 76 C4
Sanderstead Dr. M9 64 E3
Sandfield Cl. WA3 90 F8
Sandfield Cres. WA3 92 C7
Sandfield Dr. BL6 40 C6
Sandfield Rd. OL16 31 B5
Sandfold. SK5 99 E2
Sandford Ave. 3 M18 99 D6
Sandford Cl. BL2 25 E4
Sandford Rd. Orrell WN5 53 C5
Sandford Rd. Sale M33 108 F3
Sandford St. M26 44 D4
Sandford Station La. SK5 99 D2
Sandgate Ave. Droylsden M11 83 D2
Sandgate Ave. Kearsley M26 61 C7
Sandgate Cl. WN7 75 F6
Sandgate Dr. M41 95 C4
Sandgate Rd. Oldham OL9 152 B6
Sandgate Rd. Prestwich M45 63 B7
Sandham St. BL3 147 F4
Sandham Wlk. BL1 147 F4
Sandheys. M34 100 F5
Sandheys Gr. M18 99 E4
Sandhill Cl. BL1 147 F4
Sandhill La. SK6 114 E1
Sandhill St. SK14 167 F4
Sandhill Wlk. M22 121 B2
Sandhurst Ave. M20 110 A6
Sandhurst Cl. BL8 27 B3
Sandhurst Ct. BL2 42 E6
Sandhurst Dr. BL2 42 E6
Sandhurst Rd. M'ster M20 110 C2
Sandhurst Rd. Stockport SK2 124 B5
Sandhutton Rd. M9 64 D1
Sandiacre. WN6 36 E8
Sandilands Inf Sch. M23 120 D8
Sandilands Jun Sch. M33 120 D8
Sandilands Rd. M23 120 D7
Sandileigh Ave. Alt'ham WA15 119 F3
Sandileigh Ave. Brinnington SK5 112 B4
Sandileigh Ave. Cheadle SK8 123 A6
Sandileigh Ave. M'ster M20 110 B5
Sandileigh Dr. WA15 119 F3
Sandileo Ct. M7 63 A1
Sandimoss Ct. 1 M33 107 F4
Sandiway. Bredbury SK6 112 F3
Sandiway. Glossop SK13 116 F7
Sandiway. Heywood OL10 29 E2
Sandiway. Irlam M44 94 A2
Sandiway. Stockport SK7 123 E2
Sandiway Cl. SK6 125 F8
Sandiway Dr. M20 110 A3
Sandiway Pl. WA14 119 D5
Sandiway Rd. Alt'ham WA14 119 D6
Sandiway Rd. Handforth SK9 131 D5
Sandiway Rd. Sale M33 107 F4
Sandmere Wlk. 25 M9 64 E3
Sandon St. BL3 147 D4
Sandown Ave. M5 & M6 154 E2
Sandown Cl. Culcheth WA3 91 F4
Sandown Cl. 6 Oldham OL1 49 A1
Sandown Cl. Wilmslow SK9 137 D8
Sandown Cres. Little Lever BL3 43 A2
Sandown Cres. M'ster M18 99 D3
Sandown Dr. Alt'ham WA15 129 D6
Sandown Dr. Denton M34 113 B8
Sandown Dr. Sale M33 107 E3
Sandown Gdns. M41 95 A2
Sandown Rd. Bolton BL2 25 E3
Sandown Rd. Hazel Grove SK7 125 A2
Sandown Rd. Stockport SK3 123 B8
Sandown Rd. Whitefield BL9 44 F3
Sandown Rd. Whitefield BL9 & M45 45 A2
Sandown Rd. Wigan WN6 36 E3
Sandown St. M18 99 F6
Sandpiper Cl. Dukinfield SK16 101 E7
Sandpiper Cl. Farnworth BL4 59 F7
Sandpiper Cl. Newton-l-W WA12 89 C4
Sandpiper Cl. R'dale OL11 29 F7
Sandpiper Dr. SK3 170 D6
Sandpiper Rd. WN3 & WN5 54 B4
Sandra Dr. WA12 89 E3
Sandray Cl. BL3 40 F5
Sandray Gr. M5 154 E1
Sandridge Wlk. M12 164 E6
Sandringham Ave. Denton M34 100 D6
Sandringham Ave. Reddish M34 100 A3
Sandringham Ave. Stalybridge SK15 86 A3
Sandringham Cl. Adlington PR7 20 E6
Sandringham Cl. Wigan WN5 54 E5
Sandringham Ct. SK9 137 A6
Sandringham Dr. Dukinfield SK16 101 F7
Sandringham Dr. Leigh WN7 76 E7
Sandringham Dr. Milnrow OL16 32 A6
Sandringham Dr. Poynton SK12 133 D3
Sandringham Dr. Ramsbottom BL8 11 A1
Sandringham Dr. Stockport SK4 168 A1
Sandringham Grange. M25 63 E3
Sandringham Rd. Boothstown M28 78 A6
Sandringham Rd. Bredbury SK6 112 D3
Sandringham Rd. Cheadle SK8 123 A3
Sandringham Rd. Hazel Grove SK7 124 F2
Sandringham Rd. Hindley WN2 56 E4
Sandringham Rd. Horwich BL6 22 E2
Sandringham Rd. Hyde SK14 113 E7
Sandringham St. M18 99 C4
Sandringham Way. Royton OL2 48 C6
Sandringham Way. Wilmslow SK9 137 A6
Sands Ave. M24 & OL9 47 D1
Sands Cl. SK14 102 D1
Sands Wlk. SK14 102 D1
Sandsend Cl. M7 & M8 155 E5
Sandsend Rd. M41 95 C3
Sandstone Rd. Milnrow OL16 31 F7
Sandstone Rd. Wigan WN3 54 E2
Sandstone Way. M21 109 D6
Sandway. WN6 36 F2
Sandwell Dr. M33 108 B6
Sandwich Rd. M30 79 F3
Sandwich St. M28 60 D2
Sandwick Cres. BL3 145 D5
Sandwith Cl. WN3 55 B2
Sandwood Ave. BL3 40 E6
Sandy Bank. OL2 48 F8
Sandy Bank Ave. SK14 102 D1
Sandy Bank Cl. SK14 102 D1
Sandy Bank Rd. Edgworth BL7 9 D5
Sandy Bank Rd. M'ster M7 & M8 155 F8
Sandy Bank Wlk. SK14 102 D1
Sandy Brow. M9 64 D2
Sandy Brow La. WA3 90 E2
Sandy Cl. BL9 44 F4
Sandy Ct. WN7 75 A1
Sandy Gr. Dukinfield SK16 101 D8
Sandy Gr. Salford M6 154 E3
Sandy Gr. Swinton M27 79 F8
Sandy Haven Cl. SK14 102 D1
Sandy Haven Wlk. SK14 102 D1
Sandy La. Adlington PR7 20 F6
Sandy La. Alt'ham M23 120 E7
Sandy La. Charlesworth SK14 115 A4
Sandy La. Culcheth WA3 91 A1
Sandy La. Droylsden M43 84 C2
Sandy La. Dukinfield SK16 101 D8
Sandy La. Golborne WA3,WN2 75 A1
Sandy La. Golborne WA12, WA3 89 F8
Sandy La. Irlam M44 94 A2
Sandy La. Lymm WA13 117 B4
Sandy La. M'ster M21 109 C8
Sandy La. M'ster SK4 & SK5 169 E3
Sandy La. Middleton M24 65 C8
Sandy La. Orrell WN5 53 D4
Sandy La. Prestwich M25 63 A2
Sandy La. R'dale OL11 & OL12 30 C7
Sandy La. Romiley SK6 113 D3
Sandy La. Royton OL2 48 D4
Sandy La. Salford M6 154 E3
Sandy La. Stretford M32 96 C1
Sandy La. Tyldesley M29 77 A4
Sandy La. Tyldesley M29 77 B1
Sandy La. Uppermill OL3 51 B2
Sandy La. Wilmslow SK9 136 E8
Sandy Meade. M25 63 A3
Sandy Pk. WN2 57 A6
Sandy Way. WN2 56 F6
Sandy Wlk. 4 OL2 48 D4
Sandyacre Cl. BL5 59 A6
Sandybank Cl. SK14 171 E4
Sandybrook Cl. BL8 26 F6
Sandycroft Ave. 1 WN1 37 C1
Sandygate Cl. M27 79 E7
Sandyhill Rd. M9 64 B3
Sandyhills. BL3 147 E4
Sandylands Dr. M25 63 A1
Sandyshot Wlk. 4 M22 121 F3
Sandyway. M25 63 A3
Sandywell Cl. M11 99 D7
Sandywell St. M11 99 D8
Sanfold La. M18 & M19 99 C2
Sangster Ct. M5 161 A8
Sankey Gr. M9 64 B3
Sankey St. Bury BL9 140 D2
Sankey St. Golborne WA3 90 A8
Sankey St. Newton-l-W WA12 89 A3
Sankey Valley Ind Est. WA12 89 B2
Santiago St. M14 98 B3
Santley St. M12 & M18 99 A3
Santon Ave. M14 110 E8
Santon Dr. WA3 90 E8
Sapling Gr. M33 107 D2
Sapling Rd. Bolton BL3 146 C2
Sapling Rd. Swinton M27 79 D5
Sarah Ann St. M11 160 F1
Sarah Butterworth Ct. 11 OL16 31 B6
Sarah Butterworth St. 9 OL16 31 B6
Sarah St. Bacup OL13 4 C8
Sarah St. 1 Eccles M30 79 B1
Sarah St. Edenfield BL0 1 E3
Sarah St. Hindley WN2 57 B2
Sarah St. M'ster M11 164 F8
Sarah St. Middleton M24 64 F8
Sarah St. 5 R'dale OL11 31 A6
Sarah St. Shaw OL2 149 A5
Sargent Dr. M16 97 E4
Sargent Rd. SK6 112 D2
Sark Rd. M21 97 A2
Sarn Ave. M22 121 D4
Sarnesfield Cl. M12 99 A4
Sarnia Ct. M7 155 D7
Sarsfield Ave. WA3 90 D8
Satinwood Rd. WN4 72 F2
Saunton Ave. BL2 25 F3
Saunton Rd. M11 99 D8
Sautridge Cl. OL11 47 D7
Savernake Rd. SK6 113 C5
Savick Ave. BL2 42 F7
Saville Rd. Gatley SK8 122 B6
Saville Rd. Radcliffe BL8 43 F7
Saville St. Bolton BL2 148 A6
Saville St. Middleton M24 65 D7
Savio Way. M24 65 A7
Saviour CE Prim Sch. M40 156 C5
Saviours Terr. BL3 144 C5
Savoy Ct. M45 44 E2
Savoy Dr. OL2 48 D2
Savoy St. Oldham OL4 67 B5
Savoy St. R'dale OL11 & OL12 30 C8
Sawley Ave. Golborne WA3 74 D1
Sawley Ave. Littleborough OL15 16 A7
Sawley Ave. Oldham OL4 67 D4
Sawley Ave. Shevington WN6 36 F2
Sawley Ave. Whitefield M45 44 F2
Sawley Cl. WA3 92 A2
Sawley Dr. SK8 132 C6
Sawley Rd. M10 & M40 160 E4
Sawpit St. WA13 & WA14 118 A6
Sawston Wlk. M40 65 C3
Sawyer Brow. SK14 167 F4
Sawyer St. Bury BL8 27 B4
Sawyer St. 5 R'dale OL12 14 F1
Saxbrook Wlk. 3 M22 121 F3
Saxby Ave. BL7 24 F8
Saxby St. M6 80 C5
Saxelby Dr. M8 156 B7
Saxfield Dr. M23 121 C6
Saxholme Wlk. 3 M22 121 C2
Saxon Ave. Dukinfield SK16 101 C8
Saxon Ave. M'ster M8 64 A2
Saxon Cl. BL8 27 B2
Saxon Dr. Chadderton OL9 65 E8
Saxon Dr. Denton M34 100 E7
Saxon Hall L Ctr. OL16 31 C8
Saxon House. 8 M16 97 D3
Saxon Rd. OL5 68 D3
Saxon St. Denton M34 100 F3
Saxon St. Droylsden M43 84 B2
Saxon St. M'ster M10 & M40 160 E3
Saxon St. Middleton M24 65 B8
Saxon St. Oldham OL4 67 C7
Saxon St. Radcliffe M26 43 F3
Saxonholme Rd. OL11 47 C7
Saxthorpe Cl. Sale M33 107 D5
Saxthorpe Cl. Wigan WN3 54 D3
Saxthorpe Wlk. M12 164 E5
Saxwood Ave. M9 64 D1
Saxwood Cl. OL12 13 F1
Scafell Ave. OL7 84 F4
Scafell Cl. High Lane SK6 134 E8
Scafell Cl. Oldham OL1 48 F1
Scafell Dr. WN5 54 B6
Scafell Gr. WN2 56 B2
Scalby Wlk. 2 M22 121 D1
Scale St. M5 81 A1
Scarborough St. M40 83 A8
Scarcroft Rd. M12 165 A5
Scardale Ave. BL1 142 A1
Scarfield Dr. OL11 13 E1
Scargill Cl. M14 110 C8
Scargill Rd. BL3 146 A4
Scarisbrick Ave. M20 110 D3
Scarisbrick Rd. M19 110 F8
Scarisbrick St. 3 WN1 37 C1
Scarr Ave. M26 44 C2
Scarr Dr. OL12 14 F3
Scarr La. OL2 49 D7
Scarsdale Rd. M14 98 E4
Scarsdale St. M6 81 B3
Scarth Wlk. M15 162 F6
Scarthwood Cl. BL2 25 E5
Scawfell Ave. BL2 25 B2
Scawton Wlk. M9 64 B5
Sceptre Cl. WA12 89 A3
Schofield Gdns. WN7 75 E3
Schofield Hall Rd. OL15 16 C1
Schofield La. WN7 57 F3
Schofield Rd. Droylsden M43 84 B1
Schofield Rd. Eccles M30 79 A1
Schofield St. Droylsden M11 83 C2
Schofield St. Failsworth M35 83 F8
Schofield St. Haslingden BB4 1 A6
Schofield St. Heywood OL10 29 D1
Schofield St. Leigh WN7 75 E4
Schofield St. Littleborough OL15 6 D2
Schofield St. Littleborough OL15 16 C6
Schofield St. M'ster M3 158 D1
Schofield St. Milnrow OL16 32 A5
Schofield St. Oldham OL8 66 F3
Schofield St. R'dale OL11 31 A4
Schofield St. Radcliffe M26 44 B4
Schofield St. Rawtenstall BB4 2 E8
Schofield St. Royton OL2 48 D5
Scholars Way. 13 M24 46 F1
Scholefield La. WN1 151 E8
Scholes. WN1 151 D8
Scholes Bank. BL6 22 A5
Scholes Cl. M7 155 F8
Scholes Dr. M40 65 E2
Scholes La. M25 63 C3
Scholes St. Bury BL8 27 C3
Scholes St. Failsworth M35 66 A1
Scholes St. Oldham OL9 66 A4
Scholes St. 11 Oldham OL1 67 A7
Scholes St. R'dale OL11 30 C1
Scholes St. Swinton M27 80 A8
Scholes Wlk. M25 63 B3
Scholey St. BL2 & BL3 148 A5
Scholfield Ave. M41 95 F1
School Ave. Ashton-u-L OL6 85 D6
School Ave. Stretford M32 96 F3
School Ave. Wigan WN1 37 E1
School Brow. Billinge WN5 71 E5
School Brow. Bury BL9 140 E3
School Brow. Bury BL9 140 F3
School Brow. Romiley SK6 113 A2
School Brow. Worsley M28 78 F6
School Cl. SK12 133 F3
School Court No 1. M4 159 B3
School Cres. SK15 86 A4
School Ct. Bolton BL7 8 E2
School Ct. M'ster M4 159 C2
School Ct. Ramsbottom BL0 1 D2
School Ct. Stockport SK3 170 F6
School Dr. WN5 71 E5
School Gr. M'ster M20 110 D6
School Gr. Prestwich M25 63 A2
School Gr W. M20 110 C6
School Hill. BL1 145 E8
School House Flats. 1 OL8 66 C2
School La. Aspull WN2 37 E7
School La. Bury BL9 27 E8
School La. Carrington M31 106 E6
School La. Cheadle SK8 132 A8
School La. Edgworth BL7 9 D8
School La. Garswood WN4 72 C3
School La. Hollinfare WA3 105 A2
School La. Hyde SK14 113 E7
School La. Irlam M44 93 F2
School La. Irlam M44 105 D5
School La. M'ster M9 64 C2
School La. M'ster M19, M20 110 C3
School La. Mossley OL5, SK15 86 E7
School La. Orrell WN8 35 B3
School La. Orrell WN5 & WN8 53 C7
School La. Partington WA14 118 D5
School La. Poynton SK12 133 F4
School La. R'dale OL11 29 C8
School La. R'dale OL16 139 F7
School La. Reddish SK4 111 C5
School La. Romiley SK6 114 B4
School La. Standish WN6 19 D1
School La. Wigan WN1 151 D8
School Mews. SK7 132 E7
School Rd. Alt'ham WA15 119 F3
School Rd. Eccles M30 95 C8
School Rd. Failsworth M35 83 F7
School Rd. Handforth SK9 131 D3
School Rd. Oldham OL8 66 B2
School Rd. Sale M33 108 A5
School Rd. Sale M33 108 B5
School Rd. Stretford M32 96 C2
School St. Ashton-i-M WN4 73 D5
School St. Atherton M46 58 B2
School St. Bacup OL13 3 B8
School St. Bolton BL7 24 F7
School St. Bury BL9 141 B1
School St. Golborne WA3 90 A8
School St. Hazel Grove SK7 124 E2
School St. Heywood OL10 29 C2
School St. Horwich BL6 22 C3
School St. Ince-i-M WN2 151 F7
School St. Leigh WN7 75 E8
School St. Little Lever BL3 43 B3
School St. Littleborough OL15 15 E5
School St. M'ster M7 158 E4
School St. M'ster M4 159 B3
School St. Newton-l-W WA12 89 B3
School St. Oldham OL4 68 A6
School St. Oldham OL8 153 D5
School St. R'dale OL12 139 F8
School St. Radcliffe M26 44 A3
School St. Ramsbottom BL0 138 B5
School St. Tyldesley M46 76 F7
School St. Tyldesley M29 76 F8
School St. Uppermill OL3 69 B8
School St. Westhoughton BL5 57 E8
School St. Wigan WN1 151 D8
School St. Worsley M28 79 B3
School Street Ind Est. SK7 124 E2
School Terr. Golborne WA3 90 A8
School Terr. Whitworth OL12 4 D1
School View. BL7 9 D8
School Way. WN5 54 C6
School Wlk. M16 162 D5
Schools Hill. SK8 122 D3
Schools Rd. M18 99 E5
Schoolside La. M24 64 C7
Schwabe St. M24 64 C8
Scobell St. BL8 27 A5
Score St. M11 83 A1
Scorton Ave. BL2 42 F7
Scorton St. 15 BL1 144 C8
Scorton Wlk. 23 M40 65 D2
Scot La. Aspull BL6 & WN2 38 E6
Scot La. Shevington WN5 & WN6 36 E1
Scot La. Wigan WN5 54 F7
Scot Lane End CE Prim Sch. WN2 38 E7
Scot Lane Prim Sch. WN5 54 F7
Scotforth Cl. M15 162 E7
Scotia Wlk. WA3 90 F8
Scotland. M4 159 A3
Scotland Hall Rd. M40 83 C4
Scotland La. BL9 28 D8
Scotland Pl. BL0 138 C6
Scotland St. Ashton-u-L OL6 166 C2
Scotland St. Failsworth M40 83 C5
Scott Ave. Bury BL9 44 F6
Scott Ave. Eccles M30 79 C3
Scott Ave. Hindley WN2 56 E6
Scott Ave. M'ster M16 & M21 97 B2
Scott Cl. SK5 169 F4
Scott Dr. SK6 126 B8
Scott Gate. M34 100 F7
Scott House. OL14 6 A8
Scott House (Childrns Orth) Hospl. OL11 29 D8
Scott Rd. Denton M34 100 E1
Scott Rd. Droylsden M43 84 A1
Scott Rd. Golborne WA3 74 D2
Scott Rd. Prestwich M25 62 F3
Scott St. Kearsley M26 61 D7
Scott St. Leigh WN7 75 D5
Scott St. Oldham OL8 153 F5
Scott St. Salford M6 81 C4
Scott St. Tyldesley M29 77 C4
Scott St. Walsden OL14 6 A8
Scott St. Westhoughton BL5 39 E3
Scott St. Wigan WN6 37 B1
Scott St. Wigan WN6 150 B8
Scott Wlk. WA12 89 B1
Scottfield. OL8 153 F5
Scottfield Rd. OL8 153 F5
Scottia Rd. M30 95 C8
Scout Dr. M23 120 F4
Scout Rd. Bolton BL1 24 B7
Scout Rd. Edenfield BL0 2 A2
Scout View. BL8 27 A6
Scovell St. M7 155 D6
Scowcroft La. OL2 149 A6
Scowcroft St. 21 BL2 25 B1
Scroggins La. M31 105 F4
Scropton St. M40 & M9 157 D6
Seabright Wlk. 12 M11 160 F1
Seabrook Cres. M41 95 D4
Seabrook Rd. M40 83 C4
Seacombe Ave. M14 98 A1
Seacombe Gr. SK3 123 B8
Seaford Rd. Bolton BL2 25 E6
Seaford Rd. Salford M6 81 B4
Seaford Wlk. M'ster M9 64 C3
Seaford Wlk. Oldham OL9 152 B6
Seaforth Ave. M46 58 C4
Seaforth Rd. BL1 24 E5
Seaham Dr. BL8 27 C5
Seaham Wlk. 5 M14 98 B3
Seal Rd. SK7 133 A7
Sealand Cl. M33 108 E2
Sealand Dr. M30 95 A8
Sealand House. M25 63 C5
Sealand Rd. M23 108 F2
Sealand Way. 2 SK9 131 D4
Seale Ave. M34 100 D7
Seaman Way. WN2 & WN3 56 A6
Seamon's Dr. WA14 119 A6
Seamon's Rd. WA14 119 A6
Seamons Wlk. WA14 119 B5
Searby Rd. M18 99 B4
Searness Rd. M24 46 D2
Seascale Ave. M11 83 B3
Seascale Cres. WN1 37 C3
Seascales Wlk. 6 M24 46 E2
Seathwaite Cl. M29 77 A7
Seathwaite Wlk. M18 165 C5
Seatoller Ct. OL2 48 E4
Seatoller Dr. M24 46 C1
Seatoller Pl. WN5 54 B7
Seaton Cl. SK7 124 D1
Seaton Mews. OL7 84 F4
Seaton Rd. BL1 142 C2
Seaton Way. M14 98 A4
Sebastopol Wlk. 2 M4 159 C2
Second Ave. Atherton M46 58 D4
Second Ave. Bolton BL1 144 B7
Second Ave. Bury BL9 28 D4
Second Ave. Droylsden M11 83 D2
Second Ave. Little Lever BL3 42 F4
Second Ave. Mossley SK15 86 E5
Second Ave. Oldham OL8 66 D1
Second Ave. Poynton SK10 133 D1
Second Ave. Stretford M17 96 D5
Second Ave. Swinton M27 79 D5
Second Ave. Tyldesley M29 77 B4
Second Ave. Wigan WN6 37 A2
Second St. Bolton BL1 23 F4
Second St. Stretford M17 96 D5
Section St. 6 BL3 145 F6
Sedan Cl. M5 81 A1
Sedburgh Cl. M33 107 D3
Sedbury Cl. M23 108 F1
Seddon Ave. M'ster M18 99 D6
Seddon Ave. Radcliffe BL9 & M26 44 D5
Seddon Cl. M46 58 C3
Seddon Gdns. M26 61 A8
Seddon House Dr. WN6 36 E3
Seddon La. M26 61 A8
Seddon Rd. WA14 119 D2
Seddon St. Little Lever BL3 43 B3
Seddon St. M'ster M12 99 B2
Seddon St. Radcliffe M26 44 A3
Seddon St. Walkden M38 59 F5
Seddon St. Westhoughton BL5 39 E3
Seddons Ave. Bury BL8 44 A8
Sedge Cl. SK5 112 A8
Sedgeborough Rd. M16 97 E3
Sedgefield Cl. Handforth SK9 131 D1
Sedgefield Cl. Salford M5 & M6 81 A2
Sedgefield Dr. Bolton BL1 142 B3
Sedgefield Dr. Wigan WN6 36 E3
Sedgefield Pk. 1 OL4 67 D6
Sedgefield Rd. M26 62 A8
Sedgefield Wlk. M23 108 F2
Sedgeford Rd. M10, M40, M9 157 D5
Sedgely. WN6 37 A7
Sedgemoor Cl. SK8 123 B2
Sedgemoor Vale. BL2 25 F2
Sedgemoor Way. OL1 153 E7
Sedgley Ave. M'ster M25 63 C2
Sedgley Ave. R'dale OL16 31 B4
Sedgley Cl. M24 65 C7
Sedgley Dr. BL5 57 E5
Sedgley Park Cty Prim Sch. M25 63 D2
Sedgley Park Rd. M25 63 C2
Sedgley Park Trad Est. M25 63 B1
Sedgley Rd. M8 156 A8
Sedgley St. M24 65 C7
Sedgwick Cl. M46 58 E3
Sedwyn St. 7 WN1 37 E1
Seed St. BL1 144 C7
Seedfield Rd. BL9 27 F5
Seedley Ave. M38 60 B4
Seedley Park Rd. M6 154 E2
Seedley Prim Sch. M6 154 E2
Seedley Rd. M6 154 F3
Seedley St. M14 98 B3
Seedley Terr. M6 154 E3
Seedley View Rd. M6 154 E2
Seel St. OL5 68 B1
Sefton Ave. Atherton M46 58 C5
Sefton Ave. Orrell WN5 53 D5
Sefton Cl. M'ster M13 163 B6
Sefton Cl. Middleton M24 64 E8
Sefton Cl. Orrell WN5 53 D5
Sefton Cres. M33 108 B6
Sefton Ct. 8 BL1 145 E8
Sefton Dr. Bury BL9 28 A6
Sefton Dr. Handforth SK9 131 C2
Sefton Dr. Swinton M27 79 D6
Sefton Dr. Worsley M28 79 A6
Sefton Fold Dr. WN5 71 D5
Sefton Fold Gdns. WN5 71 D5
Sefton La. BL6 22 D1
Sefton Rd. Ashton-i-M WN4 72 F6
Sefton Rd. Bolton BL1 142 B2
Sefton Rd. M'ster M21 109 B8
Sefton Rd. Middleton M24 64 E8

Sterndale Ave. WN6 19 E2
Sterndale Rd.
Boothstown M28 77 F6
Sterndale Rd. Romiley SK6 113 B1
Sterndale Rd. Stockport SK3 170 E5
Sterratt St. BL1 145 D6
Stetchworth Dr. M28 78 B7
Steven Ct. M21 109 C8
Stevens St. SK9 137 A1
Stevenson Cl. WN3 150 B5
Stevenson Dr. OL1 49 E4
Stevenson Pl. M1 159 B1
Stevenson Rd. M27 61 E1
Stevenson Sq. M1 & M60 159 B1
Stevenson St. M'ster M3 158 D1
Stevenson St. Walkden M28 60 B3
Stewart Ave. BL4 60 B7
Stewart Rd. WN3 55 A3
Stewart St. Ashton-u-L OL7 84 F2
Stewart St. Bolton BL1 143 E2
Stewart St. Bury BL8 27 B3
Stewart St. Bury BL8 27 C4
Stewart St. Newhey OL16 32 B3
Stewerton Cl. WA3 73 E2
Steynton Cl. BL1 40 F8
Stile Cl. M41 94 C2
Stiles Ave. SK6 125 F7
Stiles Cl. SK14 103 E5
Stilton Dr. M11 165 A8
Stirling Ave.
Hazel Grove SK7 124 D1
Stirling Ave. Ince-i-M WN2 56 A8
Stirling Ave. M'ster M20 109 F8
Stirling Ave. 6 Marple SK6 125 F5
Stirling Cl. Leigh WN7 76 D6
Stirling Cl. Stockport SK3 123 C6
Stirling Dr. Garswood WN4 72 D4
Stirling Dr. Stalybridge SK15 86 A3
Stirling Gr. M45 63 A8
Stirling Rd. Bolton BL1 24 E5
Stirling Rd. Hindley WN2 56 F4
Stirling Rd. Oldham OL9 65 F4
Stirling St. Oldham OL9 152 C7
Stirling St. Wigan WN1 37 C2
Stirrup Brook Gr. M28 77 F5
Stitch La. SK4 169 D3
Stitch-Mi-Lane. BL2 25 F2
Stiups La. OL16 31 B4
Stobart Ave. M25 63 C2
Stock Gr. OL16 31 F7
Stock La. OL9 152 B6
Stock St. BL8 27 E5
Stock's Park Sch. BL6 22 C3
Stockburn Dr. M35 84 C7
Stockbury Cl. 6 BL1 143 F1
Stockdale Ave. SK3 170 F5
Stockdale Gr. BL2 25 F1
Stockdale Rd. M9 64 E4
Stockfield Mount. OL9 152 B6
Stockfield Rd. OL9 152 B7
Stockholm Rd. SK3 170 E6
Stockholm St. M11 83 B2
Stockland Cl. M13 163 B7
Stockley Ave. BL2 25 E2
Stockley Dr. WN6 35 E8
Stockley Wlk. 20 M15 162 D6
Stockport Coll of F & H Ed.
Stockport SK2 170 F6
Stockport Coll of F & H Ed.
Stockport SK1 170 F8
Stockport Golf Course.
SK2 125 B5
Stockport Gram Jun Sch.
SK2 124 A5
Stockport Infmy. SK3 170 E8
Stockport Rd. Alt'ham WA15 119 F5
Stockport Rd.
Alt'ham M23 & WA15 120 B6
Stockport Rd. Cheadle SK8 122 E6
Stockport Rd. Cheadle SK3 123 A7
Stockport Rd.
Denton M34 & SK14 100 F2
Stockport Rd.
Dukinfield M34 & OL7 100 F8
Stockport Rd.
Hattersley SK14 102 E2
Stockport Rd. Hyde SK14 113 D7
Stockport Rd.
M'ster M12, M13, M19 164 B3
Stockport Rd. Marple SK6 125 E6
Stockport Rd. Mossley OL5 68 C2
Stockport Rd. Romiley SK6 113 B2
Stockport Rd. Uppermill OL4 68 C5
Stockport Rd E. SK6 112 F4
Stockport Rd W. SK1 & SK6 112 D3
Stockport Sch. SK2 124 B5
Stockport Sta. SK3 170 E8
Stockport Trad Est. SK4 168 B1
Stocks Gdns. SK15 86 C1
Stocks La. SK15 86 C1
Stocks Park Dr. BL6 22 C3
Stocks St. M'ster M8 159 A4
Stocks St. R'dale OL11 30 B2
Stocks St E. M8 159 A4
Stocks The. SK14 104 A7
Stocksfield Dr. 3 M'ster M9 64 E3
Stocksfield Dr. Walkden M38 59 F5
Stockton Ave. 4 SK3 123 B8
Stockton Dr. BL8 27 B5
Stockton Pk. OL4 67 D6
Stockton Rd. Farnworth BL4 42 C2
Stockton Rd. M'ster M21 109 A8
Stockton Rd. Wilmslow SK9 136 F4
Stockton St.
Littleborough OL15 16 A5
Stockton St. 4 M'ster M15 97 E4
Stockton St. 3 Swinton M27 79 E7
Stockwell Cl. WN3 54 D3
Stockwood Wlk. M9 157 D7
Stoke Abbott Cl. SK7 132 E7
Stoke St. OL16 31 B6
Stokes St. M11 83 D1
Stokesay Cl. Bury BL9 44 F5
Stokesay Cl. Royton OL2 49 A4
Stokesay Dr. SK7 124 C1
Stokesay Rd. M33 107 E5
Stokesley Wlk. BL3 147 E3
Stokoe Ave. WA14 119 A6
Stonall Ave. M15 162 D7
Stone Breaks Rd. OL4 68 B7
Stone Cl. BL0 11 A4
Stone Cross La. WA3 90 C7
Stone Hall La. WN8 35 A5
Stone Haven. WN3 54 D2
Stone Hill La. OL12 14 A2
Stone Hill Rd. BL4 60 D6
Stone House Rd. WN5 36 D2
Stone Mead. SK6 113 E3
Stone Mead Ave. WA15 129 C7
Stone Pale. M45 62 F7
Stone Pit Cl. WA3 74 F1
Stone Pit La. WA3 90 F2
Stone Pits. BL0 1 E3
Stone Pl. M14 98 C3
Stone Row. SK6 126 A6
Stone St. Bolton BL2 25 B1
Stone St. M'ster M3 162 D7
Stone St. Milnrow OL16 31 F5
Stone St. Rawtenstall BB4 2 F8
Stoneacre. BL6 39 F8
Stoneacre Ct. M27 79 F7
Stoneacre Rd. M22 121 C2
Stonebridge Cl. BL6 40 C6
Stonechat Cl.
Boothstown M28 78 B8
Stonechat Cl. Droylsden M43 84 C3
Stonechurch. BL3 145 D5
Stonecliffe Ave. SK15 86 A2
Stonecliffe Terr. SK15 86 A3
Stoneclough Rd. BL4 & M26 61 A7
Stonecroft. 2 OL1 153 E7
Stonecroft Ct. M20 110 A4
Stonedelph Cl. BL2 26 D1
Stonefield. M29 59 C1
Stonefield Dr. M7 & M8 155 F5
Stonefield St. OL16 31 F5
Stoneflat Ct. OL12 139 D8
Stonehaven. BL3 40 F3
Stonehead St. M9 157 F7
Stonehewer St. M26 44 B2
Stonehill Cres. OL12 14 A3
Stonehill Dr. OL12 14 B3
Stonehill Rd. OL12 14 B3
Stonehouse. BL7 25 B7
Stonehouse Wlk. 3 M23 120 E7
Stonehurst Cl. M12 165 A6
Stoneleigh Ave. M33 107 E5
Stoneleigh Dr. M26 61 B7
Stoneleigh Prim Sch. OL1 49 B2
Stoneleigh Rd. OL4 68 A7
Stoneleigh St. OL1 67 B8
Stonelow Cl. M15 162 F6
Stonely Dr. OL14 6 A7
Stonemead Cl. BL3 147 F4
Stonemill Terr. SK5 169 F3
Stonepail Cl. M22 121 F5
Stonepail Rd. M22 & SK8 122 A5
Stoner Rd. PR7 20 F7
Stoneridge. SK14 103 F5
Stones Bank Rd. BL7 8 B5
Stonesby Cl. M16 97 D4
Stonesdale Cl. OL2 48 E5
Stonesteads Dr. BL7 25 A8
Stonesteads Way. BL7 25 A8
Stoneswood Dr. OL5 68 D2
Stoneswood Rd. OL3 50 F4
Stonethwaite Cl. WN3 55 A2
Stoney Bank. M26 61 C7
Stoney Brow. WN8 35 B1
Stoney Knoll. M7 155 D6
Stoney La. Adlington PR7 20 E4
Stoney La. Delph OL3 50 D7
Stoney La. Wilmslow SK9 136 F5
Stoneycroft Ave. BL6 22 D4
Stoneycroft Cl. BL6 22 D5
Stoneyfield. SK15 86 A4
Stoneyfield Cl. M16 97 F2
Stoneygate La. WN6 18 B2
Stoneygate Wlk. M11 99 D7
Stoneyhurst Cl. M15 162 F6
Stoneyhurst Cres. WA3 91 D5
Stoneyroyd. OL12 4 D1
Stoneyside Ave. M28 60 E4
Stoneyside Gr. M28 60 E4
Stoneyvale Ct. OL11 30 F4
Stonie Heyes Ave. OL12 15 B2
Stonyford Rd. M33 108 D4
Stonyhurst Ave. Bolton BL1 24 F5
Stonyhurst Ave.
Ince-i-M WN3 151 D6
Stopes Rd. BL3 & M26 43 C3
Stopford Ave. OL15 15 E4
Stopford St. Droylsden M11 99 F7
Stopford St. Ince-i-M WN2 151 F7
Stopford St. Stockport SK3 170 D8
Stopford Wlk. M13 100 F3
Stopforth St. WN6 37 A1
Stopley Wlk. M11 165 A8
Store St. Ashton-u-L OL7 85 A6
Store St. Horwich BL6 22 C4
Store St.
M'ster M1 & M4 & M60 159 C1
Store St. M'ster M11 165 B7
Store St. R'dale OL11 13 E1
Store St. Radcliffe M26 44 D4
Store St. Shaw OL2 149 C8
Store St. Stockport SK2 124 C4
Stores St. M25 63 C4
Storeton Cl. M22 121 E2
Stortford Dr. M23 109 B2
Storth Bank. SK13 115 F7
Storth Meadow Rd. SK13 115 F7
Stothard Rd. M32 96 C1
Stott Dr. M41 94 D1
Stott House. OL8 153 E5
Stott La. Bolton BL2 25 B1
Stott La. Eccles M6 & M5 80 B2
Stott La. Middleton M24 & OL10 46 F5
Stott Milne St. OL9 152 B5
Stott Rd. Failsworth OL9 65 E3
Stott Rd. Swinton M27 79 D6
Stott St. Failsworth OL8 66 A1
Stott St. Failsworth M35 83 D6
Stott St. Littleborough OL16 15 D4
Stott St. M'ster M11 160 F1
Stott St. Milnrow OL16 31 F4
Stott St. R'dale OL12 14 F1
Stott's La. M40 & M35 83 D6
Stottfield. OL2 48 B3
Stour Cl. WA14 119 C6
Stour Rd. M29 77 B7
Stourbridge Ave. M38 60 A6
Stourport St. OL1 67 A8
Stout St. WN7 75 C4
Stoveleigh Way. OL6 166 B3
Stovell Ave. M12 99 A2
Stovell Rd. M40 83 A8
Stow Cl. BL8 27 D5
Stow Gdns. M20 110 A6
Stowell Ct. BL1 143 E1
Stowell House. 7 M6 154 E1
Stowell St. Bolton BL1 143 E1
Stowell St. Salford M5 & M6 154 E1
Stowell Tech Ctr. M5 96 F8
Stowfield Cl. M9 64 B4
Stracey St. M10 & M40 160 E3
Stradbroke Cl. M18 165 C5
Strain Ave. M9 64 D4
Straits The. M29 77 C6
Strand Ave. WN4 73 B4
Strand Ct. M32 108 C8
Strand The. Ashton-i-M WN4 73 B4
Strand The. Horwich BL6 22 D3
Strand The. R'dale OL11 30 F2
Strand Way. OL1 & OL2 48 D2
Strang St. BL0 138 C6
Strange Rd. WN4 72 D3
Strange St. WN7 75 B4
Strangford St. M26 43 D4
Stranraer Rd. WN5 36 D1
Stranton Dr. M28 79 C8
Stratfield Ave. M23 108 D1
Stratford Ave. Bolton BL1 142 A1
Stratford Ave. Bury BL9 27 E8
Stratford Ave. M'ster M20 109 F5
Stratford Ave. Oldham OL8 66 F3
Stratford Ave. R'dale OL11 139 E5
Stratford Cl. BL4 147 F1
Stratford Gdns. SK6 112 F3
Stratford Rd. M24 65 B5
Stratford Sq. SK8 131 C7
Stratford St. WN6 37 A1
Strathaven Pl. OL10 28 F1
Strathblane Cl. 3 M20 110 B7
Strathfield Dr. 8 M11 83 C2
Strathmere Ave. M32 96 D3
Strathmore Ave.
Ashton-i-M WN4 73 A5
Strathmore Ave.
Denton M34 101 B2
Strathmore Ave. 4
M'ster M16 97 B2
Strathmore Cl. BL0 11 C4
Strathmore Rd. BL2 25 E1
Stratton Dr. WN2 55 F1
Stratton Gr. BL6 22 B5
Stratton Rd. M'ster M16 97 B2
Stratton Rd. Stockport SK2 124 C8
Stratton Rd. Swinton M27 61 F1
Strawberry Bank. M6 81 B3
Strawberry Cl. WA14 119 B7
Strawberry Hill. M6 81 B3
Strawberry Hill Rd. BL2 148 B5
Strawberry La.
Uppermill OL4 & OL5 68 C4
Strawberry La.
Wilmslow SK9 136 E6
Strawberry Rd. M6 81 B3
Stray St. M11 99 E8
Stray The. BL1 25 B4
Stream Terr. SK1 112 B1
Streamside Cl. WA15 120 B4
Street Bridge Rd. OL1 & OL2 48 A2
Street La. BL8 43 F8
Street Lodge. OL11 30 B1
Streetgate. Walkden M38 59 F5
Streethouse La. OL3 50 F1
Stretford Gram Sch. M32 96 E1
Stretford High Sch. M32 96 E4
Stretford House. M32 96 C1
Stretford Memorial Hospl.
M16 97 B3
Stretford Motorway Est.
M32 96 A5
Stretford Rd.
M'ster M15 & M16 161 C5
Stretford Rd. Urmston M41 95 E1
Stretford Sta. M32 96 D1
Stretton Ave. Billinge WN5 71 E5
Stretton Ave. Golborne WA3 90 E7
Stretton Ave. M'ster M20 110 C3
Stretton Ave. Sale M33 107 E4
Stretton Ave. Stretford M32 96 A3
Stretton Cl. M'ster M40 157 D5
Stretton Cl. Standish WN6 36 E8
Stretton Rd. Bolton BL3 146 B4
Stretton Rd. Ramsbottom BL0 11 A2
Stretton Way. 3 SK9 131 D5
Striding Edge Wlk. 1 OL1 49 A1
Strines Ct. SK14 167 E4
Strines Rd.
Marple SK12 & SK6 126 B3
Strines Rd. New Mills SK12 135 D8
Strines St. OL14 6 A7
Strines Sta. SK12 126 D1
Stringer Ave. SK14 102 F2
Stringer Cl. SK14 102 F2
Stringer St. Leigh WN7 75 F5
Stringer St. Stockport SK1 112 A2
Stringer Way. SK14 102 F2
Stroma Gdns. M41 95 C5
Stromness Gr. OL10 28 F1
Strong St. M7 158 E4
Strongstry Rd. BL0 1 C2
Strontian Wlk. 9 M11 83 C1
Stroud Ave. M30 79 B3
Stroud Cl. Middleton M24 65 A5
Stroud Cl. Wigan WN2 37 F2
Stuart Ave. Bacup OL13 3 D8
Stuart Ave. Hindley WN2 57 C3
Stuart Ave. Irlam M44 93 F2
Stuart Cres. WN5 71 E5
Stuart Dr. SK6 125 C7
Stuart Hampson Ct. 1
M31 105 F3
Stuart Rd. Denton SK6 112 D6
Stuart Rd. Stretford M32 96 D3
Stuart St. M'ster M11 83 A2
Stuart St. M'ster M11 160 F2
Stuart St. Middleton M24 65 C8
Stuart St. Oldham OL8 153 E5
Stuart St. R'dale OL16 31 A6
Stuart St. R'dale OL16 31 B6
Stuart St. Wigan WN1 151 D8
Stuart St E. M11 83 A2
Stuart Wlk. M24 64 F7
Stubbins Cl. M23 108 E1
Stubbins Cty Prim Sch. BL0 1 D1
Stubbins La. BL0 138 C8
Stubbins St. BL0 1 C1
Stubbins Vale Rd. BL0 1 C1
Stubbins Vale Terr. BL0 1 E1
Stubbylee La. OL13 3 F8
Stubley La. OL15 15 F4
Stubley Mill Rd.
Littleborough OL15 15 F4
Stubley Mill Rd.
Littleborough OL15 16 A5
Stubshaw Cross CE
Prim Sch. WN4 73 E5
Studforth Wlk. 3 M15 163 A5
Studland Rd. M22 121 F3
Studley Cl. OL2 49 A4
Studley Ct. Tyldesley M29 58 F1
Sturton Ave. WN3 54 E3
Styal Ave. Reddish SK5 111 F6
Styal Ave. Stretford M32 96 A3
Styal Ctry Pk. SK9 130 E3
Styal Cty Prim Sch. SK9 130 E4
Styal Gn. SK9 130 F3
Styal Gr. SK8 122 A3
Styal Rd.
Gatley M22 & SK8 & M90 & SK9 122 A3
Styal Rd. Wilmslow SK9 137 B8
Styal Rd. Wythenshawe M22 130 F7
Styal St. BL1 144 B8
Styal Sta. SK9 131 A4
Styal View. SK9 131 B2
Styhead Dr. M24 46 D3
Style St. M4 159 A3
Sudbrook Cl. WA3 90 E8
Sudbury Cl. M'ster M16 161 C5
Sudbury Cl. Wigan WN3 55 B2
Sudbury Dr. Bolton BL6 40 C6
Sudbury Dr. Gatley SK8 131 C8
Sudbury Rd. SK7 133 E8
Sudden St. OL11 30 C4
Sudell St. M10 & M40 159 B3
Sudell Street Ind Est. M4 159 B3
Sudley Rd. OL11 139 D5
Sudlow St. OL16 15 B2
Sudren St. BL8 26 F3
Sue Patterson Wlk. M40 157 D5
Suez St. WA12 89 B3
Suffield St. M24 65 A8
Suffield Wlk. 1 M22 121 D1
Suffolk Ave. M43 84 A3
Suffolk Cl. Little Lever BL3 43 B5
Suffolk Cl. Standish WN1 37 B8
Suffolk Dr. Brinnington SK5 112 C6
Suffolk Dr. Handforth SK9 131 C1
Suffolk Gr. WN7 75 C5
Suffolk Rd. WA14 119 B5
Suffolk St. Oldham OL9 66 B4
Suffolk St.
R'dale OL11 & OL16 139 F6
Suffolk St. Salford M6 81 A5
Sugar La. OL3 51 A2
Sugden Sports Ctr. M1 163 A7
Sugden St. OL6 85 D3
Sulby Ave. M32 96 E2
Sulby St. Kearsley M26 61 B7
Sulby St. M'ster M40 83 A8
Sulgrave Ave. SK12 133 F4
Sullivan St. M12 99 A3
Sullivan Way. WN1 37 D1
Sultan St. BL9 44 F8
Sulway Cl. M27 80 A7
Sumac St. M11 83 D2
Sumbland House. M27 62 B2
Summer Ave. M41 95 E2
Summer Castle. R'dale OL16 31 A7
Summer Castle. R'dale OL16 139 F7
Summer Pl. 1 M14 98 C2
Summer St. Horwich BL6 22 B4
Summer St. R'dale OL16 31 A7
Summerbottom. SK14 115 A8
Summercroft. OL9 66 B4
Summerdale Dr. BL0 11 B2
Summerfield Ave. M43 83 E3
Summerfield Ct. M21 96 F1
Summerfield Dr.
Middleton M24 47 C1
Summerfield Dr.
Tyldesley M29 77 B8
Summerfield Pl. SK9 137 A5
Summerfield Rd. Bolton BL3 42 B4
Summerfield Rd.
Worsley M28 79 A8
Summerfield Rd.
Wythenshawe M22 121 C2
Summerfields Ctr. SK9 131 D1
Summerlea. SK8 132 B8
Summers Ave. SK15 86 C2
Summers St. OL9 152 C7
Summersales Ind Est. WN3 54 C4
Summerseat Cl. Oldham OL4 68 A7
Summerseat Cl. Salford M5 161 A8
Summerseat La. BL0 11 A2
Summerseat Meth Prim Sch.
BL9 11 D2
Summerseat Sch
Limefield Bldg. BL9 27 E6
Summerseat Spec Sch. BL0 11 B2
Summerseat Sta. BL9 11 C2
Summersgill Cl. OL10 29 E1
Summershades La. OL4 68 D6
Summershades Rise. OL4 68 D6
Summerton House. 3 M5 81 A1
Summerville Ave. M9 157 F7
Summerville Prim Sch. M6 80 D5
Summerville Rd. M6 80 D5
Summerville
(Unitarian Coll). M14 98 D4
Summit Cl. BL9 28 F4
Summit St. OL10 28 F3
Sumner Ave. BL2 26 D1
Sumner Rd. M6 80 D5
Sumner St. Aspull WN2 38 D5
Sumner St. Atherton M46 58 C3
Sumner St. Bolton BL3 146 B2
Sumner St. Glossop SK13 116 C8
Sumner St. Shaw OL2 149 B5
Sumner Way. M41 95 D2
Sumners Pl. SK13 104 B1
Sun Gate. OL15 15 F1
Sun Inn Mews. OL3 33 D3
Sun St. Mossley OL5 68 C1
Sun St. Ramsbottom BL0 138 B7
Sun Vale Ave. OL14 6 B7
Sunadale Cl. BL3 144 B5
Sunbank Cl. OL12 14 D2
Sunbank La. M90 & WA15 129 E6
Sunbeam St. WA12 89 C3
Sunbeam Wlk. 10 M11 160 F1
Sunbury Cl. Handforth SK9 131 E2
Sunbury Cl. Stalybridge SK16 101 F8
Sunbury Dr. M40 83 D4
Sundance Ct. M5 96 E8
Sunderland Ave. OL6 166 C4
Sunderland Pl. WN5 36 D1
Sunderton Wlk. M12 164 E6
Sundew Pl. M24 65 D7
Sundial Cl. SK14 102 D3
Sundial Rd. SK2 124 D7
Sundial Wlk. SK14 102 D3
Sunfield. SK6 113 C3
Sunfield Ave. OL4 49 E4
Sunfield Cres. OL2 48 E3
Sunfield Dr. OL2 48 F3
Sunfield Est. OL3 51 C4
Sunfield La. OL3 51 C4
Sunfield Rd. OL1 153 E8
Sunfield Way. OL4 67 E7
Sunk La. M24 65 A7
Sunlaws St. SK13 116 B8
Sunleigh Rd. WN2 56 E6
Sunlight Rd. BL1 144 C7
Sunning Hill Cty Prim Sch.
BL3 147 D4
Sunning Hill St. 13 BL3 147 D4
Sunningdale Ave.
Droylsden M11 83 B2
Sunningdale Ave.
Radcliffe M26 43 D4
Sunningdale Ave. Sale M33 108 E3
Sunningdale Ave.
Whitefield M45 62 C7
Sunningdale Cl. Bury BL8 44 A8
Sunningdale Cl.
Dukinfield SK14 101 F5
Sunningdale Ct. M34 100 B4
Sunningdale Dr.
Bramhall SK7 133 A7
Sunningdale Dr.
Heywood OL10 46 D8
Sunningdale Dr. Irlam M44 93 F3
Sunningdale Dr.
Pendlebury M6 80 B5
Sunningdale Dr.
Prestwich M25 63 B5
Sunningdale Gr. WN7 76 D7
Sunningdale Rd.
Denton M34 101 B1
Sunningdale Rd.
Urmston M41 95 B1
Sunningdale Wlk. 1 BL1 145 D5
Sunny Ave. BL9 27 F5
Sunny Bank. Kearsley M26 61 A8
Sunny Bank. Oldham OL4 67 E5
Sunny Bank. Wilmslow SK9 136 D4
Sunny Bank. Wilmslow SK9 137 B6
Sunny Bank Ave. M43 83 F1
Sunny Bank Cl. BB4 1 A6
Sunny Bank Cty Prim Sch.
BL9 45 A3
Sunny Bank Rd.
Alt'ham WA14 128 C8
Sunny Bank Rd.
Droylsden M43 83 F1
Sunny Bank Rd.
Haslingden BB4 1 A6
Sunny Bank Rd. M'ster M13 98 E3
Sunny Bank Rd.
Whitefield BL9 45 A3
Sunny Banks. SK13 116 B8
Sunny Bower St. BL8 26 F6
Sunny Brow Rd. M'ster M18 99 C4
Sunny Brow Rd.
Middleton M24 64 E8
Sunny Dr. Orrell WN5 53 F6
Sunny Dr. Prestwich M25 62 F4
Sunny Garth. BL5 57 E8
Sunnybank Ave. Eccles M30 79 F3
Sunnybank Ave. M'ster SK4 110 F4
Sunnybank Cl. WA12 89 C4
Sunnybank Rd. Bolton BL1 142 C2
Sunnybank Rd. Tyldesley M29 77 B6
Sunnyfield Rd. M'ster SK4 110 F3
Sunnyfield Rd.
Prestwich M25 & M45 63 C7
Sunnyfields. WN3 54 C2
Sunnylea Ave. M19 110 E5
Sunnymead Ave. BL1 143 F4
Sunnymede Vale. BL0 11 A3
Sunnyside. OL7 84 F5
Sunnyside Ave. M43 83 F4
Sunnyside Cres. 8 OL6 85 D2
Sunnyside Ct. M43 83 F3
Sunnyside Gr. OL6 85 D2
Sunnyside Rd.
Ashton-i-M WN4 72 F7
Sunnyside Rd. Bolton BL1 142 C2
Sunnyside Rd. Droylsden M43 84 A3
Sunnywood Dr. BL8 27 A6
Sunnywood La. BL8 27 A6
Sunset Ave. M22 109 D2
Sunwell Terr. SK6 125 F3
Surbiton Rd. M40 83 B4
Surrey Ave. Droylsden M43 83 F3
Surrey Ave. Leigh WN7 76 E4
Surrey Ave. Shaw OL2 48 F7
Surrey Cl. BL3 43 B4
Surrey Dr. BL9 44 F8
Surrey Park Cl. OL2 149 B8
Surrey Rd. M9 64 D2
Surrey St. Ashton-u-L OL6 85 D5
Surrey St. Glossop SK13 104 C1
Surrey St. M'ster M9 64 C2
Surrey St. Oldham OL9 152 C5
Surrey Way. SK5 112 C4
Surtees Rd. M23 109 A2
Sussex Ave. Heywood OL10 28 E1
Sussex Ave. M'ster M20 110 B4
Sussex Cl. Hindley WN2 57 A5
Sussex Cl. Oldham OL9 152 B6
Sussex Cl. Standish WN1 20 B1
Sussex Cl. Swinton M27 62 A2
Sussex Dr. Bury BL9 44 F8
Sussex Dr. Droylsden M43 84 A3
Sussex Dr. Haslingden BB4 1 B8
Sussex Pl. SK14 101 F5
Sussex Rd. Irlam M44 105 C6
Sussex Rd. Partington M31 105 E2
Sussex Rd. Stockport SK3 123 B8
Sussex St. Leigh M46 76 E4
Sussex St. M'ster M7 158 D4
Sussex St. 12 M'ster M2 158 F1
Sussex St. M'ster M1 & M60 159 A1
Sussex St. R'dale OL11 139 F6
Sutch La. WA13 117 A3
Sutcliffe Ave. M12 99 B2
Sutcliffe St. Ashton-u-L OL7 84 F1
Sutcliffe St. Bacup OL13 4 C8
Sutcliffe St. Bolton BL1 143 E2
Sutcliffe St.
Littleborough OL15 16 B6
Sutcliffe St. Middleton M24 65 C8
Sutcliffe St. Oldham OL8 153 E5
Sutcliffe St. Royton OL2 49 A3
Sutcliffes Pl. 3 OL11 31 A4
Sutherland Cl. OL8 66 F1
Sutherland Gr. BL4 60 C8
Sutherland Rd. Bolton BL1 142 A1
Sutherland Rd. Heywood OL10 28 E2
Sutherland Rd. M'ster M16 97 A3
Sutherland Rd. Wigan WN3 55 A3
Sutherland St. Ashton-u-L OL6 85 E5
Sutherland St. Eccles M30 79 B3
Sutherland St. 3
Farnworth BL4 60 C8
Sutherland St. Hindley WN2 56 C5
Sutherland St. Swinton M27 61 E1
Sutherland St. 1 Wigan WN5 54 F6
Suthers St. Oldham OL9 152 C6
Suthers St. Radcliffe M26 44 C1
Sutton Ave. WA3 91 F4
Sutton Dr. M43 83 E3
Sutton House. 16 M6 154 F3
Sutton La. PR6 21 B8
Sutton Manor. 7 M21 97 A1
Sutton Rd. Alderley Edge SK9 136 F2
Sutton Rd. Bolton BL3 40 F4
Sutton Rd. M'ster M18 99 C3
Sutton Rd. M'ster SK4 168 C3
Sutton Rd. Poynton SK12 134 A2
Sutton St. M12 165 A6
Sutton Way. Hadfield SK14 104 A5
Sutton Way. 1
Handforth SK9 131 E5
Suttons La. SK6 126 A5
Swailes St. 3 OL4 67 B6
Swain St. OL12 14 E1
Swaindrod La. OL15 16 F7
Swaine St. SK3 169 E1
Swainsthorpe Dr. 15 M9 157 E8
Swale Cl. SK9 131 E2
Swale Dr. WA14 119 C6
Swalecliff Ave. M23 108 D1
Swaledale Cl. OL2 48 E5
Swallow Bank Dr. OL11 30 B3
Swallow Cl. SK15 86 F7
Swallow Dr. Bury BL9 141 B4
Swallow Dr. Irlam M44 94 A3
Swallow Dr. R'dale OL11 29 F7
Swallow La. SK15 86 F6
Swallow St. M'ster M12, M19 99 A2
Swallow St. M'ster M11 160 F1
Swallow St. Oldham OL8 66 D2
Swallow St. Stockport SK1 170 F7
Swallowfield. WN7 76 A5
Swan Cl. SK12 133 B4
Swan Ct. OL2 149 B6
Swan La. Bolton BL3 147 D4
Swan La. Hindley WN2 57 B4
Swan Meadow Rd. WN3 150 B7
Swan Rd. Ramsbottom BL8 10 F2
Swan Rd. Sale WA15 108 A1
Swan St. Ashton-u-L OL6 166 C3
Swan St. M'ster M4 159 B2
Swan St. Radcliffe M26 44 B2
Swan St. Wilmslow SK9 137 B7
Swanage Ave. Sale M23 108 D1
Swanage Ave. Stockport SK2 124 D6
Swanage Cl. BL8 27 C6
Swanage Rd. M30 79 B3
Swanbourne Gdns. SK3 123 C6
Swanhill Cl. 2 M18 99 F6
Swanley Ave. M10 & M40 157 E5
Swann Gr. SK8 123 B1
Swann La. SK8 123 B1
Swann St. WN3 150 B7
Swansea St. OL8 67 B4
Swanton Wlk. 17 M8 155 F6
Swarbrick Dr. M25 62 F2
Swarthdale House. 8 M6 154 F3
Swayfield Ave. M13 98 F3
Swaylands Dr. M33 108 B1
Sweet Briar Cl. OL12 14 E2
Sweet Briar La. OL12 14 E2
Sweetbriar Cl. OL2 149 B7
Sweetloves Gr. BL1 24 E5
Sweetloves La. BL1 24 E5
Sweetnam Dr. M11 83 B2
Swettenham Rd. SK9 131 D5
Swift Cl. SK6 113 C5
Swift Rd. Oldham OL1 49 E5
Swift Rd. R'dale OL11 29 F7
Swift St. Ashton-u-L OL6 85 D5
Swift St. Wigan WN5 150 A7

232 Swi – Thi

Swift Wlk. 2 M40 83 C5
Swiftsure Ave. M3 158 D1
Swinbourne Gr. M20 110 C7
Swinburn Gr. WN5 53 D1
Swinburn St. 2 M9 64 F1
Swinburne Ave. M43 84 A3
Swinburne Gn. SK5 99 D1
Swinburne Way. 12 M34 113 A7
Swindell's St. 6 M11 99 E7
Swindells St. SK14 101 E5
Swindon Cl. M18 99 D5
Swinfield Ave. M21 108 F8
Swinford Gr. OL2 149 A5
Swinford Wlk. 14 M9 64 E3
Swinley Chase. SK9 131 F1
Swinley La. WN1 37 C2
Swinley Rd. WN1 37 C2
Swinley St. WN1 37 C2
Swinside. WN1 37 F1
Swinside Cl. M24 46 C2
Swinside Rd. BL2 42 F8
Swinstead Ave. M40 157 E5
Swinton Cres. M45 45 A1
Swinton Gr. M13 163 C5
Swinton Hall Rd. M27 80 A8
Swinton High Sch The. M27 61 F1
Swinton Park Golf Course. M30 80 A5
Swinton Park Rd. M6 80 B5
Swinton St. Bolton BL2 42 E7
Swinton St. Oldham OL4 67 C5
Swinton Sta. M27 61 F1
Swiss Hill. SK9 137 B1
Swithemby St. BL6 22 A4
Swithin Rd. M22 130 E8
Swythamley Cl. SK3 123 A8
Swythamley Rd. SK3 123 A8
Sybil St. OL15 16 A6
Sycamore Ave. Alt'ham WA14 119 A5
Sycamore Ave. Denton M34 100 F2
Sycamore Ave. Golborne WA3 74 A1
Sycamore Ave. Heywood OL10 46 E8
Sycamore Ave. Hindley WN2 56 F3
Sycamore Ave. Newhey OL16 32 A3
Sycamore Ave. Newton-l-W WA12 89 C3
Sycamore Ave. Oldham OL9 65 F3
Sycamore Ave. Oldham OL4 67 D8
Sycamore Ave. Radcliffe M26 61 F8
Sycamore Ave. Tyldesley M29 59 D1
Sycamore Ave. Wigan WN6 36 F3
Sycamore Cl. Ashton-u-L OL6 85 E2
Sycamore Cl. Handforth SK9 131 B2
Sycamore Cl. Littleborough OL15 15 F5
Sycamore Cl. New Mills SK12 127 E1
Sycamore Cl. Stalybridge SK16 101 F8
Sycamore Cotts. OL3 50 F1
Sycamore Cres. Ashton-u-L OL6 85 C5
Sycamore Cres. Hollinfare WA3 105 B2
Sycamore Ct. 11 M'ster M16 97 D3
Sycamore Ct. M'ster M40 160 E3
Sycamore Ct. 8 Salford M6 81 A3
Sycamore Dr. Droylsden M43 84 C2
Sycamore Dr. Wigan WN3 54 C2
Sycamore Gr. M35 84 B7
Sycamore Lodge. SK7 132 F7
Sycamore Pl. M45 62 F6
Sycamore Rd. Atherton M46 58 E3
Sycamore Rd. Bury BL8 26 F5
Sycamore Rd. New Mills SK12 127 F2
Sycamore Rd. Partington M31 105 E3
Sycamore Rd. Romiley SK6 113 A4
Sycamore Rd. Worsley M28 79 A4
Sycamore St. Sale M33 108 E4
Sycamore St. Stockport SK3 123 B8
Sycamore Wlk. Cheadle SK8 122 D6
Sycamore Wlk. 1 Horwich BL6 22 E1
Sycamores The. Hadfield SK13 171 F3
Sycamores The. Kearsley M26 61 B6
Sycamores The. Mossley OL5 68 E1
Sycamores The. Oldham OL4 67 E8
Sycamores The. Stalybridge SK15 102 B8
Sydall St. M34 100 F3
Syddal Cl. SK7 132 F5
Syddal Cres. SK7 132 D4
Syddal Gn. SK7 132 D5
Syddal Park Prep Sch. SK7 132 D5
Syddal Rd. SK7 132 D5
Syddall Ave. SK8 131 D8
Syddall St. SK14 167 D2
Sydenham St. 2 OL1 49 B1
Sydenham Terr. OL12 14 D3
Sydney Ave. Eccles M30 79 D2
Sydney Ave. Leigh WN7 75 D2
Sydney Ave. Wythenshawe M90 130 A8
Sydney Gdns. OL15 6 C1
Sydney Jones Ct. M40 65 C1
Sydney Rd. SK7 132 F5
Sydney St. Failsworth M35 83 E7
Sydney St. Mossley OL5 86 D8
Sydney St. Platt Bridge WN2 56 A3
Sydney St. Salford M6 154 E2
Sydney St. Stockport SK2 124 C7
Sydney St. Stretford M32 96 D2
Sydney St. Swinton M27 79 D7
Syke La. OL12 14 F4
Syke Rd. Littleborough OL15 16 C2
Syke Rd. R'dale OL12 15 A3
Sykes Ave. BL9 45 B4
Sykes Cl. OL3 69 B5
Sykes Meadow. SK3 170 D6
Sykes St. Bury BL9 141 A3
Sykes St. Hyde SK14 167 F1
Sykes St. Newhey OL16 32 A4
Sykes St. 7 R'dale OL16 31 B6
Sykes St. Reddish SK5 111 F8
Sykes Wlk. 2 SK5 111 F8
Sylvan Ave. Failsworth M35 83 E5
Sylvan Ave. M'ster M16 97 D3
Sylvan Ave. Sale M33 108 C3
Sylvan Ave. Sale WA15 119 F8
Sylvan Ave. Urmston M41 95 D3
Sylvan Ave. Wilmslow SK9 136 F5
Sylvan Cl. M24 46 D2
Sylvan Gr. WA14 119 D5
Sylvan St. OL9 152 C7
Sylvandale Ave. M19 99 A1
Sylvester Ave. SK1 & SK2 124 B7
Sylvester Cl. SK14 102 E2
Sylvester Way. 1 Denton M34 113 A7
Sylvester Way. 9 Hattersley SK14 102 E2
Sylvia Gr. 9 SK5 111 E7
Symms St. M6 81 B4
Symond Rd. M9 64 E5
Symons Rd. M33 108 B5
Symons St. M7 155 E7
Syndall Ave. M12 164 D6
Syndall St. M12 164 D6
Synergy House. M15 163 A5
Syresham St. 1 WN2 56 B2

Taberner Cl. WN6 19 F1
Taberner St. 3 WN2 56 B2
Tabley Ave. M14 98 B2
Tabley Gdns. 3 Droylsden M43 84 B1
Tabley Gdns. Marple SK6 126 A4
Tabley Gr. M'ster M13 98 F2
Tabley Gr. Reddish SK5 111 E7
Tabley Gr. Sale WA15 120 A8
Tabley Mere Gdns. SK8 122 F3
Tabley Rd. Bolton BL3 146 B4
Tabley Rd. Handforth SK9 131 D5
Tabley Rd. Sale M33 108 E2
Tabley St. Dukinfield SK16 101 E8
Tabley St. Mossley OL5 86 D8
Tabley St. Salford M6 81 B5
Tabor St. M24 46 F2
Tackler Cl. M27 79 F7
Tadcaster Wlk. OL1 153 F7
Taddington Pl. 17 SK13 171 E1
Tadlow Wlk. 3 M40 159 C3
Tadman Gr. WA14 119 A6
Tadmor Cl. M38 59 F4
Tagore Cl. M13 98 E4
Tahir Cl. M8 156 B7
Tait Mews. SK4 110 F2
Talavera St. M7 155 D5
Talbot Ave. BL3 43 A4
Talbot Cl. Oldham OL4 67 C8
Talbot Cl. Rawtenstall BB4 1 E8
Talbot Ct. BL1 143 F4
Talbot Gr. BL9 28 A6
Talbot House Sch. SK13 104 C2
Talbot Pl. M16 161 B5
Talbot Rd. Alderley Edge SK9 137 B1
Talbot Rd. Alt'ham WA14 119 B2
Talbot Rd. Dukinfield SK14 101 F5
Talbot Rd. Glossop SK13 104 C2
Talbot Rd. M'ster M14 & M19 & M20 110 E7
Talbot Rd. Sale M33 108 E4
Talbot Rd. Stretford M16 & M32 & M15 96 F3
Talbot St. Ashton-i-M WN4 73 D4
Talbot St. Ashton-u-L OL6 166 A3
Talbot St. Eccles M30 79 E1
Talbot St. Glossop SK13 104 C1
Talbot St. Golborne WA3 90 A8
Talbot St. Hazel Grove SK7 124 E4
Talbot St. Middleton M24 47 A2
Talbot St. R'dale OL11 139 F6
Talbot St. Stockport SK1 & SK3 169 E1
Talford Gr. M20 110 A5
Talgarth Rd. M40 159 C4
Talkin Dr. M24 46 E3
Tall Trees. M7 63 D1
Tall Trees Cl. OL2 48 C4
Tall Trees Pl. SK2 124 C6
Talland Wlk. M13 164 D5
Tallarn Cl. M20 110 C7
Tallis St. M12 & M18 99 A3
Talmine Ave. M10 & M40 157 E5
Tamar Cl. BL4 61 B5
Tamar Ct. 5 M15 162 D6
Tamar Dr. M23 121 A4
Tamar Way. OL10 29 A3
Tamarin Cl. M27 61 C1
Tame Barn Cl. OL16 32 A6
Tame Cl. SK15 86 C3
Tame La. OL3 50 D7
Tame St. Denton M34 100 F4
Tame St. Dukinfield M34 100 F7
Tame St. M'ster M4 160 D1
Tame St. Stalybridge SK15 85 E1
Tame St. Uppermill OL5 68 E3
Tame St. Uppermill OL3 69 B8
Tame Valley Prim Sch. SK5 112 C7
Tame View. OL5 68 C2
Tame Water Villas. OL3 50 F1
Tame Wlk. 8 SK9 131 D2
Tamebank. OL5 68 D3
Tamer Gr. WN7 75 C8
Tamerton Dr. M7 & M8 156 A6
Tameside Coll of Tech. Ashton-u-L OL6 85 D3
Tameside Coll of Tech. Ashton-u-L OL6 166 B2
Tameside Coll of Tech. Hyde SK14 113 D7
Tameside Coll of Tech. Hyde SK14 167 E2
Tameside Ct. 5 SK14 102 E2
Tameside General Hospl. OL6 85 E4
Tameside Leisure Pk. SK14 167 F2
Tamworth Ave. Prestwich M45 63 B7
Tamworth Ave. Salford M5 161 B8
Tamworth Ave W. M5 161 A8
Tamworth Cl. Hazel Grove SK7 133 D8
Tamworth Cl. M'ster M15 162 E5
Tamworth Ct. M16 162 E5
Tamworth Dr. Bury BL8 27 C5
Tamworth Dr. Wigan WN2 37 F2
Tamworth Gn. SK1 112 B2
Tamworth St. M'ster M15 97 E4
Tamworth St. Newton-l-W WA12 89 A3
Tamworth St. Oldham OL9 152 C5
Tamworth St. Stockport SK1 112 B2
Tan House Dr. WN3 54 C2
Tan House La. WN3 54 C2
Tan Pit Cotts. WN8 35 C4
Tan Yard Brow. M18 99 E5
Tandis Ct. M30 80 A4
Tandle Hill Ctry Pk. OL2 48 A6
Tandle Hill Rd. OL2 48 B6
Tandlewood Mews. 8 M40 83 C5
Tandlewood Pk. OL2 48 B6
Tanfield Dr. M26 61 B7
Tanfield Rd. M20 122 B8
Tanfield Sch. WN2 56 E5
Tangmere Cl. M40 65 C3
Tangmere Ct. M16 97 D3
Tanhill Cl. SK2 124 E6
Tanhill La. OL8 67 A2
Tanhouse Ave. M29 77 D7
Tanhouse Rd. M41 94 D3
Tanner Brook Cl. BL3 147 E4
Tanner St. SK14 167 D3
Tanner's La. WA3 90 B8
Tanners Fold. OL8 67 A2
Tanners Gn. 15 M6 154 F3
Tanners St. Droylsden M18 99 E5
Tanners St. Ramsbottom BL0 138 B6
Tannery Way. WA14 119 E7
Tannock Rd. SK7 124 F1
Tanpit Wlk. 2 M22 121 C2
Tanpits Rd. BL9 140 E3
Tansey Gr. M7 & M8 155 F7
Tansley Ave. PR7 19 D8
Tansley Rd. M8 64 B2
Tansley Sq. WN5 54 D5
Tanworth Wlk. 27 BL1 143 E2
Tanyard Dr. WA15 129 C6
Tanyard Gn. SK5 111 F5
Tanyard La. WA15 129 A5
Tape St. BL0 138 B6
Taper St. BL0 138 B6
Tapley Ave. SK12 133 E2
Taplow Gr. SK8 122 F4
Taplow Wlk. M14 98 E3
Tarbet Dr. BL2 42 F7
Tarbet Rd. SK16 101 C7
Tarbet Wlk. M7 155 E6
Tarbolton Cres. WA15 120 C3
Tarbrook Gr. 1 SK9 131 D2
Tariff St. M1 159 B1
Tarland Wlk. 17 M11 83 C1
Tarleton Ave. M46 58 B5
Tarleton Pl. BL3 146 A3
Tarleton Wlk. M13 164 D6
Tarn Cl. WN4 73 B5
Tarn Dr. BL9 44 E6
Tarn Gr. M28 60 F1
Tarnbrook Cl. M45 63 C8
Tarnbrook Wlk. M15 163 A5
Tarnrigg Cl. WN3 54 E3
Tarns The. SK8 122 B3
Tarnside Cl. Hazel Grove SK2 124 F6
Tarnside Cl. Littleborough OL16 15 C3
Tarnside Fold. SK13 116 A7
Tarnside Rd. WN5 53 E6
Tarnway. WA3 90 F7
Tarporley Ave. M14 110 A8
Tarporley Cl. SK3 170 D5
Tarporley Wlk. SK9 131 E2
Tarran Gr. M34 101 B1
Tarran Pl. WA14 119 E6
Tarrant Cl. WN3 54 D2
Tarrington Cl. M12 165 A5
Tartan St. M11 83 B2
Tarves Wlk. M11 83 B1
Tarvin Ave. M'ster M20 110 A7
Tarvin Ave. Reddish SK4 111 D7
Tarvin Cl. WA3 90 E7
Tarvin Dr. SK6 112 E4
Tarvin Rd. SK8 123 A4
Tarvin Way. 1 SK9 131 D5
Tarvin Wlk. BL1 143 E2
Tarvington Cl. M40 156 C6
Tasle Alley. M2 158 F1
Tatchbury Rd. M35 84 A7
Tate St. OL8 67 B5
Tatham Cl. 3 M13 98 F3
Tatham St. OL16 31 A7
Tatland Dr. M22 121 F3
Tatlock Cl. WN5 71 E5
Tattenhall Wlk. 12 M14 110 D8
Tattersall Ave. BL1 23 E2
Tattersall St. OL9 153 D6
Tatton Cl. Cheadle SK8 123 A4
Tatton Cl. Hazel Grove SK7 124 F4
Tatton Ct. 4 Handforth SK9 131 E5
Tatton Ct. 8 M'ster M14 110 D8
Tatton Ct. M'ster SK4 168 C4
Tatton Dr. WN4 72 F4
Tatton Fold. M22 109 E1
Tatton Gdns. SK6 113 D5
Tatton Gr. M20 110 B6
Tatton Mere Dr. M43 84 B1
Tatton Pl. 5 M'ster M13 98 E4
Tatton Pl. Sale M33 108 B5
Tatton Rd. Denton M34 101 A1
Tatton Rd. Handforth SK9 131 E5
Tatton Rd. Sale M33 108 B5
Tatton Rd N. SK4 111 C5
Tatton Rd S. SK4 168 C4
Tatton St. Hyde SK14 113 E7
Tatton St. M'ster M15 162 D7
Tatton St. Salford M5 161 B8
Tatton St. Stalybridge SK15 86 B1
Tatton St. Stockport SK1 169 F1
Tatton Terr. 5 SK16 166 B1
Tatton View. 5 M20 110 B6
Tattonmere Gdns. SK8 123 A4
Taunton Ave. Ashton-u-L OL7 166 A4
Taunton Ave. Brinnington SK5 112 C5
Taunton Ave. Eccles M30 79 B3
Taunton Ave. Hindley WN7 57 D2
Taunton Ave. R'dale OL11 30 B7
Taunton Ave. Urmston M41 107 B8
Taunton Cl. Bolton BL1 142 C1
Taunton Cl. Hazel Grove SK7 125 A2
Taunton Dr. BL4 147 F1
Taunton Gn. OL7 84 F5
Taunton Gr. M25 & M45 63 A6
Taunton Hall Cl. OL7 84 F5
Taunton Lawns. OL7 85 A5
Taunton Pl. OL7 84 F5
Taunton Rd. Ashton-u-L OL7 166 A4
Taunton Rd. Chadderton OL9 48 A1
Taunton Rd. Sale M33 107 D4
Taunton St. M11 & M4 160 D1
Taunton Wlk. 13 M34 101 A1
Taurus St. OL4 67 C8
Tavern Court Ave. M35 84 B7
Tavern Ct. M35 84 B7
Tavery Cl. 7 M4 159 C2
Tavistock Cl. SK14 102 E2
Tavistock Dr. OL9 47 F1
Tavistock Rd. Bolton BL1 145 D6
Tavistock Rd. Hindley WN2 57 A4
Tavistock Rd. R'dale OL11 30 F2
Tavistock Rd. Sale M33 107 D5
Tavistock Sq. M9 157 D7
Tavistock St. M46 58 B4
Tawton Ave. SK14 102 E3
Taxi Rd. M90 130 B7
Tay Cl. OL8 153 E5
Tayfield Rd. M22 121 C2
Taylor Ave. OL11 29 F8
Taylor Bldgs. BL4 61 B6
Taylor Gr. WN2 57 C3
Taylor Green Way. OL4 67 F7
Taylor Holme Ind Est. OL13 3 B8
Taylor House. BL8 27 C5
Taylor Ind Est. WA3 91 F1
Taylor La. M34 100 D4
Taylor Rd. Alt'ham WA14 119 A5
Taylor Rd. Eccles M41 95 E7
Taylor Rd. Hindley WN2 57 C3
Taylor St. 8 Bolton BL3 145 F6
Taylor St. Bury BL9 141 A3
Taylor St. Chadderton OL9 152 A7
Taylor St. Denton M34 100 F4
Taylor St. Droylsden M43 84 A1
Taylor St. Golborne WN3 74 C1
Taylor St. Heywood OL10 29 C2
Taylor St. Hollingworth SK14 171 D4
Taylor St. Horwich BL6 22 B3
Taylor St. Hyde SK14 167 F3
Taylor St. Leigh WN7 75 D8
Taylor St. M'ster M14 98 C2
Taylor St. M'ster M18 165 C6
Taylor St. Middleton M24 65 A8
Taylor St. Oldham OL1 & OL4 67 C8
Taylor St. 1 Oldham OL4 67 E6
Taylor St. Prestwich M25 63 C4
Taylor St. R'dale OL12 14 F1
Taylor St. Radcliffe M26 44 A3
Taylor St. Royton OL2 48 D5
Taylor St. Stalybridge SK15 86 B1
Taylor St. Whitworth OL12 14 D8
Taylor St. Wigan WN3 150 B8
Taylor Terr. 18 SK16 166 B1
Taylor's La. Bolton BL2 43 B7
Taylor's La. Ince-i-M WN2 55 F3
Taylor's Rd. M32 96 E3
Taylors Pl. 18 OL12 14 F1
Taylorson St. M5 161 B7
Taylorson St S. M5 161 A6
Tayton Cl. M29 59 C1
Taywood Rd. BL3 40 D2
Teak Dr. M26 & M27 61 D4
Teak St. BL9 141 B2
Teal Ave. SK12 133 A4
Teal Cl. Alt'ham WA14 119 B8
Teal Cl. Hazel Grove SK2 124 F5
Teal Cl. Wigan WN3 54 B4
Teal Ct. OL11 29 F7
Teal St. BL3 147 F4
Tealby Ave. M16 97 C4
Tealby Ct. M21 97 C1
Tealby Rd. M18 99 B4
Teasdale Cl. OL9 65 E3
Tebbutt St. M4 159 B3
Ted Jackson Wlk. M11 164 F8
Tedburn Wlk. 13 M40 65 D2
Tedder Cl. BL9 & M45 45 B2
Tedder Dr. M22 130 F7
Teddington Rd. M40 65 C1
Teer St. M10 & M40 160 D2
Tees St. OL16 31 B6
Tees Wlk. OL8 153 E5
Teesdale Ave. M41 95 A4
Teesdale Cl. SK2 124 E6
Teesdale Dr. WN7 76 C5
Teesdale Wlk. 20 M9 64 E3
Teignmouth Ave. M40 159 C4
Teignmouth St. M40 159 C4
Telfer Ave. M13 98 E2
Telfer Rd. M13 98 E2
Telford Cl. M34 100 E7
Telford Cres. WN7 75 D8
Telford Rd. SK6 126 A4
Telford Sch. M9 64 C4
Telford St. Atherton M46 58 A2
Telford St. Horwich BL6 22 D2
Telford St. M'ster M8 156 C5
Telford Way. OL11 31 A2
Telford Wlk. M16 97 D4
Tell St. OL12 139 D7
Tellers Cl. M46 58 D3
Tellson Cl. M6 80 D6
Tellson Cres. M6 80 D6
Telryn Wlk. M8 156 C8
Temperance Sq. SK14 103 A4
Temperance St. Bolton BL3 145 E5
Temperance St. M'ster M12 163 C8
Temperance St. M'ster M12 164 D7
Temperance St. Mottram-i-L SK14 115 A8
Tempest Chase. BL6 40 C4
Tempest Rd. Alderley Edge SK9 137 C1
Tempest Rd. Bolton BL6 40 C4
Tempest St. BL3 146 B4
Temple Ave. SK14 104 C5
Temple Cl. OL4 67 E8
Temple Dr. Bolton BL1 142 C3
Temple Dr. Pendlebury M27 80 B7
Temple House. M8 156 A5
Temple Inf & Jun Sch. M8 156 A6
Temple La. OL15 6 D1
Temple Moor Inf Sch. M33 108 E4
Temple Rd. Bolton BL1 142 C3
Temple Rd. Sale M33 108 D4
Temple Sq. M8 156 B6
Temple St. Hadfield SK14 104 C5
Temple St. Heywood OL10 29 D2
Temple St. Middleton M24 47 B1
Temple St. Oldham OL1 67 B7
Templecombe Dr. BL1 24 E7
Templegate Cl. WN6 19 F2
Templeton Cl. Alt'ham WA14 119 B6
Templeton Cl. Westhoughton BL5 57 E8
Templeton Rd. WN2 56 B2
Temsbury Wlk. M40 157 E5
Ten Acre Ct. M45 62 D7
Ten Acre Dr. M45 62 D7
Ten Acres La. M40 83 A4
Ten Foot Cl. SK13 104 B2
Tenax Circ. M17 96 B8
Tenax Rd. M17 96 B7
Tenbury Cl. M6 154 F3
Tenbury Dr. Ashton-i-M WN4 73 A4
Tenbury Dr. Middleton M24 65 A5
Tenby Ave. Bolton BL1 142 A1
Tenby Ave. M'ster M20 110 B6
Tenby Ave. Stretford M32 96 E4
Tenby Ct. M16 161 C6
Tenby Dr. Cheadle SK8 123 B1
Tenby Dr. Salford M6 80 D5
Tenby Gr. 6 OL12 14 C1
Tenby Rd. Oldham OL8 66 B2
Tenby Rd. Stockport SK3 123 B7
Tenby St. OL12 14 C1
Tenement La. SK7 & SK8 123 C3
Tenement St. Abram WN2 56 B1
Teneriffe St. M7 155 D5
Tenham Wlk. 23 M9 64 E3
Tennis St. Bolton BL1 143 D3
Tennis St. M'ster M16 97 B4
Tennyson Ave. Bury BL9 44 F6
Tennyson Ave. Denton M34 113 A7
Tennyson Ave. Dukinfield SK16 102 B7
Tennyson Ave. Leigh WN7 75 C8
Tennyson Ave. Radcliffe M26 43 E4
Tennyson Cl. SK4 168 B2
Tennyson Dr. Orrell WN5 53 D1
Tennyson Dr. Wigan WN1 37 C3
Tennyson Gdns. M25 62 F3
Tennyson Rd. Cheadle SK8 122 F6
Tennyson Rd. Droylsden M43 84 A2
Tennyson Rd. Farnworth BL4 60 B6
Tennyson Rd. Middleton M24 47 B2
Tennyson Rd. Reddish SK5 99 D1
Tennyson Rd. Swinton M27 79 D8
Tennyson St. Bolton BL1 143 D1
Tennyson St. M'ster M13 163 C5
Tennyson St. Oldham OL1 49 C1
Tennyson St. 1 R'dale OL11 31 A5
Tennyson St. Salford M6 81 C4
Tennyson Wlk. 3 BL1 143 E2
Tensing Ave. Ashton-u-L OL7 85 B5
Tensing Ave. Atherton M46 58 C5
Tensing St. OL8 85 A8
Tenter Dr. WN6 37 B7
Tentercroft. Oldham OL1 153 E7
Tentercroft. R'dale OL12 139 E7
Tenterden St. BL9 140 D2
Tenterden Wlk. M22 121 C3
Tenterfield St. 6 BB4 2 F8
Tenterheads. BB4 2 F7
Tenterhill La. OL12 13 D2
Tenters St. BL9 140 D2
Tenth St. M17 96 D6
Terence St. M40 83 D5
Terling Wlk. M40 157 E5
Terminal Rd E. M90 130 C7
Terminal Rd N. M90 130 B7
Terminal Rd S. M90 130 B7
Tern Ave. BL4 59 F8
Tern Cl. Alt'ham WA14 119 B8
Tern Cl. Dukinfield SK16 101 E7
Tern Cl. R'dale OL11 29 F7
Tern Dr. SK12 133 B4
Ternhill Ct. BL4 60 D8
Terrace St. OL4 67 B7
Terrace The. M25 63 B3
Terrington Cl. M21 109 E7
Tetbury Dr. BL2 43 A8
Tetbury Rd. M22 121 B1
Tetlow Gr. M30 79 C1
Tetlow La. M7 & M8 155 E8
Tetlow St. Dukinfield SK14 101 E5
Tetlow St. Failsworth M40 83 D5
Tetlow St. Middleton M24 65 A8
Tetlow St. Oldham OL8 153 D6
Tetsworth Wlk. 16 M40 65 D2
Teviot St. 8 M13 98 E4
Tewkesbury Ave. Alt'ham WA15 120 C3
Tewkesbury Ave. Ashton-u-L OL6 85 C7
Tewkesbury Ave. Chadderton OL9 48 A2
Tewkesbury Ave. Droylsden M43 84 A3
Tewkesbury Ave. Middleton M24 46 F3
Tewkesbury Ave. Urmston M41 95 D4
Tewkesbury Cl. Bramhall SK8 132 B6
Tewkesbury Cl. Poynton SK12 133 D4
Tewkesbury Dr. M25 63 C2
Tewkesbury Rd. Cheadle SK3 123 B6
Tewkesbury Rd. Golborne WA3 90 B8
Tewkesbury Rd. M'ster M10 & M40 160 D3
Texas St. SK16 166 C2
Textile St. M12 165 A7
Textilose Ind Ctr. M17 96 B5
Textilose Rd. M17 96 B5
Teynham Wlk. 5 M22 121 C1
Thackeray Cl. M7 & M8 156 A6
Thackeray Gr. M43 84 A2
Thackeray Pl. WN3 150 A5
Thackeray Rd. OL1 49 C1
Thames Ave. WN7 75 F1
Thames Cl. Bury BL9 27 F7
Thames Cl. M'ster M11 165 B8
Thames Ct. 2 M15 162 D6
Thames Dr. WN5 53 F7
Thames Ind Est. M12 164 D7
Thames Rd. Culcheth WA3 92 A2
Thames Rd. Milnrow OL16 32 B6
Thames St. OL1 67 A8
Thames Steet. OL16 31 B6
Thames Trad Ctr. M44 105 F7
Thanet Cl. M7 & M8 155 E5
Thanet Gr. WN7 76 A5
Thankerton Ave. M34 84 D1
Thatch Leach. OL9 65 F5
Thatch Leach La. M45 63 A7
Thatcher St. OL8 67 A4
Thaxmead Dr. M40 83 D4
Thaxted Cl. SK2 125 A5
Thaxted Dr. SK2 125 A5
Thaxted Pl. BL1 144 C8
Thaxted Wlk. M22 130 C8
Theatre St. OL1 153 F7
Thekla St. OL9 153 D8
Thelma St. BL0 138 B6
Thelwall Ave. Bolton BL2 42 D8
Thelwall Ave. M'ster M14 110 A8
Thelwall Cl. 3 Alt'ham WA15 119 E6
Thelwall Cl. Leigh WN7 75 B4
Thelwall Rd. M33 108 E3
Theobald Rd. WA14 119 D1
Theta Cl. M11 83 B2
Thetford. 12 OL12 139 E8
Thetford Cl. Bury BL8 27 D5
Thetford Cl. Hindley WN2 56 E4
Thetford Dr. M8 156 B7
Thicketford Brow. BL2 25 D1
Thicketford Cl. BL2 25 C2
Thicketford Rd. BL2 25 C1
Thicknesse Ave. WN6 36 F3
Thimble Cl. OL12 15 D4
Thimbles The. OL12 15 D4
Third Ave. Bolton BL1 144 B7
Third Ave. Bury BL9 28 D4
Third Ave. Droylsden M11 83 C3
Third Ave. Little Lever BL3 42 F4
Third Ave. Mossley SK15 86 E6
Third Ave. Oldham OL8 66 D1
Third Ave. Poynton SK10 & SK12 133 D1
Third Ave. Stretford M17 96 D6
Third Ave. Swinton M27 79 E5
Third Ave. Tyldesley M29 77 B4
Third Ave. Wigan WN6 37 A2
Third St. BL1 23 F4
Thirkhill Pl. 2 M30 79 F2
Thirlby Dr. M22 121 D1
Thirlemere Rd. SK1 124 B7
Thirlmere Ave. Abram WN2 74 B8
Thirlmere Ave. Ashton-i-M WN4 73 C4
Thirlmere Ave. Ashton-u-L OL7 84 F4
Thirlmere Ave. Haslingden BB4 1 C8
Thirlmere Ave. Horwich BL6 22 C2
Thirlmere Ave. Ince-i-M WN2 56 B7
Thirlmere Ave. Orrell WN8 53 B7
Thirlmere Ave. Orrell WN5 53 F7
Thirlmere Ave. Standish WN6 37 A7
Thirlmere Ave. Stretford M32 96 C3
Thirlmere Ave. Swinton M27 80 A7
Thirlmere Ave. Tyldesley M29 77 A7
Thirlmere Cl. Adlington PR6 21 B8
Thirlmere Cl. Alderley Edge SK9 136 F1
Thirlmere Cl. Stalybridge SK15 86 A4
Thirlmere Dr. Bury BL9 44 E7
Thirlmere Dr. Middleton M24 46 E2
Thirlmere Dr. Walkden M38 60 A5
Thirlmere Gr. Farnworth BL4 59 E8
Thirlmere Gr. Royton OL2 48 D6
Thirlmere House. M7 158 D4
Thirlmere Mews. M24 46 E2
Thirlmere Rd. Atherton BL5 58 F7
Thirlmere Rd. Blackrod BL6 21 C3
Thirlmere Rd. Golborne WA3 74 C1
Thirlmere Rd. Hindley WN2 56 E5
Thirlmere Rd. Partington M44 105 E4
Thirlmere Rd. R'dale OL11 30 B4
Thirlmere Rd. Urmston M41 94 E3
Thirlmere Rd. Wigan WN5 54 C7
Thirlmere St. WN7 75 E5
Thirlspot Cl. BL1 24 E6
Thirlstone Ave. OL4 49 F4
Thirsfield Dr. 6 M11 83 C2
Thirsk Ave. Chadderton OL9 47 F1
Thirsk Ave. Sale M33 107 C3
Thirsk Cl. BL8 27 B5
Thirsk Mews. M7 155 D6
Thirsk Rd. BL3 43 A2
Thirsk St. M12 163 C7
Thistle Cl. SK15 102 E7
Thistle Sq. M31 105 E2
Thistle Wlk. 4 M31 105 E2
Thistledown Cl. Eccles M30 95 D8
Thistledown Cl. Wigan WN6 37 A2
Thistleton Rd. BL3 40 F3

Vavasour Ct. 5 OL16 31 B6
Vavasour St. OL16 31 B6
Vawdrey Dr. M23 108 F2
Vaynor. 15 OL12 139 E8
Vega St. M8 158 E4
Vela Wlk. M6 81 C3
Velmere Ave. M9 64 A5
Velvet Ct. M1 163 A8
Vendale Ave. M27 79 D6
Venesta Ave. M6 80 B4
Venetia St. M40 83 C5
Venice St. Bolton BL3 146 C4
Venice St. M'ster M1 163 A8
Venlow Gdns. SK8 123 B1
Ventnor Ave. Bolton BL1 143 F2
Ventnor Ave. Reddish M19 111 C8
Ventnor Ave. Sale M33 108 B6
Ventnor Ave. Whitefield BL9 45 A3
Ventnor Cl. M34 113 B8
Ventnor Rd. M'ster M20 110 C3
Ventnor Rd. M'ster SK4 168 A2
Ventnor St. M'ster M9 157 E8
Ventnor St. R'dale OL11 139 F5
Ventnor St. Salford M6 81 B4
Ventor St. M9 157 D8
Ventura Cl. M14 98 A1
Ventura Ct. SK12 127 D1
Venwood Rd. M25 62 F2
Verbena Ave. BL4 42 A1
Verbena Cl. M31 105 F3
Verda St. Abram WN2 74 B8
Verdant La. Eccles M30 94 F8
Verdant La. Eccles M30 95 A8
Verdon St. M4 159 A3
Verdun Ave. M6 80 B3
Verdun Cres. OL11 30 C8
Verdun Rd. M28 79 B4
Verdure Ave. Bolton BL1 40 E8
Verdure Ave. Sale M33 108 C1
Verdure Cl. M35 84 B7
Vere St. M5 154 F1
Verity Cl. M'ster M20 110 C6
Verity Cl. Royton OL2 48 D3
Verity Wlk. M9 64 B3
Vermont St. BL1 145 D8
Verne Ave. M27 79 E8
Verne Dr. OL1 49 E5
Verney Rd. OL2 48 E2
Vernham Wlk. BL3 147 E4
Vernon Ave. Eccles M30 79 F2
Vernon Ave. Stockport SK1 112 B2
Vernon Ave. Stretford M32 96 D1
Vernon Cl. Cheadle SK8 122 E1
Vernon Cl. Poynton SK12 133 D2
Vernon Cty Inf Sch The. SK12 133 E3
Vernon Cty Jun Sch The. SK12 133 E3
Vernon Dr. Marple SK6 125 D7
Vernon Dr. Prestwich M25 63 A2
Vernon Gr. M33 108 E3
Vernon Park Prim Sch. SK1 112 A1
Vernon Pk. WA15 120 A7
Vernon Rd. Bredbury SK6 112 E3
Vernon Rd. Droylsden M43 83 E2
Vernon Rd. M'ster M7 63 C1
Vernon Rd. Poynton SK12 133 E2
Vernon Rd. Ramsbottom BL8 11 A1
Vernon St. Ashton-u-L OL6 166 C4
Vernon St. Bolton BL1 145 E8
Vernon St. Bury BL9 140 F4
Vernon St. Farnworth BL4 42 E1
Vernon St. Hazel Grove SK7 124 D3
Vernon St. Hyde SK14 167 E2
Vernon St. Leigh WN7 75 F5
Vernon St. M'ster M7 155 D5
Vernon St. M'ster M9 157 E7
Vernon St. M'ster M16 162 D5
Vernon St. Mossley OL5 68 C2
Vernon St. Stockport SK1 169 F2
Vernon View. SK5 112 C7
Vernon Wlk. 5 Bolton BL1 145 E8
Vernon Wlk. Stockport SK1 169 E1
Verona Dr. M40 83 C4
Veronica Rd. M20 110 C3
Verrill Ave. M23 109 C1
Verwood Wlk. 9 M23 121 A5
Vesper St. M35 84 A8
Vesta St. M'ster M4 159 C1
Vesta St. Ramsbottom BL0 138 B6
Vestris Dr. M6 80 B3
Vetch Cl. WA3 105 B5
Viaduct Rd. WA14 119 D7
Viaduct St. M'ster M3 158 F2
Viaduct St. M'ster M12 164 E8
Viaduct St. Newton-l-W WA12 89 A3
Viaduct St. Stockport SK3 169 E1
Vicar's Dr. OL11 & OL16 139 F6
Vicar's Gate. OL16 139 F7
Vicarage Ave. SK8 132 B7
Vicarage Cl. Adlington PR6 21 A8
Vicarage Cl. Dukinfield SK16 101 E8
Vicarage Cl. Oldham OL4 67 F7
Vicarage Cl. Platt Bridge WN2 56 A2
Vicarage Cl. Salford M6 80 B3
Vicarage Cres. OL6 85 D5
Vicarage Dr. Dukinfield SK16 101 E8
Vicarage Dr. Littleborough OL12 & OL16 15 C3
Vicarage Gdns. SK14 167 F2
Vicarage Gr. M30 79 F2
Vicarage La. Alt'ham WA14 119 C1
Vicarage La. Middleton M24 65 D7
Vicarage La. Poynton SK12 133 E5
Vicarage La. Shevington WN6 36 A5
Vicarage Rd. Abram WN2 56 B1
Vicarage Rd. Ashton-i-M WN4 73 B2
Vicarage Rd. Ashton-u-L OL7 85 B5
Vicarage Rd. Blackrod BL6 21 D2
Vicarage Rd. Irlam M44 94 A2
Vicarage Rd. Orrell WN5 53 D4
Vicarage Rd. Stockport SK3 170 E6
Vicarage Rd. Swinton M27 79 E8
Vicarage Rd. Urmston M41 95 B4
Vicarage Rd. Walkden M28 60 C4
Vicarage Rd N. OL11 30 D1
Vicarage Rd S. OL11 30 C1
Vicarage Rd W. BL6 21 C2
Vicarage Sq. WN7 75 F5
Vicarage St. Bolton BL3 145 D5
Vicarage St. Oldham OL8 66 C3
Vicarage St. 1 Radcliffe M26 44 A3
Vicarage St. Shaw OL2 149 B7
Vicarage View. OL11 30 D1
Vicarage Way. OL2 149 A6
Vicars Hall Gdns. M28 77 F5
Vicars Hall La. M28 77 F4
Vicars Rd. M21 109 A8
Vicars St. M30 79 F2
Viceroy Ct. M20 110 B2
Vicker Cl. M27 61 F2
Vicker Gr. M20 109 F5
Vickerman St. BL1 143 D2
Vickers Row. BL4 60 B8
Vickers St. Bolton BL3 145 E5
Vickers St. M'ster M10, M40 160 E4
Victor Ave. BL9 140 E4
Victor Cl. WN5 54 D8
Victor Mann St. M11 100 A7
Victor St. Heywood OL10 46 E8
Victor St. M'ster M3 158 D2
Victor St. M'ster M40 159 C4
Victor St. Oldham OL8 66 B1
Victoria Ave. Alt'ham WA15 119 F7
Victoria Ave. Bredbury SK6 112 F3
Victoria Ave. Cheadle SK8 123 A2
Victoria Ave. Eccles M30 79 F3
Victoria Ave. Hadfield SK14 104 A5
Victoria Ave. Hazel Grove SK7 124 E3
Victoria Ave. Leigh WN2 56 E1
Victoria Ave. M'ster M9 64 C5
Victoria Ave. M'ster M20 110 A3
Victoria Ave. M'ster M19 111 A8
Victoria Ave. Swinton M27 80 A8
Victoria Ave. Whitefield M45 63 A8
Victoria Ave. Wigan WN6 37 A1
Victoria Ave E. M24, M40, M9 65 B4
Victoria Avenue Cty Prim Sch. M9 64 D5
Victoria Bridge St. M3 158 F2
Victoria Cl. Aspull WN2 38 B6
Victoria Cl. Boothstown M28 78 A6
Victoria Cl. Bramhall SK7 132 D6
Victoria Cl. Stockport SK3 170 E7
Victoria Cres. Eccles M30 79 F3
Victoria Cres. Standish WN6 36 E8
Victoria Ct. 5 Ashton-u-L OL7 166 A1
Victoria Ct. Farnworth BL4 42 C2
Victoria Ct. Horwich BL6 22 C3
Victoria Ct. M'ster M11 165 C8
Victoria Ct. Stretford M32 96 C2
Victoria Dr. M33 108 D3
Victoria Gdns. Hyde SK14 167 F4
Victoria Gdns. Shaw OL2 149 B7
Victoria Gr. Bolton BL1 142 C1
Victoria Gr. M'ster M14 110 C7
Victoria Gr. Reddish SK4 111 D5
Victoria Grange. M20 110 A4
Victoria House. Eccles M30 80 A4
Victoria House. M'ster M11 165 C8
Victoria Ind Est. WN6 37 B7
Victoria Ind Est The. M4 160 D1
Victoria La. Swinton M27 79 D8
Victoria La. Whitefield M45 62 F7
Victoria Lodge. M7 81 C5
Victoria Mews. 1 Dukinfield SK16 101 C6
Victoria Mews. Whitefield M45 & BL9 45 B2
Victoria Mkt. SK15 86 A1
Victoria Par. Rawtenstall BB4 2 E8
Victoria Par. Urmston M41 95 D2
Victoria Park Jun Sch. M32 96 D2
Victoria Pk. SK1 124 B8
Victoria Rd. Alt'ham WA15 119 D3
Victoria Rd. Alt'ham WA15 120 A6
Victoria Rd. Bolton BL1 40 D8
Victoria Rd. Dukinfield SK14 & SK16 101 C6
Victoria Rd. Eccles M30 79 E3
Victoria Rd. Eccles M6 80 A4
Victoria Rd. Garswood WN4 72 D4
Victoria Rd. Horwich BL6 22 C2
Victoria Rd. Irlam M44 93 F1
Victoria Rd. Kearsley BL4 61 A6
Victoria Rd. M'ster M16 97 D2
Victoria Rd. M'ster M19 98 F1
Victoria Rd. M'ster M14 110 B8
Victoria Rd. Newton-l-W WA12 89 C3
Victoria Rd. Platt Bridge WN2 56 A2
Victoria Rd. Sale M33 108 D3
Victoria Rd. Stockport SK1 112 B1
Victoria Rd. Stretford M32 96 D2
Victoria Rd. Urmston M41 95 B2
Victoria Rd. Wilmslow SK9 137 A6
Victoria Rd. Wythenshawe M22 121 D8
Victoria Sq. Bolton BL1 145 F7
Victoria Sq. M'ster M4 159 B2
Victoria Sq. Walkden M28 60 D3
Victoria St. Alt'ham WA14 119 D5
Victoria St. Ashton-u-L OL7 166 A1
Victoria St. Bacup OL13 3 D8
Victoria St. Blackrod BL6 21 D2
Victoria St. Boothstown M28 78 A6
Victoria St. Bury BL8 26 E7
Victoria St. Bury BL8 140 D2
Victoria St. Bury BL8 140 D3
Victoria St. Denton M34 100 F3
Victoria St. Dukinfield SK16 101 D8
Victoria St. Dukinfield SK14 102 A5
Victoria St. Failsworth M35 83 D6
Victoria St. 4 Farnworth BL4 42 B2
Victoria St. Glossop SK13 116 C8
Victoria St. Heywood OL10 29 E1
Victoria St. Leigh WN7 75 E6
Victoria St. Littleborough OL15 16 B5
Victoria St. M'ster M3 158 F2
Victoria St. M'ster M11 165 C8
Victoria St. Middleton M24 65 A8
Victoria St. Oldham OL4 67 A6
Victoria St. Oldham OL4 67 E6
Victoria St. Oldham OL8 84 F8
Victoria St. Oldham OL9 152 C8
Victoria St. Platt Bridge WN2 56 A2
Victoria St. 22 R'dale OL12 14 F1
Victoria St. 1 Radcliffe M26 44 A3
Victoria St. Ramsbottom BL0 138 B6
Victoria St. Rawtenstall BB4 2 E8
Victoria St. Shaw OL2 149 B7
Victoria St. 1 Stalybridge SK15 85 F2
Victoria St. Stalybridge SK15 86 D4
Victoria St. Westhoughton BL5 57 F8
Victoria St. Whitworth OL12 14 C8
Victoria St. Wigan WN5 54 F6
Victoria St E. OL7 166 A2
Victoria Sta. M3 159 A3
Victoria Station App. M'ster M3 & M4 159 A2
Victoria Terr. Heywood OL10 29 C4
Victoria Terr. Leigh WN2 74 F8
Victoria Terr. M'ster M12 98 F4
Victoria Terr. Milnrow OL16 32 A5
Victoria Way. Bramhall SK7 132 D6
Victoria Way. Leigh WN7 75 E7
Victoria Way. Royton OL2 48 C6
Victoria Wlk. OL9 48 C1
Victory Gr. M34 100 C7
Victory Rd. Irlam M44 105 C4
Victory Rd. Little Lever BL3 43 B4
Victory St. Bolton BL1 144 C8
Victory St. M'ster M14 98 C3
Victory Trad Est. BL3 148 A5
Vienna Rd. SK3 170 D6
Vienna Rd E. SK3 170 E6
View Cl. OL3 51 C5
View St. BL3 145 D5
Viewfield Wlk. 16 M9 157 E7
Viewlands Dr. SK9 131 D2
Vigo Ave. BL3 146 B3
Vigo St. Heywood OL10 29 E1
Vigo St. Oldham OL4 67 D5
Vigo St. 1 Wigan WN2 37 F2
Viking Cl. M11 160 F1
Viking St. Bolton BL3 42 A4
Viking St. R'dale OL11 30 C8
Villa Ave. WN6 37 A4
Villa Rd. OL8 66 F4
Village Circ. M17 96 D6
Village Ct. SK9 131 D1
Village Gn. OL3 69 B8
Village St. M7 81 C5
Village The. M31 & M41 106 F8
Village View. 2 WN7 76 B4
Village Way. SK9 131 D1
Village Wlk. 13 M11 83 C1
Villdale Ave. SK2 124 C7
Villiers Ct. M45 63 A6
Villiers Dr. OL8 153 E5
Villiers St. Ashton-u-L OL6 85 D2
Villiers St. Bury BL9 141 A3
Villiers St. Hyde SK14 167 F2
Villiers St. Salford M6 154 F4
Vinca Gr. M7 155 D6
Vincent Ave. Eccles M30 79 D4
Vincent Ave. M'ster M21 97 A1
Vincent Ave. Oldham OL4 67 C8
Vincent Ct. BL3 147 E3
Vincent St. Bolton BL1 145 D6
Vincent St. Hyde SK14 113 F8
Vincent St. Littleborough OL15 16 A6
Vincent St. M'ster M7 155 E7
Vincent St. M'ster M11 165 C8
Vincent St. Middleton M24 47 A2
Vincent St. 18 R'dale OL16 31 A5
Vincent Way. WN5 54 D8
Vine Ave. M27 80 B8
Vine Cl. Sale M33 107 C5
Vine Cl. Shaw OL2 149 B7
Vine Ct. R'dale OL16 31 B6
Vine Ct. Stretford M32 96 D1
Vine Fold. M40 65 F1
Vine Gr. Stockport SK2 124 C6
Vine Gr. Wigan WN3 150 C7
Vine Pl. OL11 139 F5
Vine St. Ashton-u-L OL6 166 C4
Vine St. Eccles M30 79 C1
Vine St. Hazel Grove SK7 124 E3
Vine St. Hindley WN2 56 D6
Vine St. M'ster M7 81 C8
Vine St. M'ster M11 & M18 99 E6
Vine St. Oldham OL9 66 B3
Vine St. Prestwich M25 63 C5
Vine St. Ramsbottom BL0 11 A4
Vine St. Wigan WN1 37 D1
Vinery Gr. M34 100 E3
Vineyard Cl. OL12 15 C7
Vineyard St. OL4 67 B7
Viola Cl. WN6 19 D2
Viola St. Bolton BL1 143 E3
Viola St. Droylsden M11 83 D2
Violet Ave. BL4 42 A1
Violet Ct. M22 121 D3
Violet Hill Ct. OL4 67 E8
Violet St. Ashton-i-M WN4 73 B2
Violet St. Droylsden M18 99 F6
Violet St. Ince-i-M WN3 151 E6
Violet St. Stockport SK2 170 F6
Violet Way. M24 65 D7
Vip Centre Ind Est. OL1 49 C1
Virgil St. M15 162 D6
Virginia Chase. SK8 131 F8
Virginia Cl. M23 120 D7
Virginia St. Bolton BL3 146 B4
Virginia St. R'dale OL11 30 E4
Virginia Way. WN5 54 C8
Viscount Dr. Alt'ham M90 & WA15 129 F7
Viscount Dr. Gatley SK8 131 D7
Viscount Rd. WN5 54 D8
Viscount St. M14 98 C3
Vista Ave. WA12 89 A4
Vista Rd. WA11 & WA12 89 A6
Vista The. M44 105 C4
Vivian St. OL11 139 E5
Vixen Cl. M21 109 E7
Voewood House. SK1 124 B8
Voltaire Ave. M6 80 B3
Vulcan Cl. WA12 89 C1
Vulcan Dr. WN1 151 D7
Vulcan Ind Est. WA12 89 D1
Vulcan Rd. WN5 54 D8
Vulcan St. OL1 & OL4 49 B1
Vyner Gr. M33 107 F6

Wadcroft Wlk. 19 M9 157 E8
Waddicor Ave. OL6 85 E6
Waddington Cl. Bury BL8 26 E2
Waddington Cl. Golborne WA3 90 F8
Waddington Fold. OL16 31 C2
Waddington Rd. BL1 142 A1
Waddington St. OL9 152 C8
Wade Bank. BL5 57 F8
Wade Hill La. OL3 & OL4 68 E8
Wade House. 8 M30 79 D1
Wade Row. OL3 69 B8
Wade St. 7 Bolton BL3 147 F3
Wade St. Middleton M24 65 D6
Wade Wlk. M11 165 A8
Wadebridge Ave. M23 120 D7
Wadebrook Gr. 4 SK9 131 D1
Wadeford Cl. M40 159 C3
Wadesmill Wlk. M13 163 B7
Wadeson Rd. M13 163 C7
Wadham Gdns. SK6 113 C5
Wadham Way. WA15 119 F1
Wadhurst Wlk. 4 M13 163 C5
Wadridge Cl. 3 BL1 25 B1
Wadsworth Cl. SK9 131 E3
Wadsworth Mews. M43 83 F1
Waggon Rd. Bolton BL2 42 D8
Waggon Rd. Mossley OL5 86 C8
Waggoners Ct. 2 M27 & M28 79 F7
Wagner St. BL1 143 D3
Wagstaffe Dr. M35 83 F7
Wagstaffe St. M24 47 A2
Wain Cl. M30 79 B2
Wain Stones Gn. SK2 124 E6
Waincliffe Ave. M20 & M21 109 D4
Wainfleet Cl. WN3 54 E2
Waingap Cres. OL12 14 D8
Waingap Rise. R'dale OL12 14 F4
Waingap Rise. Whitworth OL12 14 D7
Wainman St. M6 & M7 81 B5
Wainwright Ave. M34 99 F3
Wainwright Cl. Oldham OL4 68 A7
Wainwright Cl. Stockport SK2 124 A7
Wainwright Rd. WA14 119 C5
Wainwright St. Oldham OL8 153 E5
Wainwright St. Stalybridge SK16 85 D1
Waithlands Rd. OL16 31 B6
Wakefield Cres. Romiley SK6 113 A1
Wakefield Cres. Standish WN6 37 A6
Wakefield Dr. Kearsley M27 61 D4
Wakefield Dr. Oldham OL1 48 C1
Wakefield Rd. SK15 86 B3
Wakefield St. Golborne WA3 90 A7
Wakefield St. 2 M'ster M1 163 A7
Wakefield Wlk. M34 101 A1
Wakeling Rd. M34 112 E8
Walcot Pl. WN3 54 F2
Walcott Cl. M13 164 E5
Wald Ave. M14 110 E7
Waldeck St. 1 BL1 145 D8
Waldeck Wlk. 24 M9 64 E3
Walden Ave. OL4 49 D2
Walden Cl. M14 110 A8
Walden Cres. SK7 124 C3
Waldon Ave. SK8 122 D5
Waldon Cl. BL3 146 C4
Waldorf Cl. WN3 54 D2
Wales St. OL1 & OL4 49 C1
Walford Cl. M16 97 E4
Walford Rd. WN4 73 C3
Walk Mill Cl. OL12 15 D4
Walk The. Atherton M46 58 D3
Walk The. R'dale OL16 139 F7
Walkden Ave. WN1 & WN6 37 B2
Walkden Ave E. WN1 37 C2
Walkden High Sch. M28 60 E1
Walkden Market Pl. M28 60 D3
Walkden Rd. Walkden M27 & M28 60 D1
Walkden Rd. Worsley M28 78 E7
Walkden Sta. M28 60 D2
Walkdene Dr. M28 60 B3
Walkdens Ave. M46 58 A2
Walker Ave. Bolton BL3 147 F3
Walker Ave. Failsworth M35 84 B6
Walker Ave. Prestwich M25 & M45 63 A6
Walker Ave. Stalybridge SK15 86 C2
Walker Cl. Hyde SK14 167 F2
Walker Cl. Kearsley BL4 61 A6
Walker Fold. SK14 167 F2
Walker Fold Rd. BL1 23 D4
Walker Gn. M28 79 B5
Walker House. 9 M30 79 D1
Walker La. SK14 167 F2
Walker Rd. Failsworth OL9 65 F2
Walker Rd. Irlam M44 93 F1
Walker Rd. M'ster M9 64 E4
Walker Rd. Worsley M28 79 A4
Walker St. Bolton BL1 145 D6
Walker St. 3 Bury BL9 44 E8
Walker St. Denton M34 100 E4
Walker St. Hadfield SK14 104 A4
Walker St. Heywood OL10 29 E2
Walker St. Middleton M24 64 C7
Walker St. Oldham OL8 153 D6
Walker St. R'dale OL16 31 A7
Walker St. 4 Radcliffe M26 44 C1
Walker St. Stockport SK1 169 E1
Walker St. Westhoughton BL5 57 E8
Walker's Croft. M3 158 F2
Walker's La. OL4 68 A6
Walker's Rd. OL8 66 C2
Walkers Cl. OL3 69 B8
Walkers Ct. Farnworth BL4 60 D8
Walkers Ct. Oldham OL4 68 A6
Walkerwood Dr. SK15 86 D2
Walkway The. BL3 40 F5
Wall Hill Rd. OL3 & OL4 50 E2
Wall St. Oldham OL8 153 F5
Wall St. Salford M5 & M6 154 F2
Wall St. Shevington WN6 36 F1
Wallace Ave. M14 98 D3
Wallace La. WN1 37 E1
Wallace St. 2 OL8 66 F4
Wallasey Ave. M14 98 A1
Wallbank Dr. OL12 14 C7
Wallbank Rd. SK7 124 A1
Wallbrook Ave. WN5 53 D1
Wallbrook Cres. M38 60 B6
Wallbrook Gr. BL4 42 B2
Waller Ave. M14 110 C8
Walley St. BL1 143 E3
Wallgarth Cl. WN3 54 E2
Wallgate. WN3 & WN1 & wn6 150 B7
Wallgate Sta. WN1 150 C8
Wallingford Rd. Handforth SK9 131 C5
Wallingford Rd. Urmston M41 95 F3
Wallis St. Failsworth M40 83 C5
Wallis St. Oldham OL9 66 A4
Wallness La. M6 81 C3
Walls St. WN2 57 C2
Wallshaw Pl. OL1 67 A7
Wallshaw St. OL1 67 A7
Wallsuches. BL6 22 F4
Wallwork Cl. OL11 13 E1
Wallwork Rd. M29 77 D6
Wallwork St. Droylsden M11 99 E8
Wallwork St. Radcliffe M26 44 A4
Wallwork St. Reddish SK5 99 F2
Wallworth Ave. M18 99 D5
Wallworth Terr. SK9 136 E8
Wally Sq. M7 155 E6
Walmer Dr. SK7 124 A1
Walmer Rd. WN2 57 A5
Walmer St. M'ster M14 98 C3
Walmer St. M'ster M18 99 E6
Walmer St E. M14 98 C3
Walmersley Ct. 6 SK6 125 F6
Walmersley Golf Course. BL9 28 B8
Walmersley Old Rd. Bury BL9 27 F7
Walmersley Rd. Bury BL9 27 F6
Walmersley Rd. Failsworth M40 65 E1
Walmesley Ave. WN3 150 C6
Walmesley Dr. WN2 56 B7
Walmesley Rd. WN7 75 E5
Walmesley St. WN1 151 D7
Walmley Gr. BL3 146 C3
Walmsley Ave. OL15 15 F3
Walmsley CE Prim Sch. BL7 8 E1
Walmsley Gr. M41 95 D2
Walmsley St. 1 Bury BL8 27 B4
Walmsley St. Newton-l-W WA12 89 D4
Walmsley St. Stalybridge SK15 102 A8
Walmsley St. Stockport SK5 169 F3
Walney Rd. Wigan WN3 54 D2
Walney Rd. Wythenshawe M22 121 D4
Walnut Ave. Bury BL9 141 C3
Walnut Ave. Oldham OL4 67 D8
Walnut Ave. Wigan WN1 37 D2
Walnut Cl. Hyde SK14 102 A2
Walnut Cl. Kearsley M27 61 D4
Walnut Cl. Wilmslow SK9 137 E8
Walnut Gr. Leigh WN7 75 F8
Walnut Gr. Sale M33 108 A4
Walnut Rd. Partington M31 105 D3
Walnut Rd. Worsley M28 79 A4
Walnut St. Bolton BL1 143 F2
Walnut St. 2 M'ster M18 99 D5
Walnut Tree Rd. SK3 123 A8
Walnut Wlk. M32 96 C1
Walpole Ave. WN3 54 F3
Walpole St. OL16 31 A7
Walsall St. M6 81 A5
Walsden Est. OL14 6 B7
Walsden St. M11 83 C2
Walsh Ave. M9 64 D2
Walsh Cl. WA12 89 C5
Walsh Fold. BL7 9 D2
Walsh House. M46 58 D4
Walsh St. Horwich BL6 22 B4
Walsh St. Oldham OL9 152 B6
Walshaw Brook Cl. BL8 26 F4
Walshaw Dr. M27 79 F7
Walshaw La. BL8 26 F4
Walshaw Rd. BL8 27 B4
Walshaw Wlk. BL8 26 F5
Walshe St. BL9 140 D2
Walsingham Ave. M'ster M20 109 F4
Walsingham Ave. Middleton M24 65 A5
Walter Scott Ave. WN1 37 B5
Walter Scott St. 3 OL1 67 B8
Walter St. Ashton-i-M WN4 73 D4
Walter St. Droylsden M18 99 E6
Walter St. Leigh WN7 75 B5
Walter St. M'ster M16 97 C4
Walter St. M'ster M9 157 D8
Walter St. 3 Oldham OL1 153 F6
Walter St. Prestwich M25 62 F4
Walter St. Radcliffe M26 43 F6
Walter St. Walkden M28 60 D2
Walter St. Wigan WN5 54 D6
Waltham Ave. Glazebury WA3 92 C7
Waltham Ave. Shevington WN6 36 F2
Waltham Dr. SK8 132 B6
Waltham Gdns. M26 43 E5
Waltham Rd. M16 97 E1
Waltham St. OL4 & OL8 67 C4
Walthew House La. WN5 36 C2
Walthew La. Platt Bridge WN2 56 A2
Walton Cl. Heywood OL10 46 D8
Walton Cl. Middleton M24 46 C1
Walton Ct. BL3 147 F4
Walton Dr. Bury BL9 27 E8
Walton Dr. Marple SK6 125 D7
Walton Hall. SK5 99 D2
Walton Hall Dr. SK5 99 D1
Walton House. M35 83 F8
Walton Pl. BL4 60 E7
Walton Rd. Alt'ham WA14 119 B5
Walton Rd. Culcheth WA3 91 F3
Walton Rd. M'ster M9 64 D5
Walton Rd. Sale M33 107 F2
Walton St. Adlington PR7 21 A6
Walton St. Ashton-u-L OL7 84 F5
Walton St. Atherton M46 58 E4
Walton St. Heywood OL10 29 D1
Walton St. 1 Middleton M24 47 A2
Walton St. Stockport SK1 170 F7
Walton Way. M34 101 B1
Walworth Cl. M26 61 C7
Walwyn Cl. M32 96 E1
Wanborough Cl. WN7 75 F7
Wandsworth Ave. M11 83 D2
Wanley Wlk. 12 M9 64 E3
Wansbeck Cl. M32 96 E1
Wansbeck Lodge. M32 96 E1
Wansfell Wlk. M40 160 D2
Wansford St. M14 98 A3
Wanstead Ave. M9 65 B3
Wapping St. BL1 143 D2
War Office Rd. OL11 29 E6
Warbeck Cl. Hindley WN2 56 E3
Warbeck Cl. Reddish SK5 100 A2
Warbeck Rd. M40 65 D2
Warbreck Gr. M33 108 D3
Warburton Bridge Rd. WA13 & WA3 105 A1
Warburton Cl. Alt'ham WA15 129 D6
Warburton Cl. Lymm WA13 117 A4
Warburton Cl. Romiley SK6 113 A1
Warburton Dr. WA15 129 D6
Warburton La. Partington M31 & WA13 105 E2
Warburton La. Partington M31 105 F4
Warburton Pl. 12 M46 58 D3
Warburton Rd. SK9 131 D4
Warburton St. Bolton BL1 143 F2
Warburton St. Eccles M30 79 E1
Warburton St. 3 M'ster M20 110 B3
Warburton St. Salford M5 161 B6
Warburton View. WA3 105 A2
Warcock Rd. OL4 67 C7
Ward La. Diggle OL3 51 D3
Ward La. Disley SK12 135 F4
Ward Rd. M43 84 B1
Ward St. Bredbury SK6 112 F3
Ward St. Hindley WN2 56 E7
Ward St. Hyde SK14 167 E2
Ward St. M'ster M9 64 C2
Ward St. 1 M'ster M20 110 B3
Ward St. M'ster M40 & M9 157 F8
Ward St. Oldham OL9 152 C7
Ward St. Oldham OL1 153 D8
Ward St. Stockport SK1 124 A7
Warden La. M40 83 B6
Warden St. M40 83 B6
Wardend Cl. M38 60 A6
Wardens Bank. BL5 57 E5
Wardle Brook Ave. SK14 102 D3
Wardle Brook Wlk. SK14 102 D3
Wardle Cl. Radcliffe M26 43 E5
Wardle Cl. Stretford M32 96 E2
Wardle Ct. M33 108 C4
Wardle Edge. OL12 15 B4
Wardle Fold. OL12 15 C7
Wardle Gdns. OL12 15 C3
Wardle High Sch. OL12 15 D5
Wardle Rd. R'dale OL12 15 C4
Wardle Rd. Sale M33 108 C4
Wardle St. Bacup OL13 3 D8
Wardle St. Bolton BL2 148 C5
Wardle St. Littleborough OL15 16 A6
Wardle St. M'ster M10 & M40 160 E3
Wardley Ave. M'ster M21 97 E1
Wardley Ave. M'ster M16 & M21 109 E8
Wardley Ave. Walkden M28 60 B3
Wardley CE (VC) Prim Sch. M27 61 E2
Wardley Hall La. M28 79 A8
Wardley Hall Rd. M27 & M28 61 B1
Wardley House. M6 80 C4
Wardley Ind Est. Swinton M27 61 C1
Wardley Ind Est. Swinton M28 79 C8
Wardley Rd. M29 77 D8
Wardley Sq. M29 77 D8
Wardley St. Swinton M27 79 F8
Wardley St. Wigan WN5 54 B6
Wardlow Ave. 25 Gamesley SK13 171 D1
Wardlow Ave. Wigan WN5 36 A1
Wardlow Fold. 28 SK13 171 D1
Wardlow Gdns. 27 SK13 171 D1
Wardlow Gr. 29 SK13 171 D1
Wardlow Mews. SK13 171 D1
Wardlow St. BL3 146 B4
Wardlow Wlk. 26 SK13 171 D1
Wardour St. Atherton M46 58 C2
Wardour St. Atherton M46 58 D2
Wards Pl. 3 WN7 76 B4
Wardsend Wlk. 13 M15 162 D6
Wareham Gr. M30 79 C3
Wareham St. M8 64 B1
Wareing St. M29 76 F8
Wareing Way. BL3 145 E6
Wareings Yd. 5 OL11 31 A4
Warfield Wlk. 30 M9 64 E3
Warford Ave. SK12 134 A2
Warford La. WA16 136 B1
Warford St. M4 159 B3
Warford Terr. WA16 136 B2
Wargrave CE Prim Sch. WA12 89 C1
Wargrave House Sch. WA12 89 D1
Wargrave Mews. WA12 89 C1
Wargrave Rd. WA12 89 C2
Warham St. SK9 137 B7
Warke The. M28 78 F6
Warlands End Gate. OL14 6 F5
Warley Cl. SK8 122 E6
Warley Gr. SK16 101 C8

236 War – Wer

Warley Rd. M16 .... 97 A3
Warley St. OL15 .... 16 B5
Warlingham Cl. BL8 .... 27 B1
Warlow Crest. OL3 .... 69 A4
Warlow Dr. Leigh WN7 .... 57 D1
Warlow Dr. Uppermill OL3 .... 69 A4
Warmbly Gdns. OL8 .... 66 D1
Warmington Dr. M12 .... 164 E6
Warminster Gr. WN3 .... 54 D2
Warmley Rd. M23 .... 120 D8
Warncliffe St. 7 WN5 .... 54 D5
Warne Ave. M43 .... 84 C2
Warner Wlk. 9 M11 .... 160 F1
Warnford Cl. M40 .... 83 D4
Warnford St. 3 WN1 .... 37 C2
Warp Wlk. 3 M4 .... 159 C1
Warre St. OL6 .... 166 B3
Warren Ave. SK8 .... 122 D5
Warren Bank. M9 .... 64 D3
Warren Cl. Atherton M46 .... 58 E5
Warren Cl. Denton M34 .... 100 D2
Warren Cl. Poynton SK12 .... 133 B4
Warren Cl. Stockport SK7 .... 123 D2
Warren Dr. Alt'ham WA15 .... 129 D7
Warren Dr. Bacup OL13 .... 4 C8
Warren Dr. Newton-l-W WA12 .... 89 F4
Warren Dr. Swinton M27 .... 79 D5
Warren Hey. SK9 .... 137 E8
Warren La. OL8 .... 67 B4
Warren Lea. Poynton SK12 .... 133 E5
Warren Lea. Romiley SK6 .... 114 B2
Warren Park Prim Sch. SK1 .... 112 A2
Warren Rd. Cheadle SK8 .... 123 B2
Warren Rd. Stockport SK3 .... 170 E6
Warren Rd. Stretford M17 .... 96 B6
Warren Rd. Walkden M28 .... 60 E3
Warren St. 2 Bury BL8 .... 27 B1
Warren St. M'ster M9 .... 64 C2
Warren St. M'ster M7 .... 155 F8
Warren St. Stockport SK1 .... 169 F2
Warren Wood Prim Sch. SK2 .... 125 A6
Warrener St. M33 .... 108 D4
Warrington La. Lymm WA13 .... 117 E2
Warrington La. Wigan WN1 .... 151 D7
Warrington Rd. Abram WA3 & WN2 .... 74 B7
Warrington Rd. Ashton-i-M WN4 .... 73 B2
Warrington Rd. Fowley Common WA3 & WN7 .. 92 C5
Warrington Rd. Golborne WA12 .... 90 A6
Warrington Rd. Ince-i-M WN1,WN2,WN3,WN5 55 E5
Warrington Rd. Leigh WN7 .... 76 B3
Warrington Rd. M'ster M9 .... 64 C4
Warrington Rd. Platt Bridge WN2 .... 56 A1
Warrington Rd. Wigan WN3 & WN5 .... 54 F3
Warrington St. Ashton-u-L OL6 .... 166 B3
Warrington St. 9 Oldham OL4 .... 67 E6
Warrington St. Stalybridge SK15 .... 86 B1
Warsall Rd. M22 .... 121 E7
Warslow Dr. M33 .... 108 E1
Warsop Ave. M22 .... 121 E5
Warstead Wlk. 8 M13 .... 163 C5
Warth Fold Rd. BL9 & M26 .... 44 C6
Warth Rd. BL9 .... 44 D7
Warthenbury Wlk. M13 .... 98 E3
Warton Cl. Bramhall SK7 .... 133 A7
Warton Cl. Bury BL8 .... 26 F1
Warton Dr. M23 .... 121 A5
Warwick Ave. Ashton-i-M WN4 .... 73 D2
Warwick Ave. Denton M34 .... 100 F1
Warwick Ave. M'ster M20 .... 109 F4
Warwick Ave. Newton-l-W WA12 .... 89 E2
Warwick Ave. Prestwich M45 .... 63 B7
Warwick Ave. Swinton M27 .... 61 D2
Warwick Cl. Bury BL8 .... 27 B4
Warwick Cl. Cheadle SK8 .... 123 A4
Warwick Cl. Dukinfield SK16 .... 101 C6
Warwick Cl. Glossop SK13 .... 116 F8
Warwick Cl. Middleton M24 .... 65 A5
Warwick Cl. Prestwich M45 .... 63 A7
Warwick Cl. Ramsbottom BL8 .... 11 A1
Warwick Cl. Reddish SK4 .... 169 D4
Warwick Cl. Shaw OL2 .... 48 F7
Warwick Ct. M'ster M16 .... 97 A3
Warwick Ct. M'ster SK4 .... 168 C3
Warwick Dr. Alt'ham WA15 .... 119 F1
Warwick Dr. Hazel Grove SK7 .... 124 D1
Warwick Dr. Hindley WN2 .... 56 F6
Warwick Dr. Sale M33 .... 108 D4
Warwick Dr. Urmston M41 .... 95 B3
Warwick Gdns. BL3 .... 146 B2
Warwick Gr. M34 .... 100 C8
Warwick House. 2 M'ster M19 .... 99 A2
Warwick House. Sale M33 .... 108 D4
Warwick Mall. SK8 .... 122 D6
Warwick Rd. Alt'ham WA15 .... 119 E1
Warwick Rd. Ashton-u-L OL6 .... 85 C5
Warwick Rd. Aspull WN2 .... 38 C5
Warwick Rd. Atherton M46 .... 58 C5
Warwick Rd. Failsworth M35 .... 84 A5
Warwick Rd. Irlam M44 .... 105 D5
Warwick Rd. M'ster M16, M17 97 A4
Warwick Rd. M'ster M21 .... 97 B1
Warwick Rd. M'ster SK4 .... 168 C3
Warwick Rd. Middleton M24 .... 65 B6
Warwick Rd. Radcliffe M26 .... 43 F6
Warwick Rd. Romiley SK6 .... 113 A2
Warwick Rd. Tyldesley M29 .... 59 A2
Warwick Rd. Walkden M28 .... 60 C1
Warwick Rd S. M16 .... 97 A3
Warwick St. Adlington PR7 .... 20 F6
Warwick St. Bolton BL1 .... 143 E4
Warwick St. Leigh WN7 .... 76 E3
Warwick St. M'ster M1 & M4 & M60 .... 159 B2
Warwick St. M'ster M15 .... 162 F5
Warwick St. Oldham OL9 .... 66 C4
Warwick St. Oldham OL9 .... 152 C5
Warwick St. Prestwich M25 .... 62 F4
Warwick St. R'dale OL12 .... 15 B2
Warwick St. Swinton M27 .... 61 F1
Warwick Terr. 15 SK16 .... 166 B1
Wasdale Ave. Bolton BL2 .... 25 F1
Wasdale Ave. Urmston M41 .... 95 B3
Wasdale Dr. Gatley SK8 .... 122 B3
Wasdale Dr. Middleton M24 .... 46 E2
Wasdale Rd. WN4 .... 73 A8
Wasdale St. OL11 .... 30 C1
Wasdale Terr. SK15 .... 86 A4
Wasdale Wlk. 3 OL1 .... 67 A8
Wash Brook. OL9 .... 66 B4
Wash Fold. BL8 .... 27 B5
Wash La. Bury BL9 .... 141 B2
Wash La. Leigh WN7 .... 76 C5
Wash Terr. BL8 .... 27 B5
Washacre. BL5 .... 57 F7
Washacre Cl. BL5 .... 57 F7
Washacre Cty Prim Sch. BL5 .... 57 F7
Washbrook Ave. M28 .... 60 B1
Washbrook Ct. OL9 .... 66 B4
Washbrook Dr. M32 .... 96 B2
Washbrook House. 12 M6 .... 154 F3
Washburn Cl. BL5 .... 39 F2
Washford Dr. M23 .... 120 D8
Washington Ct. 6 BL9 .... 140 F3
Washington St. 3 Bolton BL3 .... 144 C6
Washington St. Oldham OL9 .... 152 C7
Washway Rd. Sale M33 .... 107 F2
Washway Rd. Sale M33 .... 108 A4
Washwood Cl. M28 & M38 .... 60 B6
Wasnidge Wlk. M15 .... 162 F5
Wasp Ave. OL11 .... 31 A3
Wastdale Ave. BL9 .... 45 A3
Wastdale Rd. M23 .... 121 A4
Waste St. 2 OL1 .... 67 A7
Wastwater St. 5 OL1 .... 49 A1
Watburn Rd. SK12 .... 127 D1
Watchgate Cl. M24 .... 46 D3
Water Gate. OL3 .... 69 B8
Water Grove Rd. SK16 .... 101 F7
Water La. Droylsden M43 .... 83 E1
Water La. Edenfield BL0 .... 1 D2
Water La. Farnworth BL4 .... 60 E7
Water La. Hollingworth SK14 .... 103 D5
Water La. Milnrow OL16 .... 32 A5
Water La. Radcliffe M26 .... 43 F3
Water La. Wilmslow SK9 .... 137 A7
Water Lane St. Radcliffe M26 .... 43 F3
Water Lane St. 4 Radcliffe M26 .... 44 A4
Water Rd. SK15 .... 85 F2
Water"s Reach. SK6 .... 134 E7
Water St. Adlington PR6 .... 21 A6
Water St. Ashton-u-L OL6 .... 166 B3
Water St. Atherton M46 .... 58 D3
Water St. Bolton BL7 .... 8 D2
Water St. Bolton BL1 .... 145 F7
Water St. Denton M34 .... 100 F7
Water St. Glossop SK13 .... 104 E2
Water St. Hyde SK14 .... 167 D2
Water St. M'ster M9 .... 157 D8
Water St. M'ster M3 .... 158 E1
Water St. M'ster M15 & M3 .... 162 D8
Water St. M'ster M12 .... 163 C8
Water St. 5 Middleton M24 .... 46 F1
Water St. Newton-l-W WA12 .... 89 C4
Water St. R'dale OL16 .... 31 A7
Water St. Radcliffe M26 .... 44 A3
Water St. Ramsbottom BL0 .... 138 B5
Water St. Royton OL2 .... 49 A4
Water St. Stalybridge SK15 .... 86 A2
Water St. Stockport SK1 .... 169 F3
Water St. Whitworth OL12 .... 14 C8
Water St. Wigan WN1 .... 150 C8
Water's Edge. BL4 .... 42 A2
Water's Nook Rd. BL5 .... 58 A8
Water's Reach. M17 .... 96 F6
Waterbarn La. OL13 .... 3 B8
Waterbeck Cl. WN1 .... 37 F1
Waterbridge. Worsley M28 .... 79 A5
Watercroft. OL11 .... 13 D1
Waterdale Cl. M28 .... 78 B6
Waterdale Dr. M45 .... 63 A8
Waterfield Cl. BL9 .... 27 F7
Waterfield Way. M35 .... 84 A6
Waterfold La. BL9 .... 141 C1
Waterfoot Cotts. SK14 .... 103 A4
Waterfoot Cty Prim Sch. BB4 2 F8
Waterford Ave. M'ster M20 .... 109 D3
Waterford Ave. Romiley SK6 .... 113 F2
Waterford Pl. SK8 .... 131 B8
Waterfront Quay. M5 .... 161 A7
Watergate. M34 .... 100 C8
Watergate Dr. BL5 .... 59 C7
Watergate La. Atherton BL4 & BL5 .... 59 C7
Watergate La. Atherton BL4 & BL5 .... 59 C8
Watergate Milne Ct. 6 OL4 67 D8
Waterhouse Cl. OL12 .... 15 C6
Waterhouse Rd. M18 .... 99 E4
Waterhouse St. OL12 .... 139 F8
Waterloo Ct. Bury BL9 .... 44 E8
Waterloo Ct. 3 M'ster M20 .... 110 A5
Waterloo Pk. SK1 .... 112 A1
Waterloo Prim Sch. OL7 .... 85 A5
Waterloo Rd. Ashton-u-L OL6 .... 85 B5
Waterloo Rd. Bramhall SK7 .... 132 F8
Waterloo Rd. M'ster M8 & M9 64 C1
Waterloo Rd. M'ster M7 & M8 .... 155 F6
Waterloo Rd. Poynton SK12 .... 134 A2
Waterloo Rd. Romiley SK6 .... 113 E2
Waterloo Rd. Stalybridge SK15 .... 86 A2
Waterloo Rd. Stockport SK1 .... 169 F1
Waterloo St. Ashton-u-L OL6 .... 85 D4
Waterloo St. Bolton BL1 .... 143 F1
Waterloo St. Bury BL8 .... 140 D2
Waterloo St. M'ster M8 & M9 156 C8
Waterloo St. M'ster M1 .... 163 A8
Waterloo St. Oldham OL1 & OL4 .... 67 A6
Waterloo St. 3 Wigan WN6 .... 37 A1
Waterman View. OL16 .... 31 C8
Watermans Cl. BL6 .... 22 C4
Watermead Cl. SK3 .... 123 E4
Watermede. WN5 .... 53 E3
Watermeetings La. SK6 .... 113 F1
Watermill Cl. OL16 .... 31 D6
Watermill Ct. OL7 .... 85 A5
Watermillock Gdns. BL1 .... 143 F4
Waterpark Rd. M7 .... 155 E8
Waters Meeting Rd. Bolton BL1 .... 25 A2
Waters Meeting Rd. Bolton BL1 .... 143 F3
Waters Reach. Poynton SK12 133 F5
Waters Reach. Wigan WN1 .... 151 F8
Watersedge Cl. SK8 .... 123 B3
Watersfield Cl. SK8 .... 131 F8
Watersheddings Prim Sch. OL1 .... 49 C1
Watersheddings St. OL4 .... 49 D1
Waterside. Hadfield SK14 .... 104 A6
Waterside. Hattersley SK14 .... 102 D2
Waterside. Marple SK6 .... 125 F5
Waterside. Stretford M17 .... 96 F6
Waterside Ave. 5 Marple SK6 .... 125 F5
Waterside Cl. Hattersley SK14 .... 102 D2
Waterside Cl. M'ster M21 .... 109 D4
Waterside Cl. Radcliffe M26 .... 44 D4
Waterside Cotts. OL3 .... 69 C4
Waterside Ct. SK14 .... 102 D2
Waterside La. OL16 .... 31 B8
Waterside Rd. Disley SK12 .... 135 F7
Waterside Rd. Ramsbottom BL0 & BL8 & BL9 .. 11 C3
Waterside Trad Est. 1 WN7 76 B4
Waterside Wlk. 4 SK14 .... 102 D2
Waterslea. M30 .... 79 C2
Waterslea Dr. BL1 .... 40 F7
Watersmead Cl. BL1 .... 143 F2
Watersmead St. BL1 .... 143 F2
Waterson Ave. M40 .... 83 A7
Waterton Ave. OL5 .... 68 B2
Waterton La. OL5 .... 68 B2
Waterview Cl. OL16 .... 32 B3
Waterview Pk. WN7 .... 75 E4
Waterworks Rd. OL4 .... 49 E1
Watfield Wlk. 5 M9 .... 157 D7
Watford Ave. M14 .... 98 B2
Watford Bridge Ind Est. SK12 .... 127 D1
Watford Bridge Rd. SK12 .... 127 D1
Watford Cl. 10 BL1 .... 143 E2
Watford La. SK12 .... 127 C2
Watford Rd. M'ster M19 .... 111 A6
Watford Rd. New Mills SK12 127 C2
Watkin Ave. SK14 .... 171 E4
Watkin Cl. M13 .... 163 C6
Watkin St. Hyde SK14 .... 102 A5
Watkin St. M'ster M3 .... 158 D3
Watkin St. R'dale OL16 .... 31 B4
Watkin St. Wigan WN1 .... 150 C8
Watkins Dr. M25 & M8 .... 63 F3
Watling St. Bolton BL8 .... 26 B7
Watling St. Bury BL8 .... 26 F1
Watlington Cl. OL1 .... 49 D3
Watson Ave. Ashton-i-M WN4 73 C3
Watson Ave. Golborne WA3 .... 73 F1
Watson Gdns. OL12 .... 14 D2
Watson Rd. BL4 .... 59 F8
Watson Sq. SK1 .... 169 F1
Watson St. Denton M34 .... 101 B3
Watson St. Eccles M30 .... 79 C2
Watson St. M'ster M2 .... 162 F8
Watson St. Oldham OL4 .... 67 C8
Watson St. Radcliffe M26 .... 44 A4
Watson St. Swinton M27 .... 79 F8
Watts St. Horwich BL6 .... 22 C2
Watts St. M'ster M19 .... 111 B8
Watts St. Oldham OL8 .... 66 D2
Watts St. Oldham OL9 .... 152 B7
Watts St. 1 R'dale OL12 .... 31 A8
Watts St. R'dale OL12 .... 139 F8
Waugh Ave. M35 .... 83 F7
Wavell Dr. M45 .... 45 A1
Wavell Rd. M22 .... 121 D2
Waveney Dr. WA14 .... 119 C6
Waveney Rd. Shaw OL2 .... 149 A8
Waveney Rd. Wythenshawe M22 .... 121 E4
Waverley. 23 OL12 .... 139 E8
Waverley Ave. Kearsley BL4 .... 60 F6
Waverley Ave. Stretford M32 .... 96 F3
Waverley Cres. M43 .... 84 A3
Waverley Ct. WN3 .... 54 D3
Waverley Dr. SK8 .... 132 B7
Waverley Gr. WN7 .... 76 D6
Waverley Rd. Bolton BL1 .... 143 E3
Waverley Rd. Golborne WA3 .... 74 D1
Waverley Rd. Hindley WN2 .... 56 C5
Waverley Rd. Hyde SK14 .... 113 D8
Waverley Rd. M'ster M9 .... 157 F7
Waverley Rd. Middleton M24 .... 47 A3
Waverley Rd. Pendlebury M27 80 C7
Waverley Rd. Sale M33 .... 108 C6
Waverley Rd. Stockport SK3 .... 123 C7
Waverley Rd. Walkden M28 .... 60 B1
Waverley Rd W. M9 .... 157 F7
Waverley Sq. BL4 .... 60 C6
Waverley St. Oldham OL1 .... 49 C1
Waverley St. R'dale OL11 .... 30 C1
Waverton Ave. SK4 .... 111 D7
Waverton Rd. M14 .... 98 A1
Wavertree Ave. M46 .... 58 C4
Wavertree Ct. 6 BL1 .... 145 E8
Wavertree Rd. M9 .... 64 C4
Wayfarers Dr. WA12 .... 89 E2
Wayfarers Way. M27 & M28 .... 79 F7
Wayfaring. BL5 .... 39 F2
Wayford Wlk. M9 .... 156 C7
Wayland Rd. M18 .... 99 E4
Wayland Rd S. M18 & SK5 .... 99 D3
Wayne Cl. M35 & M43 .... 84 C4
Wayne St. M11 .... 99 E8
Wayoh Croft. BL7 .... 9 D6
Wayside Dr. SK12 .... 133 C4
Wayside Gr. M28 .... 60 E4
Weald Cl. M13 .... 163 C6
Wealdstone Gr. BL2 .... 25 B2
Weardale Rd. M9 .... 64 B5
Wearhead Cl. WA3 .... 89 F7
Wearhead Row. M6 .... 154 F1
Wearish La. BL5 .... 57 C6
Weaste Dr. M38 .... 60 B4
Weaste Dr. M5 & M6 .... 154 D3
Weaste La. M5 & M6 .... 154 D3
Weaste Rd. M5 .... 154 D2
Weaste Trad Est. M5 .... 154 D2
Weatherall St N. M7 & M8 .... 155 F7
Weatherley Dr. SK6 .... 125 D6
Weaver Ave. M28 .... 60 A2
Weaver Ct. M15 .... 162 D6
Weaver Dr. BL9 .... 27 F8
Weaver Gr. WN7 .... 75 C4
Weaver House. 5 M7 .... 81 C5
Weaver Rd. WA3 .... 92 A2
Weaver Wlk. 5 M11 .... 99 D7
Weaverham Cl. 2 M13 .... 98 F3
Weaverham Way. SK9 .... 131 E4
Weaverham Wlk. M33 .... 108 E3
Weavers Ct. Bolton BL3 .... 145 E5
Weavers Ct. 11 Middleton M24 .... 46 F1
Weavers Gn. BL4 .... 60 D8
Weavers La. SK7 .... 132 D6
Weavers Rd. M24 .... 46 F1
Webb Gr. SK14 .... 102 F1
Webb La. SK1 .... 124 A8
Webb St. Bury BL8 .... 140 D3
Webb St. Horwich BL6 .... 22 C3
Webb Wlk. SK14 .... 102 F1
Webdale Dr. M40 .... 83 A7
Weber Dr. BL3 .... 145 D5
Webster Gr. M25 .... 62 F2
Webster Prim Sch. M15 .... 98 A4
Webster St. Bolton BL3 .... 148 B5
Webster St. Mossley OL5 .... 68 C2
Webster St. Oldham OL8 .... 153 F5
Webster's St. WN2 .... 56 A3
Wedgewood Dr. WN6 .... 36 D3
Wedgewood St. M10 & M40 160 F4
Wedgwood Rd. M27 .... 62 C2
Wedhurst St. OL4 .... 67 C7
Wedneshough. SK14 .... 103 C5
Weedall Ave. M5 .... 161 A6
Weeder Sq. OL2 .... 49 E8
Weedon Ave. WA12 .... 89 B5
Weedon St. OL16 .... 31 B8
Weeton Ave. BL2 .... 42 F7
Weft Wlk. 5 M4 .... 159 C1
Weint The. WA3 .... 105 B3
Weir Rd. OL16 .... 31 E7
Weir St. Failsworth M35 .... 83 E7
Weir St. M'ster M15 .... 162 E5
Welbeck Ave. Failsworth OL9 65 D3
Welbeck Ave. Littleborough OL15 .... 16 A6
Welbeck Ave. Newton-l-W WA12 .... 89 D2
Welbeck Ave. Urmston M41 .... 95 F3
Welbeck Cl. Milnrow OL16 .... 31 D6
Welbeck Cl. Whitefield M45 .... 44 F2
Welbeck Gr. M7 .... 155 E7
Welbeck House. 4 OL7 .... 166 A2
Welbeck Rd. Ashton-i-M WN4 73 C4
Welbeck Rd. Bolton BL1 .... 144 A8
Welbeck Rd. Eccles M30 .... 79 E4
Welbeck Rd. Hyde SK14 .... 167 F2
Welbeck Rd. R'dale OL16 .... 31 B4
Welbeck Rd. 1 Reddish SK5 111 F8
Welbeck Rd. Swinton M28 .... 79 B6
Welbeck Rd. Wigan WN3 .... 54 E3
Welbeck St. M18 .... 99 E6
Welbeck St N. OL6 .... 166 A2
Welbeck St S. OL7 .... 166 A2
Welbeck Terr. OL7 .... 166 A2
Welburn Ave. M22 .... 121 E3
Welburn St. OL11 .... 139 F5
Welbury Rd. M23 .... 108 F1
Welby St. M13 .... 98 D4
Welch Hill St. WN7 .... 75 E4
Welch Rd. SK14 .... 167 F4
Welcomb Cl. SK6 .... 112 F4
Welcomb St. M11 .... 165 B7
Welcomb Wlk. M45 .... 62 F7
Welcome Par. OL8 .... 67 D3
Welcroft St. SK1 .... 170 F8
Weld Rd. M20 .... 110 D7
Weldon Ave. BL3 .... 146 A2
Weldon Cres. SK3 .... 123 E4
Weldon Dr. M9 .... 64 D5
Weldon Gr. WN1 .... 37 E2
Weldon Rd. WA14 .... 119 D6
Welfold House. 3 OL4 .... 67 B5
Welford Ave. WA3 .... 90 C7
Welford Cl. SK9 .... 137 E8
Welford Gn. SK5 .... 111 F5
Welford Rd. M9 .... 63 F3
Welford St. M6 .... 81 B4
Welkin Rd. SK6 .... 112 C3
Welkin Rd Ind Est. SK6 .... 112 C3
Well Ct. WN6 .... 19 E1
Well Gate. SK13 .... 104 E2
Well Gr. M45 .... 44 E2
Well Green Prim Sch. WA15 .... 120 C2
Well i' th' La. OL11 .... 31 A4
Well La. M45 .... 44 F2
Well Mead. SK6 .... 112 E3
Well Meadow. SK14 .... 167 D4
Well Meadow La. OL3 .... 69 C8
Well Row. SK14 .... 115 A8
Well St. Ainsworth BL2 .... 26 C1
Well St. Bolton BL1 .... 148 A7
Well St. Heywood OL10 .... 29 E1
Well St. M'ster M4 & M60 .... 159 A2
Well St. 6 R'dale OL11 .... 31 A5
Well St. Tyldesley M29 .... 77 A8
Well St. Wigan WN1 .... 151 E8
Well St N. BL0 .... 1 C2
Well St W. BL0 .... 138 B5
Well-i-Hole Rd. OL3 & OL5 .... 68 F4
Wellacre Ave. M41 .... 94 D2
Wellacre High Sch. M41 .... 94 D2
Wellacre Inf Sch. M41 .... 94 D2
Wellacre Jun Sch. M41 .... 94 D2
Welland Ave. OL10 .... 29 A3
Welland Cl. M15 .... 162 D6
Welland Ct. 4 M15 .... 162 D6
Welland Rd. Ashton-i-M WN4 73 E5
Welland Rd. Shaw OL2 .... 149 A8
Welland St. Droylsden M11 .... 99 D8
Welland St. Reddish SK5 .... 99 F1
Welland The. BL5 .... 57 E8
Wellbank. SK15 .... 102 D8
Wellbank Ave. OL6 .... 85 E6
Wellbank Cl. OL8 .... 67 A4
Wellbank St. BL8 .... 26 F6
Wellbank View. OL12 .... 13 F2
Wellbeck Rd. WN4 .... 73 C5
Wellbrow Terr. OL12 .... 14 D2
Wellbrow Wlk. 10 M9 .... 64 E3
Wellcross Rd. WN8 .... 53 B6
Wellens Way. M24 .... 64 C7
Weller Ave. M'ster M21 .... 109 D7
Weller Ave. Poynton SK12 .... 133 D2
Weller Cl. SK12 .... 133 D2
Weller Gdns. M21 .... 109 D7
Wellesbourne Dr. M23 .... 120 F7
Wellesley Ave. M18 .... 99 D6
Wellesley Cl. WN5 .... 54 E8
Wellfield. SK6 .... 113 C4
Wellfield Cl. BL9 .... 44 E6
Wellfield Gdns. WA15 .... 120 C3
Wellfield Inf Sch. M33 .... 107 F6
Wellfield Jun Sch. M33 .... 107 F6
Wellfield La. WA15 .... 120 C3
Wellfield Pl. 5 OL11 .... 31 A5
Wellfield Rd. Bolton BL3 .... 144 C5
Wellfield Rd. Culcheth WA3 .... 91 F4
Wellfield Rd. Hindley WN2 .... 57 A4
Wellfield Rd. M'ster M8 .... 156 A8
Wellfield Rd. Stockport SK2 124 C6
Wellfield Rd. Wigan WN6 .... 37 A3
Wellfield Rd. Wythenshawe M23 .... 121 A7
Wellfield St. OL11 .... 31 A5
Wellgate Ave. M19 .... 111 B8
Wellgreen Cl. WA15 .... 120 C3
Wellgreen Lodge. WA15 .... 120 C3
Wellham Rd. WN3 .... 55 B3
Wellhead Cl. M15 .... 162 F5
Wellhouse Dr. M40 .... 65 C3
Welling Rd. M40 .... 83 E8
Welling St. 20 BL2 .... 25 B1
Wellington Ave. M16 .... 97 D2
Wellington Cl. Newton-l-W WA12 .... 89 A3
Wellington Cl. Sale M33 .... 108 C6
Wellington Clough. 4 OL7 .... 85 A6
Wellington Cres. M16 .... 97 C3
Wellington Ct. 6 Bury BL8 .... 27 B1
Wellington Ct. Oldham OL8 .... 66 D4
Wellington Ctr. SK16 .... 166 C2
Wellington Gdns. WA12 .... 89 A3
Wellington Gr. Ince-i-M WN3 .... 151 D5
Wellington Gr. M'ster M15 .... 162 D6
Wellington Gr. Stockport SK2 .... 170 F7
Wellington Lodge. OL15 .... 16 B6
Wellington Mill. SK3 .... 169 E1
Wellington Pl. Alt'ham WA14 .... 119 D4
Wellington Pl. 13 R'dale OL16 .... 31 A8
Wellington Rd. Alt'ham WA15 .... 119 F6
Wellington Rd. Ashton-u-L OL6 .... 166 B3
Wellington Rd. Atherton M46 58 F5
Wellington Rd. Bury BL9 .... 140 F1
Wellington Rd. Eccles M30 .... 79 F2
Wellington Rd. Edgworth BL7 .. 9 D4
Wellington Rd. High Lane SK7 .... 134 B8
Wellington Rd. M'ster M16 .... 97 E2
Wellington Rd. M'ster M20 .... 110 C8
Wellington Rd. M'ster M8 .... 156 B8
Wellington Rd. Oldham OL8 .... 153 E5
Wellington Rd. Swinton M27 .... 79 F8
Wellington Rd. Uppermill OL3 .... 69 B6
Wellington Rd N. M19 & SK3 & SK4 .... 169 D3
Wellington Rd S. SK1, SK2 .... 170 F8
Wellington Sq. 5 BL8 .... 27 B1
Wellington St. Ashton-u-L OL6 .... 166 B2
Wellington St. Bolton BL3 .... 145 E6
Wellington St. Bury BL8 .... 140 D1
Wellington St. Chadderton OL9 .... 152 B8
Wellington St. Denton M34 .... 100 F6
Wellington St. Dukinfield SK14 .... 101 C3
Wellington St. 2 Failsworth M35 .... 66 A1
Wellington St. Farnworth BL4 60 D8
Wellington St. Hazel Grove SK7 .... 124 F3
Wellington St. 1 Littleborough OL15 .... 16 B5
Wellington St. M'ster M18 .... 99 D5
Wellington St. M'ster M3 .... 158 D2
Wellington St. Milnrow OL16 .... 32 A6
Wellington St. Newton-l-W WA12 .... 89 A3
Wellington St. Oldham OL4 .... 153 F6
Wellington St. 19 R'dale OL12 .... 14 F1
Wellington St. 5 Radcliffe M26 .... 44 C4
Wellington St. Stockport SK1 & SK3 .... 169 F1
Wellington St. Stretford M32 .... 96 C1
Wellington St. Westhoughton BL5 .... 39 E2
Wellington St. Wigan WN1 .... 151 D8
Wellington St E. M7 .... 155 E7
Wellington St W. M7 .... 155 D6
Wellington Terr. 13 Dukinfield SK16 .... 166 B1
Wellington Terr. Salford M5 154 D2
Wellington Wlk. BL3 .... 145 E6
Wellmead Cl. M7 & M8 .... 155 F5
Wellock St. M10 & M40 .... 157 F5
Wellpark Wlk. 21 M40 .... 83 C5
Wells Ave. Billinge WN5 .... 71 D6
Wells Ave. Chadderton OL9 .... 48 A1
Wells Ave. M'ster M25 .... 63 C2
Wells Cl. Droylsden M11 & M43 99 F8
Wells Cl. Gatley SK8 .... 131 C7
Wells Cl. Middleton M24 .... 64 C7
Wells Cl. Tyldesley M29 .... 77 C8
Wells Ct. SK16 .... 101 C6
Wells Dr. Dukinfield SK16 .... 101 C6
Wells Dr. M'ster SK4 .... 110 E2
Wells Dr. Wigan WN2 .... 37 F2
Wells Pl. WN1 .... 151 E8
Wells Rd. OL1 .... 49 E5
Wells St. BL9 .... 140 E1
Wellside Wlk. 8 M8 .... 156 A6
Wellstock La. M38 .... 59 F6
Wellwood Dr. 11 M40 .... 83 A7
Wellyhole St. OL4 .... 67 D6
Welney Rd. M16 .... 97 B3
Welshpool Cl. M23 .... 109 B2
Welshpool Way. 9 M34 .... 101 A1
Welton Ave. M20 .... 110 C2
Welton Cl. Leigh WN7 .... 76 C5
Welton Cl. Wilmslow SK9 .... 136 F4
Welton Dr. SK9 .... 136 E4
Welton Gr. SK9 .... 136 E4
Welwyn Cl. M41 .... 95 B5
Welwyn Dr. M6 .... 80 A5
Welwyn Wlk. M40 .... 160 D2
Wem St. OL9 .... 66 A4
Wembley Gr. M14 .... 110 C8
Wembley Rd. M18 .... 99 C3
Wembury St. M9 .... 157 E8
Wembury St N. M9 .... 157 E8
Wembury Wlk. SK14 .... 102 E3
Wemsley Gr. 29 BL2 .... 25 B1
Wemyss Ave. SK5 .... 99 F1
Wendlebury Cl. WN7 .... 75 E1
Wendlebury Gn. OL2 .... 149 A5
Wendon Rd. M23 .... 121 B5
Wendover Dr. BL3 .... 40 E5
Wendover Rd. Sale M23 .... 120 D8
Wendover Rd. Urmston M41 .. 95 C1
Wenfield Dr. M9 .... 65 B3
Wenlock Ave. OL6 .... 85 B5
Wenlock Cl. Hazel Grove SK2 125 A6
Wenlock Cl. Horwich BL6 .... 22 C4
Wenlock Gr. 4 WN2 .... 56 D4
Wenlock Rd. Hindley WN2 .... 56 D5
Wenlock Rd. Leigh WN7 .... 75 E2
Wenlock Rd. Sale M33 .... 108 A2
Wenlock St. 9 Hindley WN2 56 D5
Wenlock St. Swinton M27 .... 79 D8
Wenlock Way. M12 .... 164 F6
Wenning Cl. M45 .... 45 C1
Wenning Wlk. 4 WN2 .... 56 A2
Wensley Ct. M7 .... 63 A1
Wensley Dr. Hazel Grove SK7 133 D7
Wensley Dr. M'ster M20 .... 110 B5
Wensley Rd. Cheadle SK8 .... 122 C6
Wensley Rd. Golborne WA3 .... 90 E7
Wensley Rd. M'ster M7 .... 63 A1
Wensley Rd. M'ster SK5 .... 169 F4
Wensley Way. OL16 .... 31 C6
Wensleydale Ave. SK8 .... 122 C6
Wensleydale Cl. Royton OL2 .. 48 C5
Wensleydale Cl. Whitefield BL9 .... 45 A3
Wensleydale Cl. Wythenshawe M23 .... 120 F3
Wensleydale Rd. WN7 .... 76 C5
Wentbridge Rd. BL1 .... 145 D8
Wentworth Ave. Alt'ham WA15 .... 120 A6
Wentworth Ave. Bury BL8 .... 27 B4
Wentworth Ave. Farnworth BL4 .... 60 C7
Wentworth Ave. Heywood OL10 .... 46 D8
Wentworth Ave. Irlam M44 .... 94 A3
Wentworth Ave. 8 M'ster M18 .... 99 E6
Wentworth Ave. Salford M6 .. 80 C3
Wentworth Ave. Whitefield M45 .... 62 D7
Wentworth Cl. Marple SK6 .... 125 F8
Wentworth Cl. Middleton M24 64 E8
Wentworth Cl. Radcliffe M26 43 D4
Wentworth Ct. M35 .... 83 F6
Wentworth Dr. Bramhall SK7 .... 133 A7
Wentworth Dr. Sale M33 .... 107 F5
Wentworth High Sch. M30 .... 79 F4
Wentworth Rd. Eccles M30 .... 80 A4
Wentworth Rd. Reddish SK5 .... 99 F1
Wentworth Rd. Swinton M27 79 D6
Wentworth Wlk. 2 SK14 .... 101 F5
Wenvaurn Ave. M41 .... 95 B1
Werneth Ave. Hyde SK14 .... 113 F8
Werneth Ave. M'ster M14 .... 98 B2
Werneth Cl. Denton M34 .... 100 F2
Werneth Cl. Hazel Grove SK7 124 E4
Werneth Cres. OL8 .... 66 C4
Werneth Ct. SK14 .... 167 E1
Werneth Golf Course. OL8 .... 66 E1
Werneth Hall Rd. OL8 .... 153 D5
Werneth Hollow. SK6 .... 113 B6
Werneth Inf Sch. OL8 .... 152 E5
Werneth Jun Sch. OL8 .... 152 E5
Werneth Low Ctry Pk. SK14 .... 114 A7
Werneth Low Rd. SK14 & SK6 .... 113 E5
Werneth Private Prep Sch. OL8 .... 153 D5
Werneth Rd. Glossop SK13 .... 116 A7
Werneth Rd. Hyde SK14 .... 167 F2
Werneth Rd. Romiley SK6 .... 113 C5
Werneth Rise. Hyde SK14 .... 113 F7
Werneth Sch. SK6 .... 113 A2
Werneth St. Denton M34 .... 100 F5
Werneth St. Stockport SK1 .... 112 B3

Werneth Sta. OL9 153 D6
Werneth Wlk. M34 100 F2
Wescoe Cl. WN5 53 E5
Wesley Cl. R'dale OL12 15 C3
Wesley Cl. Westhoughton BL5 39 E2
Wesley Ct. Bury BL8 26 E7
Wesley Ct. M'ster SK4 110 F2
Wesley Ct. Walkden M28 60 D4
Wesley Ct. Westhoughton BL5 39 E2
Wesley Dr. Ashton-u-L OL6 85 D6
Wesley Dr. Worsley M28 78 F8
Wesley Gn. M5 161 B8
Wesley Methodist Prim Sch. M26 43 F5
Wesley Mews. 4 BL2 148 B7
Wesley Sq. M41 95 A2
Wesley St. Atherton M46 58 E3
Wesley St. Bolton BL7 25 A8
Wesley St. Bolton BL3 145 E5
Wesley St. Bury BL8 26 E7
Wesley St. Eccles M30 79 C2
Wesley St. Failsworth M35 66 A1
Wesley St. Farnworth BL4 60 E7
Wesley St. Glossop SK13 104 E2
Wesley St. Hadfield SK14 104 A5
Wesley St. Hazel Grove SK7 124 E3
Wesley St. Heywood OL10 29 C2
Wesley St. M'ster M11 165 A8
Wesley St. Milnrow OL16 31 E6
Wesley St. R'dale OL12 15 B3
Wesley St. Royton OL2 48 E3
Wesley St. Stockport SK1 169 F1
Wesley St. Stretford M32 96 E3
Wesley St. Swinton M27 79 F8
Wesley St. Westhoughton BL5 39 E2
Wesley St. Wigan WN5 54 D5
Wessenden Bank E. SK2 124 D5
Wessenden Bank W. SK2 124 D5
Wessex Cl. WN1 20 B1
Wessex Park Cl. OL2 149 B8
Wessex Rd. WN5 36 D1
Wessington Bank. 12 SK13 171 E2
Wessington Fold. 14 SK13 171 E2
Wessington Gn. 13 SK13 171 E2
Wessington Mews. SK13 171 E2
West Ashton St. M5 154 F1
West Ave. Alt'ham WA14 119 A5
West Ave. Droylsden M18 99 E5
West Ave. Failsworth M40 65 D1
West Ave. Farnworth BL4 60 B8
West Ave. Gatley SK8 122 C1
West Ave. Golborne WA3 74 B1
West Ave. Leigh WN7 76 C3
West Ave. Littleborough OL12 15 C3
West Ave. M'ster M19 110 F7
West Ave. Stalybridge SK15 86 A3
West Ave. Walkden M28 60 C3
West Ave. Whitefield M45 44 E2
West Bank. M18 100 A7
West Bank St. Salford M5 161 C8
West Bank St. Tyldesley M46 58 E1
West Bridgewater St. WN7 75 F4
West Canteen Rd. M17, M32 96 C4
West Central Dr. M27 80 B7
West Charles St. M5 81 B1
West Church St. 9 OL10 29 C2
West Cl. M46 58 E1
West Cotts. OL4 68 F5
West Craven St. M5 161 B7
West Cres. M24 64 F7
West Croft Ind Est. M24 64 C7
West Dean St. M5 81 C1
West Downs Rd. SK8 122 F3
West Dr. Bury BL9 27 E5
West Dr. Droylsden M43 83 F1
West Dr. Gatley M22 & SK8 122 A4
West Dr. Hollingworth SK14 103 F7
West Dr. Pendlebury M27 80 B7
West Dr. Salford M6 80 E6
West Duke St. M5 158 D1
West Egerton St. M5 81 B1
West End. SK14 114 F8
West End Ave. SK8 122 A6
West End Prim Sch. Ashton-u-L OL7 84 F2
West End Prim Sch. Reddish M34 100 A3
West End St. OL9 153 D7
West Gdns. 1 OL13 3 B8
West Gn. M24 64 B7
West Gr. M'ster M13 164 D5
West Gr. 1 Mossley OL5 68 C1
West Gr. Sale M33 108 B3
West Gr. Westhoughton BL5 57 E6
West High St. M5 81 A2
West Hill Cl. SK15 85 F2
West Hill Sch. SK15 85 F2
West Hope St. M5 81 B1
West King St. M3 158 E2
West Lea. M34 101 A2
West Liverpool Street Prim Sch. M6 154 F2
West Marwood St. M7 155 E6
West Meade. Bolton BL3 147 D2
West Meade. M'ster M25 63 D2
West Meade. M'ster M21 109 A7
West Meade. Swinton M27 79 E6
West Meade. SK5 100 A1
West Mosley St. M1 & M60 159 A1
West Mount. Orrell WN5 53 F6
West Mount. Wigan WN1 37 D2
West Oak Pl. SK8 122 F1
West Over. SK6 113 A1
West Park Ave. Denton M34 101 B2
West Park Ave. Poynton SK12 133 A4
West Park Rd. Stockport SK1 112 B2
West Park Rd. Stockport SK7 123 D2
West Park St. M5 161 B7
West Pk. SK14 113 E6
West Pl. M19 110 F7
West Point Lodge. 1 M19 110 F8
West Rd. Alt'ham WA14 119 C2
West Rd. Eccles M41 95 E6
West Rd. Prestwich M25 62 F5
West Rd. Stretford M32 96 A4
West Row. M25 62 F1
West St. Alderley Edge SK9 137 A1
West St. Ashton-u-L OL6 166 B3
West St. Bolton BL1 144 C7
West St. Droylsden M11 83 B2
West St. Dukinfield SK14 101 D5
West St. Dukinfield SK16 166 B1
West St. Failsworth M35 83 F7
West St. Farnworth BL4 42 E1
West St. Heywood OL10 29 D2
West St. Hindley WN2 57 B3
West St. Hollingworth SK14 103 F7
West St. Ince-i-M WN2 56 A8
West St. Littleborough OL15 16 C5
West St. Middleton M24 47 A2
West St. Milnrow OL16 31 D7
West St. Oldham OL4 67 E5
West St. Oldham OL9 153 D6
West St. Oldham OL1 153 E7
West St. R'dale OL16 31 A8
West St. 2 Radcliffe M26 44 A3
West St. Ramsbottom BL0 138 B5
West St. Rawtenstall BB4 2 E8
West St. Stalybridge SK15 85 F2
West St. Stockport SK3 169 D1
West St. Tyldesley M46 58 E1
West St. Wigan WN6 37 B1
West Starkey St. OL10 29 C3
West Towers St. M5 & M6 154 F1
West Vale. M26 44 A5
West Vale Rd. WA15 119 F6
West View. Bacup OL13 3 B8
West View. Denton M34 100 E7
West View. Haslingden BB4 1 A7
West View. Littleborough OL15 16 C5
West View. Ramsbottom BL0 1 C2
West View Ct. M22 121 F8
West View Gr. M45 44 D1
West View Rd. M22 121 E8
West Way. Bolton BL1 25 B3
West Way. Walkden M38 60 A5
West Wlk. BL7 8 D2
West Works Rd. M17 & M32 96 C5
Westage Gdns. M23 121 A7
Westbank Rd. Bolton BL6 40 D6
Westbank Rd. M'ster M20 110 D5
Westbourne Ave. Bolton BL3 42 B3
Westbourne Ave. Kearsley M26 & M27 61 D5
Westbourne Ave. Leigh WN7 75 E7
Westbourne Ave. Leigh WN7 75 F7
Westbourne Ave. Whitefield M45 44 D1
Westbourne Dr. OL7 166 A4
Westbourne Gr. M'ster M20 110 A6
Westbourne Gr. M'ster M9 157 D8
Westbourne Gr. Reddish SK5 111 F8
Westbourne Gr. Sale M33 108 A4
Westbourne Pk. M41 95 D2
Westbourne Range. M18 & M34 99 F4
Westbourne Rd. Denton M34 100 E2
Westbourne Rd. M'ster M14 110 D8
Westbourne Rd. Swinton M28 79 B4
Westbourne Rd. Urmston M41 95 D2
Westbourne St. OL9 153 D7
Westbridge Mews. WN1 150 C7
Westbrook Ct. BL2 148 A6
Westbrook Rd. Stretford M17 96 D7
Westbrook Rd. Swinton M27 79 E7
Westbrook Sq. M12 165 A6
Westbrook St. BL2 148 A6
Westbrook Wlk. 3 M20 110 A8
Westbury Ave. Sale M33 107 C1
Westbury Ave. Wigan WN3 54 D2
Westbury Cl. Bury BL8 27 A1
Westbury Cl. Westhoughton BL5 40 A1
Westbury Dr. SK6 125 E6
Westbury Rd. M8 64 B1
Westbury St. Ashton-u-L OL6 166 C3
Westbury St. Dukinfield SK14 101 C5
Westbury Street Ind Est. SK14 101 C5
Westbury Way. OL1 & OL2 48 D2
Westby Cl. SK7 133 A7
Westby Gr. BL2 148 C8
Westcliffe House. OL12 15 D4
Westcliffe Rd. BL1 24 F6
Westcombe Dr. BL8 27 C5
Westcott Ave. M20 110 A6
Westcott Cl. BL2 25 E5
Westcott Ct. M15 162 D7
Westcott Dr. WN3 54 C4
Westcott Gr. OL2 149 A5
Westcourt Rd. Bolton BL3 147 D3
Westcourt Rd. Sale M33 108 A6
Westcraig Ave. M40 65 C3
Westcroft Rd. M19 & M20 110 D4
Westdale Gdns. M19 111 A5
Westdean Cres. M19 110 F5
Westend Ave. PR7 19 D8
Westend St. BL4 60 B8
Wester Hill Rd. OL8 67 A1
Westerdale. 1 OL4 67 C6
Westerdale Cl. M29 77 B8
Westerdale Dr. Bolton BL3 144 A5
Westerdale Dr. Royton OL2 48 C5
Westerham Ave. M5 81 A1
Westerham Cl. BL8 27 C7
Westering Wlk. 2 M21 97 E3
Western Ave. M27 62 D2
Western Circ. M19 110 F6
Western Ct. OL13 3 B8
Western Rd. Bacup OL13 3 C8
Western Rd. Urmston M41 94 E1
Western St. M'ster M18 99 E6
Western St. Salford M6 154 E3
Westerton Ct. BL3 145 D5
Westfield. M6 154 E4
Westfield Ave. Ashton-i-M WN4 73 A4
Westfield Ave. Middleton M24 65 A7
Westfield Cl. OL11 13 F1
Westfield Dr. Romiley SK6 113 C5
Westfield Dr. Uppermill OL4 68 E5
Westfield Gr. Denton M34 100 E5
Westfield Gr. Wigan WN1 37 B3
Westfield Rd. Bolton BL3 146 B2
Westfield Rd. Cheadle SK8 131 F8
Westfield Rd. Droylsden M43 83 E2
Westfield Rd. M'ster M21 97 B1
Westfield Rd. Tyldesley M46 58 E1
Westfield St. M'ster M7 63 D1
Westfield St. Oldham OL1 & OL9 48 C1
Westfield St. Oldham OL9 152 C8
Westfields. WA15 128 F8
Westgate. Alt'ham WA15 119 E2
Westgate. Sale M33 108 A4
Westgate. Urmston M41 95 B1
Westgate. Whitworth OL12 14 B7
Westgate. Wilmslow SK9 137 A5
Westgate Ave. Bolton BL1 144 C7
Westgate Ave. Bury BL9 140 E1
Westgate Ave. M'ster M9 64 C2
Westgate Ave. Ramsbottom BL0 11 A2
Westgate Cl. OL12 14 B7
Westgate Dr. Orrell WN5 53 D5
Westgate Dr. Swinton M27 79 F6
Westgate Dr. Tyldesley M29 77 C6
Westgate House. 3 OL8 66 D2
Westgate Rd. M6 80 C4
Westgate St. OL7 166 A1
Westgrove Ave. BL1 24 E6
Westhead Ave. WA3 74 E1
Westhide Wlk. 5 M9 64 F1
Westholm Ave. M19 111 B7
Westholme Ct. SK9 137 A2
Westholme Rd. M'ster M20 110 B5
Westholme Rd. Prestwich M25 63 C7
Westhorne Fold. 1 M8 63 E2
Westhoughton High Sch. BL5 57 F8
Westhoughton Parochial CE Prim Sch. BL5 57 E8
Westhoughton Prim Sch. BL5 39 F1
Westhoughton Rd. PR7 20 F8
Westhoughton Sta. BL5 39 E2
Westhulme Ave. OL1 48 D1
Westhulme St. OL1 48 D1
Westinghouse Cl. WN6 150 A8
Westinghouse Ind Est. M17 96 D5
Westinghouse Rd. Stretford M17 96 B5
Westinghouse Rd. Stretford M17 96 E5
Westlake Gr. WN2 57 B4
Westlake St. M11 165 C7
Westland Ave. Bolton BL1 142 A1
Westland Ave. Farnworth BL4 60 C6
Westland Ave. Stockport SK1 112 B1
Westland Dr. M9 64 D4
Westlands. M45 62 F6
Westlands The. M27 80 C6
Westlea Dr. M18 99 D3
Westleigh Dr. M25 63 D3
Westleigh High Sch. WN7 57 D1
Westleigh La. WN7 57 D1
Westleigh Meth Prim Sch. WN7 75 D8
Westleigh St. M9 64 F1
Westleigh St Paul's CE Prim Sch. WN7 75 E8
Westleigh View. WN7 75 E8
Westlock. WN3 150 C6
Westman Wlk. 23 M16 97 E4
Westmarsh Cl. 4 BL1 143 E1
Westmead. WN6 36 E8
Westmead Dr. M'ster M7 & M8 155 E5
Westmead Dr. Sale WA15 120 B7
Westmeade Rd. M28 60 C5
Westmere Dr. M8 & M9 156 C6
Westminster Ave. Ashton-u-L OL6 85 D7
Westminster Ave. Farnworth BL4 60 C8
Westminster Ave. M'ster M16 97 C2
Westminster Ave. Radcliffe M26 43 D4
Westminster Ave. Reddish SK5 111 E7
Westminster Ave. Royton OL2 48 C6
Westminster Ave. Whitefield M45 62 F8
Westminster Cl. Marple SK6 125 D7
Westminster Cl. Sale M33 107 D3
Westminster Cl. Shaw OL2 149 B8
Westminster Dr. Bramhall SK8 132 B6
Westminster Dr. Leigh WN7 76 E7
Westminster Dr. Wilmslow SK9 137 A4
Westminster House. M3 158 E3
Westminster Rd. Alt'ham WA15 120 A2
Westminster Rd. Bolton BL1 24 E5
Westminster Rd. Eccles M30 79 F3
Westminster Rd. Failsworth M35 84 B8
Westminster Rd. Urmston M41 95 E4
Westminster Rd. Walkden M28 60 D2
Westminster St. Bury BL9 140 E1
Westminster St. Farnworth BL4 60 C8
Westminster St. 5 M'ster M19 99 B1
Westminster St. Oldham OL1 67 B8
Westminster St. R'dale OL11 139 D5
Westminster St. Salford M15 161 C7
Westminster St. Swinton M27 61 E1
Westminster St. Wigan WN5 54 F6
Westminster Way. SK16 101 D6
Westminster Wlk. 4 BL4 60 C8
Westmoor Gables. SK4 168 A4
Westmoorland St. 3 WN1 37 E1
Westmoreland Cl. Alt'ham WA14 128 B8
Westmoreland Cl. Bury BL9 44 E6
Westmorland Ave. Ashton-u-L OL7 166 B4
Westmorland Ave. Dukinfield SK16 101 E8
Westmorland Cl. SK5 112 C6
Westmorland Dr. Brinnington SK5 112 C6
Westmorland Dr. Littleborough OL12 15 D6
Westmorland Rd. Eccles M30 80 A4
Westmorland Rd. M'ster M20 110 A2
Westmorland Rd. Partington M31 105 E2
Westmorland Rd. Sale M33 108 C2
Westmorland Rd. Tyldesley M29 59 A2
Westmorland Rd. Urmston M41 95 C1
Westmorland Wlk. 2 OL2 48 E4
Westmount Cl. M40 156 C6
Weston Ave. Failsworth M40 65 E1
Weston Ave. Swinton M27 61 F4
Weston Ave. R'dale OL16 31 B4
Weston Ave. Urmston M41 95 B1
Weston Dr. Denton M34 101 A3
Weston Dr. Stockport SK8 123 D4
Weston Gr. Reddish SK4 111 C6
Weston Gr. Wythenshawe M22 121 E8
Weston Pk. WN6 36 D3
Weston Rd. Irlam M44 94 A2
Weston Rd. Wilmslow SK9 137 E6
Weston St. Atherton M46 58 E4
Weston St. Bolton BL3 42 A4
Weston St. M'ster M10 & M40 160 D2
Weston St. Milnrow OL16 31 E6
Weston St. Reddish SK5 169 E4
Weston St. 12 Tyldesley M29 59 A1
Westover Rd. M41 95 C3
Westover St. M27 61 F1
Westpark. BL1 144 C7
Westpoint Ent Pk. M17 95 F7
Westray Cres. M5 & M6 154 E1
Westray Rd. M13 98 E2
Westrees. WN7 76 A7
Westville Gdns. M19 110 E5
Westward Ho. OL16 31 F6
Westward Rd. SK9 136 F6
Westway. Droylsden M34 100 A8
Westway. M'ster M9 64 B6
Westway. Oldham OL4 67 E5
Westway. Shaw OL2 149 B6
Westwell Gdns. 4 BL1 143 F1
Westwell Gr. 3 WN7 75 E8
Westwell St. WN7 75 E8
Westwich Terr. 17 BL1 143 E2
Westwood Ave. Alt'ham WA15 119 F7
Westwood Ave. Failsworth M40 65 E1
Westwood Ave. M'ster M7 155 E8
Westwood Ave. Urmston M41 95 F1
Westwood Ave. Walkden M28 60 A3
Westwood Bsns Ctr. OL9 153 D6
Westwood Cl. BL4 60 D8
Westwood Cres. M28 79 B4
Westwood Dr. Oldham OL9 153 D7
Westwood Dr. Pendlebury M27 80 C6
Westwood Dr. Sale M33 108 B2
Westwood Ind Est. OL9 152 C7
Westwood La. WN3 151 D5
Westwood Park Prim Sch. M30 79 B3
Westwood Prim Sch. OL9 153 D7
Westwood Rd. Bolton BL1 144 C8
Westwood Rd. Gatley SK8 131 B8
Westwood Rd. Stockport SK2 124 B4
Westwood Rd. Stretford M32 96 B2
Westwood Rd. Wigan WN3 150 C6
Westwood Terr. WN3 151 E5
Westwood Trad Est. SK6 125 E5
Westworth Cl. 11 BL1 145 D8
Wet Gate La. WA13 117 E4
Wetheral Cl. WN2 57 C3
Wetheral Dr. BL3 147 E3
Wetherall St. M19 99 B1
Wetherby Cl. WA12 89 C5
Wetherby Dr. Hazel Grove SK7 125 A2
Wetherby Dr. Royton OL2 48 D5
Wetherby St. M18 99 E7
Wexford Wlk. M22 121 E2
Wexham Gdns. WN2 56 A3
Wey Gates Dr. WA15 129 C7
Weybourne Ave. M9 65 A2
Weybourne Dr. Bredbury SK6 112 F4
Weybourne Dr. Wigan WN3 54 E3
Weybourne Gr. BL2 25 B4
Weybridge Cl. 4 BL1 145 E8
Weybridge Rd. M4 159 C2
Weybrook Rd. SK4 111 C7
Weycroft Cl. BL2 43 A6
Weyhill Rd. M23 121 A5
Weylands Gr. M6 80 B5
Weymouth Dr. WN2 57 A4
Weymouth Rd. Ashton-u-L OL6 85 F6
Weymouth Rd. Eccles M30 79 B3
Weymouth St. BL1 143 E2
Weythorne Dr. Bolton BL1 143 F4
Weythorne Dr. Bury BL9 28 F4
Whalley Ave. Bolton BL1 23 F3
Whalley Ave. Glazebury WA3 92 C7
Whalley Ave. Littleborough OL15 16 A6
Whalley Ave. M'ster M16 97 D3
Whalley Ave. M'ster M19 99 B2
Whalley Ave. M'ster M21 109 C7
Whalley Ave. Sale M33 108 C5
Whalley Ave. Urmston M41 95 E3
Whalley Cl. Alt'ham WA15 119 F8
Whalley Cl. Milnrow OL16 31 D6
Whalley Cl. Whitefield M45 44 F1
Whalley Cl. Wigan WN3 55 A2
Whalley Dr. BL8 26 F2
Whalley Gdns. OL12 14 B1
Whalley Gr. Ashton-u-L OL6 85 C7
Whalley Gr. Leigh WN7 57 D1
Whalley Gr. M'ster M16 97 D2
Whalley Range High Sch for Girls. M'ster M14 109 F8
Whalley Range High Sch for Girls. M'ster M20 110 A7
Whalley Rd. Alt'ham WA15 120 A2
Whalley Rd. Heywood OL10 29 A2
Whalley Rd. M'ster M16 97 D3
Whalley Rd. Middleton M24 46 F3
Whalley Rd. R'dale OL12 14 B1
Whalley Rd. Ramsbottom BL0 11 E7
Whalley Rd. Stockport SK2 124 C7
Whalley Rd. Whitefield M45 44 F1
Whalley St. M10 & M40 160 D2
Wham Bar Dr. OL10 29 B3
Wham Bottom La. OL12 14 D4
Wham La. OL3 33 D1
Wham St. OL10 29 B2
Wharf Cl. WA14 119 D7
Wharf Cotts. OL5 68 D1
Wharf Rd. Alt'ham WA14 119 D7
Wharf Rd. Sale M33 108 C5
Wharf St. Dukinfield SK16 166 C1
Wharf St. 2 Leigh WN7 76 A4
Wharf St. Oldham OL9 66 B3
Wharf St. Stockport SK4, SK5 169 E3
Wharf The. OL3 51 B2
Wharfedale. BL5 39 F2
Wharfedale Ave. M40 65 A1
Wharfedale Rd. SK5 111 E8
Wharfside Ave. M30 95 D8
Wharfside Bsns Ctr. M17 96 F6
Wharmton Rise. OL4 68 E6
Wharmton School Cotts. OL3 50 F1
Wharmton View. Uppermill OL5 68 E3
Wharmton View. Uppermill OL3 69 A6
Wharncliffe Cl. SK14 171 E4
Wharncliffe St. 3 WN2 56 D5
Wharton Ave. M21 109 D7
Wharton La. M38 59 E5
Wharton Lodge. M30 79 E3
Wharton Prim Sch. M38 59 E5
Wheat Cl. M13 163 C5
Wheat Croft. SK3 170 F5
Wheatcroft. SK14 171 E4
Wheater's Cres. M7 158 D4
Wheater's St. M7 158 D4
Wheater's Terr. M7 158 D4
Wheatfield. SK15 102 E7
Wheatfield Cl. Bury BL9 27 F7
Wheatfield Cl. Romiley SK6 113 A4
Wheatfield Cres. OL2 48 C3
Wheatfield House. OL2 48 D3
Wheatfield St. BL2 148 C5
Wheathill St. 4 OL11 & OL16 31 A4
Wheatlea Rd. WN3 54 F2
Wheatley Ave. WA12 89 C5
Wheatley Rd. M27 61 D2
Wheatley Wlk. M12 165 A6
Wheatsheaf Ctr The. OL16 139 F8
Wheatsheaf Ind Est. M27 62 B1
Wheeldale. OL4 67 D6
Wheeldale Cl. BL1 143 E2
Wheeldon St. M14 98 A3
Wheelock Cl. SK9 131 D1
Wheelton Cl. BL8 27 A1
Wheelwright Cl. Marple SK6 125 F8
Wheelwright Cl. R'dale OL11 30 B4
Wheelwright Dr. OL16 15 C3
Whelan Ave. BL9 44 E7
Whelan Cl. BL9 44 E7
Wheler St. M11 & M35 & M43 99 E8
Whelley. WN1 & WN2 37 E2
Whelley Hospl (General). WN1 37 E2
Whernside Ave. Ashton-u-L OL6 85 C7
Whernside Ave. M'ster M40 65 A1
Whernside Cl. SK4 169 E3
Whetmorhurst Rd. SK6 126 E4
Whetstone Hill Cl. OL1 49 B2
Whetstone Hill La. Oldham OL1 49 C1
Whetstone Hill La. 6 Oldham OL1 49 C1
Whetstone Hill Rd. OL1 49 B1
Whewell Ave. BL9 44 E5
Whewell St. 15 M29 59 A1
Whickham Cl. M14 98 B3
Whiley St. M13 98 F4
Whimberry Cl. M5 161 C7
Whimbrel Ave. WA12 89 C3
Whimbrel Rd. Hazel Grove SK2 125 A5
Whimbrel Rd. Tyldesley M29 77 C7
Whinberry Rd. WA14 119 B7
Whinberry Way. OL4 49 D4
Whinchat Ave. WA12 89 C4
Whinchat Cl. SK2 125 A4
Whinfell Dr. M24 46 C1
Whinfield Cl. WN6 150 A8
Whingroves Wlk. 3 M40 83 A6
Whinmoor Wlk. M40 83 B7
Whins Ave. BL4 59 E8
Whins Crest. BL6 40 C7
Whinslee Ct. BL1 40 C7
Whinslee Dr. BL6 40 C7
Whinstone Way. OL1 & OL9 47 E1
Whipp St. OL10 29 B3
Whirley Cl. SK4 111 D5
Whistlecroft Ct. WN3 151 F6
Whistley St. WN2 56 B3
Whiston Dr. BL2 148 C6
Whiston Rd. M'ster M8 64 B1
Whiston Rd. M'ster M8 156 B8
Whit La. Salford M6 80 F6
Whit La. Salford M6 81 A5
Whitaker St. M24 64 F8
Whitbeam Gr. WN2 56 E2
Whitbrook Way. M24 47 C5
Whitburn Ave. M13 98 E2
Whitburn Cl. Bolton BL3 40 E4
Whitburn Cl. Garswood WN4 72 D4
Whitburn Dr. BL8 27 C5
Whitburn Rd. M23 121 A4
Whitby Ave. Heywood OL10 29 C3
Whitby Ave. M'ster M16 97 D3
Whitby Ave. M'ster M14 110 E8
Whitby Ave. Salford M6 80 C3
Whitby Ave. Urmston M41 95 E2
Whitby Cl. Bury BL8 26 F2
Whitby Cl. Cheadle SK8 122 C6
Whitby Cl. Poynton SK12 133 D4
Whitby Rd. M'ster M14 110 E8
Whitby Rd. Oldham OL8 67 C4
Whitby St. Middleton M24 47 C1
Whitby St. R'dale OL11 31 A5
Whitchurch Dr. M16 162 D5
Whitchurch Gdns. 8 BL1 143 E2
Whitchurch Rd. M20 110 A7
Whitchurch St. M3 158 E3
White Bank Ave. SK5 112 C4
White Bank Rd. Oldham OL8 66 E1
White Birk Cl. BL8 10 F2
White Brook La. Uppermill OL3 69 C8
White Brook La. Uppermill OL3 69 D6
White Broom. WA13 117 B4
White Carr La. BL9 12 A1
White City Ret Pk. M16 161 A5
White City Way. M16 & M17 161 A5
White Hart Meadow. 2 M24 47 A2
White Hart St. SK14 167 D4
White Hill Cl. OL12 14 D4
White Horse Cl. BL6 22 C5
White Horse Gr. BL5 40 A2
White Horse Meadows. OL16 31 C2
White House Ave. M8 63 F3
White House Cl. OL10 46 D7
White Lady Cl. 2 M28 59 F3
White Lion Brow. BL1 145 E7
White Lodge Dr. WN4 73 D4
White Moss Ave. M'ster M21 109 D8
White Moss Gdns. M9 65 A2
White Moss Rd. M9 64 E3
White Rd. SK12 127 C2
White Slack Gate. OL14 6 A6
White St. Bury BL8 27 C1
White St. Leigh WN7 76 C4
White St. M'ster M15 162 D6
White St. Salford M6 154 E1
White St. 5 Wigan WN5 54 B6
White Swallows Rd. M27 80 B6
White Swan Ind Est. 5 OL1 67 C8
Whiteacre. WN6 19 A2
Whiteacre Rd. OL6 85 D4
Whiteacre Wlk. M15 162 E5
Whiteacres. M27 79 D7
Whitebeam Cl. Alt'ham WA15 120 E5
Whitebeam Cl. Newhey OL16 32 A3
Whitebeam Cl. Salford M6 81 A3
Whitebeam Ct. M6 81 A3
Whitebeam Wlk. Sale M33 107 D5
Whitebeam Wlk. Westhoughton BL5 39 F2
Whitebeck Ct. M9 65 A4
Whitebrook Rd. M14 98 B1
Whitecar Ave. M40 65 E1
Whitecarr La. M23 & WA15 120 E3
Whitechapel Cl. BL2 42 E7
Whitechapel St. M20 110 B3
Whitecliff Cl. M14 98 C3
Whitecroft Ave. Golborne WA3 74 E1
Whitecroft Ave. Shaw OL2 49 D7
Whitecroft Dr. BL8 26 F2
Whitecroft Gdns. 3 M19 110 E4
Whitecroft Rd. Bolton BL1 142 A1
Whitecroft Rd. Marple SK6 126 C1
Whitecroft Rd. Wigan WN3 55 B2
Whitecroft St. 12 OL1 49 C1
Whitefield. Lymm WA13 117 A4
Whitefield. Salford M6 80 D6
Whitefield. Stockport SK4 169 D3
Whitefield Ave. Newton-l-W WA12 89 E2
Whitefield Ave. R'dale OL11 29 F8
Whitefield Cl. Golborne WA3 90 A8
Whitefield Cl. Lymm WA13 117 A5
Whitefield Ct. WA3 91 F2
Whitefield Golf Course. M45 62 E7
Whitefield Gr. WA13 117 A4
Whitefield Prep Sch Ltd. M45 44 E1
Whitefield Prim Sch. M45 63 A8
Whitefield Rd. Bredbury SK6 112 E4
Whitefield Rd. Bury BL9 44 D7
Whitefield Rd. Sale M33 108 A5
Whitefield Sta. M45 44 F1
Whitefriar Ct. M3 158 E3
Whitefriars Wlk. 2 M22 130 D8
Whitegate. Bolton BL3 40 C2
Whitegate. Littleborough OL15 15 E4
Whitegate Ave. Culcheth WA3 91 F2
Whitegate Ave. Oldham OL9 65 F4
Whitegate Cl. M40 65 E1
Whitegate Dr. Bolton BL1 143 F4
Whitegate Dr. Salford M5 154 D2
Whitegate Dr. Swinton M27 62 B2
Whitegate End Prim Sch. OL9 65 E3
Whitegate La. OL9 66 A4
Whitegate Pk. M41 94 E2
Whitegate Rd. OL9 65 E3
Whitegates. SK8 122 D5
Whitegates Cl. WA15 120 B5
Whitegates La. OL4 50 B2
Whitegates Rd. Cheadle SK8 122 D5
Whitegates Rd. Middleton M24 47 C4
Whitehall Ave. WN6 35 E8
Whitehall Cl. SK9 137 A5
Whitehall La. Blackrod BL6 21 D3

Win – Woo 239

Windsor Ave. Irlam M44 94 B3
Windsor Ave. Little Lever BL3 43 A3
Windsor Ave. M'ster SK4 168 A3
Windsor Ave.
Newton-l-W WA12 89 D2
Windsor Ave. Oldham OL9 66 A4
Windsor Ave. Sale M33 108 B6
Windsor Ave. Swinton M27 62 A2
Windsor Ave. Tyldesley M29 77 A6
Windsor Ave. Urmston M41 94 F2
Windsor Ave. Walkden M38 60 B5
Windsor Ave. Whitefield M45 63 A7
Windsor Ave. Wilmslow SK9 136 F7
Windsor Cl. Poynton SK12 133 D4
Windsor Cl. Ramsbottom BL8 11 A1
Windsor Comm High Sch
The. M5 81 A2
Windsor Cres. Aspull WN2 38 D5
Windsor Cres.
M'ster M25 & M8 63 E3
Windsor Ct. Bolton BL3 147 D2
Windsor Ct. Sale M33 107 F5
Windsor Dr. Ashton-u-L OL7 84 F4
Windsor Dr. Bury BL8 44 B8
Windsor Dr. Droylsden M34 84 D1
Windsor Dr. Dukinfield SK16 101 F7
Windsor Dr. Horwich BL6 22 E2
Windsor Dr. Marple SK6 125 E5
Windsor Dr.
Newton-l-W WA11 89 A7
Windsor Dr. Sale WA14 119 F8
Windsor Dr. Stalybridge SK15 86 A3
Windsor Gr. Ashton-u-L OL6 85 C7
Windsor Gr. Bolton BL1 142 C1
Windsor Gr. Cheadle SK8 131 F8
Windsor Gr. Hindley WN2 57 B3
Windsor Gr. Kearsley M26 61 B7
Windsor Gr. Romiley SK6 113 E2
Windsor Rd. Ashton-i-M WN4 73 C1
Windsor Rd. Billinge WN5 71 F5
Windsor Rd. Bolton BL7 25 A7
Windsor Rd. Bredbury SK6 112 C3
Windsor Rd. Droylsden M43 83 E1
Windsor Rd. Failsworth M40 83 E4
Windsor Rd. Golborne WA3 90 C8
Windsor Rd. Hazel Grove SK7 124 F2
Windsor Rd. Hyde SK14 113 E7
Windsor Rd. Leigh WN7 76 E6
Windsor Rd. M'ster M25 63 E3
Windsor Rd. M'ster M19 99 A1
Windsor Rd. M'ster M9 157 E7
Windsor Rd. Oldham OL8 66 D4
Windsor Rd. Orrell WN8 53 A8
Windsor Rd. Reddish M34 100 A3
Windsor St. Failsworth M40 83 E4
Windsor St. Failsworth M35 84 A8
Windsor St. M'ster M18 99 C4
Windsor St. R'dale OL11 31 A5
Windsor St. Salford M5 81 B1
Windsor St. Stockport SK2 124 A6
Windsor St. Tyldesley M46 58 E2
Windsor St. Wigan WN1 37 D1
Windsor Terr. Milnrow OL16 31 E6
Windsor Terr. R'dale OL16 31 C7
Windsor Wlk. SK2 170 F6
Windy Bank Ave. WA3 90 E8
Windy Harbour La. BL7 25 B8
Windybank. M9 64 C5
Winfell Dr. M10 & M40 160 D3
Winfield Ave. M20 110 D6
Winfield Dr. M18 99 D6
Winfield Gr. SK6 114 B1
Winfield St. SK14 167 F2
Winford St. M9 157 E8
Wingate Ave. BL8 27 B2
Wingate Dr. Alt'ham WA15 120 B5
Wingate Dr. M'ster M20 110 C2
Wingate Dr. Whitefield M45 44 E1
Wingate Rd. M'ster SK4 168 C4
Wingate Rd. Walkden M38 60 B4
Wingate St. OL11 13 E1
Wingates Gr. BL5 39 D3
Wingates Ind Est. BL5 39 D2
Wingates La. BL5 & BL6 39 E5
Wingates Rd. WN1 37 C4
Wingates Sq. BL5 39 E3
Wingates St John's CE
Prim Sch. BL5 39 E3
Wingfield Ave. SK9 136 E6
Wingfield Dr. Pendlebury M27 80 A6
Wingfield Dr. Wilmslow SK9 136 E6
Wingfield Gr. SK13 116 F7
Wingfield St. M32 96 D4
Wingfield Villas. OL15 16 C7
Wingrove House. 3 M6 154 F2
Wings Gr. OL10 46 D7
Winhill Rd. SK12 127 C1
Winifred Ave. BL9 28 F4
Winifred Rd. Failsworth M40 83 B7
Winifred Rd. Farnworth BL4 42 A1
Winifred Rd. M'ster M20 110 B3
Winifred Rd. Stockport SK2 124 A6
Winifred Rd. Urmston M41 95 D2
Winifred St. 2 Eccles M30 79 B1
Winifred St. Hyde SK14 113 E7
Winifred St. Ince-i-M WN3 151 E6
Winifred St. R'dale OL12 14 B1
Winifred St.
Ramsbottom BL0 138 B5
Winmarith Dr. WA15 129 D7
Winmarleigh Cl. BL8 26 F1
Winmarleigh Gdns. WN7 75 E3
Winnall Wlk. 3 M40 83 C6
Winnard St. WA3 74 B2
Winnats Cl. SK13 116 F8
Winnie St. M40 83 A8
Winnington Gn. SK2 124 D6
Winnington Rd. Marple SK6 125 F7
Winnipeg Quay. M5 96 F7
Winnows The. M34 100 D3
Winscombe Dr. M40 159 C4
Winser St. M1 163 A8
Winsfield Rd. SK7 133 E8
Winsford Dr. OL11 29 F5
Winsford Gr. BL3 40 F5
Winsford Rd. M'ster M14 98 A1
Winsford Wlk. M33 108 E3
Winskill Rd. M44 106 A8
Winslade Cl. SK7 124 A2
Winsley Rd. M23 108 F2
Winslow Ave. SK14 103 A2
Winslow Pl. M19 110 F6
Winslow Rd. BL3 40 D3
Winslow St. M11 165 A8
Winson Cl. BL3 147 E4
Winstanley Cl. 6 M6 80 D5
Winstanley Coll. WN5 53 F3
Winstanley Pl. WN3 151 E6
Winstanley Prim Sch. WN3 54 C2
Winstanley Rd.
Ashton-i-M WN2 73 F8
Winstanley Rd.
Garswood WN4 &WN5 72 B6
Winstanley Rd.
M'ster M10 & M40 160 D3
Winstanley Rd. Orrell WN5 53 F3
Winstanley Rd. Sale M33 108 C5
Winstanley St. WN5 54 F6
Winster Ave. M'ster M7 81 B6
Winster Ave. M'ster M20 109 E4
Winster Ave. Stretford M32 96 A3
Winster Cl. Bolton BL2 25 F1
Winster Cl. Whitefield M45 63 B8
Winster Dr. Bolton BL2 25 F1
Winster Dr. 3 Middleton M24 46 E2
Winster Dr. Platt Bridge WN2 55 F2
Winster Gn. M30 95 B8
Winster Gr. SK2 124 A6
Winster Mews. 17 SK13 171 E2
Winster Rd. M30 95 B8
Winston Ave. Little Lever BL3 43 C3
Winston Ave.
Newton-l-W WA12 89 C3
Winston Ave. R'dale OL11 29 E6
Winston Cl. Marple SK6 125 D7
Winston Cl. Radcliffe M26 43 E5
Winston Rd. M'ster M9 64 F1
Winston Rd. M'ster M40, M9 157 F8
Winston Rd. Sale M33 107 F5
Winswell Cl. M11 83 B2
Winter Hey La. BL6 22 B3
Winter St. BL1 143 D3
Winterbottom Gr. SK14 102 F2
Winterbottom St. OL9 153 D7
Winterbottom Wlk. 4
SK14 102 F2
Winterburn Ave. M21 109 D4
Winterburn Gn. SK2 124 E5
Winterbutlee Gr. OL14 6 A8
Winterdyne St. M9 157 E7
Winterfield Dr. BL3 146 A3
Winterford Ave. M13 164 D5
Winterford Rd.
M'ster M7 & M8 155 F7
Winterford Rd. Mossley OL5 68 E1
Wintergreen Wlk. 3 M31 105 F3
Wintermans Rd. M21 109 E7
Winterslow Ave. M23 108 D1
Winterton Cl. BL5 40 A1
Winterton Rd. SK5 100 A1
Winthrop Ave. M40 & M9 157 D5
Winton Ave. Denton M34 100 D7
Winton Ave. Failsworth M40 65 D1
Winton Ave. Wigan WN5 54 D5
Winton Cl. SK7 123 D1
Winton Ct. WA14 119 C2
Winton Gn. Horwich BL6 22 F1
Winton Gr. BL3 40 E4
Winton Rd. Alt'ham WA14 119 C2
Winton Rd. Golborne WA3 90 E6
Winton Rd. Salford M6 80 D5
Winton St. Ashton-u-L OL6 166 B3
Winton St. Littleborough OL15 16 B5
Winton St. 2
Stalybridge SK15 86 B1
Winward St. Bolton BL3 146 A4
Winward St. Leigh WN7 75 B5
Winward St. 13
Westhoughton BL5 39 E1
Winwick La. WA3 90 E3
Winwick Rd. WA12 89 F1
Winwood Dr. M24 47 B1
Winwood Fold. M24 46 F4
Winwood Rd. M20 122 C8
Wirral Cl. Culcheth WA3 91 E4
Wirral Cl. Swinton M27 62 A2
Wirral Cres. SK3 123 A8
Wirral Dr. WN3 54 C2
Wisbech Dr. M23 108 F1
Wisbeck Rd. BL2 148 C8
Wiseley St. M11 164 E8
Wiseman Terr. M25 63 C4
Wishaw Sq. M21 109 E7
Wisley Cl. SK5 112 A8
Wistaria Rd. M18 99 D5
Withall House. 3 WN1 151 D8
Witham Ave. M22 121 E5
Witham Cl. Heywood OL10 29 A3
Witham Cl. Standish WN6 19 D1
Witham St. OL6 85 E4
Withenfield Rd. M23 120 F8
Withens Gn. SK2 124 E6
Withington Ave. WA3 92 A4
Withington Dr. M29 77 C7
Withington Girls Sch. M14 110 C8
Withington Gn. M24 47 A4
Withington Golf Course.
M20 109 F2
Withington Hospl. M20 109 F6
Withington La. WN2 38 C2
Withington Rd.
M'ster M16 & M21 97 D2
Withington Rd.
M'ster M16 & M21 109 D8
Withington St. Heywood OL10 46 E8
Withington St. Salford M6 81 B2
Withins Ave. M26 44 C5
Withins Cl. BL2 42 E8
Withins Dr. BL2 42 E8
Withins Gr. BL2 42 E8
Withins La. Bolton BL2 42 E8
Withins La. Radcliffe M26 44 C5
Withins Rd. Culcheth WA3 91 F3
Withins Rd. Oldham OL8 66 B2
Withins Sch. BL2 25 E2
Withins Sports Ctr. BL2 25 E2
Withins St. M26 44 C4
Withnell Dr. BL8 27 A1
Withnell Rd. M19 110 D3
Withy Gr. M4 & M60 159 A2
Withy Tree Gr. 1 M34 101 A2
Withycombe Pl. M6 81 A5
Withypool Dr. SK2 124 C5
Witley Dr. M33 107 D6
Witley Rd. OL16 31 B7
Witney Cl. 15 BL1 143 E2
Wittenbury Rd. SK4 168 B2
Witterage Cl. M12 164 F6
Witton Wlk. M7 155 F6
Woburn Ave. Bolton BL2 25 C3
Woburn Ave. Leigh WN7 57 D1
Woburn Ave.
Newton-l-W WA12 89 D2
Woburn Cl. M'ster M16 97 F3
Woburn Cl. Milnrow OL16 31 E6
Woburn Ct. SK12 133 F4
Woburn Dr. Alt'ham WA15 120 B2
Woburn Dr. Bury BL9 44 F5
Woburn Rd. M16 97 A2
Woden St. M5 161 C7
Woden's Ave. M5 161 C7
Woking Rd. SK8 132 A7
Woking Terr. BL1 143 E1
Wolfenden Gn. BB4 2 F8
Wolfenden Prim Sch. BL1 143 E2
Wolfenden St. BL1 143 E2
Wolfenden Terr. 26 BL1 143 E2
Wolford Dr. M29 59 C1
Wolfreton Cres. M27 62 A3
Wolfson Sq. WN4 72 F4
Wollaton Wlk. M34 100 E1
Wolmer St. WN4 73 A4
Wolseley House. M33 108 C6
Wolseley Pl. M20 110 B5
Wolseley Rd. M33 108 C6
Wolseley St. 1 Bury BL8 27 B1
Wolseley St. Newhey OL16 32 B4
Wolsey Cl. Ashton-i-M WN4 73 A5
Wolsey Cl. Radcliffe M26 44 A3
Wolsey Dr. WA14 119 A1
Wolsey St. Heywood OL10 29 C1
Wolsey St. Radcliffe M26 44 A3
Wolstenholme Ave. BL9 27 F6
Wolstenholme Coalpit La.
OL11 13 B2
Wolstenholme La. OL11 13 C2
Wolstenvale Cl. M24 47 B1
Wolver Cl. M38 60 B6
Wolverton Ave. OL8 66 D3
Wolverton Dr. SK9 131 D1
Wolvesey. OL11 139 E6
Wolveton St. M12 164 F7
Wood Bank Rd. OL15 16 A3
Wood Bank Terr. OL5 68 D2
Wood Brook La. OL4 68 B7
Wood Brook Rd. OL4 68 B7
Wood Cottage Cl. 4 M28 59 F3
Wood Cotts. SK6 113 A6
Wood Cres. OL4 67 E3
Wood End. SK7 123 D2
Wood Fold. BL2 25 C6
Wood Fold Prim Sch. WN6 36 D8
Wood Gdns. SK9 137 B2
Wood Gr. Denton M34 100 F4
Wood Gr. Romiley SK6 113 A5
Wood Gr. Whitefield M45 44 F3
Wood Hey Cl. M26 43 D3
Wood Hey Gr. 2
Denton M34 101 A2
Wood Hey Gr. R'dale OL12 14 F4
Wood La. Alt'ham WA15 120 B5
Wood La.
Ashton-u-L OL6 & OL7 85 B5
Wood La. Marple SK6 125 E5
Wood La. Middleton M24 65 B7
Wood La. Mobberley WA16 129 B1
Wood La. Mobberley WA16 129 D1
Wood La. Partington M31 105 D3
Wood La.
Wrightington Bar WN6 18 E8
Wood La N. SK10 134 B1
Wood La W. SK10 133 F1
Wood Lea Bank. 9 BB4 2 F8
Wood Lea Rd. BB4 2 F8
Wood Mount. WA15 120 B5
Wood Rd. M'ster M16 97 D3
Wood Rd. Sale M33 108 B1
Wood Rd N. M16 97 C3
Wood Road La. Bury BL8 27 B8
Wood Road La.
Ramsbottom BL8 & BL9 11 C1
Wood Sq. Droylsden M43 100 A8
Wood Sq. Uppermill OL3 69 B5
Wood St. Alt'ham WA14 119 D4
Wood St. Ashton-u-L OL6 166 B2
Wood St. Atherton M46 58 B4
Wood St. Bolton BL1 145 F7
Wood St. Bury BL8 27 C3
Wood St. Cheadle SK8 122 D6
Wood St. Denton M34 100 F4
Wood St. Dukinfield SK16 101 C6
Wood St. Eccles M30 79 F1
Wood St. Glossop SK13 116 C8
Wood St. Golborne WA3 90 B8
Wood St. Heywood OL10 29 E2
Wood St. Hindley WN2 57 B3
Wood St. Hollingworth SK14 103 D5
Wood St. Horwich BL6 22 C3
Wood St. Hyde SK14 167 E2
Wood St. Littleborough OL15 16 B5
Wood St. M'ster M3 158 E2
Wood St. M'ster M3 158 F1
Wood St. M'ster M11 165 B8
Wood St. Middleton M24 64 F8
Wood St. Newhey OL16 32 C4
Wood St. Oldham OL1 153 F6
Wood St. R'dale OL11 & OL16 31 A6
Wood St. Radcliffe M26 61 E8
Wood St. Ramsbottom BL0 138 B5
Wood St. Shaw OL2 48 F8
Wood St. 6 Stalybridge SK15 85 F2
Wood St. Stockport SK3 169 E1
Wood St. Tyldesley M29 77 B8
Wood St. Westhoughton BL5 57 E8
Wood St. Wigan WN5 54 F7
Wood St. Wigan WN3 150 C7
Wood Terr. BL2 26 D1
Wood Top Ave. OL11 29 F5
Wood View. Heywood OL10 29 C4
Wood View. Shevington WN6 36 B5
Wood View.
Wythenshawe M22 109 D1
Wood's Hospl. SK13 104 C3
Wood's La. WN4 73 C5
Wood's St. WN3 150 C7
Woodacres Ct. SK9 136 F6
Woodall Cl. M33 108 D4
Woodark Cl. OL4 67 F5
Woodbank. SK1 112 B1
Woodbank Ave.
Bredbury SK6 112 E3
Woodbank Ave.
Stockport SK1 124 C8
Woodbank Ct. M41 95 B3
Woodbank Rd. BL8 27 C4
Woodbank Works Ind Est.
SK1 112 B1
Woodbine Ave. M44 105 D4
Woodbine Cres. SK2 170 F7
Woodbine Rd. Bolton BL3 146 C3
Woodbine Rd. Lymm WA13 117 B4
Woodbine St. OL11 & OL16 31 A5
Woodbine St E. OL16 31 B5
Woodbourne Ct. M33 108 B2
Woodbourne Rd.
M'ster SK4 111 C6
Woodbourne Rd. Sale M33 108 A2
Woodbray Ave. M19 110 E5
Woodbridge Ave. M34 100 E7
Woodbridge Gdns. OL12 14 C2
Woodbridge Gr. M23 109 A1
Woodbridge Rd. M41 94 D3
Woodbrook Ave. Hyde SK14 167 F2
Woodbrook Ave. Oldham OL4 68 B7
Woodbrook Dr. WN3 54 D4
Woodbrook Rd. SK9 137 C1
Woodburn Dr. BL1 142 B3
Woodburn Rd. M22 121 D8
Woodbury Cres. SK16 101 B7
Woodbury Rd. SK3 123 B7
Woodchurch. WN1 37 F1
Woodchurch Cl. 3 BL1 143 E1
Woodchurch Wlk. OL9 152 B6
Woodcock Cl. Droylsden M43 84 C3
Woodcock Cl. R'dale OL11 29 F7
Woodcock Dr. WN2 56 B2
Woodcock Gr. SK13 104 E1
Woodcock House. WN1 151 D8
Woodcock Sq. M'ster M15 162 F6
Woodcock Sq. 10
Wigan WN1 150 C8
Woodcote Ave. SK7 123 C2
Woodcote Rd. Sale M33 107 A3
Woodcote Rd. Sale WA14 107 D1
Woodcote View. SK9 131 F1
Woodcote Wlk. M8 156 C8
Woodcott Gr. 3 SK9 131 E1
Woodcourt. WN3 150 B6
Woodcroft.
Appley Bridge WN6 35 E6
Woodcroft. Stockport SK2 124 D6
Woodcroft Ave. M19 110 E4
Wooddagger Cl. WN2 56 F5
Woodeaton Cl. OL2 49 A4
Wooded Cl. BL9 27 F5
Woodedge. WN4 73 A3
Woodend. OL2 149 C8
Woodend Ctr Ind Pk. OL5 68 D2
Woodend Dr. SK15 102 D6
Woodend La. Alt'ham WA16 129 E1
Woodend La. Hyde SK14 167 D1
Woodend La.
Littleborough OL12 15 D6
Woodend La.
Stalybridge SK15 102 D6
Woodend Mills. OL4 67 F5
Woodend Rd. Stockport SK3 123 F4
Woodend Rd.
Wythenshawe M22 121 D4
Woodend St. Oldham OL1 48 E1
Woodend St. Oldham OL4 67 F5
Woodend View. OL5 68 D2
Woodfield. M22 121 D3
Woodfield Ave. Hyde SK14 113 D8
Woodfield Ave. R'dale OL12 14 E2
Woodfield Ave. Romiley SK6 113 A4
Woodfield Cl.
Hollingworth SK14 103 F5
Woodfield Cl. Oldham OL8 66 C4
Woodfield Cres.
Ashton-i-M WN4 73 A2
Woodfield Cres.
Bredbury SK6 112 F2
Woodfield Ct. SK2 124 A4
Woodfield Dr. M28 78 B6
Woodfield Gr. Eccles M30 79 C1
Woodfield Gr. Farnworth BL4 60 C6
Woodfield Gr. Sale M33 108 A6
Woodfield Mews. SK14 113 D8
Woodfield Prim Sch. WN1 37 C4
Woodfield Rd.
Alt'ham WA14 119 C6
Woodfield Rd. Bramhall SK8 132 B7
Woodfield Rd. M'ster M8 64 A1
Woodfield Rd. M'ster M24 64 E6
Woodfield Rd. Salford M6 154 D4
Woodfield St. Bolton BL3 42 A3
Woodfield St. Wigan WN2 38 A3
Woodfield Terr. OL10 29 E3
Woodfold Ave. M19 99 A2
Woodfold Rd. M35 84 A7
Woodford Ave.
Dukinfield M34 101 A4
Woodford Ave. Eccles M30 79 B2
Woodford Ave. Golborne WA3 90 D7
Woodford Ave. Shaw OL2 49 D7
Woodford Ct. Droylsden M34 100 B8
Woodford Ct. 3 Hindley WN2 56 E6
Woodford Dr. M27 61 E2
Woodford Gdns. M20 110 A2
Woodford Gr. BL3 146 C4
Woodford Rd. Bramhall SK7 132 E4
Woodford Rd.
Bramhall SK12 133 B6
Woodford St. 4 Hindley WN2 56 E6
Woodford St. 8 Wigan WN5 54 B6
Woodgarth. WN7 75 C5
Woodgarth Ave. M40 83 D5
Woodgarth Dr. M27 79 E6
Woodgarth La. M28 78 F5
Woodgate Ave. Bury BL9 28 D4
Woodgate Ave. R'dale OL11 30 A6
Woodgate Cl. SK6 112 F3
Woodgate Dr. M25 63 C6
Woodgate Hill Rd. Bury BL9 28 D4
Woodgate Hill Rd. Bury BL9 141 C4
Woodgate Rd. M16 97 E1
Woodgate St. BL3 42 A3
Woodgrange Cl. 2 M6 154 E2
Woodgreen Cl. 1 WN2 56 D4
Woodgreen Dr. M26 62 A8
Woodhall Ave. M'ster M20 110 A7
Woodhall Ave. Whitefield M45 62 D6
Woodhall Cl. Bolton BL2 25 C3
Woodhall Cl. Bury BL8 27 D5
Woodhall Cl. Woodford SK7 132 E3
Woodhall Cres. SK5 112 A4
Woodhall Rd. SK5 169 F4
Woodhall St. M35 83 F8
Woodhalt Rd. M8 156 A8
Woodham Rd. M23 108 F1
Woodham Wlk. BL1 145 D5
Woodhead Cl. 11
M'ster M16 97 E4
Woodhead Cl. Oldham OL4 67 E7
Woodhead Cl.
Ramsbottom BL0 11 C4
Woodhead Dr. WA15 119 F1
Woodhead Gr. WN3 55 B2
Woodhead Rd.
Alt'ham WA15 119 F1
Woodhead Rd.
Glossop SK14 104 D4
Woodhead Rd.
Tintwistle SK14 104 B8
Woodhey Ct. M33 107 E1
Woodhey High Sch. BL0 11 A3
Woodhey Rd. BL0 11 A3
Woodheys. SK4 110 F3
Woodheys Dr. M33 107 D1
Woodheys Prim Sch. M33 107 E2
Woodheys Rd. OL15 16 A2
Woodheys St. 1 M6 154 F1
Woodhill. M24 46 F2
Woodhill Cl. M'ster M18 99 B4
Woodhill Cl. Middleton M24 46 F2
Woodhill Dr. M25 63 B3
Woodhill Fold. BL8 140 D3
Woodhill Gr. M25 63 B3
Woodhill House. 3 M6 154 F3
Woodhill Rd. Bury BL8 140 D3
Woodhill Rd. Bury BL8 140 D4
Woodhill St. BL8 140 D4
Woodhouse Ct. M41 95 A4
Woodhouse Dr. WN6 36 E2
Woodhouse Knowl. OL3 50 F4
Woodhouse La.
Partington WA14 118 C4
Woodhouse La. R'dale OL12 13 E3
Woodhouse La. Sale M33 107 C2
Woodhouse La. Sale M33 107 D2
Woodhouse La. Wigan WN6 36 E3
Woodhouse La. Wigan WN6 36 F2
Woodhouse La.
Wythenshawe M22 121 D4
Woodhouse La.
Wythenshawe M90 130 D7
Woodhouse La.
Wythenshawe M22 130 D8
Woodhouse La E.
M33 & WA15 108 A1
Woodhouse Park Prim Sch.
M22 130 D8
Woodhouse Prim Sch. M41 95 A4
Woodhouse Rd. Shaw OL2 32 C1
Woodhouse Rd. Urmston M41 94 F4
Woodhouse Rd. Urmston M41 95 A4
Woodhouse Rd.
Wythenshawe M22 130 D8
Woodhouse St. Atherton M46 58 D2
Woodhouse St. M'ster M18 99 E5
Woodhouse St.
M'ster M10 & M40 157 F5
Woodhouses CE & Free
Church Prim Sch. M35 84 C6
Woodhurst Dr. WN6 19 D1
Wooding Cl. M31 106 A4
Woodlake Ave. M21 109 C4
Woodland Ave. Bolton BL3 42 B2
Woodland Ave.
Hazel Grove SK7 124 E1
Woodland Ave. Hindley WN2 57 A3
Woodland Ave. Lymm WA13 117 A2
Woodland Ave.
Newton-l-W WA12 89 F3
Woodland Ave. Reddish M18 99 E4
Woodland Cres. M25 63 B2
Woodland Dr.
Ashton-i-M WN4 73 B5
Woodland Dr. Lymm WA13 117 A2
Woodland Dr. Standish WN6 19 E2
Woodland Gr. Bolton BL7 8 D2
Woodland Gr. Wigan WN1 37 D2
Woodland Pk. OL2 48 B6
Woodland Rd. Heywood OL10 29 E3
Woodland Rd. M'ster M19 111 A7
Woodland Rd. R'dale OL12 14 C2
Woodland Rd. Reddish M18 99 E4
Woodland Rd. Tyldesley M29 77 B7
Woodland St. Heywood OL10 29 D2
Woodland St. M'ster M12 165 B5
Woodland St. R'dale OL12 15 A2
Woodland View. BL7 25 B8
Woodland Way. M24 64 F6
Woodlands. Bolton BL2 25 D2
Woodlands. Failsworth M35 83 E4
Woodlands. 5 Urmston M41 95 C3
Woodlands Ave.
Cheadle SK8 123 A2
Woodlands Ave. Eccles M30 95 A8
Woodlands Ave.
Ince-i-M WN3 151 F6
Woodlands Ave. Irlam M44 94 A3
Woodlands Ave. Leigh WN7 75 F3
Woodlands Ave. R'dale OL11 30 A6
Woodlands Ave.
Romiley SK6 113 A5
Woodlands Ave.
Stretford M32 96 D2
Woodlands Ave. Swinton M27 79 D6
Woodlands Ave.
Urmston M41 94 C2
Woodlands Ave.
Whitefield M45 44 E1
Woodlands Cl.
Hollingworth SK14 103 F6
Woodlands Cl.
Mottram-i-L SK14 102 F1
Woodlands Cl.
Stalybridge SK15 102 D7
Woodlands Cl. Worsley M28 78 E7
Woodlands Ct.
Alt'ham WA15 119 E5
Woodlands Ct.
Stockport SK2 124 D8
Woodlands Dr. Atherton M46 58 F5
Woodlands Dr. Romiley SK6 113 A5
Woodlands Dr.
Sale M23 & M33 108 C1
Woodlands Dr.
Shevington WN6 35 F4
Woodlands Dr.
Stockport SK2 124 D8
Woodlands Gr. Bury BL8 27 B3
Woodlands Gr.
Mottram-i-L SK14 102 F1
Woodlands Hospl. M38 59 F4
Woodlands Ind Est. WA12 89 C6
Woodlands Inf Sch. M31 105 D3
Woodlands La. WA15 119 E5
Woodlands Park Rd. SK2 124 D8
Woodlands Parkway.
WA15 119 E6
Woodlands Rd.
Alt'ham WA14 & WA15 119 E5
Woodlands Rd.
Ashton-u-L OL6 85 E6
Woodlands Rd. Edenfield BL0 1 D2
Woodlands Rd.
Handforth SK9 131 E3
Woodlands Rd.
High Lane SK12 135 A6
Woodlands Rd.
M'ster M16 & M21 97 E1
Woodlands Rd. M'ster SK4 110 E2
Woodlands Rd. M'ster M8 156 B7
Woodlands Rd. Milnrow OL16 31 F5
Woodlands Rd. Sale M33 108 C4
Woodlands Rd.
Stalybridge SK15 102 D7
Woodlands Rd.
Wilmslow SK9 130 F1
Woodlands Rd. Worsley M28 78 F7
Woodlands Road Sta. M8 156 B7
Woodlands Sch. SK2 124 D8
Woodlands St. M8 156 A8
Woodlands The. Bolton BL6 40 C8
Woodlands The. Bury BL8 140 D4
Woodlands The.
Heywood OL10 46 E8
Woodlands The. Wigan WN1 37 D3
Woodlands View. BL0 138 C6
Woodlark Cl. M3 158 D1
Woodlawn Ct. M16 97 C3
Woodlea. M24 65 D7
Woodlea Ave. M19 110 E6
Woodlea Gr. M28 78 E8
Woodleigh Ct. SK9 137 A2
Woodleigh Dr. M35 & M43 84 C4
Woodleigh Rd. OL4 68 A7
Woodleigh St. M9 64 F1
Woodley Ave. M26 44 B1
Woodley Cl. SK2 124 D7
Woodley Gr. WN7 75 D5
Woodley Inf Sch. SK6 113 C5
Woodley Jun Sch. SK6 113 C5
Woodley Prec. SK6 113 A5
Woodley St. BL9 44 F8
Woodley Sta. SK6 113 B6
Woodliffe St. M16 161 C5
Woodlinn Wlk. M9 157 D7
Woodman Dr. BL9 27 E6
Woodman St. SK1 169 E2
Woodmeadow Ct. 9 OL5 68 C2
Woodmere Dr. M9 64 E3
Woodmount Cl. SK6 113 F2
Woodnook Rd. WN6 35 E8
Woodpark Cl. OL8 67 A3
Woodridge Dr. BL2 25 B1
Woodridings. WA14 119 B3
Woodrow Way. M44 105 F8
Woodrow Wlk. M12 164 F6
Woodroyd Cl. SK7 123 D1
Woodroyd Dr. BL9 141 C3
Woodruff Wlk. 7 M31 105 F3
Woodruffe Gdns. SK6 125 A8
Woodrush Rd. WN6 36 D3
Woods Ct. Middleton M24 64 C7
Woods Ct.
Newton-l-W WA12 89 A3
Woods Gr. SK8 132 B7
Woods La. Bramhall SK8 132 B7
Woods La. Uppermill OL3 51 A2
Woods Lea. BL1 40 F7
Woods Moor La. SK2 & SK3 124 A4
Woods Rd. M44 105 F8
Woods The. Alt'ham WA14 119 E6
Woods The. Oldham OL4 68 B6
Woods The. R'dale OL11 30 C3
Woodseats La. SK14 115 B6
Woodsend Circ. M41 94 D3
Woodsend Crescent Rd.
M41 94 D2
Woodsend Gn. M41 94 D3
Woodsend Prim Sch. M41 94 D3
Woodsend Rd. M41 94 E3
Woodsend Rd S. M41 94 E1
Woodshaw Gr. M28 78 C8
Woodside. M'ster SK4 110 F1
Woodside. Newhey OL16 32 C5
Woodside. Shaw OL2 49 D8

Also available in various formats

- Berkshire
- Bristol and Avon
- Buckinghamshire
- Birmingham and West Midlands
- Cannock, Lichfield Rugeley
- Cardiff, Swansea and Glamorgan
- Cheshire
- Derbyshire
- Derby and Belper
- Durham
- Edinburgh and East Central Scotland

- East Essex
- West Essex
- Glasgow and West Central Scotland
- North Hampshire
- South Hampshire
- Hertfordshire
- East Kent
- West Kent
- Lancashire
- Merseyside
- Northwich, Winsford Middlewich
- Nottinghamshire
- Oxfordshire

- Peak District Towns
- Staffordshire
- Stafford, Stone Uttoxeter
- Surrey
- East Sussex
- West Sussex
- Tyne and Wear
- Warrington, Widnes Runcorn
- Warwickshire
- South Yorkshire
- West Yorkshire

- Colour regional atlases (hardback, spiral, wire-o, pocket) ◇ Colour local atlases (paperback)
- Black and white regional atlases (hardback, softback, pocket)

◇ Paperback

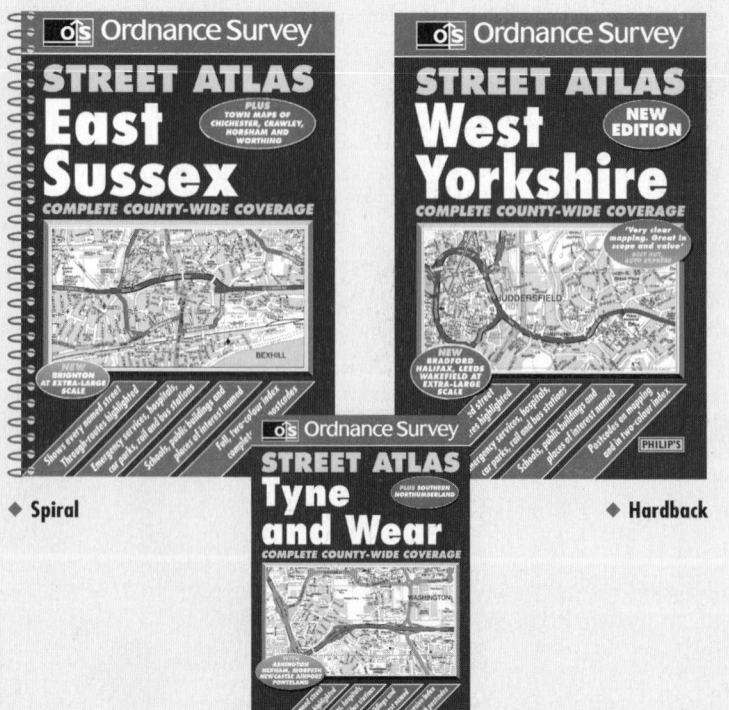

◆ Spiral

◆ Hardback

◆ Pocket